AUSTRALIA
The Law Book Company
Brisbane · Sydney · Melbourne · Perth

CANADA
Carswell
Ottawa · Toronto · Calgary · Montreal · Vancouver

AGENTS
Steimatzky's Agency Ltd., Tel Aviv;
N.M. Tripathi (Private) Ltd., Bombay;
Eastern Law House (Private) Ltd., Calcutta;
M.P.P. House, Bangalore;
Universal Book Traders, Delhi;
Aditya Books, Delhi;
MacMillan Shuppan KK, Tokyo;
Pakistan Law House, Karachi, Lahore

Bingham's Negligence Cases

By

His Honour Judge David Maddison
His Honour Judge Christopher Tetlow
Graham N. Wood, LL.B. (Hons), Barrister

FOURTH EDITION

LONDON
SWEET & MAXWELL
1996

First Edition 1961
Second Edition 1964
Third Edition 1978
Fourth Edition 1996

Published in 1996 by Sweet & Maxwell Limited of 100 Avenue Road, London NW3 3PF
Computerset by York House Typographic Ltd, London W13 8NT
Printed in England by Clays Ltd, St Ives plc

No natural forests were destroyed to make this product; only farmed timber was used and replanted

A CIP catalogue record for this book is available from the British Library

ISBN 042146500X

PREFACE

When the First Edition of this work was published in 1961 it broke new ground. Richard Bingham Q.C., its author, produced the first case book on negligence directed mainly at practitioners. The work's layout and presentation were unique, as was its aim to include every reported case within the ambit of its subject-matter from a given year (1936) and its inclusion of a substantial number of unreported decisions of the Court of Appeal.

The work was well-received, and Second and Third Editions followed. By the time of the Third Edition, Richard had been appointed to the Circuit Bench, to which he brought a rare combination of an incisive mind, sound judgement, patience and a kind heart. He retired from the Bench in 1991 and died in 1992. He is sadly missed by the many who had great respect and affection for him.

At the time of Richard's death, plans were being made for a long overdue Fourth Edition. The Third Edition appeared as long ago as 1978. The only Supplement, prepared by Richard with David Harris Q.C., was published in 1985. The present editors acknowledge with gratitude the skill and industry of both. Even since the Supplement, however, there have been a very large number of reported cases and substantial developments in the law. The task of up-dating alone has been sufficiently daunting for the present editors, and as a result the layout and method of presentation are little changed from previous editions. It is to be hoped that further thought will be given to such matters when the next edition is prepared. In this or any other regard, suggestions and comments from readers will be welcome.

That is not to say that there have been no changes. The Table of Cases now contains full references to each case. In previous editions only the year of each case was given. Liability for negligent misstatements (formerly chapter 7(5)) is now dealt with in a separate chapter (now numbered 19). The former chapter 18 has been omitted, having been rendered otiose by The Administration of Justice Act 1982. The former chapter 20 has also been omitted, chapter 20(1) having dealt with an area of law now obsolete, and chapter 20(2) for reasons stated below. There is a new chapter (now numbered 20) collecting together various miscellaneous cases which did not fit comfortably in any other chapter. The former chapter 21(2) on Remoteness has been moved to chapter 1. The former chapters 20(2), 21(1) and 22 to 25, which dealt principally with damages, practice and procedure, have been omitted for a variety of reasons. First, the impression we have obtained as users of the Third Edition, and having spoken to many other members of the legal profession, is that Bingham has always been regarded as being of most value in relation to questions of liability. Secondly, we have had to consider the size of this edition. Since the Third Edition there has been a considerable increase in the numbers in which cases on liability have been reported, and indeed in the number of law reports and journals reporting such cases. There have been similar increases in relation to damages, practice and procedure. The Fourth Edition is by some way the largest yet, and we fear that the work would have become unwieldy had its previous scope been retained. Thirdly, there are now on the market many other books dealing separately with damages, practice and procedure.

This edition, like previous editions, aims to provide a quick and convenient method of reference to the relevant case law for those considering or taking legal action involving negligence and related breaches of statutory duty. The book is essentially practical. Those looking for academic argument and original thought will be disappointed. Consisting as it does only of extracts from and/or summaries of cases, the book is to be used as a starting-point for further research, rather than as a final point of reference. A section explaining how best to make use of the book will be found at page 000.

With two exceptions, this edition aims to include every case within its subject-matter decided in England and Wales and reported since 1963, though many cases reported before that year and included in previous editions have been retained. The first exception covers a few cases on statutory provisions in the field of health and safety at work which have now long since been repealed or revoked. The second is that cases on collisions between ships have not usually been included. A few reported cases from Scotland, Northern Ireland, Eire and some Commonwealth countries have been included, as have a larger number of unreported Court of Appeal decisions. A few cases at first instance which have appeared 'ex relatione' in Current Law but are otherwise unreported have also been included. If readers know of other unreported first instance decisions which would merit inclusion in future supplements and editions, or of reported decisions overlooked by us, we would be grateful to hear from them.

This edition is intended to be up-to-date to the end of 1994. It is intended to produce annual supplements, to keep this edition far more up-to-date than was possible with previous editions.

We would like to acknowledge the invaluable assistance we have received from Mrs Raina Levy, Barrister, in gathering and providing initial summaries of unreported Court of Appeal decisions, an enormous task accomplished with great skill. Thanks are also due to Miss Sara Mann, Barrister, for her assistance on certain sections of the book. Last but by no means least we would like to thank our families for their kindness and tolerance of the hours spent in solitude preparing this edition and occasional lapses from our respective natural even-tempered demeanours.

David Maddison
Christopher Tetlow
Graham N. Wood
December 1995

HOW TO USE BINGHAM'S NEGLIGENCE CASES

This book consists of 20 chapters, each dealing with a separate branch of the law of negligence and/or related breaches of statutory duty. The first six chapters deal with general principles and the remaining 14 with particular areas of the law.

Each chapter has a number of sections and/or sub-sections, each of which usually consists of two parts, as follows:

(a) First appears an introductory table explaining in a line or two the substance of each of the cases in the section or sub-section. A good example will be found at page 67. Reported cases appear first in the table, in chronological order and numbered 1, 2, etc. Three types of print are used: **Bold upper and lower case print** indicates a decision of the House of Lords or the Privy Council. UPPER CASE PRINT indicates a decision of the Court of Appeal. Ordinary upper and lower case print indicates a decision at first instance (usually High Court but occasionally County Court) or a decision from Scotland, Northern Ireland, Eire or a Commonwealth country. Then follow any relevant unreported Court of Appeal decisions, in separate chronological order, numbered U1, U2, etc. and in *italic upper and lower case print.*

(b) After each introductory table will be found, in corresponding numerical orders, the names of the cases referred to in the table. Unless the table itself sufficiently identifies the subject matter of the case, the name of the case will be followed by a more detailed summary of and/or an extract or extracts from the case. See, for example, pages 67 to 70 where the cases corresponding with the introductory table on page 67 will be found. For convenience one or (more usually) two references for each reported case are given in the body of the text, but the Table of Cases at the front of the book will provide any further references required. Unreported Court of Appeal decisions are referred to by the serial numbers of their transcripts which are to be found in the Supreme Court Library. Bound transcripts are referred to, for example, as (1980) C.A. 123, and unbound transcripts, for example, as (1982) C.A. UB 456.

A few sections or sub-sections of chapters contain a third part, listing as examples cases which show the application to particular facts of principles of law set out earlier in the section or sub-section concerned. See, for example, Pages 131 to 134 (an introductory table) and 134 to 137 (a corresponding list of cases).

Reference to the Table of Contents at the front of the book and the Index at the book should identify the part or parts of the book of interest to the reader. The relevant introductory table(s) should then indicate at a glance cases which may be of value. The corresponding case summaries and/or extracts can then be consulted for further detail. The reader may then progress from the book to the reports or transcripts of cases identified as useful.

Those familiar with earlier editions of this book will already have their own preferred methods of using it to research cases, and new readers will quickly develop theirs. In the hope that it assists, however, one example is set out below showing how the book can be applied to a comparatively straightforward case.

EXAMPLE

The reader acts for a child aged 12 who ran from the pavement, after a ball, into the path of a passing car. The car driver should have been able to see the child with the ball on the pavement well before the accident. He did not sound his horn. He was driving at about 40 m.p.h. in a built-up area. The reader seeks guidance on the liability of the driver and, should he be liable, on the question of contributory negligence on the part of the child.

Reference to the Table of Contents at the front of the book indicates that chapters 4(1)(e) and 13(1)(e), (k) and (o) may be relevant. Using the Index at the back of the book the relevant sub-entries under 'Children', 'Contributory Negligence', 'Driver', 'Pedestrians' and 'Road Vehicles' point in similar directions.

A glance through the introductory tables at the beginning of each relevant section or sub-section will indicate the cases likely to be of assistance. These will probably include the following:

In chapter 4(1)(e) (pp. 143–145), cases 6, 10 and U2.
In chapter 13(1)(k) (pp. 401–490), cases 23, 26, 31 and U19.
In chapter 13(1)(o) (pp. 415–416), cases 4, U3 and U5.

Reference can then be made to the corresponding case summaries and/or extracts which follow the introductory tables, and to the full reports or transcripts of any cases which merit more detailed study. Though each case ultimately turns on its own facts, the use of the book in this way will assist the reader to assess the prospects of success of his action (good) and the extent of the contributory negligence likely to be found against his client.

TABLE OF CONTENTS

PART 2

PARTICULAR CLASSES

TABLE OF CASES

(*The figures in italics refer to the lists of Examples*)

Part 1

1. DUTY OF CARE

(1) General Statements of Duty

1. Donoghue v. Stevenson [1932] A.C. 562; 147 L.T. 281, H.L.

Lord Atkin (580): "The rule that you are to love your neighbour becomes in law, you must not injure your neighbour; and the lawyer's question, Who is my neighbour? receives a restricted reply. You must take reasonable care to avoid acts and omissions which you can reasonably foresee would be likely to injure your neighbour. Who, then, in law is my neighbour? The answer seems to be—persons who are so closely and directly affected by my act that I ought to have them in contemplation as being so affected when I am directing my mind to the acts or omissions which are called in question."

Approved by Lord Wright in *Bourhill v. Young*, [1943] A.C. 92, 107 as establishing "the general concept of reasonable foresight as the criterion of negligence."

2. A. C. Billings v. Riden [1957] 3 All E.R. 1; [1958] A.C. 240, H.L.

Visitor to premises injured by negligence of contractor—*Held*, contractor owed her a duty of care and was liable. Lord Reid (5 C): "That duty was the ordinary duty to take such care as in all the circumstances of the case was reasonable to ensure that visitors were not exposed to danger by their actions."

3. Fowler v. Lanning [1959] 1 All E.R. 290; 1 Q.B. 426, Diplock J.

Allegation that "plaintiff shot defendant" (and no more)—*Held*, bad, as disclosing no cause of action, inasmuch as in all cases of trespass to the person, plaintiff must prove it was either intentional or negligent, and further that "the plaintiff must today in this crowded world be considered as taking on himself the risk of inevitable injury from any acts of his neighbour which, in the absence of damage to the plaintiff, would not in themselves be unlawful . . . " (297 G).

4. Letang v. Cooper [1964] 2 All E.R. 929; [1965] 1 Q.B. 232, C.A.

Plaintiff run down while sunbathing on hotel lawn—being out of time with writ for negligence, she sued in trespass as well—*Held*, the claim was statute barred, for (a) *per* Lord Denning M.R. and Danckwerts L.J., trespass only lay for intentional acts, and for all unintentional acts the cause of action lay in negligence, so far as actions for personal injuries were concerned, and (b) in any event, on the proper construction of the Law Reform (Limitation of Actions) Act 1954, the time for bringing trespass to the person was the same as for negligence (three years).

5. Cahoon v. Franks (1967) 63 D.L.R. (2d) 274; [1968] C.L.Y. 2639, Can.Sup.Ct.

Plaintiff brought an action in negligence for damage to property—outside the limitation period he sought to amend to include a claim for damages for personal injuries—*Held*, he could do so, because there was only one cause of action. *Brunsden v. Humphrey* (1884) 14 Q.B.D. 141 *disapproved.* See 31 M.L.R. 454.

(2) Who Can Sue

(a) "Neighbours" Generally

(*N.B.* The cases and dicta grouped here are selected as showing the principles which are to be applied. For cases showing how these principles have been applied to particular sets of facts, reference should be made to:—

1. Donoghue v. Stevenson [1932] A.C. 562; 147 L.T. 281, H.L.

Lord Atkin (580): "The rule that you are to love your neighbour becomes in law, you must not injure your neighbour; and the lawyer's question, Who is my neighbour? receives a restricted reply. You must take reasonable care to avoid acts and omissions which you can reasonably foresee would be likely to injure your neighbour. Who, then, in law is my neighbour? The answer seems to be—persons who are so closely and directly affected by my act that I ought to have them in contemplation as being so affected when I am directing my mind to the acts or omissions which are called in question."

2. Bourhill v. Young [1943] A.C. 92; [1942] 2 All E.R. 396, H.L.

Lord Russell of Killowen (102): "In my opinion, such a duty (of care) only arises towards those individuals of whom it may be reasonably anticipated that they will be affected by the act which constitutes the alleged breach. . . . The appellant was not in my opinion 'so placed' (*i.e.* so placed that they may reasonably be expected to be injured)." Lord Macmillan (105): "She (the appellant) was not so placed that there was any reasonable likelihood of her being affected."

3. Best v. Samuel Fox [1952] 2 All E.R. 394; A.C. 716, H.L.

Lord Reid (400 D): "A daughter of an injured man may have to give up work which she enjoys and stay at home to nurse a father. . . . The invitor is under no duty to compensate such persons, for he owes them no duty." *But see* now the cases such as *Donnelly v. Joyce* [1973] 3 All E.R. 475.

4. Carmarthenshire C.C.v. Lewis [1955] A.C. 549; 1 All E.R. 565, H.L.

Lord Reid (572 I): "If I am right in the view . . . that injury to other road users was reasonably foreseeable if this child were allowed to escape onto the street, then the reasoning in *Bourhill* **2** is very much against the appellants (*i.e.* the defendants)."

5. A. C. Billings v. Riden [1957] 3 All E.R. 1; [1958] A.C. 240, H.L.

6. Weller v. Foot and Mouth Institute [1965] 3 All E.R. 560; [1966] Q.B. 569, Widgery J.

Defendants negligently, as was assumed for the purposes of argument, allowed virus to escape, which infected cattle, and so caused plaintiffs to lose the profits of their cattle market due to closure—*Held*, defendants not liable, as they did not owe plaintiffs any duty of care. Leaving aside cases under the *Hedley Byrne* principle (*i.e.* negligent misstatements, as to which see Chap. 19), the common law principle was that "a duty of care which arises from a risk of direct injury to person or property is owed only to those whose person or property may foreseeably be injured by a failure to take care. If the plaintiff can show that the duty was owed to him, he can recover both direct and consequential loss which is reasonably foreseeable, and for myself I can see no reason for saying that proof of direct loss is an essential part of his claim. He must, however, show that he is within the scope of the defendant's duty to take care." (570 D) In the present case, the plaintiffs as auctioneers had no proprietary interest in anything which might be damaged if the virus escaped, and they were therefore not persons to whom a duty of care was owed. *N.B.* From this case have stemmed a number of decisions on *economic loss* arising indirectly from a negligent act as to which see Chap. 1, (3) (a).

7. Home Office v. Dorset Yacht Co. [1970] 2 All E.R. 294; A.C. 1004, H.L.

Borstal escapees from Brownsea Island doing damage to yacht—due, as assumed for argument, to negligence of borstal officers in charge of party—*Held*, a duty of care was owed to prevent damage to property in the neighbourhood. Much of the argument was concerned with whether the conduct of the escapees constituted *novus actus interveniens*; it was *held* that it did not (see Chap. 1, (4) (c) **9**). On the main question of duty, all four of the Law Lords in the majority said that the fact that the defendants were acting in pursuance of statutory powers was immaterial, where, as here, the exercise of the powers was done negligently. Lord Reid (302 J) said that, if public policy was the test of the existence of a duty, he could see no grounds for giving immunity to a government department. Lord Morris doubted whether it was necessary to invoke policy as a test, and suggested that the real question was whether it was "fair and reasonable" that a duty should exist (308 A), which in this case should be answered in the affirmative. A second ground was that, applying the dictum of Dixon J. in *Smith v. Leurs* (1945) 70 C.L.R. 256 (to the effect that although in general no one was under a duty of controlling another to prevent harm to a third, there were special relations which could give rise to such a duty), there was such a special relation in the present case, arising from the right of the borstal officers to control the escapees who might well do damage to property near at hand (307 G). Lord Pearson said that prima facie the defendants came within the concept of "neighbours," and that therefore there ought to be a duty, unless there was some sufficient reason for not applying it. He considered, and dismissed, absence of proximity, act of third party, and statutory duty as being, on the facts, capable of constituting sufficient reason; and on the fourth factor, public policy, said that if this was a factor, it only went to the standard of care, and not to the existence of a duty. Lord Diplock said that the duty owed by the borstal officers was only owed to persons having property in the immediate neighbourhood, so that it could be reasonably foreseen that escapees might steal or damage such property (334 G); this limitation accords with the tenor of the other speeches.

8. Dutton v. Bognor Regis U.D.C. [1972] Q.B. 373; 1 All E.R. 462, C.A.

Local authority *held* liable to subsequent purchaser of newly-built house for the negligence of their surveyor in approving the foundations.

Approved by H.L. in *Anns* **10,** but on differently stated grounds. Overruled see *Murphy*, Chap. 18, (13) **66**.

9. Watt v. Rama [1972] V.R. 353; C.L.Y. 2408, Victoria Sup. Ct.

Duval v. Seguin (1972) 26 D.L.R. (3d) 418; C.L.Y. 2409, Fraser J. (Can.)

Held, in both cases, an action would lie. *But* the position now is regulated by the Congenital Disabilities Act 1976.

10. Anns v. Merton L.B.C. [1977] 2 W.L.R. 1024; 2 All E.R. 492, H.L.

Foundations of building defective—assumed for argument that local authority had either failed to carry out its function under the Public Health Act 1936 of inspecting the foundations or had been negligent in inspecting them—as regards (i) failure to inspect, *held*, council would not be liable unless (a) it had not exercised its discretion properly as to the making of inspections, and (b) it had failed to exercise reasonable care in its acts or omissions to secure that the by-laws concerning foundations were complied with; and as regards (ii) negligent inspection, *held*, council would be liable if the inspector, having assumed the duty of inspecting and acting otherwise than in the bona fide exercise of any discretion under the statute, failed to take reasonable care in the inspection. Lord Wilberforce (three other Law Lords concurring) said that, as a result of the *Dorset Yacht* case **7**, the existence of a duty of care no longer depended on bringing the case within some existing precedent. *In general*, the question now had to be approached in two stages: first, the question was whether there was a sufficient relationship of proximity or neighbourhood such that in the reasonable contemplation of the defendant, carelessness by him might cause damage to another; and secondly, whether there were any considerations (such as arose in the "economic loss" cases: see Chap. 1, (3) (a)) which ought to negative or limit or reduce the scope of the duty or the class of person to whom it was owed. But in the *particular* case of a public body discharging functions under statute, these tests were not enough, since the powers and duties of the public body were definable in terms of public and not private law, and it was usual for the statutes which applied in such cases to contain a large area of policy, which the courts called "discretion," and the exercise of which could not, in general, be called in question, so long as the decision was made responsibly and for reasons which accorded with the statutory purpose. But also many statutes pre-supposed the practical execution of policy decisions, so that in addition to the area of policy or discretion there was (although it was largely a matter of degree) an "operational" area as well, and the more operational a power or duty might be, the easier it was to superimpose on it a common law duty of care. For these reasons Lord Wilberforce reached the conclusions set out above. Largely overruled in *Murphy*, Chap. 18, (13) **66**.

11. Ferguson v. Home Office (1977) *The Times*, October 8, Caulfield J.

12. Ashton v. Turner [1980] 3 All E.R. 870; [1981] Q.B. 137, Ewbank J.

Held that the driver of a criminal get-away car owed no duty of care in law to the passenger. "The law of England may in certain circumstances not recognise the existence of a duty of care by one participant in a crime to another participant in the same crime, in relation to an act done in connection with the commission of that crime." (877 E).

13. The Irene's Success [1982] 1 All E.R. 218; Q.B. 481, Lloyd J.

The question was whether a shipowner owed a duty of care to the buyer of a cargo of coal afloat in his ship under a c.i.f. contract whereby the risk passed to the buyer but the ownership remained with the seller—the buyer could not sue in contract because he did not become the holder of the bill of lading—*held*, yes (for fuller details see under Chap. 7, (1)(a)**18**). In the course of the argument the defendants relied on *Weller* **6**, but the true ratio of this decision was *explained* as being "that the loss suffered by the plaintiffs, though foreseeable, was, as it were, at one remove from the damage to the cattle," and therefore exposed the defendants to claims from an almost unlimited number of potential plaintiffs (222 C).

N.B. This decision was strongly (though *obiter*) *approved* by Sheen J. in *Nea Tyhi* [1982] 1 Lloyd's Rep. 606.

14. McKay v. Essex A.H.A. [1982] 2 All E.R. 771; Q.B. 1166, C.A.

Mother in contact with German Measles early in pregnancy—as a result, child born severely disabled. Mother had contacted doctor during pregnancy and had been advised that the foetus was unaffected—alleged that had she been informed of damage to foetus, she would have undergone abortion—claim by child *inter alia* for damages for wrongful entry into life. *Held* that that aspect of the claim should be struck out as it did not disclose a reasonable cause of action. A doctor does not owe any duty to a damaged foetus to terminate its life. Such a claim for "wrongful life" would be contrary to public policy as a violation of the sanctity of human life. Furthermore it would be impossible for the court to assess damages, as this would involve a comparison between the value of non-existence and the value of existence in a disabled state.

Note. Section 4(5) of the Congenital Disabilities (Civil Liability) Act 1976 prevents any similar claim by a child born after July 22, 1976.

15. Junior Books v. Veitchi [1982] 3 All E.R. 201; [1983] A.C. 520, H.L.

Floor constructed by defendants developed cracks. Cracks did not involve any risk to person or other property, but it was necessary for the floor to be replaced. Plaintiffs sued defendants in negligence for cost of remedial work and consequential economic loss. Defendants raised preliminary point that, in the absence of a contractual relationship between the parties or risk of damage to the person or other property, the plaintiffs had not disclosed a good cause of action. *Held*, that in the circumstances the defendant owed to the plaintiffs a duty to take reasonable care to avoid acts or omissions which they ought to have known would cause the plaintiffs pure economic loss (as opposed to physical damage to the person or other property) and accordingly the plaintiffs' pleading disclosed a good cause of action. The majority of the House (Lords Fraser, Russell and Roskill) held that as (a) the proximity between the parties was so close as to fall only just short of a direct contractual relationship, (b) the defendants must have known that the plaintiffs relied on their skill and experience in laying a floor satisfying the plaintiffs' requirements, and (c) the loss sustained by the plaintiffs, although financial only, was a direct and foreseeable consequence of the alleged negligence; the duty of care owed by the defendants to the plaintiffs extended to avoiding such loss:

see particularly at 213J to 214B where Lord Roskill lists nine factors of crucial importance in establishing the necessary degree of proximity to give rise to a duty on the defendants to take reasonable care not to cause the plaintiffs financial loss. The House reserved its views as to whether a manufacturer or a contractor who provides an article which is defective but not dangerous is liable to a subsequent purchaser who suffers economic loss only. Considered in *D. & F. Estates*, Chap. 18, (6) **63**: Explained in *Murphy*, **42**.
See further 1(3)(a) **11**.

16. Fellowes v. Rother D.C. [1983] 1 All E.R. 513; C.L.Y. 2538, Robert Goff J.

Trial of preliminary issues of law in action alleging negligent exercise of statutory powers to carry out coast protection work. The judge reviewed the leading authorities, and in particular *Anns* **10**, and *said* (522 A): "From these authorities the following principles can ... be derived. Where a plaintiff claims damages for negligence at common law against a public body or official purporting to act in pursuance of a power conferred by statute or other legislation, he can only succeed if he can show (1) that the act complained of was not within the limits of a discretion bona fide exercised under the relevant power, (2) that having regard to all the circumstances, including the legislation creating the relevant power, there was sufficient proximity to create a duty of care on the defendant to avoid damage to the plaintiff of the type complained of, and no ground for negativing (or reducing or limiting) such duty of care, (3) that it was reasonably foreseeable by the defendant or by those for whom he was vicariously responsible, that the act complained of was likely to cause damage of the type in fact suffered by the plaintiff by reason of such act. In considering these questions, there is no rule that, merely because the defendant was acting under a statutory power as opposed to a statutory duty, liability is contingent on the defendant causing the plaintiff fresh or additional damage."

17. Acrecrest v. Hattrell [1983] 1 All E.R. 17; Q.B. 260, C.A.

Overruled in *Peabody* **18**

18. Governors of the Peabody Donation Fund v. Sir Lindsay Parkinson & Co. Ltd [1985] AC. 210: [1984] 3 All E.R. 529, H.L.

Plans prepared by the plaintiffs' architects and approved by the local authority, provided for the construction of a flexible system of drainage for a housing development on the plaintiffs' land. In fact a rigid system was installed by the builders on the architects' instructions. During installation the local authority's building inspector became aware of the change but did nothing. The plaintiffs sued the local authority for breach of duty of care by failing to warn them of the risk of economic loss unless a flexible system in accordance with the plans was installed—*Held*, although it might be reasonably foreseeable by the local authority that failure to invoke their powers to require compliance with the approved plans might involve economic loss to the plaintiffs, it was neither reasonable nor just to impose liability on the local authority to indemnify the plaintiffs against such loss in the circumstances in particular when the plaintiffs relied on the advice of architects, engineers and contractors; the local authority's power to require compliance was not for the purpose of safeguarding building developers against economic loss resulting from their failure to comply with approved plans. *Anns* **10** considered. *Acrecrest* **17** overruled.

19. Balsamo v. Medici [1984] 1 W.L.R. 951; [1984] 2 All E.R. 304, Walton J.

Plaintiff instructed first defendant to enter plaintiff's car in auction, and pay plaintiff proceeds of sale. Without plaintiff's knowledge, first defendant instructed second defendant to receive part of proceeds of sale and pay these to X. Second defendant, unaware of plaintiff's existence, thought he was acting only on behalf of first defendant. Second defendant carelessly paid the money to an imposter. Plaintiff sued second defendant in negligence—*Held*:

(a) The fact that second defendant was unaware of plaintiff's existence would not *per se* prevent plaintiff from suing second defendant in negligence.
(b) However, second defendant owed no duty of case to plaintiff, because there was no contract or direct relationship between the two, and because second defendant had not damaged or dissipated a specific property or identifiable fund belonging to plaintiff.

20. Page v. Read (1984) 134 New L.J. 723; [1984] C.L.Y. 1203, Stocker J.

Plaintiff, working without safety equipment, fell from roof of house he was painting and sued defendant who had the contract for the painting work, relying on the Construction (Working Places) Regulations 1966, negligence, and Occupiers' Liability Act 1957—*Held*, on the evidence, plaintiff was self-employed, thus the Regulations did not apply and there was no duty in tort is provide him with safety equipment or safe system of working. Moreover defendant owed no duty under 1957 Act because not in occupation of the site.

21. Sherrard v. British Gates (and Timber) Ltd, *The Times*, February 25 1984; [1984] C.L.Y. 2301, Kilner Brown J.

Plaintiff was injured when helping to move logs for defendant, when plaintiff had volunteered to help—*Held*, plaintiff was a neighbour of defendant and was owed some duty of care, but on the facts there was no reasonably foreseeable risk of injury.

22. Condon v. Basi [1985] 2 All E.R. 453; [1985] 1 W.L.R. 866, C.A.

Defendant, a local Sunday league footballer, lunged with studs showing 9 inches off the ground at plaintiff, on the opposing side, after plaintiff had pushed the ball away—plaintiff broke right leg—defendant sent off. Court of Appeal upheld trial Judge's decision that defendant was liable in negligence.

Per Lord Donaldson M.R.: "... there is no authority as to what is the standard of care which governs the conduct of players in competitive sports generally and, above all, in a competitive sport whose rules ... contemplate ... physical contact between the players." There would be liability "if ... the defendant failed to exercise that degree of care which was appropriate in all the circumstances, or ... acted in a way to which the plaintiff cannot be expected to have consented ... The standard is objective, but objective in a different set of circumstances. Thus there will of course be a higher degree of care required of a player in a First Division football match than of a player in a local league football match."

23. Candlewood Navigation Corp. Ltd v. Mitsui O.S.K. Lines Ltd [1986] A.C. 1; [1985] 2 All E.R. 935, P.C.

Two vessels collided owing to negligence of defendant's crew. Plaintiff had chartered other vessel involved and claimed for the hire they had to pay the owners and for loss of profits during the repair period—*Held, inter alia*, the claims failed because the plaintiff had only a contractual rather than a proprietary or possessory right to the vessel. The Privy Council adopted the following statement of principle by Scrutton L.J. in *Elliot Steam Tug Co. Ltd v. Shipping Controller* [1922] 1 K.B. 127, 139–40: "In the case of a wrong done to a chattel the common law does not recognize a person whose only rights are a contractual right to have the use of services of the chattel for purposes of making profits or gains without possession of or property in the chattel".

24. Investors in Industry Commercial Properties Ltd v. South Bedfordshire D.C. [1986] Q.B. 1034; [1986] 1 All E.R. 787, C.A.

The plaintiffs caused warehouses to be built on their land: the local authority passed plans and inspected and approved the foundation bases; the foundations proved inadequate—*Held*, the local authority in exercising their supervisory powers granted by statute owed no duty of care to an original building owner (albeit it might to a subsequent occupier) to ensure a building was erected in accordance with the relevant building regulations; it would not normally be just and reasonable to do so, in particular where it was incumbent on the building owner to ensure compliance and he had had and relied upon professional advisers. *Peabody* **18** applied. *Dennis v. Charnwood B.C.*, Chap. 18, (13) **19** distinguished.

25. Meah v. McCreamer (No. 2) [1986] 1 All E.R. 943; 136 New L.J. 235, Woolf J.

As a result of road traffic accident caused by defendant's negligence, plaintiff suffered head injuries, underwent marked personality change and developed propensity to attack women, two of whom were awarded against him damages which he now sought to recover against defendant—*Held*:

(a) Such damages were too remote a loss to be recoverable. Plaintiff's victims could not have sued defendant directly because defendant owed them no duty. Further, to allow plaintiff to recover would expose defendant and other defendants in similar cases to indefinite liability for indefinite period.
(b) It would be contrary to public policy for plaintiff to be indemnified by defendant for the consequences of plaintiff's crimes.

26. Leigh & Sillavan Ltd v. Aliakmon Shipping Co. Ltd [1986] A.C. 785; [1986] 2 All E.R. 145, H.L.

Plaintiff agreed to buy steel to be shipped from Korea to U.K. Steel badly stowed, and damaged during voyage before plaintiff acquired title to it. Plaintiff sued shipowners, *inter alia* in negligence—*Held*, a person could not claim in negligence in respect of loss of or damage to property unless he had legal ownership of or possessory title to the property when the damage occurred. Here, plaintiff had neither even if (which was doubted) it had an equitable interest in the steel when it was damaged and even though under plaintiff's c.i.f. contract with the seller of the steel, the risk had passed to plaintiff.

27. Hambro Life Assurance PLC v. White Young & Partners [1987] 2 EG LR 159; [1987] C.L.Y. 2584, C.A.

Plaintiffs purchased but never themselves occupied a building constructed some time previously; local authority conceded negligent building regulation approval and inspection of progress of work and state of building posed present and imminent danger to health and safety of occupants/licensees/visitors—*Held*, plaintiffs being mere owners and never having been occupiers were not a section of the public to whom any duty was owed.

28. Curran v. Northern Ireland Co-Ownership Housing Association Ltd [1987] A.C. 718; [1987] 2 All E.R. 13, H.L.

See for details Chap. 18, (13) **43**.

29. Ferguson v. Welsh [1987] 1 W.L.R. 1553; [1987] 3 All E.R. 777, H.L.

A council engaged contractor, S. to demolish building on site owned by council, on terms that S should not sub-contract the work without council's consent. Without such consent, S sub-contracted the work to W, who employed plaintiff. Due to unsafe system of work and breaches of statutory duty on part of W, plaintiff seriously injured. Trial judge, *inter alia*, held Council not liable as occupiers. On appeal to House of Lords, plaintiff sought re-trial against council—House of Lords dealt with appeal on basis that both council and S were occupiers of the site—*Held*:

(a) Despite limitation on sub-contracting, there was evidence capable of establishing that council had given S ostensible authority to invite W and his employees onto site, and thus that plaintiff was visitor of council on site.
(b) Council not in breach of common duty of care under section 2(2) of Occupiers' Liability Act 1957, because absence of reasonable safety arose not from physical state or use of the premises but from unsafe system of work implemented by W and followed by plaintiff.
(c) Occupier was not ordinarily under a duty to see that an independent contractor was implementing safe system of work. But by virtue of section 2(4) (b) of the Act, in special circumstances, where occupier knew or had reason to suspect that his contractor was using unsafe system, it might well be reasonable for him to take steps to see that the system was made safe, and he might therefore be liable to contractor's employee injured as a result of unsafe system. (*Per* Lords Oliver and Goff, any such liability would be as joint tortfeasor with contractor, rather than as occupier). However, on the facts, council not liable in this way.
(d) Accordingly, retrial of action against council not ordered.
(e) (*Per* Lord Goff) where two persons occupy same land, and one allows third party onto land without express or ostensible authority of other, third party will be visitor of former occupier but trespasser *vis-à-vis* the latter.

30. Transcontainer Express Ltd v. Custodian Security Ltd [1988] 1 Lloyds Rep. 128; [1988] 1 F.T.L.R. 54, C.A.

Plaintiffs contracted to carry brandy from France to Feltham, then sub-contracted the carriage to C. En route, C took the brandy to a park at which security services were provided by defendant, due to whose negligence the brandy was stolen. Plaintiff claimed for the loss in negligence—*Held*, applying *Leigh & Sillavan Ltd v. Aliakmon Shipping Co. Ltd* (Chap. 1, (2)(a) **26**) defendant owed no duty of care to plaintiff who had no proprietary or possessory title to brandy at time of theft.

Note. The Court of Appeal refused to allow plaintiff to take point not argued at first imitance that they had an immediate right to possession of the brandy at time of theft, which was sufficient to give them possessory title.

31. Calder v. H. Kitson Vickers Ltd [1988] I.C.R. 232; [1988] C.L.Y. 1952, C.A.

Plaintiff worked as labour only sub-contractor for defendant, in a team breaking up a minesweeper by a heavy metal ball dropped from crane owned by defendant and driven by defendant's employee. Part of crane's lifting equipment fell and struck plaintiff. Plaintiff knew that (i) a chain which would have secured the part had previously been damaged and not replaced and (ii) an alternative method of securing the part had been used in the past. *Held*:

(a) defendant owed plaintiff a duty of care in the circumstances, including degree of control exercised by defendant;
(b) defendant negligent in providing unsafe equipment, failing to warn plaintiff of danger and condoning unsafe system of working;

(c) plaintiff 25 per cent to blame for failing to request replacement or repair of chain or to use the alternative method, albeit at the cost of some inconvenience and loss of time.

32. Somasundaram v. M. Julius Melchior & Co. [1988] 1 W.L.R. 1394; [1989] 1 All E.R. 129, C.A.

Plaintiff claimed in civil proceedings that solicitors had been negligent in persuading him to plead guilty in criminal proceedings and in mitigating. Claim struck out; plaintiff was seeking to attack in civil proceedings the final decision of a criminal court of competent jurisdiction. *Hunter v. Chief Constable of Ltd. West Midlands Police* [1982] A.C. 529 applied.

33. Yuen Kun Yeu v. Attorney-General of Hong Kong [1988] A.C. 175; [1987] 2 All E.R. 705, P.C.

For details see Chap. 18, (2) **26**.

34. Jones v. Department of Employment [1989] Q.B.1.; [1988] 1 All E.R. 725, C.A.

Plaintiff's claim that adjudication officer was negligent in refusing him unemployment benefit thereby causing cost of successful appeal, expense, worry, distress and inconvenience struck out; to allow a common law action for negligence would be to allow a challenge to the correctness of the officer's decision, *i.e.* its finality, by a route other than that provided for by statutory provision; the officer's duty lay in the field of public law and was enforceable only by the statutory appeal procedure or judicial review (a public law remedy); thus no duty of care owed in private law and it was not just or reasonable that there should be.

35. Hill v. Chief Constable of West Yorkshire [1989] A.C. 53; [1988] 2 All E.R. 238, H.L.

Claim that but for negligent investigation plaintiff's daughter would not have been murdered by person guilty of a series of murders struck out: despite foreseeability of harm there was absent any such ingredient or characteristic as led to liability in *Dorset Yacht*, **7** or any other characteristic which would establish a duty of care; as a matter of public policy there should be immunity from suit on grounds similar to those appertaining to a barrister as in *Rondel v. Worsley*, Chap. 18, (3) **1**.

36. D. & F. Estates Ltd v. Church Commissioners for England [1989] A.C. 177; [1988] 2 All E.R. 992, H.L.

See Chap. 18, (6) **63**.

37. Gunn v. Wallsend Slipway and Engineering Company Ltd, *The Times*, January 23, 1989; [1989] C.L.Y. 2548, C.A.

Plaintiff's wife contracted mesothelioma and died as a result of inhaling asbestos dust between 1948 and 1965 when washing plaintiff's clothes which were often impregnated with dust during plaintiff's employment by defendant *Held*, defendant owed no duty of care to plaintiff's wife, because it could not reasonably have foreseen risk of injury to her from such exposure, in absence before 1965 of any relevant medical, industrial or official publications and of any approved practice as to storage and washing of working clothes.

38. Calveley v. Chief Constable of the Merseyside Police [1989] A.C. 1228; [1989] 1 All E.R. 1025, H.L.

Officers' claim for variously anxiety, vexation, depressive illness, and loss of overtime earnings during and due to suspension or dismissal caused by negligent investigation of their conduct—*Held*, contrary to public policy that any duty of care actionable; alternatively claim for economic loss; or injury not reasonably foreseeable.

39. Mills v. Winchester Diocesan Board of Finance [1989] Ch. 428; [1989] 2 All E.R. 317, Knox. J.

Assumed objects of charitable trust claimed damages from Charity Commissioners for their assumed negligent advice to trustees as to the meaning of the trust as a result of which the objects had suffered damage injury and distress—*Held*, there was no sufficient proximity between the objects and the Commissioners nor was it just or equitable for there to be a duty of care, in particular where there was a right of appeal against any action proposed on the basis of the commissioners' advice; *Hedley Byrne* of no application, there being no reliance by the objects on the advice.

40. Davis v. Radcliffe [1990] 1 W.L.R. 821; [1990] 2 All E.R. 536, P.C.

For details see Chap. 18(2) **28**.

41. R. v. H. M. Treasury, ex p. Petch [1990] C.O.D. 19: [1991] C.L.Y. 2724, Popplewell J.

Former assistant secretary dismissed from civil service; he claimed, *inter alia*, damages for anxiety and distress caused by negligent delay in dealing with claim to a pension—*Held*, *inter alia*; minister owed duty of care; there was foreseeability that delay would cause him some damage; there was a relationship of proximity "equivalent to contract" and it would not be unjust or unreasonable to impose such a duty of care; on the facts no breach.

For further detail see Chap. 18, (13) **63**.

42. Murphy v. Brentwood D.C. [1991] 1 A.C. 398; [1990] 2 All E.R. 908, H.L.

Local authority approved plans for concrete raft foundation for a building pursuant to statutory obligation and after taking advice from independent consulting engineers. Plaintiff purchased the house; the raft was inadequately designed and cracks appeared in walls and gas and soil pipes cracked; plaintiff sold at price taking account of the defects—*Held*, where defects which would render the structure dangerous are discovered in time to avert the possibility of injury or damage then the cost of repair or loss of value is pure economic loss and therefore irrecoverable. *Anns* **10** departed from in so far as it imposed any private law duty of care on local authorities in relation to their function of taking steps to secure compliance with building by laws and regulations. *Dutton v. Bognor Regis UDC* **8** overruled and all cases subsequent to *Anns* decided in reliance on it. *Per* Lord Bridge: *Junior Books* **15** understandable only on basis of a situation where, even in the absence of contract, there is a special relationship of proximity between a builder or building owner which is sufficiently akin to contract to introduce the element of reliance so that that the scope of the duty of care owed by the builder to the owner is wide enough to embrace purely economic loss.

43. Department of the Environment v. Thomas Bates & Son Ltd. [1991] 1 A.C. 499; [1990] 2 All E.R. 943, H.L.

Concrete pillars in building found to be substandard. The builders were held not liable to the sublessees for the cost of strengthening the pillars; such work was carried out to cure a defect which otherwise prevented them making full use of the building to the extent for which it was designed; there was no imminent danger to health or safety; the cost of such work was pure economic loss. *Murphy v. Brentwood D.C.*, **42** applied.

44. Pitts v. Hunt [1991] 1 Q.B. 24; [1990] 3 All E.R. 344, C.A.

Plaintiff aged 18 and friend aged 16 spent evening drinking together. Set off home on friend's motor cycle—plaintiff as pillion passenger. Friend had drunk so much he was unfit to drive, as plaintiff would have realised had he been in a proper state. Friend also unlicensed and uninsured, to plaintiff's knowledge. Friend, encouraged by plaintiff, deliberately drove in dangerous manner. Friend killed and plaintiff injured in head on collision, not fault of other driver. Plaintiff sued friend's personal representative—*Held*, plaintiff not entitled to recover on grounds of application of maxim *ex turpi causa non oritur actio* and of public policy, and because the serious circumstances precluded the Court from finding that the friend owed any duty of care to plaintiff. Further, had not section 148 (3) of the Road Traffic Act 1972 prevented defendant from raising a defence of *volenti non fit injuria*, that defence would have succeeded.

45. Gala v. Preston (1991) 172 C.L.R. 243; [1991] C.L.Y. 243, High Court of Australia

Held, driver of a vehicle which he and passenger had earlier stolen owed no duty of care to passenger injured by his careless driving, because the injury resulted from a serious criminal act in which both participated.

46. Hughes v. National Union of Mineworkers. [1991] I.C.R. 669: [1991] 4 All E.R. 278, May J.

Claim by police officer against, *inter alia*, chief constable in negligence for causing or permitting him to face picket line without support from behind as a result of which he suffered personal injury; struck out; public policy required that senior police officers should generally not be liable to their subordinates who might be injured by rioters or the like for on the spot operational decisions taken in the course of attempts to control serious public disorder.

47. Cohen v. Shaw [1991] C.L.Y. 5458

P brought an action against D in respect of death of her husband for herself and child *in utero*; on application to dismiss claim of child it was held that provided the child was born alive, *in utero* he was treated as if he had already been born whenever that was to his advantage.

48. Hewett v. Alf Brown's Transport [1992] I.C.R. 530; [1992] P.I.Q.R. P 199, C.A.

Plaintiff inhaled lead oxide powder when daily washing contaminated work clothes of her husband who was employed by defendant. Plaintiff particularly susceptible to effect of lead in her blood—*Held*, plaintiff's husband had not been exposed to significant risk of lead poisoning at work, and defendant neither negligent nor in breach of Control of Lead at Work Regulations 1980 in relation to him. Accordingly, defendant could not be liable to plaintiff, of whose susceptibility they were unaware.

49. Palmer v. London Borough of Harrow, *The Times*, April 22, 1992: [1992] 1 P.I.Q.R. P 296, Potter J.

Local authority pursuant to statutory obligations sent children with special educational needs to a boarding school whose headmaster sexually abused them. It was alleged the authority was negligent in sending or allowing them to go there—*Held*, no duty of care owed.

50. Nitrigin Eireann Teoranta v. Inco Alloys Ltd [1992] 1 W.L.R. 498; [1992] 1 All E.R. 854, May J.

Assumed facts that defendants negligent in manufacture of pipe; it was supplied and installed in plaintiff's plant; it cracked as result and was repaired by the plaintiff who did not appreciate the cause; the repair was inadequate and the pipe as a result burst and caused damage to other property namely the surrounding structure and plant—*Held*, no cause of action in negligence accrued at time of initial cracking as only loss purely economic; cause of action in negligence did accrue when pipe burst and caused damage to other property; *D. & F. Estates*, Chap. 18, (6) **63** and *Murphy v. Brentwood D.C.*, **42** considered. *Junior Books* **15** distinguished.

51. Burton v. Islington H. A. and De Martell v. Merton H. A. [1992] 3 All E.R. 833; [1992] 3 W.L.R. 637, C.A.

Plaintiffs injured when *in utero* by alleged negligence of defendant Health Authorities. As a result both suffered from considerable disabilities. On consolidated appeal—*Held*, that a child who was born suffering from disabilities caused by an injury before he had acquired legal status could bring an action in respect of such injuries because the law deemed him to be in existence at the date of the accident to his mother. Accordingly, a duty of care was owed to the unborn foetus.

52. Ephraim v. Newham L.B.C. (1993) 91 L.G.R. 412; [1993] P.I.Q.R. P 156, C.A.

Local authority pursuant to statutory duty advised plaintiff of where she might find accommodation; from that source she learnt of and found a room to rent in a house in multiple occupation; she there suffered injury due to inadequate fire precautions—*Held*, although sufficient degree of proximity it was not fair just or reasonable to impose a duty of care where the authority did not know of the inadequacy and where the imposition of such duty would oblige it to have inspected the property before giving such advice. (*Note*: Lessor held liable at first instance—for summary see Chap. 10,(1) **20**.

53. Topp v. London Country Bus (South West) [1993] 1 W.L.R. 979; [1993] 3 All E.R. 448, C.A.

Defendant's minibus left for over eight hours unlocked, unattended and with keys in at bus stop outside public house—unlawfully taken and driven into collision with cyclist—*Held*, defendant not liable—owed no duty of care to cyclist—acts of wrongdoer constituted *novus actus interveniens. P. Perl (Exporters) Ltd v. Camden L.B.C.* (Chap. 1(3)(b) **15**) followed.

54. Downsview Nominees Ltd v. First City Corporation Ltd [1993] A.C. 295; [1993] 3 All E.R. 626, P.C.
See further Chap. 18, (1) **22**.

55. Wood v. Law Society, *The Times*, July 30, 1993; [1993] C.L.Y. 3756, Otton J.

Held, the Law Society did not owe a duty of care to complainants at common law or under statute when exercising its investigative or disciplinary powers in respect of its members.

56. Hemmens v. Wilson Browne [1994] 2 W.L.R. 323; [1993] 4 All E.R. 826, Judge Moseley Q.C.

Solicitor drew a document entitling client's mistress to call for payment of £110,000; document unenforceable and client refused to pay—*Held*, not fair, just or reasonable to impose duty of care on solicitor when client still alive and able, if he wished, to put matters right. *Ross*, Chap. 18, (15) **17** and

White [1993] 3 All E.R. 481, C.A. now H.L. Chap. 18, (15) **76** distinguished. Claim failed on *Hedley Byrne* principles. *Caparo*, Chap. 18, (1) **17** applied.

57. Marc Rich & Co A.G. v. Bishops Rock Marine Co. Ltd [1994] 1 W.L.R. 1071; [1994] 12 C.L. 633, C.A.

Surveyor employed by classification society was allegedly negligent in permitting a vessel after repairs to continue her journey with the consequent loss of cargo; it was conceded the loss of the cargo was foreseeable and constituted physical damage to goods—*Held*, considerations of "proximity" and of whether it was fair just and reasonable to impose a duty of care as well as of foreseeability applied in cases involving physical damage as well as those involving pure economic loss. In the circumstances, in particular the relationship between cargo owner and ship owner and the absence of dealing between the surveyor and cargo owner there was not sufficient proximity nor was it just fair or reasonable to impose a duty of care on the surveyor in favour of the cargo owner.

Caparo, Chap. 18, (1) **17** and *Murphy v. Brentwood D.C.*, **42** applied. Affirmed, [1995] 3 W.L.R. 227, H.L.

58. M. v. Newham L.B.C. and X (Minors) v. Bedfordshire C.C. [1994] 2 W.L.R. 554; [1994] 4 All E.R. 602, C.A.

Neither an action for breach of statutory duty nor (by a majority) one for common law negligence could be maintained by a child against a local authority in respect of acts or omissions for which the authority was responsible in the exercise of its functions under child care legislation. Now in [1995] 3 W.L.R. 152, H.L.

59. Barrett v. Ministry of Defence [1995] 1 W.L.R. 1217; *The Times*, January 13, 1995, C.A.

Deceased, naval airman at base in Norway, drunk to excess, vomited, was left slumped on a chair and then carried unconscious to his cabin where he lay in coma, observed intermittently—died of aspiration of vomit. Defendant had failed to enforce disciplinary codes discouraging over-indulgence in alcohol. There were no clear orders from officers as to how deceased should have been treated after collapsing, and no adequate medical cover was available—*Held*:

(a) Defendant under no duty to take reasonable care to prevent deceased, a mature man, from abusing alcohol to extent he did. Until he became unconscious he alone was responsible for his condition. The Queen's Regulations and standing orders could not be equated with guidance given in Highway Code or factory safety pamphlets.
(b) After deceased collapsed, defendant negligent in failing properly to supervise and provide medical assistance for him.
(c) Deceased two-thirds to blame.

Note: At first instance [1993] C.L.Y. 2954, defence of *volenti* failed—deceased, with mind clouded by alcohol, had not voluntarily assumed risk of grave or fatal injury by continuing drinking.

60. White v. Jones, [1995] 2 W.L.R. 187; *The Times*, February 17, 1995, H.L.
For details see Chap. 18, (15) **76**.

(b) Abnormally Susceptible Persons

(*N.B.* See also Employers' Liability cases in Chap. 15, (2)(b).)

1. Dobbin v. Waldorf [1937] 1 All E.R. 331, Mr Comr. Proctor.

Plaintiff had bleached hair—because of this, defendant's permanent wave was liable to damage her hair—*Held*, defendant not liable for not warning plaintiff and for not carrying out a test.

2. Griffiths v. Conway [1939] 1 All E.R. 685, C.A.

Held, defendants not liable. *Applied* in **6**.

3. McLaughlin v. Trimmer (1946) 79 L1.L.R. 649, Denning J. and C.A.

Flash of light from stud-welding machine—sets up iritis—machine safe for normal user—but plaintiff had a particular susceptibility in the shape of a decayed tooth—*Held*, by Denning J., defendants not liable, but on appeal (unreported) defendants *held* liable. *N.B.* The appeal took place before transcripts were kept, so that any authority or precedent to be derived from the decision may be in doubt.

4. Pritchard v. Post Office (1950) W.N. 310; 94 S.J. 404, C.A.

Post office barrier round manhole—sufficient protection for ordinary members of the public—but plaintiff, being blind, walks into barrier—*Held*, county court judge was right in dismissing action on ground that defendants had fulfilled duty in protecting ordinary members of the public. *But* see **8**, where the ratio, though not the decision, was *disapproved*.

5. Board v. Thomas Hedley [1951] 2 All E.R. 431; [1951] W.N. 422, C.A.

Denning L.J. (432 D): "The product would, I think, be dangerous if it might affect normal users adversely, or even if it might effect adversely other users who had a higher degree of sensitivity than the normal, so long as they were not altogether exceptional."

6. Ingham v. Emes [1955] 2 Q.B. 366; [1955] 2 All E.R. 740, C.A.

Plaintiff in this case was suing on a warranty—*Held*, that the fact that the plaintiff knew, but did not disclose, that she was abnormally sensitive to the dye disabled her from suing. **2** *applied.*

7. Smith v. St. Helier H.M.C. *The Times*, May 10, 1956; [1956] C.L.Y. 5964, Devlin J.

Plaintiff washed with a strong solution of Dettol—gets dermatitis—on the evidence Dettol was normally safe to use even undiluted—plaintiff was one of a negligible number who were specially sensitive—*Held*, that as defendants could have no knowledge that plaintiff was so sensitive not liable.

8. Haley v. L.E.B. [1964] 3 All E.R. 185; [1965] A.C. 778, H.L.

Excavation in pavement—safeguards adequate for ordinary pedestrians, but not for blind persons—*Held*, defendants liable, as they owed a duty of care to blind persons as well as to ordinary people. Lord Reid (188 B) said that it would be a defence if the presence of blind persons was not reasonably foreseeable, or, if foreseeable, it was such a remote chance and protection was so difficult that it would be unreasonable to afford the latter; but on the facts neither of these applied. Lords Reid, Evershed and Hodson all cited with approval the definition of the standard of care given by Lord Sumner in *Glasgow Corporation v. Taylor* [1922] 1 A.C. 44, p. 67: "A measure of care appropriate to the inability or disability of those who are immature or feeble in body or mind is due from those who know of, or ought to anticipate, the presence of such persons within the scope and hazard of their own operations."

As a result the dictum of Lord Wright in *Bourhill v. Young* [1943] A.C. 92, p. 109, must be taken (though largely different in emphasis only) to be superseded. *Pritchard* **4** was approved as a decision in view of the fact that the defendants had erected a portable fence two feet high, but was disapproved as to its ratio that no duty was owed to blind persons as such.

9. Cook v. S [1967] 1 All E.R. 299; 1 W.L.R. 457, C.A.

Negligence of solicitor in handling divorce case for wife—as a result she developed an anxiety state and could not work—*Held*, damages therefor could not be recovered. "It was suggested in this case that the plaintiff was peculiarly liable to nervous shock. I am afraid that she was . . . . If this special circumstance had been brought home to the defendant, it might enlarge the area of foreseeability so as to make him liable; but it was not pleaded . . . . All the defendant knew was that she was a woman obviously highly strung and worried as any woman would be in the circumstances. That does not mean, however, that he should foresee that, if he was negligent, she would suffer injury to health." (Lord Denning M.R., 303 D).

10. Hewett v. Alf Brown's Transport [1992] I.C.R. 530; [1992] P.I.Q.R. P199, C.A.

Plaintiff inhaled lead oxide powder when daily washing contaminated work clothes of her husband who was employed by defendant. Plaintiff particularly susceptible to effect of lead in her blood—*Held*, plaintiff's husband had not been exposed to significant risk of lead poisoning at work, and defendant neither negligent nor in breach of Control of Lead at Work Regulations 1980 in relation to him. Accordingly, defendant could not be liable to plaintiff, of whose susceptibility they were unaware.

11. Reilly v. Mersey R.H.A. *The Independent*, April 29, 1994; [1994] C.L.Y. 1538, C.A.

Plaintiffs trapped in lift for just over one hour. Negligence against hospital occupiers alleged and proved, but plaintiffs failed on the basis that they suffered no recognisable psychiatric injury.

Claustrophobia and fear were ordinary human reactions which fell short of what was required to make the tort of negligence complete.

12. Walker v. Northumberland C. C. *The Times*, November 24, 1994; [1994] C.L.Y. 2278, Colman J.

Plaintiff, employed in defendant's social services department, came under increasingly intense pressure of work in 1980s—his requests for further staff were not met. Due to the pressure, he had a nervous breakdown in 1986. Returning in 1987 he advised his supervior that the pressure had to be relieved, but only very limited assistance was provided. Plaintiff had second breakdown later in 1987 and had to retire—*Held.*

(a) There was no logical reason for psychiatric injury to be excluded from scope of employer's duty to provide safe system of work.
(b) First breakdown not reasonably foreseeable.
(c) After plaintiff's return his supervior should have foreseen that if again exposed to same workload he was at risk of another breakdown. Continuous or substantial assistance should have been provided. Defendant negligent in not having done so, despite the constraints imposed by its budget, and although provision of further assistance might have disrupted provision of services to the public.

U1. Spedding v. Dixons Group Plc (1986) C.A. 986

Occupier of shop premises did not owe a duty of care to partially sighted elderly customer who tripped over edge of display stand.

(c) Mental Shock Cases

1. Owens v. Liverpool Corporation [1939] 1 K.B. 394; [1938] 4 All E.R. 727, C.A.

Plaintiff relatives of deceased in carriage following hearse—collision overturns coffin—*Held*, the right to damages for nervous shock extended to every case where injury by way of nervous shock resulted from negligent act of defendants.

2. Bourhill v. Young [1943] A.C. 92; [1942] 2 All E.R. 396, H.L.

Fishwife heard noise of collision forty-five feet away while she was on blind side of stationary tramcar—had a stillborn child as a result of shock and fright—*Held*, defendant not liable, as plaintiff was outside the range of persons to whom damage might reasonably be anticipated as likely to occur.

3. Dooley v. Cammell Laird [1951] 1 Lloyd's Rep. 271, Donovan J.

Held, defendants liable.

4. King v. Phillips [1953] 1 Q.B. 429; [1953] 1 All E.R. 617, C.A.

Defendant taxi-driver backs taxi over child—mother in house seventy yards away heard child scream and saw taxi back into child's tricycle—could not see child—*Held*, mother could not recover, because (*per* Singleton and Hodson L.JJ. (621 A and 624 H)) the driver could not reasonably have contemplated damage to mother from his action. **2** applied.

5. Schneider v. Eisovitch [1960] 2 Q.B. 430; [1960] 1 All E.R. 169, Paull J.

Plaintiff's husband killed and plaintiff injured by negligence of defendant—plaintiff was knocked unconscious in the accident and only knew of husband's death when told in hospital—mental shock as a result—*Held*, plaintiff could claim damages for shock, as "the difference between seeing and hearing is immaterial" (175 C).

6. Boardman v. Sanderson [1964] 1 W.L.R. 1317, C.A.

Defendant reversing his car in courtyard of garage—negligently ran over foot of boy aged eight—father of boy was in garage office at the time, having gone there at defendant's request to pay a bill—father heard screams of son and rushed out—sustains shock as a result—*Held*, defendant liable for damages (£75) for shock, as (*per* Ormerod L.J.) "all the necessary factors were present." *N.B.* One of the most important factors seems to have been that the defendant actually knew that the father was in the immediate vicinity.

7. Lawrence v. Evans (1965) 196 E.G. 407; [1965] C.L.Y. 2672, Paull J.

Held, defendants not liable.

8. Cook v. S. [1967] 1 W.L.R. 457; [1967] 1 All E.R. 299, C.A.

Held, that though action against solicitor lay in contract, damages for nervous shock were recoverable in contract, though in general it would not be reasonably foreseeable that such negligence would cause an actual breakdown in health (as opposed to mere injury to feelings, which would not in any event be recoverable), and therefore in general such a claim would fail on foreseeability. But if there was a known special propensity to nervous breakdown, this might enlarge the area of foreseeability so as to create liability. But it was not pleaded here; nor, although the plaintiff did prove that she had such a special propensity, was it proved that the defendant knew. All he was shown to know was that she was highly strung, which was not enough. Therefore, the claim failed.

9. Chadwick v. B.T.C. [1967] 1 W.L.R. 912; [1967] 2 All E.R. 945, Waller J.

Held, applying the principle in *Bourhill* **2**, defendants liable for nervous shock caused to rescuer at railway accident, even though such shock was not caused by fear for own safety or that of one's children.

10. Abramzik v. Brenner (1967) 65 D.L.R. (2d) 651, Saskatchewan C.A.

Held, no cause of action, as a reasonable man in the position of the defendant would not have foreseen shock resulting to mother, and nervous shock, other than that flowing from a physical injury, was a substantive test, and not a particular instance of damage flowing from a particular tort.

11. Carlin v. Helical Bar (1970) 9 K.I.R. 154, Rees J.

Held, defendant crane owners liable for driver's nervous shock.

12. McLoughlin v. O'Brian [1983] A.C. 410; [1982] 2 All E.R. 298, H.L.

Plaintiff's family involved in road traffic accident due to defendants' negligence. One child was killed and the rest of the family were injured. Plaintiff was then at home, two miles away. Shortly afterwards she was told of the accident and taken to hospital where she saw the injured and learnt of her child's death. As a result she suffered severe and persisting nervous shock, as was readily foreseeable. *Held*, that the defendants were liable to her. The test of liability was foreseeability of injury by shock, but their Lordships expressed different opinions as to whether this test was exclusive.

According to Lord Wilberforce, there is "a real need for the law to place some limitation on the extent of admissible claims." (304 F). There were three limiting factors: (i) the degree of relationship between the plaintiff and the victim. The law did not recognise the claim of "the ordinary bystander;" (ii) the degree of proximity of the plaintiff to the accident both in time and space; and (iii) the means by which the shock is caused. "The shock must come through sight or hearing of the event or of its immediate aftermath" (305 C).

Lords Edmund-Davies and Russell considered that, in appropriate circumstances, there might be policy factors which operated to defeat a plaintiff's claim, but there were no such factors in the present case. Lords Scarman and Bridge held that, in nervous shock cases, the sole criterion of liability was foreseeability of injury by shock, and the courts should not seek to set limits to such liability by reference to public policy. "Common law principle requires the judges to follow the logic of the 'reasonably foreseeable test' so as, in circumstances where it is appropriate to apply it, untrammelled by spatial, physical or temporal limits. Space time, distance, the nature of the injuries sustained and the relationship of the plaintiff to the immediate victim of the accident are factors to be weighed, but not legal limitations, when the test of reasonable foreseeability is to be applied." (Lord Scarman, 311 D).

13. Galt v. British Railways Board (1983) 133 New L.J. 870, Tudor Evans J.

Held that the defendants were liable in damages for the coronary attack and its consequences. They were in breach of their duty to take reasonable care not to expose the plaintiffs to injury from nervous shock.

14. Whitmore v. Euroway Expressway Coaches, *The Times*, May 4, 1984; [1984] C.L.Y. 1026, Comyn J.

Damages awarded to spouse for seeing other spouse severely injured, (but subsequently disapproved of in other cases because no identifiable psychiatric injury suffered.)

15. Brice v. Brown [1984] 1 All E.R. 997; (1984) 134 New L.J. 204, Stuart Smith J.

Once a plaintiff had established that tort complained of had caused nervous shock as a reasonably foreseeable consequence of negligence, it was immaterial that plaintiff has a highly vulnerable personality causing her to sustain very serious psychiatric condition.

16. Wigg v. British Railways Board, *The Times*, February 4, 1986; [1986] C.L.Y. 2280, Tucker J.

A train driver was entitled to succeed in a claim for damages where he came across the body of a victim struck by his train as it pulled away, and after he had descended his cab to search for him—*Held*, that whilst each nervous shock case should be tried on its own merits, a rescuer was assumed to be a person of normal disposition and it was reasonably foreseeable that the driver would behave as he did, and suffer harm accordingly—a duty of care was owed by the employers of which they were in breach.

17. Attia v. British Gas [1988] Q.B. 304; [1987] 3 All E.R. 455, C.A.

P claimed damages for psychiatric injury caused through seeing her property on fire as a result of D's negligence—*Held*, damages for nervous shock as a result of witnessing the consequences of negligence were not limited to psychiatric damage through witnessing injury to another, but could be recovered where P witnessed the destruction of property such as his home and possessions. A question of fact to be determined in each case.

18. Alcock v. Chief Constable Of South Yorkshire [1992] 1 A.C. 310; [1991] 3 W.L.R. 1057; H.L. Disaster at football stadium caused by D's negligence. Live pictures of the event had been broadcast on television, and the question arose as to whether relatives of the victims who either saw the events from other parts of the stadium, or who saw on television, or heard on radio and suffered nervous shock in consequence could recover damages—*Held*, each P. failed to show such injury was reasonably foreseeable and/or relationship between P. and victim was sufficiently close based on ties of love and affection and/or sufficient propinquity in time or space to accident or immediate aftermath.

19. Ravenscroft v. Rederiaktiebozaget Transatlantic [1991] 3 All E.R. 73, Ward J.

Held, mother can recover damages for nervous shock suffered through death of son in accident which she did not witness. But reversed [1992] 2 All E.R. 470, *The Times*, April 6, 1992, C.A., in the light of *Alcock* **18**.

20. Nicholls v. Rushton, *The Times*, June 19, 1992; [1992] C.L.Y. 3252, C.A.

A plaintiff who was involved in a road traffic accident who suffered no physical injury, but experienced a nervous reaction falling short of psychological illness was not entitled to damages for "shock and shaking up"

21. Hevican v. Ruane [1991] 3 All E.R. 65; [1992] C.L.Y. 3251, Mantell J.

Held, a parent may recover damages for nervous shock caused by death of a child in a car crash, even if he did not witness it—psychological illness is reasonably foreseeable.

22. Taylor v. Somerset Health Authority [1993] 4 Med L R 34; [1993] P.I.Q.R. P262, Auld J.

Nervous shock at viewing corpse.

23. Page v. Smith [1994] 4 All E.R. 523, C.A.

Plaintiff develops myalgic encephalitis as a result of road traffic accident—*Held*, no liability, because a plaintiff who claims damages for nervous shock as a consequence of an accident, in which there was no physical injury, had to show that a psychiatric injury was foreseeable, and would be such that would be suffered by a person of ordinary fortitude and phlegm. Reversed, [1995] 2 W.L.R. 644, H.L.

U1. Taylorson v. Shieldness Produce Ltd (1994) C.A. 145

P's son severely injured when falling off delivery wagon. Deteriorated and subsequently died in hospital. Parents claimed damages for nervous shock and mental injury upon hearing of the accident and upon witnessing the deteriorating condition of the son—*Held*, defendants not liable. *Alcock v. Chief Constable of South Yorkshire* **18** applied.

(d) Rescuers

(*N.B.* Cases of *firemen* injured on burning premises are dealt with in Chap. 10, (5) (c)

Plaintiff's van causing defendant's unbraked compressor to run downhill—no novus actus or contributory negligence. U1

1. Morgan v. Aylen [1942] 1 All E.R. 489, Cassels J.

Plaintiff escorting child of $3\frac{1}{2}$ home—child ran into road—defendant on his motor-cycle was coming too fast—plaintiff ran into road to rescue child—plaintiff hit by motor-cycle—*Held*, defendant liable. "What plaintiff did here was, in the circumstances, natural and proper" (491 A).

2. Hyett v. G.W.R. [1948] 1 K.B. 345; [1947] 2 All E.R. 264; C.A.

Plaintiff, invitee on defendants' premises, attempts to put out fire caused by defendants' negligence—*Held*, not *novus actus* and plaintiff would recover. "It is no doubt in every case relevant to consider whether or not it is life or property which is in danger. It is material to consider the relationship of the plaintiff who intervenes to the property or person in peril. It is relevant to consider the degree of danger and risk, and so forth. ... The act of plaintiff ... was the kind of act which defendants might reasonably have anticipated as likely to follow from their act of negligence ... " (266 C-F, *per* Tucker L.J.).

3. Carmarthenshire C.C. v. Lewis [1955] A.C. 549; [1955] 1 All E.R. 565, H.L.

Lord Reid (572 A): "And once the child was in the street anything might happen. It was argued that it might be reasonable to foresee injury to the child but not reasonable to foresee that the child's action would cause injury to others. I can see no force in that. One knows that every day people take risks in order to save others from being run over, and if a child wanders into the street the danger to others is almost as great as the danger to the child."

4. Baker v. Hopkins [1959] 1 W.L.R. 966; [1959] 3 All E.R. 225, C.A.

Doctor went down gas-filled well to rescue two men who due to negligence of defendant had succumbed to fumes—doctor himself is overcome and dies—*Held*, defendant liable, as it was a natural and proper consequence of defendant's negligence that someone would attempt to rescue them.

5. Videan v. British Transport Commission [1963] 2 Q.B. 650; [1963] 2 All E.R. 860; C.A.

Stationmaster killed rescuing his son who had strayed on to railway line—son could not recover, but could the stationmaster's widow?—*Held*, yes. The reasons for this decision differ, Lord Denning M.R. (868 C) holding that the right of the rescuer was independent of that of the person rescued, and the fact that the latter was a trespasser was immaterial, the criterion being whether the defendant ought to have anticipated that an emergency might arise. Pearson L.J. and Harman L.J. based their decision on the fact that the stationmaster was an employee of the defendants, whose presence on the line they ought accordingly to have anticipated, and Pearson L.J. (876 G) inclined to the view that, in an ordinary case of rescue, a rescuer could not be in any better position than the person rescued (so that, if the person rescued was a trespasser, the rescuer would ordinarily have no claim).

6. Chadwick v. British Transport Commission [1967] 2 All E.R. 945; 1 W.L.R. 912, Waller J.

Held, defendants liable for nervous shock suffered by rescuer.

7. Attorney-General for Ontario v. Keller (1978) 86 D.L.R. (3d) 426; [1979] C.L.Y. 2089, Ont. H.C.J.

8. Harrison v. British Railways Board [1981] 3 All E.R. 679, Boreham J.

Stationmaster (going off duty) tried to board moving train, recklessly endangering himself. It was foreseeable that the guard of the train would try to help him and would probably endanger himself, which is what happened. *Held*, stationmaster liable. There was no reason in principle why a person who negligently endangered himself should not owe a duty of care to a foreseeable rescuer. Also *held*, on the facts, that B.R.B. were not liable for lack of supervision and that the stationmaster was not acting in the course of his employment; and that there was 20 per cent contributory negligence for failing to apply the brakes.

9. Crossley v. Rawlinson [1981] 3 All E.R. 674; 125 S.J. 865, R.H. Tucker Q.C. as D.H.C.J.

Due to defendant's negligence, tarpaulin on his lorry caught fire. Plaintiff (an AA patrolman) ran towards the lorry with fire extinguisher, his foot went into a hole in grass verge, so that he fell. *Held*, defendant not liable, as the injury was too remote. While it was foreseeable that plaintiff would run to lorry, it was not reasonably foreseeable that he would be injured while running.

10. Knightley v. Johns [1982] 1 W.L.R. 349; [1982] 1 All E.R. 851, C.A.
See fuller statement of the law, Chap. 1(4) **15**

11. Wigg v. British Railway Board, *The Times*, February 4, 1986; [1986] C.L.Y. 2280, Tucker J
See Chap. 1, (2)(c) **16** above for summary.

12. Ogwo v. Taylor [1988] A.C. 431; [1987] 3 All E.R. 961, H.L.

Plaintiff fireman injured when answering an emergency call in premises where fire started negligently by D's workman—*Held*, D liable, because it was reasonably foreseeable that firemen would have to attend a fire negligently started, and injury was foreseeable, whether fireman was taking an ordinary or an exceptional risk.

13. Borge v. Matthews [1988] C.L.Y. 2450, H.H. Judge Watkin Powell

For summary, see Chap. 8, (4) **34**.

U1. Wilson v. British Gas Corporation (1986) C.A. 1114

Plaintiff reversed van in crowded car park making minor impact with defendant's unbraked compressor which began to roll down hill; plaintiff ran and tried to apply handbrake but was injured when hit by its towbar: defendants held liable; the minor impact was not an intervening act which destroyed the defendant's negligence; the plaintiff was not negligent in trying to stop the compressor nor was he guilty of contributory negligence.

(3) Limits of Duty of Care

(a) How Far Duty Extends to Economic Loss

(*N.B.* Liability for economic loss arising from negligent misstatements is not included here, as such liability normally flows, subject only to factors such as *novus actus* and opportunity for intermediate discovery: see Chap. 19 generally on this. Nor is liability dealt with here where there is a concurrent contractual duty: see Chap. 18 on this.)

1. Weller v. Foot and Mouth Institute [1966] 1 Q.B. 569; [1965] 3 All E.R. 560; Widgery J.

Defendants negligently, as was assumed for argument, allowed virus to escape, which infected cattle, and so caused plaintiffs to lose profits of their cattle market—*Held*, defendants not liable, as they did not owe plaintiff any duty. *Applied* in **2** and **3**. Leaving aside the cases arising from negligent misstatements, the common law principle was that a duty of care arising from a risk of direct injury to person or property "is owed only to those whose person or property may foreseeably be injured by a failure to take care. If the plaintiff can show that the duty was owed to him, he can recover both direct and consequential loss which is reasonably foreseeable, and for myself I can see no reason for saying that proof of direct loss is an essential part of his claim. He must, however, show that he is within scope of the defendant's duty to take care" (570 D.) In the present case, the plaintiffs, as auctioneers, had no proprietary interest in anything which might be damaged if the virus escaped, and they were therefore not persons to whom a duty of care was owed. The following cases were applied: *Simpson v. Thomson* (1877) 3 App. Cas. 279 (no independent right of action in insurers against tortfeasors); *Société Anonyme v. Bennetta* [1911] 1 K.B. 243 (tug could not sue ship which sank tow for loss of towage charges); *Morrison v. Greystoke Castle* [1946] 2 All E.R. 696 (cargo owners able to sue other ship for contribution, since they were liable to general average); *Best v. Samuel Fox* [1952] 2 All E.R. 394 (wife has no right to sue tortfeasor for loss of consortium).

2. Margarine Union v. Cambay Prince [1969] 1 Q.B. 219; [1967] 3 All E.R. 775; Roskill J.

Admitted negligence by shipowners in failing to fumigate ship—as a result cockroaches attacked a cargo of copra—the plaintiff was a c.i.f. purchaser and only got his title to his parcels of copra when they were separated from bulk on discharge—the negligence occurred not later than the time of loading—*Held*, no action lay, for shipowners at the time of the negligent act owed no duty of care to anyone other than the owner of the goods. *Weller* **1** *applied.*

3. Electrochrome v. Welsh Plastics [1968] 2 All E.R. 205; [1968] C.L.Y. 2662, Geoffrey Lane J.

Lorry negligently damaged water hydrant on industrial estate—as a result plaintiff factory owners lost production—*Held*, applying *Weller* **1**, defendants not liable, as plaintiffs had no proprietary or possessory interest in the damaged hydrant. *N.B.* Nothing had been physically damaged in the factory. *cf.* **4**.

4. British Celanese v. Hunt [1969] 1 W.L.R. 959; [1969] 2 All E.R. 1252, Lawton J.

Strips of metal foil floated, due to defendants' negligence, onto busbars of an electrical sub-station (belonging to electricity board)—thereby cutting off power supplies to plaintiffs' factory and causing material being processed in machines to solidify—plaintiffs claimed damages in respect of the materials so wasted—*Held*, they could recover, as the defendants by their actions had caused injury to the plaintiffs' property, namely the machines and the materials, and such injury and damage was, on the facts, reasonably foreseeable. Lawton J. *considered* the dictum of Widgery J. in *Weller* **1** where the latter said: "A plaintiff . . . cannot recover if the act or omission did not directly injure, or at least threaten to injure, the plaintiff's person or property but merely caused consequential loss, as, for example, by upsetting the plaintiff's business relations with a third party who was the direct victim of the act or omission" and said that if by "direct victim" the immediate victim only was meant, he disagreed, and said that the duty included a duty to a victim whose person or property was injured by "the operation of the laws of nature without any human intervention," and that this included the plaintiffs in the present case (1299 H). He also *considered Electrochrome* **3**, and said that the decision could be distinguished on the ground that the damage there was not foreseeable (1260 F.) *Approved* by C.A. in *S.C.M.* **5** by Lord Denning M. R. and Buckley L. J. on the ground that the negligence of the defendants did cause damage to the plaintiffs' property, albeit (*per* Lord Denning M. R.) it was indirect damage.

5. S.C.M. v. Whittall [1971] 1 Q.B. 137; [1970] 3 All E.R. 245, C.A.

Electric cable in road cut by contractors—power failure which cut off current to many factories for over seven hours—plaintiffs had molten material in their machines which solidified as a result—

Held, the plaintiffs could recover damages for the damage to the machines and for the loss of profit consequential thereon, but not for the economic loss flowing generally from the power failure, as the duty of care extended only to material damage and not to economic loss in itself. *N.B.* Strictly the judgments in dealing with economic loss in itself are *obiter*, as the plaintiff in the C.A. expressly disclaimed this part of the claim, so that the real contest was in respect of the damage to the machines and the consequential loss flowing therefrom.

6. Spartan Steel v. Martin [1973] Q.B. 27; [1972] 3 All E.R. 557, C.A.

Electric cable cut by contractors—power off for some 14 hours—plaintiffs had molten metal in a furnace which was damaged—and they lost further production during the time the power was off—*Held*, following *S.C.M.* **5**, the plaintiffs could recover for the damaged metal, but (2–1) not for the purely economic loss constituted by the loss of production. The question whether the test in this class of case lay in duty or remoteness was *discussed* by Lord Denning M. R., who said (562 G): "I think the time has come to discard these tests which have proved so elusive. It seems to me better to consider the particular relationship in hand and see whether or not as a matter of policy, economic loss should be recoverable." In this connection there were five considerations to be taken into account: (1) statutory undertakers were in a not dissimilar position, yet they were never liable for economic damage (though their liability for physical damage was not wholly clear); (2) the hazard of cutting off a power cable was one which applied to everyone, and was often due to pure accident; (3) there would be no end of claims if economic damage were recoverable; (4) the hazard was one which was better suffered by the community as a whole; and (5) the law did allow some measure of compensation in respect of the physical damage, if any.

7. Caltex Oil v. Willemstad [1979] C.L.Y. 1864; 51 A.L.J.R. 270, High Court of Australia

Pipeline belonging to X but used by plaintiff for the transport of his oil was fractured by defendant's negligence—*Held*, defendant liable to plaintiff for the economic loss caused by the extra expense of an alternative means of transport. The Court said that, while in general economic loss which was not consequential upon injury to person or property could not be claimed (even if foreseeable), yet such loss could be the subject of a claim where defendant had knowledge or means of knowledge that a particular person, not merely a member of an unascertained class, would be likely to suffer economic loss as a result of his negligence.

N.B. In *Ross v. Caunters* [1980] Ch. 297; [1979] 3 All E.R. 580, at 597 E, Megarry V.C. said, *obiter*, that this case was "plainly a *terminus a quo* for any further investigation of the subject." See below **8**.

8. Ross v. Caunters [1980] Ch. 297; [1979] 3 All E.R. 580, Megarry V.C.

Testator instructed his solicitor to draft a will giving legacy to plaintiff. Through oversight the solicitor allowed plaintiff's husband to attest the will. *Held*, solicitor owed a duty of care to the legatee and was liable (for details see Chap. 7, (1)(a) **16**); and *held*, also, the fact that the claim was purely for financial loss was no bar to liability for that loss (596 E). In deciding the latter point, the judge reviewed cases such as *S.C.M.* **5** and *Spartan* **6** and said that in time the proper test to be applied in such cases would evolve (598 D), but whichever test did evolve, the facts in the present case were sufficiently close to *Ministry of Housing v. Sharp* (Chap. 19(b)**6**) (where a local land registrar negligently issued a clear certificate to a purchaser who thereby took free from the plaintiff's incumbrance) and concluded the matter in favour of the plaintiff, particularly as in both cases (a) the defendant ought to have contemplated that his negligent omissions would injure the plaintiff, an identified or identifiable person, and (b) there was no possible liability for an indeterminate amount to an indeterminate number of persons (596 D).

N.B. As thus analysed, *Sharp* clearly is of wider authority than for negligent misstatements alone, for no misstatement was made to the plaintiff incumbrancer. At the same time the judgments show that the issue as argued turned in large part round the applicability of *Hedley Byrne* (Chap. 19(a)**1**), *i.e.* the leading case on negligent misstatements (in which field liability for economic loss, once breach of duty is established, normally flows), and perhaps because of this it does not appear that liability for economic loss was strongly contested either at first instance ([1969] 3 All E.R. 225) or in C.A. ([1970] 1 All E.R. 1009).

9. Lambert v. Lewis [1982] A.C. 225; [1981] 1 All E.R. 1185, H.L.

Manufacturer produced a defective trailer coupling, which was acquired by a dealer and sold by him to a farmer. The coupling broke when used on a road by the farmer and caused physical injuries. The dealer could not identify the person from whom he had bought the coupling, so that he could not pass on any contractual liability. The question was whether the dealer, being contractually liable to the farmer, could claim equivalent damages in tort from the manufacturer. The Court of Appeal ([1980] 1 All E.R. 978) had ruled that he could not, as damage under *D v. S* was restricted to damage by physical injury, and did not extend to economic loss. H.L. held that the dealer was not liable, on the ground that the whole fault was that of the farmer, so that the view expressed by C.A. became immaterial. Lord Diplock (all other Law Lords concurring) *said* (1192 C) *obiter* words to the effect that the House of Lords did not agree with view expressed by the Court of Appeal.

10. The Irene's Success [1982] Q.B. 481; [1982] 2 W.L.R. 422, Lloyd J.

Plaintiff was the c.i.f. buyer of a complete cargo of coal on defendant's ship. During voyage, coal was damaged, allegedly due to defendant's negligence. The plaintiff could not sue in contract because he was not the holder of a bill of lading. Issue was whether he could sue defendant in tort, even though he did not own the goods when the damage occurred—*Held*, not following *Margarine Union* **2** and distinguishing *Weller* **1**, plaintiff could sue, as there was a sufficient relationship of proximity between plaintiff as a c.i.f. buyer and defendant as the ocean carrier that defendant ought reasonably to have contemplated that carelessness on its part in carrying the coal would be likely to cause damage to plaintiff, and there were no policy factors negativing liability.

11. Junior Books v. Veitchi [1983] A.C. 520; [1982] 3 All E.R. 201, H.L.

Plaintiffs commissioned a factory. Defendants were nominated as specialist sub-contractors to lay a concrete floor in main production area. No contractual relationship between plaintiff and defendants. Floor developed cracks, allegedly due to defendants' negligence. Cracks did not involve any risk to person or other property but it was necessary for the floor to be replaced. Plaintiffs sued defendants in negligence for cost of remedial work and consequential economic loss. Defendants raised preliminary point that, in the absence of a contractual relationship between the parties or risk of damage to the person or other property, the plaintiffs had not disclosed a good cause of action—

Held, that in the circumstances the defendants owed to the plaintiffs a duty to take reasonable care to avoid acts or omissions which they ought to have known would cause the plaintiffs pure economic loss (as opposed to physical damage to person or property) and accordingly the plaintiffs' pleading disclosed a good cause of action. The majority of the House (Lords Fraser, Russell and Roskill), held that as (a) the proximity between the parties was so close as to fall only just short of a direct contractual relationship, (b) the defendants must have known that the plaintiffs relied on their skill and experience in laying a floor satisfying the plaintiffs' requirements, and (c) the loss sustained by the plaintiffs, although financial only, was a direct and foreseeable consequence of the alleged negligence, the duty of care owed by the defendants extended to avoiding such loss. See particularly at 213 J to 214 B where Lord Roskill lists nine factors of crucial importance in establishing the necessary degree of proximity between the parties to give rise to a duty to take reasonable care not to cause the plaintiff financial loss. Lord Keith held that as the plaintiffs' claim was based on their loss of profit resulting from the high cost of maintaining a defective floor, they were seeking to mitigate their loss by replacing the floor itself, and the cost of replacement was the appropriate measure of the defendants' liability. The House reserved its views as to whether a manufacturer or a contractor who provides an article which is defective but not dangerous is liable to a subsequent purchaser who suffers economic loss only as a result of the defect. As the standard required for the article may have been defined by the contract between the manufacturer or contractor and the original purchaser (including any relevant exclusion clause), it would be difficult to define the standard required to discharge any duty of care to a subsequent purchaser and such purchaser may not be entitled to any greater protection than that owed to the original purchaser. Considered in *D. & F. Estates*, Chap. 18 (6) **63**. Explained in *Murphy*, Chap. 18 (13) **66**.

12. Nicholls v. Richmond Corporation [1983] C.L.Y. 43; [1983] B.C.L.R. 169, British Columbia C.A.

13. Southern Water Authority v. Lewis & Duvivier (1984) 27 BLR 111; [1984] C.L.Y. 239, Judge Smout Q.C.

Owner of sewerage scheme built under contract between its predecessor and subcontractor sued latter in tort for negligent design, supply and installation—*Held*, although in ordinary course there was sufficient proximity between a subcontractor and building owner who had suffered damage, taking over certificates excluded all liability in tort.

14. Southern Water Authority v. Lewis & Duvivier (No. 2) (1984–85) 1 Const. L.J. 74: [1985] C.L.Y. 2331, Judge Smout Q.C.

Consulting engineers claimed subcontractor for sewerage works owed a duty of care to them in relation to the quality and fitness of the subcontract works and that they were entitled to recover as damages the damages and interest they were liable to pay the water authority for their failure properly to supervise the subcontract works—*Held*, no duty of care owed; in any event the damages were irrecoverable as being pure economic loss.

15. Victoria University of Manchester v. Hugh Wilson & Lewis Womersley & Pochin (Contractors) Ltd (1985) 2 Con L.R. 43; [1985] C.L.Y. 220, Judge Newey Q.C.

Ceramic tile cladding to reinforced concrete building in due course fell off to a large extent. It was found *inter alia* that the architect did not owe a duty of care to the main contractor in relation to inspection of the subcontractor's work; further that the subcontractor owed a duty in tort of negligence to the plaintiffs—*Junior Books* **11** relied on. For further details see Chap. 18, (6)**43**.

16. Clarke v. Bruce Lance & Co. [1988] 1 W.L.R., [1988] 1 All E.R. 364, C.A.

Testator left freehold interest in a garage to plaintiff and wife in his will; testator later instructed solicitors to draw up option to purchase garage to its lessees exercisable after death of testator and his wife. On testator's death plaintiff claimed solicitors should have advised testator that granting of option was misconceived, uncommercial and prejudicial to plaintiff—*Held*, no duty of care owed by the solicitors to plaintiff. *Yuen Kun Yeu v. Att.-Gen. of Hong Kong*, Chap. 18, (2)**26** followed. *Ross v. Caunters* **8** distinguished.

17. Simaan General Contracting Co. v. Pilkington Glass Ltd (No. 2) [1988] Q.B. 758; [1988] 1 All E.R. 791, C.A.

Defendants supplied green double glazed panels to others who incorporated them in a building as subcontractors; building owner withheld monies due to main contractor on the ground that the colouring was inconsistent—*Held*, defendants owed no duty of care to main contractors for such pure economic loss. *Junior Books* **11** distinguished.

18. Ernst & Whinney v. Willard Engineering (Dagenham) Ltd (1988) 40 BLR 67, Judge John Davies Q.C.

Consulting engineers designed and subcontractors installed airconditioning system in building for freeholders. Subsequent lessee sued both in negligence—*Held*, assuming negligence and breach of contract with freeholders, it was not just or reasonable to impose liability in tort; in any event the claim was for pure economic loss. *Junior Books* **11** and *Anns*, Chap. **1**, (2)(a) **10** considered.

19. University of Warwick v. Sir Robert McAlpine (1988) 42 BLR 1; [1989] C.L.Y. 219, Garland J.

Third defendant recommended process of resin bonding to resolve problems of defective tile cladding and became subcontractor for remedial work—*Held*, subcontractor knew or ought to have known of the risk of damage being caused by resin to tiles and was in breach of duty of care in not warning employer; the damage was not purely economic loss. *Simaan* **17** and *Greater Nottingham* **21** considered.

20. Surrey Heath Borough Council v. Lovell Construction Ltd (1988) 42 BLR 25; [1989] C.L.Y. 218, Judge Fox-Andrews Q.C.

Building owner claimed against subcontractor in tort for loss and damage caused by fire negligently caused by him. Subcontractor conceded a duty was owed to take reasonable care to avoid direct damage to the owner's property—*Held*, subcontractor liable for such damage and consequential costs so far as such sums were not recoverable by insurance; no recovery allowed for pure economic loss.

21. Greater Nottingham Cooperative Society Ltd v. Cementation Piling & Foundations Ltd [1989] Q.B. 71; [1988] 2 All E.R. 971, C.A.

Negligent piling by nominated subcontractor caused physical damage to adjoining premises for which liability admitted. Employer claimed damages for economic loss, namely, that caused by delay in deciding how to proceed to completion of piling work, additional cost to employers under main contract and for loss and expense claims caused by delay under main contract—*Held*, no liability (there being no breach of the collateral agreements between subcontractor and employer which did not relate to the manner of carrying out work); there was no assumption of responsibility by subcontractor for economic loss; any duty of care to prevent such loss was negated and, as a matter of policy, no such liability arose.

22. D. & F. Estates Ltd v. Church Commissioners for England [1989] A.C. 177; [1988] 2 All E.R. 992, H.L.

The plaintiff was tenant of a flat in a block built some time previously by the defendant's main contractor; his subcontractor had carried out defective plasterwork in the flat as a result of which it became loose and partly fell down. The plaintiff's claim for the cost of the replastering failed as being a claim for pure economic loss and outside the principle of *Hedley Byrne*; there was no room for the application of the *Donoghue v. Stevenson* principle where a hidden defect in a permanent structure was discovered before any injury to the person or damage to property other than the structure had occurred. *Quaere* whether in the case of a complex structure *Donoghue v. Stevenson* could apply where a hidden defect in one part damaged another part of such structure. (*Dutton*, Chap. 18, (13) **2** and *Anns* Chap. 18, (13) **5** considered: *Batty*, Chap. 18, (6) **18** doubted.)

23. Calveley v. Chief Constable of the Merseyside Police [1989] A.C. 1228; [1989] 1 All E.R. 1025, H.L.

Various officers claimed damages for variously anxiety, vexation, depressive illness and loss of overtime earnings during and due to periods of suspension or dismissal and allegedly due to negligent conduct of investigations into their conduct—*Held*, no cause of action: injury alleged was either not reasonably foreseeable or was pure economic loss; alternatively contrary to public policy that cause of action should arise.

24. University Court of the University of Glasgow v. William Whitfield (1988) 42 BLR 66; [1989] C.L.Y. 2539, Judge Bowsher Q.C.

Architect held liable to university for negligent advice and design of art gallery whereby leaks and condensation occurred; architect sought contribution from main contractor but held not entitled, *inter alia*, because loss claimed was pure economic loss, namely, the architect's liability to the university.

25. Cosgrove & Cosgrove v. Weeks (1989) 14 Con L.R. 119; [1990] C.L.Y. 3795, Judge Newey Q.C.

See Chap. 18, (6) **68**.

26. Reid v. Rush & Tompkins Group PLC [1990] 1 W.L.R. 212; [1989] 3 All E.R. 228, C.A.

Plaintiff employee whilst working in Ethiopia suffered injury in road traffic accident caused by a third party's negligence. He alleged his employers should either have taken out insurance to cover him against such eventuality or have advised him to do so himself, there being no compulsory third party motor insurance scheme in that country—*Held*, no term could be implied into the contract to provide or to advise taking out such insurance; there was no duty on a master to take reasonable care to protect a servant from suffering economic loss; there was no voluntary assumption of responsibility by the defendants towards the plaintiff under *Hedley Byrne* principles.

27. Murphy v. Brentwood D.C. [1991] 1 A.C. 398; [1990] 2 All E.R. 908, H.L.

Where defects which would render a structure dangerous are discovered in time to avert the possibility of injury or damage the cost of repair or loss of value is pure economic loss and irrecoverable. For further detail see Chap. 18, (13) **66**.

28. Department of the Environment v. Thomas Bates & Son Ltd [1991] 1 A.C. 499; [1990] 2 All E.R. 943, H.L.

For details see Chap. 1, (2)(a) **43**.

29. Lancashire & Cheshire Association of Baptist Churches Inc. v. Howard & Seddon Partnership [1993] 3 All E.R. 467; (1993) 65 BLR 21, Judge Kershaw Q.C.

Plaintiff's claim against architect in contract and tort for negligent design; contract claim statute barred; as to the tort claim, on the evidence the submission of drawings did not equate to a statement express or implied as to the technical qualities of the building nor did the plaintiffs rely on them as such, any reliance being upon the earlier implied term that the architect would prepare technically sound designs; *Hedley Byrne* did not therefore apply and there could be no recovery for the economic loss. *Midland Bank v. Hett Stubbs*, Chap. 18(15) **22** followed: *Tai Hing*, Chap. 18, (2) **23** and *Junior Books* **11** considered.

(b) How Far Duty Arises in Respect of Omissions to Act

1. E. Suffolk Rivers C.B. v. Kent [1941] A.C. 74; [1940] 4 All E.R. 527, H.L.

Defendants had statutory power (but *not* duty) to repair river banks—plaintiff's bank was breached and defendants went to repair it—they did this negligently, so that plaintiff's land was flooded, but not more so than if defendants had not acted—*Held*, that since defendants were under a power and not a duty to act, they would not have been liable if they had omitted to act, and having acted they were still not liable, for their negligent repairs had not added to the damage plaintiff would have suffered had they done nothing.

2. Butler v. Alcock [1941] 3 All E.R. 411, C.A.

An approved society, having *power* to institute proceedings under its rules on behalf of its members, fails to bring action within statutory period—*Held*, society not liable.

3. The Majfrid [1942] P. 145; 58 T.L.R. 385, C.A.

Plaintiff's barge moored at second defendants' wharf—first defendants improperly moved it to position of danger—second defendants stood by, saying nothing, although they knew the position was dangerous, and later took no steps to get the barge afloat in time to save serious damage—*Held*, second defendants not liable, as they were under no duty to act.

4. Deyong v. Shenburn [1946] K.B. 227; [1946] 1 All E.R. 226, C.A.

du Parcq L.J. (229 G): "It is not true to say that wherever a man finds himself in such a position that unless he does a certain act another person may suffer . . . then it is his duty . . . to be careful to do the act. Any such proposition is much too wide."

5. Goldman v. Hargrave [1967] 1 A.C. 645; [1966] 2 All E.R. 989, P.C.

Redgum tree, hit by lightning, catches fire—occupier cuts it down and leaves it to burn out—flames fanned by wind carry to adjacent premises—*Held*, occupier owed duty of care to prevent spread of fire. "In such situations the standard of care ought to be to require of the occupier what it is reasonable to expect of him in his individual circumstances" (Lord Wilberforce, 996 D).

6. Home Office v. Dorset Yacht Co. [1970] A.C. 1004; [1970] 2 All E.R. 294, H.L.

Home Office *held* liable for damage done by borstal escapees to yacht, as to which see Chap. 1, (2) (a) **7**. Lord Morris, in considering whether the Home Office were under a legal duty to control the escapees to prevent harm to strangers, cited Dixon J. in *Smith v. Leurs* (1945) 70 C.L.R. 256, p. 261:

"It is, however, exceptional to find in the law a duty to control another's actions to prevent harm to strangers. The general rule is that one man is under no duty of controlling another to prevent his doing damage to a third. There are, however, special relations which are the source of a duty of this nature."

Lord Morris went on to say that there was in the present case such a special relation in that the borstal officers were entitled to exercise control over the boys who to their knowledge might try to escape and do damage (308 G).

7. Moorgate Mercantile v. Twitchings [1976] 3 W.L.R. 66; [1976] 2 All E.R. 641, H.L.

8. Argy Trading v. Lapid Developments [1977] 1 W.L.R. 444; [1977] 3 All E.R. 785, Croom Johnson J.

9. Anns v. Merton L.B.C. [1977] 2 W.L.R. 1024; [1977] 2 All E.R. 492, H.L.

Failure (as assumed for argument) by building inspector to exercise statutory function of inspecting foundations of a building being erected—*Held*, that a decision of this nature was within the area of policy or discretion conferred by the statute, and that no duty to individuals was owed in respect of the exercise of such discretion, provided that the decision was made responsibly and for reasons which accorded with the statutory purposes; if but only if a local authority did not give proper consideration in the sense to the question of whether to inspect would an action by an individual suffering damage lie. See Chap. 1, (2) (a) **10** for further details. Largely overruled in *Murphy*, Chap. 18, (13) **66**.

10. Arnold v. Teno (1978) 83 D.L.R. (3d) 609; [1978] C.L.Y. 2064, Canada Sup.Ct.

11. Leakey v. National Trust [1980] Q.B. 485; [1980] 1 All E.R. 17, C.A.

Landslip from hill owned and occupied by defendants came onto and/or threatened the properties of the plaintiffs—landslip was entirely due to natural causes—*held*, applying *Goldman* **5**, defendants owed a duty of care, and that the standard of care required was as set out by Lord Wilberforce in *Goldman* **5**, and included "the factor of what the particular man, not the average man, could be expected to do, having regard, amongst other things, where a serious expenditure of money is required. . . . , to his means." (37 C).

12. Page Motors Ltd v. Epsom & Ewell B.C. (1982) 80 L.G.R. 337; [1982] C.L.Y. 2267, C.A.

Held, considering *Goldman v. Hargrave* **5**, and *Leakey v. N.T.* **11**, that in determining what steps the council should reasonably have taken to abate the nuisance and what was a reasonable time in which to abate it, the court was not limited to considering the council's physical and financial resources only, but was entitled to take into account broader matters arising from the council's public responsibilities.

13. Potter v. Mole Valley D.C. and Surrey C.C., *The Times*, October 22, 1982, [1982] C.L.Y. 2266, French J.

Flooding due to inadequate culvert—for which the highway authority (D2) were in any event liable—question was whether D1, who appear to have been the drainage authority, were also liable for failing to use their statutory powers under section 98 of the Land Drainage Act 1976—plaintiffs argued that the failure was due to an improper motive (namely, pique at being threatened with legal proceedings) and therefore was actionable within *Anns* **9**—*held*, this was a doubtful proposition in the circumstances, but in any event was not made out on the facts.

14. Fellowes v. Rother D.C. [1983] 1 All E.R. 513; [1983] C.L.Y. 2538, Robert Goff J.

Trial of preliminary issues of law in action alleging negligent exercise of statutory powers to carry out coast protection work. The judge reviewed the leading authorities, and in particularly *East Suffolk* **1** and *Anns* **9**, and *said* (521 G) that in *Anns* **9** Lord Wilberforce had interpreted *East Suffolk* **1** "as being a good example of a case where operational activity, at the breach in the wall, was still well within a discretionary area, so that the plaintiff's task in contending for a duty of care was a difficult one." The judge also *pointed out* (521 F) that Lord Wilberforce had also rejected an argument that there was "an absolute distinction in the law between statutory duty and statutory power, the former giving rise to possible liability, the latter not; or at least not doing so unless the exercise of the power involves some positive act creating some fresh or additional damage." As a result the *ratio* of *East Suffolk* **1** as set out in the text must be qualified accordingly.

15. Perl (P.) (Exporters) Ltd v. Camden L.B.C. [1983] 3 W.L.R. 769; [1983] 3 All E.R. 161, C.A.

Defendants let property A to plaintiffs on business tenancy—plaintiffs used basement for storage of clothing—defendants owned adjoining property, B, which was let into flats—basement flat unoccupied—defendants failed to keep basement flat secure, despite complaints about lack of security and several burglaries in block—thieves entered basement flat, broke through into plaintiffs' basement store and stole clothing—plaintiffs sued defendants for loss—defendants denied owed duty of care to act to avoid loss—*Held*, following *Home Office v. Dorset Yacht Co.* **6**) and that the defendants were not liable.

"No case has been cited to us where a party has been held liable for the acts of a third party when there was no element of control over the third party. While I do not take the view that there can never be such a case I do take the view that the absence of control must make the court approach the suggestion that there is liability for a third party who was not under the control of the defendant with caution" (Waller L.J., 164 J). And at 166 G Waller L.J. said: "Whether or not an occupier of a house can ever be liable to a neighbour for an omission to act is doubtful."

Oliver L.J. (170 H-J) said that here there was no special relationship arising from control (as there was in *Home Office v. Dorset Yacht* **6**) and that there were no other circumstances from which a duty could be inferred, apart from the fact that entry by trespassers was a foreseeable possibility; and that this latter fact was, by itself, insufficient to raise the duty.

Robert Goff L.J. (172 E) said: "I know of no case where it has been held, in the absence of a special relationship, that the defendant was liable in negligence for having failed to prevent a third party from wrongfully causing damage to the plaintiff."

16. Low v. R. J. Haddock [1985] C.I.L.L. 162; [1985] C.L.Y. 213, Judge Newey Q.C.

Houses built near to oak tree which stood on land subsequently dedicated as highway. Foundations damaged by moisture abstraction from ground by tree—*Held*, although highway authority could not initially have foreseen such damage, they later became aware of the risk and were negligent in failing to take steps to avert it by reducing size of tree. For further details see Chap. 18, (6) **41**.

17. Russell v. Barnet L.B.C. (1985) 83 L.G.R. 152; [1985] C.L.Y. 2499, Tudor Evans J.

Lessees of house claimed subsidence damage caused by roots of trees which stood on adjoining pavement; highway authority, whilst not owners of trees, had statutory powers to maintain them and to prohibit them becoming a nuisance—*Held*, authority were or ought to have been aware of risk of tree roots causing damage and were liable not only in nuisance but also for breach of duty of care.

18. Billam & Billam v. Cheltenham B.C. (1985) 3 Con. L.R. 99; [1986] C.L.Y. 198, Cyril Newman Q.C.

For details see Chap. 18, (13) **33**.

19. Denton v. United Omnibus Co. Ltd, *The Times*, May 6, 1986; [1986] C.L.Y. 2250, C.A.

Defendant's bus parked in depot with no doors or gates. Bus not immobilised—unlawfully taken and driven into collision with plaintiff's car—*Held*, defendant not liable. In the absence of a special relationship or special circumstances a party was not liable in negligence for failing to prevent the unlawful or unauthorised act of another.

20. King v. Liverpool C.C. [1986] 1 W.L.R. 890; [1986] 3 All E.R. 544, C.A.

Council dwelling flooded by activities of intruders in vacant dwelling above. Access gained through allegedly inadequate boarding—*Held, inter alia*, no liability in respect of failure to prevent actions of third parties over whom there was no control, in the absence of a special relationship. (*Perl* **15** applied). See also Chap. 2(4) **19** and Chap. 10, (7) **11** for full summary.

21. Sutcliffe v. Sayer [1987] 1 EG LR 155; [1987] C.L.Y. 2596, C.A.

For details see Chap. 18, (5) **19**.

22. Scott-Whitehead v. National Coal Board (1987) 53 P. & C.R. 263; [1987] C.L.Y. 3866, Stuart Smith J.

Plaintiffs licensed to use river water to irrigate land owned and leased by them; water became excessively saline due to coal mine workings. Water authority in breach of duty of care in failing to warn salinity might be dangerously high; coal board not liable.

23. Christchurch Drainage Board v. Brown, *Daily Telegraph*, October 12, 1987; [1987] C.L.Y. 2591, P.C.

For details see Chap. 18, (13) **45**.

24. Smith v. Littlewoods Organisation Ltd [1987] 2 W.L.R. 480; [1987] 1 All E.R. 710, H.L.

Fire started in respondent's empty cinema premises by vandals which caused damage to adjoining premises. Cinema owners were unaware of vandal activity previously, and although their premises had been left insecure, it was contended that they could not have foreseen the consequences of their alleged breach of duty. The House of Lords considered in depth the liability of an adjoining occupier for the acts of third parties—*Held*, that cinema owners could not be liable on the facts because the injury or damage was not the probable consequence of the tortfeasor's negligence, and could only have been foreseen as a mere possibility. Where damage had been caused by an independent human agency, liability could only arise where that damage was a highly likely consequence of the act or omission. (*Per* Lord Goff), liability for harm caused by third parties did not depend only on establishing a special relationship between the tortfeasor and the third party, and there were other special circumstances in which the adjoining occupier owned a duty to neighbours for such acts of third parties, *e.g.* where a source of danger had been negligently created by him and it was reasonably foreseeable that third parties might interfere and spark off the danger, causing damage. (Contrast *Perl* **15** and *King v. Liverpool City Council* **20)**

25. Re The Herald of Free Enterprise, *The Independent*, December 18, 1987; [1988] C.L.Y. 2462, D.C.

The ferry *The Herald of Free Enterprise* capsized soon after leaving Zeebrugge because the inner and outer bow doors to the main "G" deck had not been closed. The assistant bosun whose duty it was to close them had fallen asleep. His chief officer did not follow the usual practice of waiting to see the doors begin to close, but went to the bridge. There, the captain did not ask the chief officer for any report, and sailed assuming the doors had been closed. The Divisional Court dismissed the captain's appeal against a finding of the formal inquiry into the capsizing that he had been guilty of serious negligence in the discharge of his duties. He should have made a positive check that the doors were closed before putting to sea. The fact that it was not the practice of most if not all captains of such ferries to make a positive check made no difference. Though general practice was usually cogent evidence of the standard of reasonable care, here it was evidence of culpable complacency.

The standard of care to be expected of a ship's master was a high one, having regard to the number of passengers to be expected on such vessels, and risk of serious injury or death in the event of any negligence.

26. Al-Kandari v. J.R. Brown & Co. [1988] Q.B. 665; [1988] 1 All E.R. 833; C.A.

For details see Chap. 18, (15) **46**.

27. Yuen Kun Yeu v. Att.-Gen. of Hong Kong [1988] A.C. 175; [1987] 2 All E.R. 705, P.C.

For details see Chap. 18, (2) **26**.

28. Re A (A Minor) (Costs) [1988] 18 Fam. Law 339; [1988] C.L.Y. 3371, C.A.

29. Mc Intyre v. Herring Son & Daw [1988] 1 EGLR 231; [1988] C.L.Y. 3213, E.A. Machin Q.C.
For details see Chap. 18, (5) **24**.

30. Nye Saunders & Partners v. Alan E. Bristow (1987) 37 BLR 92; [1988] C.L.Y. 2421, C.A.

31. Clough v. Bussan [1990] 1 All E.R. 431; [1990] C.L.Y. 3278, Kennedy J.

See for details Chap. 18, (13) **61**.

32. Davis v. Radcliffe [1990] 1 W.L.R. 821; [1990] 2 All E.R. 536, P.C.

For details see Chap. 18, (2) **28**.

33. Bank of Nova Scotia v. Hellenic Mutual War Risks Association (Bermuda) Ltd [1990] 1 Q.B. 818; [1989] 3 All E.R. 628, C.A.

For details see Chap. 18, (4) **18**.

34. Debs v. Sibec. Developments Ltd [1990] RTR 91; [1990] C.L.Y. 4026, Simon Brown J.

Plaintiff robbed of motor car, being forced to write and sign receipt for cash; because of threats he did not report the theft for about one month during which time the car was sold eventually to defendant without notice of lack of title and after negative inquiry of H.P.I.—*Held, inter alia*, plaintiff was not under a duty of care to successive purchasers to report its loss to police. *Moorgate Mercantile v. Twitchings* **7** applied.

35. Gray v. T. P. Bennett & Son (1987) 43 BLR 63; [1990] C.L.Y. 393, Judge Sir William Stabb Q.C.

For details see Chap. 18, (6) **65**.

36. Banque Keyser Ullman S. A. v. Skandia (U.K.) Insurance Co. Ltd [1991] 2 A.C. 249; [1990] 2 All E.R. 947, H.L.

See Chap. 18, (4) **14**.

37. Barclays Bank PLC v. Khaira [1992] 1 W.L.R. 623; [1992] C.L.Y. 215, Thomas Morison Q.C.

See (Chap. 18, (2) **32**.

38. P.K. Finans International (U.K.) Ltd v. Andrew Downs & Co. Ltd [1992] 1 EGLR 172; [1992] C.L.Y. 3216, Sir Michael Ogden Q.C.

Valuer stated in his report that oral inquiries but no official search had been made as to planning consents—*Held*, not negligent in not advising that planning consents should be verified: for further details see Chap. 18, (5) **55**.

39. Deloitte Hoskins & Sells v. National Mutual Life Nominees Ltd [1993] A.C. 774; [1993] 2 All E.R. 1015, P.C.

See Chap. 18, (1) **22**.

40. Topp v. London Country Bus (South West) [1993] 1 W.L.R. 979; [1993] 3 All E.R. 448, C.A.

Defendants' minibus left for over eight hours unlocked, unattended and with keys in at bus stop outside public house—unlawfully taken and driven into collision with cyclist—*Held*, defendants not liable—owed no duty of care to cyclist—acts of wrongdoer constituted novus actus interveniens. *P. Perl (Exporters) Ltd v. Camden L.B.C.* **15** followed.

41. Alexandrou v. Oxford [1993] 4 All E.R. 328; [1990] C.L.Y. 3286, C.A.

Police attend shops premises in response to alarm; failure to inspect rear of premises allowed burglars to escape with goods—*Held*, no sufficient special relationship between shop keeper and police to give rise to a duty of care alternatively it was not fair or reasonable that the police should be under such a duty. *Hill v. Chief Constable* Chap. 18, (13) **56** followed.

42. Ancell v. McDermott [1993] RTR 235; [1993] C.L.Y. 2958, C.A.

Police noticed spillage of diesel fuel on road but took no steps to warn public of danger; driver skids an spillage and accident results—*Held*, following *Hill v. Chief Constable*, Chap. 18, (13) **56** and *Alexandrou v. Oxford* **41**, no duty of care owed.

43. Anthony v. Wright, *The Independent*, September 27, 1994; [1994] 10 C.L. 352, Lightman J.

See Chap. 18, (1) **26**.

44. Barrett v. Ministry of Defence [1995] 1 W.L.R. 1217; *The Times*, January 13, 1995, C.A.

Deceased, naval airman at base in Norway, drunk to excess, vomited, war left slumped on a chair and then carried unconscious to his cabin where he lay in coma, observed intemittently—died of aspiration of vomit. Defendant had failed to enforce disciplinary codes discouraging over-indulgence in alcohol. There were no clear orders from officers as to how deceased should have been treated after collapsing, and no adequate medical cover was available—*Held*:

(a) Defendant under no duty to take reasonable care to prevent deceased, a mature man, from abusing alcohol to extent he did. Until he became unconscious he alone was responsible for his condition. The Queen's Regulations and standing order could not be equated with guidance given in Highway Code or factory safety pamphlets.
(b) After deceased collapsed, defendant negligent in failing properly to supervise and provide medical assistance for him.
(c) Deceased two-thirds to blame.

Note: At first instance, defence of *volenti* failed—deceased, with mind clouded by alcohol, had not voluntarily assumed risk of grave or fatal injury by continuing drinking.

UI. Davies v. Cargo Fleet Iron Co. Ltd & Balfour Beatty & Co. Ltd (1956) C.A.

Denning L.J. (4 E): "A bystander is not bound to warn another whom he sees walking into danger, but it is a different matter when the danger is of his own making."

(c) No Damage Reasonably Foreseeable

Worker operating foot pedal of machine—no foreseeable risk of injury...................... U10

1. Bourhill v. Young [1943] A.C. 92; [1942] 2 All E.R. 396, H.L.

Lord Macmillan (104): "The duty is owed to those to whom injury may reasonably and probably be anticipated if the duty is not observed." And (105): "She (the appellant) was not so placed that there was any reasonable likelihood of her being affected."

2. Woods v. Duncan [1946] A.C. 401; [1946] 1 All E.R. 420, H.L.

Shipbuilders were negligent in failing to ensure that the test cock of a torpedo tube of a submarine was unblocked by paint—the tube was opened when the bow cap through some unexplained reason was open—as a result submarine sank—if the test cock had been unblocked, it would have given a warning that the bow cap was open—but this warning would have been purely incidental, for the test cock (see Lord Simonds, 444) was only intended to be used in connection with firing torpedoes—*Held*, shipbuilders not liable, because it could not reasonably have been foreseen that their negligence would result in the sinking of the submarine (and hence shipbuilders did not in respect of this failure owe a duty to deceased), and/or because the blocked test cock, being only incidentally a contributing factor, was not *the* cause, though undoubtedly *a* cause. *The* cause was the open bow cap (for which, on the facts, no one was liable either).

3. Overseas Tankship v. Morts Dock (The Wagon Mound) [1961] A.C. 388, [1961] 1 All E.R. 404; P.C.

Held, disapproving *Re Polemis* [1921] 3 K.B. 560, that reasonable foresight was the test for the recovery of damage, and not directness.

4. Hughes v. Lord Advocate [1963] A.C. 837; [1963] 1 All E.R. 705, H.L.

Post Office engineers negligently left open manhole and tent unattended which contained allurements to children—but actual accident was caused by an explosion of a paraffin lamp inside tent, which plaintiff aged eight tripped over—this explosion was unforeseeable, but it was foreseeable that plaintiff might get burnt through playing with the lamp—*Held*, that, as damage from burns and damage from explosion were *of the same kind*, defendants were liable, as liability extended to all damage of the same kind as that which could be reasonably foreseen, even though in a given case the precise type of damage and the precise type of accident were not foreseeable.

5. Doughty v. Turner [1964] 1 Q.B. 518; [1964] 1 All E.R. 98, C.A.

X, a fellow employee of plaintiff, knocked an asbestos cement cover into a cauldron of molten liquid—the extreme heat caused the asbestos cement to undergo a chemical change, which in turn caused an eruption from the cauldron, injuring plaintiff—before the accident this sequence was unsuspected and not reasonably foreseeable—but it was foreseeable that the dropping of the cover could cause a dangerous splash—*Held*, applying *Wagon Mound (No. 1)* **3** and distinguishing *Hughes* v. *Lord Advocate* **4**, plaintiff could not recover, as the cause of the accident could not be described as a variant of the perils from foreseeable splashing, but as the intrusion of a new and unexpected factor, *i.e.* the chemical change.

6. The Wagon Mound (No. 2) [1967] 1 A.C. 617; [1966] 2 All E.R. 709, P.C.

Same accident as in **3** but different evidence and different parties—*Held* that in nuisance as well as in negligence foreseeability, and not directness, of damage was the test. "It is not sufficient that the injury suffered ... was the direct result of the nuisance, if that injury in the relevant sense was unforeseeable" (Lord Reid, 717 B). Lord Reid also said (714 C) that on the authorities directness of damage, in a somewhat different and narrower sense, was the test in determining whether, in the case of a public nuisance, a plaintiff had suffered special damage "other and different from the damage caused by the nuisance to the rest of the public" (so as to found his action), but this question did not arise in the present case, as it was undisputed that the plaintiff here had suffered special damage in this sense. Applying the above, it was *held* that, on the evidence and the findings of the judge, the damage was in fact foreseeable, and that the defendants were accordingly liable. For details see Chap. 2, (3) **7**.

7. Tremain v. Pyke [1969] 1 W.L.R. 1556; [1969] 3 All E.R. 1303, Payne J.

Held, applying **4**, defendants not liable. Main authorities reviewed.

8. Old v. Eastern National Omnibus Co. [1984] C.L.Y. 2285, French J.

Plaintiff, aged four, riding bicycle in middle of pavement, wobbled into road, fell off, and was struck by bus—*Held*, bus driver not liable—not foreseeable that plaintiff would fall into road—nothing the driver could have done to avoid accident.

9. Perry v. Tendring D.C. [1985] 1 EGLR 260; [1985] C.L.Y. 192, Judge Newey Q.C.

Houses built on land subject to long term leave; local authority, consulting engineer and builder held not liable in negligence to purchasers as at time they acted they could not reasonably have known of the phenomenon.

10. Denton v. United Omnibus Co. Ltd, *The Times*, May 6, 1986; [1986] C.L.Y. 2250, C.A.

Defendant's bus parked in depot with no door or gates. Bus not immobilised—Unlawfully taken and driven into collision with plaintiff's car—*Held*, defendant not liable. In the absence of a special relationship or special circumstances a party was not liable in negligence for failing to prevent the unlawful or unauthorised act of another.

11. Flynn v. Vange Scaffolding & Engineering Co., *The Times*, March 26, 1987; [1987] C.L.Y. 2598, C.A.

Held, human error and negligence were by no means the same. Negligence required the existence and breach of a duty of care, and that the consequences were foreseeable.

12. Aldred v. Nacanco [1987] IRLR 292; [1987] C.L.Y. 1367, C.A.

In washroom of defendant's premises, employee X pushed slightly unstable washbasin against plaintiff's thigh, to startle her. Plaintiff turned quickly and in doing so injured her back which was known to defendant to be vulnerable—*Held*, defendant not liable because, *inter alia* her place of work was not unsafe—not reasonably foreseeable that condition of washbasin might cause injury.

13. Gunn v. Wallsend Slipway and Engineering Company Ltd, *The Times*, January 23, 1989; [1989] C.L.Y. 2548, C.A.

Plaintiff's wife contracted mesotheloma and died as a result of inhaling abestos dust between 1948 and 1965 when washing plaintiff's clothes which were often impregnated with dust during plaintiff's employment by defendant—*Held*, defendant owed no duty of care to plaintiff's wife, because it could not reasonably have foreseen risk of injury to her from such exposure, in absence before 1965 of any relevant medical, industrial or official publications and of any approved practice as to storage and washing of working clothes.

14. Calveley v. Chief Constable of the Merseyside Police [1989] A.C. 1228; [1989] 1 All E.R. 1025, H.L.

Various officers claimed damages for variously anxiety, vexation, depressive illness and loss of overtime earnings during and due to periods of suspension or dismissal due to negligent carrying out of investigations into their conduct—*Held, inter alia,* injury alleged was not reasonably foreseeable.

For further detail see Chap. 18, (13) **57**.

15. Petch v. Commissioners of Customs and Excise [1993] 1 C.R. 789; *The Times,* March 4, 1993, C.A.

Plaintiff, civil servant with defendant, suffered mental breakdown in October, 1974 due to manic depression. After returning to work in January, 1975, his behaviour became bizarre due to hypomania. As a result he was transferred to D.H.S.S. in June, 1975—became ill again in 1983 and was retired on medical grounds in 1986. Then claimed injury benefit under civil service scheme, claiming his illnesses were caused by pressure of work when with defendant. Following letter from defendant to Treasury concerning plaintiff and his work record, plaintiff's claim was rejected. He then claimed damages for negligence—*Held, inter alia,* that even if pressure of work caused initial breakdown, plaintiff had not proved that defendant's senior management were or should have been aware that in 1974 he was showing signs of impending breakdown or that his workload carried real risk of breakdown. Thus defendant was not in breach of its admitted duty to take reasonable care to see that plaintiff's duties did not damage his physical or mental health.

16. Topp v. London Country Bus (South West) [1993] 1 W.L.R. 979; [1993] 3 All E.R. 448, C.A.

Defendants' minibus left for over eight hours unlocked, unattended and with key in at bus stop outside public house unlawfully taken and driven into collision with cyclist—*Held,* defendants not liable—owed no duty of care to cyclist—acts of wrongdoer constituted *novus actus interveniens P. Perl (Exporters) Ltd v. Camden L.B.C.* (Chap. 1, (3)(b) **15**) followed.

17. Walker v. Northumberland C.C., *The Times,* November 24, 1994; [1994] C.L.Y. 2278, Colman J.

Plaintiff, employed in defendant's social services department came under increasingly intense pressure of work in 1980s as his requests for further staff were not met. Due to the pressure he had a nervous breakdown in 1986. Returning in 1987 he advised his superior that the pressure had to be relieved, but only very limited assistance was provided. Plaintiff had second breakdown later in 1987 and had to retire—*Held*:

(a) There was no logical reason for psychiatric injury to be excluded from scope of employer's duty to provide safe system of work.
(b) First breakdown not reasonably foreseeable.
(c) After plaintiff's return his superior should have foreseen that if again exposed to same workload he was at risk of another breakdown. Continuous or substantial assistance should have been provided. Defendant negligent in not having done so, despite the constraints imposed by its budget, and although provision of further assistance might have disrupted provision of services to the public.

U1. Jones v. Optical Industries (1984) C.A. 240

Male employee came into slight physical contact with small lightly built female employee who was off balance and fell. Had she not been off balance, degree of contact would have been insufficient to cause her to fall—*Held*, in absence of something in nature of deliberate barge, mere physical contact would not constitute negligence.

U2. Greenfield v. Tower Shipping Ltd (1984) C.A. 552

Plaintiff deckhand lowered hatch cover by pulling on rope which ran over engine-powered drum. When cover stuck, ships mate told plantiff to put an extra turn or two on drum. Engine started to labour, rope started to slip and end of rope was jerked from plaintiffs grasp, injuring his thumb—*Held*, not reasonably foreseeable that mate's instruction would put plaintiff in any danger. Plaintiff should not have carried out instruction to point that rope might jerk from his grasp.

U3. Callaghan v. Lancashire C. C. [1984] CA. 958

Worker at old people's home lightly touched patient's Zimmer frame to encourage patient to move a little quicker. Patient panicked, and fell on top of second worker who had rushed forward to prevent patient falling—*Held*, not foreseeable that first worker's actions would precipitate what happened—no liability.

U4. England v. Cleveland Potash Ltd [1986] C.A. 586

Contrary to employers' instructions, potash mine employee tried to dispose of fenobel by burning it, and was killed in ensuing explosion—*Held*, not foreseeable that deceased would embark on expressly forbidden course of conduct, and employer not liable.

U5. Winfield v. National Coal Board [1986] C.A. 651

Plaintiff tripped on step, stumbled six feet along flat concrete surface, and caught and injured foot in raised edge of metal plate in the surface. No previous complaint or mishap in relation to the plate—*Held*, place of work not unsafe. Not foreseeable someone would sustain an accident in this unusual way.

U6. Herbert v. Ermin Plant (Hire & Services) Ltd (1987) C.A. 482

Without his employer's knowledge or permission, plaintiff fixed air compressor to water tank, to improve flow of water thence to steam cleaner. Ensuing pressure caused an inspection cover to shatter, injuring plaintiff—*Held*, employer could not reasonably have foreseen plaintiff's act, and not liable.

U7. Bidwell v. North East Essex Health Authority (1988) C.A. 798

Plaintiff required to break concrete and dig trench using sledgehammer. This caused him to suffer symptoms of arthritis. He claimed a preumatic hammer or drill should have been provided—*Held*, plantiff's job was not foreseeably hazardous, and equipment provided was proper for fairly simple job. Employer not liable.

U8. Bibby v. Treacy (1989) C.A. 743

Defendant parked lorry outside general store where parking prohibited. Infant plaintiff walked, without looking, in front of lorry and into path of car—*Held*, defendant not negligent in parking where he did—did not create a reasonably foreseeable risk of danger.

U9. Tunney v. Guy (1991) C.A. 131

Defendant, driving car at 30 m.p.h. saw 76-year-old plaintiff just over centre of road, crossing from defendant's right to left, apparently oblivious to traffic. Defendant sounded horn, braked and swerved onto off-side of road. Plaintiff turned, rushed to retrace his steps and collided with defendant's car—*Held*, defendant not liable—plaintiff's reaction unforeseeable.

U10. Hill v. E. Fogarty plc (1991) C.A. 272

Plaintiff suffered Achilles tendonitis which she attributed to operating foot pedal of pillow-filling machine—*Held*, employers not liable. No evidence they knew or should have known they were exposing plaintiff to a risk of injury

(4) Remoteness

(N.B.—Headings under Duty of Care and Standard of Care to which the reader may want further to refer are:

(a) Foreseeability of Particular Damage

1. Overseas Tankship v. Morts Dock (The Wagon Mound) [1961] A.C. 388; [1961] 1 All E.R. 404, P.C.

Furnace oil from defendants' ship spilt into bay—spread to near plaintiffs' wharf—where molten metal fell on floating cotton waste—cotton waste began to smoulder—ignited oil—it was found as a fact that the defendants did not know and could not be expected to know that furnace oil could be set alight when spread on water—*Held*, disapproving *Re Polemis* [1921] 3 K.B. 560, that reasonable foreseeability, and not directness, of damage was the criterion as to whether damages were recoverable, and defendants, judged by this test, were not liable.

2. Smith v. Leech Brain [1962] 2 Q.B. 405; [1961] 3 All E.R. 1159, Lord Parker C.J.

Burn to lip—which was in pre-malignant condition—burn promoted skin cancer and subsequent death—*Held*, plaintiff could recover, as the rule that the defendant must take the victim as he found him was unaffected by the *Wagon Mound* **1**. "The J.C. were not saying . . . that a man is only liable for the extent of the damage which he could have anticipated, but the question is whether the defendants could reasonably foresee the type of injury which he suffered, namely, the burn" (1161 I-1162 G).

3. Blaikie v. British Transport Commission 1961 S.C. 44; [1961] C.L.Y. 2344, 2nd. Div.

Defect in engine causing great physical exertion on part of driver—coronary thrombosis soon after—*Held*, applying *Wagon Mound* **1**, defendants not liable.

4. Warren v. Scruttons [1962] 1 Lloyd's Rep. 497, Paull J.

Defective frayed wire rope—injuring finger—which in turn aggravated existing eye complaint—*Held*, defendants liable, as the rope could foreseeably cause injury, and therefore the defendants liable, even though the precise result of the injury could not have been foreseen.

5. Hughes v. Lord Advocate [1963] A.C. 837; [1963] 1 All E.R. 705, H.L.

Post Office engineers left an open manhole covered by a tent unattended during tea break—the site contained numerous allurements to children—including four lighted paraffin lamps—plaintiff aged eight and another boy aged ten went exploring in tent, taking one of the lamps—plaintiff tripped over lamp—which exploded and threw plaintiff in manhole, causing severe burns—the explosion was unforseeable, but it was foreseeable that the plaintiff might have burnt himself with the lamp, or fallen into manhole—defendants were negligent in leaving manhole unattended—but contended they were not liable for the damage resulting from the explosion, as it was unforeseeable—*Held*, defendants liable, because (*per* Lord Reid at 706 I) "a defender is liable, although the damage may be a good deal greater in extent than was foreseeable; he can only escape liability if the damage can be regarded as differing in kind from what was foreseeable."

6. Doughty v. Turner [1964] 1 Q.B. 518; [1964] 1 All E.R. 98, C.A.

Fellow employee of plaintiff knocked an asbestos cement cover into a cauldron of moulten cyanide sodium—this act was negligent—and could conceivably have caused a dangerous splash from the cauldron—but what, unforeseeably happened was that the asbestos cover underwent a chemical change which caused an eruption from the cauldron—this reaction was unsuspected before the accident—*Held*, applying *Wagon Mound* **1** and distinguishing *Hughes* **5**, plaintiff could not recover, as the accident could not be described as a variant of the perils of foreseeable splashing, but as the instrusion of a new and unsuspected factor, *i.e.* chemical change.

7. Overseas Tankship v. Miller SS Co. (The Wagon Mound No. 2) [1967] 1 A.C. 617; [1966] 2 All E.R. 709, P.C.

Same incident as in **1**, but in this case damaging plaintiff's vessels—plaintiff sued both in negligence and nuisance, contending that in nuisance directness of damage was still the test—*Held*, not so, and that reasonable foreseeability was the criterion for recovering damages in nuisance as well as in negligence (although in determining whether plaintiff had suffered special damage so as to enable him to sue for a public nuisance directness of damage was probably the proper test). (*N.B.* The plaintiff, nevertheless, won, although the plaintiff in **1** lost. This was because the evidence in the present case was different, and established that the risk of oil spread on water igniting was foreseeable—as to which see Chap. 2,(3) **7**).

8. Bradford v. Robinson Rentals [1967] 1 W.L.R. 337; [1967] 1 All E.R. 267, Rees J.

9. Wielan v. Cyril Lord Carpets [1969] 3 All E.R. 1006; [1969] C.L.Y. 1054, Eveleigh J.

Neck injury caused by negligence of defendants—plaintiff had to wear a collar—in consequence was unable to use her bi-focal spectacles properly—as a result of which she fell descending stairs—*Held*, the second injury was attributable to the original negligence.

10. McKew v. Holland & Hannan [1969] 3 All E.R. 1621; 1970 S.L.T. 68, H.L.

Leg injury caused by negligence of defendants—leg subsequently gave way while he was descending steep staircase without hand-rail by himself—*Held*, in the circumstances this was unreasonable conduct by the plaintiff, so that the chain of causation was broken, and the defendants were not liable for the second injury.

11. Malcolm v. Broadhurst [1970] 3 All E.R. 508, Geoffrey Lane J.

Husband and wife both injured in same accident—husband unable to continue self-employed occupation—so that wife lost a part-time job as his secretary—*Held*, no claim lay. *N.B.* The wife succeeded on a claim for temporary loss of a full-time job due to the effect of her husband's post-accident irritability on her own vulnerable (or "egg-shell") personality—as to which see Chap. 1, (4) (b) **6**.

12. Pyne v. Wilkinfeld [1981] C.L.Y. 1856; 26 S.A.S.R. 441

Accident requiring cervical collar which restricted P's vision so that she tripped—*Held*, referring to *Wielan* **9**, D liable for further injuries, as they arose causally from first accident.

13. Walker v. Mullen, *The Times*, January 19, 1984; [1984] C.L.Y. 1045, Comyn J.

Adult child seriously injured. Instead of returning to his job in Jordan, father stayed in England to be with child and mother whilst child in hospital. Father claimed resultant loss of earnings. *Held*, following *Kirkham*, [1958] 2 Q.B. 338, that although the father's action had been reasonable his loss was not recoverable. It could not reasonably have been within the contemplation of the tortfeasor and was therefore too remote.

14. Ward v. Cannock Chase D. C. [1986] Ch. 546; [1985] 3 All E.R. 537, Scott J.

D's property untenanted and uninhabited. Damage by thieves and vandals over a period of time to plaintiff's adjoining property as a consequence. Liability in negligence admitted, but question arose as to extent of liability for subsequent damage—*Held*, test of whether or not act of stranger too remote depended on (a) what might reasonably have been foreseen as consequence of the original act or omission, (b) whether damage sufficiently connected with the original act or omission to be recoverable and (c) whether intervening act was very thing which was likely to happen as a result of original act or omission. Here, the chain of causation leading from the council's breach of duty to the damage to the house belonging to P not broken and damage was not too remote as to be recoverable.

15. Meah v. McCreamer (No. 2) [1986] 1 All E.R. 943; 136 New L.J. 235, Woolf J.

As a result of road traffic accident caused by defendant's negligence, plaintiff suffered head injuries, underwent marked personality change and developed propensity to attack women, two of whom were awarded against him damages which he now sought to recover against defendant—*Held*:

(a) Such damages were too remote a loss to be recoverable. Plaintiff's victims could not have sued defendant directly because defendant owed them no duty. Further, to allow plaintiff to recover would expose defendant and other defendants in similar cases to indefinite liability for indefinite period.
(b) It would be contrary to public policy for plaintiff to be indemnified by defendant for the consequences of plaintiff's crimes.

16. Michael Sallis & Company Ltd v. E.C.A. Calil. (1988) 4 Const. L.J. 125; [1988] C.L.Y. 2420, Judge Fox-Andrews Q.C.

Architect held to owe a duty to act impartially towards main contractor in respect of such matters as certificates and extensions of time and in so far as damages could be established as having been caused by unfairness in respect of matters about which under the contract they were required to act impartially, damages were recoverable and not too remote.

17. Devlin v. Strathclyde Regional Council [1992] C.L.Y. 6065; 1993 S.L.T. 699

Child jumping through skylight on school roof. Accident of this type not foreseeable. For summary see Chap. 10, (5)(e) **22**.

18. Petch v. Commissioners of Customs and Excise [1993] 1 C.R. 789; *The Times*, March 4, 1993, C.A.

Plaintiff, civil servant with defendant, suffered mental breakdown in October, 1974 due to manic depression. After returning to work in January, 1975, his behaviour became bizarre due to hypomania. As a result he was transferred to D.H.S.S. in June, 1975—became ill again in 1983 and was retired on medical grounds in 1986. Then claimed injury benefit under civil service scheme, claiming his illnesses were caused by pressure of work when with defendant. Following letter from defendant to Treasury concerning plaintiff and his work record, plaintiff's claim was rejected. He then claimed damages for negligence—*Held, Inter alia,* that even of pressure if work caused initial breakdown, plaintiff had not proved that defendant's senior management were or should have been aware that in 1974 he was showing signs of impending breakdown or that his workload caused real risk of breakdown. Thus defendant was not in breach of its admitted duty to take reasonable care to see that plaintiff's duties did not damage his physical or mental health.

19. Walker v. Northumberland C.C. *The Times*, November 24, 1994; [1994] C.L.Y. 2278, Colman J.

Plaintiff, employed in defendant's social services department came under increasingly intense pressure of work in 1980s—his requests for further staff were not met. Due to the pressure he had a nervous breakdown in 1986. Returning in 1987 he advised his superior that the pressure had to be relieved, but only very limited assistance was provided. Plaintiff had second breakdown later in 1987 and had to retire—*Held*:

(a) There was no logical reason for psychiatric injury to be excluded from scope of employer's duty to provide safe system of work.
(b) First breakdown not reasonably foreseeable.
(c) After plaintiff's return his superior should have foreseen that if again exposed to same workload he was at risk of another breakdown. Continuous or substantial assistance should have been provided. Defendant negligent in not having done so, despite the contraints imposed by its budget, and although provision of further assistance might have disrupted provision of services to the public.

U1. Majewski v. Cementation Co. (1961) C.A. 322.

Colliery wire rope broke—piece of wire strand flew into plaintiff's eye—*Held*, defendants liable. 'Whatever *Wagon Mound* **1** does decide, it certainly does not state that the precise way in which the damage is caused should be foreseeable in order that the act causing it may be said to be negligent. It is sufficient if damage of that kind might be foreseen' (Diplock L.J., 13 E).

U2. Rowark v. National Coal Board (1986) C.A. 45.

Plaintiff developed tenosynovitis of wrist in course of his employment. Trial judge held that although a sprain, twist or strain of wrist was foreseeable, tenosynovitis was not, and dismissed claim—*Held*, allowing plaintiff's appeal, that tenosynovitis was within ambit of injuries found to be foreseeable—the precise injury did not need to be foreseen if its general nature could.

(b) Taking Victim as Found

(*N.B.*—In some cases reference may also be needed to Chap. 1, (2)(b). The distinction sought to be drawn here between the two classes is that in the cases of Abnormal Susceptibility *no* damage would have resulted but for the susceptibility, so that the issue is one of duty *vel non*. In the cases listed here *some* damage could foreseeably have arisen from the negligent act, but the question is whether the particular damage resulting from the plaintiff's antecedent condition is recoverable.)

Antecedent condition	*Contributing to*		*Liable or not*
Pre-malignant state of lip	Skin cancer promoted by burn	1	Yes
Proneness to thrombosis	Coronary thrombosis from physical exertion to overcome defect in engine	2	No
Eye complaint	Aggravated by injury to finger	3	Yes
Poliomyelitis virus in body	Poliomyelitis precipitated by electric shock	4	Yes
PRONENESS TO ANXIETY STATE	ANXIETY STATE RESULTING FROM NEGLIGENCE OF SOLICITOR	5	No
Pre-existing nervous depression	Exacerbation caused by complex results of accident	6	Yes
Fear of operative treatment	Refusal to undergo operation after accident	7	No
ALLERGY TO ANTITETANUS SERUM	ENCEPHALITIS FROM ADMINISTRATION OF SERUM AFTER ACCIDENT	8	Yes
Highly vulnerable personality	Psychiatric injury from witnessing accident	9	Yes
Highly vulnerable to pressure of work	Second nervous breakdown	10	Yes

1. Smith v. Leech Brain [1962] 2 Q.B. 405; [1961] 3 All E.R. 1159, Lord Parker C.J.

Burn to lip—which was in pre-malignant condition—burn promoted skin cancer and subsequent death—*Held*, plaintiff could recover, as the rule that the defendant must take the victim as he found him was unaffected by the *Wagon Mound* (Chap. 1, (4)(a) **1**). "The question is whether these defendants could reasonably foresee the type of injury which he suffered, namely the burn. What, in the particular case, is the amount of damage depends on the characteristics and constitution of the victim" (1161–2).

2. Blaikie v. British Transport Commission, 1961 S.C. 44; [1961] C.L.Y. 2344, 2nd. Div.

Defect in engine causing great physical exertion on the part of the driver—coronary thrombosis soon after—*Held*, applying *Wagon Mound* (Chap. 1, (4)(a) **1**), defendants not liable.

3. Warren v. Scruttons [1962] 1 Lloyd's Rep. 497, Paull J.

Defective frayed wire rope injured plaintiff's finger, which in turn aggravated an existing eye complaint—*Held*, defendants liable for the latter, as the wire rope could foreseeably cause injury, and therefore the defendants were liable, even though the precise result of the injury could not have been foreseen.

4. Sayers v. Perrin [1967] C.L.Y. 1198; [1966] Q.L.R. 89, Full Court (Queensland).

Plaintiff had a poliomyelitis virus in his body—electric shock caused him to develop poliomyelitis—*Held*, defendants liable for the test, applying *Wagon Mound* (Chap. 1, (4)(a) **1**), was not whether the actual result was reasonably foreseeable, but whether an injury of the type which might directly result in the condition complained of was reasonably foreseeable.

5. Cook v. S [1967] 1 W.L.R. 457; [1967] 1 All E.R. 299, C.A.

Negligence by solicitor in allowing divorce to go undefended—plaintiff wife claimed (*inter alia*) for damages for a resulting anxiety state—*Held*, this was not reasonably foreseeable. During argument it was alleged that the plaintiff had a special propensity to an anxiety state. *Held*, if this was so, it should have been pleaded, and in addition this propensity should have been brought home to the defendant, in which case the area of foreseeability might have been enlarged. *N.B.* The case was argued on the basis that the cause of action lay in contract only. See also *Heywood*, Chap. 18, (15) **21**.

6. Malcolm v. Broadhurst [1970] 3 All E.R. 508, Geoffrey Lane J.

Husband and wife both injured in same accident by defendant's negligence—wife had been under the doctor for some years for nervous disturbance—after the accident this was exacerbated by the pronounced irritability of the husband resulting from an injury to his head—so that wife for a time had to give up her full-time employment—*Held*, that damages for this were recoverable by the wife. "The defendant must take the wife as he finds her and there is no difference in principle between an egg-shell skull and an egg-shell personality. Exacerbation of her nervous depression was a readily foreseeable consequence of injuring her. Does the fact that it was caused, or caused to continue, by reaction to the husband's pathological bad-temper (itself the result of the defendant's negligence) put a stop to the defendant's liability? I think not. Once damage of a particular kind, in this case psychological, can be foreseen, as here it could, the fact that it arises or is continued by reason of an unusual complex of events does not avail the defendant": *Hughes* Chap. 1, (4) (a) **5**.

7. Morgan v. Wallis [1974] 1 Lloyd's Rep. 165; [1974] C.L.Y. 855, Browne J.

8. Robinson v. Post Office [1974] 1 W.L.R. 1176; [1974] 2 All E.R. 737, C.A.

9. Brice v. Brown [1984] 1 All E.R. 997 (1984) 134 New L.J. 204, Stuart Smith J.

Once a plaintiff had established that tort complained of had caused nervous shock as a reasonably foreseeable consequence of negligence, it was immaterial that plaintiff has a highly vulnerable personality causing her to sustain very serious psychiatric condition. See also Chap. 1 (2)(c) 15.

10. Walker v. Northumberland C. C. *The Times*, November 24, 1994; [1994] C.L.Y. 2278, Colman J.

Plaintiff, employed in defendant's social services department came under increasingly intense pressure of work in 1980s—his requests for further staff were not met. Due to the pressure he had a nervous breakdown in 1986. Returning in 1987 he advised his superior that the pressure had to be relieved, but only very limited assistance was provided. Plaintiff had second breakdown later in 1987 and had to retire—*Held*:

(a) There was no logical reason for psychiatric injury to be excluded from scope of employer's duty to provide safe system of work.
(b) First breakdown not reasonably foreseeable.
(c) After plaintiff's return his superior showed have foreseen that if again exposed to same workload he was at risk of another breakdown. Continuous or substantial assistance should

have been provided. Defendant negligent in not having done so despite the constraints imposed by its budget, and although provision of further assistance might have disrupted provision of services to the public.

(c) Novus Actus Interveniens

		N.A.I. or not
COLLISION AT SEA—CAPTAIN ORDERING CREW INTO BOAT WHICH CAPSIZES	1	No
EMERGENCY—REACTION THERETO—WHETHER NOVUS ACTUS	1	
NOVUS ACTUS INTERVENIENS DEFINED	1	
HOUSE LEFT UNLOCKED BY BUILDING CONTRACTOR—THIEF GETS IN	2	No
INFLAMMABLE MATERIAL DELIVERED WITHOUT WARNING—SET ALIGHT BY CIGARETTE	3	No
TRAM CONDUCTOR AWAY FROM PLATFORM—PASSENGER RINGING BELL TO START	4	No
DANGEROUSLY STOWED TIMBER—NO PRACTICAL ALTERNATIVE BUT TO ACCEPT DANGER WHEN UNLOADING	5	No
Subsequent negligent medical treatment—when novus actus	6	
NEGLIGENT ADVICE NOT TO SELL HOUSE—HOUSE BURNT DOWN	7	Yes
Negligence by solicitor—mistaken advice by counsel on action to remedy same	8	No
Negligent supervision of Borstal trainees—who escape and do damage	9	No
Act of third party—must be "very likely" if chain not to be broken	9	No
Cyclist falling off through defendant's negligence—is run down by following car	10	No
ACCIDENT—FOLLOWED BY NEGLIGENT MEDICAL TREATMENT—BUT OF NO CAUSATIVE EFFECT	11	No
Defective gate at football ground—unruly mob surge through same and trample plaintiff	12	No
Failure to prevent escape of boy remanded to community home—boy escapes and does damage	13	No
NEGLIGENT DAMAGE TO HOUSE—WHICH HAS TO BE VACATED—INVASION BY SQUATTERS	14	Yes
TRAFFIC ACCIDENT—FOLLOWED BY NEGLIGENT REACTION OF POLICE—RESULTING IN SECOND ACCIDENT	15	Yes
Unidentified person shouting "go", causing boat driver to pull inexperienced water-skier away at full power	16	No
HUMAN INTERVENTION: BETWEEN BREACH OF STATUTORY DUTY AND INJURY—WHAT PLAINTIFF MUST PROVE	17	No
UNKNOWN PERSON TAKING INSECURE BUS AND DRIVING IT INTO COLLISION WITH CAR—BUS OWNER NOT LIABLE	18	Yes
Insurer's failure to notice clause in reinsurance contract had a cut-off clause of which brokers negligently failed to inform them	19	No
Hooligans at football ground—broken concrete thrown at police officers	20	No
UNKNOWN PERSON TAKING MINIBUS LEFT WITH KEYS IN, AND DRIVING IT INTO COLLISION WITH CYCLIST—MINIBUS OWNER NOT LIABLE	21	Yes
NEGLIGENT OVERVALUATION—LOSS DUE TO FALL IN MARKET WHERE LENDER WOULD NOT HAVE LENT IF PROPER VALUATION MADE	22	No
Negligent bonfire—fire brigade failing to extinguish embers properly	U1	No

Tortious accident—leaving neck vulnerable—neck exacerbated by subsequent non-tortious accident	U2	No
Plaintiff's van causing defendant's unbraked compressor to run downhill	U3	No
Pedestrian without looking collides with bus which stops—driver then moves forward over plaintiffs foot	U4	No

1. The Oropesa [1943] P. 32; [1943] 1 All E.R. 211, C.A.

Collision at sea—captain ordered some of crew into a boat—which capsized—*Held*, not *novus actus interveniens*. "They were acting in an emergency. If they did something which was outside the exigencies of the emergency, whether it was from miscalculations or from error or, if you like, from mere wilfulness, they would be debarred from saying there had not intervened a new cause. The question is not whether there was new negligence, but a new cause" (Lord Wright, 215 F). "It must be shown that there is something which I will call ultroneous, something unwarrantable, a new cause coming in to break the sequence of events, something that can be described as either unreasonable or extraneous or extrinsic. I doubt whether the law can be stated more precisely than that" (Lord Wright, 215 G).

2. Stansbie v. Troman [1948] 2 K.B. 48; [1948] 1 All E.R. 599, C.A.

Building contractor, in negligent breach of contract, left plaintiff's house empty and unlocked for two hours—thief got in—*Held*, act of thief usually *novus actus interveniens*, but not, as here, when "the very act of negligence itself" consisted of failing to guard against "the very thing that in fact happened" (Tucker L.J., 600 H).

3. Philco v. Spurling [1949] 2 K.B. 33; [1949] 2 All E.R. 882, C.A.

Delivery of inflammable celluloid film—negligent because no warning given—typist explodes same with lit cigarette—*Held*, not such a conscious act of volition as would break chain of causation. Singleton L.J. (887 H) expressly and Jenkins L.J. (888 E) by implication said that the onus of proof was on the defendant.

4. Davies v. Liverpool Corporation [1949] 2 All E.R. 175; [1949] W.N. 268, C.A.

Held, not *novus actus interveniens*, as "an unauthorised or wrongful act of a third person does not break the chain of causation if it might reasonably have been foreseen" (Denning L.J., 177 F).

5. Denny v. Supplies, etc. Co. [1950] 2 K.B. 374; [1950] 1 T.L.R. 1168, C.A.

Plaintiff injured unloading dangerously stowed timber—*Held*, conduct of plaintiff and his employers in unloading the timber did not break the chain of causation, as there was no practical alternative but to accept the danger, and therefore loading stevedores were liable. For other bad stowage cases see Chap. 7, (2) (d). Since H.L. decision in *Billings v. Riden*, Chap. 1, (4)(d) **7** the test may now be whether the subsequent conduct was reasonable rather than whether there was a practical alternative to accepting the danger.

6. Hogan v. Bentinck Collieries [1949] 1 All E.R. 588; [1949] W.N. 109, H.L.

Workmen's compensation case, in which the previous authorities are fully reviewed, Lord Simonds (592 C) said that negligent or inefficient medical treatment may constitute a new cause, but in each case it is a question of fact.

7. Simmons v. Pennington [1955] 1 W.L.R. 183; [1955] 1 All E.R. 240, C.A.

8. Cook v. S [1966] 1 W.L.R. 635; [1966] 1 All E.R. 248, Lawton J.

Solicitor negligently allowed divorce petition to go through undefended—counsel then mistakenly, but not negligently, advised against a motion to set aside—*Held*, this did not break the chain of causation. *N.B.* On appeal [1967] 1 All E.R. 299 this point was not canvassed, being apparently treated as correctly decided.

9. Dorset Yacht Co. v. Home Office [1970] A.C. 1004; [1970] 2 All E.R. 294, H.L.

Borstal escape case—*Held*, the act of the escapees in taking a boat and damaging it in the course of their escape did not break the chain of causation. Lord Reid (300 E) said that where human action was concerned, "that action must at least have been something very likely to happen if it is not to be regarded as *novus actus interveniens*... I do not think that a mere foreseeable possibility is or should be sufficient, for then the human action can more properly be regarded as a new cause than as a consequence of the original wrong-doing. But if the intervening action was likely to happen I do not think it can matter whether that action was innocent or tortious or criminal."

10. West v. Hughes of Beaconsfield [1971] R.T.R. 298, Mocatta J.

11. Robinson v. Post Office [1974] 1 W.L.R. 1176; [1974] 2 All E.R. 737, C.A.

Slip from ladder, causing wound in left shin—anti-tetanus serum given—which because plaintiff was allergic to same caused encephalitis—doctor administering the serum should have administered test dose first in a particular way—but instead did it in a negligent way—*Held*, since the allergy would not have been discovered even if the test dose had been given properly, it was not *novus actus interveniens.*

12. Hosie v. Arbroath F.C. [1978] C.L.Y. 2068; 1978 S.L.T. 122, Outer House

13. Vicar of Writtle v. Essex C.C. (1979) 77 L.G.R. 656; [1979] C.L.Y. 1865, Forbes J.

Boy, 12, remanded in care. Suspected of history of arson. Placed in community home. Staff at home negligently not informed of arson suspicion. Accordingly did not keep him under close observation and he escaped and set fire to nearby church—

Held, the boy's actions did not break the chain of causation resulting from the defendant's negligence in permitting him to escape. Applying the test laid down in *Dorset Yacht Co.* **9**, the actions of the boy were "something very likely to happen" and "a manifest and obvious risk." The test of liability for failing to control the acts of a third party is the same whether the third party is or is not responsible in law for his own acts, but it is easier to infer *novus actus interveniens* in the case of an adult.

14. Lamb v. Camden L.B.C. [1981] 1 Q.B. 625; [1981] 2 All E.R. 408, C.A.

Defendants damaged water main causing plaintiff's house to subside. House vacant pending repairs. Squatters entered and caused substantial damage. Squatters' actions foreseeable but not likely—*Held*, damage too remote. All L.JJ. said in terms that, in the case of intervening human action, it might not be possible to determine remoteness on the sole basis of reasonable foreseeability of damage, and all three declined to apply Lord Reid's *dicta* in *Dorset Yacht* **9**.

Per Oliver L.J., "the hypothetical reasonable man in the position of the tortfeasor cannot be said to foresee the behaviour unless that behaviour is such as would, viewed objectively, be very likely to occur" (418 E), and indeed there may be circumstances in which the court would require a degree of likelihood amounting almost to inevitability (419 F).

Per Lord Denning M.R., as a matter of public policy it was the plaintiff's responsibility to take precautions against squatters and the loss should fall on her or her insurers (if any) (414–415).

Per Watkins L.J., if the features of the act in question (including matters of public policy) suggested that the event or act "is not on any practical view of it remotely connected with the original act of negligence" it should be regarded as too remote (421 G); otherwise, the criterion of reasonable foreseeability laid down in *Wagon Mound (No. 2)* (Chap. 1, (4)(a)**7**) should be applied without any gloss (421 E).

15. Knightley v. Johns [1982] 1 W.L.R. 349; [1982] 1 All E.R. 851, C.A.

Accident in tunnel due to negligence of D1. D4, a police inspector, negligently failed to close tunnel as soon as possible and also negligently directed P, a police motor-cyclist, to ride through tunnel against oncoming traffic to close it. P sustained collision with oncoming car—*Held*, negligence of inspector (D4) was *novus actus interveniens* to negligence of D1. In considering whether the chain of causation between a tort and subsequent damage had been broken by a *novus actus interveniens*, the test to be applied was whether the damage was natural and probable and therefore reasonably foreseeable, in the sense that the damage was "of a kind or class which might normally be foreseen or contemplated, though the particular accidents could not be expected" (Stephenson L.J., 860 H). "Negligent conduct is more likely to break the chain of causation than conduct which is not; positive acts will more easily constitute new causes than inaction. Mistakes and mischances are to be expected when human beings, however well trained, have to cope with a crisis; what exactly they will be cannot be predicted, but if those which occur are natural the wrongdoer cannot, I think, escape responsibility . . . simply by calling them improbable or unforeseeable" (865 H).

16. Pawlack v. Doucette and Reinks [1985] 2 W.W.R. 588; [1985] C.L.Y. 2337, British Columbia Supreme Court

First defendant invited plaintiff to water ski. Knowing plaintiff had no experience, first defendant explained, from a position on shore, how plaintiff should position himself in water. Unidentified person on shore shouted "go". Second defendant, boat driver who had not asked whether plaintiff was experienced, applied full power. Plaintiff grabbed at rope. His fingers became entangled and were severed—*Held, inter alia*:

(a) First defendant negligent in failing properly to execute the supervisory role he had assumed.
(b) Second defendant negligent in failing to ascertain whether plaintiff experienced, and applying full power in response to shout from shore.
(c) Defence of *volenti non fit injuria* did not arise. Not an obvious and necessary risk that second defendant would accelerate before plaintiff ready and without establishing system of communication.
(d) Intervention of unidentified person did not affect or reduce liability of first and second defendants.
(e) Plaintiff 15 per cent contributorily negligent in grabbing moving rope.
(f) First and second defendants 55 per cent and 30 per cent liable respectively. (*Note*, the approach to contribution would be different in England and Wales—see *Fitzgerald v. Lane*, summarised on a different point at Chap. 13, (1)(k) **30**)

17. McGovern v. British Steel Corporation [1986] I C.R. 608; [1986] I R.L.R. 411, C.A.

Plaintiff tripped on displaced toe-board on walkway 20 metres below which molten metal was being moved, bent down to move it so no-one else would trip on it, and injured his back because the board was jammed—*Held*:

(a) Defendant in breach of absolute duty imposed by regulation 30(2) of Construction (Working Places) Regulations 1966 to keep gangway free from unnecessary obstruction.
(b) Where, as here, there had been some human intervention (by plaintiff himself or a third party) between breach of statutory duty and injury, plaintiff had to prove that the intervention:
  (i) was a natural and probable consequence of the breach; and
  (ii) had not broken the chain of causation.
  Here, he had done so, having regard to height of walkway and occasional presence of molten metal beneath it.
(c) Regulation 30(2) was intended to protect workmen against risk of injury, and was not confined to preventing risks resulting from colliding with or tripping over an obstruction.

18. Denton v. United Omnibus Co. Ltd, *The Times* May 6, 1986; [1986] C.L.Y. 2250, C.A.

Defendant's bus parked in depot with no door or gates. Bus not immobilised—unlawfully taken and driven into collision with plaintiff's car—*Held*, defendant not liable. In the absence of a special relationship or special circumstances a party was not liable in negligence for failing to prevent the unlawful or unauthorised act of another.

19. Youell v. Bland Welch & Co. Ltd (No. 2) [1990] 2 Lloyd's Rep. 431, Phillips J.

Brokers arranging reinsurance failed to inform insurers that, unlike the original insurance, the reinsurance on offer and subsequently effected was subject to a 48 month cut off clause or to take appropriate action once they knew there was a risk of the period of reinsurance being exceeded—*Held*, the brokers' duties did not lie exclusively in contract, there being concurrent remedies in contract and tort; the brokers were in breach of duty of care; the insurers' own negligence in failing to notice the clause did not breach the chain of causation but amounted to contributory negligence to the extent of 20 per cent.

20. Cunningham v. Reading Football Club [1992] P.I.Q.R. p.141; [1991] C.L.Y. 3413, Drake J.

Actions of hooligans at football ground did not amount to *novus actus interveniens*. For summary see Chap. 10(6)(a) **13**.

21. Topp v. London Country Bus (South West) [1993] 1 W.L.R. 979; [1993] 3 All E.R. 448, C.A.

Defendant's minibus left for over eight hours unlocked, unattended and with keys in at bus stop outside public house—unlawfully taken and driven into collision with cyclist—*Held*, defendant not liable—owed no duty of care to cyclist—acts of wrongdoer constituted *novus actus interveniens. P. Perl (Exporters) Ltd v. Camden L.B.C.* (Chap. 1, (3)(b) **15**) followed.

22. Banque Bruxelles Lambert S.A. v. Eagle Star Insurance Co. Ltd and other appeals [1995] 2 W.L.R. 607; [1995] New L.J. 343, C.A.

U1. Smith v. Hodge (1974) C.A. 194.

Bonfire negligently lit by defendant near plaintiff's yacht—fire brigade put it out—but later (as assumed) some embers revive and burn out yacht—defendant argued that the negligence of the fire brigade in not extinguishing the embers properly was *novus actus interveniens*—*Held*, not so, and defendant liable.

U2. Rawson v. Clark (1980) C.A. 784.

Injury in April 1973 to P's cervical spine caused by B's negligence. As a result P's neck was more vulnerable to further trauma than it otherwise would have been and it was foreseeable that if his neck was subjected to further trauma the consequences would be more serious than before the injury. In September 1973 before he had fully recovered from the injury, P (who was a traffic examiner) told C in the course of a driving test to do an emergency stop. C skidded and P sustained a severe jerk to his neck which exacerbated its condition. C was held not to have been negligent in skidding—*Held*, that B was liable for the exacerbated condition of P's neck. "The problem, whether it be described as remoteness or causative, applying the principles of *novus actus interveniens*, is dominated by the question whether the injuries sustained in the second event were foreseeable as a consequence of the injuries caused by the first event" (Cumming-Bruce L.J., 14 B), and as it was eminently foreseeable that in the course of a driving test there was likely to be sudden movements in the vehicle such that the neck was likely to be subjected to further trauma (15 B), B was liable for the totality of the injuries to P. "The injuries sustained by P in September were due to the operation of two concurrent causes which combined to produce the damage . . . . . . As C was not negligent, the result in law in that B, the author of one of the two concurrent causes, is responsible for the whole of the damage" (16 B–D).

U3. Wilson v. British Gas Corporation (1986) C.A. 1114.

Plaintiff reversed van in crowded car park making minor impact with defendant's unbraked compressor which began to roll down hill; plaintiff ran and tried to apply hand brake but was injured when hit by its towbar: defendants held liable; the minor impact was not an intervening act which destroyed the defendant's negligence; the plaintiff was not negligent in trying to stop the compressor nor was he guilty of contributory negligence.

U4. Borromeo v. London Buses Ltd (1993) C.A. 863.

Plaintiff stepped from pavement into collision with bus with without looking. Bus driver stopped immediately—was told someone trapped under rear nearside wheel. Without investigating, drove forward, and ran over plaintiff's foot—*Held*, driver negligent in not going to see what the situation was. Plaintiff one-third to blame—chain of causation from her original negligence not broken.

(d) Novus Actus of Plaintiff

		Whether defendant liable or not
Motor-cyclist going too fast—rescuing child	1	Yes
FIRE—ATTEMPTING TO PUT IT OUT	2	Yes
UNSAFE STOWAGE—NO PRACTICAL ALTERNATIVE BUT TO UNLOAD	3	Yes
Collision at sea—reasonable refusal of tow	4	Yes
Accident—suicide	5, 6	Yes
Obstruction—plaintiff going on deviation	7	Yes
IMPRISONED IN LAVATORY—CLIMBING OUT	8	Yes
GAS-FILLED WELL—DOCTOR GOING TO RESCUE	9	Yes
Reasonable foresight the test, not directness	10	—

Physical exertion to remedy defect—causing coronary thrombosis	11	No
Second injury—caused by plaintiff's unreasonable conduct—is novus actus qua original negligence	12	No
Accident causing orthopaedic injuries—suicide	13	No
Hospital patient growing depressed—suicide attempt..............	14	No
Negligent sterilisation—decision not to undergo abortion..............	15	Yes
Intervention by plaintiff between breach of statutory duty and injury—what plaintiff must prove..............	16	Yes
Defective foundations—chain of causation broken by plaintiff's engineer's remedial works	17	No
Trespassing dog—plaintiff falling while running to eject it..............	U1	No
Plaintiff's van causing defendant's unbraked compressor to run downhill..............	U2	Yes

1. Morgan v. Aylen [1942] 1 All E.R. 489, Cassels J.

Defendant motor-cyclist going too fast—plaintiff escorting child of three-and-a-half home—child moved into roadway—plaintiff ran in to rescue child—struck by motor-cycle—*Held*, defendant liable.

2. Hyett v. Great Western Railway [1948] 1 K.B. 345; [1947] 2 All E.R. 264, C.A.

Plaintiff invitee on defendants' premises, attempts to put out fire caused by defendants' negligence—*Held*, not *novus actus* and plaintiff could recover. "It is no doubt in every case relevant to consider whether or not it is life or property which is in danger. It is material to consider the relationship of the plaintiff who intervenes to the property or person in peril. It is relevant to consider the degree of danger and risk, and so forth. . . . The act of plaintiff . . . was the kind of act which defendants might reasonably have anticipated as likely to follow from their act of negligence. . . . " (266 C-F, *per* Tucker L.J.).

3. Denny v. Supplies, etc., Co. [1950] 2 K.B. 374; [1950] 1 T.L.R. 1168, C.A.

Plaintiff a dock labourer injured when unloading dangerously stowed timber—sues his employers and the loading stevedores—action failed against employers (apparently because there was no safe method of unloading the timber at all—see T.L.R. 1170) but succeeded against loading stevedores—on appeal *held inter alia* that, as there was no practical alternative but to accept the danger, not *novus actus interveniens.* For other bad stowage cases see Chap. 7, (2) (d). *But* since H.L. decision in *A. C. Billings v. Riden* **7**, the test must be taken to be whether plaintiff's conduct was reasonable rather than whether there was a practical alternative to accepting the danger.

4. The Guildford [1956] P. 364; [1956] 2 All E.R. 915, Lord Merriman P.

Collison at sea—plaintiff reasonably refused tow—*Held*, applying, Chap. 1, (4) (c) **I**, not *novus actus.*

5. Cavanagh v. London Transport, *The Times*, October 23, 1956, [1956] C.L.Y. 5824, Devlin J.

Held, as suicide was a direct result of injuries caused in accident, plaintiff's widow could recover for death of deceased. *But* see **10**.

6. Pigney v. Pointers Transport [1957] 1 W.L.R. 1121; [1957] 2 All E.R. 807, Pilcher J.

Accident causing nervous depression as a result of which deceased committed suicide—*Held*, applying **5** and the *Polemis* test, widow could claim under the Fatal Accidents Acts as the death was "directly traceable" to the physical injury (810 G). *Held* further that *Beresford v. Royal Insurance* [1938] A.C. 586 did not bar the claim because a claim under the Fatal Accidents Acts was not derived from, nor did the damages form part of, the deceased's estate. *Held* further, that although deceased was sane within the M'Naughten Rules, public policy did not bar the claim. *But* judge went on to award damages under the Law Reform Act as well as under the Fatal Accidents Acts. *But* see **10**.

7. A. C. Billings v. Riden [1958] A.C. 240; [1957] 3 All E.R. 1, H.L.

Defendant makes obstruction and plaintiff deviates to get round—*Held*, defendant liable, as plaintiff's conduct was reasonable, and this was the proper test where act of plaintiff was concerned.

8. Sayers v. Harlow U. D. C. [1958] 1 W.L.R. 623; [1958] 2 All E.R. 342, C.A.

Held, plaintiff's conduct was not unreasonable and therefore damages not too remote.

9. Baker v. Hopkins [1959] 1 W.L.R. 966; [1959] 3 All E.R. 225, C.A.

Held, not *novus actus*, as the principle did not apply where the act in question, *i.e.* the rescue—was the very thing that was likely to happen as a result of the negligence, *i.e.* filling the well with gas.

10. Overseas Tankship v. Morts Dock (The Wagon Mound) [1961] A.C. 388, [1961] 1 All E.R. 404, P.C.

Held, disapproving *Re Polemis* [1921] 3 K.B. 560, that reasonable foresight was the test for recovery of damage, not directness. In view of this decision, the decisions in *Cavanagh v. London Transport* **5** and *Pigney v. Pointers Transport* **6** (suicide after accident) may require caution, in so far as they are based on the decision in *Polemis.*

11. Blaikie v. British Transport Commission, 1961 S.C. 44; 1961 S.L.T. 189, 2nd Div.

Defect in engine causing great physical exertion on part of driver—coronary thrombosis soon after—*Held*, applying *Wagon Mound* **10**, defendants not liable.

12. McKew v. Holland & Hannen [1969] 3 All E.R. 1621; 8 K.I.R. 921, H.L.

Leg injury—leg subsequently gave way while plaintiff was descending steep staircase without handrail—*Held*, defendants not liable for second injury, as plaintiff's conduct was sufficiently unreasonable to break the chain of causation. *Cf. Wieland v. Cyril Lord Carpets* [1969] 3 All E.R. 1066, where Eveleigh J. held defendants liable for a subsequent fall which was due to the fact that as a result of the original accident plaintiff had to wear a collar which prevented her using her bifocal lenses properly.

13. Swami v. Lo (1979) 105 D.L.R. (3d) 451; [1980] C.L.Y. 1904, Brit. Col. Sup. Ct.

So *held*. The Court suggested the result might have been different, had the accident caused head injuries resulting in mental disturbance and culminating in suicide.

14. Hyde v. Tameside A. H. A., *The Times*, April 16, 1981; [1981] C.L.Y. 1854, C.A.

P admitted to hospital with painful shoulder. Wrongly believed he had cancer and became increasingly depressed and attempted suicide. It was *held* that there had been no want of care by the hospital, but (*per* Lord Denning M. R., *obiter*), even if there had been, the suicide attempt was not a reasonably foreseeable consequence thereof, and the policy of the law should be to discourage actions in respect of suicide or attempted suicide.

15. Emeh v. Kensington, Chelsea And Westminster H.A. [1985] Q.B. 1012; [1984] 3 All E.R. 1044, C.A.

Sterilisation failed through negligence of D—*Held*, decision not to have an abortion did not amount to a *novus actus* on the part of the plaintiff. For full summary see Chap. 18, (11) **29**.

16. McGovern v. British Steel Corporation [1986] I.C.R. 608; [1986] I.R.L.R. 411, C.A.

Plaintiff tripped on displaced toe-board on walkway 20 metres below which molten metal was being moved, bent down to move it so no-one else would trip on it, and injured his back because the board was jammed—*Held*:

(a) Defendant in breach of absolute duty imposed by regulation 30(2) of Construction (Working Places) Regulations 1966 to keep gangway free from unnecessary obstruction.
(b) Where, as here, there had been some human intervention (by plaintiff himself or a third party) between breach of statutory duty and injury, plaintiff had to prove that the intervention.
    (i) was a natural and probable consequence of the breach; and
    (ii) had not broken the chain of causation.

    Here, he had done so, having regard to height of walkway and occasional presence of molten metal beneath it.
(c) Regulation 30(2) war intended to protect workman against risk of injury, and was not confined to preventing risks resulting from colliding with or tripping over an obstruction.

17. Frost v. Moody Homes Ltd; Hoskisson v. Donald Moody Ltd (1990) 6 Const. L.J. 43: [1990] C.L.Y. 3253, Judge Newey Q.C.

Plaintiffs purchased house on estate developed by first and second defendants; cracks subsequently appeared in house—*Held, inter alia*, structural engineer acting on behalf of the plaintiffs and their insurers was negligent in assessing that expensive foundation works were necessary and that broke the chain of causation of damage. Far further details see Chap. 18, (6) **72**.

U1. Bard v. O'Connor (1960) C.A. 56, *The Times*, February 4, 1960

Defendant's dog escaped through an unfenced boundary into plaintiff's garden and attacked plaintiff's dog—plaintiff in going to intervene fell down some steps and broke his ankle—*Held*, that defendant was not liable, since the damage was not a direct consequence of the dog-fight, and was therefore too remote. (*But, per* Lord Goddard (2 C), if the plaintiff had been injured as a direct consequence of the dog-fight, "clearly he would have been entitled to damages").

U2. Wilson v. British Gas Corporation (1986) C.A. 1114

Plaintiff reversed van in crowded car park making minor impact with defendant's unbraked compressor which began to roll down hill; plaintiff ran and tried to apply handbrake but was injured when hit by its towbar: defendants held liable; the minor impact was not an intervening act which destroyed the defendant's negligence; the plaintiff was not negligent in trying to stop the compressor nor was he guilty of contributory negligence.

(5) Whether Duty Arises in Tort or Contract

1. Davie v. New Merton Board Mills [1959] A.C. 604; [1959] 1 All E.R. 346; H.L.

"The same act or omission by an employer may support an action in tort or for breach of an implied term of the contract of employment, but it can only lead to confusion if, when the action is in tort, the court embarks on the controversial subject of implied contractual terms" (Viscount Simonds, 350 D).

2. Matthews v. Kuwait Bechtel [1959] 2 Q.B. 57; [1959] 2 All E.R. 345; C.A.

Plaintiff employee having sustained injuries abroad wished to sue out of the jurisdiction—which he could only do if the action was in respect of a breach of contract rather than tort—*Held*, the duty of an employer in regard to the safety of an employee in the course of his work arose either in tort or in contract, at the option of the employee. The authorities relied on as the basis of the above were the dicta set out in **1** and certain dicta from *Lister v. Romford* [1957] 1 All E.R. 125, including the following by Lord Radcliffe:

"But it (*i.e.* the duty of an employer) is certainly, I think, as much contractual as tortious . . . It is a familiar position in our law that the same wrongful act may be made the subject of an action either in contract or tort at the election of the claimant, and, although the course chosen may have certain incidental consequences which would not have followed had the other course been adopted, it is a mistake to regard the two kinds of liability as themselves necessarily exclusive of each other" (349 I).

3. Hedley Byrne v. Heller [1964] A.C. 465; [1963] 2 All E.R. 575 H.L.

Question was whether an action lay for negligence in a bankers' reference for creditworthiness where there was no contract between the giver and recipient of the reference—*Held*, yes. For details of the basis of such a duty in tort, see chap. 19(a).

4. Clark v. Kirby Smith [1964] Ch. 506; [1964] 2 All E.R. 835; Plowman J.

Negligent failure by a solicitor to give a notice on behalf of a tenant—on the issue of damages plaintiff claimed that the action was founded in tort—*Held*, not so. "A line of cases going back for nearly 150 years shows, I think, that the client's cause of action is in contract and not in tort." The judge also said (837 F) that he did not accept that the *Hedley* **3** case was an authority for saying that the liability of a solicitor to his client for negligence was a liability in tort. *But* see also *Cook v. S.* (Chap. 1, (2) (c) **8**). *Disapproved* by Lord Denning M.R. in *Esso* **13**.

5. Bagot v. Stevens Scanlon [1966] 1 Q.B. 197; [1964] 3 All E.R. 577, Diplock L.J.

Alleged negligent supervision by deft architects, leading to settlement of foundations and cracking of drains—if the action lay in contract only it was statute-barred—*Held*, the action was one which was founded on contract alone.

"Now I could accept that there may be cases where a similar duty is owed under the contract and independently of the contract. I think that on examination all these will turn out to be cases where the law in the old days recognised something in the nature of a status like a public calling (such as common carrier, common innkeeper, or a bailor and bailee) or the status of master and servant. There it can properly be said, as it was in such cases as *Lister v. Romford Ice* [1957] 1 All E.R. 125, that independently of contract, there existed from the mere status a relationship which gave rise to a duty of care not dependent on the existence of a contract between the parties; but I do not think that that principle applies to professional relationships of the kind with which I am concerned here, where someone undertakes to exercise by contract his professional skill in relation to the matter" (580 E-F). *Disapproved* by Lord Denning M.R. in *Esso* **13**.

6. Building Holidays Scheme v. Post Office [1966] 1 Q.B. 247; [1965] 1 All E.R. 163 C.A. Lord Denning M.R. (167 F-G):

> "At common law bailment is often associated with a contract, but this is not always the case . . . An action against a bailee can often be put, not as an action in contract, nor in tort, but as an action of its own, *sui generis*, arising out of the possession had by the bailee of the goods . . . Suffice it to say at the present day that if goods, which have been delivered to a bailee, are lost or damaged while in his custody, he is liable to the person damnified (who may be the owner or the bailor) unless the bailee proves that the loss or damage is not due to any fault on his part . . . "

7. Lee Cooper v. Jenkins [1967] 2 Q.B. 1; [1965] 1 All E.R. 280 Marshall J.

Plaintiff owners of goods contracted with A, forwarding agents, to arrange to consign same—A in turn contracted with D *as principals*—D's driver negligently left vehicle unattended, so that goods were stolen—*Held*, plaintiffs could sue deft under *Donoghue v. Stevenson*, because the deft knew that the plaintiffs, and not A, were the owners of the goods. *N.B.* **6** was not cited.

8. Weller v. Foot and Mouth Institute [1966] 1 Q.B. 569; [1965] 3 All E.R. 560 Widgery J.

Held, that apart from the *Hedley* type cases the duty of care in tort was limited to cases arising from a risk of direct injury to persons or property. For full details, see Chap. 1, (3) (a) **1**.

9. Quinn v. Burch [1966] 2 Q.B. 370; [1965] 3 All E.R. 801, Paull J.

Plaintiff sub-contractor for labour only—deft contractors failed to provide a stepladder as requested—to save time plaintiff used a trestle which was unsafe unless footed—it slipped while unfooted—plaintiff sued in contract for breach of implied term to provide equipment—*Held (obiter)*, Contributory Negligence Act 1945 did not permit plaintiff to recover partial damages, since the breach of contract by defts did not constitute a "fault" within CNA 1945, s. 4. *Applied* in **12**. *N.B.* The decision was affirmed by C.A. [1966] 2 All E.R. 283 without this point being mentioned.

10. Cook v. S. [1967] 1 W.L.R. 457; [1967] 1 All E.R. 299, C.A.

See under 1 (2) (c) **8**. See also *Esso* **13**.

11. Heaven v. Mortimore (1968) 205 E.G. 767; [1968] C.L.Y. 2660, C.A.

Cracks appeared in negligently built houses—son, on behalf of father who built houses, bored some trial boreholes, and negligently filled them in—*Held*, son was liable for damage resulting therefrom. At first instance Karminski J. *held*, applying *Wagon Mound* (No 2) (Chap. 1 (3) (c) **6**), that son was liable both in nuisance and negligence, as his duty lay in tort: the son had argued that any liability was contractual only and lay against father. The C.L.Y. report of the case before C.A. does not specifically refer to the point, beyond saying that the son was held liable in negligence.

12. Sole v. Hallt [1973] 1 Q.B. 574; [1973] 1 All E.R. 1032, Swanwick J.

Held, that subcontractor for labour only could sue in tort under Occupiers' Liability Act 1957, although he entered under contract. *N.B.* The advantage here in suing in tort was to avoid the consequences of *Quinn v. Burch* (Chap. 4, (1)(a) **14**), which decided that contributory negligence was a complete bar to a claim for breach of contract.

13. Esso Petroleum v. Mardon [1976] Q.B. 801; [1976] 2 All E.R. 5, C.A.

Negligent estimate of likely petrol sales to be expected from a new garage site—representee induced to take tenancy of site—*Held*, the duty in tort co-existed with the duty arising under the contract of tenancy. Lord Denning M.R. (15 A-G) said that negligence by a professional man arose not only in contract, but was also actionable in tort, in the same way as in the master and servant cases; and he disapproved *Clark* **4** and *Bagot* **5**, citing Lord Haldane in *Nocton v. Ashburton* [1914] A.C. 932, at 956, and Lord Campbell in *Boorman v. Brown* (1844) 11 Cl. & Fin. 1, at 42, as authorities for the proposition that liability, both in professional and in master and servant cases arose either in contract or in tort. *But in Cook* **10** Lord Denning M.R. (302 I) said: "The cause of action, it must be remembered, is one for breach of contract. An action against a solicitor is always one for breach of contract, as was held in *Groom v. Crocker* [1939] 1 K.B. 194."

14. Midland Bank Trust Co. v. Hett Stubbs & Kemp [1979] Ch. 384; [1978] 3 All E.R. 571, Oliver J.

Held, following *Esso*, **13**, and not following *Clark*, **4**, and *Bagot*, **5**, a claim against a solicitor could be framed in tort as well as in contract.

15. Batty v. Metropolitan Property [1978] Q.B. 554; [1978] 2 All E.R. 445, C.A.

So *held*, following *Esso* **13**. Doubted in *D & F. Estates*, Chap. 18(6) **63**.

16. Power v. Halley [1979] C.L.Y. 2562; (1978) 88 D.L.R. (3d) 381, Nfld.Sup.Ct.

So *held*, applying *Esso* **13** and disapproving *Bagot* **5**.

17. Ross v. Caunters [1980] Ch. 297; [1979] 3 All E.R. 580, Megarry V.C.

18. Hill (Wm.) Organisation v. Sunley (1982) 22 Build.L.R. 1; [1982] C.L.Y. 252, C.A.

19. Equitable Debenture Assets Corporation Ltd v. William Moss Group [1983] 2 Con L.R.1; [1985] C.L.Y. 221, Judge Newey Q.C.

Architect employed to design and supervise erection of curtain walling to be erected by subcontractor—*Held*, architect owed to employer a duty of care in negligence as well as in contract to precisely the same extent and was liable for faulty design and poor workmanship of the scheme: main contractor also held in breach of implied term and of duty of care owed to employer and architect to inform latter of design defects known to main contractor. For further details see Chap. 18, (6) **39**.

20. Rees Hough Ltd v. Redland Reinforced Plastics Ltd (1985) 27 BLR 136; [1984] C.L.Y. 390, Judge Newey Q.C.

See Chap. 4, (2)(a) **20**.

21. Victoria University of Manchester v. Hugh Wilson & Lewis Womersley & Pochin (Contractors) Ltd [1985] 2 ConLR 43; [1985] C.L.Y. 220, Judge Newey Q.C.

Ceramic tile cladding to reinforced concrete building in due course fell off to a large extent. The following findings *inter alia* were made; the architect owed similar duties in contract and tort and should have warned the plaintiffs of the dangers inherent in the method of fixing the tiles; the subcontractor owed main contractor a duty in tort as well as in contract to fix the tiles properly. For further details see Chap. 18, (6) **43**.

22. Thake v. Maurice [1986] Q.B. 644; [1986] 1 All E.R. 497, C.A.

Claim for breach of contractual guarantee as to success of vasectomy failed. See Chap. 18, (8) **31**.

23. Forsikringsaktieselskapet Vesta v. Butcher [1988] 3 W.L.R. 565, C.A.; [1988] 2 All E.R. 43, C.A.

Insurance brokers acting for Norwegian insurance company placed reinsurance with London underwriters—*Held*, liable not only in contract but also for breach of duty of care in failing to act on telephone call from insurance company that a term of the reinsurance was unacceptable. Deduction for contributory negligence permissible albeit claim laid in contract. (Appeal on a different point to H. L. dismissed [1989] A.C. 852).

24. Tai Hing Cotton Mill Ltd v. Liu Chong Hing Bank Ltd [1986] A.C. 80; [1985] 3 W.L.R. 317, P.C.

Judgment [1985] 3 W.L.R. 317 at p. 330.

> "Their Lordships do not believe that there is anything to the advantage of the law's development in searching for a liability in tort where the parties are in a contractual relationship. This is particularly so in a commercial relationship ... their Lordships believe it to be correct in principle and necessary for the avoidance of confusion in the law to adhere to the contractual analysis; on principle ... and for the avoidance of confusion because different consequences do follow according to whether liability arises from contract or tort, *e.g.* in the limitation of action ... Their Lordships do not, however, accept that the parties' mutual obligations in tort can be any greater than those to be found expressly or by necessary implication in their contract."

See also Chap. 18, (2) **23**. Considered in *Hendersen v. Merrett Syndicates* **38**.

25. Surrey Health Borough Council v. Lovell Construction Ltd (1988) 42 BLR 25; [1989] C.L.Y. 218, Judge Fox-Andrews Q.C.

Building owner claimed against main contractor in contract and tort for loss and damage by fire caused by negligence of subcontractor—*Held*, there was no room for a parallel duty in tort since the contract expressly dealt with the subject matters of the claim; the claim in tort failed: there could be no claim for loss and damage save that recoverable in contract.

26. University Court of the University of Glasgow. v. William Whitfield (1988) 42 BLR 66; [1989] C.L.Y. 2539, Judge Bowsher Q.C.

University sued architect for negligent advice and design of art gallery whereby leaks and condensation occurred—*Held* architect under a duty in contract and tort to exercise all due and proper professional care and skill.

27. Gray v. T.P. Bennett & Son (1987) 43 BLR 63; [1990] C.L.Y. 393, Judge Sir William Stabb Q.C.

For details see Chap. 18, (6) **65**.

28. Richard Roberts Holdings Ltd v. Douglas Smith Stimson Partnership (1988) 46 BLR 50; [1990] C.L.Y. 392, Judge Newey Q.C.

Architects held liable in contract and tort to plaintiffs for recommending and permitting installation of unsuitable lining for effluent tank albeit no fee was charged for this part of their work and they were ignorant in the field of linings. Contractor also held liable in contract and tort for poor design and workmanship.

29. Caparo Industries PLC v. Dickman [1990] 2 A.C. 605; [1990] 2 W.L.R. 358, H.L. *Per* Lord Bridge at [1990] 2 W.L.R. 366C.

30. Youell v. Bland Welch & Co Ltd. (No. 2) [1990] 2 Lloyd's Rep. 431, Phillips J.

Brokers arranging reinsurance failed to inform insurers that unlike the original insurance the reinsurance on offer and subsequently effected was subject to a 48 month cut off clause or to take appropriate action once they knew there was a risk of the period of reinsurance being exceeded—*Held*, their duties did not lie exclusively in contract, there being concurrent remedies in contract and tort and the brokers were in breach of duty of care; the insurers' own negligence in failing to notice the clause did not break the chain of causation but amounted to contributory negligence to the extent of 20 per cent.

31. Pfeiffer v. E. & E. Installations [1991] 1 EGLR 162, C.A.

Heating engineer instructed to inspect heating plant at house plaintiff proposed to buy; failure to discover cracks in heat exchanger—*Held*, whether case put in contract or tort the duty was to test and inspect and report with the reasonable skill and care to be expected of a competent heating engineer; liable.

32. Barclays Bark PLC v. Khaira [1992] 1 W.L.R. 623; [1992] C.L.Y 215, Thomas Morison Q.C. For further details see Chap. 18, (2) **32**.

33. Barclays Bank PLC v. Quincecare Ltd [1992] 4 All E.R. 363; [1988] C.L.Y. 2200, C.A. For details see Chap. 18, (2) **30**.

34. Hiron v. Pynford South Ltd [1992] 2 EGLR 138; [1993] C.L.Y. 2997, Judge Newey Q.C.

Structural engineer advised insurers of property as to its underpinning; building surveyor likewise advised owners; each pursuant to contract—*Held*, in neither case was there owed in addition a duty in tort; further the engineer did not owe a duty of care to the owners.

35. Heatley v. William H. Brown Ltd [1992] 1 EGLR 289; [1992] C.L.Y. 1549, Judge Bowsher Q.C.

Structural surveyor held to be negligently in breach of contract; in view of the detailed terms of the contract there was no room for liability in tort. *Tai Hing*, Chap. 18, (2) **23** followed.

36. Lancashire & Cheshire Association of Baptist Churches Inc. v. Howard & Seddon Partnership [1993] 3 All E.R. 467; (1993) 65 BLR 21, Judge Kershaw Q.C.

Plaintiffs' claim against architect in contract and tort for negligent design: contract claim statute barred—*Held*, in law there could be a duty of care actionable in the tort of negligence where the parties were in a contractual professional relationship but not in all such cases. Plaintiffs' claim in tort failed: for details see Chap. 18, (6) **79**.

37. Bailey v. London Borough of Newham [1993] C.L.Y. 3796, H.H. Judge Cooke.

See Chap. 10, (8)(a) **30**.

38. Henderson v. Merrett Syndicates Ltd [1994] 3 W.L.R. 761, H.L.

Where a tortious duty arose under *Hedley Byrne* principles, such arose irrespective of whether there was a contractual relationship between the parties; unless precluded by contract, a plaintiff who had available to him concurrent remedies in contract and tort might choose that remedy which appeared to him to be the most advantageous. For further details see Chap. 19, (a) **22**.

39. Barclays Bank PLC v. Fairclough Building Ltd. [1995] P.I.Q.R. P 152; [1995] 5 C.L. 253, C.A.

Contract to carry out maintenance work on building; subcontractor undertakes to do part of the work including cleaning of asbestos roofs; cleaning of roofs sub-subcontracted—*Held*, sub-subcontractor was in breach of contract in failing to take precautions which a careful and competent contractor would have taken whereby the subcontractor had suffered economic loss namely damages payable to the main contractor. *Further held*, applying *Henderson v. Merrett Syndicate*, **38**, the sub-subcontractor as a skilled contractor undertaking maintenance work assumed responsibility to the subcontractor no less than did a financial or other professional adviser undertaking work and as such owed a concurrent duty in tort to avoid causing economic loss by failing to exercise the care and skill of a competent contractor. *Further held*, in such circumstances it was permissible to reduce (by half) the damages suffered by the subcontractor under the Law Reform (Contributory Negligence) Act 1945 on the ground that the damage was suffered partly as a result of the subcontractor's own fault in that it also failed, as it ought, to have appreciated the risk of contamination from asbestos dust.

2. STANDARD OF CARE

(1) "Reasonable"

1. Glasgow Corporation v. Muir [1943] A.C. 448; [1943] 2 All E.R. 44, H.L.

Lord Macmillan (48): "The reasonable man is presumed to be free both from over-apprehension and over-confidence."

2. Daborn v. Bath Tramways [1946] 2 All E.R. 333, C.A.

"In determining whether a party is negligent, the standard of reasonable care is that which is reasonably to be demanded in the circumstances. A relevant circumstance to take into account may be the importance of the end to be served by acting in this way or that. As has often been pointed out, if all the trains in this country were restricted to a speed of 5 m.p.h., there would be fewer accidents, but our national life would be intolerably slowed down. The purpose to be served, if sufficiently important, justifies the assumption of abnormal risk." (Asquith L.J. at 336 E.) Cited with approval in **3** by Singleton L.J.

3. Watt v. Herts C.C. [1954] 1 W.L.R. 835; [1954] 2 All E.R. 368, C.A.

Denning L.J. (371 B): "It is always a question of balancing the risk against the end," and he also said there was a very considerable difference between commercial end to make profit and human end to save life or limb.

4. Hayward v. P.L.A. [1954] 2 Lloyd's Rep. 363, McNair J.

Question was whether means of escape for persons immersed in dock were "reasonably adequate" (Docks Regs. 2)—defendants argued that since they had had a standard practice since 1904, this must be taken to be reasonable. To this judge (370, col. 1) said: "This argument, if accepted would lead to the conclusion that the dock authorities are to be the sole judges of the extent of the obligation imposed on them by the Reg. I accordingly reject the argument, though I am prepared to accept that the practice of other good authorities may be some evidence of reasonableness." This case went to the House of Lords [1956] 2 Lloyd's Rep. 1, where above dictum was not commented on, except that in argument (p. 6, col. 1) Lord Tucker appears to have agreed therewith.

5. A. C. Billings v. Riden [1958] A.C. 240; [1957] 3 All E.R. 1, H.L.

Lord Reid (8 H, Lords Simonds and Cohen concurring): "But in considering what a reasonable person would realise or do in a particular situation, we must have regard to human nature as we know it, and if one thinks that in a particular situation the great majority would have behaved in one way, it would not be right to say that a reasonable man would or should have behaved in a different way. A reasonable man does not mean a paragon of circumspection." Lord Somervell (14 C): "The duty being a general duty to use reasonable care, reasonableness is the test of the steps to be taken."

6. Hardy v. M.I.B. [1964] 2 Q.B. 745; [1964] 2 All E.R. 742, C.A.

"Normally . . . the reasonable man is an idealised average man, behaving always as the average man behaves in his good moments. The average man may have his bad moments. . . . The reasonable man, as normally understood, has no such bad moments." (Pearson L.J., 748 B).

7. Goldman v. Hargrave [1967] 1 A.C. 645; [1966] 2 All E.R. 989, P.C.

Occupier of premises had a red gum tree which was hit by lightning and caught fire—he did nothing to prevent spread of fire to other premises—*Held*, he was liable, as owing a duty of care to prevent spread, but that the standard of care required was "what it was reasonable to expect of him in his individual circumstances" (Lord Wilberforce, 996 D).

8. Budden v. B.P. (1980) J.P.L. 586; [1980] C.L.Y. 1902, C.A.

Plaintiff sued for alleged injury to children through ingesting petrol fumes containing organo-lead additives—*Held*, action would be struck out, as the defendants had complied with the statutory standards and therefore could not be negligent.

9. Leakey v. National Trust [1980] Q.B. 485; [1980] 1 All E.R. 17, C.A.

Landslip from hill owned and occupied by defendants came onto and/or threatened the properties of the plaintiffs. The landslip was entirely due to natural causes—*Held*, applying *Goldman* **7**, defendants owed a duty of care, and that the standard of care required was set out by Lord Wilberforce in *Goldman*, and included "the factor of what the particular man, not the average man, could be expected to do, having regard, amongst other things, where a serious expenditure of money is required. . . . , to his means." (37 C).

10. Page Motors Ltd v. Epsom & Ewell B.C. (1982) 80 L.G.R. 337; [1982] C.L.Y. 2267, C.A.

Held, considering *Goldman v. Hargrave* **7**, and *Leakey v. N. T.* **9**, that in determining what steps the council should reasonably have taken to abate the nuisance and what was a reasonable time in which to abate it, the court was not limited to considering the council's physical and financial resources only, but was entitled to take into account broader matters arising from the council's public responsibilities.

11. Condon v. Basi [1985] 1 W.L.R. 866; [1985] 2 All E.R. 453, C.A.

Defendant, a local Sunday league footballer, lunged with studs showing nine inches off the ground at Plaintiff, on the opposing side, after plaintiff had pushed the ball away—plaintiff broke right leg—defendant sent off. Court of Appeal upheld trial Judge's decision that D was liable in negligence.

Per Lord Donaldson M.R.: " ... there is no authority as to what is the standard of care which governs the conduct of players in competitive sports generally and, above all, in a competitive sport whose rules ... contemplate ... physical contact between the players." There would be liability "if ... the defendant failed to exercise that degree of care which was appropriate in all the circumstances, or ... acted in a way to which the plaintiff cannot be expected to have consented ... The standard is objective, but objective in a different set of circumstances. Thus there will of course be a higher degree of care required of a player in a First Division football match than of a player in a local league football match."

12 Cook v. Square D. Ltd [1992] P.I.Q.R. P33, [1992] I.C.R. 262, C.A.

Plaintiff, engineer employed by first defendant, sent to work at premises in Saudi Arabia occupied by second defendant, at which third defendant was main contractor. Plaintiff's foot went through hole, of which he was aware, caused by the moving of a tile in floor of control room where he worked, probably by a subcontractor—*Held*, first defendant not liable. Where employee injured on premises occupied by third party, circumstances to be taken into account in determining extent of employers' duty to employee included:-

(a) place where work is to be done;
(b) nature of the building (if any) on the site;
(c) experience of employee;
(d) nature of his work on the premises;
(e) degree of control the employer can reasonably exercise; and
(f) employer's knowledge, if any, of defective state of premises.

Here, first defendant knew second and third defendants were reliable and responsible companies; could not be responsible for daily events in Saudi Arabia; and was under no duty to advise second and third defendants to take precautions against kind of hazard which plaintiff encountered.

13. Morrell v. Owen, *The Times*, December 14, 1993; [1993] C.L.Y. 2957, Mitchell J.

Archery and discus competitions for paraplegic athletes held simultaneously in sports hall, divided by net. Stray discus hit net. Net billowed out and discus hit plaintiff, an archer on other side, on temple. Plaintiff unaware of discus event. Archers received no safety instructions and coaches had taken no special safety precautions—*Held*, archery and discus coaches liable. Accident was entirely foreseeable. Coaches owed a greater duty of care to participants than would have done had they been able bodied.

U1. Edwards v. Nobbs (1963) C.A. 307

"It is possible that the perfect and most expert driver might have done a little better. The standard, however, is not that of the perfect driver, but the driver using ordinary skill and care" (Willmer L.J., 8 B).

U2. Wiltshire v. Foote (1968) C.A. 428

Stranger visiting Birmingham got trapped on traffic island which any local person would have avoided—*Held*, not contributory negligence on her part, as although the standard of care was an objective one, the ordinary reasonable pedestrian was not necessarily a local inhabitant.

U3. James v. Alger (1986) C.A. 229

Boy aged seven and another boy darted onto pelican crossing when taxi driver, approaching at 30 m.p.h. and for whom the lights were green, was only a few feet away. Taxi struck seven year old—*Held*, taxi driver not liable. It would be unreasonable to impose a duty to drive so slowly that a motorist could avoid a child in such circumstances—the motorist would otherwise have to drive at 5 m.p.h.

U4. Armstrong v. British Steel Corporation (1989) C.A. 118

Security officer patrolling derelict site at 2 a.m. using torch tripped over debris on ground—*Held, inter alia*, employer not liable at common law. It would be unreasonable to require pointless cleaning of the debris with which the area was strewn—provision of torch sufficient.

(2) Whether Ordinary or Expert Knowledge Required

1. Phillips v. Whiteley [1938] 1 All E.R. 566, Goddard J.

Jeweller piercing ears—plaintiff gets abscess—*Held*, defendant not liable, as plaintiff had not proved cause of abscess, and in any event defendant was only required to show the ordinary care expected of a jeweller, not the expert care one would expect from a surgeon.

2. Caminer v. London and Northern Trust [1951] A.C. 88; [1950] 2 All E.R. 486, H.L.

Roots of 130-year-old elm tree affected by elm butt rot—this was not apparent and could only have been detected by methods additional to the methods usually employed when disease suspected (494 B, Lord Normand)—crown was about thirty-five feet wide, which was not exceptional—argument in House of Lords turned mainly on whether evidence showed tree should have prudently been lopped—*Held*, not, bearing in mind that defendants' duty was only to take the care of an ordinary prudent landowner, not that of an expert (Lord Porter at 490 H). "It (the standard of care) postulates some degree of knowledge . . . short of the knowledge possessed by scientific arboriculturists but which surely must be greater than the knowledge possessed by the ordinary urban observer of trees or even of the countryman not practically concerned with their care" (Lord Normand, 493 F). Lord Reid on the other hand thought the standard of care was that of "a reasonable and careful owner without expert knowledge but accustomed to dealing with his trees and having a countryman's general knowledge about them" (499 D). He also (499 E) did not think it necessary on the evidence that defendants should have called in an expert.

3. Griffiths v. Arch Engineering [1968] 3 All E.R. 217, Chapman J.

Plaintiff workman injured by defect in portable grinding machine which had been hired from plant contractors—defendant hirers *held* liable, though possessing no sufficient expert knowledge to discover defect. For details, see Chap. 7, (2) (a) **15**.

(3) Anticipation of Danger Generally

1. Bolton v. Stone [1952] A.C. 850; [1951] 1 All E.R. 1078, H.L.

Cricket ball case—*Held*, no negligence. "It is not enough that the event should be such as can reasonably be foreseen. The further result that injury is likely to follow must also be such as a reasonable man would contemplate before he can be convicted of actionable negligence. Nor is the remote possibility of injury occurring enough. There must be sufficient probability to lead a reasonable man to anticipate it. The existence of some risk is an ordinary incident of life, even when all due care has been, as it must be, taken" (Lord Porter at 1081 A). *But* see Lord Reid's comment in **3**.

2. Basted v. Cozens & Sutcliffe [1954] 1 W.L.R. 1069; [1954] 2 All E.R. 735, Devlin J.

Sudden descent of load suspended from crane due to failure of hoist brake—no clear evidence as to cause—no evidence as to system for maintaining brakes—defendants rely on complaints from operators—*Held*, applying *Barkway v. South Wales Transport* (Chap. 13, (1) (f) **1**), defendants liable.

3. Carmarthenshire C.C. v. Lewis [1955] A.C. 549; [1955] 1 All E.R. 565, H.L.

Lord Reid (572 C), considering dictum in **1**, said: "But in my view *Bolton v. Stone* establishes that if an event is foreseeable, the antithesis of its being reasonably probable is that the possibility of its happening involves a risk so small that a reasonable man would feel justified in disregarding it." See also **7**.

4. Sayers v. Harlow U.D.C. [1958] 1 W.L.R. 623; [1958] 2 All E.R. 342, C.A.

Plaintiff immured in W.C. by negligence of defendants—is injured trying to climb out—*Held*, plaintiff's conduct not unreasonable and therefore damage not too remote.

5. Close v. Steel Company of Wales [1960] 2 Q.B. 299; [1960] 2 All E.R. 657, C.A.

Issue was breach of statutory duty in failing to fence, but Lord Evershed M.R., in delivering the judgment of the court, when considering whether the danger was reasonably foreseeable, said (661 D): "The plaintiff's accident was not one which could or would be reasonably foreseeable in the ordinary course, though it was one which those responsible, if they had closely reflected on it, would have said could happen though the chances were extremely remote." Defendants were *held* not liable, as danger not reasonably foreseeable. (Case later went to H.L., but on statutory duty only).

6. Brown v. N.C.B. [1962] A.C. 574; [1962] 1 All E.R. 81, H.L.

"The common law does not require a man to provide security against a *possible* cause of injury, even though it is foreseeable (see *Bolton v. Stone*)" (Lord Denning at 89 H).

7. The Wagon Mound (No. 2) [1967] 1 A.C. 617; [1966] 2 All E.R. 709, P.C.

Due to carelessness of ship's engineers furnace oil overflowed and floated across Sydney Bay, and eventually caught fire and caused damage to property—plaintiff sued in nuisance and negligence—judge held that the damage was unforeseeable, but was caused directly—he also held that foreseeability was the test in negligence, and directness in nuisance, and therefore gave judgment for the plaintiff on the issue of nuisance—the Privy Council (see Chap. 1, (3) (c) **6**) held that foreseeability was the test in nuisance as well as negligence, but also *held* that on the primary findings of the judge the damage here was foreseeable. The judge found that the risk of fire could reasonably have been considered possible, but only becoming an actuality in very exceptional circumstances, and that the chance of this happening while the oil was spread on the water could reasonably be considered remote. In analysing the question, Lord Reid (718 B) said that before *Bolton v. Stone* **1** the cases fell into two classes, those where the risk was a mere possibility which would never occur to the mind of a reasonable man, and those where there was a real and substantial risk that something like the event which happened might occur. But in *Bolton v. Stone* there was a new problem; the risk of a ball hitting a person in the road was plainly foreseeable but the chance of it happening was infinitesimal; and it was accordingly held that the risk was so small that a reasonable man would be justified in disregarding it. But it did not follow that it was always justifiable to disregard a risk of very small magnitude (718 F). A reasonable man would only do so if he had some valid reason for doing so. He would weigh the risk against the difficulty of eliminating it. If the activity, for example, in *Bolton* had been unlawful, a different result would have followed. In the present case, not only was the discharge of oil unlawful, but there was no balance of advantage to weigh against the risk. In these circumstances, the defendants could not excuse themselves by putting the smallness of the risk against the difficulty of eliminating it, and the only question was whether, on the findings of the judge, a reasonably qualified ship's engineer would have known that there was a real risk of the oil on the water catching fire. This question was to be answered in the affirmative, and the defendants were accordingly liable.

8. Bradford v. Robinson Rentals [1967] 1 W.L.R. 337; [1967] 1 All E.R. 267, Rees J.

Held, defendants liable.

9. Knightley v. Johns [1982] 1 W.L.R. 349, [1982] 1 All E.R. 851, C.A.

"There is no difference between what is natural and probable and what is reasonably foreseeable either in the act of rescue or in the steps taken to accomplish it. If it is natural and probable that someone will come to the rescue it is also foreseeable; if it is foreseeable that in doing so he may take a particular kind of risk or cope with the emergency in ways not precisely foreseeable, his acts will also be natural and probable consequences of the wrongful act which created the emergency" (Stephenson L.J., 860 J).

N.B. This *dictum* is addressed to rescue cases, but, *mutadis mutandis*, may be of wider application.

10. Morrell v. Owen, *The Times*, December 14, 1993; (1993) C.L.Y. 2957, Mitchell J.

Archery and discus competitions for paraplegic athletes held simultaneously in sports hall, divided by net. Stray discus hit net. Net billowed out and discus hit plaintiff, an archer on other side, on temple. Plaintiff unaware of discus event. Archers received no safety instructions and coaches had taken no special safety precautions—*Held*, Archery and discus coaches liable. Accident was entirely foreseeable. Coaches owed a greater duty of care to participants than would have done had they been able bodied.

U1. Hulse v. Manchester City Council [1986] C.L.Y. Unrep Cases 41; (1986) C.A. 59

Particular accident which befell plaintiff not reasonably foreseeable and therefore no measures taken in respect of overhanging tree branches reasonable.

(4) Anticipation of Dangerous Acts of Others

1. Wells v. Metropolitan Water Board [1937] 4 All E.R. 639, Humphreys J.

Plaintiff tripped over cover plate of valve box in road—it was not fitted with any locking device and could be opened quite easily—someone, probably a child, had opened it and left it projecting—*Held*, defendants liable for failing to anticipate and guard against this danger.

2. Coates v. Rawtenstall B.C. [1937] 3 All E.R. 602, C.A.

Defendants leave chain unsecured at bottom of chute which is put to dangerous use by children—*Held*, defendants liable, as they knew of this likelihood.

3. Simons v. Winslade [1938] 3 All E.R. 774; 159 L.T. 408, C.A.

Plaintiff going across yard of public-house to W.C. slips on some vomit—yard unlit—defendant had swept out yard at 6 p.m.—during two previous years only one other customer had vomited in yard—*Held*, defendant could not be expected to guard against danger.

4. Canter v. Gardner [1940] 1 All E.R. 325; 56 T.L.R. 305, Tucker J.
Head contractor makes hole, hands it over to defendants, the sub-contractors—unknown person removes cover—head contractor not liable because no control and no knowledge—*Held*, defendants not liable because they had left cover securely fixed—*Aliter* if not securely fixed, when they would have had a duty to inspect and warn.

5. Glasgow Corporation v. Muir [1943] A.C. 448; [1943] 2 All E.R. 44, H.L.

Child scalded by water from urn—the children were in a party, and for a fee the organisers were using defendants' tea room, themselves making and distributing the tea—it was alleged defendants should have removed the children while the urn was being moved—*Held*, not so, as a reasonable person would not have anticipated danger. "As the permitted operation was intrinsically innocuous, I do not think any obligation rested on (defendants' servant) to attempt to supervise how it was carried out" (Lord Wright at 53 D).

6. Rochman v. Hall [1947] 1 All E.R. 895, Birkett J.

Landlord employed competent engineers to look after lift—between visits someone tampered with safety device—*Held*, there was no real evidence of any foreseeable danger against which landlord should guard.

7. L.P.T.B. v. Upson [1949] A.C. 155; [1949] 1 All E.R. 60, H.L.

Lord Uthwatt: "I . . . dissent from the view that drivers are entitled to drive on the assumption that other users of the road, whether drivers or pedestrians, will behave with reasonable care. It is common experience that many do not. A driver is not of course bound to anticipate folly in all its forms, but he is not, in my opinion, entitled to put out of consideration the teachings of experience as to the form those follies commonly take." See **9**.

8. Davies v. Liverpool Corporation [1949] 2 All E.R. 175; [1949] W.N. 268, C.A.

Tram passenger rang bell to start tram while conductor absent from platform—*Held*, chain of causation from conductor's negligent absence not broken. "An unauthorised or wrongful act of a third person does not break the chain of causation if it might reasonably have been foreseen" (Denning L.J. at 177 F).

9. Berrill v. R.H.E. [1952] 2 Lloyd's Rep. 490, Slade J.

"You are not bound to foresee every extremity of folly which occurs on the road. Equally, you are certainly not entitled to drive on the footing that other users of the road, either drivers or pedestrians, will exercise reasonable care. You are bound to anticipate any act which is reasonably foreseeable, that is to say, anything which the experience of road users teaches them that people do, albeit negligently" (492, "paraphrasing" Lord Uthwatt in **7**).

10. Cuttress v. Scaffolding Ltd [1953] 1 W.L.R. 1311; [1953] 2 All E.R. 1075, C.A.

Held, as defendants could not reasonably have foreseen the probability of the events which caused the scaffold to fall, not liable. *Bolton v. Stone* (Chap. 2, (3) **1**) applied.

11. Smith v. Marriott [1954] 2 Lloyd's Rep. 358, Ormerod J.

Held, res ipsa loquitur, but claim failed because defendants showed they had moored barge properly and taken reasonable care to maintain moorings. Approved in *Newby v. General Lighterage* **12**.

12. Newby v. General Lighterage [1955] 1 Lloyd's Rep. 273, C.A.

Held, defendants liable, as there was a possibility third parties might interfere, and defendants had not established they had taken reasonable precautions against such interference. Parker L.J. (279, col. 1): "It is not enough for them (defendants) to prove that the cause was wrongful interference. Here the whole question is whether they should, as reasonable people, have anticipated that interference." (Compare with *Smith v. Marriott* **11**, where on not dissimilar facts defendants were held not liable.)

13. Perry v. Kendricks Transport [1956] 1 W.L.R. 85; [1956] 1 All E.R. 154, C.A.

Held, defendants had taken all reasonable precautions to safeguard their parked lorry, and that they were not liable in negligence, nor in *Rylands v. Fletcher* (*q.v.* under Chap. 8) for an accident caused by two boys throwing a lighted match in petrol tank.

14. Adcock v. Loveridge, *The Times*, June 21, 1956; C.L.Y. 5902, Pearce J.

Defendant occupier of site where she parked derelict lorries—plaintiff, an infant, threw match in petrol tank—*Held*, plaintiff was a trespasser, but if child had been licensee, defendant would still not have been liable, as accident was not reasonably foreseeable by her. See also **13**.

15. Hayman v. L.T.E. [1981] C.L.Y. 1834, D/Circuit Judge Krikler

16. Foskett v. Mistry [1984] R.T.R. 1; (1983) 80 L.S. Gaz. 2683, C.A.

Plaintiff aged 16 ran from parkland to the left of defendant's approaching car, across 10 foot wide pavement and some 10 feet into road, where struck by car, defendant not having seen plaintiff until then—*Held*, defendant liable—should have seen plaintiff as he ran from park-land, appreciated he presented a potential hazard and sounded his horn or braked. Plaintiff 75 per cent contributorily negligent—it was putting it a little too high to say that he should be treated or a fully grown adult man.

17. Old v. Eastern National Omnibus Co. [1984] C.L.Y. 2285, French J.

Plaintiff, aged four, riding bicycle in middle of pavement, wobbled into road, fell off, and struck by bus—*Held*, bus driver not liable—not foreseeable that plaintiff would fall into road—nothing the driver could have done to avoid accident.

18. Ward v. Cannock Chase D. C. [1986] Ch. 546; [1985] 3 All E.R. 537, Scott J. See Chap. 10, (6)(a) **12** for summary.

19. King v. Liverpool C.C. [1986] 1 W.L.R. 890; [1986] 3 All E.R. 544, 2260 C.A.

Tenant of local authority flat asked landlord to secure the flat above against vandals; any steps then taken were ineffective and as a result tenant's flat damaged by water ingress; council held not liable in negligence.

20. Denton v. United Omnibus Co. Ltd, *The Times*, May 6, 1986; [1986] C.L.Y. 2250, C.A.

Defendant's bus parked in depot with no door or gates. Bus not immobilised—unlawfully taken and driven into collision with plaintiff's car—*Held*, defendant not liable. In the absence of a special relationship or special circumstances a party was not liable in negligence for failing to prevent the unlawful or unauthorised act of another.

21. Smith v. Littlewoods Organisation Ltd [1987] 2 W.L.R. 480; [1987] 1 All E.R. 710, H.L.

For summary see Chap. 1, (3)(b) **24** Case qualifying *Perl* Chap. 1 (3)(b) **15** and *King* **19**.

22. Topp v. London Country Bus (South West) [1993] 1 W.L.R. 979; [1993] 3 All E.R. 448, C.A.

Defendant's minibus left for over eight hours unlocked, unattended and with keys in at bus stop outside public house—unlawfully taken and driven into collision with cyclist—*Held*, defendant not liable—owed no duty of care to cyclist—acts of wrongdoer constituted *novus actus interveniens. P. Perl (Exporters) Ltd v. Camden L.B.C.* (Chap. 1, (3)(b) **15**) followed.

23. Armstrong v. Cottrell [1993] P.I.Q.R. P 109; [1993] C.L.Y. 2956, C.A.

Defendant in offside of three lanes of busy carriageway. From 400 yards saw plaintiff, aged 12, and three other girls "hovering" on road side to his left. Then plaintiff and one other girl advanced to middle lane and hesitated. Defendant decelerated but when his car was very close the two girls suddenly darted into offside lane and impact occurred—*Held*, defendant liable. Having seen girls "hovering" and hesitating, should have reduced speed sufficiently to prevent accident and sounded horn. Plaintiff one-third contributorily negligent, having regard to her age.

24. Connaire v. McGuire [1994] C.L.Y. 3343, Michael Wright J.

Plaintiff and M crossed A13 dual carriageway at junction controlled by traffic lights where no pedestrian facilities and where pedestrians rarely crossed. Second carriageway had four lanes. First was empty. In second and third was traffic to left of plaintiff and M, held by red lights. M crossed second carriageway slightly ahead of plaintiff. When plaintiff in second lane, lights to his knowledge changed to green. Defendant, in fourth lane to get flying start, accelerated away and struck plaintiff. M had completed his crossing—*Held*, defendant liable—should have noticed and been put on guard by M, should also have noticed plaintiff, and should have heeded the fact that traffic to his offside had not moved when lights changed to green. Plaintiff 40 per cent contributorily negligent. Not negligent for crossing where he did, but having decided to do so, had a duty to take considerable care—should have looked left before venturing into fourth lane.

U1. Trevor v. Cole (1984) C.A. 529

Groups of young men on either side of road. One ran across and defendant, approaching in car, braked to avoid him. Plaintiff then left pavement to defendant's nearside. Defendant did not see him, and car struck him—*Held*, defendant liable—having seen groups on pavements and previous man crossing, should have kept very careful look-out and slowed down to be able to avoid any other negligent pedestrians (At first instance, plaintiff found guilty of contributory negligence, but amount not specified in Court of Appeal).

U2. Mason v. Essex L.C. (1988) C.A. 295

Plaintiff knocked down in youth camp by bus driven by volunteer who had been told only to load it and not to drive it—*Held*, defendant not liable for the volunteer's driving.

U3. White v. Estate of Matteo Constantino, deceased (1989) C.A. 1010

Plaintiff crossed road from central island at junction controlled by traffic lights. As he passed in front of stationary traffic in the offside of two lanes, lights changed from red to green. Defendant, in nearside lane, went through lights at moderate speed and struck plaintiff—*Held*, defendant liable—should have anticipated someone might be crossing, from stationary traffic to his offside, and slowed down or warned of his approach. Plaintiff 40 per cent contributorily negligent.

U4. Souter v. Barcal Design & Engineering Ltd (1989) C.A. 1055

Plaintiff, self-employed painter on building site erected and lashed ladder to steelwork in order to gain access to work; whilst working someone unlashed and removed the ladder and then returned it but did not relash it. Thereafter as plaintiff descended the ladder slipped and he was injured. Defendants held not liable.

U5. Channer v. Lucas (1990) C.A. 96

Plaintiff, aged 65, crossed road "at a sort of run, not very fast." Having got over centre line, she saw defendant's motor-cycle approaching from her left at 30 m.p.h., and stopped. Had she not done so, defendant would have passed behind her. In the event, he hit her—*Held*, defendant liable—failed to anticipate likely movement or reaction of elderly pedestrian confronted by an approaching motor cycle. Plaintiff 75 per cent to blame—failed to see defendant's motor cycle when began to cross, and gave no warning of her intention to stop.

U6. Bookham v. Unusual Rigging Co. Ltd (1990) C.A. 114

First defendant, engaged by second defendant to suspend circular frames from wires, decided tower scaffold without outrigger would suffice. Plaintiff was on scaffold when it began to tilt. Two employees of second defendant climbed and leant on it to try to steady it, but in the event caused it to overbalance—*Held*, first and second defendants respectively two-thirds and one-third to blame. First defendant should have provided outrigger. It was foreseeable that should scaffold tilt, others might climb on it and affect its stability. Second defendants' employees should have realised their actions would jeopardise plaintiff's safety.

U7. Parsons v. Pullman Foods Ltd (1991) C.A. 194

Plaintiff, aged 12, crossed road in front of bus into path of overtaking lorry. Lorry driver had previously stopped behind bus, knew children were alighting and had seen one child run across front of his lorry—*Held*, lorry driver liable—should have sounded horn. Plaintiff one-third to blame.

U8. Thistlethwaite v. Watts (1991) C.A. 952

Defendant car driver saw plaintiff, a 16-year-old girl, and another girl on grass verge with back to road, hopping up and down and throwing arms in air. Defendant slowed down, but as he drew level plaintiff rushed into road, giving defendant no chance to avoid collision—*Held*, defendant not liable—no duty in the circumstances to sound his horn.

(5) Anticipation of Gravity of Injury

1. Paris v. Stepney B.C. [1951] A.C. 367; [1951] 1 All E.R. 42, H.L.

Lord Normand (49 A): "The learned editor of *Salmond on the Law of Torts* . . . says:

> 'There are two factors in determining the magnitude of a risk—the seriousness of the injury risked, and the likelihood of the injury being in fact caused.' "

Lord Morton (51 E): "In considering generally the precautions which an employer ought to take . . . it must in my view be right to take into account both elements, the likelihood of an accident happening and the gravity of the consequences. . . . The more serious the damage which will happen . . . the more thorough are the precautions which an employer must take."

2. Jones v. Vauxhall Motors [1955] 1 Lloyd's Rep. 152, Stable J.

"The precautions which he (the employer) has to take are, of course, to some extent measured by the incident of the risk, and the incident of the risk may really fall under two categories: (1) the numerical chance of the thing happening at all, and (2) the gravity of the result if a thing does happen" (153, col. 2).

3. Morris v. West Hartlepool S.N. [1956] A.C. 552; [1956] 1 All E.R. 385 H.L.

Lord Reid (399 D): "Apart from cases where he may be able to rely on general practice, it is the duty of an employer, in considering whether some precaution should be taken against a foreseeable risk, to weigh on the one hand the magnitude of the risk, the likelihood of an accident happening, and the possible seriousness of the consequences if an accident does happen, and on the other hand the difficulty and expense and any other disadvantage of taking the precaution."

4. Bailey v Rolls Royce (1971) Ltd [1984] I.C.R. 688; [1984] C.L.Y. 2282, C.A.

Plaintiff injured back exerting force of about 100 lbs when manoeuvring a component. Plaintiff, to defendants' knowledge, had exhibited predisposition to back injury.—*Held, inter alia*, that defendant not liable in negligence—on the evidence, under no duty to stop plaintiff from doing the job, warn him of risk of injury or instruct him to ask for help, in view of the extent of the risk of injury and the extent of likely injury should the risk materialize.

5. Re The Herald of Free Enterprise, *The Independent*, December 18, 1987; [1987] C.L.Y. 2462, D.C.

The ferry *The Herald of Free Enterprise* capsized soon after leaving Zeebrugge because the inner and outer bow doors to the main "G" deck had not been closed. The assistant bosun whose duty it was to close them had fallen asleep. His chief officer did not follow the usual practice of waiting to see the doors begin to close, but went to the bridge. There, the captain did not ask the chief officer for any report, and sailed assuming the doors had been closed. The Divisional Court dismissed the captain's appeal against a finding of the formal inquiry into the capsizing that he had been guilty of serious negligence in the discharge of his duties. He should have made a positive check that the doors were closed before putting to sea. The fact that it was not the practice of most if not all captains of such ferries to make a positive check made no difference. Though general practice was usually cogent evidence of the standard of reasonable care, here it was evidence of culpable complacency. The standard of care to be expected of a ship's master was a high one, having regard to the number of passengers to be expected on such vessels, and risk of serious injury or death in the event of any negligence.

(6) Practicability of Measures to Avoid Danger

1. Daborn v. Bath Tramways [1946] 2 All E.R. 333, C.A.

"In determining whether a party is negligent, the standard of reasonable care is that which is reasonably to be demanded in the circumstances. A relevant circumstance to take into account may be the importance of the end to be served by acting in this way or that. As has often been pointed out, if all the trains in this country were restricted to a speed of 5 m.p.h., there would be fewer accidents, but our national life would be intolerably slowed down. The purpose to be served, if sufficiently important, justifies the assumption of abnormal risk." (Asquith L.J. at p. 336 E.) Cited with approval in **4** by Singleton L.J.

2. Brookes v. L.P.T.B. [1947] 1 All E.R. 506, Henn Collins J.

Underground train starts with door open—*Held*, negligence. Defendants plead reasonable owing to exigencies of traffic. Judge said he knew there was an ever-increasing tendency to say individual must be sacrificed to majority, but nevertheless defendants must do their duty.

3. Latimer v. A.E.C. [1953] A.C. 643; [1953] 2 All E.R. 449, H.L.

Lord Asquith (662), in dealing with a suggestion that a factory should have been closed down because the floor was flooded and in patches slippery: "What evidence the learned judge had before him suggests to my mind that the degree of risk was too small to justify, let alone require, closing down."

4. Watt v. Herts C.C. [1954] 1 W.L.R. 835; [1954] 2 All E.R. 368, C.A.

Denning L.J. (371 B): "It is always a question of balancing the risk against the end," and he also said there was a very considerable difference between commercial end to make profit and human end to save life or limb.

5. Stockley v. Metropolitan Borough of Knowsley [1986] 2 E.G.L.R. 141; [1986] C.L.Y. 2249, C.A.

In frozen conditions where water supply could not be switched off through lack of resources it was practical for landlords at least to advise tenant of this fact and how to turn off water.

6. Lewis v. Buckpool Golf Club, 1993 S.L.T. (Sh. Ct.) 43; [1992] C.L.Y. 6076

Defendant, a 24-handicap golfer, mis-hit ball from tee and struck plaintiff on adjacent green—*Held*, defendant liable. All he had to do war wait for plaintiff to finish putting. Risk of a golfer of defendant's level of skill mis-hitting not so small that a reasonable man would disregard it. There was no basis for a plea of *volenti non fit injuria.*

UI. Priestly v. Nottingham H.A. (1986) C.A. 37

Plaintiff hospital worker slipped on ice or slush in delivery yard at 9.15 a.m.—*Held*, defendant not liable. Test was whether reasonable and practicable steps were taken, having regard to circumstances including the use of the yard, the hours of work and available finance. No system could ensure that at all times all parts of a large complex were always being treated with salt and cleared.

(7) Common Practice

(*N.B.* See also Employers' Liability cases in Chap. 15, (2) (h).)

1. Mahon v. Osborne [1939] 2 K.B. 14; [1939] 1 All E.R. 535, C.A.

MacKinnon L.J. (556 H), citing Maugham L.J. in *Marshall v. Lindsey C. C.* [1935] 1 K.B. 516, 540: "An act cannot in my opinion be held to be due to want of reasonable care if it is in accordance with the general practice of mankind. . . . A defendant charged with negligence can clear himself if he shows that he has acted in accord with general and approved practice."

2. Barkway v. South Wales Transport [1950] A.C. 185; [1950] 1 All E.R. 392, H.L.

Bus accident through tyre-burst for which defendants *held* liable. For details, see Chap. 13, (3) **8.** Lord Normand (402 D) cited Lord Dunedin in *Morton v. William Dixon*, 1909 S.C. 809, saying that the principle, though enunciated in a master and servant case, was of general application: "Where the negligence of the employer consists of what I may call a fault of omission, I think it is absolutely necessary that proof of that fault of omission should be one of two kinds—either to show that the thing which he did not do was a thing which was commonly done by other persons in like circumstances, or to show that it was a thing which was so obviously wanted that it would be folly in anyone to neglect to provide it."

3. Whiteford v. Hunter (1950) C.L.C. 6864; [1950] W.N. 553, H.L.

Plaintiff claimed damages resulting from erroneous diagnosis of defendant that he had cancer of the bladder—the argument revolved mainly round whether defendant should have used one or other of two special cystoscopes, neither of which he had and both of which at the time were difficult to obtain—*Held*, in the circumstances he was not negligent, approving the dictum of Maugham L.J. in *Marshall v. Lindsey C.C.* [1935] 1 K.B. 516, 540 that "a defendant charged with negligence can clear himself if he shows that he acted in accordance with general and approved practice."

4. Wright v. Cheshire C.C. [1952] 2 All E.R. 789; [1952] W.N. 466, C.A.

Question was whether it was negligence to have a boy and not an adult at the end of a vaulting buck—*Held*, it was not. Singleton L.J. at 792 G: "There may well be some risk in everything one does or in every step one takes, but in ordinary everyday affairs the test of what is reasonable care may well be answered by experience from which arises a practice adopted generally and followed successfully over the years so far as the evidence in this case goes."

5. Simmons v. Pennington [1955] 1 W.L.R. 183; [1955] 1 All E.R. 240, C.A.

Solicitor answers a requisition in "stock form"—saying that there are restrictive covenants and appear to have been breaches in the past, but no notice of breach has been served—in reality the covenants were obsolete but solicitor did not say so, and as a result purchaser rescinded—*Held*, this was not negligence, as the solicitor was following general practice (but, see 243 H, it might well be negligence in future).

6. Bolam v. Friern Hospital Management Committee [1957] 1 W.L.R. 582; [1957] 2 All E.R. 118, McNair J. and jury.

Plaintiff sustained fractures while having electro-convulsive treatment to which he had consented—alleged defendants negligent in not warning of risk, not using relaxant drugs, or manual control—*Verdict* not guilty. Judge said, as to warning, plaintiff must show he would have refused treatment if warned; and as to other allegations defendants not negligent if they acted in accordance with practice accepted as proper by a responsible body of medical men skilled in that particular art, merely because there is another body taking opposite view.

7. Cavanagh v. Ulster Weaving Co. [1960] A.C. 145; [1959] 2 All E.R. 745, H.L.

So *held* by four out of five Law Lords, who said in effect that "folly" meant no more than "unreasonable or imprudent," and that the phrase must not be used to detract from the ordinary test of reasonable care. This was a master and servant case—for fuller details, see Chap. 15, (2) (h) **8.**

8. Re. The Herald of Free Enterprise, *The Independent*, December 18, 1987, [1988] C.L.Y. 2462, D.C.

The ferry *The Herald of Free Enterprise* capsized soon after leaving Zeebrugge because the inner and outer bow doors to the main "G" deck had not been closed. The assistant bosun whose duty it was to close them had fallen asleep. His chief officer did not follow the usual practice of waiting to see the doors begin to close, but went to the bridge. There, the captain did not ask the chief officer for any report, and sailed assuming the doors had been closed. The Divisional Court dismissed the captain's appeal against a finding of the formal inquiry into the capsizing that he had been guilty of serious negligence in the discharge of his duties. He should have made a positive check that the doors were closed before putting to sea. The fact that it was not the practice of most if not all captains of such ferries to make a positive check made no difference. Though general practice was usually cogent evidence of the standard of reasonable care, here it was evidence of culpable complacency. The standard of care to be expected of a ship's master was a high one, having regard to the number of passengers to be expected on such vessels, and risk of serious injury or death in the event of any negligence.

9. Cope v. Cassells [1990] C.L.Y. 3296, H. H. Judge Owen

Defendant, an "Aikido" teacher, demonstrating a technique with plaintiff, a pupil—delivered what was intended as a shadow blow with his knee, but hit plaintiff in abdomen.
—*Held*, defendant not liable. Defendant had acted with appropriate care, and plaintiff should have contemplated the use of the shadow blow. Neither practice nor necessary to warn of such a move.

10. Nilsson v. Redditch B.C. [1994] C.L.Y. 2299, C.A.

Plaintiff dustman injured by glass protruding from refuse sack. Judge held defendant liable on ground that it should have used the "wheelie bin" rather than the "black bag" system of collection—*Held*, allowing the appeal, the judge had tried to overturn an established system of work on wholly insufficient evidence. The mere fact that a system of work was hazardous did not make it unsafe. The judge had failed to weigh the gravity of the risk against the consequences of overturning an established system.

(8) Remedying Danger

(*N.B.* See also cases relating to Dangerous Premises in Chap. 10, (4) (c)).

1. Blackman v. Railway Executive [1954] 1 W.L.R. 220; [1953] 2 All E.R. 323, C.A.

Patch of oil dripped from mail barrow—foreman saw it—at once told man to get sawdust and tried to stop people passing that way—*Held*, defendants had taken all reasonable care and were not liable.

2. O'Connor v. B.T.C. [1958] 1 W.L.R. 346; [1958] 1 All E.R. 558, C.A.

Per Lord Evershed M.R. (567 B): "A decision to abandon a particular design of coach in favour of a newer model by reason of a risk of danger ... does not itself demand the immediate and total withdrawal of the first class of vehicle."

3. Wells v. Cooper [1958] 2 Q.B. 265; [1958] 2 All E.R. 527, C.A.

Defendant refixed screws in door handle himself—handle came away when plaintiff, an invitee, pulled it—*Held*, defendant not liable, as (a) the task of repair was not one which called for an expert and (b) on the facts he had used reasonable care in doing the job. Jenkins L.J. (529 I): "No doubt some kinds of work involve such highly specialised skill and knowledge, and create such serious dangers if not properly done, that an ordinary occupier ... would fail in that (*i.e.* his) duty if he undertook such work himself. But the work here in question was not of that order. It was a trifling domestic replacement well within the competence of a householder accustomed to doing small, carpentering jobs about his home ...."

(9) Warning

(*N.B.* See also cases relating to Dangerous Chattels, Occupier liability and Employers liability in Chaps. 7, 10 and 15)

1. Russell v. Criterion Films [1936] 3 All E.R. 627; 53 T.L.R. 117, Porter J.

Porter J. at p. 633: "No doubt the defendants through Mr. Wilson did warn the performers to keep their eyes down and not to look at the lights, but this was not a warning that they might suffer seriously if they did not look down. It was rather an assurance that if they did refrain from looking at the lights ... they would escape any severe injury."

2. Burfitt v. Kille [1939] 2 K.B. 743; [1939] 2 All E.R. 372, Atkinson J.

Sale of a toy pistol and blank ammunition to boy of nine—seller *held* liable for damage subsequently caused to another boy through the use of the pistol. "A warning is not a sufficient discharge of duty if the person to whom the chattel is delivered is not a competent person."

3. Wilkinson v. Rea [1941] 1 K.B. 688; [1941] 2 All E.R. 50, C.A.

Ship suddenly plunged in darkness—defendant had uncovered a hatch below—defendants' foreman heard plaintiff (who was not employed by defendants) coming, called out to him, and took hold of jamb of doorway to prevent plaintiff coming. Plaintiff, not understanding warning, pushed by and fell down hatch—*Held*, not adequate action by defendants' foreman, who could and should have stood in doorway.

4. Clarke v. Adams (1950) C.L.C. 6673; 94 S.J. 599, Slade J.

Physiotherapy treatment, containing some danger: "When I turn on the machine I want you to experience a comfortable warmth, and nothing more; if you do, I want you to tell me"—*Held*, inadequate warning.

5. Gough v. N.C.B. [1954] 1 Q.B. 191; [1953] 2 All E.R. 1283, C.A.

Held, that a specific warning of the danger was no defence if the child was not of a sufficient age to appreciate the danger of what he was doing.

6. Catherall v. Cunard [1954] 2 Lloyd's Rep. 303, Jones J.

Unauthorised use of conveyor belt on ship—defendants *held* not liable. "It is perfectly true that there was no notice to that effect, but why should there be? It is just ordinary common sense that they should not be used in this way" (308, col. 1).

7. Dyer v. Ilfracombe U.D.C. [1956] 1 W.L.R. 218; [1956] 1 All E.R. 581, C.A.

"Nor do I think it is their duty to put up notices to the effect that children under five—or whatever the age may be—are not permitted on the chutes or swings. If they did so, children would not take much notice, and if an accident happened, it would be said: 'What is the good of putting up notices unless you see they are observed?"' (Singleton L.J. at 589 F.)

8. A. C. Billings v. Riden [1958] A.C. 240; [1957] 3 All E.R. 1, H.L.

Contractor negligently executes works on premises—plaintiff, a visitor, knew of danger—*Held*, defendants liable. Lord Reid (6 I, Lords Simonds and Cohen concurring): "There is no magic in giving a warning. If plaintiff knew the danger, either because he was warned or from his own knowledge and observation, the question is whether the danger was such that, in the circumstances, no sensible man would have incurred it or, in other words, whether the plaintiff's exposing himself to the danger was a want of common and ordinary prudence on his part. If it was not, then the fact that he voluntarily or knowingly incurred the danger does not entitle defendants to escape from liability."

9. Ashdown v. Samuel Williams [1957] 1 Q.B. 409; [1957] 1 All E.R. 35, C.A.

Plaintiff, a licensee, run down by a negligently shunted truck—warning notice at entrance which plaintiff saw but only read first three lines thereof—first three lines only dealt with condition of land, but later on notice also exempted negligent acts—*Held*, plaintiff was bound by the terms of the notice as a whole, just as she would be in contract. Although it did not arise in present case, Parker L.J. (47 H) said: "A mere reference to negligence without a warning as to the user of the land might well be insufficient."

10. Sargent v. Gee Stevedoring [1957] 1 Lloyd's Rep. 357, Ashworth J.

"The nature of the complaint was, on plaintiff's own evidence, anything but forceful. What he said was: 'Someone will be getting hurt.' It seems to me that if a workman contents himself with that sort of remark, it is not to be laid against defendants that they failed to treat that as a substantial complaint calling for an alteration in their system" (359, col. 2).

11. Bolam v. Friern Hospital Management Committee [1957] 1 W.L.R. 582; [1957] 2 All E.R. 118, McNair J. and jury.

Plaintiff sustained fractures while having electro-convulsive treatment to which he had consented—alleged defendant negligent in not warning of risk, not using relaxant drugs or manual control—*Verdict*, not guilty. Judge said, as to warning, plaintiff must show he would have refused treatment, if warned.

12. Willis v. Unimarine [1958] 2 Lloyd's Rep. 436, Diplock J.

"I think that Mr. Evensen probably shouted 'stand clear' . . . There seems to me to be little doubt that the plaintiff and Robertson did not stand clear, and that they were standing in the middle of the hatch as large as life for Evensen to see if he had bothered to look. But he did not bother to look . . . " Defendants *held* liable.

13. Smith v. Austin Lifts [1959] 1 W.L.R. 100; [1959] 1 All E.R. 81, H.L.

Lord Simonds (83 D): "In each of the routine reports the same remark was made: 'Machine house door broken.' In the letter it was said: 'The machine room doors need fixing in position.' There was, I think, nothing in these reports to suggest any danger, and I would suppose they were a warning to the occupiers that, if the doors were not repaired, the machinery would be exposed to the weather."

14. Baker v. Hopkins [1959] 1 W.L.R. 966; [1959] 3 All E.R. 225, C.A.

15. Cope v. Cassells [1990] C.L.Y. 3296, H.H. Judge Owen

Defendant, an "Aikido" teacher, demonstrating a technique with plaintiff, a pupil—delivered what was intended as a shadow blow with his knee, but hit plaintiff in abdomen—*Held*, defendant not liable. Defendant had acted with appropriate care, and plaintiff should have contemplated the use of the shadow blow. Neither practice nor necessary to warn of such a move.

16. Eastman v. South West Thames A.H.A. [1991] R.T.R. 389; [1992] P.I.Q.R. P42, C.A.

Plaintiff travelled as a passenger accompanying patient in defendant's ambulance, in which a notice said "For your own safety use seat belts provided." Some seats had belts but plaintiff sat in one that did not—plaintiff injured when ambulance braked suddenly—*Held*, defendants not liable—entitled to let plaintiff decide whether or not to occupy a seat with a belt—no duty on attendant to draw notice to plaintiff's attention or exhort her to use a belt. There is no general duty on the driver of a vehicle to exhort a passenger to use a seat belt.

U1. Pounder v. South Durham Steel (1961) C.A. 52

Movement of wagons prohibited by regulation 16 of Locomotives and Waggons on Sidings Regulations "until warning has been given by the person in charge to persons whose safety is likely to be endangered."—Plaintiff argued that this imported a duty to ensure that warning was received—*Held*, not so, and defendants not liable. Devlin L. J. (9 D): "There is no obligation on defendants to ensure that such a warning is heard and understood. Provided it is a reasonable and adequate warning, they have discharged their duty."

U2. Farrow v. Turner (1962) C.A. 429

Plaintiff, employee of 17, told not to grind tools a certain way—but not warned of physical danger of disobeying—*Held*, defendants liable.

U3. British Gas Corporation v. Derbyshire C.C. (1981) C.A. U.B. 331

Plaintiffs supplied defendants with plan of gas mains—written warning on plan that plaintiffs did not accept responsibility for inaccuracies in plan—defendants ignored warning and excavated in accordance with plan—due to inaccuracy of plan defendants damaged gas main—*Held*, that the defendants were solely to blame for ignoring the warning. "The efficacy of the warning on the plan depends entirely on the circumstances." (Templeman L.J., 4).

3. PROOF OF NEGLIGENCE

(1) Generally

(a) Standard of Proof

1. Miller v. Ministry of Pensions [1947] 2 All E.R. 372; [1947] W.N. 241, Denning J.

"If the evidence in a civil case is such that the tribunal can say: 'We think it more probable than not,' the burden is discharged, but if the probabilities are equal, it is not" (374 A).

2. Hornal v. Neuberger Products [1957] 1 Q.B. 247; [1956] 3 All E.R. 970, C.A.

3. The Hebridean Coast [1961] A.C. 545; [1961] 1 All E.R. 82, H.L.

Lord Reid (84 I): "Proof may be by direct evidence or inference, and the standard of proof in civil cases is that the fact to be proved must be made to appear more probable than not."

U1. Mulvaine v. Joseph (1969) C.A. 277 A

"It is generally accepted that if one finds, in a case of this kind (road traffic), negligence by one defendant of less than 10 *per cent.* it can be disregarded on the principle of *de minimis*, or on the principle that one must look on the matter not as a theoretical exercise but from a practical point of view" (Salmon L.J., 4 F).

(b) Proof by Inference where Cause of Accident Unexplained

1. Grant v. Australian Knitting Mills [1936] A.C. 85; 52 T.L.R. 38, P.C.

Lord Wright (101): "If excess sulphites were left in the garment, that could only be because someone was at fault. The appellant is not required to lay his finger on the exact person in all the chain who was responsible, or to specify what he did wrong. Negligence is found as a matter of inference from the existence of the defects taken in conjunction with all the known circumstances ... "

2. Youngman v. Pirelli [1940] 1 K.B. 1; 109 L.J.K.B. 420, C.A.

Held, defendant not liable, as the accident was perfectly consistent with deceased having touched live wire. See Chap. 15, (3) **1**.

3. Dollman v. Hillman [1941] 1 All E.R. 355, C.A.

Lord Greene M.R. at 358 D: "The court has to consider in a question of this kind the probabilities, and only that degree of proof which the circumstances permit is required. There are all kinds of ways in which a piece of fat might get onto the pavement. Some malicious person might have picked it up from a place where he had no right to go and thrown it there. In the present case it is not speculation which leads to the selection of these two alternatives (*i.e.* the ones creating liability), but a probability upon which a judicial decision may properly be founded. Those were the suggestions put to the witnesses . . . and there was evidence that the piece of fat could have got onto the pavement in one or other of those ways. Those were obviously the most likely ways. It is no part of the duty of plaintiff in a case of this kind to track back the history of this identical piece of fat and prove how it got there by some perfectly conclusive chain of evidence."

4. Henley v. Cameron (1949) 65 T.L.R. 17; [1948] W.N. 468, C.A.

Tucker L.J. (18, col. 2): " ... it appears to me, failing any evidence to the contrary, a natural and reasonable inference to draw that the failure to provide the required light was a cause contributing to the accident."

5. O'Flaherty v. A.E. Smith Coggins (1951) C.L.C. 6775; 95 S.J. 685, C.A.

Plaintiff member of gang handling heavy crate which is dropped on plaintiff—cause of accident unexplained—*Held*, defendants not liable (reversing Donovan J.).

6. Brundell v. Vianda S.S. Co. [1952] 2 Lloyd's Rep. 277, Hilbery J. and jury.

"He (plaintiff) does not tell me anything except that he assumes that that must have happened. It cannot be said that that is a reasonable inference to be drawn. There is no established fact from which that would be an inference. An inference is a deduction from an established fact, and an assumption or guess is something quite different, but not necessarily related to any established fact" (280).

7. Brophy v. Bradfield [1955] 1 W.L.R. 1148; [1955] 3 All E.R. 286, C.A.

Deceased was found dead in boilerhouse—*Held*, the facts did not call on defendants for an answer, but if they did, the fact that the boiler had worked satisfactorily in the boilerhouse for twenty-five years was an answer to any inference of negligence.

8. Webster v. Knohr and Buchard [1956] 1 Lloyd's Rep. 271, C.A.

Held, county court judge was justified in finding that bad stowage was not cause of accident Denning L.J. (272): "Certainly if there was no evidence of any other likely cause (other than bad stowage), it would be the inevitable inference (that it was the cause of the accident). But in this case there was evidence that other causes might cause a slip of the bags."

9. Moore v. Metcalf Motor Coasters [1958] 2 Lloyd's Rep. 179, Ashworth J.

Judge cites following extract from Lord Macmillan's speech ("albeit a dissenting one") in *Jones v. Great Western* (1930) 47 T.L.R. 39:

> "The dividing line between conjecture and inference is often a very difficult one to draw. A conjecture may be plausible, but it is of no legal value, for its essence is that it is a mere guess. An inference, in the legal sense, on the other hand, is a deduction from the evidence, and if it is a reasonable deduction it may have the validity of legal proof. The attribution of an occurrence to a cause is, I take it, always a matter of inference. The cogency of a legal inference of causation may vary in degree between practical certainty and reasonable probability. Where the coincidence of cause and effect is not a matter of actual observation there is necessarily a hiatus in the direct evidence, but this may be legitimately bridged by an inference from the facts actually observed and proved."

This case subsequently went to appeal [1959] 1 Lloyd's Rep. 264, when decision in favour of defendants was upheld without comment on above.

10. Lush v. T.F. Maltby [1959] 1 Lloyd's Rep. 46, Devlin J.

"The best way in which the case on this point can be put for the plaintiff is to say that it is a borderline case ... and no one can begin to consider that fairly and draw the inference whether there was negligence or not, unless he is satisfied that he has got a complete detailed and truthful account from the witnesses of the exact circumstances in which the matter occurred. It is only with such a basis that it would be proper to begin to draw inferences ... " (56).

11. Houghland v. R.R. Low [1962] 1 Q.B. 694; [1962] 1 All E.R. 159, C.A.

Motor coach trip—suitcase of plaintiff put in boot—lost—*held*, failure of defendants to return suitcase established a prima facie case of negligence, and as this had not been rebutted, defendants were liable.

12. Dwyer v. Roderick, *The Times*, November 12, 1983; [1983] C.L.Y. 2557, C.A.

Held, that "it was to shut one's eyes to the obvious if one denied that the burden of achieving something more than the mere balance of probabilities was greater when one was investigating the complicated and sophisticated actions of a qualified and experienced lawyer, doctor, accountant, builder or motor engineer than when one was enquiring into the momentary inattention of the driver of a motor car in a simple running-down action." (May L.J.).

13. Chisholm v. State Transport Authority (1987) 46 S.A.S.R. 148; [1989] C.L.Y. 2591

Plaintiff asked court to infer negligence from nature of injuries received when he was struck by train and expert evidence that such was possibly compatible with an accident negligently caused—*Held*, not sufficient evidence so to infer.

14. Clowes v. National Coal Board, *The Times*, April 23, 1987; [1987] C.L.Y. 2565, C.A.

Plaintiff got off train which had taken him and other miners to lift at end of shift, fell and was trampled on by other miners—could not say how fell, but contended must have been pushed by other men. There was evidence that men would get off train while still moving and run to lift, despite defendant's efforts to stop this practice—*Held*, in absence of any other explanation, Judge entitled to infer that indisciplined conduct of other miners, for which defendant vicariously liable, had caused accident.

15. Carter v. Sheath, *The Times*, August 10, 1989; [1990] RTR 12, C.A.

Defendant, a good and careful driver, approached pelican crossing in well-lit road at night, at about 30 m.p.h. Lights green in defendant's favour. At or near crossing car's nearside front corner struck plaintiff, a 13-year-old boy. Neither defendant nor his wife, an experienced driver in front passenger seat, had seen plaintiff before impact, and plaintiff had no recollection of what happened—*Held*, on the evidence the accident was inexplicable and plaintiff had failed to discharge burden of proving that defendant was negligent.

U1. Chapman v. Copeland (1966) C.A. 121 A

"When a man is dead and cannot give evidence, I am ready to make every reasonable assumption in his favour" (Lord Denning M.R., 4 C).

U2. Miller v. E. K. Cole (1968) C.A. 11

"When the learned judge said that he was quite unable to say what was wrong, but he was convinced on a balance of probabilities that something was wrong, one feels that in a sense that was almost a contradiction in terms. It should be possible to indicate at least the general character of a defect as being the probable explanation of the malfunctioning of a piece of equipment if one is going to drive home a charge that there was a defect that ought not to have been there" (Winn L.J., 11 B).

(c) Relevance of Pre-Accident Events

(*N.B.* See also Employers' Liability cases in Chap. 15, (2)(f).)

1. Bolton v. Stone [1951] A.C. 850; [1951] 1 All E.R. 1078, H.L.

Lord Porter (1081 F): "I cannot accept the view that it would tend to exonerate the appellants if it were proved that they had considered the matter and decided the risks were very small and that they need not do very much. In such a case I can imagine it being said that they entertained an altogether too optimistic outlook. They seem to me to be in a stronger position if the risk were so small that it never even occurred to them."

2. Board v. Thomas Hedley [1951] 2 All E.R. 431; [1951] W.N. 422, C.A.

Held, that on issue of danger of product, complaints were very relevant, and must be disclosed both before and after accident.

3. Michaels v. Browne and Eagle [1955] 2 Lloyd's Rep. 433, McNair J.

"... the absence of accidents over a course of years, the absence of any complaints by trade union officials or factory inspectors are very relevant evidence, although of course by no means conclusive" (437).

4. Edmiston v. B.T.C. [1956] 1 Q.B. 191; [1955] 3 All E.R. 823, C.A.

After some complicated preliminaries, defendants swore an affidavit disclosing very little by way of previous accidents—plaintiff then put in another affidavit saying, in general terms, that defendants had documents relating to similar accidents—*Held*, plaintiff's application for discovery relating to previous similar accidents would be refused, because his affidavit did not *specify* any particular documents, and because the application itself was too widely phrased. *Aliter*, perhaps, if plaintiff could have shown there had been recent similar accidents of his particular type and/or that there was good ground for saying that there were reports of such cases (826 D).

5. Kilgollan v. W. Cooke & Co. Ltd [1956] 1 W.L.R. 527; [1956] 2 All E.R. 294, C.A.

Large numbers of previous accidents (600) but all of them fairly trivial—Singleton L.J. (301 D): "Defendants ... if they knew there were accidents were under a duty to consider how these accidents could be lessened in number. They owe a duty to their workpeople, and it cannot be right for them to say: 'Well, the injuries were mostly cuts on the hands, or cuts on the legs, or a scratch or abrasion on the body somewhere, and the people were not off work for more than three days. Therefore there was no duty on us to do anything because they were trivial injuries.' That is not the right approach. ... One would have thought it would occur to someone that if there are all these accidents through flailing wire some day there would be a serious one, but that does not appear to have been considered"—defendants *held* liable.

(d) Relevance of Post-Accident Events

1. Board v. Thomas Hedley [1951] 2 All E.R. 431; [1951] W.N. 422, C.A.

Held, that on issue of danger of product, complaints were very relevant, and must be disclosed both before and after accident.

2. Pipe v. Chambers Wharf [1952] 1 Lloyd's Rep. 194, Streatfield J.

After the accident a mobile crane was used instead of manhandling—*Held*, defendants not liable "Nothing is so perfect it cannot be improved. If after every accident some improvement is inaugurated it does not follow from that that the system originally followed was a breach of duty" (195).

3. Gray v. Admiralty [1953] 1 Lloyd's Rep. 14, Ormerod J.

Plaintiff employed by defendants tripped on a staircase (which was found to be safe) and put hand through glass panel of door—after accident defendants put stouter glass in panel—*Held*, this was no evidence of negligence *re* old panel.

(e) *Where Two Defendants are Sued*

1. Baker v. Market Harborough [1953] 1 W.L.R. 1472; 97 S.J. 861, C.A.

Head-on collision—both drivers killed—offside wheel of one or other vehicle, or perhaps both, over white line—*Held*, it was more likely that both drivers were to blame than one only, and since both were to blame, and there were no means of distinguishing between them, 50–50 against each.

2. Roe v. Ministry of Health [1954] 2 Q.B. 66; [1954] 2 All E.R. 131, C.A.

Case where an injection of local anaesthetic caused permanent paralysis—*Held*, there was no negligence, but Denning L.J. (136 H) said the facts called for an explanation, and the fact there were two defendants did not mean that both could avoid giving an explanation "by the simple expedient of each throwing responsibility on the other," and he cited *Baker v. Market Harborough* **1** as authority therefor. The other two L.JJ., Somervell and Morris, were more non-committal on both points (136 A and 138 H respectively).

3. Price v. Price, *The Times*, February 12, 1954, C.A.

Collision between bus and motor-cycle—pillion passenger sued bus before Oliver J., who found motor-cyclist solely to blame—pillion passenger then sued motor-cyclist before Devlin J., who found bus solely to blame—*Held*, C.A. could not interfere. Pillion passenger (who was father of motor-cyclist) should have sued both in one action.

4. Salt v. I.C.I., *The Times*, February 1, 1958; [1958] C.L.Y. 2251, C.A.

Drum of caustic soda escapes through hole—carrier and manufacturer sued—*Held*, neither liable, as this was not a case where one or other defendant must have been negligent, and the cause of the hole was unexplained.

5. Walsh v. Holst [1958] 1 W.L.R. 800; [1958] 3 All E.R. 33, C.A.

Brick from building under repair strikes plaintiff on highway—plaintiff sues occupier and contractor—*Held*, *res ipsa loquitur* against both, because contractor was in control and occupier was liable for negligence of contractor except for casual or collateral negligence (which neither defendant tried to set up), *but* defendants not liable, because although the cause of the accident was completely unexplained defendants had shown they had taken all reasonable care (Morris L.J. dissenting on this point), and this, following *Woods v. Duncan* (Chap. 3, (2)(b) **1**), was sufficient to absolve defendants.

6. Wilks v. Cheltenham Motor Cycle Club [1971] 1 W.L.R. 668; [1971] 2 All E.R. 369, C.A.

Motor cycle scramble—rider left track—went through or over ropes—and injured spectator—rider and organisers both sued—judge found rider liable and exonerated organisers—rider appealed—and on appeal he was *held* not liable. But Lord Denning M.R. said that in his view prima facie one or the other was liable, as "this was the sort of accident which ought not to occur if all those concerned use proper care" (670 B).

(f) Identifying Servant of Defendant Responsible

1. Grant v. Australian Knitting Mills [1936] A.C. 85; 52 T.L.R. 38, P.C.

Lord Wright (101): "If excess sulphites were left in the garment, that could only be because someone was at fault. The appellant is not required to lay his finger on the exact person in all the chain who was responsible, or to specify what he did wrong. Negligence is found as a matter of inference from the existence of the defects taken in conjuction with all the known circumstances . . . ."

2. Cassidy v. Ministry of Health [1951] 2 K.B. 343; [1951] 1 All E.R. 574, C.A.

Operation on fingers—rigid splint for fourteen days—hand found to be useless owing to too tight and too prolonged bandaging—*Held*, that this raised a prima facie case of negligence against defendants, which defendants had not displaced by evidence, and that it was not necessary for plaintiff to prove that a particular doctor or nurse was negligent, as all the people by whom he was treated were servants of defendants.

(g) When Onus Shifts to Defendant

1. Polkington v. Lambeth B.C. [1938] 1 All E.R. 339; 54 T.L.R. 345, C.A.

Defendants erect bollard—under continuing duty to light—plaintiff runs into it—*Held*, plaintiff need only prove bollard unlit, whereupon onus shifted to defendants to prove light was extinguished for some cause for which they were not responsible in law.

2. Turner v. Arding & Hobbs [1949] 2 All E.R. 911; 93 S.J. 756, Lord Goddard C.J.

Unexplained vegetable on shop floor—defendants *held* liable. "If an unusual danger is present, of which the injured person is unaware, and the danger is one which would not be expected and ought not to be present, the onus of proof is on defendants to explain how the accident happened" (912 A).

3. Barkway v. South Wales Transport [1950] A.C. 185; [1950] 1 All E.R. 392; H.L.

Case where tyre of bus burst due to previous impact fracture and defendants were *held* liable for failing to have a proper system for their drivers to report impact fractures. Although only Lord Radcliffe expressly says so, it seems implicit in the decision that proof by plaintiff of the tyre-burst threw on defendants the onus of proving that they had taken all reasonable care to prevent burst, and this view of the decision was applied by Devlin J. in *Basted v. Cozens & Sutcliffe* **8**.

4. Rysdale v. Blackfriars Lighterage [1952] 2 Lloyd's Rep. 31, Barry J.

Plaintiff proves that his accident occurred because a hatch cover was defective and gave way—no explanation or evidence as to how the accident came about—*Held*, plaintiff succeeded. "It is not of course for plaintiff to satisfy me affirmatively how this could have happened" (37).

5. Evans v. Bustard [1952] 1 Lloyd's Rep. 81, C.A.

Breast rope (*i.e.* rope between ship's rails and top of gangway) too low—defendants say in accordance with general practice—*Held*, defendants had not proved this, and were liable (see Birkett L.J. at 87).

6. Birchall v. Bibby [1953] 1 All E.R. 163; [1953] 1 Lloyd's Rep. 175, Jones J.

Hoist rope breaks—*res ipsa loquitur* but on the facts *held* that defendants had proved rope was maliciously cut by unknown person and were therefore not liable.

7. Tillett v. Doig [1953] 2 Lloyd's Rep. 707, C.A.

Staging collapses because wedge removed—defendants plead it was done by some unauthorised person—*Held*, since defendants were in control of staging, onus of proving this was on them, and as they had failed to discharge it, therefore they were liable.

8. Basted v. Cozens & Sutcliffe [1954] 1 W.L.R. 1069; [1954] 2 All E.R. 735n., Devlin J.

Sudden descent of load due to defect in crane brake—defendants offer no evidence of cause or of system of maintenance—defendants (crane-owners, but not employers of plaintiff) *held* liable. "Once it is established there was a defect . . . whether the rule of *res ipsa loquitur* applies or not I do not really think needs to be considered . . . [Defendants], and they alone, have the knowledge of the facts which would show whether they have exercised due care or not, and it is for them to lay that information before the court and, I think, to satisfy the court that they had a proper system of maintenance in force." **3** applied.

9. Smith v. Marriott [1954] 2 Lloyd's Rep. 358, Ormerod J.

Held, defendants not liable as they had discharged onus of showing they had moored barge properly and taken reasonable care to maintain moorings. Approved in **10**.

10. Newby v. General Lighterage [1955] 1 Lloyd's Rep. 273, C.A.

Unattended barge adrift—defendants' case was that third party had cast adrift—defendants *held* liable because there was the possibility that some malicious third party would interfere, and defendants had not proved they had taken reasonable precautions against such interference.

11. Mason v. Williams & Williams [1955] 1 W.L.R. 549; [1955] 1 All E.R. 808, Finnemore J.

Defendant manufacturers *held* liable for defective chisel. Judge says (810 C) that when plaintiff has proved chisel was too hard, and has eliminated any intermediate interference, "that is really as far as any plaintiff can be expected to take his case."

12. Moore v. R. Fox & Sons [1956] 1 Q.B. 596; [1956] 1 All E.R. 182, C.A.

Dictum of Asquith L.J. in *Barkway v. South Wales Transport* [1948] 2 All E.R. 460 approved (188 G):

> "(i) If defendants' omnibus leaves the road and falls down an embankment, and this without more is proved, then *res ipsa loquitur*, there is a presumption that the event is caused by negligence on the part of defendants, and plaintiff succeeds unless defendants can rebut this presumption. (ii) It is no rebuttal for defendants to show, again without more, that the immediate cause of the omnibus leaving the road is a tyre-burst, since a tyre-burst *per se* is a neutral event consistent, and equally consistent, with negligence or due diligence on the part of defendants. When a balance has been tilted one way, you cannot redress it by adding an equal weight to each scale. The depressed scale will remain down . . . (iii) To displace the presumption, defendants must go further and prove (or it must emerge from the evidence as a whole) either (a) that the burst itself

was due to a specific cause which does not connote negligence on their part but points to its absence as more probable, or (b) if they can point to no such cause, that they used all reasonable care in and about the management of their tyres: *Woods v. Duncan.*"

13. Steer v. Durable Rubber Co. *The Times*, November 20, 1958; [1958] C.L.Y. 2250, C.A.

Scalding water bursts out of hot water bottle three months old—*Held*, defendants liable because, the onus being on them either to show they had not been negligent or to give some explanation of the cause of the accident which did not connote negligence, they had not discharged onus on them.

14. Smith v. Austin Lifts [1959] 1 W.L.R. 100; [1959] 1 All E.R. 81, H.L.

Lord Simonds (85 A): "The premises were theirs; the duty to repair the doors was theirs, though they tried to shift it; the responsibility for what was done (*i.e.* to make the doors defective) must be theirs, unless they can prove it lay with another." *But* the other Lords did not deal directly with this point; Lords Morton and Somervell found that the defect was attributable to the occupiers on a balance of probabilities; and Lord Denning said that it did not matter, as the defect was directly caused by the original want of repair.

15. Fowler v. Lanning [1959] 1 Q.B. 426; [1959] 1 All E.R. 290, Diplock J.

16. Brown v. Rolls-Royce [1960] 1 W.L.R. 210; [1960] 1 All E.R. 577; H.L.

Industrial dermatitis from oil—plaintiff proved defendants did not supply barrier cream, and that other employers commonly did—he argued that this shifted the onus to defendants, and that it was then for them to show they had not been negligent—*Held*, not so, as there were other material facts (such as that defendants' doctor advised against barrier cream), and that it was for plaintiff to show, on the sum of these facts, that defendants had been negligent. Lord Denning (581 I) said it was important "to distinguish between a *legal* burden, properly so called, and a *provisional* burden which is raised by the state of the evidence. The *legal* burden in this case was imposed by law on the appellant (plaintiff). ... In order to discharge the burden ... the appellant (plaintiff) proved that barrier cream is commonly supplied by employers to men doing such work as the appellant was doing. This was a cogent piece of evidence and raised no doubt a 'presumption' or a 'prima facie' case in this sense, that, if nothing more appeared, the court might well infer defendants were negligent, and in that sense it put a burden on defendants to answer it. But this was only a *provisional* burden which was raised by the state of the evidence as it then stood."

17. Gardiner v. Motherwell Machinery Co. [1961] 1 W.L.R. 1424; [1961] 3 All E.R. 831, H.L.

Dermatitis—plaintiff demolition worker working among dirt and grease—question was whether dermatitis was due to working conditions—plaintiff had never had dermatitis before—the dirt and grease were capable of causing dermatitis—and the onset of the disease had been typical of dermatitis caused by such conditions—*Held*, these facts established a prima facie presumption that the disease was due to the working conditions. "When a man who has not previously suffered from a disease contracts that disease after being subjected to conditions likely to cause it, and when he shows that it starts in a way typical of disease caused by such conditions, he establishes a prima facie presumption that his disease was caused by those conditions" (Lord Reid at 832 I).

18. Cunningham v. Port of Liverpool Stevedoring [1962] 2 Lloyd's Rep. 49, C.A.

Held, prima facie either an unsafe system of slinging or negligent operation of system by employer's servants. New trial ordered.

19. Pearce v. Round Oak Steel Works [1969] 1 W.L.R. 595; [1969] 3 All E.R. 680, C.A.

Bolt in machine broke through metal fatigue—machine manufactured circa 1930 and bought secondhand by defendants in 1959—defendants called no evidence—*Held*, liable, as the burden was on the defendants to show that they had taken reasonable precautions, and this they had failed to do.

20. Henderson v. Henry E. Jenkins [1970] A.C. 282; [1969] 3 All E.R. 756, H.L.

Brake fluid pipe of lorry collapsed through corrosion—lorry five years old—the part of the pipe affected could not be seen on visual inspection, and removal of the pipe was not advocated except after 300,000 miles—the evidence was that something unusual must have happened to the pipe from outside—defendants called evidence to prove regular inspections and maintenance—*Held*, they were liable, because they had not called evidence to show that there had been no unusual occurrence (such as spillage of acid) of which they should have known. Lord Reid (758 D) suggested that it would probably have been enough to prove that there was a proper system for drivers to report any unusual occurrences affecting lorries.

21. Ward v. Tesco [1976] 1 W.L.R. 810; [1976] 1 All E.R. 219, C.A.

Slipping on yoghurt—*Held*, this raised a prima facie case against the defendants, not in the sense that they had to disprove negligence, but as throwing a burden on them "either of explaining how this thing got on the floor or of giving (the Court) far more evidence than they have as to the state of the floor and the watch that was kept on it immediately before the accident" (applying *Turner* **2**).

22. Clark v. MacLennan [1983] 1 All E.R. 416; [1983] C.L.Y. 2548, Peter Pain J.

Plaintiff developed severe stress incontinence following childbirth—operation on bladder was performed one month after birth—normal practice was not to perform such operation until at least 3 months after birth—in order to reduce the risk of haemorrhage. Plaintiff did suffer haemorrhaging during operation. This caused the operation to fail—and plaintiff was left with permanent stress incontinence. The question was whether the haemorrhage causally resulted from operating only one month after birth—*Held*, defendants were liable, as the onus of proof had shifted to them and they had failed to discharge it. "It seems to me that it follows from *McGhee* (Chap. 3(3)**3**) that where there is a situation in which a general duty of care arises and there is a failure to take a precaution, and that very damage occurs against which the precaution is designed to be a protection, then the burden lies on the defendant to show that he was not in breach of duty as well as to show that the damage did not result from his breach of duty." (427 G).

23. Kaye v. Alfa Romeo (Great Britain) Ltd (1984) 134 New L.J. 126 and 451; [1984] C.L.Y. 2295, Hutchinson J.

Plaintiffs car left road and hit trees. He sued car's manufacturers and suppliers who admitted liability for faulty seat belt anchorage but alleged contributory negligence—*Held*, plaintiff had not explained accident in a way that negatived negligence and was one-third to blame.

24. Ng Chun Piu v. Lee Chuen Tat [1988] RTR 298; *The Times*, May 25, 1988, P.C.

Defendant's coach crossed central reservation and onto opposite carriageway. Plaintiffs, passengers in coach, called no evidence and relied on *res ipsa loquitur*. Defendant proved that a car had pulled into his path causing him to brake and swerve, whereupon the coach skidded—*Held*, the prima facie case of negligence had been displaced. Plaintiffs had failed to discharge the burden of proof which remained on them throughout.

25. Worsley v. Hollins [1991] RTR 252; *The Times*, March 22, 1991, C.A.

Van owned by second defendant collided with rear of plaintiff's stationary vehicle when brakes failed due to split pin becoming detached from brake linkage. Trial Judge ruled *res ipsa loquitur* applied. Second defendant said he had had van fully serviced by automobile engineer six weeks before accident, and produced M.O.T. certificate dated four weeks before accident—*Held*, when *res ipsa loquitur* applied, production of M.O.T. certificate by owner not enough by itself to displace prima facie case against him, since it was his duty to see that vehicle was properly maintained. However, on the totality of his unchallenged evidence, second defendant had displaced prima facie case.

U1. Mirchandani v. Pyrene (1968) C.A. 256

Bursting of fire extinguisher on being filled—alleged failure to test under pressure beforehand—plaintiff proved (1) extinguisher had burst at 500 pressure, (2) it should have been tested at 750, and (3) by interrogatory, defendants were unable to say whether it had been tested or not—*Held*, plaintiff had established a prima facie case, which in default of answer entitled him to judgment.

U2. Hopper v. Haynes (1973) C.A. 17

Tyre-burst—car then hit baulk of wood on side of road—which swung into path of plaintiff's car—*Held*, applying dictum of Asquith L.J. in *Barkway* (see *Moore* **12**), defendant liable, as he had failed to satisfy the judge that, with reasonable care, he could not have avoided hitting the baulk. Although the tyre-burst was in itself a neutral event, the onus still lay on defendant to explain how the whole incident happened without negligence on his part.

U3. Sutton v. Jones (1985) C.A. 624

Held, to drive a vehicle in foggy conditions with only one of two rear lights working raised a presumption of negligence against the driver, which could be displaced by driver's explaining how light came to be off without negligence on his part.

U4. McPherson v. Devon A.H.A. (1985) C.A. 810

As nurse put down tray carrying pot of boiling water onto table, pot fell off into plaintiff's lap and plaintiff was scalded—*Held, res ipsa loquitur* applied, and nurse having given no explanation, liability was established against him. Health authority vicariously liable for his negligence.

U5. Mackay v. Holmes and Hunt (1992) C.A. 1226

Motorist accelerated at point where there was reversal of camber on road and deposits of oil from lorries from adjoining haulage company premises—lost control and skidded off road—*Held, res ipsa loquitur* applied, and motorist had failed to show any explanation consistent with lack of fault on her part. She used road regularly and knew or should have known of hazards.

(2) Res Ipsa Loquitur

(a) What is and what is not Res Ipsa Loquitur

		Whether R.I.L. or not
Operation—tube left in bladder	1	No
OPERATION—SWAB LEFT IN BODY	2	No
RAILWAY CARRIAGE DOOR FLYING OPEN	3	No
Inrush of water into submarine	4	Yes
Fire escaping from domestic grate	5	No
Tooth extraction—fractured jaw	6	No
Vegetable on shop floor	7	Yes
Fire—in bilge of motor launch	8	Yes
COLLIERY HAULAGE ROPE BREAKING	9	Yes
OPERATION—HAND RENDERED STIFF	10	Yes
Hoist rope breaking	11	Yes
TOOTH EXTRACTION—CHOKED BY SWAB	12	Yes
CRANE—PLAINTIFF IN HOLD HIT BY FALL	13	No
OPERATION—PARALYSIS FROM ANAESTHETIC	14	?
Barge adrift unattended	15	Yes
Hatch cover falling into hold	16	Yes
Crane—plaintiff in hold hit by fall	17	No
Child of four escaping onto road	18	Yes
BARGE ADRIFT UNATTENDED	19	Yes
Bus—passenger thrown off platform	20	No
EXPLOSION IN GAS TANK—OPERATED BY PLAINTIFF	21	Yes
Bad stowage—plaintiff in stowing gang	22	No
RAIL TRANSIT—-INJURY TO HORSE	23	No
OBJECT FALLING INTO ROAD FROM BUILDING	24	Yes
Crane—fall suddenly dropping 2–3 feet	25	No
TRESTLE FALLING ON PLAINTIFF DURING DISMANTLING	26	No
Dock worker dropping crate	27	No
Gas main exploding—due to action of frozen ground expanding and pressing down on it	28	?
Aircraft—crashing	29	Yes
Loud explosion in oxygen pipe in steel works	30	Yes
BOLT IN MACHINE BREAKING	31	Yes?
Aircraft—disappearing without trace	32	No
Fire—in factory	33	No
MOTOR CYCLIST AT MOTOR SCRAMBLE—LEAVING TRACK	34	No
GAS EXPLOSION AT METER	35	Yes, if . . .
YOGHURT ON SHOP FLOOR	36	Yes (in effect)
EPIDURAL ANAESTHETIC CAUSING QUADRIPLEGIA	37	Yes

LOSSES ON COMMODITY MARKET	38	No
Car leaving road and hitting tree	39	Yes
Coach crossing central reservation	40	Yes
VAN BRAKES FAILING DUE TO DETACHMENT OF PIN	41	Yes
Sciatic damage during hip replacement	42	Yes
Brain damage through hypoxia	43	Yes
Fall on escalator	44	No
Cardiac arrest under anaesthesia	45	Yes
Lump of metal falling from factory table	U1	Yes
Operation—to lung—paralysis of arm	U2	No
Teeth scaling—tongue cut	U3	No
Electric switch—blowing up when turned on	U4	No
Object falling on plaintiff during moving	U5	No
Factory floor—overflow of syrup	U6	Yes
Colliery haulage rope breaking	U7	Yes
Floor—slipping	U8	No
Tyre-burst	U9	No, but . . .
Driving in fog with one rear light not working	U10	Yes
Pot of boiling water falling from tray carried by nurse	U11	Yes
Asphyxia and brain damage to second twin	U12	Yes
Escape of water from loft into tenant's flat	U13	Yes
Fire emanating from gas heating appliance in house	U14	Yes
Motorist losing control and skidding off road	U15	Yes

1. Morris v. Winsbury-White [1937] 4 All E.R. 484, Tucker J.

Held, not *res ipsa loquitur* against the surgeon, as nurses and others had also adjusted tube.

2. Mahon v. Osborne [1939] 2 K.B. 14; [1939] 1 All E.R. 535, C.A.

Held, not *res ipsa loquitur* in the case of a complicated operation. *But* see **10**.

3. Easson v. L.N.E.R. [1944] K.B. 421; [1944] 2 All E.R. 425, C.A.

Held, not *res ipsa loquitur*, as door not continuously under sole control of defendants.

4. Woods v. Duncan [1946] A.C. 401; [1946] 1 All E.R. 420, H.L.

Held, *res ipsa loquitur* (but on the facts defendants discharged onus).

5. Sochacki v. Sas [1947] 1 All E.R. 344, Lord Goddard C.J.

Held, not *res ipsa loquitur*. "Everyone knows that fires occur through accidents which happen without negligence on anyone's part" (345 D).

6. Fish v. Kapur [1948] 2 All E.R. 176; 64 T.L.R. 328, Lynskey J.

7. Turner v. Arding & Hobbs [1949] 2 All E.R. 911; 93 S.J. 756, Lord Goddard C.J.

Held, *res ipsa loquitur* (though not in terms).

8. Reed v. Dean [1949] 1 K.B. 188; (1948) 64 T.L.R. 621, Lewis J.

Plaintiff hired a motor launch—two hours later liquid in bilge caught fire—*Held, res ipsa loquitur.*

9. Turner v. N.C.B. (1949) 65 T.L.R. 580, C.A.

Held, res ipsa loquitur (but on the facts defendants discharged onus).

10. Cassidy v. Ministry of Health [1951] 2 K.B. 343; [1951] 1 All E.R. 574, C.A.

Plaintiff went into hospital to be cured of two stiff fingers—came out with four stiff fingers after operation—*Held, res ipsa loquitur.*

11. Birchall v. Bibby [1953] 1 All E.R. 163; [1953] 1 Lloyd's Rep. 175, Jones J.

Held, res ipsa loquitur, but on the facts defendants had proved that rope had been maliciously cut by some third person, and were therefore not liable.

12. Garner v. Morrell, *The Times*, October 31, 1953; [1953] C.L.Y. 2538, C.A.

Held, the facts called for an explanation; as defendants had failed to give a satisfactory one, therefore they were liable.

13. Watts v. Shaw Savill [1953] 2 Lloyd's Rep. 430, C.A.

Followed in *Bagshaw* **17**.

14. Roe v. Ministry of Health [1954] 2 Q.B. 66; [1954] 2 All E.R. 131, C.A.

Case where an injection of local anaesthetic caused permanent paralysis—*Held,* there was no negligence, but Denning L.J. (136 H) said that the facts called for an explanation, and the fact there were two defendants did not mean that both could avoid giving an explanation by throwing responsibility on each other. Somervell and Morris L.JJ. were more non-committal (136 A and 138 H).

15. Smith v. Marriott [1954] 2 Lloyd's Rep. 358, Ormerod J.

Held, res ipsa loquitur, but claim failed because defendants showed that they had moored barge properly and taken reasonable precautions to maintain moorings. Approved in **19**.

16. Hinson v. Morgan Scanlon [1954] 2 Lloyd's Rep. 564, McNair J.

Held, res ipsa loquitur. (*N.B.* Hatch cover was one which had not been removed).

17. Bagshaw v. P.L.A. [1954] 2 Lloyd's Rep. 572, Ashworth J.

Held, following **13**, not *res ipsa loquitur* for a man in a hold to be struck by crane tackle, but where as here there was evidence that tackle was coming down too fast, a prima facie case was made out.

18. Carmarthenshire C.C. v. Lewis [1955] A.C. 549; [1955] 1 All E.R. 565, H.L.

Held, onus on defendants (school) to explain escape, and as they had not done so, therefore liable.

19. Newby v. General Lighterage [1955] 1 Lloyd's Rep. 273, C.A.

Held (probably inferentially), *res ipsa loquitur* and defendants liable. **12** approved.

20. Johnstone v. Western S.M.T. (1955) 105 L.J. 762, Lord Walker.

21. Moore v. R. Fox [1956] 1 Q.B. 596; [1956] 1 All E.R. 182; C.A.

Plaintiff employed to immerse objects in gas-heated tank—explosion—*Held* (Romer L.J. *dubitante*), *res ipsa loquitur*, despite the fact that plaintiff was operating the tank at the time.

22. Allars v. Glen Line [1956] 1 Lloyd's Rep. 51, Roxburgh J.

23. Langton v. B.T.C., *The Times*, October 17, 1956; [1956] C.L.Y. 7211, C.A.

24. Walsh v. Holst [1958] 1 W.L.R. 800; [1958] 3 All E.R. 33, C.A.

Brick from building under repair struck plaintiff on highway—Held, *res ipsa loquitur* against both occupier and contractor, but on the facts neither defendant liable because they had shown they had taken all reasonable steps, and therefore, following *Woods v. Duncan* **4**, they had discharged the onus on them.

25. Roberts v. T. Wallis [1958] 1 Lloyd's Rep. 29, Barry J.

Winch fall holding timber suddenly dropped two to three feet and struck other timber in hold of barge—*Held*, although the cause was quite unexplained, it was not a case of *res ipsa loquitur*.

26. Graham v. Grayson Rollo [1959] 2 Lloyd's Rep. 359, C.A.

Plaintiff was one of a gang of four taking down a large trestle—while he was moving away the trestle fell on him—the three members of the gang who were holding trestle gave confused evidence—plaintiff then claimed to rely on *res ipsa loquitur*—*Held*, it was not a case of *res ipsa loquitur*, as when a gang were handling a heavy object, there was a possibility that it would slip despite all due care, and even if slipping was ordinarily consistent with negligence, here plaintiff had called all available witnesses, who gave an explanation which was not necessarily consistent with negligence.

27. Alderton v. Lamport and Holt [1963] 2 Lloyd's Rep. 541, Edmund Davies J.

Held, not res ipsa loquitur.

28. Pearson v. N.W.G.B. [1968] 2 All E.R. 669, Rees J.

Judge did not decide whether *res ipsa loquitur* applied, as he found that in any event defendants had proved that there was no reasonable step open to them to safeguard the public against an explosion of this nature.

29. Cox v. Northwest Airlines [1967] 2 Lloyd's Rep. 451; [1968] C.L.Y. 158, U.S.C.A.

30. Colvilles v. Devine [1969] 1 W.L.R. 475; [1969] 2 All E.R. 53 H.L.

31. Pearce v. Round Oak Steel Works [1969] 1 W.L.R. 595; [1969] 3 All E.R. 680 C.A.

Bolt in machine broke, so that machine fell on plaintiff—it was *held* that this raised a presumption of negligence (though perhaps not *res ipsa loquitur* in full sense).

32. National Trust Co. v. Wong [1969] 2 Lloyd's Rep. 340, Can.Sup.Ct.

33. Flanagan v. British Dyewood, 1969 S.L.T. (O.H.) 223, O.H.

34. Wilks v. Cheltenham Cycle Club [1971] 1 W.L.R. 668; [1971] 2 All E.R. 369, C.A.

Held, not *res ipsa loquitur* against the cyclist, though Lord Denning M.R. indicated that an accident of this sort indicated that prima facie either the organisers or the cyclist would be liable.

35. Lloyde v. West Midlands Gas Board [1971] 1 W.L.R. 749; [1971] 2 All E.R. 1240, C.A.

Gas explosion in outhouse of house—causing meter and pipe between meter and main tap to disintegrate—*Held,* that this could be *res ipsa loquitur,* but only if the plaintiff could establish an improbability of any outside interference with it.

36. Ward v. Tesco [1976] 1 W.L.R. 810; [1976] 1 All E.R. 219 C.A.

Held, res ipsa loquitur (though not in terms), applying *Turner* **7**.

37. Brown v. Merton A.H.A. [1982] 1 All E.R. 650; [1982] C.L.Y. 800, 1344; C.A.

Admitted on the pleadings that *res ipsa loquitur* applied.

38. Merrill Lynch Futures Inc. v. York House Trading Ltd, *The Times,* May 24, 1984 [1984] C.L.Y. 2288, C.A.

Held, losses made on the commodity market were not of themselves evidence of negligence.

39. Kaye v. Alfa Romeo (Great Britain) Ltd (1984) 134 New L.J. 126 and 451; [1984] C.L.Y. 2295, Hutchison J.

See Chap 3, (1)(g) **23** for further details.

40. Ng Chun Piu v. Lee Chuen Tat [1988] R.T.R. 298; *The Times,* May 25, 1988, P.C.

Presumption of negligence displaced on the facts—see Chap. 3, (1)(g) **24** for further details.

41. Worsley v. Hollins [1991] R.T.R. 252; *The Times,* March 22, 1991, C.A.

Presumption of negligence displaced on the facts—see Chap. 3, (1)(g) **25** for further details.

42. Bentley v. Bristol & Western H.A. (No.2) [1991] 3 Med L R 1; [1992] C.L.Y. 3244, Waterhouse J.

See Chap. 18, (11) **43**.

43. Coyne v. Wigan H.A. [1992] 2 Med L R 301; [1992] C.L.Y. 3231 Rose J.

P's hypoxia caused post operatively could not have occurred without negligence on the part of D because if cause of injury had been silent regurgitation, as D alleged, this should have been detected through signs of laryngeal or broncho-spasm. *Res ipsa loquitur* applied.

44. Sherlock v. London Underground [1993] C.L.Y. 3001, Judge Quentin-Edwards.

Plaintiff fell on escalator allegedly due to its jolting; *res ipsa* relied on—*Held,* not liable.

45. Saunders v. Leeds Western H.A. [1993] 4 Med L R 355; [1994] C.L.Y. 3367, Mann J.

D offered no explanation for cardiac arrest under anaesthesia—*Held* could not have been caused without negligence, therefore *res ipsa loquitur* applied. See Chap. 18, (11) **52**.

U1. Smith v. Woodward (1954) C.A. 32 C

U2. Miller v. N.E. Metropolitan Regional H.B. (1954) C.A. 48

U3. Young v. Partridge (1956) C.A. 240

Scaling teeth—electric brush slipped and cut plaintiff's tongue—plaintiff sitting in proper position with head and tongue motionless—*Held*, defendant negligent. Not a case of *res ipsa loquitur*, but plaintiff proved negligence by showing that he was undergoing straightforward operation, with no risk given a modicum of skill, and was injured though he did not move. *Fish v. Kapur* **6** distinguished as there is always a possibility of jaw fracture on extraction of tooth. *Potter v. Buxton* (1948) December 6, unreported, also referred to, where a fragment of tooth went down throat during anaesthetic, and it was held that this did not establish negligence.

U4. Vaughan v. Coldair (1957) C.A. 194

U5. Longhurst v. London Electricity Board (1957) C.A. 305 A

Erecting scaffolding—plaintiff handed up ledger—which later fell on his head—*Held*, not *res ipsa loquitur*, as the operation was a combined one.

U6. Bond v. Sanitas (1959) C.A. 150

Held, res ipsa loquitur, and defendant liable to plaintiff (who slipped on the syrup while going round as a night watchman).

U7. Majewski v. Cementation Co. (1961) C.A. 322

U8. Hutchinson v. Fairey Engineering (1965) C.A. 137

Plaintiff slipped in factory—no witness had seen any slippery substance—but judge held defendants liable on basis that there must have been something slippery—*Held*, defendants not liable, as to hold otherwise "would be introducing into the law a new maxim, *lapsus ipse loquitur*" (Diplock L.J., 3 A).

U9. Hopper v. Haynes (1973) C.A. 17

Tyre-burst—car then hit baulk of wood at side of road—causing baulk to swing into path of plaintiff's car—*Held*, although the tyre-burst was in itself a neutral event, the onus was nevertheless on defendant to satisfy the judge that the whole incident had occurred without negligence on his part, and that as he had failed to discharge this onus, he was liable.

U10. Sutton v. Jones (1985) C.A. 624

See Chap. 3, (1)(g) **U3** for further details.

U11. McPherson v. Devon Area Health Authority (1985) C.A. 810

See Chap. 3, (1)(g) **U4** for further details.

U12. Bull v. Devon A.H.A. (1989) C.A. 235

See Chap. 18, (11) **U4**.

U13. King v. Liverpool City Council (1990) C.A. 885

Plaintiff's ground floor flat in block owned by council flooded by escape of water from loft—*Held*, landlord liable: *res ipsa loquitur*.

U14. Whyte v. Grimsby B.C. and British Gas PLC (1992) C.A. 1027

U15. Mackay v. Holmes and Hunt (1992) C.A. 1226

See Chap. 3, (1)(g) **U5** for further details.

(b) Rules Relating to Res Ipsa Loquitur

1. Woods v. Duncan [1946] A.C. 401; [1946] 1 All E.R. 420, H.L.

Held, that where *res ipsa loquitur* applied, defendant did not necessarily have to explain cause of accident; all he had to do was to show he was not negligent. Followed in **3**.

2. The Aralia (1949) 82 Ll.L.R. 884, Willmer J.

Held, following *Ballard v. N.B. Ry.*, 1923 S.C. (H.L.) 43 and *The Kite* [1933] P. 154, that in such circumstances the cogency of the fact of the accident by itself disappears, and plaintiff is under ordinary onus of proving negligence.

3. Turner v. N.C.B. (1949) 65 T.L.R. 580, C.A.

Defendants had regularly inspected rope and found no defect—but could not explain precisely why it broke—*Held*, following **1**, not liable.

4. Barkway v. South Wales Transport [1950] A.C. 185; [1950] 1 All E.R. 392, H.L.

Held, that as the cause of the accident was known *res ipsa loquitur* did not apply.

5. Bolton v. Stone [1951] A.C. 850; [1951] 1 All E.R. 1078, 1081 H, H.L.

6. Moore v. R. Fox [1956] 1 Q.B. 596; [1956] 1 All E.R. 182, C.A.

Plaintiff employed to immerse objects in gas-heated tank—explosion—*Held* (Romer L.J. *dubitante*) that this was *res ipsa loquitur*, despite the fact that plaintiff was at the time operating the tank. *Held* further, that although defendants had shown ways in which it was possible for the accident to have happened without negligence, this did not amount to discharging onus which *res ipsa loquitur* cast on them, which was to show that the accident was not attributable to want of care on their part. Dictum of Asquith L.J. in *Barkway v. South Wales Transport* [1948] 2 All E.R. 460 approved (188 G):

> "(i) If defendants' omnibus leaves the road and falls down an embankment, and this without more is proved, then *res ipsa loquitur*, there is a presumption that the event is caused by negligence on the part of defendants, and plaintiff succeeds unless defendants can rebut this presumption. (ii) It is no rebuttal for defendants to show, again without more, that the immediate cause of the omnibus leaving the road is a tyre-burst, since a tyre-burst *per se* is a neutral event consistent, and equally consistent, with negligence or due diligence on the part of defendants. When a balance has been tilted one way, you cannot redress it by adding an equal weight to each scale. The depressed scale will remain down ... (iii) To displace the presumption, defendants must go further and prove (or it must emerge from the evidence as a whole) either (a) that the burst itself was due to a specific cause which does not connote negligence on their part but points to its absence as more probable, or (b) if they point to no such cause, that they used all reasonable care in and about the management of their tyres: *Woods v. Duncan.*"

But see **12**.

7. Allars v. Glen Line [1956] 1 Lloyd's Rep. 51, Roxburgh J.

Bad stowage by one of a gang which included plaintiff—*Held, res ipsa loquitur* did not apply. *But cf.* **6**.

8. Walsh v. Holst [1958] 1 W.L.R. 800; [1958] 3 All E.R. 33, C.A.

Brick from building under repair strikes plaintiff on highway—plaintiff sues occupier and contractor—*Held, res ipsa loquitur* against both, because contractor was in control and occupier was liable for negligence of contractor except for casual or collateral negligence (which neither defendant tried to set up), *but* defendants not liable, because although the cause of the accident was completely unexplained defendants had shown they had taken all reasonable care (Morris L.J. dissenting on this point), and this, following **1**, was sufficient to absolve defendants.

9. Colvilles v. Devine [1969] 1 W.L.R. 475, [1969] 2 All E.R. 53; H.L.

Loud explosion in oxygen pipe in steel works—causing plaintiff to jump in fear from platform——*res ipsa loquitur*—defendants give as probable explanation the presence of particles in oxygen stream—but give no evidence of any steps to prevent particles, such as inspecting filter—*Held*, defendants had not discharged onus on them. The explanation in order to exculpate them must be one which was consistent with no negligence on their part.

10. Bennett v. Chemical Construction [1971] 1 W.L.R. 1571; [1971] 3 All E.R. 822, C.A.

11. Lloyde v. West Midlands Gas Board [1971] 1 W.L.R. 749; [1971] 2 All E.R. 1240, C.A.

"I doubt whether it is right to describe *res ipsa loquitur* as a 'doctrine'. I think it is no more than an exotic, though convenient, phrase to describe what is in essence no more than a commonsense approach, not limited by technical rules, to the assessment of the effect of the evidence in certain circumstances. It means that a plaintiff prima facie establishes negligence where: (i) it is not possible for him to prove precisely what was the relevant act or omission which set in train the events leading to the accident; but (ii) on the evidence as it stands at the relevant time it is more likely than not that the effective cause of the accident was *some* act or omission of the defendant or of someone for whom the defendant is responsible, which act or omission constitutes a failure to take proper care for the plaintiff's safety" (Megaw L.J., 1246 D).

12. Turner v. Mansfield Corporation (1975) 119 S.J. 629; [1975] C.L.Y. 2346, C.A.

Lord Denning M.R.: "*Res ipsa loquitur* is a rule as to the weight of evidence from which negligence can be inferred, not a doctrine. *Moore v. Fox* (**6**) should be relegated to the background."

13. Pritchard v. Clwyd C.C. [1993] P.I.Q.R. P21; [1993] C.L.Y. 3002, C.A.

The maxim *res ipsa loquitur* could only apply if event complained of was more consistent with failure to carry out duties, or to take care, or that it pointed to a particular one of two defendants being at fault. See Chap. 12, (1) (a) **51**.

14. Moore v. Worthing D.H.A. [1993] 3 Med LR 431; [1993] C.L.Y. 3003, Owen J.

Res ipsa loquitur in the context of medical negligence. P cannot establish negligence on this basis unless it can be shown that injury could only have occurred through negligence and no other means.

15. Saunders v. Leeds Western H.A. [1993] 4 Med L.R. 355; [1994] C.L.Y. 3367, Mann J.

Medical negligence—P does not need to establish the cause of the cardiac arrest, because no explanation had been given which did not amount to negligence.

U1. Hopper v. Haynes (1973) C.A. 17

Tyre-burst—car then hit baulk of wood at side of road—which swung into path of plaintiff's car—*Held*, applying dictum of Asquith L.J. cited in *Moore v. Fox* **6**, defendant liable, as he had failed to satisfy the judge that, with reasonable care, he could not have avoided hitting the baulk. Although the tyre-burst was neutral in itself, the onus still lay on defendant to explain how whole incident happened without negligence on his part.

(3) Proof of Causation

(*N.B.* See also Employers' Liability (Statutory Duty) cases in Chap. 16, (3) (b) and (c).)

1. Heskell v. Continental Express [1950] 1 All E.R. 1033; [1950] W.N. 210, Devlin J.

"Where the wrong is a tort, it is clearly settled that the wrongdoer cannot excuse himself by pointing to another cause. It is enough that the tort should be a cause and it is unnecessary to evaluate competing causes and ascertain which of them is dominant."

2. Bonnington Castings v. Wardlaw [1956] 1 A.C. 613; [1956] 1 All E.R. 615, H.L.
Nicholson v. Atlas Steel [1957] 1 W.L.R. 613; [1957] 1 All E.R. 776, H.L.

These two cases (both dealing with Factories Acts, breach of statutory duty in connection with silica dust in foundries) taken together are authority for the propositions (i) that liability will ensue if the tort made a "material contribution" to the injury and (ii) "a contribution is material unless the maxim *de minimis* can be applied to it" (see Lord Simonds in *Nicholson v. Atlas Steel* at 778 B).

3. McGhee v. National Coal Board [1973] 1 W.L.R. 1; [1972] 3 All E.R. 1008, H.L.

No washing facilities—which, together with conditions of work, materially increased risk of dermatitis—but, in the present state of medical knowledge, it could not be said that the plaintiff's dermatitis did not arise from some other cause—*Held*, applying **2**, defendants were liable.

4. Harrington v. Essex A.H.A. [1984] C.L.Y. 2325, Beldam J.

In a medical negligence action the plaintiff had not discharged the burden of proof if he could not lead the court to select one of two possible explanations for complications occurring to him after operation.

5. Wilsher v. Essex A.H.A. [1988] 2 W.L.R. 557; [1988] 1 All E.R. 871, H.L.

House of Lords held that notwithstanding any negligence (as found by the Court of Appeal), where the plaintiff's injury was attributable to a number of possible causes, the combination of defendant's breach of duty and P's injury did not give rise to a presumption that D had caused the injury. The burden remained on the plaintiff to prove a positive link between such negligence and his injury and the plaintiff had failed to discharge the burden of proof to establish the causal link between the retinal condition suffered and the excess oxygen dose, as condition was attributable to a number of other possible causes. For full summary see Chap. 18(11)**32**.

6. Kay v. Ayrshire and Arran Health Board [1987] 2 All E.R. 417; [1987] C.L.Y. 2564, H.L.

Infant plaintiff admitted to hospital suffering from pneumococcal meningitis, and during treatment negligent overdose of penicillin was given. Recovered from meningitis, but found to be suffering from deafness—*Held*, hospital not liable, because it could not be ascertained from two competing causes of damage, the meningitis, or the overdose, which had been responsible. It was necessary to first prove that a tortious cause was capable of causing and likely to have caused the damage before a presumption in favour of the injured plaintiff could be made, in accordance with *McGhee v. National Coal Board* **3**.

7. Hotson v. East Berkshire H.A. [1987] A.C. 750; [1987] 2 All E.R. 909, H.L.

Infant plaintiff could not recover for the loss of a 25 per cent chance of recovery through negligence of defendant. It was necessary to show, on balance of probabilities, that injury had actually been caused by acts complained of. See Chap. 18(11)**34**.

8. Bryce v. Swan Hunter Group plc [1988] 1 All E.R. 659; [1987] 2 Lloyd's Rep. 426, Phillips J.

Deceased worked as painter in shipyards from time to time between 1937 and 1942, 1946 and 1950 and 1958 and 1970. Limited exposure to asbestos dust during first period, substantial exposure during second and third. Died of mesothelioma in 1981, as a result of exposure to asbestos dust. Widow sued three former employers, for whom deceased had worked for total of 399 days in 1947, between 1958 and 1962 and in 1970—*Held*, *inter alia*:

(a) Defendants in breach of common law duty of care to deceased and of various statutory duties.
(b) Deceased's additional exposure to asbestos dust due to defendants' breaches of duty was significant, but less than he would have experienced in any event during his working life.
(c) Widow could not prove on balance of probabilities that additional fibres inhaled by deceased due to breaches of duty of any one of the defendants caused the mesothelioma; neither could any defendant prove to same standard that its breaches of duty were not at least a contributory cause of the mesothelioma.
(d) Widow entitled to invoke principle in *McGhee v. National Coal Board* **3**, that if conduct of a particular kind creates or inceases a risk of injury to another, and a defendant owes to a plaintiff a duty not to conduct himself in that way, then if defendant is in breach of such duty and plaintiff suffers such injury, the injury is taken to have been caused by the breach of duty even though the existence or extent of the contribution made by the breach cannot be ascertained.
(e) In the instant case, defendants' breaches of duty increased risk of deceased's developing mesothelioma, whether by adding to the number of possible initiators of the condition or producing cumulative effect on reduction of deceased's body defence mechanism. Deceased in fact developed mesothelioma. Each defendant must accordingly be taken to have caused the mesothelioma by its breach of duty.

9. Goorkani v. Tayside Health Board (O.H.), 1991 S.L.T. 94; [1991] C.L.Y. 4879

No different course of treatment would have been adopted if P had been warned of risk of failure. See Chap. 18(11) **41**.

10. Wright v. Lodge; Kerek v. Lodge [1993] 4 All E.R. 299; [1993] RTR 123, C.A.

At night, S's car in which D was rear seat passenger stopped in nearside lane of unlit dual carriageway because engine petered out. Fog reduced visibility to 60 yards. About three minutes later L, driving at 60 m.p.h. a lorry subject to a limit of 50 m.p.h., caught rear of car a glancing blow. Lorry went out of control into opposite carriageway and overturned. There, cars driven by W and K collided with it—*Held*, trial Judge entitled to find that sole legal cause of collisions involving W and K was the negligence of L (who admitted liability) rather than negligence of S in failing to push car onto verge. Not every "but for which" cause was necessarily a relevant legal cause. Which were and which were not had to be determined by application of common sense. A distinction could be drawn between negligent and reckless driving. An obstruction which was only a danger to a reckless driver was not a relevant cause. The foregoing applied even though the trial Judge also found that S's negligence *was* a legal cause of first impact (ordering S to contribute 10 per cent to D's claim against L) though (*per* Parker L.J.) "I am far from sure that I would have reached the same conclusion" and (*per* Woolf L.J.) "the question as to whether [S] caused even the initial collision was highly debatable."

11. Gunter v. John Nicholas & Sons (Port Talbot) Limited [1993] P.I.Q.R. P 67; [1993] C.L.Y. 2938, C.A.

Plaintiff's right hand came into contact with unguarded wood cutter which had continued to revolve for some $3\frac{1}{2}$ minutes after machine switched off. Trial judge held defendants negligent in failing to provide brake for cutter (not challenged on appeal) and in breach of regulation 5 of Woodworking Machines Regulations 1974, but declined to make a finding as to position of plaintiff's hand when it came into contact with cutter—*Held*:

(a) On the evidence, a guard complying with regulation 5 would have left $1\frac{3}{4}$ inches of cutter exposed. Having declined to determine position of plaintiff's hand, judge cannot have found that breach of regulation 5 was causative of the accident.
(b) Plaintiff, experienced machinist and familiar with machine, two-thirds to blame for failing to observe cutter was still moving.

U1. Rawson v. Clark (1980) C.A. 784

In April 1973 P's neck was injured due to B's negligence, and was abnormally vulnerable to further trauma—in September P was conducting a driving test of C when C skidded—jerking P's neck and exacerbating its condition—C was held not to have been negligent—*Held*, B liable for the exacerbated condition of P's neck. For further details see Chap. 1(4)(c)**U2**.

U2. Bradley v. Tinsley (1987) C.A. 449

Defendant's car turned right having signalled to do so. Motorcycle driven at speed collided with rear offside of car. Defendant had not seen motorcycle before impact—*Held*, defendant not liable. His failure to see motor cycle not causative of accident. There was ample room for the motorcycle to have passed on near-side.

4. DEFENCES

(1) Contributory Negligence

(a) General Principles

1. Caswell v. Powell Duffryn [1940] A.C. 152; [1939] 3 All E.R. 722, H.L.

Lord Porter at 186 said that the word "contributory" must be taken as expressing "something which is a direct cause of the accident." Lord Wright (172): "If the defendants' negligence is established as causing the death, the onus is on the defendants to establish that the plaintiff's contributory negligence was a substantial or material co-operating cause."

2. Porter v. Jones [1942] 2 All E.R. 570, C.A.

Dangerous ceiling in house falls on tenant—defendant landlord claims that plaintiff's continued user of room with knowledge of danger debarred him from recovery—*Held*, that, as plaintiff's continued user was not unreasonable, plaintiff could recover.

3. Boy Andrew v. St. Rognvald (owners) [1948] A.C. 140; [1947] 2 All E.R. 350, H.L.

St. Rognvald at fault in overtaking too close—*Boy Andrew* at fault in altering course while being overtaken—was the former guilty of contributory negligence? *Held*, yes, as both acts were causes of the accident. Lord Simon (149): "The suggested test of last opportunity seems to me inaptly phrased and likely in some cases to lead to error, as the Law Reform Committee said in their report: 'In truth, there is no such rule—the question, as in all cases of liability for a tortious act, is, not who had the last opportunity of avoiding the mischief, but whose act caused the wrong."' His lordship goes on to explain *Davies v. Mann* as a case where the negligence of the donkey owner was not a fault contributing to the accident, but merely a *causa sine qua non.*

4. Davies v. Swan Motor Co. [1949] 2 K.B. 291; [1949] 1 All E.R. 620, C.A.

Case of a dustman riding by clinging onto side of dustcart—run into by overtaking bus—*Held*, dustman guilty of contributory negligence, because (i) contributory negligence did not depend on a breach of duty to defendants, but on lack of care by plaintiff for his own safety (Bucknill L.J. at 309), and (ii) the doctrine of last opportunity did not exist (312, 318, 321), and the question was simply one of causation. Approved by P.C. in **6**.

5. The Older [1949] W.N. 488; 66 T.L.R. (Pt. 1) 105, C.A.

Bucknill L.J.: "It is a very salutary principle . . . that when one man by his negligence puts another in a position of difficulty the court ought to be slow to find that other man negligent merely because he may have failed to do something which, looking back on it afterwards, might possibly have reduced the amount of the damage."

6. Nance v. British Columbia Elec. Ry. [1951] A.C. 601; [1951] 2 All E.R. 448, P.C.

Deceased run down by a streetcar. Lord Simon (611 near top): "But when contributory negligence is set up as a defence, its existence does not depend on any duty owed by the injured party to the party sued, and all that is necessary to establish such defence is to prove . . . that the injured party did not in his own interests take reasonable care of himself and contributed, by this want of care, to his own injury." **4** approved.

7. Workington H. & D.B. v. Towerfield (or The Towerfield) [1951] A.C. 112; [1951] 2 All E.R. 414, H.L.

Ship went aground in harbour, sustaining damage and causing damage to harbour—pilot (for whom owners were vicariously liable) and harbour authority both negligent—accident took place before Contributory Negligence Act 1945—claim and counterclaim, insofar as each based on negligence, each failed—but harbour authority also claimed under s. 47 of Harbours, Docks and Piers Act 1847 (which provides that shipowners shall be answerable for damage done to a harbour dock or pier)—to this claim shipowners pleaded contributory negligence—*Held*, it was no defence, as liability under the Act arose independently of fault (see Lord Porter, 135). The distinction between this case and those cases where contributory negligence is available as a defence to breach of statutory duty would seem to be that here there was no duty the breach of which would give a right to damages and constitute a "fault," but merely a statutory responsibility for damage done, and as such would be more akin to a civil debt than to a claim for damages: *cf.* Lord Radcliffe at 160. *But* it was suggested by Lord Normand (148) and Lord Radcliffe (160) that where the harbour authority alone had been negligent a counterclaim might avail the shipowner to claim back the sum due under the statute. *Quaere* how far this would apply to partial negligence in cases arising after the Contributory Negligence Act 1945. See now **U1**.

8. Jones v. Livox [1952] 2 Q.B. 608; [1952] 1 T.L.R. 1377, C.A.

Denning L.J. (1383, 615): "It can now be safely asserted that the doctrine of last opportunity is obsolete; and also that contributory negligence does not depend on the existence of a duty. But the troublesome question of causation still remains to be solved. Although contributory negligence does not depend on a duty of care, it does depend on foreseeability. Just as actionable negligence requires the foreseeability of harm to others, so contributory negligence requires the foreseeability of harm to oneself. . . . "

9. Greene v. Chelsea B. C. [1954] 2 Q.B. 127; [1954] 2 All E.R. 318, C.A.

Dangerous ceiling in requisitioned house—Denning L.J. *said* (325 G) that plaintiff's knowledge of danger did not bar her claim, because she was not free to avoid the danger. *But* Singleton and Morris L.JJ. both said that in their view plaintiff did not know of the danger, so they expressed no opinion on above point. See now **11**.

10. Trevett v. Lee [1955] 1 W.L.R. 113; [1955] 1 All E.R. 406, C.A.

Case of hosepipe across road—defendant *held* not liable. "It does not necessarily follow that, because the learned judge held on the negligence claim that any liability of the defendant in negligence was wholly extinguished by the conduct or fault of plaintiff, therefore, in so far as the claim is based on nuisance, there should be a similar extinguishment of plaintiff's claim" (412 H).

11. A. C. Billings v. Riden [1957] A.C. 240; [1957] 3 All E.R. 1, H.L.

Lord Reid (9 H, Lords Simonds and Cohen concurring): "It is sometimes said that, when a visitor goes on knowing the risk, the test is whether he was free to choose or acted under some constraint. . . . If this test leads to the same answer as the question whether, in all the circumstances, the visitor acted reasonably, well and good; but if not, I think that, in cases like the present, reasonableness is the better test and more in accordance with principle. Defendant is bound to take reasonable care, but he is entitled to expect that a visitor will behave in a reasonable manner."

12. Dawrant v. Nutt [1961] 1 W.L.R. 253; [1960] 3 All E.R. 681, Stable J.

Plaintiff side-car passenger in motor-cycle combination driven by husband—to knowledge of plaintiff and husband headlight on combination was broken—collision with defendant's vehicle for which husband and defendant equally to blame—in action by plaintiff for her own personal injuries *held*, that the plaintiff owed a duty to defendant to take reasonable care for her own safety, and that she was in breach of that duty in knowingly travelling in the unlit combination, so that her claim would be reduced by 25 per cent in respect of her own contributory negligence. But, in so far as this decision is based on a breach of duty owed by the passenger, see **4** and **6**.

13. Baxter v. Woolcombers (1963) 107 S.J. 553; [1963] C.L.Y. 2320, C.A.

Plaintiff of low intelligence found guilty of contributory negligence in disobeying orders—*Held*, in dismissing appeal, that the standard to be applied was that of a reasonable man, and not the standard of plaintiff's intelligence. *Aliter*, however, when it came to the duty owed by the employer to the employee.

14. Quinn v. Burch [1966] 2 Q.B. 370; [1965] 3 All E.R. 801, Paull J.

Plaintiff sub-contractor for labour only—defendant contractors failed to provide a stepladder as requested—to save time plaintiff used a trestle which was unsafe unless footed—it slipped while unfooted—plaintiff sued in contract for breach of an implied term to provide equipment—*Held obiter*, that Contributory Negligence Act 1945, did not permit plaintiff to recover partial damages, since the breach of contract (if any) did not constitute a "fault" within s. 4. *N.B.* The decision in the case was later affirmed by C.A., [1966] 2 All E.R. 283, without this point being mentioned.

15. Sole v. Hallt [1973] 1 Q.B. 574; [1973] 1 All E.R. 1032, Swanwick J.
So held, applying *Quinn* **14**.

16. Bell Can v. Cope [1980] 11 C.C.L.T. 170; [1980] C.L.Y. 1874, Ont.High Ct.

17. Rowe v. Turner Hopkins [1980] N.Z.L.R. 550; [1981] C.L.Y. 1852, N.Z. High Ct.

18. Basildon D.C. v. J.E. Lesser (Properties) Ltd [1985] 1 Q.B. 839; [1985] 1 All E.R. 20, H.H. Judge Newey Q.C., O.R.
Held, The effect of sections 1(1) and 4 of the Law Reform (Contributory Negligence) Act 1945 was that a defendant could raise the defence of contributory negligence only if the plaintiff's claim was based on negligence, breach of statutory duty or other act or omission giving rise to liability in tort. Accordingly contributory negligence was not available as a defence to an action for damages for brearch of contract above.

19. Victoria University Manchester v. Wilson and Womersley [1984] C.I.L.L. 126; [1985] C.L.Y. 220, H.H. Judge Newey Q.C., O.R.

So *held*, applying *Basildon D.C. v. Lesser*, **18** above.

20. A.B. Marintrans v. Comet Shipping Co. Ltd [1985] 1 W.L.R. 1270; [1985] 3 All E.R. 442, Neill L.J.
Held, on a true construction of the 1945 Act, its apportionment provisions do not apply to a claim in contract. They are directed to tortious liabilities alone and are not apt to cover breaches of contractual duties of care or breaches of statutory duty which give rise to liabilities other than tortious liabilities.

21. Wasson v. Chief Constable of the R.U.C. [1987] 8 N.I.J.B. 34; [1988] C.L.Y. 2664, Hutton J.

22. Tennant Radiant Heat Ltd v. Warrington Development Corporation [1988] 1 EGLR 41; [1988] C.L.Y. 2034, C.A.

Landlord let unit in warehouse to tenant, the majority of the other units remaining unlet. The warehouse roof became flooded due to rain water outlets becoming blocked by bird droppings, feathers etc. and as a result that part of roof over tenant's unit collapsed and water damage ensued; the landlord's architects had warned the landlord of the problem posed by the birds—*Held*, lessee in breach of its covenant to keep roof above its unit cleansed and maintained; landlord, in the absence of any implied covenant was liable in negligence and nuisance for foreseeable loss and damage to lessee's goods save in so far as lessee's own breach absolved it from liability. Further *held*, in the circumstances the Law Reform (Contributory Negligence) Act 1945 did not apply but as a matter of causation of damage 90 per cent of damage to lessee's goods caused by lessor's negligence and nuisance, 10 per cent of damage to lessor's building caused by lessee's breach of covenant.

23. Alliance and Leicester Building Society v. Edgestop Ltd [1993] 1 W.L.R. 1462; [1994] 2 All E.R. 38, Mummery J.

24. Barclays Bank PLC v. Fairclough Building Ltd [1995] P.I.Q.R. p.152; [1995] 5 C.L. 253, C.A.

Contract to carry out maintenance work on building; subcontractor undertakes to do part of the work including cleaning of asbestos roofs; cleaning of roofs sub-subcontracted—*Held*, sub-subcontractor was in breach of contract in failing to take precautions which a careful and competent contractor would have taken whereby the subcontractor had suffered economic loss namely damages payable to the main contractor.

Further *held*, applying *Henderson v. Merrett Syndicates* (Chap. 19(a) **22**) the sub-subcontractor as a skilled contractor undertaking maintenance work assumed responsibility to the subcontractor no less than did a financial or other professional adviser undertaking work and as such owed a concurrent duty in tort to avoid causing economic loss by failing to exercise the care and skill of a competent contractor.

Further *held*, in such circumstances it was permissible to reduce (by half) the damages suffered by the subcontractor under the law Reform (Contributory Negligence) Act 1945 on the ground that the damage was suffered partly as a result of the subcontractor's own fault in that it also failed, as it ought, to have appreciated the risk of contamination from asbestos dust.

U1. British Waterways Board v. Benham (1963) C.A. 129

Lorry damaged a canal bridge—bridge owners claimed cost of repairs as a sum due under statute (Locomotive Act 1861, s. 7)—lorry alleged contributory negligence (insufficient warning notice on bridge)—*Held*, applying **7**, contributory negligence was no defence.

(b) Rules Governing Apportionment

Contributory negligence very small in degree—as compared with fault of defendant—contributory negligence apportioned as nil U1

1. Henley v. Cameron (1949) 65 T.L.R. 17, p. 19 (*per* Tucker L.J.), C.A.

2. Davies v. Swann Motor Co. [1949] 2 K.B. 291; [1949] 1 All E.R. 60, C.A.

Denning L.J. (326): "Whilst causation is the decisive factor in deciding whether there should be a reduced amount payable to the plaintiff, nevertheless the amount of the reduction does not depend solely on the degree of causation. The amount of the reduction . . . involves a consideration, not only of the causative potency of a particular factor, but also of its blameworthiness."

3. Wemborn v. Harland & Wolff [1952] 1 Lloyd's Rep. 255, Sellers J.

So *held*, following *Weaver v. Commercial Process*, (1947) 63 T.L.R. 466, a case of joint tortfeasors.

4. Stapley v. Gypsum [1953] A.C. 663; [1953] 2 All E.R. 478, H.L.

Lord Reid (682): "The claimant's share in the responsibility for the damage cannot, I think, be assessed without considering the relative importance of his acts in causing the damage apart from his blameworthiness."

5. Cavanagh v. London Transport, *The Times*, October 23, 1956; [1956] C.L.Y. 5824, Devlin J.

Traffic accident between plaintiff and defendants' bus—*Held*, the causative potency of the accident was shared 50–50, but defendants' driver was only 20 per cent blameworthy, and defendants were liable for one-third.

6. McMath v. Rimmer Brothers [1962] 1 W.L.R. 1; [1961] 3 All E.R. 1154, C.A.

"As there is no preponderance of culpability or causative potency on either side, the responsibility should be shared equally" (Pearson L.J. 1159 B).

7. Brown v. Thompson [1968] 1 W.L.R. 1003; [1968] 2 All E.R. 708, C.A.

8. Jayes v. I.M.I. (Kynoch) Ltd [1985] I.C.R. 155; [1985] C.L.Y. 2330, C.A.

Plaintiff, an experienced supervisor, held rag to stop grease spreading from belt of a machine being tested without guards after attention to a lubrication problem. Rag became caught, and plaintiff's finger pulled into machine and partially amputated. Plaintiff claimed breach of section 14 of Factories Act, 1961 and regulation 5 of Operations at Unfenced Machinery Regulations, 1938. He admitted he had done a very foolish thing—*Held*, there was no principle of law that there could not be a case of 100 per cent contributory negligence, even when the intention of the statute concerned is, *inter alia*, to protect against folly on the part of workmen. There comes a point at which the degree of fault is so great that the Court ceases to make fine distinctions, and holds that, in practical terms, the fault is entirely that of the plaintiff. Assuming that there had been breaches of statutory duty, the judge was entitled to take that view of this case.

U1. Cullip v. Horsham D.C. (1981) C.A. UB 9

Plaintiff motor-cyclist came round blind bend in daylight—and collided with stationary dust cart—*Held*, plaintiff had been negligent in riding so as to collide, but his fault in so riding was so small in comparison to the fault of the dust cart driver in parking where he did that the plaintiff's share of the blame would be assessed at nil.

(c) Particular Instances

(N.B.—For cases involving road traffic and pedestrians see Chap. 13). For cases involving employees see Chaps. 4(1)(d) and 16(4)(g) and (h)).

		C.N. or not
Platform—falling off in fog	1	No
FOOTWALK—OPEN CELLAR FLAP	2	No
OPEN LIFT SHAFT—WALKING INTO	3	Yes
NIGHT—WALKING ALONG PATH WITH NO LIGHT AND NO MOON	4	Yes
Shop forecourt—tripping over broken concrete	5	No
GUTTER OF ROAD—TRIPPING ON HEAP OF SLATES	6	No
Pedestrian—need not constantly look down at feet	7	
Bus—boarding in motion	8	Yes
ROAD—HOSEPIPE ACROSS—TRIPPING OVER	9	Yes
Railway platform—no duty to look down at feet	10	No
Railway platform—struck by train door	11	No
Night—falling into hole	12	Yes
GAS-FILLED WELL—RESCUE	13	No
Passenger—travelling at night in car known to have no lights	14	Yes
Pedestrian on pavement—need not keep eyes to ground	15	No
Passenger—knowing driver unfit through drink	16	Yes
PASSENGER IN MINICAB—TRIPPING OVER SEAT BELT ON GETTING OUT	17	No
Power failure—power failure warning detector not operating—baby chicken farm	18	Yes
Passenger—knowing driver intoxicated—no seat belt—knowing driver might drive recklessly	19	Yes
Pedestrian crossing road—tripping over hole	20	No
Welding—near to gas oil discharged into harbour	21	No
PEDESTRIAN ON KERB—LEANING OUT SLIGHTLY—HIT BY CAR'S WING MIRROR	22	No
Bus started with jerk—passenger not firmly gripping hand rail	23	No
Canteen assistant crossing railway line despite notice forbidding	24	Yes
Inexperienced water skier grabbing moving rope	25	Yes
Accepting lift from drunken driver	26	Yes
Solicitor's failure to ensure policy taken out—client's failure to pay premium	27	Yes
Valuer—liability not excluded by written warnings as to extent of report—no contributory negligence in not having structural survey	28	No
Prisoner—attacked in prison—failure to heed advice that he needed protection	29	Yes
MOPED RIDER WEARING BUT FAILING TO FASTEN CRASH HELMET	30	Yes
House purchaser—no contributory negligence for failure to have survey	31	No
Surveyor—accident at premises surveyed—surveyor warned of danger	32	Yes
Insurers—failure to notice limitation in reinsurance	33	Yes
Golfer on wrong fairway struck by ball	34	Yes

Licensed deposit taker—failure to instruct solicitors to check planning consents	35	Yes
Taxi driver not wearing seat belt	36	No
Valuer—whether lending finance company contributorily negligent in failing to comply with own rules and guidelines	37	No
Accepting lift from drunken driver	38	Yes
Plaintiff riding as passenger in own car driven, at plaintiff's instigation, by drunk and inexperienced driver	39	Yes
Taxi driver not wearing seat belt	40	No
Contractor—failure to check architect's survey or to conduct his own	41	No
NAVAL AIRMAN—DIED WHEN DRUNK DUE TO INHALATION OF VOMIT	42	Yes
Valuer—effect of knowledge of lender as to risks of lending	43	Maybe
Valuer—failure to take account of comparable rents—whether bank contributorily negligent in making loan	44	No
Valuer—negligent valuation—failure of bank to enquire as to disparity between sale price and valuation	45	Yes
Valuer—negligent valuation—whether lender negligent in lending too much	46	Yes
Dark room—falling downstairs	U1	No
Dark room—wandering to find light	U2	Yes
Night—not seeing hole in path	U3	No
Dark room—falling downstairs	U4	No
Plaintiff's van causing defendants' unbraked compressor to run downhill	U5	No
Motorcyclist removing rope entangled in wheel during race	U6	No
Deceased intoxicated—falling over retaining wall	U7	Yes

1. Schlarb v. L. N. E. R. [1936] 1 All E.R. 71; 80 S.J. 168, Atkinson J.

2. Daniel v. Rickett Cockerell [1938] 2 K.B. 322; [1938] 2 All E.R. 631, C.A.

Held, plaintiff was entitled to expect footwalk to be in ordinary condition of safety and was under no duty to keep a special look-out for cellar flaps which might be open.

3. Kerry v. Keighley Engineering Co. [1940] 3 All E.R. 399; 163 L.T. 97, C.A.

So *held*, disapproving *obiter dictum* to the contrary by Horridge J. in *Morgan v. Girls Friendly Society* [1936] 1 All E.R. 404.

4. Gibby v. East Grinstead Gas Co. [1944] 1 All E.R. 358; 170 L.T. 250, C.A.

5. Howard v. Walker [1947] K.B. 860; [1947] 2 All E.R. 197, Lord Goddard C.J.

"It is true she knew the place and it is true she knew, if she had thought about it at the time, that the concrete was broken, but a person who enters or leaves a shop in the evening can hardly be expected to keep her eyes on the ground" (198 A).

6. Almeroth v. Chivers [1948] 1 All E.R. 53; 92 S.J. 71, C.A.

Plaintiff crossing road tripped on heap of slates lying by kerb in gutter—kerb was 4–6 inches high and top of heap was below kerb level—*Held*, not contributory negligence, as a man crossing a road did not fail to take reasonable care if he did not constantly look down at his feet. *Approved* by H.L. in **15**.

7. Stowell v. Railway Executive [1949] 2 K.B. 519; [1949] 2 All E.R. 193, Lynskey J.

"It would not be reasonable to require that those using the platforms should be looking down at their feet at every step they take" (525).

8. Guinnear v. L. P. T. B. (1948) 92 S.J. 350; [1948] C.L.C. 6620, Lynskey J.

9. Trevett v. Lee [1955] 1 W.L.R. 113; [1955] 1 All E.R. 406, C.A.

10. Rossi v. P. L. A. [1956] 1 Lloyd's Rep. 478, Lynskey J.

"There is no obligation on a person walking along say a railway platform or in a ballroom to watch where he is placing his feet. He is entitled to rely on the general condition of the area" (480, col. 1).

11. Hare v. B. T. C. [1956] 1 W.L.R. 250; [1956] 1 All E.R. 578, Lord Goddard C.J.

12. A. C. Billings v. Riden [1958] A.C. 240; [1957] 3 All E.R. 1, H.L.

13. Baker v. Hopkins [1959] 1 W.L.R. 966; [1959] 3 All E.R. 225, C.A.

14. Dawrant v. Nutt [1960] 1 W.L.R. 253; [1960] 3 All E.R. 681, Stable J.

15. Haley v. L. E. B. [1965] A.C. 778; [1964] 3 All E.R. 185, H.L.

Lord Reid (187 G): "I agree with Somervell L. J. (in *Almeroth* **6**) that a person walking along a pavement does not have to keep his eyes to the ground to see whether or not there is an obstacle in his path."

16. Owens v. Brimmell [1977] 2 W.L.R. 943; [1976] 3 All E.R. 765, Watkins J.

Pub crawl—driver and passenger both drank a great deal—accident on way home—*Held*, 20 per cent contributory negligence against passenger.

17. McCready v. Miller [1979] R.T.R. 186, C.A.

P, a passenger in a minicab, tripped over the loop of a seat belt suspended from a hook when she was getting out. She had never been in vehicle before, it was night time and the minicab driver neither warned P nor switched on interior light—*Held*, no contributory negligence. *Donn v. Shacter* [1975] R.T.R. 238 distinguished (and possibly disapproved); in this latter case the facts were similar, save that it was a friend's car in which P had travelled previously, and the trial judge found that P was solely to blame.

18. Heeney v. Beer (1979) 108 D.L.R. (3d) 766; [1980] C.L.Y. 1875, Ont. C.A.

Plaintiff 25 per cent to blame. The court *said* that the failure was analogous to a failure to wear seat belt.

19. Ashton v. Turner [1981] Q.B. 137; [1980] 3 All E.R. 870, Ewbank J.

Held, no duty of care owed (see Chap. 1, (2)(a) **12** and Chap. 4, (3) **33**), but if there had been, 50 per cent contributory negligence by passenger.

20. Hymanson v. Greater Manchester Council (1981) C.A. 89

Plaintiff failed to notice $2\frac{1}{2}$ inch deep hole when crossing road carrying "quite a lot of traffic."—*Held*, no contributory negligence.

21. The Arzew [1981] 1 Lloyd's Rep. 142; [1981] C.L.Y. 1838, Sheen J.

Held, no contributory negligence, as it would have been difficult for P to notice the gas oil on the water.

22. Chapman v. Post Office [1982] R.T.R. 165; [1982] C.L.Y. 2136, C.A.

23. Azzopardi v. State Transport Authority 30 S.A.S.R. 434; [1983] C.L.Y. 2515, Sup. Ct. of South Australia

24. Umek v. London Transport Executive (1984) 134 New L.J. 522; [1984] C.L.Y. 2313, McNeill J.

Canteen assistant killed whilst crossing line to defendant's depot, ignoring, as others had, notice forbidding such conduct and advising use of footbridge whilst subway blocked by flooding—*Held*, defendants were aware of such conduct and should have warned train drivers accordingly; 75 per cent contributory negligence of deceased.

25. Pawlack v. Doucette and Reinks [1985] 2 W.W.R. 588; [1985] C.L.Y. 2337, British Columbia Supreme Court

First defendant invited plaintiff to water ski. Knowing plaintiff had no experience, first defendant explained, from a position on shore, how plaintiff should position himself in water. Unidentified person on shore shouted "go". Second defendant, who had not asked whether plaintiff was experienced, applied full power. Plaintiff grabbed at rope. His fingers became entangled and were severed—*Held, inter alia*:

(a) First defendant negligent in failing properly to execute the supervisory role he had assumed.
(b) Second defendant negligent in failing to ascertain whether plaintiff experienced, and applying full power in response to shout from shore.
(c) Plaintiff 15 per cent contributorily negligent in grabbing moving rope.

26. Meah v. McCreamer [1985] 1 All E.R. 367; 135 New L.J. 80, Woolf J.

Plaintiff accepted lift from defendant, with whom he had been drinking for a considerable time. Had plaintiff not been affected by drink it would have been obvious to him that defendant was unfit to drive. Plaintiff injured when defendant lost control of car—*Held*, plaintiff 25 per cent contributorily negligent.

27. McClellan v. Fletcher (1987) 137 New L.J. 593; [1987] C.L.Y. 3559, Anthony Lincoln J.

Solicitor held negligent in failing to ensure a life insurance policy had been taken out where the policy was part of the security on which a mortgage was advanced for purchase of house by deceased; deceased had lost the contingent interest in such policy less the premium payable; 75 per cent deduction for deceased's contributory negligence in not paying premium.

28. Davies v. Parry [1988] 1 EGLR 147; [1988] C.L.Y. 2457, Mc Neill J.
For details see Chap. 18, (5)**22**.

29. Steele v. Northern Ireland Office (1988) 12 N.I.J.B.1.; [1989] C.L.Y. 2706, Kelly J., N.I.

Sex offender attacked whilst on remand—*Held*; duty on defendant to exercise reasonable care for prisoner's safety *a fortiori* where sex offender; breach of duty found but reduced by one third for plaintiff's contributory negligence in failing to heed advice given to him that he needed protection.

30. Capps v. Miller [1989] 1 W.L.R. 839; [1989] 2 All E.R. 333, C.A.

Defendant's car ran into plaintiff's moped. Plaintiff wearing crash helmet but, contrary to regulation 4 of the Motor Cycles (Protective Helmets) Regulations 1980, the chinstrap was unfastened, and helmet came off before plaintiff's head struck road—*Held*, because it was less blameworthy to wear a helmet unfastened than not to wear a helmet at all, plaintiff was 10 per cent contributorily negligent rather than the 15 per cent he would have been had he worn no helmet.

31. Kijowski v. New Capital Properties Ltd (1990) 15 Con LR 1, [1990] C.L.Y. 398, Judge Esyr Lewis Q.C.

Held, inter alia, that builder was negligent in and about construction of house whereby differential settlement occurred and was liable to the house owner; owner was not contributorily negligent in failing to have a survey carried out at time of purchase.

32. Rae (Geoffrey) v. Mars U.K. [1990] 3 E.G. 80; [1990] C.L.Y. 3309, H.H.J. White

P, experienced surveyor, injured when falling down drop in unlit storeroom. A warning had been given of the danger—*Held*, this was inadequate. D was liable because further steps should have been taken, but P also negligent for not using torch or looking down.

33. Youell v. Bland Welch & Co. Ltd (No. 2) [1990] 2 Lloyd's Rep. 431; [1991] C.L.Y. 3288, Phillips J.

Whilst the insurance brokers were in breach of duty of care in failing to inform insurers of a limitation clause in reinsurance policy, the insurers were held 20 per cent to blame for their negligence in failing to notice that clause or make enquiry about it. For further details see Chap. 18,(4) **19**.

34. Feeny v. Lyall, 1991 S.L.T. 156; [1991] C.L.Y. 5298, (O.H.)

Plaintiff struck golf ball onto wrong fairway—when recovering it, was struck by ball driven by another golfer from the tee of that fairway—*Held*, had the other golfer seen P, P would have been 25 per cent contributorily negligent for failing to check on the actions of golfers on that tee.

35. P.K. Finans International (U.K.) Ltd v. Andrew Downs & Co. Ltd [1992] 1 EGLR 172: [1992] C.L.Y. 3216. Sir Michael Ogden Q.C.

Valuer stated in his report he had made oral inquiries but no official search as to planning consents—*Held*, not negligent in not advising planning consents should be verified; if there had been negligence, then recipients, licensed deposit takers, were contributorily negligent in failing to instruct solicitors to verify the position: for further detail see Chap 18, (5) **55**.

36. Pace v. Cully, 1992 S.L.T. 1073 (O.H.); [1992] C.L.Y. 5645

Taxi driver injured in accident for which liability admitted. Had not been wearing seat belt on police advice that it was safer not to, having regard to risk of attack from passengers—*Held*, not contributorily negligent.

37. HIT Finance Ltd v. Lewis & Tucker Ltd [1993] 2 EGLR 231, Wright J.

Defendant valuers were admittedly negligent in overvaluing property; they alleged that the plaintiff finance company was contributorily negligent in failing to follow its own rules and guidelines on lending—*Held*, although the lender had taken a somewhat relaxed attitude to these matters, it was entitled to do so given the valuation provided and the extent of the security shown thereby; the lender did not fall below the standard of the prudent lender of the kind the plaintiff was. Further *held*; the plaintiff's solicitors were, having regard to the nature and extent of their instructions, under no duty to the plaintiff to make inquiries which would have revealed matters which might cause concern as to the transaction and hence the plaintiff was not fixed with such presumed knowledge.

38. Stinton v. Stinton and M.I.B. [1993] P.I.Q.R. P 135; [1993] C.L.Y. 2939, Simon Brown J.

Plaintiff was passenger in brother's car. Both had been on lengthy drinking session. Brother drove vehicle into lamp post—admitted liability—*Held*, plaintiff contributorily negligent by one third accepting lift from a driver whose ability was impaired by drink. The case involved "blameworthiness . . . to the highest extent possible short of direct participation in the actual performance." (*N.B.* The case was taken to appeal—*The Times*, November 23, 1994—but only on the liability of the M.I.B.)

39. Donelan v. Donelan and General Accident [1993] P.I.Q.R. P205; [1994] C.L.Y. 3341, H. H. Judge Askill, sitting as a High Court Judge

First defendant driving and plaintiff passenger in plaintiff's 2,000 c.c. automatic car, when first defendant negligently crashed it. First defendant had driven at instigation of plaintiff who was the older and dominant party, knew that first defendant was drunk (as was he) and knew or should have known of the risks of her driving given than she had never before driven a car so powerful or with automatic transmission—*Held*, on the wholly exceptional facts, plaintiff 75 per cent contributorily negligent.

40. Jones v. Morgan [1994] C.L.Y. 3344, Dyson J.

Taxi driver injured in accident for which liability admitted. Had not been wearing seat belt—*Held*, not contrubutorily negligent. One relevant matter was that taxi drivers are legally exempt from wearing sear belts when carrying fare-paying passengers. Moreover, taxi driver had just picked up barmaid not known to him at midnight, and he and his employer were concerned about risk of attack from passengers—easier to evade if seatbelt off. However, there should be no invariable policy for taxi drivers not to wear seat belts—time of day and nature of passenger were relevant features.

41. Cardy & Son v. Taylor [1994] NPC 30; [1994] 12 C.L. 82, Judge Bowsher Q.C.

Employer counterclaimed damages *inter alia* for defective design against contractor who joined unqualified architect, who had designed alterations to premises, as third party—*Held*, duty of care owed by an architect was the same whether he was qualified or not; contractor not guilty of contributory negligence in failing to check the architect's survey or in failing to conduct his own survey.

42. Barrett v. Ministry of Defence [1995] 1 W.L.R. 1217; *The Times*, January 13, 1995, C.A.

For details see Chap 18, (13)**79**.

43. Craneheath Securities Ltd v. York Montague Ltd [1994] 1 EGLR 159; [1995] 1 C.L. 287, Jacob J.

Plaintiff bank lent on security of restaurant in reliance on audited and management accounts and on valuation by defendant valuers—*Held*, valuer not negligent; the open market value basis of valuation assumed a static market and the valuer did not have to take account of the possible collapse of property prices; the valuation was one which a competent valuer could properly have reached. Had the defendant been negligent the plaintiff would very likely have been held partly to blame as he had more information than valuer, and knew it, about matters affecting the valuation.

44. United Bank of Kuwait v. Prudential Property Services Ltd [1994] 2 EGLR 100; [1995] 1 C.L. 284, Gage J.

Valuers held negligent in valuing commercial premises by assessing market rents incorrectly through failure to take into account comparable rents in the locality; the bank lending on their valuation would not have proceeded had a proper valuation been provided. The bank was not guilty of contributory negligence; it had not fallen below the standard required of a reasonably competent banker in making the loan. *HIT Finance v. Lewis & Tucker*, **37** relied on. Appeal on quantum [1995] New L.J. 343.

45. Banque Bruxelles Lambert SA v. Eagle Star Insurance Co. Ltd [1994] 2 EGLR 108; [1995] 1 C.L. 285, Phillips J.

Plaintiff bank lent 90 per cent of value of various properties and obtained mortgage indemnity guarantees giving 100 per cent cover against loss. The defendant valuers were involved *inter alia* in three such properties—*Held*, the plaintiff's claim against the valuers was in tort; the defendants had overvalued the properties in particular by not investigating and giving due weight to the marketing history of the properties and were negligent, but that in one case the plaintiff had not substantially relied upon the defendant's advice whether directly or indirectly. The plaintiff was guilty of contributory negligence to the extent of 30 per cent in that it had fallen below the standard of care to be expected of a merchant bank in protecting its own interests by failing to make inquiries as to the disparity between sale prices and valuations. Defendants were also held following *Smith v. Eric Bush*, Chap. 18, (13) **66** and *Caparo*, Chap. 18, (1), **17** to owe a duty of care to the guarantors who had relied on their valuations and thereby suffered loss. Much of the lengthy judgment was concerned with the assessment of damages, including loss represented by a collapse in market prices which latter was the subject of appeal [1995] 2 W.L.R. 607.

46. Nyckeln Finance Co Ltd v. Stumpbrook Continuation Ltd [1994] 2 EGLR 143; [1995] 1 C.L. 282, H.H. Judge Fawcus

Plaintiff finance company lent monies on security of office premises. The defendant valuers admitted valuation was higher than a reasonably competent surveyor could have provided at the time—*Held*, plaintiff had relied on valuation in deciding to lend; it was reasonable for it to rely on the same; the plaintiff would not have proceeded had a proper valuation been given; the defendants were liable in contract and tort. Further, following *Banque Bruxelles v. Eagle Star* **45**, the plaintiff was contributorily negligent to the extent of 20 per cent since no reasonably prudent finance company would have lent as much as the plaintiff did.

U1. Bartle v. Theatre Royal (1952) C.A. 123

U2. Smith v. Sheppard (1955) C.A. 107

U3. Ramage v. Francis Jackson (1959) C.A. 109

U4. Parker v. Charalambou (1961) C.A. 198

U5. Wilson v. British Gas Corporation (1986) C.A. 1114

Plaintiff reversed van in crowded car park making minor impact with defendant's unbraked compressor which began to roll downhill; plaintiff ran and tried to apply handbrake but was injured when hit by its towbar: defendants held liable; the minor impact was not an intervening act which destroyed the defendant's negligence; the plaintiff was not negligent in trying to stop the compressor nor was he guilty of contributory negligence.

U6. Butler v. Vann (1991) C.A. 702

15-year-old in motor cycle race got rope from improperly erected marker fence entangled in his rear wheel when he went off the track; he resumed the race without realising but had later to stop and unravel it but whilst doing so was hit by another competitor. Defendants held liable; no contributory negligence by plaintiff resuming race without checking rear wheel or acting as he subsequently did.

U7. Scollen v. Leisure Holidays Ltd (1992) C.A. 214

Deceased held 25 per cent to blame for fall which led to fatal injuries, when falling over unlit retaining wall in darkness at holiday camp. He had been intoxicated and had been venturing unseen into an area of darkness.

(d) Employees

(N.B. — The cases listed here deal solely with what is, or may be, contributory negligence by an employee. The cases dealing with the problem of an employer who has been guilty of a technical breach or minor default and an employee whose contributory negligence has been the real cause are dealt with in (Chap. 16 (4) (c), *q.v.*)

1. Caswell v. Powell Duffryn [1940] A.C. 152; [1939] 3 All E.R. 722, H.L.

Lord Wright at 174 expressly approves dictum of Lawrence J. in *Flower v. Ebbw Vale Steel* [1934] 2 K.B. 132, 139: "It is not for every risky thing which a workman in a factory may do in his familiarity with the machinery that a plaintiff ought to be held guilty of contributory negligence." Also approved by Lord Reid in *Summers v. Frost* [1955] 1 All E.R. 870, 887 I, H.L. *But* now see *Staveley v. Jones* **14**.

2. Homes v. Hadfield [1944] K.B. 275; [1944] 1 All E.R. 235; C.A.

Defendant in breach of statutory duty in allowing travelling crane to come too near plaintiff — allege plaintiff guilty of contributory negligence in giving faulty signal — *Held*, no contributory negligence, for defendants were in effect substituting a private signalling arrangement for the absolute prohibition in Factories Acts, and if the signals were misunderstood, defendants must be responsible.

3. Callaghan v. Fred Kidd [1944] 1 K.B. 560; [1994] 1 All E.R. 525, C.A.

Scott L.J. at 563: " . . . the judge was obviously right in acquitting him of negligence in failing to observe the collection of rusty iron bars . . . as he walked round from the grindstone . . . As the judge says, he would be intent on his job, with his eyes up and not down."

4. Gallagher v. Dorman Long [1947] 2 All E.R. 38; 177 L.T. 143, C.A.

Wrottesley L.J. at 42 E: "It is not every mistake or inadvertence that amounts to contributory negligence. If a man exercising his skill and knowledge to the best of his ability makes a mistake, particularly as in this case in estimating what would be a safe lift, it does not in our view amount to contributory negligence."

5. Hopwood v. Rolls Royce (1947) 176 L.T. 514, C.A.

"Contributory negligence does not mean mere error of judgment, nor does it mean that sort of degree of inattention which a workman in a factory may in the ordinary course of his work be expected to show in circumstances that are familiar to him" (Lord Greene M.R.). *But* now see **14**.

6. Jerred v. Dent [1948] 2 All E.R. 104; 81 Ll.L.R. 412, Atkinson J.

Duty of securing hatch beams under reg. 42 not discharged — defendants (or rather third party) tries to argue that as the duty is laid generally on those carrying on the processes, plaintiffs (stevedores) just as much to blame as anyone — *Held*, not so, though judge said result might have been different if plaintiffs had known reg. was being broken (109 H).

7. Donovan v. Cammell Laird [1949] 2 All E.R. 82; (1949) L1.L.R. 642, Devlin J.

Plaintiff fell down unguarded tank top on ship. " . . . the plaintiff's behaviour was due to a momentary lapse from alertness such as might affect the ordinary prudent workman of his grade . . . " (86 B). *Held*, not contributory negligence.

8. General Cleaning Contractors v. Christmas [1953] A.C. 180; [1952] 2 All E.R. 1110, H.L.

Lord Jowitt L.C. at 1113 B cites Denning L.J. [1952] 1 All E.R. 42 with approval: "You cannot blame the man for not taking every precaution which prudence would suggest. It is only too easy to be wise after the event. He was doing the work in the way which the employers expected him to do it . . . "

9. Laszczyk v. N.C.B. [1954] 1 W.L.R. 1426; [1954] 3 All E.R. 205, Pearson J.

Coal mining case — defendants negligent but was plaintiff? — he was acting in contravention of various regs. but was doing so on instructions of the deputy — *Held*, proportion of contributory negligence in these circumstances would only be 5 per cent.

10. Hodkinson v. Henry Wallwork [1955] 1 W.L.R. 1195; [1955] 3 All E.R. 236, C.A.

Unfenced transmission belt nine feet above ground — stoppage — plaintiff unauthorised went up ladder to adjust — *Held*, plaintiff acting in defiance of accepted practice and was going to a place where no one expected him to go, and he was 90 per cent liable.

11. Honeyman v. Orient S.N. [1955] 2 Lloyd's Rep. 27, Hilbery J.

"Lastly, it is not without some significance that for some time there was put, and there remained, upon the record of the court an allegation that in the alternative plaintiff was himself guilty of contributory negligence in failing to use a lifeline. That seems to me to involve this: it involves really saying that a reasonable man, knowing the danger of working outboard without a lifeline would have provided himself with a lifeline and used it, and if that is to be said, even in the alternative, against plaintiff, it must have equal force if plaintiff says: "You, the defendants, knew the risk of my working outboard without a lifeline and you failed to provide one" (33, col. 2).

12. Davison v. Apex Scaffolds [1956] 1 Q.B. 551; [1956] 1 All E.R. 473, C.A.

Collapse of scaffold causing death of chargehand erector—due to use of "foreign" coupler which was defective through having too long a bolt—defendants admittedly in breach of statutory duty, and also negligence (485 F) for having mixed a "foreign" coupler with their own—question was whether deceased was himself to blame, either at common law or for his own breach of statutory duty under reg. 4 of Building Regulations 1948—four allegations were made against deceased:

(a) He should have rejected the coupler as a foreigner;
(b) he should have discovered the bolt was too long;
(c) he should have followed an alleged drill of coupling the vertical first;
(d) he should have put in a second coupler as a safety precaution.

Singleton L.J. said (481 I) that deceased was in breach of statutory duty under (iii) and (iv); Jenkins L.J. said (486 H) that deceased was guilty of contributory negligence under (i), but did not go into question of whether this contributory negligence was at common law or breach of statutory duty; Hodson L.J. said no contributory negligence at all. As a result *held*, deceased 20 per cent. to blame.

13. Simmons v. Bovis [1956] 1 W.L.R. 381; [1956] 1 All E.R. 736, Barry J.

Case where plaintiff stepped onto trap end of scaffold—plaintiff *held* 10 per cent. to blame. " . . . without really having time to direct his mind specifically to the sort of questions which he might have asked himself in other circumstances, he ducked under the guardrail and trod on this platform. The instinctive, or semi-instinctive, nature of the act also weighs with me . . . " (743 F).

14. Staveley Iron and Chemical v. Jones [1956] A.C. 627; [1956] 1 All E.R. 403, H.L.

Lord Tucker (413 F), with whom Lords Morton, Porter and Cohen concurred, after referring to the dicta in *Flower v. Ebbw Vale Steel* and *Caswell v. Powell* **1** to the effect that it is not every risky thing which plaintiff in his familiarity with work may do which amounts to contributory negligence, said: " . . . while accepting without question this and other dicta to a similar effect which have been used in this House in relation to cases under the Factories Acts and other statutes imposing absolute obligations on employers and occupiers of premises, I doubt very much whether they were ever intended to be applied, or could properly be applied, to a simple case of common law negligence, such as the present, where there is no evidence of work-people performing repetitive work under strain or for long hours at dangerous machines." And at 414 C: "This (the application of the dicta) is not so illogical as may appear at first sight, when it is remembered that contributory negligence is not founded on breach of duty . . . and that in cases under the Factories Acts the purpose of imposing the absolute obligation is to protect the workmen against those very acts of inattention which are sometimes relied on as constituting contributory negligence, so that too strict a standard would defeat the object of the statute."

15. I.R.C. v. Hambrook [1956] 2 Q.B. 641; [1956] 3 All E.R. 338, C.A.

Denning L.J. (340 D): "If the owner of a motor-car sends it out with a driver and, whilst he is driving it in the course of his employment, the car is damaged by the fault of both drivers, the owner must take responsibility, for his own driver's negligence. He only gets reduced damages. If however the driver takes the car out on a frolic of his own, outside the course of his employment, the owner recovers full damages for the car because he is then not responsible for his driver's negligence."

16. Pead v. Furness Withy [1956] 2 Lloyd's Rep. 149, Slade J.

Plaintiff slips on steel deck slippery from spilt grain—*Held,* not contributory negligence. "A court ought not to be too astute to find contributory negligence merely because the employee does not, every time he comes across a situation of extra hazard caused to him by his employer, [refuse to work further]" (155).

17. Williams v. Port of Liverpool Stevedoring [1956] 1 W.L.R. 551; [1956] 2 All E.R. 69, Lynskey J.

Improper method of stowage adopted by gang of six, plaintiff being one—*Held,* plaintiff's share of blame 50 per cent. "I think plaintiff was equally responsible with the other five men in the gang in carrying out this wrong method of work, because it required the consent of all the gang to carry it out, and plaintiff could have stopped it if he had wanted" (74 A).

18. Hicks v. B.T.C. [1958] 1 W.L.R. 493; [1958] 2 All E.R. 39, C.A.

"The fact, of course, is that inadvertence may itself amount to negligence or it may not" (Lord Evershed M.R., 47 H).

19. Campbell v. Harland & Wolff [1959] 1 Lloyd's Rep. 198, Gorman J.

Staging too narrow—plaintiff did not report it—*Held*, breach of Shipbuilding Reg. 53 (a) and contributory negligence at common law. Contributory negligence assessed at one-sixth.

20. Quintas v. National Smelting Co. [1961] 1 W.L.R. 401; [1961] 1 All E.R. 630, C.A.

Sellers L.J. (636 E): "It has often been held that there is a high responsibility on a defendant who fails to comply with his statutory duty which is absolute and has penal sanctions. A workman is not to be judged so severely."

21. Johnson v. Rea [1962] 1 Q.B. 373; [1961] 3 All E.R. 816, C.A.

Plaintiff lorry driver (not employed by defendants) slipped on floor of dock shed made slippery by negligence of defendants' stevedores—plaintiff had to carry keg across the floor and knew the floor was slippery—*Held*, no contributory negligence, as it could not be said that he was at fault in continuing with his work, nor had it been proved that he walked carelessly on the floor.

22. Foley v. Enso-Gutzeit Osakeyhtio [1962] 1 Lloyd's Rep. 247, Gorman J.

Foreman stevedore tripped on obstruction on deck which he had no reason to expect—*Held*, one-third contributory negligence as, "if a man is working on a ship in a space of this kind, he must keep his eyes open" (252, col. 1).

23. Holmes v. T. & J. Harrison [1962] 1 Lloyd's Rep. 455, C.A.

Fork-lift truck used as mobile crane by suspending load from top of truck—admittedly unsafe system—*Held*, defendants liable, and plaintiff (although a hatch foreman) not liable for contributory negligence because he was only putting into operation something which he had seen done from time to time before.

24. O'Malley v. Sheppard [1963] 1 Lloyd's Rep. 189, C.A.

Plaintiff an insurance inspector who had come to test a crane—during the tests crane toppled and fell on plaintiff—cause was insufficient ballast, of which plaintiff should have known—*Held*, plaintiff guilty of one-third contributory negligence.

25. Machray v. Stewart & Lloyds [1965] 1 W.L.R. 602; [1964] 3 All E.R. 716, McNair J.

Plaintiff used rope block instead of chain block, because latter not available—*Held*, no contributory negligence. "When I find a workman ... adopting a course of conduct not for the sake of saving himself trouble, but in order to get on with the employer's business, and when I find that he has been prevented from doing the work in the way he would have preferred to do it by the employer's breach in not providing him with the proper tackle, I am very slow to put any blame on him ... " (721 F). *Adopted* by C.A. in **U11**.

26. Kansara v. Osram [1967] 3 All E.R. 230, C.A.

Machine being adjusted by mechanical fitter—who is not concerned with electrical side at all, other than to switch current on—while working, his long screwdriver touched a bare wire—admitted breach of Electricity Regulations—*Held*, reversing county court judge, no contributory negligence.

27. Mullard v. Ben Line [1970] 1 W.L.R. 1414; [1971] 2 All E.R. 424, C.A.

"What happened indeed was exactly of the nature intended to be guarded against by the precautions prescribed by the regulations; and when a defendant's liability stems from such a breach the courts must be careful not to emasculate those regulations by the sidewind of apportionment. Moreover, the more culpable and continuing the breach of the regulation, the higher the proportion of blame that must fall on the defendant" (Sachs L.J., 1418 E). Dicta in *Staveley* **14** and *Quintas* **20** applied. Facts were that plaintiff, a ship repairer, went from a lighted into a dark compartment without a torch and fell down an unlit unfenced hatch—clear breaches of Shipbuilding Regulations 1960—judge held plaintiff 50 per cent contributorily negligent for going without torch—C.A. *held* proportion should be reduced to 33 per cent.

28. O'Keefe v. Stewart [1979] 1 Lloyd's Rep. 182; [1979] C.L.Y. 2474, Kenneth Jones J.

P, footing ladder, went up same to help fellow employee who was in danger of falling—ladder slewed and threw P—*Held*, no contributory negligence, as the risk taken by P was far outweighed by the danger to the fellow employee.

29. McMullen v. N.C.B. [1982] I.C.R. 148; [1982] C.L.Y. 2121, Caulfield J.

Plaintiff, with others, jumped off moving man-rider in mine—fell in crush and was severely injured. The men had been properly instructed not to leave man-rider whilst in motion. Plaintiff in breach of statutory duties—*Held*, applying *I.C.I. v. Shatwell* (Chap. 15,(8)**27**) that the claim failed, as the plaintiff's conduct in disobeying his instructions was the sole cause of the accident.

30. Johns v. Martin Simms [1983] 1 All E.R. 127; [1983] I.C.R. 305, Lawson J.

Plaintiff checking unfenced radiator fan in excavator engine—hand trapped—defendants in breach of statutory duty—*Held*, no c.n. "... this is the sort of accident that can happen by inadvertence and that is one of the reasons why regulations made under this statute are made, because workmen who are concentrating on doing a job may inadvertently get their hands in a position of danger by reason of a dangerous part of the machine, and that is why the law requires the dangerous part to be fenced" (130 E-F).

31. Jayes v. I.M.I. (Kynoch) Ltd [1985] I.C.R. 155; [1985] C.L.Y. 2330, C.A.

Plaintiff, an experienced supervisor, held rag to stop grease spreading onto belt of a machine being tested without guards after attention to a lubrication problem. Rag became caught, and plaintiff's finger pulled into machine and partially amputated. Plaintiff claimed breach of section 14 of Factories Act 1961 and regulation 5 of Operations at Unfenced Machinery Regulations 1938. He admitted he had done a very foolish thing—*Held*, there was no principle of law that there could not be a case of 100 per cent contributory negligence, even when the intention of the statute concerned is, *inter alia*, to protect against folly on the part of workmen. There comes a point at which the degree of fault is so great that the Court ceases to make fine distinctions, and holds that, in practical terms, the fault is entirely that of the plaintiff. Assuming that there had been breaches of statutory duty, the judge was entitled to take that view of this case.

U1. Cross v. Segal (1952) C.A. 257

Plaintiff puts his hand behind bars to adjust insecurely fenced transmission belt in motion—a conscious and deliberate act on the part of the plaintiff—*Held*, 50: 50.

U2. Burrows v. Metal Box Co. (1956) C.A. 347

Plaintiff minder of colour printing machine—had to clean rollers from time to time—no fence—warned that must stop machine to clean it—practice in factory not to stop machine to clean rollers, though dangerous, to save trouble—men knew they should not clean machine when running—*Held*, defendants in breach of Factories Acts—50 per cent contributory negligence against plaintiff for doing not only what told not to do but also what no sensible person would do.

U3. Robinson v. Pearce (1960) C.A. 267 A

Plaintiff bricklayer sent to private house to repair chimney—defendant employers send him his equipment separately by lorry—ladder and cat ladder—but no rope for lashing them—plaintiff goes up unlashed cat ladder which slips—trial judge apportioned two-thirds blame against employers, one-third against plaintiff—*Held*, plaintiff 75 per cent to blame as he erected and went up an obviously dangerous cat ladder, without having checked or queried the absence of rope with the lorry driver and without having rung up employers to ask for rope to be sent.

U4. Hogg v. Modern Heating Co. (1961) C.A. 144

Passageway of unsecured planks on first floor of building site—clear breaches of Building Regulations—plaintiff thrown when plank tilted—*Held* (reversing county court judge), no contributory negligence because it was a passageway in common and frequent use, and in such circumstances it was not contributory negligence merely because plaintiff had failed to look and see the danger.

U5. Burgon v. Nottingham Evening News (1962) C.A. 256

Unfenced machine. "Provision must be made for the fact that from time to time, human nature being what it is, there is some falling off in the concentration of the person using the machine. . . . It would appear to me that in those circumstances 'inadvertence' is much nearer the true word to use than 'negligence'."

U6. Dalton v. Sankey Sugar (1962) C.A. 231

Unfenced transmission shaft fifteen feet up—foreman went up pipes on wall to replace belt while in motion—instead of stopping shaft and using inching button—but to adopt latter method would have held up production—*Held*, 50: 50.

U7. Ryan v. Manbre (1970) C.A. 251 A

Step slippery from damp sugar—known to plaintiff—*Held*, in the absence of any unreasonable act by him, not contributory negligence.

U8. Stocker v. Norprint (1970) C.A. 460A (also (1971) 10 K.I.R. 10

Guillotine machine admittedly insecurely fenced—but judge held plaintiff 100 per cent. liable for contributory negligence—*Held*, this was not possible, except in a *Ginty* type of case (*i.e.* where plaintiff also owed a statutory duty—see Chap. 16, (4)(d) **5**). In addition, plaintiff's fault here was only inadvertence, so that defendants were 100 per cent liable.

U9. Lynch v. Key Engineering (1971) C.A. 84

Salmon L.J. (6C): "One ought not to approach a case of this kind on the basis that, once it has been shown against a defendant that he is in breach of section 14 of the Act (*i.e.* the fencing provisions), then you must rigidly apply a rule that in no circumstances can the plaintiff be as much as 50 per cent to blame." Facts were that plaintiff was acting both foolishly and contrary to instructions in relation to a dangerous nip.

U10. Leavey v. Foster Wheeler (1972) C.A. 382A

Plaintiff steel erector going up long ladder bangs head against piece of tubular steel which someone had put there in unknown circumstances—judge held 50: 50—but C.A., applying *Mullard* **27**, *reduced* plaintiff's share to 33 per cent.

U11. Pilling v. Matto (1973) C.A. 99

Plaintiff, painting external fire escape, puts up makeshift scaffold—having been left to own devices—and falls—*Held*, adopting dictum of McNair J. in *Machray* **25**, no contributory negligence.

U12. Vause v. English Sewing Ltd (1981) C.A. UB 361

Plaintiff, night manager at a cotton mill, failed to isolate machine before clearing blockage manually near dangerous moving parts—*Held*, plaintiff 40 per cent contributory negligent.

U13. Weir v. Bedford Commercial Vehicles (1988) C.A. 574

Release mechanism on plaintiff's drilling machine stuck due to a defect of which he had informed the defendants, who had not rectified it. To free the drill bit, he struck the chuck with his left hand, without holding the bit with his right hand, and the bit fell and injured his left-hand—*Held*, defendants liable for their failure to maintain the machine. Although plaintiff acknowledged it would have been sensible to hold the bit with his right hand, no contributory negligence found. When a workman was doing his best on a repetitive job and suffered an accident due to his employers' fault, the court would not be astute to find contributory negligence against him.

Examples

CONTRIBUTORY NEGLIGENCE OF WORKMAN

Contributory Negligence		*No Contributory Negligence*	
GANTRY AT NIGHT—NO LIGHT	1	TRIPPING—INTENT ON JOB	2
DARK PART SHIP—NO LIGHT	3	UNDERESTIMATING WEIGHT OF CRANE LOAD	6
Gangway about to move—warning	4	Unsafe system—following example	8
ADJUSTING CIRCULAR SAW TOO HIGH	5	Not seeing open tank top	9
ADJUSTING CIRCULAR SAW TOO HIGH	7	TESTING UNGUARDED FAN	12
Not inspecting oxy-acetylene tool	10	**Window cleaner—not securing sash**	15
BARRIER CREAM—NOT PROCURING	11	Missing bilge board—fall while working	18
REMOVING GUARD OF MACHINE	13	Dry dock—stumbling over debris	19
NOT DISCLOSING EPILEPTIC	14	Falling from steel girder	20
ERECTING AND GOING UP INSECURE LADDER	16	Bogie—mounting unstable bogie	22
Unlighted 'tween deck	17	Lifting cover of machine to feel inside	25
PUTTING HAND UNDER GUARD	21	HAND INADVERTENTLY TRAPPED IN COAL CHUTE	28
STRAIGHTENING UPRIGHT OF SCAFFOLD	23	Tripping—over unlit towbar of machine	29
Mine—doing part of shotfirer's job	24	Ladder—slipping from	30

<u>*Contributory Negligence*</u>	
Insecure fencing—conscious and deliberate interference by plaintiff	U4
Insecure fencing—plaintiff putting in hand without cutting power off	U5
Using faulty rope to hang scaffold	U6
Ladder—using when plaintiff knew rung missing	U7
Machine—removing guard	U8
Cleaning unfenced machine in motion	U9
Removing machine cover and cleaning when in motion	U10
Circular saw—using when guard too high	U11
Unfooted ladder—foreman going up	U12
Toolsetter—adjusting machine in motion	U14
Roof—going up without proper ladders	U15
Unfenced shaft—adjusting in motion rather than stop production	U18
Tripping—obstruction on factory floor 8in. high	U19
Putting hand in machine to free jam	U22
Unfooted ladder—no one available—urgent work on piece rates—plaintiff aware of risk	U25
Ladder—hitting head on obstruction going up	U26
Mill manager—failing to isolate machine before clearing block-age	U27
Using insecure ladder	U28
Stepping on slippery slab while cutting undergrowth	U29
Descending insecure ladder, having unlashed the top	U30
Driving over-loaded crane which toppled over	U31
Tripping over batten in ill-lit passage, not having switched on light	U32
Putting hand near snagged chain	U33
Slipping on water leaked from fire-fighting machine	U35
Pulling at jammed metal bar while on stepladder	U36
Glazier not wearing gauntlets	U37
Fireman falling off flat roof during practice drill	U38
Descending staircase carrying tray—catching foot on obstruction	U39
Manoeuvring heavy steel member in restricted space	U40

Contributory Negligence

Failing to notice planks missing from means of access	U41
Man injured by falling chip-boards when unloading van	U42
Failing to secure ladder at its base	U43
Climbing/descending un-footed ladder	U44
Falling from unguarded tower scaffold	U45

	% C.N. v. Plaintiff
1. Gibby v. East Grinstead Gas Co. [1944] 1 All E.R. 358; 170 L.T. 250, C.A.	
2. Callaghan v. Fred Kidd [1944] K.B. 560; 1 All E.R. 525, C.A.	
3. O'Flaherty v. Shaw Savill (1945) 78 L1.L.R. 435, C.A.	
4. Romain v. E. & H. Green (1945) 78 L1.L.R. 421, Hallett J.	
5. Cakebread v. Hopping [1947] 1 All E.R. 389; K.B. 641, C.A.	50
6. Gallagher v. Dorman Long [1947] 2 All E.R. 38; 177 L.T. 143, C.A.	
7. Beal v. Gomme (1949) 65 T.L.R. 543; W.N. 235, C.A.	80
8. Barcock v. Brighton Corporation [1949] 1 All E.R. 251; 1 K.B. 339, Hilbery J.	
9. Donovan v. Cammell Laird [1949] 2 All E.R. 82; 82 L1.L.R. 642, Devlin J.	
10. Shotter v. R. H. Green & Silley Weir [1951] 1 Lloyd's Rep. 329, Lynskey J.	
11. Clifford v. Charles Challen [1951] 1 All E.R. 72; 1 K.B. 495, C.A.	50
12. Thurogood v. Van den Bergh [1951] 2 K.B. 535; 1 All E.R. 682, C.A.	
13. Norris v. Syndi [1952] 1 All E.R. 935; 2 Q.B. 135, C.A.	20
14. Cork v. Kirby Maclean [1952] 2 All E.R. 402; 2 T.L.R. 217, C.A.	50
15. General Cleaning v. Christmas [1952] 2 All E.R. 1110; [1953] A.C. 180, H.L.	
16. Manwaring v. Billington [1952] 2 All E.R. 747; 2 T.L.R. 689, C.A.	
17. Wenborn v. Harland & Wolff [1952] 1 Lloyd's Rep. 255, Sellers J.	75
18. Byrne v. Clan Line [1952] 2 Lloyd's Rep. 598, Ormerod J.	
19. Welch v. Admiralty [1952] 2 Lloyd's Rep. 520, Havers J.	
20. Sheppey v. Matthew T. Shaw [1952] 1 T.L.R. 1272; W.N. 249, Parker J.	
21. Smith v. Chesterfield Co-op. [1953] 1 All E.R. 447; 1 W.L.R. 370, C.A.	60
22. Rouse v. P.L.A. [1953] 2 Lloyd's Rep. 179, Parker J.	
23. Norris v. Wm. Moss [1954] 1 All E.R. 324; 1 W.L.R. 346, C.A.	100
24. N.C.B. v. England [1954] 1 All E.R. 456; A.C. 403, H.L.	
25. Charles v. S. Smith [1954] 1 All E.R. 499; 1 W.L.R. 451, Hilbery J.	
26. Johnson v. Croggon [1954] 1 All E.R. 121; 1 W.L.R. 195, Pilcher J.	99
27. Laszczyk v. N.C.B. [1954] 3 All E.R. 205; 1 W.L.R. 1426, Pearson J.	5
28. Gibbons v. N.C.B. [1954] 1 Lloyd's Rep. 181, C.A.	
29. Ryan v. Maltby [1954] 1 Lloyd's Rep. 196, Hilbery J.	
30. Cheeseman v. Orient S.N. [1954] 2 Lloyd's Rep. 231, Slade J.	
31. Davey v. Howes [1954] 2 Lloyd's Rep. 553, Ashworth J. (Reversed—see **38**).	100
32. Crockett v. Royal Mail [1954] 2 Lloyd's Rep. 576, Lynskey J.	50
33. Jones v. Richards [1955] 1 All E.R. 463; 1 W.L.R. 444, Barry J.	33
34. Hurley v. Sanders [1955] 1 All E.R. 833; 1 W.L.R. 470, Glyn-Jones J.	25
35. John Summers v. Frost [1955] 1 All E.R. 870; A.C. 740, H.L.	
36. Williams v. Sykes & Harrison [1955] 3 All E.R. 225; 1 W.L.R. 1180, C.A.	80
37. Hodkinson v. Henry Wallwork [1955] 3 All E.R. 236; 1 W.L.R. 1195, C.A.	90
38. Davey v. H. W. Howes [1955] 1 Lloyd's Rep. 95, C.A.	50

39. Davison v. Apex Scaffolding [1956] 1 All E.R. 473; 1 Q.B. 551, C.A. 20
40. Simmons v. Bovis [1956] 1 All E.R. 736; 1 W.L.R. 381, Barry J. 10
41. Williams v. Port of L'pool Stevedoring [1956] 2 All E.R. 69; 1 W.L.R. 551, Lynskey J.. 50
42. Reilly v. B.T.C. [1956] 3 All E.R. 857; [1957] 1 W.L.R. 76, Donovan J. 33
43. Jeyes v. Currie Line [1956] 2 Lloyd's Rep. 87, Pearce J. 50
44. Pead v. Furness Withy [1956] 2 Lloyd's Rep. 149, Slade J.
45. Lilly v. N.Z. Shipping Co. [1956] 2 Lloyd's Rep. 157, Pilcher J. 80
46. Trznadel v. B.T.C. [1957] 3 All E.R. 196; 1 W.L.R. 1002, C.A. (*semble*). 100
47. Smith v. Hovey [1957] 1 Lloyd's Rep. 372, Stable J. 25
48. Driscoll v. Lange Bell [1957] 1 Lloyd's Rep. 377, Byrne J. 25
49. Barnes v. P.L.A. [1957] 1 Lloyd's Rep. 486, Byrne J. 33
50. Blakeley v. C. & H. Clothing [1958] 1 All E.R. 297; 1 W.L.R. 378, Lynskey J. 33
51. Hicks v. B.T.C. [1958] 2 All E.R. 39, 1 W.L.R. 493, C.A. 50
52. Bush v. Colonial Wharves [1958] 1 Lloyd's Rep. 533, Pearson J. 40
53. White v. Ben Line Steamers [1958] 1 Lloyd's Rep. 541, Paull J. 50
54. Lynch v. Furness Withy [1958] 2 Lloyd's Rep. 360, Diplock J. 33
55. Willis v. Unimarine [1958] 2 Lloyd's Rep. 436, Diplock J. 33
56. Brown v. Scruttons [1958] 2 Lloyd's Rep. 440, Gorman J.
57. Snaith v. Glen Line [1958] 2 Lloyd's Rep. 546, Donovan J.
58. Smith v. Austins Lifts [1959] 1 All E.R. 81; 1 W.L.R. 100, H.L.
59. Jenner v. Allen West [1959] 2 All E.R. 115; 1 W.L.R. 554 C.A. 66
60. Baker v. Hopkins [1959] 3 All E.R. 225; 1 W.L.R. 966, C.A. 10
61. Rushton v. Turner Asbestos [1959] 3 All E.R. 517; [1960] 1 W.L.R. 96, Ashworth J.... 100
62. Tomlinson v. Ellermans Wilson [1959] 1 Lloyd's Rep. 141, L.C.J. 33
63. Campbell v. Harland & Wolff [1959] 1 Lloyd's Rep. 198, Gorman J. 17
64. Hodgson v. P.L.A. [1959] 1 Lloyd's Rep. 389, Gorman J. 50
65. Westcott v. Structural & Marine Engineers [1960] 1 All E.R. 775; 1 W.L.R. 349, Lord Parker C.J.
66. Wiggins v. Caledonia Stevedoring [1960] 1 Lloyd's Rep. 18, C.A.
67. Johnson v. J. Stone [1961] All E.R. 869; 1 W.L.R. 849, Hinchcliffe J. 33
68. Quintas v. National Smelting [1961] 1 All E.R. 630; 1 W.L.R. 401, C.A. 50
69. Johnson v. Rea [1961] 3 All E.R. 816; [1962] 1 Q.B. 373, C.A.
70. Foley v. Enzo-Gutzeit [1962] 1 Lloyd's Rep. 247, Gorman J. 33
71. Holmes v. T. & J. Harrison [1962] 1 Lloyd's Rep. 455, C.A.
72. O'Malley v. Sheppard [1963] 1 Lloyd's Rep. 189, C.A. 33
73. Barry v. Cleveland Bridge Co. [1963] 1 All E.R. 192, Lyell J. 50
74. Coles v. English Abrasive Co. [1965] C.L.Y. 2651, Lawrence J. 60
75. Field v. Jeavons [1965] 2 All E.R. 162; 1 W.L.R. 996, C.A. 25
76. Uddin v. A.P.C. [1965] 2 All E.R. 213; 2 Q.B. 582, C.A. 80
77. Thompson v. British Oxygen (1965) 109 S.J. 194, C.A. 33
78. Leach v. Standard Telephones [1966] 2 All E.R. 523; 1 W.L.R. 1392, Browne J. 75
79. Astell v. L.T.B. [1966] 2 All E.R. 748; 1 W.L.R. 1047, C.A. 25
80. Maguire v. Thomas Fraser (1966) S.J. 269; C.L.Y. 5091, C.A. 80
81. Lovelidge v. Anselm Olding [1967] 1 All E.R. 459; 2 Q.B. 351, Widgery J. 50
82. McArdle v. Andmac [1967] 1 All E.R. 583; 1 W.L.R. 356, C.A.
83. Kansara v. Osram [1967] 3 All E.R. 230, C.A. (reversing CCJ)
84. Wright v. Richard Thomas & Baldwins (1966) 1 K.I.R. 327; [1967] C.L.Y. 2653, C.A.
85. Kerry v. Carter [1969] 3 All E.R. 723; 1 W.L.R. 1372, C.A. 66
86. Moran v. Kitching (1969) C.A. 288. 25
87. Mullard v. Ben Lines (1970) 1 W.L.R. 1414; [1971] 2 All E.R. 424, C.A. 33

88. Rawding v. London Brick Co. (1970) 9 K.I.R. 194, James J. 33
89. Stocker v. Norprint (1971) 10 K.I.R. 10, C.A.
90. McGuiness v. Key Markets (1973) 13 K.I.R. 249; C.L.Y. 1449, C.A. 66
91. Westwood v. Post Office [1973] 3 All E.R. 184; [1974] A.C. 1, H.L.
92. Bux v. Slough Metals [1973] 1 W.L.R. 1358; [1974] All E.R. 262, C.A.* 40
93. Ridgway v. P. D. Wharfage [1973] 2 Lloyd's Rep. 511, Wien J. 33
94. O'Keefe v. Stewart (1979) 1 Lloyd's Rep. 182; C.L.Y. 2474, Kenneth Jones J.
95. Turner v. Lancashire C.C. [1980] C.L.Y. 1886, Arnold J.
96. Cox v. Angus (H.C.B.) [1981] I.C.R. 683, Lloyd J. 50
97. *Saunders v. S.E. Electricity Board* [1981] C.A. 0525.
98. Wheeler v. Copas [1981] 3 All E.R. 405, Chapman J. 50
99. Sanders v. Lloyd (1982) I.C.R. 360; C.L.Y. 1365, Drake J.
100. Storey v. N.C.B. [1983] 1 All E.R. 375, Mustill J. 75
101. Johns v. Martin Simms [1983] 1 All E.R. 127; I.C.R. 305, Lawson J.
102. Jayes v. I.M.I. (Kynoch) Ltd. [1985] I.C.R. 155; C.L.Y. 2330, C.A. 100
103. Allen v. Avon Rubber Co. Ltd. [1986] I.C.R. 695; [1987] I.R.L.R. 22, C.A. 50
104. Calder v. H. Kitson Vickers Ltd. [1988] I.C.R. 232; C.L.Y. 1952, C.A. 25
105. Crouch v. British Rail Engineering [1988] I.R.L.R. 404; *The Times*, March 10, 1988, C.A. 50
106. Smith v. Stages [1989] A.C. 928; 1 All E.R. 833, H.L.
107. Mearns v. Lothian Regional Council [1991] S.L.T.; C.L.Y. 5693 50
108. Gunter v. John Nicholas & Sons (Port Talbot) limited 66
109. King v. Smith The Times, 3rd November, 1994; [1994] C.L.Y. 2284, C.A. 30
110. Barrett v. Ministry of Defence [1995] 1 W.L.R. 1217; *The Times*, **January 13, 1995, C.A.** **66**
U1. *Goodman v. Kay & Whiting (1951) C.A. 156.* *60*
U2. *Stubbinton v. Fortress Ironworks (1951) C.A. 320.* *50*
U3. *Morris v. William Willett (1952) C.A. 133.* *100*
U4. *Cross v. Segal (1952) C.A. 257.* *50*
U5. *Lonie v. Rego Clothiers Ltd. (1952) C.A. 303.* *66*
U6. *Crawford v. Erection Services (1953) C.A. 254.* *50*
U7. *Kelly v. Thomas & Edge (1953) C.A. 266 A.* *80*
U8. *Taylor v. Cass (1954) C.A. 262.* *90*
U9. *Burrows v. Metal Box Co. (1956) C.A. 347.* *50*
U10. *Woods v. Crittall Manufacturing Co. Ltd. (1957) C.A. 46.* *100*
U11. *White v. Post Office (1957) C.A. 189.* *60*
U12. *Smith v. R. Smith (Horley) Ltd. (1957) C.A. 273 A.* *100*
U13. *Reynolds v. Goffe (1958) C.A. 134.*
U14. *Broughton v. Joseph Lucas Ltd. (1958) C.A. 330 A.* *25*
U15. *Robinson v. Pearce (1960) C.A. 267 A.* *75*
U16. *Hogg v. Modern Heating (1961) C.A. 144.*
U17. *Burgon v. Nottingham Evening News (1962) C.A. 256.*
U18. *Dalton v. Sankey Sugar (1962) C.A. 231.* *50*
U19. *Bell v. Dorman Long (1963) C.A. 80.* *50*
U20. *Savage v. B.T.C. (1965) C.A. 301 A.*
U21. *Brown v. Watkins & Bradfords (1966) C.A. 119.*
U22. *Finucanes v. Southall (1968) C.A. 128.* *33*
U23. *Ryan v. Manbre (1970) C.A. 251 A.*

* Defendants were liable for acquiescing in habitual non-user of goggles provided (see 15 (2) (e) **22**).

(e) Children

1. Yachuk v. Oliver Blais [1949] A.C. 386; [1949] 2 All E.R. 150, P.C.

Child of nine lies to pump attendant to get petrol—then sets light to it and burns himself—*Held*, not contributory negligence, as on the evidence "the boy had no knowledge of the peculiarly dangerous quality of gasoline," but "if the evidence had showed that the infant plaintiff in the present case had in fact greater knowledge than one would normally impute to a child of his age, a more debatable question would have arisen" (154 C, *per* Lord du Parcq).

2. Hughes v. Lord Advocate [1963] A.C. 837; [1963] 1 All E.R. 705, H.L.

Held, not contributory negligence for boy of eight and (*semble*) his companion of ten to be meddling with lamps and impedimenta at an unguarded and unfenced open manhole site in a public street (708 I).

3. French v. Sunshine Holiday Camp (1963) 107 S.J. 595, Glyn-Jones J.

Child of six at holiday camp—she three times climbed on low wall surrounding flower bed with glass lights in it—each time ordered down by attendants—eventually she got up again and fell off wall on to glass—*Held*, defendants liable and no contributory negligence, as child too young to appreciate danger from glass.

4. Gough v. Thorne [1966] 1 W.L.R. 1387; [1966] 3 All E.R. 398, C.A.

Held, not contributory negligence for girl of 13, when beckoned across road by lorry driver, not to look forward and see whether anything else was coming. "A very young child cannot be guilty of contributory negligence. An older child may be; but it depends on the circumstances. A judge should only find a child guilty of contributory negligence if he or she is of such an age as reasonably to be expected to take precautions for his or her own safety; and then he or she is only to be found guilty if blame should be attached to him or her" (Lord Denning M.R., 399 H).

5. Jones v. Lawrence [1969] 3 All E.R. 267, Cumming-Bruce J.

6. Waller v. Lawton [1982] C.L.Y. 2132, Michael Davies J.

Held, boy 40 per cent to blame.

7. Minter v. D. & H. Contractors, *The Times*, June 30, 1983; [1983] C.L.Y. 2544, Tudor Evans J.

Held, plaintiff was 20 per cent contributory negligent. He was normally a "good rider" on his bicycle and was capable of contributory negligence.

8. Foskett v. Mistry [1984] R.T.R. 1; [1984] C.L.Y. 2286, C.A.

Plaintiff aged 16 ran from parkland to the left of defendant's approaching car, across 10 foot wide pavement and some 10 feet into road, where struck by car, defendant not having seen plaintiff until then—*Held*, defendant liable—should have seen plaintiff as he ran from park-land, appreciated he presented a potential hazard and sounded his horn or braked. Plaintiff 75 per cent contributorily negligent—it was putting it a little too high to say that he should be treated as a fully grown adult man.

9. Ducharme v. Davies [1984] 1 W.W.R. 699; [1984] C.L.Y. 2291, Saskatchewan Court of Appeal

Held, three-year-old infant incapable of contributory negligence in not wearing a seat belt. Any negligence on parents' part not to be imputed to infant.

10. Morales v. Eccleston [1991] R.T.R. 151; [1992] C.L.Y. 3189, C.A.

Defendant driving at 20 m.p.h. Steady stream of rush hour traffic both ways. Plaintiff, aged 11, followed ball which rolled into road from defendant's off-side pavement. Plaintiff not looking in either direction—caused a driver coming from his right to swerve—continued over centre of road and struck by car of defendant, who did not see him until impact—*Held*, defendant liable, but plaintiff 75 per cent contributorily negligent. Defendant had only limited opportunity to see plaintiff before impact—the fact that he had not seen plaintiff crossing defendant's off-side of the road did not necessarily connote failure to keep a proper look-out.

11. Armstrong v. Cottrell [1993] P.I.Q.R. P.109; [1993] C.L.Y. 2956, C.A.

Defendant in offside of three lanes of busy carriageway. From 400 yards saw plaintiff, aged 12, and three other girls "hovering" on road side to his left. Then plaintiff and one other girl advanced to middle lane and hesitated. Defendant decelerated but when his car was very close the two girls suddenly darted into offside lane and impact occurred—*Held*, defendant liable. Having seen girls "hovering" and hesitating, should have reduced speed sufficiently is prevent accident and sounded horn. Plaintiff one-third contributorily negligent, having regard to her age.

U1. Jones v. Maggi (1954) C.A. 267

Two children ten and eight and a half step into busy street together—elder child was in charge—*Held*, elder child 75 per cent to blame, younger child nil.

U2. Dexter v. Ellis (1968) C.A. 190

Boy of 13 ran across 25 foot street in heavily built-up area—run down by car going too fast when a few feet from far kerb—*Held*, 35 per cent contributory negligence.

U3. Parsons v. Pullman Foods Ltd (1991) C.A. 194

Plaintiff, aged 12, crossed road in front of bus into path of overtaking lorry. Lorry driver had previously stopped behind bus, knew children were alighting and had seen one child run across front of his lorry—*Held*, lorry driver liable—should have sounded horn. Plaintiff one-third to blame.

U4. Roberts v. Pearson (1991) C.A. 335

Plaintiff, boy of 12, crossing from central reservation, struck by motorcycle of defendant, who was driving too fast and not keeping proper look-out—*Held*, defendant liable, plaintiff one-third to blame. At the age of 12, a boy is not able to assess the speed of an approaching vehicle as well as an adult, and tends to be less inhibited.

(2) Express Exemption of Negligence

(*N.B.* (1) Causes of action arising after February 1, 1978 are substantially affected by the Unfair Contract Terms Act 1977. (2) Disclaimers of responsibility in *Hedley Byrne* cases are dealt with under Chap. 19 (a), *q.v.*)

(a) When Plaintiff Bound by Conditions

1. Chapelton v. Barry U.D.C. [1940] 1 K.B. 532; [1940] 1 All E.R. 356, C.A.

Plaintiff received two chairs from attendant, paid fee and received two tickets—on the back of the tickets was an exemption clause—there was a notice by the chairs which merely advertised them for hire and gave the rate—*Held*, defendants liable, as in the circumstances plaintiff was entitled to assume that all conditions were contained in the notice by the chairs. *N.B.* In **4** Denning L.J. treated this case as authority for the general proposition that a notice on a receipt for money would not suffice to exempt, see p. 549.

2. Sugar v. L.M.S. [1941] 1 All E.R. 172, Lord Caldecote C.J.

Held, plaintiff not bound by conditions on back.

3. Henson v. L.N.E.R. [1946] 1 All E.R. 653, C.A.

Held, the giving and acceptance of the pass, which was non-contractual, were not sufficient notice of the exemption to bind plaintiff. *Held*, also—probably *obiter*—that even if the pass were contractual, plaintiff would still not be bound. Dicta in this case were criticised in *Ashdown v. Samuel Williams*, Chap. 4, (2) (b) **4.**

4. Olley v. Marlborough Court [1949] 2 K.B. 532; [1949] 1 All E.R. 127, C.A.

Plaintiff received as guest—goes upstairs to bedroom where exempting notice displayed—*Held*, defendants could not rely on notice because contract had been made before plaintiff could see notice. Denning L.J. at 549 near top: "Now people who rely on a contract to exempt themselves from their common law liability must prove that contract strictly. Not only must the terms of the contract be clearly proved, but also the intent to create legal relations—the intent to be legally bound—must also be clearly proved. The best way of proving it is by a written contract signed by the party to be bound. Another way is by handing him before or at the time of the contract a written notice specifying its terms and making clear to him that the contract is on those terms. A prominent public notice which is plain for him to see when he makes the contract or an express oral stipulation would, no doubt, have the same effect. But nothing short of one of these three ways will suffice."

5. Curtis v. Chemical Cleaning [1951] 1 K.B. 805; [1951] 1 All E.R. 631, C.A.

6. J. Spurling v. Bradshaw [1956] 1 W.L.R. 461; [1956] 2 All E.R. 121, C.A.

7. Cockerton v. Naviera Aznar, S.A. [1960] 2 Lloyd's Rep. 450, Streatfeild J.

Held, distinguishing *Olley v. Marlborough Court* **4**, that the shipping company could rely on the exemption clause, as there was no binding contract until the ticket was issued and the shipping company had taken all reasonable steps to draw the attention of the plaintiff, who was a fairly experienced traveller, to the conditions on the ticket.

8. McCutcheon v. David Macbrayne [1964] 1 W.L.R. 125; [1964] 1 All E.R. 430, H.L.

Plaintiff's agent went to defendant's office to arrange transport of plaintiff's car—the freight was quoted to the agent, who paid it, and who was then given a printed receipt, which contained exempting conditions, which he did not read—there was also one or more notices in the office containing exempting conditions—but plaintiff, who had frequently shipped goods, had never read them—on previous occasions he had also signed a risk note, which also contained them, and which also he had never read—on this occasion no risk note was made out—*Held*, liability for negligence was not excluded. The ticket cases did not apply, as it was essential that there should be a contractual document of some description for them to apply. "There is not so much as a peg on which to hang any terms which are not expressed in the contract nor a phrase which is capable of expansion": Lord Devlin, 438 F. The previous dealings were irrelevant, for "previous dealings are only relevant if they prove knowledge of the terms, actual and not constructive, and assent to them": Lord Devlin, 437 B. The printed receipt was irrelevant, for it was "handed over after the contract was completed, and cannot be treated as an offer": Lord Hodson, 434 D. The posting of four copies of the conditions on the pier and three on the ship was also irrelevant: Lord Hodson, 434 D. Generally, *per* Lord Devlin (436 C):—

"It would be a strangely generous set of conditions in which the persistent reader, after wading through the verbiage, could not find something to protect the carrier against 'any loss ... ', ... and it is conceded that if the form had been signed as usual the appellant would have had no case. By a stroke of ill luck for the respondents it was on this day of all days that they omitted to get M to sign the conditions. What difference does that make? If it were possible for your Lordships to escape from the world of make-believe, which the law has created, into the real world in which transactions of this sort are actually done, the answer would be short and simple. It would make no difference whatever. This sort of document is not meant to be read, still less to be understood."

9. Sydney City Council v. West [1966] C.L.Y. 536; (1965) 39 A.L.J.R. 324, High Ct.

Municipal car park—ticket issued to owner contained clause exempting municipality from loss or damage however caused and contained a notice that the ticket must be presented to the attendant to secure release of the car—a third party persuaded the car-park attendants to let him have the car, saying that he had lost his ticket—*Held*, defendants could not rely on exemption clause, since their act in delivering car to stranger was entirely outside the authority of the contract.

10. Gore v. Van der Lann [1967] 2 Q.B. 31; [1967] 1 All E.R. 360, C.A.

Bus authority applied to stay action against their conductor, on the ground that the action was a fraud on them—*Held*, application would be refused.

11. Garnham Harris v. Ellis [1967] 1 W.L.R. 940; [1967] 2 All E.R. 940, Paull J.

12. Mendelssohn v. Normand [1970] 1 Q.B. 177; [1969] 2 All E.R. 1215, C.A.

Customer leaving car in garage subject to exempting conditions—attendant assured customer that he would lock car—but did not—result goods stolen from car—*Held*, exemptions did not apply.

13. Thornton v. Shoe Lane Parking [1971] 2 Q.B. 163; [1971] 1 All E.R. 686, C.A.

14. B.G. Transport v. Marston Motor [1971] 1 Lloyd's Rep. 371, Bean J.

Theft of van and load from car park—owner had parked it for one day and received a receipt with exempting conditions—next day he did the same—during latter period van was stolen—*Held*, owner was bound by conditions.

15. Hollier v. Rambler Motors [1972] 2 Q.B. 71; [1972] 1 All E.R. 399, C.A.

So *held* by C.A. in judgments which review the previous cases.

16. British Crane Hire v. Ipswich Plant Hire [1975] Q.B. 303; [1974] 1 All E.R. 1059, C.A.

Both parties hirers-out of plant—defendant hired a machine from plaintiff—which sustained non-negligent damage before a copy of plaintiff's conditions reached defendant—*Held*, that as both parties were of equal bargaining power and as defendant knew that plaintiff would attach some conditions, defendant was bound by the actual conditions.

17. Evans v. Andrea Merzario [1976] 1 W.L.R. 1078; [1976] 2 All E.R. 930, C.A.

Defendant forwarding agents orally promised plaintiff shippers that cargo would be shipped below deck—by mistake it was not and was washed overboard—defendants tried to rely on exemption in their printed conditions—*Held*, following **12**, they could not do so.

18. Hollingworth v. Southern Ferries (1977) 2 Lloyd's Rep. 70, Deputy Judge Ogden.

19. The Dragon [1979] 1 Lloyd's Rep. 257; [1979] C.L.Y. 1869, Brandon J.

So *held. Cockerton* **7** expressly not followed.

20. Rees Hough Ltd v. Redland Reinforced Plastics Ltd (1985) 27 BLR 136; [1984] C.L.Y. 390, Judge Newey Q.C.

Manufacturers of pipes supplied to plaintiff—*Held*, express or implied term that the pipes would be fit for the purpose of "jacking"; further held there was sufficient proximity for manufacturers to owe plaintiff a duty of care in negligence, *i.e.* to exercise reasonable care in the design of pipes which they were to supply for jacking. Further the manufacturers' standard terms which were incorporated into the contract excluded the terms and also liability in negligence but manufacturers had failed to prove their standard terms were reasonable under the Unfair Contract Terms Act 1977.

21 Phillips Products Ltd v. Hyland [1987] 1 W.L.R. 659; [1987] 2 All E.R. 620, C.A.

See Chap. 4, (2)(c) **31** for further details.

22. Thompson v. T. Lohan (Plant Hire) Ltd [1987] 1 W.L.R. 649; [1987] 2 All E.R. 631 C.A.

See Chap. 4, (2)(c) **32** for further details.

23. Norwich C.C. v. Harvey [1989] 1 W.L.R. 828; [1989] 1 All E.R. 1180, C.A.

Under contract between owner of swimming pool and builder, owner accepted risk of fire: fire caused by subcontractor's negligence—*Held*; any duty of care otherwise owed by the builder did not arise in the contractual circumstances.

24. Dorset C. C. v. Southern Felt Roofing Co. (1990) 9 T.L.R. 96; [1990] C.L.Y. 636, C.A.

25 McConkey v. AMEC, *The Times*, February 28, 1990; [1990] C.L.Y. 3325, C.A.

See Chap. 4, (2)(c) **34** for further details.

26 E.E. Caledonia Ltd, v. Orbit Valve plc [1994] 1 W.L.R. 1515; [1995] 1 All E.R. 174, C.A.

See Chap. 4, (2)(c) **35** for further details.

(b) Notices

(*N.B.* The Unfair Contract Terms Act 1977, which came into force on February 1, 1978, materially alters the law relating to exemption notices.)

1. The Humorist (1944) 77 Ll.L.R. 189, Pilcher J. *Held*, notice ineffective.

2. Olley v. Marlborough Court [1949] 2 K.B. 532; [1949] 1 All E.R. 127, C.A.

Plaintiff received as guest—goes upstairs to bedroom where exempting notice displayed—*Held*, defendants could not rely on notice because contract had been made before plaintiff could see notice. Denning L.J. at 549 near top: "Now people who rely on a contract to exempt themselves from their common law liability must prove that contract strictly. Not only must the terms of the contract be clearly proved, but also the intent to create legal relations—the intent to be legally bound—must also be clearly proved. The best way of proving it is by a written contract signed by the party to be bound. Another way is by handing him before or at the time of the contract a written notice specifying its terms and making clear to him that the contract is on those terms. A prominent public notice which is plain for him to see when he makes the contract or an express or oral stipulation would, no doubt, have the same effect. But nothing short of one of these three ways will suffice."

3. The Cawood III [1951] P. 270, Willmer J.

Plaintiff's lighter damaged by defective condition of defendants' jetty—defendants had put an exempting notice on jetty—*Held*, notice ineffective, because contract had already been made and in any case the lighterman was not an agent of plaintiff for the purpose of varying the contract.

4. Ashdown v. Samuel Williams [1957] 1 Q.B. 409; [1957] 1 All E.R. 35, C.A.

Plaintiff a licensee run down by a negligently shunted truck—warning notice at entrance which plaintiff saw but only read first three lines thereof—first three lines only dealt with condition of land, but later on notice also exempted negligent acts—*Held*, plaintiff was bound by the terms of the notice as a whole, just as she would be in contract. Although it did not arise in present case, Parker L.J. (47 H) said: "A mere reference to negligence without a warning as to the user of the land might well be insufficient."

5. Adams v. Trust Houses [1960] 1 Lloyd's Rep. 380, Mr. Comr. Fenton Atkinson.

Held, (*obiter*) that an exempting notice on the wall of a garage had not been sufficiently brought to plaintiff's attention. "There is authority for saying that the more unreasonable a condition is, the more must be done to bring it to the notice of the other party. If that condition contained in the notice on the garage wall really means that the hotel night porter can deliberately destroy or damage the customer's motor-car . . . it seems to me that that sort of condition should be printed in letters a foot high with an arrow pointing towards them" (387).

6. McCutcheon v. David Macbrayne [1964] 1 W.L.R. 125; [1964] 1 All E.R. 430, H.L.

Held, none of the notices excluded liability. For details, see Chap. 4, (2) (a) **8**.

7. Burnett v. Westminster Bank [1966] 1 Q.B. 742; [1965] 3 All E.R. 81, Mocatta J.

Held, conditions not binding.

8. Lisi v. Alitalia [1966] 2 Lloyd's Rep. 328, U.S. District Ct.

Aircraft crash near Shannon airport—on the tickets and baggage checks delivered to the plaintiffs the provisions of the Warsaw Convention (limiting liability) were printed in such small type as to be virtually invisible—*Held*, the defendants could not limit their liability.

9. Smith v. Taylor [1966] 2 Lloyd's Rep. 231, Blain J.

Held, plaintiff had not visited garage often enough to be taken to know of the notice.

10. Buckpitt v. Oates [1968] 1 All E.R. 1145; [1968] C.L.Y. 2736, John Stephenson J.

Held, notice exempted driver from liability to passenger, as it was shown that the plaintiff, an infant, was aware of notice at all material times.

11. Bennett v. Tugwell [1971] 2 Q.B. 267; [1971] 2 All E.R. 248, Ackner J.

Held, negligence was exempted. For details see Chap. 4, (3) **24**.

12. Geier v. Kujawa [1970] 1 Lloyd's Rep. 364, Brabin J.

German girl who did not see or read notice—spoke little English—*Held*, not bound by conditions.

13. Hollier v. Rambler Motors [1972] 2 Q.B. 71; [1972] 1 All E.R. 399, C.A.

So *held* by C.A. in judgments which review most of the previous cases on the subject.

14. Birch v. Thomas [1972] 1 W.L.R. 294; [1972] 1 All E.R. 905, C.A.

15. White v. Blackmore [1972] 2 Q.B. 651; [1972] 3 All E.R. 158, C.A.

Facts are somewhat particular because deceased went to arena at different times and in different capacities—but eventually was there as a spectator, and was killed as a result of defective safety arrangements—*Held*, defendants were not liable by reason of exempting warning notices.

16. Burnett v. British Waterways Board [1973] 1 W.L.R. 700; [1973] 2 All E.R. 631, C.A.

Plaintiff lighterman employed by Charrington Lighterage injured by rope snapping due to negligence of defendants—at the time plaintiff's barge was being warped by defendants' staff—at defendants' dock office there was a notice, which the plaintiff had read some time previously, which was sufficient in its wording to exempt the defendants from this type of negligence—*Held*, the test was whether the plaintiff had, expressly or impliedly, agreed to be bound by the terms of the notice. This was generally so in the car notices cases (*e.g. Buckpitt* **10**, *Bennett* **11** and *Birch* **14**), and in cases where the plaintiff with the permission of the occupier went on land where dangerous operations were taking place (*e.g. Ashdown* **4** and *White* **15**). But here the plaintiff had no choice, being an employee of a third party, and so no agreement could be imputed to him. Equally *volenti* was here no defence (see Chap. 4, (3) **28**). Defendants *held* liable.

17. Mendelssohn v. Normand [1970] 1 Q.B. 177; [1969] 2 All E.R. 1215, C.A.

"A notice is not imported into the contract unless it is brought home so prominently to the party that he must be taken to have known of it and agreed to it" (Lord Denning M.R.).

18. Canadian Pacific Airlines v. Montreal Trust [1977] 2 Lloyd's Rep. 80; [1977] C.L.Y. 2033, Can.Sup.Ct.

Held, interpreting the Hague Protocol, the notice purporting to limit liability was ineffectual to do so, as it was printed in the same type as the other printed matter.

19. Umek v. London Transport Executive (1984) 134 New L.J. 522; [1984] CLY 2313, McNeill J.

Canteen assistant killed whilst crossing line to defendant's depot, ignoring, as others had, notice forbidding such conduct and advising use of footbridge whilst subway blocked by flooding—*Held*, defendants were aware of such conduct and should have warned train drivers accordingly; 75 per cent contributory negligence of deceased.

20. Eastman v. South West Thames A.H.A. [1991] R.T.R. 389; [1992] P.I.Q.R. P42, C.A.

Plaintiff travelled as a passenger accompanying patient in defendants' ambulance, in which a notice said "For your own safety use seat belts provided." Some seats had belts but plaintiff sat in one that did not—Plaintiff injured when ambulance braked suddenly—*Held*, defendants not liable—entitled to let plaintiff decide whether or not to occupy a seat with a belt—no duty on attendant to draw notice to plaintiff's attention or exhort her to use a belt. There is no general duty on the driver of a vehicle to exhort a passenger to use a seat belt.

(c) Construction of Exemption Clauses

1. Ashby v. Tolhurst [1937] 2 K.B. 242; 2 All E.R. 837; [1937] C.A.

"The proprietors do not take any responsibility for the safe custody of any cars or articles therein"—*Held*, wide enough to exempt attendants' negligence.

2. Beaumont Thomas v. Blue Star [1939] 3 All E.R. 127, C.A.

Held, words wide enough to exempt defendants from negligence.

3. Alderslade v. Hendon Laundry [1945] K.B. 189; [1945] 1 All E.R. 244; C.A.

Held, as laundry only under a duty to take reasonable care, to hold that exempting words did not apply to negligence would deprive them of any force, and therefore negligence was exempted. Lord Greene M.R. said:

> "Where the head of damage in respect of which limitation of liability is sought to be imposed by such a clause is one which rests on negligence and nothing else, the clause must be construed as extending to that head of damage, because it would otherwise lack subject-matter. Where, on the other hand, the head of damage may be based on some other ground than that of negligence, the general principle is that the clause must be confined in its application to loss occurring through that other cause, to the exclusion of loss arising through negligence."

The above passage was approved by Lord Morton in *Canada S.S. Co. v. R.* [1952] A.C. 1, P.C.

4. Clement Shaw v. Mount & Co. (1949) 82 L1.L.R. 992, Lord Goddard C.J.

Held, words "owner's risk" exempted from negligence.

5. Olley v. Marlborough Court [1949] 1 K.B. 532; [1949] 1 All E.R. 127, C.A.

Held, these words did not exempt defendants from liability for negligence, but only from liability in the absence of negligence (see 550).

6. White v. John Warwick [1953] 1 W.L.R. 1285; [1953] 2 All E.R. 1021 C.A.

"Nothing in this agreement shall make the owners liable for any personal injuries to the riders of the machines"—saddle of tricycle allegedly slipped, causing plaintiff injury—*Held*, these words were wide enough to exempt defendants for breach of contract, but they did not exempt from liability for the tort of negligence.

7. Farr v. Admiralty [1953] 1 W.L.R. 965; [1953] 2 All E.R. 512; Parker J.

Distinction between an exemption for "any loss" (which ordinarily will not exempt negligence) and "any loss however caused" (which will) *applied* in terms laid down by Phillimore L.J. in *Joseph Travers v. Cooper* [1915] 1 K.B. 73.

8. James Archdale v. Comservices [1954] 1 W.L.R. 459; [1954] 1 All E.R. 210, C.A.

Somervell L.J. (211 F): "General words in an exception clause do not ordinarily except the party seeking to rely on the exception from liability for his own negligence or that of his servants. There is an exception to what I may call the prima facie approach if, looking more closely into the subject matter, it is found that substantially the only scope for the operation of the exception clause is the negligence of the servant of the person who is seeking the benefit of it.

9. Adler v. Dickson [1955] 1 Q.B. 158; [1954] 3 All E.R. 397, C.A.

Held, servant not exempt, as employers were not contracting as agents for their negligent servant (who was sued personally), and the servant was not a party to the contract—nor should a term exempting the servant be implied in the contract.

10. Woolmer v. Delmer Price [1955] 1 Q.B. 291; [1955] 1 All E.R. 377, Mc Nair J.

Plaintiff leaves fur coat with defendants for storage—"all goods left at customer's risk"—loss of coat—defendants put forward no acceptable explanation for loss (beyond saying they had re-delivered coat, which was rejected) and rely on exemption alone—*Held*, liable, because they had to establish either that loss occurred in some way not involving their negligence or alternatively that loss did occur by their negligence, and apart from these two possibilities loss might have been due (i) to accidental sale of coat by defendants or (ii) to storage by defendants with an independent contractor—which would have been a fundamental breach of contract. See **11**.

11. J. Spurling v. Bradshaw [1956] 1 W.L.R. 461; [1956] 2 All E.R. 121, C.A.

Held, the words in question exempted defendants in delivering goods in a damaged condition caused by negligence—but not (*per* Denning L.J. at 124 H) if they had been guilty of a breach going to the root of the contract. Observations *passim* on burden of proof and pleading in such cases. **10** distinguished, probably because (*per* Parker L.J. at 128 E) the only fault alleged here by plaintiff was negligence causing damage, whereas in **10** there was a failure to redeliver and plaintiff relied on this at large, so that defendants had to try to bring themselves within the exemption—and failed.

12. Karsales v. Wallis [1956] 1 W.L.R. 936; [1956] 2 All E.R. 866, C.A.

Car incapable of self-propulsion—*Held*, fundamental breach, against which exemption clause of no avail.

13. B. Kilroy Thompson v. Perkins [1956] 2 Lloyd's Rep. 49; [1956] C.L.Y. 1497, Sellers J.

Held, the excepting words only applied to pilferage or theft without negligence on the part of defendants, and since defendants were negligent, therefore liable.

14. Ashdown v. Samuel Williams [1957] 1 Q.B. 409; [1957] 1 All E.R. 35, C.A.

Held, words were wide enough to exempt defendants from negligent act of shunter. Parker L.J. (47 I): "A mere reference to negligence without a warning as to the user of the land might well be insufficient."

15. Akerib v. Booth [1961] 1 W.L.R. 367; [1961] 1 All E.R. 380, C.A.

Held, wide enough to exempt negligence.

16. The Ballyalton [1961] 1 W.L.R. 929; [1961] 1 All E.R. 459, Karminski J.

Notice in incoming vessels contained words: "(Defendants) will not be responsible for and will repudiate any liability in respect of any damage . . . resulting from using quays"—*Held*, these words were wide enough to exempt from negligence.

17. L. Harris v. Continental Express [1961] 1 Lloyd's Rep. 251, Paull J.

"Shall not be responsible for any goods carried deposited or left in any vehicles. . . . "—theft of goods through negligence of carrier—*Held*, that as the only liability of the carrier towards the owner lay in negligence, the exempting words could have no effect apart from negligence, and applying *Rutter v. Palmer* [1922] 2 K.B. 87 at p. 92, the exempting words were sufficiently wide enough to cover the loss.

18. Producer Meats v. Thomas Borthwick [1965] 1 Lloyd's Rep. 130, C.A. (N.Z.)

Held, words related to accidental damage only, and did not exempt from negligence (N.Z.)

19. John Carter v. Hanson Haulage [1965] 2 Q.B. 495; [1965] 1 All E.R. 113, C.A.

It was *held* (123 B and 129 B) that liability for theft was excluded by the words used, albeit the theft of the carrier's own driver; but this was primarily based on the ground that it had not been pleaded or argued in the lower court to the contrary; Russell L.J. however expressly said (129 B) that the exclusion of "loss" excluded loss by theft. As to the failure to check antecedents, admittedly negligent, it appears (125 I) to have been conceded that the exempting words excluded liability from ordinary negligence, but it was argued that they did not exempt from "personal" antecedent negligence, such as a failure to check antecedents—*Held* (Sellers L.J. dissenting), that no such distinction could be drawn.

20. Morris v. C. W. Martin [1966] 1 Q.B. 716; [1965] 2 All E.R. 725, C.A.

Cleaners stipulated that all goods "belonging to customers" should be at customer's risk—the owner of a fur sent it to furriers to clean—they sent it to cleaners as principals, where it was stolen—*Held*, the exemption did not apply, because the customer of the cleaners was the furrier, as he was acting as principal, and the fur did not belong to him.

21. Suisse Atlantique v. N.V. Rotterdamsche [1967] 1 A.C. 361; [1966] 2 All E.R. 61, H.L.

So *held*, disapproving dicta to contrary in *Karsales* **12**. See **25**.

22. Anglo-Continental Holidays v. Typaldos (1967) 111 S.J. 599; 2 Lloyd's Rep. 61, C.A.

Held, defendants liable, as the provision for alteration could not be used to alter the substance of a transaction.

23. Hill v. Ashington Piggeries [1969] 3 All E.R. 1496, C.A.

24. Budd v. P & O [1969] 2 Lloyd's Rep. 262, Paull J.

25. Harbutts Plasticine v. Wayne Tanks [1970] 1 Q.B. 447; [1970] 1 All E.R. 225, C.A.

Lord Denning M.R., explaining *Suisse Atlantique* **21**, said that there were three cases: (1) where the innocent party elected to disaffirm the contract as a result of the fundamental breach; (2) where the fundamental breach automatically terminated the contract, *e.g.* by destruction of the subject matter; and (3) where the innocent party elected to affirm the contract. In the first two cases any exemption clauses automatically went, but in the third case (which was what happened in *Suisse Atlantique*) it was a matter of construction whether the exemption clause covered the breach which had been committed.

26. Kenyon v. Baxter Hoare [1971] 1 W.L.R. 519; [1971] 2 All E.R. 708, Donaldson J.

Nuts in warehouse eaten by rats—in holding that exemption clause applied judge *said* that the only kind of breach of contract which disentitled a party from relying on an exemption clause was performance totally different from that contemplated in the contract.

27. White v. Blackmore [1972] 2 Q.B. 651; [1972] 3 All E.R. 158, C.A.

28. Levison v. Patent Steam Carpet [1977] 3 W.L.R. 90; [1977] 3 All E.R. 498, C.A.

29. Photo Productions v. Securicor [1980] A.C. 827; [1980] 1 All E.R. 556, H.L.

So *held*, overruling *Harbutt* **25**.

30. Spriggs v. Sotheby Parke Bernet & Co. Ltd [1986] 1 EGLR 13; [1986] C.L.Y. 136, C.A.

Diamond placed by plaintiff in 1977 with auctioneers for sale was stolen whilst in their care; the Court of Appeal did not accept the system for viewing of jewellery was a reasonably safe system in the circumstances or that such a system was functioning properly but held exclusion clause excluded liability.

31. Phillips Products Ltd v. Hyland [1987] 1 W.L.R. 659; [1987] 2 All E.R. 620, C.A.

Plaintiff hired excavator and driver (the first defendant) from the second defendant. Clause 8 of the contract provided that the first defendant "shall . . . be regarded or the [servant or agent] of the hirer who alone shall be responsible for all claims arising in connection with the operation of the plant by the [first defendant] . . . ". First defendant negligently drove excavator into plaintiff's buildings and did considerable damage. No personal injury was caused—*Held*:

(a) In determining whether there had been negligence for the purposes of section 1(1) of the Unfair Contract Terms Act 1977, the contract term relied on by the defence as defeating the plaintiff's claim had to be left out of account.
(b) Clause 8 was one to which section 2(2) of the 1977 Act applied. Though the clause purported to transfer liability for the first defendant from the second defendant to the plaintiff, and did not in terms "exclude or restrict" the second defendant's liability for negligence, the purported transfer of liability would necessarily exclude a liability that would otherwise fall on the second defendant.
(c) The second defendant had not in the circumstances of the case proved that Clause 8 satisfied the requirement of reasonableness as defined in section 11(1) of the 1977 Act. (See further [1987] 2 All E.R. 629 e–630 b).
(d) Accordingly, the second defendant was not entitled to rely on Clause 8 as against plaintiff.

32. Thompson v. T. Lohan (Plant Hire) Ltd [1987] 1 W.L.R. 649; [1987] 2 All E.R. 631 C.A.

Second defendant hired excavator and driver from first defendant. Clause 8 of the contract was the same as in *Phillips v. Hyland* **31**. Due to driver's negligence, plaintiff's husband was killed. Plaintiff sued first and second defendants and obtained judgment against the former, who now claimed indemnity against the latter in reliance on Clause 8—*Held*, distinguishing *Phillips v. Hyland*, in this case Clause 8 was not one to which the 1977 Act applied. It did not purport to exclude or restrict any liability to the plaintiff, but only to provide as between the two defendants who should bear the consequences of the driver's negligence. Thus Clause 8 was effective, and the first defendant was entitled to its indemnity.

33 Dorset C. C. v. Southern Felt Roofing Co. Ltd (1989) 48 BLR 96; [1990] C.L.Y. 636, C.A.

The contract provision that the employer should "bear the risk of loss or damage in respect of the Works and . . . the existing structure and contents . . . by fire . . . " did not exclude the contractor's liability for damage caused by fire on assumption that the fire had been caused by the contractor's negligence.

34 M[c]Conkey v. AMEC Plc, *The Times*, February 28, 1990; [1990] C.L.Y. 3325, C.A.

Owners of crane hired it under contract which provided that they should also "supply a person competent in operating the plant", such person "to be regarded as the [servant] or [agent] of the hirer . . . who alone shall be responsible for all claims arising in connection with the operation of the plant by the said [driver] or [operator]". When crane was operated by a driver whom trial judge held to be incompetent, fly-jib buckled and crane's load fell onto plaintiff—*Held*, since operator was not competent, contractual provisions referred to above did not apply; thus owner remained vicariously liable for driver's negligence; and hirers not liable to indemnify owners in respect of their liability to plaintiff.

35 E.E. Caledonia Ltd v. Orbit Valve plc, [1994] 1 W.L.R. 1515; [1995] 1 All E.R. 174, C.A.

Defendant agreed to supply to plaintiff a service engineer to work on Piper Alpha platform, which was operated and jointly owned by plaintiff. The contract provided *inter alia* that "each party . . . shall indemnify . . . the other . . . from and against any claim, demand, cause of action, loss, expense or liability . . . arising by reason of any injury to or death of any employee . . . of the indemnifying party, resulting from or in any way connected with this Order." Due to plaintiff's negligence and breach of statutory duty, a fire started on the platform, in which the service engineer was killed. Plaintiff settled claims by engineer's estate and dependants, and now sought to recover the settlement sum from defendant under the indemnify provision—*Held*;

(a) Since that provision did not contain words clearly relieving any party of liability for its negligence, plaintiff could not rely on the provision in relation to such liability.
(b) Neither was plaintiff entitled to indemnity in relation to its liability for breach of statutory duty since that duty ran concurrently with its liability in negligence.

U1. Chuter v. British Mouldex (1954) C.A. 205 B.

Held, liability for negligence not excluded.

(d) Effect on Third Parties

1. Grant v. Australian Knitting Mills [1936] A.C. 85, P.C.

Lord Wright (106): "Equally irrelevant is any question of liability between the retailers and the manufacturers on the contract of sale between them. The tort liability is independent of any question of contract."

2. Fosbroke-Hobbs v. Airwork [1937] 1 All E.R. 108, Lord Goddard C.J.

Charter of private plane by host—*Held*, guests were bound by exemption in charter.

3. Herschtal v. Stewart & Ardern [1939] 3 All E.R. 124, Tucker J.

Plaintiff signs exempting receipt presented to him by defendant dealer—signs "for and on behalf of" hire-purchase company—*Held*, whatever effect this might have between hire-purchase company and defendant, it could not affect position between plaintiff and defendant.

4. Haseldine v. Daw [1941] 2 K.B. 343; [1941] 3 All E.R. 156, C.A.

Plaintiff visiting premises injured in lift—defendant owners seek to rely on exemption in their contract with lift repairers—*Held*, they could not do so, because the duty of defendants to plaintiff arose quite independently of their contract with the lift repairers.

5. Scruttons v. Midland Silicones [1962] A.C. 446; [1962] 1 All E.R. 1, H.L.

Defendant stevedores negligently damaged cargo when unloading—in an action by the cargo owners they claimed that their liability was limited to 500 dollars per package, this being the limit of the shipowner's liability under the bill of lading—*Held*, following *Dunlop v. Selfridge* [1915] A.C. 847, that the stevedores, not being parties to the contract contained in the bill of lading, were not entitled to the benefit of a stipulation in the contract, and further that the contract of carriage had not been entered into by the shipowners as agent for the stevedores so as to enable the latter to claim the benefit of its terms, nor was there any basis for implying a contract between the stevedores and the consignees limiting the liability of the stevedores to that in the contract of carriage. *Elder Dempster v. Paterson Zochonis* [1924] A.C. 522 distinguished on its facts. See also *Adler v. Dickson* (Chap. 4, (2) (c) **9**).

6. Morris v. C. W. Martin [1966] 1 Q.B. 716; [1965] 2 All E.R. 725, C.A.

Owner of fur sent it to furriers to clean—in turn, with consent of owners and as principals, they sent it to defendant cleaners, where it was stolen—in accepting fur from furriers, cleaners imposed exempting conditions (which however did not apply; see Chap. 4 (2) (c) **20**)—on the question whether owner would have been bound, *held* Yes, because she impliedly consented to the furriers making a contract for cleaning on terms usually current in the trade.

7. Gore v. Van der Lann [1967] 2 Q.B. 31; [1967] 1 All E.R. 360, C.A.

Held, corporation who had issued bus pass were not entitled to restrain plaintiff from suing servant of corporation directly, as the pass contained no undertaking by plaintiff not to sue servant, and, *semble*, if it had, such an undertaking would have been a contractual provision, which would have been avoided by Road Traffic Act 1960, s. 151.

8. Hollingworth v. Southern Ferries (1977) 2 Lloyd's Rep. 70, Deputy Judge Ogden

Held, that as friend was acting as agent for plaintiff in booking ticket any knowledge of exemptions which the friend had would be imputed to plaintiff (though here, on the facts, there was none).

9. Southern Water Authority v. Carey [1985] 2 All E.R. 1077; [1985] C.L.Y. 195, Judge Smout Q.C. (Also as **Southern Water Authority v. Lewis & Duvivier** (1984) 27 BLR 111)

Main contract clause provided "The contractor's liability under this clause shall be in lieu of any condition or warranty implied by law as to the quality or fitness for any particular purpose of any portion of the works taken over. . . . and save as in this clause expressed neither the contractor nor his subcontractors servant or agents shall be liable whether in contract, tort or otherwise in respect of defects in or damage to such portion or for any injury damage or loss of whatsoever kind attributable to such defects or damage. For the purpose of this sub-clause the contractor contracts on his own behalf and on behalf of and as trustee for his subcontractors servants and agents"—*Held*: a subcontractor whose works had been so completed as to be the subject of a valid taking over certificate was protected from any liability in tort to the employer of the main contractor.

(3) Volenti Non Fit Injuria/Ex Turpi Causa Non Oritur Actio

(*N.B.* Also see Unfair Contract Terms Act 1977, s. 2(3) which limits further the scope of volenti.)

1. Dann v. Hamilton [1939] 1 K.B. 509; [1939] 1 All E.R. 59, Asquith J.

Held, plaintiff entitled to succeed, for although she knew driver drunk, she did not thereby impliedly consent to any subsequent negligence by him. *Approved* by C.A. in *Slater v. Clay Cross* **11**. *But see* **14** and **25**.

2. D'Urso v. Sanson [1939] 4 All E.R. 26, Simonds J.

Through defendant's negligence building catches fire—defendant's night watchman goes back into fire—defendant pleads *volenti—Held*, not applicable, as defendant not a volunteer but acting in the course of his employment. Simonds J. at p. 29 H: "That (*volenti*) has no reference whatever to the case where the actor is a person who does what he does in pursuance of the duty which his employer imposes on him."

3. Taylor v. Sims [1942] 2 All E.R. 375; 58 T.L.R. 339, Lewis J.

Workmen working in bomb-damaged house—*Held*, that by continuing to work there without question and with full knowledge of risk he voluntarily incurred the risk. But this is doubtful, because there were two grounds for the decision.

4. Bowater v. Rowley Regis B.C. [1944] K.B. 476; [1944] 1 All E.R. 465, C.A.

Held, volenti no defence. Goddard L.J. at p. 467 A: "The maxim *volenti non fit injuria* is one which in the case of master and servant is to be applied with extreme caution. Indeed I would say that it can hardly ever be applicable where the act to which plaintiff is said to be *volens* arises out of his ordinary duty, unless the work for which plaintiff is engaged is one in which danger is necessarily involved."

5. Murray v. Harringay Arena [1951] 2 K.B. 529; [1951] 2 All E.R. 320n., C.A.

Held, plaintiff could not recover because he took the risks incidental to a game of ice-hockey.

6. O'Dowd v. Frazer Nash (1951) C.L.C. 6778; [1951] W.N. 173, McNair J.

No contractual duty—defendants had issued deceased with handbook warning him of danger of sport—*Held*, defendants not liable.

7. Merrington v. Ironbridge Metal Works [1952] 2 All E.R. 1101; 1953 S.L.T. 97, Hallett J. *Held*, not *volenti.*

8. General Cleaning Contractors v. Christmas [1953] A.C. 180; [1952] 2 All E.R. 1110, H.L. *Held*, not *volenti.*

9. Leathley v. Mersey Insulation [1954] 1 Lloyd's Rep. 349, C.A.

In lower court Donovan J. (see 351, col. 1) said *obiter*: " . . . if four men deliberately decided to use the one method (of removing hatch cover section) which does entail an element of risk, then they must be regarded as having decided voluntarily to run that risk"—but C.A. did not deal with the point in their judgments affirming decision of Donovan J.

10. Honeyman v. Oriental S.N. [1955] 2 Lloyd's Rep. 27, Hilbery J.

Held, not *volenti.*

11. Slater v. Clay Cross [1956] 2 Q.B. 264; [1956] 2 All E.R. 625, C.A.

Plaintiff licensee in railway tunnel run down by a train driven negligently—plaintiff knew of risk of walking in tunnel—defendants say she was therefore *volenti—Held*, not, approving **1**, as plaintiff only voluntarily accepted the risk of a train driven in ordinary way, not negligently.

12. Behrens v. Bertram Mills [1957] 2 Q.B. 1; [1957] 1 All E.R. 583, Devlin J.

Held, plaintiff not *volenti* because the risk from elephants was not such an obvious danger that he ought not to have gone into booth.

13. A.C. Billings v. Riden [1958] A.C. 240; [1957] 3 All E.R. 1, H.L.

See Chap. 10, (6) (c) **13**.

14. Davies v. Jones (1958) 108 L.J. 58, McNair J. [1958] C.L.Y. 2308, *The Times*, April 1, C.A. *Held*, by McNair J. following **1**, that *volenti* was no defence: however, *Settled coram* C.A. at lower figure, as plaintiff's counsel expressed some doubt as to correctness of **1**.

15. Fowler v. Lanning [1959] 1 Q.B. 426; [1959] 1 All E.R. 290, 297 G, Diplock J.

16. Baker v. Hopkins [1959] 1 W.L.R. 966; [1959] 3 All E.R. 225, C.A.

Doctor went down gas-filled well to rescue two men—*Held, volenti* no defence, as rescue attempt was foreseeable.

17. I.C.I v. Shatwell [1965] A.C. 656; [1964] 2 All E.R. 999, H.L.

Held, volenti was a defence to claim of each plaintiff, (i) as regards statutory duty, because the employer was not himself in breach of any statutory duty, and was not vicariously in breach of any statutory duty through the neglect of someone of superior rank to the plaintiff; and (ii) as regards negligence at common law, because there was a genuine full agreement between the plaintiffs, free from any kind of pressure, to assume the risk of loss (Lord Pearce, 1013 B-D, Lord Radcliffe concurring).

18. O'Reilly v. National Rail and Tram [1966] 1 All E.R. 499, Nield J.

Semble, this was *volenti* within *Shatwell* **17**.

19. Bolt v. William Moss (1966) 110 S.J. 385; [1966] C.L.Y. 1102, Cantley J.

Held, defendants not liable, as plaintiff and co-employee had combined to disobey orders, and following *Shatwell* **17**, *volenti* was a complete defence.

20. Morley v. Dubinski [1967] C.L.Y. 2668; (1966) 59 D.L.R. (2d) 217, Nova Scotia Supreme Ct.

21. Rootes v. Shelton (1967) 41 A.J.L.R. 172; [1967] C.L.Y. 2672, Aust. High Ct.

Skier injured in collision with stationary boat, near which driver had gone without warning—jury found negligence—*Held,* verdict should stand, as it was a case where all the circumstances had to be considered, including the extent to which risks could be inferred as having been accepted by the fact of participation; the rules of the game were a relevant, but not a determining, circumstance. So far as *volenti* was concerned, the onus was on the defendant to establish voluntary acceptance of a risk not inherent in the pastime.

22. Buckpitt v. Oates [1968] 1 All E.R. 1145; [1968] C.L.Y. 2726, John Stephenson J.

Held, volenti was a defence to claim by infant passenger.

23. Simms v. Leigh Rugby F.C. [1969] 2 All E.R. 923, Wrangham J.

24. Bennett v. Tugwell [1971] 2 Q.B. 267; [1971] 2 All E.R. 248, Ackner J.

Notice in car: "Warning. Passengers travelling in this vehicle do so *at their own risk*"—in fact the son of the owner put it there in order to protect his father—a friend was injured—the friend knew of the notice but believed it meant that he would not be able to sue the defendant but merely the insurance company—*Held,* on the facts the friend had assented to being carried in the car "at his own risk", and since the test was an objective one, the defence succeeded.

25. Nettleship v. Weston [1971] 2 Q.B. 691; [1971] 3 All E.R. 581, C.A.

A friend agreed to take a learner out to give her instruction—she panicked and caused him injury—before going out, the instructor had made enquiries about insurance to make sure he was covered—*Held*, in these circumstances he was not *volenti*. "Knowledge of the risk of injury is not enough. Nor is willingness to take the risk of injury. Nothing will suffice short of an agreement to waive any claim for negligence" (Lord Denning M.R., 377 D). Lord Denning also said that a professional instructor might not be able to sue, because there might well be implied in the contract an agreement to waive any claim for injury (377 H). Megaw L.J. *said* that he doubted if *Dann v. Hamilton* **1** was correctly decided, but Lord Denning referred to it with apparent approval.

26. White v. Blackmore [1972] 2 Q.B. 651; [1972] 3 All E.R. 158, C.A.

So *held, but* defendants *not liable* because adequate exempting notices displayed (see Chap. 4, (2) (b) **15**).

27. Birch v. Thomas [1972] 1 W.L.R. 294; [1972] 1 All E.R. 905, C.A.

Notice in car: "Passengers ride at their own risk and on condition that no claims shall be made against driver or owner"—words were small, but driver had pointed to notice, saying that he was not insured for passenger liability—*Held*, defendant not liable. N.B.—This case was decided on exemption of negligence rather than *volenti*, though the difference between the two in notice cases (see **28**), is very small.

28. Burnett v. British Waterways Board [1973] 1 W.L.R. 700; [1973] 2 All E.R. 631, C.A.

Plaintiff lighterman employed by Charrington Lighterage injured while warping his barge with assistance of defendants' employees—injury due to negligence of latter—defendants had exhibited a notice, which plaintiff had read some time previously, exempting them from negligence—*Held*, that no agreement sufficient to found *volenti* could possibly be implied. *N.B.* It was also held, for similar reasons, that since plaintiff had no choice but to have his barge warped, the notice would not operate to exempt negligence, since the test was whether the plaintiff had expressly or impliedly agreed to be bound by the terms of the notice (see Chap. 4, (2) (b) **16**).

29. Bridgeford v. Weston [1975] R.T.R. 189; [1975] C.L.Y. 3000, Waller J.

30. Hugh v. N.C.B. 1972 S.C. 252; [1977] C.L.Y. 2051, Lord Keith, O.H.

In breach of regulations and despite reasonable efforts by defendants to prevent the practice, plaintiff and others jumped off moving train in mine—plaintiff injured in ensuing rush—*held*, applying *Shatwell* **17**, plaintiff was *volens* and action failed.

31. Gregory v. Kelly [1978] R.T.R. 426; [1978] C.L.Y. 2610, Kenneth Jones J.

Held, section 148(3) of the Road Traffic Act 1972 deprived the defendant of any defence of *volenti*. *N.B.* section 148(3) in effect avoids any agreement to contract out of certain specified risks, including those arising from "the condition of the vehicle".

Not followed and *distinguished* by Ewbank J. in *Ashton* **33** (see [1980] 3 All E.R. 878 G-J).

32. Belton v. Toone [1978] C.L.Y. 2055, Judge Leonard

33. Ashton v. Turner [1981] Q.B. 137; [1980] 3 All E.R. 870, Ewbank J.

34. Harrison v. Vincent [1982] R.T.R. 8; [1982] C.L.Y. 2159, C.A.

35. Latchford v. Spedeworth International Ltd, *The Times*, October 11, 1983; [1983] C.L.Y. 2584, Hodgson J.

Held, not *volenti*, applying *Harrison* **34**.

36. Marshall v. Osmond [1983] Q.B. 1034; [1983] 2 All E.R. 225, C.A.

Held, that the defence of *volenti non fit injuria* is not really applicable in the case of the police pursuing a suspected criminal.

37. M^c^Ginlay or Titchener v. B.R.B. [1983] 1 W.L.R. 1427; [1983] 3 All E.R. 770, H.L.

Plaintiff, then 15, taking short cut along railway line got onto line through long-standing gap in fence. Defendants knew people used gap to cross line. Plaintiff had done so on previous occasions and knew of danger. She was run down by train being driven properly—*Held*, that the defendants had discharged their duty of care to the plaintiff and any breach of duty was not causative of the accident. Also *held* that the defendants were exempted from liability by virtue of section 2(3) of the Occupiers' Liability (Scotland) Act 1960 (the equivalent of section 2(5) of the Occupiers' Liability Act 1957) as the plaintiff fully appreciated the risk she took in crossing the line, and since the train that injured her had not been negligently driven, the risk that materialised was one of the risks the plaintiff had accepted.

38. Condon v. Basi [1985] 1 W.L.R. 866; [1985] 2 All E.R. 453, C.A.

Defendant, a local Sunday league footballer, lunged with studs showing 9 inches off the ground at plaintiff, on the opposing side, after plaintiff had pushed the ball away—plaintiff broke right leg—defendant sent off. Court of Appeal upheld trial Judge's decision that defendant was liable in negligence. *Per* Lord Donaldson M.R.:

> "... there is no authority as to what is the standard of care which governs the conduct of players in competitive sports generally and, above all, in a competitive sport whose rules ... contemplate ... physical contact between the players." There would be liability "if ... the defendant failed to exercise that degree of care which was appropriate in all the circumstances, or acted in a way in which the plaintiff cannot be expected to have consented ... The standard is objective, but objective in a different set of circumstances. Thus there will of course be a higher degree of care required of a player in a First Division football match than of a player in a local league football match."

39. Paulette v. Doucette and Lainks [1985] 2 W.W.R. 588; [1985] C.L.Y. 2337, British Columbia Supreme Court.

First defendant invited plaintiff to water ski. Knowing plaintiff had no experience, first defendant explained, from a position on shore, how plaintiff should position himself in water. Unidentified person on shore shouted "go". Second defendant, who had not asked whether plaintiff was experienced, applied full power. Plaintiff grabbed at rope. His fingers became entangled and were severed. *Held*, *inter alia*:

(a) First defendant negligent in failing properly to execute the supervisory role he had assumed.
(b) Second defendant negligent in failing to ascertain whether plaintiff experienced, and applying full power in response to shout from shore.
(c) Defence of *volenti non fit injuria* did not arise. Not an obvious and necessary risk that second defendant would accelerate before plaintiff ready and without establishing system of communication.

40. Kirkham v. Chief Constable of the Greater Manchester Police [1990] 2 Q.B. 283; [1990] 3 All E.R. 246, C.A. For further details see Chap. 18, (13) **65**.

41. Pitts v. Hunt [1991] 1 Q.B. 24; [1990] 3 All E.R. 344, C.A.

Plaintiff aged 18 and friend aged 16 spent evening drinking together. Set off home on friend's motorcycle—plaintiff as pillion passenger. Friend had drunk so much he was unfit to drive, as plaintiff would have realised had he been in a proper state. Friend also unlicensed and uninsured, to plaintiff's knowledge. Friend, encouraged by plaintiff, deliberately drove in dangerous manner. Friend killed and plaintiff injured in head-on collision, not fault of other driver. Plaintiff sued friend's personal representative—*Held*, plaintiff not entitled to recover on grounds of application of maxim *ex turpi causa non oritur actio* and of public policy, and because the serious circumstances precluded the Court from finding that the friend owed any duty of care to plaintiff. Further, had not section 148 (3) of the Road Traffic Act, 1972 prevented defendant from raising a defence of *volenti non fit injuria*, that defence would have succeeded.

42. Morris v. Murray [1991] 2 Q.B. 6, [1991] 3 All E.R. 801, C.A.

After drinking alcohol plaintiff and deceased decided to go on a flight in deceased's light aircraft; the deceased acted as pilot, the plane crashed and the plaintiff was injured. It was found that the plaintiff was aware the deceased had been drinking heavily and was capable of appreciating the nature of the risk he was taking—*Held*, the maxim *volenti non fit injuria* applied. *Dann v. Hamilton* (**1**), *Slater v. Clay Cross* (**11**), *Wooldridge v. Sumner* (Chap. 10, (5)(a) **31**) and *Nettleship v. Weston* (**25**) considered.

43. Gala v. Preston (1991) 172 C.L.R. 243; [1991] C.L.Y. 243, High Court of Australia

Held, driver of a vehicle which he and passenger had earlier stolen owed no duty of care to passenger injured by his careless driving, because the injury resulted from a serious criminal act in which both participated.

44. Weir v. Wyper, 1992 S.L.T. 579; [1992] C.L.Y. 6068.

Plaintiff, aged 16 was passenger in car driven by defendant, whom plaintiff knew to be unqualified and unsupervised. Defendant alleged he owed her no duty of care—relied on maxim *ex turpi causa non oritur actio*. Plaintiff said there had earlier been a qualified driver in car—he had get out and not returned. It being late at night and in country road she had become anxious and was being driven home by defendant when accident occurred—*Held*, in circumstances alleged by plaintiff, it was hard to see that she was participating in any significant criminal activity or that public policy would deny her a right to recover.

45. Lewis v. Buckpool Golf Club, 1993 S.L.T. (Sh. Ct.) 43; [1992] C.L.Y. 6076

Defendant, a 24-handicap golfer, mishit ball from tee and struck plaintiff on adjacent green—*Held*, defendant liable. All he had to do was wait for plaintiff to finish putting. Risk of a golfer of defendant's level of skill mis-hitting not so small that a reasonable man would disregard it. There was no basis for a plea of *volenti non fit injuria*.

46. Barrett v. Ministry of Defence [1995] 1 W.L.R. 1217; *The Times*, January 13, 1995, C.A.

Deceased, naval airman at base in Norway, drank to excess, vomited, was left slumped on a chair and then carried unconscious to his cabin where he lay in coma, observed intermittently—died of aspiration of vomit. Defendant had failed to enforce disciplinary codes discouraging over-indulgence in alcohol. There were no clear orders from officers as to how deceased should have been treated after collapsing, and no adequate medical cover was available—*Held*:

(a) Defendant under no duty to take reasonable care to prevent deceased, a mature man, from abusing alcohol to extent he did. Until he became unconscious he alone was responsible for his condition. The Queen's Regulations and standing orders could not be equated with guidance given in Highway Code or factory safety pamphlets.
(b) After deceased collapsed, defendant negligent in failing properly to supervise and provide medical assistance for him.
(c) Deceased two-thirds to blame.

Note: At first instance, defence of *volenti* failed—deceased, with mind clouded by alcohol, had not voluntarily assumed risk of grave or fatal injury by continuing drinking.

U1. Whitford v. Monkman (1983) C.A. 926

P injured when participating with D in flying of radio controlled gliders. Although P had accepted risks inherent in the sport, this did not excuse negligence of D who had flown his machine carelessly.

(4) Crown Immunity

1. Bell v. Secretary of State for Defence [1986] Q.B. 322; [1985] 3 All E.R. 661, C.A.

For details see Chap. 18, (13) **42** but overruled in *Pearce* **2** below.

2. Pearce v. Secretary of State for Defence [1988] A.C. 755; [1988] 2 All E.R. 348, H.L.

Plaintiff alleged that whilst in the forces he was exposed to dangerous radiation due to negligence of UKAEA's nuclear weapons testing; liabilities of UKAEA transferred to defendants by Act of 1973—*Held*, the Act did not admit of construction that liability was deemed always to be that of the defendants and hence they could not rely on section 10 of the Crown Proceedings Act 1947 so as to take away any accrued rights. In any event section 10(1) did not provide a defence but section 10(2) would have; the words "any suffered" in section 10(1) and (2) related to the casualty or other event caused by the acts or omissions from which personal injury or death resulted and not to the acts or omissions themselves; *Bell* **1** wrongly decided.

3. Welsh v. Chief Constable of the Merseyside Police [1993] 1 All E.R. 692; [1993] C.L.Y. 2943, Tudor Evans J.

Plaintiff claimed damages against *inter alias* Crown Prosecution Service alleging negligent failure to ensure magistrates' court was informed that two offences for which he was on trial had been taken into consideration in the Crown Court; as a result of the failure he was arrested—*Held*, claim would not be struck out as disclosing no reasonable cause of action; section 2(5) of the Crown Proceedings Act 1947 did not provide C.P.S. with immunity from prosecution.

5. LIABILITY FOR ACTS OF OTHERS

(1) Servants

(a) Who is Servant

		Whether servant or not
Commercial traveller	1	No
Variety dancer—in show produced by defendant	2	No
House surgeon	3	Yes
Hospital pharmacist	3	Yes
Consultant surgeon	3	No
THEATRE NURSE	4	Yes
HOUSE SURGEON	4	Yes
CONSULTANT SURGEON	4	No
Consultant physician	5	?
PART-TIME VISITING ANAESTHETIST	6	Yes
CONSULTANTS GENERALLY	6	?
CONSULTANTS UNDER NATIONAL HEALTH SERVICE	7	Probably
Police constable	8	No
Director under contract of service	9	Yes?
Co-adventurers on fishing voyage	10	No
Scoutmaster—not a servant of Boy Scouts' Association	11	No
Tree feller	12	No
PUPIL DETAILED TO DELIVER MILK TO CLASSROOMS	13	No
WORKING SUB-CONTRACTOR—ON THE "LUMP"—MAY STILL BE EMPLOYEE—DESPITE THE LABEL	14	Yes
Hunt servants, agents and mounted followers	15	Yes
Employee of parent company of defendant	16	No
Compulsory pilot—not servant of harbour authority	17	No
Pilot—not servant of port authority	18	No

1. Egginton v. Reader [1936] 1 All E.R. 7; 52 T.L.R. 212, Lewis J.

Commercial traveller—owner-driver—commission plus £1 per week towards petrol—could take orders from other firms as well—*Held*, not servant or agent of defendant. Tests propounded by McCardie J. in *Performing Right Society v. Mitchell* [1924] 1 K.B. 762 applied.

2. Fraser-Wallas v. Waters [1939] 4 All E.R. 609, Lord Hewart C.J.

Dancer in variety programme produced by defendant kicks heel into audience—*Held*, that in the circumstances dancer was not servant of defendant.

3. Collins v. Herts. C.C. [1947] K.B. 598; [1947] 1 All E.R. 633, Hilbery J.

Held, house surgeons and pharmacists were, and consulting surgeons were not, servants of hospital for whom hospital would be liable.

4. Cassidy v. Ministry of Health [1951] 2 K.B. 343; [1951] 1 All E.R. 574, C.A.

Held, hospital would be liable for negligence of house surgeons and even of nurses who were under the direction of consulting surgeon in operating theatre, but not for negligence of consulting surgeons. But *see* **6**, where the position of consultants and visiting anaesthetists is further considered.

5. Higgins v. N.W. Met. Regional Hospital Board [1954] 1 W.L.R. 411; [1954] 1 All E.R. 414, Pilcher J.

Issue was whether a consultant physician could take advantage of Public Authorities Protection Acts—*Held*, he could. In the course of his judgment judge (422 G): "He was certainly acting as an agent for the Board at the material time. He would, no doubt, be properly described as an officer of the Board. He may have been the servant of the Board. . . . He was a person acting on behalf of the Hospital Board in the execution . . . of a public duty." *Approved* in **7**.

6. Roe v. Ministry of Health [1954] 2 Q.B. 66; [1954] 2 All E.R. 131, C.A.

Court considered position of a part-time visiting anaesthetist at a voluntary hospital (pre-National Health Service), but decided in the event there was no negligence anyway—Somervell L.J. said hospital were liable for him, as he was part of the permanent staff, like the orthopaedic surgeon in *Cassidy* **4**—he also said that "the position of surgeons and others under the National Health Service Act will have to be decided when it arises" (135 H), and that "the position of hospitals under that Act may or may not be different from when they were voluntary or municipal hospitals."—*Held*, that a visiting anaesthetist at a voluntary hospital who was not employed by the patient was a servant or agent of the hospital.

7. Razzel v. Snowball [1954] 1 W.L.R. 1382; [1954] 3 All E.R. 429, C.A.

Issue was whether a consultant under National Health Service Acts could take advantage of Public Authorities Protection Acts—*Held*, he could, approving **5**, but Denning L.J. also said, probably *obiter*, that all consultants under the National Health Service Acts were members of the hospital staff.

8. Att.-Gen. for N.S.W. v. Perpetual Trustee Co. [1955] A.C. 457; [1955] 1 All E.R. 846, P.C.

Held, Crown could not sue for loss of service of police constable, and *said* (857 1) that the service relationship of a police constable to Crown was same as soldier.

9. Lee v. Lee's Air Farming [1961] A.C. 12; [1960] 3 All E.R. 420, P.C.

Held, that the governing director of a company principally owned by himself could be a servant of that company under a contract of service.

10. Parker v. Walker, 1961 S.L.T. 252, O.H.

Injury to engineer on fishing boat—crew and owners had agreed to share proceeds of catch—*Held*, this made the voyage a joint adventure, and that there was no master and servant relationship—so that owners were not liable.

11. Murphy v. Zoological Society *The Times*, November 14, 1962; [1962] C.L.Y. 68, Fenton Atkinson J.

12. Inglefield v. Macey (1967) 2 K.I.R. 146; [1962] C.L.Y. 2726, Ashworth J.

13. Watkins v. Birmingham C.C. *The Times*, August 1, 1975; [1975] C.L.Y. 2338, C.A.

14. Ferguson v. John Dawson [1976] 1 W.L.R. 1213; [1976] 3 All E.R. 817, C.A.

Held, in a case where the "self-employee" was seeking to sue under the Construction Regulations as a "workman employed." See Chap. 16, (8) (b) for further details and other similar cases (not always so decided).

15. League Against Cruel Sports v. Scott [1986] Q.B. 240; [1985] 2 All E.R., 489, Park J.

Master of hounds is vicariously liable for hunt servants, agents and mounted followers.

16. McDermid v. Nash Dredging Ltd [1987] A.C. 906; [1987] 2 All E.R. 878, H.L.

Plaintiff was sent by his employer the defendant to work on tug owned by and the master of which was employed by defendant's parent company. In breach of master's own system of working, he reversed tug before plaintiff had finished unmooring it, and a rope swept plaintiff into water—*Held*, defendant not vicariously liable for negligence of master, who was not its employee, but was liable personally for breach of duty to ensure that plaintiff was provided with safe system of work, that duty being non-delegable in sense that employer could not escape liability for performance of the duty which had in fact been delegated to another and had not been properly performed.

17. Esso Petroleum Co. v. Hall Russell Co. [1989] A.C. 643; [1989] 1 All E.R. 37, H.L.

Fire broke out on tug designed and built by defendant, as it was helping to berth oil tanker owned by plaintiff. Tow line from tug to tanker was cast off, and tanker crashed into jetty. Ensuing damage led to escape of oil which polluted foreshore and harmed sheep owned by local crofters. Plaintiff compensated crofters under a voluntary agreement. Plaintiff claimed damages, *inter alia*, for sums they had paid the crofters. Defendant alleged accident caused, *inter alia*, by fault of compulsory pilot employed by harbour authority, who had been aboard the tanker—*Held, inter alia*:

(a) Payments to crofters were made voluntarily and not recoverable from defendants. In any event, claims for such payments, beeing by subrogation, could only be made in names of crofters.
(b) Harbour authority not vicariously liable for any negligence on pilot's part because:
 (i) pilot is independent professional man who navigates a ship as a professional and not as a servant of his general employer;
 (ii) effect of the Pilotage Act 1913, s. 15(1) was to render master or owner of vessel with pilot on board liable for loss or damage caused by vessel or any fault in navigation of vessel.

18. Oceangas (Gibraltar) Ltd v. Port of London Authority ("The Cavendish") [1993] 2 Lloyds Rep. 292; *The Times*, May 24, 1993

Held, defendant not vicariously liable for any negligence on part of a pilot provided by it pursuant to the Pilotage Act 1987, s. 2(3), which required it to supply properly authorised pilots but did not impose on it a duty to pilot ships.

(b) Course of Employment

(*N.B.* For cases where one employee is injured by practical joking of other employees, see Chap. 15, (8).)

		Whether in course of employment or not
Crew inviting stevedores to load onto hatch covers	1	No
FRAUD OF SERVANT—SOLICITOR'S CLERK PRODUCING FORGERY TO PLAINTIFF	2	Yes
Driver throwing away lighted match while delivering petrol	3	Yes
Using own car instead of defendants' vehicle as instructed	4	Yes
Using car instead of going by train as instructed	5	Yes
DRIVER GIVING LIFT—FORBIDDEN TO DO SO	6	No
Assaulting customer	7	No
General principles stated	8	
DRIVER GIVING LIFT—FORBIDDEN TO DO SO	9	No
FOREMAN ARRANGING LORRY FOR WORKMEN	10	Yes
Ordinary miner firing shot	11	No
GARAGE HAND DRIVING CAR	12	Yes
EXPOSING NAKED LIGHT NEAR PETROL	13	Yes
Workmen's compensation cases not a good guide	14	
Frolic—starting ship's conveyor belt	15	No
Lorry driver going to café	16	No
Using own car	17	Yes
Going to draw wages within factory premises	18	Yes
Theft by servant—lorry driver stealing goods of consignor in transit	19	Yes
Using own vehicle—to get tools and/or meal while on outside job	20	Yes
Miner smoking—causes explosion	21	No
Apprentice—moving plant—moves van on premises	22	Yes
Ship's donkeyman—operating throttle lever—no part of duty—but might reasonably be expected to do so	23	Yes
Ship's crew—returning to ship from shore leave in hired rowing boat	24	No
Employee driving employer's van to get refreshment with permission of employer	25	No
Permission of employer to do act—test is still whether servant doing act which he is employed to do	25	
DANCE HALL STEWARD—ASSAULTING PATRON	26	Yes/No
PLAYFUL PAT ON BUTTOCKS	27	No

Driver—allowing someone else to drive	28	Yes
Throwing away lighted match	29	No
Theft by servant—employed to clean fur	30	Yes
Urging plaintiff to do act of folly—to hit a shell with a sledge hammer	31	No
Driver deviating—at instigation of boys being taken home from summer camp	32	Yes
Factory hand trying to move lorry blocking warehouse entrance—reverses it into driver	33	Yes
Driver provided by employer with car—to drive other workmates to work	34	No
Travelling from home to work	35	No
Driving fellow employee to work	36	No
Employee passenger grabbing wheel from employee driver	37	No
One employee driving other home—after evening of joint sales canvassing	38	Yes
Bus conductor—driving bus inside depot—to help get own bus on road	39	No
Bus conductor—striking passenger in quarrel—no general disorder	40	No
Prohibition—licensee of inn allowing guests to remain well after closing time—contrary to express orders	41	Yes
Driving in company's car park	42	Yes
Driver giving lift when forbidden—milkman giving lift to boy helping him	43	Yes
Doing prohibited act—general principles explained	43	
Driver deviating—to get glasses from home	44	Yes
Stationmaster—boarding moving train after finishing work	45	No
Employee doing act of the class which he is authorised to do—but wholly for own purposes and in own time	46	No
Employee on course hacking with chisel at other trainees' work	47	No
Employee on course grabbing chisel (above) and precipitating struggle	47	Yes
Employee, for a "joke", pushing trolley so as to upset duckboard on which plaintiff standing	48	Yes
Employee pushing slightly unstable wash basin against another, in order to startle the other	49	No
Employees travelling from place at which sent to work, in paid travelling time	50	Yes
Manager at licensed premises seizing customer to protect himself from robber	51	No
Radio mechanic moving radio at householder's request—after repairing it	U1	No
Presumption that man falling from place of work was acting in course of employment	U2	Yes
Driver of coal truck deviating to sell coal for own benefit	U3	No
Employer lending employee lorry—so that employee can convey own car away from employer's premises	U4	No
Driver deviating to go to public-house and to drop friend	U5	Yes
Miners stampeding to get into pit cage	U6	No
Farmworker harvesting—takes gun which goes off	U7	Yes
Driver giving lift—forbidden to do so—plaintiff riding on running board	U8	No

Horseplay—cutting apron strings of co-employee	U9	No
Worker at leisure centre inviting guests into centre out of normal opening hours	U10	No

1. Hillen v. I.C.I. [1936] A.C. 65, H.L.

Plaintiff, a stevedore, at the suggestion or invitation of member of crew, uses hatch cover to load cargo onto and from—it gave way—*Held*, shipowner not liable as plaintiff was a trespasser. Lord Atkin (70): "It (any invitation by crew to use hatch cover) was wholly without the authority of the owners, and quite outside the ostensible scope of authority of the crew. The owner of a barge does not clothe the crew with apparent authority to use it or any part of it for purposes which are known to be extraordinary or dangerous. The crew could not within the scope of their authority convert it into a dancing-hall or drinking-booth. They could not invite stevedores to work the engines or take part in the navigation. The most that could be said of the engineer is that, if he saw a trespasser unwittingly entering into danger upon the employer's property, he might owe a moral duty to the trespasser to warn him. But for breach of a servant's moral duty, an employer is not vicariously liable."

2. Uxbridge Building Society v. Pickard [1939] 2 All E.R. 344, C.A.

Solicitor's managing clerk produces to plaintiff a deed which he must have known to be forged—*Held*, master was liable because clerk was acting within his ostensible authority.

3. Century Insurance v. Northern Ireland R.T.B. [1942] A.C. 509; [1942] 1 All E.R. 491, H.L.

4. McKean v. Raynor Bros. [1942] 2 All E.R. 650, Hilbery J.

Held, that as servant was doing an authorised act the fact that he was doing it in an unauthorised manner would not relieve defendants. Followed in **20**.

5. C.P.R. v. Lockhart [1942] A.C. 591; [1942] 2 All E.R. 464, P.C.

Held, acting in course of employment. The act, *i.e.* going, was authorised and it was immaterial if the method of doing it was prohibited. Followed in **20**.

6. Twine v. Beans Express (1946) 175 L.T. 131; 62 T.L.R. 458, C.A.

Held, outside course of employment. Applied in **9**. See **43**.

7. Warren v. Henly's (1948) 92 S.J. 706; [1948] 2 All E.R. 935, Hilbery J.

Defendants employed B as a garage pump attendant—row between B and P, a customer—B knocked P unconscious—*Held*, B's assault had no connection with the discharge of any duty for defendants, and defendants not liable.

8. Marsh v. Moores [1949] 2 K.B. 208; [1949] 2 All E.R. 27, Lynskey J.

"It is well-settled law that a master is liable even for acts which he has not authorised provided that they are so connected with the acts which he has authorised that they may rightly be regarded as modes, although improper modes, of doing them. On the other hand, if the unauthorised and wrongful act of the servant is not so connected with the authorised act as to be a mode of doing it, but is an independent act, the master is not responsible, for in such a case the servant is not acting in the course of his employment but has gone outside it."

9. Conway v. George Wimpey [1951] 2 K.B. 266; [1951] 1 All E.R. 363, C.A.

Work on aerodrome—defendants had a lorry to transport their men—defendants' driver forbidden to carry any but defendants' men—notice in cab to that effect—driver gives plaintiff (not employed by defendants) a lift—accident—*Held*, driver was performing an act which he was not employed to perform at all, and therefore defendants not liable. **6** applied.

10. Young v. Edward Box [1951] 1 T.L.R. 789, C.A.

Defendants' foreman without authority arranged for lorry to take men, including plaintiff, home—*Held*, the act was within the ostensible authority of the foreman, and defendants were liable.

11. Alford v. N.C.B. [1952] 1 All E.R. 754; [1952] W.N. 144, H.L.

12. L.C.C. v. Cattermoles [1953] 1 W.L.R. 997; [1953] 2 All E.R. 582, C.A.

Garage hand, employed, *inter alia*, to move cars by hand in garage, drives car onto highway to turn it, although forbidden to do so—*Held*, acting in course of employment.

13. Dunk v. Hawker Saunders *The Times*, October 27, 1953; [1953] C.L.Y. 2508, C.A.

14. N.C.B. v. England [1954] A.C. 403; [1954] 1 All E.R. 546, H.L.

Held, in course of employment. "Where no question of (workmen's) compensation arises, a different approach is, I think, justified . . . " (Lord Porter at 552 A). *But* see **34**.

15. Catherall v. Cunard [1954] 2 Lloyd's Rep. 303, Jones J.

16. Crook v. Derbyshire Stone [1956] 1 W.L.R. 432, [1956] 2 All E.R. 447, Pilcher J.

Lorry driver stopped (as he was permitted to do) and went across road to café to get cup of tea—while walking across he caused an accident—*Held*, not acting in course of employment, as the obtaining of refreshment, though permitted, was not something which he was employed to do.

17. Trust Company v. De Silva [1956] 1 W.L.R. 376; [1956] 1 Lloyd's Rep. 309 P.C.

Plaintiff a passenger injured by negligence of X driving Y's car on business of defendants—Y employed by defendants—plaintiff was being driven to make a medical examination on behalf of defendants (an insurance company)—*Held*, Y, though not driving, was in control of car, and was using car on the business of defendants, who were therefore vicariously liable.

18. Staton v. N.C.B. [1957] 1 W.L.R. 893; [1957] 2 All E.R. 667, Finnemore J.

Servant bicycling across defendants' bus park to draw his wages, as he was required to do—*Held*, acting in course of employment, but *aliter* (*semble*) if servant had not been on defendants' premises at the time (671 E).

19. United Africa Co. v. Saka Owoade [1955] A.C. 130; [1957] 3 All E.R. 216, P.C.

Lorry driver stole goods of consignor in transit—*Held*, acting in course of employment and therefore master liable.

20. Harvey v. O'Dell [1958] 2 Q.B. 78; [1958] 1 All E.R. 657, McNair J.

Held, that, following **4** and **5**, servant was acting in course of employment, as his journey was properly part of or fairly incidental to his day's work and, that being so, it was irrelevant whether or not the means of transport had been expressly authorised.

21. Kirby v. N.C.B., (1958) S.C. 514; (1959) S.L.T. 7, 1st Div.

22. Mulholland v. Wm. Reid, (1958) S.C. 290; (1958) S.L.T. 285, 1st Div.

Apprentice moving equipment on employer's premises—found van impeding way—drove it a short distance within premises—no authority to drive—fellow-workman killed as a result—*Held*, employers liable, as conduct of apprentice in driving was reasonably incidental to his work.

23. Tomlinson v. Ellerman's Wilson [1959] 1 Lloyd's Rep. 141, Lord Parker C.J.

Held, defendants liable to plaintiff donkeyman for not warning him throttle lever might kick owing to an erratic governor.

24. Bradford v. Boston Deep Sea Fisheries [1959] 1 Lloyd's Rep. 394, Finnemore J.

25. Hilton v. Burton [1961] 1 W.L.R. 705; [1961] 1 All E.R. 74, Diplock J.

Deceased, H and X all employed by defendants at demolition site—H drove them to a café seven miles away in employers' van to get tea—deceased killed by negligent driving of H—director of defendants said in evidence that he permitted employees to use van for any reasonable purpose, including going to get refreshments—*Held*, the test was not whether the servant was using the vehicle with his master's permission, but whether the servant was doing something which he was employed to do. On the facts H was plainly not doing something which he was employed to do and therefore defendants were not liable.

26. Daniels v. Whetstone Entertainments [1962] 2 Lloyd's Rep. 1, C.A.

Dance hall steward struck plaintiff in dance hall—plaintiff went outside and while talking to friends was struck again by steward—shortly before second assault dance hall manager had seen steward outside in a rage and had told him to go back inside—*Held*, employers of steward liable for first assault, but not for second. Davies L.J. cited with approval the test laid down in *Salmond on Torts* (13th ed.), pp. 122, 123, and said that although the steward's authority did not necessarily terminate at the threshold, here the facts showed that the plaintiff had left and had no intention of returning, and the steward had repudiated the manager's order to return and had instead assaulted the plaintiff as a private act of retaliation; these facts constituted "a complete break between the steward's authorised province of operation and the subsequent events" (8, col. 2). Leading cases are summarised in the judgments.

27. Sidwell v. British Timken (1962) 106 S.J. 243; [1962] C.L.Y. 1137, C.A.

28. Ilkiw v. Samuels [1963] 1 W.L.R. 991; [1963] 2 All E.R. 879, C.A.

S (not employed by defendants) was allowed by defendants' driver to move lorry a few yards—S was quite incompetent and ran down plaintiff—*Held, per* Willmer and Danckwerts L.JJ., lorry driver was negligent in allowing S to drive without inquiry, but in so allowing S he was acting in course of employment, so that defendants were liable. Diplock L.J. arrived at the same result on a somewhat different ground, that is, that the defendants, having put the driver in charge of the lorry, remained liable for the driving of that lorry (except on a frolic), whether it was driven by the driver or by someone whom the driver permitted to drive. With regard to this latter view, Willmer L.J. (883 H) said that this might be correct on the authority of *Ricketts v. Tilling* [1915] 1 K.B. 644, where a bus driver allowed a conductor to drive and the employers were held liable.

29. British Transport Commission v. Maxine [1963] 107 S.J. 1024; [1963] C.L.Y. 1263, McNair J.

Servant under notice went round saying good-bye to workmates—dropped lighted match—*Held*, not in course of employment.

30. Morris v. C. W. Martin [1966] 1 Q.B. 716; [1965] 2 All E.R. 725, C.A.

Held, defendants vicariously liable. "When a principal has in his charge the goods or belongings of another in such circumstances that he is under a duty to take all reasonable precautions to protect them from theft or depredation, then if he entrusts that duty to a servant, he is answerable for the manner in which that servant or agent carries out his duty. If the servant or agent is careless so that they are stolen by a stranger, the master is liable. So also if the servant himself steals them or makes away with them" (Lord Denning M.R., 732 E). Diplock L.J. based his decision on the two duties of a bailee for reward—not to convert the goods and to take reasonable care of them; if he entrusted the goods, and therefore these duties, to a servant, the master would be liable. He emphasised that he was only dealing with a bailee for reward; and reserved the question of a gratuitous bailee. Salmon L.J., in concurring, emphasised that the liability of the master depended solely on the fact that it was the dishonest servant through whom the defendants had chosen to discharge their duty to take reasonable care of the plaintiff's fur. "A theft by a servant who is not employed to do anything in relation to the goods bailed is entirely outside the scope of his employment and cannot make the master liable . . . It might be otherwise if the master knew or ought to have known that his servant was dishonest, because then the master could be liable in negligence for employing him" (74 G-H). *Cheshire v. Bailey* [1905] 1 K.B. 237 *overruled.*

31. O'Reilly v. National Rail and Tramway [1966] 1 All E.R. 499, Nield J.

32. A. & W. Hemphill v. Williams [1966] 2 Lloyd's Rep. 101; [1966] C.L.Y. 4430, H.L. (Scottish case)

33. Kay v. I.T.W. [1968] 1 Q.B. 140; [1967] 3 All E.R. 22, C.A.

A borderline case—O was employed as a general warehouse assistant, and in such employment he normally drove trucks and small vans—O came to the warehouse entrance with a fork-lift truck—found entrance blocked by a lorry not belonging to defendant employers—to clear entrance, O got into lorry and started it up—but it had been left in reverse, because of the slope of the ramp—and the lorry driver and plaintiff, who was employed by defendant, were at the back unloading it—lorry ran down plaintiff—*Held*, O was acting in the course of his employment. Sellers L.J. said it was near the borderline (27 B), but was not so gross and extreme to take the act outside what O was employed to do. Test in *C.P.R. v. Lockhart* **5** applied ("a master is liable for acts which he has not authorised provided that they are so connected with acts which he has authorised that they may rightly be regarded as modes—albeit improper modes—of doing them").

Beard v. L.G.O.C. [1900] 2 Q.B. 530 was considered by Sellers L.J. (25 G; Sachs L.J. concurring, 29 C), and was explained on the basis that the conductor in driving the horse bus may have been regarded as going on an unauthorised jaunt, and that this may have been the reason for holding that he was outside the course of his employment.

34. Vandyke v. Fender [1970] 2 Q.B. 292; [1970] 2 All E.R. 335, C.A.

Held, the driver was not acting "in the course of his employment", for in interpreting this phrase the Workmen's Compensation cases must be followed; but, nevertheless, the employers were liable for the driver's negligence, for he was driving for their purposes and was therefore their agent. **14** was not cited.

35. Boag v. Rogers [1970] N.Z.L.R. 261, Compensation Court

Held, that employee was not in course of employment, even though he was paid a travelling time allowance.

36. Nottingham v. Aldridge [1971] 2 Q.B. 739; [1971] 2 All E.R. 751, Eveleigh J.

37. Stitt v. Woolley (1971) 115 S.J. 708; [1971] C.L.Y. 8041, C.A.

38. Elleanor v. Cavendish Woodhouse (1972) 117 S.J. 14; [1973] 1 Lloyd's Rep. 313, C.A.

39. Iqbal v. London Transport *The Times*, June 7, 1973; [1973] C.L.Y. 2319, C.A.

40. Keppel Bus Co. v. Sa'ad bin Ahmad [1974] 1 W.L.R. 1082; [1974] 2 All E.R. 700, P.C.

"There was no evidence which would justify the ascription of the act of the conductor to any authority, express or implied, vested in him by his employers" (Lord Kilbrandon, 704 E).

41. Stone v. Taffe [1974] 1 W.L.R. 1575; [1974] 3 All E.R. 1016, C.A.

Manager of inn, in breach of express instructions, allowed a party to continue well after closing time—*Held*, he was acting in the course of his employment. Stephenson L.J. (1022 D) adopted the distinction drawn by Lord Dunedin in *Plumb v. Cobden* [1914] A.C. 62 at 67 between "prohibitions which limit the sphere of employment and prohibitions which deal only with conduct within the sphere of employment", and said that the manager's conduct here fell in the second category. But it *seems* (1022 B) that had the prohibition been known, or even if the prohibition was likely to have been known, to the injured party (who fell down unlit stairs), the result would have been different.

42. Compton v. McClure [1975] I.C.R. 378, May J.

M, late for work, drove from factory gates onto factory car park in such a way as to run down plaintiff—*Held*, M was acting in course of employment once he had passed through boundary gates of factory and employers were liable (*sed quaere*).

43. Rose v. Plenty [1976] 1 W.L.R. 141; [1976] 1 All E.R. 97, C.A.

Boy injured when riding on milk float—*Held*, driver was acting in course of employment when giving boy lift, because the prohibited act of allowing the boy to ride was done so that the boy could assist, albeit in a prohibited way, in the job entrusted by the employers to the milkman (Scarman L.J., 104 E). Both Lord Denning M.R. and Scarman L.J. (the other member, Lawton L.J. dissented) *said* that the first question to ask in such cases was whether the employee was himself liable; seen in this light, any question of the boy trespassing on the float became irrelevant, and then to ask whether the employer should shoulder this responsibility. Lord Denning M.R. (101 A) said the answer to this question depended very much on the purpose of the prohibited act; if it was done for the employers' business, the employers would usually be liable. Scarman L.J. said that the test was whether the act of the servant was a mode, albeit a prohibited mode, of doing the job with which he was entrusted, and the answer in the present case (which distinguished it from *Twine* **6** and *Conway* **9**) was Yes (104 D). As a result of the difference between the two L.JJ. in putting the test, Scarman L.J. expressly approved *Iqbal* **39** (inasmuch as a conductor is not entrusted with the job of driving a bus), whereas Lord Denning M.R. thought that the decision was" out of line".

44. Angus v. Glasgow Corporation, 1977 S.L.T. 206; [1977] C.L.Y. 2040, First Div.

45. Harrison v. B.R.B. [1981] 1 All E.R. 679; [1981] C.L.Y. 1833, Boreham J.

46. Kooragang Investments v. Richardson [1982] A.C. 462; [1981] 3 All E.R. 65, P.C.

R, a valuer employed by respondents, became a director of GB at the same time. Respondents had instructed all their valuers (including R) not to do further valuations for GB (because of unpaid bills). R took a sheet of respondents' notepaper and prepared at GB's premises a valuation on the faith of which the appellants lent money to GB. The valuation was negligent and the appellants suffered loss. The respondents knew nothing of the valuation—*Held*, R was acting outside the scope of his employment as a valuer, and the respondents were not liable. "Where, as here, there was no dealing with the servant or agent, and where the issue is one of actual authority or total absence of authority, the case (*i.e. Uxbridge* **2**) gives no support for an argument that authority need not be proved but is to be inferred from the fact that the acts done are of a class which the master could himself have done or entrusted to the servant" (Lord Wilberforce, 71 D).

47. Duffy v. Thanet D.C. (1984) 134 New L.J. 680; [1984] C.L.Y. 2344, McCowan J.

Plaintiff, A and B sent by their employer on course at technical school. B hacked with a chisel at a wooden arch which plaintiff and A were constructing. A grabbed chisel. B let go after a struggle, and chisel hit plaintiff's eye—*Held*:

(a) A negligent in grabbing chisel and precipitating struggle close to other people. A's employers vicariously liable—had arch been dented by chisel, A's marks could have been downgraded, which would not have been in his employers' interests—it was a case of a stupid mode of doing an authorised act for A's employers' business. (*Rose v. Plenty* (**43** above) applied).
(b) B's act was unauthorised and independent of his employment. His employers not vicariously liable. (*O'Reilly v. National Rail and Tramway* (**31** above) applied).

48. Harrison v. Michelin Tyre Co. Ltd [1985] I.C.R. 696; [1985] 1 All E.R. 918, Comyn J.

An employee at defendant's factory, for what he saw as a joke, pushed truck some two inches outside the bounds of a marked passageway under a duckboard on which plaintiff was standing. Duckboard tipped up—plaintiff fell and was injured. Considering whether defendant vicariously liable, Comyn J. asked whether incident was "part and parcel of the employment in the sense of being incidental to it although and albeit unauthorised or prohibited" or "so divergent from the employment as to be plainly alien to and wholly distinguishable from the employment"—*Held*, on the facts, the former applied and thus defendant was vicariously liable.

49. Aldred v. Nacanco [1987] I.R.L.R. 292; [1987] C.L.Y. 1367, C.A.

In washroom of defendant's premises, employee X pushed slightly unstable washbasin against plaintiff's thigh, to startle her. Plaintiff turned quickly and in doing so injured her back which was known to defendant to be vulnerable—*Held*, defendant not liable because:

(a) Place of work not unsafe—not reasonably foreseeable that condition of washbasin might cause injury.
(b) X's act was unauthorised and wrongful, unconnected with X's employment, for which defendant not vicariously liable. *Per* Lawton L.J. (at 295, paragraph 15): " . . . the correct principle of law . . . is that set out in the 18th edition of *Salmond on Torts* at p. 437 . . . : 'a master is responsible not merely for what he authorises his servant to do, but also for the way in which he does it. If a servant does negligently that which he was authorised to do carefully, or if he does fraudulently that which he was authorised to do honestly, or if he does mistakenly that which he was authorised to do correctly, his master will answer for that negligence, fraud or mistake. On the other hand, if the unauthorised and wrongful act of the servant is not so connected with the authorised act as to be a mode of doing it, but is an independent act, the master is not responsible: for in such a case the servant is not acting in the course of his employment, but has gone outside of it." ' *Per* Lord Donaldson M.R. (at 295–296): the test in *Salmond* (above) is to be preferred to that formulated by Comyn J. in *Harrison v. Michelin Tyre Co. Ltd* (**48** above).

50. Smith v. Stages [1989] A.C. 928; [1989] 1 All E.R. 833, H.L.

Plaintiff and fellow employee sent from the Midlands to do urgent work at a power station in Wales—paid travelling time, but mode of travel left to them. They went in fellow employee's car. Having worked 19 of the 24 hours before finishing the job, they drove straight back. As they did so, car left road due to fellow employee's negligence—*Held*:

(a) by Court of Appeal, plaintiff not contributorily negligent in travelling with fellow employee knowing he had insufficient rest;
(b) by Court of Appeal and House of Lords, the mens' employers were vicariously liable for fellow employee's negligence. The men were paid wages to travel and the travel was part of their duties performed in the cause of their employment. *Per* Lord Lowry at 851b: "The paramount rule is that an employee travelling on the highway will be acting in the course of his employment if and only if he is at the material time going about his employer's business. One must not confuse the duty to turn up for one's work with the concept of already being 'on duty' while travelling to it." (More detailed prima facie propositions are set out at 851c–f.)

51. Reilly v. Ryan [1991] 2 I.R. 247; [1992] C.L.Y. 3263, Blayney J.

During robbery at licensed premises, manager seized plaintiff customer to protect himself from robber and plaintiff was stabbed. Plaintiff sued manager's employers—*Held*, manager's acts fell outside class of acts impliedly authorised—employers not vicariously liable.

U1. Shapiro v. Jay (1954) C.A. 311

Defendant asked to repair plaintiff's wireless set—sent round boy to do so—plaintiff later asked boy to move it—boy put it on metal shelf connected with towel rail in bathroom so that plaintiff had electric shock when touching rail—*Held*, defendant not liable as boy not acting within scope of authority as he was sent to repair and not move wireless set.

U2. Colving v. Charles Griffiths Ltd (1956) C.A. 289

Parker L.J. (11): 'Where a workman is found during working hours having fallen from his place of work, the scale must go down, in the first instance at any rate, very heavily in favour of his having been acting in the course of his employment.'

U3. Peel Ltd v. Cartwright (1957) C.A. 197

U4. Pentonville Motors v. Thompson (1958) C.A. 75

Held, employee neither acting in course of employment nor as agent for employer (even though employer benefited by removal of employee's car from his premises).

U5. Stallard v. William Whiteley (1960) C.A. 312

Driver made small deviation on his way to depot to stop at public-house and to drop a friend at his house—*Held*, still acting in course of employment.

U6. Pickard v. National Coal Board (1961) C.A. 165

Stampede to get into pit cage about to go up—plaintiff injured—*Held*, defendants not liable, as (a) stampede not foreseeable, and therefore no failure of system, and (b) the men stampeding were not doing an authorised act in an unauthorised way, but were doing a wholly unauthorised act, and therefore defendants were not vicariously liable.

U7. Spencer v. Curtis (1962) C.A. 170

Harvesting—defendant's servant takes a gun with him which goes off in circumstances unexplained—*Held*, defendant liable for negligence of servant.

U8. Tyler v. Condray (1965) C.A. 162B

U9. O'Connor v. United Bisuits (1982) C.A. U.B. 542

U10. Stenner v. Taff-Ely B.C. (1987) C.A. 534

Gymnastic coach employed by defendant invited plaintiff to defendant's leisure centre when closed to the public. The centre's manager gave permission. Plaintiff, who made no payment, was injured using a trampette—*Held*, the coach was not acting in the course of his employment, and defendant not liable.

(c) Ostensible Scope of Authority

		Whether within scope of authority or not
Ship's crew—inviting stevedores to load onto hatch covers	1	No
Servant inviting plaintiff to make extraordinary use of premises	1	No
SOLICITOR'S CLERK—PRODUCING DEED	2	Yes
ADMISSION—MADE BY SERVANT BEFORE HEARING	3	No
admission—made by servant in evidence	4	No
FOREMAN—ARRANGING TRANSPORT FOR WORKMEN	5	Yes
Knowledge of manual employee of danger—not to be imputed to employing company	6	
Knowledge of chargehand of defect—to be imputed to employing company	7	

Radio mechanic moving radio at householder's request—after repairing it .... UI No

1. Hillen v. I.C.I. [1936] A.C. 65, H.L.

Plaintiff a stevedore at the suggestion or invitation of member of crew used hatch cover to load cargo onto and from—it gave way—*Held*, shipowner not liable as plaintiff was a trespasser. Lord Atkin (70): "It (any invitation by crew to use hatch cover) was wholly without the authority of the owners, and quite outside the ostensible scope of authority of the crew. The owner of a barge does not clothe the crew with apparent authority to use it or any part of it for purposes which are known to be extraordinary or dangerous. The crew could not within the scope of their authority convert it into a dancing hall or drinking booth. They could not invite stevedores to work the engines or take part in the navigation. The most that could be said of the engineer is that, if he saw a trespasser unwittingly entering into danger upon the employer's property, he might owe a moral duty to the trespasser to warn him. But for breach of a servant's moral duty, an employer is not vicariously liable."

2. Uxbridge Building Society v. Pickard [1939] 2 All E.R. 344, C.A.

Solicitor's managing clerk produces to plaintiff a deed which he must have known to be forged—*Held*, master was liable because clerk was acting within his ostensible authority.

3. Burr v. Ware R.D.C. [1939] 2 All E.R. 688, C.A.

Plaintiff in a running-down case sought to interrogate defendants' driver as to what he had said at inquest—driver was not joined as a defendant—*Held*, interrogatories would not be allowed. Sir Wilfrid Greene M.R. (689 G): "... admissions by the lorry driver would not be evidence against the defendants in the absence of proof to that effect (*i.e.*, that driver was an agent to make admissions)."

4. Glasgow Corporation v. Muir [1943] A.C. 448; [1943] 2 All E.R. 44, H.L.

In evidence defendants' servant said that, if she had been warned, she "certainly would have got them (the children) from the entrance" (451). On this, Lord Thankerton (455) said: "It is not an admission in the sense that it can bind the appellants, though it may be of some little value as to what the ordinary person would regard a reasonable standard of care. For myself, I regard it of little value ... in assisting the court. ..."

5. Young v. Edward Box [1951] 1 T.L.R. 789, C.A.

Defendants' foreman without authority arranged for lorry to take men, including plaintiff, home—*Held*, the act was within the ostensible authority of the foreman, and defendants were liable.

6. O'Reilly v. National Rail and Tramway [1966] 1 All E.R. 499, Nield J.

Place of work alleged to be unsafe, because a live shell was delivered with some scrap—presence of shell was known to two manual labourers, but not to any chargehand or foreman—*Held*, that such knowledge could not be imputed to the employing company.

7. Taylor v. Rover [1966] 1 W.L.R. 1491; [1966] 2 All E.R. 181, Baker J.

Defective chisel—previous accident to chargehand from same chisel—*Held*, that employers were liable for failure of chargehand to take action to withdraw chisel after his accident.

U1. Shapiro v. Jay (1954) C.A. 311 A

Defendant asked to repair plaintiff's wireless set—sent round boy to do so—plaintiff later asked boy to move it—boy put it on metal shelf connected with towel rail in bathroom so that plaintiff had electric shock when touching rail—*Held*, defendant not liable as boy not acting within scope of authority as he was sent to repair and not move wireless set.

(d) Loan of Servant

(*N.B.* For cases where the servant himself is plaintiff, see under Chap. 15, (1) (c).)

		Whether general (G) or temporary (T) employer liable
HIRE OF LORRY AND DRIVER	1	G
Carrying goods under running agreement	2	G
HIRE OF LORRY AND DRIVER	3	G
Hire of crane and driver	4	G
General principles stated	4	
Terms of contract of hiring—irrelevant	4	
Loan of driver by motor repairers to drive plaintiff in own car	5	G
Test may be different when servant himself is injured—instead of third party	6	G
Terms of contract of hiring—may determine liability of employers *inter se*	7	
Tug and tow—position of tugmaster	8	G
Control the test—not contract of service	8	
Hire of crane and driver	9	G
Loan of driver—to drive lorry owned by person borrowing driver	10	T
EMPLOYEES OF SUB-CONTRACTOR FOR LABOUR ONLY—MAY BE TEMPORARY SERVANTS OF MAIN CONTRACTOR	11	T?
LOAN OF EXCAVATOR AND DRIVER—BORROWER GIVING DETAILED INSTRUCTIONS AS TO METHOD OF WORK	12	G
Temporary employer only liable if he has entire and absolute control	13	
LOAN OF CRANE AND OPERATOR	14	G

1. Willard v. Whiteley [1938] 3 All E.R. 779, C.A.

Held, that driver during hire of lorry still continued to be employed by owners, being his general employers.

2. Century Insurance v. Northern Ireland R.T.B. [1942] A.C. 509; [1942] 1 All E.R. 491, H.L.

Defendants were hauliers carrying petrol for X under a running agreement (not an agreement for hiring) whereby defendants' drivers were to accept and obey all orders given by X—*Held*, driver was still defendants' servant, being only subject to X's orders as far as was necessary to enable defendants to carry out contract.

3. Bontex v. St. Johns [1944] 1 All E.R. 381, C.A.

4. M.D.H.B. v. Coggins & Griffiths [1947] A.C. 1; [1946] 2 All E.R. 345, H.L.

Held, driver remained servant of general employer. The agreement of hiring was immaterial, as the question depended on the circumstances of the case. Lord Simon (348 H) said the test turned on where the authority lay to direct, or to delegate to, the workman the manner in which the vehicle was driven. "The ultimate question is not what specific orders, or whether any specific orders, were given, but who is entitled to give the orders as to how the work should be done" (Lord Porter, 351 G). Applied by H.L. in **9**.

5. Chowdary v. Gillot [1947] 2 All E.R. 541; 63 T.L.R. 569, Streatfeild J.

Plaintiff took car for repair—after handing it over asked for "lift" to station—defendants, repairers, supplied driver to drive plaintiff in own car—*Held*, following **4**, defendants having received car were bailees, and plaintiff having no right to control bailees' servants, the driver remained servant of defendants.

6. Garrard v. Southey [1952] 2 Q.B. 174; [1952] 1 All E.R. 597, Parker J.

Suggested that the test in cases where servant injured self might be different from those where third party has been injured. See further under Chap. 15, (1) (c) **2**.

7. Herdman v. Walker [1956] 1 W.L.R. 307; [1956] 1 All E.R. 429, Pearce J.

8. The Panther [1957] P. 143; [1957] 1 All E.R. 641, Willmer J.

Tugowners attempt to say not liable for negligence of master, as master was *pro hac vice* servant of tow—*Held*, not so, whatever the contract of towage might say. "The position would, I apprehend, be different if the faulty manoeuvre were one within the province of the pilot or officer in charge of the tow, *e.g.*, if the tug failed to carry out an order, or negligently executed without orders a manoeuvre which it was within the province of those in charge of the tow to order" (648 B).

9. John Young v. O'Donnell, 1958 S.L.T. 46, H.L.

Held, applying **4**, crane driver remained servant of general employer.

10. McGregor v. Duthie, 1966 S.L.T. 133; [1966] C.L.Y. 4434, Ct. of Sess.

Driver in general employment of partnership who were engaged in sawing timber for a company—driver was lent to drive company lorry on company business—*Held*, he was *pro hac vice* employed by company.

11. McArdle v. Andmac [1967] 1 W.L.R. 356; [1967] 1 All E.R. 583, C.A.

Sellers L.J. *obiter* suggested this (586 I), but the point was not pleaded.

12. County Plant Hire v. Jackson (1970) 8 K.I.R. 989; [1970] C.L.Y. 1877, C.A.

Loan of excavator and driver by L to J—J wanted driver to use excavator as a lifting device to move a loader-screener—gave driver detailed instructions as to how to do it—which driver negligently disobeyed—and damaged loader-screener—J sued L for the damage—*Held*, L was liable. A transfer of employment could not occur merely because J gave driver more detailed instructions than he was entitled to give.

13. Bhoomidas v. Port of Singapore [1978] 1 All E.R. 956, P.C.

". . . partial control by the hirer is not enough but . . . entire and absolute control is necessary in order to transfer liability . . . " (Lord Salmon, 959 G).

14. McConkey v. AMEC Plc *The Times*, February 28 1990; [1990] C.L.Y. 3325, C.A.

Owners of crane hired it under contract which provided that they should also "supply a person competent in operating the plant", such person "to be regarded as the [servant] or [agent] of the hirer . . . who alone shall be responsible for all claims arising in connection with the operation of the plant by the said [driver] or [operator]." When crane was operated by a driver whom trial judge held to be incompetent, fly-jib buckled and crane's load fell onto plaintiff—*Held*, since driver was not competent, contractual provisions referred to above did not apply; thus owners remained vicariously liable for drivers' negligence; and hirers not liable to indemnify owners in respect of their liability to plaintiff.

(2) Agents

		Whether agent or not
Commercial traveller—driving own car	1	No
Driver—owner not in car	2	No
DRIVER—OWNER NOT IN CAR	3	No
Driver—owner not in car	4	Yes
BUYER'S CREW—SHIP DOING TRIALS—STILL IN BUILDER'S HANDS	5	No
DRIVER—OWNER NOT IN CAR	6	Yes
Driver—owner-passenger	7	Yes
LICENSED PORTER—DRIVING DEFENDANT'S BOGIE	8	No
Party of four going on trip—driver is agent for each member	9	Yes
Scoutmaster—not an agent for Boy Scout's Association	10	No
Builder—building house for local authority	11	No
FATHER ARRANGING THAT EMPLOYEE DRIVE SON IN EVENINGS	12	Yes
EMPLOYER—PROVIDING EMPLOYEE WITH CAR TO DRIVE OTHERS TO WORK	13	Yes
Presumption—is that car is driven on behalf of owner	14	
Friend—borrowing car without consent—told to return it—accident while doing so	15	No
Employer—one employee driving another to work—in own car—whether agent of employer	16	No
Permission—not to be equated with agency—agency only if principal authorised act—and authorised on own behalf	17	
Wife—lending husband car—husband getting friend to drive him home because of drink—whether friend agent of wife	17	No
POLICEMAN—ACTING MINISTERIALLY ON AUTHORISATION OF DEFENDANT	18	Yes
FATHER—BOOKING HOLIDAY FOR FAMILY—IS NOT THEIR AGENT—BUT IS ABLE TO RECOVER DAMAGES FOR THEIR LOSS	19	

1. Egginton v. Reader [1936] 1 All E.R. 7; 52 T.L.R. 212, Lewis J.

Commercial traveller—owner-driver—commission plus £1 per week towards petrol—could take orders from other firms as well—*Held*, not servant or agent of defendant. Tests propounded by McCardie J. in *Performing Right Society v. Mitchell* [1924] 1 K.B. 762 applied.

2. Daniels v. Vaux [1938] 2 K.B. 203; [1938] 2 All E.R. 271, Humphreys J.

Mother lends car to son to drive more or less as his own—*Held*, son not the agent of mother.

3. Hewitt v. Bonvin [1940] 1 K.B. 188; 56 T.L.R. 43, C.A.

Father lends car—son driving for own purposes—*Held*, son not agent of father.

4. Smith v. Moss [1940] 1 K.B. 424; [1940] 1 All E.R. 469, Charles J.

Car belonged to mother-in-law of driver—driver drove her and his own wife from party—dropped mother-in-law—then proceeded home with wife—while doing so had accident causing injury to wife—*Held*, driver was agent for mother-in-law, who was accordingly liable. *N.B.* The point in this case arose from the rule that a wife could not sue husband in tort, but this rule has been abolished, in respect of causes of action arising on or after August 1, 1962, by the Law Reform (Husband and Wife) Act 1962, s. 1.

5. Hobson v. Bartram [1950] 1 All E.R. 412; [1950] W.N. 174, C.A.

Buyer's crew leave hatch open during trials—*Held*, they were not agents of defendants, who consequently were not liable. See Chap. 5 (3)(a) **6**, which was distinguished by C.A.

6. Ormrod v. Crosville Motor Services [1953] 1 W.L.R. 1120; [1953] 2 All E.R. 65, C.A.

Driver was driving car to Monte Carlo where owner would meet it and take it over to enter in rally—accident on way down—*Held*, as car being used wholly or partly for purposes of owner, driver was agent of owner. *Approved* in **17**.

7. Trust Company v. De Silva [1956] 1 W.L.R. 376; [1956] 1 Lloyd's Rep. 309, P.C.

8. Norton v. Canadian Pacific Steamships [1961] 1 W.L.R. 1057; [1961] 2 All E.R. 795, C.A.

A licensed self-employed porter at Liverpool landing stage negligently drove a bogie into plaintiff—the bogie, which was owned by the defendants, was one of a number provided by shipowners and others for the porters to use—*Held*, the porter in question was not the agent of the defendants, and the defendants were not liable for his negligence. *Ormrod v. Crossville* **6** distinguished on the ground that there the journey was for the joint purposes of both, whereas the user of the bogie in the present case was not. "There was no delegation of the driving of the bogies, which was the basis of the decisions in *Hewitt v. Bonvin* **3** and *Ormrod v. Crosville* **6**" (Sellers L. J. at 788 H).

9. Scarsbrook v. Mason [1961] 3 All E.R. 767, Glyn Jones J.

Car struck plaintiff on pavement—it had been taken away without consent of owner—defendant was one of the passengers, who had been picked up without knowing how car had been acquired—invited to go in a party to Southend, paying towards cost of petrol—*Held*, driver was acting as agent for each and all members of the party, and accordingly defendant was liable for negligent driving of driver.

10. Murphy v. Zoological Society *The Times*, November 14, 1962; [1962] C.L.Y. 68, Fenton Atkinson J.

11. Sharpe v. Sweeting [1963] 1 W.L.R. 665; [1963] 2 All E.R. 455, Nield J.

Builder building house for local authority *held* to be independent contractor and not agent. *N.B.* In *Travers v. Gloucester Corporation* [1946] 2 All E.R. at 513 it was, on similar facts, conceded that the builder was an agent.

12. Carberry v. Davies [1968] 1 W.L.R. 1103; [1968] 2 All E.R. 817, C.A.

13. Vandyke v. Fender [1970] 2 Q.B. 292; [1970] 2 All E.R. 335, C.A.

14. Ramburran v. Gurrucharran [1970] 1 W.L.R. 556; [1970] 1 All E.R. 749, P.C.

15. Klein v. Calouri [1971] 1 W.L.R. 619; [1971] 2 All E.R. 701, Lyell J.

16. Nottingham v. Aldridge [1971] 2 Q.B. 739; [1971] 2 All E.R. 751, Eveleigh J.

17. Morgans v. Launchbury [1973] A.C. 127; [1972] 2 All E.R. 606, H.L.

Wife lent husband car—having previously asked that if husband had too much to drink he should get friend to drive—husband did both these—friend had collision—*Held*, friend was not agent of wife, as it was merely a case of giving permission, which was not the same as agency. *Ormrod* **6** expressly approved. Dictum of du Parcq L. J. in *Hewitt* **3** approved as providing proper test:

> "The driver of a car may not be the owner's servant, and the owner will nevertheless be liable for his negligence if it be proved that at the material time he had authority, express or implied, to drive on the owner's behalf. Such liability depends not on ownership, but on the delegation of a task or duty."

18. Ansell v. Thomas [1974] Crim. L.R. 31, C.A.

19. Jackson v. Horizon Holidays [1975] 1 W.L.R. 1468; [1975] 3 All E.R. 92, C.A.

20. S. v. Walsall M. B. C. [1985] 1 W.L.R. 1150; [1985] 3 All E.R. 294, C.A.

Child taken into care and boarded out to foster parents by local authority pursuant to statutory powers; there child suffered severe burns to feet—*Held*, relationship between child and local authority regulated solely by statutory scheme and foster parents therefore were not to be treated as its agents and it was not vicariously liable for the negligence of either foster parent.

U1. Pentonville Motors v. Thompson (1958) C.A. 75

Held, employee neither acting in course of employment nor as an agent for employer (even though employer benefited by removal of employee's car from his premises).

U2. Whittington v. Emile (1963) C.A. 302 B

Held, applying *Ormrod* **6**, son was agent of father, as father had dual interest in journey (a) in finding out if car was suitable for son, and (b) in getting son to come to office, in order to interest him in family business. *But* now see **17**.

U3. Britter v. Robert Marriott (1974) C.A. 75

Employee of labour-only sub-contractors drove defendants' dumper in order to unload lorry for defendants—*Held*, defendants liable for negligence of employee as their agent.

U4. Boston v. Karayiannis (1975) C.A. 144

Owner lent driver van so that (a) driver could go to inspect a van he wanted to buy, and (b) driver could also drive owner home—*Held*, the dual purpose of the journey did not prevent driver from being agent of owner. *N.B.* In any event, owner was in van at the time of the accident.

U5. Stephenson v. John Williams (1977) C.A. 112

Lorry driver collecting steel from stockist—helps stockists' men to carry load to lorry—is negligent in doing so—*Held*, lorry driver was not agent of stockist. Megaw L.J. (14 F) *said* that in a case like this the question of control was really vital, and that there was no question here of the stockist having control over the lorry driver.

(3) Independent Contractors

(a) General Principles

(*N.B.* Formerly the liability of an occupier for acts of an independent contractor was in doubt; see *Thomson v. Cremin* **10** on the one hand and *Haseldine v. Daw* **4** on the other. Since January 1, 1958 the Occupiers' Liability Act 1957, s. 2(4) has in effect confirmed *Haseldine* and overruled *Thomson v. Cremin*, so far as the latter relates to the duty of an occupier. For cases on the liablility of employers for independent contractors, see also 15(1)(d).)

1. Daniel v. Rickett Cockerell [1938] 2 K.B. 322; [1938] 2 All E.R. 631, C.A.

Coal supplier leaves flap in pavement open—plaintiff falls down—*Held*, occupier liable, as act of independent contractor no defence. *Approved* and *explained* in **3**.

2. Paine v. Colne Valley Elec. [1938] 4 All E.R. 803; 106 L.T. 124, Goddard L.J.

Workman killed by live busbar—*Held*, defendants, the employers, could not delegate their duty of providing a safe place of work and therefore it was no defence to say that they had employed competent contractors to instal the plant.

3. Wilkinson v. Rea [1941] 1 K.B. 688; [1941] 2 All E.R. 50, C.A.

Coal contractors negligent in removal of hatch cover, and failure to guard hatch—are shipowners liable to their invitee? *Held*, yes, following *Daniel v. Rickett Cockerell* **1**, the *ratio decidendi* being explained by Luxmoore L.J. as being that the contractors were employed by the shipowners to do a job which created a danger, and therefore owners were liable, but *aliter* if the job involved no inherent danger, but only became dangerous because of some casual neglect by the contractors (60 H). 75 per cent. against contractor, 25 per cent. against shipowners. *Approved* by H.L. in **10**.

4. Haseldine v. Daw [1941] 2 K.B. 343; [1941] 3 All E.R. 156, C.A.

Visitor to flat injured by landlord's lift—landlord employs competent lift repairers—*Held*, that if plaintiff invitee (which was doubtful) landlord not liable, and *a fortiori* if plaintiff licensee. *Distinguished* in *Bloomstein*, Chap. 5, (3) (b) **12**. *Followed* in **12** below.

5. The Pass of Ballater [1942] P. 112; [1942] 2 All E.R. 79, Langton J.

Shipowner, relying on certificate of safety given by independent contractors, allows workmen on board—petrol vapour causes explosion—*Held*, certificate no defence and defendants liable.

6. Woodward v. Mayor of Hastings [1944] 2 All E.R. 565, C.A.

Negligent school cleaner—school governors say she was an independent contractor—*Held*, that she was still performing a duty which was incumbent on defendants, and therefore defendants could not rely on defence of independent contractor. See *Hobson*, Chap. 5 (2) **5**, where it was distinguished by C.A.

7. Spicer v. Smee [1946] 1 All E.R. 489, Atkinson J.

Held, act of independent contractor no defence in nuisance.

8. Darling v. Att.-Gen. [1950] 2 All E.R. 793, Morris J.

9. Waddle v. Wallsend Shipping [1952] 2 Lloyd's Rep. 105, Devlin J.

Sinking of ship—member of crew drowned—judge found ship not as safe as she might have been, due to (a) an oversight during building by the Lloyd's surveyor, and (b) a failure during subsequent repairs by the repairers to give adequate information to the Lloyd's surveyor—*Held*, that the shipowners were not liable for (a), but were liable for (b).

10. Thomson v. Cremin [1956] 1 W.L.R. 103, [1953] 2 All E.R. 1185; H.L.

Wooden shore insecurely fixed by shipwrights in Australia—falls on plaintiff when unloading ship—*Held*, shipowners were liable for negligence of shipwrights. **3** approved. The H.L. treated the case as one of fact rather than law but Lord Simon (with whose speech Lord Romer concurred) and Lord Wright both said, in effect, that it was no defence for the shipowner to rely on independent contractor and Lord Wright (1191 H) went further and said that the invitor could never rely on defence of independent contractor with regard to unsafety of premises. This has been criticised, and it is suggested that defence of independent contractor is still available where independent contractor is employed to do technical work of a character usually entrusted to independent contractors. Followed in *Keen*, Chap. 5, (3) (b) **15**. This decision has been criticised in **14**, and Lord Wright's dicta are no longer binding.

11. Balfour v. Barty-King [1957] 1 Q.B. 496; [1957] 1 All E.R. 156, C.A.

See Chap. 8, (2) (b) **7**.

12. Green v. Fibreglass [1958] 2 Q.B. 245; [1958] 2 All E.R. 521, Salmon J.

Defendants were tenants of offices since 1951—had premises rewired by competent electricians—plaintiff an invitee injured when touching an electric fire which though off was live—defendants had no reason to suspect defect—did not regularly inspect wiring—*Held*, defendants not liable, as they had discharged their duty by employing competent independent contractors, since electric wiring required technical knowledge which defendants could not possess themselves. **4** followed. **10** distinguished and dictum of Lord Wright therein at 1191 H criticised. *Re* employer's duty, "the master too owes special duties to his servant which he cannot delegate" (525 D).

13. Walsh v. Holst [1958] 1 W.L.R. 800; [1958] 3 All E.R. 33; C.A.

For details see Chap. 3, (1)(e) **5**—Hodson L.J. (36 G) cites with approval following extract from *Penny v. Wimbledon U.C.* [1899] 2 Q.B. 72, 78:

> "When a person through a contractor does work which from its nature is liable to cause injury to others, there is a duty on his part to take all reasonable precautions against such danger, and he does not escape from liability for the discharge of that duty by employing the contractor if the latter does not take these precautions . . . Accidents arising from . . . casual or collateral negligence . . . do not come within this rule."

Morris L.J. (38 B), who agreed on this point but dissented on main issue, cited Denning L.J. in *Cassidy v. M/H* [1951] 1 All E.R. 574, 586:

> " . . . Where a person is himself under a duty to use care he cannot get rid of his responsibility by delegating the performance of it to someone else, no matter whether . . . to a servant . . . or an independent contractor."

14. Davie v. New Merton Board Mills [1959] A.C. 604; [1959] 1 All E.R. 346; H.L.

The question was whether an employer was liable for the negligence of a manufacturer in the manufacture of a defective tool. Lord Reid *examined* the decision in *Thomson v. Cremin* **10** and (367 B) pointed out that the shipowner never pleaded act of independent contractor as a defence, and therefore any observations on the matter must be *obiter*. He thought that the decision was probably explicable on the ground that the shipowner knew or ought to have known of the negligence of the independent contractor, and that for this reason the shipowner admitted he could not rely on act of independent contractor. At 367 G he expressed doubt whether Lord Wright's dicta could be reconciled with the duty of an invitor as laid down in *Indermaur v. Dawes*, but left this point open for decision when it should arise.

15. Sullivan v. Gallagher, 1959 S.C. 243, 2nd Div.

Defective electric truck causes injury to driver—trucks were hired out by J.S. to employers to be driven by employees of latter—*Held*, following *Davie* **14**, employers not liable for negligence of J.S.

16. Wingfield v. Ellerman's Wilson [1960] 2 Lloyd's Rep. 16, C.A.

Plaintiff employed by defendant shipowners to unload tomatoes from ship to lighter—lightermen had erected ladder from ship to lighter which was insecure—ladder slipped and threw plaintiff—*Held*, defendants were liable, as the safety of access from ship to lighter was something which should have been attended to by employers. Defendants argued that the fact that it was the invariable practice of the lightermen to provide the ladder relieved them of liability—*Held*, not. On this Devlin L.J. (22, col. 2) said: "In my view it (the practice) makes no difference at all. An invariable practice is only an agreement which has lasted for a considerable time . . . Since the provision of a ladder comes within those things which a prudent employer would order or require to be done before he is satisfied that arrangements have been made for the safety of his men, then it follows that a person acting in pursuance of that agreement is his agent *pro hac vice* for discharging his duty."

17. Riverstone Meat Co. v. Lancashire Shipping Co. [1961] A.C. 807; [1961] 1 All E.R. 495, H.L.

Held, that shipowners were liable, under their statutory duty (arising from the Hague Rules) to exercise due diligence to make the ship seaworthy, for the negligence of a fitter employed by ship repairers. Lord Simonds said that no one doubted that in some cases a defendant would not be liable for the negligence of an independent contractor, while in others he would, and that, without attempting to reconcile all the cases on the subject, it was patent that here the obligation of the shipowner came into the latter category.

18. Summer v. Wm. Henderson [1964] 1 Q.B. 450; [1963] 1 All E.R. 408, Phillimore J.

Shop fire—death of employee—plaintiff husband of employee alleged that start of fire was due to negligent electrical installation, and that spread of fire was due to negligent construction of premises—on the assumption, agreed between the parties for the purpose of argument, that these allegations were well founded, an issue was raised as to whether in such circumstances, the employer shopkeepers were liable for the negligence of the contractors responsible—*Held*, defendants were liable for the negligence (if any) of (a) consultant electrical engineer, (b) electrical contractors, (c) architect, and (d) builders, but not for that (if any) of the manufacturer of the cable in question. On appeal [1963] 2 All E.R. 712, the order was *discharged* on the ground that the issue, being based on hypothetical facts, was premature. No opinion was expressed by C.A. on merits of issue.

19. Sharpe v. Sweeting [1963] 1 W.L.R. 665; [1963] 2 All E.R. 455, Nield J.

Held, independent contractor.

20. John Carter v. Hanson Haulage [1965] 2 Q.B. 495; [1965] 1 All E.R. 113, C.A.

Sellers L.J. (119 F), *obiter*: "*Wilsons v. English* [1938] A.C. 57 establishes the position between master and servant. The duty is there described as a personal duty of the master to take reasonable care for the safety of his workmen and the general duty is conveniently described as comprising three obligations, one of which is to select proper and competent persons to perform the employer's work. This duty cannot be delegated in the sense that the extent of the duty is such that it is not performed if reasonable care has not been taken either by the employer himself or by anyone to whom the task has been delegated. The employer cannot divest himself of responsibility by leaving it to others. Lord Wright pointed out, however, that there may be in the case of plant mere misuse or failure to use proper plant and appliances by a servant's negligence or a failure to keep in order or adjust it and he described this as casual negligence of servants, in contrast to 'personal negligence,' the direct responsibility of the employer."

21. Taylor v. Rover [1966] 1 W.L.R. 1491; [1966] 2 All E.R. 181, Baker J.

22. B.R.S. v. Arthur Crutchley [1968] 1 All E.R. 811, C.A.

All three L.JJ. expressly *agreed* (although the question was strictly *obiter*) that a bailee warehouseman was liable for the negligence of an independent contractor or his servants whom the bailee had engaged to patrol his premises.

23. Cook v. Broderip (1968) 112 S.J. 193; [1968] C.L.Y. 2690, O'Connor J.

Owner of flat employed independent contractor to put in new switch fuse—latter failed to test for reversed polarity—with result that cleaner employed by flatowner got an electric shock—*Held*, flatowner not liable for negligence of independent contractor. *Green* **12** and *Davie* **14** *applied*.

24. Salsbury v. Woodland [1970] 1 Q.B. 324, [1969] 3 All E.R. 863; C.A.

Held, houseowner was not liable for negligence of independent contractor. *Per* Widgery L.J., the cases where a principal had been liable for negligence of independent contractor in similar cases were all either examples of "extra-hazardous acts" or where the work was being done under statutory powers and would have constituted a nuisance but for the statutory powers.

25. Bluett v. King Core Demolition (1973) 227 E.G. 503; [1974] C.L.Y. 2598, Boreham J.

Building developers engaged contractors to do demolition work—which they did so negligently as to damage plaintiff's property—it was claimed that the work was "extra-hazardous" so that the developers also would be liable—*Held*, not, since for the extra-hazardous exception to apply there must be inherent danger, so that however careful the operator is the danger still subsists.

26. Rogers v. Night Riders [1983] R.T.R. 324; [1983] C.L.Y. 2549, C.A.

Defendants held themselves out as providing private hire-taxi service. They did not own vehicles, but operated through a network of independent owner/drivers. Plaintiff's mother booked minicab for plaintiff with defendants—plaintiff injured in course of journey due to fault in minicab. Argued that defendants could not be liable for default of independent contractor—*Held*, that the defendants were under a primary duty to the plaintiff to take reasonable care to provide her with safe transport and, as the duty was non-delegable, they were liable.

27. Equitable Debenture Assets Corporation Ltd v. William Moss Group [1983] 2 Con L.R.1; [1985] C.L.Y. 221, Judge Newey Q.C.

Architect employed to design and supervise erection of curtain walling to be erected by subcontractor. In the absence of agreement, he could not delegate such duties to others.
For further details see Chap. 18(6) **39**.

28. Cynat Products Ltd v. Landbuild (Investment & Property) Ltd [1984] 3 All E.R. 513; [1984] C.L.Y. 2283, Judge Sir William Stabb Q.C.

See, for details, Chap. 18(6) **36**.

29. D. & F. Estates Ltd v. Church Commissioners for England [1989] A.C. 177; [1988] 2 All E.R. 992, H.L.

Mere fact of main contractor employing sub-contractor does not import the concept that he has assumed a personal duty to all the world to ensure that the building should be free of dangerous effects and that he is under a non-delegable duty.

30. Borge v. Matthews [1988] C.L.Y. 2450, Judge Watkin Powell

D liable for tort of independent contractor in respect of fire where his contractor negligently causes fire to escape from D's land and damage adjoining property See also Chap. 8, (4) **34** and Chap. 1, (2)(d) **13**.

31. Luxmoore-May v. Messenger May Baverstocks [1990] 1 W.L.R. 1009, [1990] 1 All E.R. 1067, C.A.

Auctioneer and valuer being asked to value paintings took advice from their consultant, an independent contractor; he advised a value of between £30 and £40, the paintings were sold at auction by the defendants for £840 and subsequently at Sothebys as the work of George Stubbs for £88,000—*Held, inter alia*, that, a personal duty of care having been assumed, it was not discharged by employing an independent contractor unless he himself was not personally negligent; further that the consultant had not in the circumstances been proved negligent and the plaintiff's claim failed. For further details see Chap. 18, (5) **45**.

32. Alcock v. Wraith (1992) 59 B.L.R. 16, [1992] C.L.Y. 3264, C.A.

Terrace house owners employ independent contractor to reroof using tiles instead of slates; difficulty and failure to effect waterproof join with neighbour's roof; owners held to be under non-delegable duty to ensure the roofing work was done with proper care.

U1. Smith v. Storey (1980) C.A. 504

Held, following *Green* **12**, defendants not liable.

(b) Particular Instances

(*N.B.* Pre-1958 occupier cases are starred, as the law since January 1, 1958 is governed by the Occupiers' Liability Act 1957, s. 2(4).)

Defendant	*Independent contractor*	*Fault complained of*		*Liable for I.C. or not*
Occupier*	Lift repairer	Faulty lift door	1	No
Shipowner*	Ship repairer	Ship's valve	2	No
Occupier*	Electrician	Scaffold breaking	3	No
Employer	Supplier	Live busbar	4	?
OWNER OF CELLAR FLAP	COAL MERCHANT	OPEN HOLE IN FOOTWALK	5	Yes
Car owner	Repairer	Wheel hitting pedestrian	6	No
SHIPOWNER*	COAL MERCHANT	OPEN HATCH	7	Yes
OCCUPIER*	LIFT REPAIRER	OPEN LIFT DOOR	8	No
Shipowner*	Ship's surveyor	Certificate of safety from petrol vapour	9	Yes
OCCUPIER*	SCHOOL CLEANER	FROZEN SNOW ON STEP	10	Yes

Adjacent owner	Electrician	Fire from bad wiring	11	Yes
Occupier*	Weighing machine repairers	Projecting nut	12	Yes
Employer	Ship's surveyor	Errors in surveying	13	Yes/No
Shipowner*	**Shipwright**	**Loose wooden shore**	14	Yes
Shipowner*	Loading stevedore	Bad Stowage	15	Yes
Shipowner*	Repairer	Moving hatch cover	16	No
Shipowner*	Loading stevedore	Bad stowage	17	No
Occupier*	Electrician	Faulty wiring	18	No
Employer	Supplier	Electric truck faulty	19	No
Employer*	**Supplier**	**Faulty tool**	20	No
EMPLOYER	LIGHTERMAN	ERECTING UNSAFE LADDER	21	Yes
Shipowner	**Repairer**	**Loose nut causing damage to cargo**	22	Yes
Shipowner	Loading stevedore	Bad stowage	23	Yes
Employer	Builder, architect and electrician	Fire in shop	24	Yes?
Employer	Manufacturer	Faulty cable	24	No?
POLICE	GARAGE TOWING CAR AWAY	NEGLIGENT TOWING	25	No
Developers	Engineer	Foundations	26	No
Shopkeeper	*Shopfitter*	*Wrong glass used in door*	U1	No
Education authority	*Taxi firm*	*Setting down child at dangerous spot*	U2	No

1. Morgan v. Girls Friendly Society [1936] 1 All E.R. 404, Horridge J.
2. Howard v. Furness Houlder (1936) 80 S.J. 554; [1936] 2 All E.R. 781, Lewis J.
3. Clelland v. Edward Lloyd [1938] 1 K.B. 272; [1937] 2 All E.R. 605, Goddard J.
4. Paine v. Colne Valley Elec. [1938] 4 All E.R. 803; 106 L.T. 124, Goddard L.J.
5. Daniel v. Rickett Cockerell [1938] 2 K.B. 322; [1938] 2 All E.R. 631, C.A.
6. Stennett v. Hancock [1939] 2 All E.R. 578, Branson J.
7. Wilkinson v. Rea [1941] 1 K.B. 688; [1941] 2 All E.R. 50, C.A.
8. Haseldine v. Daw [1941] 2 K.B. 343; [1941] 3 All E.R. 156, C.A.
9. The Pass of Ballater [1942] P. 112; [1942] 2 All E.R. 79, Langton J.
10. Woodward v. Mayor of Hastings [1944] 2 All E.R. 565, C.A.
11. Spicer v. Smee [1946] 1 All E.R. 489, Atkinson J.
12. Bloomstein v. Railway Executive [1952] 2 All E.R. 418; [1952] W.N. 378, Parker J.
13. Waddle v. Wallsend Shipping [1952] 2 Lloyd's Rep. 105, Devlin J.
14. Thomson v. Cremin [1956] 1 W.L.R. 103; [1953] 2 All E.R. 1185, H.L.
15. Keen v. Lykiardopoulo [1953] 2 Lloyd's Rep. 349, Jones J.
16. Thompson v. Anglo-Saxon Petroleum [1955] 2 Lloyd's Rep. 363, Oliver J.
17. Jeyes v. Currie Line [1956] 2 Lloyd's Rep. 87, Pearce J.
18. Green v. Fibreglass [1958] 2 Q.B. 245; [1958] 2 All E.R. 521, Salmon J.
19. Sullivan v. Gallagher, 1959 S.C. 243, 2nd Div.
20. Davie v. New Merton Board Mills [1959] A.C. 604; [1959] 1 All E.R. 346, H.L.
21. Wingfield v. Ellerman's Wilson [1960] 2 Lloyd's Rep. 16, C.A.
22. Riverstone Meat Co. v. Lancs. Shipping [1961] A.C. 807; [1961] 1 All E.R. 495, H.L.
23. Shepherd v. Ellerman's Wilson [1962] 2 Lloyd's Rep. 291, Sachs J.
24. Sumner v. Wm. Henderson [1964] 1 Q.B. 450; [1963] 1 All E.R. 408, Phillimore J.
25. Rivers v. Cutting [1982] 1 W.L.R. 1146; [1982] 3 All E.R. 69 C.A.
26. Frost v. Moody Homes Ltd; Hoskisson v. Donald Moody Ltd (1990) 6 Const. L.J. 43; [1990] C.L.Y. 3253, Judge Newey Q.C. (for details, see Chap. 18(6) **72**).

U1. *Smith v. Storey* (1980) C.A. 504.
U2. *Myton v. Woods* (1980) C.A. 646.

(4) Liability of parent and the like for child

1. Donaldson v. McNiven [1952] 1 All E.R. 1213, Pearson J.; [1952] 2 All E.R. 691, C.A.

Held, that a parent would be negligent if he allowed a child to have an airgun and took no reasonably necessary precautions about its use, but on the facts of the present case (child 13—steps taken to restrict use of rifle to place of safety), defendant was not negligent. *Upheld* by C.A., who say there was no evidence of lack of supervision, and that a parent, not being able to supervise child all the time, could do no more than extract a promise of safe user from child.

2. Carmarthenshire C.C. v. Lewis [1955] A.C. 549; [1955] 1 All E.R. 565 H.L.

Case of child of four escaping from school, but H.L. speeches (*vide* Lord Reid, 573 A) show same principle applies to parents—*Held*, the escape itself, in the case of children too young to have sufficient "road sense" to go to school unattended (*vide* Lord Tucker, 573 I), raised a presumption of negligence which put onus on defendants—who on the facts did not discharge it and were liable. But Lord Reid, in speaking of standard of care, said no one could expect mother to be in two places at once, or that a young child had always to be cooped up. The standard was that of a reasonable and prudent mother (573 B).

3. Newton v. Edgerley [1959] 3 All E.R. 337, Lord Parker C.J.

Held, defendant parent liable for accident when son shot another boy.

4. Court v. Wyatt *The Times*, June 25, 1960: [1960] C.L.Y. 882, Donovan J.

Boy of 15 shot plaintiff with an airgun—*Held*, defendant father liable as father knew the boy was of such a disposition as not to be trusted with the gun, and therefore father was negligent.

5. Gorely v. Codd [1967] 1 W.L.R. 19; [1966] 3 All E.R. 891, Nield J.

Held, in the circumstances, father was not negligent in allowing son aged 16½ to have airgun. The judge attached some importance to the fact that there was no infringement of any of the provisions of the Air Guns and Shot Guns Act 1962; and to the fact that the accident occurred in a field in a sparsely populated country district.

6. Gambino v. Di Leo (1971) 17 D.L.R. (3d) 167, Ontario High Ct.

7. Home Office v. Dorset Yacht Co. [1970] A.C. 1004; [1970] 2 All E.R. 294, H.L.

Case dealing with liability for escaping Borstal inmates—in the course of their speeches four Law Lords referred with specific approval to the judgment of Dixon J. *in Smith v. Leurs* (1945) 70 C.L.R. 256:

> "The general rule is that one man is under no duty of controlling another to prevent his doing damage to a third. There are however special relations which are the source of a duty of this nature. It appears now to be recognised that it is incumbent on a parent who maintains control over a young child to take reasonable care so to exercise that control as to avoid conduct on his part exposing the person or property of others to unreasonable danger. Parental control, where it exists, must be exercised with due care to prevent the child inflicting intentional damage on others or causing damage by conduct involving unreasonable risk of injury to others."

8. Partington v. Wandsworth L.B.C. *The Independent*, November 8, 1989; [1989] C.L.Y. 2563, Schiemann J.

For details, see Chap. 18 (13) **62**.

9. Porter v. Barking & Dagenham L.B.C. *The Times*, April 9, 1990; [1990] C.L.Y. 3268, Simon Brown J.

School caretaker allowed his son and plaintiff to practice putting the shot on school property outside school hours; an accident occurred—*Held*, the caretaker's duty had been to take care to the standard of a reasonably prudent parent; his conduct was not to be regarded as imprudent given the boys were 14 and by all accounts sensible and well behaved.

10. Surtees v. Kingston-upon-Thames B.C. [1991] 2 F.L.R. 559; [1992] C.L.Y. 3198, C.A.

For details see Chap, 18 (13) **68**.

U1. Simpson v. Shafi (1984) C.A. 710

Mother released 16-month-old child from pushchair in congested shop where injured—*Held* shopkeeper not liable. "The responsibility for the safety of little children must rest primarily upon the parents; it is their duty to see that such children are not allowed to wander about by themselves, or, at the least, to satisfy themselves that the places to which they do allow their children to go unaccompanied are safe for them to go to" Devlin J. in *Phipps v. Rochester Corporation* [1955] 1 All E.R. 129 at 143 3 H.

6. STATUTORY DUTY

(1) Generally

(*N.B.* See also the Employers' Liability cases under Chaps. 15 (2) (k) and 16.)

1. Provender Millers v. Southampton C.C. [1939] 3 All E.R. 882, Farwell J.

Defendants in exercise of statutory power rebuilt a culvert which decreased flow of water in plaintiffs' stream—*Held*, onus was on defendants to show there was no other reasonably possible way of doing work, which onus they had failed to discharge.

2. Barnes v. Irwell Valley Water Board [1939] 1 K.B. 21, [1938] 2 All E.R. 650, C.A.

Action for breach of statutory duty in failing to supply pure water and negligence at common law—water was pure in the pipes, but absorbed lead after being in contact therewith for a time—no breach of statutory duty on wording of Act. *Held*, defendants liable at common law under *D. v. S.* See Slesser L. J. at 45 (bottom). See also *Read v. Croydon Corporation* (Chap. 6. (2) **1**).

3. Caswell v. Powell Duffryn Collieries [1940] A.C. 152; [1939] 3 All E.R. 722, H.L.

Held, that contributory negligence on the part of the plaintiff was a defence to an action for breach of statutory duty.

4. Knight v. Sheffield Corporation [1942] 2 All E.R. 411; 167 L.T. 203, Hilbery J.

Held, defendants liable. Leading cases conveniently summarised by judge.

5. Longhurst v. M.W.B. [1948] 2 All E.R. 834; 64 T.L.R. 579, H.L.

Leak from stopcock percolating to and loosening paving stone some distance away—*Held*, no liability in the absence of negligence, as defendants were acting under statutory powers.

6. Marriage v. East Norfolk Rivers C.B. [1950] 1 K.B. 284; [1949] 2 All E.R. 1021, C.A.

Defendants deposited soil on bank of river, preventing overflow water escaping in time of flood—work done under powers in Land Drainage Act—*Held*, since no negligence established, no cause of action.

7. Cooper v. Railway Executive [1953] 1 W.L.R. 223; [1953] 1 All E.R. 477, Devlin J.

Held, that the liability of the railway to fence under Railways Clauses Consolidation Act 1845, s. 68, was to erect an ordinary fence against cattle straying, and did not include a duty to fence against cattle using some exceptional force. *Obiter* at 479 G: "The section creates, of course, an absolute obligation in the sense that defendants are absolutely bound to maintain a fence, and it is no answer to say that some accident or act of a trespasser made it defective."

8. Farrell v. John Mowlem [1954] 1 Lloyd's Rep. 437, Devlin J.

Obiter at 439, col. 2 (bottom): "[A person] doing work which he is entitled to do by Act of Parliament is entitled of course to do whatever is necessary and reasonable for the carrying out of that work, even if he thereby causes an obstruction on the highway."

9. Anns v. Merton L.B.C. [1977] 2 W.L.R. 1024; 2 All E.R. 492, H.L.

Held, that generally and subject to provisos a local authority would not be liable to a house owner if it failed to inspect the foundations altogether during construction, but similarly would be liable if an inspection was made negligently. *N.B.* This case is strictly not concerned with breach of statutory duty as such, but with breach of common law duty of care imposed on someone having a statutory function to discharge. For fuller details see Chap. 1, (2) (a) **10** largely overruled in *Murphy*, Chap. 18, (13) **66**.

(2) When an Action for Breach of Statutory Duty Lies

Impure water	1	Waterworks Clauses Act 1847, s. 35	Yes/no
Permitting driving uninsured	2	Road Traffic Act, 1960, s. 201	Yes/no
RAILWAY BRIDGE—RUT	3	Railway Clauses Act 1845, s. 46	Yes
TRAM-TRACK—NONFEASANCE	4	Tramway Act 1870, s. 25	Yes
Sale of car—bad brakes	5	Road Traffic Act 1960, s. 68	No
No rear light on car	6	Road Transport Lighting Act 1957	No
Water co.—making up road	7	Waterworks Clauses Act 1847, s. 32	Yes
Pedestrian on crossing	8	Pedestrian Crossing Regs. 1941	Yes
General principle stated	9	Betting & Lotteries Act 1934, s. 11	—
Permitting driving uninsured	10	Road Traffic Act, 1960, s. 201	Yes
Car not maintained	11	Construction & Use Regs. 1941	No
Tyres not maintained	12	Construction & Use Regs. 1941	No
Driver—epileptic	13	Road Traffic Act 1960	No

Sale of dangerous machinery	14	Factories Act 1961, s. 17(2)	No
Dog at large in park	15	Local by-law	No
Inadequate fire escape	16	London Building Act 1939, s. 133	Yes
Danger on dock estate	17	Port of London Bye-laws	No
CELLAR FLAP—NON-FEASANCE	18	Public Health, etc. Act 1890, s. 35	?
PEDESTRIAN ON CROSSING	19	Pedestrian Crossing Regs.	Yes
Land drains—non-repair	20	An Inclosure Act of 1800	Yes
Pedestrian on crossing	21	Pedestrian Crossing Regs.	Yes
Embankment—non-repair	22	Private Act	Yes
EXCEEDING SPEED LIMIT	23	Road Traffic Act 1960	No?
Learner driver—unaccompanied	24	Road Traffic Act 1960, s. 102	No
School glass door	25	Education Act 1944, s. 10	Yes
School glass door	26	Education Act 1944, s. 10	Yes
STREET WORKS—NOT FENCING OR LIGHTING	27	Public Utilities Street Works Act 1950, s. 8 (1) (a)	No
Shower on ship scalding seaman	28	Merchant Shipping (Crew Accommodation) Regs. 1953, s. 24	Yes
FLAGSTONE OVER CELLAR	29	Highways Act 1959, s. 154 (5)	No/but
Defect in steering	30	Construction and Use Regs. (Malaysia)	No
PARKING ON A CLEARWAY	31	Various Trunk Roads Order 1963	No
Permitting driving uninsured	32	Road Traffic Act 1960, s. 201	Yes
LAND REGISTRY ISSUING FALSE CERTIFICATE OF SEARCH FOR LOCAL LAND CHARGE	33	Land Charges Act 1925, s. 15	Yes and no
NEGLIGENT APPROVAL OF FOUNDATIONS BY COUNCIL SURVEYOR	34	Public Health Acts 1936 and 1961	Yes
RAILWAY—STILE OF PUBLIC FOOTPATH IN DISREPAIR	35	Railway Clauses Consolidation Act 1845, s. 61	Yes
Negligent approval of foundations by council surveyor	36	Public Health Act 1936	Yes, provided . . .
Failure of council surveyor to inspect foundations	36	Public Health Act 1936	No, provided . . .
POOR FACILITIES FOR SICK PERSON	37	Chronically Sick etc. Persons Act 1970	No
Negligent approval of damp-proofing by council surveyor	38	London Building Acts (Amendment) Act 1939, s.82	Yes
HOMELESS PERSON: NOT HOUSED BY LOCAL AUTHORITY	39	Housing (Homeless Persons) Act 1977, s.3	Yes
Failure to use statutory powers—to prevent flooding—failure alleged to be due to improper motive	40	Land Drainage Act 1976, s.98	Probably no
Negligent inspection of defective foundation	41	Public Health Act 1936	Yes, provided . . .
Failure of local authority to make inquiries as to status of applicant's homelessness	42	Housing Act 1985, s. 62	No
FAILURE OF DIRECTORS TO EFFECT EMPLOYERS' LIABILITY INSURANCE	43	Employers' liability (Compulsory Insurance) Act 1969	No

Whether Local Authority liable to individuals under child care legislation	44	Children and Young Person's Act 1969, Child Care Act 1980, Children Act 1989	No
Flooding from watercourse	U1	Private Act of 1765	Yes
Health Authority's application to cancel nursing home registration	U2	Registered Homes Act 1984, s. 30	No

1. Read v. Croydon Corporation [1938] 4 All E.R. 631; 55 T.L.R. 212, Stable J.

In breach of Waterworks Clauses Act 1847, s. 35, defendants supplied water which contained typhoid bacilli—in consequence daughter of a ratepayer got typhoid fever—*Held*, no action for breach of statutory duty, as the statutory duty was only owed to ratepayers. *But* a claim at common law succeeded.

2. Daniels v. Vaux [1938] 2 K.B. 203; [1938] 2 All E.R. 271, Humphreys J.

Fatal claim against mother of negligent driver for permitting him to drive her car uninsured—driver subsequently died and any claim against his estate was out of time—*Held*, action against mother failed, as the cause of plaintiff's loss was not the breach of duty to insure, but the plaintiff's failure to sue driver in time.

3. Swain v. Southern Railway [1939] 2 K.B. 560; [1939] 2 All E.R. 794, C.A.

4. Simon v. Islington B.C. [1943] K.B. 188; [1943] 1 All E.R. 41, C.A.

Held, cause of action for breach of statutory duty would lie, even without aid of s. 55 (which apparently gives express right to damages) (193 (middle)).

5. Badham v. Lambs [1946] K.B. 45; [1946] 2 All E.R. 295, du Parcq L.J.

Held, no action for breach of statutory duty, as aim of legislation was not to protect purchasers.

6. Clarke v. Brims [1947] K.B. 497; [1947] 1 All E.R. 242, Morris J.

Held, duty to light imposed by statute was a public duty only, and plaintiff could not found an action for breach of statutory duty.

7. Longhurst v. M.W.B. [1948] 2 All E.R. 834; 64 T.L.R. 579, H.L.

Said (probably *obiter*) that water board liable for failure to reinstate properly (Lord Porter 839 H, 840 A).

8. L.P.T.B. v. Upson [1949] A.C. 155; [1949] 1 All E.R. 60, H.L.

Driver approached a controlled pedestrian crossing showing lights in his favour, but owing to part of crossing being obscured by vehicle his approach was in breach of Pedestrian Crossing Regulations 1941 (made under Road Traffic Act 1934, s. 18)—*Held*, liable because he was in breach of the Regulations. See also **19** and **21**.

9. Cutler v. Wandsworth Stadium [1949] A.C. 398; [1949] 1 All E.R. 544, H.L.

10. Corfield v. Groves [1950] 1 All E.R. 488; [1950] W.N. 116, Hilbery J.

First defendant driving insured with permission (but not as agent) of second defendant the owner—negligently kills plaintiff—first defendant without means—plaintiff sues both—second defendant claims that as Motor Insurers' Bureau will satisfy any judgment against first defendant, plaintiff has suffered no damage from second defendant's breach of statutory duty—*Held*, not so and second defendant liable, inasmuch as the cause of action against second defendant (since first defendant was impecunious) accrued to plaintiff at the very moment of the tortious act.

11. Winter v. Cardiff R.D.C. [1950] 1 All E.R. 819; [1950] W.N. 193, H.L.

Lord Porter: "The statement of claim also contained an allegation that the respondents had been guilty of a breach of statutory duty in that the requirements of (now reg. 72 of the Motor Vehicles (Construction and Use) Regulations 1951, relating to the maintenance of vehicle and avoidance of overloading) had not been complied with. This last contention was, however, not persisted in save as providing a standard with reference to which the requisite care to be observed could be estimated. So regarded, it merges in the question whether the respondents were guilty of negligence . . . "

12. Barkway v. South Wales Transport [1950] A.C. 185; [1950] 1 All E.R. 392, H.L.

Lord Normand: "It (now reg. 77 of 1951 Regulations, relating to maintenance of tyres) gives no right of action to persons injured by the breach of it" (400 F).

13. Balmer v. Hayes, 1950 S.C. 477; 1950 S.L.T. 388

14. Biddle v. Truvox [1952] 1 K.B. 101; [1951] 2 All E.R. 835, Finnemore J.

Held, no action against seller for breach of statutory duty.

15. Newman v. Francis [1953] 1 W.L.R. 402; 97 S.J. 134

By-law prohibiting dogs being brought into park—defendant's Alsatian jumps fence and injures plaintiff in park—*Held*, no action for breach of statutory duty.

16. Solomons v. Gertzenstein [1954] 2 Q.B. 243; [1954] 1 All E.R. 1008, Lord Goddard C.J.

Plaintiff employed in a building of which defendants were the lessees—fire—fire escape not complying with London Building Acts—plaintiff had to climb out of a window and was injured—*Held*, defendants liable, since statutory duty was not imposed for benefit of public generally, but for a particular class of which plaintiff was one. *N.B.* The Acts provided a penalty for default.

17. Ryan v. Maltby [1954] 1 Lloyd's Rep. 196, Hilbery J.

18. Macfarlane v. Gwalter [1959] 2 Q.B. 332; [1958] 1 All E.R. 181, C.A.

Question whether plaintiff could sue on the statute mentioned (185 A) but not decided, as defendant was found liable in nuisance.

19. Bassett v. Victoria Wine Co. *The Times*, February 6, 1958, C.A.

Car parked within 45 feet of pedestrian crossing—plaintiff crossed on crossing in front of car—was run down by defendant as she crossed into his path—plaintiff sued defendant at common law only (not under Pedestrian Crossing Regulations)—*Held*, defendant not liable, as his speed and lookout were reasonable. But *semble* defendant would have been liable if sued under the Regulations, and parked car also, if sued.

20. Att.-Gen. v. St. Ives R.D.C. [1960] 1 Q.B. 312; [1959] 3 All E.R. 371, Salmon J.

21. Kozimor v. Adey [1962] 105 S.J. 431, [1962] C.L.Y. 2646, Megaw J.

Held, driver not negligent, but 25 per cent liable for breach of regulations.

22. Sephton v. Lancashire River Board [1962] 1 W.L.R. 623; [1962] 1 All E.R. 183, Lawton J.

River bank broke owing to failure by defendants to maintain it—by the Scarisbrick Estate Drainage Agreement of 1924 commissioners had the duty of maintaining the embankment—by later Acts the functions of the commissioners were transferred to the defendants—*Held*, plaintiff was entitled to recover damages from defendants for breach of statutory duty.

23. Barna v. Hudes Merchandising Corporation (1962) 106 S.J. 194; [1962] Crim. L.R. 321, C.A.

Defendant doing 30–40 m.p.h. in built-up area—*Held*, exceeding speed limit was not in itself negligence (and, therefore, it would seem, did not give rise to an action for breach of statutory duty either, though this was not apparently pleaded).

24. Verney v. Wilkins (1962) 106 S.J. 879, Winn J.

L driver unaccompanied by qualified driver—has accident—*Held*, that breach of statutory duty with regard to learner drivers did not in itself afford a cause of action.

25. Lyes v. Middlesex C.C. (1962) 61 L.G.R. 443; [1962] C.L.Y. 2425, Edmund Davies J.

26. Reffell v. Surrey C.C. [1964] 1 W.L.R. 358; [1964] 1 All E.R. 743; Veale J.

27. Keating v. Elvan Reinforced Concrete [1968] 1 W.L.R. 722; [1968] 2 All E.R. 139, C.A.

28. Foulder v. Canadian Pacific [1969] 1 All E.R. 283; [1968] 2 Lloyd's Rep. 366, Caulfield J.

29. Scott v. Green [1969] 1 W.L.R. 301; [1969] 1 All E.R. 849, C.A.

"The Act does not by itself give a cause of action, but it forms the basis on which the common law can build a cause of action. The Act clearly gives the occupier a sufficient degree of control of the flagstone . . . so as to enable him to repair it, no matter whether it is dedicated to the public or not. Being in control of it, the common law says that he is under a duty to those passing by. He must use reasonable care to see that it is safe . . . " (Lord Denning M.R. 750 G).

30. Tan Chye Choo v. Chong Kew Moi [1970] 1 W.L.R. 147; [1970] 1 All E.R. 266, P.C.

31. Coote v. Stone [1971] 1 W.L.R. 279; [1971] 1 All E.R. 266, C.A.

So *held*, overruling *Kelly v. W.R.N.* [1968] 1 All E.R. 369 Ashworth J.

32. Martin v. Dean [1971] 2 Q.B. 208; [1971] 3 All E.R. 279, John Stephenson J.

Uninsured driver only able to satisfy his liability to plaintiff by instalments—owner who had permitted driver to drive uninsured argued that since the driver was able to satisfy the liability, albeit by instalments, plaintiff had suffered no damage from the statutory breach—*Held*, not so, and owner liable.

33. Ministry of Housing v. Sharp [1970] 2 Q.B. 223; [1970] 1 All E.R. 1009, C.A.

Registrar of local land charges issued erroneous certificate of search—but no negligence on his part—*Held*, (2–1), the Act did not impose an absolute duty to issue an accurate certificate, and therefore registrar was not liable. But all three L.JJ. were of the opinion that there was an actionable statutory duty to use reasonable care.

34. Dutton v. Bognor Regis U.D.C. [1972] Q.B. 373; [1972] 1 All E.R. 462, C.A.

Held, Defendant council liable to subsequent purchaser of house for negligence of their surveyor in approving the foundations when house being built in 1958. The decision has been *upheld* in *Anns* **36**, though on somewhat different grounds to those expressed by C.A. in present case. *N.B.* This case and *Anns* **36** are not strictly cases of breach of statutory duty at all, but of breach of the common law duty of care which is held to arise, in these two cases, when the exercise of a statutory function is being carried out. Overruled: See *Murphy*, Chap. 18 (13) **66**.

35. Thomas v. B.R.B. [1976] Q.B. 912; [1976] 3 All E.R. 15, C.A.

36. Anns v. Merton L.B.C. [1977] 2 W.L.R. 1024; [1977] 2 All E.R. 492, H.L.

This case is, in effect, an appeal against *Dutton* **34**. For purpose of argument it was assumed that the inspector had either failed to inspect the foundations at all or else had been negligent in inspecting—as to (i) failure to inspect it was held that there would be no liability for a failure to inspect, provided always that this was the result of a decision responsibly made and for reasons which accorded with the purpose of the statute (but *aliter* if this proviso did not apply); and as to (ii) negligent inspection—*Held*, in general there would be liability, provided that the person making the inspection was acting otherwise than in the bona fide exercise of any discretion under the statute. Largely overruled in *Murphy*, Chap. 18 (13) **66**.

37. Wyatt v. Hillingdon L.B.C. (1978) 122 S.J. 349; 76 L.G.R. 727, C.A.

38. Marsh v. Betstyle and G.L.C. [1979] C.L.Y. 1875, Judge Lewis Hawser Q.C.

39. Thornton v. Kirklees [1979] Q.B. 626; [1979] 2 All E.R. 349, C.A.

40. Potter v. Mole Valley D.C. and Surrey C.C., *The Times*, October 22. 1982; [1982] C.L.Y. 2266, French J.

For details see Chap 1 (3) (b) **13**.

41. Bluett v. Woodspring D.C. [1983] J.P.L. 242; [1983] C.L.Y. 2513, Judge Stabb Q.C.

Held, that a cause of action only arises against a local authority under the principles laid down in *Anns* **36**, "when the state of the building was such that there was present or imminent danger to the health or safety of persons occupying it" (244). But now see *Murphy*, Chap. 18(13) **66**.

42. R. v. Northavon D.C., ex p. Palmer, *The Independent*, February 22, 1994; *The Times*, March 16, 1994, Roger Toulson Q.C.

43. Richardson v. Pitt-Stanley [1995] 2 W.L.R. 26; [1994] C.L.Y. 2281, C.A.

Company's employees injured at work—injury caused by its breach of statutory duty—company's failure to insure for such liability—*Held*, by a majority, there was no express provision creating civil liability on the part of employees or directors, nor was the Act intended to create such liability—directors not liable in damages.

44. M. v. Newham L.B.C.; X (Minors) v. Bedforshire C.C. [1994] 2 W.L.R. 554; [1994] 4 All E.R. 602, C.A.

Neither an action for breach of statutory duty nor (by a majority) one for common Law negligence could be maintained by a child against a local authority in respects of acts or omissions for which the authority was responsible in the exercise of its functions under child care legislation. Now see [1995] 3 W.L.R. 152, H.L.

U1. Rippingale Farms v. Black Sluice I.D. Board (1963) C.A. 268 (unreported)

Flooding from a watercourse—Act of 1765 provided that commissioners should keep it in repair—*Held*, that this imposed a positive duty giving rise to a cause of action, and this duty had by virtue of Land Drainage Act 1930 passed to defendants, who were liable.

U2. Martine v. South East Kent H.A., *The Times*, March 8, 1993; [1993] C.L.Y. 2947, C.A.

The power of an area health authority to make application under the Act to cancel a nursing home's registration did not give rise to a cause of action in negligence at the suit of the proprietor.

Part 2: Particular Classes

7. LIABILITY FOR DANGEROUS OPERATIONS, PRODUCTS, ETC.

In this edition, the title of this chapter has been changed and is closer to that in earlier editions. Although liability in this area still stems from *Donoghue v. Stephenson* for the most part, categories of negligence have been much more closely defined in recent years (*Junior Books, D. & F. Estates, Caparo,* etc.), and specific instances of breach of duty can be found in different chapters in this edition, especially Chap. 18. New cases are therefore largely confined to product or operations liability, and "Negligent misstatements" now appear in a new chapter section, Chap. 19, The Consumer Protection Act 1987 is now relevant to this area of law.

(1) Duty of Care

(a) General Scope and Limits

(*N.B.* Negligent misstatements see Chap. 19 Economic Loss see Chap. 1, (3) (a) Damage not resonably foreseeable see Chap. 1, (3) (c) and for fuller extracts from some of the leading cases citing dicta on the principles to be applied in deciding whether a duty of care exists see Chap. 1 (2) (a).)

1. Donoghue v. Stevenson [1932] A.C. 562; 147 L.T. 281, H.L.

Lord Atkin (580): "The rule that you are to love your neighbour becomes in law, you must not injure your neighbour; and the lawyer's question, Who is my neighbour?, receives a restricted reply. You must take reasonable care to avoid acts and omissions which you can reasonably foresee would be likely to injure your neighbour. Who, then, in law is my neighbour? The answer seems to be—persons who are so closely affected by my act that I ought to have them in contemplation as being so affected when I am directing my mind to the acts or omissions which are called in question."

2. Hindustan SS Co. v. Siemens [1955] 1 Lloyd's Rep. 167, Willmer J.

3. Carmarthenshire C.C. v. Lewis [1955] A.C. 549; [1955] 1 All E.R. 565, H.L.

For liability, in particular, of parent for child see Chap. 5 (4), and of schoolmasters see Chap. 18 (13) (a).

4. A.C. Billings v. Riden [1958] A.C. 240; [1957] 3 All E.R. 1, H.L.

5. Creed v. McGeoch [1955] 1 W.L.R. 1005; [1955] 3 All E.R. 123, Ashworth J.

Held, applying *Buckland v. Guildford Gas Co.* (Chap. 7 (2) (e) **1**) *q.v.* for fuller details. These three cases were expressly approved by two of the Law Lords in *B.R.B. v. Herrington* (Chap. 7 (2) (c) **14**).

6. Weller v. Foot and Mouth Institute [1966] Q.B. 569; [1965] 3 All E.R. 560; Widgery J.

Defendants negligently, as was assumed for the purposes of argument, allowed virus to escape, which infected cattle, and so caused plaintiffs to lose the profits of their cattle market due to closure—*Held*, since the plaintiffs as auctioneers had no proprietary interest in anything which might be damaged if the virus escaped, no duty of care was owed to them by the defendants. *N.B.* From this case have stemmed a number of decisions on *economic loss* arising indirectly from a negligent act (chiefly in connection with loss of production by a factory), as to which see Chap. 1, (3) (a).

7. Lee Cooper v. Jenkins [1967] 2 Q.B. 1; [1965] 1 All E.R. 280; Marshall J.

Goods stolen in transit due to negligence of defendants' driver—the contract of carriage had been made between the defendants and a firm of forwarding agents who were found to have contracted as principals and not as agents for the owners of the goods—*Held*, the defendants owed a duty under *Donoghue v. Stevenson* to the owners, who could accordingly recover for the loss in tort. One factor in this decision may have been that the defendants knew that the forwarding agents as such frequently handled goods belonging to their customers. *But Building Holidays Scheme v. P.O.* [1965] 1 All E.R. 163 was not cited, in which Lord Denning M.R. (167 F) said:

> "At common law bailment is often associated with a contract, but this is not always the case . . . An action against a bailee can often be put, not as an action in contract nor in tort, but as an action on its own, *sui generis*, arising out of the possession had by the bailee of the goods . . . Suffice it to say that at the present day if goods which have been delivered to a bailee are lost or damaged while in his custody, he is liable to the person damnified (who may be the owner or the bailor) unless the bailee proves that the loss or damage is not due to any fault on his part . . . "

8. Margarine Union v. Cambay Prince [1969] 1 Q.B. 219; [1967] 3 All E.R. 775, Roskill J.

Shipowners negligently failed to fumigate a ship—copra attacked by cockroaches as a result—plaintiff was a c.i.f. purchaser and only acquired title to his copra when it was separated from bulk on discharge—the negligence had occurred not later than the time of loading—*Held*, plaintiff could not recover in tort, as at the time of the negligent act no duty of care was owed to anyone other than the then owner of the goods. Dicta in *Weller* **6** *applied*.

9. Home Office v. Dorset Yacht Co. [1970] A.C. 1004; [1970] 2 All E.R. 294, H.L.

Borstal escapees on Brownsea Island damage yacht—*Held*, Borstal authorities owed a duty of care "to persons whom (they) could reasonably foresee had property situate in the vicinity of the place of detention . . . which the detainee was likely to steal or to appropriate and damage in the course of eluding immediate pursuit and recapture" (Lord Diplock, 334 G). Lord Morris (307 J) suggested that the test of whether a duty arose in a particular situation was whether it was "fair and reasonable," and that this would obviate using "policy" as a main test. Lord Pearson (321 C) said that a main question was whether it was "fair and just" that a duty should arise, and that since the case prima facie came within the *Donoghue v. Stevenson* principle, a duty should arise unless there was some sufficient reason to the contrary. In this connection he examined, and rejected, absence of proximity (321 D), act of third party (321 E), statutory authority (322 B) and public policy (322 H) as capable of constituting sufficient reason, and concluded that a duty of care limited in the way put forward by Lord Diplock was owed.

10. Watt v. Rama [1972] V.R. 343; [1972] C.L.Y. 2408, Victoria Sup. Ct.

Duval v. Seguin (1972) 26 D.L.R. (3d) 418; [1972] C.L.Y. 2409, Fraser J. (Can.)

Held, in both cases, an action would lie. *N.B.* The situation is now regulated by the Congenital Disabilities Act 1976.

11. Smith v. Scott [1973] Ch. 314; [1972] 3 All E.R. 645, Pennycuick V.-C.

12. Moorgate Mercantile v. Twitchings [1976] 3 W.L.R. 66; [1976] 2 All E.R. 641, H.L.

Held, (3–2) although both the plaintiffs and the defendant were members of HP Information (this fact being one which allegedly created the proximity needed for a *Donoghue v. Stevenson* relationship), the rules of HPI have now been changed, and all members undertake that they will register all hp agreements.

13. Bryson v. Northumbria Police (1977) C.L.Y. 2042, Reeve J.

14. Batty v. Metropolitan Property [1978] Q.B. 554; [1978] 2 All E.R. 445, C.A.

Builders retained by developers negligently built house on unstable hillside. Developers sold house to P who later found that, because of the danger of sudden collapse, house was valueless—builders argued, *inter alia*, that liability under *D v. S* extended only to damage consequential on putting an article into circulation, and did not extend to the loss of the value of the article itself—*Held*, not so. *Dicta* by Stamp L.J. in *Dutton*, Chap. 7, (2)(c) **15** disapproved. Doubted in *D. & F. Estates*, Chap. 18(4)(b) **63**.

15. Vicar of Writtle v. Essex C.C. (1979) 77 L.G.R. 656; [1979] C.L.Y. 1865, Forbes J.

Boy, 12, remanded in care, suspected of history of arson was placed in community home. Staff at home not informed of arson suspicion; at the time unsupervised, the boy escaped from home and set fire to local church—*Held*, following *Anns* (Chap. 18, (6) **13**) and *Dorset Yacht Co.* **9**, that the defendants were liable in negligence: (a) There was a sufficient proximity between the parties to give rise to a duty of care. (b) The undoubted discretion in the defendants to deal with the boy as appropriate in the light of the various conflicting interests potentially served to limit the duty. "In a case such as this the courts cannot substitute their views of proper treatment of the child for any arrived at bona fide by the authority" (672). (c) Because the relevant information was not passed on to the staff, the defendants did not exercise any discretion, and accordingly the potential limitation on the duty of care did not apply. (d) It was "highly probable" that, if the boy escaped, he would cause damage by fire. The defendants should have foreseen that the failure of communication was very likely to result in damage by fire and, had the information been communicated, the staff would have kept a closer observation on the boy which would probably have prevented him from escaping.

16. Ross v. Caunters [1980] Ch. 297; [1979] 3 All E.R. 580, Megarry V.-C.

Testator instructed his solicitor to draft will giving legacy to plaintiff. Through oversight the solicitor allowed plaintiff's husband to attest the will—*Held*, solicitor owed duty of care to legatee and was liable. The judge reviewed the main cases and *said* that the true basis of liability in the present case (where there was no misstatement to the plaintiff and hence no reliance by him) was *Donoghue v. Stevenson* **1** (593 B), and that here (a) there was close proximity between solicitor and legatee, (b) this proximity was not casual, but was a product of the duty of care owed by the solicitor to the testator and (c) the duty of care if imposed in no way imposed on the solicitor an uncertain or unlimited liability, but was to the plaintiff alone (587–588); and hence there was a duty of care.

17. Hayman v. L.T.E. [1981] C.L.Y. 1834, D/Circuit Judge Krikler.

18. The Irene's Success [1982] Q.B. 481; [1982] 1 All E.R. 218, Lloyd J.

P bought a cargo of coal under a c.i.f. contract when it was afloat on D's ship. P never became holder of bill of lading (so could not sue in contract) *but*, by reason of the contract, the coal was at P's risk, although P did not become the owner. The question was whether P could sue D for negligent damage to the coal—*Held*, yes. The primary test, as laid down by Lord Wilberforce in *Anns* (Chap. 1, (2)(a) **10**), was to ask whether there was a sufficient relationship of proximity or neighbourhood such that in the reasonable contemplation of the defendant carelessness on his part might be likely to cause damage to the plaintiff; and in the present case there was such a relationship. Secondly, the court had to ask whether there were any considerations of policy or otherwise for negativing or limiting the scope of the duty. One such consideration might arise if the duty, if imposed, might create an indeterminate liability to an indeterminate class; but here that was not the case, and, there being no other such considerations, D were under a duty of care to P. *Margarine Union* **8** not followed.

The true ratio of *Weller* **6** was *explained* as being "that the loss suffered by the plaintiffs, though foreseeable, was, as it were, at one remove from the damage to the cattle", and therefore exposed the defendants to claims from an almost unlimited number of potential plaintiffs (222 C).

N.B. The above decision was strongly (though *obiter*) *approved* by Sheen J. in *Nea Tyhi* [1982] 1 Lloyd's Rep. 606.

19. Standard Chartered Bank v. Walker [1982] 1 W.L.R. 1410; [1982] 2 All E.R. 938, C.A.

To secure overdraft a company gave the plaintiff bank a debenture and the defendant directors gave personal guarantees. Later the bank appointed a receiver. There was evidence that the bank had interfered in the sale by the receiver of the company's assets, so that the sale took place at a gross undervalue. The bank sued the defendants on the guarantees and applied for summary judgment under O.14. *Held*, that a receiver, as the agent of the company, owes a duty of care in the disposal of the company's assets both to the company and to the guarantors. A debenture holder "is not responsible for what the receiver does except in so far as he gives him directions or interferes with his conduct of the realisation. If it does so, then it too is under a duty to use reasonable care towards the company and the guarantor" (Lord Denning M.R., 942 J).

As there was evidence of negligent interference in the sale by the plaintiff bank, summary judgment was *refused*.

20. D. & F. Estates Ltd v. Church Commissioners for England [1989] A.C. 177; [1988] 2 All E.R. 992, H.L.

For details, see Chap. 1, (3)(a) **22**.

21. Clarke v. Bruce Lance & Co. [1988] 1 W.L.R. 881; [1988] 1 All E.R. 364, C.A.

Testator left freehold interest in a garage to plaintiff and wife in his will; he later instructed solicitors to draw up an option to purchase to lessees of the garage exercisable after the death of the testator and his wife. On testator's death, plaintiff claimed solicitors should have advised testator that granting of the option was misconceived uncommercial and prejudicial to the plaintiff—*Held*, no duty of care owed by the solicitors to him: *Yuen Kun Yen v. A. G.–of Hong Kong* followed; *Ross v. Caunters* **16** distinguished.

U1. Burrough v. Berkshire Fire Authority (1971) C.A. 40

Plaintiff volunteered to help fire brigade to fight barn fire—by using tractor to drag straw bales out—*Held*, as plaintiff thereby came under the control of the defendants, they owed him a duty of care and were liable for not providing him with a helmet (which was readily available).

(b) Chattels "Dangerous Per Se"

1. Donoghue v. Stevenson [1932] A.C. 562; 147 L.T. 281, H.L.

Lord Macmillan (611): "I rather regard this type of case as a special instance of negligence where the law exacts a degree of diligence so stringent as to amount practically to a guarantee of safety." Lord Atkin (596): "The nature of the thing may very well call for different degrees of care, and the person dealing with it may well contemplate persons as being within the sphere of his duty . . . who would not be sufficiently proximate with less dangerous goods."

2. Wray v. Essex C.C. [1936] 3 All E.R. 97, C.A.

Lord Wright M.R. (101): "The case of things dangerous in themselves . . . is a case separate and distinct and holds a special place in the law of negligence."

3. Howard v. Furness Houlder (1936) 80 S.J. 554; [1936] 2 All E.R. 781, C.A.

Plaintiff welder working on ship—injured by escape of steam from defective valve—defendants the repairers plead valve not dangerous *per se* and therefore not within *Donoghue v. Stevenson—Held*, this was irrelevant and that what mattered was that valve as repaired was dangerous, and therefore defendants liable.

4. North Western Utilities v. London Guarantee [1936] A.C. 108, P.C.

Gas leak in supply pipes under street caused by action of third party (the City Corporation of Edmonton) in constructing a storm sewer and causing pipe to sag—the gas company maintained the pipe under statutory authority—*Held*, (a) the gas in the pipe was a dangerous thing to which *Rylands v. Fletcher* liability would ordinarily apply (118); (b) the fact that defendants were acting under statutory authority was a defence to a claim under *Rylands v. Fletcher* (121); (c) the defendants were, however, liable in negligence, as gas was a dangerous commodity, and it was defendants' duty to watch all operations in the vicinity of their mains which were likely to affect the same: "their duty . . . was at the lowest to be on watch and be vigilant; they do not even pretend to have done as much as that" (Lord Wright, 127).

5. Burfitt v. Kille [1939] 2 K.B. 743; [1939] 2 All E.R. 372, Atkinson J.

Sale of toy pistol and blank ammunition to boy of 12—*Held*, a chattel dangerous *per se*, and defendant liable for selling it to boy. Judge said:

(a) "If A places in the hands of B a chattel which belongs to a class of things dangerous in themselves in the hands of such a person as B . . . a duty of care rests upon A, not only towards the recipient, but towards all such persons as may reasonably be contemplated as likely to be endangered" (374 H);
(b) "The duty resting upon him may in some cases be discharged by a warning. If it cannot, the duty must be to refrain from the sale" (375 E);
(c) "A warning is not a sufficient discharge of duty if the person to whom the chattel is delivered is not a competent person" (375 G).

6. The Pass of Ballater [1942] 2 All E.R. 79, Langton J.

Held, having regard to dangerous nature of substance "no precaution which was commercially practicable ought to have been omitted, and any omission of a practicable precaution would constitute a failure of duty" (84 G).

7. Glasgow Corporation v. Muir [1943] A.C. 448, [1943] 2 All E.R. 44, H.L.

A case turning on the liability of an occupier for acts of other visitors (see under Chap. 10, (4) (e) **1**). Lord Wright (463–464): "A distinction has been drawn in some cases between things intrinsically dangerous and/or dangerous *per se* and other things which are not dangerous in the absence of negligence. The correctness or value of that distinction has been doubted by eminent judges. I think, however, there is a real and practical distinction between the two categories. Some things are obviously and necessarily dangerous unless the danger is removed by appropriate precautions. These are things dangerous *per se*. Other things are only dangerous if there is negligence. Thus, to introduce, not a tea urn, but a savage animal . . . would have been of the former class. Another illustration of the same class may be afforded by the performance in the circus of the flying trapeze . . . "

8. Ball v. L.C.C. [1949] 2 K.B. 159; [1949] 1 All E.R. 1056, C.A.

Held, defendants not liable, because boiler not dangerous *per se*. This decision criticised and *overruled* by H.L. in *A. C. Billings v. Riden* (Chap. 7, (2) (a) **12**) in so far as it was based on the absence of any duty of care owed by a contractor to a tenant.

9. Yachuk v. Oliver Blais [1949] A.C. 386; [1949] 2 All E.R. 150, P.C.

Held, defendant liable for selling petrol to boy of nine.

10. Donaldson v. McNiven [1952] 1 All E.R. 1213, Pearson J.; [1952] 2 All E.R. 691, C.A.

Case of parent allowing a child of 13 to use an airgun—*Held*, by Pearson J. not negligence as airgun was not dangerous *per se* and father had taken sufficient steps to confine use to place of safety.

Upheld by C.A. on ground that there was no negligence by father: Pearson J.'s judgment appears impliedly to have been accepted.

11. Beckett v. Newalls Insulation [1953] 1 W.L.R. 8; [1953] 1 All E.R. 250, C.A.

Shipworker injured by calor gas cylinder exploding—*held* dependants liable—for full facts see Chap. 15, (5) **9**—in course of judgment Singleton L.J. quotes with approval argument of Sir Hartley Shawcross A.-G. in *Read v. Lyons* [1947] A.C. 156: "This case (*Read v. Lyons*) is not within *Rylands v. Fletcher*, which is really founded on the idea that defendant did what he should not have done. It depends on negligence, though the greater the danger, the greater the care required of him. In the authorities the application of the standard of things called dangerous in themselves has no logic in it . . . The true question is not whether a thing is dangerous in itself but whether, by reason of some extraneous circumstances, it may become dangerous. There is really no category of dangerous things: there are only some things which require more and some which require less care" (254 D).

12. Behrens v. Bertram Mills [1957] 2 Q.B. 1; [1957] 1 All E.R. 583, Devlin J.

"In the case of dangerous chattels, for example, the law has recognised, although it is not perhaps now of much importance, the distinction between chattels that are dangerous in themselves and chattels that are dangerous when used for certain purposes" (590 F).

13. Todman v. Victa [1982] V.R. 849; [1983] C.L.Y. 253b, Supreme Ct. of Victoria

Whilst mowing lawn, plaintiff struck in eye by unidentified object allegedly propelled by the lawnmower blades—*held*, in action against manufacturer that the lawnmower was not dangerous *per se*, but it was doubtful whether the common law still recognised a distinction between liability for things which were dangerous in themselves and things which were not. The manufacturer's duty was to design and construct the mower with a degree of care appropriate to the dangers attendant upon its use so as to minimise the risk of injury and to warn prospective users of its dangerous propensities.

(c) When Duty Ceases

1. Buckner v. Ashby [1941] 1 K.B. 321, C.A.

Plaintiff trips over soleplate—*Held*, contractor not liable as intermediate examination and acceptance by building owner had taken place, and the effective cause was the failure of the building owner to light.

2. Haseldine v. Daw [1941] 3 All E.R. 156, C.A.

Visitor to premises injured in lift—*Held*, lift repairers liable. Goddard L.J. (at 185 H) said that to render a repairer or contractor liable there must be "a want of care on his part *and* circumstances which show that employer will be left in ignorance of the danger which the lack of care has created."

3. Hartley v. Mayoh [1954] 1 Q.B. 383; [1954] 1 All E.R. 375, C.A.

4. Hobbs (Farms) v. Baxenden Chemical Company Gerber Foods (Holdings) v. E. Hobbs (Farms) [1992] 1 Lloyd's Rep. 54; [1992] C.L.Y. 3204

In main and third party actions liability of occupier of barn for fire which spread to adjoining buildings was considered, as well as liability of manufacturer of foam which caused the fire to spread—*Held* manufacturer of foam substantially to blame as its duty did not cease when the goods were sold and if it realised that an omission to warn past customers about newly discovered risk might cause injury to them.

(2) Standard of care

(a) Standard Required of Particular Persons

Fire brigade—owe duty of care to volunteer fire fighter—who puts himself under their control.......... U1

1. Donoghue v. Stevenson [1932] A.C. 562; 147 L.T. 281, H.L.

"A manufacturer of products, which he sells in such a form as to show that he intends them to reach the ultimate consumer in the form in which they left him with no reasonable possibility of intermediate examination, and with the knowledge that the absence of reasonable care in the preparation or putting up of the products will result in an injury to the consumer's life or property, owes a duty to the consumer to take that reasonable care" (Lord Atkin).

2. North Western Utilities v. London Guarantee [1936] A.C. 108, P.C.

Gas leak in supply pipes under street caused by action of third party (the City Corporation of Edmonton) in constructing a storm sewer and causing pipe to sag—the gas company maintained the pipe under statutory authority—*Held*, (a) the gas in the pipe was a dangerous thing to which *Rylands v. Fletcher* liability would ordinarily apply (118); (b) the fact that defendants were acting under statutory authority was a defence to a claim under *Rylands v. Fletcher* (121); (c) the defendants were, however, liable in negligence, as gas was a dangerous commodity, and it was defendants' duty to watch all operations in the vicinity of their mains which were likely to affect the same: "their duty . . . was at the lowest to be on watch and be vigilant: they do not even pretend to have done as much as that" (Lord Wright, 127).

3. Burfitt v. Kille [1939] 2 K.B. 743; [1939] 2 All E.R. 372, Atkinson J.

Sale of toy pistol and blank ammunition to boy of 12—*Held*, a chattel dangerous *per se*, and defendant liable for selling it to boy. Judge said:

(a) "If A places in the hands of B a chattel which belongs to a class of things dangerous in themselves in the hands of such a person as B . . . a duty of care rests upon A, not only towards the recipient, but towards all such persons as may reasonably be contemplated as likely to be endangered" (374 H);
(b) "The duty resting upon him may in some cases be discharged by a warning. If it cannot, the duty must be to refrain from the sale" (375 E);
(c) "A warning is not a sufficient discharge of duty if the person to whom the chattel is delivered is not a competent person" (375 G).

4. Watson v. Buckley [1940] 1 All E.R. 174, Stable J.

Hair dye contained 10 per cent. instead of 4 per cent. chromic acid, causing dermatitis—*Held*, distributor liable, as he was not buying from an established manufacturer of repute, but through an agent who had "emerged from Spain", and he should therefore have taken care to see that the product was safe. In addition, the product, even at its proper strength of 4 per cent., was potentially dangerous, and special care was needed to see that it was safe. *N.B.* The hairdresser was also liable in contract.

5. The Pass of Ballater [1942] 2 All E.R. 79, Langton J.

Held, having regard to dangerous nature of substance, "no precaution which was commercially practicable ought to have been omitted, and any omission of a practicable precaution would constitute a failure of duty" (84 F).

6. Barkway v. South Wales Transport [1950] A.C. 185; [1950] 1 All E.R. 392, H.L.

Skid caused by burst tyre—all allegations of negligence were negatived, excluding failure to have a system of reporting blows likely to cause an impact fracture—*Held*, on this ground defendants were liable. Lord Porter (399 A) said the duty of a transport company was "to take all reasonable precautions for the safety of their passengers and not to leave them in danger of a risk against which some precautions, at any rate, can be taken." Lord Radcliffe (403 H) said it was "to provide a carriage which was as free from defects as the exercise of all reasonable care can make it."

7. Board v. Thomas Hedley [1951] 2 All E.R. 431; 2 T.L.R. 779, C.A.

Denning L.J. (432 D): "The product would, I think, be dangerous if it might affect normal users adversely or even if it might adversely affect other users who had a higher degree of sensitivity than the normal, so long as they were not altogether exceptional."

8. Basted v. Cozens & Sutcliffe [1954] 1 W.L.R. 1069; [1954] 2 All E.R. 735, Devlin J.

Sudden descent of load suspended from crane due to failure of hoist brake—no clear evidence as to cause—no evidence as to system for maintaining brakes—defendants rely on complaints from operators—*Held*, applying **6**, defendants liable.

9. Sellars v. Best [1954] 1 W.L.R. 913; [1954] 2 All E.R. 389, Pearson J.

Held, the installers were liable. *Ball* (Chap. 7, (1) (b) **8**) is not mentioned in the report, but the boiler in the present case was an electric one—*Held*, also that the electricity suppliers were not liable under *Donoghue v. Stevenson* for omitting to ensure that the boiler was in a fit state to receive supply of electricity.

10. Whitehorn v. P.L.A. [1955] 1 Lloyd's Rep. 54, Morris J.

"Now the obligation of one invitee to a fellow invitee cannot be any higher than that of an invitor to an invitee" (57, col. 1). *But* see **11**.

11. Sullivan v. Lipton, *The Times*, February 23, 1955; [1955] C.L.Y. 1789, Parker L.J.

Plaintiff, a child, was standing on 2 feet 6 inches high wall of unoccupied garden when another child in garden threw a phial of sulphuric acid at her—the phial was one of a number which burglars had thrown about and which defendant had looked for—*Held*, that plaintiff was a trespasser, and the same principles applied to dangerous chattels as to premises, and that if defendant did owe any duty to plaintiff they had discharged it by their search for the phials. *N.B.* In this case as distinct from *Buckland v. Guildford Gas Co.* (Chap. 7, (2) (c) **2**) and *Davis v. St. Mary's Demolition* (Chap. 7, (2) (c) **4**), defendant was the occupier.

12. A. C. Billings v. Riden [1958] A.C. 240; [1957] 3 All E.R. 1, H.L.

Question of duty of contractor towards licensee—*Held*, duty was ordinary duty to take reasonable care to ensure visitors not exposed to danger by their actions. "In the present case, I see no reason why the contractor . . . should be entitled to rely on any speciality in law of licensor and licensee."—*Held*, also that *Malone v. Laskey* [1907] 2 K.B. 141 and *Ball v. L.C.C.* (Chap. 7, (1) (b) **8**), in so far as the latter was based on the contractor owing no duty of care owing to absence of contractual relationship, were wrong, and contractor owed ordinary duty of care to residents in house.

13. Goodchild v. Vaclight, *The Times*, May 22, 1965; [1965] C.L.Y. 2669, Hinchcliffe J.

Held, distributor of foreign vacuum cleaners liable, as he was "more than a mere distributor", servicing and guaranteeing and having his name on the goods.

14. Taylor v. Rover [1966] 1 W.L.R. 1491; [1966] 2 All E.R. 181, Baker J.

Defect in chisel due to negligent hardening—manufacturer sent chisels to independent contractor to be hardened—factory worker injured by splinter—*Held*, manufacturer not liable, as he was entitled to rely on the competence of the independent contractor in the same way as the employer was entitled to rely on competence of manufacturer, and in the circumstances there was no duty on manufacturer to examine or test chisels after hardening.

15. Griffiths v. Arch Engineering [1968] 3 All E.R. 217, Chapman J.

Portable grinding machine—defective because speed was too great for diameter of wheel which was fitted—defendants A had hired machine for use on docks—plaintiff, engaged on other dock repair work and not employed by A, asked A's foreman if he could borrow it—was injured—A's manager had assumed that, as the machine was hired from reputable plant-hiring contractors, it would be in safe working order (222 H)—no one in firm A had any real technical knowledge sufficient to see that speed of wheel was unsafe—*Held*, A liable:

> "If a person professing to handle or control such a machine does not have the engineering knowledge to enable him to say whether it is correctly set up, so much the worse for him. He can hardly be heard to say 'Although I profess to be an engineer, in fact I am an ignoramus and simply did not know that it was dangerous.' If he does not know, then his duty must, in my view, extend to enquiring so as to find out" (220 H–I).

16. McCarthy v. Wellington City [1966] N.Z.L.R. 481, Sup. Ct.

Theft of explosives—*Held*, act of thief on distributing explosives was not a *novus actus interveniens* such as would relieve the possessor from liability to person injured by explosives.

17. Kingzett v. B.R.B. (1968) 112 S.J. 625; [1968] C.L.Y. 2655, C.A.

Theft of detonators by trespassing boys—*Held*, defendants bound to use reasonable care to keep detonators safely, but on the facts the theft by the boys could not reasonably have been foreseen.

18. Rootes v. Shelton (1967) 41 A.L.J.R. 172; [1962] C.L.Y. 2672, Aust. High Ct.

19. Smith v. Scott [1973] Ch. 314; [1972] 3 All E.R. 645, Pennycuick V.-C.

20. Bryson v. Northumbria Police [1977] C.L.Y. 2042, Reeve J.

21. Hill v. Crowe, *The Times*, May 17, 1977 Mackenna J.

22. Cowan v. Blackwill [1978] R.T.R. 421, C.A.

Car repairer left P's vehicle locked in street, where it was stolen—*Held*, not liable, as the duty was no more than that of a reasonable car owner.

23. Arnold v. Teno (1978) 83 D.L.R. (3d) 609; [1978] C.L.Y. 2064, Canada Sup. Ct.

24. Idnani v. Elisha [1979] R.T.R. 488; [1979] C.L.Y. 143, C.A.

Held, defendants not liable.

25. Harrison v. Vincent [1982] R.T.R. 8; [1982] C.L.Y. 2159, C.A.

D rider and P sidecar passenger of motor cycle combination engaged in race. Accident due to defective brakes—D was negligent in causing or permitting defect—but he argued that, since the accident happened in a race, he only owed P a modified duty not to be reckless for his safety—*Held*, that D owed P an ordinary duty of care and was liable. The modified duty laid down in *Wooldridge v. Sumner* (Chap. 10(5)(a)**25**) was appropriate to acts or omissions "in the flurry and excitement of the sport", and not, as here, to those "in the relative calm of the workshop".

26. Nightingale v. Tildsley [1980] C.L.Y. 134, Judge Chetwynd Talbot

Held, D had sufficiently discharged duty by keeping vehicle outside but within locked premises, as with their own vehicles. They had no duty to make regular inspections, and over the years deterioration was inevitable.

27. Kaye v. Alfa Romeo (1984) 174 New L.J. 126; [1984] C.L. 2295, Hutchison J.

Held, that the defendants were liable, but the plaintiff was one-third to blame as his negligent driving had caused the accident.

28. William Hill Organisation Ltd. v. Bernard Sunley & Sons Ltd. (1983) 22 B.L.R. 1; [1983] C.L.Y. 252, C.A.

Plaintiffs engaged defendants to construct office block under R.I.B.A. form of contract—clause 24 defined circumstances in which final certificate to be conclusive evidence work properly carried out and completed in accordance with contract. A conclusive final certificate was issued. Many years later, serious defective workmanship was discovered. Plaintiff, *inter alia*, sought to circumvent the final certificate by suing defendants in negligence—*Held*, that as the contract circumscribed the boundaries of the duty of care and defined its context, the plaintiffs were not entitled to claim a remedy in tort wider than the obligations assumed by the defendants under the contract. "It is not open to the plaintiffs in effect to disregard those clauses of the contract which provided for the conclusive effect of the Final Certificate but to claim a remedy for breaches which were only capable of ascertainment by reference to the contract itself." (Cumming-Bruce, L.J., 29). In principle, as Lord Roskill suggested in *Junior Books v. Veitchi* (Chap. 1(3)(a) **11**), an exclusion clause in a contract may be relevant in determining the duty of care in tort.

U1. Burrough v. Berkshire Fire Authority (1971) C.A. 40

Plaintiff volunteered to help fire brigade to fight barn fire—by using tractor to drag straw bales out—*Held*, as plaintiff thereby came under defendants' control, they owed him a duty of care and were liable for not providing him with a helmet (which was readily available).

(b) To Members of Public

1. Burfitt v. Kille [1939] 2 All E.R. 372, Atkinson J.

Defective pistol sold to boy—owing to defect plaintiff bystander injured—*Held*, defendant liable.

2. Stennett v. Hancock [1939] 2 All E.R. 578, Branson J.

Pedestrian injured by car owing to repairers' having failed to fix flange of wheel securely—*Held*, repairers liable.

3. Ricketts v. Erith B.C. [1943] 2 All E.R. 629, Tucker J.

Held, sellers not liable.

4. Donaldson v. McNiven [1952] 2 All E.R. 691, C.A.

Held, father had not been guilty of negligence in allowing child to use airgun, and therefore defendant not liable.

U1. Whitford v. Monkman (1983) C.A. 926

Plaintiff and defendant flying their radio-controlled gliders in recognised area. P injured by D's glider. Although a willing participant who accepted risks inherent in the sport, P had been injured by a careless flying of glider by D.

(c) To Persons on Private Premises

(*N.B.* (1) The immunity of a building owner in tort towards subsequent purchasers was abolished by the Defective Premises Act 1972 which also imposes duties of care on those doing work for the provision of a dwelling both towards the building employer and subsequent purchasers.
(2) *Dutton* **15** and *Anns* **16** are included in this section for reasons of historical perspective only, and must now be read in the light of *D.F. Estates v. Church Commissioners* and other subsequent cases more fully set out in Chap. 1, (2)(a), 1, (3)(a) and (18.)

1. Haseldine v. Daw [1941] 2 K.B. 343; [1941] 3 All E.R. 156, C.A.

Held, repairers liable. See Chap. 7(1)(c) **2**.

2. Buckland v. Guildford Gas Co. [1949] 1 K.B. 410; [1948] 2 All E.R. 1086, Morris J.

Girl trespasser climbs tree—electrocuted by power cable—*Held*, girl was a "neighbour" within *Donoghue v. Stevenson* to the power company (who were not occupiers), and latter were liable. *Followed* in **4** and **6**.

3. Ball v. L.C.C. [1949] 2 K.B. 159; [1949] 1 All E.R. 1056, C.A.

Relative of tenant injured when boiler blew up which had been put in by defendant installers—C.A. (erroneously, as H.L. held in **8**) held that a duty of care only arose in such circumstances if the boiler was a thing dangerous *per se*—*Held*, that, on the evidence, a boiler without a safety valve was not dangerous *per se*. This decision was influenced by the fact that the tenant lit the boiler when the pipes were frozen and by the possibility that safety valves were in short supply during the war. With a wider definition of duty and more modern standards the decision might today not go the same way.

4. Davis v. St. Mary's Demolition Co. [1954] 1 W.L.R. 592; [1954] 1 All E.R. 578, Ormerod J.

Demolition site—on a Sunday, children dislodge some loose bricks and bring down wall—*Held*, following **2**, children were neighbours of defendant contractors (who were not occupiers), and the latter were liable for failing to take precautions.

5. Sellars v. Best [1954] 1 W.L.R. 913; [1954] 2 All E.R. 389, Pearson J.

Held, the installers were liable to the relative of the owner who was injured. **3** is not mentioned in the report, but the boiler in the present case was an electric one—*Held*, also, the electricity authorities were not liable under *Donoghue v. Stevenson* for omitting to ensure that the boiler was in a fit state to receive a supply of electricity.

6. Creed v. McGeoch [1955] 1 W.L.R. 1005; [1955] 3 All E.R. 123, Ashworth J.

Defendants were contractors not in occupation of land in question (on this point see Chap. 10, (1)**5**—left trailer—trespassing children known to play—plaintiff aged five injured when playing see-saw on trailer—*Held*, following **2** and **4**, defendants owed a duty under *Donoghue v. Stevenson*, and on the facts were liable—*Held*, also, the defence of trespass on an object was not available to them in a case where they "negligently left a dangerous and attractive object in a place where children are known to play" (128 D). *N.B.*—In *Aldrich v. Boyer* (1960) C.A. 14 (unreported) Hodson L.J. (*obiter*) expressed doubt whether it was correct that the relationship between the occupier and the trespasser was irrelevant in considering the duty owed in a case such as the present, and suggested that this question might need consideration in the C.A.

7. Uctkos v. Mazzetta [1956] 1 Lloyd's Rep. 209, Ormerod J.

Held, person using blowlamp was liable for blowing up yacht.

8. A.C. Billings v. Riden [1958] A.C. 240; [1957] 3 All E.R. 1, H.L.

Defendant contractors employed to make a path and steps to front door of No. 25—this made it necessary for visitors to No. 25 to deviate onto No. 26 to get to the front door—visitor to care-taker of No. 25 fell at night into concealed danger when on deviation—*Held*, contractors owed plaintiff the ordinary duty of care, and were liable for failing to take steps to mitigate the danger—*Held*, also, that the fact that the occupier under the law of licensor and licensee might not have been liable was irrelevant. *Ball* **3**, in so far as it decided that a person doing work on premises owed only a limited duty of care to visitors and the like, impliedly overruled.

9. Samways v. Westgate Engineers (1962) 106 S.J. 937; [1962] C.L.Y. 2012, C.A.

Dustman collecting carton of rubbish from house—piece of glass protruding—injuring hand—dustman had been provided with special gloves, but had taken them off because it was hot—*Held*, householder liable, but 50 per cent. contributory negligence.

10. Sharpe v. Sweeting [1963] 1 W.L.R. 665; [1963] 1 All E.R. 455, Nield J.

Builder so constructed canopy over doorway of house he was building for local authority that it collapsed on wife of tenant—*Held*, liable.

11. McBrien v. Arden (1963) 107 S.J. 791; [1963] C.L.Y. 2373, C.A.

Defective electric fire in bedroom of hotel waitress—when it did not go on, she touched it and was burned—*Held*, defendants liable, but 50 per cent. contributory negligence.

12. Brewer v. Delo [1967] 1 Lloyd's Rep. 488; 117 New L.J. 575, Hinchcliffe J.

Held, on the facts, risk of injury from hooking so slight that it could be ignored, and therefore defendants not liable.

13. Petrovitch v. Callingham [1969] 2 Lloyd's Rep. 386, John Stephenson J.

14. British Railways Board v. Herrington [1972] A.C. 877; [1972] 1 All E.R. 749, H.L.

The case which re-defined the duty of an occupier towards trespassers (see Chap. 10, (5) (f) **1**). In the course of speeches certain dicta fell, *obiter*, on the duty of a non-occupier towards a trespasser (see **2**, **4** and **6**): see Lord Wilberforce (772 A), and Lord Diplock (797 E), whose comments approve these three cases.

15. Dutton v. Bognor Regis U.D.C. [1972] Q.B. 373; [1972] 1 All E.R. 462, C.A.

Held, a council surveyor was liable to a subsequent purchaser for negligent inspection of the foundations of a house under construction. However, see now *D. & F. Estates v. Church Commissioners* and other subsequent cases (Chaps. 1, (3) (a) and 18.

16. Anns v. Merton L.B.C. [1977] 2 W.L.R. 1024; [1977] 2 All E.R. 492, H.L.

Defective foundations of house—it was assumed for argument that either the council had failed altogether to exercise their function under the Public Health Act 1936 of inspecting the foundations or else had made a negligent inspection—*Held*, that ordinarily and subject to provisos the council would not be liable for a failure to inspect, but would be liable for a negligent inspection. But see new cases in Chaps. 1, (3) (a) and 18.

17. Bluett v. Woodspring D.C. [1983] J.P.L. 242; [1983] C.L.Y. 2513, Judge Stabb Q.C.

18. Munn v. Porthkerry Park, *The Times*, March 9, 1984, Beldam J.

Deceased drinking at cliff-top leisure centre—subsequently climbed over high fence at edge of site and fell to death—*Held*, that although a licensee may be under a duty of care not to serve a customer if he is aware that the customer would become so intoxicated as to be incapable of protecting himself from an immediate hazard, there was no evidence that the deceased was so intoxicated or that the licensee served him knowing he would become so.

19. Rimmer v. Liverpool C.C. [1984] 1 All E.R. 930. C.A.

For details, see Chap. 10, (8)(a).

20. Rigby v. Chief Constable Of Northamptonshire [1985] 2 All E.R. 985; [1985] C.L.Y. 2327, Taylor J.

CS gas cylinder fired into plaintiff's shop to flush out dangerous psychopath set premises ablaze, and P sued the Chief Constable in negligence and in trespass, in respect of the first on the basis that D had been negligent in not purchasing new type of cylinder which did not carry with it a fire risk—*Held*, no negligence in relation to purchase and use because decision had been made bona fide and could not be impugned; further, defence of necessity succeeded in relation to action in trespass and *R.v.F* in the absence of negligence in the firing itself as police had no alternative but to fire cylinder, but were negligent in not having firefighting equipment to hand in the light of the real fire risk. See also *Rylands v. Fletcher*.

U1. Whyte v. Grimsby BC and British Gas Plc [1992] C.A. 1027

(d) To Persons At Place of Work

(*N.B.* Cases here are where persons other than the employer has been sued. This is likely to be a diminishing category in the aftermath of the Employer's Liability (Defective Equipment) Act 1969. Otherwise, see Chaps. 15 and 16.)

1. Paine v. Colne Valley Elec. [1938] 4 All E.R. 803; 106 L.T. 124, Goddard L.J.

Faulty construction of electric kiosk causing electrocution of deceased—*Held*, manufacturers not liable, as there had been ample opportunity for examination by the electric supply company.

2. Burley v. Stepney Corporation [1947] 1 All E.R. 507, Hallett J.

Held, not negligence, because swarf not obviously abnormal or dangerous and defendants could not reasonably have realised danger.

3. Marshall v. Cellactite (1947) 63 T.L.R. 456; [1947] C.L.Y. 6697, C.A.

General permission by factory owner to contractor to borrow plant—*Held*, there was no representation of safety as to any particular piece of plant, and therefore defendants not liable. *Followed* in **11**.

4. Philco v. Spurling [1949] 2 K.B. 33; [1949] 2 All E.R. 882, C.A.

Defendant in error delivered to plaintiff some scrap celluloid film which can be, and is, ignited with a cigarette end—no warning—*Held*, defendants liable.

5. Denny v. Supplies etc. Co. [1950] 2 K.B. 374; 1 T.L.R. 1168, C.A.

Plaintiff a dock labourer injured when unloading dangerously stowed timber—sues his employers and the loading stevedores—the action failed against employers (apparently because there was no safe method of unloading the timber at all (see T.L.R. 1170), *sed quaere*) but succeeded against loading stevedores—*Held*, on appeal by latter, that they were liable as the dangerous stowage came within *Donoghue v. Stevenson*, and (distinguishing *Farr v. Butters* [1932] 2 K.B. 606) the fact that plaintiff had knowledge of the danger and/or opportunity for examination was no defence where as here there was no practical alternative but to accept the danger (T.L.R. 1173), and furthermore since there was no practical alternative to the unloading, there was no *novus actus interveniens*. Applied in **8**.

6. Pratt v. Richards [1951] 2 K.B. 208; [1951] 1 All E.R. 90n., Barry J.

Faulty scaffold supplied and erected by defendants—plaintiff employed by another employer injured while working thereon—*Held*, defendants liable. It would appear judgment was largely based on liability of defendants as occupiers of and invitors onto scaffold, but it also appears second ground of judgment was that defendants were liable under *Donoghue v. Stevenson* as suppliers (213 and 214, bottom).

7. Twiss v. W. H. Rhodes [1951] 1 Lloyd's Rep. 333, Gorman J.

Plaintiff dock labourer employed by first defendants unloading timber—injured—*Held*, barge had been wrongly stowed by second defendants, but first defendants were solely liable because they had opportunity to inspect, but did not inspect, stowage, nor did they properly supervise unloading. **5** *followed*.

8. Wickens v. Associated Portland Cement [1951] 1 Lloyd's Rep. 162, Cassels J.

Plaintiff dock labourer injured when unloading timber—*Held*, due to improper method of stowage by first defendants and not to any improper method of unloading by second defendants.

9. Beckett v. Newalls Insulation [1953] 1 W.L.R. 8, [1953] 1 All E.R. 250; C.A.

Plaintiff working on a ship—defendants bring on a calor gas cylinder which if a valve or regulator is turned will emit gas which is liable to explode on contact with a naked flame—plaintiff looking for something lights match—explosion—not known how gas escaped—*Held*, defendants liable, as they should have taken precautions by warning and/or instructions as to how it should be moved, as it was patently dangerous if moved.

10. Keen v. Lykiardopoulo [1953] 2 Lloyd's Rep. 349, Jones J.

Plaintiff dock labourer injured when unloading badly stowed cargo from defendants' ship—*Held*, defendants not liable, as although there was a danger it was a usual danger. *N.B.* in this case defendants had not loaded, and they were sued solely as invitors, it being admitted that under *Thomson v. Cremin* (Chap. 10 (5)(d) **6**, (*sed q.v.*) that defendants would be vicariously liable for any negligence of those who loaded.

11. Johnson v. Croggan [1954] 1 W.L.R. 195; [1954] 1 All E.R. 121, Pilcher J.

Facts similar to **3** and for same reasons—*Held*, defendants not liable.

12. Basted v. Cozens & Sutcliffe [1954] 1 W.L.R. 1069; [1954] 2 All E.R. 735, Devlin J.

Sudden descent of load suspended from defendants' crane—due to failure of hoist brake—cause uncertain—*Held*, it was defendants' duty, all the knowledge of the facts being with them, to satisfy the court they had a proper system of maintenance, which they had failed to do, and were therefore liable.

13. Whitehorn v. P.L.A. [1955] 1 Lloyd's Rep. 54, Morris L.J.

Plaintiff a tally clerk had to pass through a narrow way left between stacked hatch covers and hatch coamings and tripped in a loop of rope left by defendants who were stevedores—*Held*, defendants not liable. The judge said (57, col. 1) that the obligation of one invitee to a fellow invitee could not be any higher than that of an invitor to an invitee, and that neither the narrowness of the passage (for which defendants were responsible) nor the loop of rope were unusual dangers or traps. "Plaintiff knew quite well the nature of the place and he was aware of the general unavoidable risks of the work of those engaged in unloading ships" (63, col. 1). *Sed quaere* now—see *A. C. Billings v. Riden* (Chap. 7, (2) (a) **12**).

14. Simmons v. Bovis [1956] 1 W.L.R. 381; [1956] 1 All E.R. 736, Barry J.

Plaintiff, employed by main contractors, stepped onto a very defective scaffold erected by sub-contractors, defendants—*Held*, defendants liable, as they ought to have foreseen that plaintiff might use scaffold.

15. Jeyes v. Currie Line & P.L.A. [1956] 2 Lloyd's Rep. 87, Pearce J.

Overstowed barrels which were dangerous to unload unless special measures taken—unloading stevedores who employed plaintiff found liable—*Held* shipowners not liable, because they had no reason to suppose the barrels were a danger (92). In addition, on the facts, the unloading stevedores were aware of the danger.

16. Dukelow v. Scruttons [1956] 2 Lloyd's Rep. 631, Lloyd-Jacob J.

Held, loading stevedores liable for unstable stowage, and that unloading stevedores were entitled to assume that the bags had been stowed in accordance with normal safe practice.

17. Gledhill v. Liverpool Abattoir [1957] 1 W.L.R. 1028; [1957] 3 All E.R. 117, C.A.

Held defendants not liable. See Chap. 7, (4) (d) **17**.

18. Roberts v. T. Wallis [1958] 1 Lloyd's Rep. 29, Barry J.

Set of timber suspended from winch suddenly drops 2–3 feet and strikes timber in hold—*Held*, defendants not liable, as not *res ipsa loquitur*, and in addition, of the two causes suggested, *i.e.* broken con rod and riding turn on winch barrel, the first would be met by defence of latent defect, and the second would not in itself constitute negligence.

19. Johnson v. Rea [1962] 1 Q.B. 373; [1961] 3 All E.R. 816, C.A.

Plaintiff lorry driver (not employed by defendants) slipped on dock shed floor when carrying a keg—defendants' stevedores were in control (but not in law occupiers) of dock shed—floor was slippery through discharge of soda ash from bags being moved by defendants—defendants took no steps to remove danger—plaintiff was aware the floor was slippery—*Held*, defendants liable, as their duty was not merely to warn, but to take reasonable steps to obviate danger.

20. Vandersteen v. P.L.A. [1962] 1 Lloyd's Rep. 126, Edmund Davies J.

Plaintiff dock labourer injured when unstacking dangerously stacked jibs of cranes—sues employers (Port of London Authority) and shipowners who stacked the jibs—after stacking shipowners handed over stack to employers—shipowners claimed that in accordance with *Denny v. Supplies and Transport Company* **5** their liability ended with the handing over of the stack to the employers who could and should have made an intermediate examination and discovered the defects, if any—*Held*, not so, and that both shipowners and employers were liable to plaintiff.

21. Moorhead v. Thomas Smith [1963] 1 Lloyd's Rep. 164, Hinchcliffe J.

Held, cause of accident was that chisel was in bad condition and harder than hammer head, and that hammer was properly tempered and hardened. Makers of hammer not liable. Observations *passim* on proper standards for making hammers: on this topic see also judgment of Ashworth J. in *Davie v. New Merton Board Mills* [1957] 2 Q.B. 368 and *Mason v. Williams and Williams* [1955] 1 All E.R. 808.

22. Clay v. Crump [1964] 1 Q.B. 633; [1963] 3 All E.R. 687, C.A.

Patently unsafe wall left by demolition contractors—passed by architect as safe—rebuilding started without any further precautions by new contractors, who employed plaintiff—on whom wall fell—

Held, all three defendants liable (notwithstanding, *qua* first two, that new contractors had opportunity for examination—see Chap. 7 (4) (d) **22**).

23. Taylor v. Rover [1966] 1 W.L.R. 1491; [1966] 2 All E.R. 181, Baker J.

Held, manufacturer not liable, as he was entitled to rely on competence of independent contractor in the same way as an employer who bought defective equipment from a reputable source (see *Davie v. New Merton* (Chap. 15 (1) (d) **5**)). *N.B.* Since the Employer's Liability (Defective Equipment) Act 1969 abrogates the immunity of employers *only* under *Davie*, this decision is not affected thereby.

24. Quinn v. Burch [1966] 2 Q.B. 370; [1966] 2 All E.R. 283, C.A.

Held, defendants not liable, because their breach of contract merely provided the occasion which brought about the plaintiff's conduct, but in no way caused it: "If the defendants . . . had to comply with the duties arising between master and servant, the position would have been different" (Sellers L.J., 287 D).

25. McArdle v. Andmac [1967] 1 W.L.R. 356; [1967] 1 All E.R. 583, C.A.

P, employed by subcontractors, pouring bitumen on roof—fell through open skylight left unfenced by other subcontractors—main contractors supplied no labour—but their engineer was on the site in charge, giving out jobs and instructions to other subcontractors—*Held*, main contractors and both subcontractors all liable. One-third against each.

26. Griffiths v. Arch Engineering [1968] 3 All E.R. 217, Chapman J.

P, employed on docks doing some repair work, borrowed a portable grinding machine from D1, who also had men working on the docks—machine was defective in that it rotated too fast for size of wheel fitted—P injured—D1 had hired machine from D2, who were plant contractors—*Held*, D1 and D2 both liable equally: the fact that D1 had no specialist knowledge enabling them to recognise defect was of no avail (see Chap. 7, (2) (a) **15**); and D2 could not rely on intermediate examination, because they had no reason to suppose D1 would make one (see Chap. 7, (4) (d) **24**). On the question of liability for plant gratuitously loaned, *Marshall* **3** and *Johnson* **11** were apparently not cited in argument.

27. Barry v. Black-Clawson (1966) 2 K.I.R. 237; [1966] C.L.Y. 2678, C.A.

Held, main contractor not liable, as he had obtained the equipment from a reputable supplier, and had no reason to suspect defect. *N.B.* This decision is unaffected by the Employer's Liability (Defective Equipment) Act 1969, which applies to employers and employees only.

28. Jones v. Minton (1973) 15 K.I.R. 309; [1974] C.L.Y. 2599, Thompson J.

Defendant main contractor made available to working subcontractor a cement mixer which was patently defective in that it had no safety guard on it—*Held*, defendant not liable.

29. Hill v. Crowe, *The Times*, May 17, 1977, MacKenna J.

30. Kealey v. Heard [1983] 1 W.L.R. 573; [1983] 1 All E.R. 973, Mann J.

Defendant decided to convert properties into flats. Instead of engaging a general contractor, he engaged specialist tradesmen individually, including plaintiff, a self-employed plasterer. Plaintiff injured when planks on scaffold erected by unknown workman collapsed—*Held*, that the defendant was in breach of his duty of care to the plaintiff. He was not entitled to rely on the tradesmen to provide safe scaffolding: "If a person chooses to build by the method selected by the defendant then ought he to provide at least some form of superintendence either by himself or by another in order that his common law duty may be discharged" (976 J).

31. Wheeler v. Copas [1981] 3 All E.R. 405, Chapman J.

P was doing bricklaying for D, a farmer, as a labour-only contractor. At one stage he needed a longer ladder and was shown two by D, one with 35 rungs was probably too long. P took the other which was a fruit ladder and too flimsy so that it collapsed in use—*Held*, D was under a duty of care in providing the ladder and was liable (but 50 per cent. contributory negligent).

U1. Curtis v. Hermit Industries Ltd. (1957) C.A. 102

Plaintiff repairing defect in switchboard—director of defendants said all right to set machine in motion—door fell open while rotating and broke plaintiff's leg—*Held*, defendants not liable. Following *Bates v. Parker* (Chap. 10, (4) (d) **3**) defendants owed no duty to plaintiff—occupier through director saying all right to set machine in motion was not representing it was safe to do so—plaintiff might have action against someone else but not against defendants. Jenkins L.J. (8 D): "In my view, the defendants were in no way concerned as to the manner in which the experts achieved their object, and it was no part of their function to instruct the experts in the experts' own business."

U2. Mitchell v. Mills Scaffold Co. (1960) C.A. 360

Defendant builders were retained by a house owner to attend to a defective cornice—builders contracted with scaffolders to erect scaffold—while scaffold was being erected cornice collapsed injuring plaintiff employee of scaffolders—plaintiff sued and won against both builders and scaffolders—builders appealed—*Held*, builders liable, as their inspection ought to have given them knowledge of the imminent danger of collapse.

U3. Brown v. Watkins and Bradford (1966) C.A. 119

Bradfords, main contractors, installing washing machines in factory—they employed plaintiff as electrical subcontractor to connect them to the mains—space at back of machines was cramped—and Bradfords then took off back panels exposing machinery—for a reason unknown the machinery started while plaintiff was in the cramped space—Bradfords contended they owed no duty—*Held*, they did, and were liable. *Savory v. Holland Hannen* (Chap. 10, (5) (c) **14**) and *Field v. Jeavons*, which were both cases where defendants were occupiers, *applied.*

U4. Withers v. A.M. Curtis (1992) C.A. 137

Plaintiff injured when falling off scaffolding tower supplied by main contractors (D2). The ladder leading to the tower was short, unlashed and unfooted—*Held*, D not liable because a safe means of access was available to him, *i.e.* the inside framework of the tower.

Examples

Plaintiff	*Defendant*	*Fault*		*Liable or not*
Ship's welder	Ship repairer	Steam from defective valve	1	Yes
Electrician	Manufacturer	Electric kiosk	2	No

Barge hand	Consignor	Refuse containing magnesium swarf	3	No
BUILDING WORKER	FACTORY OWNER	LOAN OF FAULTY PLANT	4	No
FACTORY WORKER	CONSIGNOR	INFLAMMABLE CELLULOID MATERIAL	5	Yes
Dock worker	Crane owner	Not maintaining brakes	6	Yes
DOCK WORKER	LOADING STEVEDORES	BAD STOWAGE: TIMBER	7	Yes
Building worker	Scaffolding contractor	Faulty scaffold	8	Yes
Dock worker	Loading stevedores	Bad stowage: timber	9	No
Dock worker	Loading stevedores	Bad stowage: timber	10	Yes
SHIP WORKER	SHIP REPAIRER	GAS CYLINDER EXPLODING	11	Yes
Dock worker	Railway undertaking	Bad stowage: fishplates on railway truck	12	Yes
Dock worker	Shipowner	Bad stowage	13	No
Dock worker	Loading stevedores	Bad stowage: baled rubber	14	No
Dock worker	Crane owner	Jerking and swinging load	15	Yes
Dock worker	Crane owner	Lowering load on plaintiff	16	Yes
Tug	Bridge owner	No warning: bridge hit	17	Yes
Building worker	Factory owner	Loan of faulty plant	18	No
Dock worker	Owner of welding machine	Projecting towbar	19	Yes
Dock worker	Crane owner	Sudden descent of crane	20	Yes
Lorry driver	Stevedores	Rolling barrels onto lorry too fast	21	Yes
WORKMAN	OWNERS OF COALING PLANT	RAISING RAMP OF COAL CHUTE UNEXPECTEDLY	22	Yes
Factory worker	Manufacturer	Defective chisel	23	Yes
Dock worker	Stevedores	Loop of rope on deck	24	No
Dock worker	Lorry driver	Drum rolling off lorry	25	Yes
Dock worker	Crane owner	Eye of strop not taken inside shackle	26	Yes
Dock worker	Crane owner	Swinging too quickly	27	Yes
Building worker	Scaffolding contractor	Faulty scaffold	28	Yes
Dock worker	Shipowner	Bad stowage: barrels	29	No
Dock worker	Loading stevedores	Bad stowage: cement bags	30	Yes
VISITOR	RAILWAY UNDERTAKING	TRAIN TOO FAST IN TUNNEL	31	Yes
SLAUGHTERMAN	ABATTOIR OWNER	UNSUITABLE CHAINS FOR SLINGING	32	No
Dock worker	Lorry owner	Lorry sinking under increasing load	33	Yes
Dock worker	Loading stevedores	Gap in gratings on floor of hold	34	Yes

VISITOR	RAILWAY UNDERTAKING	SHUNTING: NO WARNING, NO LOOK-OUT	35	Yes
Dock worker	Crane owner	Load dragged in hold	36	Yes
Dock worker	Crane owner	Sudden drop of 2–3 feet in hold	37	No
DOCK WORKER	STEVEDORES	SLIPPERY DOCK SHED	38	Yes
Dock worker	Shipowner	Bad stowage: crane jibs	39	Yes
Factory worker	Manufacturer	Hammer chipping	40	No
BUILDING WORKER	DEMOLITION CONTRACTOR	UNSAFE WALL LEFT STANDING	41	Yes
BUILDING WORKER	ARCHITECT	UNSAFE WALL LEFT STANDING	41	Yes
Factory worker	Manufacturer	Chisel splintering: defendant had got competent contractor to harden	42	No
WORKING SUB-CONTRACTOR	MAIN CONTRACTOR	NO STEPLADDER PROVIDED: SO PLAINTIFF USES UNFOOTED TRESTLE	43	No
DOCK WORKER	SHIPOWNER	BAD STOWAGE: TIMBER	44	Yes
EMPLOYEE OF SUB-CONTRACTOR	MAIN CONTRACTOR	ROOF: UNFENCED OPENING	45	Yes
Building worker	Safety consultant	Passing hoist as safe	46	Yes
FACTORY WORKER	MANUFACTURER	CARCINOGENOUS CHEMICAL	47	Yes
Post Office worker	Consignor of parcels	Sending parcels over 50 lbs in weight	48	No
Working sub-contractor	Main contractor	Defendant making available concrete mixer without guard	49	No
Lorry driver	Manufacturer	Packing case stoving in when stood on	50	Yes
Labour-only contractor	Building owner	Loan of ladder: too flimsy	51	Yes
DOCK WORKER	SHIPOWNER	BAD STOWAGE: DEEP GAP IN HOLD BETWEEN BULKHEAD AND STOWED TIMBER	52	YES
Technical expert	Factory owner	Telling expert safe to start machine when not	U1	No
Dock worker	Shipowner	Mooring rope suddenly tightening	U2	No
Scaffolder	Building contractor	Building unsafe for scaffold	U3	Yes
Factory worker	Manufacturer	Drum of caustic soda spraying contents	U4	Yes

1. Howard v. Furness Houlder [1936] 2 All E.R. 781, Lewis J.
2. Paine v. Colne Valley Elec. [1938] 4 All E.R. 803; 106 L.T. 124, Goddard L.J.
3. Burley v. Stepney Corporation [1947] 1 All E.R. 507; 176 L.T. 535, Hallett J.
4. Marshall v. Cellactite (1947) 63 T.L.R. 456; (1947) C.L.Y. 6697, C.A.
5. Philco v. Spurling 2 K.B. 33, [1949] 2 All E.R. 882; (1949) C.A.
6. Spain v. Ocean S.S. (1949) 83 L1.L.R. 188, Sellers J.
7. Denny v. Supplies etc. Co. [1950] 2 K.B. 374; 1 T.L.R. 1168, C.A.
8. Pratt v. Richards [1951] 2 K.B. 208; [1991] 1 All E.R. 90n., Barry J.
9. Twiss v. W. H. Rhodes [1951] 1 Lloyd's Rep. 333, Gorman J.
10. Wickens v. Associated Portland Cement [1951] 1 Lloyd's Rep. 162, Cassels J.
11. Beckett v. Newalls Insulation 1 W.L.R. 8; [1953] 1 All E.R. 250 [1993]; C.A.
12. McDonald v. Smith Coggins & Railway Executive [1953] 2 Lloyd's Rep. 203, Devlin J.
13. Keen v. Lykiardopoulo [1953] 2 Lloyd's Rep. 349, Jones J.
14. Oliver v. Montgomerie [1953] 2 Lloyd's Rep. 672, Sellers J.
15. Gray v. Docks Executive [1953] 1 Lloyd's Rep. 558, Byrne J.
16. Ashton v. M.D.H.B. [1953] 1 Lloyd's Rep. 230, Gorman J.
17. Munday v. S.E. Gas Board [1953] 2 Lloyd's Rep. 230, Gorman J.
18. Johnson v. Croggan 1 W.L.R. 195; [1954] 1 All E.R. 121 [1994]; Pilcher J.
19. Ryan v. Maltby [1954] 1 Lloyd's Rep. 196, Hilbery J.
20. Basted v. Cozens and Sutcliffe [1954] 1 W.L.R. 1069; [1954] 2 All E.R. 735, Devlin J.
21. Mackenzie v. Leach [1954] 1 Lloyd's Rep. 158, Lord Goddard C.J.
22. Gibbons v. N.C.B. [1954] 1 Lloyd's Rep. 181, C.A.
23. Mason v. Williams and Williams 1 W.L.R. 549, [1955] 1 All E.R. 808; Finnemore J.
24. Whitehorn v. P.L.A. [1955] 1 Lloyd's Rep. 54, Morris L. J.
25. Rogers v. George Transport [1955] 1 Lloyd's Rep. 524, Hallett J.
26. Cresswell v. Harland and Wolff [1955] 2 Lloyd's Rep. 345, Lynskey J.
27. Williams v. P.L.A. [1956] 1 Lloyd's Rep. 180, Cassels J.
28. Simmons v. Bovis 1 W.L.R. 381; [1956] 1 All E.R. 736; [1956] Barry J.
29. Jeyes v. Currie Line [1956] 2 Lloyd's Rep. 87, Pearce J.
30. Dukelow v. Scruttons [1956] 2 Lloyd's Rep. 631, Lloyd-Jacob J.
31. Slater v. Clay Cross 2 Q.B. 264; [1956] 2 All E.R. 625; C.A.
32. Gledhill v. Liverpool Abattoir 1 W.L.R. 1028; [1957] 3 All E.R. 117; [1957] C.A.
33. Newall v. Grimditch [1957] 2 Lloyd's Rep. 457, Pearce L. J.
34. Smith v. Silvertown Services [1957] 2 Lloyd's Rep. 569, Devlin J.
35. Ashdown v. Samuel Williams 1 Q.B. 409; [1957] 1 All E.R. 35; [1957] C.A.
36. Smith v. L. J. Hovey [1957] 1 Lloyd's Rep. 372, Stable J.
37. Roberts v. T. Wallis [1958] 1 Lloyd's Rep. 29, Barry J.
38. Johnson v. Rea [1962] 1 Q.B. 373; [1961] 3 All E.R. 816; C.A.
39. Vandersteen v. P.L.A. [1962] 1 Lloyd's Rep. 126, Edmund Davies J.
40. Moorhead v. Thomas Smith [1963] 1 Lloyd's Rep. 164, Hinchcliffe J.
41. Clay v. Crump [1964] 1 Q.B. 533; [1963] 3 All E.R. 687; C.A.
42. Taylor v. Rover 1 W.L.R. 1491; [1966] 2 All E.R. 181; [1966] Baker J.
43. Quinn v. Burch [1966] 2 Q.B. 370; [1966] 2 All E.R. 283, C.A.
44. Gaffney v. Aviation and Shipping [1966] 1 Lloyd's Rep. 249, C.A.
45. McArdle v. Andmac 1 W.L.R. 356; [1967] 1 All E.R. 583; C.A.
46. Driver v. Willett [1969] 1 All E.R. 665, Rees J.
47. Cassidy v. I.C.I., *The Times*, November 2, 1972; [1972]; C.L.Y. 2381, C.A.
48. Smith v. Southwark Offsets (1974) 119 S.J. 258; [1974] C.L.Y. 2589, Bristow J.
49. Jones v. Minton (1973) 15 K.I.R. 309; [1974] C.L.Y. 2599, Thompson J.
50. Hill v. Crowe, *The Times*, May 17, 1977, MacKenna J.
51. Wheeler v. Copas [1981] 3 All E.R. 405, Chapman J.
52. The Vladimir Timofeyev [1983] 1 Lloyd's Rep. 378; [1983] C.L.Y. 2530, C.A.

U1. *Curtis v. Hermit Industries* (1957) C.A. 102
U2. *Clay v. Ministry of Transport* (1960) C.A. 178; (1960) 1 Lloyd's Rep. 517.

U3. *Mitchell v. Mills Scaffold Co.* (1960) C.A. 360
U4. *Broomhall v. British Railways Board* (1963) C.A. 110

(e) To Child (Causing Injury to Self)

1. Buckland v. Guildford Gas Co. [1949] 1 K.B. 410; [1948] 2 All E.R. 1086, Morris J.

Trespassing girl climbs tree—electrocuted by nearby overhead power cable—*Held*, power company (who were *not* occupiers) liable, as girl was a "neighbour" within *Donoghue v. Stevenson*, whose presence they should have anticipated. *Applied* in **3**. But *doubted* (*obiter*) in **U1**, *q.v.*

2. Perry v. Thomas Wrigley [1955] 1 W.L.R. 1164; [1955] 3 All E.R. 243, Oliver J.

Plaintiff surmounted a fence round hole in road and fell into pit 20 feet deep—defendants were contractors but not in occupation of road—*Held*, applying test of allurement (*sed quaere*), this was not an allurement and claim failed.

3. Creed v. McGeoch [1955] 1 W.L.R. 1005; [1955] 3 All E.R. 123, Ashworth J.

Defendants were contractors not in occupation of land in question (on this point see Chap. 10, (1) **5**)—left trailer—trespassing children known to play—plaintiff aged five injured when playing see-saw on trailer—*Held*, that, since defendants were not in occupation, they owed duty under *Donoghue v. Stevenson*, and since they were aware of the risk of injury to children and knew that it was attractive to children, they were liable; and that, by analogy with *Gough v. N.C.B.* (Chap. 10, (6) (d) **2**), the defence of trespass on an object was not available to them in a case where they "negligently left a dangerous and attractive object in a place where children are known to play" (128 D). **1** applied. But *doubted* (*obiter*) in **U1**, *q.v.*

4. Miller v. South of Scotland E.B., 1958 S.C. (H.L.) 20; [1958] C.L.Y. 2226, H.L.

House being demolished—Electricity Board reported they had turned off the electricity but failed to do so—in consequence plaintiff child was injured—*Held*, failure of Electricity Board raised a prima facie case of negligence against them, even though plaintiff was (as it seems) a trespasser.

5. Beaver v. Cohen *The Times*, May 14, 1960; [1960] C.L.Y. 2142, Stable J.

Held, defendant liable for loss of sight when firework exploded.

6. Hughes v. Lord Advocate [1963] A.C. 837; [1963] 1 All E.R. 705, H.L.

Open manhole site in street unguarded and unfenced—four lit paraffin lamps—one lamp exploded when meddling boy of eight tripped over it—*Held*, defendants liable. *N.B.* The real point in the case revolved round the unforeseeability of the explosion.

7. Arnold v. Teno (1978) 83 D.L.R. (3d) 609; [1978] C.L.Y. 2064, Canada Sup.Ct.

8. Eastham v. Eastham [1982] C.L.Y. 2141, Caulfield J.

Plaintiff aged $9\frac{1}{2}$ playing tig with other children by hotel swimming pool—able to swim. Slipped on wet tiled surround and fell in, striking projecting bracket. P sues parents—*Held*, (a) the court would not expect a parent to inspect a pool, in general use, to see if it was safe; (b) it was reasonable for the parents to allow the child to play tig with instructions to be careful and (sic) act reasonably; (c) the risk of such injury was unforeseeable; and (d) not every risk of injury could be avoided by a careful parent, whose only duty was to take reasonable care. Defendant parents not liable.

9. Jauffur v. Akhbar, *The Times*, February 10, 1984; [1984] C.L.Y. 2332, Peter Pain J.

U1. Aldrich v. Henry Boyer (1960) C.A. 14

Hodson L.J. (9–10, *obiter*) said **1** and **3** might require reconsideration. But more recently in *Herrington*, Chap. 7, (2) (c) **14**, the two cases were approved *obiter* by Lords Wilberforce and Diplock.

(f) In Respect of Child Causing Injury to Others

SPOUT OF OILCAN—SCHOOLMASTER ENTRUSTING TO BOY 1
Defective pistol—shop selling to boy of 12 2
Toy bow and arrow—shop selling to child 3
Petrol—selling to child of 9 4
AIRGUN—FATHER ALLOWING BOY OF 13 TO USE 5
Demolition site—contractor not guarding against children 6
Phial of sulphuric acid—thrown by one trespassing child at another—defendant occupier of premises 7
PETROL TANK OF PARKED LORRY—CHILD THROWING MATCH IN 8
.410 shotgun—father allowing boy of 12 to have 9
Airgun—parent allowing boy of 15 to have 10

1. Wray v. Essex C.C. [1936] 3 All E.R. 97, C.A.

Schoolboy carrying oilcan for master injures another boy with spout—*Held*, master not guilty of negligence.

2. Burfitt v. Kille [1939] 2 All E.R. 372, Atkinson J.

Defective pistol sold to boy of 12—injures plaintiff bystander when discharged (because of defect)—*Held*, defendant seller liable.

3. Ricketts v. Erith B.C. [1943] 2 All E.R. 629, Tucker J.

Held, not negligent to sell toy bow and arrow to child.

4. Yachuk v. Oliver Blais [1949] A.C. 386; [1949] 2 All E.R. 150, P.C.

Held, defendant negligent for selling petrol to child of nine, even though child misrepresented purpose for which required.

5. Donaldson v. McNiven [1952] 2 All E.R. 691, C.A.

Held, defendant father had not been guilty of negligence in allowing son of 13 to use airgun.

6. Davis v. St. Mary's Demolition Co. [1954] 1 W.L.R. 592; [1954] 1 All E.R. 578, Ormerod J.

Defendant contractors (*not* occupiers) demolishing buildings—trespassing children known to play—plaintiff and other boys dislodge some loose bricks playing—*Held*, defendants liable for failing to take precautions.

7. Sullivan v. Lipton, *The Times*, February 23, 1955; [1955] C.L.Y. 1789, Parker L.J.

Held, defendant not liable. See Chap. 7, (2) (a) **11**.

8. Perry v. Kendricks Transport [1956] 1 W.L.R. 85; [1956] 1 All E.R. 154, C.A.

Defendants had parked a disused coach and emptied tank—they inspected vehicle from time to time and saw petrol cap was on—an unknown child removed cap and threw a match in, causing explosion which injured plaintiff—*Held*, defendants not liable, as this was not reasonably foreseeable.

9. Newton v. Edgerley [1959] 1 W.L.R. 1031; [1959] 3 All E.R. 337, Lord Parker C.J.

Held, defendant father liable for accident when son aged 12 shot another boy.

10. Court v. Wyatt, *The Times*, June 25, 1960; [1960] C.L.Y. 882, Donovan J.

Boy of 15 shot plaintiff with an airgun—*Held*, defendant father liable, as father knew the boy was of such a disposition as not to be trusted with the gun, and therefore father was negligent.

(g) To Ultimate Consumer

(*N.B.* The Consumer Protection Act 1987 applies to goods produced after March 1, 1988 and now provides a statutory framework for certain types of product liability claims.)

1. Evans v. Triplex [1936] 1 All E.R. 283, Porter J.

Held, manufacturers not liable. For reasons see Chap. 7(4) (d) **3**.

2. Grant v. Australian Knitting Mills [1936] A.C. 85; 52 T.L.R. 38, P.C.

Held, manufacturers liable, although (see Chap. 7, (3)**1**) plaintiff could not "lay his finger on the exact person in all the chain who was responsible."

3. Parker v. Oloxo [1937] 3 All E.R. 524, Hilbery J.

Held, manufacturers liable for hair dye which was irritant to anyone who was susceptible—*Held*, hairdresser also liable.

4. Kubach v. Hollands [1937] 3 All E.R. 907; 53 T.L.R. 1024, Lord Hewart C.J.

Explosion in school classroom due to manganese dioxide containing antimony sulphide—makers had no notice of intended user and retailers had had ample opportunity for intermediate test—*Held*, makers not liable.

5. Dransfield v. B.I. Cables [1937] 4 All E.R. 382; 54 T.L.R. 11, Hawke J.

Breakage of "bull-ring"—*Held*, although makers were negligent there was opportunity for intermediate examination by the local authority who bought it, and therefore makers not liable. This case has been criticised.

6. Daniels v. White [1938] 4 All E.R. 258, Lewis J.

Carbolic acid in lemonade—*Held*, applying dictum of Lord Wright in **2**, defendants had succeeded in disproving negligence.

7. Barnes v. Irwell Valley Water Board [1939] 1 K.B. 21, [1938] 2 All E.R. 650, C.A.

Supply of plumbo-solvent water, *i.e.* after being in contact with lead for some time, water absorbed lead—*Held*, defendants liable.

8. Read v. Croydon Corporation [1938] 4 All E.R. 631; 55 T.L.R. 212, Stable J.

Held, defendants liable for negligently supplying impure drinking water.

9. Griffiths v. Conway [1939] 1 All E.R. 685, Branson J.

Held, defendants not liable.

10. Mayne v. Silvermere Cleaners [1939] 1 All E.R. 693, Croom-Johnson J.

Held, defendants liable.

11. Stennett v. Hancock [1939] 2 All E.R. 578, Branson J.

Held, motor-car repairers liable to injured pedestrian for insecure fixing of wheel flange.

12. Herschtal v. Stewart & Ardern [1940] 1 K.B. 155; [1939] 4 All E.R. 123, Tucker J.

Second-hand car supplied on hire-purchase to plaintiff—defective—plaintiff injured—plaintiff was given an opportunity to examine but as defendants never contemplated he would use it—*Held*, liable. *Applied* in **18**.

13. Watson v. Buckley [1940] 1 All E.R. 174, Stable J.

Distributors advertised hair product as absolutely harmless and needing no preliminary test before use—*Held*, in view of this defendants liable for negligence and could not rely on defence of opportunity of examination.

14. Barnett v. Packer [1940] 3 All E.R. 575, Singleton J.

Plaintiff shopkeeper—had bought sweets from wholesaler—pricked finger on wire in sweets—*Held*, defendant manufacturers liable.

15. Holmes v. Ashford [1950] 2 All E.R. 76; [1950] W.N. 269, C.A.

Hair dye which could be dangerous to certain skins—manufacturers warned hairdresser of this danger—*Held*, they had discharged their duty, and that it was not necessary in every case to warn ultimate recipient.

16. Ingham v. Emes [1955] 2 Q.B. 366; [1955] 2 All E.R. 740, C.A.

Plaintiff in this case was suing on a warranty—*Held*, the fact that plaintiff knew but did not disclose she was abnormally sensitive to the dye disabled her from suing. **9** *applied.*

17. Hindustan S.S. Co. v. Siemens Bros. [1955] 1 Lloyd's Rep. 167, Willmer J.

Telegraph system supplied which in event of breakage put hands to "zero" which was very near "full ahead"—engineer, on breakage, mistook hands going to zero for full ahead—*Held*, design defective, and defendants would ordinarily be liable under *Donoghue v. Stevenson*, but not here, because the chain of events was unforeseeable and defendants had had abundant opportunity for examination.

18. Andrews v. Hopkinson [1957] 1 Q.B. 229; [1956] 3 All E.R. 422, McNair J.

Second-hand car supplied on hire-purchase to plaintiff by defendant—defective—*Held*, following **12**, defendant liable, as the test was whether the car *would* be examined by or on behalf of plaintiff, not whether it was possible.

19. Steer v. Durable Rubber Co., *The Times*, November 20, 1958; [1958] C.L.Y. 2250, C.A.

Held, defendant manufacturers liable because they had not discharged the onus of proof on them. See Chap. 7, (3) **5**.

20. Goodchild v. Vaclight, *The Times*, May 22, 1965; [1965] C.L.Y. 2669, Hinchcliffe J.

Held, applying *Watson* **13**, machine dangerous (but 50 per cent. contributory negligence).

21. Fisher v. Harrods (1966) 110 S.J. 133; [1966] 1 Lloyd's Rep. 500, McNair J.

Held, defendants were liable in failing to make inquiries of the manufacturer, failing to have the cleaner analysed, and marketing it without a warning.

22. Hart v. Dominion Stores (1968) 67 D.L.R. (2d) 675, Ontario High Ct.

23. Vacwell v. B.D.H. Chemicals [1971] 1 Q.B. 88; [1969] 3 All E.R. 1681, Rees J.

Held, defendants liable, but appeal was settled at 80 per cent.—see [1970] 3 All E.R. 553n.

24. Hill v. Crowe, *The Times*, May 17, 1977, MacKenna J.

A packing case gave way when stood on by a lorry driver handling same—manufacturers gave evidence of a good system of work and good supervision—and then, relying on dicta by Lewis J. in **6**, alleged that no negligence was established—*Held*, not so, and defendants were liable, as one obvious cause, not covered by defendants' evidence, was negligence by an employee.

25. Hone v. Benson [1977] C.L.Y. 2062, Judge Fay Q.C.

The defendants, being husband and wife, built a restaurant, in which they and/or a plumber working for them installed a hot water system. Some months later they sold the premises to P. In an action brought by P he alleged that (a) the defendants when building the restaurant knew that they might soon sell it; (b) the hot water system was negligently designed and installed; and (c) after conveyance the system malfunctioned, causing physical damage and loss—*Held*, the allegations if proved would make the defendants liable.

26. Murphy v. Atlantic Speedy Propane (1979) 103 D.L.R. (3d) 545; [1980] C.L.Y. 1905, Nova Scotia Sup. Ct.

Explosion of propane supplied by D to P—*Held*, D negligent in supplying propane with insufficient odour for detecting leakage.

27. Hurley v. Dyke [1979] R.T.R. 265; [1979] C.L.Y. 1867, H.L.

Held, the sellers had sufficiently discharged their duty by giving the warning at auction.

28. Junior Books v. Veitchi [1983] A.C. 520; [1982] 3 All E.R. 201, H.L.

In this case it was held that a subcontractor engaged in work for a building owner owes the owner a duty of care to avoid causing him economic loss by reason of defects in the work. For details see Chap 1, (3)(a) **11**. The House *reserved its views* as to whether a manufacturer or a contractor who provides an article which is defective but not dangerous is liable to a subsequent purchaser who suffers economic loss only as a result of the defect. As the standard required for the article may have been defined by the contract between the manufacturer or contractor and the original purchaser (including any relevant exclusion clause). it would be difficult to define the standard required to discharge any duty of care to a subsequent purchaser and such purchaser may not be entitled to any greater protection than that owed to the original purchaser.

29. Sidey v. Olsen Bros. [1984] C.L.Y. 2304, C.A.

Injury caused in coach accident due to latent defect of which previous owner had been aware—*Held* liability of present owner did not extend beyond taking of reasonable care as there were no special circumstances of which they had reason to be aware.

30. Muirhead v. Industrial Tank Specialists [1986] Q.B. 507; [1985] 3 W.L.R. 993

D1 was engaged by P to install tank for storage of lobsters in tanks which used pumps supplied by D2. Electric motors for the pumps were supplied to D2 by D3 and once installed the pumps proved to be unsuitable, causing the lobsters to die from lack of oxygen. P claimed special damages in negligence from all Ds for loss of lobsters and for economic loss—*Held*, Ds not liable for pure economic loss but D3 liable and should have reasonably foreseen some type of damage if pumps failed.

U1. Operman Ltd. v. Coker (1951) C.A. 330

Grass-drying machine which caused fire when used—*Held*, defendants liable.

U2. Crow v. Barford (1963) C.A. 102

Rotary grass cutter into the grass ejection aperture of which plaintiff put his foot—*Held*, manufacturers not liable, as the danger was apparent.

U3. Sutcliffe v. Trojan (1967) C.A. 143

U4. Winward V.T.V.R. Engineering (1992) C.A. 213

D designed and manufactured sports car with engine and component parts produced by others. P's car caught fire because of carburettor defect—*Held*, D liable although did not manufacture carburettor. Reasonable manufacturer would have appreciated push fit utilised was not good engineering practice and created risk of fire. Design defective therefore and D negligent in not modifying design or warning potential purchasers of the risk.

(3) Proof of Negligence

(*N.B.* See also, for general principles, Chap. 4.)

1. Grant v. Australian Knitting Mills [1936] A.C. 85; 52 T.L.R. 38, P.C.

Lord Wright (101): "If excess sulphites were left in the garment that could only be because someone was at fault. The appellant is not required to lay his finger on the exact person in all the chain who was responsible, or to specify what he did wrong. Negligence is found as a matter of inference from the existence of the defects taken in conjunction with all the known circumstances ... "

2. Basted v. Cozens & Sutcliffe [1954] 1 W.L.R. 1069; [1954] 2 All E.R. 735n., Devlin J.

Sudden descent of load due to defect in crane brake—defendants offer no evidence of cause or of system of maintenance—*Held*, defendants (crane owners, but not employers of plaintiff) liable. "Once it is established there was a defect . . . whether the rule of *res ipsa loquitur* applies or not I do not really think needs to be considered . . . (Defendants), and they alone, have the knowledge of the facts which would show whether they have exercised due care or not, and it is for them to lay that information before the court and, I think, to satisfy the court that they had a proper system of maintenance in force." *Barkway v. South Wales Transport* Chap. 13, (1) (b) **2**, applied. In same action employers were liable for requiring plaintiff to work under suspended load, the judge saying that, since there was no pre-accident consideration of system, onus was on defendants to establish no other system practicable.

3. Mason v. Williams & Williams [1955] 1 W.L.R. 549; [1955] 1 All E.R. 808, Finnemore J.

Held, defendant manufacturers liable for defective chisel. Judge says (810 C) that when plaintiff has proved chisel was too hard, and has eliminated any intermediate interference, "that is really as far as any plaintiff can be expected to take his case."

4. Steer v. Durable Rubber Co., *The Times*, November 20, 1958; [1958] C.L.Y. 2250, C.A.

Scalding water bursts out of hot-water bottle three months old—*Held*, defendants liable because, the onus being on them either to show they had not been negligent or to give some explanation of the cause of the accident which did not connote negligence, they had not discharged onus on them.

5. Salt v. I.C.I., *The Times*, February 1 1958; [1958] C.L.Y. 2251, C.A.

Drum of caustic soda escapes through hole—carrier and manufacturer sued—*Held*, neither liable, as this was not a case where one or other defendant must have been negligent, and the cause of the hold was unexplained.

6. Bleach v. Blue Gate Products, *The Times*, January 26, 1960; [1960] C.L.Y. 2125, McNair J.

Defective tap on cooker—stoker found dead from gas poisoning in kitchen—*Held*, onus had shifted to defendants to give innocent explanation of death, and as they had failed to do this, therefore they were liable.

(4) Defences

(a) Generally

1. Evans v. Triplex [1936] 1 All E.R. 283, Porter J.

Held, manufacturers not liable because of:

(a) lapse of time between purchase of car and accident;
(b) possibility that glass may have been strained when fitted;
(c) opportunity for examination by intermediate seller;
(d) breakage may have been due to some cause other than defect in manufacture.

2. Kubach v. Hollands [1937] 3 All E.R. 907; 53 T.L.R. 1024, Lord Hewart C.J.

Explosion in school classroom due to manganese dioxide containing antimony sulphide—makers had no notice of intended user and retailers had ample opportunity for examination—*Held*, makers not liable.

3. Marshall v. Cellactite (1947) 63 T.L.R. 456; [1947] C.L.Y. 6697, C.A.

General permission by factory owner to contractor to borrow plant—*Held*, there was no representation of safety as to any particular piece of plant, and therefore defendants not liable.

4. Holmes v. Ashford [1950] 2 All E.R. 76; [1950] W.N. 269, C.A.

Hair dye which could be dangerous to certain skins—manufacturers warned hairdresser of this danger—*Held*, that they had discharged their duty, and it was not necessary in all cases to warn the ultimate recipient.

5. Johnson v. Croggan [1954] 1 W.L.R. 195; [1954] 1 All E.R. 121, Pilcher J.

Facts similar to **3**—*Held*, for same reasons, defendants not liable. *But see* Chap. 7, (2)(d) **X**.

6. Creed v. McGeoch [1955] 1 W.L.R. 1005; [1955] 3 All E.R. 123, Ashworth J.

Defendants were contractors not in occupation of land in question—left trailer—children known to play—plaintiff aged five injured when playing see-saw on trailer—*Held*, that, since defendants were not in occupation, they owed duty under *Donoghue v. Stevenson*, and since they were aware of the risk of injury to children and knew that it was attractive to children, they were liable; and that, by analogy with *Gough v. N.C.B.* Chap. 10, (6)(d) **2**, the defence of trespass on an object was not available to them in a case where they "negligently left a dangerous and attractive object in a place where children are known to play" (128 D).

7. Roberts v. T. Wallis [1958] 1 Lloyd's Rep. 29, Barry J.

"In those circumstances can it be said that the owner of a machine of this kind, or indeed of a motor-car, is responsible if through some defect (which may well be entirely latent) of a connecting rod it breaks during the time the machine was in motion?" (38).

8. Hurley v. Dyke [1979] R.T.R. 265; [1979] C.L.Y. 1867, H.L.

Defendants sold a dangerously defective car at auction "as seen with all its faults and without warranty". Later a passenger in the car when driven by the ultimate purchaser was killed when the bodywork collapsed—*Held*, the defendants had discharged their duty of care towards ultimate users by the warning given at auction.

U1. Broomhall v. B.R.B. (1963) C.A. 110

Drum of caustic soda delivered to factory—internal and undiscoverable defect in drum whereby plaintiff employee sprayed with contents when loosening bung—but no accident would have occurred if employers had given proper instructions as to how to loosen bung—*Held*, manufacturers 60 per cent, and employers 40 per cent, liable.

(b) Abnormal Susceptibility of Plaintiff

1. Griffiths v. Conway [1939] 1 All E.R. 685, Branson J.

Held, defendant not liable.

2. Board v. Thomas Hedley [1951] 2 All E.R. 431; [1951] W.N. 422, C.A.

Denning L.J. (432 D): "The product would, I think, be dangerous if it might affect normal user adversely, or even if it might adversely affect other users who had a higher degree of sensitivity that the normal, so long as they were not altogether exceptional."

3. Ingham v. Emes [1955] 2 Q.B. 366; [1955] 2 All E.R. 740, C.A.

Plaintiff in this case was suing on a warranty—*Held*, the fact that plaintiff knew but did not disclose she was abnormally sensitive to the dye disabled her from suing. **1** applied.

(c) Knowledge of Plaintiff and Warning

1. Farr v. Butters [1932] 2 K.B. 606; 147 L.T. 427, C.A.

Defendants sent crane to buyer in parts to be assembled on the spot—the buyer's foreman saw that it was defective, but nevertheless assembled and worked it, and as a result was killed—*Held*, defendants not liable, as there had been intermediate examination and knowledge.

2. Grant v. Australian Knitting Mills [1936] A.C. 85; 52 T.L.R. 38, P.C.

Lord Wright (105): 'The principle in *Donoghue v. Stevenson* can only be applied where the defect is hidden and unknown to the consumer: otherwise the directness of cause and effect is absent. The man who consumes or uses a thing which he knows to be noxious cannot complain in respect of whatever mischief follows, because it follows from his own conscious volition . . . .' And (106): 'The decision in *Donoghue v. Stevenson* did not depend on the bottle being stoppered and sealed: the essential point in this respect was that the article should reach the consumer or user subject to the same defect it had when it left the manufacturer.'

3. Burfitt v. Kille [1939] 2 K.B. 743; [1939] 2 All 372; Atkinson J.

Sale of toy pistol and blank ammunition to boy of nine—*Held*, seller liable for damage subsequently caused to another boy through the use of the pistol. 'A warning is not a sufficient discharge of duty if the person to whom the chattel is delivered is not a competent person.'

4. Denny v. Supplies etc. Co. [1950] 2 K.B. 374; 1 T.L.R. 1168, C.A.

Plaintiff a dock labourer injured when unloading dangerously stowed timber—sues employers and loading stevedores—action fails against employers—*Held*, loading stevedores liable, as it came within *Donoghue v. Stevenson* and, distinguishing **1**, the fact that plaintiff had knowledge of the danger and there was opportunity for examination was no defence where, as here, there was no practical alternative but to accept the danger (T.L.R. 1173), and furthermore since there was no practical alternative but to unload, there was no *novus actus interveniens* (T.L.R. 1171). *Followed* in *Twiss v. W.H. Rhodes* (Chap 7, (2) (d) **7**). See now **7**.

5. Holmes v. Ashford [1950] 2 All E.R. 76; [1950] W.N. 269, C.A.

Hair dye which could be dangerous to certain skins—manufacturers warned hairdresser of this danger—*Held*, that they had discharged their duty, but it was not necessary in all cases to warn the ultimate recipient.

6. London Graving Dock v. Horton [1951] A.C. 737; [1951] 2 All E.R. 1, H.L.

Lord Porter (750), commenting on *Donoghue v. Stevenson*: 'An examination by the retail vendor, if rightly expected, could be relied upon by the manufacturer and would have been a complete answer to the claim. Still more so would knowledge by the purchaser of the true position, whether such knowledge was actual or such as the circumstances would warrant the manufacturer to assume. The defence did not have to show that the pursuer drank the contents with a full knowledge of the risk; it would have been enough if examination and consequent knowledge was to be expected.'

7. A. C. Billings v. Riden [1958] A.C. 240; [1957] 3 All E.R. 1, H.L.

See Chap. 10(5)(b) **11**—case where plaintiff, a visitor, fell down hole when making deviation necessitated by works being carried out by defendant, a contractor—*Held*, defendant liable.

8. Gledhill v. Liverpool Abattoir 1 W.L.R. 1028; [1957] 3 All E.R. 117, C.A.

Liverpool Corporation, second defendants, had an abattoir where plaintiff was employed by first defendants—due to unsuitable chains supplied by second defendants a dead pig slipped and fell on plaintiff—complaints had been made to first defendants by other employees, and plaintiff was fully aware of the condition of the chains—*Held*, second defendants were not liable to plaintiff because (a) he had full and complete knowledge of the condition of the chains, and (b) there was ample opportunity for intermediate examination of the chains by first defendants and by their employees. But, on (a), *cf.* **7**.

9. Rimmer v. Liverpool C.C. [1984] 1 All E.R. 930, C.A.

Plaintiff a council tenant who had complained of danger from glass panel in hall wall. He then tripped and fell into glass panel, injuring himself—*Held*, following *Denny* **4**, plaintiff's knowledge was no defence, as he was not free to act on such knowledge.

U1. Brown v. Watkins and Bradfords (1966) C.A. 119

Held, defendants liable, even though plaintiff subcontractor knew of and had complained of danger. For full facts, see Chap. 7, (2) (d) **U3**.

(d) Opportunity for Intermediate Examination

		Whether defendant liable or not
General statement	1	
CRANE DEFECTIVE AS ASSEMBLED	2	No
Safety glass shattering in car	3	No
Clothing containing excess sulphites	4	Yes
Not a defence if chattel intended to reach consumer in form sent out	4	
Chemicals for school use exploding	5	No
Bull-ring breaking	6	No
Live busbar in electric kiosk	7	No
Defect in car	8	Yes
Not a defence if defendant never anticipated that opportunity to examine would be used	8	

Dangerous hair product	9	Yes
Not a defence if defendants represent no test needed	9	
SOLEPLATE LEFT DEFECTIVE BY CONTRACTOR	10	Yes
UNSAFE STOWAGE	11	Yes
NOT A DEFENCE WHERE NO PRACTICAL ALTERNATIVE TO RUNNING RISK	11	
Unsafe stowage	12	No
General dictum as to when defence applies	13	
Defective chisel	14	Yes
Defect in ship's telegraph system	15	No
Not a defence if merely possible but not contemplated	16	
UNSUITABLE CHAINS TO SLING PIGS	17	No
HOLE IN FLOOR REPAIRED WITH FAULTY PLUG	18	Yes
KNOWLEDGE OF PLAINTIFF NOT NECESSARILY A DEFENCE	19	Yes
Bad stacking—stackers liable	20	Yes
Concrete canopy over doorway of house	21	Yes
NOT ALWAYS A DEFENCE—COLLAPSE OF PATENTLY UNSAFE WALL	22	Yes
Carelessness in intermediate examination—how far same will exonerate producer	23	
Not necessarily a defence—question is whether supplier reasonably expected that recipient would use opportunity to do adequate inspection	24	Yes
OPPORTUNITY FOR SUBSEQUENT SURVEY—DEFECTIVE HOUSE—WHETHER DEFENCE FOR BUILDING SURVEYOR NEGLIGENTLY APPROVING DEFECTIVE CONSTRUCTION	25	
Opportunity for subsequent survey—subsidence of house due to negligent construction	26	Yes
Not always a defence—defective gate post collapsing	U1	Yes

1. Donoghue v. Stevenson [1932] A.C. 562; 147 L.T. 281, H.L.

Lord Atkin stated the duty of the manufacturer of products in the following terms: "A manufacturer of products, which he sells in such a form as to show that he intends them to reach the ultimate consumer in the form in which they left him with no reasonable possibility of intermediate examination, and with the knowledge that the absence of reasonable care in the preparation or putting up of the products will result in an injury to the consumer's life or property, owes a duty to the consumer to take that reasonable care."

2. Farr v. Butters [1932] 2 K.B. 606; 147 L.T. 427, C.A.

Defendants sent crane to buyer in parts to be assembled on the spot—the buyer's foreman saw that it was defective, but nevertheless assembled and worked it, and as a result was killed—*Held*, defendants not liable, as there had been intermediate examination and knowledge.

3. Evans v. Triplex [1936] 1 All E.R. 283, Porter J.

Held manufacturers not liable because of:

(a) lapse of time between purchase of car and accident;
(b) possibility that glass may have been strained when fitted;
(c) opportunity for examination by intermediate seller;
(d) breakage may have been due to some cause other than defect in manufacture.

4. Grant v. Australian Knitting Mills [1936] A.C. 85; 52 T.L.R. 38, P.C.

Lord Wright (105): "The principle in *Donoghue v. Stevenson* can only be applied where the defect is hidden and unknown to the consumer: otherwise the directness of cause and effect is absent. The man who consumes or uses a thing which he knows to be noxious cannot complain in respect of whatever mischief follows, because it follows from his own conscious volition. . . . " And (106): "The decision in *Donoghue v. Stevenson* did not depend on the bottle being stoppered and sealed: the essential point in this respect was that the article should reach the consumer or user subject to the same defect it had when it left the manufacturer."

5. Kubach v. Hollands [1937] 3 All E.R. 907; 53 T.L.R. 1024, Lord Hewart C.J.

Explosion in school classroom due to manganese dioxide containing antimony sulphide—makers had no notice of intended user and retailers had ample opportunity for examination—*Held*, makers not liable.

6. Dransfield v. B. I. Cables [1937] 4 All E.R. 382; 54 T.L.R. 11, Hawke J.

Breakage of "bull-ring"—*Held*, although defendants the manufacturers were negligent there was an opportunity for intermediate examination by the local authority who bought it, and therefore defendants not liable. Lord Goddard in *Haseldine v. Daw* (Chap. 10, (4)(c) 1) said it was wrongly decided.

7. Paine v. Colne Valley Elec. [1938] 4 All E.R. 803; 55 T.L.R. 944, Goddard L.J.

Faulty construction of electric kiosk causing electrocution of deceased—plaintiff sues, *inter alia*, manufacturers—*Held*, not liable as there had been ample opportunity for examination by the electric supply company.

8. Herschtal v. Stewart and Ardern [1940] 1 K.B. 155; [1939] 4 All E.R. 123, Tucker J.

Second-hand car supplied on hire-purchase—defective—injury to plaintiff—plaintiff was given an opportunity to examine for defects but as defendants never anticipated he would use opportunity—*Held*, they were liable. "They are liable on the basis that they . . . were supplying this dangerous article for his user when, and in circumstances in which, they did not and could not reasonably have anticipated that there would be any such intermediate examination as would be likely to reveal a defect such as existed in this motor car" (136). Applied in **16** and **21**.

9. Watson v. Buckley [1940] 1 All E.R. 174, Stable J.

Distributors advertised hair product as absolutely harmless and needing no preliminary test before use—*Held*, in view of this could not rely on defence of opportunity of intermediate examination.

10. Buckner v. Ashby [1941] 1 K.B. 321; 110 L.J.K.B. 460, C.A.

Plaintiff trips over soleplate—*Held*, contractor not liable as intermediate examination by owner had taken place.

11. Denny v. Supplies etc. Co. [1950] 2 K.B. 374; 1 T.L.R. 1168, C.A.

Plaintiff a dock labourer injured when unloading dangerously stowed timber—sues employers and loading stevedores—action fails against employer—*Held* loading stevedore liable, as it came within *Donoghue v. Stevenson* and, distinguishing **2**, the fact that plaintiff had knowledge of the danger and there was opportunity for examination was no defence where, as here, there was no practical alternative but to accept the danger (T.L.R. 1173), and furthermore since there was no practical alternative but to unload, there was no *novus actus interveniens* (T.L.R. 1171). *Followed* in **12**. See now *A. C. Billings v. Riden*, Chap. 7, (4) (c) **7**.

12. Twiss v. W. H. Rhodes [1951] 1 Lloyd's Rep. 333, Gorman J.

Plaintiff dock labourer employed by first defendants unloading timber—injured—*Held*, barge had been wrongly stowed by second defendants but first defendants were solely liable because they had the opportunity to inspect but did not inspect the stowage, nor did they properly supervise the unloading. **11** *followed*. *But* see *Dukelow v. Scruttons* Chap. 7, (2) (d) **16**.

13. London Graving Dock v. Horton [1951] A.C. 737; [1951] 2 All E.R. 1, H.L.

Lord Porter (750), commenting on *Donoghue v. Stevenson*: "An examination by the retail vendor, if rightly expected, could be relied upon by the manufacturer and would have been a complete answer to the claim. Still more so would knowledge by the purchaser of the true position, whether such knowledge was actual or such as the circumstances would warrant the manufacturer to assume. The defence did not have to show that the pursuer drank the contents with a full knowledge of the risk; it would have been enough if examination and consequent knowledge was to be expected."

14. Mason v. Williams & Williams [1955] 1 W.L.R. 549; [1955] 1 All E.R. 808, Finnemore J.

Held, intermediate examination no defence, as none contemplated or intended.

15. Hindustan S. S. Co. v. Siemens [1955] 1 Lloyd's Rep. 166, Willmer J.

Held, defendants not liable. See Chap. 7, (2) (g) **17**.

16. Andrews v. Hopkinson [1957] 1 Q.B. 229; [1956] 3 All E.R. 422, McNair J.

Held, applying **8**.

17. Gledhill v. Liverpool Abattoir [1957] 1 W.L.R. 1028; [1957] 3 All E.R. 117, C.A.

Held, defendants not liable, as ample opportunity for examination.

18. Gallagher v. McDowell [1961] N.I. 26, C.A.

Injury to tenant's wife when wooden plug in floor gave way—builders had erected house for landlord—*Held*, no opportunity of intermediate examination.

19. Johnson v. Rea [1962] 1 Q.B. 373; [1961] 3 All E.R. 816, C.A.

Plaintiff lorry driver (not employed by defendants) slipped on dock shed floor when carrying a keg—defendant stevedores were in control (but not in law occupiers) of dock shed—floor was slippery through discharge of soda ash from bags being moved by defendants—defendants took no steps to remove danger—plaintiff was aware the floor was slippery—*Held*, defendants liable, as their duty was not merely to warn, but to take reasonable steps to obviate danger.

20. Vandersteen v. P. L. A. [1962] 1 Lloyd's Rep. 126, Edmund Davies J.

Plaintiff dock labourer injured when unstacking dangerously stacked jibs of cranes—sues employers (Port of London Authority) and shipowners who stacked the jibs—after stacking shipowners handed over stack to employers—shipowners claimed that, in accordance with *Denny v. Supplies and*

Transport Company **11**, their liability ended with the handing over of the stack to the employers who could and should have made an intermediate examination and discovered the defects, if any—*Held*, not so, and that both shipowners and employers were liable to plaintiff.

21. Sharpe v. Sweeting [1963] 1 W.L.R. 665; [1963] 1 All E.R. 455, Nield J.

Builder building house for local authority so constructed canopy that it collapsed on wife of tenant—*Held*, no opportunity for intermediate examination within the definition of the term given by Tucker J. in *Herschtal v. Stewart and Ardern* **8**.

22. Clay v. Crump [1964] 1 Q.B. 533; [1963] 3 All E.R. 687, C.A.

During demolition a wall was left standing as safe by demolition contractors (and by architect)—it was patently unsafe and one month later collapsed on plaintiff, employed in rebuilding—demolition contractors and architect pleaded that the contractors rebuilding had ample opportunity to examine and detect fault, and therefore they were not liable—*Held*, although rebuilding contractors did have ample opportunity, this did not exempt the others, as the absence of an opportunity to examine was not an invariable condition precedent to liability under *Donoghue v. Stevenson*: Lord Atkin had only been dealing with the particular case of an article of food.

23. Taylor v. Rover [1966] 1 W.L.R. 1491, [1966] 2 All E.R. 181; Baker J.

Defective chisel—defect known to chargehand, who did nothing about it—*Held*, that whatever the rule was where carelessness failed to reveal the defect, this was not such a case, for the defect was known, and the carelessness lay in failing to take action; accordingly, the manufacturers were not liable, for the real cause of the subsequent accident was the failure of the chargehand to take action to withdraw the chisel from use.

24. Griffiths v. Arch Engineering [1968] 3 All E.R. 217, Chapman J.

For full facts see Chap. 7, (2) (d) **26**—P employed at docks on repair work borrowed a defective portable grinding machine—it belonged to plant contractors and had been hired out to the company from whom P borrowed it—plant contractors on being sued by P pleaded opportunity for intermediate examination by hirers—*Held*, not a defence in the circumstances. Chapman J. (222 D) said: "The importance laid on the possibility—that is, the probability—of intermediate examination is merely one facet of the wider principle as it has now been formulated, namely, was there a reasonably foreseeable risk that the plaintiff in fact injured would sustain injury if no precautions were taken to guard against the risk?" He also quoted with approval passage from *Salmond on Torts* (14th ed.), pp. 435–436.

25. Dutton v. Bognor Regis U. D. C. [1972] Q.B. 373; [1972] 1 All E.R. 462, C.A.

Council building surveyor negligently approved defective foundations and was found liable to subsequent purchaser on collapse of walls—Lord Denning M. R. (474 C) said that if the defects passed by the surveyor were of the sort which a subsequent survey might disclose, then the proximity and the duty would cease as and when the opportunity for a subsequent survey arose (*e.g.* on the sale of the house). Now see cases after *D. & F. Estates v. Church Commissioners* (Chap. 18).

26. Sutherland v. Maton [1976] J.P.L. 753; [1976] C.L.Y. 87, Cobb J.

Plaintiff bought a three-year-old house—which subsided four years later due to negligence of builder—the only survey had been by building society who had advised investigating the cause of a crack—*Held*, reasonable in the circumstances not to have a full survey.

U1. Wood v. Steele (1969) C.A. 439

Gate post defectively built—collapsed while children swinging on it—house owner was a subsequent purchaser who had had building surveyed for mortgage—survey had not disclosed defect—*Held*, applying *Clay* **22**, opportunity for intermediate examination was no defence.

8. DANGEROUS THINGS UNDER RYLANDS V. FLETCHER

This chapter includes all the modern cases arising on a strict liability basis under the rule in *Rylands v. Fletcher* but, as the scope of such claims have narrowed in recent years, the majority of cited cases are in relation to the liability in negligence for the escape of dangerous things generally. Petrol and inflammable liquid is dealt with in Chap. 8, (4).

(1) Duty

(a) What are Dangerous Things within Rylands v. Fletcher

1. Greenwood Tileries v. Clapson [1937] 1 All E.R. 765; 156 L.T. 386, Branson J.

Defendants (by their predecessors in title) had removed part of a sea bank and built a wall instead—which collapsed, so that plaintiff's land was inundated—*Held*, defendants liable because "their position is really analogous to the position of the defendants in *Rylands v. Fletcher*. They have created a danger against which they must guard at all events" (771 A).

2. Hale v. Jennings Bros. [1938] 92 S.J. 193; [1938] 1 All E.R. 579, C.A.

Chair-o-plane in motion becomes detached and hits plaintiff—*Held*, defendants liable under *Rylands v. Fletcher*.

3. Mulholland v. Baker [1939] 3 All E.R. 253; 161 L.T. 20, Asquith J.

Adjoining shops—defendant has 20-gallon drum of paraffin—defendant lit some paper to smoke a rat out of pipe—fire spreads to paraffin and to plaintiff's shop—*Held*, defendant was guilty of negligence in starting fire so close to paraffin, and further the paraffin was "a thing likely to do damage unless kept under proper control," so that defendant was also liable under *Rylands v. Fletcher. sed quaere.*

4. Thomas and Evans v. Mid Rhondda Society [1941] 1 K.B. 381; [1940] 4 All E.R. 357, C.A.

Defendants removed a river wall which was on their land—river flooded onto their land and thence escaped onto plaintiff's land—*Held*, defendants not liable under *Rylands v. Fletcher* (or in nuisance or negligence either).

5. Bolton v. Stone [1951] A.C. 850; [1951] 1 All E.R. 1078, 1086 D, H.L.

Held, Rylands v. Fletcher did not apply.

6. Pride of Derby v. British Celanese [1953] Ch. 149; [1953] 1 All E.R. 179, C.A.

Evershed M.R. (195 B) appeared to be of the view that the discharge of untreated sewage into a river would come within *Rylands v. Fletcher*—but the case was mainly argued in nuisance. Denning L.J. (203 A) seems to have been of the same view.

7. Perry v. Kendricks Transport [1956] 1 W.L.R. 85; [1956] 1 All E.R. 154, C.A.

Held, this was an object within *Rylands v. Fletcher* (but action failed on defence of act of stranger: see Chap. 8, (2) (b) **6**).

8. Davey v. Harrow Corporation [1957] 2 All E.R. 305; [1958] 1 Q.B. 60, C.A.

Held, that an action for nuisance would lie for damage done by encroaching tree roots, and perhaps (though not decided) under *Rylands v. Fletcher* also. *Giles v. Walker* (1890) 24 Q.B.D. 656, which decided no cause of action for blown thistledown, criticised, so that it may no longer be good law.

9. Noel T. James v. C.E.A. (1958) 108 L.J. 250; [1958] C.L.Y. 3304, Elwes J.

Explosion in transformer releasing oil which caught fire and flowed onto plaintiff's land—*Held*, statutory authority was a defence to *Rylands v. Fletcher*, but defendants were liable in negligence.

10. Mills v. Smith [1963] 1 Lloyd's Rep. 168, Paull J.

Held, adjacent owner liable for encroaching tree roots. Liability was described as arising in nuisance (177, col. 1).

11. Miller S.S. Co. v. Overseas Tankship (Wagon Mound No. 2) [1963] 1 Lloyd's Rep. 402, Walsh J., Sup.Ct. N.S.W.

Held, no liability under *Rylands v. Fletcher*, as (a) applying *Read v. Lyons* (Chap. 8, (1) (c) **2**), the escape had to be from land, and not from a ship, and (b) user of harbour by defendants was not a non-natural user. *N.B.* This point was not raised on the appeal to P.C. [1967] 1 A.C. 617.

12. Morgan v. Khyatt [1964] 1 W.L.R. 475; 108 S.J. 236, P.C.

Held, encroaching tree roots constituted a nuisance.

13. Mitchell v. Mason (1966) 10 W.I.R. 26; [1968] C.L.Y. 2682, Jamaica C.A.

14. Smith v. Scott [1973] Ch. 314; [1972] 3 All E.R. 645, Pennycuick V.-C.

Held, landlord not liable under *Rylands v. Fletcher* for unruly tenants. *Att.-Gen. v. Corke* [1933] Ch. 89 (where a landowner who brought caravan dwellers onto his land as his licensees was held liable under *Rylands v. Fletcher*) distinguished on the ground that normally it was the occupier, as opposed to the owner, of the land who was liable. Here it was the tenant who was the occupier, while in *Corke's* case it was the landowner. The judge also said that he thought that *Corke's* case could equally well have been decided on the basis that the landowner, being in possession and occupation, was liable in nuisance for the acts of his licensees.

15. Solloway v. Hampshire C.C. (1981) 79 L.G.R. 449; [1981] C.L.Y. 2005, C.A.

Large horsechestnut tree in highway near P's house. Tree roots encroached into P's land and dehydrated clay pockets under foundations, causing subsidence which damaged house. P sued highway authority for cost of remedial work—*Held*, highway authority not liable. There were two questions to be considered: (a) was there a foreseeable risk that the encroachment of these tree roots would cause damage to P's house; and (b) were there any reasonable precautions which the authority could take to prevent or minimise the risk?

(b) Natural and Non-natural User

1. Western Engraving v. Film Laboratories (1936) 80 S.J. 165; [1936] 1 All E.R. 106, C.A.

Defendants, occupants of factory on second floor, used water in large quantities for process, which escaped onto plaintiff below—*Held*, liable under *Rylands v. Fletcher*, as this was not ordinary or natural user.

2. Mulholland v. Baker [1939] 3 All E.R. 253; 161 L.T. 20, Asquith J.

Adjoining shops—defendant has 20 gallon drum of parraffin—defendant lit some paper to smoke a rat out of pipe—fire spreads to paraffin and to plaintiff's shop—*Held*, defendant was guilty of negligence in starting fire so close to paraffin, and further the paraffin was "a thing likely to do damage unless kept under proper control," so that defendant was also liable under *Rylands v. Fletcher*. *Sed quaere.*

3. Hanson v. Wearmouth Coal Co. [1939] 3 All E.R. 47; 55 T.L.R. 747, C.A.

Held, not natural user.

4. Rouse v. Gravelworks [1940] 1 K.B. 489, [1940] 1 All E.R. 26; C.A.

Held, digging for gravel ordinary user, and therefore defendants not liable for escape.

5. Peters v. Prince of Wales Theatre [1943] K.B. 73; [1942] 2 All E.R. 533, C.A.

Held, probably *obiter*, that it was a natural user.

6. Read v. Lyons [1947] A.C. 156; [1946] 2 All E.R. 471, H.L.

Semble, it was natural user.

7. Sochacki v. Sas [1947] 1 All E.R. 344, Lord Goddard C.J.
Held, natural user.

8. Prosser v. Levy [1955] 1 W.L.R. 1224; [1955] 3 All E.R. 577, C.A.

Case where water leaked onto floor below from an open-ended pipe with a stop tap on it which could be accidentally moved—*Held* defendants were liable because there was no implied consent in such a case (see chap. 8(2) (c) **5**) and in any event there was negligence by the trustees, *but* the court throughout treated liability as arising under *Rylands v. Fletcher* and seem to have tacitly assumed that a domestic water supply, if unusual or (more probably) of negligent layout, was not ordinary user.

9. Doltis v. Braithwaite [1957] 1 Lloyd's Rep. 522, Streatfeild J.

Held, natural user.

10. Miller S.S. Co. v. Overseas Tankship (Wagon Mound No. 2) [1963] 1 Lloyd's Rep. 402, Walsh J., Sup. Ct. N.S.W.

Held, natural user.

11. Mason v. Levy Auto Parts [1967] 2 Q.B. 530; [1967] 2 All E.R. 62, MacKenna J.

Held, non-natural user.

12. Gertsen v. Municipality of Metropolitan Toronto (1973) 41 D.L.R. (3d) 646; [1974] C.L.Y. 2597, Ontario High Ct.

13. Bottoni v. Henderson (1978) 90 D.L.R. (3d) 301; [1979] C.L.Y. 2008, Ont.H.C.J.
Held, natural user, and no liability under *R. v. F.* (or at all).

14. Cambridge Water Co. v. Eastern Counties Leather [1992] N.P.C. 147; [1991] C.L.Y. 3412

Held, natural user of land to store chemicals for use in tanning industry on land in an industrial village. (But now *reversed* [1994] 2 A.C. 264; [1994] 1 All E.R. 53, H.L.)

(c) Escape

1. Hale v. Jennings Bros. (1938) 82 S.J. 193; [1938] 1 All E.R. 579 C.A.

Chair-o-plane in motion becomes detached and hits plaintiff—*Held* defendants liable under *Rylands v. Fletcher.*

2. Read v. Lyons [1947] A.C. 156; [1946] 2 All E.R. 471; H.L.

Plaintiff was invitee in explosives factory which blew up—no negligence—*Held*, plaintiff could not recover under *Rylands v. Fletcher* because there had been no escape from a place over which defendants had occupation or control to a place where he had not. *Semble*, an explosives factory was natural user.

3. Davey v. Harrow Corporation [1958] 1 Q.B. 60; [1957] 2 All E.R. 305, C.A.

Held, that an action for nuisance would lie for damage done by encroaching tree roots, and perhaps (though not decided) under *Rylands v. Fletcher* also. *Giles v. Walker* (1890) 24 Q.B.D. 656, which decided no cause of action for blown thistledown, criticised, so that it may no longer be good law.

4. Doltis v. Braithwaite [1957] 1 Lloyd's Rep. 522, Streatfeild J.

Plaintiff employed defendant contractors to install heating in the parts of a building occupied by him, namely basement, third and fourth floors—defendants to test whether third-floor chimney was clear lit a newspaper fire—this set fire to the soot—the fire spread down inter-communicating chimney (of which both plaintiff and defendant unaware) into basement—*Held, inter alia*, this did not constitute an escape within *Rylands v. Fletcher.*

5. Miller S.S. Co. v. Overseas Tankship (Wagon Mound No. 2) [1963] 1 Lloyd's Rep. 402, Walsh J., Sup. Ct. N.S.W.

Held, applying **3**, escape must be from land, and escape from a ship did not qualify. This point was not mentioned on the appeal to the P.C. [1967] 1 A.C. 617.

(d) Whether Liability Extends to Personal Injuries

1. Hale v. Jennings Bros. (1938) 82 S.J. 193; [1938] 1 All E.R. 579, C.A.

Held, plaintiff could recover damages for personal injuries under *Rylands v. Fletcher.*

2. Read v. Lyons [1947] A.C. 156; [1946] 2 All E.R. 471, H.L.

Lord Macmillan (476 A): " . . . I am of the opinion that as the law now stands an allegation of negligence is in general essential to the relevancy of an action of reparation for personal injuries." But the other Lords did not express any opinion on this point.

3. Perry v. Kendricks Transport [1956] 1 W.L.R. 85; [1956] 1 All E.R. 154, C.A.

Held, despite doubts expressed in **3**, claim would lie for personal injuries under *Rylands v. Fletcher.*

(e) Whether plaintiff must have Proprietary Interest

1. Weller v. Foot and Mouth Institute [1966] 1 Q.B. 569; [1965] 3 All E.R. 560, Widgery J.

Held, no action lay, as the plaintiff auctioneers had no interest in the property onto which the virus escaped.

(2) Defences

(a) Act of God

1. Hill v. British Airways (1936) 56 Ll.L.R. 20, Lewis J.

Held, not an act of God.

2. Greenwood Tileries v. Clapson [1937] 1 All E.R. 765; 156 L.T. 386, Branson J.

High tide—but not the highest on record—*Held*, not an act of God.

3. Ryan v. Youngs (1938) 82 S.J. 233; [1938] 1 All E.R. 522 C.A.

Held, death of driver due to sudden heart failure was act of God. *N.B.* This case arose in negligence, not under *Rylands v. Fletcher.*

4. Cushing v. Walker [1941] 2 All E.R. 693, Hallett J.

"Before wind can amount to act of God, . . . the wind must not only be exceptionally strong, but must be of such exceptional strength that no one could be reasonably expected to anticipate or provide against it" (695 A).

(b) Act of Stranger

1. North Western Utilities v. London Guarantee [1936] A.C. 108; 52 T.L.R. 93, P.C.

Gas leak in supply pipes under street caused by action of third party (the City Corporation of Edmonton) in constructing a storm sewer and causing pipe to sag—the gas company maintained the pipe under statutory authority—*Held*, the action of the City Corporation in causing the pipe to sag was the independent conscious act (119, 122) of a third party, and therefore, following *Richards v. Lothian* [1913] A.C. 263, P.C., was a defence to a claim under *Rylands v. Fletcher*.

2. Hale v. Jennings Bros. (1938) 82 S.J. 193; [1938] 1 All E.R. 579, C.A.

Chair-o-plane in motion becomes detached and hits plaintiff—*Held*, defendants liable under *Rylands v. Fletcher*. The possibility that the chair became detached because the occupant played about with it was no defence because the occupant was under the "control" of defendants.

3. Hanson v. Wearmouth Coal Co. [1939] 3 All E.R. 47; 55 T.L.R. 747, C.A.

Held, gas company liable. Goddard L.J. at 53 A: "A person who brings a dangerous thing onto his land and allows it to escape, thereby causing damage to another, is liable to that other unless he can show that the escape was due to the conscious act of a third party, and without negligence on his part."

4. Philco v. Spurling [1949] 2 All E.R. 882; 65 T.L.R. 757, C.A.

A case in negligence where defendant had negligently delivered some inflammable material to plaintiff, and plaintiff's employee had ignited it in circumstances unknown—was this a *novus actus?*—*Held*, not, because defendant had not proved that the act of the employee was a conscious act of volition. *Applied* in **5**.

5. Prosser v. Levy [1955] 1 W.L.R. 1224; [1955] 3 All E.R. 577, C.A.

Water escaped from landlord's pipe onto tenant's floor below—defendant had pleaded that the overflow was due to act of stranger—*Held*, they had not discharged the onus of so showing, and moreover the act, to be a defence, must not be mere negligence (see *Philco v. Spurling* **4**), but must be at the least "a deliberate and mischievous act" (587 D).

6. Perry v. Kendricks Transport [1956] 1 W.L.R. 85; [1956] 1 All E.R. 154, C.A.

Boys threw a lighted match in petrol tank of defendants' coach causing an explosion which injured plaintiff who was passing by—*Held*, defendants not liable, as accident was due to act of stranger over whom defendants had no control, and the fact that the stranger might have been so young as to be incapable of conscious volition was immaterial, since for this purpose a "stranger" was "a person over whose acts the occupier has no control" (Jenkins L.J. at 159 G). *Aliter, per curiam*, if defendants ought reasonably to have anticipated the act of the stranger—but then the action would have been in negligence *simpliciter* (see Jenkins L.J. at 160 G). See also Chap. 8, (4)**15** and Chap. 8, (4) **16**. *But see 7.*

7. Balfour v. Barty-King 1 Q.B. 496; [1957] 1 All E.R. 156, C.A.

Defendant's plumber negligently causes a fire which spreads to plaintiff's house—defendant will be liable for the escape unless the plumber's act was an act of stranger—*Held*, it was not, and defendant liable. Lord Goddard C.J. said (160 D) that the test of ability for the act of an independent contractor was different under *Rylands v. Fletcher* to that in negligence, and that although control may be the test, as laid down in **6**, yet "control" in this sense did not necessarily mean that the person concerned was not left to carry out the work in his own way, but was "control" in the sense that defendant "chose him, invited him to their premises to do the work, and he could have been ordered to leave at any moment" (160 F).

8. Emanuel v. G.L.C. [1971] 2 All E.R. 835; [1971] 2 Lloyd's Rep. 36, C.A.

Defendants wanted to demolish some prefabs which were on their land—they requested the Ministry of Housing to remove them—Ministry of Works entered into contract with K to do the work, stipulating that no rubbish be burnt on the site—despite this K immediately started a fire to get rid of unwanted material—sparks escaped onto P's land—K became insolvent—*Held*, defendants liable as occupiers. Lord Denning M.R. said that the defence of act of stranger would cover the act of a person who was on the land with the occupier's permission, if he acted contrary to anything which the occupier could anticipate; but in this case the defendants had control over the site and could have anticipated what happened. Accordingly, the defence of act of stranger failed—*Held*, also, defendants liable for lack of supervision.

9. King v. Liverpool C.C. [1986] 1 W.L.R. 890; [1986] 3 All E.R. 544, C.A.

See Chap. 10, (7) **11** for summary.

(c) Common Interest and/or Consent

1. North Western Utilities v. London Guarantee [1936] A.C. 108; 52 T.L.R. 93, P.C.

Gas leak in supply pipes under street caused by action of third party (the City Corporation of Edmonton) in constructing a storm sewer and causing pipe to sag—the gas company maintained the pipe under statutory authority—*Held*, the defence of common interest or consent of plaintiff did not apply, as the only fact tending to establish this defence was that the plaintiff received a domestic supply of gas through the pipe, which was insufficient to establish common interest or consent.

2. Kiddle v. City Business Properties [1942] 1 K.B. 269; [1942] 2 All E.R. 216, Lord Goddard C.J.

Plaintiff was tenant of shop leased by defendants—water from defendants' arcade roof escaped into plaintiff's shop—*Held*, defendants not liable, as plaintiff had impliedly consented to the water drainage system and/or the same was for the common benefit of plaintiff and defendants, and in the absence of negligence by defendants this was a defence. *Applied* in **5**.

3. Peters v. Prince of Wales Theatre [1943] K.B. 73; [1942] 2 All E.R. 533, C.A.

Plaintiff was tenant of part of a building leased by defendant—defendant in his part had an extensive sprinkler system which, without negligence on defendant's part, burst in frost and flooded plaintiff—at the time of the lease plaintiff knew of the sprinkler system—*Held*, following **2**, defendant not liable, as in the circumstances plaintiff had impliedly consented to the sprinkler system. *Applied* in **5**.

4. Smeaton v. Ilford Corporation [1954] Ch. 450; [1954] 1 All E.R. 923, Upjohn J.

5. Prosser v. Levy [1955] 1 W.L.R. 1224; [1955] 3 All E.R. 577, C.A.

Water escaped from landlord's pipe onto tenant's floor below—*Held*, that although consent to an ordinary water supply would normally be implied in the case of a tenant (586 G) or even where the parties occupied parts of the same building (585 E), and such consent to and/or common benefit derived from the supply would ordinarily be a defence, the defence would not be available if:

(a) the supply "is of quite an unusual kind, or is defective or dangerous, unless he knows that" (586 G), or
(b) there was no negligence on the part of defendant (586 H),
and in the present case defendants were liable on both these counts.

(d) Statutory Authority

1. North Western Utilities v. London Guarantee [1936] A.C. 108; 52 T.L.R. 93, P.C.

Gas leak in supply pipes under street caused by action of third party (the City Corporation of Edmonton) in constructing a storm sewer and causing pipe to sag—the gas company maintained the pipe under statutory authority—*Held*, the fact that defendants were acting under statutory authority was a defence to a claim under *Rylands v. Fletcher* (121).

2. Markland v. Manchester Corporation [1936] A.C. 360; 51 T.L.R. 527, H.L.

Burst water main—water escaping onto road—freezing—consequential skid by vehicle on road—*Held*, negligence on the part of the water authority, and it seems (see [1934] 1 K.B. 578, C.A.) that liability under *Rylands v. Fletcher* would also have been established but for the defence of statutory authority.

3. Longhurst v. Metropolitan Water Board [1948] 2 All E.R. 834; [1948] W.N. 418, H.L.

4. Pride of Derby v. British Celanese [1953] Ch. 149; [1953] 1 All E.R. 179, C.A.

Denning L.J. (203 A) doubted whether a local authority acting under statutory powers could ever be liable under *Rylands v. Fletcher* for damage done by sewage, but Evershed M.R. dissented (195 B), saying that it would depend on the wording of the statute in question.

5. Smeaton v. Ilford Corporation [1954] Ch. 450; [1954] 1 All E.R. 923, Upjohn J.

Held, that on a proper construction of Public Health Act 1936, statutory authority was a defence.

6. Noel T. James v. Central Electricity Authority (1958) 108 L.J. 250; [1958] C.L.Y. 3304, Elwes J.

Explosion in transformer releasing oil which caught fire and flowed onto plaintiff's land—*Held*, statutory authority was a defence to *Rylands v. Fletcher*, but defendants were liable in negligence.

7. Dunne v. North Western Gas Board [1964] 2 Q.B. 806; [1963] 3 All E.R. 916, C.A.

Water escaped from a Liverpool water main and caused a sewer underneath to collapse—the collapse of the sewer withdrew support from a gas main above it—the gas main sagged and gas escaped along and into the sewer, and finally escaped in a series of 46 explosions at manholes along the sewer—plaintiff was riding a bicycle and was injured by the explosion—Court of Passage judge found there had been no negligence, but held the Water Authority liable under *Rylands v. Fletcher*, but not in nuisance, and the Gas Board liable in nuisance, but not under *Rylands v. Fletcher*—*Held*, neither defendant liable, for (a) in the case of the Gas Board, they were supplying gas under a mandatory statutory obligation, and in such a case there could be no liability without negligence; and (b) in the case of the Water Authority, they were acting under permissive statutory powers, but the relevant statutes contained no section retaining liability for nuisance, and therefore the authority were protected under the rule in *Geddes v. Bann Reservoir* (1878) 3 App.Cas. 430 that no action lies for doing something authorised by statute, provided that there is no negligence. But in *Lowery v. Vickers Armstrong* (1969) C.A. 389 (unreported) Russell L.J. (5 A) said that in his view it was possible for a defendant such as the gas board to be guilty of nuisance without being guilty of negligence. (See also *Lowery* (1969) 8 K.I.R. 603)

(3) Electricity

1. Collingwood v. H. & C. Stores [1936] 3 All E.R. 200; 53 T.L.R. 53, C.A.

Held, electric wiring not an unusual user and *Rylands v. Fletcher* therefore not applicable. *Rylands v. Fletcher* not applicable to gas, water and electricity for ordinary domestic purposes, as opposed to storage in bulk (? and/or transmission in bulk). In the absence of negligence in the installation or maintenance of the wiring defendants would not be liable.

2. Spicer v. Smee [1946] 1 All E.R. 498, Atkinson J.

Electric wiring in defendant's house defective—nuisance—causes fire which spreads to plaintiff's house—*Held,* defendant liable, and it was no defence (a) that defendant had had wiring done by independent contractor, or (b) that defendant was not in occupation at the time.

3. Heard v. Brymbo Steel Works [1947] K.B. 692; 117 L.T. 251, C.A.

Explosion in factory—faulty switch in factory—under control of power company—breach of Electricity Supply Regulations 1937—*Held,* power company liable.

4. Buckland v. Guildford Gas Co. [1949] 1 K.B. 410; [1948] 2 All E.R. 1086, Morris J.

Girl climbing tree killed by nearby electric cable—defendants were neither owners nor occupiers—*Held,* defendants liable, even though girl trespassing. But see *Aldrich* (Chap. 7, (2) (e) **U1**).

5. Sellars v. Best [1954] 1 W.L.R. 913; [1954] 2 All E.R. 389, Pearson J.

Electric boiler installed in plaintiff's house—new circuit—electricity authority connect up new circuit to their supply—but do not test whether boiler earthed—plaintiff's wife gets fatal shock—*Held,* electricity authority not liable, as in the circumstances they owed no duty of care. But electrician was liable.

6. Miller v. South of Scotland Electricity Board 1958 S.C. (H.L.) 20; [1958] C.L.Y. 2226, H.L.

Electricity board notified town council who were about to demolish a house that electricity was cut off—council start demolition—plaintiff, a boy, entered house, touched cable and was burnt—*Held,* this raised a prima facie case of negligence against electricity board.

7. Moyle v. Southern Electricity Board [1962] 1 Lloyd's Rep. 607, C.A.

Kite in contact with 30,000-volt cable 30 feet overhead—*Held,* defendants not liable.

8. McBrien v. Arden (1963) 107 S.J. 791; [1963] C.L.Y. 2373, C.A.

Defective electric fire in hotel bedroom occupied by waitress—when it failed to function, she touched it and was burned—*Held,* defendants liable, but 50 per cent. contributory negligence.

9. McDowell v. F.M.C. (Meat) (1968) 5 K.I.R. 456; [1968] C.L.Y. 2648, C.A.

D2, occupiers and organisers of agricultural show site, allotted stand site to D1 over which an electric high tension cable passed—D1's manager was killed when he erected a flagpole over site—*Held,* D2 were liable for failing to warn of the danger of the cable, and manager was 20 per cent. contributory negligent.

10. Cook v. Broderip (1968) 112 S.J. 193; [1968] C.L.Y. 2690, O'Connor J.

Owner of flat employed independent contractor to put in new switch fuse—latter failed to test for reversed polarity—with the result that daily help at flat received an electric shock—*Held*, flatowner not liable for negligence of independent contractor.

U1. Withers v. Camp (1975) C.A. 449

33,000-volt cable 20 feet above caravan site—plaintiff contacts cable when manipulating a 20-foot ridge pole for his tent—*Held*, caravan site owner and electricity board both equally liable.

(4) Fire, Firearms and Explosives

1. Collingwood v. H. & C. Stores [1936] 3 All E.R. 200; 53 T.L.R. 53, C.A.

Held, electric wiring not an unusual user and *Rylands v. Fletcher* therefore not applicable. *Rylands v. Fletcher* not applicable to gas, water and electricity for ordinary domestic purposes as opposed to storage in bulk (? and/or transmission in bulk). In the absence of proof of negligence in the installation or maintenance of the wiring defendants would not be liable.

2. Fryer v. Salford Corporation [1937] 81 S.J. 177; [1937] 1 All E.R. 617, C.A.

Child of 11 at school cookery class—unguarded gas stove—she gets burnt—*Held*, defendants liable in negligence.

3. Mulholland v. Baker [1939] 3 All E.R. 253; 161 L.T. 20, Asquith J.

Adjoining shops—defendant has 20-gallon drum of paraffin—defendant lit some paper to smoke a rat out of pipe—fire spreads to paraffin and to plaintiff's shop—*Held*, defendant was guilty of negligence in starting fire so close to paraffin, and further the paraffin was "a thing likely to do damage unless kept under proper control," so that defendant was also liable under *Rylands v. Fletcher*.

4. The Pass of Ballater [1942] P. 112; [1942] 2 All E.R. 79, Langton J.

Defendants repairing plaintiffs' ship—blow it up—spark from oxyacetylene burner ignites petrol vapour—*Held*, defendants liable. "No precaution which was commercially practicable ought to have been omitted, and any omission of a practicable precaution would constitute a failure of duty" (84 F).

5. Century Insurance v. Northern Ireland Road Transport Board [1942] A.C. 509; [1942] All E.R. 491, H.L.

Held, that lorry driver throwing away a lighted match while his petrol lorry was discharging petrol in bulk into a storage tank was negligent.

6. Read v. Lyons [1943] A.C. 156; [1943] 2 All E.R. 471, H.L.

Plaintiff was invitee in explosives factory which blew up—no negligence—*Held*, plaintiff could not recover under *Rylands v. Fletcher* because there had been no escape from a place over which defendant had occupation or control to a place where he had not. *Semble*, an explosives factory was natural user.

7. Spicer v. Smee [1946] 1 All E.R. 498, Atkinson J.

Electric wiring in defendant's house defective—nuisance—causes fire which spreads to plaintiff's house—*Held*, defendant liable, and it was no defence (a) that defendant had had the wiring done by independent contractor, or (b) that defendant was not in occupation at the time.

8. Sochacki v. Sas [1947] 1 All E.R. 344, Lord Goddard C.J.

Held, escape of fire from an ordinary domestic fire lit in the ordinary way was not within *Rylands v. Fletcher*.

9. Yachuk v. Oliver Blais [1949] A.C. 386, [1949] 2 All E.R. 150, P.C.

Sale of petrol to boy of nine—boy gets burned using it—*Held*, negligence and defendants liable.

10. Philco v. Spurling [1949] 2 K.B. 33; [1949] 2 All E.R. 882 C.A.

A case in negligence where defendant had negligently delivered some inflammable material to plaintiff, and plaintiff's employee had ignited it in circumstances unknown—was this a *novus actus?*—*Held*, not, because defendant had not proved that the act of the employee was a conscious act of volition.

11. Donaldson v. McNiven [1952] 1 All E.R. 1213; [1952] W.N. 466, Pearson J.

Boy of 13 allowed to have air-rifle by father—boy of five injured when discharged—*Held*, an air-rifle was not a dangerous thing *per se* in the same way that a savage animal or poison or fire was (1216) but liability would depend on whether or not father had been negligent—which on the facts he had not. *Upheld* by C.A. [1952] 2 All E.R. 691, on the facts, without first point being considered.

12. Merrington v. Ironbridge Metal Works [1952] 2 All E.R. 1101; 117 J.P. 23, Hallett J.

Plaintiff a fireman going to put out fire in factory—dust explosion—*Held*, defendant factory occupiers liable.

13. Uctkos v. Mazzetta [1956] 1 Lloyd's Rep. 209, Ormerod J.

Held, user of blowlamp liable for resultant explosion.

14. Adcock v. Loveridge, *The Times*, June 21 1956; [1956] C.L.Y. 5902, Pearce J.

Defendant occupier of site where she parked derelict lorries—plaintiff an infant threw match in petrol tank—*Held*, plaintiff was a trespasser, but if child had been licensee defendant would still not have been liable, as accident was not reasonably foreseeable by her.

15. Perry v. Kendricks Transport [1956] 1 W.L.R. 85; [1956] 1 All E.R. 154, C.A.

Defendants had parked a disused coach and emptied tank—they inspected vehicle from time to time and saw that petrol cap was on—an unknown child removed cap and threw a match in, causing explosion which injured plaintiff—*Held*, defendants not liable, as this was not reasonably foreseeable.

16. Balfour v. Barty-King [1957] 1 Q.B. 496; [1957] 1 All E.R. 156, C.A.

Defendant employed a plumber to unthaw a pipe—plumber negligently used blowlamp which started a fire which spread to plaintiff's house—*Held*, defendant liable, because under the 1774 Act defendant was only protected against fires beginning accidentally, and a fire caused by negligence of someone who was not a stranger to defendant was not an accidental fire, and on the question whether or not the plumber was a stranger, whatever was the position in ordinary negligence, in cases dealing with escape of dangerous things the plumber was not a stranger.

17. Doltis v. Braithwaite [1957] 1 Lloyd's Rep. 522, Streatfeild J.

Plaintiff employed defendant contractors to install heating in the parts of a building occupied by him, namely, basement, third and fourth floors—defendants to test whether third-floor chimney was clear lit a newspaper fire—this set fire to soot—the fire spread down intercommunicating chimney (of which both plaintiff and defendants unaware) into basement—*Held*, defendants not liable either under *Rylands v. Fletcher* or in negligence, because:

(a) as to *Rylands v. Fletcher*, there was no escape in the circumstances, and lighting a fire in a grate was natural user, and
(b) as to negligence, the risk of damage was unforeseeable, since intercommunicating chimneys were a rare feature and in addition the risk of setting fire to soot was negligible.

18. Noel T. James v. Central Electricity Authority (1958) 108 L.J. 250; [1958] C.L.Y. 3304, Elwes J.

Explosion in transformer releasing oil which caught fire and flowed on to plaintiff's land—*Held*, statutory authority was a defence to *Rylands v. Fletcher*, but defendants were liable in negligence.

19. Beaver v. Cohen *The Times*, May 14, 1960; [1960] C.L.Y. 2142, Stable J.

Held, defendant liable for loss of sight when firework exploded.

20. Court v. Wyatt *The Times*, June 25, 1960; [1960] C.L.Y. 882, Donovan J.

Boy of 15 shot plaintiff with an airgun—*Held*, defendant father liable as father knew the boy was of such a disposition as not to be trusted with the gun and therefore father was negligent.

21. Overseas Tankship v. Morts Dock (Wagon Mound) [1961] A.C. 388; [1961] 1 All E.R. 404, P.C.

Oil from ship spilled into bay—molten metal from wharf fell on to floating cotton waste which began to smoulder and ignited the oil—danger of fire from oil was not reasonably foreseeable—*Held*, defendants not liable in negligence, the test being whether the damage was reasonably foreseeable.

22. Sturge v. Hackett [1962] 1 W.L.R. 1257; [1962] 3 All E.R. 166 C.A.

Tenant of flat tried to smoke out a sparrow's nest, but in doing so burnt down the house—*Held*, negligence and defendant liable as occupier. "The fire which caused the damage started on and escaped from premises of which he was the occupier. It was started negligently, and as such occupier he was liable for damage caused by its escape, quite apart from his liability as the actual person whose own negligent act started the fire" (Diplock L.J. 173 E).

23. Hughes v. Lord Advocate [1963] A.C. 837; [1963] 1 All E.R. 705, H.L.

Explosion of paraffin lamp when meddling child tripped over it—lamp was on unguarded and unfenced works site in street—*Held*, defendants liable, as the site was an allurement, and the accident, though the explosion itself was unforeseeable, was of a class and kind which was reasonably foreseeable.

24. The Wagon Mound (No. 2) [1967] 1 A.C. 617; [1966] 2 All E.R. 709, P.C.

Held, that the test for liability in nuisance was foreseeability, and not directness, of damage, and that on an analysis of the facts the damage was foreseeable, and defendants accordingly were liable.

25. Goldman v. Hargrave [1967] 1 A.C. 645; [1966] 2 All E.R. 709, P.C.

Held, that an occupier owed a duty of care to prevent hazards arising accidentally on his premises from spreading, and that the standard of care required was "what it was reasonable to expect of him in his individual circumstances" (Lord Wilberforce, 996 D)—*Held*, further, that the 1774 Act did not apply to absolve an occupier from the consequences of a fire which spread through his negligence, because the latter was a different fire from that which began accidentally.

26. Hinds v. Direct Supply Co. *The Times*, January 29 1966; [1966] C.L.Y. 5210, MacKenna J.

Held, sellers liable.

27. Gorely v. Codd [1967] 1 W.L.R. 19; [1966] 3 All E.R. 891, Nield J.

Held, father not liable.

28. Mason v. Levy Auto Parts [1967] 2 Q.B. 530; [1967] 2 All E.R. 62, MacKenna J.

Yard stacked with crates containing machinery, tarpaulins and other combustible material—fire started in unknown circumstances—spread to plaintiff's land adjacent—defendants not negligent in connection with start or spread of fire—*Held*, defendants were liable on the basis of a strict liability analogous to *Rylands v. Fletcher*, in that (a) they had brought on to their land things likely to catch fire, and had kept them in such condition that if they did catch fire, the fire was likely to spread to the plaintiff's land, and (b) they did so in the course of some non-natural use. Dicta in *Collingwood* **1** *applied.*

29. Kingzett v. B.R.B. (1968) 112 S.J. 625; *The Times*, July 10, 1968, C.A.

Held, defendant board bound to use reasonable care to keep explosives safe, but on the facts they could not have foreseen theft by boys.

30. Mitchell v. Mason (1966) 10 W.I.R. 26; [1968] C.L.Y. 2682, Jamaica C.A.

31. Emanuel v. G.L.C. [1971] 2 All E.R. 835; [1971] 2 Lloyd's Rep. 36, C.A.

Contractor removing prefabricated bungalows from council land lit a bonfire negligently which escaped and did damage—*Held*, defendants were occupiers for the purpose of liability for escape of fire, and were accordingly liable for any escape which was due to the negligence of anyone other than a stranger—defendants argued that the contractors were strangers, having been engaged by the Ministry of Works who were clearing the prefabs at the request of defendants—*Held*, contractors were not strangers. Lord Denning M.R. said that "stranger" was anyone "who in lighting a fire acts contrary to anything which the occupier would anticipate he would do" (839 A). Edmund Davies L.J. (840 J) said that the test was whether the occupier had control over the activities of the person concerned.

32. The Arzew [1981] 1 Lloyd's Rep. 142; [1981] C.L.Y. 1838, Sheen J.

D's vessel was discharging a cargo of gas oil. P's trawler was doing welding works at a nearby wharf. Some oil escaped and spread onto the water and was ignited by the welding. Other trawlers of P were damaged—*Held*, D liable (and no contributory negligence by P, as it would have been difficult to notice the oil on the water).

33. Rigby v. Chief Constable Of Northamptonshire [1985] 2 All E.R. 985; [1985] C.L.Y. 2327, Taylor J.

CS gas cylinder fired into plaintiff's shop to flush out dangerous psychopath set premises ablaze, and P sued the Chief Constable in negligence also alleging escape of a dangerous thing, nuisance and trespass—*Held*, no negligence in relation to choice because decision to purchase and use that CS gas had been made bona fide and could not be impugned. However, D was negligent in not having firefighting equipment on hand in view of real and substantial fire risk. (It was doubted that *Rylands v. Fletcher* would apply in situation of a voluntary release such as this, but if it did, defence of necessity would apply.) See also Chap. 7 (2)(c) **20**.

34. Borge v. Matthews [1988] C.L.Y. 2450, H.H. Judge Watkin Powell

D liable for tort of independent contractor in respect of fire where his contractor negligently causes fire to escape from D's land and damage adjoining property and negligence which causes fire to rage out of control within D's own land whereby passer by is induced to enter as rescuer and suffers personal injury. See also Chap. 1, (2)(d) **13**.

U1. Theresa v. Garrley Heritage & Co. (1952) C.A. 410.

Electric fire left on near corrugated paper—fire—spreading to plaintiff's premises—*Held*, defendants negligent and liable.

U2. Burrough v. Berkshire Fire Authority (1971) C.A. 40.

Plaintiff volunteered to help fire brigade to fight barn fire—by using tractor to drag straw bales clear—*Held*, as plaintiff thereby came under control of defendants, they owed him a duty of care and were liable for not providing him with a helmet (which was readily available).

U3. Smith v. Hodge (1974) C.A. 194.

Bonfire negligently lit by plaintiff near defendant's yacht—fire brigade put it out—but later (as assumed) some embers revived and burnt out the yacht—plaintiff argued that the negligence of the fire brigade in not extinguishing the embers was *novus actus*—*Held*, not so.

(5) Gas

1. North Western Utilities v. London Guarantee [1936] A.C. 108; 53 T.L.R. 93, P.C.

Gas leak in supply pipes under street caused by action of third party (the City Corporation of Edmonton) in constructing a storm sewer and causing pipe to sag—the gas company maintained the pipe under statutory authority—*Held*, (a) the gas in the pipe was a dangerous thing to which *Rylands v. Fletcher* liability would ordinarily apply (118), (b) the action of the City Corporation in causing the pipe to sag was the independent conscious act (119) (122) of a third party, and therefore, following ***Rickards v. Lothian*** [1913] A.C. 263, P.C., was a defence to a claim under ***Rylands v. Fletcher***; (c) the fact that defendants were acting under statutory authority was a defence to a claim under ***Rylands v. Fletcher*** (121); (d) the defence of common interest or consent of plaintiff did not apply, as the only fact tending to establish this defence was that the plaintiff received a domestic supply of gas through the pipe, which was insufficient to establish common interest or consent; (e) the defendants were however liable in negligence, as gas was a dangerous commodity, and it was defendants' duty to watch all operations in the vicinity of their mains which were likely to affect the same: "their duty . . . was at the lowest to be on watch and be vigilant; they do not even pretend to have done as much as that" (Lord Wright, 127).

2. Fryer v. Salford Corporation [1937] 81 S.J. 177; [1937] 1 All E.R. 617, C.A.

Child of 11 at school cookery class—unguarded gas stove—she gets burnt—*Held*, defendants liable in negligence.

3. Hanson v. Wearmouth Coal Co. [1939] 3 All E.R. 47; 55 T.L.R. 747, C.A.

Held, gas company liable. Goddard L.J. at 53 A: "A person who brings a dangerous thing onto his land and allows it to escape, thereby causing damage to another, is liable to that other unless he can show that the escape was due to the conscious act of a third party, and without negligence on his part."

4. Glemister v. London & Eastern Gas Board [1951] 2 Lloyd's Rep. 115, Lord Goddard C.J.

Held, Gas Board under no obligation to inspect gas service pipes in private premises unless they knew or should have known of defect, and in the absence of negligence they were not liable.

5. Beckett v. Newalls Insulation [1953] 1 W.L.R. 8; [1953] 1 All E.R. 250, C.A.

Plaintiff working on a ship—defendants bring on a calor gas cylinder which if a valve or regulator is turned will emit gas which is liable to explode on contact with a naked flame—plaintiff looking for something lights match—explosion—not known how gas escaped—*Held*, defendants liable, as they should have taken precautions by warning and/or instructions as to how it should be moved, as it was patently dangerous if moved.

6. O'Brien v. Bridge Marine Works [1954] 2 Lloyd's Rep. 79, Cassels J.

Yacht hired from defendants had butane gas container stored in small space only 18 inches away from engine—as a result gas expanded due to heat, causing explosion—*Held*, defendants liable for negligence.

7. Moore v. R. Fox [1956] 1 Q.B. 596; [1956] 1 All E.R. 182, C.A.

Plaintiff employed to immerse objects in gas-heated tank—explosion—*Held* (Romer L.J. *dubitante*) that this was *res ipsa loquitur*, despite the fact that plaintiff was at the time operating the tank.

8. Bleach v. Blue Gate Products *The Times*, January 26, 1960; [1960] C.L.Y. 2125, McNair J.

Kitchen cooker with defective gas tap—stoker found dead in kitchen from gas poisoning—*Held*, defendants liable, as on proof of defect onus passed to them to give innocent explanation, which they had not discharged.

9. Dunne v. North Western Gas Board [1964] 2 Q.B. 806; [1963] 3 All E.R. 916, C.A.

Escape of water from main caused collapse of sewer—which in turn caused a gas main to leak—the gas escaped into the sewer—and exploded in a series of 46 explosions along manholes in the sewer—plaintiff bicyclist was injured—*Held*, since trial judge had excluded negligence by Gas Board, they were not liable, as the latter were supplying gas under a mandatory statutory obligation, and in such a case there could be no liability without negligence.

10. Smith v. South Eastern Gas Board, *The Times*, April 17, 1964; 108 S.J. 337, Fenton Atkinson J.

Woman turned off all gas taps in her house—neighbour smelt gas in his house—sent for Gas Board officer—he checked that the meter was off in the woman's house, and made some tests, but could defect no fault—strong smell of gas outside house when he left—shortly after, explosion—*Held*, Gas Board official negligent in leaving situation as it was, which he should have appreciated was one of great danger.

11. Pearson v. North Western Gas Board [1968] 2 All E.R. 669; [1968] C.L.Y. 2721, Rees J.

Frozen soil thrust downwards on gas main—fracturing same—main exploded after gas had accumulated under floor boards of house—pipe had been laid in 1878 two feet nine inches down and was in good condition—frost was eight inches deep—judge did not decide if it was *res ipsa loquitur*—*Held, even if it was, defendants were not liable, as there was no reasonable step to protect the public from such a danger.*

12. Frederic v. Perpetual Investments (1968) 2 D.L.R. (3d) 50, Ontario High Ct.

13. King v. Sadler (1969) 114 S.J. 192, Sir Jocelyn Simon P.

14. Lowery v. Vickers Armstrong (1969) 8 K.I.R. 603; [1969] C.L.Y. 1178, C.A.

Maintenance man went to investigate a gas leak with a lighted spill and blew himself up—*Held*, Gas Board were liable for not inspecting properly a gas main which had given trouble in the past and was old (see Bar Library transcript (1969) C.A. 389), but plaintiff was 25 per cent. contributorily negligent.

15. Lloyde v. West Midlands Gas Board [1971] 1 W.L.R. 749; [1971] 2 All E.R. 1240, C.A.

16. Pusey v. Peters (1974) 119 S.J. 85; [1974] C.L.Y. 2596, Michael Davies J.

Held, Gas Board liable for failing to inspect air brick.

17. Sullivan v. South Glamorgan C.C., *The Times*, August 7, 1985; [1985] C.L.Y. 2308, C.A.

It was reasonably foreseeable that a council's negligent system of carrying out road works that involved gas pipes adjacent to a house could cause fatal injuries to the occupier resulting from the ignition of natural gas which leaked from a severed pipe detached within the house.

U1. Duncan v. Robinson Brothers (1961) C.A. 178 (unreported)

Explosion of carbon disulphide gas given off in chemical process—*Held*, defendants liable.

(6) Water

1. Tilley v. Stevenson [1939] 4 All E.R. 207, C.A.

Defendant about to go into a flat—has key—for three days before he goes in burst pipe due to frost leaks into plaintiff's flat—defendant had good reason to believe water turned off at main—*Held*, (a) following *Rickards v. Lothian* [1913] A.C. 263, *Rylands v. Fletcher* could not possibly apply and (b) as plaintiff had not proved defendant knew or ought to have known water turned on, no negligence.

2. Rouse v. Gravelworks [1940] 1 K.B. 489; [1940] 1 All E.R. 26, C.A.

Held, digging for gravel ordinary user and therefore defendants not liable for escape.

3. Sedleigh-Denfield v. O'Callaghan [1940] A.C. 880; [1940] 3 All E.R. 349, H.L.

Water pipe laid on defendants' land by third party—became blocked and overflowed onto plaintiff's land—*Held*, defendants liable for continuing a nuisance after actual or presumed knowledge thereof. *Cf. Neath R.D.C. v. Williams* [1950] 2 All E.R. 625, D.C., where the flooding was due to a naturally caused obstruction in a natural stream—*Held*, defendants were under no liability to remove the obstruction.

4. Thomas & Evans v. Mid Rhondda Society [1941] 1 K.B. 381; [1940] 4 All E.R. 357, C.A.

Defendants removed a river wall which was on their land—river flooded onto their land and thence escaped onto plaintiff's land—*Held*, defendants not liable under *Rylands v. Fletcher* (or in nuisance or negligence, either).

5. Watson v. Sutton Water Co. [1940] 3 All E.R. 502; 56 T.L.R. 979, C.A.

Plaintiff requested defendant water company to turn off his domestic water supply—defendants complied but did it in such a way that a third party (unknown) could and did turn it on again, thereby flooding plaintiff's house—*Held*, defendants liable. (*N.B.* In C.A. defendants who were appealing asked for appeal to be allowed by consent, but C.A. refused to do so, and eventually dismissed appeal.)

6. Kiddle v. City Business Properties [1942] 1 K.B. 269; [1942] 2 All E.R. 216; Lord Goddard C.J.

Plaintiff was tenant of shop leased by defendants—water from defendants' arcade roof escaped into plaintiff's shop—*Held*, defendants not liable, as plaintiff had impliedly consented to the water drainage system and/or the same was for the common benefit of plaintiff and defendants, and in the absence of negligence by defendants this was a defence.

7. Peters v. Prince of Wales Theatre [1943] K.B. 73; [1942] 2 All E.R. 533, C.A.

Plaintiff was tenant of part of a building leased by defendants—defendant in his part had an extensive sprinkler system which, without negligence on defendant's part, burst in frost and flooded plaintiff—at the time of the lease plaintiff knew of the sprinkler system—*Held*, following **6**, defendants not liable, as in the circumstances plaintiff had impliedly consented to the sprinkler system.

8. Longhurst v. Metropolitan Water Board [1948] 2 All E.R. 834; [1948] W.N. 418, H.L. See Chap. 12,(1) (a) **9**.

9. Frensham v. Shorn (1950) C.L.C. 6677; [1950] W.N. 406, Finnemore J.

Adjacent owners—escape of water from radiator owing to frost burst—*Held*, defendant liable.

10. Pride of Derby v. British Celanese [1953] Ch. 149; [1953] 1 All E.R. 179, C.A.

Evershed M.R. (195 B) appeared to be of the view that the discharge of untreated sewage into a river would come within *Rylands v. Fletcher*—but the case was mainly argued in nuisance. Denning L.J. (203 A) seems to have been of same view.

11. Prosser v. Levy [1955] 1 W.L.R. 1224; [1955] 3 All E.R. 577, C.A.

Plaintiff was tenant of part of building leased by defendant—water from defendant's pipe overflowed onto plaintiff—*Held*, defendants were liable, as consent was no defence where, as here, the water system was of quite an unusual or defective type, and/or where, as here, defendants had been negligent, and further because defendants had not established act of stranger (see Chap. 8,(2) (b) **5**).

12. Brand v. Barrow (1965) 109 S.J. 834; [1965] C.L.Y. 2648, C.A.

Business premises—plaintiff in basement, defendants in floors above—defendants left without turning off their stopcock—but plaintiff had main stopcock, which he also failed to turn off—frost, bursting pipe in defendant's part, and flooding basement—*Held*, defendants negligent, but plaintiff 50 per cent. negligent in not turning off his stopcock.

13. C.B. Printers v. P. & C. Manufacturing (1968) 206 E.G. 311; [1968] C.L.Y. 2643, C.A.

Business premises—third-floor lavatory pipe froze—on thawing water flooded basement—*Held* third-floor tenant liable, but landlord, who occupied basement, held liable for 20 per cent, contributory negligence, as he should have either cut off water supply or asked tenant's permission to do so.

14. Boxes v. British Waterways [1971] 2 Lloyd's Rep. 183, C.A.

Bank of D's canal collapsed due to barges banging against wall—*Held*, D liable, because their duty as a canal authority with statutory power to maintain a canal included a duty to prevent it becoming a danger to others, which duty included one to regulate traffic, and in this they had failed—*Held*, also, that a claim under *Rylands v. Fletcher* failed.

15. Potter v. Mole Valley D.C. and Surrey C.C., *The Times*, October 22 1982, [1982] C.L.Y. 2266, French J.

Regular flooding affecting P's premises due to inadequate culvert built by predecessors in title of highway authority (D2)—*Held*, D2 liable for public and private nuisane—*Helds* (who appear to have been the drainage authority) not liable for failing to exercise their powers under the Land Drainage Act 1976, as to which see Chap. 1, (3)(b) **13**.

16. Stephens v. Anglian Water Authority [1987] 131 S.J. 1214; [1987] 3 All E.R. 379, C.A.

Landowner who abstracts undergrounds water causes damage to adjoining land—*Held*, no liability to P because landowner was acting within his rights.

U1. King v. L.C.C. (1965) C.A. 127

Escape of water from empty flat owned by defendants—the flat was padlocked, and the door was burst down by the police, who found no evidence intruders having been in—there had been two plumbers employed by defendants in the flat doing some work—they gave evidence they had not touched the tap in question—C.C.J. on the evidence found for defendants—*Held*, defendants liable, since, on this basis, it was virtually impossible for the tap to have been turned on. *Per* Winn L. J. (citing Sherlock Holmes) (13 E): "When you have eliminated the impossible, whatever remains, however improbable, must be the truth."

U2. Downes v. Cameron (1975) C.A. 438A

U3. King v. Liverpool C.C. (1990) C.A. 885

P, tenants of ground floor flat in block of flats, flooded out from common loft in the block—*Held*, D liable. *Res ipsa loquitur* applied.

U4. Anglian Water Services Ltd v. H. G. Thurston & Co. Ltd (1993) C A 1119

Pumping station connected to sewage works by 8" asbestos concrete pipe: D1 contractors and D2 owners of land. D2 made planning application to raise an area of marshland over sewage pipes. D1 tipped soil on land which was then levelled by bulldozer. This caused a leak from asbestos pipe which had fractured and PVC pipe at one of its couplings—*Held*, neither defendant liable in negligence or nuisance. D1 not aware of existence of pipes and therefore damage to them not foreseeable and D2 knew of pipes but could not have foreseen harm arising from operation carried out by D1.

9. ANIMALS

The Animals Act 1971 establishes a strict liability for animals in certain circumstances, and abolishes the rules at common law relating to cattle trespass, whilst providing a liability for damage done by animals straying on to the highway. Accordingly, pre-1971 cases are now of limited value, save as examples of negligence. Strict liability is dealt with in Chap. 9, (1), while Chap. 9, (2) deals with negligence, but as most cases involve considerations of liability under the Animals Act as well as at common law, cross-references should be made.

(1) Strict Liability

1. Cummings v. Grainger [1976] 3 W.L.R. 842; [1977] 1 All E.R. 104, C.A.

Defendant kept an untrained Alsatian dog in his scrapyard at night to deter intruders—yard was locked at night and notices about the dog were prominently displayed—plaintiff, who knew about the dog, trespassed and was attacked—*Held*, defendant was absolved under the Animals Act 1971 s. 5(3)(b), inasmuch as it was "not unreasonable" to roam on the premises at night, and furthermore, since the plaintiff knew about the dog, she had voluntarily accepted the risk, so that the defendant was also absolved under section 5(2). But Lord Denning M.R. said that, when the Guard Dogs Act 1975 was in force, it might have the effect of making it unreasonable in civil proceedings to let a dog of this nature roam at night.

2. Kite v. Napp, *The Times*, July 1, 1982; [1982] C.L.Y. 67, Stephen Brown J.

3. Wallace v. Newton [1982] 1 W.L.R. 375; [1982] 2 All E.R. 106, Park J.

P, a groom employed by D, loading D's horse into trailer. Horse suddenly became violent and uncontrollable, injuring P—*Held*, that under section 2(2) it was sufficient for P to show that to D's knowledge the horse was unreliable and unpredictable. It was unnecessary to prove that the horse had a known vicious tendency to attack people. D liable.

4. Curtis v. Betts [1990] 1 W.L.R. 459; [1990] 1 All E.R. 769 C.A.

P lived opposite D who owned a bull mastiff with which P was friendly. Dog attacked P whilst in back of D's Land Rover—*Held* D liable to P for injury sustained, under the Animals Act 1971, s. 2(2). Subsection 2(2)(a) was satisfied if damage caused was of a kind that the dog was likely to cause if not restrained. It was not necessary to show that the dog had abnormal characteristics, as it belonged to a breed likely to cause damage. Dog also had characteristics not normally found in bull mastiffs except at certain times.

5. Hill v. Lovett, S.L.T. 994, [1992] C.L.Y. 6084, O.H.

P injured in employer's garden by dogs after being permission to enter to clean windows—*Held*, D liable as occupier and for failure to provide safe system of work.

6. Hunt v. Wallis *The Times*, May 10, 1991; [1994] P.I.Q.R. P128, Pill J.

P claimed damages in respect of injuries which she received when knocked over by D's border collie. Claimed negligence and liability under Animals Act 1971. No negligence found as a fact—*Held* in relation to strict liability claim that this border collie did not possess any characteristics not normally found in the species of border collies which were not normally dangerous dogs. Further, owners did not have any knowledge of any propensity in Bruce (the dog) to collide with people or things.

U1. Hubble v. Oughtibridge (1986) C.A. 403

Plaintiff child bitten by neighbouring dog through gap in hedge—*Held* no liability under Animals Act as no evidence of fierce and mischievous nature, and no liability in negligence as the incident of a dog putting its head through such a narrow gap was not foreseeable.

U2. Harrison v. Gledstone (1987) C.A. 635

Plaintiff thrown from horse and suffered injury—*Held*, defendant liable in negligence and under Animals Act 1971 because knew of animal's dangerous rearing characteristics, which made it unpredictable and unreliable.

U3. Cockhill v. Muff (1987) C.A. 620

Child of nine attacked by cross-bred labrador dog—*Held*, owners not liable, as not known to be dangerous dog.

U4. Smith v. Ainger [1990] C.L.Y. 3297 C.A

The keeper of a dog with a known propensity to attack other dogs is liable to a plaintiff injured in the course of an attack on P's dog.

(2) Liability for negligence

1. Pitcher v. Martin [1937] 3 All E.R. 918; 53 T.L.R. 903, Atkinson J.

Dog in street on loose lead 50 inches long—*Held*, negligent.

2. Aldham v. United Dairies [1940] 1 K.B. 507, [1939] 4 All E.R. 522, C.A.

Plaintiff attacked by unattended horse attached to milk cart—*Held*, defendants liable because negligent in leaving horse unattended, and the proper inference was the plaintiff's injuries were directly caused by that negligence. Importance was attached to the fact that the horse was known to be restive.

3. Tallents v. Bell [1944] 2 All E.R. 474, C.A.

Held, could not be said to be negligent to let dogs run just because rabbit hutch in neighbourhood.

4. Fitzgerald v. Cooke Bourne [1964] 1 Q.B. 249; [1963] 3 All E.R. 36, C.A.

Two unbroken fillies in field with public footpath running across it—playful but not vicious—one filly knocked plaintiff down by getting too close to her, but without any intention of causing damage—a hunt secretary said in evidence that he knew the fillies and would not have put them in the field—*Held*, defendants not liable, because (a) no liability under *scienter* rule (as it then was); and (b) it would impose too high a standard of duty to oblige defendants to guard against possibility of injury from fillies which were merely playful.

5. Bativala v. West [1970] 1 Q.B. 716; [1970] 1 All E.R. 332, Bridge J.

Gymkhana run by riding school—saddle of pony slipped, unseating rider—pony ran away onto highway and injured plaintiff's car—*Held*, riding proprietor was liable, because she knew (a) that there was always a danger of a saddle slipping; (b) if this happened in an event for young riders (as here), the rider would be likely to lose control; and (c) if this happened, the pony would be likely to bolt onto the road, if it could, where it was foreseeable it would cause an accident; and in such circumstances the defendant ought to have kept the gate onto the road closed during the event. *N.B.* The judge decided the case under the ordinary principles of negligence, holding that the then existing law exempting liability for animals escaping onto the highway did not apply. As to the latter, see now Animals Act 1971, s. 8.

6. Draper v. Hodder [1972] 2 Q.B. 556; [1972] 2 All E.R. 210, C.A.

Plaintiff aged three and defendant dog-breeder living in adjacent premises in the country—defendant bred Jack Russell terriers which were brought up in kennels—a pack of them went off from defendant's premises and severely bit the plaintiff—*Held*, defendants liable in negligence. The decision turned largely on the expert evidence which was to the effect that kennel dogs should always be kept confined and not allowed to roam in packs, as there was a foreseeable risk that they might get excited and attack children.

7. Andrews v. Watts [1971] R.T.R. 484, C.A.

8. Carryfast Ltd. v. Hack [1981] R.T.R. 464; [1981] C.L.Y. 1847, Ralph Gibson J.

Driver on country road overtaking horse being ridden along nearside grass verge. Horse nervous in traffic but controllable—rider accomplished horsewoman. Driver began to overtake too fast and too close—horse "danced", causing driver to brake swerve and collide with oncoming vehicle—*Held*, sole cause of accident was driver's negligence. Not negligent to take onto road a horse which is nervous in traffic, provided it is ridden with proper care. Otherwise, if horse cannot be properly controlled.

9. Haimes v. Watson [1981] R.T.R. 90; [1981] C.L.Y. 1853, C.A.

Driver about to overtake horse—horse shied, causing rider to lose control—horse moved into path of car—*Held*, although the movement of the horse across the road gave rise to an inference of negligence, this was negatived by the rider's explanation that the horse had unforeseeably shied, and the rider was not liable. There was no absolute duty on a rider to keep his horse under control.

10. Spearing v. Rapkins [1982] C.L.Y. 73, Kingdom C.C.

11. Smith v. Prendergast, *The Times*, October 18, 1984; [1984] C.L.Y. 2314.

P, child, injured in attack by guard dog which had been taken in by D as a stray—Held D, negligent in not taking any steps to ascertain whether or not dog was vicious.

12. Cullum v. Clarke [1989] C.L.Y. 2546, Mr Reg Hetherington

Duty of dog owner for labrador off lead—Held, not liable.

U1. Friend v. Facey (1963) C.A. 79A

Driving cows across busy road—one man only in charge—he opened gate, and while his attention was diverted, a cow galloped out—plaintiff's car only 40 feet away, doing 40 m.p.h.—C.C.J. found plaintiff 50 per cent. to blame for not swerving—*Held*, this was asking too much of a driver, and defendant was 100 per cent. liable for not controlling cows properly.

U2. Hunt v. Stephens (1963) C.A. 14

Local show—*Held*, organisers not liable for allowing ponies to be trotted close to entrance to horticultural tent, where mother of, and carrying, infant plaintiff stepped backwards into pony.

U3. Stannage v. Jennaway (1963) C.A. 86

Plaintiff at agricultural show knocked down by pony ridden by defendant—pony was trotting through crowded passageway—doubt as to whether plaintiff moved into path of pony—*Held*, defendant liable, as in any event people moving about at a show not bound to move in straight lines.

U4. Trevarthen v. Labrum (1965) C.A. 77B

Cattle escaped—defendant was rounding them up on road—when plaintiff ran into them—*Held*, defendant not liable, as although he owed a duty of care, he had on the facts discharged it.

U5. Davies v. Davies (1974) C.A. 246A

Sheep straying from common on to road—*Held*, owner not liable by reason of Animals Act 1971, s. 8(2).

U6. Upton v. John Reid (1977) C.A. 158

Night—car collides with two heifers—which have trampled down fence and escaped—*Held*, defendant farmer liable under Animals Act 1971, s. 8: "The fence having broken, the onus was on the defendants to show that they took all reasonable care, or, as the judge put it, 'Can the defendants show that the fence collapsed without their negligence?"' (Waller L.J., 9D).

U7. Smith v. Sudron (1981) C.A. 140

Small puppy escaped from back yard into road and caused traffic accident—*Held, obiter*, on assumption that puppy had crawled under small gap in fence, that the owner had not been negligent. "Puppies, like little girls, do grow up and it would be . . . (an) unreasonable burden on householders if they had to go to great expense to provide safeguards against the possibility that, for a period of three or four months in the early life of a puppy it could wriggle through a small opening in a fence or hedge:" (Lawton L.J., 6).

U8. Breeden v. Lampard (1985) C.A. 1035

Riding accident at clubbing meet. P injured when D's horse shuffled to left and kicked out striking P.—*Held*, D not liable as no negligence and no breach of Animal's Act 1971, s. 2.

U9. Hubble v. Oughtibridge (1986) C.A. 403

Plaintiff child bitten by neighbouring dog through gap in hedge—*Held*, no liability under Animals Act as no evidence of fierce and mischievous nature, and no liability in negligence as the incident of a dog putting its head through such a narrow gap was not foreseeable.

(3) Liability for Trespass

(*N.B.* The common law rules of cattle trespass are abolished by the Animals Act 1971. Liability for trespassing livestock is now regulated by sections 4, 5, and liability for injury done by dogs by sections 3, 5. Liability for killing or injuring a dog worrying livestock is dealt with in section 9. As a result all previous cases on cattle trespass and the like are now obsolete and are not set out below.)

1. Hoskin v. Rogers, *The Times*, January 25, 1985; [1985] C.L.Y. 2314, C.A.

Straying cattle because of inadequate fencing—Held, liability to attach to owner of cattle rather than owner of land, because when land had been let out the fencing was adeqate, and the owner of the land was not aware that anything was wrong with the fencing at the time of the accident.

2. League Against Cruel Sports v. Scott [1986] Q.B. 240; [1985] 2 All E.R. 489, Park J.

Case arising in trespass in respect of injunctive relief sought by League against master of hounds in hunt—*Held*, master liable for trespass of hounds if he was aware that there was a real risk of hounds entering on the land in pursuit of the stag, or if he was indifferent to such a risk.

3. Matthews v. Wicks, The Times, May 25, 1987; [1987] C.L.Y. 115

The grazing right for cattle does not provide a defence under the Animals Act 1971, s. 5(5) to a claim for trespass under section 4 of the Act.

U1. Taylor v. Huggins (1976) C.A. 266

Plaintiff licensed defendant to graze horses in his field—they escape from field into plaintiffs' garden—*Held*, defendant liable under Animals Act 1971, s. 4.

10. LIABILITY OF OCCUPIER FOR DANGEROUS PREMISES

The Occupiers' Liability Act 1957 came into force on January 1, 1958, establishing a common duty of care owed to all lawful visitors, and the Occupiers' Liability Act 1984, dealing with liability to trespassers (see Chap. 10(5)(f)) came into force on May 13, 1984. Earlier cases, such as those distinguishing between invitees and licensees, are included largely for example, whilst cases which are now clearly obsolete have been excluded. In many instances, there will be replication in other chapters, but the qualification for inclusion in this chapter, is the determination of liability by reference to the tortfeasor's status as occupier.

(1) Persons liable as occupier

1. Canter v. Gardner [1940] 1 All E.R. 325; 56 T.L.R. 205, Tucker J.

Building contractor makes hole and hands same over to sub-contractor—latter covers it but later the cover is removed—*Held*, building contractor not liable because not in control of the hole or aware of the danger. Not decided what would have been position if they had been not in control but aware of danger.

2. Buckner v. Ashby [1941] 1 K.B. 321; 110 L.J.K.B. 460, C.A.

Contractors employed to roof-in passage—they leave a soleplate which was dangerous unless properly lit—owners approve and accept work—but do not light—*Held*, contractors not liable as the approval and acceptance of the work by the owners amounted, to an intervening conscious agency which should have prevented mischief, and therefore defendant owed no duty to plaintiff. *Aliter per* Goddard L.J. if defect not apparent—*Held*, also that the effective cause of the accident was the bad lighting. Goddard L.J. (337) further said that the *test* in such cases was:

> "Are the terms of the contract such that an ordinarily prudent person would consider that his liability was at an end after the approval of the other party to the contract?"

3. Hartwell v. Grayson Rollo [1947] K.B. 901; [1947] L.J.R. 1038, C.A.

Dictum by Lord Oaksey L.J. at 913 to the effect that A owes duty of invitor to B when he invites B "to a place where they both have business", "no matter whether the place belongs to the invitor or is in his exclusive occupation". But this dictum may need caution—the Lord Justice repeats the proposition later, but adds the qualification that A must have a business interest or control in the premises. *And* the other two Lords Justices found defendants were in actual occupation, possession or control, so above may well be *obiter*.

4. Hawkins v. Coulsdon U.D.C. [1954] 1 Q.B. 319; [1954] 1 All E.R. 97, C.A.

Held, local authority who had requisitioned a house in which they permitted persons to live were liable as occupiers.

5. Creed v. McGeoch [1955] 1 W.L.R. 1005; [1955] 3 All E.R. 123, Ashworth J.

Defendants contractors constructing roads, sewers and paths on a council estate—leave a trailer standing, and infant plaintiff is injured thereon playing see-saw—question was whether defendants' duty was to be judged on the basis of their being occupiers or under *Donoghue v. Stevenson*—defendants were going to do work on the land where the trailer was standing, but they had not done any, nor had they fenced or marked it off from the waste-land—*Held*, in these circumstances they were not in occupation of the land in question but only of the strip actually under construction. Judge accepts dictum of Lord Oaksey L.J. in *Hartwell v. Grayson Rollo* **3**, namely that the occupation need not be exclusive (126 D), and he further said that the question of occupation could not be answered by reference to the contract in this case (though in some cases the agreement coupled with the defendants' conduct might be relevant), and/or that the agreement should be treated in the same way as an agreement for loan of servant is treated *qua* third party.

6. A.C. Billings v. Riden [1958] A.C. 240; [1957] 3 All E.R. 1, H.L.

Question of duty owed by contractors executing works to visitor to house—*Held per* Lord Reid, 4–5, Lords Simonds and Cohen concurring, that the fact that plaintiff was only a licensee *vis-à-vis* the occupier was no ground for limiting duty of contractor accordingly, but that their duty was to take reasonable care to ensure that visitors were not exposed to danger by their actions (5 C). Lord Somervell (13 D) put the duty in similar terms.

7. Hughes v. Lord Advocate [1963] A.C. 837; [1963] 1 All E.R. 705, H.L.

Post Office manhole site in street—tent over manhole—children go into tent to play—*Held*, Post Office did not have sufficient exclusive possession in any part of the roadway to constitute them as occupiers, and therefore the children were not to be treated as trespassers.

8. Kearney v. Waller Lawton J. [1967] 1 Q.B. 29, [1965] 3 All E.R. 352, Lawton J.

Plaintiff employed by painting sub-contractors fell from a scaffold erected by scaffolding subcontractors—cause was insufficient amount of staging—*Held*, main contractors were not occupiers at common law, as at the time the relevant part of the scaffold was under the supervision and control of the painting sub-contractors.

9. Fisher v. C.H.T. [1966] 2 Q.B. 475; [1966] 1 All E.R. 88, C.A.

D1, owners, allowed D**2** to operate a restaurant under licence—but D1 controlled the entrance door to the whole premises and could pass at will through the restaurant—they also had a maintenance man who was "round and about" the restaurant while some repairs were being done by D2, in the course of which a decorator (employed by D3, painting sub-contractors) was injured by a live wire in the ceiling—*Held*, D1 were occupiers as well as D2, and were 10 per cent. liable by reason of the activities of their maintenance man.

10. Wheat v. Lacon [1966] A.C. 552; [1966] 1 All E.R. 582, H.L.

Manager of public house was allowed by licence to occupy private quarters, which he furnished—the brewers had a right to do the repairs—the manager was allowed to take in guests—one of his guests fell down the back staircase in the private quarters and was killed—*Held*, that both the manager and the brewers were occupiers of the private quarters (but there was no breach of any duty on the facts). Lord Denning (595 E) said that the brewers had the same degree of residuary control as the defendants in *Green v. Chelson B.C.* [1954] 1 All E.R. 318, and as such were occupiers; Lord Pearson (601 C) said that the foundation of occupiers' liability was occupational control, and the brewers here had some sufficient degree of occupational control of the private quarters to make them occupiers. *But* all the Law Lords stressed that the extent of the duty of care might vary very greatly according to the degree of control exercised by separate occupiers: "Where separate persons are each under a duty of care the acts or omissions which would constitute a breach of that duty may vary very greatly. That which would be negligent in one may well be free from blame in the other" (Lord Pearce, 599 G). Lord Morris (599 B) said that the extent of the particular control which was exercised within the sphere of joint occupation would often be a pointer as to the nature and extent of the duty devolving on a particular occupier.

11. Smith v. Vange [1970] 1 W.L.R. 733; [1970] 1 All E.R. 249, MacKenna J.

12. Whiting v. Hillingdon London Borough Council (1970) 68 L.G.R. 437; [1970] C.L.Y. 1191, James J.

Footpath—privately owned—but local authority were under a duty to maintain it—P fell over a hidden tree stump—*Held*, that the mere fact that the local authority were liable to maintain footpath did not make them "occupiers" under the 1957 Act.

13. Ellis v. Scruttons [1975] 1 Lloyd's Rep. 564, Croom-Johnson J.

Held, on the terms of the charterparty, shipowners and not charterers in occupation of hold for the purpose of supervising loading.

14. Harris v. Birkenhead Corporation [1976] 1 W.L.R. 279; [1976] 1 All E.R. 341, C.A.

Clearance scheme—compulsory purchase order made in respect of privately rented house—local authority then served on the tenant two notices—which were somewhat inconsistent with each other but which the Court construed to mean that local authority was notionally taking possession within 14 days but would allow tenant to remain there as long as they thought fit—tenant thereupon left without notifying local authority—subsequently the house was vandalised and a young infant going in by an open door was injured—*Held*, the occupier was the local authority, applying dicta in *Wheat* **10**, inasmuch as the local authority by their notices had asserted, and (albeit unknowingly) had actually obtained, control over the premises.

15. Collier v. Anglian Water Authority, *The Times*, March 26, 1983; [1983] C.L.Y. 3641. C.A.

Held, the water authority were the occupiers within the 1957 Act, inasmuch as they had exercised control over the condition and maintenance of the structure, so that they and the local authority shared in the occupation and control of the promenade.

16. Jordan v. Achara (1988) 20 H.L.R. 607; [1989] C.L.Y. 2572, C.A.

P injured when falling down unlit common staircase in block of flats. Local authority responsible for electricity charge and not landlords—*Held*, payment by local authority of electricity charge did not excuse occupier landlord of his responsibilities, and therefore a duty of care was owed to visitors.

17. Robertson v. Ridley [1989] 1 W.L.R. 872; [1989] 2 All E.R. 474, C.A.

P, a club member, injured on club premises *Held*, cannot sue club, notwithstanding that club rules place responsibility on chairman and secretary for the conduct of the club or a group (see also Chap. 11).

18. Jones v. Northampton B.C. [1990] C.L.Y. 3274, C.A.

Duty of care owed by officer or member of a club to other members if he becomes aware of circumstances giving rise to a risk of injury (see also Chap. 11).

19. Owen v. Northampton B.C. [1992] L.G. Rev. 23; [1992] C.L.Y. 1553, C.A.

Local authority compromised claim of person injured in sports hall and brought contribution proceedings against the hirer of the sports hall—*Held* hirer liable in negligence on contributution proceedings.

20. Ephraim v. L.B. of Newham and Mirza [1993] P.I.Q.R. P156, C.A.

P living in bed and breakfast accommodation. Injured in fire caused by negligence of D2. Local authority under no duty in relation to advising unsuitable accommodation, but second defendant liable under Occupier's Liability Act, having entered into a licence agreement with a third party and aware that house would be used for multiple occupancy, for failure to take adequate precautions against the fire. See also Chap. 1 (1)(a) **52**.

21. Gesner v. Wallingford and District Labour Party Supporters Club, *The Times*, June 2, 1994; [1994] 6 C.L. 320

Duty of care owed by a club to its members (see Chap. 11)—*Held*, such a duty was owed if a club was incorporated under the Industrial and Provident Societies Act 1965, s. 3.

22. McGeown v. N.I. Housing Executive [1994] 3 All E.R. 53, Carswell L.J.

Public right of way passed over local authority land. P fell in hole and was injured—*Held*, that the old rule that the owner of land over which a public right of way passed was under no liability for negligent non-feasance towards members of the public was still good law. Paths were used as of right and not by virtue of any licence or invitation. It would be unreasonable if landowner were obliged to maintain such paths in a safe condition, and therefore no liability arose at common law or under the Occupier's Liability Act.

U1. Aldrich v. Henry Boyer (1960) C.A. 14

Contractors demolishing a building—had been given possession by the owners—*Held*, applying the test of control laid down in *Hartwell* **3**, they were the occupiers—*Held*, also that the test of occupancy for rating purposes was irrelevant (7 B).

(2) Right to Enter

Since January 1, 1958, there is no longer any distinction drawn between invitees and licensees.

(a) Creation and Nature

1. Nabarro v. Cope [1938] 4 All E.R. 565, du Parcq L.J. (sitting as an additional judge)

Held, builder owed no duty of care to building owner coming on unannounced visit.

2. Edwards v. Railway Executive [1952] A.C. 737; [1952] 2 All E.R. 430, H.L.

Railway embankment adjoining public recreation ground—railway fence separating the two—children frequently broke fence and played on the embankment—railway repaired fence whenever they saw it damaged—plaintiff aged nine got through an opening in fence in order to retrieve ball, slipped on railway line and was run over—plaintiff did not know of other boys having played on the embankment, and he had been warned by father not to go through fence—the jury found plaintiff was a licensee—*Held*, there was no evidence on which they could do so. Lord Porter (434 G): "There must be such assent to the user relied on as amounts to a licence to use . . . but in my view a court is not justified in lightly inferring it," and (435 D): " . . . the suggestion that knowledge of itself constitutes the children licensees carries the doctrine of implied licence much too far. No doubt, the owner of premises must take steps to show that he resents and will try to prevent the invasion." *N.B.* Dicta in *Herrington* (Chap. 10, (5) (f) **1**) suggest that, in view of the new and wider duty to trespassers there laid down, the courts will be more reluctant to imply licences, particularly in the case of children, than in the past.

3. Buchanan v. Motor Insurers' Bureau [1955] 1 W.L.R. 488; [1955] 1 All E.R. 607, McNair J.

Question was whether dock road in London Docks was a road for the purpose of compulsory insurance—*Held*, not, as the general public had no right of access. "It would indeed be strange to find that in any great docks as those of the P.L.A. or of M.D.H.B. it was permissible for members of the public, without any permission, to wander at large within the docks."

4. Phipps v. Rochester Corporation [1955] 1 Q.B. 450; [1955] 1 All E.R. 129, Devlin J.

Held, that in view of the facts that:

(a) defendants knew children were using the land;
(b) the children using the land constituted "a class of people who formed something of a habit";
(c) "a reasonable owner would feel that, unless he acted to stop the trespass, the belief would naturally be induced in those who used his land that they had his tacit permission to do so"; and
(d) defendants took no steps to show that they resented and would try to prevent the invasion (applying dictum from **2**), therefore children as a class were licensed to use the open space.

5. Uctkos v. Mazzetta [1956] 1 Lloyd's Rep. 209, Ormerod J.

Plaintiff went on defendant's yacht to help him paint it—*Held*, *obiter* he was a licensee. "I find it hard to distinguish between that position (of plaintiff) from the position of somebody who might call on a friend and spend a day with him in his house or his garden, and perhaps assist in the weeding of the garden or the mowing of the grass, or even in carrying out some of the domestic duties. . . . I think it would be impossible to suggest that such a person was anything more than a licensee" (214, col. 1).

6. Periscinotti v. Brighton West Pier Co. (1961) 105 S.J. 526, C.A.

Plaintiff paid to go on pier—climbed over rail to get to diving board—dived into water, which was too shallow—*Held*, plaintiff was a trespasser.

7. Hughes v. Lord Advocate [1963] A.C. 837; [1963] 1 All E.R. 705, H.L.

Held, child not a trespasser, as Post Office did not have sufficient exclusive occupation to constitute them occupiers of the site.

8. Sonnex v. London County Council, *The Times*, February 3, 1965; [1965] C.L.Y. 2665, Thompson J.

Held, children were trespassers, as hole in fence were speedily repaired, and police and defendants' servants did what they could to chase children off.

9. McGlone v. British Railways Board, 1966 S.C. (H.L.) 1; [1966] C.L.Y. 2664, H.L.

Held, defendants not liable.

10. Greenhalgh v. British Railway Board [1969] 2 Q.B. 286; [1969] 2 All E.R. 114, C.A.

11. Sole v. Hallt [1973] 1 Q.B. 574; [1973] 1 All E.R. 1032, Swanwick J.

12. Holden v. White [1982] Q.B. 679; [1982] 2 All E.R. 328, C.A.

Held, following *Greenhalgh* **10**, P was a milkman using a right of way over D's land to deliver milk to a customer in a dominant tenement.

U1. Boden v. Leeds Corporation (1955) C.A. 376

Boy, four-and-a-half, drowned in river alongside area of waste land belonging to defendants—defendants realising danger put up good fence to prevent children getting to river—repaired and inspected it from time to time as thought necessary—gap in fence through which children had been going for a long time—*Held*, boy trespasser as no express or tacit licence to go through fence to river.

U2. Ramage v. Francis Jackson (1959) C.A. 109

(b) Scope and Extent of Right

1. Hillen v. I.C.I. [1936] A.C. 65, H.L.

Held, shipowner not liable to plaintiff stevedore loading cargo on to hatch cover known to be "out of bounds." Lord Atkin (69): "This duty to an invitee only extends so long as and so far as the invitee is making what can reasonably be contemplated as an ordinary and reasonable use of the premises by the invitee for the purpose for which he has been invited. He is not invited to use any part of the premises for purposes which he knows are wrongfully dangerous and constitute an improper use." *Applied* in **8**.

2. Gould v. McAuliffe [1941] 2 All E.R. 527; 57 T.L.R. 527, C.A.

Held, plaintiff an invitee. Scott L.J. (528 C): "The gate was not locked, nor was there any notice on it that the yard was private, or that trespassers were forbidden, or that there was a dangerous dog there."

3. Pearson v. Coleman [1948] 2 K.B. 359; [1948] 2 All E.R. 274, C.A.

Child invitee to circus wanted to relieve herself and crawled into lion's tent, where she was injured by lion—*Held*, she was still an invitee because (a) there was no W.C. provided and she was naturally looking for a substitute place, and (b) the steps taken to delimit the zoo were, to a child, inadequate. Generally: " . . . in my opinion, if a landowner is minded to make part of his land a prohibited area, he must indicate this to his invitees by appropriate means" (Lord Greene M.R. at 375, middle).

4. Bates v. Stone Parish Council [1954] 1 W.L.R. 1249; [1954] 3 All E.R. 38, C.A.

Child of three-and-a-half goes to playground with child of six—*Held*, the permission given to him to enter was, on the facts, a general one and not limited to children who were either attended or old enough to appreciate danger, but the Lords Justices in their judgments indicated that a court would be ready to assume that a licence was so limited (see, *e.g.* Romer L.J. at 47 D, though Birkett L.J. (44 A) attached importance of the absence of any notice or overt prohibition as negativing any limitation). See **5**.

5. Phipps v. Rochester Corporation [1955] 1 Q.B. 450; [1955] 1 All E.R. 129, Devlin J.

"Little" child (*i.e.* one too young to be guilty of contributory negligence) falls down trench on building site—judge finds that children as a class were licensed to be on the land, but this danger was neither a trap nor an allurement, though it was imperceptible to plaintiff simply because he was not old enough to take steps to avoid it—what then was position?—*Held*, after examination of authorities, liability was not to be judged according to whether the licence was impliedly conditional (on child being escorted) or unconditional; such a concept would lead to many difficulties, and "the terms of the supposed licence would be mainly lawyers' inventions" (142 F); moreover, C.A. have never mentioned point in last 30 years, except du Parcq L.J. in *Morely v. S. Staffs* (Chap. 10, (5)(e) **1**), (but **4** was *not* cited); therefore, the test, where a condition of accompaniment would have to be implied (as opposed to where it *is* express), is not whether the licence was conditional or unconditional, but whether licensor had fulfilled his duty of care towards little children (as to which, see Chap. 10, (5)(e) **1**. Alternatively, if the test of conditional licence was the correct one—*Held*, the licence here was impliedly conditional, and therefore plaintiff a trespasser.

6. Braithwaite v. South Durham Steel [1958] 1 W.L.R. 986; [1958] 3 All E.R. 161, Edmund Davies J.

Plaintiff a licensee of railway company on a narrow walkway closely adjacent to railway company's track—while walking, a train coasts up behind him—a workmate shouts—plaintiff in looking round momentarily deviates a few inches from the walkway onto the outer part of the sleepers (and outside the area of licence) and is run down by train—*Held*, in making this small involuntary deviation he was still a licensee.

7. Perkovski v. Wellington Corporation [1959] A.C. 53; [1958] 3 All E.R. 368, P.C.

Diving board over water shallow at low tide—it was argued by defendants that the danger was in the sea outside the area occupied—and therefore the law of licensor or licensee did not apply—*Held*, not so: "The fact that the concealed danger is that of injury outside the occupied area, whether in the sea or on a highway or in adjacent property, on principle would not seem to prevent the application of the rule" (372 G). (But plaintiff lost on the facts.) *Cf.* on the other hand the position of the second defendants in *Banks v. M.D.H.B.* [1956] 1 Lloyd's Rep. 147, C.A., which would seem to imply the opposite, *q.v.* at Chap. 10, (3)(b) **2**.

8. Hourigan v. Mariblanca Navegacion [1958] 2 Lloyd's Rep. 277, C.A.

Deceased a boatman who fell into dock while leaving ship—one material issue was whether the defendant shipowners at the time still owed the deceased any duty as an invitee—if they did there was a further issue as to whether the means of leaving the ship were safe—the ship's siren had sounded some time previously as a warning that she was about to move—the deceased, who came on the ship as an invitee, had stayed on drinking coffee—*Held*, that the master did not know and had no means of knowing that the deceased would remain on board the ship for such a long time, and that accordingly the defendants no longer owed to him any duty as an invitee. Dictum of Lord Atkin in applied.

9. Hogan v. Peninsular & Oriental Steam Navigation Co. [1959] 2 Lloyd's Rep. 305, Davies J.

Plaintiff ship's rigger went on ship to look for shackle to borrow for gangway—went into semi-dark part of ship and fell down open hatch—*Held*, he was a trespasser, but (*obiter*) if permission had been given as alleged, it could only be on the basis that he could only go where he could see (309, col. 2).

10. McCullie v. Butler, *The Times*, March 19, 1959; [1959] C.L.Y. 2207, C.A.

Held, occupier entitled to assume child would remain in care of mother, and not liable.

11. Periscinotti v. Brighton West Pier Co. (1961) 105 S.J. 526, C.A.

Plaintiff paid for admission to defendants' pier—there was a bathing station on lower part of pier—which in fact was closed at time—plaintiff got to it by climbing over railings and by using a ladder—*Held*, a trespasser.

12. Videan v. British Transport Commission [1963] 2 Q.B. 650; [1963] 2 All E.R. 860, C.A.

"When the infant strayed from the platform onto the barrow crossing, and thence 10–12 feet up the line, he was a trespasser, for he went beyond the bounds of any licence he had" (Lord Denning M.R., 864 E).

13. Henry v. Mersey Ports Stevedoring [1963] 2 Lloyd's Rep. 97, C.A.

Plaintiff loading ship—is told by his stevedore employers to go to hold number one to get mats—this hold not in use and not being worked—*Held*, plaintiff in going to the hold had not become a trespasser *qua* the shipowners. "There was no defined place in the ship from which the first defendants (employers) or their servants could draw the necessary mats, and it seems to have been accepted that they were to be collected from other holds" (Sellers L.J., 106, col. 1).

14. Stone v. Taffe [1974] 1 W.L.R. 1575; [1974] 3 All E.R. 1016, C.A.

U1. Bartle v. Theatre Royal (Chatham) Ltd (1952) C.A. 123

Deceased at theatre—going through swing doors into vestibule 12 feet 6 feet—opened door on left marked "Private" mistaking it for toilet—fell down steep stairs leading to cellar—toilet up steps on other side—lighting not very good—cellar door in neglected condition—unpadlocked and easily opened—no warning—defendants occupiers of theatre—*Held*, vestibule dangerous—deceased invitee not trespasser—defendants had not taken reasonable care to make premises safe. No contributory negligence.

U2. Smith v. Sheppard (1955) C.A. 107

Plaintiff fell down flight of steps leading to cellar when finding her way to "Ladies" in publichouse—opened door without "Ladies" on it—few steps forward—felt for light switch—dark—*Held*, invitee—defendant negligent in not providing adequate lighting.

U3. Toner v. Ellis and National Coal Board (1962) C.A. 241

Plaintiff employed by first defendants to do work on premises of second defendants—he worked from a ladder placed in or near railway track—struck by train—second defendants had advised him to do work at week-end when no trains running—now argued that plaintiff was therefore a trespasser within *Hillen v. I.C.I.* **1** *Held*, not so, and second defendants liable, because the advice did not amount to a ban and in any event they knew plaintiff was working despite advice.

U4. Burke v. Cardiff C.C. (1986) C.A. 224
See Chap. 10, (5)(e) **U4**.

(3) Duty of Care

(a) Generally

1. Glasgow Corporation v. Muir [1943] A.C. 448; [1943] 2 All E.R. 44, H.L.

The duty of care, *per* Lord Wright (462), extends also "to the use which the occupier . . . permits a third party to make of the premises." *Unaffected* by 1957 Act. See cases in Chap. 10, (4) (e).

2. Tinsley v. Dudley [1951] 2 K.B. 18; [1951] 1 All E.R. 252, C.A.

"There is no warrant on the authorities, as far as I know, for holding that an invitor, where the invitation extends to goods as well as the person of the invitee, thereby by implication of law assumes a liability to protect the invitee and his goods, not merely from physical dangers arising from defects in the premises, but from the risk of the goods being stolen by some third party" (Jenkins L.J., 31). *Unaffected* by 1957 Act.

3. Buchanan v. Motor Insurers' Bureau [1955] 1 W.L.R. 488; [1955] 1 All E.R. 607, McNair J.

Question was whether a dock road in London docks was a road for the purpose of compulsory insurance—*Held*, not, as the general public had no right of access.

4. Hartley v. Mayoh [1954] 1 Q.B. 383; [1954] 1 All E.R. 375, C.A.

Firemen electrocuted when dealing with factory fire—*Held*, occupier liable in that, *inter alia*, the main switches being of an unusual type, no warning had been given of the danger presented thereby.

5. Goldman v. Hargrave [1967] 1 A.C. 645; [1966] 2 All E.R. 989, P.C.

A redgum tree was hit by lightning and began to burn—the occupier cut it down and left it to burn out—wind fanned the flames and spread them onto other property—*Held*, occupier owed a duty of care to prevent the hazard which had arisen accidentally on his premises from spreading. The standard of care in such a case "ought to be to require of the occupier what it is reasonable to expect of him in his individual circumstances" (Lord Wilberforce, 996 D).

6. Leakey v. National Trust [1980] Q.B. 485; [1980] 1 All E.R. 17, C.A.

Held, applying *Goldman* **5**.

7. Bradburn v. Lindsay [1983] 2 All E.R. 408; [1983] C.L.Y. 2741, Judge Blackett—Ord, V.C.

Held, applying *Leakey*. For details, see Chap. 10, (7)**9**.

8. Titchener v. B.R.B. [1983] 1 W.L.R. 1427; [1983] 3 All E.R. 770, H.L.

See Chap. 10, (5)(a)**40**.

9. Ogwo v. Taylor [1988] A.C. 431; [1987] 3 W.L.R. 1145, H.L.

Fireman attending emergency call at private house. See Chap. 10, (5)(e)**10** for summary.

(b) Outside Area of Occupation

1. Hartwell v. Grayson Rollo [1947] K.B. 901; 80 Ll.L.R. 381, C.A.

Dictum by Lord Oaksey L.J. to the effect that A owes duty of invitor to B when he invites B "to a place where they both have business," "no matter whether the place belongs to the invitor or is in his exclusive occupation." But this dictum may need caution—the L.J. repeats the proposition later, but adds the qualification that A must have a business interest or control in the premises. *And* the other two Lords Justices found defendants were in actual occupation, possession or control, so above may well be *obiter*.

2. Banks v. Mersey Docks and Harbour Board [1956] 1 Lloyd's Rep. 147, C.A.

Case where a ladder was left on the dock estate by a third party unknown in a dangerously defective condition—dock board were exonerated (see Chap. 10, (4) (b) **10**), but in addition the owners of a barge were sued—this barge came and moored itself at a point in the quay where the above ladder led immediately down from top of quay to deck of barge—crew of barge knew ladder was dangerous—a licensee of the barge went down ladder at night to get on barge and was killed—*Held*, that no action lay against barge owners, as they had no responsibility for the ladder. *But* see **3** and **4**.

3. A. C. Billings v. Riden [1958] A.C. 240; [1957] 3 All E.R. 1, H.L.

Plaintiff visiting house unable to leave by front path owing to obstruction created by defendant and has to deviate by a route over adjacent premises—as she entered adjacent premises she fell down unfenced hole—*Held*, defendant liable. *N.B.* Defendant here was a contractor, but same principle would seem to be applicable if he had been occupier (subject, of course, to special defences open to invitor or licensor).

4. Perkowski v. Wellington Corporation [1959] A.C. 53; [1958] 3 All E.R. 368, P.C.

Diving board over water shallow at low tide—it was argued by defendants that the danger was in the sea outside the area occupied—and therefore the law of licensor or licensee did not apply—*Held*, not so: "the fact that the concealed danger is that of injury outside the occupied area, whether in the sea or on a highway or in adjacent property, on principle would not seem to prevent the application of the rule" (372 G). (But plaintiff lost on the facts.) *Cf.* on the other hand the position of the second defendants in *Banks v. M.D.H.B.* **2**, which would seem to imply the opposite.

5. Braithwaite v. South Durham Steel [1958] 1 W.L.R. 986; [1958] 3 All E.R. 161, Edmund Davies J.

Plaintiff a licensee of railway company on a narrow walkway closely adjacent to railway company's track—while walking, a train coasts up behind him—a workmate shouts—plaintiff, in looking round, momentarily deviates a few inches from the walkway onto the outer part of the sleepers (and outside the area of licence) and is run down by train—*Held*, in making this small involuntary deviation he was still a licensee.

(c) Loan of Chattel by Occupier to Visitor

1. Marshall v. Cellactite (1947) 63 T.L.R. 456, C.A.

General permission by factory occupier to contractor to borrow plant—*Held*, there was no representation of safety as to any particular piece of plant, and therefore defendants not liable.

2. Jones v. Barclays Bank (1949) 93 S.J. 372; [1949] W.N. 267, C.A.

Held, defendant householder not liable, as it was too much to expect him to test a ladder which had no apparent defect.

3. Johnson v. Croggan [1954] 1 W.L.R. 195; [1954] 1 All E.R. 121, Pilcher J.

Similar facts to **1**—*Held*, for same reasons, defendant not liable.

(4) Standard of Care Generally

(a) Darkness and Fog (Liability of Occupiers only)

1. Simons v. Winslade [1938] 3 All E.R. 774; 159 L.T. 408, C.A.

Plaintiff going across yard of public-house to W.C. slips on vomit—yard was unlighted—defendant had swept out yard previously—during two previous years only one customer had vomited—*Held*, defendant not liable.

2. Caseley v. Bristol Corporation [1944] 1 All E.R. 14, C.A.

Plaintiff licensee passing through dock estate wanders in fog from road and falls over edge of unfenced dock basin—*Held*, defendants not liable, it not being for landowner but for plaintiff to take special precautions to deal with fog.

3. Grant v. Sun Shipping [1948] A.C. 459; [1948] 2 All E.R. 238, H.L.

Repairers leave hatch open and unlit—*Held*, shipowners liable for not ensuring repairers had done their duty.

4. Dunster v. Abbott [1954] 1 W.L.R. 58; [1953] 2 All E.R. 1572, C.A.

Held, defendant not liable. "In darkness where they cannot see whether there is danger or not, if they will walk they walk at their peril" (Somervell L.J. at 1573 F, citing Hamilton L.J. in *Latham v. Johnson* [1913] 1 K.B. 411).

5. Hawkins v. Coulsdon [1954] 1 Q.B. 319; [1953] 2 All E.R. 364, Pearson J.

Plaintiff licensee fell on a broken porch step of private house—*Held*, defendant liable. *Upheld* by C.A. [1954] 1 Q.B. 319.

6. Rae (Geoffrey) v. Mars U.K. (1990) 3 E.G. 80; [1990] C.L.Y. 3309, H.H. Judge White

P, experienced surveyor, injured when falling down drop in unlit storeroom. A warning had been given of the danger—*Held*, however, that this was inadequate. D was liable because further steps should have been taken, but P also negligent for not using torch or looking down.

U1. Bartle v. Theatre Royal (Chatham) Ltd (1952) C.A. 123

Deceased at theatre—going through swing doors into vestibule 12 ft. by 6 ft.—opened door on left marked "Private" mistaking it for toilet—fell down steep stairs leading to cellar—toilet up steps on other side—lighting not very good—cellar door in neglected condition—unpadlocked and easily opened—no warning—defendants occupiers of theatre—*Held*, vestibule dangerous—deceased invitee not trespasser—defendants had not taken reasonable care to make premises safe. No contributory negligence.

U2. Smith v. Sheppard (1955) C.A. 107

Plaintiff fell down flight of steps leading to cellar when finding her way to "Ladies" in public-house—opened door without "Ladies" on it—few steps forward—felt for light switch—dark—*Held*, invitee—defendant negligent in not providing adequate lighting.

U3. Scollen v. Leisure Holidays Ltd (1992) C.A. 214

Deceased at a holiday camp fell from retaining wall at nighttime and sustained fatal injuries. Wall not lit at night, and no restrictions imposed on holidaymakers not to walk in that area at night time—*Held*, defendants liable but deceased 25 per cent. to blame because of intoxication and venturing into darkness.

(b) "Know" and "Ought to Know"

1. Woodman v. Richardson [1937] 81 S.J. 700; [1937] 3 All E.R. 866 C.A.

Plaintiff employed by sub-contractors injured when using a defective ladder on a building site scaffold—sues main contractors—*Held* defendants not liable, as no evidence that any of defendants' servants or agents placed ladder in position or knew or ought to have known of defect.

2. Ellis v. Fulham B.C. [1938] 1 K.B. 212; [1937] 3 All E.R. 454; C.A.

Held, glass a concealed danger, and that defendants though not knowing of actual glass knew of the possibility of danger, and therefore liable.

3. Simons v. Winslade [1938] 3 All E.R. 774; 159 L.T. 408, C.A.

Plaintiff going across yard of public-house to W.C. slips on vomit—yard was unlighted—defendant had swept out yard previously—during two previous years only one customer had vomited—*Held*, defendant not liable.

4. Griffiths v. Smith [1941] A.C. 170; [1941] 1 All E.R. 66, H.L.

Collapse of school floor over 100 years old—no survey for 30 years—*Held*, negligence, but claim failed by reason of Public Authorities Protection Act 1893 (writ not issued within six months).

5. Pearson v. Lambeth B.C. [1950] 2 K.B. 353; [1950] 1 All E.R. 682, C.A.

Plaintiff using public lavatory struck head against overhead grid—grid had been moved into dangerous position by person unknown—children had been seen tampering with it frequently—defendants' servant had so seen them shortly before accident—*Held*, defendants had "actual knowledge" of danger, and were therefore liable to plaintiff (who was a licensee).

6. Cuttress v. Scaffolding [1953] 1 W.L.R. 1311; [1953] 2 All E.R. 1075, C.A.

Scaffold on building site with rope hanging 35 feet above ground—children pull it over—*Held*, not an allurement, and as defendants could not have foreseen the probability of children pulling it over, not liable. *Cf.* the case of *Davis v. St. Mary's Demolition* (Chap. 7, (2) (f) **6**), where defendants were not occupiers and were found liable.

7. Bates v. Stone Parish Council [1954] 1 W.L.R. 1249; [1954] 3 All E.R. 38, C.A.

Playground with chute having 12-foot-high platform—gap between rails of platform $13\frac{1}{2}$ in. by $13\frac{1}{2}$ in.—in 1934 a child fell through—additional rails were put up as a result, but later they disappeared—plaintiff aged three-and-a-half went to playground with child aged six—he fell through gap—*Held*, plaintiff was a licensee and defendants were liable. Romer L.J. said that, but for the 1934 accident, plaintiff's claim must have failed (49 E). *Approved* (as to last dictum): in *Dyer* (Chap 10, (5) (e) **12**), *q.v.*

8. Adcock v. Loveridge *The Times*, June 21, 1956; [1956] C.L.Y. 5902, Pearce J.

Defendant occupier of site where she parked derelict lorries—plaintiff an infant threw match in petrol tank—*Held*, plaintiff was a trespasser, but if child had been licensee defendant would still not have been liable as accident was not reasonably foreseeable by her. See also Chap. 8 (4) 14.

9. Perry v. Kendricks Transport [1956] 1 W.L.R. 85; [1956] 1 All E.R. 154, C.A.

Held, defendants had taken all reasonable precautions to safeguard their parked lorry, and that they were not liable in negligence. Nor in *Rylands v. Fletcher* (*q.v.* under Chap. **8**) for an accident caused by two boys throwing a lighted match in petrol tank.

10. Banks v. Mersey Docks and Harbour Board [1956] 1 Lloyd's Rep. 147, C.A.

Admittedly defective ladder down from quay to barge—not defendants' property and no evidence where it came from—evidence was that it had been there at least 36 hours—*Held*, there was no evidence to show that it had been in position for such a period of time as would have brought home to defendants the danger. Hodson L.J. (158, col. 2): "The property in the ladder is irrelevant to the duty of the occupier. . . . The only relevance of the ownership . . . is that it has a bearing on whether the occupier knew or ought to have known of the existence of the unusual danger . . . "

11. Melvin Franklin (1972) 71 L.G.R. 142; [1973] C.L.Y. 2293, C.A.

12. Harrison v. Vincent [1982] R.T.R. 8; [1982] C.L.Y. 2159, C.A.

Motor cycle race organisers parked a recovery vehicle so that it projected about two feet into escape road. A motor cycle combination rider got into an emergency owing to his negligence in having defective brakes and rode into escape road, colliding with vehicle and injuring his passenger—*Held*, organisers liable, for although the combination of circumstances causing the accident was unfortunate, they were not too fantastic as to be outside the reasonable contemplation of the organisers.

13. Cunningham v. Reading Football Club [1992] P.I.Q.R. p. 141; [1991] C.L.Y. 3413, Drake J.

Likelihood of injury by visiting supporters "very foreseeable". For summary see Chap. 10, (6) (a), U2.

(c) Maintenance of Premises and Remedying Defects

1. Haseldine v. Daw [1941] 2 K.B. 343; [1941] 3 All E.R. 156, C.A.

Held, occupier who had employed competent contractors to look after lift was not liable for defective state of lift. *N.B.* Contractors were held liable.

2. Griffiths v. Smith [1941] A.C. 170; [1941] 1 All E.R. 66, H.L.

Collapse of school floor over 100 years old—no survey for 30 years—*Held*, negligence, but claim failed by reason of Public Authorities Protection Act 1893 (writ not issued within six months).

3. Blackman v. Railway Executive [1954] 1 W.L.R. 220; [1953] 2 All E.R. 323, C.A.
Patch of oil dripped from mail barrow—foreman saw it—at once told man to get sawdust and tried to stop people passing that way—*Held*, defendants had taken all reasonable care and were not liable.

4. Green v. Fibreglass [1958] 2 Q.B. 245; [1958] 2 All E.R. 521, Salmon J.

Defendants were tenants of offices since 1951—had premises rewired by competent electricians—plaintiff an invitee injured when touching an electric fire which though off was live—defendants had no reason to suspect defect—did not regularly inspect wiring—*Held*, defendants not liable, as they had discharged their duty by employing competent independent contractors, since electric wiring required technical knowledge which defendants could not possess themselves.

5. Wells v. Cooper [1958] 2 Q.B. 265; [1958] 2 All E.R. 527, C.A.

Defendant refixed screws in door handle himself—handle came away when plaintiff an invitee pulled it—*Held*, defendant not liable, as (a) the task of repair was not one which called for an expert, and (b) on the facts he had used reasonable care in doing the job. Jenkins L.J. (529 I): "No doubt some kinds of work involve such highly specialised skill and knowledge, and create such serious dangers if not properly done, that an ordinary occupier . . . would fail in that (*i.e.* his) duty if he undertook such work himself. But the work here in question was not of that order. It was a trifling domestic replacement well within the competence of a householder accustomed to doing small carpentering jobs about his home . . ."

6. Lowther v. Hogarth [1959] 1 Lloyd's Rep. 171, Pilcher J.

Plaintiff slipped on patch of oil on deck from ship's winch—accident occurred at 3 p.m.—winch was working from 1 to 1.45 p.m.—then it rained—plaintiff came back at 3 p.m.—defendants' greaser went round winches about every three hours and cleared up any oil he saw—*Held*, defendants had taken reasonable care and were not liable.

7. Wood v. Moreland (1971) 115 S.J. 569; [1971] C.L.Y. 7781, Shaw J.

8. Titchener v. B.R.B. [1983] 1 W.L.R. 1427; [1983] 3 All E.R. 770, H.L.

See Chap. 10, (5)(a) **40**.

9. Jennings v. B.R.B. (1984) 134 N.L.J. 584; [1984] C.L.Y. 2312, Stocker J.

P injured after falling over rubbish left on station platform—*Held*, system of cleaning inadequate and D liable.

10. Hogg v. Historic Buildings and monuments Commission for England [1989] C.L.Y. 2573, Mr Recorder Boney

Held, when injury sustained in an ancient and historic building, its antiquity was a relevant feature in an action under the Occupier's Liability Act. D not liable.

11. Murphy v. City Of Bradford M. C. [1992] P.I.Q.R. p. 68; [1992] C.L.Y. 3255, C.A.

Plaintiff supply teacher at D's school premises slips on snow on a sloping pathway. Defendants had "excellent system for clearing of snow"—*Held*, however, on occasion of P's accident there had been a failure, because sloping pathway had called for special treatment, and county court judge had been entitled to hold that there had been a breach of duty.

12. Ward v. The Ritz Hotel (London) [1992] P.I.Q.R. p. 135; [1993] C.L.Y. 2975, C.A.

Plaintiff injured after falling over a balustrade which was six inches lower than BSI recommendation—*Held* D liable. Although British Standards were not legally binding, they provided strong evidence as to what was safe.

U1. Hawkins v. Dowdeswell (1957) C.A. 269 A

Deceased fell down stairs of club leading from first floor to pavement level—deceased guest not member—defendants occupiers of club and staircase—steps made wet by persons coming in from rain—single light on landing at top of stairs—old-fashioned staircase—treads narrow—handrails on either side—where handrail fastened to wall and where water pipe between rail and wall person could not keep hand round rail—allegation that defendants negligent as could easily have built another safer staircase as they did after accident—*Held*, defendants not negligent—staircase in good repair and no traps—Jenkins L.J. (9 A): "There is, in my view, a real distinction between dangers inherent in a particular design of staircase and dangers produced by failure to keep the staircase, such as it is, in good repair. I am not referring, of course, to matters amounting to traps, where some danger is encountered which could not reasonably be expected to be in a particular place. I am not speaking of such a case as a door opening directly upon a steep staircase with nothing to indicate what lies beyond the door."

U2. Griffith v. Salford Hospital Management Committee (1958) C.A. 180 A

Plaintiff slipped on spilled soup when visiting hospital—attendant was away getting something to mop it up—*Held*, defendants not liable.

U3. Prokop v. D.H.S.S. and Cleaners Ltd (1983) C.A. 756

Plaintiff slipped and injured because of highly polished floor surface—*Held*, second defendants, the contracted cleaners, were liable.

U4. Johnson v. G.L.C. (1985) C.A. 867

P was river worker and driver who sustained injury on D's land when clearing undergrowth after stepping on to a slab which had previously formed part of a fence—*Held*, presence of slabs increased the risk of slipping in an already slippery area and should have been removed—D liable.

U5. Priestley v. Nottingham H.A. (1986) C.A. 37

P, domestic supervisor, injured when walking across delivery yard—slipped on slushy ice—*Held*, no liability under Occupiers Liability Act or at common law. System of clearing ice adopted by D was reasonable in all the circumstances.

U6. Dove v. L.B. of Havering (1988) C.A. 979

Plaintiff, a waitress, was serving drinks when she slipped on polished dance floor—*Held*, defendants not liable. It was reasonable to keep the floor in a polished and shiny condition for dancing purposes, because of the use to which the hall was put, and there were no steps which could reasonably have been taken to prevent the accident.

U7. Watson v. South Lincolnshire H.A. (1993) C.A. 93

P injured when attempting to load hot food trolley on to a lift, where floor of lift was about 1\2 inch higher than corridor—*Held*, neither Health Authority nor lift engineer liable.

(d) Liability to Contractors doing Work to Premises

1. Vaughan v. Building Estates [1952] 2 Lloyd's Rep. 231, McNair J.

Duty of building contractor to his sub-contractor is canvassed, but somewhat indecisively because plaintiff fails whatever test is applied. Judge (235) quotes with approval dictum in *Salmond on Torts* to the effect that where the use of the premises is ancillary to the main purpose of the contract the duty is assimilated to that owed to an invitee.

2. Christmas v. General Cleaning Contractors [1952] 1 K.B. 141; [1952] 1 All E.R. 39, C.A.

Held, where a window was safe for ordinary purposes a defect in it which made it dangerous for a window cleaner was not an unusual danger for which occupier would be liable (*N.B.* This part of the decision was not appealed to H.L.). See **4**.

3. Bates v. Parker [1953] Q.B. 231; [1953] 1 All E.R. 768; C.A.

Window cleaner injured by piece of plywood coming away in his hands—he had used it before as a handhold, but just before accident plaintiff had unbolted plywood and left it *in situ*—*Held*, on appeal, defendants not liable. **2** applied: " . . . the law thus (in **2**) applied is not peculiar to window cleaners. . . . Where a householder employs an independent contractor to do work . . . the contractor must satisfy himself as to the safety or condition of that part of the premises on which he is to work . . . It was not for defendants to tell him how to do it or to call his attention to the fact that the piece of plywood was not in a condition to serve as a support . . . If the cleaner had been injured by some defect in the premises which had nothing to do with the work for which he was employed . . . it would have been the duty of the latter (*i.e.* the householder) to warn him" (Lord Goddard C. J. at 770 H-771 D). See **4**.

4. Smith v. Austin Lifts [1959] 1 All E.R. 81; [1959] 1 W.L.R. 100, H.L.

Plaintiff was a lift repairer working on defendants' premises—his work took him up an iron ladder into a machine house—fell owing to defective condition of door at top of ladder—*Held*, defendant occupiers liable. Lord Denning (92) differentiated this case from the window cleaning cases **2** and **3** on the ground that "in those cases the householders did not provide any means of access to the window" (92 E). "But, in this case, the workman was using the means of access provided by the occupiers, and that makes all the difference" (92 F).

5. Roles v. Nathan [1963] 1 W.L.R. 1117; [1963] 2 All E.R. 908, C.A.

Two chimney sweeps asphyxiated by carbon monoxide fumes from boiler flue which they had come to clean—*Held*, applying *Christmas* **2** and Occupiers' Liability Act 1957, s. 2(3)(b) (an occupier can expect that a person in the exercise of his calling will guard against special risks ordinarily incident thereto), occupier was not liable, as "a householder can reasonably expect the sweep to take care of himself so far as any dangers from the flues are concerned" (*per* Lord Denning M. R.).

6. Fisher v. C. H. T. [1966] 2 Q.B. 475; [1966] 1 All E.R. 87, C.A.

T operated a restaurant under licence from C, the owners—during re-decoration, C had a maintenance man "round and about" during the work, and T had an electrician, who switched on some bare wires in the ceiling, so that the plaintiff employed by the decorators was injured—T and C were both in law occupiers—*Held*, both were liable, though C only to a small extent.

7. Ferguson v. Welsh [1987] 1 W.L.R. 1553; [1987] 131 S.J. 1552, H.L.

P employee of independent contractor injured during demolition of D's building. Unsafe system of work and liability of D as occupier was alleged—*Held*, as it was not usual for an occupier to inspect or supervise the system of work used by an independent contractor, he could not be liable for any unsafe system, in the absence of any specific knowledge that the system of work was unsafe.

8. Dexter v. Tenby Electrical Accessories [1991] C.O.D. 288; [1992] C.L.Y. 2227, D.C.

Independent contractor injured when working in unsafe area at D's premises where D as occupier did not foresee he would work—*Held*, D owed a duty to all persons working at factory premises even if they were not his employees. (Prosecution under the 1961 Act, s. 29(i) and considered from point of view of statutory duty, but contrast with *Ferguson v. Walsh* (supra).)

U1. Curtis v. Hermit Industries Ltd. (1957) C.A. 102

Plaintiff repairing defect in switchboard—director of defendants said all right to set machine in motion—door fell open while rotating and broke plaintiff's leg—*Held*, defendants not liable. Following *Bates v. Parker* **3**, defendants owed no duty to plaintiff—occupier through director saying all right to set machine in motion was not representing it was safe to do so—plaintiff might have action against someone else but not against defendants. Jenkins L. J. (8 D): "In my view, the defendants were in no way concerned as to the manner in which the experts achieved their object, and it was no part of their function to instruct the experts in the experts' own business."

U2. Beigan v. Liverpool C. C. (1991) C.A. 1265

Deceased employee of Manweb was instructed to disconnnect electricity supply from houses to be demolished by defendants. When attempting to gain access was struck by coping stone which fell from top of bay window, because of defective condition created by vandals—*Held* D liable for failing to warn employers of deceased of inherent defect in roof when they knew that vandalism had occurred, and that deceased would attempt to remove boarding from window.

(e) In Respect of User of Premises by Other Visitors

(*N.B.* See also cases in Chap. 10, (6) (a) and Chap. 10, (6) (b).

1. Glasgow Corporation v. Muir [1943] A.C. 448; [1943] 2 All E.R. 44, H.L.

Child scalded by water from urn—the children were in a party, and for a fee the organisers were using defendants' tea room, themselves making and distributing the tea—it was alleged defendants should have removed the children while the urn was being moved—*Held*, not so, as a reasonable person would not have anticipated danger. "As the permitted operation was intrinsically innocuous, I do not think any obligation rested on (defendants' servant) to attempt to supervise how it was carried out" (Lord Wright at 53 D). The duty of care, *per* Lord Wright (462), extends not only to the structural condition of the premises, but also "to the use which the occupier . . . permits a third party to make of the premises."

2. Grant v. Sun Shipping [1948] A.C. 549; [1948] 2 All E.R. 238, H.L.

Ship repairers leave hatch uncovered and unlit—breach of statutory duty by repairers—plaintiff (not employed by either defendant) falls down hatch—sues shipowner, *inter alia*, at common law as invitor—*Held*, shipowner liable, as they were not entitled to rely on telling repairers to make secure, but must ensure it was done. It would appear that this was a case where there was a duty on the occupier to ensure that one invitee created no danger for another.

3. O'Dowd v. Fraser Nash [1951] C.L.C. 6778; [1951] W.N. 173, McNair J.

Doctor killed by car leaving track during practice—organisers had issued deceased with a handbook warning him of danger—*Held*, defendants not liable.

4. Murray v. Harringay Arena [1951] 2 K.B. 529; [1951] 2 All E.R. 320n., C.A.

Infant (paid for by adult) injured by puck watching ice-hockey—netting at ends but not at sides—*Held*, it could not be said that ice-hockey was "intrinsically dangerous" (534 top) and therefore plaintiff failed because (a) defendants took reasonable precautions, and (b) plaintiff took the risk of a danger incidental to the game.

5. Bolton v. Stone [1951] A.C. 850; [1951] 2 All E.R. 1078, H.L.

Cricket club sued for ball hit onto highway—*Held*, no negligence, but "they (the trustees of the field) are and are admitted to be responsible for the negligent action of those who use the field in the way intended that it should be used" (Lord Porter at 1080 F).

6. Dantzie v. Maxwell, *The Times*, October 18, 1955; [1955] C.L.Y. 1845, Havers J.

Plaintiff deliberately tripped by another skater—*Held*, defendants not liable, as they had no knowledge of the other skater having tripped anyone before, and they had taken reasonable steps to supervise.

7. Hilder v. Associated Portland Cement [1961] 1 W.L.R. 1434; [1961] 3 All E.R. 709, Ashworth J.

Children permitted by defendant occupiers to play football on an open space adjoining a busy highway—ball kicked onto highway into immediate path of motor-cyclist, causing accident—*Held*, applying test of Lord Reid in *Bolton v. Stone* **5**, *i.e.* "was the risk so small that a reasonable man would have thought it right to refrain from taking steps?" defendants were liable in negligence.

8. Miller v. Jackson [1977] Q.B. 966; [1977] 3 All E.R. 338, C.A.

P bought a newly built house on the edge of a cricket ground—cricket club built a 15 foot high protective fence along edge—despite this 15 balls over two years landed in P's garden—P sought an injunction—which was *refused* (2–1)—but it was also *said* (2–1) that, in view of the series of incidents, the risk of injury to persons and property was so great that, whenever a ball went over the fence and caused damage, the defendant cricket club were guilty of negligence (348 C and 349 J).

9. Evans v. Glasgow D.C., 1978 S.L.T. 17; [1978] C.L.Y. 1789, O.H.

10. Ogwo v. Taylor [1987] 3 W.L.R. 1145; [1987] 3 All E.R. 961, H.L.

Plaintiff fireman injured when answering an emergency call in premises where fire started negligently by D's workman—*Held*, D liable, because it was reasonably foreseeable that firemen would have to attend a fire negligently started, and injury was foreseeable, whether fireman was taking an ordinary or an exceptional risk. See Chap. 1, (2) (d) **12**.

11. Wheeler v. Trustees Of St Mary's Hall, Chislehurst, *The Times*, October 10, 1989, [1989] C.L.Y. 2574, Rougier J.

Parish hall hired out by D, for special use. P injured—*Held*, D under no duty to ensure premises are suitable for the intended activity.

12. Neame v. Johnson [1993] P.I.Q.R. P100; [1993] C.L.Y. 2974, C.A.

Fireman injured when falling over a pile of books at D's premises during course of answering emergency call—*Held*, in circumstances, D not liable as no reasonably foreseeable risk of personal injury. Contrast with **10** (supra).

U1. Taylor v. Plymouth Corporation (1952) C.A. 22

Plaintiff, boy of eight—children often played on embankment built up by tipping—children at top getting stones to dam stream at bottom—one boy pushed stone which rolled down bank and injured plaintiff at bottom of bank—defendants knew children played, built dams, etc., but did not know they pushed stones down—*Held*, defendants not negligent as did not know people were accustomed to push stones down. Somervell L.J. (6 F): "If it was held that people might be liable unless they kept out children from all areas where some mischievous boy could pick up a stone and throw it at another boy, it would introduce a very grave result."

U2. Morgan v. Avonhurst School Trust Ltd (1985) C.A. 982

P was cadet injured on army assault course when climbing rope after demonstration by instructors—*Held*, D not liable.

U3. Butler v. Vann (1991) C.A. 702

P injured when participating in junior moto-cross event. D liable for inadequate rope fences delineating track, which led to injury when in collision with other participants.

(5) Standard of Care to Particular Persons

(a) Members of the Public

1. Coates v. Rawtenstall B.C. [1937] 3 All E.R. 602, C.A.

Held, defendants knew chain was likely to be put to dangerous use by boys, and were negligent in leaving chain unsecured.

2. Simons v. Winslade [1938] 3 All E.R. 774; 159 L.T. 408, C.A.

Plaintiff going across yard of public-house to W.C. slips on vomit—yard was unlighted—defendant had swept out yard previously—during two previous years only one customer had vomited—*Held*, defendant not liable.

3. Gillmore v. L.C.C. [1938] 4 All E.R. 331; 55 T.L.R. 95, du Parcq L.J.

Held, defendants liable for providing a "fairly highly polished" hardwood floor for P.T. class.

4. Campbell v. Shelbourne [1939] 2 K.B. 534; [1939] 2 All E.R. 351

Hotel guest going in search of lavatory at night down unlit corridor fell down some steps—*Held*, defendants negligent for failing to light.

5. Clark v. Bethnal Green B.C. (1939) 55 T.L.R. 519

Held, that there was a duty to provide an attendant at public swimming baths.

6. Hesketh v. Liverpool Corporation [1940] 4 All E.R. 429, Stable J.

Aeroplane struck trees on landing—*Held*, the trees were a danger, and plaintiff was entitled to recover from airport for breach of statutory duty (Air Navigation Order 1923) and at common law.

7. Haseldine v. Daw [1941] 2 K.B. 343; [1941] 3 All E.R. 156, C.A.

Held, occupier who had employed competent contractors to look after lift was not liable for defective state of lift. *N.B.* Contractors were held liable.

8. Gould v. McAuliffe [1941] 2 All E.R. 527; 57 T.L.R. 527, C.A.

Dangerous dog in yard of inn—plaintiff an invitee—no warning—*Held*, defendant liable.

9. Caseley v. Bristol Corporation [1944] 1 All E.R. 135, C.A.

Held, defendants not liable. For facts see Chap. 10, (4)(a) **2**.

10. Woodward v. Mayor of Hastings [1945] K.B. 174; [1944] 2 All E.R. 565, C.A.

Step covered with frozen snow—school—defendants liable.

11. Baker v. Bethnal Green B.C. [1945] 1 All E.R. 135, C.A.

Large public inrush into air-raid shelter—no physical means of controlling crowd, only one entrance, no sliding crush bars, doors opened inward, no human control at entrance, lighting very poor, steps 10 feet wide with no handrail in centre—*Held*, defendants liable for each of these sources of danger.

12. Dalby v. West Ham Corporation (1945) 173 L.T. 191, Lynskey J.

Plaintiff invitee at defendants' public baths—when using a shower is scalded—*Held*, defendants liable for failing to mix water at safe temperature and/or for failing to show plaintiff how to do so.

13. Howard v. Walker [1947] K.B. 860; [1947] 2 All E.R. 197, Lord Goddard C.J.

Question as to whether plaintiff could sue landlord as well as tenant—*Held*, that as plaintiff was invitee of tenant coming *from* shop instead of highway-user deviating onto forecourt, could not sue landlord. *N.B.* Forecourt was in occupation of tenant.

14. Turner v. Arding and Hobbs [1949] 2 All E.R. 911; 93 S.J. 756, Lord Goddard C.J.

Plaintiff shopping, slips on piece of vegetable matter—defendants offer no explanation of how it got onto floor or what their system was—*Held*, defendants liable in the absence of a satisfactory explanation.

15. Protheroe v. Railway Executive [1951] 1 K.B. 376; [1950] 2 All E.R. 1093, Parker J.

Paving-stones at edge of platform defective because uneven—*Held*, contractual duty at any rate extended to the part of the platform which plaintiff would have to pass to board train and therefore defendants liable—but judge said he would have had some difficulty in finding for plaintiff if only an invitee.

16. Pearson v. Lambeth B.C. [1950] 2 K.B. 353; [1950] 1 All E.R. 682, C.A.

Plaintiff using public lavatory struck head against overhead grid—grid had been moved into dangerous position by person unknown—children had been seen tampering with it frequently—defendants' servant had so seen them shortly before accident—*Held*, defendants had "actual knowledge" of danger, and were therefore liable to plaintiff (who was a licensee).

17. Warren v. Railway Executive (1950) 94 S.J. 457, Finnemore J.

Plaintiff enters unlit railway carriage—sits down where there should be a seat—but is in fact empty space—*Held*, defendants liable.

18. Mumford v. Naylor (1951) 95 S.S. 742; [1951] W.N. 579, C.A.

Plaintiff a licensee—depression about 18 inches wide in concrete of shop forecourt, having worn down to hole in centre—*Held*, viewed objectively, this was not a concealed danger, whatever it was to the particular person at the particular time.

19. Murray v. Harringay Arena [1951] 2 K.B. 529; [1951] 2 All E.R. 320n., C.A.

Infant (paid for by adult) injured by puck watching ice-hockey—netting at ends but not at sides—*Held*, it could not be said that ice-hockey was "intrinsically dangerous" (534 top) and therefore plaintiff failed because (a) defendants took reasonable precautions, and (b) plaintiff took the risk of a danger incidental to the game. Singleton L.J (533 middle): "I assume the infant plaintiff is to be regarded as having entered into a contract with defendants." See also *O'Dowd* (Chap. 10, (6)(c) **2**).

20. Blackman v. Railway Executive [1954] 1 W.L.R. 220; [1953] 2 All E.R. 323, C.A.

Patch of oil dripped from mail barrow—foreman saw it—at once told man to get sawdust and tried to stop people passing that way—*Held*, defendants had taken all reasonable care and were not liable.

21. Slade v. Battersea Hospital Committee [1955] 1 W.L.R. 207; [1955] 1 All E.R. 429, Finnemore J.

Defendants *Held*, liable: "It would be obvious, I suppose, if one walked down the ward with one's eyes fixed on the ground . . . but that is not what people are supposed to do when they walk along the ward of a hospital" (431 F).

22. Banks v. Mersey Docks and Harbour Board [1956] 1 Lloyd's Rep. 147, C.A.

Held, defendants not liable as ladder only proved to have been there for 36 hours, and this was not long enough to fix defendants with knowledge. See Chap. 10, (4)(b) **10**.

23. Dyer v. Ilfracombe U.D.C. [1956] 1 W.L.R. 218; [1956] 1 All E.R. 581, C.A.

Child falls from chute on playground—*Held*, defendants not liable, because there was no trap or concealed danger, and (*per* Singleton L.J. at 589 G) "there was nothing that was not obvious to a child aged four-and-a-half." The Lord Justice also said (589 E) it was not necessary in the case of a small recreation ground to provide an attendant, and that it was no good putting up notices because children would not read them.

24. Newman v. E. J. Rose, *The Times*, November 16, 1961; [1961] C.L.Y. 5818, Thompson J.

Plaintiff fell down steps leading to toilet—steps rather steep and prone to get wet—public house—*Held*, defendants not liable under Occupiers' Liability Act.

25. Wooldridge v. Sumner [1963] 2 Q.B. 43; [1962] 2 All E.R. 978, C.A.

"In my opinion, a competitor or player cannot, at least, in the normal case of competition or game, rely on the maxim *volenti non fit injuria* in answer to a spectator's claim, for there is no liability unless there is negligence, and the spectator comes to witness skill and with the expectation that it will be exercised. But, provided that the competition or game is being performed within the rules and requirement of the sport and by a person of adequate skill and competence, the spectator does not expect his safety to be regarded by the participant. If the conduct is deliberately intended to injure someone whose presence is known, or is reckless and in disregard of all safety of others, so that it is a departure from the standards which might reasonably be expected in anyone pursuing the competition or game, then the performer might well be held liable for any injury his act caused" (Sellers L.J. 983 H).

26. Stracstone v. London Transport Board, *The Times*, January 21, 1966; [1966] C.L.Y. 8317, Phillimore J.

Gap between train and platform on curve at tube station—*Held*, defendants not negligent.

27. Blackett v. British Railways Board, *The Times*, December 19, 1967; [1967] C.L.Y. 2664, Phillimore J.

Held, defendants liable (but one-third contributory negligence).

28. Carroll v. Garford, *The Times*, November 22, 1968; [1968] C.L.Y. 2649, Paull J.

29. Simms v. Leigh Rugby F.C. [1969] 2 All E.R. 923; [1969] C.L.Y. 2400, Wrangham J.

30. King v. Sadler (1970) 114 S.J. 192, Sir Jocelyn Simon P.

31. Wilks v. Cheltenham Cycle Club [1971] 1 W.L.R. 668; [1971] 2 All E.R. 369, C.A.

Spectator injured by motor cycle at scramble which left track—and went through or over the ropes—both rider and organisers were sued—the judge exonerated the organisers, because they had complied with all the safety requirements of the Auto Cycle Union, and found the rider liable for excessive speed—the rider appealed—*Held*, he was not liable, because there was no evidence of excessive speed. Edmund Davies L.J. (674 H) said that it was not a case to which *res ipsa loquitur* could apply. Lord Denning M.R. (670 B) said that prima facie, in an accident of this sort, either the organisers or the rider were liable, since it was the sort of accident which ought not to occur with proper care; and it may be that he would have found the organisers liable (671 C). *Wooldridge* **25** considered Edmund Davies L.J. said that the "reckless disregard" test there laid down was wrong, and that the test was whether the spectator had been injured "by an error of judgment that a reasonable competitor, being the reasonable man of the sporting world, would not have made" (674 A). Lord Denning M.R. (670 D) said that a reasonable man would do everything he could to win, but he would not be foolhardy. Phillimore L.J. (676 A) however said that he was attracted by the *Wooldridge* test, provided it was remembered that the basic test was negligence.

32. Reid v. Galbraith, 1970 S.L.T. (Notes) 83, O.H.

Held, defendants not liable.

33. Wood v. Morland (1971) 115 S.J. 569, Shaw J.

Held, nothing could have been done to render the forecourt less dangerous in the conditions prevailing, and D not liable. To have made a path through the snow might have been worse than useless.

34. White v. Blackmore [1972] 2 Q.B. 651; [1972] 3 All E.R. 158, C.A.

35. Ward v. Tesco (1976) 1 W.L.R. 810; [1976] 1 All E.R. 219, C.A. (see *also* **U10**).

36. Harrison v. Vincent [1982] R.T.R. 8; [1982] C.L.Y. 2159, C.A.

N.B. This is not a spectator v. occupier case, but the principles are analogous.

Motor cycle combination race. Rider negligently road with defective brakes and got into emergency and as a result rode into escape road, where he collided with a recovery vehicle parked by organisers and projecting two feet into escape road, thereby injuring passenger. Rider argued that he only owed passenger a modified duty not to be reckless for his safety—*Held*, not so, and the rider was liable. The modified duty laid down in *Wooldridge* **25** was appropriate to acts or omissions "in the flurry and excitement of the sport", and not, as here, to those "in the relative calm of the workshop"—*Held*, also, that the organisers were liable, as although the combination of circumstances was unfortunate, they were not so fantastic as to be outside their reasonable contemplation.

37. Cunningham v. O'Brien [1982] 4 N.I.J.B.; [1983] C.L.Y. 2692, Northern Ireland C.A.

Held, that the defendants were liable. When they negligently caused the fire, they ought reasonably to have foreseen that it could well present an unusual source of danger to a trained and skilled fireman.

38. Latchford v. Spedeworth International Ltd, *The Times*, October 11, 1983; [1983] C.L.Y. 2584, Hodgson J.

Held, that the defendants were negligent in not shielding concrete flower beds near to the track and using a dangerous method of demarcating the track. "It was the duty of the organiser of such events not unnecessarily to add to the hazards inherent in the sport. The defendant had been aware of the dangers . . . and was negligent in allowing them to continue."

39. Brayshaw v. Leeds C.C. [1984] 1 C.L.Y. 2331, McCullough J.

School grounds frequented by public after school hours which contained a trench. Plaintiff, 14-year-old pupil, attempted to jump over trench, fell and was injured—*Held*, that the defendants were not liable. It was impracticable for a watchman to have been employed or for the trench to have been boarded. There ought to have been a warning of the trench, but the sole cause of the accident was the plaintiff's unnecessary decision to jump over the trench.

40. Titchener v. B.R.B. [1983] 1 W.L.R. 1427; [1983] 3 All E.R. 770, H.L.

Plaintiff, then 15, taking short cut along railway line. Got onto railway line through long-standing gap in fence. Defendants knew people used gap to cross line, plaintiff had done so on previous occasions and knew of dangers. Run down by train being driven properly—*Held*, defendants were not liable. They did not owe the plaintiff a duty to maintain the fence in any better condition. "The existence and extent of a duty to fence will depend on the circumstances of the case including the age and intelligence of the particular person entering on the premises; the duty will tend to be higher in a question with a very young or very old person than in a question with a normally active and intelligent adult or adolescent. The nature of the locus and the obviousness or otherwise of the railway line may also be relevant" (Lord Fraser, 775 A). As the plaintiff was aware of the railway line and its dangers and could have kept a proper look-out, the defendants had discharged the duty they owed to her. Furthermore, as she would probably have climbed over a fence in good condition, any breach of duty by the defendants did not cause the accident—*Held*, also, that the plaintiff was *volens*, as to which see Chap. 4(3).

N.B. This was a Scottish case decided in accordance with the duty of care imposed by the Occupiers' Liability (Scotland) Act 1960 towards persons "entering premises". This duty as worded is similar to the duty owed in England and Wales to visitors, and it seems that the status of the plaintiff would in England and Wales have been that of a visitor, but this point did not specifically arise in the present case, since (so it is understood) the distinction between a trespasser and a visitor is not a rigid one in Scottish law.

41. Morgan v. Blunden, *The Times*, February 1, 1986; [1986] C.L.Y. 2264, C.A.

Duty of care of managers of adventure playground was limited to risks within their reasonable contemplation. Accordingly, there was no liability for injury sustained by children from an abandoned smouldering car which exploded, as their had been no duty to inspect.

42. Horne & Marlow v. R.A.C. Motor Sports Association [1989] C.L.Y. 2592 C.A.

Negligence of stewards at car rally cause injury to plaintiffs—*held*, rally organisers liable as stewards did not advise Ps to move from a dangerous part of the ground where they were injured.

43. Banks v. Bury B. C. [1990] C.L.Y. 3284

P dived into shallow end of swimming pool and fractured spine on pool floor. The only sign said ".9 metres" at side of pool, easily observed by others. P conceded a degree of contributory negligence, and it was held that design guidelines had not been followed, making D 30 per cent liable.

44. Green v. Building Scene Ltd [1993] P.I.Q.R. P259, C.A.

P injured when falling down short stairway in shop premises, where no central handrail had been installed contrary to Building Regulations—*Held*, no liability: *Ward v. Ritz Hotel* (*supra*, chap. 10(4)(c) **12**, contrasted.

45. Cotton v. Derbyshire Dales D.C., *The Times*, June 20, 1994; [1994] 7 C.L. 432, C.A.

Absence of warning notice of dangerous cliffs held not to be breach of duty of care of owner of land under the Occupiers' Liability Act 1957, s. 2(1).

U1. Parker v. Charalambou (1951) C.A. 198

Plaintiff going to ladies' toilet in restaurant—enters ante-room which is dark and contains staircase leading off—while feeling for lightswitch plaintiff falls down staircase—*Held*, defendants liable. *N.B.* The decision turned largely on whether plaintiff had behaved reasonably in staying in anteroom and feeling for switch, and it was held that in the circumstances she had.

U2. Bartle v. Theatre Royal (Chatham) Ltd (1952) C.A. 123

Deceased at theatre—going through swing doors into vestibule 12 feet by 6 feet—opened door on left marked "Private" mistaking it for toilet—fell down steep stairs leading to cellar—toilet up steps on other side—lighting not very good—cellar door in neglected condition—unpadlocked and easily opened—no warning—defendants occupiers of theatre—*Held*, vestibule dangerous—deceased invitee not trespasser—defendants had not taken reasonable care to make premises safe. No contributory negligence.

U3. Woosey v. Cannon Breweries (1953) C.A. 276

Plaintiff entering public house trips on horizontal bar across doorway . . . from ground—*Held*, defendants not liable, because, although the bar was a danger, there was no evidence defendants knew or ought to have known it was down. But *cf. Smith v. Austin Lifts* (Chap. 10, (6) (a)**9**).

U4. Smith v. Sheppard (1955) C.A. 107

Plaintiff fell down flight of steps leading to cellar when finding her way to "Ladies" in public house—opened door without "Ladies" on it—few steps forward—felt for light switch—dark—*Held*, invitee—defendant negligent in not providing adequate lighting.

U5. Craggs v. Hutchinson (1955) C.A. 346

Firework display—enclosure provided—people warning boys not to try to get through—tried to get them back—jumping crackers fired from middle of enclosure—plaintiff infant hit by jumping cracker when trying to get into enclosure—*Held*, defendant not liable.

U6. Higginson v. Manchester Corporation (1957) C.A. 261

Plaintiff invitee slipped on wet floor of public washhouse—being swilled by attendant—instructions were that floor should (in order to avoid risk of slipping) only be swilled when public had left—*Held*, defendants liable.

U7. Griffith v. Salford Hospital Management Committee (1958) C.A. 180A

Plaintiff slipped on spilled soup when visiting hospital—attendant was away getting something to mop it up—*Held*, defendants not liable.

U8. Hunt v. Stephens (1963) C.A. 14

Local show—*Held*, organisers not liable for allowing ponies to be trotted close to entrance to horticultural tent, where mother of, and carrying, infant plaintiff stepped backwards into pony.

U9. Stannage v. Jennaway (1963) C.A. 86

Plaintiff at agricultural show knocked down by pony ridden by defendant—pony was trotting through crowded passageway—doubt as to whether plaintiff moved into path of pony—*Held*, defendant liable, as in any event people moving about at a show not bound to move in straight line.

U10. Gibson v. C. & A. (1976) C.A. 269

Vinyl tile in shop slightly curled up—over which plaintiff tripped—*Held*, as there was no evidence, expert or otherwise, that the defendants ought to have foreseen and guarded against the contingency that such tiles were likely to curl up, defendants were not liable. *Ward* **35** distinguished on the ground that there the danger was something which had been dropped on to the floor, which was a foreseeable risk against which there should have been precautions.

U11. Smith v. Storey (1980) C.A. 804

U12. Gear v. De Vere Hotels and Restaurants plc (1985) C.A. 1111

Plaintiff slipped and sustained serious injury on dance floor at D's banqueting suite. No evidence as to any spillage, but if there had been it had been caused accidentally when waitress collided with dancer, and there was a system for immediate clearance of spillages. Therefore D not liable.

U13. Marshall v. East Yorkshire H.A. (1987) C.A. 720

Held, Authority ought to have been aware of defective vinyl floor covering through system of cleaning, and therefore liable.

U14. Stimpson v. Wolverhampton B.C. (1990) C.A. 515

P injured by golf ball in park where persons often practised golf—*Held*, D liable. They knew park was used for such purposes, and failed to take any active measures to prevent use.

U15. Preece v. Home Office (1990) C.A. 895

P slipped on shingle on concrete. No libaility because this was "the kind of hazard which any ordinary pedestrian meets with out of doors"; no duty to provide system of clearance.

U16. Kehoe v. Adshel Ltd (1991) C.A. 424

P leant against place where middle glass panel in bus shelter should have been, but missing. Fell and sustained injury D responsible for maintaining bus shelters under agreement with transport executive—*Held*, D not liable because no evidence of broken glass having been swept up by D rather than city in exercise of street cleansing responsibility, and as D had a system of inspection that was reasonable, P had failed to discharge burden of proof.

U17. Seymour v. Flynn (1992) C.A. 87

P, care assistant injured when falling down step at home of elderly and infirm occupier—*Held* estate of occupier (since deceased) not liable as deceased had no duty to warn of trap on account of her mental infirmity.

U18. Roberts v. Vale of Glamorgan B.C. (1993) C.A. 999

P fell down bank in country park when walking dogs—stepped back to avoid approaching vehicle—*Held*, D not liable for failure to fence bank. Cause of accident had been P's failure to keep a lookout for approaching vehicle, and not condition of bank.

U19. Merritt v. National Car Parks Ltd (1994) C.A. 645

P returning to car distracted by "Mind your head" sign referring to hazard around corner—did not see six-inch kerb clearly delineated by white line—*Held*, not liable—kerb not a danger.

U20. O'Shea v. Royal Borough of Kensington (1994) C.A. 1412

Plaintiff dived into swimming pool and struck his head on bottom in area of pool where diving was unsafe. Suffered very serious injuries—*Held*, although plaintiff had been acting ill-advisedly in not checking the depth, liability lay with the defendants because an unsafe diving area had not been properly designated.

Examples

Liable

Example	No.
HOSPITAL: MAT ON POLISHED FLOOR	1
Station: stairs to platform edge	2
Diving board: shallow water	3
PADDLING POOL: GLASS	4
CHUTE: BOYS INTERFERE WITH CHAIN	5
P.T.: highly polished floor	6
AIR-RAID SHELTER: ENTRANCE	9
Theatre: bombed ceiling	10
Shop: vegetable on floor	11
Station: uneven platform edge	12
Railway carriage: unlit: no seat	13
Station: projecting nut	17
Hospital: polish spread on floor	23
Ship: no weatherboards in storm	28
Lift: latticework gates without mid-bar pickets	32
DIVING BOARD: SEA TOO SHALLOW	33
STAIRCASE: STEP AND UNLIT: IN PUBLIC HOUSE	34
SHOP: YOGHURT ON FLOOR	35
Shop: failure to warn of full length window next to exit	36
Restaurant: no light in W.C. ante-room	U2
Theatre: no light in access to W.C.	U3
Public house: no light in access to W.C.	U6
Washhouse: floor slippery from swilling	U8
Path: digging hole	U10
Hostel: bed too near window: plaintiff falls out	U11
Caravan site: high tension cable 20 feet above ground	U15
Hotel forecourt: frozen snow	U14
Shop: vinyl tile curling up	U17
Passage in Public house: broken glass	U18
Private use of leisure centre out of hours	U21

Not Liable

Example	No.
PUBLIC HOUSE: VOMIT IN YARD	7
DOCK: UNFENCED: FOG	8
SHOP FORECOURT: DEPRESSION	14
ICE-HOCKEY: SPECTATOR HURT	15
Car race: spectator hurt	16
Racecourse: marquee tent peg	18
STATION: SUDDEN SNOWFALL	19
HOTEL: SLIPPERY DRIVE	20
STATION: OIL: PROMPT STEPS	21
Steps on cliff: slippery	22
Sports stand: empty bottles lying	24
Ship: quoits board put out in rough weather	25
Ship: disembarkation arrangements	26
DOCK: DEFECTIVE LADDER LEFT BY THIRD PARTY	27
Diving board: shallow water (sea)	29
Public house: steep steps to toilet	30
HORSE SHOW: VISITOR RUN DOWN BY HORSE	31
Trench in school grounds: frequented by public: plaintiff trying to jump across	37
Descending underground escalator when jolted	38
public house: low bar across doorway near opening time	U1
Public house: low bar across doorway	U4
Garage: unguarded inspection pit	U5
Firework display: spectator encroaching too close	U7
Hospital: soup spilled on floor	U9
Local show: pony runs down visitor	U12
Local show: pony collides with visitor	U13
Public house: door with glass panel 1/8 in. thick	U16
Fall over dimly lit retaining wall in park	U19
Public park: hit by golf ball	U20
Arts Centre: wall clock falling during decoration	U22
Swimming pool steps slippery	U23

1. Weigall v. Westminster Hospital [1936] 1 All E.R. 232, C.A.
2. Schlarb v. L.N.E.R. [1936] 1 All E.R. 71.
3. Simmonds v. Mayor of Huntingdon [1936] 1 All E.R. 596.
4. Ellis v. Fulham B.C. [1937] 3 All E.R. 454, C.A.
5. Coates v. Rawtenstall B.C. [1937] 3 All E.R. 602, C.A.
6. Gillmore v. L.C.C. [1938] 4 All E.R. 331, du Parcq J.
7. Simons v. Winslade [1938] 3 All E.R. 774, C.A.
8. Caseley v. Bristol Corporation [1944] 1 All E.R. 14, C.A.
9. Baker v. Bethnal Green B.C. [1945] 1 All E.R. 135, C.A.
10. Pope v. St. Helens Theatre [1947] K.B. 30; [1946] 2 All E.R. 440, Sellers J.
11. Turner v. Arding & Hobbs [1949] 2 All E.R. 911, Lord Goddard C.J.
12. Protheroe v. Railway Executive [1951] 1 K.B. 376; [1950] 2 All E.R. 1093, Parker J.
13. Warren v. Railway Executive [1950] C.L.C. 6703; 94 S.J. 457, Finnemore J.
14. Mumford v. Naylor 1951 95 S.J. 742; [1951] W.N. 579, C.A.
15. Murray v. Harringay Arena [1951] 2 K.B. 529; [1951] 2 All E.R. 320, C.A.
16. O'Dowd v. Fraser Nash [1951] C.L.C. 6778; [1951] W.N. 178, McNair J.
17. Bloomstein v. Railway Executive [1952] 2 All E.R. 418; [1952] W.N. 378, Parker J.
18. Higgins v. R.C.B. Control Board [1952] 1 All E.R. 294, Ormerod J.
19. Tomlinson v. Railway Executive [1953] 1 All E.R. 1, C.A.
20. Bell v. Travco Hotels [1953] 1 All E.R. 638; [1953] 1 Q.B. 473, C.A.
21. Blackman v. Railway Executive [1953] 2 All E.R. 323; [1954] 1 W.L.R. 220, C.A.
22. Blakeley v. Newquay U.D.C. [1953] C.P.L. 715; [1953] C.L.Y. 2456, Barry J.
23. Slade v. Battersea Hospital Committee [1955] 1 W.L.R. 207; [1955] 1 All E.R. 429, Finnemore J.
24. Holloway v. London Stadium *The Times*, April 26, 1955; [1955] C.L.Y. 1795, Wynn-Parry J.
25. Glyn v. Royal Mail Lines [1955] 2 Lloyd's Rep. 35, Gorman J.
26. Barling v. B.T.C. [1955] 2 Lloyd's Rep. 393, Devlin J.
27. Banks v. M.D.H.B. [1956] 1 Lloyd's Rep. 147, C.A.
28. Austin v. B.T.C. [1956] 2 Lloyd's Rep. 353, Pilcher J.
29. Perkowski v. Wellington Corporation [1959] A.C. 53, [1958] 3 All E.R. 388, P.C.
30. Newman v. E.J. Rose, *The Times*, November 16, 1961; [1961] C.L.Y. 5818, Thompson J.
31. Wooldridge v. Sumner [1962] 2 Q.B. 43; [1962] 2 All E.R. 978, C.A.
32. Sandford v. Eugene (1970) 115 S.J. 33; [1970] C.L.Y. 7782, Hinchcliffe J.
33. Davies v. Tenby Corporation [1974] 2 Lloyd's Rep. 469; [1974] C.L.Y. 849, C.A.
34. Stone v. Taffe 1 W.L.R. 1575; [1974] 3 All E.R. 1016, C.A. (but 25 per cent. contributory negligence, C.N.).
35. Ward v. Tesco [1976] 1 W.L.R. 810; [1976] 1 All E.R. 219, C.A.
36. Vollans v. Simco Supermarkets [1982] C.L.Y. 2142, Pickles J.
37. Brayshaw v. Leeds C.C. [1984] C.L.Y. 2331, McCullough J.
38. Sherlock v. London Underground [1993] C.L.Y. 3001, H.H. Judge Quentin Edwards.

U1. *Marshall v. Wheeler* (1951) C.A. 83
U2. *Parker v. Charalambou* (1951) C.A. 198
U3. *Bartle v. Theatre Royal (Chatham)* (1952) C.A. 123
U4. *Woosey v. Cannon Breweries* (1953) C.A. 276
U5. *Paterson v. Morris* (1954) C.A. 185
U6. *Smith v. Sheppard* (1955) C.A. 107
U7. *Craggs v. Hutchinson* (1955) C.A. 346
U8. *Higginson v. Manchester Corporation* (1957) C.A. 261
U9. *Griffith v. Salford H.M.C.* (1958) C.A. 108A
U10. *Ramage v. Francis Jackson* (1959) C.A. 109
U11. *Hughes v. Laing* (1960) C.A. 190
U12. *Hunt v. Stephens* (1963) C.A. 14
U13. *Stannage v. Jennaway* (1963) C.A. 86
U14. *Wood v. Morland* (1972) C.A. 49A
U15. *Withers v. Camp* (1975) C.A. 449

U16. *Gurney v. Everards Brewery* (1975) C.A. 518
U17. *Gibson v. C. & A.* (1976) C.A. 269
U18. *Brocken v. Allied Breweries* (1987) C.A. 1252
U19. *Jones v. Leeds D.M.C.* (1986) C.A. 980
U20. *Stimpson v. Wolverhampton B.C.* (1990) C.A. 515
U21. *Stenner v. Toff Ely B.C.* (1990) C.A. 534
U22. *Burns v. Thameside B.C.* (1991) C.A. 1061
U23. *Baines v. York C.C.* (1992) C.A. 461

(b) Private Visitors to Houses

1. Pitt v. Jackson [1939] 1 All E.R. 129

Plaintiff, guest in house, slips on polished linoleum—*Held*, defendant not liable, as not a trap or concealed danger.

2. Haseldine v. Daw [1941] 2 K.B. 343; [1941] 3 All E.R. 156, C.A.

Held, occupier who had employed competent contractors to look after lift was not liable for defective state of lift. *N.B.* Contractors were held liable.

3. Glasgow Corporation v. Muir [1943] A.C. 448; [1943] 2 All E.R. 44, H.L.

Held, defendants not liable for act of one of the visitors in spilling tea urn over another, See Chap 10, (4)(e) **1** for full facts.

4. Devine v. London Housing Society [1950] 2 All E.R. 1173; 66 T.L.R. (Pt. 2) 1012

Unlit common staircase of block of flats—tenant falls—*Held*, since there was no unusual danger, defendant landlord was under no duty to light and was not liable.

5. Dunster v. Abbott [1954] 1 W.L.R. 58; [1953] 2 All E.R. 1572, C.A.

Held, defendant not liable.

6. Hawkins v. Coulsdon U.D.C. [1954] 1 Q.B. 319, [1954] 2 All E.R. 318, C.A.

Held, defendant liable.

7. Greene v. Chelsea B.C. [1954] 2 Q.B. 127, [1954] 2 All E.R. 318, C.A.

Dangerous ceiling in requisitioned house—*Held*, defendants liable.

8. McKenna v. Bune *The Times*, February 8, 1995, [1955] C.L.Y. 1831, Streatfeild J.

Held, defendant not liable.

9. Andrews v. Pattullo *The Times*, December 16, 1955, [1955] C.L.Y. 1835, Morris L.J.

Held, defendant not liable.

10. Uctkos v. Mazzetta [1956] 1 Lloyd's Rep. 209, Ormerod J.

Held, de fendant not liable.

11 A. C. Billings v. Riden [1958] A.C. 240, [1957] 3 All E.R. 1, H.L.

A contractor (*not an occupier*) who was remaking a front path of a private house was sued—his works had obstructed the ordinary front access so that visitors were obliged to deviate off the premises to gain access—the deviation contained a danger—plaintiff injuired thereby—*Held*, contractor liable (*N.B.* For contractor cases generally, see Chap. 7)

12. Wells v. Cooper [1958] 2 Q.B. 265; [1958] 2 All E.R. 527, C.A.

Door handle repaired by defendant himself comes off when plaintiff pulls it—*Held*, defendant not liable. See Chap. 10(4) (c) **5** for details.

13. Green v. Fibreglass [1958] 2 Q.B. 245, [1958] 2 All E.R. 521, Salmon J.

Defendants were tenants of offices since 1951—had premises rewired by competent electricians—plaintiff an invitee injured when touching an electric fire which though off was live—defendants had no reason to suspect defect—did not regularly inspect wiring—*Held*, defendants not liable, as they had discharged their duty by employing competent independent contractors, since electric wiring required technical knowledge which defendants could not possess themselves. *See* now the Occupiers' Liability Act, s. 2, which in effect confirms this decision.

14. Wheat v. Lacon [1966] A.C. 552; [1966] 1 All E.R. 582 H.L.

Held, on the facts no breach of duty by either the manager or the brewers, who owned the premises. The manager was absolved at first instance, and there was no appeal from this finding. In the H.L. the brewers were held to be occupiers as well as the manager (see Chap. 10, (1) **10**), but on the facts were not liable.

U1. Hawkins v. Dowdeswell (1957) C.A. 269 A

Deceased fell down stairs of club leading from first floor to pavement level—deceased guest not member—defendants occupiers of club and staircase—steps made wet by persons coming in from rain—single light on landing at top of stairs—steep old-fashioned staircase—treads narrow—handrails on either side—where hand-rail fastened to wall and where water pipe between rail and wall person could not keep hand round rail—allegation that defendants negligent as could easily have built another safer staircase as they did after accident—*Held*, defendants not negligent—staircase in good repair and no traps.

U2. Leech v. Newcastle-on-Tyne C.C. (1982) C.A.U.B. 766

Held, applying *Herrington* 10(5)(f)1, defendants liable for falling to take steps to prevent access to what was an obvious attraction to children.

U3. Marsden v. L.B. of Harvering (1984) C.A. 114

Plaintiff injured when door knocker came away in hand due to defect which landford knew; D liable.

(c) Workers (Other than on Ships and Docks)

(*N.B.* In these cases, the "workers" were not employed by the defendants.)

1. Clelland v. Edward Lloyd [1938] 1 K.B. 272; [1937] 2 All E.R. 605; Goddard J.

Occupier of premises employs electrical contractors to do work on his premises—scaffold breaks—*Held*, occupier not liable *qua* occupier.

2. Woodman v. Richardson 81 S.J. 700; [1937] 3 All E.R. 866; (1937) C.A.

Plaintiff employed by sub-contractors injured when using a defective ladder on a building site scaffold—sues main contractors—*Held* defendants not liable, as no evidence that any of defendants' servants or agents placed ladder in position or knew or ought to have known of defect.

3. Howard v. Farmer [1938] 2 All E.R. 296, C.A.

Plaintiff (employed on building site by third party) went up partly built staircase—fell owing; to missing tread—*Held*, defendants not liable.

4. Canter v. Gardner [1940] 1 All E.R. 325; 56 T.L.R. 305, Tucker J.

Defendant sub-contractors had securely fixed cover to hole—cover removed by person unknown—plaintiff employed by another sub-contractor falls down—*Held*, defendants not liable, as they had left cover securely fixed. *Aliter* if they had not, as they would then have had a duty to inspect and/or warn.

5. Whitby v. Burt, Boulton K.B. 918; [1947] 2 All E.R. 324; [1947] Denning J.

Factory occupier employed by independent contractor to repair roof—plaintiff employed by independent contractor—working on roof when one of the timbers collapsed—*Held*, occupier was not liable at common law (though he was under Factories Act 1937, s. 26).

6. Pratt v. Richards [1951] 2 K.B. 208; [1951] 1 All E.R. 90n., Barry J.

Plaintiff sub-contractors' employee injured on scaffold of defendants' main contractors due to no guard rail—*Held*, defendants liable as invitors. *N.B.* This decision was largely based on *London G.D. v. Horton* [1950] 1 K.B. 421 as decided by C.A. before it went to H.L.

7. Vaughan v. Building Estates [1952] 2 Lloyd's Rep. 231, McNair J.

Duty of building contractor to his sub-contractor is canvassed, but somewhat indecisively because plaintiff fails whatever test is applied. Judge (235) quotes with approval dictum in *Salmond on Tarty* to the effect that where the use of the premises is ancillary to the main purpose of the contract the duty is assimilated to that owed to an invitee.

8. Christmas v. General Cleaning Contractors 1 K.B. 141; [1952] 1 All E.R. 39 [1952], C.A.

Held, that where a window was safe for ordinary purposes a defect in it which made it dangerous for a window cleaner was not an unusual danger for which occupier would be liable. (*N.B.* This part of the decision was not appealed to H.L.).

9. Bates v. Parker [1953] Q.B. 231; [1953] 1 All E.R. 768, C.A.

Window cleaner injured by piece of plywood coming away in his hands—he had used it before as a handhold, but just before accident defendant had unbolted plywood and left it *in situ*—on appeal defendant *held* not liable. **8** *applied*. "... the law thus (in **8**) applied is not peculiar to window cleaners ... Where a householder employs an independent contractor to do work ... the contractor must satisfy himself as to the safety or condition of that part of the premises on which he is to work ... It was not for defendant to tell him how to do it or to call his attention to the fact that the piece of plywood was not in a condition to serve as a support ... If the cleaner had been injured by some defect in the premises which had nothing to do with the work for which he was employed ... it would have been the duty of the latter (*i.e.* the householder) to warn him" (Lord Goddard C.J. at 770 H-771 D). See *Smith v. Austin Lifts* (Chap. 10(4)(d)**4**).

10. Wingrove v. Prestige 1 W.L.R. 524; [1954] 1 All E.R. 576; [1974] C.A.

Plaintiff clerk of works (and invitee) on building site—hits head on low pole across passageway—*Held*, a danger, but as plaintiff had full knowledge thereof, claim failed.

11. Hartley v. Mayoh 1 Q.B. 383; [1954] 1 All E.R. 375; [1954] C.A.

Firemen electrocuted when dealing with factory fire—*Held, inter alia*, factory occupier was liable in that, the main switches being of an unusual type, no warning had been given of the danger presented thereby.

12. Gledhill v. Liverpool Abattoir 1 W.L.R. 1028; [1957] 3 All E.R. 117; [1959] C.A.

Held, defendants not liable. See Chap. 10, (6)(c). **13**.

13. Smith v. Austin Lifts 1 W.L.R. 100; [1959] 1 All E.R. 81; [1959] H.L.

Held, defendants liable, as it was proved that the defect was attributable to them, and that plaintiff did not have "full appreciation" of the danger.

14. Savory v. Holland Hannen [1964] 1 W.L.R. 1158; [1964] 3 All E.R. 18, C.A.

Plaintiff was doing the blasting on a building site—occupier was to provide flagmen, but did not provide enough—as a result plaintiff undertook to do the work himself, as well as the blasting—while proceeding from one job to other, he slipped on a steep bank—he could have gone another way—*Held*, occupier not liable. "Warnings have already gone out from the House of Lords as to not extending the nursemaid school of negligence. I certainly would not extend it in this case to a duty to advise someone who is the servant of an independent contractor" (Diplock L.J. 22 H).

15. Field v. Jeavons [1965] 1 W.L.R. 996; [1965] 2 All E.R. 162, C.A.

Defendant factory occupiers got in contractors to connect up electric saw—plaintiff employed by contractors did this, and then switched on the saw to check—saw was in dangerous condition and advanced on plaintiff, since blade was in contact with bed—*Held*, defendants liable (but 25 per cent. contributorily negligent for not asking permission to switch on first).

16. Fisher v. C.H.T. [1966] 2 Q.B. 475; [1966] 1 All E.R. 87, C.A.

Two occupiers, C and T—C had a maintenance man who was "round and about"—T had an electrician, who switched on current to some bare wires in ceiling, thereby injuring plaintiff who was employed by decorators on the premises—*Held*, C and T both liable, but C only to a small extent.

17. Woolins v. British Celanese (1966) 110 S.J. 686; 1 K.I.R. 438, C.A.

Held, this was not a risk incidental to plaintiff's calling, within the 1957 Act, s. 2(3)(b) but a risk incident to the premises, and the defendants were liable.

18. Sibbald v. Sher (1980) 124 S.J. 117; [1980] C.L.Y. 1877, H.L.

Held, occupiers not liable. The duty to visitors varied with the character of the visitor, and the duty towards a fireman was lower than that towards other visitors. Here, there was no duty to provide the fireman with an exit route which would remain safe throughout the fire (Scottish case).

19. Hartley v. B.R.B., *The Times*, February 2, 1981; [1981] C.L.Y. 1836, C.A.

Railway station—employee negligently stoked up stove and then left premises without telling anyone. There was a fire. Plaintiff fireman went on roof to search for employee and was injured—*Held*, defendant Railway Board liable, being in breach of duty to take reasonable care not to subject plaintiff to unnecessary risk. It was irrelevant that the plaintiff might have to accept the risk of going onto a roof at other times in the course of service.

20. Salmon v. Seafarer Restaurant [1983] 1 W.L.R. 1264; [1983] 3 All E.R. 729, Woolf J.

Chip fryer was negligently left overnight with bottom heat on. Oil in chip fryer caught fire and set light to the premises. Plaintiff fireman attended and was injured by gas exploding as a result of the fire—*Held*, defendant occupiers liable. "In deciding whether the negligent act could foreseeably cause injury to a fireman, it is necessary to take into account the skills that are ordinarily expected to be shown by firemen . . . Where it can be foreseen that the fire which is negligently started is of the type which could, first of all, require firemen to attend and where, because of the very nature of the fire, when they attend they will be at risk even though they exercise all the skill of their calling, there seems no reason why a fireman should be at any disadvantage when the question of compensation for his injuries arises" (735 J–736 B). Here the explosion was directly caused by the negligence of the defendants, and the sort of sequence of events which occurred was by no means unique or unusual, so that the negligence gave rise to a liability to the plaintiff who, it was readily foreseeable, would be required to attend and be at risk of such injuries (736 F).

In the course of his judgment the judge analysed the main previous authorities, and *said* that *Merrington v. Ironbridge* [1952] 2 All E.R. 1101 was not a case of negligence in *starting* the fire, but of exposing the plaintiff to an exceptional and serious risk of an explosion from accumulated dust (733 D). Similarly, no question of negligence in starting the fire arose in *Sibbald* **18** (733 H), while in *Hartley v. B.R.B.* **19**, although the issue could have been considered on the basis of original negligence in starting the fire, it was in fact decided on the basis of the responsibilities of an occupier towards firemen generally and irrespectively of original negligence (735 C).

21. Hemmings v. British Aerospace [1986] C.L.Y. 2265, Swinton Thomas J.

Injury caused by ice on factory path used by P on his way to attend a union meeting—*Held*, purpose of use immaterial, as path was a means of access to a place of work and D was liable in negligence and for breach of statutory duty.

22. Ogwo v. Taylor [1987] 3 W.L.R. 1145, H.L.
See Chap. 10, (5)(e) **10** for summary.

23. Capitano v. Leeds C.C. [1989] C.L.Y. 3522, Otton J.

P security officer was injured when patrolling premises in dark at night—*Held*, the provision of a torch was a sufficient discharge of the duty of care.

U1. Priestley v. Nottingham H.A. (1986) C.A. 37 (unreported)

P, domestic supervisor, injured when walking across delivery yard—slipped on slushy ice—*Held*, no liability under Occupiers' Liability Act or at common law. System of clearing ice adopted by D was reasonable in all the circumstances.

Examples

Liable

Factory on fire: dust explosion 5
Goods truck: projecting buffers 8
FACTORY: MAIN SWITCH UNRECOGNISABLE.. 11
LIFT: THIRD PARTY STARTING DURING INSPECTION 17
FACTORY: ELECTRIC SAW LEFT IN DANGEROUS CONDITION 19
BUILDING SITE: OCCUPIER ALLOWING BARE WIRES IN CEILING TO BECOME LIVE 20
FACTORY ROOF: POST OFFICE ENGINEER FALLING THEREFROM 21
Cleaner: private house: floor too slippery 23
Lift: permitting overloading 24
Building site: welding cable left suspended nine inches from ground... 25
Lift: folding lattice gates with no mid-bar pickets 26
Sub-contractor: not provided with boards to cover stair well of house being built.. 17
FACTORY: UNSUITABLE CHAINS TO SLING PIGS 16
Window cleaner: private house: ornamental trellis giving way 22
Floor: bolts protruding while building being altered.................................. U1
Fire station: investigating officer slips on water in unlit area U4
Building site: missing handrail on scatfolding...................................... U6
Scaffolder injured by · unsafe scaffolding...................................... U7

Not Liable

BUILDING SITE: UNFINISHED STAIRCASE .... 1[1]
Collapse of factory roof: employee of independent contractor injured 2
FACTORY: LOAN OF EQUIPMENT 3
PRIVATE HOUSE: LOAN OF LADDER 4
Building site: plank in long grass 6
WINDOW CLEANING: DEFECTIVE SASH 7
Door: needing force to slide open 9
WINDOW CLEANING—LOOSE PIECE OF PLYWOOD 10
Factory: loan of equipment................ 12
LOW POLE ACROSS PASSAGE....................... 13
Factor: debris on floor........................ 14
DOCK: DEFECTIVE LADDER LEFT BY THIRD PARTY 15
BUILDING SITE: PLAINTIFF SUB-CONTRACTOR BLASTING: INSUFFICIENT FLAGMEN PROVIDED BY OCCUPIER 18
Vinolay in factory canteen: slippery: caterers' employee slipping............. U3
Cylinder: tilting while being painted . U2
Security officer falling on derelict site: provision of torch adequate discharge of duty U5

1. Howard v. Farmer [1938] 2 All E.R. 296, C.A.

2. Whitby v. Burt, Boulton [1947] K.B. 918; [1947] 2 All E.R. 324, Denning J.
3. Marshall v. Cellactite (1947) 63 T.L.R. 456, C.A.
4. Jones v. Barclays Bank (1949) 93 S.J. 372; [1949] W.N. 267, C.A.
5. Merrington v. Ironbridge Metal Works [1952] 2 All E.R. 1101; 117 J.P. 23, Hallett J.
6. Vaughan v. Building Estates [1952] 2 Lloyd's Rep. 231, McNair J.
7. Christmas v. General Cleaning Contractors [1952] 1 K.B. 141; [1952] 1 All E.R. 39, C.A.
8. Shevlin v. M.D.H.B. [1953] 1 Lloyd's Rep. 288, Barry J.
9. Culling v. P.L.A. [1953] 2 Lloyd's Rep. 117, Pilcher J.
10. Bates v. Parker [1953] 2 Q.B. 231; [1953] 1 All E.R. 768, C.A.
11. Hartley v. Mayoh [1954] 1 Q.B. 383; [1954] 1 All E.R. 375, C.A.
12. Johnson v. Croggan [1954] 1 W.L.R. 195; [1954] 1 All E.R. 121, Pilcher J.
13. Wingrove v. Prestige [1954] 1 W.L.R. 524; [1954] 1 All E.R. 567, C.A.
14. Prince v. Carrier Engineering [1955] 1 Lloyd's Rep. 401, Parker L.J.
15. Banks v. M.D.H.B. [1956] 1 Lloyd's Rep. 147, C.A.
16. Gledhill v. Liverpool Abattoir [1957] 1 W.L.R. 1028; [1957] 3 All E.R. 117, C.A.
17. Gibbs v. Fresh Productions, *The Times*, May 14, 1957; [1957] C.L.Y. 2352, C.A.
18. Savory v. Holland Hannen [1964] 1 W.L.R. 1158; [1964] 3 All E.R. 18, C.A.
19. Field v. Jeavons [1965] 1 W.L.R. 996; [1965] 2 All E.R. 162, C.A.
20. Fisher v. C.H.T. [1966] 1 All E.R. 87, C.A.
21. Woolins v. British Celanese (1966) 110 S.J. 686; [1966] C.L.Y. 8133, C.A.
22. Caddis v. Gettrup (1967) 202 E.G. 517; [1967] C.L.Y. 2669, Swanwick J.
23. Adams v. S. J. Watson (1967) 117 New L.J. 130; *The Times*, January 20, 1967.
24. Gallen v. Seigals (1968) 209 E.G. 587; [1969] C.L.Y. 2405, Hinchcliffe J.
25. Smith v. Vange [1970] 1 W.L.R. 733; [1970] 1 All E.R. 249, MacKenna J.
26. Sandford v. Eugene (1970) 115 S.J. 33, Hinchcliffe J.
27. Sole v. Hallt [1973] 1 Q.B. 574; [1973] 1 All E.R. 1032, Swanwick J.

U1. *Hammond v. Standard Telephones* (1952) C.A. 104.
U2. *Zelowbowski v. Long* (1963) C.A. 116.
U3. *Rabbits v. Tubes* (1966) C.A. 318.
U4. *Jones v. London Fire and Civil Defence Authority* (1988) C.A. 1004.
U5. *Armstrong v. B.S.C.* (1989) C.A. 118.
U6. *Gillinghan v. Ash Scaffolding Company Ltd* (1990) C.A. 516.
U7. *Linge v. Grayston Scoffolding* (1984) C.A. 729.

(d) Workers on Ships and Docks

(*N.B.* In these cases, the "workers" were not employed by the defendants.)

1. Wilkinson v. Rea [1941] 1 K.B. 688; [1941] 2 All E.R. 50, C.A.

Unguarded hatch down which plaintiff, a ship repairer fell—sued defendant shipowners—hatch had been left open by independent contractors who were loading coal—*Held*, defendants liable, as act of independent contractor no defence.

2. Jerred v. Dent [1948] 2 All E.R. 104; 81 Ll.L.R. 412, Atkinson J.

Shipowners assured stevedores they had secured hatch beams—statutory duty on stevedores—*Held*, shipowners liable as invitors.

3. Grant v. Sun Shipping [1948] A.C. 549; [1948] 2 All E.R. 238, H.L.

Repairers leave hatch open and unlit—*Held*, shipowners liable for not ensuring repairers had done their duty.

4. Love v. Canadian Pacific [1953] 2 Lloyd's Rep. 478, Pearson J.

Held, defendants not liable.

5. Mancktelow v. B.I.S.N. [1955] 1 Lloyd's Rep. 172, Finnemore J.

Plaintiff dock labourer trips over lugs protruding from cargo in defendants' ship—*Held*, defendants not liable. "... is not this the sort of thing that people who are stowing cargo have to be ready for? Is it not the essence of the business that there will be projections and protuberances and gaps?" (174).

6. Thomson v. Cremin [1956] 1 W.L.R. 103n.; [1953] 2 All E.R. 1185, H.L.

Wooden shore in ship insecurely fastened by stevedores who loaded ship in Australia—plaintiff dock labourer injured thereby in unloading—*Held*, shipowner was liable as occupier for the negligence of his independent contractor, the loading stevedores. *Followed* in—but see criticisms of the decision in Chap. 10, (6)(b) **8**.

7. Keen v. Lykiardopoulo [1953] 2 Lloyd's Rep. 349, Jones J.

Plaintiff dock labourer injured when unloading badly stowed cargo from defendants' ship—plaintiff was not employed by defendants, nor had defendants done the loading—*Held*, defendants not liable, as although there was a danger, it was a usual danger. It was apparently *admitted* that defendants would be liable for the negligence of any of the loading stevedores. *But* see **11**, which indicates the contrary, and cases generally in Chap. 10, (6)(b).

N.B. In this case and in **11** the defendant was sued for dangerous stowage solely in his capacity as occupier. Usually it will be either the loading stevedore or the unloading stevedore (who will ordinarily be the plaintiff's employer) who is sued. The liability of the loading stevedore arises under *Donoghue v. Stevenson* and is dealt with in Chap. 7; that of the employer is dealt with under Chap. 15.

8. Browne v. P. & O. [1954] 1 Lloyd's Rep. 159, Cassels J.

Held, defendants not liable. "The engine room of a ship ... is not to be compared with an hotel or dance floor" (161, col. 1).

9. Whitehorn v. Port of London Authority [1955] 1 Lloyd's Rep. 54, Morris L.J.

Held, defendants not liable. *N.B.* This was a case between fellow invitees but judge applied invitor's standard of care. "You cannot expect the deck of a ship by a hold that is being unloaded to be like a ballroom floor or like a corridor of an hotel . . . Anyone working on the deck of a ship in these circumstances must expect to find pieces of rope lying about or expect to find something like a loop of rope by a ring, or must know that there are rings in the deck and be prepared to expect the existence of such things" (62, col. 1).

10. Banks v. Mersey Docks and Harbour Board [1956] 1 Lloyd's Rep. 147, C.A.

Held, defendants not liable, as ladder only there for 36 hours, which was not long enough to fix defendants with knowledge.

11. Jeyes v. Currie Line & Port of London Authority [1956] 2 Lloyd's Rep. 87, Pearce J.

Unloading of barrels—barrels overstowed with consequent danger to unloading stevedores—latter, plaintiff's employers, found liable for failing to safeguard plaintiff—*Held*, shipowner not liable, because (92) they had "no reason to suppose there was any unusual danger for the dockers." The question of shipowner's liability for the loading stevedores was not even canvassed. See **9**, and note thereto on dangerous stowage generally.

12. Richards v. W.F. White [1957] 1 Lloyd's Rep. 367, Ashworth J.

Held, defendant shipowners not liable, as patch of oil had only been there for five to 35 minutes, which was not long enough to say that it should reasonably have been "caught" by a reasonable system of inspection.

Examples

Liable

- HATCH: LEFT OPEN BY REPAIRERS 1
- Winch: shipowner's, not stevedore's duty, to see safe 3, 5
- Hatch beams: failure to secure 4
- Open hatchway: at ladder bottom 7
- Hatch cover: giving way 8
- Goods truck: projecting buffers 11
- Bogie: overbalancing when stood on 15
- Scalding water: in pump 16
- Inadequate winch platform 19
- **Shoring: insecurely fastened** 20
- Loose guard rail of ship 22
- Badly stowed cargo 23
- Greasy dunnage and poor lighting in ship 26
- Hatch cover (unmoved) falling into hold 27
- Barge ladder: 2 feet 6 in. drop from bottom 28

Not Liable

- Dock: rough surface: bogie skids 2
- Stepping on pile of hatch covers 6
- Dock: uneven railway lines 9
- Lugs protruding from cargo: on ship. 10
- STEERING GEAR OF TUG: TRAPS FOOT 12
- Door: needing force to slide open 13
- Stepping on pile of hatch covers 14
- Badly stowed cargo 17
- Hatch: bolts protruding round 18
- Catwalk: edge unguarded 21
- Defective batten: in hold of ship 24
- Dock: edge of quay unmarked in fog 25
- Rope loop lying in narrow passage: in ship 29
- 2 feet 10 in. drop from ladder to deck 31
- Access to ship: gangplanks $25\frac{1}{2}$ in. wide 32

Hatchway: open near access to hold of barge 30
Floor grating: laid upside down in barge 34
Hole in floor: barge 36
Ladder: rope wound round rung 39
Quay: bundle of netting just outside shed door 43
Dock road: slippery from wet cornflour 44
*Deck cargo: lashed while stevedores working 45
Dock shed: broken step 47
*Bilge boards: hole in 48
*Bight of wire protruding from coil 50
*Deck: bottles lying thereon 51
TIMBER IN HOLD: DEEP GAP BETWEEN TIMBER AND BULKHEAD 53
dock: defective ladder left by third party 33
Dock: hosepipe across road at night. 35
Hatch: locking bars put near winch .. 37
Patch of oil left by third party on ship 38
CATWALK: EDGE UNGUARDED 40
Dock: patch of ice in early morning .. 41
Dock: berthing edge unfenced 41
*Patch of oil on deck: reasonable precautions taken 42
*Dock shed: loose peas 46
*Cargo: trap end of overhanging case: plaintiff stepping on 49
*Cargo: casks stowed on sides behind others stowed upright 52

1. Wilkinson v. Rea [1941] 1 K.B. 688; [1941] 2 All E.R. 50, C.A.
2. Chappell v. Smith (1946) 80 Ll.L.R. 92, Sellers J.
3. Butler v. Hogarth (1946) 80 Ll.L.R. 84, Morris J.
4. Jerred v. Dent [1948] 2 All E.R. 104; 81 Ll.L.R. 412, Atkinson J.
5. Lawday v. France Fenwick (1950) 84 Ll.L.R. 458, Ormerod J.
6. Kerr v. Whimster (1950) 83 Ll.L.R. 399, Hilbery J.
7. Jones v. Shaw Savill [1951] 2 Lloyd's Rep. 33, Finnemore J.
8. Rysdale v. Blackfriars Lighterage [1952] 2 Lloyd's Rep. 31, Barry J.
9. Smith v. P.L.A. [1953] 1 Lloyd's Rep. 6, Barry J.
10. Mancktelow v. B.I.S.N. [1953] 1 Lloyd's Rep. 172, Finnemore J.
11. Shevlin v. M.D.H.B. [1953] 1 Lloyd's Rep. 288, Barry J.
12. Wiseman v. Rea [1953] 2 Lloyd's Rep. 1, C.A.
13. Culling v. P.L.A. [1953] 2 Lloyd's Rep. 117, Pilcher J.
14. Osgood v. Thames Stevedoring [1953] 2 Lloyd's Rep. 134, Gorman J.
15. Rouse v. P.L.A. [1953] 2 Lloyd's Rep. 179, Parker J.
16. Cushway v. Mills and Knight [1953] 2 Lloyd's Rep. 272, Streatfeild J.
17. Keen v. Lykiardopoulo [1953] 2 Lloyd's Rep. 349, Jones J.
18. Love v. Canadian Pacific [1953] 2 Lloyd's Rep. 478, Pearson J.
19. Nelson v. P.S.N. [1953] 2 Lloyd's Rep. 685, Gerrard J.
20. Thomson v. Cremin [1956] 1 W.L.R. 103n.; [1953] 2 All E.R. 1185, H.L.
21. Browne v. P. & O. [1954] 1 Lloyd's Rep. 159, Cassels J.
22. Dongworth v. Houlder Bros. [1954] 1 Lloyd's Rep. 272, Hilbery J.
23. Hurley v. Hollandsche Stoomboot [1954] 2 Lloyd's Rep. 194, Cassels J.
24. Hurley v. B.T.C. [1954] 2 Lloyd's Rep. 343, Pilcher J. (*obiter*).
25. Hayward v. P.L.A. [1954] 2 Lloyd's Rep. 363, McNair J.
26. Young v. Royal Mail Lines [1954] 2 Lloyd's Rep. 419, Wynn-Parry J.
27. Hinson v. Morgan Scanlon [1954] 2 Lloyd's Rep. 564, McNair J.
28. Crockett v. Royal Mail [1954] 2 Lloyd's Rep. 576, Lynskey J.
29. Whitehorn v. P.L.A. [1955] 1 Lloyd's Rep. 54, Morris L.J.
30. Howard v. Thames Steam Tug Co. [1955] 2 Lloyd's Rep. 37, Gorman J.
31. Martin v. City Lighterage [1955] 2 Lloyd's Rep. 136, Sellers J.
32. Nolan v. G.S.N. [1955] 2 Lloyd's Rep. 751, Gorman J.

(* Denotes causes under Occupiers' Liability Act 1957.)

33. Banks v. M.D.H.B. [1956] 1 Lloyd's Rep. 147, C.A.
34. Tarrant v. Thames Steam Tug & Lighterage [1956] 1 Lloyd's Rep. 526, Pearson J.
35. Cowhig v. P.L.A. [1956] 2 Lloyd's Rep. 306, Pearce J.
36. Warren v. P.L.A. [1957] 1 Lloyd's Rep. 23, Hinchcliffe J.
37. Shanley v. West Coast Stevedoring [1957] 1 Lloyd's Rep. 144, Glyn-Jones J.
38. Richard v. W. F. White [1957] 1 Lloyd's Rep. 367, Devlin J.
39. Mace v. R. H. Green [1959] 2 Q.B. 14; [1959] 1 All E.R. 655, Lord Parker C.J.
40. Swales v. I.C.I. [1959] 1 Lloyd's Rep. 23, Pilcher J.; [1960] 1 Lloyd's Rep. 124, C.A.
41. Wilczek v. Gardiner & Tidy [1959] 1 Lloyd's Rep. 91, Pearson J.
42. Lowther v. Hogarth [1959] 1 Lloyd's Rep. 171, Pilcher J.
43. Swan v. Scruttons [1959] 2 Lloyd's Rep. 388, Pilcher J.
44. Berry v. P.L.A. [1960] 2 Lloyd's Rep. 233, Thesiger J.
45. Foley v. Enzo-Gutzeit [1962] 1 Lloyd's Rep. 247, Gorman J.
46. Gerrard v. Blue Star Line [1962] 2 Lloyd's Rep. 294, Phillimore J.
47. Fisher v. P.L.A. [1962] 1 All E.R. 458; 1 W.L.R. 234, Stevenson J.
48. Coughlin v. Navigation Bulgare [1963] 1 Lloyd's Rep. 113, Roskill J.
49. Richards v. Brooks Wharf [1965] 2 Lloyd's Rep. 304, Thompson J.
50. Lines v. Harland & Wolff [1966] 2 Lloyd's Rep. 400, Geoffrey Lane J.
51. Bird v. King Line [1970] 2 Lloyd's Rep. 349, Cantley J.
52. Crawley v. Gracechurch Line [1971] 2 Lloyd's Rep. 179, MacKenna J.
53. The Vladimir Timofeyev [1983] 1 Lloyd's Rep. 378; [1983] C.L.Y. 2530, C.A.

(e) Children

1. Morley v. Staffs C.C. [1939] 4 All E.R. 92, C.A.

Heap of sand and heap of metal on road—child after playing with sand collided with stack of metal—*Held*, if the sand was an allurement, it had no causal connection with accident and claim failed. The metal was "as much, or as little, dangerous as barbed wire along a fence" (*per* Mackinnon L.J. at 95 A).

2. Holdman v. Hamlyn [1943] K.B. 664; [1943] 2 All E.R. 137, C.A.

Boy of 10 helping at threshing machine—pushes sheaf into aperture with his foot—which is trapped—*Held*, defendants liable.

3. Sutton v. Bootle Corporation [1947] 1 K.B. 359; [1947] 1 All E.R. 92, C.A.

Not expressly decided whether swing allurement, because defendants' lack of knowledge of defect—*Held* good defence in any event.

4. Pearson v. Coleman [1948] 2 K.B. 359; [1948] 2 All E.R. 274, C.A.

Child invitee at fair—wanting to relieve herself, wanders under side flap of tent—tent unfortunately contains lions—*Held*, defendants liable, because plaintiff still an invitee. See chap 10, (2) (b) **3** for reasons why plaintiff invitee.

5. Williams v. Cardiff Corporation [1950] 1 K.B. 514; [1950] 1 All E.R. 250, C.A.

Broken glass on rubbish tip where children permitted to play—*Held*, defendants liable, it being their duty to keep the ground clear of things like broken glass, "the danger to be apprehended from which would not be clearly apparent to persons of tender years" (Jenkins L.J. at 252 H).

6. Cuttress v. Scaffolding [1953] 2 All E.R. [1953] 2 All E.R. 1075, C.A.

Scaffold on building site with rope hanging 35 feet above ground—children pull it over—*Held*, not an allurement, and as defendants could not have foreseen the probability of children pulling it over, not liable. *Cf.* the case of *Davis v. St. Mary's Demolition* (chap 7, (2) (f) **6**), where defendants were not occupiers and were found liable.

7. Gough v. National Coal Board [1954] 1 Q.B. 191, [1953] 2 All E.R. 1283, C.A.

Held, slow moving colliery trucks were an allurement and a trap—*Held*, further that no defence to say that child, though a licensee on the land, was a trespasser on the truck. "Such a contention destroys the whole doctrine of allurement to children" (*per* Hodson L.J. at 1295 A). *Held*, also that a specific warning of the danger was no defence if the child was not of a sufficient age to appreciate the danger of what he was doing.

8. Perry v. Thomas Wrigley [1953] 1 W.L.R. 1164; [1953] 3 All E.R. 243, Oliver J.

Held, not an allurement.

9. Bates v. Stone Parish Council [1954] 1 W.L.R. 1249; [1954] 3 All E.R. 38; C.A.

Playground with chute having 12 foot high platform—gap between rails of platform $13\frac{1}{2}$ in.—in 1934 a child fell through—additional rails were put up as a result, but later they disappeared—plaintiff aged three-and-a-half went to playground with child aged six—he fell through gap—*Held*, plaintiff was a licensee and defendants were liable. It was contended plaintiff was a trespasser on the chute but C.A., approving **7**, rejected this as "impossible" (Somervell L.J., 41 H). Romer L.J. said that, but for the 1934 accident, plaintiff's claim must have failed (49 E). This last dictum was expressly approved by Singleton L.J. in **12** at 589 D.

10. Phipps v. Rochester Corporation [1955] 1 Q.B. 450; [1955] 1 All E.R. 129, Devlin J.

"Little" child (*i.e.* too young for contributory negligence) falls down trench on building site—judge holds children as a class licensed to play (see chap 10, (2) (a) **4**, and finds that the trench while neither an allurement nor a trap, was yet a danger imperceptible, because he was not old enough to be able to avoid it—judge propounded four alternative tests of liability:

(a) children must expect no higher standard than adults;
(b) the parents must accept the burden of contributory negligence which the child cannot himself bear;
(c) the licence may be impliedly conditional on child being escorted;
(d) the licensor is not entitled to assume that all children will, unless they are allured, behave like adults; but he is entitled to assume that normally little children will in fact be accompanied by a responsible adult, and discharge his duty accordingly (135 C-G).

After consideration—*Held* (d) was the right test, and plaintiff's claim failed. For reasons rejecting (c) see chap 10 (2) (b) **5** and for amplification of duty under (d), see 143 E-I in judgment. This case was considered by Singleton L.J. in **12**, but no view as to its correctness was expressed.

11. McKenna v. Bune *The Times*, February 8, 1955 C.L.Y. [1955] 1831, Streatfeild J.

Held, defendant not liable.

12. Dyer v. Ilfracombe U.D.C. [1956] 1 W.L.R. 218, [1956] 1 All E.R. 581, C.A.

Child falls from chute on playground—*Held*, defendants not liable, because there was no trap or concealed danger, and (*per* Singleton L.J. at 589 G) "there was nothing that was not obvious to a child aged four-and-a-half". The Lords Justices also said (589 E) it was not necessary in the case of a small recreation ground to provide an attendant, and that it was no good putting up notices because children would not read them.

13. Adcock v. Loveridge *The Times*, June 21 [1956; [1956] C.L.Y. 5902, Pearce J.

Defendant occupier of site where she parked derelict lorries—plaintiff an infant threw match in petrol tank—*Held*, plaintiff was a trespasser, but if child had been licensee defendant would still not have been liable, as accident was not reasonably foreseeable by her.

14. Peters v. Hill *The Times*, March 29, 1957, [1957] C.L.Y. 2367, C.A.

Held defendant liable for not having adequate supervision to see that plaintiff, aged seven, came down the tree by the ladder, which was left accessible for children.

15. O'Connor v. British Transport Commission [1958] 1 W.L.R. 346; [1958] 1 All E.R. 558, C.A.

Railway case—see chap 14 (**33**)—Held, railway company entitled to assume child passenger would be accompanied.

16. Prince v. Gregory [1959] 1 W.L.R. 177; [1959] 1 All E.R. 133.

Held, not negligence by defendants, and statement of claim would be struck out as disclosing no cause of action.

17. McCullie v. Butler *The Times*, March 19, 1959; [1959] C.L.Y. 2207, C.A.

Held, defendants not liable when child injured by machine.

18. Nicholson v. Zoological Society *The Times*, February 26, 1960; [1960] C.L.Y. 2127, Hinchcliffe J.

Plaintiff aged four at zoo with father—outside llama pen plaintiff put finger in hasp of gate—keeper kicked door open believing child in safe position—finger trapped—*Held*, defendants not liable, as keeper had not been negligent, and no one was in a better position than the father to see whether plaintiff's finger was in danger.

19. Hughes v. Lord Advocate [1963] A.C. 837, [1963] 1 All E.R. 705, H.L.

Unattended open manhole in street covered by tent and surrounded by lit paraffin lamps—*Held*, an allurement to two boys of eight and 10, and defendants consequently liable for damage caused by paraffin lamp to one of the boys. *N.B.* The real point in the case was whether the fact that the explosion of the lamp was unforeseeable barred liability.

20. French v. Sunshine Holiday Camp [1963] 107 S.J. 595, Glyn-Jones J.

Girl of six at holiday camp—three times climbed on low wall surrounding flower bed with glass lights in it—each time ordered down by attendants—eventually she got up again and fell off wall into glass—*Held*, defendants liable, as they should have foreseen danger from wall. No contributory negligence.

21. Simkiss v. Rhondda B.C. (1983) 81 L.G.R. 460; [1983] C.L.Y. 3640, C.A.

Plaintiff, seven, and friend, 10, playing on very steep natural bluff occupied by defendant council and situated opposite council flats where plaintiff lived. Plaintiff slid down slope on blanket and fell 30–40 feet—*Held*, applying *Phipps* **10** and *Dyer* **12** defendants were not liable. The bluff was an obvious danger to adults, and the defendants were "entitled to assume that adult parents would act reasonably and not permit their children to play there unless the parents were satisfied that the children would not do stupid things on the bluff" (Dunn L.J., 467).

22. Devlin v. Strathclyde R.C. [1992] C.L.Y. 6065

Child killed when jumps through skylight in school roof—*Held* although there were reasonable and practicable steps which could have been taken to reduce the risk of injury, action of deceased child in jumping from five feet on to skylight could not have been foreseen, and therefore D was not liable.

23. Adams v. Southern Electricity Board, *The Times*, October 21, 1993; [1993] 11 C.L.Y. 2994

Liability owed by electricity board to child trespasser. See Chap. 10, (5) (f) **9**.

U1. Gurney v. Everards Brewery (1975) C.A. 518

Children's room in public house—double doors glazed from 2 feet 6 in up with panels $7\frac{1}{2}$ in. × $10\frac{1}{2}$ in.—glass $\frac{1}{8}$ in. thick—panels had been there over 30 years without incident—by 1966 British Standard Code of Practice C.P. 152 of 1966 required such panels to be of toughened glass—plaintiff aged nine put hand through panel during play—*Held*, defendants not liable. *Reffell v. Surrey C.C.* (Chap. 18(13)(b) **5**) *distinguished* on the facts, inasmuch as there (a) it was a swing door leading to the lavatory, (b) the panel was $8\frac{1}{4}$ in. × 15 in., and (c) the evidence showed it was an obvious danger.

U2. Issitt v. L.B. of Tower Hamlets (1983) C.A. 933

For summary, see Chap. 10, (8), U3.

U3. Moss v. Frank J. Privett Ltd and Portsmouth C.C. (1986) C.A. 463

P, 10 years of age, injured on waste site where building operations were being carried out by D1. Aerosol can thrown onto smouldering bonfire and exploded. D1 primarily liable—*Held*, however, D2 also to blame as owners and occupiers of site. As such, they should have known that children would be attracted to the area, and should have carried out regular inspections to ensure that the site was safe.

U4. Burke v. Cardiff C.C. (1986) C.A. 224

P, aged 10, severely injured after getting into difficulties in deep end at D's swimming pool. Life guard had not been looking at time and had his attention drawn to the incident—*Held*, D liable. Implied invitation to children not supervised by their parents to use deep end of swimming pool and standard of reasonable care demanded included reasonable supervision of young people. Brain damage could have been avoided by early and proper supervision.

U5. Meehan v. Lancashire C.C. (1988) C.A. 1006

Swing doors at school closing quickly and cause injury to pupil—*Held*, D not liable, as no evidence of any defect.

U6. Allen v. Stoke On Trent C.C. (1989) C.A. 127

10-year-old boy injured on glass on piece of land not a designated open space or playground, but on which children were known to play—*Held*, it was adequate discharge of duty for council to inspect twice a year and to respond to specific complaints. Therefore, no liability attached.

U7. Smith v. Liverpool C.C. (1990) C.A. 832

Schoolchild running along corridor at break time—hand went through glass door—*Held*, education authority liable. Although Codes of Practice required toughened glass in new buildings, and this glass had been *in situ* for many years without incident, authority ought to have known it was inappropriate for location. *Reffell v. Surrey*, Chap. 18, (13)(b) **5** applied.

(f) Trespassers

(*N.B.* Post-1984 cases are now decided under the Occupiers' Liability Act 1984. Pre-*Herrington* cases are now obsolete.)

1. British Railways Board v. Herrington [1972] A.C. 877; [1972] 1 All E.R. 749, H.L.

Trodden footpath across open National Trust property leading to railway—track having third live line—near railway the path branched to the right, leading to a footbridge over railway—but another trodden track went straight on for a short way towards railway fence—fence had been down for some time, and clearly people were using latter track as short cut across railway—children had been seen trespassing through broken fence—plaintiff aged six wandered from his playmates on the National Trust property and received severe injuries on contacting third rail—*Held*, defendants were liable. In the course of the speeches the duty and standard of care of an occupier towards trespassers were both newly stated, so that all previous cases on the subject are now obsolete.

Lord Reid said that the duty was a duty not to act culpably towards trespassers, and that culpability was akin to recklessness and had a subjective meaning (767 D). The standard of care was that of a conscientious humane man, and would vary according to the knowledge, ability and resources which he possessed; and to this extent the trespasser had to take the occupier as he found him. Provided the occupier acted in a humane manner according to his knowledge, ability and resources he was not required to do more (758 E).

Lord Morris said that the circumstances in the present case, all of them obvious and well known, were such as to impose a duty to take such steps as common sense or common humanity would dictate (767 H). But the duty was a limited one: it did not include ensuring that trespassers would not trespass, nor making surveys to find out what dangers might exist (767 F). Where the duty did arise, it was a duty of acting with common humanity towards trespassers (767 D).

Lord Wilberforce said that any duty had to arise from the proximity of the danger to places of access, from the continuous nature of the danger and from its lethal nature, and from the fact that children might not appreciate the danger (777 F). An occupier was under no general duty to fence out trespassers (save perhaps where there was a danger adjacent to a public place), nor was he under any duty to foresee trespass (777 B). Where the duty arose, the standard of care demanded a compromise between the demands of humanity and the avoidance of undue burdens on occupiers. What was reasonable depended on the degree of danger, the difficulty and expense of precautions, and on this aspect the means and resources of the occupier, viewed subjectively, were relevant (777 H). In any event, the duty could not arise unless the occupier knew of the presence of a trespasser or knew that such presence was "extremely likely" (776 F).

Lord Pearson said that where the presence of a trespasser was known or was reasonably to be anticipated, a duty was owed, but the duty was lower than the duty of common care owed to a visitor. It was a duty to treat the trespasser with common humanity (779 G). Reasonable measures to deter trespassers, such as by fencing, warning and the like, would ordinarily be enough (780 A), and a trespasser who entered despite such measures ordinarily could not sue, subject to the proviso that if an occupier knew or as good as knew that some emergency had arisen so as to put the trespasser in imminent danger, common humanity would require further steps (780 D).

Lord Diplock said that the duty did not arise until the occupier actually knew either of the presence of the trespasser or of facts which made it likely that the trespasser would come onto the land (796 B). In addition, to impose a duty, the occupier had to have actual knowledge of the condition of, or of activities on, his land which allegedly were dangerous (796 B). Actual knowledge in the above senses were essential to the existence of a duty, but once facts were actually known indicating likely presence or likely risk, the test whether they did indicate likely presence or risk was the objective one of the reasonable man (796 B). When the duty arose, the standard of care was limited to taking reasonable steps to enable the trespasser to avoid the danger, and in this connection more steps might be needed with children (796 C). The duty (or the standard) would vary according to the likelihood, as known to the occupier, of the trespasser going to a place when and where it was dangerous. If the degree of likelihood was such as would impel a man of ordinary humane feelings to take steps, then the duty arose (796 D).

N.B. It will be seen that Lord Reid and Lord Wilberforce (but not the other three Law Lords) both said in terms that the standard of care would fall in some cases to be judged by the subjective means and resources of the occupier himself rather than by the objective standards normally applied. As far as is known, the only other instance of such a standard being postulated is that of the Privy Council decision in *Goldman v. Hargrave* (Chap. 10(3)(a) **5**).

2. Pannett v. McGuiness [1972] 2 Q.B. 599; [1972] 3 All E.R. 137, C.A.

Defendant contractors in occupation of warehouse which they were demolishing—when work nearly complete, they took down hoardings and lit fires—knowing the fires would attract children (who played in an adjacent public park), they employed three men to keep the children away—but the men left the job, and the infant plaintiff was burned—*Held*, applying **1**, defendants were liable. Lord Denning M.R. and Lawton L.J. adopted the test as formulated by Lord Morris in **1** (to take such steps as common sense or common humanity would dictate). Edmund Davies L.J. (143 H) adopted Lord Reid's formulation as set out in **1** (including the subjective element in the test). Lord Denning M.R. (141 A) said that there were four important elements to be considered: (a) the nature of the hazard, inasmuch as the greater the hazard, the more the need to take steps, (b) the character of the trespass, inasmuch as a straying child was in a different position to a poacher or a burglar (c) the nature of the place, since an electrified railway line or a warehouse being demolished would require more precautions than a private house and (d) the knowledge which the defendant has, or ought to have (*sed quaere*: see Lord Diplock's speech in **1**), of the likelihood of trespassers being present, since the more likely they were, the more precautions might be needed.

3. Southern Portland Cement v. Cooper [1974] A.C. 623; [1974] 1 All E.R. 87, P.C.

High-voltage cable on poles—defendants gradually tipped waste round poles—thereby raising ground level until it was possible to touch cable—plaintiff aged 13 trespassed in area of poles to take a short cut to a play area where he would also have been trespassing on defendants' land (but without defendants objecting)—touched cable—*Held*, defendants liable. Lord Reid (delivering opinion of Board, of whom the other members were Lords Morris of Borth-y-Gest, Wilberforce, Simon and Salmon) reformulated the law relating to trespassers, saying that the Board believed that this reformulation was "substantially in line with the development in English law as expressed by the House of Lords" in *Herrington* **1**. In the course of his opinion Lord Reid said:

> "The nature and extent of an occupier's duty to a trespasser must be based on considerations of humanity (96 H) . . . But in applying that passage (*i.e.* Lord Atkin's classic passage in *Donoghue v. Stevenson* to trespassers it must be remembered that the neighbourhood relationship has been forced on the occupier . . . and it would therefore be unjust to subject him to the full obligations resulting from it in the ordinary way. The rights and interests of the occupier must have full consideration. No unreasonable burden can be put on him. With regard to dangers which have arisen on his land without his knowledge he can have no obligation to make enquiries or inspection. With regard to dangers of which he has knowledge but which he did not create he cannot be required to incur what for him would be large expense. If the occupier creates the danger when he knows that there is a chance that trespassers will come that way and will not see or realise the danger he may have to do more. There may be difficult cases where the occupier will be hampered in the conduct of his own affairs if he has to take elaborate precautions . . . The more serious the danger the greater is the obligation to avoid it. And if the dangerous thing or something near it is an allurement to children that may greatly increase the chance that children will come there" (97 H–98 B).

Lord Reid (98 C) observed that the duty to a trespasser was owed when the occupier knew facts showing a "substantial chance" that trespassers might come. The standard of care might be higher if the anticipated trespassers were children, because here mere warning was generally of little value (98 E). In the end, "the problem . . . is to determine what would have been the decision of a humane man with the financial and other limitations of the occupier" (98 F).

N.B. Herrington **1** was hardly mentioned as an authority, perhaps because Australian law which, in general, still retains the old law of invitee and licensee was alone involved. But it would seem that in reality the opinion of the Board is an amplification of *Herrington* **1**. If this is so, the partially subjective test of an occupier's standard of care has been endorsed (see note to **1** above).)

4. Penny v. Northampton B.C. (1974) 118 S.J. 628; 72 L.G.R. 733, C.A.

Defendants, owners of rubbish tip, took precautions to chase children off, but to erect effective fence would have been prohibitively expensive—*Held*, defendants not liable, as they had not acted contrary to the dictates of common sense and common humanity.

5. Harris v. Birkenhead Corporation [1976] 1 W.L.R. 279; [1976] 1 All E.R. 341. C.A.

Local authority occupiers of empty house which became vandalised—at the time they were not aware that the old occupier had left in pursuance of notices served by them—infant plaintiff aged four-and-a-half wandered in through open front door—went upstairs and fell out through window (which was either smashed or open)—the local authority contended that they could not owe a duty to the plaintiff (which they would ordinarily have performed by bricking up the doors), as they had no actual knowledge of the situation and thus, applying Lord Diplock's words in *Herrington* **1**, could not be liable—*Held*, not so, as they had served the notices on the old occupier, and were thus put on notice that the house was likely to become empty, and moreover they had officers who were moving about in the clearance area at the time and who, if they had looked, could have seen that the house was empty and derelict; moreover the local authority well knew that derelict houses in the area would quickly become vandalised. "It has long been accepted that a man cannot claim he has no knowledge when he shuts his eyes to the obvious. Nor can he claim that he has no knowledge when he has knowledge of what are sometimes called primary facts and has not drawn the inferences which can reasonably be drawn from those primary facts . . . It seems to me . . . that the knowledge which the corporation was proved to have was the kind of 'actual knowledge' which Lord Diplock envisaged in *Herrington* **1**" (Lawton L.J., 352 E and H).

6. Lowry v. Buchanan [1980] 3 N.I.J.B.; [1980] C.L.Y. 1973, N.I.C.A.

P trespassed into partly burnt house; and a board gave way—*Held* occupier not liable. The duty of an occupier was to act with common humanity, and this only arose when the occupier knew of the facts constituting the dagner, and the trespasser did not.

7. Davies v. B.R.B. (1984) 134 New L.J. 888; [1984] C.L.Y. 2309, Farquharson J.

Child trespasser on a railway line—*Held*, repair left something to be desired, but D not failing in its duty. See Chap. 14, 56.

8. Hulse v. Manchester C.C. (1986) (Unreported) C.A. 59; C.L.Y. (unrep. cases) 41 C.A.T. 59

Infant plaintiff who had been playing outside school fence climbed overhanging branches to retrieve a stick used to obtain acorns, and fell sustaining injury—*Held*, accident of special kind and not reasonably foreseeable. Defendants were entilted to regard the risk as so remote as not to call upon them to take any special measure to avoid it. Tree had been climbed not to gain access but to dislodge a piece of wood that had been thrown into the tree.

9. Adams v. Southern Electricity Board, *The Times*, October 21, 1993; [1993] 11 C.L.Y. 2994

Electricity Board owed a duty to an intelligent teenage boy to ensure that he was effectively prevented from climbing up a pole-mounted high-voltage electricty installation. The Board was in breach of its duty to take reasonable care for the safety of the plaintiff. (Liability arose because of regulations requiring anti-climbing device)

U1. Ward v. Norweb Plc (1991) C.A.

Boy of 15 gained access to roof of electricity substation and suffered severe burning injury—*Held* defendants were not liable as occupiers under 1984 Act because precautions taken to protect against intruders were reasonable in all the circumstances.

U2. Wiltshire v. B.R.B. (1992) C.A. 1243

Boy, aged 14, climbed on to stationary railway carriage roof and severely injured by electrical burns from cable overhead—*Held*, D not liable, as no reasonable occupier could have done more. *Parnett v. McGuiness* (supra) **2** considered.

(6) Defences

(*N.B.* The cases listed here are those where an *Occupier* is sued. More generally, reference should be made to Chap. 2, Chap. 4 and Chap. 5. See also sections dealing with defences under Chap. 15 and 16, Chap. 7 and Chap. 8, which may in appropriate cases provide analogies).

(a) Act of Stranger (Including Children)

1. Woodman v. Richardson (1937) 81 S.J. 700; [1937] 3 All E.R. 866, C.A.

Plaintiff employed by sub-contractors injured when using a defective ladder on a building site scaffold—sues main contractors—*Held*, defendants not liable, as no evidence that any of defendants' servants or agents placed ladder in position or knew or ought to have known of defect.

2. Coates v. Rawtenstall B.C. [1937] 3 All E.R. 602, C.A.

Defendants leave chain unsecured at bottom of chute which is put to dangerous use by children—*Held*, defendants liable, as they knew of this likelihood.

3. Canter v. Gardner [1940] 1 All E.R. 325; 56 T.L.R. 305, Tucker J.

Held, defendants not liable, as they had fixed cover securely. If they had not, their duty would have been to inspect and/or warn.

4. Rochman v. Hall [1947] 1 All E.R. 895, Birkett J.

Landlord employed competent engineers to look after lift—between visits someone tampered with safety device—*Held*, there was no real evidence of any foreseeable danger against which landlord should guard.

5. Cuttress v. Scaffolding [1953] 1 W.L.R. 1311; [1953] 2 All E.R. 1075, C.A.

Scaffold on building site with rope hanging 35 feet above ground—children pull it over—*Held*, not an allurement, and as defendants could not have foreseen the probability of children pulling it over, not liable. *cf.* the case of *Davis v. St. Mary's Demolition* (Chap. 7, (2)(f) **6**), where defendants were not occupiers and were found liable.

6. Birchall v. Bibby [1953] 1 All E.R. 163; 1 Lloyd's Rep. 175, Jones J.

Held, res ipsa loquitur, but on the facts defendants had proved rope had been maliciously cut by some unknown person, and therefore not liable.

7. Banks v. Mersey Docks and Harbour Board [1956] 1 Lloyd's Rep. 147, C.A.

Held, defendants not liable, as ladder only proved to have been there for 36 hours, and this was not long enough to fix defendants with knowledge. See Chap. 10, (4)(b) **10**.

8. Richards v. W. F. White [1957] 1 Lloyd's Rep. 367, Ashworth J.

Held, defendant shipowner not liable, as patch of oil had only been there for five to 55 minutes, which was not long enough to say that it should reasonably have been "caught" by a reasonable system of inspection. *Cf.* **7**

9. Smith v. Austin Lifts [1959] 1 W.L.R. 100; [1959] 1 All E.R. 814, M.L.
Lord Simonds (85 A): "The premises were theirs; the duty to repair the door was theirs, though they tried to shift it; the responsibility for what was done must be theirs, unless they can prove that it lay with another." *But* the other Law Lords did not deal directly with this point; Lords Morton and Somervell thought that the defect was attributable to an act of the occupiers' servants on a balance of probabilities; Lord Denning thought that the defect was directly attributable to an original want of repair.

10. Tynan v. Bailey (1972) 116 S.J. 922; [1972] C.L.Y. 2348, C.A.

Held, defendants (who were owners of private road) not liable.

11. Harris v. Birkenhead Corporation [1976] 1 W.L.R. 279; [1976] 1 All E.R. 341, C.A.

Local authority became occupiers of empty house awaiting demolition (see Chap. 10, (1) (**14**)—was then vandalised and became dangerous—*Held*, local authority liable. For further details see Chap. 10, (5)(f) **5**.

12. Ward v. Cannock Chase D. C. [1986] Ch. 546; [1985] 3 All E.R. 537, Scott J.

D's property untenanted and uninhabited. Damage by thieves and vandals over a period of time to plaintiff's adjoining property as a consequence. Liability in negligence admitted, but question arose as to extent of liability for subsequent damage—*Held*, test of whether or not act of stranger too remote depended on: (a) what might reasonably have been foreseen as a consequence of the original act or omission, (b) whether damage sufficiently connected with the original act or omission to be recoverable and (c) whether intervening act was very thing which was likely to happen as a result of original act or omission. Here, the chain of causation leading from the council's breach of duty to the damage to the house belonging to P not broken and damage was not too remote as to be recoverable.

13. Cunningham v. Reading Football Club [1992] P.I.Q.R. P141; [1991] C.L.Y. 3413, Drake J.

Plaintiff police officers injured at football match by concrete thrown from terraces by rival fans from Bristol—*Held*, in a claim brought under the Occupiers' Liability Act 1957, Reading Football Club were liable as occupiers, having learnt at earlier match that concrete could easily be broken up and used as missiles, and that no reasonable steps had been taken to prevent a recurrence. A prudent occupier would have taken steps to remove or minimise the risk, which was clearly foreseeable, and by implication the chain of causation was not broken by the activities of the hooligan element, (*Lamb v. Camden London B.C.* [1981] 2 All E.R. 408 and dicta of Oliver L.J. applied). See also Chap. 1, (5)(c), 20.

U1. Beigan v. Liverpool C.C. (1991) C.A. 1265

See Chap. 10, (4)(d), U2.

(b) Act of Independent Contractor

(*N.B.* The law here is now governed by the Occupiers' Liability Act 1957, s.2(4)(b), which in effect confirms *Haseldine v. Daw* **2** and *Green v. Fibreglass* **14**, and overrules the dicta in *Thomson v. Cremin* **8**.)

		Whether occupier liable
Repairs by I.C.—lift—left defective	1	No
REPAIRS BY I.C.—LIFT—LEFT DEFECTIVE	2	No
HATCH LEFT UNCOVERED BY I.C.	3	Yes
MAINTENANCE BY I.C.—SNOW LEFT ON STEPS	4	Yes
REPAIRS BY I.C.—FAULTY WIRING AMOUNTING TO NUISANCE	5	Yes
Hatch left uncovered by I.C.	6	Yes
Statutory duty to make safe resting on I.C.—duty of occupier to ensure done—open hatch	6	
Repairs by I.C.—nut on weighing machine projecting	7	Yes
Shoring insecurely fixed by I.C.	8	Yes
Defence of I.C. never available to occupier	8	
Bad stowage on ship by I.C.—dangerous to unload	9	N.A.
Danger left on ship by I.C.	10	Yes
Hatch cover interfered with by I.C.	11	No
Bad stowage on ship by I.C.—dangerous to unload	12	No
Patch of oil—left by I.C.	13	No
Repairs by I.C.—faulty wiring	14	No
GENERAL RESTATEMENT OF PRINCIPLES	15	
Proposition that defence of I.C. never available to occupier criticised	16	
Repairs by ship repairer—nut left loose causing leak and damage to cargo	17	Yes
Dangerous glass in door constructed by I.C.	U1	No
Warehouse repair work by I.C.	U2	No

1. Morgan v. Girls' Friendly Society [1936] 1 All E.R. 404; 80 S.J. 323, Horridge J.

Plaintiff a licensee of defendant, owner of premises—lift door open but no lift inside—plaintiff goes down shaft—defendant employed independent contractors to look after lift—*Held*, negligence was that of independent contractors only and defendant neither knew nor ought to have known of danger.

2. Haseldine v. Daw [1941] 2 K.B. 343; [1941] 3 All E.R. 156, C.A.

Held, occupier who had employed competent contractors to look after lift was not liable for defective state of lift. *N.B.* Contractors were held liable.

3. Wilkinson v. Rea [1941] 1 K.B. 688; [1941] 2 All E.R. 50, C.A.

Coal contractors negligent in removal of hatch cover and failure to guard hatch—are shipowners liable to their invitee?—*Held*, yes, the *ratio decidendi* being explained by Luxmoore L.J. as being that the contractors were employed by the shipowners to do a job which created a danger, and therefore owners were liable, but *aliter* if the job involved no inherent danger, but only became dangerous because of some casual neglect by the contractors (60 H). 75 per cent. against contractor, 25 per cent. against shipowners. Approved by H.L. in **8**.

4. Woodward v. Mayor of Hastings [1945] K.B. 174; [1944] 2 All E.R. 565, C.A.

Negligent school cleaner—school governors say she was an independent contractor—*Held*, that if she was she was still performing a duty which was incumbent on defendants, and therefore defendants could not rely on defence of independent contractor.

5. Spicer v. Smee [1946] 1 All E.R. 489, Atkinson J.

Held, act of independent contractor no defence in nuisance.

6. Grant v. Sun Shipping [1948] A.C. 549; [1948] 2 All E.R. 238, H.L.

Ship repairers leave hatch uncovered and unlit—breach of statutory duty by repairers—plaintiff (not employed by either defendant) falls down hatch—sues shipowner, *inter alia*, at common law as invitor—*Held*, shipowner liable, as they were not entitled to rely on telling repairers to make secure, but must ensure it was done. It would appear that this was a case where there was a duty on the occupier to ensure that one invitee created no danger for another.

7. Bloomstein v. Railway Executive [1952] 2 All E.R. 418; [1952] W.N. 378, Parker J.

Projecting nut on weighing machine in railway station—defendants plead they employed a competent independent contractor—*Held*, distinguishing **2**, no defence, because the principle in **2**, only applied to cases where defendant "cannot properly perform his duties because he has not got the technical knowledge and experience, without an independent contractor".

8. Thomson v. Cremin [1956] 1 W.L.R. 103; [1953] 2 All E.R. 1185, H.L.

Wooden shore insecurely fixed by shipwrights in Australia—falls on plaintiff when unloading ship—*Held*, shipowners were liable for negligence of shipwrights. approved. The H.L. treated the case as one of fact rather than law, but Lord Simon (with whose speech Lord Romer concurred) and Lord Wright both said, in effect, that it was no defence for the shipowner to rely on independent contractors, and Lord Wright (1191 H) went further and said that the invitor could never rely on defence of independent contractor with regard to unsafety of premises. Followed in **9**. See criticism of decision by H.L. in **16**.

9. Keen v. Lykiardopoulo [1953] 2 Lloyd's Rep. 349, Jones J.

Plaintiff dock labourer injured when unloading dangerously stowed cargo on defendants' ship—*Held*, defendants were not liable on the ground that it was a usual danger, but it was admitted that, following **8**, defendants would be liable for negligence of loading stevedores, and could not rely on act of independent contractor. See **8**.

10. Norton v. Straits S.S. Co. [1954] 2 Lloyd's Rep. 635, Streatfeild J.

Held, perhaps *obiter*, that, applying **8**, shipowner would be liable to invitees for default of independent contractors.

11. Thompson v. Anglo-Saxon Petroleum [1955] 2 Lloyd's Rep. 363, Oliver J.

Casual negligence by independent contractors of shipowner in interfering with a hatch cover—*Held*, shipowner not liable, though if there had been evidence from which it could have been inferred that they knew or ought to have known, they would have been liable (367, col. 1). The judge referred to the difficulty of reconciling *Haseldine v. Daw* **2** with *Thomson v. Cremin* **8**.

12. Jeyes v. Currie Line & Port of London Authority [1956] 2 Lloyd's Rep. 87, Pearce J.

Unloading of barrels—barrels overstowed with consequent danger to unloading stevedores—latter, plaintiff's employers, found liable for failing to safeguard plaintiff—*Held*, shipowner not liable, because (92) they had "no reason to suppose there was any unusual danger for the dockers." The question of shipowners' liability for the loading stevedores was not canvassed. See **9**.

13. Richards v. W. F. White [1957] 1 Lloyd's Rep. 367, Ashworth J.

Held, defendant shipowner not liable, as patch of oil had only been there for five to 55 minutes, which was not long enough to say that it should reasonably have been "caught" by a reasonable system of inspection. *Cf. Banks v. M.D.H.B.* (Chap. 10,(6) (a)7).

14. Green v. Fibreglass [1958] 2 Q.B. 245; [1958] 2 All E.R. 521, Salmon J.

Defendants were tenants of offices since 1951—had premises rewired by competent electricians—plaintiff an invitee injured when touching an electric fire which though off was live—defendants had no reason to suspect defect—did not regularly inspect wiring—*Held*, defendants not liable, as they had discharged their duty by employing competent independent contractors, since electric wiring required technical knowledge which defendants could not possess themselves. **8** *distinguished* and dictum of Lord Wright therein at 1191 H *criticised.*

15. Walsh v. Holst [1958] 1 W.L.R. 800; [1958] 3 All E.R. 33, C.A.

Brick from building under repair struck plaintiff on highway—occupier and contractor sued—*Held*, occupier liable for negligence of contractor (except for casual or collateral negligence—which neither defendant tried to set up), but on the facts defendants had taken all reasonable care and neither liable. Hodson L.J. (36 G) cited with approval following extract from *Penny v. Wimbledon U.C.* [1899] 2 Q.B. 72 at 78: "When a person through a contractor does work which from its nature is liable to cause injury to others, there is a duty on his part to take all reasonable precautions against such danger, and he does not escape from liability for the discharge of that duty by employing the contractor if the latter does not take these precautions ... Accidents arising from ... casual or collateral negligence ... do not come within this rule." Morris L.J. (38 B), who agreed on this point but dissented on main issue, cited Denning L.J. in *Cassidy v. M/H* [1951] 1 All E.R. 574 at 586 " ... Where a person is himself under a duty to use care, he cannot get rid of his responsibility by delegating the performance of it to someone else, no matter whether ... to a servant ... or an independent contractor."

16. Davie v. New Merton Board Mills [1959] A.C. 604; [1959] 1 All E.R. 346, H.L.

A master and servant case—but in course of judgment Lord Reid said defendants never pleaded act of independent contractor in **8** and therefore on this question it was *obiter*. Lord Keith agreed and said it might no longer be binding.

17. Riverstone Meat Co. v. Lancashire Shipping Co. [1961] A.C. 807; [1961] 1 All E.R. 495, H.L.

A ship leaked because a fitter employed by ship repairers had negligently failed to tighten a nut during repairs—cargo was damaged as a result—cargo owners sued shipowners under a term imported into the bill of lading by the Hague Rules, that the shipowners should exercise due diligence to make ship seaworthy, this term being very much the same as a duty to take reasonable care—*Held*, shipowners were liable for the default of the independent contractor. Lord Simonds said that no one doubted that in some cases a defendant would not be liable for the negligence of an independent contractor, while in others he would, and that, without attempting to reconcile all the cases on the subject, it was patent that here the obligation of the shipowner came into the latter category.

U1. Smith v. Storey (1980) C.A. 504

Plaintiff leaving defendant's shop collided with plate glass panel in door. Panel broke, injuring plaintiff. Defendant had engaged competent shop-fitters to install shop front. Shop-fitters had installed plate glass in breach of B.S.I. Code of Practice—*Held*, defendant had discharged common duty of care by entrusting work to shop-fitters. There was nothing to put him on inquiry that the glass was dangerous.

U2. Dyson v. L.E. Sims & Partners Ltd (1984) C.A. 1004

Defendants, owners of warehouse had acted reasonably in entrusting repair work to contractors who were competent, and had taken all necessary steps to see that the work was done: Occupiers' Liability Act 1957, s. 2(4).

(c) Knowledge of Plaintiff and Warning

(*N.B.* The law here is governed by the Occupiers' Liability Act 1957, s. 2(4)(a), which provides that a warning does not necessarily in itself absolve the occupier. Warning and knowledge of the danger are merely two of the factors to be considered in deciding whether, in all the circumstances, reasonable care has been taken by the occupier.)

1. Gould v. McAuliffe [1941] 2 All E.R. 527; 57 T.L.R. 527, C.A.

Dangerous dog in yard of inn—plaintiff an invitee—no warning—*Held*, defendant liable.

2. O'Dowd v. Fraser Nash [1951] C.L.C. 6778; [1951] W.N. 173, McNair J.

Doctor killed by car leaving track during practice—organisers had issued deceased with a handbook warning him of danger—*Held*, defendants not liable.

3. London Graving Dock v. Horton [1951] A.C. 737; [1951] 2 All E.R. 1, H.L.

4. Gough v. National Coal Board [1954] 1 Q.B. 191; [1953] 2 All E.R. 1283, C.A.

Child licensee injured by slow-moving colliery truck—*Held*, defendants liable, as, *inter alia*, a specific warning was "no defence if child was not old enough to appreciate the danger of what he was doing".

5. Greene v. Chelsea B.C. [1954] 2 Q.B. 127; [1954] 2 All E.R. 318, C.A.

Dangerous ceiling in requisitioned house—Denning L.J. *said* (325 G) that plaintiff's knowledge of danger did not bar her claim, because she was not free to avoid the danger. See now **12**.

6. Wingrove v. Prestige [1954] 1 W.L.R. 524; [1954] 1 All E.R. 576, C.A.

Plaintiff clerk of works (and invitee) on building site—hits head on low pole across passageway—*Held*, a danger, but as plaintiff had full knowledge thereof, claim failed.

7. Catherall v. Cunard [1954] 2 Lloyd's Rep. 303, Jones J.

Unauthorised use of conveyor belt on ship—*Held*, defendants not liable: "It is perfectly true that there was no notice to that effect, but why should there be? It is just ordinary common sense that they should not be used in this way" (308, col. 1).

8. McKirdy v. Royal Mail Lines (1955) 105 L.J. 586

Held, that the onus of proving plaintiff knew of the danger was on defendants.

9. Uctkos v. Mazzetta [1956] 1 Lloyd's Rep. 209, Ormerod J.

Held, defendant not liable, as, whether plaintiff was an invitee or licensee, defendant's warning to plaintiff was an ample discharge of his duty.

10. Dyer v. Ilfracombe U.D.C. [1956] 1 W.L.R. 218, [1956] 1 All E.R. 581, C.A.

See Chap. 10, (5)(e) **12**—"nor do I think it is their duty to put up notices to the effect that children under five—or whatever the age may be—are not permitted on the chutes or swings. If they did so, children would not take much notice, and if an accident happened, it would be said: 'What is the good of putting up notices unless you see they are observed?" ' (Singleton L.J. at 589 F).

11. Ashdown v. Samuel Williams [1957] 1 Q.B. 409; [1957] 1 All E.R. 35, C.A.

Plaintiff a licensee run down by a negligently shunted truck—warning notice at entrance which plaintiff saw but only read first three lines thereof—first three lines only dealt with condition of land, but later on notice also exempted negligent acts—*Held*, plaintiff was bound by the terms of the notice as a whole, just as she would be in contract. Although it did not arise in present case, Parker L.J. (47 H) said: "A mere reference to negligence without a warning as to the user of the land might well be insufficient."

12. A. C. Billings v. Riden [1957] A.C. 240, [1957] 3 All E.R., H.L.

Lord Reid (9 H, Lords Simonds and Cohen concurring): "It is sometimes said that, when a visitor goes on knowing the risk, the test is whether he was free to choose or acted under some constraint.... If this test leads to the same answer as the question, whether in all the circumstances, the visitor acted reasonably, well and good; but if not, I think that, in cases like the present, reasonableness is the better test and more in accordance with principle. Defendant is bound to take reasonable care, but he is entitled to expect that a visitor will behave in a reasonable manner." *N.B.* In this case it was a contractor, and not the occupier, who was sued.

13. Gledhill v. Liverpool Abattoir [1957] 1 W.L.R. 1028; [1957] 3 All E.R. 117, C.A.

Liverpool Corporation were the occupiers of abattoir in which plaintiff was employed by other defendant—unsuitable chains provided by corporation for slinging pigs—on the basis (which was not decided) that liability of corporation to plaintiff must be judged as between invitor and invitee—*Held*, corporation not liable, because (following *Horton* **3**) plaintiff had full knowledge of the danger. *But cf.* **12**.

14. Smith v. Austin Lifts [1959] 1 W.L.R. 100; [1959] 1 All E.R. 81, H.L.

Plaintiff gave a door a tug—thought it seemed safe enough as it would not budge—then used it as a handhold to pull himself up to the top of a ladder—the door gave way—*Held*, plaintiff was entitled to recover as he had not got "full appreciation of the danger." Lord Simonds (85 B): "He had, it is true, some apprehension of risk, but he did not appreciate, nor could he reasonably have been expected to appreciate, that ... the door would give way if pressure was applied higher up." Lord Morton expressed doubt, but did not dissent. Lord Somervell (93 C) agreed in effect with Lord Simonds, but added that the test was a purely subjective one as to what the particular plaintiff thought (as opposed to the objective test of what a reasonable man would appreciate), with which Lord Reid (91 C) and Lord Denning (93 D) agreed. Lord Denning said (93 E): "If a man, faced with a dangerous means of getting across a gap, mistakes the risk, saying to himself: 'I know it is a bit risky, but so long as I am careful, I shall be all right,' he is under no disability. But if he truly measures the risk, saying: 'No matter how careful I am, it is very likely I shall fall,' and still goes on, he cannot recover."

15. Bunker v. Charles Brand [1969] 2 Q.B. 480; [1969] 2 All E.R. 59, O'Connor J.

(d) Trespass on an Object

1. Hillen v. I.C.T. [1936] A.C. 65, H.L.

Held, as plaintiff trespasser on hatch cover defendant shipowner not liable as no duty of care as occupier owed. *But* see *Herrington* (Chap. 10(5)(f) **1**).

2. Gough v. National Coal Board [1954] 1 Q.B. 191; [1953] 2 All E.R. 1283, C.A.

Held, slow-moving colliery trucks were an allurement and a trap—*Held*, further, that no defence to say that child, though a licensee on the land, was a trespasser on the truck. "Such a contention destroys the whole doctrine of allurement to children" (*per* Hodson L.J. at 1295 A).

3. Bates v. Stone Parish Council [1954] 1 W.L.R. 1249; [1954] 3 All E.R. 38, C.A.

Playground with chute having 12-foot-high platform—gap between rails of platform $13\frac{1}{2}$ in. by $131\frac{1}{2}$ in.—in 1934 a child fell through—additional rails were put up as a result, but later they disappeared—plaintiff aged three-and-a-half went to playground with child of six—he fell through gap—*Held*, plaintiff was a licensee and defendants were liable. It was contended plaintiff was a trespasser on the chute, but C.A., approving **2**, rejected this as "impossible" (Somervell L.J., 41 H).

4. Creed v. McGeoch [1955] 1 W.L.R. 1005; [1955] 3 All E.R. 123, Ashworth J.

Defendants were contractors not in occupation of land in question—left trailer—children known to play—plaintiff aged five injured when playing see-saw on trailer—*Held*, that, since defendants were not in occupation, they owed duty under *Donoghue v. Stevenson*, and since they were aware of the risk of injury to children and knew that it was attractive to children, they were liable; and that, by analogy with **2**, the defence of trespass on an object was not available to them in a case where they "negligently left a dangerous and attractive object in a place where children are known to play" (128 D).

(7) Liability of Occupier to Persons on Adjoining Premises

(*N.B.* In respect of the escape of dangerous things, see also Chap. 8.)

1. Shirvell v. Hackwood Estates [1938] 2 K.B. 577; [1938] 2 All E.R. 1, C.A.
A landlord and tenant case—*Held*, landlord was not liable for fall of overhanging branch from his land onto demised premises, because danger existed at date of demise (see Chap. 10, (8)(a) **1** for full details). At 594 Greer L.J. referred to *Cunard v. Antifyre* [1933] 1 K.B. 551, D.C. (where landlord was held liable to sub-tenant for failing to repair dangerous gutter on landlord's part of premises) and said that the decision was due to the fact that the defect only arose after the date of the lease; if defect existed at date of lease, decision was wrong inasmuch as it meant that the landlord's duty towards tenants was the same as that of ordinary adjacent occupier. See Chap. 10, (8), *passim*.

2. Taylor v. Liverpool Corporation [1939] 3 All E.R. 329

Defective chimney stack, known by defendants to be so, injures tenant of three rooms in house and daughter while they are in yard—*Held*, yard not part of demised premises, so that both plaintiffs can recover in any case, but even if it was, the fact that chimney not part of demise would enable both plaintiffs to recover under *Cunard v. Antifyre* [1933] 1 K.B. 551.

3. Wringe v. Cohen [1939] 4 All E.R. 241; [1940] 1 K.B. 229, C.A.

Held, knowledge of want of repair immaterial. Atkinson J. at 243 F: "In our judgment, if owing to want of repair, premises upon a highway become dangerous and therefore a nuisance, and a passer-by or adjoining owner suffers damage by their collapse, the occupier, or owner if he has undertaken the duty to repair, is answerable, whether or not he knew or ought to have known of the danger . . . On the other hand if the nuisance is created not by want of repair, but for example by the act of a trespasser, or by a secret and unobservable operation by nature, such as a subsidence . . . neither an occupier nor an owner . . . is answerable, unless with knowledge or means of knowledge he allows the danger to continue."

4. Courage v. Meakers Garages [1948] C.L.C. 6676; 98 L.J. 163, Roxburgh J.

Held, defendants liable.

5. Goldman v. Hargrave [1967] 1 A.C. 645; [1966] 2 All E.R. 989, P.C.

Redgum tree hit by lightning—caught fire—occupier cut it down and left it to burn itself out—wind fanned flames and carried them onto adjacent premises—*Held*, occupier owed a duty of care to prevent fire spreading, and the standard was to do "what it was reasonable to expect of him in his individual circumstances" (Lord Wilberforce, 996 D).

6. McDowell v. F.M.C. (1968) 5 K.I.R. 456; [1968] C.L.Y. 2648, C.A.

Defendants, occupiers of site of agricultural show, were aware of a live overhead cable 22 feet above site—deceased manager of one of the stands erected a flagpole which fell against the cable and electrocuted him—*Held*, defendants liable as occupiers and organisers of show for not warning of danger, but manager was guilty of 20 per cent, contributory negligence.

7. Knight v. Hext (1979) 253 E.G. 1227; [1980] C.L.Y. 1884, C.A.

8. Leakey v. National Trust [1980] Q.B. 485; [1980] 1 All E.R. 17, C.A.

Landslip from hill owned and occupied by defendants came onto and/or threatened the properties of the plaintiffs. Landslip was entirely due to natural causes. *Held*, applying *Goldman* **5**, defendants owed a duty of care, and the standard of care required was as set out by Lord Wilberforce in *Goldman*, and included "the factor of what the particular man, not the average man, could be expected to do, having regard, amongst other things, where a serious expenditure of money is required . . . to his means." (37 C).

9. Bradburn v. Lindsay [1983] 2 All E.R. 408; [1983] C.L.Y. 2741, Judge Blackett-Ord, V.C.

P owned and occupied one and D the other of semi-detached properties built as a unit. D allowed her property to become derelict, due partly to dry rot. D's property demolished by local authority, leaving party wall largely unsupported. In addition to loss of support, P's property was exposed to damage from dry rot and decay as result of D's failure to repair. P sued D in negligence and nuisance—*Held*, applying *Leakey v. National Trust* **8**, that D was liable. She should have appreciated the dangers to P's property from dry rot and disrepair in her own property and taken the reasonable precautions open to her to prevent damage.

10. Tutton v. A. D. Walter Ltd [1986] Q.B. 61; [1985] 3 All E.R. 757, Denis Henry Q.C.

Bees on adjoining land of P were killed by pesticide which had been sprayed on rapeseed crop belonging to defendant farmer—*Held*, as it was known to D that the particular pesticide which he had used was harmful to bees, and as spraying the crop in full flower presented a foreseeable risk of injury to the bees nearby, D owed P a duty of care, and was in breach of that duty in not giving P adequate notice, and in failing to heed warnings about best time in which to spray crops.

11. King v. Liverpool C.C. [1986] 1 W L R 890; [1986] 3 All E.R. 544, C.A.

Plaintiff's council flat premises were flooded by water which escaped from vacant premises above after vandals had entered and removed plumbing installations. Action based upon a claim that defendant landlord should have secured vacant premises when it knew of risk to other tenants in building from vandals—*Held*, duty of landlord generally restricted in the circumstances because damage occasioned by third parties over whom landlord had no control and specifically, because landlord could not take effective steps to defeat activities of vandals, as even steel sheeting would not keep out the determined vandal. (*Quaere*: should the effectiveness of the steps to comply determine whether a duty exists in the first place?)

12. Stephens v. Anglian Water Authority [1981] 131 SJ. 1214; [1987] 3 All E.R. 379, C.A.

Landowner who abstracts underground water causes damage to adjoining land—*Held*, no liability to P because landowner was acting within his rights.

13. Smith v. Littlewoods Organisation Ltd [1987] 2 W L R 480; [1987] 1 All E.R. 710, H.L.

Fire started in respondent's empty cinema premises by vandals which caused damage to adjoining premises. Cinema owners were unaware of vandal activity previously, and although their premises had been left insecure, it was contended that they could not have foreseen the consequences of their alleged breach of duty. The House of Lords considered in depth the liability of an adjoining occupier for the acts of third parties—*held*, cinema owners could not be liable on the facts because the injury or damage was not the probable consequence of the tortfeasor's negligence, and could only have been foreseen as a mere possibility. Where damage had been caused by an independent human agency, liability could only arise where that damage was a highly likely consequence of the act or omission. *Per* Lord Goff; liability for harm caused by third parties did not depend only on establishing a special relationship between the tortfeasor and the third party, and there were other special circumstances in which the adjoining occupier owed a duty to neighbours for such acts of third parties, *e.g.* where a source of danger had been negligently created by him and it was reasonably foreseeable that third parties might interfere and spark off the danger, causing damage. See Chap. 1(3)(b) **24** and 5(5).

14. Hawkins v. Dhawan And Mishiku (1987) 19 H.L.R. 232; [1987] C.L.Y., 2909, C.A.

Blocked overflow pipe on D's premises caused flooding to P's premises—*Held* not liable. It would impose too high a duty on an occupier to inspect a waste outlet at regular intervals, and in the absence of anything which ought to have alerted his attention to the possibility of an overflow, there was no liability. Further, the tenant's (D's) obligations to his landlords were not analagous to those owed to his neighbour.

15. E. Hobbs (Farms) v. Baxenden Chemical Company Gerber Foods (Holdings) v. E. Hobbs (Farms) (1992) 1 Lloyd's Rep. 54; [1992] C.L.Y. 3204, Sir Michael Ogden Q.C.

In main and third party actions liability of occupier of barn for fire which spread to adjoining buildings was considered, as well as liability of manufacturer of foam which caused the fire to spread—*Held* in relation to adjoining occupier, not too remote.

(8) Liability of lessor or landlord

(a) For Condition of Demised Premises and Approaches Thereto

1. Shirvell v. Hackwood Estates [1938] 2 K.B. 577; [1938] 2 All E.R. 1, C.A.

Tenant took lease of farm which had a number of dangerous branches projecting from landlord's adjacent premises—five months later branch fell and killed tenant's servant—*Held*, defendants not liable, because servant could not be in better position than tenant himself (*Cavalier v. Pope* [1906] A.C. 428 at 430 followed), and any claim by tenant was barred by the rule that, fraud apart, a tenant took premises as they stood at the date of lease (*Robbins v. Jones* (1863) 15 C.B.(N.S.) 221 and Lord Macnaghten's speech in *Cavalier v. Pope* (*supra*) followed). *Cunard v. Antifyre* [1933] 1 K.B. 551, D.C. (which held a landlord liable to a sub-tenant for failure to repair guttering on landlord's part of premises) distinguished (594) on the ground that in *Cunard* defect was not in existence at the date of lease and/or that the attention of Divisional Court was not drawn to the difference between the liability of an occupier and that of a lessor in respect of adjacent premises.

2. Davis v. Foots [1940] 1 K.B. 116; [1939] 4 All E.R. 4, C.A.

Landlord lets unfurnished flat to tenant, removing gas fire—result tenant is gassed when gas turned on at mains—*Held*, tenant's widow had no cause of action in tort, nor, on the facts, any in contract (18).

3. Travers v. Gloucester Corporation [1947] K.B. 71; [1946] 2 All E.R. 506, Lewis J.

Tenant's lodger dies from inhaling gas fumes from geyser—*Held*, landlord under no liability for dangerous state of premises, although landlord had installed the geyser and knew of the defect.

4. Howard v. Walker [1947] K.B. 860; [1947] 2 All E.R. 197, Lord Goddard C.J.

Shopper injured on defective shop forecourt which was in occupation of tenant—tenant of shop liable, but is landlord?—no obligation to repair on either landlord or tenant, but landlord has power to repair and did in fact repair forecourt after accident—*Held*, landlord not liable, as (following dictum in *Wilchick v. Marks* [1934] 2 K.B. 66) "no duty was owed by landlord to visitors any more than to tenant." *Quaere* what would have been the position if plaintiff had merely used forecourt to deviate from highway and not to shop. See *Mint v. Good* (Chap. 12, (2) **9**. See **8**.

5. Hart v. Liverpool Corporation (1949) 65 T.L.R. 677; [1949] W.N. 412, C.A.

Held, tenant invitee on access road, and defendants liable for usual danger (hole).

6. Anderson v. Guinness Trust [1949] 1 All E.R. 530; [1949] W.N. 127, Hilbery J.

Irregular surface in courtyard—*Held*, this could not be described as a concealed danger, and as wife was only a licensee, claim failed.

7. Ball v. L.C.C. [1949] 2 K.B. 159; [1949] 1 All E.R. 1056, C.A.

During tenancy defendant landlords put in a new boiler which had no safety valve—it blew up when pipes became frozen and injured tenant's daughter—*Held*, defendants not liable because, although it was true that a landlord doing repairs during tenancy had no immunity as such and stood in same position as an ordinary contractor, *Malone v. Laskey* [1907] 2 K.B. 141, C.A. was binding authority for saying that a contractor repairing a house was not liable for negligence to a stranger to the contract, unless the work involved something which was "dangerous *per se*," which a boiler was not. Now *overruted* by *Billings v. Riden* (Chap. 7, (2) (a) **10**).

8. Jacobs v. L.C.C. [1950] A.C. 361; [1950] 1 All E.R. 737, H.L.

Held, plaintiff was only licensee of landlord, and as landlord did not know of danger on forecourt, plaintiff could not recover. It would appear that if landlord *had* known he would have been liable.

9. Turner v. Waterman [1961] 105 S.J. 1011; [1961] C.L.Y. 5840, Veale J.

Dry rot—landlord liable for repairs—tenant injured by collapse of floor board—landlord had recently replaced adjacent flooring on account of dry rot—*Held*, landlord liable as he should have known that wood adjacent to dry rot was liable to become infected and he should have inspected frequently.

10. Gallagher v. McDowell [1961] N.I.26, C.A.

Wife of tenant injured when heel of her shoe went through floor—*Held*, new trial must be ordered. Liability of landlord under *Donoghue v. Stevenson* examined and discussed.

11. Sharpe v. Sweeting [1963] 1 W.L.R. 665; [1963] 1 All E.R. 455, Nield J.

Builder building house for local authority so constructed canopy over doorway that it collapsed on wife of tenant—*Held*, builderh liable. **10** *approved.*

12. Appah v. Parncliffe Investment [1964] 1 W.L.R. 1064; [1964] 1 All E.R. 838, C.A.

Self-contained flatlet occupied by plaintiff as licensee, and not as tenant, of defendant—there had been a previous break in—as a result defendant had provided a mortice lock—but he did not give key of this lock to plaintiff, nor warn her of previous break in—plaintiff used vale lock—only—break in occurred again—*Held*, defendant was negligent. It was *conceded* that defendant would only owe a duty if plaintiff was a licensee, and not a tenant.

13. Irving v.L.C.C. (1965) 109 S.J. 157; C.L.Y. 2666, Paull J.

Plaintiff tenant of a flat slipped on slippery object on common staircase—which was unlit due to faulty time switch—*Held*, defendants had taken all reasonable care and were not liable. "The proposition that there is a duty on landlords to light common staircases at all times is too wide."

14. Wheat v. Lacon [1966] A.C. 552; [1966] 1 All E.R. 582, H.L.

Visitor lodging with manager in private quarters of public house was killed falling down back stairs—dusk—lighting sufficient during daylight—no electric light at bottom—and bulb at top missing—for bottom three steps walls receded and hand-rail on one side ceased—Winn J. found no negligence on the part of the manager as occupier, and there was no appeal from this—in H.L. brewers were held to be occupiers as well as manager (see Chap. 10 (1) **10**)—*Held*, on the above facts, they were not negligent either.

15. Moloney v. Lambeth B.C. (1966) 110 S.J. 406; *The Times*, May 19, 1966, Brabin J.

Held, defendants liable. Balustrade consisted of three horizontal rails $10\frac{1}{2}$ inches apart, supported by uprights four to five feet apart.

16. Brown v. Liverpool Corporation [1969] 3 All E.R. 1345, C.A.

Held, defendants liable, since the steps were an essential part of the means of access to the house and thus constituted part of the "building" so as to attract the duty to repair under the Housing Act 1961, s. 32 *Cf.* **U2**.

17. Smith v. Scott [1973] Ch. 314; [1972] 3 All E.R. 645, Pennycuick V.-C.

18. O'Brien v. Robinson [1973] 1 All E.R. 583; [1973] A.C. 912, H.L.

19. Liverpool C.C. v. Irwin [1976] 2 W.L.R. 562; [1976] 2 All E.R. 39 H.L.

Held, in the absence of any express stipulation, there must be implied into the contract of tenancy of a high-rise flat (a) an easement for the tenants and their licensees to use the stairs, (b) a right in the nature of an easement to use the lifts, and (c) an easement to use the rubbish chutes, and that the implication of these easements and rights also involved, again in the absence of express stipulation, an obligation on the landlord to take reasonable care to keep the facilities in question in reasonable repair and usability (Lord Wilberforce, 43 J and 45 J). But "the tenants themselves have their responsibilities. What is reasonable to expect of a landlord has a clear relation to what a reasonable set of tenants should do for themselves" (46 A)—*Held*, on the facts the landlords were not in breach of their obligations, but they were in breach of the covenant implied by the Housing Act 1961 s. 32, in respect of a water closet which overflowed on being used.

20. Campden Hill Towers v. Gardner [1977] A.C. 239 C.A.

21. Ryan v. L.B. of Camden (1983) 13 Fam. Law 81; [1983] C.L.Y. 2545, C.A.

Six month-old infant plaintiff rolled off bed and became trapped against heating pipes. It was alleged that the pipes ought to have been boxed or insulated as they constituted a danger to very young children. Heating system in common use and no record of previous accidents—*Held*, that the defendants were neither negligent nor in breach of the Defective Premises Act 1972 s 4. "Although it was not difficult to point to the hypothetical risks presented by the heating system, the experience of the local authority justified them in thinking that such risks as existed, that a small child might trap herself and get burnt, were in fact avoided by the precautions that parents in fact took" (Cumming-Bruce, L.J., 82). The local authority was entitled to expect parents to devise means of safeguarding their children against dangers resulting from the heating pipes. See also *Simkiss v. Rhondda B.C.*

22. Rimmer v. Liverpool C.C. [1985] Q.B. 1 [1984] 1 All E.R. 930, C.A.

Defendants designed and built flats in 1959 with dangerously thin glass panels in hall wall Plaintiff became tenant in 1974 and tripped and fell against panel, injuring self—*Held*, defendants liable *qua* designer/builders. Although it was still the law that a "bare" landlord letting unfurnished premises did not owe any common law duty of care (as per *Cavalier v. Pope* [1906] A.C. 428), he did owe a duty of care if responsible as designer or builder for creating a danger to those foreseeably affected by it! "The landowner who designs or builds a house or flat is no more immune from personal responsibility for faults of construction than an architect simply because he has disposed of his house or flat by letting or selling it . . . (The defendants) owed him, not as tenant, but, like his wife or his child, as a person who might reasonably be expected to be affected by the provision of a glass panel in the flat, a duty to take such care as was reasonable in all the circumstances to see that he was reasonably safe from personal injury caused by the glass panel" (Stephenson L.J., 938 A-C). However, to impose on a landlord a duty of care at common law *qua* landlord may be so great a change as to require legislation.

23. Collins v. N.I. Housing Executive [1985] C.L.Y. 2412 Carswell J.

Held, a duty of care was not owed to a the wife of tenant by a landlord to avoid causing her inconvenience or discomfort.

24. Stockley v. Knowsley M.B.C. (1986) 279 E.G. 677; [1986] C.L.Y. 2249, C.A.

P, tenant of council flat reported frozen pipes to landlords who did not attend to turn off water supply or to advise P how to do this *Held*, defendant landlord owed a duty of care to tenant to in respect of installations, and if it had not been practical to attend because of workload, should at least have advised the tenant how to isolate her water supply and prevent the serious consequences of a burst and subsequent thaw and flood.

25. Dear v. L.B. of Newham (1988) 20 H.L.R. 348; [1989] C.L.Y. 2551 C.A.

P injured by rubbish left uncollected on balcony of demised premises by local authority landlords. Liability of local authority considered under Public Health Act 1936 as well as under Occupiers' Liability Act 1957—*Held*, the rubbish in question did not come within the definition in the Public

Health Act 1936, s. 72, and as there was no obligation to remove, there could be no liability at common law, nor did any obligation arise under the Occupiers' Liability Act 1957: D not liable.

26. Jordan v. Achara (1988) 20 H.L.R. 607; [1989] C.L.Y. 2572, C.A.

P injured when falling down unlit common staircase in block of flats. Local authority responsible for electricity charge and not landlords—*Held*, payment by local authority of electricity charge did not excuse occupier landlord of his responsibilities, and therefore a duty of care was owed to visitors.

27. McNerney v. Lambeth L.B.C. (1988) H.L.R. 188; [1990] C.L.Y. 2871, C.A.

Held, landlord of unfurnished premises is not under a duty to ensure that the premises are reasonably safe for the tenant at the beginning of the letting.

28. Targett v. Torfaen B.C. (1991) 24 H.L.R. 164; [1992] C.L.Y. 3199, C.A.

P, tenant, fell down faulty steps leading to council house—*Held*, local authority liable because of negligent design and construction of the steps.

29. Mcauley v. Bristol CC [1992] Q.B. 134; [1992] 1 All E.R. 749, C.A.

P injured when she fell on broken concrete steps at her council house—*Held* landlords liable as a duty was owed under the Defective Premises Act 1972 s.4. The landlord had a right to enter the premises for the purposes of repair, and such a right carried with it an analogous duty of care.

30. Bailey v. L.B. of Newham [1993] C.L.Y. 3796, H.H. Judge Cooke

Landlord not under any higher duty in tort beyond obligations implied by statue or imposed in contract, therefore not liable to make flat premises reasonably secure.

U1. Cohen v. Erlichman (1952) C.A. 333

Plaintiff visitor to flat—hit by falling plaster on staircase—defendant knew plaster defective—*Held*, defendant liable.

U2. Hopwood v. Rugeley U.D.C. (1974) C.A. 394A; *The Times*, December 14, 1974

Sunken paving stone in back yard of house—over which plaintiff tripped—*Held*, applying the *ratio decidendi* of *Brown* **16**, the yard, since it was not an essential part of the means of access to the house, was not part of the "building" so as to attract the repairing duty under the Housing Act 1961, s. 32.

U3. Issit v. L.B. of Tower Hamlets (1983) C.A. 933

Boy of 26 months fell out of bathroom window immediately above wash hand basin—catch defective with missing screw—*Held*, defendant landlords not liable as it was not foreseeable that the absence of the screw rendered the window unsafe. Defect could have been rendered safe by the parents, and one does not expect small children to be completely unsupervised throughout the house. See also Chap. 10, (5)(e) U2.

U4. McDonagh v. Kent Area H.A. (1985) C.A. 553

D landlords, were owners of tenanted premises where P fell down steep staircase in her home—*Held*, D not occupiers of house within meaning of Occupiers Liability Act 1957 and owed no duty under Defective Premises Act 1972 in the absence of any inherent defect, previous accident or report of danger.

U5. Bamforth v. Jones (1991) C.A. 252

D was absentee owner of premises where ambulanceman injured when descending icy steps outside premises, carrying elderly patient—*Held*, D liable. Failed to discharge duty by relying on the voluntary activities of an elderly tenant to sweep snow of steps to keep them safe. This was an ordinary use of the premises and it was foreseeable that some heavy object could be carried down steps.

(b) For Dangers Arising from Lessor's Part of Premises

1. Shirvell v. Hackwood Estates [1938] 2 K.B. 577; [1938] 2 All E.R. 1, C.A.

Tenant took lease of farm which had a number of dangerous branches projecting from landlord's adjacent premises—five months later branch fell and killed tenant's servant—*Held*, defendants not liable, because servant could not be in better position than tenant himself (*Cavalier v. Pope* [1906] A.C. 428 at 430 followed), and any claim by tenant was barred by the rule that, fraud apart, a tenant took premises as they stood at the date of lease (*Robbins v. Jones* (1863) 15 C.B. (N.S.) 221 and Lord Macnaghten's speech in *Cavalier v. Pope* (*supra*) followed). *Cunard v. Antifyre* [1933] 1 K.B. 551, D.C. (which held a landlord liable to a sub-tenant for failure to repair guttering on landlord's part of the premises), distinguished (594) on the ground that in *Cunard* defect was not in existence at the date of lease and/or that the attention of Divisional Court was not drawn to the difference between the liability of an occupier and that of a lessor in respect of adjacent premises.

2. Taylor v. Liverpool Corporation [1939] 3 All E.R. 329, Stable J.

Defective chimney stack, known by defendants to be so, injures tenant of three rooms in house and daughter while they are in yard—*Held*, yard not part of demised premises, so that both plaintiffs can recover in any case, but even if it was, the fact that chimney not part of demise would enable both plaintiffs to recover under *Cunard v. Antifyre* [1933] 1 K.B. 551.

3. Kiddle v. City Business Premises [1942] 1 K.B. 269; [1942] 2 All E.R. 216, Goddard L.J. (sitting as an additional judge).

Held, no liability in the absence of negligence.

4. Peters v. Prince of Wales Theatre [1943] K.B. 73; [1942] 2 All E.R. 533, C.A.

Extensive sprinkler system extending both over landlord's and tenant's parts of same building—owing to frost landlord's part leaks onto tenant's part—*Held*, there being no negligence, defendants not liable. *Explained* that the reason for the rule derived from the implied consent of tenant at the time of going into occupation. Goddard L.J. *cites* a case, *Thomas v. Lewis* [1937] 1 All E.R. 137, where plaintiff had two fields, one rented from defendants, a quarry owner, and the other his own: the quarry caused damage to both fields: "as a tenant plaintiff had no cause of action, as an adjoining owner he had" (538 E).

5. Prosser v. Levy [1955] 1 W.L.R. 1224; [1955] 3 All E.R. 577, C.A.

Water escaped from landlord's pipe onto tenants' floor below—*Held*, that although consent to an ordinary water supply would normally be implied in the case of a tenant (586 G) or even where the parties occupied parts of the same building (585 E), and such consent to and/or common benefit derived from the supply would ordinarily be a defence, the defence would not be available if:

(a) "the supply is of quite an unusual kind, or is defective or dangerous, unless he knows of that" (586 G), or
(b) there was negligence on the part of defendant (586 H), and in the present case defendants were liable on both these counts.

Defendants had pleaded that the overflow was due to act of stranger—*Held*, however, they had not discharged the onus of so showing, and moreover the act, to be a defence, must not be mere negligence (see *Philco v. Spurling* (Chap. 8, (2) (b) **4**), but must be at least "a deliberate and mischievous act" (587 D). *Kiddle v. City Business* **3** and *Peters v. P.O.W.* **4** applied.

6. Evans v. Glasgow D.C. 1978 S.L.T. 17; [1978] C.L.Y. 1789, O.H.

Block of flats owned by D. Some left empty and unsecured. Vandals entered one and caused damage to P's flat *Held*, D, knowing of the risk of vandalism, were under a duty to secure empty flats, and were liable.

7. King v. Liverpool C.C. [1986] 1 WLR 379; [1986] 3 All E.R. C.A.

(9) Current Operations on Premises

1. Chettle v. Denton (1951) 95 S.J. 802; [1951] C.L.C. 6747, C.A.

Held, defendant negligent because although plaintiff was visible, defendant was concentrating on pigeon and did not look to see if plaintiff in line of fire.

2. Davis v. St. Mary's Demolition Co. [1954] 1 W.L.R. 592; [1954] 1 All E.R. 578, Ormerod J.

Defendants (*not* occupiers) demolishing buildings on site where trespassing children known to play—on Sunday plaintiff and other boys dislodge some loose bricks and bring wall down—*Held*, following *Buckland v. Guildford Gas Co.* (Chap. 7, (2)(c) **2**), plaintiff was a "neighbour," and defendants were liable for failing to take precautions.

3. Slater v. Clay Cross [1946] 2 Q.B. 264; [1946] 2 All E.R. 625, C.A.

Held, defendants liable for negligence of their engine driver in running down plaintiff in a tunnel in which she was a licensee. The negligence consisted of not stopping at entrance, not whistling and going at 8 m.p.h.

4. A. C. Billings v. Riden [1958] A.C. 240; [1957] 3 All E.R. 1, H.L.

Question of duty owed by contractors executing works to visitor to house—*Held* (*per* Lord Reid 4–5, Lords Simonds and Cohen concurring) that the fact that plaintiff was only a licensee *vis-á-vis* the occupier was no ground for limiting duty of contractor accordingly, but that their duty was to take reasonable care to ensure that visitors were not exposed to danger by their actions (5 C). Lord Somervell (13 D) put the duty in similar terms.

5. Doltis v. Braithwaite [1957] 1 Lloyd's Rep. 522, Streatfeild J.

See Chap. 8, (4) **21**—*Held* defendants not liable.

6. Miller v. South of Scotland Electricity Board, 1958 S.C. (H.L.) 20; [1958] C.L.Y. 2226, H.L.

Held, the failure of Electricity Board to switch current off (after they had reported they had done so) raised a prima facie case of negligence against Electricity Board, even though plaintiff boy was (it seems) a trespasser.

7. Commissioner for Railways v. McDermott [1966] 1 A.C. 169; [1966] 2 All E.R. 162, P.C.

Level crossing in Australia in bad condition—plaintiff stumbled and fell—and was run down by train coming round curve—plaintiff was a licensee—no Occupiers' Liability Act in Australia—it was argued that plaintiff, being a licensee, could not recover, as she knew the state of the crossing—*Held*, not so. There were two duties owed by the defendants, their duty as occupier and their duty as persons carrying on positive operations on their land. Any exemption from their duty under the first head would not affect their duty under the second, and here it was dangerous to run trains fast round the curve *when* the level crossing was in such a dangerous condition.

8. McArdle v. Andmac [1967] 1 W.L.R. 356, [1967] 1 All E.R. 583, C.A.

Held, main contractors owed a duty and were liable to employee of sub-contractors who fell down opening in roof left unfenced by other sub-contractors. Edmund Davies L.J. (592 B), relying on *Billings* **4**, said that the duty was closely analogous with that owed by an occupier.

11. CLUBS

1. Prole v. Allen [1950] 1 All E.R. 476; 209 L.T. 183, Pritchard J.

Held, no action lay against committee, but an action would and did lie against steward.

2. Shore v. Ministry of Works [1950] 2 All E.R. 227, C.A.

Held, no action would lie against committee; *sed quaere* if it had been a proprietary club.

3. Campbell v. Thompson [1953] 1 Q.B. 445; [1953] 1 All E.R. 831, Pilcher J.

Plaintiff a cleaner sued assistant honorary secretary and chairman of house committee—*Held*, representation order could properly be made authorising defendants to defend on behalf of members. On the facts however the claim failed.

4. Carroll v. Hibbert, The Times, March 22, 1967; [1967] C.L.Y. 429, John Stephenson J.

5. Robertson v. Ridley [1989] 1 W.L.R. 872 [1989] 2 All E.R. 474, C.A.

P. a club member, was injured on his club premises—*Held*, applying—cannot sue club, notwithstanding that club rules place responsibility on chairman and secretary for the conduct of the club or group.

6. Jones v. Northampton B.C. [1990] C.L.Y. 3274, C.A.

Duty of care owed by officer or member of a club to other members if he becomes aware of circumstances giving rise to a risk of injury.

7. Gesner v. Wallingford and District Labour Party Supporters Club, *The Times*, June 2, 1994; [1994] 6 C.L. 320

Duty of care owed by a club to its members—*Held*, such a duty was owed if a club was incorporated under the Industrial and Provident Societies Act 1965, s. 3.

U1. Hawkins v. Dowdeswell (1957) C.A. 269 A

Deceased fell down stairs of club leading from first floor to pavement level—deceased guest not member—defendants occupiers of club and staircase—steps made wet by persons coming in from rain—single light on landing at top of stairs—steep old-fashioned staircase—treads narrow—hand-rails on either side—where hand-rail fastened to wall and where water pipe between rail and wall person could not keep hand round rail—allegation that defendants negligent as could easily have built another safer staircase as they did after accident—*Held*, defendants not negligent—staircase in good repair and no traps.

12. HIGHWAY DANGERS

Most modern highway cases will concern the Highways Act 1959 or 1980 where the defendant is the highway authority, but older cases have been included for examples. The liability of statutory undertakers other than highway authorities is also dealt with in Chap. 12(1)(a), whilst those cases in Chap. 12, (1)(b) and Chap. 12, (2) are largely decided in negligence/nuisance.

(1) Dangers on Highway

(a) Statutory Undertaker as Defendant

1. Polkinghorn v. Lambeth B.C. [1938] 1 All E.R. 339; 54 T.L.R. 345, C.A.

Plaintiff runs into unlighted bollard at end of tram refuge—*Held*, defendants under a continuing duty to keep it lit, and were therefore liable. *Approved* in **6**.

2. Wells v. M.W.B. [1937] 4 All E.R. 639; 54 T.L.R. 104, Humphreys J.

Held, defendants liable to plaintiff for injuries sustained when she fell over upright lid.

3. Withington v. Bolton B.C. [1937] 3 All E.R. 108, Goddard J.

Stopcock box—projecting above level of unmade highway—protected by rammed earth round it—but earth weathered away leaving original projection—*Held*, defendants liable.

4. Simon v. Islington B.C. [1943] K.B. 188; [1943] 1 All E.R. 41, C.A.

Tramway company abandon a defective tramtrack to local authority—after transfer plaintiff injured thereby—*Held*, local authority liable, as (a) they took the tramtrack together with any liability for continuing nuisance or negligent disrepair (196 bottom), and (b) non-feasance was no defence, as it only applied to non-repair of road *qua* road.

5. Lewys v. Burnett [1945] 2 All E.R. 458; 61 T.L.R. 527, C.A.

Local authority, by raising road surface by six inches, reduce clearance from 9 feet 3 in. to 8 feet 9 in.—*Held*, negligent, despite warning notices.

6. Fisher v. Ruislip—Northwood U.D.C. [1945] K.B. 584; [1945] 2 All E.R. 458, C.A.

1, followed—*Held*, duty to light existed, and was part of general duty to take care to prevent obstruction becoming a danger to public. *Applied* in **8**.

7. Morris v. Luton Corporation [1946] 1 K.B. 114; [1946] 1 All E.R. 1, C.A.

Defendants had painted corners white, but had not lit it—*Held*, liable.

8. Whiting v. Middlesex C.C. [1948] 1 K.B. 162; [1947] 2 All E.R. 758, Croom-Johnson J.

Held, that the fact the street lighting was on did not necessarily absolve defendants from lighting unlit structure, unless street lighting is "so effective and so clear that anyone driving along the highway with due care and attention would find the shelter duly illuminated." **6** *applied*.

9. Longhurst v. Metropolitan Water Board [1948] 2 All E.R. 834; [1948] W.N. 418, H.L.

Stopcock leaked (which defendants remedied) causing percolation which loosened paving-stone some distance away over which plaintiff tripped—no evidence that defendants knew or ought to have known of this danger—*Held*, no negligence, and no liability in the absence of negligence. Lord Porter at 839 A: "My Lords, even in the case of a private individual, liability for nuisance without negligence or deliberate act is not readily established, apart of course from cases of the *Rylands v. Fletcher* type."

10. Wilson v. Kingston-upon-Thames Corporation [1949] 1 All E.R. 679; [1949] W.N. 121, C.A.

Cyclist injured by defective road surface—no repairs done except occasional patching up with tarmac—*Held*, condition of road due to non-feasance, and defendants not liable. *N.B.* There was no evidence tarmac patching had been negligently done. *Approved* in **13**.

11. Rider v. Metropolitan Water Board [1949] 2 K.B. 378; [1949] 2 All E.R. 97, Devlin J.

A very complicated case, turning mainly on the fact that the highway authority had undertaken some of the reinstatement, and on the application of the Metropolis Management Act 1855, s. 114.

12. Baxter v. Stockton-on-Tees Corporation [1959] 1 Q.B. 441; [1958] 2 All E.R. 675, C.A.

Awkward approach to roundabout—accident—judge finds roundabout was negligently designed—it had been designed and built by county council who had transferred the road under statutory powers to the defendants—on the assumption (which C.A. doubted) that there was negligence in design—*Held*, defendants were not liable, as they had not created the danger and therefore non-feasance was a defence. The C.A. were asked to say defendants were under a duty to light and warn similar to that in. **1** and **6**, but said *no*, because in the present case the difference was the defendants had not created the danger. C.A. also *held* (probably *obiter*) that an action would lie against a highway authority which failed to take reasonable care to construct a reasonably safe road.

13. Burton v. West Suffolk C.C. [1960] 2 Q.B. 72; [1960] 2 All E.R. 26, C.A.

Plaintiff skidded on ice—alleged due to negligence of defendant highway authority in that (a) the condition of the road was due to bad drainage, and this in turn was due to misfeasance, the defendants having done some work to improve the drainage, but not enough to remove all danger, and (b) they had not exhibited red lights or other warning of danger—*Held*, defendants not liable, as (a) what they had done had not created any danger actual or potential and so was not misfeasance (28 C), and (b) they were under no duty to warn of a danger which they had not created. On (a), *Wilson v. Kingston Corp.* **10** *applied* and *approved.*

14. Hughes v. Lord Advocate [1963] A.C. 837; [1963] 1 All E.R. 705, H.L.

Children eight and 10 meddling with unfenced and unguarded open manhole site—accident with one of the lamps—*Held*, defendants liable. *N.B.* The real point in the case was whether the fact that the explosion of the lamp was unforeseeable prevented recovery.

15. Haley v. London Electricity Board [1965] A.C. 778; [1964] 3 All E.R. 185, H.L.

This case decided that street undertakers owed a duty of care to blind persons as such where, as here, their presence was reasonably foreseeable (see Chap. 1, (2) (b))—*Held*, unanimously, by H.L., that a punner hammer laid horizontally so that it was at ground level at outside of pavement and at height of two feet at inside was not a sufficient discharge of this duty. On the other hand, it *seems* that they regarded the portable fence two feet high used by Post Office in *Pritchard* (Chap 1,(2) (b)**4**) as adequate.

16. Griffiths v. Liverpool Corporation [1967] 1 Q.B. 374; [1966] 2 All E.R. 1015, C.A.

Flagstone dangerous because it protruded half an inch and rocked (*N.B.* C.A. by themselves might not have found it dangerous)—defendants gave evidence that they could not get sufficient tradesmen to repair flagstones—but they gave no evidence as to what steps they had taken to get tradesmen; and in any event they had carried out no systematic inspections (which could be carried out by labourers, who were not in short supply); and in addition this flagstone could have been repaired by a labourer, or could have been roped off—*Held*, accordingly, that the defendants had not proved the statutory defence under the Act of 1961 s. 1(2) and (3). Salmon L.J. (1024 H) *said* that the words "such care as was reasonably required" meant "reasonably required of the highway authority" and not "reasonably necessary".

17. Murray v. Southwark London B.C. (1966) 65 L.G.R. 145; [1967] C.L.Y. 2691, MacKenna J.

18. Meggs v. Liverpool Corporation [1968] 1 W.L.R. 689; [1968] 1 All E.R. 1137

Held, that judge was right in finding a projection of [1/4] inch was not dangerous. "Everyone must take account of the fact that there may be unevenness here and there. There may be a ridge of [1/2] in. or [3/4] in. occasionally, but that is not the sort of thing which makes it dangerous or not reasonably safe" (Lord Denning M.R., 1139I).

19. Littler v. Liverpool Corporation [1968] 2 All E.R. 343; 66 L.G.R. 660, Cumming-Bruce J.

Held, defendants not liable, following *Meggs* **18**: "It is a mistake to isolate and emphasise a particular difference in levels unless that difference is such that a reasonable person who noticed and considered it would regard it as presenting a real source of danger" (345 D). Applied in **50**.

20. Burnside v. Emerson [1968] 1 W.L.R. 1490; [1968] 3 All E.R. 741, C.A.

Pool of water in road after rain—causing defendant's car to swerve to offside and into plaintiff's car—*Held*, local authority one-third to blame and swerving car two-thirds. Lord Denning M.R. said that in an action for failure to maintain a highway, there were three things: (a) that the road was in such a condition as to be dangerous, and in deciding this foreseeability was an essential element, in that the state of affairs had to be such that injury could be anticipated to persons using the highway; (b) that the dangerous condition was due to a failure to maintain, and in this connection the existence of a transient danger due to the elements was no evidence of a failure to maintain; and (c) if there was a failure to maintain, the highway authority was prima facie liable, and could only escape if it proved that it took such care as was in all the circumstances reasonable. On the facts of the case, the highway authority were at fault, for the road was always flooding in rain, and the highway authority were at fault in the drainage arrangements made.

21. Lilley v. British Insulated Callenders Construction (1968) 67 L.G.R. 224; [1968] C.L.Y. 2429, C.A.

Residential road in Bromley—defendants left excavation properly lit at 8.30 p.m.—by 10.50 p.m. the barriers and lights had been interfered with, so that plaintiff was injured—no previous interference—*Held*, on the facts defendants were not under a duty to inspect the excavation periodically during the night.

22. Greenhalgh v. British Railways Board [1969] 2 Q.B. 286; [1969] 2 All E.R. 114, C.A.

23. Levine v. Morris [1970] 1 W.L.R. 71; [1970] 1 All E.R. 144, C.A.

Held, Ministry liable for siting a road sign so as to constitute a hazard.

24. Bright v. Attorney-General [1971] 2 Lloyd's Rep. 68; [1971] R.T.R. 253, C.A.

Held, groove was dangerous for motor-cyclists, and since it was a trunk road (A1), the Ministry of Transport were vicariously liable for negligent work done on their behalf. *N.B.* The fact that the nominal defendant was the Attorney-General was due to the disappearance of the Ministry of Transport on the setting up of the Department of the Environment.

25. Whiting v. Hillingdon L.B.C. (1970) 68 L.G.R. 437; [1970] C.L.Y. 1191, James J.

Footpath—privately owned but local authority under duty to maintain it—plaintiff stepped into grass and foliage on edge in order to allow other pedestrians to pass—and caught her ankle against a hidden tree stump—the tree had been felled since the authority's last inspection shortly before the accident—and there was no reason to expect the authority to carry out another inspection by the time the accident took place—*Held*, defendants not liable. They were not in breach of their duty under the Highways Act 1959; and they had established a defence under the Highways Act 1961, s. 1.

26. Pridham v. Hemel Hempstead Corporation (1970) 114 S.J. 884; 69 L.G.R. 523, C.A.

Held, that a highway authority established its defence under the 1961 Act, s. 1(2), if it showed that its system of inspection was reasonable, and the fact that it might be practicable to inspect more frequently was immaterial. The facts were that the defendants employed a full-time inspector on their 106 miles of roads—busy roads were inspected monthly, less busy ones every two months, housing roads (such as the one in question) quarterly, and field paths annually—there was also a follow-up system for dealing with defects—*Held*, a proper system.

27. Davies v. Carmethenshire C.C. [1971] R.T.R. 112, C.A.

See Chap 13,(1)(e)**6**.

28. Bramwell v. Shaw [1971] R.T.R. 107, Ackner J.

29. Rider v. Rider [1973] 1 Q.B. 505; [1993] R.T.R. 178, C.A.

30. Farrell v. Northern Ireland Electricity [1977] N.I. 39; [1977] C.L.Y. 1971, Lord Lowry C.J.

P fell in street because street light not working—*Held*, defendants as the statutory undertakers were liable. Where an authority provided lighting under statutory powers it was under a duty to take reasonable care to maintain the lighting to the standard provided.

31. Haydon v. Kent C.C. [1978] Q.B. 343; [1978] 2 All E.R. 97, C.A.

Lord Denning M.R. *said* (105 A) that the highway authority were only liable for non-repair, which did not include clearing snow and ice and/or gritting: Goff L.J. *said* (107 F) that the duty did include such measures; and Shaw L.J. (109 E) *said* that there could be "extreme cases in special circumstances where a liability for failure to maintain not related to want of repair may arise". *But* all L.JJ. *agreed* that, on the facts, any duty had not been breached.

32. Pitman v. Southern Electricity [1978] 3 All E.R. 901; [1978] C.L.Y. 2054, C.A.

N.B. The essence of the decision is that the plate was *unlit* during darkness.

33. Trappa v. District of Surrey (1978) 95 D.L.R. (3d) 107; [1979] C.L.Y. 1890, Br.Col.Sup.Ct.

34. Cohen v. British Gas Corporation [1978] C.L.Y. 2053, Judge Lymbery Q.C.

N.B. But in addition the judge *found* that P did not trip as alleged.

35. Bird v. Pearce [1979] R.T.R. 369; [1980] C.L.Y. 1333, C.A.

"Give way" marking obliterated during re-surfacing. The topography did not indicate to the minor road driver that he was coming to a major road junction—*Held*, highway authority one-third liable. Having created a traffic flow system under their statutory powers, they were under a duty to see that the system did not deteriorate so as to become a hazard, and they should have erected temporary warning signs.

36. Tarrant v. Rowlands [1979] R.T.R. 144; [1979] C.L.Y. 1361, Cantley J.

Facts very similar to *Burnside* **20** *Held*, applying this case, highway authority 50 per cent. to blame and swerving driver also 50 per cent. to blame.

37. Allison v. Corby D.C. [1980] R.T.R. 111, Peter Pain J.

Held, that:

(a) even if the defendants owed a duty to road users to take reasonable care to eliminate or reduce the number of stray dogs, it was not in breach of such duty as it had carefully considered, and taken reasonable steps to deal with the problem;
(b) the presence of stray dogs did not constitute a failure to maintain the highway under the Highways Act 1959; ss. 44(1) and 295(1);
(c) the dogs did not amount to an obstruction of the highway under the 1959 Act, s. 116(3).

38. Hughlock v. Dept. of Transport [1981] C.L.Y. 1281, Mars Jones J.

39. Whittaker v. West Yorkshire M.C.C. [1982] C.L.Y. 1435, H.H. Judge Bennett, Q.C.

Held, obiter, that in the absence of evidence as to available resources and the practice of other highway authorities, it did not amount to negligence or breach of statutory duty not to operate a system of defect inspections or to employ street inspectors.

40. Capper and Lamb v. Department of Environment for Northern Ireland [1984] C.L.Y. 2403

P's lorry damaged after skidding on icy patch in area where improvement works had been carried out and drains opened up—*Held*, D highway authority liable for not making provision for drainage of water away from road area.

41. Ellis v. Tyne & Wear C.C. [1984] C.L.Y. 1022, Judge Percy

12-year-old plaintiff slipped on ice and snow which had been lying in place for approximately four weeks—*Held*, local authority under a duty under Highways Act to clear ice and snow.

42. Jacobs v. Hampshire C.C. *The Times*, May 28, 1984, [1984] C.L.Y. 2315

Highways—frequency of inspection—*Held*, where a roadway was particularly susceptible to water penetration, a six-monthly inspection was inadequate and highway authority could not rely upon the statutory defence under section 58 to a claim for damages.

43. McKenna v. Scottish Omnibus (1984) 134 New L.J. 681, [1985] C.L.Y. 2307

P travelling on motor coach owned by D1 which skids on icy road—injured. P sued D1 and D2, highway authority responsible—*Held*, highway authority not to blame. D2 was only given an indication of overnight fost on the previous evening, and a duty to maintain the roads does not include a duty to prevent ice forming on roads 24 hours per day. Statutory defence made out.

44. Bartlett v. Department Of Transport (1984) 83 L.G.R. 579; [1985] C.L.Y. 1598, C.A.

No snow and ice clearance because of industrial action—*Held*, where industrial action not condoned, Department of Transport not in breach of statutory duty to clear the road.

45. Sullivan v. South Glamorgan C.C. *The Times*, August 7, 1985; [1985] C.L.Y. 2308, C.A.

For summary, see Chap. 8, (5) **17**.

46. West v. Buckinghamshire C.C. (1985) 83 L.G.R. 449; [1985] C.L.Y. 1603

Action brought by third party for indemnity in respect of claim by estate of deceased in road traffic accident—*Held*, that no duty of care was owed by the council to road users in respect of the failure to place double white lines on a road where it was said that they were required.

47. Reid v. British Telecommunications *The Times*, June 27, 1987, [1987] C.L.Y. 2618, C.A.

Statutory undertaker is not negligent in relying on highway authority's six-monthly road inspection rather than inspecting manhole covers itself. However, undertaker will be assumed to have the same knowledge that it would or should have had if it had inspected the cover at the same time the local authority had so inspected.

48. Brady v. Department of Environment for Northern Ireland [1988] C.L.Y. 2598

P tripped at edge of highway, but no liability because, *inter alia*, particular piece of ground where defect lay had not been adopted.

49. Lavis v. Kent C.C. (1992) 90 L.G.R. 416; [1993] C.L.Y. 2949, C.A.

Cause of action against local authority alleging failure to erect signs as to warning in bends in road not struck out—decision to erect signs cannot always be categorised as a policy decision.

50. Mills v. Barnsley M.B.C. [1992] P.I.Q.R. P291; [1993] C.L.Y. 2967, C.A.

The plaintiff shipped when she caught her heel in a hole in the pavement, 2 in. at its widest and 1[¼] in. deep, where the corner of a paving brick had broken away—*Held*, that a mechanical test based purely on dimensions of defect was to be discouraged. It would not be right to say that a depression of one inch will never be dangerous, as the test of danger is one of reasonable foresight of harm, with each case turning on it own facts. Here, the defect was minor, and the highway not dangerous.

51. Pritchard v. Clwyd C.C. [1993] P.I.Q.R. P21; [1993] 12 C.L. 529, C.A.

Plaintiff slipped in flooded street, when wading through water—*Held*, mere collection of water did not in itself indicate a failure of the statutory undertaker, or highway authority and the maxim *res ipsa loquitur* could only apply if event complained of was more consistent with failure to carry out duties, or to take care, or that it pointed to a particular one of two defendants being at fault.

52. James v. Preseli Pembrokeshire D.C. [1993] P.I.Q.R. 114; [1993] C.L.Y. 2966, C.A.
If the particular spot where the plaintiff fell was not dangerous, it was irrelevant that there were other spots nearby which were dangerous or that the area as a whole was due for resurfacing (*Whitworth v. Manchester Corporation* (1971) C.A. 212 (unreported) applied (**U7**) 20 mm trip was not dangerous. The danger must be that which an authority may reasonably be expected to guard against. There must be a reasonable balance between private and public interest.

53. Misell v. Essex C.C., *The Times*, December 16, 1994; [1995] 1 C.L. 297, C.A.
Where authority responsible for maintaining highway failed to clean the road adequately, to secure that those responsible for mud on the lorries which dropped on to the road cleaned their lorries, failed to widen the road, reinforce the banks or erect warning signs it was in breach of its duty of care.

U1. Swift v. Ankerdine (1951) C.A. 70

Pile of earth in roadway—warning notice 50 yards down road—not lit—night collision—*Held*, defendant, liable as unlit warning notice was of little if any value at night.

U2. Stewart v. Manchester Corporation (1952) C.A. 358

Held, defendants liable.

U3. Gregson v. Watkins (1953) C.A. 94

Held, defendant liable.

U4. Schrader v. Crosville Motor Services Ltd. (1959) C.A. 10

Held, not negligence and not nuisance.

U5. Birmingham v. East Ham County Borough (1961) C.A. 331; *The Times*, October 20, 1961

Plaintiff trips in 6-in. cavity in highway—caused by rats—defendants had recently reinstated surface—*Held*, not liable.

U6. Murray v. Liverpool Corporation (1969) C.A. 218 B

Electricity grid projecting $\frac{3}{4}$ in.—had been there some considerable time—no complaints—*Held*, defendants not liable. "The plaintiff must give evidence that the pavement was in such a condition as to be dangerous for traffic" (Lord Denning M.R., 3 B).

U7. Whitworth v. Manchester Corporation (1971) C.A. 212

Held, a $\frac{3}{4}$ in. trip in a pavement was not dangerous. *But* Edmund Davies L.J. *said* (6 F) that the citation of tripping cases needed to be carefully controlled, and that one case was at best only a guide to another; in his view, in *some* circumstances, it was not inconceivable that a trip of $\frac{3}{4}$ inch could be a danger.

U8. Swaine v. Post Office (1972) C.A. 395B

Widish shallow hole some $\frac{5}{8}$ in. below general level of pavement—*Held*, not dangerous.

U9. Hymanson v. Greater Manchester Council (1981) C.A

U10. Lawman v. Waltham Forest Corpn. (1980) C.A. 25

Plaintiff must show not merely disrepair, but dangerous disrepair. On the evidence, the trial judge was entitled to find that the trip did not render the highway dangerous.

U11. Jones v. Mayor and Burgers of L.B. of Newham (1985) C.A. 36

P allegedly tripped on remains of litter bin which had been reduced to a pile of rubbish—Held, in ordering a new trial, there was an evidential burden on P to show that such an appalling hazard was the cause of the fall and not the kerbstone.

U12. Beyga v. M.B. of Knowsley (1989) C.A. 729

P fell over on pavement when his foot "canted" on edge of pavement which projected 2–3 inches above adjacent verge—*Held*, no liability as highway authority, because such a projection or drop, did not render the pavement dangerous to pedestrians.

U13. Anderton v. Shropshire C.C. (1990) C.A. 18

No duty to provide warning signs.

U14. Pike v. Isle of Wight (1991) C.A. 229

Kerb projected above pavement by half an inch, causing P to trip, and to fall into road, injuring herself—*Held*, D was in breach of its statutory duty under section 41 despite a small projection. There was a foreseeable risk of injury, and the defect was not isolated, being in a substantial area of uneven and cracked footway. P tripped at the very edge of the pavement and therefore there was the added danger of falling into the highway.

U15. Winter v. Spelthorne B. C. (1992) C.A. 1131

Pothole one to one and a half inches deep did not pose a foreseeable risk of injury to cyclist.

(b) Private Person as Defendant

1. Dollman v. Hillman [1941] 1 All E.R. 355, C.A.

Plaintiff slips on piece of fat outside defendant's shop (butcher's)—*Held*, defendant liable because on the facts correct inference was that defendant either caused the fat to jump into the street or they allowed it to drop in their shop in such a place that it might be picked up on a customer's shoe and carried outside; and so were guilty of negligence and nuisance.

2. Longhurst v. Metropolitan Water Board [1948] 2 All E.R. 834; [1948] W.N. 418, H.L.

Stopcock leaked (which defendants remedied) causing percolation which loosened paving-stone some distance away over which plaintiff tripped—no evidence that defendants knew or ought to have known of this danger—*Held*, no negligence, and no liability in the absence of negligence. Lord Porter at 839 A: "My Lords, even in the case of a private individual, liability for nuisance without negligence or deliberate act is not readily established, apart of course from cases of the *Rylands v. Fletcher* type."

3. Bolton v. Stone [1951] A.C. 850; [1951] 1 All E.R. 1078, H.L.

Cricket club are sued in nuisance and negligence—no negligence (see Chap. 2, (3)), and *conceded* (1082 G, All E.R.) that liability could not be established in this case without proof of negligence.

4. Farrell v. John Mowlem [1954] 1 Lloyd's Rep. 437, Devlin J.

Defendants as contractors for L.C.C. lay a compressor pipeline across footwalk over which plaintiff trips—*Held*, a nuisance and defendants liable. In the course of his judgment judge enunciates following propositions:

(a) Statutory authority was not pleaded, and therefore defendants' liability must be judged as if they were ordinary members of the public.
(b) As ordinary members of the public their position was different from that of statutory undertakers, who were entitled to create an obstruction if it was the necessary and reasonable way of doing the work.
(c) Their position was also different from that of an adjacent occupier, who was entitled, if it was reasonable, to create obstructions in pursuance of his right of access and/or his right to repair his property.
(d) Proof of negligence was not necessary to found an action for nuisance brought against the person creating the nuisance, though different considerations would arise if the nuisance was merely on defendants' property.
(e) Since *any* obstruction was prima facie a nuisance, defendants in the above circumstances had no defence. Dictum (a) approved in **5**.

5. Trevett v. Lee [1955] 1 W.L.R. 113; [1955] 1 All E.R. 406, C.A.

Defendant an adjacent owner laid a [1/2]-inch garden hosepipe across road to draw water—plaintiff tripped on it—negligence was disproved by county court judge, but plaintiff appealed on nuisance—*Held*, even assuming it was a sufficient obstruction to be a nuisance, which was doubtful (409 I), the user by defendant of the highway for this purpose was reasonable (**4**, dictum (c), *approved*), and claim failed.

6. Esso Petroleum v. Southport Corporation [1956] A.C. 218, [1955] 3 All E.R. 864, H.L.

Held, (perhaps *obiter*, by Lord Tucker (873 F) and perhaps Lord Radcliffe (872 C).

7. Penney v. Berry [1955] 1 W.L.R. 1021; [1955] 3 All E.R. 182, C.A.

As a result of pavement remaking, defendant's cellar flap was left protruding [3/4] inch above pavement, and plaintiff tripped over it—*Held*, defendant not liable, as he had no power to go onto pavement to put it right, and also because his duty under the Public Health Acts Amendment Act 1890, s. 35(1), was to keep the cellar flap and surrounds in good condition and repair, and that he had done this, and that what was wrong was the "design or layout" when the pavement was re-constructed.

8. Coburn v. Williams, *The Times*, May 17, 1956; [1956] C.L.Y. 6168, C.A.

Plaintiff was alleging a defective forecourt was part of highway—*Held*, he had not proved this.

9. Macfarlane v. Gwalter [1959] 2 Q.B. 332; [1958] 1 All E.R. 181, C.A.

Cellar flap out of repair to knowledge of owner who failed to repair—it formed part of highway—*Held*, owner liable. Ormerod L.J. (185 B, others concurring): "The position is that there was a structure on the highway, and it was the duty of defendant (by reason of the Public Health Acts Amendment Act 1890, s. 35(1) to keep it in repair. Whether that duty arose by statute or from any other circumstances does not appear to be relevant."

10. Prince v. Gregory [1959] 1 W.L.R. 177; [1959] 1 All E.R. 133, C.A.

Held, statement of claim should be struck out as disclosing no cause of action.

11. Parish v. Judd [1960] 1 W.L.R. 867; [1960] 3 All E.R. 33, Edmund Davies J.

Lights on defendant's car failed totally—defendant got a tow from lorry—lorry driver stopped near street lamp to see whether defendant was all right—when stopped defendant's car was about six yards from the lamp post, was close into the kerb and had three reflectors at the rear—visible from about 100 yards away—plaintiff ran into rear—sued defendant in negligence and nuisance—*Held*, (a) as regards nuisance, plaintiff had to show that the vehicle was not merely an obstruction on the road but that it was a danger on the road, and that on the facts this was not so; and (b) as regards negligence, while it was true that an unlit vehicle on a road at night raised a presumption of negligence, this had been rebutted both as regards place and as regards maintenance, and that therefore the claim failed.

12. British Road Services v. Slater [1964] 1 W.L.R. 498; [1964] 1 All E.R. 816, Lord Parker C.J.

Defendants acquired certain land in 1926—at that date there was a tree on the land with a branch projecting over the road at a height of 16 feet—defendants allowed branch to remain—plaintiffs lorry, being over 16 feet high, collided with it—*Held*, the branch was a nuisance because it prevented the convenient use of the highway, but defendants were not liable because following *Sedleigh-Denfield v. Callaghan* (Chap. 8, (6) **3**), defendants did not have sufficient knowledge of it as would render them liable in law to remedy it. As regards knowledge, the branch was clear to see, but defendants could not reasonably have realised it was a nuisance until the accident happened, as it was so unlikely.

13. Lamond v. Glasgow Corporation, 1968 S.L.T. 291; [1968] C.L.Y. 2673, Ct. of Session

Narrow public lane ran between golf course and railway embankment—pedestrian hit on head by golf ball—6,000 shots a year were hit onto lane from golf course—no one previously injured—*Held*, defendants liable, as risk was clearly foreseeable, it was not impracticable for defendants to redesign the course and there was no duty in the circumstances on the pedestrian to take evasive action.

14. Scott v. Green [1969] 1 W.L.R. 301; [1969] 1 All E.R. 849, C.A.

Cellar flap run over by lorry, shortly after which plaintiff walks onto flap and goes down into cellar—*Held*, occupier not liable, as his duty was to use reasonable care—*Held*, also, that the Highways Act 1959, s. 154(5), did not give rise to an action for breach of statutory duty, but operated to give the occupier sufficient control over the flap, whether the pavement was dedicated or not, so as to enable him to repair it, and from this stemmed his duty to use reasonable care.

15. Dymond v. Pearce [1972] 1 Q.B. 496; [1972] 1 All E.R. 1142, C.A.

Lorry in road—not liable because whole fault was that of motor-cyclist (see Chap. 13, (1)(j) **8**)—but Edmund Davies L.J. said that an obstruction, which was a nuisance, had to be a danger to be actionable, and there had to be evidence of lack of reasonable care. Following this, there have been three cases of leaving skips on roads at night, with the following results:

(a) *Wills v. Martin* [1972] R.T.R. 368, Foster J.: Not liable.
(b) *Drury v. Camden L.B.C.* [1972] R.T.R., May J.: 50 percent liable.
(c) *Saper v. Hungate* [1972] R.T.R. 380, Cantley J.: 60 percent liable.

16. Miller v. Jackson [1977] Q.B. 966; [1977] 3 All E.R. 338, C.A.

Plaintiff a house owner, but principles may be applicable to highway cases. See Chap. 10, (4)(e) **11** for details.

17. Cartwright v. McLaine [1977–1979] 143 C.L.R. 549; [1982] C.L.Y. 2269, Aust. High Ct.

18. Trappa Holdings v. District of Surrey (1978) 95 D.L.R. (3d) 107; [1979] C.L.Y. 1890, Brit. Col. Sup. Ct.

19. Tysoe v. Davis *The Times*, June 21, 1983; [1983] C.L.Y. 2740, Skinner J.

Held, defendant liable in negligence and public nuisance.

20. Diboll v. City of Newcastle [1993] P.I.Q.R. P16 [1993] C.L.Y. 3795, C.A.

For summary, see Chap. 13 (e)(8).

21. McGeown v. Northern Ireland Housing Executive [1994] 3 All E.R. 53, Carswell L.J.

Private landowner not liable for negligent non-reasance in respect of public right of way. See Chap. 10, (1) **22** for details.

U1. Gordon v. Portsmore (1984) C.A. 964

Pile of shingle left by defendant causes plaintiff to lose control of van—*Held*, defendant liable.

(2) Dangers Adjoining Highway

1. Wringe v. Cohen [1940] 1 K.B. 229; [1939] 4 All E.R. 241, C.A.

Collapse of house onto adjoining house due to want of repair—*Held*, knowledge of want of repair immaterial. Atkinson J. giving judgment of court (243 F): "In our judgment, if owing to want of repair, premises upon a highway become dangerous and therefore a nuisance, and a passer-by or adjoining owner suffers damage by their collapse, the occupier, or owner if he has undertaken the duty to repair, is answerable, whether or not he knew or ought to have known of the danger . . . On the other hand if the nuisance is created not by want of repair, but for example by the act of a trespasser, or by a secret and unobservable operation of nature, such as a subsidence . . . neither an occupier nor an owner is answerable, unless with knowledge or means of knowledge he allows the danger to continue."

2. Slater v. Worthington Cash Stores [1941] 1 K.B. 488; [1941] 3 All E.R. 28, C.A.

Large accumulation of snow and ice on roof—remains there for four days—then falls and injures plaintiff—*Held*, defendants liable in nuisance and negligence.

3. Howard v. Walker [1947] K.B. 860; [1947] 2 All E.R. 197, Lord Goddard C.J.

Question whether plaintiff could sue landlord of shop as well as tenant—*Held*, could not, as on the facts plaintiff was invitee of tenant on forecourt. "No doubt it is difficult for a layman to understand why, if he is walking along the road and slips into an excavation at the side of it, he should be entitled to recover, whereas if he slips into the excavation as he is endeavouring to get onto the road, he is not . . . " (199 G). See Chap. 10, (8) (a) **4** for reasons why landlord not liable to invitee of tenant. *Approved* in q.v.

4. Brown v. Harrison (1947) 177 L.T. 281; [1947] W.N. 191, C.A.

Dying tree—apparent from dead branches at top—*Held*, defendant liable, as he ought "as an ordinary landowner to have known it was dangerous".

5. Holling v. Yorkshire Traction [1948] 2 All E.R. 662; 206 L.T. 240, Oliver J.

Dense steam emitted from defendants' coke ovens across road causing accident—*Held*, defendants liable in nuisance and negligence! "His artificial fog had no business on the road at all" (664 F).

6. Jacobs v. L.C.C. [1950] A.C. 361; [1950] 1 All E.R. 737, H.L.

Held, that if plaintiff was deliberately leaving highway to go elsewhere (as here), he could not sue on the ground of a danger adjoining the highway, but must sue as invitee or licensee, if at all.

7. Caminer v. London and Northern Trust [1951] A.C. 88; [1950] 2 All E.R. 486, H.L.

Roots of 130-year-old elm tree affected by elm butt rot—this was not apparent and could only have been detected by methods additional to the methods usually employed when disease suspected (494 B, Lord Normand)—crown was about 35 feet wide, which was not exceptional—argument in House of Lords turned mainly on whether evidence showed tree should have prudently been lopped—*Held*, not, bearing in mind that defendants' duty was only to take the care of an ordinary prudent landowner, not that of an expert (Lord Porter at 490 H). "It (the standard of care) postulates some degree of knowledge . . . short of the knowledge possessed by scientific arboriculturists but which surely must be greater than the knowledge possessed by the ordinary urban observer of trees or even of the countryman not practically concerned with their care" (Lord Normand, 493 F). Lord Reid on the other hand thought the standard of care was that of "reasonable and careful owner without expert knowledge but accustomed to dealing with his trees and having a countryman's general knowledge about them" (499 D). He also (499 E) did not think it necessary on the evidence that defendants should have called in an expert.

8. Lambourn v. London Brick [1950] C.L.C. 6810; 156 E.G. 146, Finnemore J.

Elm trees blown down across road—*Held*, as there was nothing to indicate they were dangerous, defendants not liable.

9. Mint v. Good [1951] 1 K.B. 517; [1950] 2 All E.R. 1159, C.A.

Held, that landlord would be liable not only where he had expressly covenanted to repair or expressly reserved a right of entry to repair, but also where he had an implied right of entry (which would ordinarily be the case with a weekly tenancy which was silent about repairing). Denning L.J. (1166 F) went even further, and said landlord would be liable where he had in practice taken the structural repairs on himself.

10. Bolton v. Stone [1951] A.C. 850; [1950] 1 All E.R. 1078, H.L.

Cricket club are sued in nuisance and negligence—no negligence (see Chap. 2, (3) **1**), and *conceded* (1082 B, All E.R.) that liability could not be established in this case without proof of negligence.

11. Morton v. Wheeler *The Times*, February 1, 1956; [1956] C.L.Y. 6164, C.A.

A shop near a football ground fitted spikes to the window-sill to prevent people sitting on it while waiting to go in—a pedestrian fell ill and in falling fell with his face on to spike so that he died—*Held*, defendant not liable, as not reasonably foreseeable.

12. Coburn v. Williams *The Times*, May 17, 1956; [1956] C.L.Y. 6168, C.A.

Held, that forecourt was not part of highway, and that plaintiff's claim failed (probably because of).

13. Walsh v. Holst [1958] 1 W.L.R. 800, [1958] 3 All E.R. 33, C.A.

Held, res ipsa loquitur, but on facts defendants had discharged onus and were not liable. For details see Chap. 3 (2) (b) **8**.

14. Rollingson v. Kerr [1958] C.L.Y. 2427, Cassels J.

Dense smoke from defendant's bonfire of hedge clippings rolled across road—collision in smoke—*Held*, defendant liable in negligence and in nuisance.

15. Hilder v. Associated Portland Cement [1961] 1 W.L.R. 1434; [1961] 3 All E.R. 709, Ashworth J.

Children permitted by defendant occupiers to play football on an open space adjoining a busy highway—ball kicked onto highway into immediate path of motor-cyclist, causing accident—*Held*, applying test of Lord Reid in *Bolton v. Stone* **10**, *i.e.* "was the risk so small that a reasonable man would have thought it right to refrain from taking steps?" defendants were liable in negligence.

16. Quinn v. Scott [1965] 1 W.L.R. 1004; [1965] 2 All E.R. 588; Glyn-Jones J.

Held, defendants liable. Test in *Caminer* **7** *applied*.

17. Lamond v. Glasgow Corporation, 1968 S.L.T. 291; [1968] C.L.Y. 2673, Ct. of Session.

Narrow public lane running between golf course and railway embankment—pedestrian hit by golf ball—about 6,000 shots a year were hit on to lane from golf course—no one previously injured—*Held*, defendants liable, as the risk was clearly foreseeable, it was not impracticable to re-design course, and the pedestrian was under no duty in the circumstances to take evasive action.

18. Salsbury v. Woodland [1970] 1 Q.B. 324; [1969] 3 All E.R. 863, C.A.

Held, owner of land on which tree stood not liable for negligence of his independent contractor.

19. Perkins v. Glyn [1976] C.L.Y. 179, Wimborne C. C.

Held, on the facts, no liability in negligence or nuisance, mainly because the defendant in firing the stubble had formed an incombustible strip 60 feet wide, and because the smoke could be seen from a distance, so that there was no concealed trap.

20. Woolfall v. Knowsley B.C. The Times, June 26, 1992; [1992] C.L.Y. 3229, C.A.

P injured by rubbish falling onto highway—Held, no defence that rubbish could not be collected because of industrial action.

21. Diboll v. City of Newcastle-upon-Tyne and often [1993] P.I.Q.R. p 16; [1993] C.L.Y. 3795 C.A. see Chap. 13 (e)(8) for summary

22. Stovin v. Wise (Norfolk C.C. Third Party), [1994] 1 W.L.R. 1124; [1994] 3 All E.R. 467, C.A.

Impaired visibility through obstruction on land adjoining highway—held, there is no statutory duty owed by a highway authority to alleviate such a danger to highway users but a duty is owed at common law to take appropriate steps.

U1. Radstock Co-op v. Norton-Radstock U.D.C. (1968) C.A. 41; [1968] Ch. 605

Sewerage case—probably *obiter*, Russell L.J. (15 A) explained ratio in *Slater* **2** as being based on a failure to remove snow which was obviously dangerous and which *could* have been removed.

U2. Jenkins v. City Of Birmingham C. C. (1983) C.A. 668

P walking along a pavement when polythene bag some three feet long and one foot wide, wrapped itself around her leg, causing her to fall. Bag came from building site controlled by D—held, no reasonable system for clearing up site—D liable.

13. ROAD VEHICLES

(1) Liability of Ordinary Driver

(a) Generally

1. Bourhill v. Young [1943] A.C. 92; [1942] 2 All E.R. 396, H.L.

"A blind or deaf man who crosses the traffic on a busy street cannot complain if he is run over by a careful driver who does not know of and cannot be expected to observe and guard against the man's infirmity" (Lord Wright at 405 G).

2. Farrugia v. Great Western Ry. [1947] 2 All E.R. 565; 204 L.T. 310, C.A.

Lorry laden with large box—driver went under bridge which was too low and box fell off, injuring plaintiff who was running behind lorry at the time—plaintiff had been on lorry before and was running behind in order to try to get on again—*Held*, (a) even if plaintiff a trespasser *qua* owner of subsoil, defendants not thereby discharged from duty of care, and (b) defendants owed duty of care to anyone who might be on the highway in the near neighbourhood when the danger they had created materialised, whether he was there lawfully or unlawfully, and the duty was not confined to someone whom they could have reason to expect to be there at the time.

3. London Passenger Transport Board v. Upson [1949] A.C. 155; [1949] 1 All E.R. 60, H.L.

Lord Uthwatt: "I . . . dissent from the view that drivers are entitled to drive on the assumption that other users of the road, whether drivers or pedestrians, will behave with reasonable care. It is common experience that many do not. A driver is not of course bound to anticipate folly in all its forms, but he is not, in my opinion, entitled to put out of consideration the teachings of experience as to the form those follies commonly take." See **5**.

4. Nance v. British Columbia Electric Ry. [1951] A.C. 601; [1951] 2 All E.R. 448, P.C.

Lord Simon at 611, line 27: "Generally speaking, when two parties are so moving in relation to one another as to involve risk of collision, each owes to the other a duty to move with due care, and this is true whether they are both in control of vehicles, or both proceeding on foot, or whether one is on foot and the other controlling a moving vehicle." Dictum of Denning L.J. to the contrary in *Davies v. Swan* [1949] 2 K.B. 291, 324, *disapproved.*

5. Berrill v. Road Haulage Executive [1952] 2 Lloyd's Rep. 490, Slade J.

"You are not bound to foresee every extremity of folly which occurs on the road. Equally, you are certainly not entitled to drive on the footing that other users of the road, either drivers or pedestrians, will exercise reasonable care. You are bound to anticipate any act which is reasonably foreseeable, that is to say, anything which the experience of road users teaches them that people do, albeit negligently" (492, "paraphrasing" Lord Uthwatt in **3**).

6. Esso Petroleum v. Southport Corporation [1956] A.C. 218; [1955] 3 All E.R. 864, H.L.

So *held*, by Lord Tucker at 873 F (perhaps *obiter*). See also Lord Radcliffe at 872 C.

7. Randall v. Tarrant [1955] 1 W.L.R. 255; [1955] 1 All E.R. 600, C.A.

Defendant's farm vehicle unsuccessfully tries to squeeze past plaintiff's car which is parked in lane while plaintiff is trespassing—*Held*, car not in these circumstances trespassing and defendant liable as having failed to disprove negligence. Question of what would have been position if car had been trespassing *left open.*

8. Letang v. Cooper [1965] 1 Q.B. 232; [1964] 2 All E.R. 929, C.A.

9. Mitchell v. Mason (1966) 10 W.I.R. 26, Jamaica C.A.

10. Nettleship v. Weston [1971] 2 Q.B. 691; [1971] 3 All E.R. 581, C.A.

Held (2–1), that learner driver owed full reasonable standard of care, not only to the public at large, but also to an instructor–friend who knew of her lack of competence. Lord Denning M.R. thought that a claim by a professional instructor would probably be excluded because there might be implied in the contract an agreement to waive any claim.

11. West v. Hughes of Beaconsfield [1971] R.T.R. 298; [1971] C.L.Y. 7738, Mocatta J.

12. McCready v. Miller [1979] R.T.R. 186; [1979] C.L.Y. 1863, C.A.

In alighting from a minicab in which she had not previously travelled, P caught foot in loop of seat belt hanging loose from hook—night time—*Held*, minicab driver liable, in that he ought to have tied back the seat belt or switched interior light on or warned P—*Held*, also, no contributory negligence on the part of P. *Donn v. Shacter* [1975] R.T.R. 238 distinguished (and possibly disapproved); in this latter case the facts were similar, save that it was a friend's car in which P had travelled previously, and the trial judge found that P was solely to blame.

13. Awad v. Pillai, *The Times*, June 6, 1981; [1982] R.T.R. 266, C.A.

Plaintiff car owner took car to garage for re-spray. Garage owner (who later disappeared) lent car to defendant, giving her the impression that he owned car and that she would be covered by insurance. The defendant damaged car by negligent driving—*Held*, defendant owed a duty of care to plaintiff and was liable.

14. R. v. Preston JJ., ex p. Lyons [1982] R.T.R. 173; [1982] C.L.Y. 2757, Div. Ct.

Instructor directed pupil to execute emergency stop without first checking that road behind was clear. A following motor cyclist collided with the car. Justices convicted pupil of careless driving—*Held*, dismissing application for judicial review, "a prudent driver would, despite what the instructor said, have looked in his mirror before jamming on his brakes" (Lord Lane C. J., 176 D).

U1. Bowen v. Lathan (1959) C.A. 273 A.

Defendant misjudged speed of plaintiff ("had I known it was going so fast I would have waited")—*Held*, approving words of Donovan J., "an error of judgment of this sort is not necessarily negligence", and defendant not liable.

U2. Rothwell v. Davies (1963) C.A. 145; [1963] 107 S.J. 436

Stationary car scraped by lorry—incensed car driver followed lorry, hooting and flashing lights—lorry driver, distracted ran into another vehicle—*Held*, car driver 75 per cent. negligent.

U3. Dumpleton v. Holden (1963) C.A. 111

Car pulled up suddenly because lorry ahead decided to turn right—motor-cycle, following car, ran into same—*Held*, car and motor-cycle equally to blame, car because of insufficient look-out, and motor-cycle for failing in his duty to anticipate that the vehicle ahead might have to pull up suddenly.

U4. Brooks v. Graham (1964) C.A. 77

For facts, see Chap. 13, (1) (1) **U3**.

U5. Wiltshire v. Foote (1968) C.A. 428

Visitor to Birmingham got trapped on dangerous traffic island which local person would probably have avoided—*Held*, no contributory negligence on her part, as although the standard of care was an objective one, the ordinary reasonable pedestrian was not necessarily a local inhabitant. *N.B.* Conforming with *Haley* (Chap. 13, (1) (k) **4**), the approach in such cases would seem to be to ask first whether the class to which the person belonged could reasonably be foreseen and, if so, to judge the person concerned by the standard requisite to that class. One exception may be the learner or novice driver.

U6. Evans v. King (1973) C.A. 165

"I am not prepared to assent to the proposition that a stranger to a locality must be regarded and have his behaviour treated more indulgently than a person familiar with the location where an accident occurs" (Edmund Davies L. J., 3 H).

U7. Mayers v. Gilbert (1981) C.A. U.B. 227

D driving slowly towards factory gate. Pickets on his right shouted and D looked towards them. As he did so, P, another picket on his left, stepped off kerb in front of car and was hit by near side front of car—*Held*, D not liable.

U8. Trevor v. Cole (1984) C.A. 529

Groups of young men on either side of road. One ran across and defendant, approaching in car, braked to avoid him. Plaintiff then left pavement to defendant's nearside. Defendant did not see him, and car struck him—*Held*, defendant liable—having seen groups on pavements and previous man crossing, should have kept very careful look-out and slowed down to be able to avoid any other negligent pedestrians. (At first instance, plaintiff found guilty of contributory negligence, but amount not specified in Court of Appeal).

U9. Channer v. Lucas (1990) C.A. 96

Plaintiff, aged 65, crossed road "at a sort of run, not very fast". Having got over centre line, she saw defendant's motor cycle approaching from her left at 30 m.p.h., and stopped. Had she not done so, defendant would have passed behind her. In the event, he hit her—*Held*, defendant liable—failed to anticipate likely movement or reaction of elderly pedestrian confronted by a approaching motor cycle. Plaintiff 75 per cent. to blame—failed to see defendant's motor cycle when began to cross, and gave no warning of her intention to stop.

(b) Emergencies

(*N.B.* For the following specific types of emergency, see separate subsections:

1. Parkinson v. Liverpool Corporation [1950] 1 All E.R. 367; [1950] W.N. 43, C.A.

Dog runs across bus—driver brakes causing passengers who are standing to fall—*Held*, in the circumstances not negligence. C.A. endorse Pritchard J. in saying: "This is not a case which can be argued ... on the lines ... whether the driver owed a duty to the dog or a greater duty to his passenger. The simple test to be applied in the circumstances of this case which took place is: Did the driver act reasonably or unreasonably by doing something which a reasonable person would not do and leaving undone something a reasonable person would do?" This case was considered by H.L. in **3**, when it was neither affirmed nor disapproved.

2. Barkway v. South Wales Transport [1950] A.C. 185; [1950] 1 All E.R. 392, H.L.

Skid caused by burst tyre—all allegations of negligence were negatived, except failure to have a system of reporting blows likely to cause an impact fracture—*Held*, on this ground, defendants were liable.

3. Glasgow Corporation v. Sutherland [1951] 95 S.J. 204; [1951] W.N. 111, H.L.

Dog running in front of tramcar—driver applied magnetic brake (which produced almost instantaneous stop)—plaintiff who was moving to a seat, having just boarded, thrown—*Held*, on the facts, negligence on the part of driver. *Parkinson* **1** *considered*, but neither affirmed nor disapproved.

4. Ng Chun Piu v. Lee Chuen Tat [1988] R.T.R. 298; *The Times*, May 25, 1988, P.C.

Coach driven along offside lane of dual carriageway. Car in nearside lane suddenly pulled out in front of coach. Coach driver braked and swerved right. Coach crossed central reservation and struck bus coming the other way—*Held*, coach driver not liable. Faced with the emergency, he had acted with the alertness, skill and judgment reasonably to be expected in the circumstances.

U1. Roberts v. Arnold (1967) C.A. 173

Car at night halted on wrong side of 18-foot road with headlights full on—driver from opposite direction breasted hill 75 yards from stationary car, did not brake until 10 yards away and then ran into the latter—dazzled by latter's headlights—*Held*, moving driver free from blame "on the basis of the agony of collision rule" (Willmer L.J., 5 F).

U2. Hopper v. Haynes (1973) C.A. 17

Tyre burst—car then hit baulk of wood on side of road—which swung into path of plaintiff's car—*Held*, applying dictum of Asquith L.J. in *Barkway* (see Chap. 3, (2)(b) **6**), defendant liable, as he had failed to satisfy the judge that, with reasonable care, he could not have avoided hitting baulk. Although the tyre burst was neutral, the onus still lay on the defendant to explain how the whole incident happened without negligence on his part.

U3. Cam v. Munks (1974) C.A. 363

Mini driver negligently got onto wrong carriageway of dual carriageway—dark—lorry driver on meeting her flashed and hooted and stopped on his nearside—Mini driver pulled up on her nearside—plaintiff, coming on scene shortly after, saw Mini sidelights, and thought Mini was in *other* carriageway—pulled out to pass lorry—then realised Mini was on his carriageway—swerved left—but hit lorry, which was 25 yards on beyond Mini—*Held*, plaintiff could not be blamed for his reactions, and fault was entirely that of the Mini driver.

U4. Howe v. Kershaw (1983) C.A. 653

Taxi driver attacked by two assailant—one got out but other resumed attack—in heat of moment, trying to defend himself, taxi driver's foot came off depressed clutch—taxi shot back and struck assailant who had got out previously—*Held*, taxi driver not liable.

U5. Turner v. Crittal Windows Ltd (1984) C.A. 557

Plaintiff's lorry went over centre line in road close to a bend to overtake cyclists. Defendant, driving lorry in opposite direction, braked and tried to mount nearside kerb to avoid collision. Defendant's trailer rebounded into plaintiff's lorry—*Held*, defendant not liable.

U6. Barry v. Greater Manchester Passenger Executive and Sindrey (1984) C.A. 610

Dog, which bus driver had seen on pavement, suddenly ran in front of but driver who braked—two standing passengers fell over—*Held*, driver not liable.

U7. Reardon v. Fall (1984) C.A. 1005

D1 went round sharp bend on motorcycle at proper speed—confronted by D2 well over central line, passing D3's parked car. D1 lost control, swerving to avoid D2's car and crashed, killing pillion passenger—*Held*, D1 not liable, D2 and D3 each 50 per cent. to blame.

U8. Church v. Baker (1987) C.A. 378

D2 confronted by D1's vehicle wholly on D2's side of road. D2 steered right. At same time, D1 moved back to correct side. Head-on collision ensured—*Held*, D1 wholly liable—D2 had acted reasonably in emergency.

(c) Sudden Failure of Health

1. Ryan v. Youngs (1938) 82 S.J. 233; [1938] 1 All E.R. 522, C.A.

Held, not liable: "An apparently healthy, apparently competent man, in charge of a competent machine, is suddenly struck down, and that is a matter which no one can anticipate" (Slesser L.J. at 524 H).

2. Watmore v. Jenkins [1962] 2 Q.B. 572; [1962] 2 All E.R. 868, D.C.

Dangerous driving case—defence was that owing to an excess of bodily and injected insulin defendant was in a state of automatism while driving and therefore not responsible for his acts—*Held*, defence could not succeed, as defendant had driven five miles and it was unreasonable to say that the whole of his driving over this distance had been unconscious or involuntary.

3. Waugh v. Allan [1964] 2 Lloyd's Rep. 1; 1964 S.C.(H.L.) 162, H.L.

Held, no evidence that driver had been guilty of negligence in driving shortly after one of his gastric attacks.

4. Jones v. Dennison [1971] R.T.R. 174; [1971] C.L.Y. 1038, C.A.

D, an epileptic, had a sudden black-out while driving—he had had similar black-outs previously of which, though known to his wife, he was completely unaware—*Held*, D was not, and could not reasonably have been, aware of the tendency, and he had displaced the presumption of negligence against him.

5. Roberts v. Ramsbottom [1980] 1 All E.R. 7; [1980] R.T.R. 261, Neill J.

Defendant suffered stroke which impaired his awareness of surroundings and ability to control car. D able to drive purposefully albeit inefficiently and collided with stationary vehicle—*Held*, defence of automatism failed and defendant liable. A "driver will be able to escape liability if his actions at the relevant time were wholly beyond his control . . . But if he retained some control, albeit imperfect control, and his driving, judged objectively, was below the required standard, he remains liable" (at 15). Also, defendant negligent in continuing to drive when he should have known that he was unfit to do so.

6. Moses v. Winder [1981] R.T.R. 37; [1980] Crim. L.R. 232, C.A.

D, knowing that he was about to have an attack of diabetic coma, drove on after taking sugar sweets. Coma came on, causing accident—*Held*, D had not taken proper precautions and was guilty of careless driving.

7. Kaye v. Alfa Romeo (1984) 134 New L.J. 126; [1984] C.L.Y. 2295, Hutchison J.

U1. Cullen v. Hardy (1958) C.A. 53

Plaintiff knocked down by lorry—driver taking injured man bleeding profusely to surgery—driver apt to faint at sight of blood and had fainted seven years ago—driver felt queer but pulled himself together and feeling passed off for a while—fainted and knocked down plaintiff—*Held*, no negligence.

(d) Lights on Vehicles

(*N.B.* Cases dealing with Unlit Stationary Vehicles are grouped in Chap. 13, (1) (q), and cases on the extent to which a driver must be able to stop within the limits of his vision are set out in Chap. 13, (1) (g).)

1. Dawrant v. Nutt [1960] 1 W.L.R. 253; [1960] 3 All E.R. 681, Stable J.

Husband driver of, and wife passenger in, motor-cycle combination which has (as they both know) broken headlight—collision with defendant's car, husband and defendant being equally to blame—*Held*, in action by wife, that her claim would be reduced by 25 per cent. for contributory negligence in travelling in vehicle which she knew had inadequate lights.

2. Rowlands v. Street, *The Times*, November 22, 1962; [1962] C.L.Y. 2035, C.A.

Defendant following plaintiff's car at a little distance in fast lane of four-lane highway—plaintiff's car developed stoppage in feed system and slowed right down—at this moment a car going in opposite direction dazzled and blinded defendant—when he recovered plaintiff's car was just ahead of him—collision—*Held*, reversing county court judge, defendant liable, as the failure of plaintiff's car was a foreseeable emergency and defendant should have anticipated it might have slowed down or stopped while he was dazzled.

3. Chisman v. Electromation (1969) 6 K.I.R. 456; [1969] C.L.Y. 2393, C.A.

Similar facts to **U1**, but innocent driver had 700 yards of straight visibility, and driver of stationary vehicle flashed headlights at him as he approached—*Held*, 50: 50.

4. Jordan v. North Hampshire Plant Hire [1970] R.T.R. 212; [1970] C.L.Y. 2565, C.A.

Held, defendants liable for a most dangerous manoeuvre, despite the fact that there was no statutory requirement that the sides of long lorries should be lit at night.

U1. Roberts v. Arnold (1967) C.A. 173

Held, driver of stationary car was wholly liable, although oncoming car had 75 yards of intervisibility: "I can think of few things more dangerous than to park a car in a narrow road on the wrong side and to leave the headlights on. I make that observation regardless of whether the head-lights are dipped or full on" (Willmer L.J., 4E).

U2. Pickett v. Hall (1968) C.A. 23

Similar facts to **U1**, but innocent driver had 300–400 yards of straight visibility and tried to steer to his offside of stationary car—C.A. *upheld* trial judge's finding that stationary car wholly to blame.

U3. Harwin v. Thurlow (1984) C.A. 940

Defendant drove without lights during hours of darkness so slowly and close to kerb as to be indistinguishable from parked car to other moving traffic, then pulled out into plaintiff's path. Plaintiff struck rear of defendant's car—*Held*, defendant liable in full.

U4. Sutton v. Jones (1985) C.A. 624

Held, to drive a vehicle in foggy conditions with only one of two rear lights working raised a presumption of negligence against the driver, which could be displaced by driver's explaining how light came to be off without negligence on his part.

(e) Look-out

(*N.B.* See also the cases in Chap. 13(1) (g), (h), (j), (k), (l), (p) and (q), in which questions of look-out often arise).

		Whether liable for bad look-out
CROSSING ON GREEN AT TRAFFIC LIGHTS	1	No
TURNING RIGHT—NOT LOOKING IN MIRROR	2	Yes
Approaching minor road—seeing traffic thereon	3	Yes
PULLING UP—GLANCING ONCE IN MIRROR	4	No
Crossing on green at traffic lights	5	Yes
SETTING SUN—HIGHWAY AUTHORITY MUST TAKE REDUCED LOOK-OUT INTO ACCOUNT	6	
Overtaking vehicle behind another emitting dense smoke	7	Yes
HORIZONTAL POLE PROJECTING ABOVE HIGHWAY	8	Yes
Crossing on green at lights—which then go amber	U1	No
Pedestrian hurrying into front offside of car	U2	No
Drivers cannot look everywhere at once	U2	No
Turning away at roundabout—not looking in mirror	U3	Yes
Pulling up—not looking in mirror	U4	Yes
Turning right—not looking ahead	U5	Yes

Driver under no duty to keep look-out for possible side roads	U6	No
Turning right—motor cycle approaching from behind	U7	No
Lorry—blind spot	V8	No

1. Joseph Eva v. Reeves [1938] 2 K.B. 393; [1938] 2 All E.R. 115, C.A.

Defendant at lights which turn green—he pulls out onto offside to overtake stream ahead—X comes across lights at red and collides with defendant—*Held*, defendant not negligent. He owed no duty to traffic crossing in disobedience to the lights beyond that if he saw such traffic in fact he should take reasonable steps to avoid a collision. *Explained* in **U1**. *Also* see **5**.

2. Davies v. Swan Motor Co. [1949] 2 K.B. 291; [1949] 1 All E.R. 620, C.A.

Lorry turned across path of overtaking bus—*Held*, driver of lorry negligent for not using mirror (and not giving signal to turn).

3. Lang v. London Transport Executive [1959] 1 W.L.R. 1168; [1959] 3 All E.R. 609, Havers J.

Deceased motor-cyclist emerging from minor onto major road—"Slow Major Road Ahead" sign—approached at 20 m.p.h. and entered major road without slowing down—defendant bus driver on major road collided with him—"Slow" sign on major road—defendant saw there was traffic moving along minor road as he approached—but did not look again—knew minor road had "Major Road Ahead" sign—also knew that vehicles do suddenly emerge when unwise to do so—*Held*, defendant negligent in not looking further at side road as he approached. One-third against defendant, two-thirds against deceased.

4. Flack v. Withers, *The Times*, March 22, 1960, C.A.

Jury case—jury found for plaintiff—C.A. (Sellers L.J. dissenting) held defendant not liable—ultimately case was settled *coram* H.L. (see [1961] 3 All E.R. 388)—for approximately 50 per cent. of full value—case was one where plaintiff cyclist ran into preceding car as it pulled up behind stationary vehicle—defendant driver said that he looked in his inside mirror but did not see anyone behind as he was about to pull up—Ormerod L.J., in holding that this was not negligent, *said* that a driver could not give more than an occasional glance in his mirror.

5. Godsmark v. Knight Bros, *The Times*, May 12, 1960; [1960] C.L.Y. 2152, Barry J.

Collision at traffic lights—lorry crossed at amber—car going slightly faster crossed at green to it—car hit lorry on offside at right angles—neither driver had infringed the regulations—car driver relied on *Eva v. Reeves* **1**—*Held*, car one-third, and lorry two-thirds to blame; *Eva v. Reeves* was a case where the defendant had crossed at red; different considerations applied where a vehicle crossed at amber.

6. Davies v. Carmarthenshire C.C. [1971] R.T.R. 112, C.A.

D highway authority, in widening a main road, left a lamp-post in what had become the centre of the road—only sign was one saying "Road Works Ahead"—normally lamp-post could be seen 100 yards away, but owing to setting sun plaintiff was dazzled—*Held*, defendants 80 per cent. to blame.

7. Tysoe v. Davies [1984] R.T.R. 88; [1984] C.L.Y. 2338, Skinner J. *Held*, overtaking driver 20 per cent. to blame for failing to keep a proper look-out. For further details, see Chap. 13,(1) (h) **14**.

8. Diboll v. City of Newcastle upon Tyne [1993] P.I.Q.R. P1; [1993] C.L.Y. 3795, C.A.

Plaintiff was passenger in refuse vehicle owned by first defendant and driven by their employee. Plaintiff injured when vehicle collided with horizontal pole projecting above highway. This had formed part of stall in market which had been held in area through which highway ran. Area, of which first defendants had overall control, had seen closed to traffic until market had closed, about 40 minutes before accident. By time of accident, second defendant, who had erected stall, should have dismantled it. Third defendant, stallholder, had left scene having removed canopy from projecting poles. Trial judge held first defendant vicariously liable for negligence of driver in failing to see pole, and all three defendants liable for nuisance on highway. On appeal as to contribution, the Court of Appeal held that negligence of driver and nuisance on highway were respectively 75 per cent. and 25 per cent. responsible for accident. On the facts, first defendants less to blame for the nuisance than second and third defendants. Total contributions, therefore, 80 per cent., 10 per cent. and 10 per cent. by first, second and third defendants, respectively.

U1. Rowlands v. George Fisher (1959) C.A. 203

Defendant crossed stop line when lights at green—as he got onto junction he saw lights go to amber—he went on—plaintiff (who was crossing from defendant's nearside) moved off on red and amber—the mutual views were obscured by a large van on plaintiff's right, which also started on red and amber but stopped in time—collision between plaintiff and defendant—*Held*, defendant not liable.

Eva v. Reeves **1**, *per* Hodson L.J. (8 C), does not absolve drivers crossing with lights in their favour from keeping a lookout, but (7 D) "it (*i.e.* the decision) does not cast a heavy burden on them of anticipating such danger as might arise from the action of someone who is unlawfully on the crossing"—*Held*, also that defendant was under no duty to go onto the crossing "tenderly" (as Thesiger J. had held) in case the lights went to amber while he was crossing.

U2. Brown v. Bramley (1960) C.A. 145

"The human vision, although it is very remarkable and takes in a very wide field, cannot take in everything at the same time. The driver has to look not only in front but to right and to left and in his mirror behind. But he cannot look at all these places at the same time. His primary duty is to look at the part of the road in which he is himself travelling. That does not mean that he is absolved from keeping observation even on pavements as well as on the other half of the road. But that is a matter really of degree" (Hodson L.J., 4 F)—*Held*, that defendant driver was not liable for failing to see a pedestrian who hurried or ran into the front offside mudguard of defendant's car: car was on crown of 90-foot road and pedestrian was coming from defendant's offside.

U3. Sleater v. Marshall (1960) C.A. 299

Ormerod L.J. (5 A): "It is surely part of the duty of anybody driving a car in modern conditions of traffic, to keep an eye on his driving mirror and to know what is coming behind him, especially if he is driving into a roundabout of this kind and running into another road heading away from the roundabout."

U4. Hilling v. Ferris (1962) C.A. 404

Van stopped suddenly in road eight feet out from kerb to give friend a lift—driver failed to look in mirror—motor-cyclist following collided—*Held*, van driver negligent in not looking (25 per cent. to blame).

U5. Davies v. Kermode Jones (1962) C.A. 354

Plaintiff autocyclist turning right on main road—defendant motor-cyclist, going too fast and no look-out, ran into plaintiff from opposite direction—defendant was found wholly liable by Nield J.—*Held*, on appeal, 50:50, as plaintiff must either have failed to look, or, if he crossed when his view was obstructed, he ought to have waited until view was clear.

U6. Rea v. Difolco (1973) C.A. 241

Defendant emerged from side road—on plaintiff's offside—side road was not indicated by any signpost on major road—*Held*, plaintiff not liable at all, as she was under no duty to look to her right for possible side roads as she went along.

U7. Bradley v. Tinsley (1987) C.A. 449

Defendant's car turned right having signalled to do so. Motorcycle driven at speed collided with near offside of car. Defendant had not seen motor cycle before impact—*Held*, defendant not liable. His failure to see motor cycle not causative of accident. There was ample room for the motorycle to have passed on nearside.

U8. Archer v. Brown (1988) C.A. 831

On a congested roundabout, plaintiff drove into a gap to nearside of defendant's lorry. Plaintiff's path then blocked. Defendant steered left and hit plaintiff's car, which he had not seen because it was in a blind spot—*Held*, defendant not liable.

(f) Mechanical and Other Defects

1. Barkway v. South Wales Transport [1950] A.C. 185; [1950] 1 All E.R. 592, H.L.

Skid caused by burst tyre—all allegations of negligence were negatived except failure to have a system of reporting blows likely to cause an impact fracture—Held, on this ground, defendants were liable.

2. Roberts v. T. Wallis [1958] 1 Lloyd's Rep. 29, Barry J.

"In those circumstances, can it be said that the owner of a machine of this kind, or indeed the owner of a motor-car, is responsible if through some defect (which may well be entirely latent) of a connecting rod it breaks, during the time the machine is in motion?" (38).

3. Henderson v. Henry E. Jenkins [1970] A.C. 282; [1969] 3 All E.R. 756, H.L.

Brake-fluid pipe of lorry collapsed through corrosion—the corrosion was on the inside and could not have been seen without removal of pipe—it was not advocated that pipes should be removed except at major overhaul after about 300,000 miles—it was probable that something unusual must have happened to cause the corrosion—defendants called no evidence—*Held*, they were liable, for the onus of proving latent defect was on them, and it might have been, for example, that something unusual had happened, of which they knew or ought to have known. From Lord Reid's speech (758 H), it seems probable that the defendants would have exculpated themselves if they proved they had a proper system for drivers reporting unusual occurrences.

4. Tan Chye Choo v. Chong Kew Moi [1970] 1 W.L.R. 147; [1970] 1 All E.R. 266, P.C.

Held, driver not liable, as the defect was latent and all proper maintenance had been carried out—*Held*, further, that no action for breach of statutory duty arising under the Construction and Use Rules would lie, although "it may well be that statutory obligations will often indicate a standard of care which must be reached" (154 F).

5. Rees v. Saville [1983] R.T.R. 332; [1983] C.L.Y. 2537, C.A.

Defendant purchased used car with valid M.O.T. certificate issued three or four months previously—as there was nothing to indicate any serious defect in the car, defendant did not have it examined by an engineer. Three or four weeks after purchase, suspension failed causing car to collide with plaintiff's car—*Held*, that the defendant had not been at fault. Although the M.O.T. test system does not relieve the owner of his duty to use reasonable care in relation to the maintenance of his vehicle, there was nothing to indicate any risk if the defendant postponed expert examination and service for a month or two after purchasing the car, and he was not therefore negligent in failing to discover and remedy the defect in time.

6. Tysoe v. Davis [1984] R.T.R. 88; [1984] C.L.Y. 2338, Skinner J.

Held, defendant liable in negligence and public nuisance.

7. R. v. Bristol Crown Court, ex p. Jones (1986) 83 Cr. App. R. 109; [1986] R.T.R. 259, D.C.

Lights on lorry suddenly failed at unlit section of M4. Driver took foot off accelerator and immediately pulled onto hard shoulder, where he struck another vehicle he could not see in the darkness—*Held*, driver not guilty of driving without due care and attention—had done what was reasonable given that he had been confronted suddenly by an emergency.

8. Worsley v. Hollins [1991] R.T.R. 252; *The Times*, March 22, 1991, C.A.

Van driven by first defendant and owned by second defendant collided with rear of plaintiff's stationary vehicle. First defendant established that brakes had failed because a split pin had become detached from the brake linkage and held not liable at first instance. Second defendant said he had had van fully serviced by automobile engineers six weeks before accident, and produced M.O.T. certificate dated four weeks before accident—*Held*, on the basis of his unchallenged evidence, second defendant not liable.

U1. McMinn v. Spath (1961) C.A. 187 B

Driver to passenger: "I do not think your door is properly shut"—passenger puts hand on door handle—door flies open—passenger thrown out—*Held*, defendant not liable.

U2. Elliott v. Chiew (1966) C.A. 150

U3. Sutcliffe v. Trojan (1967) C.A. 143

U4. Hopper v. Haynes (1973) C.A. 17

Tyre burst—car then hit baulk of timber on side of road—which swung into plaintiff's car—*Held*, applying dictum of Asquith L.J. in *Barkway* (see Chap. 3, (2) (b) **6**), defendant liable, as he had failed to show that, with reasonable care, he could not have avoided hitting baulk. Although the tyre burst was in itself a neutral event, the onus still lay on the defendant to explain how the whole incident occurred without negligence on his part.

U5. Ancliffe v. Tams (1990) C.A. 106

Plaintiff on motor cycle came round bend to be confronted by lorry overtaking defendants' parked lorry. Plaintiff braked, but road wet, plaintiff going too fast and rear tyre partially devoid of tread—lost control and crashed—*Held*, defendants liable for parking on bend; plaintiff one-third to blame.

U6. Jeevanjee v. Russell (1991) C.A. 894

Collision between first and second defendants, travelling in opposite directions at night. First defendant driving at speed, overtook without checking road ahead was safe. Second defendant's offside headlight not working—*Held*, first defendant 75 per cent. to blame; second defendant 25 per cent., for failing to notice headlight not working.

(g) Night, Fog and Ice

(*N.B.* The following types of cases are dealt with in separate subsections:

1. Morris v. Luton Corporation [1946] 1 K.B. 114; [1946] 1 All E.R. 1, C.A.

Held, not a proposition of law that driver must be able to pull up within limits of vision, but each case must depend on own circumstances.

2. Burton v. West Suffolk C.C. [1960] 2 Q.B. 72; [1960] 2 All E.R. 26, C.A.

Formation of paper-thin coating of ice on road for distance of 58 feet—temperature had fallen from 38 at noon to 30.7 at 6 p.m. and 32.1 at 9 p.m.—driver skidded on the ice at 9 p.m.—going reasonable speed—*Held*, not negligent, as a reasonably prudent driver would not have been able to control skid.

3. Powell v. Phillips [1972] 3 All E.R. 864; [1973] R.T.R. 19, C.A.

Pedestrian walking in left-hand gutter at night at places where the pavement was impassable due to snow—*Held*, not contributory negligence (but result might have been different if defendant's driving had not been so unreasonable: see Stephenson L.J. at 6 C). *Applied* in **4**.

4. Kerley v. Downes [1973] R.T.R. 189, C.A.

Plaintiffs, father and young son, walking on nearside of 19-foot unlit road when struck from behind—nearside verge too rough to walk on—but on the offside there was a footpath—*Held*, applying **3** and **U2**, no contributory negligence.

5. Lancaster v. H.B. and H. Transport [1979] R.T.R. 380, C.A.

Main road driver ran into side of long lorry as latter was crossing the second dual carriageway. It was just after dawn with drifting fog limiting visibility to 50–100 yards—*Held*, lorry driver solely liable. For details see Chap. 13 (2) **12**.

6. Lloyd's Bank v. Budd [1982] R.T.R. 80; [1982] C.L.Y. 2154, C.A.

Lorry broke down on A1 road due to burnt out clutch—left overnight in lay-by—next day, in fog, it was driven off for repairs—and broke down again due to clutch—causing multiple collision—*Held*, lorry driver had been "very blameworthy" in driving back onto A1 in fog when he knew of the risk of further breakdown, and was 40 per cent liable.

7. Wright v. Lodge; Kerek v. Lodge [1993] 4 All E.R. 299; [1993] R.T.R. 123, C.A.

At night, S's car, in which D was rear seat passenger stopped in nearside lane of unlit dual carriageway because engine petered out. Fog reduced visibility to 60 yards. About three minutes later L, driving at 60 m.p.h. a lorry subject to a limit of 50 m.p.h., caught rear of car a glancing blow. Lorry went out of control into opposite carriageway and overturned. There, cars driven by W and K collided with it—*Held*, trial judge entitled to find that sole legal cause of collisions involving W and K was the negligence of L (who admitted liability) rather than negligence of S in failing to push car onto verge. Not every "but for which" cause was necessarily a relevant legal cause. Which were and which were not had to be determined by application of common sense. A distinction could be drawn between negligent and reckless driving. An obstruction which was only a danger to a reckless driver was not a relevant cause. The foregoing applied even though the trial judge also found that S's negligence *was* a legal cause of first impact (ordering S to contribute 10 per cent. to D's claim against L) though (per Parker L.J.) "I am far from sure that I would have reached the same conclusion" and (*per* Woolf L.J.) "the question as to whether [S] caused even the initial collision was highly debatable".

U1. Scott v. Edwards Motors (1961) C.A. 416

Icy road—lorry loaded with four-and-a-half tons travelling at 20 m.p.h. suddenly skidded across road—*Held*, speed too fast for conditions and driver negligent.

U2. Parkinson v. Parkinson (1963) C.A. 74

Two pedestrians in country road walking on left-hand side at night—taking up four feet six inches of roadway—no available footpath—Streatfeild J. held no contributory negligence—*Held*, by C.A., not without some doubt, they would not disturb judgment. *Applied* in **4**.

U3. Barber v. British Road Services (1964) C.A. 289, *The Times*, November 18, 1964

Defendant lorry reversing broadside across trunk road at night—headlights on—*Held*, plaintiff two-thirds, defendant one-third, to blame (reversing trial judge, who exonerated defendant).

U4. Burgess v. Hearn (1965) C.A. 93; *The Guardian*, May 25, 1965

Fog—visibility 10–15 yards—16-foot road—two damaged vehicles on plaintiff's nearside 15 yards apart—plaintiff pulled out to pass at 25 m.p.h.—hit defendant's car coming in opposite direction—defendant had only sidelights on—judge (Faulks J.) found 50 : 50—*Held*, defendant was probably at fault in having sidelights only, but it had no causative effect on the accident, and plaintiff was solely to blame.

U5. Woodward v. P.O. (1967) C.A. 188

Fog—visibility varying, but difficult at times to see kerb—P on motor-cycle overtaking car, while from opposite direction D in van overtakes electric delivery van—collision—D just on own side of white line—P just on wrong side—*Held*, 50 : 50, as in such conditions D was clearly "wrong, ill-advised and negligent" in overtaking so as to bring him so close to white line.

U6. Norman v. Allied Breweries (1982) C.A. 85

Fog—visibility 30 yards—main road 25 feet wide—van delivering newspapers stopped in road with hazard lights on—van driver could (as was inferred) have got off road—a lorry negligently overtook the van and collided with oncoming plaintiff—*Held*, van driver also negligent (25 per cent).

U7. Sutton v. Jones (1985) C.A. 624

Held, to drive a vehicle in foggy conditions with only one of two rear lights working raised a presumption of negligence against the driver, which could be displaced by driver's explaining how light came to be off without negligence on his part.

(h) Overtaking

1. Joseph Eva v. Reeves [1938] 2 K.B. 393; [1938] 2 All E.R. 115, C.A.

Defendant at lights which turn green—he pulls out onto offside to overtake stream ahead—X comes across lights at red and collides with defendant—*Held*, defendant not negligent. But see *Godsmark* (Chap. 13, (1) (e) **5**) and *Rowlands* (Chap. 13, (1) (e) **U1**).

2. Dorrington v. Griff Fender [1953] 1 W.L.R. 690; [1953] 1 All E.R. 1177, C.A.

Collision between plaintiff emerging from side road (in order to turn left) and defendant overtaking another vehicle (both coming from plaintiff's nearside)—*Held*, defendant was 25 per cent. at fault in passing where he knew there was a side road.

3. Holdack v. Bullock (1965) 109 S.J. 238; [1965] C.L.Y. 2683, C.A.

Held, no need to hoot when overtaking vehicle going straight along road. *Aliter*, if vehicle makes movement to put overtaking driver on inquiry.

4. Powell v. Moody (1966) 110 S.J. 215; *The Times*, March 10, 1966, C.A.

Motor-cycle overtaking stationary queue on offside—collides with vehicle emerging from nearside through gap in queue—*Held*, motor cycle 80 per cent. to blame.

5. Tocci v. Hankard (1966) 110 S.J. 835; [1966] C.L.Y. 8213, C.A.

Held, as the side road did not form a "road junction" in the sense used in the Highway Code, it was not negligent to overtake. *Cf. Dorrington* **2.**

6. Clarke v. Winchurch [1969] 1 W.L.R. 69; [1969] 1 All E.R.275, C.A.

Bus at head of slow-moving stream stopped to let parked vehicle pull out from nearside—moped driver overtook stream on off-side and collided with car as it slowly pulled out—*Held*, moped driver solely to blame. *Powell* **4** *distinguished* on the ground that in that case the driver pulling out through gap had not concentrated his look-out to the right as he inched his way out. *N.B.* At first instance bus driver was also sued for failing to ensure that moped driver got warning, but this was negatived on the ground that, although the bus driver had flashed his lights to the pulling-out car, his signal meant no more than "Come on as far as I am concerned", and he owed no duty to moped driver.

7. Burns v. Ellicott (1969) 113 S.J. 490; [1969] C.L.Y. 2424, Paull J.

8. R. v. Blything Justices [1970] R.T.R. 218; [1970] C.L.Y. 2596, D.C.

Said *obiter* that if a motorist being overtaken accelerated improperly so as to cause overtaking vehicle to cross double white lines, that might afford a defence to a charge of crossing white lines.

9. Challoner v. Williams [1975] 1 Lloyd's Rep. 124, C.A.

D1 moved into centre of road preparatory to turning right—did not see D2 who was overtaking—*Held*, reversing trial judge, D2 solely liable on the facts.

10. H. L. Motorworks v. Alwahli [1977] R.T.R. 276, C.A.

Three lanes of traffic—inner two lanes stopped to let car out of side road on left—D on outer third lane overtook the two inner stationary lanes—and collided with emerging car—*Held*, D solely liable.

11. Worsfold v. Howe [1980] 1 W.L.R. 1175; [1980] 1 All E.R. 1028, C.A.

D, emerging from station yard in order to turn right, inched his way in front of stationary tanker in nearside lane. Tanker was in queue but had stopped to allow gap. P on motor cycle travelling in outer lane overtook tanker and collided with D. Judge said that he would have found 50:50 but for the decision in *Clarke* **6** and applied *Clarke* to hold P entirely to blame—*Held*, that there were certain differences in the facts of the two cases, and that in any event *Clarke* was no authority for any principle in law that a driver who inched forward very slowly was entitled to emerge blind from a minor road. In the circumstances the judge's apportionment of 50:50 would be restored (though the Court said that they would not necessarily have reached such an apportionment themselves).

12. Carryfast Ltd. v. Hack [1981] R.T.R. 464; [1981] C.L.Y. 1847, Ralph Gibson J.

N.B. See also Chap. 9, (2) **8**.

13. Haimes v. Watson [1981] R.T.R. 90; [1981] C.L.Y. 1853, C.A.

Driver about to overtake horse. Horse shied, causing driver to lose control. Horse moved into path of car—*Held*, that, although the movement of the horse across the road gave rise of an inference of negligence, this was negatived by the rider's explanation that the horse had unforeseeably shied, and the rider was not liable. There was no absolute duty on a rider to keep his horse under control.

14. Tysoe v. Davies [1984] R.T.R. 88; [1984] C.L.Y. 2338, Skinner J.

Defendant's vehicle, emitting dense smoke, closely followed by Land Rover. Plaintiff, on moped behind, thinking smoke was from Land Rover, overtook it, to be confronted by defendant vehicle which he struck—*Held*, defendant liable. Plaintiff 20 per cent. to blame for failure to keep proper look-out.

15. Madden v. Quirk [1989] 1 W.L.R. 702; [1989] R.T.R. 304, Simon Brown J.

Plaintiff riding in open back section of first defendant's pick-up vehicle. First defendant overtook another vehicle when approaching a side road to his off-side, before reaching which he forced an oncoming Ford Escort to swerve to its nearside, due to his central position in road. Second defendant turned to his left from the side road, having looked first left and then right. As second defendant turned, struck by the pick-up. Further collisions ensued—*Held*, in terms of driving negligence, first and second defendants 80 per cent. and 20 per cent. to blame, respectively. The Escort would have masked second defendant's view of the pick-up as second defendant began to emerge, but shortly thereafter pick-up would have come into his view had he kept a proper look-out. However, because first defendant was also carrying plaintiff in a position of potential danger contrary to regulation 100(1) of the Road Vehicles (Construction and Use) Regulations, 1986, first defendant's contribution increased to 85 per cent., and second defendant's contribution reduced accordingly to 15 per cent.

U1. Saunders v. Pearce (1960) C.A. 141

Road 24 feet wide, narrowed to 16 feet by parked car—deceased motor-cyclist moved to his offside to overtake this car on his nearside—in doing so moved over to wrong side, being about central in the available roadway—defendant motor-cyclist on correct side of road collided with him in this position—*Held*, as each party could see each other, both to blame equally.

U2. Creber v. Ashenden (1962) C.A. 123

Plaintiff overtaking at road junction on offside—defendant turning right into junction without any signal—*Held*, defendant two-thirds and plaintiff one-third to blame (upholding judgment). Davies L.J. expressed doubt whether he would have put plaintiff's share as high as one-third.

U3. Drugnick v. United Service Transport (1963) C.A. 281

Van pulled out into outer of three lanes in order to turn right—pile up from following traffic in outer lane ensues—*Held*, van one-quarter to blame, for having meandered into far lane without regard for other traffic.

U4. Gardner v. Gains (1966) C.A. 83

Held, reversing trial judge (who exonerated overtaking car), 50:50.

U5. Teakel v. Rayner (1967) C.A. 204

Three-lane road—D in act of overtaking lorry when P on motor-cycle pulls from opposite direction to overtake tanker—*Held*, D not liable.

U6. Rainshaw v. Stockwell (1970) C.A. 114

Cyclist suddenly wobbled or swerved while being overtaken in inner lane—forcing overtaking car into outer lane—car in outer lane being driven carefully collides—London traffic—*Held*, overtaking motorist liable, as she had ignored car in outer lane. (*N.B.* Bicyclist was not traced.)

U7. Grace v. Lamoureaux (1977) C.A. 31

Wide road—D travelling east and P west. P pulled out to overtake stationary car but remaining just on his side of the road. D, travelling on crown of road (for no reason), remained on crown and collided with P—*Held*, D solely liable. A driver placed like P was "entitled to assume that there will be a measure of sanity in the driver coming the other way that will cause him to move from the position in the road which he occupies" (Cairns L.J., 6 G).

U8. Crawford v. Jennings (1981) C.A. U.B. 272

Defendant intending to turn right into main road. Nearside lane of main road contained stationary queue of traffic. First driver in queue flashed on defendant who edged across and collided with plaintiff who was overtaking queue at moderate speed in offside lane—*Held*, that the judge had been entitled to find the defendant solely to blame for the accident. As had been said in *Worsfold v. Howe* **11**, *Clarke v. Winchurch* **6**, did not lay down any principle of law and each case has to be decided on its own facts.

U9. Curtis v. R.D.B. Freight Lines Ltd (1984) C.A. 131

Plaintiff, a cyclist, looked round, put out her right arm and began to turn right when defendant's lorry was only 30 yards behind her. Defendant tried to pass her on offside, but struck her outstretched arm and she fell from bicycle—*Held*, defendant liable—had seen plaintiff look round and reacted belatedly. Plaintiff 75 per cent. contributorily negligent, for doing what she did when lorry so close.

U10. Davies v. Price (1985) C.A. 844

Defendant's car overtook plaintiff, a 14-year-old cyclist, giving an insufficiently wide berth. Plaintiff veered into car's path—*Held*, defendant liable, plaintiff 30 per cent. contributorily negligent.

U11. Nugent v. James (1988) C.A. 1062 (unreported)

Defendant's car emerged from side road, though gap left in queue of traffic, intending to turn right. Collided with plaintiff's motor cycle which was overtaking queue. Defendant had looked right but had not seen plaintiff. Plaintiff going too fast and keeping no careful look-out—*Held*, defendant liable, but plaintiff 75 per cent. contributorily negligent.

U12. Farrell v. Rothon (1989) C.A. 300 (unreported)

Defendant's car emerged from side road, through gap left in queue of traffic, intending to turn right. When protuding a short distance beyond offside line of the queue, collided with plaintiff's moped which was overtaking queue—*Held*, defendant liable, plaintiff 50 per cent. contributorily negligent.

U13. Lewis v. Lieberman (1990) C.A. 164

Plaintiff overtook defendant approaching blind bend. Realising he would not make it, plaintiff braked to pull back in, but defendant also braked, and head on collision ensued—*Held*, plaintiff solely to blame.

U14. Emmett v. Block (1992) C.A. 621

Plaintiff, motor cyclist with "L" plates, looked back for friends and wobbled. Defendant, about to overtake, hit plaintiff—*Held*, defendant liable—had not seen "L" plates and did not give plaintiff clearance he would have done, had he seen them. Plaintiff 50 per cent. to blame.

(j) Parking

(*N.B.* See also the "stopping" cases in 13 (m), some of which are analagous).

1. David Taylor v. Bowden Transport [1966] 1 Lloyd's Rep. 287, Winn L.J.

Held, negligence.

2. Kelly v. W.R.N. [1968] 1 W.L.R. 921; [1968] 1 All E.R. 369, Ashworth J.

Overruled by **9**.

3. Cohen v. Plaistow [1968] 2 Lloyd's Rep. 587, MacKenna J.

Held, negligent (*obiter*).

4. Chisman v. Electromation (1969) 6 K.I.R. 456; [1969] C.L.Y. 2393, C.A.

Similar facts to **U1**, but moving driver had 700 yards of visibility, and stationary driver flashed headlights as former approached—*Held*, 50: 50.

5. B. G. Transport v. Marston Motor [1970] 1 Lloyd's Rep. 371, Bean J.

Held, D. not liable as car-park owners, as the van was only parked under a licence, in that the presentation of the parking ticket was not a prerequisite to withdrawing the vehicle.

6. Stevens v. Kelland [1970] R.T.R. 445, Waller J.

7. Watson v. Heslop [1971] R.T.R. 308, C.A.

D parked his car at night, showing a single parking light only, on a busy main road 22 feet 8 inches wide—plaintiff was blinded by an oncoming car's headlights and ran into parked car—*Held*, plaintiff 70 per cent., defendant 30 per cent. to blame.

8. Dymond v. Pearce [1972] 1 Q.B. 496; [1972] 1 All E.R. 1142, C.A.

Held, lorry driver not liable to motor cyclist who ran into lorry. C.A. said that parking such a lorry in the manner done made an obstruction, which was in turn a nuisance, but the real cause of the accident was the negligence of the motor cyclist. Edmund Davies L.J. *said* that an obstruction on a road constituting a nuisance had to be a danger to be actionable, and in addition it must be shown that the defendant did not use reasonable care; but if it was a danger, then the defendant was liable unless he had sufficient justification or excuse.

9. Coote v. Stone [1971] 1 W.L.R. 279; [1971] 1 All E.R. 657, C.A.

So *held*, overruling *Kelly* **2** (where it had been held that an action lay for breach of statutory duty in not observing parking regulations).

10. Denton v. United Omnibus Co. Ltd, *The Times*, May 6, 1986; [1986] C.L.Y. 2250, C.A.

Defendants' bus parked in depot with no door or gates. Bus not immobilised—unlawfully taken and driven into collision with plaintiff's car—*Held*, defendant not liable. In the absence of a special relationship or special circumstances, a party was not liable in negligence for failing to prevent the unlawful or unauthorized act of another.

11. Topp v. London Country Bus (South West) [1993] 1 W.L.R. 979; [1993] 3 All E.R. 448, C.A.

Defendant's minibus left for over eight hours unlocked, unattended and with keys in at bus stop outside public house—unlawfully taken and driven into collision with cyclist—*Held*, defendants not liable—owed no duty of care to cyclist—acts of wrongdoer constituted *novus actus interveniens. P. Perl (Exporter) Ltd v. Cambden L. B. C.* (Chap. 1, (3) (b) **15**) followed.

U1. Roberts v. Arnold (1967) C.A. 173

"I can think of few things more dangerous than to park a car in a narrow road on the wrong side and to leave the headlights on. I make that observation regardless of whether the headlights are dipped or full on" (Willmer L.J., 4 E)—*Held*, oncoming driver was free from blame, although he had 75 yards of intervisibility, "on the basis of the agony of collision rule" (per Willmer L.J., 5 F).

U2. Pickett v. Hall (1968) C.A. 23

Similar facts to U1, but innocent driver had 300–400 yards of straight road and tried to steer to his offside of stationary car—*Held*, stationary driver wholly to blame.

U3. Gilbert v. Hay (1968) C.A. 403 B

Parking on nearside of 18-foot road just round blind corner—*Held*, clearly negligent.

U4. Cullip v. Horsham D.C. (1981) C.A. U.B. 9

Dust cart parked round blind bend. Plaintiff motor cyclist collides with cart. *Held*, both parties negligent, but fault of dust cart driver was so much greater that plaintiff's share of blame would be assessed at nil.

U5. Reardon v. Fall (1984) C.A. 1005

D1 went round sharp bend on motor cycle at proper speed—confronted by D2 well over central line, passing D3's car parked partly on road and partly on driveway. D1 lost control, swerving to avoid D2 and crashed, killing pillion passenger—*Held*, D1 not liable, D2 and D3 each 50 per cent to blame.

U6. Bibby v. Treacy (1989) C.A. 743

Defendant parked lorry outside general store where parking prohibited. Infant plaintiff walked, without looking, in front of lorry and into path of car—*Held*, defendant not negligent in parking where he did—did not create a reasonably foreseeable risk of danger.

U7. Ancliffe v. Tams (1990) C.A. 106

Plaintiff on motor cycle came round bend to be confronted by lorry overtaking defendants' parked lorry. Plaintiff braked, but road wet, plaintiff going too fast and near tyre partially devoid of tread—lost control and crashed—*Held*, defendants liable for parking on bend, plaintiff one-third to blame.

(k) Pedestrians

1. Daly v. Liverpool Corporation [1939] 3 All E.R. 142

Driver saw pedestrian crossing—allowed him sufficient clearance on the assumption pedestrian would move with normal speed—pedestrian was infirm and could not move normally—collision—*Held*, driver liable.

2. Bourhill v. Young [1943] A.C. 92, [1942] 2 All E.R. 396, H.L.

'A blind or deaf man who crosses the traffic on a busy street cannot complain if he is run over by a careful driver who does not know of and cannot be expected to observe and guard against the man's infirmity' (Lord Wright at 405 G). *But* see **4**.

3. Carmarthenshire C.C. v. Lewis [1955] A.C. 549; [1955] 1 All E.R. 565, H.L.

Held, Defendant school liable.

3A. Kozimor v. Adey (1962) 106 S.J. 431, Megaw J.

4. Haley v. London Electricity Board [1965] A.C. 778; [1964] 3 All E.R. 185, H.L.

Pavement excavation was fenced adequately for ordinary, but not for blind, persons—*Held*, defendants liable, as a duty of care was owed to blind persons as such when their presence was reasonably foreseeable. Dictum in *Bourhill* **2** is therefore no longer correct.

5. Neal v. Bedford [1966] 1 Q.B. 505; [1965] 3 All E.R. 250, D.C.

6. Watson v. Whitney [1966] 1 W.L.R. 57; [1966] 1 All E.R. 122, C.A.

Held, reversing registrar who tried case, driver 100 per cent. liable.

7. Burns v. Bidder [1967] 2 Q.B. 227; [1966] 3 All E.R. 29, D.C.

This judgment contains a helpful summary of earlier cases on and explanation of the duty under what is now regulation 8 of Zebra Pedestrian Crossing Regulations, 1971.

8. Barry v. MacDonald (1966) 110 S.J. 56; *The Times*, January 15, 1966, MacKenna J.

9. Baker v. Willoughby [1970] A.C. 467; [1969] 3 All E.R. 1528; H.L.

Held, pedestrian 25 per cent. to blame: "It is quite possible that the motorist may be very much more to blame than the pedestrian" (Lord Reid, 1531 A).

10. Snow v. Giddins (1969) 113 S.J. 229; *The Times*, February 28, 1969, C.A.

11. Green v. Hills (1969) 113 S.J. 385; *The Times*, April 22, 1969, James J.

12. Maynard v. Rogers (1970) 114 S.J. 320, Mocatta J.

Plaintiff at last moment, without looking and without having shown any signs of wanting to cross, stepped onto crossing—*Held*, pedestrian might have jumped back if defendant had hooted, although there was little else he could have done: one-third against defendant.

13. Jankovic v. Howell [1970] C.L.Y. 1863, Ormrod J.

Held, pedestrian was wholly to blame, as it was superfluous for a motorist to hoot or take evasive action every time a pedestrian approached a centre bollard.

14. Hurt v. Murphy [1971] R.T.R. 186, Talbot J.

P looked when starting to cross—nothing coming for 100 yards—as she crossed D approached at over 60 m.p.h. in a built up area and hit her—she did not look to her left after starting to cross—*Held*, 20 per cent. contributory negligence.

15. Mulligan v. Holmes [1971] R.T.R. 179, C.A.

Two pedestrians crossed at a well-lit junction on a crossing marked by studs—lights were green to traffic—D drove his car to crossing very fast—overtook another car—and hit pedestrians—*Held*, in the circumstances too much attention should not be paid to fact that lights were green to D, and pedestrians were only 20 per cent. liable.

16. Powell v. Phillips [1972] 3 All E.R. 864; [1973] R.T.R. 19, C.A.

Held, not negligent in the circumstances. Judgments indicate that if driver had not been going so fast, some negligence by pedestrian could well have been found.

17. Williams v. Needham [1972] R.T.R. 387; [1972] C.L.Y. 3080, Judge Stabb Q.C.

18. Kerley v. Downes [1973] R.T.R. 189, C.A.

Held, pedestrians not guilty of contributory negligence, even though there was a footpath on other side. **U2** *applied.*

19. Davies v. Journeaux [1976] R.T.R. 111; [1975] 1 Lloyd's Rep. 483, C.A.

20. Moore v. Poyner [1975] R.T.R. 127; [1975] C.L.Y. 2321, C.A.

21. Clifford v. Drymond [1976] R.T.R. 134; [1976] C.L.Y. 2434, C.A.

P went 10 feet onto crossing—and was hit by car which was circa 85 feet away when she stepped on—car was going at 26–30 m.p.h.—*Held*, (a) if she had *not* looked, she was clearly guilty of contributory negligence, and (b) if she *had* looked, she would have seen the danger. 20 per cent. contributory negligence.

22. Chapman v. Post Office [1982] R.T.R. 165; [1982] C.L.Y. 2136, C.A.

Held that defendant was 100 per cent. to blame. Plaintiff was not at fault merely because she was at the edge of or leaning out slightly from pavement.

23. Waller v. Lawton [1982] C.L.Y. 2132, Michael Davies J.

Defendant driving at 40 m.p.h. in 60 m.p.h. restricted area, saw plaintiff (almost 11) standing at kerbside holding a milk bottle. Plaintiff ran out, defendant braked, but collided with plaintiff—*Held*, that the defendant had been negligent in assuming that the plaintiff had seen him and in not sounding his horn. However, the plaintiff was held 40 per cent. to blame.

24. Skolimowski v. Haynes [1983] C.L.Y. 2525, Cantley J.

P began to cross when "green man" showing. P slightly disabled. As he was crossing "red man" came on which P did not notice. Traffic in first two lanes moved off but slowed to allow P to pass. As P moved into third lane, looking away from traffic, he was hit by D's car coming in third lane—*Held*, D negligent, there being a high duty of care owed when pedestrians were foreseeable, and, in particular, where there was only a short delay between the pedestrian light turning red and the traffic light turning green—as here—*Held*, however, P was one-third to blame. (*N.B.* As to which latter, *cf. Shephard v. West* **U1**, which was not appealed when the case later went to House of Lords on damages only).

25. Kilminster v. Rule (1983) 32 S.A.S.R. 39; [1983] C.L.Y. 2520, Sup.Ct. of South Australia

Held, that the trial judge had been wrong in disregarding the intoxication as a factor in the apportionment of responsibility. The reduction for contributory negligence should be increased from 20 per cent. to 35 per cent.

26. Foskett v. Mistry [1984] R.T.R. 1; [1984] C.L.Y. 2286, C.A.

Plaintiff aged 16 ran from parkland to the left of defendant's approaching car, across 10-foot wide pavement and some 10 feet into road, where struck by car, defendant not having seen plaintiff until then—*Held*, defendant liable—should have been plaintiff as he ran from parkland, appreciated he presented a potential hazard and sounded his horn or braked. Plaintiff 75 per cent. contributorily negligent—it was putting it a little too high to say that he should be treated as a fully grown adult man.

27. Old v. Eastern National Omnibus Co. [1984] C.L.Y. 2285, French J.

Plaintiff, aged four, riding bicycle in middle of pavement, wobbled into road, fell off, and struck by bus—*Held*, bus driver not liable—not foreseeable that plaintiff would fall into road—nothing the driver could have done to avoid accident. (*N.B.* Case included here because of its similarity to the "pedestrian" cases).

28. Donoghoe v. Blundell [1986] C.L.Y. 2254, H.H. Judge Lewis Hawser Q.C., O.R.

Plaintiff lying in road drunk, run over by car—*Held*, plaintiff two-thirds contributorily negligent.

29. Tremayne v. Hill [1987] R.T.R. 131, *The Times*, December 11, 1986, C.A.

Plaintiff crossed road diagonally at busy junction controlled by traffic lights—did not use nearby pelican crossing—struck by defendant's car which entered junction through red lights—*Held*, defendant wholly liable. Plaintiff not under a duty to look in direction from which defendant came, since plaintiff knew the lights were red. Plaintiff not under a duty to use pelican crossing. A pedestrian can cross the road where he likes, as long as he takes reasonable care for his own safety.

30. Fitzgerald v. Lane [1988] 3 W.L.R. 356; [1988] 2 All E.R. 961, H.L.

Plaintiff walked onto pelican crossing over two-lane carriageway when lights red against him. Passed between stationary traffic in congested nearside lane, but struck by first defendant's car travelling at about 30 m.p.h. in free-flowing offside lane, thrown onto opposite carriageway and struck again by second defendant's car—*Held*, on the facts, both defendants liable. H.L. upheld C.A. is ruling that plaintiff was 50 per cent. contributorily negligent, describing the ruling as generous, and plaintiff as substantially the author of his own misfortune.

31. Morales v. Eccleston [1991] R.T.R. 151; [1992] C.L.Y. 3189, C.A.

Defendant driving at 20 m.p.h. Steady stream of rush-hour traffic both ways. Plaintiff, aged 11, followed ball which rolled into road from defendant's offside pavement. Plaintiff not looking in either direction—caused a driver coming from his left to swerve—continued over centre of road and struck by car of defendant, who did not see him until impact—*Held*, defendant liable, but plaintiff 75 per cent. contributorily negligent. Defendant had only limited opportunity to see plaintiff before impact—the fact that he had not been plaintiff crossing defendant's offside of the road did not necessarily connote failure to keep a proper look-out.

32. Armstrong v. Cottrell [1993] P.I.Q.R. P 109; [1993] C.L.Y. 2956, C.A.

Defendant in offside of three lanes of busy carriageway. From 400 yards saw plaintiff, aged 12, and three other girls "hovering" on road side to his left. Then plaintiff and one other girl advanced to middle lane and hesitated. Defendant decelerated but when his car was very close the two girls suddenly darted into offside lane and impact occurred—*Held*, defendant liable. Having seen girls "hovering" and hesitating, should have reduced speed sufficiently to prevent accident and sounded horn. Plaintiff one-third contributorily negligent, having regard to her age.

33. Saleem v. Drake [1993] P.I.Q.R. P 129, [1993] C.L.Y. 2955, C.A.

Plaintiff, boy of six, held onto and ran round sapling in pavement three feet from kerb. Suddenly let go and was catapulted into collision with defendant's car travelling at 10 to 15 m.p.h. Defendant had seen plaintiff playing. Only issue was whether defendant should have sounded horn—*Held*, defendant not liable. Not incumbent on prudent motorist to sound horn on seeing children playing on pavement unless it could reasonably be anticipated that one or more might run into road.

34. Sweeney v. Westerman and Burton Coaches [1993] C.L.Y. 2941, H.H. Judge Wolton Q.C., sitting as a High Court Judge.

First defendant came out of public house at night and crossed road on which were patches of light and dark, to offside of second defendant's coach, where he spoke to a passenger before turning right to front of coach. Struck by plaintiff's motor cycle, overtaking coach. Plaintiff had had view of public house and coach for 528 yards—*Held*, first defendant negligent in placing himself in position of danger in reduced light and failing to keep proper look-out for traffic. Plaintiff one-third contributorily negligent. Second defendant not liable.

35. Hayes v. Robinson [1993] C.L.Y. 3004, Drake J.

Plaintiff, aged four, ran quickly in daylight from pavement directly into path of defendant's car. Defendant braked and swerved but unable to avoid collision—*Held*, defendant not liable—had done everything a prudent motorist could have done to avoid collision.

36. Ebanks v. Collins and M.I.B. [1994] C.L.Y. 3401, C.A.

Defendant's car struck plaintiff, aged six, who had run from defendant's offside pavement, between parked cars—*Held*, defendant not liable.

37. Pollard v. Curcic [1994] C.L.Y. 3402, H.H. Judge Stockdale, Watford County Court

Plaintiff crossed road in front of stationary bus into path of defendant's motorcycle overtaking bus at 15 m.p.h. Defendant braked and swerved but unable to avoid collision—*Held*, defendant not liable.

38. Connaire v. McGuire [1994] C.L.Y. 3343, Michael Wright J.

Plaintiff and M crossed A13 dual carriageway at junction controlled by traffic lights where no pedestrian facilities and where pedestrians rarely crossed. Second carriageway had four lanes. First was empty. In second and third was traffic to left of plaintiff and M, held by red lights. M crossed second carriageway slightly ahead of plaintiff. When plaintiff in second lane, lights to his knowledge changed to green. Defendant, in fourth lane to get flying start, accelerated away and struck plaintiff. M had completed his crossing—*Held*, defendant liable—should have noticed and been put on guard by M, should also have noticed plaintiff, and should have heeded the fact that traffic to his offside had not moved when lights changed to green. Plaintiff 40 per cent. contributorily negligent. Not negligent for crossing where he did but, having decided to do so, had a duty to take considerable care—should have looked left before venturing into fourth lane.

U1. Shephard v. West (1962) C.A. 326

Mother and child started to cross Euston Road when lights to traffic at red—as they crossed lights changed to amber and then green—bus on mother's left "whirred"—mother took step beyond front of bus and was run down by lorry coming up on left of bus—*Held*, lorry wholly liable, and mother not guilty of contributory negligence, as when she stepped off kerb lights were at red to traffic, "and one does not know when lights are going to turn to amber and green." *N.B.* It is not quite clear whether lights were at amber or green when lorry hit mother, but the negligence of lorry was not seriously in dispute, and the real point was whether mother was guilty of any contributory negligence. Decision of lower court, and facts, are reported in (1962) 106 S.J. 391.

U2. Parkinson v. Parkinson (1963) C.A. 74

Two pedestrians in country road walking on left-hand side at night, taking up four and a half feet of roadway—no pavement or footpath—*Held*, by Streatfield J., no contributory negligence—Held, by C.A., not without some doubt, they would not disturb judgment.

U3. Newbold v. Mason (1965) C.A. 243

Pedestrian run down when over halfway across—never kept car approaching from left in sight while going across—*Held*, 50 per cent. contributory negligence (reversing trial judge, who exonerated pedestrian).

U4. Heeley v. Birmingham Omnibus Co. (1967) C.A. 116

Held, reversing trial judge (who had exonerated bus driver), bus driver one-third to blame for breach of statutory duty (only). Applying *Burns v. Bidder* 7, a driver owed an absolute obligation "unless his control of the vehicle has been lost in some way through no fault of his own" (Willmer L.J., 7B).

U5. Frank v. Cox (1967) C.A. 138A

Held, driver of vehicle wholly liable. (See also (1967) 111 S.J. 670.)

U6. McGowan v. Warne Wright (1966) C.A. 287

4.45 p.m. in November in Birmingham—dark and raining—P halfway across road when run down—bad look-out by both parties—and D going too fast—trial judge found D had no lights on, and awarded 75 per cent. against him—C.A. disagreed and said he had lights on—*Held*, in these circumstances 50:50.

U7. Massey v. Part (1968) C.A. 409

Night—pedestrian 24 feet across first part of dual carriageway—run down from her right—*Held*, 60:40 against pedestrian.

U8. Wiltshire v. Foote (1968) C.A. 428

Visitor to Birmingham got trapped on dangerous traffic island, which a local resident would probably have avoided—*Held*, no contributory negligence as although the standard of care was an objective one, the ordinary reasonable pedestrian was not necessarily a local resident.

U9. Milson v. Curtis (1970) C.A. 69

Pedestrian wearing dark clothes wheeling bicycle across country road at night—*Held*, 80 per cent. to blame for accident.

U10. Trevor v. Cole (1984) C.A. 529

Groups of young men on either side of road. One ran across and defendant, approaching in car, braked to avoid him. Plaintiff then left pavement to defendant's nearside. Defendant did not see him, and car struck him—*Held*, defendant liable—having seen groups and previous man crossing, should have kept very careful look-out and slowed down to be able to avoid any other negligent pedestrians. (At first instance, plaintiff found guilty of contributory negligence, but amount not specified in Court of Appeal.)

U11. James v. Alger (1986) C.A. 229

Boy aged seven and another boy darting onto pelican crossing when taxi driver approaching at 30 m.p.h. and for whom the lights were green was only a few feet away. Taxi struck seven-year-old—*Held*, taxi driver not liable. It would be unreasonable to impose a duty to drive so slowly that a motorist could avoid a child in such circumstances—the motorist would otherwise have to drive at 5 m.p.h.

U12. Gore v. Naylor (1987) C.A. 389

Plaintiff and two friends, crossed road on Halloween, two of the three wearing witches' masks. Defendant motorcyclist approached to be confronted by "witches" prancing about in middle of road—braked and swerved but hit plaintiff's leg—*Held*, defendant liable, but plaintiff two-thirds contributorily negligent.

U13. Shaw v. Evans (1989) C.A. 34

Plaintiff crossed road having only looked left. Struck by defendant's taxi. Defendant had not seen plaintiff, but should have done so from about 80 feet—*Held*, defendant liable—should have slowed down and given warning of his approach.

U14. White v. Estate of Matteo Constantino, deceased (1989) C.A. 1010

Plaintiff crossed road from central island at junction controlled by traffic lights. As he passed in front of stationary traffic in the offside of two lanes, lights changed from red to green. Defendant, in nearside lane, went through lights at moderate speed and struck plaintiff—*Held*, defendant liable—should have anticipated someone might be crossing, from stationary traffic to his offside, and slowed down or warned of his approach. Plaintiff 40 per cent contributorily negligent.

U15. Pockett v. Simmonds (1989) C.A. 1011 (unreported)

Plaintiff, aged three, ran through gateway, across lay-by and onto road in front of defendant's car. Defendant did not see plaintiff until half-second before impact, when plaintiff at edge of road—*Held*, defendant not liable

U16. Channer v. Lucas (1990) C.A. 96

Plaintiff, aged 65, crossed road "at a sort of run, not very fast". Having got over centre line, she saw defendant's motorcycle approaching from her left at 30 m.p.h., and stopped. Had she not done so, defendant would have passed behind her. In the event, he hit her—*Held*, defendant liable—failed to anticipate likely movement or reaction of elderly pedestrian confronted by approaching motor cycle. Plaintiff 75 per cent: to blame—failed to see defendant's motor cycle when began to cross, and gave no warning of her intention to stop.

U17. Tunney v. Guy (1991) C.A. 131

Defendant, driving car at 30 m.p.h., saw 76-year-old plaintiff just over centre of road, crossing from defendant's right to left, apparently oblivious to traffic. Defendant sounded horn, braked and swerved onto offside of road. Plaintiff turned, rushed to retrace his steps and collided with defendant's car—*Held*, defendant not liable—plaintiff's reaction unforeseeable.

U18. Parsons v. Pullman Foods Ltd (1991) C.A. 194

Plaintiff, aged 12, crossed road in front of bus into path of overtaking lorry. Lorry driver had previously stopped behind bus, knew children were alighting and had seen one child run across front of his lorry—*Held*, lorry driver liable—should have sounded horn. Plaintiff one-third to blame.

U19. Roberts v. Pearson (1991) C.A. 335

Plaintiff, boy of 12, crossing from central reservation, stuck by motor cycle of defendant, who was driving too fast and not keeping proper look-out—*Held*, defendant liable, plaintiff one-third to blame. At the age of 12, a boy is not able to assess the speed of an approaching vehicle as well as an adult, and tends to be less inhibited.

U20. Thistlethwaite v. Watts (1991) C.A. 952

Defendant car driver saw plaintiff, a 16-year-old girl, and another girl on grass verge with backs to road, hopping up and down and throwing arms in air. Defendant slowed down, but as he drew level plaintiff rushed into road, giving defendant no chance to avoid collision—*Held*, defendant not liable—no duty in the circumstances to sound his horn.

(l) Road Junctions and Turning

(*N.B.* For Traffic Light cases, see Chap. 13, (1) (p).

1. France v. Parkinson [1954] 1 W.L.R. 581, [1954] 1 All E.R. 739, C.A.

2. MacIntyre v. Coles [1966] 1 W.L.R. 831; [1966] 1 All E.R. 723, C.A.

Y junction—D was going up main stem of Y, to bear right at junction—P was coming down left upper limb of Y—there was a bollard in the centre of the mouth of his road, and there were some indications (though no signs) that traffic following D's course had priority over P—in addition, Sellers L.J. (724 A) said: "It is a well-recognised rule, that where vehicles are approaching like that in risk of collision or where there is some doubt as to priority, the vehicle which has the other on its right-hand side is the vehicle to give way. It may not be established as obligatory, but it is a very salutary guiding rule."—*Held*, accordingly, that P was solely to blame. *N.B.* The rule about giving way to traffic on the right has, under the Traffic Signs Regulations, been made obligatory in the case of roundabouts.

3. Jordan v. North Hampshire Plant Hire [1970] R.T.R. 212; [1970] C.L.Y. 2565, C.A.

Held, a most dangerous manoeuvre, and defendants liable, despite the absence of any statutory requirement that sides of long lorries should be lit.

4. H.L. Motorworks v. Alwahbi [1977] R.T.R. 276; [1977] C.L.Y. 2021, C.A.

P coming from side road wanted to turn right. Both lanes of traffic coming from his right on main road stopped to let him out but D, also coming from P's right, overtook the two waiting lanes and hit P as he emerged—*Held*, D solely liable. P was entitled to assume no one would overtake in such circumstances.

5. Lancaster v. H.B. and H. Transport [1979] R.T.R. 380, C.A.

Held, lorry solely liable. For details see Chap. 13, (2)**12**.

6. Worsfold v. Howe [1980] 1 W.L.R. 1175; [1980] 1 All E.R. 1028, C.A.

Held, emerging driver and motor cyclist equally to blame. For fuller details see Chap. 13, (1)(h) **11**.

7. Truscott v. McLaren [1982] R.T.R. 34; [1982] C.L.Y. 2155, C.A.

Second defendant driving at 40 m.p.h. on major road. Fifty yards from crossroads saw first defendant's car approaching at 50–55 m.p.h. about 75 yards away on minor road. Second defendant relied on his right of way and took no evasive action. Collision at crossroads, injuring plaintiff at roadside—*Held*, that the first defendant was 80 per cent. and the second defendant 20 per cent. to blame.

8. Hardy v. Walder [1984] R.T.R. 312; [1984] C.L.Y. 2287, C.A.

Defendant drove from minor road at a junction 100–150 yards from which, to defendant's right on the main road, was a blind bend. Defendant had looked left and right, but was looking left as he emerged. Collided with plaintiff's motor cycle approaching from defendant's right at excessive speed, having overtaken a car on the blind bend—*Held*, defendant liable, plaintiff two-thirds to blame.

9. Banfield v. Scott and Ranzetta (1984) 134 New L.J. 550; [1984] C.L.Y. 2329, Croom-Johnson J.

First defendant drove from a side road into path of second defendant's car, followed by deceased's motor cycle, both approaching from first defendant's right. Second defendant braked and steered right. This caused deceased to pass second defendant on offside. Deceased lost control, hit a lorry coming the other way and was killed—*Held*, accident entirely the fault of first defendant, whose look-out and estimation of second defendant's speed were at fault.

10. Winter v. Cotton [1985] C.L.Y. 2978, H.H. Judge Clapham, Gravesend County Court

Held, driver giving false indication wholly liable for ensuing collision. For further details see Chap. 13, (1)(m) **10**.

11. Madden v. Quirk [1989] 1 W.L.R. 702; [1989] R.T.R. 304, Simon Brown J.

Held, in terms of driving negligence, driver emerging from side road 20 per cent, to blame, driver overtaking on main road 80 per cent. For further details see Chap. 13, (1)(h) **15**.

U1. Scott v. Lavis (1961) C.A. 347

Defendant driving on main road collided with cyclist emerging from side road whom he never saw—could have seen him for 100 feet before accident—*Held*, defendant one-third and cyclist two-thirds to blame.

U2. Creber v. Ashenden (1962) C.A. 123

Plaintiff overtaking at road junction on offside—defendant turning right into junction without any signal—*Held*, defendant two-thirds and plaintiff one-third to blame (upholding judgment). Davies L.J. expressed doubt whether he would have put plaintiff's share as high as one-third.

U3. Brooks v. Graham (1964) C.A. 77 A

D1 on major road entered crossroads at 15 m.p.h.—D2 entered from D1's left at 20 m.p.h., having ignored halt sign—D2 hit D1 on middle of nearside—D1 never saw D2 before impact—as he entered crossroads, he saw there was no vehicle on halt line, and went on—Winn J. found D1 25 per cent. to blame—*Held*, D1 was not to blame at all. As to D1's failure to see D2, Willmer L.J. (4 A) said that as D1 entered, D2 must have been some way down minor road, and if D1 had seen him, he would have been justified in assuming D2 would stop: "The judge has treated the case as though it were one of a collision at an uncontrolled crossroads, or a crossroads subject only to a slow sign. It seems to me that when one is dealing with a crossroads subject to a halt sign, wholly different considerations apply. If a vehicle on the major road fails to observe the halt sign, it would mean that it would have to slow down to little more than walking pace . . . That . . . would represent a wholly unrealistic view of the requirements of present-day traffic conditions" (4 D-E). Willmer L.J. also said (5 C), referring to the dictum in *Upson* (Chap. 13, (1) (a) **3**), that to require the major road driver to expect that the minor road driver would not stop at halt sign would require him to anticipate folly in a wholly unreasonable form.

U4. Nettleship v. Atkinson (1967) C.A. 180

P emerging from minor road—30 yards visibility to his right—D coming too fast on major road from P's right—P looked right, saw nothing, then had a long look to left as he emerged, and only looked right again when D on top of him—*Held*, P two-thirds to blame: "If . . . there is only a 30 yards visibility to your right . . . your eyes, until you get to the middle of the road, ought to be glued to the right so that as soon as something appears you stop and you will give him a chance of steering across the road and avoiding you" (Salmon L.J., 6 A).

U5. McLachlan v. Brooking (1968) C.A. 68

Held, applying the rule in the *Bywell Castle*, the non-turning vehicle should not be blamed for a wrong reaction.

U6. Rea v. Difolco (1973) C.A. 241

D. emerged from side road—which was on offside of P going along main road—no signpost to indicate side road—*Held*, P not liable at all, as she was under no duty to look to the side for possible side roads as she went along.

U7. Crawford v. Jennings (1981) C.A. U.B. 272

Defendant intending to turn right into main road—nearside lane of main road contained stationary queue of traffic. First driver in queue flashed on defendant. Defendant edged across and collided with plaintiff who was overtaking queue at moderate speed in offside lane—*Held*, that the judge had been entitled to find the defendant solely to blame for the accident. *Clarke v. Winchurch* (Chap. 13, (1)(m) **4**) did not lay down any principle of law and each case has to be decided on its own facts.

U8. Reeves v. Mackie (1985) C.A. 891

Defendant emerged from side road and stopped about one foot beyond line of parked cars on main road, so he could see to his right. Plaintiff, approaching from defendant's right at 25–30 m.p.h. on 30 m.p.h. limit main road, which was wet, braked and skidded into collision with defendant's car—*Held*, defendant liable, but plaintiff 80 per cent. contributorily negligent. A 30 m.p.h. speed limit is a prohibition against driving at a greater speed, but is not an indication that it is safe to drive at or below that speed.

U9. Wark v. Kawasaki Motors (U.K.) Ltd (1988) C.A. 1112

Defendant waiting to turn right from minor road. Car approached from defendant's right, indicating to turn left into the minor road. As it was doing so, defendant emerged and collided with plaintiff motor cycle which had been following the car close to its offside, going at excessive speed, and unsighting itself from any traffic that might emerge from the minor road—*Held*, defendant liable; plaintiff 40 per cent. contributorily negligent.

U10. Upshall v. Scowcroft (1990) C.A. 311

Defendant, with blood alcohol level slightly over the limit, turned right from minor road across path of plaintiff, who was going too fast. Collision ensued—*Held*, defendant liable; plaintiff 25 per cent. contributorily negligent.

U11. Adey v. Simpson (1990) C.A. 616

Defendant emerged carefully from side road intending to turn right—visibility to right obstructed by parked cars—pulled out so that her car projected 8 to 12 inches beyond outer line of parked cars, and stopped. Plaintiff, driving very fast on the main road, collided with defendant's car—*Held*, defendant not liable.

U12. Turk v. Murison and Jenkins (Third Party) (1991) C.A. 470

Facts similar to **U11**, but main-road driver approaching at reasonable speed—*Held*, main-road driver liable—failed to keep sufficient look-out for emerging vehicles.

U13. Morrison v. Burns (1994) C.A. 224.

Plaintiff entered junction from minor road and collided with defendant on major road. Give-way road markings obliterated by road-works and no other signs indicating priority. Defendant accelerating and not keeping proper look-out as approached junction—*Held*, defendant liable, but plaintiff two-thirds to blame.

(m) Signalling and Stopping

1. White v. Broadbent [1958] Crim.L.R. 129, C.A.

Held, negligent to wave following vehicle to pass when unsafe to do so. *Followed* in **3**.

2. Jungnickel v. Laing (1966) 111 S.J. 19; [1966] C.L.Y. 2693, C.A.

3. Grange Motors v. Spencer [1969] 1 W.L.R. 53; [1969] 1 All E.R. 340, C.A.

Post Office van parked on bend—driver gave following vehicle signal to overtake—collision—*Held*, driver of Post Office van wholly to blame.

4. Clarke v. Winchurch [1969] 1 W.L.R. 69; [1969] 1 All E.R. 274, C.A.

Bus driver at head of slow-moving queue stopped and flashed lights to let car on nearside out—collision between car as it emerged and moped overtaking bus—*Held*, the action of the bus driver in flashing lights and stopping meant no more than "Come on as far as I am concerned", and he was not liable for ensuing collision, as he owed no further duty. See *also* Chap. 13, (2) **U2**.

5. Leeson v. Bevis [1972] R.T.R. 373, C.A.

6. Thompson v. Spedding [1973] R.T.R. 312; [1973] C.L.Y. 2286, C.A.

Held, reversing trial judge who had found braking car wholly to blame, following vehicle was 50 per cent. liable for following too close.

7. Goke v. Willett [1973] 117 S.J. 468; [1973] R.T.R. 422, C.A.

Said that, even if stop lights and indicators were working correctly, it could still be negligent, if driver was performing an unusual or hazardous manoeuvre, to omit to give hand signals.

8. Lee v. Lever [1974] R.T.R. 35; [1974] C.L.Y. 2557, C.A.

9. Elizabeth v. M.I.B. [1981] R.T.R. 405; [1981] C.L.Y. 2368, C.A.

Held, that a driver who brakes suddenly and thereby causes an accident is subject to the burden of showing that he had good reason for his sudden braking.

10. Winter v. Cotton [1985] C.L.Y. 2978, H.H. Judge Clapham, Gravesend County Court.

Plaintiff stopped on minor road at T junction, intending to turn right. Defendant approached on main road from plaintiff's right, travelling slowly and indicating left. Plaintiff pulled out, assuming defendant turning left. Defendant went straight on, and collided with plaintiff—*Held*, defendant wholly liable.

11. Wright v. Lodge; Kerek v. Lodge [1993] 4 All E.R. 299; [1993] R.T.R. 123, C.A.

At night, S's car, in which D was rear seat passenger, stopped in nearside lane of unlit dual carriageway when engine petered out. Fog reduced visibility to 60 yards. About three minutes later, L, driving too fast, struck car with his lorry. L admitted liability. Trial judge ordered S to contribute 10 per cent. towards D's claim against L, as a result of S's negligence in failing is push car onto verge. (For further details, see Chap. 13, (1)(g) **7**.)

U1. Budd v. Standing (1987) C.A. 274

Defendant ran out of petrol in borrowed van, petrol gauge of which showed one-quarter full. Got van as close to nearside as possible. Plaintiff came round nearby blind bend on motor cycle at excessive speed, swerved, lost control and crashed—*Held*, plaintiff entirely responsible.

U2. Cartledge v. Hudsons of Mudley Ltd (1993) C.A. 371

First defendant stopped lorry on A40 to investigate defective window at 7 a.m. in February—lorry displayed near lights, reflectors and nearside indicator, but hazard lights not put on. Second defendant's lorry collided with rear of stationary lorry—*Held*, first and second defendants 20 and 80 per cent. to blame, respectively. Court observed that on a relatively fast, clear dual carriageway it is easy to assume that the tail lights you can see in the lane ahead are moving.

(n) Skidding

1. Barkway v. South Wales Transport [1950] A.C. 185; [1950] 1 All E.R. 392, H.L.

Skid caused by burst tyre—all allegations of negligence were negatived, except failure to have a system of reporting blows likely to cause an impact fracture—*Held*, on this ground, defendants were liable.

2. Burton v. West Suffolk C.C. [1960] 2 Q.B. 72; [1960] 2 All E.R. 26, C.A.

"Paper-thin" coating of ice which had formed across road for distance of 58 feet—temperature had fallen from 38 degrees at noon to 30.7 at 6 p.m. and 32.1 at 9 p.m.—driver (who was suing council for defective drainage) skidded on the ice at 9 p.m.—going reasonable speed—*Held*, not negligent, as not to blame for skid, nor would any reasonably prudent driver have been able to control it.

U1. Scott v. Edwards Motors (1961) C.A. 416

Icy road—lorry loaded with four-and-a-half tons travelling at 20 m.p.h. suddenly skidded across road—*Held*, speed too fast for conditions and driver negligent.

(o) Speed

(*N.B.* See also the cases in Chap. 13 (1)(e), (h), (k) and (l), in which questions of speed often arise.)

1. Morris v. Luton Corporation [1946] 1 K.B. 114; [1946] 1 All E.R. 1, C.A.

Held, not a proposition of law that driver must be able to pull up within limits of vision, but each case must depend on own circumstances.

2. Gaynor v. Allen [1959] 2 Q.B. 403; [1959] 2 All E.R. 644, McNair J.

3. Tribe v. Jones (1961) 105 S.J. 931; [1961] Crim.L.R. 835, D.C.

Held, that a speed of between 45 m.p.h. and 65 m.p.h. in a restricted area was not automatically dangerous contrary to the Road Traffic Act 1960, s. 2.

4. Barna v. Hudes Merchandising Corporation (1962) 106 S.J. 194; [1962] Crim.L.R. 321, C.A.

Defendant doing 30–40 m.p.h. in built-up area—*Held*, exceeding speed limit was not in itself negligence, and in the circumstances the speed was not excessive, and defendant not liable.

5. Hurlock v. Inglis, *The Times*, November 29, 1963; [1963] C.L.Y. 2349, Havers J.

Held, it was not negligent in itself to do 100 m.p.h. on motorway, but the facts called for an explanation from driver, and as he had not satisfactorily explained them, he was liable.

6. Kite v. Nolan [1983] R.T.R. 253; [1983] C.L.Y. 2524, C.A.

Defendant driving at 15 m.p.h. through gap between ice-cream van at offside kerb and parked cars at nearside kerb. Child ran from between cars and was hit by defendant's car. Accident only avoidable if defendant reduced speed to 5 m.p.h.—*Held*, defendant not negligent.

7. Cornwell v. A.A. [1989] C.L.Y. 2535, H.H. Judge Lee, Slough County Court

Plaintiff travelling at 60 m.p.h. collided with rear of AA van travelling at 15 m.p.h. in slow lane of motorway, having entered that lane from hard shoulder—*Held*, 15 m.p.h. too slow in circumstances—driver of van solely responsible.

U1. Scott v. Edwards Motors (1961) C.A. 416

Icy road—lorry loaded with four-and-a-half tons travelling at 20 m.p.h. suddenly skidded across road—*Held*, speed too fast for conditions and driver negligent.

U2. Stryzyk v. Hughes (1978) C.A. U.B. 121

Police officer driving at over 60 m.p.h. at 2 a.m. on dual carriageway with 30 m.p.h. limit on his way to an accident. Collided with plaintiff emerging from side road—*Held*, police officer not negligent for speeding in circumstances, but negligent in failing to appreciate the risk of plaintiff emerging. Plaintiff held two-thirds to blame.

U3. Reeves v. Mackie (1985) C.A. 891

Held, 30 m.p.h. speed limit is a prohibition against driving at a greater speed, but is not an indication that it is safe to drive at or below that speed. (For further details see Chap. 13, (1) (l) **U8**.)

U4. James v. Alger (1986) C.A. 229

See Chap. 13, (1) (k) **U11** for further details.

U5. Hamied v. Estwick (1994) C.A. 1277

Defendant drove from side road onto main road with 30 m.p.h. speed limit—collided with plaintiff approaching on main road at 35–40 m.p.h.—*Held*, defendant liable. Plaintiff 20 per cent. to blame—by driving faster than should have in circumstances, deprived himself of opportunity of taking avoiding action.

(p) Traffic Lights

1. Joseph Eva v. Reeves [1938] 2 K.B. 393; [1938] 2 All E.R. 115, C.A.

Defendant at lights which turn green—he pulls out onto offside to overtake stream ahead—X comes across lights at red and collides with defendant—*Held*, defendant not negligent. He owed no duty to traffic crossing in disobedience to the lights beyond that if he saw such traffic in fact he should take reasonable steps to avoid a collision. See **3** and **U1**.

2. Watt v. Herts C.C. [1954] 1 W.L.R. 835; [1954] 2 All E.R. 368, C.A.

Denning L.J. (371 B): "I quite agree that fire engines, ambulances and doctors' cars should not shoot past the traffic lights when they show a red light. That is because the risk is too great to warrant the incurring of the danger."

3. Godsmark v. Knight Bros, *The Times*, May 12, 1960; [1960] C.L.Y. 2152, Barry J.

Collision at crossroads with traffic lights—lorry crossed at amber—car going slightly faster crossed at green to it—car hit lorry on offside at right angles—neither driver had infringed the regulations—car driver relied on *Eva v. Reeves*—*Held*, car driver one-third and lorry driver two-thirds to blame; *Eva v. Reeves* was a case where the equivalent of the lorry driver had crossed at red; but different considerations applied where a vehicle crossed at amber.

4. Tingle Jacobs v. Kennedy [1964] 1 W.L.R. 638; [1964] 1 All E.R. 888, C.A.

5. Knight v. Wiper Supply (1965) 109 S.J. 358; *The Times*, April 15, 1965, Havers J. *Held*, applying *Eva v. Reeves* **1**.

6. Davis v. Hassan, *The Times*, January 13, 1967; [1967] C.L.Y. 2685, C.A.

Held, driver crossing at green not guilty of any negligence. Bar Library transcript ((1967) C.A. 3) shows that the C.A. *expressed* the view that *Eva v. Reeves* **1** laid down no rule of law, but said that on the facts of the present case the driver crossing at green was not negligent in not seeing the other car, although it was well visible if she had looked, because up to entering the junction her attention would be on the lights, and the collision happened very shortly after.

7. Frank v. Cox (1967) 111 S.J. 670; *The Times*, May 11, 1967, C.A.

8. Ryan v. Smith [1967] 2 Q.B. 893; [1967] 1 All E.R. 611, D.C.

9. Radburn v. Kemp [1971] 1 W.L.R. 1502, [1971] 3 All E.R. 249, C.A.

Defendant's car, entering at green, hit plaintiff cyclist coming from his offside—latter had also entered at green—but in view of light phase could not get across in time—*Held*, applying and approving **3**, defendant was solely liable.

10. Sudds v. Hanscombe [1971] R.T.R. 212, C.A.

Plaintiff, entering at green, collides with defendant, who was already on the junction, having entered at green from plaintiff's offside and having been obstructed from further progress by turning traffic—defendant when way was clear proceeded without paying attention to change in lights—*Held*, defendant solely to blame. While it was true that all that plaintiff, on entering at green, was entitled to assume was that no fresh traffic would enter junction against him, here the defendant's car had been obstructed and stopped so far back in the junction that the plaintiff was entitled to regard him as not being a hazard when he entered the junction.

11. Ramoo v. Gan Soo Swee [1971] 1 W.L.R. 1014; [1971] 3 All E.R. 320, P.C.

Collision at junction where lights were at green to both—both drivers had clear view of lights for some way back, and each could have seen that the lights were out of order and functioning erratically—*Held*, both drivers negligent, and *Eva v. Reeves* **1** did not apply to a case where the lights were in this sort of condition.

12. Hopwood Homes v. Kennerdine [1975] R.T.R. 82; [1975] C.L.Y. 2304, C.A.
Miller v. Evans [1975] R.T.R. 70; [1975] C.L.Y. 2305, C.A.

Two cases with basically the same facts—driver at lights wanting to turn right moves on green into junction and waits until lights go red to oncoming traffic—then turns right—in each case is hit by car coming from oncoming queue—which car in each case is going across red lights—in each case trial judge found a small percentage of contributory negligence against turning driver—*Held*, wrong, and that the turning driver was not liable for making no allowance for another approaching vehicle travelling so fast as to be unable (or, *sic*, unwilling) to stop.

13. Skolimowski v. Haynes [1983] C.L.Y. 2525, Cantley J.

P began to cross when "green man" showing. Slightly disabled. As he was crossing "red man" came on which P did not notice. Traffic in first two lanes moved off but slowed to allow P to pass. As P moved into third lane, looking away from traffic, he was hit by D's car coming in third lane—*Held*, D negligent, there being a high duty of care owed when pedestrians were foreseeable, and, in particular, where there was only a short delay between the pedestrian light turning red and the traffic light turning green—as here—*Held*, however, P one third to blame. (*N.B.* As to which latter, *cf. Shephard v. West* **U2**, which was not appealed when the case later went to House of Lords on damages only.)

14. Tremayne v. Hill [1986] R.T.R. 131; *The Times*, December 11, 1986, C.A.

Held, driver wholly liable. Plaintiff not obliged to use pelican crossing. (For further details see Chap. 13, (1) (k) **29**.)

15. Fitzgerald v. Lane [1988] 3 W.L.R. 356; [1988] 2 All E.R. 961, H.L.

For further details see Chap. 13, (1) (k) **30**.

16. Connaire v. McGuire [1994] C.L.Y. 3343, Michael Wright J.

Held, pedestrian 40 per cent. contributorily negligent. (For further details see Chap. 13, (1) (k) **38**.)

U1. Rowlands v. George Fisher (1959) C.A. 203

Defendant crossed stop line when lights at green—as he got onto junction he saw lights go to amber—he went on—plaintiff (who was crossing from defendant's nearside) moved off on red and amber—the mutual views were obscured by a large van on plaintiff's right, which also started on red and amber but stopped in time—collision between plaintiff and defendant—*Held*, defendant not liable. *Eva v. Reeves* **1**, *per* Hodson L.J. (8 C), does not absolve drivers crossing with the lights in their favour from keeping a lookout, but (7 D) "it (*i.e.* the decision) does not cast a heavy burden on them of anticipating such danger as might arise from the action of someone who is unlawfully on the crossing"—*Held*, also that defendant was under no duty to go onto the crossing "tenderly" (as Thesiger J. had held) in case the lights went to amber while he was crossing.

U2. Shephard v. West (1962) C.A. 326

Mother and child started to cross Euston Road when lights to traffic at red—as they crossed lights changed to amber and then green—bus on mother's left "whirred"—mother took step beyond front of bus and was run down by lorry coming up on left of bus—*Held*, lorry wholly liable, and mother not guilty of contributory negligence, as when she stepped off kerb lights were at red to traffic, "and one does not know when lights are going to turn to amber and green". *N.B.* It is not quite clear whether lights were at amber or green when lorry hit mother, but the negligence of lorry was not seriously in dispute, and the real point was whether mother was guilty of any contributory negligence. Decision of court of first instance, and facts, are reported in (1962) 106 S.J. 391.

U3. White v. Estate of Matteo Constantino, deceased (1989) C.A. 1010

Held, pedestrian 40 per cent. contributorily negligent. (For further details see Chap. 13, (1) (k) **U14**.)

U4. Wood v. B.R.B. (1990) C.A. 966

Plaintiff entered junction through amber traffic lights. Defendant entered from plaintiff's left, through red and amber, and did not look right—collision ensued—*Held*, defendant liable; plaintiff 40 per cent. to blame.

(q) Unlit Stationary Vehicles

Road Conditions	*Moving Driver*	*% to blame*	*Stationary Driver*	*% to blame*	
Night	Bad look-out	100	Lights failure: proper steps taken	0	1
NIGHT	BAD LOOK-OUT	100	LIGHTS FAILURE: PROPER STEPS TAKEN	0	2
NIGHT	DIPPED LIGHTS	50	TRAILER LEFT IN COUNTRY ROAD	50	3
NIGHT	BAD LOOK-OUT	100	STOPPING TO MEND FUSE	0	4
Night	Bad look-out	100	Broken down on clearway with rear lights on	0	5
NIGHT	DIPPED LIGHTS	20	LORRY LEFT UNLIT ON DARK ROAD	80	6
NIGHT	BAD LOOK-OUT	75	LORRY JACK-KNIFED ACROSS MOTORWAY: LIT BY HEADLIGHTS OF ANOTHER LORRY AT SCENE	25	7
NIGHT	DIPPED LIGHTS	40	BROKEN DOWN: USE OF STARTER DIMMING REAR LIGHTS	60	8
NIGHT	BAD LOOK-OUT	50	LIGHTS FAILED ON LIGHTED CLEARWAY: NO WARNING SIGN WHILE DRIVER AWAY	50	9
NIGHT	BAD LOOK-OUT	75	PARKED ON WELL-LIT ROAD	25	10
Night	*Lights dipped unnecessarily*	30	*Lights failure: driver mending at bad place*	70	U1
Lighting-up time	*Bad look-out*	100	*Stopped unlit temporarily*	0	U2
Night	*Overtaking on crest at 50 m.p.h.*	20	*Parked with front unlit*	80	U3
Night	*Blameless*	0	*Parked unlit on road*	100	U4

Early a.m.	*Blameless*	0	*Stopped unlit temporarily*	100	U5
Night	*Bad look-out*	66	*Lorry reversing broadside: headlights on*	33	U6
Night	*Dazzled*	30	*Parked at awkward place with parking lights on*	70	U7
Night	*Dipped lights*	20	*Rear lights U/S: no reflector: breaking down just before dusk: no torch carried*	80	U8
Night	*Bad look-out*	100	*Parked unlit outside own house*	0	U9
Night	*Blameless: 30–40 m.p.h.*	0	*Left unlit round bend*	100	U10

1. Parish v. Judd [1960] 1 W.L.R. 867; [1960] 3 All E.R. 33, Edmund Davies J.

Lights on defendant's car failed totally—defendant got a tow from a lorry—lorry driver stopped near a street lamp to see whether defendant was all right—when stopped defendant's car was about six yards from the lamp post, was close into the kerb and had three reflectors at the rear—visible from about 100 yards away—plaintiff ran into rear—sued defendant in negligence and nuisance—*Held*, (a) as regards nuisance, plaintiff had to show that the vehicle was not merely an obstruction on the road but that it was a danger on the road, and that on the facts this was not so; and (b) as regards negligence, while it was true that an unlit vehicle on a road at night raised a presumption of negligence, this had been rebutted both as regards place and as regards maintenance, and that therefore the claim failed.

2. Jones v. Price and Jago, *The Guardian*, March 1, 1963; [1963] C.L.Y. 2316, C.A.

Short-circuit in first defendant's car at night—second defendant stopped to help—drew up in front of and facing car with own headlights on—plaintiff drove his car into them—*Held*, defendants not liable.

3. Hill v. Phillips (1963) 107 S.J. 890; [1963] C.L.Y. 2355, C.A.

Unlit trailer in country road—left by lorry driver while he went to get lights—following driver, using dipped headlights, only saw trailer a car's length away—lorry driver negligent in not carrying proper equipment—judge found lorry driver wholly to blame—*Held*, 50:50, as following driver should have seen trailer earlier.

4. Moore v. Maxwells [1968] 1 W.L.R. 1077; [1968] 2 All E.R. 779, C.A.

Lorry driver, in consequence of signal from another lorry, stopped to mend fault in plug to trailer—in doing so, all lorry lights fused—driver did not think it would take long to mend—could not get onto verge because verge too soft for load—700 yards further on road was lit, but driver did not know this—he sent mate to rear to warn traffic—but a lorry, keeping bad look-out, ran into trailer—owners of stationary lorry called no evidence of servicing lorry—but driver had tested lights before setting out and again before lighting up time—*Held*, defendants not liable.

5. Butland v. Coxhead, *The Times*, May 8, 1968; [1968] C.L.Y. 2681, Browne J.

6. Brown v. Thompson [1968] 1 W.L.R. 1003; [1968] 2 All E.R. 708, C.A.

7. Rouse v. Squires [1973] Q.B. 889; [1973] 2 All E.R. 903, C.A.

8. Young v. Chester [1974] R.T.R. 70; [1974] C.L.Y. 2556, C.A.

9. Lee v. Lever [1974] R.T.R. 35; [1974] C.L.Y. 2557, C.A.

Plaintiff's lights failed—car pushed to side of well-lit clearway—plaintiff went to garage to re-charge battery—some 20 minutes later defendant collided—judge found wholly for defendant—*Held*, both liable, defendant for bad look-out and plaintiff for failing to display warning sign.

10. Hannam v. Mann [1984] R.T.R. 252; [1984] C.L.Y. 2293, C.A.

Plaintiff on motorcycle on well-lit road at night, behind car with offside indicator flashing. Thought the car was turning right, and moved to overtake on nearside. In fact, car was overtaking defendant's unlit parked car with which defendant collided—*Held*, defendant liable, plaintiff 75 per cent. Contributorily negligent.

U1. Arkless v. R.A.H. Transporters (1960) C.A. 170

Lorry A was warned by flashes from oncoming lorries that his lights were defective—he went on, looking for a suitable place to pull in—eventually pulled partly on to grass verge just short of an unofficial lay-by which was muddy—his vehicle projected three feet on to the road—overhanging trees made it difficult to see his lorry—he could have switched on his headlights—lorry B with dipped headlights showing only 10 yards ahead ran into him—trial judge awarded 70 per cent. against A, 30 per cent. against B—*Held*, this apportionment would not be disturbed (but Upjohn L.J. would have found B more to blame).

U2. Benton v. M.R.C.E. Farms (1960) C.A. 296

Time "round about lighting-up time"—farm tractor and trailer stopped temporarily in street—no rear light—motor-cycle ran into rear of trailer—*Held*, driver of farm tractor not liable, as on the evidence the trailer could be seen by anyone driving along the road.

U3. Bell v. Ives and Smith (1961) C.A. 344

Road 24 feet wide—lorry left broken down at night with offside 15 feet out—line of red hurricane lamps on offside—but no lights or lamps to front—plaintiff driving van in opposite direction came over crest 200 feet away somewhat on wrong side (after overtaking) at about 50 m.p.h.—*Held*, plaintiff 20 per cent. to blame.

U4. Fotheringham v. Prudence *The Times*, May 16, 1962; (1962) C.A. 185

Unlit stationary lorry—no reflectors and only one rear lamp, and that out—motor-cyclist ran into rear—some but not very adequate street lighting—*Held*, lorry 100 per cent. liable.

U5. Duffin v. Young (1962) C.A. 38 (unreported)

Lighting-up time ended 6.50 a.m.—at 6 a.m. defendant lorry driver pulled up on nearside of main road—turned out lights—went to shop—no streetlighting—deceased motor-cyclist ran into rear—*Held*, defendant 100 per cent. liable.

U6. Barber v. British Road Services (1964) C.A. 289

U7. Watson v. Heslop (1971) 115 S.J. 308; [1971] R.T.R. 308

U8. Jordan v. Smith (1971) C.A. 309

U9. Griffiths v. Dacre (1980) C.A. 86

Unlit van parked for night by D outside his house; in residential road—*Held*, this was reasonable user and D was not liable.

U10. Draycott v. Clayton (1982) C.A. U.B. 808

(r) White Lines

1. Kirk v. Parker (1938) 60 Ll.L.R. 129, C.A

Defendant's wheels were slightly over the offside of white line—*Held*, that that was not in itself negligence if it was clear that, by driving in that position, any collision with oncoming vehicles would be avoided.

U1. Quinn v. Head (1952) C.A. 203

Head-on collision in centre lane of three-lane road—at night—plaintiff's car was overtaking vehicle in his nearside lane—defendant's motor-cycle had no reason to travel in centre lane—could have gone in nearside lane—*Held*, defendant solely responsible.

U2. Devlin v. Sunter Bros. Ltd. (1957) C.A. 136

Tractor driven by defendants projected 9–10 inches over white line at bend due to width—still ample room for oncoming traffic—plaintiff's vehicle being driven on own side collides—*Held*, plaintiff solely to blame, as too near white line.

U3. Dunn v. Brown (1989) C.A. 205

Head-on collision between plaintiff's motor cycle or wrong side of road and defendants car astride centre line. Each could and should have been on own side—*Held*, defendant liable; plaintiff 80 per cent. contributorily negligent.

U4. Bushell v. Southall (1993) C.A. 107

Collision between plaintiff's motor cycle, going round bend in country lane at high speed and out of control, and defendant's van, travelling slowly in opposite direction with offside wheels a matter of inches over centre line of road—*Held*, defendant not liable—plaintiff had plenty of room to pass in safety.

(2) Liability of Drivers of Special Vehicles

(*N.B. Buses* are dealt with in Chap. 13, (3). *Crash helmets* for motor-cyclists are in Chap. 13, (6).)

1. Ward v. L.C.C. [1938] 2 All E.R. 341, Charles J.

2. Pope v. Fraser (1939) 55 T.L.R. 324

3. Ferrugia v. G.W.R. [1947] 2 All E.R. 565; 204 L.T. 310, C.A.

4. Watts v. Herts C.C. [1954] 1 W.L.R. 835; [1954] 2 All E.R. 368, C.A.

"I quite agree that fire engines, ambulances and doctors' cars should not shoot past the traffic lights when they show a red light. That is because the risk is too great to warrant incurring the danger" (Denning L.J., 371 B).

5. Gaynor v. Allen [1959] 2 Q.B. 403; [1954] 2 All E.R. 644, McNair J.

Applied in Wardell-Yarburgh **9**.

6. Amos v. Glamorgan C.C. (1967) 112 S.J. 52; 66 L.G.R. 166, C.A.

Motor-cyclist in heavy rain during daytime collided with fire engine parked by kerb at scene of fire, where it had arrived two minutes earlier—blue lights flashing—no warning lights put out to warn approaching traffic—*Held*, fire engine not liable.

7. Jordan v. North Hampshire Plant Hire [1970] R.T.R. 212; [1970] C.L.Y. 2565, C.A.

Lorry, 35 feet long driven out of drive at night across main road—at point where there were double white lines and gradual bend—P going at 60 m.p.h. drove into side of lorry, which being unlit he did not see in time—*Held*, lorry liable, as this was a most dangerous manoeuvre, despite the absence of any statutory requirement that the sides of lorries should be lit.

8. Buckoke v. G.L.C. [1971] 1 Ch. 655; [1971] 2 All E.R.254, C.A.

Application for injunction by fire brigade members on account of instructions tacitly permitting drivers to ignore lights at red—the application failed, but the judgments contain accounts of the procedure adopted by the defendant fire authority for dealing with the situation.

9. Wardell-Yarburgh v. Surrey C.C. [1973] R.T.R. 462; [1974] C.L.Y. 3329, Brabin J.

Held, applying *Gaynor* **5**, that the driver of an emergency vehicle owed the same duty of care to the public as any other driver.

10. Wood v. Richards [1977] R.T.R. 201; [1977] C.L.Y. 2606, D.C.

So held, in a careless driving case; Divisional Court did not, however, wholly exclude a defence of necessity in some types of emergency.

11. Arnold v. Teno (1978) 83 D.L.R. (3d) 609; [1978] C.L.Y. 2064, Canada Sup. Ct.

Infant P, having bought ice cream from van, moved out into road and into passing car. Van driver could have seen car approaching through his glass rear window—*Held*, van driver owed duty of care to P, and on the facts was liable.

12. Lancaster v. H.B. and H. Transport [1979] R.T.R. 380, C.A.

Just after dawn with drifting fog limiting visibility to 50–100 yards D drove 49½ foot long lorry across both dual carriageways of the Great North Road. The central reservation was only 32 feet wide. When lorry was about half way over second carriageway P's car ran into the side of the lorry. Trial judge found that D had not been negligent—*Held*, D was liable, as the manoeuvre was one on which he should never have embarked, although once he had embarked on it no amount of care could have cured the situation (384 K)—*Held*, also, no contributory negligence proved against car driver.
N.B. C.A. also said that there was a safer alternative open to D (*i.e.* turning left onto the main road and using a slip road and flyover bridge to turn back onto the second carriageway), but it would not seem that this was a factor in the decision to hold D liable.

13. Lincoln v. Hayman [1982] 1 W.L.R. 488; [1982] R.T.R. 336, C.A.

14. Marshall v. Osmond [1983] Q.B. 1034; [1983] 2 All E.R. 225, C.A.

P passenger in car which he knew was stolen. There was a police chase. The stolen car stopped in layby and the police driver braked with the intention of stopping alongside. Because of error of judgment, driver of police car skidded slightly and collided with stolen car, injuring P who was attempting to escape—*Held*, police driver had not been negligent. He owed P the normal duty of care but on the facts he was not in breach of that duty.

15. Cox v. Dixon (1984) 134 New L.J. 236; [1984] C.L.Y. 2310, Kilner Brown J.

Police driver chasing motor cyclist, driving at 60 m.p.h. at night on inside lane of main road in 30 m.p.h. area. D drove out from side road—collision—*Held*, D one-third and police driver two-thirds to blame.

U1. Crossgrove v. Barkers (1967) C.A. 89

Held, in the absence of any explanation from driver as to, *e.g.* alternatives available, negligent.

U2. Metters v. Gill (1968) C.A. 53

A traffic control officer (whom C.A. equated with a police officer), on private industrial estate, driving illuminated car, stopped to allow bulldozer to cross from right to left—car overtook and crashed into bulldozer as it crossed—*Held*, traffic control officer not negligent, as he was not controlling traffic, but was acting primarily as a driver, in which latter case his action in stopping conveyed no assurance to the bulldozer that it was safe to cross.

U3. Stryzyk v. Hughes (1978) C.A. U.B. 121

Police driver going to scene of accident at 2 a.m. doing 60 m.p.h. on dual carriageway in 30 m.p.h. area. He collides with plaintiff emerging from side road—*Held*, police officer not negligent for speeding in the circumstances, but was negligent in failing to appreciate risk of plaintiff emerging. Plaintiff two-thirds to blame.

U4. Ree v. Hill (1983) C.A. 732

Plaintiff drove police car at excessive speed under instruction on advanced during course. Defendant turned right from a side street on plaintiff's right. Plaintiff tried to go through on nearside instead of braking and going round offside—collided with rear of defendant's car—*Held* defendant not liable.

U5. Young v. Commissioner of Police for the Metropolis (1983) C.A. 769

Plaintiff's van turned right from minor road at T-junction. Struck by police car on main road, answering emergency call, going at 55 m.p.h., on dipped headlights, blue lights flashing and two-tone horn sounding—*Held*, plaintiff solely responsible for accident.

U6. Cameron v. Commissioner of Police for the Metropolis (1985) C.A. 948

Similar facts to **U5**—*Held*, police driver not liable.

U7. Calder v. Howlett (1988) C.A. 955

Plaintiff's car collided head-on with fire engine travelling on wrong side of road, but with lights flashing, bell and siren sounding and headlights on. Plaintiff did not see fire engine until it was almost on top of her—*Held*, defendant liable. Plaintiff 50 per cent. contributorily negligent, for failing earlier to appreciate the need for avoiding action.

(3) Liability of Bus and Coach Operatives

1. Mottram v. South Lancs. Transport [1942] 2 All E.R. 452, C.A.

Held, it would be putting too high a duty on conductress to say she should be on platform when passengers alighting.

2. Western Scottish Motor Co. v. Allam [1943] 2 All E.R. 742; [1943] W.N. 223, H.L.

Held, defendants liable, the duty of care being owed to standing as well as sitting passengers.

3. Wilkie v. London Passenger Transport Board [1947] 1 All E.R. 258; 63 T.L.R. 115, C.A.

Held, negligence for a bus to start while passenger boarding had only one foot on the step.

4. Askew v. Bowtell [1947] 1 All E.R. 883; 63 T.L.R. 316, D.C.

Conductor prosecuted for endangering passenger through negligence—tram driver had approached compulsory stop, slowed down, and then accelerated, thus throwing plaintiff off platform—conductor had remained upstairs—*Held*, conductor not negligent, as his duty was only to see that it was safe to start tram again—he was entitled to assume driver would stop at compulsory stop.

5. Hale v. Hants & Dorset Motor Services Ltd [1947] 2 All E.R. 628, C.A.

Bus brushing past tree branch—glass damaged on upper deck injuring plaintiff—*Held*, bus driver negligent. *N.B.* The local authority, who were responsible for the tree, were also held liable. Two-thirds against local authority, one-third against bus driver.

6. Guinnear v. London Passenger Transport Board (1948) 92 S.J. 350, Lynskey J.

Plaintiff falls from bus while boarding it at request stop—bus driver had signalled to plaintiff that he was going to stop a little further down, and accelerated as he moved past stop—at this moment plaintiff tried to get on—*Held*, both equally negligent.

7. Davies v. Liverpool Corporation [1949] 2 All E.R. 175; [1949] W.N. 268, C.A.

Plaintiff injured by tram starting on an unauthorised signal given by a passenger while the conductor was away from platform—he was away an appreciable time without reasonable excuse—*Held*, defendants liable. The Lords Justices all said, in differing language, that it was the duty of the conductor to be on the platform at a stop unless it was impracticable for him to be there.

8. Barkway v. South Wales Transport [1950] A.C. 185; [1950] 1 All E.R. 392, H.L.

Skid caused by burst tyre—all allegations of negligence were negatived, except failure to have a system of reporting blows likely to cause an impact fracture—*Held*, on this ground, defendants were liable. Lord Porter (399 A) said the duty of a transport company was "to take all reasonable precautions for the safety of their passengers and not to leave them in danger of a risk against which some precautions, at any rate, can be taken."

9. Glasgow Corporation v. Sutherland (1951) 95 S.J. 204; [1951] W.N. 111, H.L.

Dog running in front of tramcar—driver applied magnetic brake (which produced almost instantaneous stop)—plaintiff who was moving to a seat, having just boarded, thrown—*Held*, on the facts, negligence on the part of driver. *Parkinson* (Chap. 13, (1) (b) **1**) considered, but neither affirmed nor disapproved.

10. Prescott v. Lancashire Transport [1953] 1 W.L.R. 232; [1953] 1 All E.R. 288, C.A.

Plaintiff through her husband told conductor she wished to get off at next request stop—short of this stop bus stopped for traffic—plaintiff tried to alight but was injured as bus moved off—conductor had previously told plaintiff to wait till bus next stopped—but he did not warn plaintiff, when it did stop, that it was not at a stop—*Held*, in these circumstances, defendants liable.

11. Nicholson v. Goddard [1954] Crim. L.R. 474; [1954] C.L.Y 2297, D.C.

Held, this raised a very strong case for defendant to answer on a charge of failing to take all reasonable precautions for safety of passengers alighting.

12. Hatton v. London Transport Executive *The Times*, May 3, 1956; [1956] C.L.Y. 6032, McNair J.

Plaintiff thrown against window on upper deck when bus started with a jerk—*Held*, defendants liable.

13. Franklin v. Edmonton Corporation (1965) 109 S.J. 876; [1965] C.L.Y. 2720, Lawrence J.

14. Scottish Omnibuses v. Wyngrove *The Times*, June 24, 1966; [1966] C.L.Y. 8067, H.L.

15. Gore v. Van Der Lann [1967] 2 Q.B. 31; [1967] 1 All E.R. 360, C.A.

16. Wooller v. London Transport Board [1967] R.T.R. 206; [1967] C.L.Y. 247, C.A.

Lorry stopped suddenly for pedestrian at crossing—bus behind lorry followed suit—no accident—but passenger who was standing ready to get off thrown—*Held*, reversing judge, bus not liable, as in modern traffic conditions it was a counsel of perfection that a bus should always preserve a gap sufficient to enable driver to brake at leisure.

17. Fury v. Cardiff C.C. [1977] C.L.Y. 2031, Thompson J.

One-man-operated bus—plaintiff got in and paid her fare—bus at once started—but driver had to brake sharply to avoid a motor-cyclist emerging from crossroads at speed—plaintiff thrown before she reached her seat—*Held*, defendants not liable. The braking was necessary, and in the case of passengers who appeared to be able-bodied it was reasonable to start the bus before passengers had reached their seats.

18. Thrower v. Thames Valley Bus Co. [1978] R.T.R. 271; [1978] C.L.Y. 2094, C.A.

P's car 5 feet 5 in. wide—bus 8 feet 2 in—road 17 feet 6 in.—collision. P alleged that D should have taken some special precautions in view of the width of the bus—*Held*, not so.

19. Hayman v. L.T.E. [1981] C.L.Y. 1834, D/Circuit Judge Krikler

20. Azzopardi v. State Transport Authority (1983) 30 S.A.S.R. 434; [1983] C.L.Y. 2515, Sup. Ct. of South Australia

Held, defendants liable; no contributory negligence.

21. Sweeney v. Westerman and Burton Coaches [1993] C.L.Y. 2941, H.H. Judge Wolton Q.C., sitting as a High Court judge

First defendant struck by plaintiff's motor cycle on offside of second defendant's coach, which first defendant was about to board having come from public house—*Held*, *inter alia*, second defendant not liable—not his duty to see passengers safety onto his coach—his duty did not extend beyond the inside of the coach and its exit. (See also Chap. 13, (1) (k) **34**.)

U1. Royston v. Barton Transport Ltd. (1953) C.A. 116

Bus conductor opened mechanical doors 70 yards before stop—plaintiff fell out—*Held*, defendants liable (but 10 per cent. contributory negligence).

U2. Furlong v. Liverpool Corporation (1960) C.A. 4

Conductor on platform—failed to press bell for bus to stop at next stop—a passenger gave emergency signal near stop—bus pulled up quickly—plaintiff thrown—*Held*, assuming conductor was negligent within *Davies v. Liverpool Corporation* **7**, defendants not liable, as it could not be foreseen that as a result a passenger would give the emergency signal.

U3. Fletcher v. Ribble Motor Services (1961) C.A. 12

Single decker bus with door leading straight into body of coach—no platform—door left open between stops by conductor—deceased fell out—*Held*, defendants liable, it being conductor's duty to keep door closed "unless there be some good reason for leaving it open".

U4. Wragg v. Grout (1966) C.A. 110

Held, reversing trial judge, that in the absence of evidence of some quite exceptional lurch or sway, an ordinary sway which caused a passenger to lose balance was not negligence; and defendants were not liable. *Western Scottish* case **2** *explained* as being a decision which turned solely on the excessive speed of the bus.

U5. Grant v. L.T.B. (1970) C.A. 100 B

U6. Parry v. L.T.B. (1970) C.A. 444

Plaintiff passenger in bus mistakenly alighted at what she thought was a stop—while doing so, bus drove off—conductor was sitting in front with back to passengers—*Held*, conductor negligent, as it was his duty to be on the platform. 25 per cent. contributory negligence.

U7. Bentley v. Bradford Corporation (1975) C.A. 546

U8. Carling v. McCullagh (1980) C.A. 390

Held, 50:50.

U9. Borromeo v. London Buses Ltd (1993) C.A. 863

Plaintiff stepped from pavement into collision with bus without looking. Bus driver stopped immediately—was told someone trapped under rear nearside wheel. Without investigating, drove forward, and ran over plaintiff's foot—*Held*, driver negligent in not going to see what the situation was. Plaintiff one-third to blame—chain of causation from her original negligence not broken.

(4) Liability of Owners

1. Ormrod v. Crosville Motor Services [1953] 1 W.L.R. 1120, [1953] 2 All E.R. 65, C.A.

Driver was driving car to Monte Carlo where owner would meet it and take it over to enter in rally—accident on way down—*Held*, as car being used wholly or partly for purposes of owner, driver was agent of owner.

2. Lampert v. Eastern National Omnibus [1954] 1 W.I.R. 1047; [1954] 2 All E.R. 719n, Hilbery J.

Wife owner of and passenger in car driven by husband—collision injuring wife—husband and defendants 50:50 to blame—*Held*, as wife had right and duty to control husband's driving she could only recover at 50 per cent, against defendants.

3. Trust Company v. De Silva [1956] 1 W.L.R. 376, P.C.

Question was whether defendants were vicariously liable for negligent driving of X—X was driving Y's car on defendants' business—Y was employed by defendants and was a passenger in car—*Held*, that defendants were vicariously liable for Y, and as Y was in control as owner–passenger, they were liable for the negligent driving of the car. Lord Tucker: "It is now well settled that the person in control of a . . . vehicle—though not actually driving—is liable for the negligence of the driver over whom he has the right to exercise control."

4. Ilkiw v. Samuels [1963] 1 W.L.R. 991; [1963] 2 All E.R. 879, C.A.

Held, per Willmer and Danckwerts L.JJ., Diplock L.J. *dubitante*, that it was negligent to allow a volunteer to drive a lorry without making inquiry as to his competence.

5. Carberry v. Davies [1968] 1 W.L.R. 1103; [1968] 2 All E.R. 817, C.A.

6. Vandyke v. Fender [1970] 2 Q.B. 292; [1970] 2 All E.R. 335, C.A.

7. Ramburran v. Gurrucharran [1970] 1 W.L.R. 556; [1970] 1 All E.R. 749, P.C.

8. Morgans v. Launchbury [1973] A.C. 127; [1972] 2 All E.R. 606, H.L.

Wife lent husband car—having previously asked that if husband had too much to drink he should get friend to drive—husband did both these—friend had collision—*Held*, friend was not agent of wife, as it was merely a case of giving permission which was not the same as agency. *Ormrod* **1** expressly *approved*. Dictum of du Parcq L.J. in *Hewitt v. Bonvin* [1940] 1 K.B. 188 approved as providing proper test:

"The driver of a car may not be the owner's servant, and the owner will nevertheless be liable for his negligence if it be proved that at the time he had authority, express or implied, to drive on the owner's behalf. Such liability depends not on ownership, but on the delegation of a task or duty."

9. Norwood v. Navan [1981] R.T.R. 457; [1981] C.L.Y. 1861, C.A.

Held, following *Morgans* **8**, husband not liable. The plaintiff had not proved that the wife was driving for the purpose of a task or duty delegated to her by the husband, and no inference of agency could arise from the mere fact that some part of the journey was for the purpose of family shopping.

10. Ansin v. R. & D. Evans [1982] 1 N.Z.L.R. 184; [1983] C.L.Y. 2583, High Ct. of New Zealand

Wife B owner of family car which was usually driven by husband C.C, on his way to collect B, called at X's house and X requested lift. On arriving where B was, C felt ill and X offered to drive. C went in to collect B and on return with her found X in driving seat. C explained that X was driving and got into front passenger seat, B got into back. X drove 100 yards and had a collision—*Held*, B was not vicariously liable for X's negligence, there being no basis for saying that she was in control of her car or of X's manner of driving. The evidence did not show any communication by B to X authorising him to drive her car, and on the facts she did not expressly or impliedly authorise X to drive.

U1. Pentonville Motors v. Thompson (1958) C.A. 75

Held, employee neither acting in course of employment nor as agent for owner, who was therefore not liable.

U2. Whittington v. Emile (1963) C.A. 302 B

Held, applying *Ormrod*, **1** son was agent of father, as father had dual interest in the journey, (a) in finding out if the car was suitable for the son, and (b) in getting son to come to the office, in order to interest him in the family business.

(5) Liability of and to passengers

1. Lampert v. Eastern National Omnibus [1954] 1 W.L.R. 1047; [1954] 2 All E.R. 719n., Hilbery J.

Wife owner of and passenger in car driven by husband—collision injuring wife—husband and defendants 50:50 to blame—*Held*, as wife had right and duty to control husband's driving she could only recover at 50 per cent, against defendants.

2. Trust Company v. De Silva [1956] 1 W.L.R. 376, P.C.

Question was whether defendants were vicariously liable for negligent driving of X—X was driving Y's car on defendants' business—Y was employed by defendants and was a passenger in car—*Held*. that defendants were vicariously liable for Y, and as Y was in control as owner–passenger, they were liable for the negligent driving of the car. Lord Tucker: "It is now well settled that the person in control of a . . . vehicle—though not actually driving—is liable for the negligence of the driver over whom he has the right to exercise control."

3. Dawrant v. Nutt [1960] 1 W.L.R. 253; [1960] 3 All E.R. 681, Stable J.

Plaintiff side-car passenger in motor-cycle combination driven by husband—night—to knowledge of plaintiff and husband headlight on combination was broken—collision with defendant's vehicle for which husband and defendant equally to blame—*Held*, in action by the plaintiff for own personal injuries, that the plaintiff owed a duty to defendant to take reasonable care for her own safety, and that she was in breach of that duty in knowingly travelling in the unlit combination, so that her claim would be reduced by 25 per cent. in respect of her own contributory negligence. But, in so far as this decision is based on a breach of duty owed by the passenger, see cases in Chap. 4, (1) (a).

4. Scarsbrook v. Mason (1961) 105 S.J. 889; [1961] 3 All E.R. 767, Glyn-Jones J.

Car struck plaintiff on pavement—car had been taken away without owner's consent—defendant a passenger, picked up without knowing how car acquired—invited to go in a party to Southend paying towards cost of petrol—*Held*, driver was acting as agent for each and all the members of the party, and accordingly defendant was liable for negligent driving of driver.

5. Owens v. Brimmell [1976] 3 All E.R. 765, Watkins J.

Pub crawl—driver and passenger both drinking a great deal—accident on way home—*Held*, 20 per cent. contributory negligence against passenger.

6. Gibbons v. Priestley [1979] R.T.R. 4; [1979] C.L.Y. 2368, Judge Lymbery Q.C.

Held driving instructor not liable for allowing learner driver, at her stage of her instruction, to drive a car without dual controls—*Held*, also, negligent for instructor not to advise use of seat belt (but this was not causative of accident).

7. Ashton v. Turner [1981] Q.B. 137; [1980] 3 All E.R. 870, Ewbank J.

Held, no duty of care owed (see Chap. 1, (2)(a) **12** and Chap. 4, (3) **33**) but, if there had been, 50 per cent. contributory negligent.

8. Campbell v. Jelley [1984] C.L.Y. 2296, Judge Hall as D.H.C.J.

Defendant drove passenger home from public house. There was an accident en route in which passenger was killed. Passenger knew defendant had been drinking—*Held*, defendant had not discharged onus of proof in showing that the passenger was negligent in accepting the lift on the basis of the apparent condition of the defendant.

9. Meah v. McCreamer [1985] 1 All E.R. 367; 135 New L.J. 80, Woolf J.

Plaintiff accepted lift from defendant, with whom he had been drinking for a considerable time. Had plaintiff not been affected by drink it would have been obvious to him that defendant was unfit to drive. Plaintiff injured when defendant lost control of car—*Held*, plaintiff 25 per cent. contributionly negligent.

10. Pitts v. Huat [1991] 1 Q.B. 24; [1990] 3 All E.R. 344, C.A.

Plaintiff aged 18 and friend aged 16 spent evening drinking together. Set off home on friend's motor cycle—plaintiff as pillion passenger. Friend had drunk so much he was unfit to drive, as plaintiff would have realised had he been in a proper state. Friend also unlicensed and uninsured, to plaintiff's knowledge. Friend, encouraged by plaintiff, deliberately drove in dangerous manner. Friend killed and plaintiff injured in head-on collision, not fault of other driver. Plaintiff sued friend's personal representative—*Held*, plaintiff not entitled to recover, on grounds of application of maxim *ex turpi causa non oritur actio* and of public policy, and because the serious circumstances precluded the court from finding that the friend owed any duty of care to plaintiff. Further, had not the Road Traffic Act 1972, s. 148(3), prevented defendant from raising a defence of *volenti non fit injuria*, that defence would have succeeded.

11. Gala v. Preston (1991) 172 C.L.R. 243; [1991] C.L.Y. 243, High Court of Australia

Held, driver of a vehicle which he and passenger had earlier stolen, owed no duty of care to passenger injured by his careless driving, because the injury resulted from a serious criminal act in which both participated.

12. Weir v. Wyper, 1992 S.L.T. 579; [1992] C.L.Y. 6068

Plaintiff, aged 16, was passenger in car driven by defendant, whom plaintiff knew to be unqualified and unsupervised. Defendant alleged he owed her no duty of care—relied on maxim *ex turpi causa non oritur actio.* Plaintiff said there had earlier seen a qualified driver in car—he had got out and not returned. It being late at night and in country road she had become anxious and was being driven home by defendant when accident occurred—*Held*, in circumstances alleged by plaintiff, it was hard to see that she was participating in any significant criminal activity or that public policy would deny her a night to recover.

13. Stinton v. Stinton and M.I.B. [1993] P.I.Q.R. P. 135; [1993] C.L.Y. 2939, Simon Brown J.

Plaintiff was passenger in brother's car. Both had been on lengthy drinking session. Brother drove vehicle into lamp post—admitted liability—*Held*, plaintiff contributionly negligent by one-third in accepting lift from a driver whose ability was improved by drink. The case involved "blameworthiness . . . to the highest extent possible short of direct participation in the actual performance". (*N.B.* The case was taken to appeal—*The Times*, November 23, 1994—but only on the liability of the M.I.B.)

14. Donelan v. Donelan and General Accident [1993] P.I.Q.R. P. 205; [1994] C.L.Y. 3341, H. H. Judge Astill, sitting as a High Court judge.

First defendant driving and plaintiff passenger in plaintiff's 2,000 c.c. automatic car, when first defendant negligently crashed it. First defendant had driven at instigation of plaintiff who was the older and dominant party, knew that first defendant was drunk (as was he) and knew or should have known of the risks of her driving, given that she had never before driven a car so powerful or with automatic transmission—*Held*, on the wholly exceptional facts, plaintiff 75 per cent contributorily negligent.

U1. Furlong v. Liverpool Corporation (1960) C.A. 4

Conductor on platform—failed to press bell for bus to stop at next stop—a passenger gave emergency signal near stop—bus pulled up quickly—plaintiff thrown—*Held*, defendants not liable, as it could not be foreseen that as a result a passenger would give the emergency signal.

U2. McMinn v. Spath (1961) C.A. 187 B

Driver to passenger: "I do not think your door is properly shut"—passenger puts hand on door handle—door flies open—passenger thrown out—*Held*, defendant not liable in action by passenger.

(6) Liability for Not Using Safety Equipment

(*N.B.* The statutory provisions governing the wearing of seat belts are currently to be found in the Road Traffic Act, 1988, ss. 14 and 15, the Motor Vehicles (Wearing of Seat Belts) Regulations, 1993 and the Motor Vehicles (Wearing of Seat Belts by Children in Front Seats) Regulations, 1993.)

1. O'Connell v. Jackson [1972] 1 Q.B. 270; [1971] 3 All E.R. 129, C.A.

Current Highway Code exhorted wearing crash helmet, but no enforcing regulations as yet in force at the time—moped rider doing 20 m.p.h. in urban area in collision with car—head injury—*Held*, moped rider 15 per cent. contributorily negligent.

> "It must be borne in mind that, for so much of the injuries and damage as would have resulted from the accident even if a crash helmet had been worn, the defendant is wholly to blame, and the plaintiff not at all. For the additional injuries and damage which would not have occurred if a crash helmet had been worn, the defendant, as solely responsible for the accident, must continue in substantial measure to be held liable, and it is only in the last field of additional injuries and damage that the contributory negligence of the plaintiff has any relevance" (Edmund Davies L.J., 133 A).

2. Lee v. Lever [1974] R.T.R. 35; [1974] C.L.Y. 2557, C.A.

Plaintiff, his lights having failed, went to garage to take battery to be re-charged—some 20 minutes later defendant ran into stationary car—judge found wholly for defendant—*Held*, both liable, defendant for bad look-out, and plaintiff for failing to display warning sign.

3. Froom v. Butcher [1976] Q.B. 286; [1975] 3 All E.R. 520, C.A.

"Sometimes the evidence will show that the failure made no difference. The damage would have been the same, even if a seat belt had been worn. In such cases the damages should not be reduced at all. At other times the evidence will show that the failure made all the difference. The damage would have been prevented altogether if a seat belt had been worn. In such cases I would suggest that the damages should be reduced by 25 per cent. But often the evidence will show that the failure made a considerable difference. Some injuries to the head, for instance, would have been a good deal less severe if a seat belt had been worn, but there would still have been some injury to the head. In such a case, I would suggest that the damages attributable to the failure to wear a seat belt should be reduced by 15 per cent" (Lord Denning M.R., 528 B, with whose judgment the other two concurred). This judgment supersedes many previous, and conflicting, decisions at first instance.

4. Roberts v. Sparks [1977] C.L.Y. 2643, Dunn J.

Passenger door ripped off—and plaintiff passenger thrown out—if he had been wearing seat belt, he would probably have sustained *other*, but less serious, injuries—*Held*, 20 per cent. contributory negligence.

5. Barker v. Murdoch [1977] C.L.Y. 2013; S.L.T. 75, Lord Grieve

6. Trayner v. Donovan [1978] C.L.Y. 2612, Sheldon J.

7. Hoadley v. Dartford D.C. [1979] R.T.R. 359, C.A.

P's vehicle not required by statute to be fitted with seat belts—none fitted. P injured in collision—*Held*, not negligent *per se* to fail to fit seat belts. Having called no evidence as to the practicality of fitting seat belts, D had failed to discharge the onus of proving contributory negligence.

8. Mackay v. Borthwick, 1982 S.L.T. 265; [1982] C.L.Y. 2157, O.H.

Plaintiff not wearing seat belt—injured. Gave evidence that she had a hiatus hernia and seat belt in question ran across her chest causing her discomfort. She wore a seat belt in car for longer journeys, but not for short journeys—*Held*, that the case was exceptional and the plaintiff had not been negligent in failing to use the seat belt.

9. Patience v. Andrews [1983] R.T.R. 447; [1982] C.L.Y. 789, Croom-Johnson J.

Plaintiff passenger in car—not wearing seat belt—car collided with another vehicle—as a result, plaintiff thrown forwards and to left against roof pillar, suffering fracture of the skull—and then flung from car so that suffered fractured cervical vertebra—would not have suffered these injuries had he been wearing seat belt. Argued that his damages should not be reduced by the full 25 per cent. under *Froom* **3**, as he would still have suffered same injuries, even if he had been wearing a seat belt—*Held*, rejecting argument, that the court's task was to examine the injuries actually suffered and then to make a deduction depending on the extent to which those injuries had been caused or contributed to by the plaintiff's failure to wear a seat belt, and it was not open to the court to reduce that deduction by investigating what injuries might have been, but had not in fact been, caused in circumstances which had not arisen.

10. Salmon v. Newland, *The Times*, May 16, 1983; [1983] C.L.Y. 1655, Michael Davies J.

Plaintiff passenger in car involved in head-on collision. Suffered severe facial and eye injuries and anxiety state. Injuries would have been "a good deal less severe" if she had been wearing a seat belt—*Held*, that it was open to the court in appropriate cases to reduce the damages by more than the 15 per cent. suggested in *Froom* **3**; the appropriate reduction in this case was 20 per cent.

11. Ducharme v. Davies [1984] 1 W.W.R. 699; [1984] C.L.Y. 2291, Saskatchewan Court of Appeal

Held, infant, aged 3, incapable of contributory negligence in failing to wear seat belt. Any negligence on parent's part not to be imputed to the infant.

12. Capps v. Miller [1989] 1 W.L.R. 839; [1989] 2 All E.R. 333, C.A.

Defendant's car ran into plaintiffs moped. Plaintiff wearing crash helmet but, contrary to regulation 4 of the Motor Cycles (Protective Helmets) Regulations 1980, the chinstrap was unfastened, and helmet came off before plaintiff's head struck road—*Held*, because it was less blameworthy to wear a helmet unfastened than not to wear a helmet at all, Plaintiff was 10 per cent. contributorily negligent rather than the 15 per cent. he would have been had he worn no helmet.

13. Madden v. Quirk [1989] 1 W.L.R. 702; [1989] R.T.R. 304, Simon Brown J.

Held, driver's contribution increased from 80 to 85 per cent. because of manner in which passenger carried contrary to regulation 100(1) of Road Vehicles Construction and the Regulation 1986. (For further details see Chap. 13, (1)(h) **15**.).

14. Eastman v. South West Thames Area H.A. [1991] R.T.R. 389; [1992] P.I.Q.R. P42, C.A.

Plaintiff travelled as a passenger accompanying patient in defendant's ambulance, in which a notice said "For your own safety use seat belt provided". Some seats had belts but plaintiff sat in one that did not—plaintiff injured when ambulance braked suddenly—*Held*, defendant not liable—entitled to let plaintiff decide whether or not to occupy a seat with a belt—no duty on attendant to draw notice to plaintiff's attention or exhort her to use a belt. There is no general duty on the driver of a vehicle to exhort a passenger to use a seat belt.

15. Pace v. Cully, 1992 S.L.T. 1073; [1992] C.L.Y. 5645, O.H.

Taxi driver injured in accident for which liability admitted. Had not been wearing belt on police advice that it was safer not to, having regard to risk of attack from passengers—*Held*, not contributorily negligent.

16. Jones v. Morgan [1994] C.L.Y. 3344, Dyson J.

Taxi driver injured in accident for which liability admitted had not been wearing seat belt—*Held*, not contributorily negligent. One relevant matter was that taxi drivers are legally exempt from wearing seat belts when carrying fare-paying passengers. Moreover, taxi driver had just picked up barmaid not known to him at midnight, and he and his employer were concerned about risk of attack from passengers—easier to evade if seat belt off. However, there should be no invariable policy for taxi drivers not to wear seat belts—time of day and nature of passenger were relevant features.

(7) Proof and Presumption of Negligence

1. Morris v. Luton Corporation [1946] 1 K.B. 114; [1946] 1 All E.R. 1, C.A.

Held, not a proposition of law that driver must be able to pull up within limits of vision, but each case must depend on own circumstances.

2. Barkway v. South Wales Transport [1950] A.C. 185; [1950] 1 All E.R. 392, H.L.

Case where bus ran off road due to burst tyre which in turn was due to pre-existing impact fracture—*Held*, defendant bus company liable. Lord Porter: "Omnibuses, it is said, which are properly serviced do not burst tyres without cause, nor do they leave the road along which they are being driven. If the evidence stopped there, the statement is unexceptionable."

3. Bray v. Palmer [1953] 1 W.L.R. 1455; [1953] 2 All E.R. 1449, C.A.

Judge dismissed both claim and counterclaim, being unable to decide which party was to blame—*Held*, new trial must be ordered as judge must not exclude possibility that both were in some measure to blame.

4. Baker v. Market Harborough Industrial Co-op. [1953] 1 W.L.R. 1472; 97 S.J. 861, C.A.

Head-on collision—both drivers killed—offside wheel of one or other vehicle, or perhaps both, over white line—*Held*, it was more likely that both drivers were to blame than one only, and since both were to blame, and there were no means of distinguishing between them, 50:50 against each. See **5** and **22**.

5. France v. Parkinson [1954] 1 W.L.R. 581; [1954] 1 All E.R. 739, C.A.

Plaintiff had lent his car to X (who had disappeared and who was not plaintiff's agent)—X and defendant collide at crossroads of equal status—both cars on correct side of their road—defendant does not give evidence—*Held*, there was a presumption that each driver was negligent and therefore defendant liable.

6. Carmarthenshire C.C. v. Lewis [1955] A.C. 549; [1955] 1 All E.R. 565, H.L.

Held, defendant school liable.

7. Randall v. Tarrant [1955] 1 W.L.R. 255; [1955] 1 All E.R. 600, C.A.

Defendant's farm vehicle unsuccessfully tries to squeeze past plaintiff's car which is parked in lane while plaintiff is trespassing—*Held*, car not in these circumstances trespassing and defendant liable as having failed to disprove negligence. Question of what would have been position if car had been trespassing *left open.*

8. Shiner v. Webster, *The Times*, April 27, 1955; [1955] C.L.Y. 1849, C.A.

One party killed, other severely concussed—trial judge dismissed claim and counterclaim for want of evidence—*Held*, there was evidence of negligence against each, and blame should be equally shared.

9. Roberts v. T. Wallis [1958] 1 Lloyd's Rep. 29, Barry J.

"In those circumstances, can it be said that the owner of a machine of this kind, or indeed the owner of a motor-car, is responsible if through some defect (which may well be entirely latent) of a connecting rod it breaks during the time the machine is in motion?" (38).

9A. Bassett v. Victoria Wine Co. *The Times*, February 6, 1958, C.A.

10. Qualcast v. Haynes [1959] A.C. 743; [1959] 2 All E.R. 38, H.L.

Lord Denning (45 A): "It contains many propositions of good sense which may be taken into account in considering whether reasonable care has been taken, but it would be a mistake to elevate them into propositions of law."

11. Parish v. Judd [1960] 1 W.L.R. 867; [1960] 3 All E.R. 33, Edmund Davies J.

Lights on defendant's car failed totally—defendant got a tow from a lorry—lorry driver stopped near a street lamp to see whether defendant was all right—when stopped defendant's car was about six yards from the lamp post, was close into the kerb and had three reflectors at the rear—visible from about 100 yards away—plaintiff ran into rear—sued defendant in negligence and nuisance—*Held*, (a) as regards nuisance, plaintiff had to show that the vehicle was not merely an obstruction on the road but that it was a danger on the road, and that on the facts this was not so; and (b) as regards negligence, while it was true that an unlit vehicle on a road at night raised a presumption of negligence, this had been rebutted both as regards place and as regards maintenance, and that therefore the claim failed.

12. Tribe v. Jones (1961) 105 S.J. 931; [1961] Crim. L.R. 835, D.C.

Held, that a speed of between 45 m.p.h. and 65 m.p.h. in a restricted area was not automatically dangerous contrary to the Road Traffic Act 1960, s. 2.

13. Verney v. Wilkins (1962) 106 S.J. 879, Winn J.

13A. Kozimor v. Adey (1962) 106 S.J. 431; [1962] Crim. L.R. 564, Megaw J.

14. Tingle Jacobs v. Kennedy [1964] 1 W.L.R. 638; [1964] 1 All E.R. 888, C.A.

Both sides claimed lights were green—county court judge unable to decide—found 50:50—*Held*, new trial, as it was judge's duty to decide who was right. *Cf.* **3**, **4**, **5** and **8** (which were not apparently cited).

15. Chapman v. Copeland (1966) 110 S.J. 569; *The Times*, May 7, 1966, C.A.

Plaintiff widow proved that her deceased husband had been seen waiting to cross major road, and that major-road driver left tyre marks 184 feet long—*Held*, this evidence (defendant electing not to give evidence) was sufficient evidence of major-road driver's negligence, but there was insufficient evidence to show that deceased had also been negligent.

16. Ludgate v. Lovett [1969] 1 W.L.R. 1016; [1969] 2 All E.R. 1275, C.A.

17. Davison v. Leggett (1969) 133 J.P. 552; [1969] C.L.Y. 2417, C.A.

18. Ramburran v. Gurrucharran [1970] 1 W.L.R. 556; [1970] 1 All E.R. 749, P.C.

19. O'Connell v. Jackson [1972] 1 Q.B. 270; [1971] 3 All E.R. 129, C.A.

20. Powell v. Phillips [1972] 3 All E.R. 864; [1973] R.T.R. 19, C.A.

"In law a breach of the Highway Code has a limited effect . . . A breach creates no presumption of negligence calling for an explanation, still less a presumption of negligence making a real contribution to causing an accident or injury. The breach is just one of the circumstances on which one party is entitled to rely in establishing the negligence of the other and its contribution towards causing the accident or injury" (Stephenson L.J., 868 B-D).

21. Howard v. Bemrose [1973] R.T.R. 32; [1973] C.L.Y. 2982, C.A.

Said by Stephenson L.J. that the *Baker v. Market Harborough* **4** principle does not apply where the accident takes place on the wrong side of one driver's road; in such a case an explanation was only called for from that driver.

22. Knight v. Fellick [1977] R.T.R. 316; [1977] C.L.Y. 2010, C.A.

P, street sweeper, was hit by D's car on a dark morning—C.A. *upheld* judge's inference that P had moved from the pavement at the last moment, and dismissed P's appeal. *But* P also argued that the presumption in *Baker* **4** applied, and that since D could not satisfactorily explain how his car and P came into contact (since he barely, if at all, saw P), D must be liable, at least partially—*Held*, not so. The principle in *Baker* **4** was not to be extended beyond the ambit of the circumstances which gave rise to that case, and where, as here, there was evidence enabling the court to draw a distinction between the parties, it could not apply in any event, even if the circumstances had been within the ambit of the *Baker* **4** principle. *N.B.* In the result it seems that the *Baker* principle is to be confined to head-on collisions in the middle of the road (and similar situations), where there is no evidence enabling the court to draw a distinction between the parties.

23. Haimes v. Watson [1981] R.T.R. 90; [1991] C.L.Y. 1853, C.A.

Held, that the sudden movement of a horse across a road and into the path of an overtaking car gave rise to an inference of negligence (but on the facts of the case an inference was negatived).

24. Elizabeth v. M.I.B. [1981] R.T.R. 405; [1981] C.L.Y. 2368, C.A.

25. Kaye v. Alfa Romeo (Great Britain) Ltd (1984) 134 New L.J. 126, 451; [1984] C.L.Y. 2295, Hutchison J.

Plaintiff's car left road and hit trees. He sued car's manufacturer and supplier who admitted liability for faulty seat belt anchorage but alleged contributory negligence—*Held*, plaintiff had not explained accident in a way that negatived negligence and was one-third to blame.

26. Ng Chun Piu v. Lee Chuen Tat [1988] R.T.R. 298; *The Times*, May 25, 1988, P.C.

Defendant's coach crossed central reservation and onto opposite carriageway. Plaintiffs, passengers in coach, called no evidence and relied on *res ipsa loquitur*. Defendant proved that a car had pulled into his path causing him to brake and swerve, whereupon the coach skidded—*Held*, the prima facie case of negligence had been displaced. Plaintiffs had failed to discharge the burden of proof which remained on them throughout.

27. Carter v. Sheath [1990] R.T.R. 12; *The Times*, August 10, 1989, C.A.

Defendant, a good and careful driver, approached pelican crossing in well-lit road at night, at about 30 m.p.h. Lights green in defendant's favour. At or near crossing car's nearside front corner struck plaintiff, a 13-year-old boy. Neither defendant nor his wife, an experienced driver in front passenger seat, had seen plaintiff before impact, and plaintiff had no recollection of what happened—*Held*, on the evidence the accident was inexplicable and plaintiff had failed to discharge burden of proving that defendant was negligent.

28. Worsley v. Hollins [1991] R.T.R. 252; *The Times*, March 22, 1991, C.A.

Van owned by second defendant collided with rear of plaintiff's stationary vehicle when brakes failed due to split pin becoming detached from brake linkage. Trial judge ruled *res ipsa loquitur* applied. Second defendant said he had had van fully serviced by automobile engineer six weeks before accident, and produced M.O.T. certificate dated four weeks before accident—*Held*, when *res ipsa loquitur* applied, production of M.O.T. certificate by owner not enough by itself to displace prima facie case against him, since it was his duty to see that vehicle was properly maintained. However, on the totality of his unchallenged evidence, second defendant had displaced prima facie case.

U1. Bowen v. Lathan (1959) C.A. 273 A

Defendant misjudged speed of plaintiff ("had I known it was going so fast I would have waited")—*Held*, approving words of Donovan J., "an error of judgment of this sort is not necessarily negligence," and defendant not liable.

U2. Kirby v. Leather (1965) C.A. 86 B

Defendant van driver pulled out to overtake bus—collided with plaintiff motor scooter coming in opposite direction—judge said that on the evidence he could not say what the cause of the accident was and dismissed the claim—*Held*, applying *Baker v. Market Harborough* **4**, this was a case where one or other or both parties were to blame, and there was therefore no longer a burden of proof on the plaintiff, but it was simply a matter of inferring from the facts who was to blame. Defendants two-thirds, plaintiff one-third to blame. *N.B.* This case is reported [1965] 2 All E.R. 441, but on a point of limitation only.

U3. Horowitz v. Shillabeer (1966) C.A. 62

Collision—P. and D. both sustain damage—deputy county court judge dismisses both claims because not satisfied either had proved negligence—*Held*, question of fact, and C.A. could not interfere. *But* see **U2**, which was not cited.

U4. Mulvaine v. Joseph (1969) C.A. 277 A

"It is generally accepted that if one finds, in a case of this kind (road traffic), negligence by one defendant of less than 10 per cent., it can be disregarded on the principle of *de minimis*, or on the principle that one must look on the matter not as a theoretical exercise but from a practical point of view" (Salmon L.J., 4 F).

U5. Hopper v. Haynes (1973) C.A. 17

Tyre burst—car then hit baulk of timber at side of road—which swung into path of plaintiff's car—*Held*, applying dictum of Asquith L.J. in *Barkway* (as to which, see Chap. 3, (2) (b) **6**), defendant liable, as he had failed to show that, with reasonable care, he could not have avoided hitting the baulk. Although the tyre burst was in itself a neutral event, the onus still lay on the defendant to explain how the whole incident occurred without negligence on his part.

U6. Sutton v. Jones (1985) C.A. 624

Held, to drive a vehicle in foggy conditions with only one of two rear lights working raised a presumption of negligence against the driver, which could be displaced by driver's explaining how light came to be off without negligence on his part.

U7. Mackay v. Holmes and Hunt (1992) C.A. 1226

Motorist accelerated at point where there was reversal of camber on road and deposits of oil from lorries from adjoining haulage company premises—lost control and skidded off road—*Held*, *res ipsa loquitur* applied, and motorist had failed to show any explanation consistent with lack of fault on her part. She used road regularly and knew or should have known of hazards.

14. RAILWAYS

(*N.B.* This chapter includes all cases dealing with railways, with the exception of employees' actions for breach of statutory duty, as to which see Chap. 16, (15).)

Plaintiff		Liable or not	
Passenger	Platform—falling over edge in fog	Yes	1
Farmer	Private crossing—cows run down in mist	No	2
PASSENGER	DOOR—FLIES OPEN IN MOTION	No	3
Landowner	Sparks—from engine	Yes	4
Landowner	Sparks—from engine	Yes	5
FARMER	PRIVATE CROSSING—DUTY OF RAILWAY	No	6
Passenger	Door—not closed on starting	Yes	7
Ganger	Run down—lookout too near tunnel	Yes	8
Pedestrian	Private crossing—frequent user by public—duty	—	9
Pedestrian	Public crossing—duty of railway	—	10
PASSENGER	DOOR—SLAMMED ON HAND	Yes	11
ENGINE DRIVER	PUBLIC CROSSING—CAR RAMMING GATE	?	12
Motorist	Public crossing—stopped up but unlit	Yes	13
—	Private crossing—road later made public—duties of users and of railway	—	14
Passenger	Platform—defective edge	Yes	15
Passenger	Carriage—unlit	Yes	16
MOTORIST	PUBLIC CROSSING—NO WHISTLE BOARD—NO GATEKEEPER	Yes	17
Trespasser	**Live electric rail—electrocution**	No	18
PASSENGER	PLATFORM—OILY PATCH—PROMPT STEPS TAKEN	No	19
PASSENGER	PLATFORM—SUDDEN SNOWFALL	No	20
Motorist	Dock crossing—bad lookout by fireman	Yes	21
Dock worker	Wagon—hole in floor	Yes	22
EMPLOYEE	LIVE ELECTRIC RAIL—EMPLOYEE HAS TO CROSS	Yes	23
PEDESTRIAN	RUN DOWN—IN TUNNEL	Yes	24
Visitor	Platform—guard's van door open as train moves off	Yes	25
MOTORIST	PRIVATE CROSSING—NO WHISTLE BOARD	No	26
MOTORIST	PRIVATE CROSSING—FOG	No	27
EMPLOYEE	RUN DOWN—DUTY OF ENGINE DRIVER	No	28

PEDESTRIAN	SHUNTING—NO LOOK-OUT, NO WARNING	Yes	29
Employee	Shunting—riding on engine—caught by obstruction	Yes	30
Employee	Shunting by hand—wagons left unbraked	Yes	31
EMPLOYEE	SHUNTING—RIDING ON ENGINE—CAUGHT BY OBSTRUCTION	Yes	32
CHILD PASSENGER	DOOR—CHILD CAUSES IT TO FLY OPEN	No	33
Motorist	Private crossing—fog	No	34
Pedestrian	Run down—on track	Yes	35
Engine driver	Coronary thrombosis—while rectifying defect	No	36
PORTER	DOOR—PASSENGER JUMPING IN AND NOT SHUTTING IN TIME	Yes	37
EMPLOYEE	RUN DOWN—RESCUING TRESPASSER ON TRACK	Yes	38
CHILD VISITOR	RUN DOWN—TRESPASSING ON TRACK	No	38
Employee	Violent bang during shunting—causing plaintiff to jump into path of wagon	Yes	39
Passenger	Gap between train and platform—tube station	No	40
Passenger	Platform trolley—bag falling and causing passenger to trip	Yes	41
EMPLOYEE	ENGINE REVERSING AT NIGHT DOWN UP-TRACK—NO SUFFICIENT WARNING BY WHISTLE	Yes	42
Employee	Signal near bridge with unusually narrow clearance—engine going in reverse	Yes	43
Passenger	Train stopping short at station	Yes	44
Motorist	Accommodation crossing—gates constantly left open—no other precautions	Yes	45
Trespasser	**Fence broken—electrified railway track**	Yes	46
Cattle killed	Accommodation crossing—constructed by third party across railway which was not within the 1845 Act—railway board have no duty to maintain	No	47
Employee	Ganger—stepping from place of safety into path of second train—no whistle	Yes	48
CHILD OF TWO	WALKING ONTO CROSSING—PUBLIC RIGHT OF WAY—STILE IN DISREPAIR	Yes	49
Motorist	Unmanned level crossing—restricted view	Yes	50
Intended passenger	Fell onto and was struck on track due to epileptic fit—not trespasser on track	Yes	51
Rescuer	Station master boarding moving train—after finishing work	Yes	52
Pedestrian	**Run down—on track—taking short cut—passed through gap in fence**	No	53
Visitor	Delivering packages—trip in parcels department	Yes	54
Employee	Killed crossing line—despite notice forbidding	Yes	55
Trespasser	Hole in fence—burnt on conductor rail	No	56
ADJOINING OWNER	NO DUTY TO ADJOINING OWNER TO ERECT FENCE CAPABLE OF PREVENTING CHILDREN AND DOGS GETTING ON TO RAILWAY	No	57

Train driver	Guard allowing train to start when door open—passenger dragged under train and killed—nervous shock of driver	Yes	58
Pedestrian	Injured when struck by train—whether negligence to be inferred	No	59
Employee	Slipped on oil and water on plat form	No	60
Passenger	Fall on escalator due to its jolting	No	61
Employee	*Run down—by train on unusual track*	No	U1
Railway co.	*Door—left open by passenger jumping on train—damage to door*	Yes	U2
Passenger	*Door—mechanical door opened too early*	Yes	U3
Passenger	*Platform—gap between platform and train*	No	U4
Employee	*Shunting—squashed during loose shunting*	No	U5
Employee	*Shunting—squashed while coupling up*	Yes	U6
Employee	*Shunting—engine in rear—no continuous look-out*	No	U7
Employee	*Run down—on track*	No	U8
Employee	*Run down—on track at night*	Yes	U9
Employee	*Run down—on track—habitual practice of employees to walk in four-foot way*	No	U10
Employee	*Run down—on track*	No	U11
Employee	*No canting bar to turn over flat bottomed rail*	No	U12
Employee	*Walking along sleeper ends on foggy day*	No	U13
Engine driver	*Floor of brake compartment of diesel engine—slippery through oil leakage*	Yes	U14
Passenger	*Platform—gap between platform and train at bend in platform*	No	U15
Guard	*Falling from train*	No	U16
Motorist	*Private crossing—night—no special lights on train*	No	U17
Trespasser	*Electrical burns when climbing on carriage*	No	U18

1. Schlarb v. London and North Eastern Railway [1936] 1 All E.R. 71; (1936) 80 S.J. 168, Atkinson J.

Plaintiff descends staircase onto platform—fog and bad lighting—she falls over platform edge three yards from staircase—*Held,* negligence. No contributory negligence.

2. Knight v. Great Western Railway [1943] K.B. 105; [1942] 2 All E.R. 286, Tucker J.

Engine driver going at 30 m.p.h., being a speed at which owing to mist he could not pull up within limits of vision—*Held,* not negligent.

3. Easson v. London and North Eastern Railway [1944] K.B. 421; [1944] 2 All E.R. 425, C.A.

Door opens in motion—child falls out—child could not have opened door from outside (only way of opening it)—cause of opening unknown—door in good working order—*Held,* defendants not liable.

4. Parker v. London and North Eastern Railway (1945) 175 L.T. 137; [1946] W.N. 63, Denning J.

Held, defendants negligent for not fitting most modern type of spark arrester.

5. Sellwood v. London, Midland and Scottish Railway (1946) 175 L.T. 366, Hallett J.

Held, defendants not liable for not fitting modern arrester, but were liable for defendants' fireman's negligent firing.

6. Liddiatt v. Great Western Railway [1946] K.B. 545; [1946] 1 All E.R. 731, C.A.

Held, defendants under no duty to employ keeper at an accommodation crossing, or to give signalman instructions to keep a special lookout for people on accommodation crossing.

7. Brookes v. London Passenger Transport Board [1947] 1 All E.R. 506, Henn Collins J.

8. Dyer v. Southern Railway [1948] 1 K.B. 608; [1948] 1 All E.R. 516, Humphreys J.

9. Smith v. Railway Executive [1948] W.N. 276; [1948] 1 C.L.C. 8234, Hilbery J.

Held, defendants under duty at common law to render crossing safe, and in particular to see that there was nothing in the nature of a trap.

10. Smith v. London, Midland and Scottish Railway, 1948 S.L.T. 235; [1948] 1 C.L.C. 8235, Ct. of Session

Held, that at every level crossing where public had a right to be, there was a duty to take all reasonable precautions in train operation (and perhaps in other respects) to reduce the danger to a minimum. *Cliff v. Midland Rly.* (1870) L.R. 5 Q.B. 258 *applied.*

11. Bird v. Railway Executive (1949) 93 S.J. 357; [1949] W.N. 196, C.A.

12. Knapp v. Railway Executive [1949] 2 All E.R. 508, C.A.

13. Law v. Railway Executive (1949) 65 T.L.R. 288; [1949] W.N. 172, Hallett J.

14. Copps v. Payne [1950] 1 K.B. 611; [1950] 1 All E.R. 246, D.C.

Defendant prosecuted for failing to shut gates after crossing—pleaded that the road had subsequently become a public highway, and therefore duty to shut gates was on railway and not on him—*Held*, duty remained on person using a crossing where (as here) the crossing had been *provided* as a private crossing, even though the character of the road had subsequently changed. *N.B.* This case contains a useful summary of the statute law appertaining to private crossings.

15. Protheroe v. Railway Executive [1951] 1 K.B. 376; [1950] 2 All E.R. 1093, Parker J.

Paving-stones at edge of platform defective because uneven—*Held*, contractual duty at any rate extended to the part of the platform which plaintiff would have to pass to board train and therefore defendants liable—but judge said he would have had some difficulty in finding for plaintiff if only an invitee.

16. Warren v. Railway Executive (1950) 94 S.J. 457

Plaintiff enters unlit railway carriage—sits down where there should be a seat—but is in fact empty space—*Held*, defendants liable.

17. Lloyds Bank v. Railway Executive [1952] 1 All E.R. 1248; [1952] W.N. 215, C.A.

Held, that even if owing to the absence of dedication the statutory obligations of a public crossing did not attach, defendants were under a common law duty to take all reasonable precautions, "by whistles, warning and so forth" to safeguard members of the public who habitually used the crossing.

18. Edwards v. Railway Executive [1952] A.C. 737; [1952] 2 All E.R. 430, H.L.
See **46**.

19. Blackman v. Railway Executive [1954] 1 W.L.R. 220; [1953] 2 All E.R. 323, C.A.

Patch of oil dripped from mail barrow—foreman saw it—at once told man to get sawdust and tried to stop people passing that way—*Held*, defendants had taken all reasonable care and were not liable.

20. Tomlinson v. Railway Executive [1953] 1 All E.R. 1, C.A.

21. Jones v. Port of London Authority [1954] 1 Lloyd's Rep. 489, Devlin J.

490, col. 1: "I find that keeping a lookout from an engine is not quite the same thing as keeping a lookout from a car, and there may be reasons which cause an engine driver or fireman to have their attention diverted because they have something to do with the engine, but ten seconds, unaccounted for by any specific operation, is in my judgment too long to be allowed for in that way."

22. McDonald v. British Transport Commission [1955] 1 W.L.R. 1323; [1955] 3 All E.R. 789, Pilcher J.

23. Nizniekiewicz v. British Transport Commission, *The Times*, February 5, 1955; [1955] C.L.Y. 1899, C.A.

24. Slater v. Clay Cross [1956] 2 Q.B. 264; [1956] 2 All E.R. 625, C.A.

Held, defendants liable for negligence of their engine driver in running down plaintiff in a tunnel in which she was a licensee. The negligence consisted of not stopping at entrance, not whistling and going at 8 m.p.h.

25. Hare v. British Transport Commission [1956] 1 W.L.R. 250; [1956] 1 All E.R. 578, Lord Goddard C.J.

26. Lloyds Bank v. British Transport Commission [1956] 1 W.L.R. 1279; [1956] 3 All E.R. 291, C.A.

27. Kemshead v. British Transport Commission [1958] 1 W.L.R. 173n., [1958] 1 All E.R. 119n., C.A.

Held, defendants not liable, as it was the duty of persons using accommodation crossings to take special precautions.

28. Trznadel v. British Transport Commission [1957] 1 W.L.R. 1002; [1957] 3 All E.R. 196n., C.A.

Held, engine driver not liable for running down railwayman going along track. Morris L.J. (198 B): "An engine driver's duties are entirely different [from duties of road drivers]. The engine driver is driving on fixed tracks; he is driving on private property; he has of course to watch for the signals, and he has to have in mind that he is driving to a schedule of time. He must take all reasonable steps that he can to ensure that he stops if there is an obstacle ahead. It is not however like a roadway; and those who have permission to use a railway track with the knowledge that a train may be coming which is being driven at speed and cannot be pulled up in a very short space of time ... " The Lord Justice also said a driver could not lean out to see all the time, nor could he be expected to whistle merely because there *might* be someone walking on track. *Cf.* **35**.

29. Ashdown v. Samuel Williams [1957] 1 Q.B. 409; [1957] 1 All E.R. 35, C.A.

Held, defendant railway were negligent in shunting, but escaped liability because of an exempting notice (see Chap. 4 (2) (b) **4**).

30. Barnes v. Port of London Authority [1957] 1 Lloyd's Rep. 486, Byrne J.

31. Gibbs v. United Steel [1957] 1 W.L.R. 668; [1957] 2 All E.R. 113, Streatfeild J.

32. Hicks v. British Transport Commission [1958] 1 W.L.R. 493; [1958] 2 All E.R. 39, C.A.

33. O'Connor v. British Transport Commission [1958] 1 W.L.R. 346; [1958] 1 All E.R. 558, C.A.

Child of four and mother in guard's van while passing down train—child operates internal handle and falls out—*Held*, defendants not negligent, as they were entitled to assume child would be accompanied by someone capable of looking after it.

34. Hazell v. British Transport Commission [1958] 1 W.L.R. 169; [1958] 1 All E.R. 116, Pearson J.

Held, following **27**, and facts being similar, defendants not liable.

35. Braithwaite v. South Durham Steel [1958] 1 W.L.R. 986; [1958] 3 All E.R. 161, Edmund Davies J.

Known and permitted practice for certain licensees to walk down walkway very close to a secondary railway track—plaintiff run down by train going at 5–8 m.p.h. with guard's van in front—night-time—poor lighting—guard said he could see 40 yards and train could be pulled up in 20 yards—*Held*, guard was not keeping a proper lookout and accordingly defendants were liable *Cf.* **28**.

36. Blaikie v. British Transport Commission, 1961 S.C. 44; 1961 S.L.T. 189, 2nd Div.

Defect in engine causing great physical exertion on part of driver—coronary thrombosis soon after—*Held*, applying *Wagon Mound* (Chap. 1(4) (a) **1**) defendants not liable, as injury not reasonably foreseeable.

37. Booker v. Wenborn [1962] 1 W.L.R. 162; [1962] 1 All E.R. 431, C.A.

Train moving off—defendant jumped in—before he could shut door it had struck plaintiff porter—*Held*, defendant liable.

38. Videan v. British Transport Commission [1963] 2 Q.B. 650; [1963] 3 All E.R. 860, C.A.

Infant son of village stationmaster strayed from platform onto track—and was run down by a power-driven rail trolley—stationmaster killed in rescuing child—*Held*, child a trespasser and therefore could not recover; but widow could recover for death of stationmaster, as the right of action was independent to that of the trespasser, and trolley driver was going too fast and keeping bad look-out. *But* now see **46**.

39. Slatter v. B.R.B. (1966) 1 K.I.R. 336; [1967] C.L.Y. 2675, Sachs J.

40. Stratstone v. London Transport Board, *The Times*, January 21, 1966; [1966] C.L.Y. 8317, Phillimore J.

41. Blackett v. B.R.B., *The Times*, December 19, 1967 [1967] C.L.Y. 2664, Phillimore J.

42. Geddes v. B.R.B. (1968) 4 K.I.R. 373; [1968] C.L.Y. 2653, C.A.

43. McArthur v. B.R.B. (1968) 112 S.J. 1006; [1968] C.L.Y. 2700, Eveleigh J.

Driver of railway engine obliged to lean out to observe signal placed near bridge with unusually narrow clearance—was killed—engine was travelling in reverse—*Held*, defendants liable, in failing to route engine so that it would travel forwards, and in failing to use different type of engine, and in failing to put warning on tender.

44. Struthers v. B.R.B. (1969) 113 S.J. 268; *The Times*, March 11, 1969, James J.

45. Walker v. B.R.B. [1971] C.L.Y. 8006, O'Connor J.

46. B.R.B. v. Herrington [1972] A.C. 877; [1992] 1 All E.R. 749, H.L.

Child trespasser wandering through dilapidated fence onto electrified railway track—*Held*, as the presence of the trespasser was known to defendants or was to be anticipated by them, they owed a duty of common humanity to him, and were in breach. In the course of the speeches the duty towards a trespasser was re-defined, and *Edwards* **18** *and Videan* **38** must accordingly be read in the light of the duty as newly defined. For full details, see Chap. 10, (5) (f) **1**.

47. Short v. B.R.B. [1974] 1 W.L.R. 781, [1974] 3 All E.R. 28, Latey J.

48. Trotman v. B.R.B. (1974) 119 S.J. 65; [1975] K.I.L.R. 161, Bridge J.

Gangers' look-out man whistled for gang to go to place of safety—which they did—train passed—then look-out signalled approach of another train—signal not acknowledged by gang—deceased, one of gang, stepped into path of second train—*Held*, interpreting the railway Rules for Observance by Employees, no negligence in failing to ensure that an acknowledgment of the warning signal was given by persons who were already in a place of safety; but, on the facts, the driver of the second train was negligent is not whistling (two-thirds contributory negligence).

49. Thomas v. B.R.B. [1976] Q.B. 912; [1976] 3 All E.R. 15, C.A.

Public footpath across railway line—stile had fallen into disrepair so that people could walk through it—child aged two wandered onto line—judge had held that as the railway had come into existence before the footpath there was no duty under the 1845 Act, s. 61, to keep the stile in repair—*Held*, this made no difference, and the Railway Board were liable both for breach of section 61 and at common law.

50. Skeen v. B.R.B. [1976] R.T.R. 281; [1976] C.L.Y. 1859, Latey J.

Unmanned level crossing—view of motorists along line restricted—*Held*, Railway Board wholly liable, as there was no practicable step which the driver could have taken. *Lloyd's Bank* **17** followed.

51. Public Transport Commission of N.S.W. v. Perry (1977) 137 C.L.R. 107; [1979] C.L.Y. 1888, Aust. High Court

52. Harrison v. B.R.B. [1981] 3 All E.R. 679; [1981] C.L.Y. 1833, Boreham J.

53. Titchener v. B.R.B. [1983] 1 W.L.R. 1427; [1983] 3 All E.R. 770, H.L.

Plaintiff, then 15, taking short cut along railway line, got onto line through long-standing gap in fence. Defendants knew people used gap to cross line; plaintiff had done so on previous occasions and knew of danger. P run down by train being driven properly—*Held*, that the defendants were not liable. They did not owe the plaintiffs a duty to maintain the fence in any better condition: "The existence and extent of a duty to fence will depend on the circumstances of the case including the age and intelligence of the particular person entering on the premises; the duty will tend to be higher in a question with a very young or a very old person than in a question with a normally active and intelligent adult or adolescent. The nature of the locus and the obviousness or otherwise of the railway line may also be relevant." (Lord Fraser, 775 A). As the plaintiff was aware of the railway line and its dangers and could have kept a proper look-out, the defendants had discharged the duty they owed to her. Furthermore, as she probably would have climbed over a fence in good condition, any breach of duty by the defendants did not cause the accident. *N.B.* This was a Scottish case.
Also held that the plaintiff was *volens*: see Chap. 4, (3) **37**.

54. Jennings v. B.R.B. (1984) 134 New L.J. 584; [1984] C.L.Y. 2312, Stocker J.

Printer's employee delivering packages to parcels department of Euston station tripped over piece of tape concealed amongst paper and rubbish on floor; inadequate system of cleaning—*Held*, liable.

55. Umek v. London Transport Executive (1984) 134 New L.J. 522; [1984] C.L.Y. 2313, McNeill J.

Canteen assistant killed whilst crossing line to defendant's depot, ignoring, as others had, notice forbidding such conduct and advising use of footbridge whilst subway blocked by flooding—*Held*; defendants were aware of such conduct and should have warned train drivers accordingly; 75 per cent. contributory negligence of deceased.

56. Davies v. B.R.B. (1984) 134 New L.J. 888; [1984] C.L.Y. 2309, Farquharson J.

12-year-old boy got through hole in chain link fence to retrieve ball on railway embarkment; he tripped and got badly burnt when he fell on conductor rail—*Held*, duty to trespasser less than duty of care propounded in *Donoghue v. Stevenson*: system of checking and effecting repairs, though improveable, was adequate; defendants not liable.

57. Proffitt v. B.R.B., *The Times*, February 4, 1985; [1985] C.L.Y. 2302, C.A.

Held, a plaintiff whose garden was next to a railway and marked off by a fence had no cause of action against the defendant requiring it to erect a fence sufficient to prevent teenage children and dogs getting on to the railway, the defendant's duties being limited to marking off its property; declaration refused.

58. Wigg v. B.R.B., *The Times*, February 4, 1986, [1986] C.L.Y. 2280, Tucker J.

Passenger getting on to train as it moved off and caused by open door to be dragged under train and killed—*Held*, guard should have seen open door and was negligent in causing the train to start—*Held*, also, train driver entitled to recover for nervous shock and trauma when he came across the body on basis of *Mc Loughlin v. O'Brian* [1983] 1 A.C. 410.

59. Chisholm v. State Transport Authority (1987) 46 S.A.S.R. 148; [1989] C.L.Y. 2591, Sup. Ct. of South Australia

Plaintiff asked court to infer negligence from nature of injuries received when struck by train and expert evidence that such was possibly compatible with an accident negligently caused—*Held*, not sufficient evidence so to infer.

60. Hanlon v. B.R.B., 1991 S.L.T. 228; [1991] C.L.Y. 5303, O.H.

Employee slipped on puddle of oil and water on platform; at best, the substance could only have been a film whose origin was unknown and whose presence was not proved to have been of more than the shortest duration; there was no evidence of similar substances or accidents therefrom there or elsewhere—*Held*, that pursuer failed to establish circumstances in which a duty of care regularly to inspect platforms to see that they were free from greasy and oily substances could be said to arise.

61. Sherlock v. London Underground [1993] C.L.Y. 3001, Judge Quentin Edwards

Plaintiff fell on escalator allegedly due to its jolting; *res ipsa loquitur* relied on—*Held*, not liable.

U1. Bent v. London Transport Executive (1952) C.A. 76

U2. London Transport Executive v. Lawson (1952) C.A. 199

U3. Royston v. Barton Transport Ltd (1953) C.A. 116

Bus conductor opened mechanical doors 70 yards before stop—plaintiff fell out—*Held*, defendants liable (but 10 per cent. contributory negligence).

U4. Bellamy v. Railway Executive (1954) C.A. 140

Plaintiff passenger on new double-decker train—no running-board as in old-type coach—distance to platform same—gap between platform and train as often happens with other trains—plaintiff alighting stepped into gap thinking there was a running-board—*Held*, defendants not negligent in not taking special precautions as no increased risk—passengers should keep lookout realising new type of coach different—passengers get into coach before alighting and should realise no running-board.

U5. Donnelly v. British Transport Commission (1955) C.A. 246

Plaintiff shunter squeezed when loose shunted coach is run into end of train—*Held*, defendants not liable, for although loose shunting dangerous unless there were strict rules as to when to go between buffers to couple up, in this case there were such rules in existence.

U6. Clark v. British Transport Commission (1955) C.A. 5

U7. Jenkinson v. British Transport Commission (1960) C.A. 140

U8. Collyer v. British Transport Commission (1960) C.A. 121

Electric train coming into Blackfriars Station—driver saw deceased who was a railwayman near the track and blew his whistle—then concentrated on the signals—while he was doing so deceased stepped onto track—*Held*, driver not negligent in failing to keep a proper look-out, as it was his primary duty to concentrate on the signals.

U9. Foard v. British Transport Commission (1960) C.A. 226

Chargehand ganger run down by railway engine at night—*Held*, engine driver negligent (but only 20 per cent., deceased ganger had failed to post look-out).

U10. Lloyd v. British Transport Commission (1961) C.A. 128

Plaintiff lengthman run down by engine while walking in four-foot way of track—this was a very common practice in daytime and defendants must have known of it to the point of acquiescence, notwithstanding it was in breach of rules—but plaintiff was walking at first light in weather which was foggy with rain—*Held*, defendants not liable, as they could not be taken to have acquiesced in practice in such conditions.

U11. Talbot v. British Transport Commission (1963) C.A. 113

Deceased chargehand ganger crushed while standing in blind area in front of engine—*Held*, defendants not liable.

U12. Galloway v. B.R.B. (1968) C.A. 292

U13. Vidgen v. B.R.B. (1974) C.A. 317

Deceased, employee of contractors to defendants, walking along sleeper ends on foggy day—visibility 60–70 yards—run down by train going at 60 m.p.h.—the side of the line was rough with ballast—but passable—there was also the top of a grass bank which was wet and slippery but passable—*Held*, defendants not liable.

U14. Burns v. B.R.B. (1977) C.A. 278 A

U15. Newbold v. B.R.B. (1980) C.A. 297

Because of bend in platform, there was a gap of 17 inches between platform and running board of one of coaches. To warn, defendants had painted platform edge white and illuminated it. Plaintiff did not keep proper look-out and foot went down gap—*Held*, risk of injury was not so great as to require further precautions.

U16. Webb v. B.R.B. (1982) C.A. 339

Railway guard fall from open door of empty passenger train which began to be moved to station—*Held*, defendants not negligent in not having a system of signals between guard and driver in such circumstances or otherwise at fault.

U17. Smith v. B.R.B. (1983) C.A. 412

U18. Wiltshire v. B.R.B. (1992) C.A. 1243

14-yr-old boy suffered burns from overhead electrical cable when he climbed onto roof of carriage in sidings—*Held*, defendants not liable as occupiers. *Pannett v. Mc Guinness* [1992] 2 Q.B. 599 applied. See Chap. 10, (5)(f) **2**.

15. EMPLOYERS' LIABILITY—COMMON LAW

(1) Duty of Care

(a) General Scope of Duty

(*N.B.* The cases listed in this subsection are selected as representative from many others.)

1. Wilsons and Clyde Coal Co. v. English [1938] A.C. 57; [1937] 2 All E.R. 628, H.L.

Lord Wright (640 C): "The obligation is threefold, the provision of a competent staff of men, adequate material and a proper system and effective supervision." But see **4**.

2. Paris v. Stepney B.C. [1951] A.C. 367; [1951] 1 All E.R. 42, H.L.

Lord Oaksey (50): "The duty of an employer . . . is to take reasonable care for his servant's safety in all the circumstances of the case." "The respondents' duty of care is a duty owed to their employees as individuals" (Lord Normand, 48 F).

3. Woods v. Durable Suites [1953] 1 W.L.R. 857; [1953] 2 All E.R. 393, C.A.

Singleton L.J. (393 E) cited Lord Herschell in *Smith v. Baker* [1891] A.C. 362: "It is quite clear that the contract between employer and employed involves on the part of the former the duty of taking reasonable care to provide proper appliances, and to maintain them in a proper condition, and so to carry on his operations as not to subject those employed by him to unnecessary risk." *N.B.* This dictum was also endorsed by Lord MacDermott in *Paris v. Stepney Borough Council* [1951] 1 All E.R. 42 at 54 C. (See, however, **4**.)

4. Wilson v. Tyneside Window Cleaning [1958] 2 Q.B. 110; [1958] 2 All E.R. 265, C.A.

Pearce L.J. (271 D): "Now it is true that in *Wilsons and Clyde v. English* **1** Lord Wright divided up the duty of a master for convenience of definition or argument; but all three are ultimately only manifestations of the same duty of the master to take reasonable care so to carry out his operations as not to subject those employed by him to unnecessary risk." Parker L.J. (272 H): "This case is a very good example of the difficulties one gets into in treating the duty owed at common law by a master to his servant as a number of separate duties," and: "The master's duty is general, to take all reasonable steps to avoid risk to his servants."

5. Davie v. New Merton Board Mills [1959] A.C. 604; [1959] 1 All E.R. 346, H.L.

Lord Simonds (351 A) referred with approval to the *Smith v. Baker* definition of duty, for terms of which see **3**.

6. Cavanagh v. Ulster Weaving [1960] A.C. 145; [1959] 2 All E.R. 745, H.L.

Lord Somervell (751 I, Lord Tucker concurring): "Now that common employment has been abolished those distinctions need no longer be drawn. I suggest with all respect that courts of first instance ... will proceed more satisfactorily if what I have called the normal formula—that is reasonable care in all the circumstances—is applied whatever the circumstances."

7. Matthews v. Kuwait Bechtel [1959] 2 W.L.R. 702; [1959] 2 All E.R. 345, C.A.

Plaintiff employee wished to sue in contract so as to get leave to serve writ out of jurisdiction—*Held*, he could do so, as (following dicta in **1** and **5**) duty arose either in tort or in contract.

8. Brown v. Rolls-Royce [1960] 1 W.L.R. 210; [1960] 1 All E.R. 577, H.L.

Lord Cohen (579 G), citing Lord Keith in *Cavanagh v. Ulster Weaving* **6**: "The ruling principle is that the employer is bound to take reasonable care for the safety of his workmen and all other rules or formulas must be taken subject to this principle."

(b) Scope of Duty in Particular Cases

1. Deyong v. Shenburn [1946] K.B. 227: [1946] 1 All E.R. 226, C.A.

Held, not. "There never has been a decision that a master must, merely because of the relationship which exists between a master and a servant, take reasonable care for the safety of his servant's belongings" in the sense that he must ensure so far as he can that they are not stolen (229 H). *But* du Parcq L.J. said that this decision did not mean that a claim for damage to clothing sustained in the course of personal injury was barred (229 G). And Tucker J. (232 A) said that if a master orders an act which may imperil servant's property known by him to be in a certain place, he may be liable as the servant's neighbour. Applied in **6**.

2. Gregory v. Ford [1951] 1 All E.R. 121, Byrne J.

Negligent driving of servant—master not insured—question was whether servant had to indemnify master—*Held*, not, because although master owed no statutory duty under Road Traffic Act 1930, s. 35, to servant to insure, there was an implied term in contract of service that master would not require servant to perform unlawful act, which had been broken by the failure to insure. "from which it would follow that the servant would be indemnified by insurers for any damage caused by his negligence" (124 A—but this is no longer valid—see 7), and although servant was negligent. "it is owing to breach of statutory duty by master that the damages in respect of which they claim indemnity falls on them" (124 B).

3. Semtex v. Gladstone [1954] 1 W.L.R. 945; [1954] 2 All E.R. 206, Finnemore J.

Held, see Chap. 17, **3**—approved by H.L. in **7**.

4. Smith v. Ocean S.S. [1954] 2 Lloyd's Rep. 482, Gorman J.

Native coolie knifed a ship's officer—Held, on the facts defendants not liable, but judge seems to have assumed that a duty of care did exist. See cases in Chap. 15 (8).

5. Hayden v. M.D.H.B. [1956] 2 Lloyd's Rep. 497, Jones J.

Held, defendants not liable.

6. Edwards v. West Herts Group Hospital M.C. [1957] 1 W.L.R. 415; [1957] 1 All E.R. 541, C.A.

Held, applying **1**, defendants not liable for theft of effects from bedroom of resident house physician, because no duty of care owed.

7. Lister v. Romford Ice Co. [1957] A.C. 555; [1957] 1 All E.R. 125, H.L.

Defendant employed by plaintiff negligently drove lorry into X in course of employment—X a fellow employee—X successfully sues plaintiff—plaintiff starts action against defendant to be indemnified —*Held*, defendant liable (3–2), because the only implied term which was relevant was that plaintiff should insure sufficiently to avoid requiring defendant to perform an illegal act, which plaintiff had done, and there was no further term to be implied, either to insure plaintiff generally or to indemnify him out of insurance moneys or otherwise. **3** approved.

8. Tomlinson v. Ellerman's Wilson [1959] 1 Lloyd's Rep. 141, Lord Parker C.J.

Ship's throttle lever dangerous owing to erratic governor—plaintiff donkeyman injured moving it—no part of his duty to do so—but in the circumstances he might reasonably be expected to move it—*Held*, defendants owed plaintiff duty of care and were liable for not warning him.

9. Bradford v. Boston Deep Sea Fisheries [1959] 1 Lloyd's Rep. 394, Finnemore J.

Deceased was returning from shore leave to ship in hired dinghy when he was drowned—the skipper of the ship was in the dinghy at the same time—cause of the drowning was overloading—*Held*, defendant employers not liable as they owed no duty: "A sailor's employment is on or about the ship, or on shore if he goes there on ship's business. If he goes on shore on leave he is during that time away from his employment, and does not come again within the scope of his employment until he has reached the ship on his return. Apart from any special arrangements, he is responsible to get back to the ship from his leave. While on the quay, if the ship is in port, he is still outside the course of his employment, and he regains it only when he goes on board ship or is in the act of going on board. If the ship is at anchor and he goes by boat, he is still away from his employment, in my view, until the boat reaches the ship and he proceeds to climb on board or attempts to do so" (393, col. 1).

10. Quinn v. Burch [1966] 2 Q.B. 370; [1966] 2 All E.R. 283, C.A.

Working sub-contractor, finding that main contractor had failed, in breach of contract, to provide stepladder, used an unfooted trestle which slipped—*Held*, main contractor not liable, as his failure only provided the occasion for the plaintiff's conduct, and in no way caused it. Sellers L.J. (287 D) said that the position would have been different if the defendant had owed a master and servant duty.

11. McPhee v. General Motors (1970) 8 K.I.R. 885; [1970] C.L.Y. 187, Lyell J.

Held, defendants liable for failure to warn plaintiff.

12. Jones v. Minton (1973) 15 K.I.R. 309; [1974] C.L.Y. 2599, Thompson J.

13. Sole v. Hallt [1973] 1 Q.B. 574; [1973] 1 All E.R. 1032, Swanwick J.

Working sub-contractor fixing ceilings in houses being built by defendant main contractor—the work involved walking backwards on upper floor—plaintiff fell down unguarded staircase well hole—guard rails should have been made available by defendant—if plaintiff had been suing in contract, his claim would have been defeated by his own contributory negligence (see *Quinn v. Burch* Chap., 4, (1) (a)**14**)—*Held*, however that although he entered house under contract he could sue under Occupiers' Liability Act, and that defendants were 66 per cent. liable.

14. Page v Read (1984) 134 New L.J. 723; [1984] C.L.Y. 1203, Stocker J.

Plaintiff, working without safety equipment, fell from roof of house he was painting and sued defendant who had the contract for the painting work, relying on the Construction (Working Places) Regulations 1966, negligence, and Occupiers' Liability Act, 1957—*Held*, on the evidence, plaintiff was self-employed; thus, the Regulations did not apply and there was no duty in tort to provide him with safety equipment or safe system of working. Moreover, defendant owed no duty under 1957 Act because not in occupation of the site.

15. Hemmings v. British Aerospace [1986] C.L.Y. 2265, Swinton Thomas J.

Plaintiff slipped on ice using a path to attend a union meeting in the canteen. The path was also a means of access to places of work—*Held*, defendant negligent. It was immaterial that plaintiff going to a union meeting.

16. Ferguson v. Welsh [1987] 1 W.L.R. 1553; [1987] 3 All E.R. 777; H.L.

A council engaged contractor, S, to demolish building on site owned by council, on terms that S should not sub-contract the work without council's consent. Without such consent, S sub-contracted the work to W, who employed plaintiff. Due to unsafe system of work and breaches of statutory duty on part of W, plaintiff seriously injured. Trial judge, *inter alia*, held council not liable as occupiers. On appeal to House of Lords, plaintiff sought retrial against council—House of Lords dealt with appeal on basis that both council and S were occupiers of the site—*Held*;

(a) Despite limitation on sub-contracting, there was evidence capable of establishing that council had given S ostensible authority to invite W and his employees onto site, and thus that plaintiff was visitor of council on site.
(b) Council not in breach of common duty of care under The Occupiers' Liability Act 1957, s. 2 (2), because absence of reasonable safety arose not from physical state or use of the premises but from unsafe system of work implemented by W and followed by plaintiff.
(c) Occupier was not ordinarily under a duty to see that an independent contractor was implementing safe system of work. But, by virtue of section 2 (4) (b) of the Act, in special circumstances, where occupier knew or had reason to suspect that his contractor was using unsafe system, it might well be reasonable for him to take steps to see that the system was made safe, and he might therefore be liable to contractor's employee injured as a result of unsafe system. *Per* Lords Oliver and Goff, any such liability would be as joint tortfeasor with contractor, rather than an occupier. However, on the facts, council not liable in this way.

(d) Accordingly, retrial of action against council not ordered.
(e) *Per* Lord Goff: where two persons occupy same land, and one allows third party onto land without express or ostensible authority of other, third party will be visitor of former occupier but trespasser *vis-à-vis* the latter.

17. Calder v. H. Kitson Vickers Ltd [1988] I.C.R. 232; [1988] C.L.Y. 1952, C.A.

Plaintiff worked as labour-only sub-contractor for defendant, in a team breaking up a minesweeper by a heavy metal ball dropped from crane owned by defendant and driven by defendant's employee. Part of crane's lifting equipment fell and struck plaintiff. Plaintiff knew that (a) a chain which would have secured the part had previously been damaged and not replaced, and (b) an alternative method of securing the part had been used in the past—*Held*,

(a) defendant owed plaintiff a duty of care in the circumstances, including degree of control exercised by defendant;
(b) defendant negligent in providing unsafe equipment, failing to warn plaintiff of danger and condoning unsafe system of working;
(c) plaintiff 25 per cent. to blame for failing to request replacement or repair of chain or to use the alternative method, albeit at the cost of some inconvenience and loss of time.

18. Ali v. Furness Withy (Shipping) Ltd [1988] 2 Lloyd's Rep. 379; [1989] C.L.Y. 2553, Tudor Evans J.

Deceased showed signs of mental illness on board vessel, anchored about $1\frac{1}{2}$ miles from port. Master ordered him to be restrained on stretcher and kept in locked and guarded cabin. Cabin door then found to have been locked from inside. Master key would not open it from outside. By the time access finally gained, deceased had gone through port-hole, believing he was fleeing his delusions—*Held*,

(a) On the medical evidence, Master not negligent in failing to diagnose mental illness earlier, to keep deceased in ship's hospital or to sedate him further;
(b) Master negligent in that deceased not properly secured to stretcher and kept in cabin with no ready means of observation from outside; and, having diagnozed illness, in failing to take immediate steps to get deceased ashore.
(c) Defendant negligent in failing adequately to inspect the locks on the ship.

19. Smith v. Stages [1989] A.C. 928; [1989] 1 All E.R. 833, H.L.

Plaintiff and fellow employee sent from the Midlands to do urgent work at a power station in Wales—paid travelling time, but mode of travel left to them. They went in fellow employee's car. Having worked 19 of the 24 hours before finishing the job, they drove straight back. As they did so, car left road due to fellow employee's negligence—*Held*,

(a) by Court of Appeal, plaintiff not contributorily negligent in travelling with fellow employee knowing he had had insufficient rest;
(b) by Court of Appeal and House of Lords, the mens' employers were vicariously liable for fellow employee's negligence. The men were paid wages to travel and the travel was part of their duties performed in the course of their employment. *Per* Lord Lowry at p 851b: "The paramount rule is that an employee travelling on the highway will be acting in the course of his employment if and only if he is at the material time going about his employer's business.

One must not confuse the duty to turn up for one's work with the concept of already being 'on duty' while travelling to it." (More detailed prima face propositions are set out at 851 C–f.)

20. Reid v. Rush & Tompkins Group plc [1990] 1 W.L.R. 212; [1989] 3 All E.R. 228, C.A.

Plaintiff injured in road accident in Ethopia, where he had been sent by his employers, due to negligence of unidentified driver. Being unable to recover compensation, he claimed his employer negligent in failing to insure him against such an eventuality or advising him to insure himself—*Held*, employer owed no duty to protect plaintiff from economic loss. Any such duty could only arise from contract of employment.

21. Petch v. Commissioners of Customs and Excise [1993] I.C.R. 789; *The Times*, March 4, 1993, C.A.

Plaintiff, civil servant with defendant, suffered mental breakdown in October 1974 due to manic depression. After returning to work in January, 1975, his behaviour became bizarre due to hypomania. As a result he was transferred to D.H.S.S. in June, 1975—became ill again in 1983 and was retired on medical grounds in 1986. Then claimed injury benefit under civil service scheme, claiming his illnesses were caused by pressure of work when with defendant. Following letters from defendant to Treasury concerning plaintiff and his work record, plaintiff's claim was rejected. He then claimed damages for negligence—*Held, inter alia*:

(a) Even if pressure of work caused initial breakdown, plaintiff had not proved that defendant's senior management were or should have been aware that in 1974 he was showing signs of impending breakdown or that his workload carried real risk of breakdown. Thus defendant was not in breach of its admitted duty to take reasonable care to see that plaintiff's duties did not damage his physical or mental health.
(b) On the evidence, defendant had not caused the hypomania and its treatment of and decision to transfer plaintiff thereafter were proper and not negligent.

22. Walker v. Northumberland C.C., *The Times*, November, 24, 1994; [1994] C.L.Y. 2278, Colman J.

Plaintiff, employed in defendant's social services department, came under increasingly intense pressure of work in 1980s; his requests for further staff were not met. Due to the pressure he had a nervous breakdown in 1986. Returning in 1987 he advised his supervisor that the pressure had to be relieved, but only very limited assistance was provided. Plaintiff had second breakdown later in 1987 and had to retire—*Held*,

(a) There was no logical reason for psychiatric injury to be excluded from scope of employer's duty to provide safe system of work.
(b) First breakdown not reasonably foreseeable.
(c) After plaintiff's return his supervisor should have foreseen that if again exposed to same work load he was at risk of another breakdown. Continuous or substantial assistance should have been provided. Defendant negligent in not having done so, despite the constraints imposed by its budget, and although provision of further assistance might have been disruptive to provision of services to the public.

23. Barrett v. Ministry of Defence, *The Times*, January 13, 1995, C.A.

Deceased, naval airman at base in Norway, drank to excess, vomited, was left slumped on a chair and then carried unconscious to his cabin where he lay in a coma, observed intermittently—died of aspiration of vomit. Defendant had failed to enforce Queen's Regulations and standing orders discouraging over-indulgence in alcohol. There were no clear orders from officers as to how deceased should have been treated after collapsing, and no adequate medical cover was available—*Held*,

(a) Defendant under no duty to take reasonable care to prevent deceased, a mature man, from abusing alcohol to extent he did. Until he became unconscious he alone was responsible for his condition. The Queen's Regulations and standing orders could not be equated with guidance given in Highway Code or factory safety pamphlets.
(b) After deceased collapsed, defendant negligent in failing properly to supervise and provide medical assistance for him.
(c) Deceased two-thirds to blame.

N.B. At first instance, defence of *volenti* failed—deceased, with mind clouded by alcohol, had not voluntarily assumed risk of grave or fatal injury by continuing drinking.

U1. Grosvenor v. Gerrard & Sons Ltd (1954) C.A. 19

Deceased employed by defendants as general roof maintenance man—fell through roof at place where no reason for him to be—*Held*, defendants not liable, as no duty owed under Building Regulations or at common law.

U2. Marsden v. L.B. of Havering (1983) C.A. 114

Social worker visiting defendant's flat injured when door knocker came away as she pulled on it to close door. Defendant's estate officer knew the knocker were insufficiently robust for use in closing door—*Held*, defendants liable for fitting such a knocker in the first place, alternatively for failing to inspect knocker periodically to see it was strong enough.

U3. O'Neill v. Boddingtons Brewery Ltd (1986) C.A. 160

Plaintiff, an experienced driver and driver's mate, jumped from a moving delivery lorry and injured his foot—*Held*, defendant not liable. Even if there was a common practice for employees to jump from lorries in this way, there was no evidence that defendant knew of it, to enable it to devise a system of work to counteract it. Plaintiff should have informed defendant's management of the malpractice.

U4. Walker v. Reigate and Banstead B.C. (1986) C.A. 312

Plaintiff, lorry driver, was injured lifting a pavement cornerstone weighing 220 lbs in the course of unloading it from his lorry. The normal practice was to roll such stones along the floor of the lorry—*Held*, defendant not negligent and not in breach of regulation 55 of Construction (General Provisions) Regulations 1966. Plaintiff was employed to move the cornerstone, not to lift it.

U5. England v. Cleveland Potash Ltd (1986) C.A. 586

Contrary to employer's specific instructions, deceased tried to dispose if a quantity of fenobel by burning it, and was killed in ensuing explosion—*Held*, defendant not liable—deceased's action not foreseeable. Mines and Quarries Act 1954, s. 88, did not apply.

U6. Walkey v. Aluminium Storefront Components Ltd (1986) C.A. 809

Plaintiff shopfitter, a sub-contractor of first defendant, was provided with tower scaffold by first defendant, who had obtained it from a supplier together with literature directing that outriggers should be used if the working platform was above a specified height, and that toe boards and guard rails should always be provided on the platform. First defendant did not show the literature to plaintiff. Plaintiff used platform above the specified height. Outrigger were not used, and no guard rail was fitted to one side of the platform. First defendant's foreman saw this but said nothing. The scaffold tipped and plaintiff was injured—*Held*, first defendants negligent in failing to inform plaintiff of the safety directions in the literature. Plaintiff contributorily negligent and in breach of regulation 28(1) of the Construction (Working Places) Regulations 1966 for not fitting complete guard rail. Plaintiff one-third to blame.

U7. Sinclair v. Electrolux Ltd (1986) C.A. 1025

Plaintiff crossed a public road from defendants factory to the canteen at 2 a.m. when he slipped on ice. Defendant had not gritted the public road. The road was well used and camed a bus route—*Held*, defendant was not in breach of duty of care in failing to grit the public road. Had the road been public only in the technical sense but effectively used only by their employees, it might have been defendant's duty to grit the road.

U8. Herbert v. Ermin Plant (Hire & Services) Ltd (1987) C.A. 482

Without his employer's knowledge or permission, plaintiff fixed air compressor to water tank, to improve flow of water thence to steam cleaner. Ensuing pressure caused an inspection cover to shatter, injuring plaintiff—*Held*, employer could not reasonably have foreseen plaintiff's act, and not liable.

U9. Angell v. W. F. Button & Son Ltd (1987) C.A. 624

Demolition worker cut his knee on broken glass in a window frame when climbing down from a roof—*Held*, defendant not liable in negligence or for search of regulation 6 (2) of Construction (Working Places) Regulations 1966—defendant had not provided or adopted the window frame or a means of access/egress.

U10. Bristow v. A. H. Gore Ltd (1987) C.A. 915

Lorry driver stacking sacks of malt waste onto his lorry. Each sack should have weighed 50 kg. One weighed 75 kg. Plaintiff, realising it was heavier than the others, tried to lift it on top of five other sacks. He fell with the sack—*Held*, defendant not liable. Accident not reasonably foreseeable—plaintiff was an experienced man, well able to assess difficulty presented by overweight sack, which he could have put on the platform of the lorry to start a new stack.

U11. Cox v. Aiton & Co. Ltd (1989) C.A. 1056

Plaintiff, steel erector, climbed over guard rails to an opening created to accomodate chain hoists and not for access—fell when trying to descend through the opening—*Held*, defendant not liable—accident caused solely by plaintiff's decision to descend by unauthorised and obviously dangerous route.

U12. Bookham v. Unusual Rigging Co. Ltd (1990) C.A. 114

First defendant, engaged by second defendant to suspend circular frames from wires, decided tower scaffold without outrigger would suffice. Plaintiff, a self-employed rigger, was on scaffold when it began to tilt. Two employees of second defendant climbed and leant on it to try to steady it, but in the event caused it to overbalance—*Held*, first and second defendants respectively two-thirds and one-third to blame. First defendant should have provided outrigger. It was foreseeable that, should scaffold tilt, others might climb on it and affect its stability. Second defendants' employeer should have realized their actions would jeopardise plaintiff's safety.

U13. Scaife v Imperial Inns and Taverns Plc (1990) C.A. 617

Plaintiff injured when lifting a 22-gallon beer container weighing 2 cwt. in the cellar of a public house. The container had been left by the delivering brewery on top of a smaller container—*Held* neither employer nor brewery liable. The accident was not foreseeable. The simple method of moving the larger container was by "collapsing it", *i.e.* pulling it from the other, and letting it fall to the ground. Specific instructions from employers as to how to move one container from the top of another were not necessary.

U14. Carr v. R. W. Construction (Stockport) Ltd (1993) C.A. 662

Plaintiff was employed by subcontractor on a building site on which defendant was main contractor. Plaintiff climbed a ladder placed against blockwork left behind when a wall had been demolished by defendant. Because two of the blocks were displaced, the ladder twisted as plaintiff climbed it and he fell—*Held*, defendant liable—should have foreseen that the blockwork might have been rendered unstable and should have inspected its condition after the demolition operation.

(c) Loan of Employee—Which Employer Liable

(*N.B.* The cases here are those where the employee is plaintiff–for cases where a third party is plaintiff suing for the negligence of the employee, see Chap. 5, (1).)

1. Holt v. W.H. Rhodes (1949) 93 S.J. 399; [1949] 1 All E.R. 478, C.A.

Plaintiff crane driver loaned with crane to stevedores—accident through faulty system of work—the faulty system consisted of casual piling of goods round a pillar, making it impossible for plaintiff to get to pillar safely—*Held*, general employers could not be liable for a faulty system *of this sort*, but there would have to be a new trial on question whether stevedores were plaintiff's master *pro hac vice.*

2. Garrard v. Southey [1952] 2 Q.B. 174; [1952] 1 All E.R. 597, Parker J.

Held, that plaintiff had become servant of factory occupier, following *M.D.H.B. v. Coggins* [1946] 2 All E.R. 345, because he "was entitled to tell, and did tell, plaintiff how to do the work". Judge went on to say that test might not be the same, in loan of servant cases, where servant injured someone else, and where servant was himself injured.

3. Johnson v. Beaumont [1953] 2 Q.B. 184; [1953] 2 All E.R. 106, McNair J.

The question was whether there had been a sufficient transfer of plaintiff's services as a trimmer to the wharf-owners for plaintiff's ordinary employers to be able to say they were not carrying on the process of unloading by their workmen for the purpose of the Dock Regulations—the wharf-owners had general control and supplied the signaller and the crane driver—*Held*, following *M.D.H.B. v. Coggins* [1946] 2 All E.R. 345, there had been no sufficient transfer to exempt the ordinary employers of plaintiff from their duty under Dock Regulations.

4. O'Reilly v. I.C.I. [1955] 1 W.L.R. 1155; [1955] 3 All E.R. 382, C.A.

Plaintiff a lorry driver employed by British Road Services—B.R.S. put plaintiff and plaintiff's lorry at full-time disposal of I.C.I.—accident while plaintiff unloading drums due to unsafe system of I.C.I.—action would fail if plaintiff merely an invitee since he was well aware of the danger—but would succeed if plaintiff was an employee of I.C.I.—it was not established that B.R.S. had delegated to I.C.I. right to give orders on how plaintiff's work was to be done or that plaintiff was bound to obey such orders from I.C.I.—*Held*, I.C.I. did not owe plaintiff duty of employers, since plaintiff had not discharged the heavy onus of proving a relationship of employer and employee *pro hac vice.*

5. Denham v. Midland Employers Association [1955] 2 Q.B. 437; [1955] 2 All E.R. 561, C.A.

X lent Y, an employee of theirs, to Z to assist them—Y negligently killed by Z—if Y was under a contract of service with Z when he was killed insurers A were liable—if not, insurers B—plaintiff had to take orders about his work (which was unskilled) from Z's foreman—in other respects, such as pay and dismissal, plaintiff remained servant of X—*Held*, that Z would have been liable as master for the negligence of Y (564 H and 566 H) and also owed to Y the duty owed by a master (on the principle that "the right of control carries with it the burden of responsibility"—Denning L.J. 564 I), but these considerations were irrelevant in deciding whether Y was under a contract of service to Z, and that on this question he was clearly not under a contract of service to Z, but to X.

6. The Panther [1957] P. 143; [1957] 1 All E.R. 641, Willmer J.

Owners of negligent tug argue that their master was *pro hac vice* servant of tow—*Held*, not so, whatever the contract of towage might say. (*N.B.* This was a case where plaintiff was a third party.)

7. Gibb v. United Steel [1957] 1 W.L.R. 668; [1957] 2 All E.R. 110, Streatfeild J.

Held, that although under the dock labour scheme the harbour board was the general employer of a dock labourer, he became *pro hac vice* the servant of the master stevedores when working a cargo for them.

8. Savory v. Holland Hannen [1964] 1 W.L.R. 1158; [1964] 3 All E.R. 18, C.A.

Held, the blaster did not become the servant *pro hac vice* of the building contractors, because they had no right to dictate to him how to do the actual blasting. *N.B.* Lord Denning M.R. pointed out (21 D) that *O'Reilly* **4** would be decided according to a different test since the Occupiers' Liability Act 1957. *N.B. also* Diplock L.J. said (22 B) that since Lord Somervill's formulation of the general duty of care ("reasonable care in all the circumstances") in *Cavanagh v. Ulster Weaving* (Chap. 15, (1) (a) **6**), the rules concerning master and servant *pro hac vice* were obsolete where the servant was plaintiff, for whether he was or was not servant *pro hac vice*, the quasi-employer would owe him the same duty of "reasonable care in all the circumstances".

9. McArdle v. Andmac [1967] 1 All E.R. 583, C.A.

Suggested *obiter* by Sellers L.J. (586 I), the point not being pleaded.

10. Morris v. Breaveglen Ltd [1993] I.C.R. 766; [1993] P.I.Q.R. P 294, C.A.

Defendant supplied plaintiff to S under labour-only sub-contract, requiring defendant, *inter alia*, to insure against employer's liability, indemnify S against all such claims and perform all obligations placed on employers by statute or common law, though in practice S controlled plaintiff's work. Plaintiff instructed by S to tip soil from a dumper truck in area in part of which was steep unprotected overhang. Truck went over the edge, probably because plaintiff inadvertently took foot off clutch—he had not been trained properly in driving dumper truck—*Held*,

(a) System of work plaintiff was following was unsafe—no marks indicating how far to proceed when approaching overhang, and no physical barrier to prevent truck from going over edge.
(b) Defendant liable for the unsafe system at common law—had not delegated its duty of care, but chosen to perform it through S.
(c) Defendant also negligent in failing properly to train plaintiff in driving dumper truck.
(d) Through the plaintiff, defendant was "using" the truck within meaning of regulation 3 of Construction (General Provisions) Regulation 1961 and was thus liable for admitted breaches of regulations 32 and 37.

(d) Liability for Independent Contractors and Suppliers

(*N.B.* (1) See, more generally, cases listed in Chap. 5 (3) (a). (2) The decision in *Davie v. New Merton Board Mills* has been *reversed* by the Employers' Liability (Defective Equipment) Act 1969 in, but only in, cases where an "employee" sustains personal injury in the course of his employment in consequence of equipment provided by the employer for the purposes of the employer's business, "employee" being defined as a person employed under a contract of service for the purposes of a business (which includes activities carried on by any public body) carried on by the employer. For persons not within this definition, such as domestic servants and working subcontractors, the law as laid down in *Davie* **5** still applies).

1. Wilsons and Clyde Coal Co. v. English [1938] A.C. 57: [1937] 2 All E.R. 628, H.L.

Lord Thankerton (65): "In my opinion the master cannot 'delegate' his duty in this sense" (*i.e.* appointing a competent person to perform his duty of providing safe system, etc., so as to absolve himself from that duty). Lord Macmillan (75): "The owner (*i.e.* employer) remains vicariously responsible for the negligence of the person whom he has appointed to perform his obligation (*i.e.* as to safe system, etc.) . . . If the owner's duty has not been performed, no matter how competent the agent selected by the owner to perform it for him, the owner is responsible."

2. Paine v. Colne Valley Electricity [1938] 4 All E.R. 803; 106 L.T. 124, Goddard L.J.

Workman killed by live busbar—*Held*, defendants, the employers, could not delegate their duty of providing a safe place of work, and therefore it was no defence to say that they had employed competent contractors to instal the plant. *But* see comments of Phillimore J. in *Summer* **8** at 414 H.

3. Waddle v. Wallsend Shipping [1952] 2 Lloyd's Rep. 105, Devlin J.

Held, shipowners were not liable for an error of a Lloyd's surveyor during building, but were liable for a failure by repairers during subsequent repairs to pass certain information to Lloyd's surveyor.

4. Walsh v. Holst [1958] 1 W.L.R. 800; [1958] 3 All E.R. 33, C.A.

Morris L.J. cited Denning L.J. in *Cassidy v. Ministry of Health* [1951] 1 All E.R. 574 at 586: "Where a person is himself under a duty to use care, he cannot get rid of his responsibility by delegating the performance of it to someone else, no matter whether . . . to a servant . . . or an independent contractor."

5. Davie v. New Merton Board Mills [1959] A.C. 604; [1959] 1 All E.R. 346, H.L.

Defect in drift (for details of defect, see [1957] 2 Q.B. 368) manufactured in 1946 and sold to B who in same month resold to defendant employers—thereafter drift seldom used—in 1953 piece of drift flew in plaintif's eye when he struck it with hammer—both manufacturers and employers were held liable—employers appealed—*Held* not liable, because (*per* Lord Simonds, 354 D) it could not be said "that it was as the delegate or agent of the employer that the manufacturer failed to exhibit due skill and care" and (*per* Lord Morton, 357 B) "the doctrine of vicarious liability ... has never been extended ... to a case where a master has ordered a standard tool from a reputable supplier." All Law Lords agreed that the manufacturer could not be an independent contractor in the circumstances. *N.B.* This decision has been largely *reversed* by the Employers' Liability (Defective Equipment) Act 1969: see note at head of subsection.

6. Sullivan v. Gallagher, 1959 S.C. 243, 2nd Div.

Held, following **5**, employers not liable. But today decision would have been different as a result of the Employers Liability (Defective Equipment) Act 1969: see note at head of subsection.

7. Wingfield v. Ellerman's Wilson [1960] 2 Lloyd's Rep. 16, C.A.

Plaintiff employed by defendant shipowners to unload tomatoes from ship to lighter—lightermen had erected ladder from ship to lighter which was insecure—ladder slipped and threw plaintiff—*Held*, defendants were liable, as the safety of access from ship to lighter was something which should have been attended to by employers. Defendants argued that the fact that it was the invariable practice of the lightermen to provide the ladder relieved them of liability—*Held*, not. On this, Devlin L.J. (22. col. 2) said: "In my view, it (*i.e.* the practice) makes no difference at all. An invariable practice is only an agreement which has lasted for a considerable time ... Since the provision of a ladder comes within those things which a prudent employer should order or require to be done before he is satisfied that arrangements have been made for the safety of his employees, then it follows that a person acting in pursuance of that agreement is his agent *pro hac vice* for discharging his duty."

8. Sumner v. Hendersons [1964] 1 Q.B. 450; [1963] 1 All E.R. 408, Phillimore J.

Shop fire—death of employee—plaintiff alleged start of fire due to negligent electrical installation and spread due to negligent construction of premises—on a preliminary question to determine liability of shop for the negligence (if any) of others—*Held*, shop would be liable for (a) consultant electrical engineer, (b) electrician contractor, (c) architect and (d) builders, but *not* for manufacturer of cable in question. This judgment was however later *discharged* by C.A. [1963] 2 All E.R. 712, on ground that the facts until found were too hypothetical. N.B. That part of the decision exonerating the employer in respect of any defect in the cable as manufactured now has to be read in the light of the Employers' Liability (Defective Equipment) Act 1969: see note at head of subsection.

9. John Carter v. Hanson Haulage [1965] 2 Q.B. 495; [1965] All E.R. 113, C.A.

Sellers L.J. (119 F, *obiter*), after referring with approval to the threefold nature of the personal duty of the employer as set out in *Wilsons* **1**, said: "This duty cannot be delegated in the sense that the extent of the duty is such that it has not been performed if reasonable care has not been taken either by the employer himself or by anyone to whom the task has been delegated. The employer cannot divest himself of responsibility by leaving it to others."

10. Taylor v. Rover [1966] W.L.R. 1491; [1966] 2 All E.R. 181, Baker J.

Chisel negligently hardened by independent contractor of manufacturer—purchased by employer—then chipped on more than one occasion—eventually causing injury to plaintiff employee—*Held*, employer liable by reason of the previous history of chipping (and would today in any event have been liable by reason of the Employers' Liability (Defective Equipment) Act 1969), but, by analogy with *Davie* **5**, the manufacturer was not liable, for he had contracted with a reputable independent contractor to do the hardening.

11. Barry v. Black-Clawson (1966) 2 K.I.R. 237; [1967] C.L.Y. 2678, C.A.

Deceased sheeter, a working subcontractor of defendant R, had fatal fall when, due to a hidden defect, an item of equipment collapsed—R was erecting gantry in factory under contract with factory owner—he had ordered the item of equipment through a reputable source—*Held*, following *Davie* **5**, R not liable, since he had obtained the item through reputable suppliers. Nor were either R or the factory owner liable under the Building Regulations 1948, since the deceased was a sub-contractor and not an employee. *N.B.* Since the deceased was not an employee, this decision is not affected by the Employers' Liability (Defective Equipment) Act 1969.

12. Cook v. Broderip (1968) 112 S.J. 193; [1968] C.L.Y. 2690, O'Connor J.

Cleaner employed by owner of flat got electric shock due to reversed polarity on a switch—owner had employed I.C. to replace switch—I.C. had failed to test for reversed polarity—*Held*, applying *Green v. Fibreglass* (Chap. 5, (3) (a) **12**) and *Davie* **5**, flat owner not liable. *N.B.* Since, as appears, the switch was not being provided by the flatowner for any business purpose, this decision is not affected by the 1969 Act: see note at head of subsection.

13. Pearce v. Round Oak Steel Mills [1969] 1 W.L.R. 595; [1969] 3 All E.R. 680, C.A.

Bolt of tensile testing machine broke due to metal fatigue—the machine had been made circa 1930 and had been brought secondhand by the defendants in 1959—defendants called no evidence—*Held*, defendants liable, as the circumstances raised a presumption of negligence on their part which they had not rebutted by evidence, *e.g.* to show no want of care at the time of purchase. *N.B. Quaere* whether the 1969 Act would now require the rebutting evidence also to exclude any fault by a third party, *e.g.* the manufacturer or a previous user.

14. Kondis v. State Transport Authority [1984] 154 C.L.R. 672; [1986] C.L.Y. 2262, High Court of Australia

During manual extension of crane jib, defendant's independent contractor deliberately dropped crane part without giving warning or keeping proper look-out—part fell on plaintiff, defendant's employee, whose foreman had failed to instruct plaintiff not to stand under jib during extension—*Held*, in view of foreman's failure, defendant was in breach of duty to provide safe system of work, and independent contractor's failure to adopt safe system constituted further breach by defendant of his non-delegable duty to provide safe system.

15. Clarkson v. William Jackson & Sons Ltd, *The Times*, November 21, 1984; [1984] C.L.Y. 2341, C.A.

The Court of Appeal observed that the Employer's Liability (Defective Equipment) Act 1969 did not give employees a new cause of action, but prevented an employer from escaping liability where the fault in the equipment was not his but that of the supplier or manufacturer.

16. McDermid v. Nash Dredging Ltd [1987] A.C. 906; [1987] 2 All E.R. 878, H.L.

Plaintiff was sent by his employer, the defendant, to work on tug owned by and the Master of which was employed by defendant's parent company. In breach of Master's own system of working, he reversed tug before plaintiff had finished unmooring it, and a rope swept plaintiff into water—*Held*, defendant not vicarously liable for negligence of Master, who was not its employee, but was liable personally for breach of duty to ensure that plaintiff was provided with safe system of work, that duty being non-delegable in the sense that employer could not escape liability for performance of the duty, even though the duty had in fact been delegated to another and had not been properly performed.

17. Coltman v. Bibby Tankers Ltd—The Derbyshire, [1988] A.C. 276; [1987] 3 All E.R. 1068, H.L.

Defendant's bulk carrier sank with loss of all hands. Personal representatives of third engineer sued defendant, claiming that defective design and construction of vessel's hull led to sinking, and relying on Employers' Liability (Defective Equipment) Act 1969—*Held*, the vessel was "equipment" within section 1(1) of the Act, even though vessels were not specifically referred to in section 1(3), which provided illustrations, but not a comprehensive definition, of "equipment".

18. Knowles v. Liverpool C.C. [1993] 1 W.L.R. 1428; [1993] 4 All E.R. 921, H.L.

Pavement flagger injured finger when flagstone he was manhandling broke, due to defect in flagstone's manufacture which defendant, flagger's employer, could not reasonably have discovered before accident—*Held*, flagstone was "equipment" within the Employers' Liability (Defective Equipment) Act 1969, s. 1, and defendant was accordingly liable to plaintiff. Section 1 was to be widely continued to embrace every article of any kind furnished by the employer for the purposes of his business, and not merely for the use of his employees. *Coltman v. Bibby Tankers* (**17** above) applied.

19. Morris v. Breaveglen Ltd, [1993] I.C.R. 766; [1993] P.I.Q.R. P 294, C.A.

See Chap. 15, (1) (c) **10** for further details.

U1. Williams v. Trimm Rock Quarries (1965) C.A. 134A, also reported at 109 S.J. 454

Demonstration at employer's quarry of large drilling machine—with a view to purchase by employers—due to defect (for which makers were in any event liable) machine fell over onto plaintiff, an employee at the quarry—it was *conceded* in C.A. (by W.L. Mars Jones Q.C.) that employers would also be liable "because they employed the makers as independent contractors to give all necessary instructions about the machine, and they were not given (Lord Denning M.R.6 D). *But* employers got 100 per cent. indemnity from the makers.

U2. Fullwood v. Stoke-on-Trent Corporation (1975) C.A. 388

Question was whether employers were liable under Employer's Liability (Defective Equipment) Act 1969 for an obstruction jamming the cylinder of a skip loading vehicle which they had bought—obstruction prevented the jib from fully retracting (so that jib caught the underside of a bridge)—

Held, no. "Even if there was a 'defect,' the question is whether it was attributable to the fault of the third party (*i.e.* the maker of the vehicle), which ... means attributable to their negligence. This involves the problem whether they ought reasonably to have foreseen that the defect might cause an accident to the drivers of these vehicles" (Megaw L.J., 20 C).

(2) Standard of Care

(a) Generally

1. Paris v. Stepney B.C. [1951] A.C. 367; [1951] 1 All E.R. 42, H.L.

One-eyed man hammering rusty bolts under car without goggles—*Held,* (3–2) defendants were liable for not providing goggles. Lord Normand (49 A) cited *Salmond on Torts* (10th ed.), p. 438: "There are two factors in determining the magnitude of a risk—the seriousness of the injury risked, and the likelihood of the injury being in fact caused," to which he added (49 D) that there may be other factors: "for example, Asquith L. J. pointed out in *Daborn v. Bath Tramways* (Chap. 13, (1) **13**), that it is sometimes necessary to take account of the consequence of not assuming a risk." Lord MacDermott (54 F) said that "risk" must "connote consequences as well as causes," and that the employer's duty of care "must be related to both the risk and the degree of injury" (55 A).

2. Thorogood v. Van den Berghs [1951] 2 K.B. 537; [1951] 1 All E.R. 682, C.A.

Plaintiff employed by defendants took a fan to maintenance shop to test it—tested it in motion on the floor unguarded—plaintiff's hand somehow got caught in it—*Held,* defendants negligent. Asquith L. J. (691 F): "Then again although reasonable foresight is the true criterion where negligence *vel non* is the issue, an employer who has created or permitted a dangerous condition to arise is reasonably expected to foresee and provide against the possibility of injury arising therefrom even though it results through the intermediation of an act of inadvertence by the employee and even though that act of inadvertence be of a character which cannot be precisely forecast and remains in the event 'unexplained'."

3. Newman v. Harland & Wolff [1953] 1 Lloyd's Rep. 114, Lynskey J.

"As has been pointed out in many cases, there are certain operations which are dangerous and in which the element of danger cannot be eliminated. As long as the employer takes reasonable care to carry out that work in a reasonably safe way, his obligation is complete" (118).

4. Latimer v. A.E.C. [1953] A.C. 643; [1953] 2 All E.R. 449, H.L.

"Phenomenal" rainstorm flooding factory and leaving floor slippery despite three tons of sawdust applied. Plaintiff slips—*Held*, defendants not liable. Lord Tucker (455 C) said there was no evidence to suggest that factory should have been closed down, though such a step might be required "if the peril was sufficiently grave". He also said it was "desirable in these days, when there are in existence so many statutes and statutory regulations imposing absolute obligations on employers, that the courts should be vigilant to see that the common law duty owed by a master to his servants should not be gradually enlarged until it is barely indistinguishable from his absolute statutory obligations." Lord Oaksey (453 B) said that "an error of judgment in circumstances of difficulty" did not amount to negligence.

5. Hayward v. P.L.A. [1954] 2 Lloyd's Rep. 363, McNair J.

On question whether means of escape from dock for person immersed were "reasonably adequate", defendants argued that since they had had a standard practice since 1904, this must be taken to be reasonable. To this judge said (370, col. 1): "This argument, if accepted, would lead to the conclusion that the dock authorities are to be the sole judges of the extent of the obligation imposed on them by the regulation. I accordingly reject the argument, though I am prepared to accept that the practice of other good authorities may be some evidence of reasonableness." Lord Tucker partly agreed with this in H.L. during argument at p. 6, col. 1. See [1956] 2 Lloyd's Rep. 1, H.L.

6. Watt v. Herts C.C. [1954] 2 All E.R. 368, C.A.

Fireman travelling to accident hurt by shifting jack which could not be secured in vehicle available—*Held*, defendants not liable. Dictum of Asquith L.J. in *Daborn v. Bath Tramways* (Chap. 2 (6) **1**) cited with approval by Singleton L.J. (370 F). Denning L.J. said (371 B): "It is always a question of balancing the risk against the end," and he also said there was a very considerable difference between commercial end to make profit and human end to save life or limb.

7. Jones v. Richards [1955] 1 W.L.R. 444; [1955] 1 All E.R. 463, Barry J.

Held, defendants liable for breach of statutory duty in failing to fence a threshing machine: "One must always guard against making industry impossible and against slowing down production by setting unduly high standards or by placing wholly unreasonable requirements on the makers and owners of machinery of this kind" (470 D).

8. Jones v. Vauxhall Motors [1955] 1 Lloyd's Rep. 152, Stable J.

"The precautions which he (the employer) has to take are, of course, to some extent measured by the incident of the risk, and the incident of the risk may really fall under two categories:

(1) the numerical chance of the thing happening at all, and
(2) the gravity of the result if a thing does happen" (153, col. 2).

9. Harman v. Mitcham Works, *The Times*, June 22, 1955; [1955] C.L.Y. 1894, C.A.

Manufacture of fluorescent lighting tubes—plaintiff handling beryllium oxide—causes chronic poisoning—*Held*, (2–1) that as defendants had no knowledge of danger at time and no reason to suspect it, not liable.

10. Michaels v. Browne & Eagle [1955] 2 Lloyd's Rep. 433, McNair J.

" . . . an employer does not warrant that the system of work operated is absolutely safe, or that no accident will occur during its operation . . . nor is the employer necessarily liable on proof that the system . . . contains some remote element of risk which was absent from some other available system of work" (437).

11. Staveley Iron and Chemical Co. v. Jones [1956] 1 All E.R. 403, H.L.

Lord Tucker (414 A), with whom Lords Cohen and Porter concurred: " . . . I do not consider that . . . the standard (of care) can differ according to whether the workman is being sued personally or his employer is being sued in respect of his acts or omissions in the course of his employment. It is true that there may be cases, such as those involving breach of statutory duty, where an employer . . . cannot be heard to say, as against his own servant, that some risky act due to familiarity . . . amounts to contributory negligence. In this respect it is possible that the same act may have different consequences when the injured man is the plaintiff suing his employers, and where the employer is being sued by a third party (including another employee) in respect of the same act or omission . . . . This doctrine cannot be used to require any modification in the standard of care required from a workman in relation to his fellow servants or other third parties or the resulting liability of his employers."

12. Szumczyk v. Associated Tunnelling [1956] 1 W.L.R. 98; [1956] 1 All E.R. 126, Ashworth J.

Plaintiff was employed by defendants who were tunnelling in coal mine under contract with N.C.B.—fall of roof—N.C.B. were liable under Coal Mines Act 1911, but were defendants liable at common law?—N.C.B. had laid down the method of support—*Held*, that in view of this and the fact that N.C.B. were under absolute statutory duty to support, defendants could not be said to be negligent in failing to insist on another method of support. *N.B.* This decision was *upheld* by C.A. (unreported).

13. Morris v. West Hartlepool S.N. [1956] A.C. 552; [1956] 1 All E.R. 385, H.L.

Lord Reid (399 D): "Apart from cases where he may be able to rely on general practice, it is the duty of an employer, in considering whether some precaution should be taken against a foreseeable risk, to weigh on the one hand the magnitude of the risk, the likelihood of an accident happening, and the possible seriousness of the consequences if an accident does happen, and on the other hand the difficulty and expense and any other disadvantage of taking the precaution."

14. Cusack v. T. & J. Harrison [1956] 1 Lloyd's Rep. 100, C.A.

Held, defendants not liable for using a latticed metal tray to discharge cartons. Singleton L.J. (104): "But, on the whole, they (the employers) are the best judges of the tackle and appliances which should be used. If they adopt some method which is fraught with danger, in the ordinary course some workman or some officer of the union—a safety officer, for instance—will probably point out the danger therefrom, and they will take warning."

15. Meah v. H. Hogarth [1958] 1 Lloyd's Rep. 523, Devlin J.

Question was whether ship's officer was justified in setting plaintiff to washing paintwork in heavy sea—in the result a large wave came and injured plaintiff—*Held*, defendants not liable. "I think it is a case which is near the borderline, and I therefore necessarily find it important . . . to have regard to the views of the men on the spot and to attach more importance to them, provided I am satisfied that they are and were genuinely held, than to criticism which is made afterwards of what the men on the spot decided to do" (526, col. 2).

16. Croxford v. Scruttons [1958] 2 Lloyd's Rep. 492, Hilbery J.

Roll of stacked lino fell onto plaintiff in dock shed—difficult to devise any system of stacking which would be wholly safe—26 previous accidents in seven years—during same time 1,400,000 rolls of lino moved in and out of shed—*Held*, defendants not liable. "It is of course of the highest importance that men should not be unfairly exposed to unnecessary risk in the work they are employed to do. On the other hand, it is of importance that the court should not insist on standards of care . . . which will render the work quite impracticable or impossible, unless of course the risks involved . . . are such that, if those risks cannot be eliminated, the work ought to stop completely" (494, col. 2).

17. Smith v. Austin Lifts [1959] 1 All E.R. 81, H.L.

Lord Simonds (85 E): "I deprecate any tendency to treat the relation of employer and skilled workman as equivalent to that of a nurse and imbecile child." Lord Morton (87 G) cited the words of Lord Oaksey in **1** at 50: "The standard of care which the law demands is the care which an ordinarily prudent employer would take in all the circumstances."

18. Davie v. New Merton Board Mills [1959] 1 All E.R., 346, 355E, H.L.

19. Close v. Steel Company of Wales [1960] 2 All E.R. 657, C.A.

Issue was breach of statutory duty in failing to fence, but Lord Evershed M.R., in delivering the judgment of the court, when considering whether the danger was reasonably foreseeable, said (661 D): "The plaintiff's accident was not one which could or would be reasonably foreseeable in the ordinary course, though it was one which those responsible, if they had closely reflected on it, would have said could happen though the chances were extremely remote."—*Held*, Defendants were not liable, as danger not reasonably foreseeable.
This case subsequently went to H.L. [1961]2 All E.R. 953, on issue of statutory duty only.

20. Bill v. Short Brothers *The Guardian*, May 22, 1962; [1962] C.L.Y. 2014, H.L.

Plaintiff fell over rubber hose lying on floor of passage at his place of employment—he knew of two previous such accidents—*Held*, plaintiff's knowledge of the danger did not exonerate defendants from their duty of care, though it would sound in contributory negligence.

21. Doughty v. Turner [1964] 1 Q.B. 518; [1964] 1 All E.R. 98, C.A.

Asbestos and cement compound cover dropped into cauldron of molten cyanide sodium—explosion injuring plaintiff employee—*Held*, defendant employers not liable, as the consequences of the cover being dropped were not reasonably foreseeable.

22. Stokes v. Guest Keen [1968] 1 W.L.R. 1776; [1968] C.L.Y. 2701, Swanwick J.

23. McCafferty v. Metro. Police Receiver [1977] 1 W.L.R. 1073; [1977] 2 All E.R. 756, C.A.

P, a police ballistics expert, suffered ear damage from testing firearms in a confined room—D had made no inquiry from experts as to whether any precautions were needed—such inquiry, if made, would have indicated that ear muffs should be provided and soundproof materials installed in room—*Held*, D liable, as the standard of care required included taking "steps to keep (himself) informed of developments and increased knowledge in the sphere in which he operates" (Geoffrey Lane L.J., 773 J).

24. Thompson v. Smiths Shiprepairers [1984] Q.B. 405; [1984] 1 All E.R. 881, Mustill J.

Industrial deafness developing over long period (for details see Chap. 15(2)(h)**14**)—in the course of his judgment the judge *cited* (888 J) a passage from the judgment of Swanwick J. in *Stokes* **22** as correctly setting out the standard of care required of an employer in such circumstances:

> "The overall test is still the conduct of the reasonable and prudent employer, taking positive thought for the safety of his workers in the light of what he knows or ought to know; where there is a recognised and general practice which has been followed for a substantial period in similar circumstances without mishap, he is entitled to follow it, unless in the light of common sense or newer knowledge, it is clearly bad; but, where there is developing knowledge, he must keep reasonably abreast of it and not be too slow to apply it; and where he has in fact greater than average knowledge of the risks, he may thereby be obliged to take more than the average or standard precautions. He must weigh up the risks in terms of the likelihood of injury occurring and the potential consequences if it does; and he must balance against this the probable effectiveness of the precautions that can be taken to meet it and the expense and inconvenience they involve. If he is found to have fallen below the standard to be properly expected of a reasonable and prudent employer in these respects, he is negligent."

25. Bailey v. Rolls Royce (1971) Ltd [1984] I.C.R. 688; [1984] C.L.Y. 2282, C.A.

Plaintiff injured back exerting force of about 100 lbs when manoeuving a component. Plaintiff, to defendants' knowledge, had exhibited predisposition to back injury—*Held, inter alia* that defendant not liable in negligence—on the evidence, under no duty to stop plaintiff from doing the job, warn him of risk of injury or instruct him to ask for help, in view of the extent of the risk of injury and the extent of likely injury should the risk materialise.

26. Bacon v. Jack Tighe (Offshore) and Cape Scaffolding [1987] C.L.Y. 2568, H.H. Judge Whitehead, Lincoln County Court

Plaintiff, employed by first defendant, tripped on scaffolding clip left on oil rig catwalk by second defendant—*Held*, plaintiff solely to blame. Working place such as an oil rig was fraught with potential hazards. Plaintiff was not required to look where putting his feet, but his normal progress should have enabled him to see clip.

27. Bryce v. Swan Hunter Group plc [1988] 1 All E.R. 659; [1987] 2 Lloyd's Rep. 426, Phillips J.

Deceased worked as painter in shipyards from time to time between 1937 and 1942, 1946 and 1950 and 1958 and 1970. Limited exposure to abestos dust during first period, substantial exposure during second and third. Died of mesothelioma in 1981, as a result of exposure to asbestos dust. Widow sued three former employers, for whom deceased had worked for total of 399 days in 1947, between 1958 and 1962 and in 1970—*Held, inter alia*, that, having regard to Factories Inspectorate literature between 1932 and 1956, defendants should have appreciated at times of plaintiff's employments by them that exposure to asbestos dust was likely to be injurious to employees, and were under a duty at common law, of which they were in breach, to reduce, though not altogether to prevent, such exposure.

28. Crouch v. British Rail Engineering [1988] I.R.L.R. 404; *The Times*, March 10, 1988, C.A.

Fragment of metal flew into plaintiff's eye as he was using hammer and chisel to separate a nut and bolt at a location about five minutes walk from his department. Goggles were available on request from chargehand, foreman or stores—*Held*, extent of duty to provide protective equipment or clothing depended on circumstances including risk and gravity of possible injury, difficulty of providing such equipment or clothing, distance employee had to go to get it, how often he might need it and his experience and skill. In instant case, defendent negligent in failing to provide goggles into hands of plaintiff when sending him to work at location of accident. Plaintiff 50 per cent. to blame for failing is provide himself with goggles when he knew risk of working without them.

29. Baxter v. Harland & Wolff plc [1990] I.R.L.R. 516; [1991] C.L.Y. 1878, N.I. C.A.

The plaintiff was employed without protection for his ears in conditions of excessive noise in the defendant's Belfast shipyard from 1937 to 1944 and 1946 to 1962, and developed noise-induced deafness as a result—*Held*, *inter alia*, differing from Thompson (**24** above) that the defendant was liable in negligence for damage to the plaintiff's ears caused by exposure to noise from January, 1954 onwards prior to which the claim was statute-barred. The defendant was negligent in failing to consider or take any steps to deal with or reduce the harmful effects of noise which they knew was injuring their employees. There was sufficient medical, scientific and legal knowledge available prior to 1963 (the Thompson "year of liability") to have brought home to reasonable employers that some kind of protection was required. It was no defence that the attitude of others in the industry was the same as that of the defendant; or that during the relevant period (1954 to 1962) there were no complaints from unions or employees and no guidance from the Factory Inspectorate. The employer was responsible for taking the initiative in matters of safety. A relevant feature was that the defendant was dealing with worker whose hearing had already been partially damaged by noise.

30. Gitsham v. C.H. Pearce & Sons [1992] P.I.Q.R. P57; *The Times*, February 11, 1991, C.A.

Plaintiff slipped on snow and ice when crossing road on defendant's six-acre weather-exposed site in harsh weather conditions. Defendant treated snow and ice by mechanical salt and sand spreader—process should have finished by time of accident—*Held*, defendant not in breach of the Factories Act 1961, s. 29(1), or negligent. Even if relevant area had not been treated (as to which trial judge made no finding) judge was entitled to find that defendant was doing everything reasonably practicable, taking into account severity of weather and size of site. *Per* Stocker L.J.: "The fact that the system might for one reason or another have been running late does not itself in my view establish that the system was not being properly put into effect."

31. Pape v. Cumbria C.C. [1992] I.C.R. 132; [1992] 3 All E.R. 211, Waite J.

Plaintiff cleaner contracted dermatitis on hands due to repeated contact with a variety of chemical cleaning agents—she had not been warned of danger of dermatitis and though provided with rubber gloves had not been instructed to wear them and rarely did so—*Held*, danger of dermatitis from such contact was well enough known for a reasonable employer to appreciate it, but not so well known for it to be obvious to his staff without warning or instruction. Thus it was defendant's duty to warn plaintiff of danger and instruct her always to wear gloves provided.

32. Bowman v. Harland & Wolff plc [1992] I.R.L.R. 349; [1992] C.L.Y. 3222, Carswell J., N.I.

Plaintiffs employed at defendant's Belfast shipyard during 1950s and 1960s—regularly used hand-held pneumatic caulking hammers, vibration from which caused them to suffer from Raynaud's Phemonenon also known as "vibration white finger" (V.W.F.)—*Held*,

(a) Having regard to medical publications and other literature about V.W.F. (referred to in detail in judgment), defendant should have appreciated the existence of the problem and instituted preventative measures by January 1, 1973, and was negligent in having failed to do either.
(b) Damages available only in respect of deterioration in plaintiffs' conditions from January 1, 1973 to date of issue of proceedings in 1988.

U1. Webb v. Greaseproof Paper Mills Ltd (1954) C.A. 135

Plaintiff went underneath moving rollers to remove paper—*Held.* defendants not liable. Denning L.J. (18 A): "I take it to be plain that the dryermen, by adopting a dangerous system themselves, cannot make the employers liable if the employers did not know of it or acquiesce in it, or there is nothing to impute it to the employers. A practice such as this can only be imputed to employers if it has been carried on so long, or so frequently, or so openly, so that the employers should be made responsible for it."

U2. Roberts v. Dixon (1957) C.A. 268 A

Parker L.J. (9 C): "It seems to me when you are dealing with a case such as this where, if an accident does occur, the result is almost certain death, if there are two methods and one is really substantially safer than the other, it is the duty of employers to take steps to see that their employees use that safer method."

U3. Vizor v. Multi-Spring (1962) C.A. 189

Plaintiff clearing wire jammed in machine by pulling with pliers—pliers cut wire which jumped up into the plaintiff's eye—blunt pliers subsequently provided—*Held*, reversing Paull J., defendants not liable, as, applying dictum of Lord Porter in *Bolton v. Stone* (Chap. 2, (3) **1**), accident not reasonably foreseeable.

U4. Higham v. Lloyd (1967) C.A. 221

"That test (*i.e.* the *Bletchley Fletton* test for the statutory meaning of 'safe' and 'dangerous') is whether there is a reasonably foreseeable cause of injury to anyone acting in a way in which a human being may be reasonably be expected to act in circumstances which may reasonably be expected to occur. It seems to me that, in deciding whether an employer is negligent at common law (as to place of work) precisely the same test has to be applied" (Willmer L.J., 7 E, Diplock and Winn L.JJ. concurring). *Sed quaere*: the *Bletchley Fletton* test, as formulated, says "possible cause of injury," and not "reasonably foreseeable cause," and in this form it was reiterated by the majority of the House of Lords in *Summers v. Frost* (Chap. 16, (2) (a) **4**). The substitution of "reasonably foreseeable cause" was suggested by Lord Reid. Moreover, the *Bletchley Fletton* test is a test of "dangerous" and "safe", which words are often qualified statutorily by words such as "so far as is reasonably practicable," and in this qualified form they have often been said to import the same standard (subject to onus of proof) as the common law standard of taking reasonable care. If then the qualified form equals the common law standard, how can the unqualified form do so also, unless the qualification means nothing?

U5. Crawford v. Post Office (1984) C.A. 45

Plaintiff injured back when twisting a drum unloaded from delivery lorry. Defendants appreciated that such twisting involved risk of injury and since accident had introduced hydraulic device for this process—*Held*, defendants liable. Known risk of injury could have and had since been avoided by steps not requiring disproportionate expense and trouble.

U6. Priestly v. Nottingham H.A. (1986) C.A. 37

Plaintiff hospital worker slipped on ice or slush in delivery yard at 9.15 a.m.—*Held*, defendant not liable. Test was whether reasonable and practicable steps were taken, having regard to circumstances including the use of the yard, the hours of work and available finance. No system could ensure that at all times all parts of a large complex were always being treated with salt and cleared.

U7. Rowark v. N.C.B. (1986) C.A. 45

Plaintiff developed tenosynovitis of wrist in course of his employment. Trial judge held that although a sprain, twist or strain of wrist was foreseeable, tenosynovitis was not, and dismissed claim—*Held*, allowing plaintiff's appeal that tenosynovitis was within ambit of injuries found to be foreseeable. The precise injury did not need to be foreseen if its general nature could.

U8. Graham v. Esso Petroleum Ltd (1986) C.A. 614

Plaintiff tanker driver, working from walkway running along the top of the tank, used both hands to open a valve. In doing so, fell 12 feet to the ground. He argued that guard rail should have been provided—*Held*, defendant not negligent in providing no guard rails. Plaintiff's task would normally be done with one hand, using the other to hold onto the walkway. No record of previous similar accidents. General practice in industry was not to fit guard rails. There was a respectable body of opinion that such rails would increase the risk of accidents. Trades unions, government agencies and the Health and Safety Executive had not pressed for or recommended guard rails.

U9. Winfield v. N.C.B. (1986) C.A. 651

Plaintiff tripped on step, stumbled six feet along flat concrete surface, and caught and injured foot in raised edge of metal plate in the surface. No previous complaint or mishap in relation to the plate—*Held*, place of work not unsafe. Not foreseeable someone would sustain an accident in this unusual way. Defendant liable neither in negligence nor for breach of the Mines and Quarries Act 1954, s. 98(1).

U10. Bidwell v. North East Essex H.A. (1988) C.A. 798

Plaintiff required to break concrete and dig trench using sledgehammer. This caused him to suffer symptoms of arthritis. He claimed a preumatic hammer or drill should have been provided—*Held*, plaintiff's job was not foreseeably hazardous, and equipment provided was proper for fairly simple job. Employer not liable.

U11. Armstrong v. B.S.C. (1989) C.A. 118

Security officer patrolling direct site at 2 a.m. using torch tripped over debris on ground—*Held, inter alia*, employer not liable at common law. It would be unreasonable to require pointless clearing of the debris with which the area was strewn—provision of torch sufficient.

U12. Hill v. E. Fogarty plc (1991) C.A. 272

Plaintiff suffered Achilles tendonitis which she attributed to operating foot pedal of pillow-filling machine—*Held*, employers not liable. No evidence they knew or should have known they were exposing plaintiff to a risk of injury.

(b) Abnormal Susceptibility of Employee

1. McLaughlin v. Trimmer (1946) 79 Ll.L.R. 649, Denning J. and C.A.

Flash of light from stud-welding machine—sets up iritis—machine safe for normal user—but plaintiff had an extraordinary susceptibility in the shape of a decayed tooth—*Held*, defendants not liable—*Held*, however, on appeal (unreported), defendants liable.

2. Clayton v. Caledonian Engineering (1948) 81 Ll.L.R. 332, Cassels J.

Dermatitis from handling ammonium chloride in transit—no evidence that anyone had ever got dermatitis from such a cause—the manufacturers said that they had never had a case—*Held*, the defendants not liable, as the cause of the accident was that plaintiff (a dock labourer) had a hypersensitive skin.

3. Paris v. Stepney B.C. [1951] A.C. 367; [1951] 1 All E.R. 42, H.L.

One-eyed man employed to hammer rusty bolts under car—no goggles provided—piece of metal enters good eye—*Held*, (3–2) defendants negligent, as whether or not they should have provided goggles for two-eyed men (which was not decided but probably not), they were under a special duty to plaintiff to do so. Lord MacDermott (55 A) " . . . the known circumstances that a particular workman is likely to suffer a graver injury than his fellows from the happening of a given event is one that must be taken into consideration in assessing the nature of the employer's obligation to that workman."

4. Board v. Thomas Hedley [1951] 2 All E.R. 431; [1951] W.N. 422, C.A.

Not a master and servant case (issue was whether a detergent product was dangerous under *Donoghue v. Stevenson*), but in his judgment Denning L.J. (432 D) said: "The product would, I think, be dangerous if it might affect normal users adversely, or even if it might affect other users who had a higher degree of sensitivity than the normal so long as they were not altogether exceptional."

5. Cork v. Kirby Maclean [1952] 2 All E.R. 402; [1952] W.N. 399, C.A.

Workman falls from scaffold in epileptic fit—scaffold was not adequately fenced—workman had not disclosed he was an epileptic—*Held*, the failure to fence and the non-disclosure were two contributing causes, and responsibility would be apportioned equally between deceased and defendants.

6. Ebbs v. James Whitson [1952] 2 Q.B. 877, C.A.

Plaintiff woodworker idiosyncratic to monsonia wood dust—causing dermatitis—danger at time unknown—*Held*, defendants not liable.

7. Heapy v. Cheshire C.C. (1955) 105 L.J. 410; [1955] C.L.Y. 1895, Donovan J.

Held, defendants liable for providing plaintiff with unsuitable tool and for failing to protect his eye, plaintiff being one-eyed.

8. Parkes v. Smethwick Corporation (1957) 121 J.P.415; [1957] C.L.Y. 2425, C.A.

Held, defendants not liable for further hernia sustained by plaintiff, as plaintiff's previous hernia was unknown to them.

9. Withers v. Perry Chain [1961] 3 All E.R. 676, C.A.

Dermatitis from grease—as a result plaintiff stopped work in April 1956, employers having taken proper precautions and not being to blame therefore—in May 1956 plaintiff returned and asked for job—employers gave her driest job available, though some contact with grease still entailed—thereafter plaintiff contracted dermatitis on three occasions, on each occasion stopping work and returning and asking for job and being given same (*i.e.* driest available) job back—plaintiff now alleged that defendants were negligent in permitting her to continue with the work which it was known entailed, for her, a risk of dermatitis—*Held*, defendants not liable as it was not their duty to dismiss or refuse to employ her merely because she wished to do a job which entailed some risk to her. *Aliter* perhaps (*per* Devlin L.J. at 680 H), if the employer were to conceal the risk or fail to give the employee information which he had and which might help her to evaluate it properly: "It may be also (on the principle of *Paris v. Stepney Borough Council*) that when the susceptibility of an employee to dermatitis is known there is a duty on the employer to take extra or special precautions to protect such an employee. But it is not suggested that there were any extra or special precautions here which could have been taken." (Devlin L.J., 680 I.)

10. Porteous v. N.C.B., 1967 S.L.T. 117; [1967] C.L.Y. 2720, Ct. of Sess.

Plaintiff was blind in one eye—vision in other defective—while plunging a drain a twig went in the defective eye, causing total blindness—*Held*, applying *Paris* **3**, defendants were negligent in employing plaintiff on outside labouring work.

11. Hawkins v. Ian Ross [1970] 1 All E.R. 180, Fisher J.

Plaintiff and young untrained Indian labourer carrying box of molten metal—plaintiff stumbled and shouted to Indian to stop—but Indian, not fully understanding, went on—metal spilt over plaintiff's foot—judge decided the case on breach of statutory duty but *said* (186 D) that the employment of such a labourer cast light on the standard of care to be followed by defendants in the layout of the work and in the precautions taken to avoid accidents.

12. Darvill v. Hampton (1973) 13 K.I.R. 275; [1973] C.L.Y. 2318, Rees J.

Severe dermatitis through working in oil coolant—then discovered that plaintiff was constitutionally susceptible—employers were aware of risk and had provided gloves and barrier cream, which were ineffective in plaintiff's case—*Held*, not liable, as the risk was small, and there was no satisfactory evidence that employers had failed to take reasonable precautions.

13. Kossinski v. Chrysler (1973) 15 K.I.R. 225; [1974] C.L.Y. 1227, C.A.

14. Bailey v Rolls Royce (1971) Ltd [1984] I.C.R. 688; [1984] C.L.Y. 2282, C.A.

Plaintiff injured back exerting force of about 100 lbs when manoeuving a component. Plaintiff, to defendants' knowledge, had exhibited predisposition to back injury—*Held, inter alia*, defendant not liable in negligence—on the evidence, under no duty to stop plaintiff from doing the job, warn him of risk of injury or instruct him to ask for help, in view of the extent of the risk of injury and the extent of likely injury should the risk materialise.

15. Whitfield v. H. & R. Johnson (Tiles) Ltd, [1990] 3 All E.R. 426; [1990] I.R.L.R. 525, C.A.

Plaintiff was required each day to lift between about 270 and 360 batches of tiles each weighing about 25 lbs from trolley onto conveyor belt. Was vulnerable to back injury because of congenital condition of which defendant knew nothing, but had had no previous problems with the lifting until, one day, she felt pain in back and leg when lifting—*Held, inter alia,* defendant not negligent.

16. Baxter v. Harland & Wolff plc [1990] I.R.L.R. 516; [1991] C.L.Y. 1878, N.I. C.A.

For further details, see Chap. 15, (2)(a) **29**.

U1. Jones v. Lionite Specialities (1961) C.A. 406

Deceased foreman addicted to inhaling trichlorethylene fumes in a tank—employers knew of his addiction and frequently remonstrated with him—as a result deceased died from heart failure—*Held*, defendants not liable as all they could have done was to dismiss him which (following *Withers v. Perry Chain* **9**) they were not called on to do.

U2. Pettitt v. Layfield Oura (1961) C.A. 136 A

Inhalation of trichlorethylene fumes—C.C.J. found ventilation inadequate for purposes of Factories Act 1937, s. 4, but that plaintiff had intentionally leaned over tank and inhaled fumes, and that against conduct of this nature good ventilation would have been of no effect—and therefore, following *Bonnington* (Chap. 16, (3)(b) **7**), plaintiff had not proved injury was due to breach—*Held*, by C.A. this was right, and defendants not liable. See also *Peebles v. Armstrongs Patents* (Chap. 15, (2)(d) **U6**).

U3. Barnes v. Fine Tubes Ltd (1984) C.A. 549

Plaintiff injured back lifting bin of steel dust with another employee. Weight of bin safe for two fit people. Plaintiff had had back disability in past, but for seven years before incident had been regarded as fully fit—*Held*, defendant not liable.

U4. Wakefield v. Basildon and Thurrock H.A. (1990) C.A. 595

Nursing auxiliary suffered epileptic attack. Plaintiff catering assistant injured her back trying to roll the auxiliary to a position in which she would not suffocate—*Held*, defendant not liable—such risk as there was to plaintiff did not make it their duty to have dismissed the auxiliary because of her epilepsy.

U5. Bowfield v. South Sefton (Merseyside) H.A. (1991) C.A. 290

Plaintiff, a nurse in a stroke rehabilitation unit, was assisting a patient weighting 15 stones to move from a chair to a bed using a recognised technique, during which the patient jumped. Plaintiff took his full weight and injured her back. Plaintiff had a history of back trouble, but had been discharged with a medical certificate stating "fit to return to work", had considered himself able to return to the same unit as before, had played sports without restriction and had worked for 14 months without mishap—*Held*, defendant not liable. It was reasonable to leave plaintiff to assess the patient's capacity to co-operate. He had fully co-operated in the past. Moreover, in the circumstances it was not negligent to allow him to return to work in the unit.

(c) Carelessness and Indifference on the Part of Employees

(*N.B.* See also (d) and (e))

1. Rooney v. Aberdeen Lines (1945) 78 L1.L.R. 511, C.A.

"I am not prepared to assent to the proposition that in providing safe conditions . . . the master is entitled to disregard the possibilities of those slips, those errors of judgment, that momentary forgetfulness to which any ordinary human workman is subject . . . " (Lord Greene M.R., 513–514).

2. Clifford v. Charles Challen [1951] 1 K.B. 495; [1951] 1 All E.R. 72, C.A.

Synthetic glue causing dermatitis—*Held*, defendants liable for not adequately providing barrier cream. For facts see Chap. 15, (7) **5**. Denning L.J. (75 A) said "the foreman should have seen, as far as he could, that the workmen used it (the cream)," and at 74 G: "He (employer) must remember that men doing a routine task are often heedless of their own safety, and may become careless about taking precautions. He must therefore by his foreman keep them up to the mark and not tolerate any slackness." *But* these dicta were qualified in *Woods v. Durable Suites* (Chap. 15, (2) (e) **2**), *q.v.*.

3. Thorogood v. Van den Berghs [1951] 2 K.B. 537; [1951] 1 All E.R. 682, C.A.

Plaintiff employed by defendant took a fan to maintenance shop to test it—tested it in motion on the floor unguarded—plaintiff's hand somehow got caught in it—*Held*, defendants negligent. Asquith L.J. (691 F): "Then again although reasonable foresight is the true criterion where negligence *vel non* is the issue, an employer who has created or permitted a dangerous condition to arise is reasonably expected to foresee and provide against the possibility of injury arising therefrom even though it results through the intermediation of an act of inadvertence by the employee and even though that act of inadvertence be of a character which cannot be precisely forecast and remains in the event 'unexplained'."

4. General Cleaning Contractors v. Christmas [1953] A.C. 180; [1952] 2 All E.R. 1110, H.L.

Window-cleaning case—for details see (Chap. 15, (4) (b) **3**)—*Held*, defendants liable. Lord Oaksey (1114 E): "It is I think well known that . . . workpeople are very frequently, if not habitually, careless about the risks which their work may involve. It is in my opinion for that very reason that the common law demands that employers should take reasonable care to lay down a reasonably safe system of work. Employers are not exempted from this duty by the fact that their men are experienced and might, if they were in the position of an employer, be able to lay down a reasonably safe system of work themselves. Workmen are not in the position of employers. Their duties are not performed in the calm atmosphere of board-rooms with the advice of experts. They have to make their decisions on narrow window-sills and other places of danger, and in circumstances in which the dangers are obscured by repetition." Lord Reid at 1117 B; "Where the problem varies from job to job it may be reasonable to leave a great deal to the man in charge, but the danger in this case is one which is constantly found and it calls for a system to meet it. Where a practice of ignoring an obvious danger has grown up, I do not think that it is reasonable to expect an individual workman to take the initiative in devising and using precautions. It is the duty of the employer to consider the situation, to devise a suitable system, to instruct his men what they must do, and supply any implements that may be required ... No doubt he cannot be certain that men will do as they are told when they are working alone. But if he does all that is reasonable to ensure that his safety system is operated, he will have done what he is bound to do." *N.B.* Dictum of Lord Oaksey is not of universal application: see **19** and **21**.

5. Woods v. Durable Suites [1953] 1 W.L.R. 857; [1953] 2 All E.R. 393, C.A.

Singleton L.J. (395 H), after citing Lord Herschell's dictum in *Smith v. Baker* as to general extent of duty of master (see Chap. 15, (1) (a) **3**), said: "If there are young people or trainees employed in a factory, obviously the need for watching them is greater than in the case of skilled and experienced men."

6. Stockton v. P.L.A. [1954] 1 Lloyd's Rep. 125, Hilbery J.

Held, defendants not liable because plaintiff failed to prove plank defective, *but* "if ... this plank was defective in that way ... any court would have found ... that defendants failed to provide reasonably safe equipment ... more especially as defendants would know that the men were working on piecework, and therefore less likely to be taking the care for themselves that they ought ordinarily to take. It is no good blinking the fact that there is a great difference in entering a shop where people are working piecework and a shop ... on timework" (127, col. 1). See **16.**

7. Marshall v. Hull Fishing Vessel Owners [1954] 2 Lloyd's Rep. 495, Parker J.

Accident unloading ship due, as plaintiff alleged, to use of rope instead of chain sling for bringing fish boards out of hold—frequent previous accidents due to boards slipping out of ropes—safety committee set up—use of chains advocated—but men resent and/or refuse change—further meeting—after which men throw away chains—*Held*, employers had done all that could reasonably be expected of them, and it was unreasonable to expect that enforcement should go as far as taking disciplinary action.

8. Leathley v. Mersey Insulation [1954] 1 Lloyd's Rep. 349, C.A.

Four experienced riggers, of whom plaintiff was one, told to remove hatch cover section—which they do by raising it up with derrick and standing on hatch cover to push—plaintiff falls down hold while pushing—*Held*, that employers were justified in leaving method of removal to the men, and therefore were not liable for failure to provide safe system, although there were at least three safer ways than that adopted. *But* from judgments it would appear that this was a borderline case, and in view of accident defendants would be under obligation to lay down safer system.

9. Honeyman v. Orient S.S. [1955] 2 Lloyd's Rep. 27, Hilbery J.

Plaintiff working outboard on ship without a lifeline—*Held*, defendants liable: "The fact that men themselves, in their familiarity with risk, cease almost to regard the matter as one of risk does not determine the questions that arise in such a case as this when it comes into a court of law" (31, col. 1).

10. Qualcast v. Thorpe [1955] C.L.Y. 1896, H.L.

Iron foundry—defendants provided safety spats free of charge but plaintiff preferred to wear his own foundry boots—*Held*, no evidence of negligence, and defendants not liable.

11. Schofield v. Glen Line [1955] 2 Lloyd's Rep. 350, Glyn-Jones J.; [1955] 2 Lloyd's Rep. 719, C.A.

Held, defendants not liable. *Upheld* by C.A. without mentioning this point.

12. Stringer v. Automatic Woodturning [1956] 1 W.L.R. 138; [1956] 1 All E.R. 327, C.A.

Girl of 18 tending circular saw (properly guarded)—Singleton L.J. (331 I): "I believe that if employers do put a young girl in charge of such a machine, they are under a duty of giving special instructions to her. Furthermore (even if they have provided a statutory guard), they ought in compliance with their duty at common law to have taken some additional means to protect a young girl such as this." *N.B.* The course of this case was confusing—*Held*, by Oliver J., defendants not liable at common law, but liable for breach of statutory duty—*Held*, by C.A., defendants not liable for breach of statutory duty, but ordered new trial on common law issue. Both parties appealed to H.L.—*Held* [1957] A.C. 544, [1957] 1 All E.R. 90, defendants not liable at common law or for breach of statutory duty. The dictum cited above was not considered by H.L.

13. Norcott v. Glen Line [1956] 2 Lloyd's Rep. 108, Pilcher J.

"Having regard to the way labour is recruited now it seems to me to be virtually impossible for an employer . . . to know what his experience may be and what it would be proper to tell him . . . . I think it must be left to the man . . . to gather from his companions what the risks normally incidental to the ordinary occupation of a dock labourer are" (112).

14. Bastable v. Eastern Electricity Board [1956] 1 Lloyd's Rep. 586, C.A.

Held, defendants not liable for failing to carry out periodical inspections of chisel issued to plaintiff, which became blunt in use—Denning L.J. (588, col. 2): "It seems to me that the system which the employers had of remedying any bluntness as soon as it was reported was a perfectly good system. These men, who had been doing this kind of work for years, were as well able as anyone to know whether a chisel was blunt: they could inspect for themselves."

15. Wheeler v. London & Rochester Trading [1957] 1 Lloyd's Rep. 69, Gorman J.

Held, defendants liable for not instructing young seaman how to put fender out.

16. Pike v. Trinity Wharf [1957] 2 Lloyd's Rep. 122, Hilbery J.

"The key . . . is of course the fact that the crane driver and the men in the barge were working on piecework. Piecework done in such circumstances is done as fast as the men doing it can manage it. A long experience of these cases has persuaded me that those are precisely the circumstances in which sometimes risks are taken and what would otherwise be routine conduct is not observed" (123, col. 2). See **6.**

17. Shanley v. West Coast Stevedoring [1957] 1 Lloyd's Rep. 144, Glyn-Jones J.; 1 Lloyd's Rep. 391, C.A.

Plaintiff hatchman stood on side of coamings nearest winch—some hatch cover locking bars had been placed there which got caught in winch causing injury to plaintiff—*Held*, defendants not liable.

"An experienced hatchman may take up his place anywhere round the hatch where he thinks it convenient, but in so doing, he must have due regard for his own safety, and if he chooses to go and stand in a place where the ship's company quite legitimately and properly put these locking bars, and if in consequence an accident happens—I do not say there is any contributory negligence on his part; he may not have foreseen this very unusual and very unexpected accident . . . I think he must bear the consequences if an accident happens" (149, col. 2). *Upheld* by C.A. in similar terms.

18. Wilson v. International Combustion [1957] 3 All E.R 505n. C.A.

Held, defendants liable. Morris L.J.: " . . . it must be something perilous to proceed along steel joists when there is an open space on either side . . . It is of no avail to say that the appellant was only doing what steel erectors often do, or to say that the appellant was running risks which steel erectors generally regard as slight. The failure of these respondents (to provide a ladder) directly brought it about that the appellant was subjected to those risks which result when a steel erector goes along girders . . . His injuries resulted from risks which he was unnecessarily running, and they were . . . caused by the respondents' negligence."

19. Wilson v. Tyneside window Cleaning [1958] 2 Q.B. 110; [1958] 2 All E.R. 265, C.A.

Defective sash handle comes away in window cleaner's hand—*Held*, defendant employers not liable. Parker L.J. (274 C): " . . . I cannot think that 'reasonable care' demands a repeated warning to skilled men in a case at any rate such as this, where the dangers involved are patent. It is not a case . . . of the danger of silicosis from particles of dust which are quite invisible and cannot be seen. I do not know, but it may well be that in such cases reasonable care would demand that the employer should warn and exhort the men constantly to wear masks. However, there, as I have said, the danger is not patent."

20. Smith v. Austin Lifts [1959] 1 All E.R. 81, H.L.

Lord Simonds (85 E): "I deprecate any tendency to treat the relation of employer and skilled workman as equivalent to that of a nurse and imbecile child."

21. Jenner v. Allen West [1959] 1 W.L.R. 554; [1959] 2 All E.R. 115, C.A.

Deceased (ordinarily a plumber) put in charge of roof work—which he had done before at irregular intervals—he fell due to there being no crawling boards—he knew crawling boards should be used for roof work—but there was no sufficient evidence that the task was within his experience and competence—defendants relied solely on him and gave him no specific instructions as to how the task, which was awkward, should be performed—*Held*, that although the dicta in **4** certainly did not apply in all cases where the workman was highly skilled or experienced, yet here the employers were at fault in all the circumstances (but deceased was found two-thirds to blame).

22. Joseph v. Ministry of Defence; *The Times*, March 4, 1980; [1980] C.L.Y. 1891, C.A.

23. Bell v D.H.S.S. *The Times*, June 13, 1989; [1989] C.L.Y. 2547, Drake J.

Defendant provided hot water for employees to make drinks in kitchen on top floor of four-storey office block. Spillages from mugs or cups carried thence to employees' places of work were common. Defendant's bulletins regularly encouraged staff to take more care. Plaintiff slipped on liquid probably spilt by another employee on imitation marble floor outside lift with manually operated door—*Held*,

(a) On the evidence, defendant's system of inspection was reasonable, however:
(b) Defendant negligent and in breach of duties under the Occupiers' Liability Act 1957, s. 2, and the Offices, Shops and Railway Premises Act 1963, s. 16 because:
  (i) set against history of spillages, entreaties in bulletins did not discharge defendant's duties;
  (ii) defendant should have provided distribution point for hot water on each floor, appropriate saucers, cups and trays and a suitable non-slip surface over the imitation marble.

24. King v. Smith, *The Times*, November 3, 1994; [1994] C.L.Y. 2284, C.A.

Plaintiff window-cleaner fell from outside sill from which he had had to clean window, because of the position of a desk inside the room served by the window and because the top half of the window could not be opened from the inside—*Held*, employer liable. Since *General Cleaning Contractors v. Christmas* (**4** above) it had become well appreciated that it was a dangerous practice to clean a window by standing on an outside sill. Employer should have forbidden plaintiff to do this unless harness anchor points were available, and should have told customer to have window in proper working order before they were cleaned. (At first instance, Waller J. found plaintiff 30 per cent to blame.)

U1. Hartley v. Howard and Bullough (1961) C.A. 150

Dermatitis from non-soluble mineral oil—barrier cream and washing facilities provided—but there had been a number of previous casualties and employees including plaintiff had become slack about washing—*Held*, upholding C.C.J., defendants liable, but plaintiff one-third to blame. Holroyd Pearce L.J.: "One knows that insidious dangers are more easily forgotten by workmen than dramatic and obvious dangers. The prudent employer will do his best to keep the thought of insidious dangers alive in the minds of the men, whether by notices or instructions or in any other way that may help to that end, particularly so when it seems from a heavy incidence of the disease that precautions are being forgotten" (7 F).

U2. Farrow v. Turner (1962) C.A. 429

Plaintiff aged 17 told not to grind tools in a certain way—but not told of danger of disobedience—*Held*, defendants liable when plaintiff did disobey.

U3. O'Neill v. Boddingtons Brewery Ltd (1986) C.A. 160

Plaintiff, an experienced driver and driver's mate, jumped from a moving delivery lorry and injured his foot—*Held*, defendant not liable. Even if there was a common practice for employees to jump from lorries in this way, there was no evidence that defendant knew of it, to enable it to devise a system of work to counteract it. Plaintiff should have informed defendant's management of the malpractice.

U4. Wyeth v. Thames Case Ltd (1986) C.A. 533

Plaintiff developed tenosynovitis of right wrist during employment by defendant. She was one of a team of three employees who respectively assembled, stitched and stacked cardboard boxes. The assembly job involved the greatest number of repetitive movements. Defendant had a system of rotating the three jobs, set quotas for the manufacture of boxes after which employees were not required to produce more, and warned its employees that working rapidly might cause injury. However, employees failed to operate the rotation system and persisted in working rapidly—*Held*, defendant not liable—their systems were reasonable and they had made every reasonable effort to see that their systems were followed.

(d) Instructions and Warnings

1. Rees v. Cambrian Wagon Works (1946) 175 L.T. 220; [1946] W.N. 139, C.A.

Held, defendants liable for failing to give instructions as to method of work and/or supervise same. *Approved* in **4**, *q.v.*

2. Gallagher v. Dorman Long [1947] 2 All E.R. 38; 177 L.T. 143, C.A.

Crane topples over due to overloading—plaintiff one of the loaders injured—plaintiff received no instructions as to what was a safe load save that he was expected to judge the load in accordance with a printed notice on the crane which gave various tonnage figures at various radii—*Held*, plaintiff not properly instructed as to limits of safety of crane and defendants liable.

3. Barcock v. Brighton Corporation [1949] 1 K.B. 339; [1949] 1 All E.R. 251, Hilbery J.

Plaintiff injured in explosion during test which, following example of others, he carried out in unsafe way—had been told to read regulations—*Held*, defendants liable: "The employers contend that they had provided a safe system, but I do not think that one devises a system of work by saying to the workman: 'Read the Regulations and do not break them.' In my view, that is not devising a system of work" (255 B).

4. Winter v. Cardiff R.D.C. [1950] 1 All E.R. 819; [1950] W.N. 193, H.L.

Held, defendants not liable for leaving method of work to gang. **1** approved (although facts very similar).

5. General Cleaning Contractors v. Christmas [1953] A.C. 180; [1952] 2 All E.R. 1110, H.L.

Window cleaning case—for details see Chap. 15, (4) (b) **3**—*Held*, defendants liable. Lord Reid at 1117 B: "Where the problem varies from job to job it may be reasonable to leave a great deal to the man in charge, but the danger in this case is one which is constantly found and it calls for a system to meet it. Where a practice of ignoring an obvious danger has grown up. I do not think that it is reasonable to expect an individual workman to take the initiative in devising and using precautions. It is the duty of the employer to consider the situation, to devise a suitable system, to instruct his men what they must do, and supply any implements that may be required ... No doubt he cannot be certain that men will do as they are told when they are working alone. But if he does all that is reasonable to ensure that his safety system is operated, he will have done what he is bound to do." See qualifications to this decision made in **U3** and **U4**.

6. Rands v. McNeil [1955] 1 Q.B. 253; [1954] 3 All E.R. 593, C.A.

Experienced farm worker going into loose box of dangerous bull—had not actually had instructions in way to tackle it—*Held* defendant not liable: "Even if he had not actually been instructed to use the method above described (safe method), his common sense would tell him to keep outside until bull had been tethered ... " (Jenkins L.J., 602 B) " ... he met his accident because ... he did something in a way he knew was irregular and unauthorised" (Morris L.J., 606 C).

7. Leathley v. Mersey Insulation [1954] 1 Lloyd's Rep. 349, C.A.

Four experienced riggers, of whom plaintiff was one, told to remove hatch cover section—which they do by raising it up with derrick and standing on hatch cover to push—plaintiff falls down hold while pushing—*Held*, that employers were justified in leaving method of removal to the men, and therefore were not liable for failure to provide safe system although there were at least three safer ways than that adopted—*but* from judgments it would appear that this was a borderline case, and in view of accident defendants would be under obligation to lay down safer system.

8. Catherall v. Cunard [1954] 2 Lloyd's Rep. 303, Jones J.

Unauthorised use of conveyor belt on ship—*Held* defendants not liable: "It is perfectly true that there was no notice to that effect, but why should there be? It is just ordinary common sense that they should not be used in that way" (308, col. 1).

9. Williams v. Newton S.S. Co. [1955] 1 Lloyd's Rep. 88, Pilcher J.

Plaintiff a greaser—is warned that bilge pump in ship's engineroom is broken and dangerous and must not go near it—does—*Held*, defendants not liable, as since only greasers would be likely to go near it, warning was adequate, and there was no need to fence it off.

10. Jones v. A. E. Smith Coggins [1955] 2 Lloyd's Rep. 17, C.A.

Plaintiff employed by defendants struck a suspended load in hatch which was sticking—county court judge found for plaintiff on ground that defendants should have instructed plaintiff in such circumstances to have the load lowered—*Held*, by C.A. that defendants not liable because this allegation was not pleaded, but Denning L.J. (19 col. 1) and Birkett L.J. (20, col. 1) both commented that there could be no need to give instructions when plaintiff already knew what was the proper thing to do.

11. Prince v. Carrier Engineering Co. [1955] 1 Lloyd's Rep. 401, Parker L.J.

Plaintiff walking backwards with load fell on debris littering floor—*Held*, defendant employers not liable: "Now, that (the duty of employers to lay out job) is all very well when you are dealing with operations which are of proved danger—window cleaning, climbing ladders and that sort of thing—but for my part I think it would be absurd to say that there were no jobs which could be left to the initiative of men, especially when they are skilled men . . . " (404, col.2).

12. Stringer v. Automatic Woodturning [1956] 1 W.L.R. 138; [1956] 1 All E.R. 327, C.A.

Girl of 18 tending circular saw (properly guarded)—Singleton L.J. (331 I) "I believe that if employers do put a young girl in charge of such a machine, they are under a duty of giving special instructions to her. Furthermore (even if they have provided a statutory guard), they ought in compliance with their duty at common law to have taken some additional means to protect a young girl such as this." *N.B.* The course of this case was confusing—*Held*, by Oliver J., defendants not liable at common law, but liable for breach of statutory duty—*Held*, by C.A., defendants not liable for breach of statutory duty, but ordered new trial on common law issue. Both parties appealed to H.L.—*Held* ([1957] A.C. 544; [1957] 1 All E.R. 90), that defendants not liable at common law or for breach of statutory duty. The dictum cited above was not considered by H.L.

13. Ashley v. Esso [1956] 1 Lloyd's Rep. 240, Roxburgh J.

"Then again ought plaintiff to have been given specific instructions how to carry out this routine job? Surely it would be impracticable, and would be regarded by a skilled man as an insult, to give to every fitter precise instructions how to carry out every routine job of maintenance because if he departed from the accepted method of doing the job his departure might involve an element of danger" (241–242).

14. Morris v. Cunard [1956] 2 Lloyd's Rep. 132, Pilcher J.; [1956] 2 Lloyd's Rep. 583, C.A.

Held, that as plaintiff had some grounds for assuming he was not precluded from using electric winch (which was dangerous), and as defendants had failed to prove they had given him effective warning not to do so, therefore defendants liable. *Upheld* by C.A. who however disapprove of judge's view that onus lay on defendants to prove they had given warning.

15. Wheeler v. London & Rochester Trading [1957] 1 Lloyd's Rep. 69, Gorman J.

Held, defendants liable for not instructing young seaman how to put fender out.

16. Lewis v. High Duty Alloy [1957] 1 W.L.R. 632; [1957] 1 All E.R. 740, Ashworth J.

Judge found there was quite a widespread practice of oiling machines in motion if the circumtances of the work rendered it inconvenient to wait for a stoppage—*Held*, defendants liable for failing to issue proper instructions and/or to take proper steps to ensure instructions carried out.

17. Nicholson v. Shaw Savill [1957] 1 Lloyd's Rep. 162, Pilcher J.

Cleaning ship's funnel—liable to give off gases—*Held*, defendants liable for failing to give instructions.

18. Nolan v. Dental Manufacturing [1958] 1 W.L.R. 936; [1958] 2 All E.R. 449, Paull J.

Held, that defendants were liable for failing to give strict orders that goggles were to be used and to supervise their employees to a reasonable extent to see orders obeyed. *Haynes v. Qualcast* [1958] 1 All E.R. 441 applied, but *quaere* as this decision has now been reversed by H.L.: see—Chap. 15, (7) **13**.

19. See cases in Chap. 15, (4)(b).

20. Graves v. J. & E. Hall [1958] 2 Lloyd's Rep. 100, Barry J.

Plaintiff working on ship is required by defendant employers to borrow rope for job from ship's stores—selects coir instead of manila or sisal, not being able to tell difference—it breaks—*Held*, defendants liable for not instructing plaintiff (a) to contact storeman before borrowing, (b) how to differentiate between types of ropes.

21. Jenner v. Allen West [1959] 1 W.L.R. 554; [1959] 2 All E.R. 115, C.A.

Deceased (ordinarily a leading plumber) put in charge of roof work—which he had done before at irregular intervals—he fell due to there being no crawling boards—he knew crawling boards should be used for roof work—there was no sufficient evidence that the task, which was awkward, was within his experience and competence—defendants relied solely on him and gave him no specific instructions as to how the task was to be performed—*Held*, the defendants were negligent for failing to give instructions (though only for one-third).

22. Baker v. Hopkins [1959] 3 All E.R. 225, C.A.

Gas-filled well—"don't go down that bloody well till I get there"—*Held*, defendants liable for not giving a clearer warning whereby "the nature of the peril was explained and described" (232 B).

23. Shah v. P. & O. [1959] 2 Lloyd's Rep. 646, Havers J.

Plaintiff was newly employed as seaman on ship—told to go down tank—ladder was oily and gave toehold only—tank was deep and poorly lit—plaintiff slipped—*Held*, defendants should have given plaintiff proper instructions about lay-out and method of going down into tank.

24. Anderson v. Tyne Improvement Commission [1961] 1 Lloyd's Rep. 226, Havers J.

Operation of a mobile vertical hoist on docks, known as a doodle-bug—shortage of experienced operators—plaintiff dock labourer given 20 minutes' instruction and demonstration—worked it for one hour and then got foot crushed—*Held*, defendants liable for failing to instruct plaintiff sufficiently.

25. Watts v. Empire Transport [1963] 1 Lloyd's Rep. 262, Hinchcliffe J.

Boy's hand trapped when seaman let go of side ropes holding drum—*Held*, defendants liable, as boy should have been instructed not to hold on to his tail rope.

26. Ross v. Associated Portland Cement [1964] 1 W.L.R. 768; [1964] 2 All E.R. 452, H.L.

Issue was breach of statutory duty (safe work place) but the question was whether plaintiff or defendants were responsible for an admitted breach of F.A. 1937, s. 26, in using a ladder to repair a cableway instead of a mobile tower, and on this Lord Reid (456 B) said: "But it is his (defendant's) responsibility to see that proper instructions are given and proper equipment is available. Where the work is to be done by a person fully skilled in that type of work, he may say: 'Go and plan out the work and come back and discuss the matter if you have any difficulty, or cannot find the equipment you need.' But here Ross was only a chargehand, the respondents had no reason to suppose that he had ever done a job of this kind before, and there is nothing to show the chief engineer gave him any encouragement to come back and discuss the matter. No account has been taken of the reluctance which a man in Ross's position would naturally feel in going to a chief engineer uninvited to ask for extra equipment . . . ".

27. James v. Hepworth & Grandage [1968] 1 Q.B. 98; [1967] 2 All E.R. 829, C.A.

New foundry worker given four weeks' training—but is not told about wearing safety spats—mainly because instructor did not believe in them (this being a not unreasonable view)—spats were available on request, and there were notices up saying so—but plaintiff could not read—some men did wear them—*Held*, reversing C.C.J., defendants not liable.

28. Broaders v. James Fisher [1968] 1 Lloyd's Rep. 255, James J.

Plaintiff slipped off a gangway after he had been told to hurry—*Held*, defendants not liable as an instruction to hurry did not mean he was expected to do so at personal risk to himself.

29. Herton v. Blaw Knox (1968) 112 S.J. 963; [1968] C.L.Y. 2699, Willis J.

30. Stokes v. Guest Keen [1968] 1 W.L.R. 1776; [1968] C.L.Y. 2701, Swanwick. J.

31. Thompson v. N.C.B. [1982] I.C.R. 15; [1982] C.L.Y. 2019, C.A. (2)

Deceased employed primarily as pump attendant and tippler operator in colliery. He occasionally worked as wagon lowerer if there was a shortage of labour, but had had no adequate instructions and was not competent to do the work unsupervised. Being conscientious, he responded to a tannoy message for a wagon lowerer and was killed attempting to lower wagons—*Held*, defendants liable, in that, not having given him adequate instructions, they ought to have foreseen that he might attempt to lower wagons unsupervised and to have warned him against doing so. Deceased one-third to blame.

32. Burgess v. Thorn, *The Times*, May 16, 1983; [1983] C.L.Y. 1060, Bristow J.

P suffered tenosynovitis (inflammation of a tendon) as a result of employment. D had received guidance from Health and Safety Executive and Department of Employment on the subject—*Held*, D liable for failing to warn P, as, if the condition had been caught early enough, permanent damage to P would have been avoided.

33. Bailey v. Rolls Royce (1971) Ltd [1984] I.C.R. 688; [1984] C.L.Y. 2282, C.A.

Plaintiff injured back exerting force of about 100 lbs when manoeuvring a component. Plaintiff, to defendants' knowledge, had exhibited predisposition to back injury—*Held, inter alia*, defendant not liable in negligence—on the evidence, under no duty to stop plaintiff from doing the job, warn him of risk of injury or instruct him to ask for help, in view of the extent of the risk of injury and the extent of likely injury should the risk materialise.

34. White v. Holbrook Precision Castings Ltd [1985] I.R.L.R. 215; [1985] C.L.Y. 2312, C.A.

In 1973, plaintiff began work as a grinder. In about 1976 he was found to be suffering from vibration-induced white finger (V.W.F.)—taken off grinding and offered another job at a lower wage. He claimed he should have been warned of the risk of developing V.W.F. when offered the job, and periodically examined to see how the condition was developing—*Held*,

(a) Plaintiff knew of risk when accepting the job, and would have accepted it even if warned.
(b) In any event, defendant was not under duty to warn plaintiff. *Per* Lawton L.J. at 218: "If a job has risks to health and safety which are not common knowledge but of which an employer knows or ought to know and against which he cannot guard by taking precautions, then he should tell anyone to whom he is offering the job what those risks are if, on the information then available to him, knowledge of those risks would be likely to affect the decision of a sensible, level-headed prospective employee about accepting the offer." Had defendant possessed all relevant information, it would have concluded that plaintiff would have regarded risk of V.W.F. or of no consequence in deciding to take on the job.
(c) In the circumstances, defendant was not under a duty to carry out periodic medical checks.

35. Smith v. Scot Bowyers Ltd [1986] I.R.L.R. 315; *The Times*, April 16, 1986, C.A.

Plaintiff worked where there was an inherent risk of greasy water on floor, rendering it slippery. Defendants therefore provided employees with diamond ridge-soled boots, renewed on request when soles wore smooth. Plaintiff slipped when wearing boots which he knew had smooth soles. He had not requested a new pair. Had the boots had ridged soles he probably would not have slipped—*Held*, defendants not liable—were not under a duty to instruct employees to inspect boots' soles, warn them of danger of wearing boots with worn soles, or encourage them to obtain replacement boots where necessary.

36. Calder v. H. Kitson Vickers Ltd [1988] I.C.R. 232; [1988] C.L.Y. 1952, C.A.

See Chap. 15, (1)(b) **17** for further details.

37. Mearns v. Lothian R.C., 1991 S.L.T. 338; [1991] C.L.Y. 5693

Plaintiff injured when awkwardly shaped valve weighing 98 lbs slipped as he carried it up a ladder on vessel on which he worked—no one else immediately available to help him, and defendant had given no instruction what to do if no assistance—*Held*, a safe system of work would involve telling employee not to perform such a task himself but to seek assistance—defendant negligent. Plaintiff 50 per cent. to blame.

38. Pape v. Cumbria C.C. [1992] I.C.R. 132; [1992] 3 All E.R. 211, Waite J.

Plaintiff cleaner contructed dermatitis on hands due to repeated contact with a variety of chemical cleaning agents—she had not been warned of danger of dermatitis and though provided with rubber gloves had not been instructed to wear them and rarely did so—*Held*, danger of dermatitis from such contact was well enough known for a reasonable employer to appreciate it, but not so well known for it to be obvious to his staff without warning or instruction. Thus it was defendant's duty to warn plaintiff of danger and instruct her always to wear gloves provided.

39. Ping v. Essette-Letraset [1992] C.L.Y. 3211, H.H. Judge Griffiths

The nine plaintiffs carried out bench work including knocking up, collating and labelling papers. They developed various injuries including tenosynovitis, carpal tunnel syndrome, tennis elbow and trigger thumb. The longest-serving employee began work in July 1970. They claimed that their injuries were brought about by the repetitive twisting and gripping movements involved in their jobs—*Held*, the plaintiffs' injuries were thus caused, and were foreseeable. Their employers were negligent. Their duty could have been discharged by warning employees before they commenced the risk-bearing work to report and seek medical advice at once on any pain in the wrist or arm; by explaining why such steps were necessary; and by educating employees regularly as to how to reduce the risks, having regard to the nature of their work. No adequate warnings had been given in the present case.

40. Morris v. Breaveglen Ltd [1993] I.C.R. 766; [1993] P.I.Q.R. P294, C.A.

see Chap. 15, (1)(c)**10** for further details.

41. Woolger v. West Surrey and North East Hampshire H.A. *The Times*, November 8, 1993; [1993] C.L.Y. 2948, C.A.

Held, the method by which a trained nurse lifted a patient was a matter for the nurse's individual judgment, and the hospital authority was not under a duty to warn the nurse against the use of a method which caused her a back injury.

42. Colclough v. Staffordshire C.C. [1994] C.L.Y. 2283; Mr. Reorder Beeston, Birmingham County Court

Plaintiff, social worker in elderly care team, went to home of elderly 15-stone man, to find him very distressed and halfway out of bed. Injured back trying to lift him back in with help of neighbour—*Held*, defendants liable—should have warned plaintiff not to lift in such emergency situations, which were reasonably foreseeable.

43. King v. Smith, *The Times*, November 3, 1994; [1994] C.L.Y. 2284, C.A.

See Chap. 15, (2)(c)**24** for further details.

U1. London v. Steel Breaking and Dismantling Co. Ltd (1952) C.A. 30

Plaintiff teenager employed by defendants to demolish top of double-decker bus—panel collapsed suddenly when plaintiff hit side with 14 lb hammer and plaintiff and hammer went through—*Held*, defendants negligent in failing to instruct plaintiff as work dangerous if not carried out with care.

U2. Green v. Courtaulds (1955) C.A. 172

Morris L.J. (15 C): "The defendants, having held these lectures, and having in the course of them prescribed what was the right method, did what reasonable and careful employers could do in order to institute a safe and effective system of work."

U3. Roberts v. Summers (1959) C.A. 77, C.A.

Two men holding a long rod at the far end of which a heavy ladle was balanced—the man at the extreme end suddenly detached his part of the rod so that the ladle went down and the remainder of the rod came up trapping the fingers of plaintiff who was holding it—trial judge found defendants liable for not giving instructions as to when extension rod to be detached (following *Christmas*

5)—*Held*, by C.A., however, defendants not liable, as this operation did not call for instructions. Hodson L.J. (5 F) said that the H.L. in *Christmas* were undoubtedly much impressed by the fact that window cleaning was a very dangerous operation—which was not the case here.

U4. Dwornicki v. B.T.H. (1959) C.A. 271 A

Plaintiff crane slinger sustained injury to toe when load descended after being slightly lifted—plaintiff alleged that, as load heavy, there should have been a foreman to instruct—*Held*, not so, and defendants not liable. Hodson L.J. (4 D): "It is not in itself a dangerous operation in which the plaintiff was employed, and I think there is a difference between this case and the *Christmas* window cleaning case . . . (**5**) where the court was considering an operation of an exceptionally dangerous nature, and perhaps it may be said that they were astute to find a defect in the system of working against the employers . . . "

U5. Ferner v. Kemp Bros (1960) C.A. 176 A

Plaintiff an experienced plumber fell through asbestos roof because his crawling board was not positioned at both ends over purlins—*Held*, defendants not liable: "An experienced workman must know the ordinary risks of the work which he does and which he is employed to do. In the doing of that work he is expected to take the ordinary routine precautions which are common to that work, and should not be expected to be told by his employer of every danger which might arise and every step that should be taken in order to counteract that danger" (Ormerod L.J., 9 F).

U6. Peebles v. Armstrongs Patents (1962) C.A. 135

Dermatitis from trichlorethylene—known danger—*Held*, defendants liable for failing to warn plaintiff.

U7. Farrow v. Turner (1962) C.A. 429

Plaintiff aged 17 was told not to grind tools in a certain way, but was not told that this was because it was dangerous—he disobeyed and the danger materialised—*Held*, defendants not liable.

U8. Forsdike v. Meek (1963) C.A. 92

Held, defendants liable for failing to give plaintiff instructions how to place ladder securely.

U9. Gilks v. James Edwards (1974) C.A. 64 A

Five men moving boiler section weighing 2–4 cwt—plaintiff's finger crushed as section moved past rack—*Held*, employers not negligent in not appointing someone to give instructions.

U10. Williams v. Birlee (1974) C.A. 190

Plaintiff aged 19 allowed to work at controls of a RB 22 excavator in order to learn how to drive same—no instruction or supervision—on getting out of cabin with engine running, caught foot in wire drum—*Held*, defendants 75 per cent. liable for allowing plaintiff at controls without instruction.

U11. Greenfield v. Tower Shipping Ltd (1984) C.A. 552

Plaintiff deckhand lowered hatch cover by pulling on rope which ran over engine-powered drum. When cover stuck, ship's mate told plaintiff to put an extra turn or two on drum. Engine started to labour, rope started to slip and end of rope was jerked from plaintiff's grasp, injuring his thumb—

Held, not reasonably foreseeable that mate's instruction would put plaintiff in any danger. Plaintiff should not have carried out instruction to point that rope might jerk from his grasp.

U12. Ellston v. Stockports Area H.A. (1984) C.A. 902

Plaintiff was a district nurse, having previously worked on a hospital. She damaged her neck while lifting a patient in a "baby lift", *i.e.* by cradling the patient in her arms—*Held*, defendant not liable. Lifting was a basic skill for nurses and plaintiff was sufficiently trained to decide how best to lift the patient. She should not have used the "baby lift", which was known to be dangerous. She could have used the face-to-face method.

U13. Flowerday v. Visionhire Ltd (1987) C.A. 1162

Television service engineer injured back lifting a TV set he was collecting from a house—*Held*, defendant not liable—reasonable to expect experienced employee to lift sets up to 22 inches unaided, but in any event defendant's system was for technicians to contact their manager should they need assistance. Instructions as to how to lift a TV set were unnecessary.

U14. Shearman v. Oldham M.B.C. (1988) C.A. 548

Street cleaner was provided with handcart with two large wheels and small one at front. He parked it in a tipped-forward position with all three wheels on the ground and it ran away. He was injured trying to retrieve it—*Held*, defendant not liable. It was obvious that cart should not have been parked in that way, and no instructions from defendant were needed as to how to park it.

U15. Simox v. B.S.C. (1988) C.A. 769

Plaintiff was injured when using a high pressure hose for the first time—*Held*, defendant liable for failing to instruct him how to control the hose by an overhand grip—but not necessary for defendant to provide a second man or to warn plaintiff of the obvious fact that the hose would generate powerful back pressure.

U16. Scaife v. Imperial Inns and Taverns Plc (1990) C.A. 617

Plaintiff injured when lifting a 22-gallon beer container weighing 2 cwt in the cellar of a public house—The container had been left by the delivering brewery on top of another container—*Held*, neither employers nor brewery liable. The accident was not foreseeable. The simple method of moving the larger container was by "collapsing it", *i.e.* pulling it from the other, and letting it fall to the ground. Specific instructions from employers as to how to move one container from the top of another were not necessary.

U17. Kitson v. K. & A. Engineering (Cheltenham) Ltd (1992) C.A. 1143

Plaintiff failed properly to attach one of two hooks to a drum to be lifted by a machine. When machine took the load, the hook became disengaged and the drum fell onto plaintiff's foot—*Held*, defendant not liable—not necessary to instruct plaintiff to attack hooks securely—it was common sense to do so.

(e) Supervision and Enforcement of Precautions

1. Clifford v. Charles Challen [1951] 1 K.B. 495; [1951] 1 All E.R. 72, C.A.

Synthetic glue causing dermatitis—*Held*, defendants liable for not adequately providing barrier cream. For facts, see Chap. 15, (7) **2**. Denning L. J. (75 A) said "the foreman should have seen, as far as he could, that the workmen used it (the cream)," and at (74 G): "He (employer) must remember that men doing a routine task are often heedless of their own safety, and may become careless about taking precautions. He must therefore by his foreman keep them up to the mark and not tolerate any slackness." *But* these dicta are qualified in **2**.

2. Woods v. Durable Suites [1953] 1 W.L.R. 857; [1953] 2 All E.R. 391, C.A.

Barrier cream case—*Held*, defendants not liable. For facts, see under Chap. 15, (7) **5**. Plaintiff relied chiefly on dicta in **1** as imposing a duty on defendants to see that precautions were observed. Court however decided **1** could not be applied to present facts, and the case did not mean that foreman was legally liable if he did not stand over workmen to ensure precautions observed. It was said that the basis of **1** was that foreman there did not believe in use of barrier cream himself (395 E)—and perhaps because there plaintiff was a young trainee, whereas here he was an experienced man of 56.

3. McDonald v. Smith Coggins [1953] 2 Lloyd's Rep. 203, Devlin J.

Plaintiff unloading dangerously stowed railway truck—*Held*, defendant employers liable for not providing "a man in the position of hatch foreman or ship's foreman who would be able to decide on a plan of action and make decisions and be there constantly."

4. Marshall v. Hull Fishing Vessel Owners [1954] 2 Lloyd's Rep. 495 Parker J.

Accident unloading ship due, as plaintiff alleged, to use of rope instead of chain sling for bringing fish boards out of hold—frequent previous accidents due to boards slipping out of ropes—safety committee set up—use of chains advocated—but men resent and or refuse change—further meeting—after which men throw away chains—*Held*, employers had done all that could reasonably be expected of them, and it was unreasonable to expect that enforcement should go as far as taking disciplinary action.

5. Crookall v. Vickers Armstrong [1955] 1 W.L.R. 659; [1955] 2 All E.R. 12, Glyn-Jones J.

Steel foundry—known risk of silicosis—masks available but no attempt to induce men to wear them—*Held*, defendants liable: "Workmen however find it very uncomfortable to do heavy work wearing masks and are reluctant to wear them. The difficulty created by this reluctance was discussed in the judgment of Parker J. in *Adsett's Case* [1953] 1 W.L.R. 773 . . . Nevertheless, there is in my opinion a halfway house between, on the one hand, merely providing masks and leaving it to the men to decide whether or not they will use them, and on the other hand proceeding to the length of dismissing a man caught working without a mask. Once the employer knows or ought to know (of the risk) and that the risk can be markedly diminished, if not eliminated, by the wearing of masks, he must take all reasonable steps, by clearly warning the men . . . and by encouragement and exhortation, to seek to persuade them to do so" (16 C-E).

6. Rogers v. George Transport [1955] 1 Lloyd's Rep. 524, Hallett J.

Plaintiff employed as a dock labourer by defendants to load large drums onto a lorry—owing to failure of lorry driver (not employed by defendants) to secure load after lowered onto lorry a drum rolled off and injured plaintiff—plaintiff alleged defendants were under a duty to see lorry driver secured load properly—*Held*, not so, and defendants not liable.

7. Qualcast v. Thorpe [1955] C.L.Y. 1896, H.L.

Iron foundry—defendants provided safety spats free of charge but plaintiff preferred to wear his own foundry boots—*Held*, no evidence of negligence and defendants not liable.

8. Morris v. Cunard [1956] 2 Lloyd's Rep. 132, Pilcher J.; [1956] 2 Lloyd's Rep. 583, C.A.

Held, that as plaintiff had some grounds for assuming he was not precluded from using electric winch (which was dangerous), and as defendants had failed to prove they had given him effective warning not to do so, therefore defendants liable. *Upheld* by C.A. who however disapprove of judge's view that onus lay on defendants to prove they had given warning.

9. Lewis v. High Duty Alloys [1957] 1 W.L.R. 632; [1957] 1 All E.R. 740, Ashworth J.

Judge found there was quite a widespread practice of oiling machines in motion if the circumstances of the work rendered it inconvenient to wait for a stoppage—*Held*, defendants liable for failing to issue proper instructions and/or to take proper steps to ensure instructions carried out.

10. Nolan v. Dental Manufacturing [1958] 1 W.L.R. 936; [1958] 2 All E.R. 449, Paull J.

Held, that defendants were liable for failing to give strict orders that goggles were to be used and to supervise their employees to a reasonable extent to see orders obeyed: *Haynes v. Qualcast* [1958] 1 All E.R. 441 applied, but *quaere* as this decision has now been reversed by H.L.; see **13**.

11. Wilson v. Tyneside Window Cleaning [1958] 2 Q.B. 110; [1958] 2 All E.R. 265, C.A.

Defective sash handle comes away in window cleaner's hand—*Held*, defendant employers not liable. Parker L.J. (274 C): " . . . I cannot think that 'reasonable care' demands a repeated warning to skilled men in a case at any rate such as this, where the dangers involved are patent. It is not a case . . . of the danger of silicosis from particles of dust which are quite invisible and cannot be seen. I do not know, but it may well be that in such cases reasonable care would demand that the employer should warn and exhort the men constantly to wear masks. However, there, as I have said, the danger is not patent."

12. Wylde v. Royal Mail Lines [1958] 2 Lloyd's Rep. 526, Barry J.

"I am bound to say that for a fitter, under whom a fitter's mate was working, to make no effort to instruct his mate not to embark on a hazardous enterprise of this kind does amount to a serious lack of proper supervision" (531, col. 2).

13. Qualcast v. Haynes [1959] A.C. 743; [1959] 2 All E.R. 38, H.L.

Plaintiff injured by molten metal splashing on his legs—an allegation that the employers failed to provide him with spats having been negatived, plaintiff also alleged that defendants should have exhorted or instructed him to use the spats provided—he was an experienced workman—county court judge found that prima facie this did not constitute lack of reasonable care in the circumstances—but he felt obliged on the authority of previous similar cases to hold that defendants were negligent—*Held*, defendants not liable. Lord Radcliffe (40 C): "The courts should be circumspect in filling out that duty (of providing protective equipment) with the much vaguer obligation of encouraging, exhorting or instructing workmen . . . to make regular use of what is provided . . . An experienced workman dealing with a familiar and obvious risk may not reasonably need the same attention or the same precautions as an inexperienced man who is likely to be more receptive of advice or admonition."

14. Batten v. Harland and Wolff [1961] 1 Lloyd's Rep. 261, Salmon J.

Rung of iron ladder dangerous because pipe running behind restricted toehold to two inches—chargehand present and footing ladder—able to see defect—*Held*, liability should be shared equally.

15. McWilliams v. Sir William Arrol & Co. [1962] 1 W.L.R. 295; [1962] 1 All E.R. 623, H.L.

16. Snell v. John Shelbourne (1965) 109 S.J. 270; [1965] C.L.Y. 2723, Streatfeild J.

17. Franklin v. Edmonton Corporation (1965) 109 S.J. 876; [1965] C.L.Y. 2720, Lawrence J.

Held, defendants liable for not adhering to system.

18. Lovelidge v. Anselm Olding [1967] 1 All E.R. 459, Widgery J.

19. James v. Hepworth & Grandage [1968] 1 Q.B. 94; [1967] 2 All E.R. 829, C.A.

20. Kerry v. Carter [1969] 1 W.L.R. 1372; [1969] 3 All E.R. 723, C.A.

Held, employers one-third to blame for not further verifying experience of plaintiff.

21. Hawkins v. Ian Ross [1970] 1 All E.R. 180, Fisher J.

22. Bux v. Slough Metals [1973] 1 W.L.R. 1358; [1974] 1 All E.R. 262, C.A.

Goggles had been provided, but the employees, who were on piecework, had discarded them, because of misting up—judge said that in effect the defendants had acquiesced in their non-user—and that the least they should have done was to "institute a system and at least endeavour to make it a rule that goggles will be worn"—*Held*, correct, although the question whether instruction, persuasion or insistence on wearing protective equipment was called for would always depend on the particular facts of the case, and that one of the most important factors was the nature and degree of risk. Another factor would be whether the plaintiff, if exhorted, would ever have worn the protective equipment.

23. Thompson v. N.C.B. [1982] I.C.R. 15; [1982] C.L.Y. 2019, C.A.

Deceased employed primarily as pump attendant and tippler operator in colliery. Occasionally he worked as a wagon lowerer if there was shortage of labour but had had no adequate instructions and was not competent to do the work unsupervised. Deceased, being conscientious, responded to a tannoy message for a wagon lowerer and was killed while attempting to lower wagon—*Held*, defendants liable in that they ought to have foreseen that the deceased might attempt to lower wagons unsupervised and to have warned him against doing so. Deceased one-third to blame.

24. Smith v. Scot Bowyers Ltd [1986] I.R.L.R. 315; *The Times*, April 16, 1986, C.A.

For further details see Chap. 15, (2)(d) **35**.

25. Crouch v. British Rail Engineering [1988] I.R.L.R. 404; *The Times*, March 10, 1988, C.A.

For further details see Chap. 15, (2)(a) **28**.

U1. Pugh v. Sheffield Corporation (1952) C.A. 29

U2. Knight v. Mutual Mills Ltd (1952) C.A. 242

U3. Ergin v. Marmite Food Extract Co. (1955) C.A. 217

Dictum by Birkett L.J. (6 E): "I do not think it has ever been laid down that if a safe system of work as such is inaugurated it is incumbent at all times on the employers that they shall have supervisors there to see people do that which they know it is their duty to do. It is quite true that the employers when men are working with dangerous articles or machinery must be alert to see that their system is maintained and their workmen follow it."

U4. Broughton v. Joseph Lucas Ltd (1958) C.A. 330 A

Plaintiff toolsetter employed by defendants—plaintiff testing machine—put in hand to make slight adjustment—uncovenanted stroke—plaintiff's hand injured—*Held*, defendants in breach of Factories Act 1937, s. 16—plaintiff in breach of Factories Act 1937, s. 119—toolsetters thought immune from Factories Act 1937, s. 16 until C.A. decision in 1947—see Chap. 16, (6)(f) **2**—defendants drew clear attention of everyone concerned to obligation by putting up notice and getting all toolsetters including plaintiff to sign copy of notice—unpopular as slowed down work affecting bonuses—defendants took no steps by disciplinary insistence or rearrangement of wages or time to make it practicable for precautions to be carried out—defendants 75 per cent. to blame—25 per cent. contributory negligence against plaintiff.

U5. Wilson v. Nuffield Metal Products (1960) C.A. 206

Armlets provided but frequently not worn—defendants issued a safety booklet urging employees to use the protective equipment issued—but did not exhort them directly to wear the armlets—*Held*, following *Qualcast v. Haynes* **13**, defendants not liable.

U6. Lloyd v. B.T.C. (1961) C.A. 128

Plaintiff lengthman run down by engine while walking in four foot way of track—this was a very common practice in daytime and defendants must have known of it to the point of acquiescence, notwithstanding it was in breach of Rules—but plaintiff was walking at first light in weather which was foggy with rain—*Held*, defendants not liable, as they could not be taken to have acquiesced in practice in such conditions.

U7. Speechley v. Aveling Barford (1970) C.A. 198

U8. Williams v. Birlee (1974) C.A. 190

Held, defendants 75 per cent. liable for allowing youth of 19 to work controls of RB 22 excavator without providing instruction and/or supervision.

U9. Cremin v. Hanwell Glass Co. Ltd (1989) C.A. 35

Glazier was cut by glass when replacing skylights. Not wearing gauntlets provided. Defendant aware that employees frequently did not wear gauntlets, but failed to give plaintiff clear instructions to wear them—*Held*, defendant liable. Plaintiff one-third to blame.

(f) Relevance of Previous Accidents and Complaints

1. Latham v. Ross and Marshall (1946) 79 Ll.L.R. 561, Lord Goddard C.J.

Badly installed petrol pump in ship. At 565: "A proper precaution can often be omitted and no accident occur over a long period of time, but if the precaution is one that ought to be taken, it is no answer to say: 'I successfully ignored this precaution for a long time, and therefore it is unnecessary'."

2. Board v. Thomas Hedley [1951] 2 All E.R. 431; 2 T.L.R. 779, C.A.

Interlocutory appeal on discovery—manufacturers were being sued by retail purchaser under *Donoghue v. Stevenson*—*Held*, that while post-accident complaints were irrelevant to defendants' state of knowledge at material time, they were very relevant to the issue whether the article was in fact dangerous.

3. Marshall v. Hull Fishing Vessel Owners [1954] 2 Lloyd's Rep. 495, Parker J.

Accident unloading ship due, as plaintiff alleged, to use of rope instead of chain sling for bringing fish boards out of hold—frequent previous accidents due to boards slipping out of ropes—safety committee set up—use of chains advocated—but men resent and/or refuse change—further meeting—after which men throw away chains—*Held*, employers had done all that could reasonably be expected of them, and it was unreasonable to expect that enforcement should go as far as taking disciplinary action.

4. Brophy v. Bradfield [1955] 3 All E.R. 286, C.A.

Deceased was found dead in boilerhouse—*Held*, the facts did not call on defendants for an answer, but if they did, the fact that the boiler had worked satisfactorily in the boilerhouse for 25 years was an answer to any inference of negligence.

5. Michaels v. Browne and Eagle [1955] 2 Lloyd's Rep. 433, McNair J.

" . . . the absence of accidents over a course of years, the absence of any complaints by trade union officials or factory inspectors are very relevant evidence, although of course by no means conclusive" (437).

6. Edmiston v. B.T.C. [1955] 1 Q.B. 191; [1955] 3 All E.R. 823, C.A.

Interlocutory appeal on interrogatories—Singleton L.J. (826 C): "If plaintiff could show there had been recent accidents to employees of defendants engaged on type of work he was doing, and the men engaged on that kind of work slipped in the way he slipped, and fell and were injured, evidence to that effect would be admissible in the action . . . "

7. Atkinson v. Tyne-Tees S.S. [1956] 1 Lloyd's Rep. 244, Streatfeild J.

Plaintiff run down by travelling crane while accompanying it to steady load—*Held*, defendants liable for unsafe system: "It does not follow that one must wait for an accident . . . before a system can be condemned as an unsafe one. There are many systems which are common enough where the danger involved, if one gives one's mind to it, is perfectly obvious, and if a danger is quite obvious and is a foreseeable danger, then it is the duty in law of an employer to apply his mind to it and to evolve a reasonable safe system and to see that it is carried out" (247).

8. Kilgollan v. W. Cooke [1956] 2 All E.R. 294, C.A.

Plaintiff employed by defendants at wire-winding machine which wound wire strands from 18 bobbins onto rotating barrel—strand of wire snapped—particle entered plaintiff's eye causing blindness—in the previous three years there had been six hundred cases of strands breaking and causing some injury which was usually trivial and never serious—in some 10 cases the face had been struck—but there had never been an eye injury or one comparably serious—defendants took no precautions—*Held*, that defendants were liable, in that in view of the accident record defendants ought in fact to have anticipated the risk of serious damage and taken precautions.

As part of the defence defendants showed that 32 other factories adopted the same methods as defendants, but to this Singleton L.J. (303 B) said: "I do not know what their experience was; I have no particulars on which to go; I have only the evidence in this case in regard to the defendants."

9. Cusack v. T. & J. Harrison [1956] 1 Lloyd's Rep. 100, C.A.

Held, defendants not liable for using a latticed metal tray to discharge cartons. Singleton L.J. (104): "But on the whole, they (the employers) are the best judges of the tackle and appliances which should be used. If they adopt some method which is fraught with danger, in the ordinary course some workmen or some officer of the union—a safety officer, for instance—will probably point out the danger therefrom, and they will take warning."

10. Sargent v. Gee Stevedoring [1957] 1 Lloyd's Rep. 357, Ashworth J.

"The nature of the complaint was, on the plaintiff's own evidence, anything but forceful. What he said was: 'Someone will be getting hurt.' It seems to me that if a workman contents himself with that sort of remark, it is not to be laid against the defendants that they failed to treat that as a substantial complaint calling for an alteration in their system" (359, col. 2).

11. Hardy v. Briggs Motor, *The Times*, March 19, 1957; [1957] C.L.Y. 2427, C.A.

Held, defendants not liable for failing to provide gloves, despite plaintiff's previous request for them to be provided.

12. Croxford v. Scruttons [1958] 2 Lloyd's Rep. 492, Hilbery J.

Dock labourer injured in dock shed when roll of lino fell from stack—in seven years there had been 26 accidents to men from falling rolls—usually injuries very slight—but "occasions when men have had a fracture of their big toe" (496)—during the seven years 1,400,000 rolls of lino had been moved in and out of shed—*Held*, in view of this, and the fact that injuries were usually slight, the hazard was not sufficiently great to constitute negligence, having regard to the difficulty of devising any safe method of stacking lino rolls.

13. Ratcliffe v. Shell Petroleum [1959] 1 Lloyd's Rep. 36, Streatfeild J.

"Of course, as the case of *Morris v. West Hartlepool* (Chap. 15, (2)(h) **5**) shows, it does not follow that, because an accident of a particular sort has not happened before, that it is not an accident which carries the result of negligence" (39, col. 1).

14. Birnie v. Ford Motor Co., *The Times*, November 22, 1960, Glyn-Jones J.

Two plaintiffs, press operators, cut their wrists handling sharp steel panels—in 1956—accident rate was one in 10,000 pressings—but that meant three to four such accidents a day—defendants' precautions, in the shape of mittens and sleeves, were as good as, if not better than, any other employer—but they left wrist vulnerable—in 1957 defendants devised an improved protection—*Held*, despite general practice of industry, defendants were negligent in not providing improved protection earlier.

15. Davies v. Manchester Ship Canal [1960] 2 Lloyd's Rep. 11, C.A.

Spade hook (called a slipper) slipped from paper reel which was being pulled upright—as a result reel fell back onto plaintiff—after the accident deeper hooks were used—during previous 25 years six to eight minor injuries from same cause—but joint safety committee had never suggested using different hooks—*Held*, defendants not liable.

16. McKenna v. Pressed Steel Co. [1960] C.L.Y. 1271, Lloyd C.C.J.

Complaints by plaintiff to shop steward as to dangerous condition of floor—*Held*, such complaints were not complaints made to the employers so as to fix the employers with knowledge thereof.

17. Hayes v. British Oil and Cake Mills [1962] 2 Lloyd's Rep. 288, Phillimore J.

Unloading barges moored to each other—one barge riding five feet higher than next—plaintiff had to climb onto hatch covers to get onto higher barge—barges bumped and plaintiff thrown into hold—*Held*, defendants not liable, as, following customary method, they had left it to the men to complain if distance was too high.

18. Lovelidge v. Anselm Olding [1967] 2 Q.B. 351; [1967] 1 All E.R. 459, Widgery J.

Widgery J. (464 D): " . . . in this day and age every careful employer must realise that high speed unfenced shafts are things which will only be tolerated in circumstances where it cannot really be avoided. I am not unmindful of the fact that this machine has been used in this condition for 20 years without complaint, but that, in a sense, only explains why nothing has been done before. It may be that if these machines were designed today, matters of this kind would be taken into account because views have advanced in the last 20 years; but if a machine is made to an old design which does not give serious trouble, there is the danger (into which I think the present defendants have fallen) of thinking that all is well and of not applying that enquiring mind to the machinery which a reasonably minded employer should apply." Case was one where plaintiff's loose tie got caught in shaft—*Held* defendants liable both at common law and for breach of statutory duty, but 50 per cent. contributory negligence.

19. Bell v. D.H.S.S. *The Times*, June 13, 1989; [1989] C.L.Y. 2547, Drake J.

See Chap. 15, (2) (c) **23** for further details.

20. Baxter v. Harland & Wolff plc [1990] I.R.L.R. 516; [1991] C.L.Y. 1878, N.I.C.A.

See Chap. 15, (2) (a) **29** for further details.

21. Hollier v. Denholm Ship Management [1993] P.I.Q.R. P104; [1993] C.L.Y. 3292, C.A.

First defendant operated system whereby its employee, the deceased, walking backwards and, signalling, guided into position trailers pushed onto a ferry by tractor driven by second defendant's employee. Deceased gave hand and sound signals to stop trailer, but tractor driver did not notice them, and deceased was crushed to death. Owen J. held both defendants liable. First defendant's system obviously potentially dangerous, despite absence of previous accidents. Second defendant vicariously liable for inattention of its driver. Defendants 75 per cent. and 25 per cent. to blame respectively. Court of Appeal dismissed first defendant's appeal against this apportionment.

22. Holmes v. Tees and Hartlepool Port Authority [1993] C.L.Y. 2020, H.H. Judge Stroyan Q.C.

Plaintiff claimed to have suffered injury from repeatedly carrying onto ships one at a time 2 cwt. bags of fertilizers lifted onto his shoulders by two other employees. No complaints had ever been made by plaintiff or his workmates and the system was a common one—*Held*, plaintiff's injuries did not result from his work, but had they done so defendants would not have been negligent.

23. Fishwick v. Lin Pak [1994] C.L.Y. 3340, Grimsby County Court

Plaintiff left his right thumb on spindle of reel of paper as he was locating it onto stub of a machine, and thumb was trapped—*Held*, defendant not liable. Plaintiff had done this job hundreds of times before without accident, and it was common sense to keep hands clear of spindle.

U1. Britton v. Ministry of Defence (1983) C.A. 767

Plaintiff tripped in crack in floor of gangway. Crack $\frac{3}{8}$ in. deep and $\frac{1}{2}$ in. wide. There had been a number of complaints in the preceding two years—*Held*, defendant liable at common law.

U2. Masterman v. Humberside C.C. (1984) C.A. 622

Plaintiff, a care assistant at a special school, and a colleague were putting a grossly disabled pupil on the lavatory when pupil had an epileptic fit and plaintiff injured her back—*Held*, defendant not liable. Two experienced workers were carrying out routine operation using a system which had been used for many years without mishap.

U3. Pickford v. Control Data (1984) C.A. 720

Plaintiff tripped on 2 feet square tile, one corner of which was "something not more than $\frac{1}{4}$ inch proud" of the adjacent tiles. There were 5,500 such tiles on the floor, which was heavily used. Defendant relied on those using the floor to report loose tiles, which were then promptly attended to. No evidence that anyone had noticed anything wrong with the tile in question before the accident, and no evidence of any previous tripping accident—*Held*, defendants not liable in negligence and not in breach of the Factories Act 1961, s. 29.

U4. Graham v. Esso Petroleum Ltd (1986) C.A. 614

See Chap. 15, (2)(a) **U8** for further details.

U5. Winfield v. N.C.B. (1986) C.A. 651

See Chap. 15, (2)(a) **U9** for further details.

(g) Danger Alleged to have been Unknown at Time

1. Ebbs v. James Whitson [1952] 2 Q.B. 877; [1952] 2 All E.R. 192, C.A.

Monsonia wood dust causing dermatitis—not a recognised cause of dermatitis at time—evidence was that in 1935 and 1936 Chief Inspector of Factories had referred to the wood as having noxious properties, and in 1936 he reported that the skin of some people might be sensitive to it—the wood was not used in substantial quantities until after the war and there were only two cases of dermatitis attributed to it—*Held*, defendants not negligent for failing to recognise danger.

2. Adsett v. K. and L. Steelfounders [1953] 1 W.L.R. 773; [1953] 2 All E.R. 320, C.A.

Pneumoconiosis from sand in iron foundry—*Held*, by Parker J., defendants not liable at common law because danger unknown, and this was not discussed on appeal, but in discussing statutory duty and "practicable" precautions Singleton L.J. (322 D) said: "In deciding whether practicable measures were taken one must have regard to the state of knowledge at the material time and particularly to the knowledge of scientific experts."

3. Gregson v. Hicks Hargreaves [1955] 1 W.L.R. 1252; [1955] 3 All E.R. 507, C.A.

Common law negligence not alleged, probably because danger quite unknown—but plaintiff succeeds eventually under Factories Act, 1937, s. 47—see Chap. 16 (7) (d) **5**.

4. Harman v. Mitcham Works, *The Times*, June 22, 1955; [1955] C.L.Y. 1894, C.A.

Manufacture of fluorescent lighting tubes—plaintiff handling beryllium oxide—causes chronic poisoning—*Held*, (2–1) that as defendants had no knowledge of danger at time and no reason to suspect it, not liable.

5. Balfour v. Wm. Beardmore, 1956 S.L.T. 205, O.H.

Held, since publication of interim report of Committee on Dust in Steel Foundries in 1944 defendants could not plead that they could not reasonably have foreseen the danger.

6. Graham v. Wholesale Co-op. Society [1957] 1 W.L.R. 511; [1957] 1 All E.R. 654, Devlin J.

Dermatitis from West African mahogany—not then recognised as a cause of dermatitis—Chief Inspector of Factories in 1935 had referred to monsonia wood as a possible cause of dermatitis, but defendants had never used monsonia and only started to use West African hardwood in quantity after the Second World War—*Held*, defendants not liable. Judge applied the "folly" test by saying (657 E) defendants' duty was to acquire that degree of knowledge which was common in the trade, and not to be guilty of obvious neglect. On this test, defendants were not liable, as they received and read the bulletins ordinarily supplied by the trade, and had not been guilty of any obvious neglect. If, however, the bulletins had been proved to contain any reference to the danger, defendants would probably have been liable (657 I). As to the desirability of interrogatories in a case of this sort, see 657 I.

7. Tremain v. Pike [1969] 1 W.L.R. 1586; [1969] 3 All E.R. 1303, Payne J.

Held, defendant not liable, because (a) there was no evidence to suggest that farmers knew or ought reasonably to have known of the disease, or alternatively (b) if the hazard from the disease should have been foreseen, it was at most a remote possibility. The judgment contains a number of facts about the incidence of the disease, and it may be that the same result would not follow in the case of a fish worker or sewer man, where the incidence is higher and is recognised.

U1. Nash v. Parkinson Cowan (1962) C.A. 121

Silicosis from rubbing slipstones for valves on fine sand—*Held*, defendants not liable because danger not foreseeable by a "reasonably informed employer".

U2. Wrigglesworth v. B.S.C. (1972) C.A. 167A

Plaintiff cutting cobble (*i.e.* a steel beam rejected during rolling) into lengths with propane gas cutter—when part fractured with great force—*Held*, defendants not liable, as danger was at the time not foreseeable.

(b) General Practice of Industry

1. Barkway v. South Wales Transport [1950] A.C. 185; [1950] 1 All E.R. 392, H.L.

Bus accident through tyre-burst—*Held* defendants liable. Lord Normand (402 D) cited Lord Dunedin in *Morton v. William Dixon*, 1909 S.C. 809, saying that the principle, though enunciated in a master and servant case, was of general application: "Where the negligence of the employer consists of what I may call a fault of omission, I think it is absolutely necessary that proof of that fault of omission should be one of two kinds—either to show that the thing which he did not do was a thing which was commonly done by other persons in like circumstances, or to show that it was a thing which was so obviously wanted that it would be folly in anyone to neglect to provide it." *But* see now **8** and **10**.

2. Paris v. Stepney B.C. [1951] A.C. 367, [1951] 1 All E.R. 42; H.L.

Defendants—*Held* liable for failing to provide goggles to a one-eyed man. For details, see Chap. 15, (2)(b) **3**. Lord Normand (49 G), with whom Lord Oaksey (50 G) concurred, restated the *Morton* dictum as set out in **1** above.

3. General Cleaning Contractors v. Christmas [1953] A.C. 180; [1952] 2 All E.R. 1110, H.L.

Window cleaning case in which defendants were *held* liable for failing to instruct plaintiff in precautions against the danger of a sash moving. The evidence appears to have been that it was regular and/or general practice to take no such precautions. Lord Reid (1116 A) said: "A plaintiff who seeks to have condemned as unsafe a system of work which has been generally used for a long time in an important trade undertakes a heavy onus . . . "; and then at 1116 F: "The need to provide against the danger of a sash moving unexpectedly appears to me to be so obvious that, even if it were proved that it is the general practice to neglect this danger, I would hold that it ought not to be neglected and that precautions should be taken."

4. Hurley v. Sanders [1955] 1 W.L.R. 470; [1955] 1 All E.R. 833, Glyn-Jones J.

Dangerous access to bottom of dry-dock down steep altar courses—no precautions (such as safety belts or lines)—defendants were following universal practice of industry—*Held*, defendants liable. "... I hesitate very much to find that the universal practice of the trade is negligent, yet the risk seems to me so clear that I feel bound to find that some precautions such as the provision of a safety belt and line should have been taken, and I think it was for the employer to satisfy me that it would not be practicable to do so, and this he has not done" (836 I).

5. Morris v. West Hartlepool S.N. [1956] A.C. 552; [1956] 1 All E.R. 385, H.L.

'Tween deck hatch unfenced at sea—defence of general practice—*Held*, (3–2) no defence because, *per* Lord Tucker (400 F), "it (the risk) was obvious, its consequences were likely to be calamitous, and the remedy was simple and available." Lord Cohen (401 I) said the word "folly" in Lord Dunedin's test in **1** did not mean "ridiculous." All three majority Lords thought that evidence of general practice was "of great value and sometimes decisive" (Lord Tucker at 400 F), and that it "weighs heavily in the scale on the side of defendants" (Lord Cohen at 402 A), and from the doubts expressed by Lord Reid (399 B), Lord Tucker (400 C) and Lord Cohen (402 B) as to the cogency of the evidence of general practice adduced, it seems possible that if the evidence had been clearer on this point, the issue, which was a narrowly balanced one, might have gone the other way.

6. Kilgollan v. W. Cooke [1956] 1 W.L.R. 527; [1956] 2 All E.R. 294, C.A.

Held, defendants liable. Singleton L. J. (303 A): "I have not forgotten the evidence given by the defendants' witnesses that thirty-two factories in Sheffield adopted the same method as defendants and that only one had guards of the kind which the factory inspector recommended. I do not know what their experience was; I have no particulars on which to go; I have only the evidence in this case in regard to the defendants."

7. Welsford v. Lawford Asphalte Co. [1956] C.L.Y. 5984, Diplock J.

See Chap. 15, (7) **11**—*Held* defendants liable.

8. Cavanagh v. Ulster Weaving Co. [1960] A.C. 145; [1959] 2 All E.R. 745, H.L.

Plaintiff had slipped coming down a roof ladder—defendants' expert gave evidence that the "set-up" was in perfect accord with good practice—this evidence was not challenged—the jury found for the plaintiff—the Northern Ireland Court of Appeal reversed this finding on the ground that, since there was unchallenged evidence that the defendants had acted in accordance with good general practice, the "folly" test must apply to exculpate them—*Held*, not so, and verdict for plaintiff must be restored.

Lord Tucker (Lords Simonds, Somervell and Jenkins concurring) at 748 H said, in connection with the folly test: "I would however desire to express my agreement with ... Lord Cohen in *Morris's* case **5** where ... he said: 'I think that the effect of their lordships' observations is that when the court finds a clearly established practice 'in the circumstances,' the practice weighs heavily in the scale on the side of the defendants and the burden of establishing negligence, which the plaintiff has to discharge, is a heavy one.' Later (*ibid*) he equates the word 'folly' as used by Lord Dunedin and Lord Normand to 'unreasonable or imprudent,' thereby emphasising that Lord Dunedin could not have been intending to extend the employers' common law liability beyond that which had been laid down in *Smith v. Baker* (Chap. 15, (1) (a) **3**) and many subsequent cases in this House. To give the word 'folly' any other meaning would necessarily have this result."

9. Qualcast v. Haynes [1959] A.C. 743; [1959] 2 All E.R. 38, H.L.

Lord Keith, in referring to the precautions contained in the Iron and Steel Foundries Regulations, 1953, said (43 A): "This is in no sense conclusive of the scope of an employer's duty, but it has some evidential value in a case otherwise lacking in evidence of practice in this direction."

10. Brown v. Rolls-Royce [1960] 1 W.L.R. 210; [1960] 1 All E.R. 577, H.L.

Industrial dermatitis from oil—defendants did not supply barrier cream—but it was proved that other employers commonly did—*Held*, this was not necessarily conclusive, and that the ultimate test was lack of reasonable care for the safety of the workman in all the circumstances of the case, and in all the circumstances defendants were not liable. Lord Cohen (579 H) said the "folly" test was "only a prima facie guide".

11. Birnie v. Ford Motor Co., *The Times*, November 22, 1960, Glyn-Jones J.

Two plaintiffs, press operators, cut their wrists handling sharp steel panels—in 1956 accident rate was one in 10,000 pressings—but that meant three to four such accidents a day—defendants' precautions, in the shape of mittens and sleeves, were as good as, if not better than, any other employer—but they left the wrist vulnerable—in 1957 defendants devised an improved protection—*Held*, despite general practice of industry, defendants were negligent in not providing improved protection earlier.

12. Brown v. John Mills (1970) 8 K.I.R. 702; [1970] C.L.Y. 1873, C.A.

13. Williams v. Gwent Area H.A. [1983] C.L.Y. 2551, Stephen Brown J.

Held, that the defendants were negligent. For details see Chap. 15, (4)(b) **28**.

14. Thompson v. Smiths Shiprepairers [1984] Q.B. 405; [1984] 1 All E.R. 881, Mustill J.

Plaintiffs worked in shipyards over long periods—exposed to excessive noise which damaged their hearing. Employers knew of risk of noise induced hearing loss, but failed to provide protection against noise until early 1970s. Prior to 1963 industry generally apathetic in relation to industrial deafness and defendants' failure to take precautions in line with common approach—*Held*, applying *Morris* **5** and dictum in *Stokes* set out in Chap. 15, (2)(a) **24**, the test to be applied in determining the point of time at which an employer's failure to provide protection against industrial noise constituted actionable negligence was what would have been done at any particular time by a reasonable and prudent employer who was properly but not extraordinarily solicitous for his workers' safety in the light of what he knew or ought to have known at the time. Accordingly, an employer was not negligent if at any given time he followed a recognised practice which had been followed throughout the industry as a whole for a substantial period, even though the practice may not have been without mishap, and at that particular time the consequences of a particular type of risk were regarded as an inescapable feature of the industry: "The standard of what is negligent is influenced though not decisively by the practice of the industry as a whole. In my judgement, this principle applies not only where the breach of duty is said to consist of a failure to take precautions known to be available as a means of combating a known danger, but also where the omission involves an absence of initiative in seeking out knowledge of facts that were not in themselves obvious. The employer must keep up to date but the court must be slow to blame him for not ploughing a lone furrow" (889 E). On the facts, the dividing line was 1963. Prior to that, the employer's failure to provide protection against noise in the yards did not constitute actionable negligence, but after that date it did.

N.B
In an unreported case, *Kellet v. B.R.B.*, heard by Popplewell J. at Chester on and after May 3, 1984, it was held that, in a similar claim arising from noise over a long period in railway workshops, liability commenced in 1955 in view of the special facts and circumstances adduced in evidence. (*N.B.* Shortland writers were Nightingale of Liverpool.)

15. Grioli v. Allied Building Company Ltd, *The Times*, April 10, 1985; [1985] C.L.Y. 1152/3, C.A.

Held, employer who failed to provide wrist and forearm gauntlets for carpenter employed by them not liable for injury to his right wrist from glass which shattered when he was glazing a door—there was no significant practice amongst carpenters to use such gauntlets.

16. Re The Herald of Free Enterprise, *The Independent*, December 18, 1987; [1988] C.L.Y. 2462, D.C.

The ferry *The Herald of Free Enterprise* capsized soon after leaving Zeebrugge because the inner and outer bow doors to the main "G" deck had not been closed. The assistant bosun, whose duty it was to close them, had fallen asleep. His chief officer did not follow the usual practice of waiting to see the doors begin to close, but went to the bridge. There, the captain did not ask the chief officer for any report, and sailed assuming the doors had been closed. The Divisional Court dismissed the captain's appeal against a finding of the formal inquiry into the capsizing that he had been guilty of serious negligence in the discharge of his duties. He should have made a positive check that the doors were closed before putting to sea. The fact that it was not the practice of most if not all captains of such ferries to make a positive check made no difference. Though general practice was usually cogent evidence of the standard of reasonable care, here it was evidence of culpable complacency. The standard of care to be expected of a ship's Master was a high one, having regard to the numbers of passengers to be expected on such vessels, and risk of serious injury or death in the event of any negligence.

17. Baxter v. Harland Wolff plc [1990] I.R.L.R. 516; [1991] C.L.Y. 1878, N.I.C.A.

See Chap. 15, (2) (a) **29** for further details.

18. Holmes v. Tees and Hartlepool Port Authority [1993] C.L.Y. 2020, H.H. Judge Stroyan Q.C.

Plaintiff claimed to have suffered injury from repeatedly carrying onto ships one at a time 2 cwt, bags of fertilizers lifted onto his shoulders by two other employees. No complaints had ever been made by plaintiff or his workmates and the system was a common one—*Held*, plaintiff's injuries did not result from his work, but had they done so defendants would not have been negligent.

19. Nilsson v. Redditch B.C. [1994] C.L.Y. 2299, C.A.

Plaintiff dustman injured by glass protruding from refuse sack. Judge held defendant liable on ground that it should have used the "wheelie bin" rather than the "black bag" system of collection—*Held*, allowing the appeal, the judge had tried to overturn an established system of work on wholly insufficient evidence. The mere fact that a system of work was hazardous did not make it unsafe. The judge had failed to weigh the gravity of the risk against the consequences of overturning an established system.

U1. Lavelle v. George Adlam Ltd. (1961) C.A. 82

Plaintiff lathe operator cut hand on emitted swarf—alleges lathe should have had a chip breaker which would have broken coils of swarf as emitted into little flakes—*Held*, applying "folly" test (see 6 E, *per* Holroyd Pearce L.J.), defendants not liable, as use of chip breaker was not common practice, nor "folly" in sense used by Lord Normand.

U2. Downer v. Eastern Gas Board (1975) C.A. 15

Chipping tar from gas pipes—finger caught when tar gives way—only one minor accident in over 30 years—*Held*, applying test in *Brown* **12**, the established system of work created such a remote possibility of risk that it could not be negligent.

U3. Gandy v. Clarke Chapman (1976) C.A. 412

Fitter testing diesel compressor—tightening injector nut after testing injector—nut 8–10 inches from fan (which was running)—spanner slipped—finger caught by fan—plaintiff was doing work in accordance with the general practice of industry—*Held*, notwithstanding general practice, method was obviously dangerous, and plaintiff should have been instructed to shut off engine before tightening. Dictum of Edmund Davies L.J. in *Brown v. Mills* **12**, approved (citing Munkman (8th ed.), p. 48): "General and approved practice in an industry is the primary guide in determining the standard of care: but it is not inflexible and may be departed from when there is a failure to take account of some proved danger." *N.B.* The same considerations did not apply to loosening the nut at the start, as there the spanner was moved away from the fan.

U4. Masterman v. Humberside C.C. (1984) C.A. 622

See Chap. 15, (2)(f) **U2** for further details.

U5. Graham v. Esso Petroleum Ltd (1986) C.A. 614

See Chap. 15, (2)(a) **U8** for further details.

U6. Taylor v. British Gas Corporation (1986) C.A. 906

An experienced gas fitter was dealing with a gas leak in a residential street. When stepping bachwards out of the hole he was excavating he fell into another nearby hole about 3 feet deep—*Held*, defendant not liable in negligence and not in breach of Construction (Working Places) Regulations 1966, reg. 6(2). The place of work was not unsafe. Alternatively, if it was unsafe, the erection of barriers between the closely proximate holes was not reasonably practicable, and was not normal practice.

U7. Thomson v. Peglers Ltd (1987) C.A. 522

Plaintiff, foundry worker, was struck in the chest by a small piece of metal from a heavy hammer being used by another employee. The hammer had crazing on its face which would not normally be found on visual examination, and had not been noticed by the employee using it. Defendant had no formal system for inspecting hammers, but relied on the experience and common sense of their employees to spot defects. Crazing rarely occurred on hammer heads. Crazing would have been visible had the hammer been wiped clean with solvent and then inspected, but both processes would require adequately trained staff and this was not a practice adopted by prudent employees generally—*Held*, defendant not liable—system of work was safe.

(j) Relevance of Official and Trade Publications

1. Clifford v. Charles Challen [1951] 1 K.B. 495; [1951] 1 All E.R. 72, C.A.

Dermatitis from synthetic glue—a government factory notice calling attention to this danger and prescribing precautions was put before court—*Held*, the notice afforded "a safe basis on which the common law can build" (*per* Denning L.J., 74 A), and the defendants liable for failing to take adequate precautions.

2. Dickson v. Flack [1953] 2 Q.B. 464; [1953] 2 All E.R. 840, C.A.

Question was whether defendants were in breach of fencing duty under Factories Acts and Woodworking Regulations—two pamphlets were produced to judge (Safety Pamphlet No. 8, issued in 1928 by Home Office, and Form No. 279, issued in 1935 and reprinted in 1947 by Ministry of Labour)—the particular danger in question (a cutter flying out) was recognised in both pamphlets—*Held*, this showed that the machine was foreseeably dangerous. As regards precautions, defendants had fitted a "Shaw guard" which was described in one or both of the pamphlets, but others were also described which C.A. thought might give better protection—*Held*, accordingly, defendants liable for not fencing securely and failing to fit most "efficient" guard.

3. Balfour v. Wm. Beardmore, 1956 S.L.T. 205, O.H.

Held, since publication of interim report of Committee on Dust in Steel Foundries in 1944 defendants could not plead that they could not reasonably have foreseen the danger.

4. Graham v. Co-op. Wholesale Society [1957] 1 W.L.R. 511; [1957] 1 All E.R. 654, Devlin J.

Dermatitis from West African mahogany—not then recognised as a cause of dermatitis—Chief Inspector of Factories in 1935 had referred to monsonia wood as a possible cause of dermatitis, but defendants had never used monsonia and only started to use West African hardwood in quantity after the Second World War—*Held*, defendants not liable. Judge applied the "folly" test by saying (657 E) defendants' duty was to acquire that degree of knowledge which was common in the trade and not to be guilty of obvious neglect. On this test, defendants were not liable, as they received and read the bulletins ordinarily supplied by the trade, and had not been guilty of any obvious neglect. If however the bulletins had been proved to contain any reference to the danger, defendants would probably have been liable (657 I). As to the desirability of interrogatories in a case of this sort, see 657 I.

5. Wallhead v. Ruston and Hornsby (1973) 14 K.I.R. 285; [1973] C.L.Y. 737, Bagnall J.

Plaintiff worked in iron foundry from 1924 to 1964—developed bronchitis and emphysema—condition not caused, but aggravated, by dust from foundry sand—in 1950 a book was issued which led to the danger becoming generally recognised—*Held*, from 1950 on defendants were in breach of duty. (A statutory duty case.)

6. Cartwright v. G.K.N. Sankey (1973) 14 K.I.R. 349; [1973] C.L.Y. 1445, C.A.

Arc welder exposed to injurious fumes—judge dismissed action because of insufficient indication from medical and other literature—but in 1965 Ministry had issued pamphlet containing ceiling limits—*Held*, in a statutory duty case, defendants, being under duty to take "all practicable measures", had to consider all safety literature, and in view of the 1965 pamphlet they were liable.

7. Burgess v. Thorn, *The Times*, May 16, 1983; [1983] C.L.Y. 1060, Bristow J.

P suffered tenosynovitis (inflammation of a tendon) as a result of employment. D had received guidance from Health and Safety Executive on the subject—*Held*, D liable for failing to warn P, as, if the condition had been caught early enough, permanent damage to P would have been avoided.

8. Thompson v. Smiths Shiprepairers [1984] Q.B. 405; [1984] 1 All E.R. 881, Mustill J.

See Chap. 15, (2) (h) **14** for further details.

9. Bryce v. Swan Hunter Group plc [1987] 2 Lloyd's Rep. 426; [1988] 1 All E.R. 659, Phillips J.

See Chap. 15, (2) (a) **27** for further details.

10. Gunn v. Wallsend Slipway and Engineering C. Ltd, *The Times*, January 23, 1989; [1989] C.L.Y. 2548, C.A.

Plaintiff's wife contracted mesothelioma and died as a result of inhaling asbestos dust between 1948 and 1965 when washing plaintiff's clothes which were often impregnated with dust during plaintiff's employment by defendant—*Held*, defendant owed no duty of care to plaintiff's wife, because it could not reasonably have foreseen risk of injury to her from such exposure, in absence before 1965 of any relevant medical, industrial or official publications and of any approved practice as to storage and washing of working clothes.

11. Baxter v. Harland Wolff plc [1990] I.R.L.R. 516; [1991] C.L.Y. 1878, N.I.C.A.

The plaintiff was employed without protection for his ears in conditions of excessive noise in the defendant's Belfast shipyard from 1937 to 1944 and 1946 to 1962, and developed noise-induced deafness as result—*Held, inter alia*, and differing from Thompson (**8** above) that the defendant was liable in negligence for damage to the plaintiff's ears caused by exposure to noise from January 1, 1954 onwards, prior to which the claim was statute-barred. The defendant was negligent in failing to consider or take any steps to deal with or reduce the harmful effects of noise which they knew was injuring their employees. There was sufficient medical, scientific and legal knowledge available prior to 1963 (the Thompson "year of liability") to have brought home to reasonable employers that some kind of protection was required.

12. Bowman v. Harland & Wolff plc [1992] I.R.L.R. 349; [1992] C.L.Y. 3222, Carswell J., N.I.

Plaintiffs employed at defendant's Belfast shipyard during 1950s and 1960s—regularly used hand-held pneumatic caulking hammers, vibration from which caused them to suffer from Raynaud's Phemonenon, also known as "vibration white finger" (V.W.F.)—*Held*,

(a) Having regard to medical publications and other literature about V.W.F. (referred to in detail in judgment) defendant should have appreciated the existence of the problem and instituted preventative measures by January 1, 1973, and was negligent in having failed to do either.
(b) Damages awardable only in respect of deterioration in plaintiffs' condition from January 1, 1973 to date of issue of proceedings in 1988.

13. Wilebore v. St Edmundsbury B.C. [1994] C.L.Y. 2282, Tucker J.

Plaintiff claimed that hand and wrist movements during his work as an abbattoir meat inspector had caused straining injury to his thumbs—*Held*, on the medical evidence, plaintiff's condition was unrelated to his work. In any event his work did not involve the kind of rapid repetitive twisting and gripping envisaged in D.H.S.S. Guidance Note MS10 which might reasonably foreseeably cause straining injury. Defendant not liable.

14. Barrett v. Ministry of Defence, *The Times*, January 13, 1995, C.A.

See Chap. 15, (1)(b) **23** for further details.

U1. Foster v. British Electricity Authority (1952) C.A. 200

Electrocution of linesman—breach by defendants of own Safety Rules in putting warning pennants on wrong part of pylon—*Held*, this breach was evidence of negligence, and defendants liable.

U2. Dibley v. Welbecson Press Ltd (1955) C.A. 238

Plaintiff compositor employed by defendants contracted dermatitis from paraffin used to clean formes—isolated case in factory and trade—there were Stationery Office pamphlets in regard to industrial dermatitis showing that paraffin can cause dermatitis, but not dealing with this trade or risk—wide in their scope—*Held*, paraffin (apart from fire risk) not dangerous *per se*—defendants not negligent—did not know of risk and no reason to know of risk.

U3. Collyer v. B.T.C. (1956) C.A. 123

Denning L.J. (17 D): "It (rule book) is not, to my mind, part of the contract. It has no statutory force. It cannot limit the rules of the common law as to the duties of an employer to his servants, because the rules of the common law have been developed over the last hundred years and exist apart from contract altogether. The rule book is only a book of instructions, compiled as a result of experience, showing what, in the opinion of the Commission, ought to be done for the proper working of the railway. Failure by the Commission or its servants to obey the rules is evidence of negligence against them. Failure by a man to observe the rules which are drawn to his attention may be evidence of contributory negligence by him. But the rules are only a guide: they cannot set the bounds to the common law."

U4. Graham v. Esso Petroleum Ltd (1986) C.A. 614 (unreported)

See Chap. 15, (2)(a) **U8** for further details.

(k) How Far Statutory Code Relevant

Statutory provisions may be "exhaustive definition" of duty	1	Coal Mines Act 1911
COMPLIANCE WITH STATUTORY PROVISIONS—MAY REBUT COMMON LAW LIABILITY	2	Grinding of Metals, etc., Regulations 1925
BREACH OF STATUTORY DUTY—HOW FAR COMMON LAW NEGLIGENCE	2	Grinding of Metals, etc., Regulations 1925
Compliance with statutory provisions—common law liability may still exist—shotfiring	3	
Breach of statutory duty—how far common law negligence	4	Coal Mines Act 1911
BREACH OF STATUTORY DUTY—HOW FAR COMMON LAW NEGLIGENCE	5	Factories Act 1937
COMPLIANCE WITH STATUTORY PROVISIONS—HOW FAR REBUTS COMMON LAW NEGLIGENCE	6	Building, etc., Regulations 1948
CIRCUMSTANCES "JUST OUTSIDE" STATUTORY PROVISIONS—PROVISIONS IRRELEVANT TO COMMON LAW NEGLIGENCE	6	Building, etc., Regulations 1948
COMPLIANCE WITH STATUTORY PROVISIONS—YOUNG PEOPLE—COMMON LAW LIABILITY MAY STILL EXIST	7	Woodworking Regulations 1922
Compliance with statutory provisions—will not necessarily rebut common law negligence—but a factor to be considered	8	Horizontal Milling Machines Regulations 1928
Statutory provisions may be good guide to what is reasonable standard of care	9	
Regulations may not be exhaustive code of whole duty for sphere in which they operate	10	Coal Mines (Sidings) Regulations 1956

1. Caulfield v. Pickup [1941] 2 All E.R. 510, Asquith J.

Suggested that Coal Mines Act was an "exhaustive statutory definition of what constitutes safe working system" in coal mines.

2. Franklin v. Gramophone Co. [1948] 1 K.B. 542; [1948] 1 All E.R. 353, C.A.

Inhalation of dust over period causing fatal pneumoconiosis—claim under statutory Regulations failed because deceased was not "wholly or mainly employed" in the process—if he had been, a hood, duct or fan would have been required—*Held*, however, defendants were liable at common law.

Somervell L.J.: "It is of course relevant to consider the Regulations, and in very many cases it would be difficult, if not impossible, to maintain that an employer who had complied with the Regulations had been guilty of negligence at common law. In this case however it is the regulation itself, coupled with the evidence, which I find establishes negligence. The regulation . . . is an indication that danger is to be apprehended by . . . (the circumstances causing the accident) . . . It is the regulation, of which the employers' officers were aware, which is itself a warning . . . " (360 A–C).

3. Nicol v. N.C.B. (1952) 102 L.J. News. 357.

4. N.C.B. v. England [1954] A.C. 403; [1954] 1 All E.R. 546, H.L.

Shotfirer in breach of statutory duty fires prematurely—some doubt as to whether breach of statutory duty was personal to shotfirer so as to exclude vicarious liability—in which case, does the breach of statutory duty also constitute common law negligence for which defendants *would* be liable—majority find common law negligence independently, but Lord Porter (550 G) *said*: "Nor do I think the existence of the Regulations can be neglected . . . (They) must have been known to all mineworkers and if known must have made it abundantly clear that an accident might happen."

5. Hartley v. Mayoh [1954] 1 Q.B. 383; [1954] 1 All E.R. 375, C.A.

Held, factory occupier liable to widow of electrocuted fireman for failing to have main switches of the usual type and recognisable as such. No statutory liability, as statutory duty did not extend to firemen, but Jenkins L.J. (384 D) said that the fact that there was a statutory duty with regard to type of main switch (which was broken) was strong support for inferring that factory occupier ought to have known his unusual main switch was a source of danger.

6. Chipchase v. British Titan Products [1956] 1 Q.B. 545; [1956] 1 All E.R. 613, C.A.

Plaintiff fell off staging which if 6 inches higher would have been a breach of statutory duty—*Held*, Regulations were irrelevant and claim failed at common law. Morris L.J. (614 D): "That case (*i.e.* **2**) showed that whether an owner is relieved of his common law duty by some regulation depends on the particular regulation in each case. That case also shows that the fact that the occupier of a factory has complied with all the requirements of (statutory duty), which may be of limited scope, will not necessarily absolve him from liability for negligence at common law." Dictum in **2** cited and approved.

7. Stringer v. Automatic Woodturning [1956] 1 W.L.R. 138; [1956] 1 All E.R. 327, C.A.

Girl of 18 tending circular saw (properly guarded)—Singleton L.J. (331 I): "I believe that if employers do put a young girl in charge of such a machine, they are under a duty of giving special instructions to her. Furthermore (even if they have provided a statutory guard), they ought in compliance with their duty at common law to have taken some additional means to protect a young girl such as this." *N.B.* The course of this case was confusing—*Held*, by Oliver J., defendants not liable at common law, but liable for breach of statutory duty—*Held*, by C.A., defendants not liable for breach of statutory duty, but ordered new trial on common law issue. Both parties appealed to H.L.—*Held*, [1957] A.C. 544; [1957] 1 All E.R. 90, that defendants not liable at common law or for breach of statutory duty. The dictum cited above was not considered by H.L.

8. Quinn v. Horsfall [1956] 1 W.L.R. 652; [1956] 1 All E.R. 777, Glyn-Jones J.

Question whether a milling cutter should have been guarded—no statutory duty, because it was being used for automatic profiling and was therefore exempt—"I think the truth is that the common law obligation to fence is concealed or masked by the wider obligations imposed by statute, and, if for any reason the wider statutory obligation disappears the common law duty once more arises . . . Although . . . I do not think that the existence of the Regulations relieves the employer from any common law duty to fence, the fact that the Regulations exist is a fact to be considered in assessing whether or not a reasonable employer would think it necessary to do so" (782 B–D).—*Held*, on the facts, defendants were not liable at common law or for breach of statutory duty, but this was reversed on both counts by C.A. ([1956] 1 W.L.R. 652; [1956] 2 All E.R. 467) without any comment on above dictum.

9. Qualcast v. Haynes [1959] A.C. 743; [1959] 2 All E.R. 38, H.L.

Question at issue was to what extent defendants should have seen that plaintiff wore protective spats in a foundry. Lord Radcliffe, after saying that properly to measure that obligation would require fuller details than were contained in the evidence, then went on (40 D): "Particularly would that be so, I think, when, as here, there had only just come into force an enactment, the Iron and Steel Regulations, 1953, which though containing a regulation expressly devoted to the subject of 'protective equipment' made no reference at all to the provision or use of protective spats."

Lord Keith (42 I): "It is not insignificant that regulation 8 of the Iron and Steel Foundries Regulations, 1953, while requiring the provision of other safety equipment requires no provision of boots, spats, or other protective foot or leg equipment."

10. Smith (or Westwood) v. N.C.B. [1967] 1 W.L.R. 871; [1967] 2 All E.R. 593, H.L.

11. Bux v. Slough Metals [1973] 1 W.L.R. 1358; [1974] 1 All E.R. 262, C.A.

U1. Palmer v. Wagon Repairs (1951) C.A. 20

Eye case—the turning machines in question were not included in the Regulations made under the Factories Act 1937, s. 49—Cohen L.J. (5 E): "If there was other evidence to show that the danger was not reasonably foreseeable, the fact that those machines had been left out of these Regulations was, at any rate, consistent with that view."

U2. Williams v. William Press (1959) C.A. 104 A

Defendants *held*, liable for unfooted ladder at common law, but not under Building Regulations (which did not apply). Ormerod L.J. (9 A): "The Regulations must be regarded to some extent as a guide to the standard of care that a wise employer should take for the safety of his work people."

U3. Denman v. Gibson (1965) C.A. 263

Plaintiff was repairing a wagon on a dock siding—using chisel to free rusted nut—piece flew in his eye—under Protection of Eyes Regulations 1938, "cutting out or cutting off cold rivets or bolts from boilers or other plant" would in a factory require goggles—judge said that since this was an analogous risk, it afforded some ground for saying that goggles should have been provided—*Held*, per Willmer and Danckwerts L.JJ., this was right. *But* Winn L.J. was doubtful whether the two processes were analogous.

(l) Ordinary Risks of Service

1. Field v. Perry's [1950] 2 All E.R. 521; [1950] W.N. 320, Devlin J.

Held, ordinary risk of service. See Chap. 15, (5) **2**.

2. General Cleaning Contractors v. Christmas [1953] A.C. 180; [1952] 2 All E.R. 1110, H.L.

Held, defendants liable.

3. Michie v. Shenley H.M.C., *The Times*, March 19, 1952; [1952] C.L.Y. 2411, Barry J.

Held, defendants not liable, as ordinary risk of service.

4. Burke v. Ellerman and Papayanni [1953] 1 Lloyd's Rep. 295, Barry J.

Held, defendants not liable, as this was "the sort of hazard which a man cleaning a deck must expect" (297, right column).

5. Pease v. B.I.S.N. [1953] 1 Lloyd's Rep. 207, Lord Goddard C.J.
See **6**.

6. Watts v. Shaw Savill [1953] 1 Lloyd's Rep. 407, McNair J.

Two loose hooks on sling containing boxed motor-cars—one of these caught in coaming, slipped off. and, coming down, struck plaintiff—*Held, res ipsa loquitur* applied, but on the evidence a reasonable explanation was afforded, which was that this was "one of those unfortunate accidents which do from time to time happen in the course of stevedoring operations, in the course of handling heavy cargo, which of necessity involves certain risks . . . " (410). Judge also quoted (410) Lord Chief Justice in **5** to the effect that "accidents can happen and do happen, and everyone knows in the ordinary experience of life that accidents happen in everyday life in which it would be quite wrong to attribute negligence to anybody."

7. Scanlan v. Maltby [1953] 2 Lloyd's Rep. 122, Lord Goddard C.J.

Held, defendants not liable: "I dare say it was a bit awkward when this lower part of the Jacob's ladder was, so to speak, hanging free, but it is just one of those awkward things that any stevedore would be accustomed to and would meet as an ordinary incident in his daily work" (124).

8. Watt v. Herts C.C. [1954] 1 W.L.R. 835; [1954] 2 All E.R. 368, C.A.

Plaintiff a fireman injured when a heavy jack being carried in fire tender to accident shifted and trapped plaintiff who was travelling in tender—there was no way of securing jack in this particular vehicle, so that there was an inherent risk of shifting—defendants did have a proper vehicle for the jack, but it was not available at the time—*Held*, that defendants not liable, as the risk was undertaken in an emergency and was one that might normally be encountered in the fire service (370 H).

9. Rands v. McNeil [1955] 1 Q.B. 253; [1954] 3 All E.R. 593, C.A.

Morris L.J. (604 G): "It may well be that if someone is employed as the custodian of a bull with dangerous propensities, he voluntarily accepts such risks as are involved in such employment." *But* not, as Lord Justice emphasised, the risks of negligence on the part of employers.

10. Drummond v. British Building Cleaners [1954] 1 W.L.R. 1434; [1954] 3 All E.R. 507, C.A.

"In the present case defendants seem to have been content to accept the view that a window cleaner's job is inherently risky in the absence of eyes fitted into the wall, and to have given no consideration at all to further methods of making it safe" (Parker L.J., 512 H).

11. Hurley v. Sanders [1955] 1 W.L.R. 470; [1955] 1 All E.R. 833, Glyn-Jones J.

"A great deal of work which has to be done is dangerous, and if it is not reasonably practicable for the master to eliminate or diminish the danger, then the risk is a necessary incident of this employment and a risk which the servant is paid to take" (836 F)—*Held*, defendant liable. For full details see Chap. 15,(2)(h)**4**.

12. Davie v. P.L.A. [1955] 1 Lloyd's Rep. 135, Pilcher J.

"I do not think that one must expect them (cold-store workers) to be ready for patches of slippery ice such as the patch which I have found to exist in this case" (140, col. 1).

13. Lewis v. Union Castle [1955] 1 Lloyd's Rep. 480, Barry J.
Held, defendants not liable.

14. Gibbons v. Regent Stevedoring [1955] 2 Lloyd's Rep. 273, Pearce J.
Held, defendants not liable.

15. Pollendine v. Orient S.N. [1955] 2 Lloyd's Rep. 409, Lord Goddard C.J.

Held, defendants not liable.

16. Morris v. West Hartlepool S.N. Co. [1956] A.C. 552; [1956] 1 All E.R. 385, H.L.

Lord Tucker (400 E): "Sailors are of course necessarily exposed to many risks by the very nature of their calling, and no one would suggest that the courts should be ready to interfere with the practice based on past experience with regard to such occupational risks, but the risk in the present case was not of that nature."

17. Rudkin v. Maltby [1956] 1 Lloyd's Rep. 416, Pearce J.

"The presence of loose lentils among the sacks was a normal risk inherent in the unloading of lentils" (420)—*Held*, defendants not liable.

18. Norcott v. Glen Line [1956] 2 Lloyd's Rep. 108, Pilcher J.

See Chap. 15,(2) (c)**13**.

19. Wilson v. International Combustion [1957] 3 All E.R. 505n., C.A.

See Chap. 15,(5)**12**.

20. Trznadel v. B.T.C. [1957] 1 W.L.R. 1002; [1957] 3 All E.R. 196n., C.A.

Held, defendants not liable, as ordinary risk of service.

21. Shanley v. West Coast Stevedoring [1957] 1 Lloyd's Rep. 144, Glyn-Jones.; [1957] 1 Lloyd's Rep. 391, C.A.

Plaintiff hatchman stood on side of coamings nearest winch—some hatch cover locking bars had been placed there which got caught in winch causing injury to plaintiff—*Held*, defendants not liable: "An experienced hatchman may take up his place anywhere round the hatch where he thinks it convenient, but in so doing, he must have due regard for his own safety, and if he chooses to go and stand in a place where the ship's company quite legitimately and properly put these locking bars, and if in consequence an accident happens—I do not say there is any contributory negligence on his part; he may not have foreseen this very unusual and very unexpected accident . . . I think he must bear the consequences if an accident happens" (149, col. 2). *Upheld* by C.A. in similar terms.

22. Sargent v. Gee Stevedoring [1957] 1 Lloyd's Rep. 357, Ashworth J.

Plaintiff had to stand on greasy pipes in hold to unload same—*Held*, defendants not liable: "Stevedores . . . unloading tubes would be the first to admit that they are not entitled to expect conditions to be altogether level and even. The very nature of the work which they undertake exposes them to the task of working in awkward places" (359, col. 2).

23. Middleditch v. Union Castle [1957] 1 Lloyd's Rep. 530, Finnemore J.

Held, defendants not liable.

24. Freeman v. Furness Withy [1957] 2 Lloyd's Rep. 586, Barry J.

Held, defendants not liable: "It is inevitable, when an operation of this kind is being carried out ... that a number of these dried peas ... will be lying on the quayside ... and in various parts of the shed."

25. Adamson v. Bickle Bros [1957] C.L.Y. 2426, Pearson J.
Held, defendants not liable, as, *inter alia*, it was an ordinary risk of service.

26. Wilson v. Tyneside Cleaning Co. [1958] 2 Q.B. 110; [1958] 2 All E.R. 265, C.A.

Held, defendants not liable.

27. Oughton v. Perkins [1958] 1 Lloyd's Rep. 626, Donovan J.

Held, defendants not liable: "A wet deck, as such, must be commonplace in a barge and certainly by itself is not evidence of negligence, and I think the same is true of the slope of the deck" (629. col. 2).

28. Ali v. Ellerman & Bucknall Co. [1958] 1 Lloyd's Rep. 630, Slade J.

Held, defendants not liable.

29. Ashford v. Scruttons [1958] 2 Lloyd's Rep. 223, C.A.

Plaintiff dock labourer guiding load of pipes into hold got hand caught when load struck stanchion, causing pipes to shift—*Held*, defendants not liable. Hodson L.J. (228, col. 1): "The man caught his hand and it seems to me that that is the sort of risk which must necessarily be run by anybody who is guiding a suspended cargo with his hand."

30. Croxford v. Scruttons [1958] 2 Lloyd's Rep. 493, Hilbery J.
Held, defendants not liable: "This is a type of work which has, like so many types of work ... a hazard connected with it" (499, col. 2).

31. Smith v. Hovey [1960] 1 Lloyd's Rep. 457, Hilbery J.

Plaintiff stevedore injured when bale of woodpulp he was manhandling in hold of ship slipped—plaintiff complained that the stowage of bales of woodpulp on top of bundles of steel rods caused a dangerously uneven working surface in hold—*Held*, defendants not liable, as the method of stowage was a customary one, and there had never been any complaints about it. In addition, the judge, in negativing negligence, took into account the fact that when awkward parts of the cargo were reached in the course of unloading, the piecework rates were adjusted on the spot.

32. Blackwell v. Port of London Stevedoring [1962] 2 Lloyd's Rep. 245, Glyn-Jones J.

Held, defendants not liable.

33. Mawson v. Unilever [1963] 2 Lloyd's Rep. 198, Scarman J.

Held, ordinary risk of occupation, and defendants not liable for not stopping the work.

34. Jones v. Freight Conveyors [1966] 1 Lloyd's Rep. 593, C.A.

35. White v. Holbrook Precision Castings Ltd [1985] I.R.L.R. 215; [1985] C.L.Y. 232, C.A. See Chap. 15, (2) (d) **34** for further details.

36. Bacon v. Jack Tighe (Offshore) and Cape Scaffolding [1987] C.L.Y. 2568, H.H. Judge Whitehead, Lincoln County Court. See Chap. 15, (2) (a) **26** for further details.

37. Nilsson v. Redditch B.C. [1994] C.L.Y. 2299, C.A.
See Chap. 15, (2) (h) **19** for further details.

U1. Ferner v. Kemp Bros (1960) C.A. 176 A

Plaintiff an experienced plumber fell through asbestos roof because his crawling board was not positioned at both ends over purlins—*Held*, defendants not liable: "An experienced workman must know the ordinary risks of the work which he does and which he is employed to do. In the doing of that work he is expected to take the ordinary routine precautions which are common to that work, and should not be expected to be told by his employer of every danger which might arise and every step that should be taken in order to counteract that danger" (Ormerod L.J., 9 F).

U2. Vernon v. Morland Stevedoring (1961) C.A. 297

Held, defendant stevedores not liable for requiring plaintiff to discharge a Russian ship whose deck cargo consisted of irregular pieces of pig-iron strewn all over deck.

U3. Baker v. White's Window Clearing (1962) C.A. 69

Plaintiff window cleaner fell when ring attached to sash of window broke—the rings were known to both plaintiff and defendants to be treacherous and liable to break—defendants had complained to owners—*Held*, defendants two-thirds liable as they should have given express instructions to plaintiff not to put any strain on the rings. *N.B.* Court of Appeal in upholding judgment regarded case as a borderline one.

U4. Jones v. Combined Optical Industries (1984) C.A. 240

Male employee came into slight physical contact with small lightly built female employee who was off balance and fell. Had she not been off balance, degree of contact would have been insufficient to cause her to fall—*Held*, in absence of something in nature of deliberate barge, mere physical contact would not constitute negligence.

U5. Masterman v. Humberside C.C. (1984) C.A. 622

See Chap. 15, (2) (f) **U2** for further details.

U6. Taylor v. British Gas Corporation (1986) C.A. 906

See Chap. 15, (2) (h) **U6** for further details.

U7. Chrost v. B.S.C. (1987) C.A., 575

Plaintiff slipped on Swarfega that had fallen from a wall dispenser. His job was to clean the floor—*Held*, defendant not negligent and not in breach of the Factories Act 1961, s. 28(1). Some Swarfega would have got on floor even had the dispensers been located over the sinks.

U8. Babinski v. Atlantic Steam Navigation Co. Ltd (1988) C.A. 462

Plaintiff was crossing loading bay of the ro-ro ferry on which he worked when he was struck by a juggernaut—*Held*, defendant ferry operator not liable. They provided specific places for persons to cross the loading bay and warning by flashing lights and sirens when vehicles were loading. Moreover, the juggernauts were difficult to miss.

U9. Bundell v. Portsea Island Mutual Co-operation Society Ltd (1988) C.A. 791

Plaintiff warehouseman ascended a ladder to put a ticket in a roll of carpet shelved 12 feet above the floor. While he was holding onto a shelving upright, the ladder slipped and he fell. Ladder was not secured or footed—*Held*, defendant not liable. In the circumstances, the ladder was a proper means of access for the plaintiff's task. Many people such as painters, window cleaners, library workers and housewives would use a ladder in similar circumstances.

U10. Folawiyo v. Riverside H.A. (1988) C.A. 1010

Plaintiff, an experienced nurse, injured her spine when lifting a patient who resisted her efforts into a sitting position. The patient had had a cerebral vascular accident. Such patients were known to plaintiff to be prone to difficult, unco-operative and aggressive behaviour—*Held*, defendant not liable. Plaintiff knew of the patient's propensity. No warning was necessary. Help was available in case of need.

U11. Armstrong v. B.S.C. (1989) C.A. 118

Security officer patrolling direct site at 2 a.m. using torch tripped over debris on ground—*Held*, *inter alia*, employer not liable at common law. It would be unreasonable to require pointless clearing of the debris with which the area was strewn—provision of torch sufficient.

U12. Gilbert v. Lane's Storage and Removals Ltd (1991) C.A. 767

Plaintiff stepped down 12 inches from tailgate of furniture removal vehicle to the ground when unloading sofa, and fell—*Held*, defendant not liable—not unreasonable to expect a removal man to cope with a 12-inch drop.

U13. Minogue v. The London Residuary Body (1994) C.A. 934

Plaintiff slipped in school kitchen on water spilt on floor as dishes were transferred from one sink to another. Staff were instructed to mop up spillages immediately, and mops, buckets, floor-cloths and non-slip shoes were provided—*Held*, defendant not liable—the system of work was safe.

(m) Where Work Carried On on Others' Premises

		Liable or not
Bomb-damaged house	1	No
Ship under repair—defective staging	2	No
Ship under repair	3	No
Ship under repair—several repairers—open tank top	4	Yes
Jetty—hole causing bogie to overturn	5	Yes
FACTORY—PAINTING CRANES—ASKING IF SAFE	6	No
Houses—cleaning windows	7	Yes
Unloading ship—bad light and open hole in hold	8	Yes

Unloading ship—dangerous hole in hold	9	No
Unloading ship—defective wooden shore	10	No
Unloading—slippery dock shed	11	Yes
Ship under repair—repair of circulating pump	12	No
Unloading ship—unsafe winch platform	13	Yes
Private house—plumber electrocuted in loft	14	No
Dock—dangerous projection from machine	15	No
Unloading barge—defective batten	16	No
Unloading ship—defective hatch cover	17	No
Tunnelling in mine—owner laying down method of support—fall of roof	18	No
ROUTE ACROSS TO WORK—SAFE LONG ROUTE—ALSO SHORT ROUTE PROVING UNSAFE	19	No
FACTORY—OCCUPIED BY THIRD PARTY—UNSUITABLE LIFTING CHAINS SUPPLIED BY THIRD PARTY	20	Yes
Unloading ship—bad stowage—generally	21	
Unloading ship—bad stowage—standard of care to be observed by unloading stevedores	22	No
BUILDING SITE—OTHER WORKMEN—CAUSING MATERIAL TO FALL DOWN SHAFT WHERE PLAINTIFF WORKING	23	No
DUTY ON OTHERS' PREMISES RESTATED GENERALLY	24	
PRIVATE HOUSE—WINDOW CLEANING—DEFECTIVE SASH HANDLE	24	No
Duty on others' premises restated generally	25	
Machine house—lift repairer—door defective	25	Yes
Employer ordinarily entitled to assume other premises safe—unless put on inquiry	25	
Ship—defective ladder to hold	26	No
BARGE—NARROW UNFENCED CATWALK	27	No
SHIP—INSECURE LADDER TO LIGHTER	28	Yes
Transit shed—broken step	29	No
SHIP—SENDING DOCK WORKER TO UNLIT HOLD WITH UNFENCED HATCH	30	Yes
FACTORY—WORK ON GIRDERS—PLAINTIFF LEFT TO MAKE OWN ARRANGEMENTS	31	Yes
Sub-contractor—liable to own employee for not complaining to main contractor of untidiness of site	32	Yes
EMPLOYEE SENT TO WORK IN SAUDI ARABIA—HOLE IN FLOOR—PRINCIPLES RESTATED	33	No
WINDOW CLEANER—EMPLOYER SHOULD WARN NOT TO WORK FROM OUTSIDE SILL UNLESS HARNESS ANCHOR POINTS AVAILABLE	34	Yes
Employer must satisfy himself as to safety of outside premises	U1	Yes

1. Taylor v. Sims [1942] 2 All E.R. 375; [1942] W.N. 124, Lewis J.

Held, defendant employers not liable, as there was "very great difficulty" in holding that they were under any duty to see house—not occupied by them—was safe. Applied in **14.** Disapproved by C.A. in **24.**

2. Hodgson v. British Arc Welding [1946] 1 K.B. 302; [1946] 1 All E.R. 95, Hilbery J.

Held, defendats (who were sub-contractors) not liable, because they were not in occupation nor responsible for the staging which caused accident. Approved by C.A. in **24**, *q.v.* for correct *ratio decidendi.*

3. Breedon v. London Graving Dock (1946) 79 Ll.L.R. 329, Lewis J.

Held, employers (who had sent plaintiff, a chargehand, to ship) not liable: "In my view it is not the law that when a person sends workmen to premises occupied by someone else, over which he has no control, it is the duty of the employer to see that the premises are reasonably safe, much less first to ensure they are safe" (332).

4. Donovan v. Cammell Laird [1949] 2 All E.R. 82; 82 Ll.L.R. 642, Devlin J.

Cammell Laird were engaged in repairing ship along with other repairers—they were not occupiers of ship, but there was an open tank top near where plaintiff, employed by Cammell Laird, was working—down which he fell—*Held*, Cammell Laird liable because they failed "to provide a safe system of work and a safe place of work" (84 H). "No one exercised any co-ordinating function or final supervision to see that the place was safe to work in" (86 A). The question of Cammell Laird not being occupiers was not apparently raised, but that may be because they were treated as being in occupation of the relevant part of the ship, or because Cammell Laird's fault was as much system as place of work, or because (apparently, though judge does not expressly say so) Cammell Laird's men had lowered a lifeline round the tank top.

5. Bright v. Thames Stevedoring [1951] 1 Lloyd's Rep. 116, Pritchard J.

Plaintiff bogie driver thrown from bogie by hole in jetty—jetty not owned or occupied by defendants—*Held*, defendants liable for not putting light on bogie (so that this may be an example of unsafe plant rather than workplace).

6. Bott v. Prothero Steel Tube (1951) 95 S.J. 834; [1951] W.N. 595, C.A.

Contractors going to paint factory cranes ask if safe—are told yes—one moves while being painted—*Held*, contractors not liable, as they had laid out work properly, and that factory owners were solely liable.

7. General Cleaning Contractors v. Christmas [1953] A.C. 180; [1952] 2 All E.R. 1110, H.L.

Held, defendants, window cleaning employers, liable for failing to devise a safe system on premises which might contain defects of a known type (*i.e.* defective sashes). See Chap. 15, (4) (b) **3**.

8. Byrne v. Clan Line [1952] 2 Lloyd's Rep. 598, Ormerod J.

Bad lighting in hold and missing bilge boards, creating an open hole—shipowners were liable under Dock Regulations—*Held*. stevedores (employers) were also liable in failing to have a safe system of work whereby the defects would have been remedied.

9. Coppin v. Butlers Wharf [1952] 2 Lloyd's Rep. 307, Pearson J.

Dangerous hole in hold of ship—concealed by large quantity of straw—plaintiff employed by stevedores injured—stevedores alone sued—*Held*, they were not negligent in not having straw cleared as work progressed, and although hole was a dangerous trap, that was the responsibility of shipowners alone.

10. Thomson v. Cremin [1956] 1 W.L.R. 103n.; [1953] 2 All E.R. 1185, H.L.

Defective wooden shore falls on plaintiff unloading ship—*Held*, the stevedore employers were not liable, as in the absence of special circumstances of suspicion, they were under no duty to inspect the structure of the ship. Applied in **17** and **18**.

11. Reid v. Elder Dempster [1953] 1 Lloyd's Rep. 347, Barry J.

Floor of dock shed slippery with unswept groundnuts—plaintiff slips—employed by defendants who are using shed for discharge of cargo—but defendants are not occupiers—*Held*, defendants liable for failure to provide safe place of work: "This is not a case where defendants came to this berth for the first time on the morning of November 14, 1949. Had it been such a case, a very different consideration would arise. It might well be unreasonable to say that before sending any of their men onto a berth of this kind they should conduct a detailed examination of the floor . . . " (351). In fact defendants had been discharging at the berth for 18 months, and had discharged previous ship there.

12. Cushway v. Mills and Knight [1953] 2 Lloyd's Rep. 273, Streatfeild J.

Plaintiff employed by defendant repairers to repair circulating pump on ship—on removal of cover plate scalding water came out—*Held*, defendants' duty was merely to report to ship work was going to be done, and to rely on ship's engineer to see that the necessary valves were turned off, and since defendants had so reported, therefore not liable (*N.B.* Ship was held liable.)

13. Nelson v. P.S.N. [1953] 2 Lloyd's Rep. 685, Gerrard J.

Held, employers (as well as ship) liable for causing or permitting plaintiff to work on a winch platform which was not reasonably safe (689). Platform was small, unfenced and 41 inches high. *But* both defendants were represented by same counsel, and extent of duty on employer may not have been fully canvassed.

14. Cilia v. James [1954] 1 W.L.R. 721; [1954] 2 All E.R. 9, Byrne J.

Plumber's mate electrocuted in loft of empty house—*Held*, applying **1**, that defendant employer was under no duty to take reasonable steps to see that premises were reasonably safe. Dictum of Denning L.J. in C.A. to the contrary in **7** not applied. *But* judge went on to find that, even if there was a duty, plaintiff must fail on the facts, as the danger was not foreseeable. Applied in **17**. Disapproved on first point by C.A. in **24**.

15. Ryan v. Maltby [1954] 1 Lloyd's Rep. 196, Hilbery J.

Welding machine left unlit at night on dockside with towbar projecting into passageway—*Held*, defendant employers not liable (but owners of machine were).

16. Hurley v. B.T.C. [1954] 2 Lloyd's Rep. 343, Pilcher J.

Held (*obiter*, because batten was found not defective) that it could not be supposed defendant employers were under a duty to inspect when they had not the slightest idea there was a defect (351, col. 1).

17. Hinson v. Morgan Scanlon [1954] 2 Lloyd's Rep. 564, McNair J.

Held, defendant stevedores not liable for failing to inspect: " . . . unless there is some very special circumstances or something manifestly wrong with the barge and its fitments, the master stevedores are entitled to take the barge as they find it, and are under no general duty of taking reasonable care to see that the barge and its fitments are safe" (571, col. 1). **10** and **14** applied.

18. Szumczyk v. Associated Tunnelling [1956] 1 W.L.R. 98; [1956] 1 All E.R. 126, Ashworth J.

See Chap. 15, (2)(a) **12**—*Held*, defendant employers not liable—dictum in **10** applied. *Upheld* (unreported) by C.A.

19. Ashdown v. Samuel Williams [1957] 1 Q.B. 409; [1957] 1 All E.R. 35, C.A.

A longer safe route provided—short route commonly used proves unsafe but defendants could not have foreseen this—casual act of negligence by servant of occupiers—*Held*, defendant employers not liable.

20. Gledhill v. Liverpool Abattoir [1957] 1 W.L.R. 1028; [1957] 3 All E.R. 117, C.A.

Employers of plaintiff engaged in slinging pigs in abattoir owned and occupied by corporation—corporation supply unsuitable chains—other employees complain to employers—accident—*Held*, employers liable. *N.B.* This part of the case was not appealed.

21. See cases in Chap. 7, (2)(d).

22. Fittock v. Shaw Savill [1957] 2 Lloyd's Rep. 149, Glyn-Jones J.

Bad stowage of sacks calling for extra exertion by men unloading—plaintiff sustains hernia unloading—sues his employers—*Held*, not liable: "A shipowner (*i.e.* here the employer of plaintiff in unloading) cannot be expected to say that (not to unload) unless as a reasonable man he could foresee that the work he is setting his stevedores to do is calculated to cause an injury, in other words, that it would involve such excessive exertion that any reasonable man could foresee not only the remote possibility of injury but a reasonable risk . . . "

23. Baily v. Ayr Engineering [1958] 2 W.L.R. 882; [1958] 2 All E.R. 222, C.A.

Held, employers not liable as not reasonably foreseeable.

24. Wilson v. Tyneside Window Cleaning [1958] 2 Q.B. 110; [1958] 2 All E.R. 265, C.A.

Whole question of employers' duty to servants working on other premises reviewed—*Cilia v. James* **14** and *Taylor v. Sims* **1**, which laid down that an employer owed no duty, disapproved; equally, dicta to the other extreme by Denning L.J. in the *Christmas* case **7** in the C.A. disapproved—*Held*, that the correct position was that the employers' duty in such circumstances was merely one aspect of his general duty to use reasonable care, and that what was reasonable would vary with the circumstances, and one important circumstance in this respect was whether the premises were under control of employer. Pearce L.J. (271 E): "Whether the servant is working on the premises of the master or on those of a stranger, that duty is still the same; but as a matter of common sense its performance and discharge will probably be vastly different in the two cases. The master's own premises are under his own control . . . If however a master sends his plumber to mend a leak in a respectable private house, no one could hold him negligent for not visiting the house himself . . . Additional safeguards intended to reinforce the man's own knowledge and skill in surmounting difficulties or dangers may be reasonable in the former case (on master's own premises) but impracticable and unreasonable in the latter. So viewed the question whether the master was in control of the premises ceases to be a matter of technicality and becomes merely one of the ingredients, albeit a very important one, in a consideration of the question of fact whether in all the circumstances the master took reasonable steps. That is the reasoning of this court in *Biddle v. Hart* [1907] 1 K.B. 649." Parker L.J. (273 H): "In so far as . . . the making of the premises safe cannot be fully performed, as when they are in possession of a third party, it behoves the master to exercise all the more care in regard to his system of working." The facts were that a window handle of a house frequently cleaned by plaintiff, an experienced man, came away in his hand—*Held*, defendant employer not liable, as in the circumstances defendant was not in breach of his duty as to safety of premises, nor as to system, inasmuch as he was not at fault in failing to inspect, nor was there any need to warn experienced men against this danger, nor was it established that instructions should have been given as to the method of cleaning. *Approved* in **25**. *Applied* in **26**.

25. Smith v. Austin Lifts [1959] 1 W.L.R. 100; [1959] 1 All E.R. 81, H.L.

Plaintiff lift repairer injured when defective door on third party premises gives way—had several times reported to defendant employers it was defective—but the defect on occasion of accident was a different one (door jammed so as to be a trap)—*Held*, in these circumstances defendants liable (Lord Reid dissenting, Lord Simonds *dubitante*). Lords Morton and Denning based their decision on the reports made by plaintiff to defendants—Lord Somervell did likewise, but in language ("I am not prepared to disagree with this finding") which showed some degree of doubt. **24** expressly approved by Lords Reid and Denning. Lord Denning (94 E) said that in the absence of plaintiff's reports defendants "would have been entitled to assume that the means of access provided by the occupiers was reasonably safe."

26. Mace v. R.H. Green [1959] 2 Q.B. 14; [1959] 1 All E.R. 655, Lord Parker C.J.

Held, defendant employers not liable as (following **24**) there was nothing to suggest that a reasonable employer should have to go and inspect the ladder (657 H).

27. Swales v. I.C.I. [1960] 1 Lloyd's Rep. 124, C.A.

Plaintiff stevedore working on catwalk 18 inches wide—protected by hatch covers stacked outboard—bargeowners removed some covers leaving a gap through which plaintiff fell—*Held*, defendant employers not liable, as no evidence they knew or ought to have known of danger (but bargeowners were liable).

28. Wingfield v. Ellerman's Wilson [1960] 2 Lloyd's Rep. 16, C.A.

Plaintiff employed by shipowner defendants to unload tomatoes from ship to lighter—lightermen erected insecure ladder which slipped and threw plaintiff—*Held*, defendants liable. Devlin L.J. (22):

> "I think that formulation of the question 'What would a prudent employer order or require to be done before he was satisfied that arrangements had been made for the safety of his employees' puts the point in the way in which I should like to put it in this case . . . It is normally unreasonable to expect an employer to examine and test tools bought from a reputable manufacturer, it is unreasonable to expect him to go and inspect established buildings or public transport, but in my judgment it is not at all unreasonable to expect him to look into the means of access to a lighter on which his men have to work."

29. Fisher v. P.L.A. [1962] 1 All E.R. 458, Stevenson J.

Plaintiff tally clerk employed by shipping company slipped on broken step of transit shed owned and controlled by Port of London Authority—*Held*, shipping company not liable to plaintiff (but P.L.A. were).

30. Henry v. Mersey Ports Stevedoring [1963] 2 Lloyd's Rep. 97, C.A.

Loading ship—employing stevedores sent plaintiff to 'tween deck which was in darkness and contained unfenced hatch—*Held*, employers liable.

31. Thompson v. British Oxygen (1965) 109 S.J. 194, C.A.

Plaintiff, an experienced man, sent by defendants to assist in installing oxygen pipes in a factory—to do so he had to go up on to girders—he trod on a small unsuitable plank which broke—there should have been staging—*Held*, it was the defendants' duty, as in window-cleaning cases, to lay out the work and give proper instructions, and they were liable (but one-third contributory negligence).

32. Smith v. Vange [1970] 1 W.L.R. 733; [1970] 1 All E.R. 249, MacKenna J.

33. Cook v. Square D. Ltd [1992] I.C.R. 262; [1992] P.I.Q.R. P33, C.A.

Plaintiff, engineer employed by first defendant, sent to work at premises in Saudi Arabia occupied by second defendant, at which third defendant was main contractor. Plaintiff's foot went through hole, of which he was aware, caused by the moving of a tile in floor of control room where he worked, probably by a sub-contractor—*Held*, first defendant not liable. Where employee injured on premises occupied by third party, circumstances to be taken into account in determining extent of employers' duty to employee included (a) place where work is to be done, (b) nature of the building (if any) on the site, (c) experience of employee, (d) nature of his work on the premises, (e) degree of control the employer can reasonably exercise and (f) employer's knowledge, if any, of defective state of premises. Here, first defendant knew second and third defendants were reliable and responsible companies; could not be responsible for daily events in Saudi Arabia; and was under no duty to advise second and third defendants to take precautions against kind of hazard which plaintiff encountered.

34. King v. Smith, *The Times*, November 3, 1994; [1994] C.L.Y. 2284, C.A.

See Chap. 15, (2)(c) **24** for further details.

U1. Zelowbouski v. Long (1963) C.A. 116

Plaintiff was sent to paint the lid of a large cylinder which tilted and threw him—*Held*, defendant employers liable. Dictum of Lord Goddard C.J. in *Bates v. Parker* [1953] 1 All E.R. 768 at 770 H, applied: "Where a householder employs an independent contractor to do work . . . the contractor must satisfy himself as to the safety or condition of that part of the premises on which he is to work."

(3) Proof of Negligence

(*N.B.* Generally see also Chap. 3, (1).)

1. Youngman v. Pirelli [1940] 1 K.B. 1; 109 L.J.K.B. 420, C.A.

Deceased a linesman up pole—on reaching tie bar he collapsed and died—no evidence as to how body came into contact with current—*Held*, no evidence of negligence, as accident was perfectly consistent with deceased having touched live wire.

2. O'Flaherty v. E. Smith Coggins (1951) 95 S.J. 685; [1951] C.L.C. 6775, C.A.

Plaintiff a member of gang handling heavy crate which is dropped on plaintiff—cause of accident unexplained—*Held*, defendants not liable (reversing Donovan J.).

3. Rysdale v. Blackfriars Lighterage [1952] 2 Lloyd's Rep. 31, Barry J.

Plaintiff proves that his accident occurred because a hatch cover was defective and gave way—no explanation or evidence as to how the accident came about—*Held*, plaintiff succeeded: "It is not of course for plaintiff to satisfy me affirmatively how this could have happened" (37).

4. Pipe v. Chambers Wharf [1952] 1 Lloyd's Rep. 194, Streatfeild J.

After the accident a mobile crane was used instead of manhandling—*Held*, defendants not liable: "Nothing is so perfect it cannot be improved. If after every accident some improvement is inaugurated it does not follow from that that the system originally followed was a breach of duty" (195).

5. Evans v. Bustard [1952] 1 Lloyd's Rep. 81, C.A.

Breast rope (*i.e.* rope between ship's rails and top of gangway) too low—defendants say in accordance with general practice—*Held*, defendants had not proved this, and were liable (see Birkett L.J. at 87).

6. Gray v. Admiralty [1953] 1 Lloyd's Rep. 14, Ormerod J.

Plaintiff employed by defendants tripped on a staircase (which was found to be safe) and put hand through glass panel of door—after the accident defendants put stouter glass in door—*Held*, this was no evidence of negligence in the original condition of the door.

7. Birchall v. Bibby [1953] 1 All E.R. 163; [1953] 1 Lloyd's Rep. 175, Jones J.

Hoist rope breaks—*res ipsa loquitur*—*Held*, on the facts, that defendants had proved rope was maliciously cut by unknown person and were therefore not liable.

8. Tillett v. Doig [1953] 2 Lloyd's Rep. 707, C.A.

Staging collapses because wedge removed—defendants plead it was done by some unauthorised person—*Held*, since defendants were in control of staging onus of proving this was on them, and as they had failed to discharge it, therefore they were liable.

9. Basted v. Cozens and Sutcliffe [1954] 2 Lloyd's Rep. 132, Devlin J.

Plaintiff required by defendants to work under suspended load of crane (which falls on plaintiff)—defendants try to say no practicable alternative—*Held*, liable: "Once I am satisfied, as I am satisfied, that no system of work looking towards the safety of the employee was properly considered, the burden passes to defendants to establish that, even if such consideration had been given, it would not have mattered because they had adopted the only system that in the circumstances could possibly have been adopted" (145, col. 2). *N.B.* In this same case, the craneowners were also sued and found liable, and judge said words to the effect that once a defect, such as a sudden descent of the fall of a crane, was established, where defendants alone had knowledge of the facts, the onus lay on defendants to make all information available to the court and to establish that a proper system of maintenance was in force.

10. Hurley v. Sanders [1955] 1 W.L.R. 470; [1955] 1 All E.R. 833, Glyn-Jones J.

Plaintiff slipped while descending altar courses of dry dock—judge found this method of access without safety devices was dangerous—*Held*, therefore, onus passed to defendants to establish not practicable to avert danger, which onus defendants had not discharged and were therefore liable.

11. McDonald v. B.T.C. [1955] 1 W.L.R. 1323; [1955] 3 All E.R. 789, Pilcher J.

Railway wagon with dangerous hole in it—*Held*, defendants liable: "If a situation of danger is shown to exist and the onus rests under the Factories Acts on an employer to show that he has done what was reasonably practicable ... I do not see why the same onus should not rest on an employer at common law to show in parallel circumstances that he has exercised due care for the safety of his servants" (791 F).

12. Brophy v. Bradfield [1955] 1 W.L.R. 1148; [1955] 3 All E.R. 286, C.A.

Held, defendants not liable, as proof of accident did not shift onus to them, and if it did, the fact boiler had worked satisfactorily for 25 years was an answer.

13. Moore v. R. Fox and Sons [1956] 1 Q.B. 596; [1956] 1 All E.R. 182, C.A.

Held, defendants liable. See Chap. 3, (1) (g) **12**, particularly for statement of standard of proof required of defendants to discharge onus.

14. Webster v. Knohr and Buchard [1956] 1 Lloyd's Rep. 271, C.A.

Held, county court judge was justified in finding that bad stowage was not cause of accident. Denning L.J. (272): "Certainly if there was no evidence of any other likely cause (other than bad stowage), it would be the inevitable inference (that it was the cause of the accident). But in this case there was evidence that other causes might cause a slip of the bags."

15. Balfour v. Wm. Beardmore, 1956 S.L.T. 205. O.H.

Held, since publication of interim report of Committee on Dust in Steel Foundries in 1944 defendants could not plead they could not reasonably have foreseen the danger of pneumoconiosis from foundry dust.

16. Graham v. C.W.S. [1957] 1 W.L.R. 511; [1957] 1 All E.R. 654, Devlin J.

See Chap. 15, (2) (g) **6** for full details.

17. Brown v. Rolls-Royce [1960] 1 W.L.R. 210; [1960] 1 All E.R. 577, H.L.

Industrial dermatitis from oil—plaintiff proved defendants did not supply barrier cream, and that other employers commonly did—he argued that this shifted the onus to defendants, and that it was then for them to show they had not been negligent—*Held*, not so, as there were other material facts (such as that defendants' doctor advised against barrier cream), and that it was for plaintiff to show on the sum of these facts that defendants had been negligent. Lord Denning (581 I) said it was important "to distinguish between a *legal* burden, properly so called, and a *provisional* burden which is raised by the state of the evidence. The *legal* burden in this case was imposed by law on the appellant (plaintiff) ... In order to discharge the burden ... the appellant (plaintiff) proved that barrier cream is commonly supplied by employers to men doing such work as the appellant was doing. This was a cogent piece of evidence and raised no doubt a 'presumption' or a 'prima facie' case in this sense, that, if nothing more appeared, the court might well infer defendants were negligent, and in that sense it put a burden on defendants to answer it. But this was only a *provisional* burden which was raised by the state of the evidence as it then stood."

18. Davies v. Manchester Ship Canal [1960] 2 Lloyd's Rep. 11, C.A.

Spade hook (called a slipper) slipped from paper reel which was being pulled upright—as a result fell back onto plaintiff—after accident deeper hooks were used—during previous 25 years six to eight minor injuries from same cause—but joint safety committee had never suggested using different hooks—*Held*, defendants not liable.

19. Gardiner v. Motherwell Machinery Co. [1961] 1 W.L.R. 1424; [1961] 3 All E.R. 831, H.L.

Dermatitis—plaintiff demolition worker working among dirt and grease—question was whether dermatitis was due to working conditions—plaintiff had never had dermatitis before—the dirt and grease were capable of causing dermatitis—and the onset of the disease had been typical of dermatitis caused by such conditions—*Held*, these facts established a prima facie presumption that the disease was due to the working conditions. "When a man who has not previously suffered from a disease contracts that disease after being subjected to conditions likely to cause it, and when he shows that it starts in a way typical of disease caused by such conditions, he establishes a prima facie presumption that his disease was caused by those conditions"—(Lord Reid, 831 I).

20. Vernon v. British Transport Docks Board [1963] 1 Lloyd's Rep. 55, C.A.

Sellers L.J. (60): "I do not myself attach importance to the fact in itself that after the accident some extra precaution was taken. It is never, I think, quite reliable evidence in itself . . . "

21. Pearce v. Round Oak Steel Works [1969] 1 W.L.R. 595; [1969] 3 All E.R. 680 C.A.

Bolt in machine broke through metal fatigue—machine manufactured circa 1930 and bought secondhand by defendants in 1959—defendants called no evidence—*Held*, liable, as burden was on defendants to show that they had taken reasonable precautions, and this they had failed to do.

22. McGhee v. N.C.B. [1973] 1 W.L.R. 1; [1972] 3 All E.R. 1008, H.L.

Plaintiff working in clouds of abrasive brick dust—no washing facilities—dermatitis—but no positive evidence that it was more probable than not that he would not have got dermatitis if adequate washing facilities provided—the failure to provide washing facilities was a breach of duty (as found) owed by the defendants—*Held*, the failure by the defendants had on the evidence materially increased the risk of dermatitis, which for practical purposes was equal to a finding that the failure had materially contributed to the risk, and defendants were therefore liable.

23. Clowes v. N.C.B., *The Times*, April 23, 1987; [1987] C.L.Y. 2565, C.A.

Plaintiff got off train which had taken him and other miners to lift at end of shift, fell and was trampled on by other miners—could not say how fell, but contended must have been pushed by other men. There was evidence that men would get off train while still moving and run to lift, despite defendant's efforts to stop this practice—*Held*, in absence of any other explanation, judge entitled to infer that undisciplined conduct of other miners, for which defendant vicariously liable, had caused accident.

24. Bryce v. Swan Hunter Group plc [1987] 2 Lloyd's Rep. 426; [1988] 1 All E.R. 659, Phillips J.

Deceased worked as painter in shipyards from time to time between 1937 and 1942, 1946 and 1950 and 1958 and 1970. Limited exposure to abestos dust during first period, substantial exposure during second and third. Died of mesothelioma in 1981, as a result of exposure to asbestos dust. Widow sued three former employes, for whom deceased had worked for total of 399 days in 1947, between 1958 and 1962 and in 1970—*Held*,

(a) Having regard to Factories Inspectorate literature between 1932 and 1956 defendants should have appreciated at times of plaintiff's employments by them that exposure to asbestos dust was likely to be injurious to employees, and were under a duty at common law, of which they were in breach, to reduce, though not altogether to prevent, such exposure.
(b) Defendants also in breach of statutory duty.
(c) Deceased's additional exposure to asbestos dust due to defendants' breaches of duty, was significant, but less than he would have experienced in any event during his working life.
(d) Widow could not prove on balance of probabilities that additional fibres inhaled by deceased due to breaches of duty of any one of the defendants caused the mesothelioma: neither could any defendant prove to same standard that its breaches of duty were not at least a contributory cause of the mesothelioma.
(e) Widow entitled to invoke principle in *McGhee v. N.C.B.* (**22** above) that if conduct of a particular kind creates or increases a risk of injury to another, and a defendant owes to a plaintiff a duty not to conduct himself in that way, then if defendant is in breach of such duty and plaintiff suffers such injury, the injury is taken to have been caused by the breach of duty even though the existence or extent of the contribution made by the breach cannot be ascertained.
(f) In the instant case, defendants' breaches of duty increased risk of deceased's developing mesothelioma, whether by adding to the number of possible initiators of the condition or producing cumulative effect on reduction of deceased's body defence mechanism. Deceased in fact developed mesothelioma. Each defendant must accordingly be taken to have caused the mesothelioma by its breach of duty.

25. Hanlon v. B.R.B., 1991 S.L.T. 228; [1991] C.L.Y. 5303

Railwoman slipped in puddle of water and oil or grease on railway platform—*Held*, she had failed to establish that substance had been present for such a time that a reasonable system of inspection, maintenance and cleaning would have led to its discovery and removal before the accident.

26. Gitsham v. C.H. Pearce & Sons [1992] P.I.Q.R. P57; *The Times*, February 11, 1991, C.A.

Plaintiff slipped on snow and ice when crossing road on defendant's six-acre weather-exposed site in harsh weather conditions. Defendant treated snow and ice by mechanical salt and sand spreader—process should have finished by time of accident—*Held*, defendants not in breach of the Factories Act 1961, s. 29(1), or negligent. Even if relevant area had not been treated (as to which trial judge made no finding) judge was entitled to find that defendant was doing everything reasonably practicable, taking into account severity of weather and size of site. *Per* Stocker L.J. "The fact that the system might for one reason or another have been running late does not itself in my view establish that the system was not being properly put into effect."

27. Flagg v. Kent C.C. [1993] P.I.Q.R. P389, C.A.

Plaintiff, a senior fire officer, who had agreed to act as second safety officer while other officers performed exercise in smoke chamber, had to make his way to his position in the chamber in the dark. In doing so, he tripped over a steel rod protruding downwards to the floor from the side of a pipe through which those on the exercise had to crawl—*Held*, defendant liable in negligence and under Occupier's Liability Act 1957. It was defendant's duty not to place unnecessary hazards in plaintiff's way when not performing the exercise. Defendant should have removed protruding rods, or warned plaintiff about them, or put lights on. *Per* Glidewell L.J.: the trial judge should have taken into account that after accident defendant had removed protruding rods, even if he had then concluded that this was with benefit of hindsight and of little weight.

U1. Foster v. British Electricity Authority (1952) C.A. 200

Deceased linesman electrocuted up pylon—some conductors thereon live some cut off—warning pennants were out but were in wrong place—*Held*, defendants liable, as it could be inferred that the position of the pennants was a cause of the accident.

U2. Jackson v. Post Office (1953) C.A. 80

Plaintiff a linesman employed by Post Office to do a job called rodding (*i.e.* joining long rods)—while using spanner to tighten rod, backlash occurred so that spanner was flung into plaintiff's eye—defendants admitted that backlash was to be expected and that it was a dangerous operation—but called no evidence as to precautions taken or the practicability of other precautions—*Held*, defendants liable.

U3. Fowler v. Hoffman Manufacturing Co. (1960) C.A. 311

Sellers L.J. (3A): "The learned judge stated, and I think rightly stated, that because the condition had been improved that ought not to be regarded as showing a breach of duty or negligence at some previous time."

U4. Mirchandani v. Pyrene (1968) C.A. 256

Bursting of fire extinguisher on being filled—alleged failure to test under pressure beforehand—plaintiff proved (a) extinguisher had burst at 500 pressure, (b) it should have been tested at 750, and (c), by interrogatory, defendants were unable to say whether it had been tested or not—*Held*, plaintiff has established prima facie case which in default of answer entitled him to judgment.

U5. Reynolds v. B.S.C. (1977) C.A. 128

Sheeting up railway wagon—plaintiff thrown when rope suddenly broke—defendants called no evidence—*Held*, applying *Henderson v. Henry Jenkins* (Chap. 3, (1) (g) **20**, plaintiff's evidence had made it more probable than not that the rope broke because of some defect which the defendants with reasonable care might have discovered, and therefore in the absence of any defence evidence, defendants were liable.

U6. Cousins v. Lambeth, Southwark and Lewisham Area H.A. (1986) C.A. 225

Plaintiff, a hospital ward receptionist, slipped on water on the floor and injured herself. The floor was cleaned twice daily. If a nurse spilled water she would be expected to mop it up immediately—*Held*, the judge was entitled to infer that a nurse had spilled the water and failed to mop it up, and that defendant was therefore liable for nurse's negligence.

(4) System of Work

(a) Generally

1. Speed v. Swift [1943] 1 All E.R. 539, C.A.

Failure to remove rail while using married gear—*Held* faulty system. "It (system) includes in my opinion, or may include according to circumstances, such matters as the physical layout of the job, the setting of the stage (so to speak), the sequence in which the work is to be carried out, the provision in proper cases of warnings and notices, and the issue of special instructions" (Lord Greene M.R., 542 A).

2. Colfar v. Coggins & Griffiths [1945] 1 All E.R. 326, H.L.

System is "the practice and method adopted in carrying on the master's business of which the master is presumed to be aware," contrasted with "those isolated or day-to-day acts of the servant of which the master is not presumed to be aware" (Lord Simon L.C. at 329 B).

3. Donovan v. Cammell Laird [1949] 2 All E.R. 82 Ll.L.R. 642, Devlin J.

See Chap. 15 (2) (m) **4** for full details—case of a workman employed by one repairer of a number repairing a ship falling down an open tank top—*Held*, defendant employers liable for failing to organise system: "In this there was no system or method at all. What was everybody's business became nobody's business . . . No one exercised any co-ordinating function or final supervision to see that the place was safe to work in" (85–86).

4. Barcock v. Brighton Corporation [1949] 1 K.B. 339; [1949] 1 All E.R. 251, Hilbery J.

Plaintiff injured in explosion during test which following example of others, he carried out in unsafe way—had been told to read regulations—*Held*, defendants liable: "The employers contend that they had provided a safe system, but I do not think that one devises a system of work by saying to the workman: 'Read the regulations, and do not break them.' In my view, that is not devising a system of work" (255 B).

5. Winter v. Cardiff R.D.C. [1950] 1 All E.R. 819; [1950] W.N. 193, H.L.

Held, that the job of lashing down a load on a lorry was not a matter for which the master had to lay down a system. Lord Reid (825 C): "A system of working normally implies that the work consists of a series of similar or somewhat similar operations and the conception of a system of working is not easily applied to a case where only a single act of a particular kind is to be performed. Recently however this obligation has been extended to cover certain cases where only a single operation is involved. I think that the justification for this is that, where an operation is of a complicated or unusual character, an employer careful of the safety of his men would organise it before it was begun and in that sense provide a safe system of working for it. Where such organisation is called for, the employer must provide it, and he cannot delegate his responsibility for it, but cases in which such a duty has been found to exist are comparatively few and it has never even been suggested that such an obligation arises in every case where a group of the employer's servants are doing some work which may involve danger if negligently performed."

6. Basted v. Cozens & Sutcliffe [1954] 2 Lloyd's Rep. 132, Devlin J.

Plaintiff required by defendant employers to work under suspended load of crane (which falls on plaintiff)—defendants try to say no practicable alternative but they had not considered any safe system before the accident—*Held*, defendants liable: "Once I am satisfied, as I am satisfied, that no system of work looking towards the safety of the employee was properly considered, the burden passes to defendants to establish that, even if such consideration had been given, it would not have mattered because they had adopted the only system that in the circumstances could possibly have been adopted" (145, col. 2).

7. Prince v. Carrier Engineering Co. [1955] 1 Lloyd's Rep. 401, Parker L.J.

Plaintiff walking backwards with load fell on debris littering floor—*Held*, defendant employers not liable: "Now, that (the duty of employer to lay out job) is all very well when you are dealing with operations which are of proved danger—window cleaning, climbing ladders and that sort of thing—but for my part I think it would be absurd to say that there were no jobs which could be left to the initiative of men, especially when they are skilled men ... " (404, col. 2).

8. Michaels v. Browne & Eagle [1955] 2 Lloyd's Rep. 433, McNair J.

" ... an employer does not warrant that the system of work operated is absolutely safe, or that no accident will occur during its operation ... nor is the employer necessarily liable on proof that the system ... contains some remote element of risk which was absent from some other available system of work" (437).

9. Cusack v. T. & J. Harrison [1956] 1 Lloyd's Rep. 100, C.A.

Held, defendants not liable for using a latticed metal tray to discharge cartons. Singleton L.J. (104): "But on the whole, they (the employers) are the best judges of the tackle and appliances which should be used. If they adopt some method which is fraught with danger, in the ordinary course some workman or some officer of the union—a safety officer, for instance—will probably point out the danger therefrom, and they will take warning." But see Chap. 15 (2) (a) **5**.

10. Wilson v. Tyneside Window Cleaning [1958] 2 Q.B. 110; [1958] 2 All E.R. 265, C.A.

Parker L.J. (273 H): " ... in so far as ... the making the premises safe cannot be fully performed, as when they are in the possession of a third party, it behoves the master to exercise all the more care in regard to his system of working." *Approved* by Lord Denning in *Smith v. Austin Lifts* (Chap. 15 (2) (m) **25**).

11. Jenner v. Allen West [1959] 1 W.L.R. 554; [1959] 2 All E. R. 115, C.A.

Fatal roof fall due to crawling boards not being used—deceased ordinarily a plumber but was in charge of roofing work, as he had been before—task was unusually awkward and although in general deceased knew boards should be used he had had no instructions from defendants as to how to do work—defendants left it solely to him—no sufficient evidence that task within his competence and experience—*Held*, defendants liable (but two-thirds contributory negligence).

12. Qualcast v. Haynes [1959] 2 W.L.R. 510; [1959] 2 All E.R. 38, H.L.

Lord Denning (45 G): "What is a 'proper system of work' is a matter for evidence, not for the law books. It changes as the conditions of work change. The standard goes up as men become wiser. It does not stand still as the law sometimes does."

13. Kinsella v. Lebus (1963) 108 S.J. 14, C.A.

Defendants had a system for weight lifting whereby an employee could call on another without the latter losing piecework time—the weight in question was 145 lbs—plaintiff tried to lift it himself and sustained injury—*Held*, not a safe system of work, as it could "readily lead to a man hurting himself by merely trying to see if the load was within his capacity" (Willmer L.J.). Pearson L.J. said that, for intermediate weights, such as 145 lbs, *some* system was required from employers, and that the one devised was not adequate, since, if a system of this nature was to be relied on, the help must be readily available, which was not so in the present case. Diplock L.J., however, while not dissenting, indicated that he would have been prepared to find for defendants. See also Chap. 15 (4) (b) **25**.

14. Ross v. Associated Portland Cement [1964] 1 W.L.R. 768; [1964] 2 All E.R. 452, H.L.

Question was whether plaintiff or defendants were responsible for an admitted breach of Factories Act 1937, s. 26 (use of ladder instead of mobile tower)—on this Lord Reid (456 B) said:

> "But it is his (defendant's) responsibility to see that proper instructions are given and proper equipment is available. Where the work is to be done by a person fully skilled in that type of work, he may say: 'Go and plan out the work and come back and discuss the matter if you have any difficulty, or cannot find the equipment you need.' But here Ross was only a chargehand, the respondents had no reason to suppose that he had ever done a job of this sort before, and there is nothing to show that the chief engineer gave him any encouragement to come back and discuss the matter. No account has been taken of the reluctance which a man in Ross's position would naturally feel in going to a chief engineer uninvited to ask for extra equipment ..."

15. McGhee v. N.C.B. [1973] 1 W.L.R. 1; [1972] 3 All E.R. 1008, H.L.

Plaintiff working in clouds of abrasive brick dust—no washing facilities—dermatitis—but no positive evidence that it was more probable than not that he would not have got dermatitis if adequate washing facilities provided—the failure to provide washing facilities was a breach of duty owed by defendants—*Held*, defendants liable, as on the evidence the failure had materially increased the risk of dermatitis, which for practical purposes was equal to a finding that the failure had materially contributed to the risk.

U1. Arlen v. I.C.I. (1955) C.A. 353

Winding of tubs in mine—plaintiff gets caught in curve of rope between two tubs—*Held*, defendants liable for unsafe system. Parker L.J. (20 C): "The defendants were saying that really the system was that the men were trained never to get into what is called the curve of the rope. But all that that means really is that the defendants were relying on the workmen each taking care for their own safety. Bearing in mind the fallibility of human nature, I do not think the employer in those circumstances is entitled in effect to have no system at all, merely relying on the men looking after themselves, each for himself."

(b) In Particular Instances

(*N.B.* See also the cases listed as Examples, below.)

1. Rees v. Cambrian Wagon Works (1946) 175 L.T. 220, C.A.

Held, defendants liable for failing to give instructions as to method of work and/or supervise same. *Approved* in **2**.

2. Winter v. Cardiff R.D.C. [1950] 1 All E.R. 819; [1950] W.N. 193, H.L.

Held, defendants not liable for leaving method of work to gang. **1** approved (although facts very similar).

3. General Cleaning Contractors v. Christmas [1953] A.C. 180; [1952] 2 All E.R. 1110, H.L.

Window cleaner falls when sash providing hand-hold closes and when other sash is already closed—*Held*, that defendants were not negligent on the evidence in not providing ladders or hooks for safety belts but they were negligent in failing to instruct plaintiff to test windows and/or always to keep one sash open and/or in failing to provide wedges. For extracts from speeches on general principles see Chap. 15, (2) (c) **4**.

4. Drummond v. British Building Cleaners [1954] 1 W.L.R. 1434; [1954] 3 All E.R. 507, C.A.

Held, applying **3**, defendants liable for failing to instruct plaintiff in the transom method (attaching safety belt to transom).

5. Leathley v. Mersey Insulation [1954] 1 Lloyd's Rep. 349, C.A.

Four experienced riggers, of whom plaintiff was one, told to remove hatch cover section—which they do by raising it up with derrick and standing on hatch cover to push—plaintiff falls down hold while pushing—*Held*, that employers were justified in leaving method of removal to the men, and therefore were not liable for failure to provide safe system, although there were at least three safer ways than that adopted—*but* from judgments it would appear that this was a borderline case, and in view of accident defendants would be under obligation to lay down safer system.

6. Kerner v. Amal. Window Cleaning, *The Times*, March 17, 1954; [1954] C.L.Y. 2284, L.C.J.
Held, applying **3**, defendants liable.

7. Rands v. McNeil [1955] 1 Q.B. 253; [1954] 3 All E.R. 593, C.A.

Experienced farmworker going into loose box of dangerous bull—had not actually had instructions in way to tackle it—*Held*, defendant not liable. "Even if he had not actually been instructed to use the method above described (safe method), his common sense would tell him to keep outside until bull had been tethered ..." (Jenkins L.J., 602 B). "... he met his accident because ... he did something in a way he knew was irregular and unauthorised" (Morris L.J., 606 C).

8. Honeyman v. Orient S.N. [1955] 2 Lloyd's Rep. 27, Hilbery J.

Held, defendants liable.

9. Schofield v. Glen Line [1955] 2 Lloyd's Rep. 350, Glyn-Jones J.; [1955] 2 Lloyd's Rep. 719, C.A.

Held defendants not liable. *Upheld* by C.A., without mentioning this point.

10. Lewis v. High Duty Alloys [1957] 1 W.L.R. 632; [1957] 1 All E.R. 740, Ashworth J.

11. Flatman v. J. Fry [1957] 1 Lloyd's Rep. 73, Paull J.

Discharge of timber from ship to barge—timber varied from 8 feet to 35 feet long, 3 inches to 4 inches thick, 8 inches to 9 inches wide—several lengths lifted by single sling—one drops out of sling and hits plaintiff in barge—*Held*, defendants liable, because although system as system was safe, it required special care in making up sling to see that lengths, especially short lengths not gripped by sling, did not fall out, and in centring sling so that it went into barge hold approximately level.

12. Parkes v. Smethwick Corporation (1957) 121 J.P. 415; [1957] C.L.Y. 2425, C.A.

13. Wilson v. Tyneside Cleaning [1958] 2 Q.B. 110; [1958] 2 All E.R. 265, C.A.

Accident when defective sash handle came away—plaintiff argues a safe system would have included (a) repeated warnings. (b) periodic inspections by defendants and (c) general instructions as to how to clean sash window—*Held*, no, and defendants not liable.

14. Ellis v. Ocean S.S. [1958] 2 Lloyd's Rep. 373, C.A.

Plaintiff, seaman aged 17, washed overboard when cleaning scupper pipe on unfenced deck—*Held*, he should have had someone to help him, and defendants liable.

15. Lee v. John Dickinson (1960) 110 L.J. 317, Pilcher J.

Plaintiff fell down stairs through being pushed by a surge of other workers leaving the workroom—*Held*, defendants liable.

16. Bell v. Blackwood, 1960 S.C. 11; 1960 S.L.T. 145, 1st Div.

Held, defendants liable.

17. Clements v. General Services, *The Times*, March 10, 1961; [1961] C.L.Y. 5947, Paull J.

Plaintiff window cleaner was climbing back into room through window when window frame fell out owing to latent defect—*Held*, defendants not liable, as the defect was a latent one, and the failure of defendants to provide safety hooks or a ladder was immaterial as before the accident the plaintiff had been standing on the balcony.

18. Houghton v. Hackney Corporation *The Times,* May 18 1961; [1961] C.L.Y. 5929; Diplock J.
Rent collector injured due to assault in the course of robbery—*Held,* in the circumstances defendant employers not negligent.

19. Hardaker v. Huby (1962) 106 S.J. 327; [1962] C.L.Y. 2076, C.A.

Foreman sent to deliver 2 cwt bath single-handed—he obtained some (inadequate) assistance—*Held*, defendant employers liable for resultant injury.

20. Percival v. Leicester Corporation [1962] 2 Lloyd's Rep. 43, Finnemore J.
Held, defendant fire authority not liable for death of fireman drowned in gravel-pit while practising aqua-lung swimming.

21. Kinsella v. Lebus (1963) 108 S.J. 14, C.A.

Willmer L.J. *said* that he was disposed to agree with C.C.J. that a weight of 145 lbs was not, as a matter of weight alone, likely to cause injury to a man accustomed to moving weights of this sort; and therefore defendants were not liable under Factories Act 1961, s. 56 (1). *But* plaintiff won at common law, on ground of unsafe system: see Chap. 15(4)(a) **13**.

22. Walden v. Court Line (1965) 109 S.J. 151; [1965] C.L.Y. 2716, Glyn-Jones J.

Attack on P by H, another crew member—H had a history of assaults and violent conduct on board—*Held,* on the facts, it was not negligent of the captain, who had taken over after H's previous misdeeds, not to have got rid of H.

23. Stokes v. Guest Keen [1968] 1 W.L.R. 1776; [1968] C.L.Y. 2701, Swanwick J.

24. Hawkins v. Ian Ross [1970] 1 All E.R. 180, Fisher J.

25. Peat v. Muschamp (1969) 7 K.I.R. 469; [1970] C.L.Y. 900. C.A.

P, a one-legged man who to D's knowledge had suffered back strain, was employed to lift heavy lengths of chain—he had been told to ask for help should he ever need it—*Held,* D were entitled to permit P to judge whether he needed help or not, since he was the best and only judge of his capacity, and accordingly the system of work was safe. Widgery L.J. indicated that if the loads were of differing sizes an employer might be expected to give guidance as to when assistance should or should not be sought.

26. Charlton v. Forrest Printing [1980] I.R.L.R. 331; [1980] C.L.Y. 1890, C.A.

Plaintiff factory manager attacked by robbers when collecting wages. Previous snatches had occurred and defendant employers had reviewed wages collection policy, emphasising the need to vary collecting arrangements weekly, but after a time these instructions had become ignored—*Held,* reversing trial judge, defendants not liable. They had taken reasonable steps to reduce the risk of robbery, and in such circumstances it was not necessary for a small firm to employ a security firm.

27. Black v. Carricks [1980] I.R.L.R. 448; [1980] C.L.Y. 919, C.A.

P shop manageress of D's shop. Assistants all off ill unexpectedly. Necessary for bread trays to be unloaded, normally lifted by two women. P phoned superior who instructed her to get on with her job as best she could and if she needed help to ask a customer. Implicit that P could leave load if no help available. P injured while lifting tray by herself—*Held,* D not liable. They "could not reasonably have foreseen that P's predicament in being temporarily deprived of assistance would bring about a situation in which under some constraint imposed by her work, she would expose herself to the risk of the kind of injury she suffered in the circumstances which brought it about" (Shaw L.J., 451).

28. Williams v. Gwent Area H.A. [1983] C.L.Y. 2551, Stephen Brown J.

Plaintiff employed by defendants as S.E.N. at hospital. She suffered back injury whilst engaged with another S.E.N. in lifting heavy disabled patient from bed to geriatric chair. The lifting method involved moving the patient to the side of the bed and then raising her with each nurse supporting her with an arm under the patient's armpit and the nurse's free hand resting on the bed to give purchase. During the lift, the patient made an unexpected movement, and the plaintiff was injured—*Held,* that the defendants were negligent. They had failed to take proper precautions to deal with the foreseeable risk of injury (revealed by agreed statistics) to nurses involved in handling patients. Further, the method of lifting adopted by the plaintiff and her colleague, although approved at the hospital, was unsafe and negligent, involving extra strain upon the spine.

29. Thompson v. Smiths Shiprepairers [1984] Q.B. 405; [1984] 1 All E.R. 881, Mustill J.

Held, on the facts, defendants liable for excessive noise in shipyards from 1963 onwards, but not for earlier period. The judgment contains an exhaustive analysis of the development of precautions in recent years against industrial deafness. As to how far general practice of industry may be a defence in such cases, see Chap. 15, (2)(h)**14**.
N.B. In an unreported case, *Kellet v. B.R.B.*, decided by Popplewell J. at Chester in May 1984, it was held, in a similar claim arising from noise in railway workshops, liability commenced in 1955 in view of the special facts and circumstances adduced in evidence. (*N.B.* Shorthand writers were Lee and Nightingale of Liverpool.)

30. Yates v. Rockwell Graphic Systems Ltd [1988] I.C.R. 8; [1988] C.L.Y. 1739, Steyn J.

From 1956, plaintiff's hands were regularly in contact with contaminated coolant, from which arose a known and substantial risk of dermatitis. Notices warned employees regularly to wash their hands and use barrier cream, but there was no system of inspecting or cleaning the coolant until 1987. Plaintiff developed dermatitis in 1978—*Held,* defendants liable at common law and for breach of the Factories Act 1961, s. 29(1). *Per* Steyn J. at 14, "place" in section 29(1) did not simply mean the floor space within a factory: "One has to have regard to the permanently installed machinery and the regular activities carried on in the factory in order to decide whether the place is safe." Reasonably practicable steps were available to make the place safe, namely regular inspection and cleaning of coolant such as was introduced in 1987.

31. McSherry v British Telecommunications; Lodge v. British Telecommunications [1992] 3 Med. L.R. 129; [1992] C.L.Y. 1552, H.H. Judge Byrt Q.C.

Plaintiffs developed repetitive strain injury in cause of employment as data processing officers—*Held,*

(a) Defendant liable in negligence—Plaintiffs' condition caused by repetitive movements of unsupported hands and arms. Strain aggravated because defendant's bonus system caused plaintiffs to push themselves to limit; by plaintiffs' poor posture which defendant should have corrected; and by seating which was unsuitable because not properly adjustable.
(b) Defendant also in breach of the Shops, Offices and Railway Premises Act 1963, s. 14.

32. Mughal v. Reuters Ltd, [1993] I.R.L.R. 571; *The Times*, November 10, 1993, H.H. Judge Prosser Q.C.

Plaintiff alleged he had developed repetitive strain injury from use of computer keyboards and visual display units during employment as journalist—*Held*, plaintiff had not proved causal connection between his condition and his work. In any event, defendants not negligent. They had provided British Standard equipment and it was for each employee to find most comfortable position and method in and by which to work. *Per* H.H. Judge Prosser Q.C.: "R.S.I. is in reality meaningless, in that it has no pathology ... Its use by doctors can only serve to confuse ... where a condition like tenosynovitis, peritendonitis crepitans or tennis elbow and the like are referred to, each has a definite pathology ... Each has attributable causes, some of which can be attributed to the patient's work and often ... the employer is guilty of failing to protect his employee from work conditions which cause injury ... In such a case the employer knows what has to be done and failure, causing injury to the employee, results in liability."

U1. Green v. British Insulated Callenders Cables Ltd (1953) C.A. 77

Plaintiff steel erector—plaintiff placed ladder in position—attempted to climb it and slipped—ladder not in safe position—safe system provided by employers that labourer footed and supervised—*Held*, defendants not liable—accident happened because plaintiff "did not take care that the ladder properly placed, not through fault of defendants or lack of supervision".

U2. Donnelly v. B.T.C. (1955) C.A. 246

Plaintiff shunter squeezed when loose shunted coach is run into end of train—*Held*, defendants not liable, for although loose shunting dangerous unless there were strict rules as to when to go between buffers to couple up, in this case there were such rules in existence.

U3. Parkes v. Ramoneur (1956) C.A. 198

Plaintiff window cleaner employed by defendants—ladder slipped—defendants had not supplied proper rubber footings for ladder and had not instructed plaintiff in best way of doing work—left him to do it with wet swab as had done before—defendants' practice did not conform to practice in other firms—*Held*, defendants liable.

U4. Wilson v. International Combustion Ltd (1956) C.A. 218

Plaintiff steel erector employed by defendants—primary air heaters being erected on twin girders at a height—told to put wire over girder so that ducting could be raised—plaintiff investigating how to do it when fell from steel joist—nothing to prevent falling from joist—safe way was to use ladder lashed to girder but no ladder provided—no proper scheme of work—no supervision—*Held*, defendants negligent—argued by defendants that negligence did not cause accident as plaintiff only doing what steel erectors often do and running risks steel erectors regard as slight—defendants liable as negligence caused plaintiff to go on an exploring and improvising expedition in which exposed to risks unnecessarily.

U5. Ioannou v. Fishers Foils Ltd (1957) C.A. 216

Plaintiff machine operator employed by defendants—slipped disc caused by lifting in position on machine reel of foil weighing 420 lb—lifted into position one end at a time so that lifted more than half that weight—crow-bars on premises and could have been used for lifting—plaintiff never instructed to use crow-bars and did not know there for that purpose—never instructed to obtain assistance from someone else—*Held*, defendants negligent, applying folly test laid down in *Paris v. Stepney* (Chap. 15, (7) **3**).

U6. Hall v. Petter McLaren Service Ltd (1958) C.A. 110

Plaintiff stoker employed by defendants—developed hernia—work hard and strenuous—no serious complaint made—*Held*, defendants not negligent—could not foresee hernia or other injury to workman—Jenkins L.J. (9 B): "It is a possibility that anyone whose work involves lifting heavy weights or the like may unfortunately contract that complaint (hernia). But when employers engage a stoker and set him to fire boilers, they must, I think, assume that he is the best judge of his own capabilities. If he makes any real complaint of the conditions on the score that they make the doing of the work dangerous, or are liable to cause injury to him in the way of strain, then it may very well be that if employers ignore such a complaint, they will do so at their peril."

U7. Ashcroft v. Harden & Sons Ltd (1959) C.A. 63A

Plaintiff turner employed by defendants—working on lathe 3 feet $4\frac{1}{2}$ inches from ground—components to be put on lathe usually weighed 80–140 lb—lifted on and off about once a day—no lifting tackle provided although complaints made—practice to ask other labourers for assistance if thought component too heavy to manage alone—five labourers available to help turners—might have to wait up to half an hour—component weighing 150 lb had to be put on lathe—plaintiff could not find labourer to help him—after waiting 25 minutes attempted to lift component himself although knew beyond his capacity—sustained rupture—*Held*, defendants not negligent.

U8. Williams v. William Press (1959) C.A. 104A

Plaintiff fell carrying pipe with chargehand up unfooted ladder—*Held*, in the circumstances negligence and defendants liable. *But* Ormerod L.J. (9 C) emphasised that whether or not a ladder should be footed must depend on the circumstances of each case.

U9. Baker v. White's Window Cleaning (1962) C.A. 69

Plaintiff window cleaner fell when ring attached to sash of window broke—the rings were known to both plaintiff and defendants to be treacherous and liable to break—defendants had complained to owners—*Held*, defendants two-thirds liable, as they should have given express instructions to plaintiff not to put any strain on the rings. *N.B.* Court of Appeal in upholding judgment regarded case as a borderline one.

U10. Peebles v. Armstrongs Patents (1962) C.A. 135

Dermatitis from trichlorethylene—known danger—*Held*, defendants liable for failing to warn plaintiff. See also Chap. 15, (7) Ex. **U28**.

U11. Hooley v. Mason (1962) C.A. 364

Two men to manhandle $3\frac{1}{2}$ cwt roll of paper round corner—no accidents in 25 years—*Held*, reversing C.C.J., defendants not liable.

U12. Brennan v. Techno Constructors (1962) C.A. 336

Plaintiff steel erector sent by defendant employers to a brewery to fit up a conveyor—on completion it became necessary to remove a block and tackle from roof trusses—plaintiff climbed up trusses (as he had done to fix block at start)—overbalanced and fell—plaintiff complained that he should have had a ladder—*Held*, defendants not liable, as they had rightly left decisions as to the manner of the work to plaintiff, who was an experienced man and could have taken steps to procure ladder. Window cleaning cases and *Wilson v. International Combustion* **U4** distinguished, the latter on the ground that there the chargehand had not laid the work out properly (4 A).

U13. Shepherd v. George Mason (1974) C.A. 20

Woman shop assistant aged 47 slipped disc lifting 50 lb cartons—no evidence was led that such weight was likely to damage woman of 47—*Held*, although the court might take judicial notice of danger with much heavier weights, evidence on the question was essential in the present case, and accordingly judge's decision in favour of plaintiff must be reversed.

U14. Gilks v. James Edwards (1974) C.A. 64 A

Five men moving boiler section weighing 2–4 cwt,—*Held*, employers not negligent in not appointing someone to superintend operation.

U15. Gleave v. B.R.S. (1978) C.A. 757

Plaintiffs roping load on lorry. Rope unexpectedly breaks. Defendants relied on employees to report worn ropes—*Held*, no further precautions were required and defendants were not liable.

U16. Walls v. N.C.B. (1980) C.A. 582

Plaintiff, with three others, lifting and manoeuvring tray weighing $6\frac{1}{4}$ cwt. Plaintiff unfamiliar with operation and not used to such weights suffered back injury—*Held*, defendants negligent.

U17. Saunders v. Rushmoor B.C. (1982) C.A. U.B. 435

Two dustmen manhandling very heavy container up ramp. Employers had standing arrangement with customer that customer would provide assistance if requested. No request made and one dustman injured in manhandling—*Held*, that the employers were not liable. Their system of work, including the arrangement for assistance, was reasonable.

U18. Towers v. Cambridge Area H.A. (1982) C.A. U.B. 435

Two ambulancemen lifting heavy sweating restless patient at defendants' hospital—not, however, employed by defendants—requested lifting assistance of nursing staff, but no assistance provided. One ambulanceman lost grip and other suffered injury as result—*Held*, that the defendants were liable, as they ought to have provided assistance, if necessary from nursing staff.

Examples

(i) Moving cargo

Safe		*Unsafe*	
Yard arm of derrick: no preventer wire	4	Married gear: not removing ship's rail	1
Stowage: timber	6	Pig iron in nets	2
LIFTING PIPES: CRANE AND SNOTTER	7	Wire leg spliced to rope fall	3
Winch fall down hold: no lookout man	9	Stowage: timber	5
		Lifting hatch covers: no supervision	8
		Stowage: unsafely stowed	16

Safe	
STOWAGE: BALE FALLING	10
NO SUPERVISION IN HOLD	10
Dog hooks to free jammed cases	11
Load crushing dunnage	12
Hatch covers: standing on to replace	13
Loose hook liable to catch in coamings	14
Using cargo to secure other cargo	15
Reel of paper rolling	17
Rolling large paper reels	19
Lump falling from mound	21
Crate toppling on landing	22
Spillage: reasonable precautions	23
SLIDING CHESTS ONTO TROLLEY	24
Slinging two bales of wool	25
FAIRLEAD TO LOWER GOODS	26
Manhandling cases from lorry	28
Slinging four tea chests	29
Stowage: cement bag falls	32
Slinging several lengths of timber	33
Lifting pipes: union purchase gear	34
Stowage: woodpulp bales on top of steel rods	37
MOVING PAPER REELS: IRON HOOKS AND ROPES	38
Lifting paper reels: ship's derrick instead of shore crane	39
Cargo: case disintegrates on handling	40
Lifting tackle: leaving skilled man to select	44

Unsafe	
Working under suspended load	18
Slinging unstable stack of logs	20
Man walking by travelling crane to steady load	27
Stowage: dangerous wall in square of hatch	30
Married gear: swinging	31
Slinging long timber in three slings: no steps to protect plaintiff against collapse on unfastening	35
MARRIED GEAR: NOT REMOVING SHIP'S RAIL	36
SLING: OBJECT FALLING FROM	41
Discharging grain by trunk: no look-out to warn men on quay of trunk jamming while being lowered	42
Winch: putting ship's cook in charge without proper instructions	43
Crane: no look-out man	45
Removing hatch boards: not enough men	46
Winch: no system of communication between man winding rope and winch driver	47
Lifting cases: unevenly shared load	48

1. Twiss v. W. H. Rhodes [1951]1 Lloyd's Rep. 333, Gorman J.
2. Handley v. Cunard White Star (1944) 77 Ll.L.R. 543, Gorman J.
3. Porter v. Liverpool Stevedoring (1944) 77 Ll.L.R. 411, Hilbery J.
4. Roberts v. Holt (1945) 61 T.L.R. 289, Singleton J.
5. Twiss v. W. H. Rhodes [1951] 1 Lloyd's Rep. 333, Gorman J.
6. Wickens v. A.P.C. [1951] 1 Lloyd's Rep. 162, Cassels, J.
7. Tierney v. Gupwell [1951] 2 Lloyd's Rep. 55, C.A.
8. Campbell v. P.L.A. [1952] 1 Lloyd's Rep. 399, Gorman J.
9. Spalding v. Bradley Forge [1952] 1 Lloyd's Rep. 461, Lloyd-Jacob J.
10. Walker v. Bowaters [1952] 2 Lloyd's Rep. 299, C.A.
11. Holford v. P.L.A. [1953] 1 Lloyd's Rep. 152, Byrne J.
12. Pease v. B.I.S.N. [1953] 1 Lloyd's Rep. 207, Goddard L.C.J.
13. Atherton v. Pace [1953] 1 Lloyd's Rep. 353, Stable J.

14. Watts v. Shaw Savill [1953] 1 Lloyd's Rep. 407, McNair J.
15. Bishop v. W. H. Howes [1953] 1 Lloyd's Rep. 603, Finnemore J.
16. McDonald v. Smith Coggins [1953] 2 Lloyd's Rep. 202, Devlin J.
17. Taylor v. Convoys [1953] 2 Lloyd's Rep. 578, Sellers J.
18. Basted v. Cozens & Sutcliffe [1954] 2 Lloyd's Rep. 132, Devlin J.
19. Perry v. Convoys [1954] 2 Lloyd's Rep. 258, Jones J.
20. Arter v. P.L.A. [1955] 1 Lloyd's Rep. 179, Pilcher J.
21. Copas v. P.L.A. [1955] 1 Lloyd's Rep. 295, Sellers J.
22. Carvin v. Smith Coggins [1955] 1 Lloyd's Rep. 339, Ashworth J.
23. Wakeford v. Scruttons [1955] 1 Lloyd's Rep. 584, Streatfeild J.
24. Schofield v. Glen Line [1955] 2 Lloyd's Rep. 350, Glyn-Jones J.; [1955] 2 Lloyd's Rep. 719, C.A.
25. Michaels v. Browne & Eagle [1955] 2 Lloyd's Rep. 433, McNair J.
26. Martin v. A. B. Dalzell [1956] 1 Lloyd's Rep. 94, C.A.
27. Atkinson v. Tyne-Tees S.S. [1956] 1 Lloyd's Rep. 244, Streatfeild J.
28. Shadwell v. B.T.C. [1956] 1 Lloyd's Rep. 285, Sellers J.
29. Smith v. P.L.A. [1956] 2 Lloyd's Rep. 35, Pearce J.
30. Spring v. J. J. Mack [1956] 2 Lloyd's Rep. 558, Jones J.
31. Eggleston v. P.L.A. [1956] 2 Lloyd's Rep. 612, Ormerod J.
32. Dukelow v. Scruttons [1956] 2 Lloyd's Rep. 631, Lloyd-Jacob J.
33. Flatman v. J. Fry [1957] 1 Lloyd's Rep. 73, Paull J.
34. Sargent v. Gee Stevedoring [1957] 1 Lloyd's Rep. 357, Ashworth J.
35. Snaith v. Glen Line [1958] 2 Lloyd's Rep. 546, Donovan J.
36. Wiggins v. Caledonia Stevedoring [1960] 1 Lloyd's Rep. 18, C.A
37. Smith v. Hovey [1960] 1 Lloyd's Rep. 457, Hilbery J.
38. Davies v. Manchester Ship Canal [1960] 2 Lloyd's Rep. 11, C.A.
39. Bird v. Scruttons [1960] 2 Lloyd's Rep. 402, Elwes J.
40. Ellis v. Scruttons [1961] 1 Lloyd's Rep. 304, Edmund Davies J.
41. Cunningham v. Port of Liverpool Stevedoring [1962] 2 Lloyd's Rep. 49, C.A.
42. Munday v. P.L.A. [1967] 1 Lloyd's Rep. 550, McKenna J.
43. Antcliffe v. Alfred Bannister [1967] 1 Lloyd's Rep. 429, O.R.
44. Richardson v. Stephenson Clark [1969] 3 All E.R. 705, Nield J.
45. Wattson v. P.L.A. [1969] 1 Lloyd's Rep. 95, Megaw J.
46. Warner v. Royal Mail [1970] 2 Lloyd's Rep. 353, Bridge J.
47. Clay v. South Coast Shipping [1970] 2 Lloyd's Rep. 146, Eveleigh J.
48. Fricker v. Benjamin Parry (1973) 16 K.I.R. 356; [1979] C.L.Y. 1880, Bridge J.

Examples

(ii) Other cases

Safe

Mine: haulage and men travelling on same road 2
SHIP: ERECTING SCAFFOLD AT SEA 3
Man making own defective tool 7
Loading lorry: leaving to men 10
ASKING IF OTHER'S CRANE SAFE TO PAINT ... 11
Lifting: 84 lb bundles of canes 13
SHIP: ONE MAN TO HOLD STERN ROPE 14

Unsafe

Intense light used: no warning 1
Rolling plate on barrel 4
LIFTING LOAD: LEAVING TO MEN 5
SAFE CRANE LOAD: NO INSTRUCTIONS AS TO 6
Railway: lookout man too near tunnel 8
Merely telling plaintiff to read regulations 9
Window cleaner: no drill for sashes 12

Safe

Unsafe

Safe

Lifting: two men for 1–5 cwt U8
Shunting: engine in rear: no continuous lookout U10
Lifting: one man for 100 lb U14
Lifting: full milk churns to top deck of lorry U21
Cobble burning: with propane gas cutter U22
Lifting hose: up ladder of milk tanker: unaided U23
Lifting: 50 lb carton for woman shop assistant U24
Gang moving boiler section: no one in charge U25
Lifting: plaster cast 55–60 lb out of mould U26
Chipping tar from gas pipes with chisel U27
Lifting—113lb—help available U29
Roping load: rope breaks U30
Dustman manhandling container: assistance available from customer on request U32
Empty train taken from sidings to stations: no signals between driver and guard U34
Special school: care assistant and colleague assisting of epileptic pupil ... U35
Female employee lifting cartons each weighing 24 lbs without help U38
Moving metal weighing 54 lbs U39
Two employees lifting pipe weighing 240 lbs U40
Tenosynovitis: assembling, stitching and stacking cardboard boxes U41
No inspections of hammer face U42
Lifting TV set unaided U43
Using high pressure lose unaided U44
Nurse lifting unco-operative patient .. U45
Lifting wheelbarrow containing nylon weighing 123 lbs U46
Nurse unaided assisting 15-stone patient from chair to bed U48
Two men lifting cabin weighing 286 lbs U49
System for clearing water spilt on kitchen floor U51

Unsafe

Carrying heavy valve up ladder unaided 64
Tools causing vibration white finger—no preventative measures 65
Repetitive strain injury: data processing officers 66
Repetitve strain injury: bench workers 67
GUIDING TRAILER ONTO FERRY, WALKING BACKWARDS 68
DRIVING DUMPER TRUCK CLOSE TO UNPROTECTED OVERHANG 70
Pressure of work: second nervous breakdown 73
WINDOW CLEANER: NO HARNESS ANCHOR POINTS: WORK FROM OUTSIDE SILL 76
Winding tubs: loose curve of rope formed U2
Window cleaning: no adequate instruction in proper method U3
Manhandling 500 lb flywheel: instead of using crane U4
Lifting: 420 lb unaided U5
Unfooted ladder: carrying pipe up U9
Lifting: one man for 278 lb U11
Window cleaner: fragile rings on sashes U12
Lifting: five men to move long 15 cwt pipe up muddy slope U13
Opening drum of caustic soda: inadequate instructions U15
Noise: plaintiff at machine unable to communicate properly with mate controlling button U16
Lifting: 140 lb battery into front of van unaided U17
Drop hammer: no instructions to prop when not in use U18
Tree feeling: not telling novice to keep clear U19
Two-handed job from ladder: replacing air filter U20
Tightening nut near revolving engine fan U28
Manhandling 6¼ cwt by gang of four: plaintiff unused to operation U31
Ambulancemen lifting patient: assistance required U33
Plater fixing channel unaided U36

Unsafe
Plaintiff securing heavy radiator: inadequate assistance U37
Two nurses lifting patient prone to spasm and panic U47
Carrying bucket of molten bitumen weighing 24 lbs up ladder U50

1. Russell v. Criterion Films (1936) 53 T.L.R. 117.
2. Wilsons v. English [1938] A.C. 57, H.L.
3. Rooney v. Aberdeen Line (1945) 78 Ll.L.R. 511, C.A.
4. Wilkins v. R. H. Green (1946) 79 Ll.L.R. 243, Denning J.
5. Rees v. Cambrian Wagon (1946) 175 L.T. 220, C.A.
6. Gallagher v. Dorman Long [1947] 2 All E.R. 38; 177 L.T. 143, C.A.
7. Franklin v. Bristol Aeroplane [1948] W.N. 341.
8. Dyer v. Southern Railway [1948] 1 K.B. 608; [1948] 1 All E.R. 516, Humphreys J.
9. Barcock v. Brighton Corporation [1949] 1 K.B. 339; [1949] 1 All E.R. 251, Hilbery J.
10. Winter v. Cardiff R.D.C. [1950] 1 All E.R. 819; [1950] W.N. 193, H.L.
11. Bott v. Prothero Steel Tube [1951] C.L.C. 6849; [1951] W.N. 595, C.A.
12. General Cleaning Contractors v. Christmas [1952] A.C. 180; [1952] 2 All E.R. 1110, H.L.
13. Pipe v. Chambers Wharf [1952] 1 Lloyd's Rep. 194, Streatfeild J.
14. Martin v. Manchester Ship Canal [1952] 1 Lloyd's Rep. 539, C.A.
15. Rutherford v. T. J. Harrison [1952] 2 Lloyd's Rep. 493, Jones J.
16. Holtum v. W. J. Cearns, *The Times*, July 23, 1953, C.A.
17. Douglas v. M.D.H.B. [1953] 1 Lloyd's Rep. 93, Ormerod J.
18. Calnan v. London Graving Dock [1953] 1 Lloyd's Rep. 149, Barry J.
19. Hegarty v. Rye Arc [1953] 1 Lloyd's Rep. 465, Pilcher J.
20. Hook v. Consolidated Fisheries [1953] 2 Lloyd's Rep. 647, C.A.
21. Rands v. McNeill [1955] 1 Q.B. 253; [1954] 3 All E.R. 593, C.A.
22. Drummond v. British Building Co. [1954] 1 W.L.R. 1434; [1954] 3 All E.R. 507, C.A.
23. Pasfield v. Hays Wharf [1954] 1 Lloyd's Rep. 150, Hilbery J.
24. Noble v. Tankers [1954] 2 Lloyd's Rep. 33, Pilcher J.
25. Basted v. Cozens & Sutcliffe [1954] 2 Lloyd's Rep. 132, Devlin J.
26. Smith v. Ocean S.S. [1954] 2 Lloyd's Rep. 482, Gorman J.
27. Kerner v. Amal. Window Cleaning, *The Times*, March 17, 1954; [1954] C.L.Y. 2284, L.C.J.
28. Honeyman v. Orient S.N. [1955] 2 Lloyd's Rep. 27, Hilbery J.
29. Ashley v. Esso [1956] 1 Lloyd's Rep. 240, Roxburgh J.
30. Lewis v. High Duty Alloys [1957] 1 All E.R. 740, Ashworth J.
31. Gibbs v. United Steel [1957] 1 W.L.R. 668; [1957] 2 All E.R. 113, Streatfeild J.
32. Wilcock v. B.T.C. [1957] 1 Lloyd's Rep. 360, Ashworth J.
33. Lawes v. Nicholl, *The Times*, May 8, 1957; [1957] C.L.Y. 2419, Salmon J.
34. Wilson v. Tyneside Window Cleaning [1958] 2 Q.B. 110; [1958] 2 All E.R. 265, C.A.
35. White v. Bowker [1958] 1 Lloyd's Rep. 318, Diplock J.
36. Graham v. Copthall Shipping Co. [1958] 2 Lloyd's Rep. 366, Ashworth J.
37. Clements v. General Services, *The Times*, March 10, 1961; [1961] C.L.Y. 5947, Paull J.
38. Kinsella v. Lebus (1963) 108 S.J. 14, C.A.
39. Walden v. Court Line (1965) 109 S.J. 151; [1965] C.L.Y. 2716, Glyn-Jones J.
40. Jones v. N.C.B. [1965] 1 W.L.R. 532; [1965] 1 All E.R. 221, Nield J.
41. Aberan v. Philip Leonard, *The Times*, December 3, 1965; [1965] C.L.Y. 2692, Browne J.
42. Bradford v. Robinson Rentals [1967] 1 All E.R. 267, Rees J.
43. Lovelidge v. Anselm Olding [1967] 1 All E.R. 459, Widgery J.
44. Price v. P.L.A. [1967] 1 Lloyd's Rep. 559, Roskill J.
45. Williams v. Grimshaw (1967) 112 S.J. 14; *The Times*, December 6, 1967, Phillimore J.
46. Porteous v. N.C.B., 1967 S.L.T. 117; [1967] C.L.Y. 2720, Ct. of Sess.

47. Birch v. Indestructive Paint Co. (1968) 118 New L.J. 421; [1968] C.L.Y. 2661, Phillimore J.
48. Houghton v. Hackney B.C. (1967) 3 K.I.R. 615; [1968] C.L.Y. 2706, Diplock J.
49. Tremain v. Pike [1969] 3 All E.R. 1303, Payne J.
50. Peat v. Muschamp (1969) 7 K.I.R. 469; [1970] C.L.Y. 900, C.A.
51. Brown v. John Mills (1970) 8 K.I.R. 702; [1970] C.L.Y. 1873, C.A.
52. Cassidy v. I.C.I., *The Times*, November 2, 1972; [1972] C.L.Y. 2381, C.A.
53. Payne v. Bennie (1973) 14 K.I.R. 395; [1973] C.L.Y. 2323, Shaw J.
54. Upson v. Temple Engineering (1975) K.I.R. 171; [1975] C.L.Y. 1431, Judge Richards Q.C.
55. Black v. Carricks [1980] I.R.L.R. 448; [1980] C.L.Y. 919, C.A.
56. Thompson v. Smiths Shiprepairers [1984] Q.B. 405; [1984] 1 All E.R. 881, Mustill J.
57. Kondis v. State Transport Authority (1984) 154 C.L.R. 672; [1986] C.L.Y. 2262. High Court of Australia (see Chap. 15, (1)(d) **14**).
58. McDermid v. Nash Dredging Ltd [1987] A.C. 906; [1987] 2 All E.R. 878, H.L. (see Chap. 15, (1)(d) **16**).
59. Bryce v. Swan Hunter Group plc [1987] 2 Lloyd's Rep. 426; [1988] 1 All E.R. 659, Phillips J. (see Chap. 15,(2)(a) **27**).
60. Yates v Rockwell Graphic Systems Ltd [1988] I.C.R. 8; [1988] C.L.Y. 1739, Steyn J. (see Chap. 15, (4)(b) **30**).
61. Calder v. H. Kitson Vickers Ltd [1988] I.C.R. 232; [1988] C.L.Y. 1952, C.A. (see Chap. 15, (1)(b) **17**).
62. Baxter v. Harland Wolff plc [1990] I.R.L.R. 516, [1991] C.L.Y. 1878, N.I.C.A. (see Chap. 15, (2)(a) **29**).
63. Whitfield v. H. & R. Johnson (Tiles) Ltd. [1990] 3 All E.R. 426; [1990] I.R.L.R. 525, C.A. (see Chap. 15, (2)(b) **15**).
64. Mearns v. Lothian R.C., [1991] S.L.T. 338; [1991] C.L.Y. 5693 (see Chap. 15, (2)(d) **37**).
65. Bowman v. Harland & Wolff plc. [1992] I.R.L.R. 349; [1992] C.L.Y. 3222, Carswell J., N.I. (see Chap. 15, (2)(j) **12**).
66. McSherry v. British Telecommunications; Lodge v. British Telecommunications [1992] 3 Med. L.R. 129; [1992] C.L.Y. 1552, H.H. Judge Byrt Q.C. (see Chap. 15, (4)(b) **31**).
67. Ping v. Esselte Letraset [1992] C.L.Y. 3211, H.H. Judge Griffiths (see Chap. 15, (2)(d) **39**).
68. Hollier v. Denholm Ship Management [1993] P.I.Q.R. P104; [1993] C.L.Y. 3292, C.A. (see Chap. 15, (2)(f) **21**).
69. Holmes v. Tees and Hartlepool Port Authority [1993] C.L.Y. 2020, H.H. Judge Stroyan Q.C. (see Chap. 15, (2)(f) **22**).
70. Morris v. Breaveglen Ltd [1993] I.C.R. 766; [1993] P.I.Q.R. P 294, C.A. (see Chap. 15, (1)(c) **10**).
71. Woolger v. West Surrey and North East Hampshire H.A., *The Times* November 8, 1993; [1993] C.L.Y. 2948, C.A. (see Chap. 15, (2)(d) **41**).
72. Mughal v. Reuters Ltd [1993] I.R.L.R. 571; *The Times*, November 10 1993, H.H. Judge Prosser Q.C. (see Chap. 15, (4)(b) **32**).
73. Walker v. Northumberland C.C., *The Times*, November 24, 1994; [1994] C.L.Y. 2278, Colman J. (see Chap. 15, (1)(b) **22**).
74. Wilebore v. St Edmundsbury B.C. [1994] C.L.Y. 2282, Tucker J. (see Chap. 15, (2)(j) **13**).
75. Nilsson v. Redditch B.C. [1994] C.L.Y. 2299, C.A. (see Chap. 15, (2)(h) **19**).
76. King v. Smith, *The Times*, November 3, 1994; [1994] C.L.Y. 2284, C.A. (see Chap. 15, (2)(c) **24**).

U1. *Ward v. Pillinger* (1951) C.A. 355.
U2. *Arlen v. I.C.I.* (1955) C.A. 353.
U3. *Parkes v. Ramoneur Co. Ltd* (1956) C.A. 198.
U4. *Lucin v. Ruston & Hornsby Ltd* (1956) C.A. 358.
U5. *Ioannou v. Fishers Foils Ltd* (1957) C.A. 216.
U6. *Hall v. Petter McLaren Service Ltd* (1958) C.A. 110.
U7. *Pickering v. Gloster Aircraft Co. Ltd* (1958) C.A. 230.
U8. *Plant v. Bamfords Ltd* (1959) C.A. 52.
U9. *Williams v. William Press* (1959) C.A. 104 A.
U10. *Jenkinson v. B.T.C.* (1960) C.A. 140.
U11. *Crane v. Robinson* (1961) C.A. 365.
U12. *Baker v. Whites* (1962) C.A. 69 .
U13. *Rankin v. Simmons and Walker* (1962) C.A. 412.
U14. *Johnson v. Pressed Steel Co.* (1963) C.A. 76.

U15. *Broomhall v. B.R.B.* (1963) C.A. 110.
U16. *Bolton v. Cradley* (1965) C.A. 298.
U17. *Smithers v. Brazil* (1966) C.A. 36 A.
U18. *Hanson v. Thomas Smith* (1966) C.A. 208.
U19. *Newell v. Evans* (1968) C.A. 75.
U20. *Bell v. G.L.C.* (1969) C.A. 391 (but 25 per cent. contributory negligence).
U21. *Evans v. South Caernarvon Creameries* (1971) C.A. 355.
U22. *Wriggleworth v. B.S.C.* (1972) C.A. 167 A.
U23. *Williams v. Milk Marketing Board* (1972) C.A. 336.
U24. *Shepherd v. George Mason* (1974) C.A. 20 (see Chap. 15, (4) (b) **U13**).
U25. *Gilks v. James Edwards* (1974) C.A. 64 A.
U26. *Sleightholme v. Ideal Standard* (1974) C.A. 285.
U27. *Downer v. Eastern Gas Board* (1975) C.A. 15.
U28. *Gandy v. Clarke Chapman* (1976) C.A. 412.
U29. *Pilkington v. Mersey Regional H.A.* (1978) C.A. 717.
U30. *Gleave v. B.R.S.* (1978) C.A. 757.
U31. *Walls v. N.C.B.* (1980) C.A. 582.
U32. *Saunders v. Rushmoor B.C.* (1982) C.A. U.B. 435.
U33. *Towers v. Cambridgeshire Area H.A.* (1982) C.A. U.B. 435.
U34. *Webb v. B.R.B.* (1982) C.A. 339.
U35. *Masterman v. Humberside C.C.* (1984) C.A. 622 (see Chap. 15, (2) (f) **U2**).
U36. *Hogg v. S.L.P. Fabricating Engineers Ltd* (1984) C.A. 652.
U37. *Porteous v. City and East London Area H.A.* (1984) C.A. 660.
U38. *Chessum v. Lesley U.K. Sales Ltd* (1984) C.A. 669.
U39. *Turner v. British Leyland (U.K.) Ltd* (1984) C.A. 698.
U40. *Shaw v. Cleveland Bridge & Engineering Co. Ltd* (1985) C.A. 1060.
U41. *Wyeth v. Thames Case Ltd* (1986) C.A. 533 (see Chap. 15, (2)(c) **U4**).
U42. *Thomson v. Peglers Ltd* (1987) C.A. 522 (see Chap. 15, (2)(h) **U7**).
U43. *Flowerday v. Visionhire Ltd* (1987) C.A. 1162 (see Chap. 15, (2)(d) **U13**).
U44. *Simox v. B.S.C.* (1988) C.A. 769 (see Chap. 15, (2)(d) **U15**).
U45. *Folawiyo v. Riverside H.A.* (1988) C.A. 1010 (see Chap. 15(2)(l) **U10**).
U46. *Frank v. Halls Barton Ropery* (1990) C.A. 369.
U47. *Fitzsimmons v. Northumberland H.A.* (1990) C.A. 968.
U48. *Barfield v. South Sefton (Merseyside) H.A.* (1991) C.A. 290 (see Chap. 15, (2)(b) **U5**).
U49. *Loynton v. Dinefwr B.C.* (1991) C.A. 451.
U50. *Wray v. Kirklees Rock Asphalt Ltd* (1991) C.A. 553.
U51. *Minogue v. The London Residuary Body* (1994) C.A. 934 (see Chap. 15, (2)(l) **U13**).

(5) Place of Work (including Access)

(*N.B.* See also the cases listed as Examples, below.)

SLIPPERY DUCKBOARD—CONSTANTLY SPLASHED FROM VAT 1
Building site—loose planks lying about—night watchman 2
Factory floor flooded by storm—residue of slippery oil and water 3
Dock shed—slippery through unswept groundnuts 4
DOCK—SOME OBSTRUCTIONS ON FLOOR TO BE EXPECTED 5
Ship's deck—dunnage lying about—plaintiff well able to remove it himself 6
BOILERMAKER'S YARD—DEBRIS LYING ABOUT TO BE EXPECTED 7
ROOF—UNGUARDED EDGE—PLAINTIFF MUST REMEMBER 8
Dry dock—steep altar courses dangerous 9
Access—duty of employer includes 9

1. Davidson v. Handley Page [1945] 1 All E.R. 235; 61 T.L.R. 178, C.A.

Plaintiff washing teacup at tap slips on duck-board constantly splashed from vat—defendants had put sawdust down but at the time none available—*Held*, liable.

2. Field v. Perry's [1950] 2 All E.R. 521; [1950] W.N. 320, Devlin J.

Held, defendants not liable. "One would expect that on a building site there would be obstructions and obstacles such as the plank in question, and a night watchman must take the risk of them."

3. Latimer v. A.E.C. [1953] A.C. 643; [1953] 2 All E.R. 449, H.L.

Held, defendants not liable, as they had taken all reasonable steps short of closing down the factory.

4. Reid v. Elder Dempster [1953] 1 Lloyd's Rep. 347, Barry J.

Floor of dock shed slippery with unswept groundnuts—plaintiff slips—employed by defendants who are using shed for discharge of cargo—but defendants are not occupiers—*Held*, defendants liable for failure to provide safe place of work. Defendants had in fact been discharging at berth for 18 months and had discharged previous ship. "This is not a case where defendants came to this berth for the first time on the morning of November 14, 1949. Had it been such a case, very different considerations would arise. It might well be unreasonable to say that before sending any of their men onto a berth of this kind they should conduct a detailed examination of the floor . . . " (351).

5. Moncreiff v. Swan Hunter [1953] 2 Lloyd's Rep. 149, C.A.

"As Pritchard J. said on one occasion, you cannot expect the floor of a dock to be as free from obstruction as a dance floor" (Denning L.J., 150, col. 2).

6. Lynch v. Harland & Wolff [1953] 2 Lloyd's Rep. 536; Glyn-Jones J.

Plaintiff employed to paint ship's funnel by defendants has to go round base of funnel undoing ropes—while doing so is caused to fall by pieces of dunnage lying about—he had already been round funnel once—*Held*, defendants not liable: "If and in so far as these pieces of dunnage on the deck constituted a risk plaintiff himself or any of the workpeople could have picked them up and put them on one side and that would have avoided the accident. Therefore this action fails" (539, col. 2).

7. Williams v. M.D.H.B. [1954] 2 Lloyd's Rep. 221, C.A.

Plaintiff trips over piece of metal lying near dump in boilermaker's yard—*Held*, defendants not liable: "I do not see how it can possibly be said that because in a boilermaker's yard within two feet or thereabouts of a dump of metal, there is a piece of metal on the ground, that is evidence of negligence against anyone. Nobody would expect this place to be kept as tidy as a gentleman's drive or a garden path. It is a place where tools, bits of metal, rubbish and one thing and another would naturally be found" (Lord Goddard C.J., 223, col. 2).

8. Montgomery v. A. Monk [1954] 1 W.L.R. 258; [1954] 1 All E.R. 252, C.A.

(The fuller report on common law liability is in W.L.R.) Plaintiff erecting flat root stepped back over edge—*Held*, defendants not liable. Somervell L.J. at 259 bottom: "It would of course have been quite impossible to provide guard rails, as they would have to be moved as the work proceeded. It seems to me that it was one of those cases where although the work was at a height, one cannot say that it was an unsafe place because if those working there did not remember there was an edge off which they could fall they might meet with an accident."

9. Hurley v. Sanders [1955] 1 W.L.R. 470; [1955] 1 All E.R. 833, Glyn-Jones J.

Plaintiff employed to paint ship's bottom in dry-dock slipped when going down the steep altar courses—the universal practice of the industry was not to provide safety devices such as a safety belt or net or line—*Held*, employers' duty extends to means of access as well as to working place, and that despite the universal practice the altar courses were a dangerous means of access (*Bath v. B.T.C.* [1954] 2 All E.R. 542, C.A.: see Chap. 15 (5) Ex (i) **26**, taken into consideration on this point), and since the access was dangerous, onus passed to defendants to establish not practicable to avert danger, which onus they had not discharged and therefore were liable.

10. Prince v. Carrier Engineering [1955] 1 Lloyd's Rep. 401, Parker L.J.

Held, defendants not liable. See Chap 15, (2)(d) **11**.

11. Lewis v. Union-Castle [1955] 1 Lloyd's Rep. 481, Barry J.

"In a storm at sea articles such as these are always liable to come adrift, and the fact that they do so . . . does not in my judgment establish any prima facie case of negligence" (485, col. 1).

12. Wilson v. International Combustion [1957] 3 All E.R. 505n., C.A.

Held, defendants liable. Morris L.J.: " . . . it must be something perilous to proceed along steel joists when there is an open space on either side . . . it is of no avail to say that the appellant was only doing what steel erectors often do, or to say that the appellant was running risks which steel erectors generally regard as slight. The failure of these respondents (to provide a ladder) directly brought it about that the appellant was subjected to those risks which result when a steel erector goes along girders . . . His injuries resulted from risks which he was unnecessarily running, and they were . . . caused by the respondents' negligence." *Distinguished* in **U9**.

13. Kennedy v. Lamport and Holt [1957] 1 Lloyd's Rep. 425, Devlin J.

14. Tickner v. Glen Line [1958] 1 Lloyd's Rep. 468, Devlin J.

Employers put two men in addition to shed-man onto sweeping up loose spilled marbles—plaintiff trod on one—*Held*, defendants had taken reasonable steps, and were not liable.

15. Baker v. Hopkins [1959] 3 All E.R. 225, C.A.

Held, defendants liable, for all defendants had done was to say: "Don't go down that bloody well till I get there", which in view of the lethal hazard created by defendants was not an adequate discharge of their duty. (10 per cent. contributory negligence against workman.)

16. Bradford v. Boston Deep Sea Fisheries [1959] 1 Lloyd's Rep. 394, Finnemore J.

Deceased was drowned returning from shore leave in a hired dinghy—due to overloading of dinghy—*Held*, defendant employers not liable, as they did not owe him any duty at the time (see Chap 15, (1) (b) **9** as to when duty of Master commences for sailors rejoining ship). *Held*, further, that where there were boats available to take seamen back to ship at anchor, the shipowner owed no duty to supply special transport to take them back.

17. Lee v. John Dickinson (1960) 110 L.J. 317, Pilcher J.

Plaintiff fell down stairs through being pushed from behind by a surge of other workers leaving the workroom—*Held*, defendants liable.

18. Batten v. Harland & Wolff [1961] 1 Lloyd's Rep. 261, Salmon J.

Rung of iron ladder giving only 2 inches of toehold owing to pipe running behind—*Held*, not a safe foothold on which to work, and defendants liable. *N.B.* Plaintiff was an experienced man, and if he had gone up this ladder to do the work by himself, he would have been wholly responsible; but as it happened, the chargehand was footing the ladder and could have seen the danger—liability was shared equally.

19. Carolan v. Redpath Brown [1964] 108 S.J. 136; [1964] C.L.Y. 2543, C.A.

Experienced steel erector working on underside of roof 35 feet above ground—no tackle provided—*Held*, defendants liable, as they had exposed him to unnecessary risk.

20. Vinnyey v. Star Paper [1965] 1 All E.R. 175, Cumming-Bruce J.

Held, defendants not liable.

21. O'Reilly v. National Rail and Tramway [1965] 1 All E.R. 499, Nield J.

At 11.15 a.m. scrap was delivered which contained a live shell—the shell was seen and handled by two manual labourers—at about 1 p.m. plaintiff hit the shell with a sledgehammer and blew himself up—*Held*, defendants not liable for unsafe place of work, as the knowledge of the two manual labourers could not be imputed to them.

22. Fildes v. International Computers [1984] C.L.Y. 2316, C.A.

Plaintiff slipped on ice on factory car park one acre in area, during several days' freezing weather. Only way to make car park safe would have been to cover it with sand and salt twice a day. Defendant did not treat car park at all, but gave priority to more frequently used areas elsewhere on its premises—*Held*, defendants not in breach of the Factories Act 1961, s. 29(1) and not liable in negligence.

23. Darby v. G.K.N. Screws & Fasteners Ltd [1986] I.C.R. 1; [1986] C.L.Y. 2266, Peter Pain J.

After snowy night, plaintiff slipped on untreated ice in front of a door to defendant's factory, just before 7.45 a.m. shift. Salt-spreading gang came on duty at 7.30 a.m. and salted most used and dangerous parts first—*Held*, defendants neither negligent nor in breach of duty under the Factories Act 1961, s. 29, to provide safe means of access—had taken all reasonably practicable steps by its system, and no basis for finding that any individual employee had negligently failed to salt the relevant area earlier.

24. Davies v. Massey Ferguson Perkins [1986] I.C.R. 580; [1986] C.L.Y. 1539, Evans J.

Plaintiff on night shift missed footing when descending outside steel staircase, the light at the bottom of which was not working—stumbled and injured back—*Held*, defendant in breach of duty under the Factories Act 1961, s. 5(1), to maintain sufficient and suitable lighting, which was absolute. Also in breach of section 29(1)—system for repairing lighting defects once reported was satisfactory, but for discovering and reporting defects was not, depending on periodic patrols of parts of factory site by security guard or reports of defects by individual workmen. On available evidence, plaintiff had not proved that defendant negligent.

25. Aldred v. Nacanco [1987] I.R.L.R. 292; [1987] C.L.Y. 1367, C.A.

In washroom of defendant's premises, employee X pushed slightly unstable washbasin against plaintiff's thigh, to startle her. Plaintiff turned quickly and in doing so injured her back which was known to defendant to be vulnerable—*Held*, defendant not liable because, *inter alia*, place of work not unsafe—not reasonably foreseeable that condition of washbasin might cause injury.

26. Hewett v. Alf Brown's Transport [1992] I.C.R. 530; [1992] P.I.Q.R. P199, C.A.

Plaintiff inhaled lead oxide powder when daily washing contaminated work clothes of her husband who was employed by defendant. Plaintiff particularly susceptible to effects of lead in her blood—*Held*, plaintiff's husband had not been exposed to significant risk of lead poisoning at work, and defendant neither negligent nor in breach of Control of Lead at Work Regulations 1980 in relation to him. Accordingly, defendant could not be liable to plaintiff, of whose susceptibility they were unaware.

27. Hill v. Lovett 1992 S.L.T. 994; [1992] C.L.Y. 6084

Vet's receptionist entered vet's private garden to clean surgery windows, with vet's permission—bitten on leg by one of vet's two dogs, neither of which had attacked a stranger before, but which were pugnacious, inclined to guard their territory jealously and prone to nip—*Held*, vet must have been aware of dogs' vicious tendencies, and liable for failing to provide safe place of work for receptionist.

28. Dixon v. London Fire and Civil Defence Authority, *The Times*, February 22, 1993; [1993] C.L.Y. 2025, C.A.

Plaintiff slipped on water which had leaked onto tiled floor of fire station from valve of pump on fire appliance—*Held*, plaintiff had not shown that defendant had failed to take reasonable steps to prevent the leaking, or had failed to provide a proper floor.

U1. Potts v. Churchill Redman Ltd (1952) C.A. 201

Plaintiff turner—on night shift in factory—trod on sharp steel cutting on way to W.C.—steel cuttings did get on floor especially at night—labourer employed at night to sweep up—at the time this was only piece of metal on floor—*Held*, defendants had done what was reasonably practicable and not liable.

U2. Freeman v. Robinson Bros Ltd (1955) C.A. 12

Explosion caused by overheated methalyl escaping over partition to place where naked jet was burning—deceased had let methalyl overheat while he went to get tea—he knew of danger—*Held*, defendants liable, as they should have had airtight barrier between flame and methalyl, and/or thermostatic control. No contributory negligence because mere error of judgment or forgetfulness.

U3. Thornley v. Manchester Abattoirs Products Co. Ltd (1955) C.A. 161

Plaintiff slipped on floor which was slimy and wet—floor washed every evening at 4.40 p.m. and cleaned so that dry next morning—if floor became unreasonably slimy foreman detailed persons to clean it—people automatically cleaned floor themselves if rather messy—done for 200–300 years—

possible to build wall round receptacle where gut washed and to have something within wall to drain away water and slimy matter—*Held*, defendants not negligent.

U4. Beard v. Industrial Engineering Ltd (1957) C.A. 7

Morris L.J. (13 C): "Those who have to work on roofs cannot. I think, expect absolute safety in the sense that every conceivable possibility must be provided against."

U5. Wolstenholme v. Briggs Motor Bodies Ltd (1958) C.A. 26

Plaintiff slipped on grease in gangway—grease dripped from metal sheets when removed from presses—six cleaners to sweep and clean grease from gangways—*Held*, unreasonable and unnecessary to wipe grease from sheets when removed from presses—no failure to provide proper system of cleaning gangways—but defendants liable for negligence of cleaners in failing to see and remove grease which had been on floor for a few hours.

U6. Smallwood v. Lamport and Holt (1960) C.A. 917

Plaintiff boatswain clambered over dunnage on port side of hatch and slipped and fell because it was greasy—starboard side was quite clear—*Held*, defendants not liable, as they could not have foreseen that plaintiff would choose that route instead of starboard side.

U7. Skinner v. Steeplejack Company (1961) C.A. 186 A

Plaintiff steeplejack required to work on top of 250-foot chimney, which was in use, sitting on the capping 30 inches wide—overcome by carbon dioxide fumes from chimney—ordinarily place of work would have been safe for steeplejacks—*Held*, however, owing to danger from fumes, defendants liable for breach of regulation 5 of 1948 Regulations and at common law in failing to provide scaffold.

U8. Fenn v. London Transport Executive (1961) C.A. 243

Plaintiff slipped on grease deposit in canteen—defendants swept and washed floor with soda daily—every three months a special squad cleaned it with caustic soda—*Held*, precautions adequate and defendants not liable.

U9. Brennan v. Techno Constructors (1962) C.A. 336

Plaintiff steel erector sent to fit up a conveyor at a brewery—he climbed up steel trusses—overbalanced and fell—complained he should have had a ladder—*Held*, defendants not liable, as they had rightly left manner of work to plaintiff who was experienced. *Wilson* **12** distinguished on ground that there chargehand had not laid out work properly.

U10. Turner v. Salford Area H.A. (1984) C.A. 1286

Plaintiff nurse deliberately leaned against two substantial wrought iron gates at the top of a staircase at defendant's hospital while talking to fellow employees. The gates gave way as a securing bolt was not properly in its socket. Plaintiff fell down the staircase and was injured—*Held*, defendant liable. It was foreseeable that someone would lean against the gates or use them as support, since outwardly they appeared safe.

U11. Smith v. B.R.B. (1985) C.A. 577

Employees regularly had to gain access to storage area 10 feet above ground level, using any available ladder. Plaintiff was injured when unfastened and unfooted ladder he was using for this purpose slipped—*Held*, defendants liable in negligence and in breach of the Factories Act 1961, s. 29—means of access were unsafe—a permanently fastened ladder, or means of easily fastening a ladder, were called for—it was plainly foreseeable that men would use an insecure ladder. Plaintiff 50 per cent. to blame, for stepping on a rung that protruded above the level of the storage area, knowing the ladder to be insecure.

U12. Johnson v. G.L.C. (1985) C.A. 867

River worker cutting undergrowth on banks of ditch slipped on slab which had formed part of a fence but now lay under the undergrowth, hidden from view—*Held*, defendant liable. The slab increased the risk of slipping and defendant should have removed it. Plaintiff 25 per cent. to blame.

U13. Harvey v. Compair Industries Ltd (1986) C.A. 870

Plaintiff was injured when jumping 4 feet to the ground from the back of a lorry he was employed to drive, and which he was unloading. No form of step down was provided. The back of the lorry platform was not infrequently slippery as a result of rain, oil or grease—*Held*, defendant liable, for not providing a step down or a suitable alternative.

U14. Carter v. British Aerospace plc (1987) C.A. 708

Plaintiff caught his foot on an air-line at his place of work, slipped and fell. The line had not been there when he began work, there was no need for it to have been placed there, and no one warned plaintiff of its presence—*Held*, defendant liable.

U15. Barker v. Brook Motors Ltd (1987) C.A. 996

Plaintiff tripped over wooden batten on floor of a passage in defendant's factory. Passage was ill-lit but plaintiff had not switched on the light—*Held*, defendant liable in negligence and for breach of the Factories Act 1961, s. 28(1). Plaintiff 50 per cent. to blame.

U16. Jones v. London Fire and Civil Defence Authority (1988) C.A. 1004

Fire officer slipped on water that had leaked from fire-fighting machine—*Held*, defendant negligent and in breach of duty under the Occupiers' Liability Act 1957, s. 2, in failing to prevent the presence of water on the floor. Plaintiff one-third to blame.

U17. Dwyer v. Welsh Water Authority (1988) C.A. 1009

Plaintiff stood on step ladder to free a blockage of coke or coal in a conveyor, using 12 foot bar which became jammed. Plaintiff pulled bar as hard as he could—bar suddenly freed, and plaintiff fell, bringing step ladder with him. A solid working platform surrounded by a cage would have prevented the accident and could have been provided at insignificant expense—*Held*, defendant negligent and in breach of The Factories Act 1961, s. 29(1). Accident circumstances were foreseeable. Plaintiff one-third to blame, for failing to take the greatest possible precaution to see he would not lose his balance if bar came away.

U18. Carzana v. West 'n' Welsh Windows Ltd (1989) C.A. 349

Glass-cutter was moving large sheet of glass in confined space when it struck part of a glass rack and shattered—*Held*, defendant not negligent or in breach of The Factories Act 1961, s. 29. Place of work not unsafe.

U19. Ditchfield v. Mabey and Johnson Ltd (1989) C.A. 1098

Welder rolled steel member weighing 175 lbs over to gain access to another part of it. Crushed his thumb between it and a previously welded member which restricted available work space—*Held*, defendant liable in negligence and in breach of The Factories Act 1961, s. 29—failed to provide crane to remove previously welded member and provided work-place so restricted in space as to present a foreseeable risk of the kind of accident that happened. Plaintiff 25 per cent. to blame—should have checked whether there was room to roll the member.

U20. Shore v. Royal Ordnance plc (1989) C.A. 1177

When plaintiff lifted a table at defendant's factory a cast iron radiator stored beneath the table fell on him—*Held*, defendant not liable at common law—no foreseeable danger. Not in breach of The Factories Act 1961, s. 28—radiator was not an obstruction—and not in breach of section 29 of same Act.

U21. Wright v. British Gypsum Ltd (1990) C.A. 158

Plaintiff descended from tracked excavator vehicle by standing on the track, where he slipped on mud and on oil from a fractured hydraulic pipe. The step down had been missing from the vehicle for four months. The vehicle had been satisfactorily repaired the day before—*Held*, on the facts the defendant was not negligent in relation to the leaking oil. The sole cause of the accident was plaintiff's choice of an unsafe means of egress. There were safer means of egress available than that which the plaintiff took.

U22. Hemming v. St Helens and Knowsley H.A. (1991) C.A. 432

Hospital gardener slipped on what he knew to be a mossy path. To his knowledge, there was also a moss-free tarmacadam path he could have used, but he used the mossy path because he reached it first—*Held*, defendant not liable.

U23. Atherton v. Mersey H.A. (1993) C.A. 149

Plaintiff, an assistant nurse in a hospital, banged her knee against a bedside locker behind a curtain as she was hurrying to assist a patient—*Held*, defendant not liable. The place of work was not unsafe.

U24. Disney v. South Western Egg Products (1993) C.A. 938

Plaintiff carried tray of loaves down ramp with 1:4 slope at shop where she worked, to which the loaves had been delivered. She slipped on a few seeds from loaves she had carried by hand immediately beforehand. Ramp was swept after deliveries complete and items delivered had been carried into the shop—*Held*, defendant not negligent and not in breach of the Offices, Shops and Railway Premises Act 1963, s. 16.

Examples

(i) Ships, Docks and Shipyards

Safe

- BELOW DECK: CANDLES TO LIGHT WAY 2
- Below deck: closing door with bars ... 6
- FIREFLOAT: PLAINTIFF FALLING OFF 7
- Cofferdam: no ladder out of 8
- Hatch: 'tween deck hatch part open while moving crate: no lifeline 10
- Hatch: 'tween deck hatch open: no work 13
- Hold: straw over hole 14
- Deck: oily patch 15
- Access: Jacob's ladder swinging free .. 19
- Repairers giving notice of repairs to ship 20
- Deck: pieces of dunnage lying about. 21
- Crane: fall swinging in hold 23
- Hold: uneven landing platform 24
- Hold: load lowered to crush dunnage 24
- Hatch covers: standing on to replace . 25
- Access: 3 foot 6 in. drop from gunwale of barge 27
- Access: plaintiff assuming ladder secured 28
- Hold: ladder as egress 32
- Cargo: securing in storm 34
- Deck: hosepipe cover 35
- DECK: OILY WITH SACKS DOWN 37
- Cargo: lump falling from sugar mound on quay 39
- Cargo: crate toppling over on landing 40
- Deck: loaded with scrap iron 41
- Deck: somewhat slippery with oil 42
- Cargo: articles coming adrift in storm 43
- Cargo: spillage from sacks: reasonable precautions 44
- ACCESS: UNFOOTED LADDER AS ACCESS TO SHIP 47
- Cargo: plaintiff walking across timber which moves 48
- Saloon: steward slipping on saloon floor 49
- Stokehold: sludge and débris on floor 50
- Access: across steel deck of barge 51

Unsafe

- CARGO: NO BARRIER TO STOP CARGO ROLLING OFF 1
- HOLD: NO LIFELINE FOR PLATFORM 3
- Tank top: unguarded 4
- Jetty: hole in it 5
- BREAST ROPE: TOO LOW 9
- Hold: no bilge board and bad lighting 11
- Cargo: stowing greasy drums: slipping 12
- Dock shed: slippery floor 16
- Hatch: only part covered 17
- Deck: slippery with oil and water 18
- Winch platform: small and 41 in. high 22
- DRY DOCK: UNFENCED ALTAR LEDGE 26
- Workplace: under suspended load 29
- Hold: greasy substance 30
- Hold: greasy dunnage 31
- Dry dock: unfenced altar ledge 33
- Cargo: unstable stack of logs on quay 36
- Cargo: tilting when stepped on 38
- Outboard work: no lifeline 45
- Hold: palm oil not cleaned from floor 46
- **Hatch: 'tween deck hatch unfenced at sea** 53
- Deck: steel deck slippery from grain spilt 56
- Cargo: dangerous "wall" in square of hatch 58
- Trawler: no lifeline: trawling in storm 59
- Ship's funnel: liable to give off gases . 61
- UNFENCED DECK AT SEA: NO ASSISTANT 67
- Hold: inadequate lighting 73
- Staging: 27 in. wide but part overhung by propeller 77
- Ladder in hold: banging head on beam 80
- Ladder from quay to lighter: liable to slip 81
- LADDER FROM BULWARKS TO DECK: UNFENCED 86

Safe

Access: gangplanks $25\frac{1}{2}$ in wide	52
Cargo: loose lentils on floor while unloading	54
Cargo: overstowed barrels liable to slip	55
Passageway: steward having to cross 21 in high casing	57
HATCH: LOCKING BARS LYING NEAR WINCH	60
Cargo: greasy pipes in hold	62
Hold: dunange tipping up	63
Access: hosepipe laid on one side of gangway	64
Ship: cramped space for repair work	65
Cargo: bad stowage: sacks	66
DECK: GUNWALE REMOVED FOR LOADING	68
Access: no handrail on ship;s internal ladder	69
Dock shed: loose marbles on floor	70
Ship at sea: washing paintwork in heavy weather	71
Deck (of barge): wet and sloping	72
Cargo: bags of graphite slipping	74
Dock shed: roll of lino falling	75
Seaman: washed overboard on trawler	76
Dock shed: ingot falling from stack	78
Ship: brass coupling of hosepipe across doorway sill	79
Dunnage on deck: plaintiff clambering over	82
ACCESS TO SHIP: CLIMBING OVER SHIP'S RAIL 3 foot 6 in. high	83
CARGO: STACKING GLASS CRATES AGAINST WALL	84
CATWALK: HOSEPIPE RUNNING ALONG	85
Dock road: gap between railway lines	87
Staging: painting engine room on 9 in. plank in calm sea	94
Heat in engine room: fitter collapsing	96
Icy patch: refrigerated hold	97
Hold: oily patch from crated engines	98
Hold: slippery from copra and rainwater	99
Loading bank: oil spilled	101
Ship's ladder: foot two feet above quay	104
Cargo: trap end of overhanging case: plaintiff steps on	105

Unsafe

Gunwale of barge: standing on to paint ship	88
Staging: no guard rail	89
Quayside: plaintiff caught in loop of rope	90
Hatch coaming: debris from previous voyage	91
Vertical ladder: 2-inch toehold	92
Vertical ladder: lashed but not bolted at top	93
Gantry: collapse due to heart rot in wood	95
Deck at sea: seaman on after deck swept by sea	100
Deck: no safety net round hold: slippery from frost	102
Gangway: unsecured	103
Hatch: covered by tarpaulin, but no hatch cover	106
Deck: dunnage athwartships	107
Gantry: edge unfenced: plaintiff hoisting therefrom	108
Gunwale of barge: obstruction thereon	110
Gunwale of barge: slippery liquid from paint thinners	111
Shower: scalding seaman	114
GANGWAY: NO RAILING FOR LAST 3 FEET	116
Hold: insufficient dunnage	117
Hovercraft deck: vibrating	118
Excessive noise in shipyards	120,122
Asbestos dust in shipyards	121
Hold: Unfooted ladder	U2
Jacob's ladder from ship to cutter in swell: ship not forming lee	U3

1. Grantham v. N.Z. Shipping [1940] 4 All E.R. 258, Lewis J.
2. Hill v. Harland & Wolff (1944) 78 L1.L.R. 4, C.C.
3. Mahoney v. A.E. Smith (1945) 78 L1.L.R. 82, Lynskey J.
4. Donovan v. Cammell Laird [1949] 2 All E.R. 82; 82 L1.L.R. 642, Devlin J.
5. Bright v. Thames Stevedoring [1951] 1 Lloyd's Rep. 116, Pritchard J.
6. Maddock v. Scruttons [1951] 1 Lloyd's Rep. 181, Donovan J.
7. Hutchinson v. L.C.C. [1951] 2 Lloyd's Rep. 401, C.A.
8. Daley v. R.H. Green & Silley Weir [1951] 1 Lloyd's Rep. 64, Pritchard J.
9. Evans v. Bustard [1952] 1 Lloyd's Rep. 81, C.A.
10. Green v. N.Z. Shipping [1952] 1 Lloyd's Rep. 318, Gorman J.
11. Byrne v. Clan Line [1952] 2 Lloyd's Rep. 598, Ormerod J.
12. Sullivan v. Antwerp S.S. Co. [1952] 1 Lloyd's Rep. 318, Gorman J.
13. Wenborn v. Harland & Wolff [1952] 1 Lloyd's Rep. 255, Sellers J.
14. Copping v. Butlers Wharf [1952] 2 Lloyd's Rep. 307, Pearson J.
15. Burke v. Ellerman & Papayanni [1953] 1 Lloyd's Rep. 295, Barry J.
16. Reid v. Elder Dempster [1953] 1 Lloyd's Rep. 347, Barry J.
17. Gray v. Docks Executive [1953] 1 Lloyd's Rep. 558, Parker J.
18. Day v. Harland & Wolff [1953] 2 Lloyd's Rep. 58, Pearson J.
19. Scanlon v. Maltby [1953] 2 Lloyd's Rep. 122, Lord Goddard C.J.
20. Cushway v. Mills and Knight [1953] 2 Lloyd's Rep. 272, Streatfeild J.
21. Lynch v. Harland & Wolff [1953] 2 Lloyd's Rep. 536, Glyn-Jones J.
22. Nelson v. P.S.N. [1953] 2 Lloyd's Rep. 685, Gerrard J.
23. Carroll v. P.L.A. [1953] 1 Lloyd's Rep. 66, Parker J.
24. Pease v. B.I.S.N. [1953] 1 Lloyd's Rep. 207, Lord Goddard C.J.
25. Atherton v. Pace [1953] 1 Lloyd's Rep. 353, Stable J.
26. Bath v. B.T.C. [1954] 1 W.L.R. 1013; [1954] 2 All E.R. 542, C.A.
27. Hales v. P.L.A. [1954] 1 Lloyd's Rep. 116, Cassels J.
28. Lusk v. Harland & Wolff [1954] 1 Lloyd's Rep. 346, Parker J.
29. Basted v. Cozens & Sutcliffe [1954] 2 Lloyd's Rep. 132, Devlin J.
30. Cheeseman v. Orient S.N. [1954] 2 Lloyd's Rep. 231, Slade J.
31. Young v. Royal Mail Lines [1954] 2 Lloyd's Rep. 419, Wynn-Parry J.
32. Bryan v. G.S.N. [1951] 1 Lloyd's Rep. 495, Lynskey J.
33. Hurley v. Sanders [1955] 1 All E.R. 833; [1995] 1 Lloyd's Rep. 199, Glyn-Jones J.
34. Mayers v. Laurentian Marine [1955] 1 Lloyd's Rep. 1, C.A.
35. Fairey v. R. H. Green & Silley Weir [1955] 1 Lloyd's Rep. 30, Pilcher J.
36. Arter v. P.L.A. [1955] 1 Lloyd's Rep. 179, Pilcher J.
37. Ravera v. Ellerman & Papayanni [1955] 1 Lloyd's Rep. 45, C.A.
38. Matthews v. Glen Line [1955] 1 Lloyd's Rep. 396, Ormerod J.
39. Copas v. P.L.A. [1955] 1 Lloyd's Rep. 295, Sellers J.

40. Carvin v. Smith Coggins [1955] 1 Lloyd's Rep. 339, Ashworth J.
41. Nevill v. P.L.A. [1955] 1 Lloyd's Rep. 448, Lord Goddard C.J.
42. Downham v. Royal Mail [1955] 1 Lloyd's Rep. 450, McNair J.
43. Lewis v. Union Castle [1955] 1 Lloyd's Rep. 481, Barry J.
44. Wakeford v. Scruttons [1955] 1 Lloyd's Rep. 584, Streatfeild J.
45. Honeyman v. Orient S.N.[1955] 2 Lloyd's Rep. 27, Hilbery J.
46. Buckley v. Ocean S.S. [1955] 2 Lloyd's Rep. 97, Jones J.
47. Robinson v. J. & R. Griffiths [1955] 2 Lloyd's Rep. 101, C.A.
48. Gibbons v. Regent Stevedoring [1955] 2 Lloyd's Rep. 273, Pearce J.
49. Pollendine v. Orient S.N. [1955] 2 Lloyd's Rep. 409, Lord Goddard C.J.
50. Mosettig v. Wm. France Fenwick [1955] 2 Lloyd's Rep. 632, Hallett J.
51. D'wan v. Charles Hay [1955] 2 Lloyd's Rep. 651, Sellers J.
52. Nolan v. G.S.N. [1955] 2 Lloyd's Rep. 751, Gorman J.
53. Morris v. West Hartlepools [1956] A.C. 532; [1956] 1 All E.R. 385, H.L.
54. Rudkin v. Maltby [1956] 1 Lloyd's Rep. 416, Pearce J.
55. Jeyes v. Currie Line [1956] 2 Lloyd's Rep. 87, Pearce J.
56. Pead v. Furness Withy [1956] 2 Lloyd's Rep. 149, Slade J.
57. Perel v. MacAndrews [1956] 2 Lloyd's Rep. 362, Pilcher J.
58. Spring v. J. J. Mack [1956] 2 Lloyd's Rep. 558, Jones J.
59. Lyell v. Boyd Line [1956] 2 Lloyd's Rep. 660, Willmer J.
60. Shanley v. West Coast Stevedoring [1957] 1 Lloyd's Rep. 391, C.A.
61. Nicholson v. Shaw Savill [1957] 1 Lloyd's Rep. 162, Pilcher J.
62. Sargent v. Gee Stevedoring [1957] 1 Lloyd's Rep. 357, Ashworth J.
63. Middleditch v. Union Castle [1957] 1 Lloyd's Rep. 531, Finnemore J.
64. McLean v. Bowring S.S. Co. [1957] 2 Lloyd's Rep. 38, Slade J.
65. Broughton v. Royal Mail [1957] 2 Lloyd's Rep. 44, Lloyd-Jacob J.
66. Fittock v. Shaw Savill [1957] 2 Lloyd's Rep. 149, Glyn-Jones J.
67. Ellis v. Ocean S.S. [1958] 2 Lloyd's Rep. 373, C.A.
68. Lawler v. A. E. Smith Coggins [1958] 1 Lloyd's Rep. 1, C.A.
69. White v. Bowker [1958] 1 Lloyd's Rep. 318, Diplock J.
70. Tickner v. Glen Line [1958] 1 Lloyd's Rep. 468, Devlin J.
71. Meah v. H. Hogarth [1958] 1 Lloyd's Rep. 523, Devlin J.
72. Oughton v. Perkins [1958] 1 Lloyd's Rep. 626, Donovan J.
73. Lynch v. Furness Withy [1958] 2 Lloyd's Rep. 360, Diplock J.
74. Brown v. Scruttons [1958] 2 Lloyd's Rep. 440, Gorman J.
75. Croxford v. Scruttons [1958] 2 Lloyd's Rep. 492, Hilbery J.
76. Jessop v. Newington Steam Trawling [1959] 1 Lloyd's Rep. 118, Karminski J.
77. Campbell v. Harland & Wolff [1959] 1 Lloyd's Rep. 198, Gorman J.
78. Norton v. Hay's Wharf [1959] 1 Lloyd's Rep. 219, McNair J.
79. O'Neill v. B.I.S.N. [1959] 2 Lloyd's Rep. 21, Glyn-Jones J.
80. Wilkins v. William Cory [1959] 1 Lloyd's Rep. 98, Gorman J.
81. Wingfield v. Ellerman's Wilson [1959] 2 Lloyd's Rep. 205, Diplock J.
82. Smallwood v. Lamport and Holt [1959] 2 Lloyd's Rep. 213, Slade J.
83. Ahmed v. Everard [1959] 2 Lloyd's Rep. 466, C.A.
84. Watts v. T. & J. Harrison [1960] 1 Lloyd's Rep. 24, C.A.
85. Ratcliffe v. Shell Petroleum [1960] 1 Lloyd Rep. 30, C.A.
86. Davies v. F. T. Everard [1960] 1 Lloyd's Rep. 59, C.A.
87. Sullivan v. P.L.A. [1960] 1 Lloyd's Rep. 567, Streatfeild J.
88. Manning v. Wright [1960] 2 Lloyd's Rep. 95, Donovan J.
89. King v. Swan Hunter [1960] 2 Lloyd's Rep. 195, Hinchcliffe J.
90. Warwick Deeping [1961] 1 Lloyd's Rep. 30, Karminski J.
91. Dingwall v. J. Wharton [1961] 2 Lloyd's Rep. 213, H.L.
92. Batten v. Harland & Wolff [1961] 1 Lloyd's Rep. 261, Salmon J.
93. Williamson v. Houlder Brothers [1962] 2 Lloyd's Rep. 199, Mocatta J.
94. Wood v. Stag Line [1962] 2 Lloyd's Rep. 132, Elwes J.

95. Jackson v. William Gray [1962] 2 Lloyd's Rep. 156, Sachs J.
96. Adamson v. Ayr Engineering [1963] 1 Lloyd's Rep. 117, Donovan L.J.
97. Roper v. Scruttons [1963] 1 Lloyd's Rep. 120, Donovan L.J.
98. Weller v. Thomas Wallis [1963] 1 Lloyd's Rep. 178, Megaw J.
99. Mawson v. Unilever [1963] 2 Lloyd's Rep. 198. Hewson J.
100. Connell v. Hellyer [1963] 2 Lloyd's Rep. 249, Hewson J.
101. Mahoney v. Hay's Wharf [1963] 2 Lloyd's Rep. 312, Fenton Atkinson J.
102. Stafford v. Antwerp S.S. [1965] 2 Lloyd's Rep. 104, McKenna J.
103. Jolliffe v. Townsend Bros. [1965] 2 Lloyd's Rep. 19, Atkinson J.
104. Beattie v. N.Z. Shipping Co. [1965] 2 Lloyd's Rep. 382, Ct. of Sess.
105. Richards v. Brooks Wharf [1965] 2 Lloyd's Rep. 304, Thompson J.
106. Dyckhoff v. Vokins [1966] 1 Lloyd's Rep. 284, Hinchcliffe J.
107. Day v. Harland & Wolff [1967] 1 Lloyd's Rep. 136, Waller J. (*N.B.* New trial was ordered by C.A. because of fresh evidence.)
108. Jarvis v. Hay's Wharf [1967] 1 Lloyd's Rep. 329, Mocatta J.
109. Paramor v. Dover Harbour Board [1967] 2 Lloyd's Rep. 107, C.A. (reversing trial judge).
110. Fox v. Ardley [1967] 2 Lloyd's Rep. 383, Waller J.
111. Durrell v. Cords & Buck [1967] 2 Lloyd's Rep. 387, Brabin J.
112. McCarthy v. Hellenic Lines [1968] 1 Lloyd's Rep. 537. Willis J.
113. Sullivan v. Temple Steamship [1968] 2 Lloyd's Rep. 95, Hinchcliffe J.
114. Foulder v. Canadian Pacific [1968] 2 Lloyd's Rep. 366, Caulfield J.
115. Attridge v. Hovey Antwerp [1968] 2 Lloyd's Rep. 597, Blain J.
116. Philpott v. B.R.B. [1969] 2 Lloyd's Rep. 180, C.A.
117. Robertson v. Ellerman Lines [1974] 2 Lloyd's Rep. 161, Geoffrey Lane J.
118. Noseda v. Hoverlloyd [1974] 1 Lloyd's Rep. 448, Judge Richards Q.C.
119. Parker v. Vickers [1979] C.L.Y. 1876, Talbot J.
120. Thompson v. Smiths Shiprepairers [1984] Q.B. 405; [1984] 1 All E.R. 881, Mustill J. (see, *e.g.* Chap. 15, ((2)(a)**24**).
121. Boyce v. Swan Hunter Group plc [1988] 1 All E.R. 659; [1987] 2 Lloyd's Rep. 426, Phillips J. (see Chap. 15, ((2)(a)**27**).
122. Baxter v. Harland & Wolff plc [1990] I.R.L.R. 516; [1991] C.L.Y. 1878, N.I.C.A. (see Chap. 15, (2)(a)**29**).

U1. *Chunnoo Meah v. Hogarth* (1959) C.A. 80.
U2. *Preece v. Condrons* (1972) C.A. 91.
U3. *Weston v. British Transport Docks Board* (1975) C.A. 147 A.

Examples

(ii) Places Other Than Ships, Docks and Shipyards

Safe

- Building site: loose plan 7
- Floor: slippery from grease and/or rainwater 8
- FLOOR: AIR LINE LYING ACROSS 9
- **Floor: slippery: sudden storm** 15
- Glass door: at staircase end 17
- Dismantling staging: plaintiff falls in gap 19
- ACCESS: ICY SURFACE FROM SUDDEN SNOWFALL 21
- Private house: electrical fault in loft 22
- WORK 8 FEET UP: NO STAGING 23

Unsafe

- Electric kiosk: live busbar 1
- Boiler: combustible material near 2
- FLOOR: SLIPPERY DUCKBOARD AT TAP 3
- Building: no examination of old supports 4
- LADDER: LEFT BEHIND UNGUARDED DOOR 5
- FACTORY: NO EXTRACTOR FOR DUST 6
- Scaffold: no guard rail 10
- Platform: no ladder 11
- Staging: liable to swing 12
- Steel framework: access along girders 13

Safe

Unsafe

Safe

Unsafe

Safe

Unsecured ladder giving access to carpet shelf 12 feet high U51
Movement of large sheet of glass in confined space U54
Nurse tripping on masking tape at edge of carpet in nursing home U56
Radiator stored beneath table: fell when table moved U57
Descent from excavator by standing on slippery track: safer means of egress available U58
Gardener slipping on mossy path: moss-free path available U59
12-in. drop from tailgate of removal vehicle U61
Bedside locker behind certain at hospital U62
Seeds from loaves on bread: shop floor U63

Unsafe

Two routes: one unsafe: plaintiff following senior employee on latter ... U17
Steel girders: no precautions against fall U19
Gangway: grease regularly dripping. U22
Access: crate left obstructing passageway U23
Access: sulphuric acid spilling on concrete U25
Factory yard: open gully 8 in. wide. 4 in. deep U26
Floor: piece of greasy paper U28
Railway: sidewalk in cutting uneven and overgrown U32
Access: climbing up to mend machine: makeshift assemblage of odd boxes U34
Vinolay in canteen: slippery U35
Cross pieces in college loft: too flimsy to walk on U36
Crack $\frac{3}{8}$ in. deep and $\frac{1}{2}$ in. wide in gangway floor U37
Insecure gates at top of hospital staircase U39
Insecure ladder to raised storage area U40
Slippery slab in ditch bank undergrowth U41
4 foot drop from back of lorry: no step U47
Airline causing tripping accident U48
Wooden batten on ill-lit passage floor U49
Water leaking from fire-fighting machine U52
Plaintiff on step-ladder trying to free blockage on conveyor U53
Movement of heavy steel member in confined space U55
Carrying bucket of molten bitumen up long ladder U60

1. Paine v. Colne Valley [1938] 4 All E.R. 803; 55 T.L.R. 181.
2. D'Urso v. Sanson [1939] 4 All E.R. 26.
3. Davidson v. Handley Page [1945] 1 All E.R. 235; 61 T.L.R. 178, C.A.
4. Whitby v. Burt Boulton [1947] K.B. 918; [1947] 2 All E.R. 324, Denning J.
5. Spencer v. R. H. Green & Silley Weir (1947) 80 Ll.L.R. 217, C.C.
6. Franklin v. Gramophone Co. [1948] 1 K.B. 542; [1948] 1 All E.R. 353, C.A.
7. Field v. Perry's [1950] 2 All E.R. 521; [1950] W.N. 320, Devlin J.

8. Davies v. De Havilland [1951] 1 K.B. 50; [1950] 2 All E.R. 582; Somervell L.J.
9. Taylor v. R. H. Green & Silley Weir [1951] 1 Lloyd's Rep. 345, C.A.
10. Pratt v. Richards [1951] 2 K.B. 208; [1951] 1 All E.R. 90, Barry J.
11. Daniels v. Frederick Leyland [1951] 1 Lloyd's Rep. 59, Pritchard J.
12. Taylor v. Ellerman Wilson [1952] 1 Lloyd's Rep. 144, Ormerod J.
13. Sheppey v. Matthew Shaw [1952] 1 T.L.R. 1272, Parker J.
14. Harris v. Brights Contractors [1953] 1 Q.B. 617; [1953] 1 All E.R. 395, Slade J.
15. Latimer v. A.E.C. [1953] A.C. 643; [1953] 2 All E.R. 449, H.L.
16. Rowden v. Gosling [1953] C.L.Y. 2420, Morris L.J.
17. Gray v. Admiralty [1953] 1 Lloyd's Rep. 14, Ormerod J.
18. Tillett v. Doig [1953] 2 Lloyd's Rep. 707, C.A.
19. Calnan v. London Graving [1953] 1 Lloyd's Rep. 149, Barry J.
20. Flynn v. Harland & Wolff [1953] 1 Lloyd's Rep. 339, McNair J.
21. Thomas v. Bristol Aeroplane [1954] 2 All E.R.1, C.A.
22. Cilia v. James (1954) 98 S.J. 320; [1954] 2 All E.R. 9, Byrne J.
23. Reading v. Harland & Wolff [1954] 1 Lloyd's Rep. 131, C.A.
24. Swift v. Mountstuart Dry Docks [1954] 2 Lloyd's Rep. 1, C.A.
25. Basted v. Cozens & Sutcliffe [1954] 2 Lloyd's Rep. 132, Devlin J.
26. Williams v. M.D.H.B. [1954] 2 Lloyd's Rep. 221, C.A.
27. Copeland v. R. H. Green & Silley Weir [1954] 2 Lloyd's Rep. 315, Finnemore J.
28. Montgomery v. A. Monk [1954] 1 W.L.R. 258; [1954] 1 All E.R. 252, C.A.
29. Murray v. Walnut Cabinet Works [1954] C.L.Y. 1320, C.A.
30. Jones v. Richards [1955] 1 W.L.R. 444; [1955] 1 All E.R. 463, Barry J.
31. Downham v. Royal Mail Lines [1955] 1 Lloyd's Rep. 450, McNair J.
32. McDonald v. B.T.C. [1955] 1 W.L.R. 1323; [1955] 3 All E.R. 789, Pilcher J.
33. Walsh v. N.C.B. [1955] 1 Q.B. 511; [1955] 3 All E.R. 632, C.A.
34. Gemmell v. P.L.A. [1955] 1 Lloyd's Rep. 5, C.A.
35. Davey v. P.L.A. [1955] 1 Lloyd's Rep. 135, Pilcher J.
36. Prince v. Carrier Engineering [1955] 1 Lloyd's Rep. 401, Parker L.J.
37. Niznikiewicz v. B.T.C., *The Times*, February 2, 1955; [1955] C.L.Y. 1899, C.A.
38. Davison v. Apex Scaffolding [1956] 1 All E.R. 473, 485 F, C.A.
39. Chipchase v. British Titan [1956] 1 Q.B. 545; [1956] 1 All E.R. 613, C.A.
40. Simmons v. Bovis [1956] 1 W.L.R. 381; [1956] 1 All E.R. 736, Barry J.
41. Moore v. R. Fox [1956] 1 Q.B. 569; [1956] 1 All E.R. 182, C.A.
42. Sidor v. Associated Tunnelling [1956] C.L.Y. 5536, McNair J.
43. Hayden v. M.D.H.B. [1956] 2 Lloyd's Rep. 497, Jones J.
44. Carrington v. John Summers [1957] 1 W.L.R. 504; [1957] 1 All E.R. 457, Streatfeild J.
45. Wilson v. International Combustion [1957] 3 All E.R. 505n., C.A.
46. Trznadel v. B.T.C. [1957] 1 W.L.R. 1002; [1957] 3 All E.R. 196, C.A.
47. Barnes v. P.L.A. [1957] 1 Lloyd's Rep. 486, Byrne J.
48. Mitchell v. N.C.B. [1957] C.L.Y. 2193; 107 L.J. 265, Glyn-Jones J.
49. Nicholls v. Reemer [1957] C.L.Y. 2351; 107 L.J. 378, McNair J.
50. Lawes v. Nicholl, *The Times*, May 8, 1957; [1957] C.L.Y. 2419, Salmon J.
51. Baily v. Ayr Engineering [1958] 2 All E.R. 222, C.A.
52. Wilson v. Tyneside Window Cleaning [1958] 2 Q.B. 110; [1958] 2 All E.R. 265, C.A.
53. Hicks v. B.T.C. [1958] 1 W.L.R. 493; [1958] 2 All E.R. 39, C.A.
54. Braithwaite v. South Durham Steel [1958] 1 W.L.R. 986; [1958] 3 All E.R. 161, Davies J.
55. Machin v. Cravens (1958) 108 L.J. 633; [1958] C.L.Y. 1319, Salmon J.
56. Smith v. Austin Lifts [1959] 1 All E.R. 81, H.L.
57. Jenner v. Allen West [1959] 1 W.L.R. 554; [1959] 2 All E.R. 115, C.A.
58. Baker v. Hopkins [1959] 3 All E.R. 225, C.A.
59. Burke v. New Fresh Wharf [1959] 1 Lloyd's Rep. 57, Jones J.
60. Kimpton v. Steel Company of Wales [1960] 2 All E.R. 274, C.A.
61. Braithwaite v. Caulfield, *The Times*, May 5, 1961; [1961] C.L.Y. 5928, H.L.
62. Laing v. Royal Mail Lines [1960] 2 Lloyd's Rep. 33, Donovan J.

63. Quintas v. National Smelting Co. [1961] 1 W.L.R. 401; [1961] 1 All E.R. 630, C.A.
64. Batten v. Harland & Wolff [1961] 1 Lloyd's Rep. 261, Salmon J.
65. Bill v. Short Brothers [1963] N.I. 1; [1962] C.L.Y. 2014, H.L.
66. Blades v. B.B.C; *The Times*, December 2, 1961; [1961] C.L.Y. 5989, Barry J.
67. Carolan v. Redpath Brown (1964) 108 S.J. 136; [1964] C.L.Y. 2542, C.A.
68. Fisher v. C.H.T. [1966] 2 Q.B. 475; [1966] 1 All E.R. 87, C.A.
69. Vinnyey v. Star Paper [1965] 1 All E.R. 175, Cumming Bruce J.
70. Donaghey v. O'Brien [1966] 2 All E.R. 822, C.A. (see [1967] 2 All E.R. 1014, H.L.).
71. Sanderson v. Millom Hematite [1967] 3 All E.R. 1050, Cantley J.
72. Thornton v. Fisher & Ludlow [1968] 1 W.L.R. 655; [1968] 2 All E.R. 241, C.A.
73. Pisicani v. P.O., *The Times*, May 11 1967; [1967] C.L.Y. 2706, C.A.
74. Kendrick v. Cozens and Sutcliffe (1968) 5 K.I.R. 469; [1968] C.L.Y. 334, C.A.
75. Birch v. Indestructive Paint (1968) 118 New L.J. 421; [1968] C.L.Y. 2661, Phillimore J.
76. Collier v. Hall & Ham River (1968) 4 K.I.R. 628; [1968] C.L.Y. 2693, Waller J.
77. Houghton v. Hackney B.C. (1967) 3 K.I.R. 615; [1968] C.L.Y. 2706; Diplock J.
78. Maher v. Hurst (1969) 6 K.I.R. 95; 67 L.G.R. 367, C.A.
79. Baxter v. St. Helena Group H.M.C., *The Times*, February 15, 1972; [1972] C.L.Y. 2365, C.A.
80. Stanley v. Concentric (1971) 11 K.I.R. 260, C.A.
81. Busby v. Watson (1973) 13 K.I.R. 498; [1973] C.L.Y. 2321, Forbes J.
82. Thompson v. Bowaters (1975) K.I.R. 47; [1975] C.L.Y. 1427, C.A.
83. Venus v. Peters Ice Cream (1976) 14 S.A.S.R. 247; [1977] C.L.Y. 2036, Sup. Ct. of South Aust.
84. Godden v. Brewer[1977] C.L.Y. 2028, Michael Davies J.
85. McCafferty v. Metropolitan Police District Receiver [1977] 1 W.L.R. 1073; [1977] 2 All E.R. 756, C.A.
86. Bell v. Vaughan [1979] C.L.Y. 1299, Hodgson J.
87. Woodward v. Renold [1980] I.C.R. 387; [1980] C.L.Y. 1274, Lawson J.
88. Sanders v. Lloyd[1982] I.C.R. 360; [1982] C.L.Y. 1365, Drake J.
89. Halsey v. South Bedfordshire D.C., *The Times*, October 13, 1983; [1983] C.L.Y. 2564, Kilner Brown J.
90. Kondis v. State Transport Authority (1984) 154 C.L.R. 672; [1984] C.L.Y. 2262, High Court of Australia (see Chap. 15, (1)(d) **14**).
91. Fildes v. International Computers [1984] C.L.Y. 2316, C.A. (see Chap. 15, (5) **22**).
92. Hemmings v. British Aerospace [1986] C.L.Y. 2265, Swinton Thomas J. (see Chap. 15, (1)(b) **15**).
93. Darby v. G.K.N. Screws & Fasteners Ltd [1988] I.C.R. 1; [1986] C.L.Y. 2266, Peter Pain J. (see Chap. 15, (5) **23**).
94. Davies v. Massey Ferguson Perkins[1986] I.C.R. 580; [1986] C.L.Y. 1539, Evans J. (see Chap. 15, (5) **24**).
95. Aldred v. Nacanco [1987] I.R.L.R. 292; [1987] C.L.Y. 1367, C.A. (see Chap. 15, (5) **25**).
96. Bacon v. Jack Tighe (Offshore) and Cape Scaffolding [1987] C.L.Y. 2568, H.H. Judge Whitehead, Lincolm County Court (see Chap. 15, (2)(a) **26**).
97. Yates v. Rockwell Graphic Systems Ltd [1988] I.C.R. 8; [1988] C.L.Y. 1739, Steyn J. (see Chap. 15, (4)(b) **30**).
98. Bell v. D.H.S.S., *The Times*, June 13, 1989; [1989] C.L.Y. 2547, Drake J. (see Chap. 15, (2)(c) **23**).
99. Hanlon v. B.R.B., 1991 S.L.T. 228; [1991] C.L.Y. 5303 (see Chap. 15, (3) **25**).
100. Gitsham v. C.H. Pearce and Sons [1992] P.I.Q.R. P57; *The Times*, February 11, 1991, C.A. (see Chap. 15, (2)(a) **30**).
101. Hewett v. Alf Brown's Transport [1992] I.C.R. 530; [1992] P.I.Q.R. P199, C.A. (see Chap. 15, (5) **26**).
102. Hill v. Lovett, 1992 S.L.T. 994; [1992] C.L.Y. 6084, (see Chap. 15, (5) **27**).
103. Dixon v. London Fire and Civil Defence Authority, *The Times*, February 22, 1993; [1993] C.L.Y. 2025, C.A. (see Chap. 15, (5) **28**).
104. Flagg v. Kent C.C. [1993] P.I.Q.R. P389, C.A. (see Chap. 15, (3) **27**).

U1. *Evison v. Mayor of Peterborough* (1951) C.A. 233.
U2. *Devenny v. Moore* (1951) C.A. 357.
U3. *Senior v. Fowler* (1952) C.A. 69.
U4. *Bent v. London Transport Executive* (1952) C.A. 76.
U5. *Cryer v. Deepdale Labour Club* (1952) C.A. 240.
U6. *Quinn v. Lambeth Group Hospital Management Committee* (1953) C.A. 31.

U7. *Pryde v. Wright, Anderson & Co. Ltd* (1953) C.A. 232 C.
U8. *Ackerley v. Fearnall* (1954) C.A. 27.
FU9. *Longworth v. Hughes* (1954) C.A. 29 A.
U10. *Rendell v. Bournemouth Corporation* (1954) C.A. 79.
U11. *Herraghty v. Riley and Neate Ltd* (1954) C.A. 297 A.
U12. *Payne v. Clarke Chapman & Co.* (1955) C.A. 33.
U13. *Thornely v. Manchester Abattoirs Products Ltd* (1955) C.A. 161.
U14. *Cendrowski v. Fairford Concrete Products Ltd* (1955) C.A. 340.
U15. *Shelley v. Binns Ltd* (1956) C.A. 65 A.
U16. *Moss v. Belsham & Fairburn* (1956) C.A. 66.
U17. *Wright v. N.C.B.* (1956) C.A. 74.
U18. *Cole v. Berk & Co. Ltd* (1956) C.A. 76.
U19. *Wilson v. International Combustion Ltd* (1956) C.A. 218.
U20. *Brading v. Guest Keen Iron & Steel Co. Ltd* (1957) C.A. 85.
U21. *Lannen v. Weston Biscuit Co. (Wales) Ltd* (1957) C.A. 192.
U22. *Wolstenholme v. Briggs Motor Bodies Ltd* (1958) C.A. 26.
U23. *Price v. N.C.B.* (1959) C.A. 228.
U24. *Bramwell v. Jacksons Industries* (1960) C.A. 152.
U25. *Oakley v. Steel Company of Wales* (1960) C.A. 179 A.
U26. *Mullinder v. Gasel* (1960) C.A. 209.
U27. *Green v. N.C.B.* (1960) C.A. 281.
U28. *Fletcher v. Steel Company of Wales* (1960) C.A. 248.
U29. *Brennan v. Techno Constructors* (1962) C.A. 336.
U30. *Thomas v. Birds Eye Foods* (1962) C.A. 371.
U31. *Clayton v. Worcester Royal Porcelain* (1963) C.A. 136 A.
U32. *Smith v. British Railways* (1964) C.A. 272.
U33. *Eley v. Avery* (1965) C.A. 113 B.
U34. *Horton v. Chubb* (1966) C.A. 60.
U35. *Rabbits v. Tubes* (1966) C.A. 318.
U36. *Astbury v. West Riding C.C.* (1970) C.A. 443.
U37. *Britton v. Ministry of Defence* (1983) C.A. 767 (see Chap. 15, (2) (f) **U1**).
U38. *Pickford v. Control Data* (1984) C.A. 720 (see Chap. 15, (2) (f) **U3**).
U39. *Turner v. Salford Area H.A.* (1984) C.A. 1286 (see Chap. 15, (5) **U10**).
U40. *Smith v. B.R.B.* (1985) C.A. 577 (see Chap. 15, (5) **U11**).
U41. *Johnson v. G.L.C.* (1985) C.A. 867 (see Chap. 15, (5) **U12**).
U42. *Priestly v. Nottingham H.A.* (1986) C.A. 37 (see Chap. 15, (2) (a) **U6**).
U43. *Graham v. Esso Petroleum* (1986) C.A. 614 (see Chap. 15, (2) (a) **U8**).
U44. *Harvey v. Compair Industries Ltd* (1986) C.A. 870 (see Chap. 15, (5) **U13**).
U45. *Taylor v. British Gas Corporation* (1986) C.A. 906 (see Chap. 15, (2) (h) **U6**).
U46. *Sinclair v. Electrolux Ltd* (1986) C.A. 1025 (see Chap. 15, (1) (b) **U7**).
U47. *Chrost v. B.S.C.* (1987) C.A. 575 (see Chap. 15, (2) (l) **U7**).
U48. *Carter v. British Aerospace plc* (1987) C.A. 708 (see Chap. 15, (5) **U14**).
U49. *Barker v. Brook Motors Ltd* (1987) C.A. 996 (see Chap. 15, (5) **U15**).
U50. *Babinski v. Atlantic Steam Navigation Co. Ltd* (1988) C.A. 462 (see Chap. 15, (2) (l) **U8**).
U51. *Bundell v. Portsea Island Mutual Co-operative Society Ltd* (1988) C.A. 791 (see Chap. 15, (2) (l) **U9**).
U52. *Jones v. London Fire and Civil Defence Authority* (1988) C.A. 1004 (see Chap. 15, (5) **U16**).
U53. *Dwyer v. Welsh Water Authority* (1988) C.A. 1009 (see Chap. 15, (5) **U17**).
U54. *Carzana v. West 'n' Welsh Windows Ltd* (1989) C.A. 343 (see Chap. 15, (5) **U18**).
U55. *Ditchfield v. Mabey and Johnson Ltd* (1989) C.A. 1098 (see Chap. 15, (5) **U19**).
U56. *Walton v. Joyce and Joyce* (1989) C.A. 1134.
U57. *Shore v. Royal Ordnance plc* (1989) C.A. 1177 (see Chap. 15, (5) **U20**).
U58. *Wright v. British Gypsum Ltd* (1990) C.A. 158 (see Chap. 15, (5) **U21**).
U59. *Hemming v. St. Helens and Knowsley H.A.* (1991) C.A. 432 (see Chap. 15, (5) **U22**).
U60. *Wray v. Kirklees Rock Asphalt Ltd* (1991) C.A. 553 (see Chap. 15, (4) **U50**).
U61. *Gilbert v. Lane's Storage and Removals Ltd* (1991) C.A. 767 (see Chap. 15, (2) (l) **U12**).

U62. *Atherton v. Mersey Regional H.A.* (1993) C.A. 149 (see Chap. 15, (5) **U23**).
U63. *Disney v. South Western Egg Products* (1993) C.A. 938 (see Chap. 15, (5) **U24**).

(6) Plant and Appliances

(*N.B.* See also the cases listed as Examples, below. For fuller details of cases dealing with equipment and plant which is defective when brought by the employer, see Chap. 15, (1)(d)).

1. Naismith v. London Film Productions [1939] 1 All E.R. 794; [1939] W.N. 86 C.A.

Greene M.R. (796 G): "The obligation of defendants . . . was to provide proper equipment for their employees. That does not mean of course that they were not entitled to supply equipment which was in fact dangerous, but if they supplied equipment which was in fact dangerous, that would impose on them, as a matter of law, the further duty to take whatever steps were reasonable and proper to ensure that the danger should be minimised as far as possible."

2. O'Melia v. Freight Conveyors [1940] 4 All E.R. 516

Defendants had provided sound rope—but it disappeared and someone else's unsound rope was used—*Held*, defendants not liable "for want of proper system".

3. Lovell v. Blundells [1944] 1 K.B. 502; [1944] 1 All E.R. 53, Tucker J.

No system for obtaining materials for staging—plaintiff left to find for himself—collapse of staging—*Held*, defendants liable.

4. Norris v. Syndic [1952] 2 Q.B. 135; [1952] 1 All E.R. 935, C.A.

For details see Chap. 16, (2) (f) **5**—one of the questions was whether a guard fitted to a machine without any instructions for its use was an "appliance provided" within the Factories Act 1937, s. 119—*Held*, it was.

5. Marshall v. Hull Fishing Vessel Owners [1954] 2 Lloyd's Rep. 495, Parker J.

See Chap. 15, (2) (e) **4**.

6. Brophy v. Bradfield [1955] 1 W.L.R. 1158; [1955] 3 All E.R. 286, C.A.

Unexplained accident—lorry driver found suffocated in boiler house where he had no right to be—*Held*, proof of accident did not shift onus to defendants, and if it did, the fact that the boiler had worked satisfactorily for 25 years was an answer.

7. Harman v. Mitcham Works, *The Times*, June 22, 1955; [1955] C.L.Y. 1894, C.A.

Manufacture of fluorescent lighting tubes—plaintiff handling beryllium oxide—causes chronic poisoning—*Held*, (2–1), that as defendants had no knowledge of danger at time and no reason to suspect it, not liable.

8. Quinn v. Horsfall [1956] 1 W.L.R. 652; [1956] 2 All E.R. 467, C.A.

9. Cusack v. T. & J. Harrison [1956] 1 Lloyd's Rep. 100, C.A.

Held, defendants not liable for using a latticed metal tray to discharge cartons. Singleton L.J. (104): "But, on the whole, they (the employers) are the best judges of the tackle and appliances which should be used. If they adopt some method which is fraught with danger, in the ordinary course some workman or some officer of the union—a safety officer, for instance—will probably point out the danger therefrom, and they will take warning."

10. Bastable v. Eastern Electricity Board [1956] 1 Lloyd's Rep. 586, C.A.

Held, defendants not liable for failing to carry out periodical inspections of chisel issued to plaintiff, which became blunt in use—Denning L.J. (588, col. 2): "It seems to me that the system which the employers had of remedying any bluntness as soon as it was reported was a perfectly good system. These men, who had been doing this kind of work for years, were as well able as anyone to know whether a chisel was blunt; they could inspect for themselves."

11. Roberts v. T. Wallis [1958] 1 Lloyd's Rep. 29, Barry J.

Set of timber suspended from winch fell 2–3 feet onto floor of hold—*Held*, defendants not liable, as not *res ipsa loquitur*, and the only two causes suggested were (a) breaking of connecting rod of winch, which would probably be latent defect, and (b) a riding turn on barrel of winch, which would not be negligence in itself.

12. Graves v. J. & E. Hall [1958] 2 Lloyd's Rep. 100, Barry J.

Plaintiff fitter's mate employed by defendant refrigeration engineers to remove condensers from a ship—plaintiff is left to borrow suitable rope from ship's store to lift condensers—plaintiff, not being able to tell difference, borrows a coir rope (instead of manila or sisal)—it breaks—plaintiff injured—*Held*, defendants not negligent in leaving plaintiff to borrow from ship, but they were negligent in not instructing plaintiff (a) to contact storeman when borrowing, and/or (b) how to differentiate between different types of rope. Defendants liable.

13. Davie v. New Merton Board Mills [1959] 1 All E.R. 346, H.L.

Held, defendants not liable, as duty only to take reasonable care, and the defect in the tool was not reasonably discoverable by defendants. See cases in Chap 15 (1) (d). *N.B.* The effect of this decision is now largely *reversed* by the Employers' Liability (Defective Equipment) Act 1969.

14. Close v. Steel Company of Wales [1962] A.C. 367; [1961] 2 All E.R. 953, H.L.

"If in a factory there is a machine which it is known from experience has a tendency to throw out parts of the machine itself or of the material on which it is working, so as to be a danger to the operator, the absence of a shield to protect him may well afford him a cause of action at common law" (Lord Goddard, 961 D).

15. Harriman v. Martin [1962] 1 W.L.R. 739; [1962] 1 All E.R. 225, C.A.

Slicing 9-inch planks with circular saw protruding $4\frac{3}{4}$ inches—impracticable to fence—plaintiff pulling plank through by himself when plank kicked and his right hand was caught in the saw—*Held*, defendants liable, as they should have (a) supplied a second man to pull off planks, or (b) provided a larger saw which could have been fenced.

16. Ross v. Associated Portland Cement [1964] 1 W.L.R. 768; [1964] 2 All E.R. 452; H.L.

Issue was breach of statutory duty (safe workplace), but the question was whether plaintiff or defendants were responsible for an admitted breach of the Factories Act 1937, s. 26, in using a ladder to repair a cableway instead of a mobile tower, and on this Lord Reid (456 B) said: "But it is his (defendant's) responsibility to see that proper instructions are given and proper equipment is available. Where the work is to be done by a person fully skilled in that type of work, he may say: 'Go and plan out the work and come back and discuss the matter if you have any difficulty, or cannot find the equipment you need.' But here Ross was only a chargehand, the respondents had no reason to suppose that he had ever done a job of this kind before, and there is nothing to show the chief engineer gave him any encouragement to come back and discuss the matter. No account has been taken of the reluctance which a man in Ross's position would naturally feel in going to a chief engineer univited to ask for extra equipment ... ".

17. Taylor v. Rover [1966] 2 All E.R. 181, Baker J.

Chisel defective when bought—due to negligent hardening by independent contractor employed by manufacturers to harden chisels for them—employer became aware of defect, but allowed chisel to remain in use—*Held*, employer liable, but manufacturer was not, because (a) the keeping of the chisel in use broke the chain of causation, so far as manufacturers were concerned, and (b) the manufacturers, having got a competent hardener to do the hardening for them, were entitled to assume that the hardening was done properly and had no duty to examine or test for themselves.

18. Barry v. Black-Clawson (1966) 2 K.I.R. 237; [1966] C.L.Y. 2678, C.A.

See Chap. 15, (1) (d) **11** for details. *N.B.* Plaintiff was in fact an independent contractor.

19. Pearce v. Round Oak Steel Works [1969] 1 W.L.R. 595; [1969] 3 All E.R. 680, C.A.

Bolt in machine broke through metal fatigue, and machine fell on plaintiff—*Held*, the breaking of the bolt raised a presumption of negligence, and that as the defendants had called no evidence, they were liable.

20. McPhee v. General Motors (1970) 8 K.I.R. 885; [1970] C.L.Y. 187, Lyell J.

Cabinet consisting of a hood with a door—the hood was raised and lowered on four pillars—there was a safety device which ensured that so long as the door was open the hood could not come down—but the apparatus had behaved temperamentally for some time—it finally refused to work—and P, a maintenance fitter employed by defendants, was called to attend to it—he was not told of its temperamental history—while he was inspecting it, the hood suddenly came down—*Held*, defendants liable, as they should have warned P of previous history of machine.

21. Sumner v. P.L.A. [1974] 2 Lloyd's Rep. 92; [1974] C.L.Y. 2568, Mocatta J.

Load of angle iron slipped from sling and killed fork lift driver—*Held*, employers of driver not liable for failing to provide a headguard, as purpose of headguard was to prevent packages falling back onto driver, and in any event plaintiff had failed to show that a headguard would have saved driver.

U1. Broaster v. Curlwood (1951) C.A. 97

Overhand planing machine—statutory requirements complied with—defect developed—repair—but no further inspection—left to plaintiff to report if defect developed again—plaintiff injured when it did—*Held*, defendant liable.

U2. Stevenson v. Birkett & Roberts Ltd (1952) C.A. 116

Plaintiff electrician injured when repairing wheel of bread-setter—plaintiff alleged defendants negligent in not providing right tools—*Held*, defendants not liable, as plaintiff experienced and able to ask for any tools he required.

U3. Howlett v. Lacey (1953) C.A. 218

Plaintiff joiner putting up rod over staircase window—no vehicle or truck available to take materials from defendants' premises—told to borrow equipment next door—fell from dangerous erection made with borrowed ladder and step-ladder—*Held*, defendants not liable, as plaintiff's negligence in not getting plank caused accident.

U4. Flaherty v. Carter Horsley (1954) C.A. 258

Plaintiff told by foreman to get ladder for job—cannot find one—there was one available—plaintiff falls—*Held*, defendants not liable.

U5. Goulding v. Ministry of Works (1955) C.A. 175 A

Held, defendants liable.

U6. Barker v. Hardman Ltd (1956) C.A. 182 A

Plaintiff supervisor at erection of school—second-hand concrete mixer used—inspected by someone who said it was all right—machine stopped—plaintiff trying to start—handle came away and struck plaintiff in eye—defendants no reason to know machine not in suitable condition for use—*Held*, defendants not liable.

U7. Wall v. Barker (1957) C.A. 305

Raised body of tipping lorry collapsed—mechanism defective—before accident new coupling had been fitted as old coupling defective—*Held*, defendant negligent, as no general practice of inspecting mechanism at periodic intervals but only when defects reported and no testing of repaired mechanism before sending vehicle out.

U8. Robinson v. Pearce (1960) C.A. 267 A

Plaintiff bricklayer sent to a private house to repair chimney—defendant employers send him his equipment separately by lorry—ladder and cat ladder—but no rope for lashing them—plaintiff goes up unlashed cat ladder, which slips—trial judge apportioned blame two-thirds against employer, one-third against plaintiff—*Held*, plaintiff 75 per cent. to blame, as he erected and went up an obviously dangerous cat ladder without having checked or queried the absence of rope with the lorry driver and without having rung up employers to ask for rope to be sent.

U9. Dickie v. Brighton Lighting (1962) C.A. 367

Piece of metal in eye of plaintiff from improvised punch used by fellow-workman—*Held*, defendants not liable, as hardness of punch lay between .9 and 1.3 per cent. of carbon, and expert metallurgist put permissible limits at .95 and 1.25 per cent.

U10. O'Connor v. Gerrard (1964) C.A. 30

Chisel of mechanical breaker broke—bringing machine down on plaintiff's foot—D, employers, had bought chisel from reputable suppliers—break was due to fatigue stress which was only discoverable with magnetic test equipment or by X-rays—*Held*, it was unreasonable to expect D to carry out such tests, and claim failed.

U11. Ford v. Higgins (1968) C.A. 432 A

Held, applying *dicta* in *Bastable* **10.**

U12. Reynolds v. B.S.C. (1977) C.A. 128

Sheeting up railway wagon—plaintiff thrown when rope broke—defendants called no evidence—*Held*, applying *dicta* of Lord Pearson in *Henderson v. Jenkins* (Chap. 3, (1) (g) **20**), the plaintiff's evidence made it more probable than not that the rope broke because of some defect which the defendants with reasonable care might have discovered, and therefore in the absence of evidence from them, they were liable.

U13. Halewood v. A.E. O'hare & Partners Ltd (1984) C.A. 972

Plaintiff, an electrician, attempted to remove a bolt by means of a second bolt which he had previously removed, and which he struck with a hammer. The hammer deflected off the second bolt and struck his finger. Had he used an instrument known as a "podger" the risk of injury would have been far less. He had asked for one, but none was available—*Held*, defendant liable at common law.

U14. Arthur v. Geever Tin Miner Ltd (1986) C.A. 417

Plaintiff working in defendant's mine was attempting to clear broken rock which had become blocked in a box-hole shaft above him, using a metal pinch bar. Some rock fell onto the bar which in turn struck and pinched plaintiff—*Held*, defendant liable—there was a foreseeable risk of injury from the work the plaintiff was doing. Further the use of "grizzly" bars at the top of the shaft—common practice in other mines—would have substantially reduced the risk of oversized pieces of material getting into and blocking the shaft.

U15. Weir v. Bedford Commercial Vehicles (1988) C.A. 574

Release mechanism on plaintiff's drilling machine stuck due to a defect of which he had informed the defendants, who had not rectified it. To free the drill bit, he struck the chuck with his left hand, without holding the bit with his right hand, and the bit fell and injured his left hand—*Held*, defendants liable for their failure to maintain the machine. Although plaintiff acknowledged it would have been sensible to hold the bit with his right hand, no contributory negligence found. When a workman was doing his best on a repetitive job and suffered an accident due to his employers' fault, the court would not be astute to find contributory negligence against him.

U16. Smith v. Post Office (1989) C.A. 931

Plaintiff, motor mechanic, jacked up van with jack which was not suitable but could have been used with care. Van slipped off jack and struck plaintiff. There were five suitable jacks on defendants premises, none of which were then available—*Held*, defendant not liable—had provided enough jacks for all reasonably foreseeable contingencies—Plaintiff could have waited for a suitable jack to become available.

U17. Treacher v. B.B.C. (1992) C.A. 136

Plaintiff seriously injured when brakes of truck he was driving failed. Truck was more than five years old but brake fluid had never been examined or changed—*Held*, defendant liable for failing reasonably to maintain the vehicle.

Examples

Safe		Unsafe	
Torch for security officer patrolling derelict site	U35	*Unmarked open can: petrol in it*	U4
Unsuitable vehicle jack: plaintiff could have waited for suitable one: no liability	U36	*Ladder for window cleaning: no rubber footings*	U5
		Overhand planing machine: no jig or holder for chair wings	U8
		Tipping mechanism of lorry: body collapsing when raised	U9
		Carbon disulphide gas exploding	U12
		Continuously fed metal strip: nip unguarded	U13
		Wire rope: finger cut by frayed strand	U14
		Circular saw: offcuts projected from rear	U16
		Fire extinguisher: bursting during charging	U19
		Lorry tyre: no cage or remote control airline to inflate from very low pressure	U21
		Rope breaking when sheeting up railway wagon	U22
		Circular saw: no pullstick	U23
		Inadequate insulation to lag connecting live wires on electricity pole	U24
		Lathe producing swarf: no chip breaker provided	U25
		Twisting drum: hydraulic device should have been provided	U26
		Attempting to remove bolt: "podger" not providedv	U27
		"Grizzly" bar not fitted to shaft in mine: plaintiff injured cleaning ensuing blockage	U28
		4-foot drop from back of lorry: no step provided	U30
		Release mechanism on drilling machine defective	U32
		High pressure hose: instructions on how to hold and control necessary.	U33
		Truck brakes failing	U37

1. Naismith v. London Film Productions [1939] 1 All E.R. 794; [1939] W.N. 86, C.A.
2. Russell v. Criterion Films [1936] 3 All E.R. 627; 53 T.L.R. 117.
3. Speed v. Swift [1943] 1 K.B. 557; [1943] 1 All E.R. 539, C.A.
4. Platt v. Alfred Holt (1944) 77 Ll.L.R. 296, Birkett J.
5. Handley v. Cunard White Star (1944) 77 Ll.L.R. 543, Croom-Johnson J.
6. Porter v. Liverpool Stevedoring (1944) 77 Ll.L.R. 411, Hilbery J.
7. Roberts v. Alfred Holt (1945) 78 Ll.L.R. 236, Singleton J.

8. Bailey v. G.W.R. (1946) 79 Ll.L.R. 321, Hallett J.
9. Vaughan v. Ropner (1947) 80 Ll.L.R. 119, C.A.
10. Pratt v. Richards [1951] 2 K.B. 208; [1951] 1 All E.R. 90n., Barry J.
11. Daniels v. Frederick Leyland [1951] 1 Lloyd's Rep. 59, Pritchard J.
12. Daley v. R. H. Green and Silley Weir [1951] 1 Lloyd's Rep. 64. Pritchard J.
13. Bryan v. G.S.N. [1951] 1 Lloyd's Rep. 495, Lynskey J.
14. Coulam v. Consolidated Fisheries [1951] 1 Lloyd's Rep. 135, Finnemore J.
15. Bright v. Thames Stevedoring [1951] 1 Lloyd's Rep. 116, Pritchard J.
16. Shotter v. R. H. Green and Silley Weir [1951] 1 Lloyd's Rep. 329, Lynskey J.
17. Pearce v. Armitage (1950) 83 Ll.L.R. 361, C.A.
18. Tierney v. Gupwell [1951] 2 Lloyd's Rep. 55, C.A.
19. General Cleaning Contractors v. Christmas [1952] 2 All E.R. 1110, H.L.
20. Rutherford v. T. & J. Harrison [1952] 2 Lloyd's Rep. 493, Jones J.
21. Holford v. P.L.A. [1953] 1 Lloyd's Rep. 162, Byrne J.
22. Watts v. Shaw Savill [1953] 1 Lloyd's Rep. 407, McNair J.
23. Gatehouse v. John Summers [1953] 1 W.L.R. 742, [1953] 2 All E.R. 117, C.A.
24. Scanlon v. Maltby [1953] 2 Lloyd's Rep. 122, Lord Goddard C.J.
25. Watt v. Herts C.C. [1954] 1 W.L.R. 835; [1954] 2 All E.R. 368, C.A.
26. Moore v. West Coast Stevedoring [1954] 2 Lloyd's Rep. 447, Pearce J.
27. Hurley v. B.T.C. [1954] 2 Lloyd's Rep. 343, Pilcher J.
28. James v. Vauxhall Motors [1955] 1 Lloyd's Rep. 152, Stable J.
29. Kiernan v. R. H. Green and Silley Weir [1955] 1 Lloyd's Rep. 454, Pilcher J.
30. Jones v. Richards [1955] 1 W.L.R. 444; [1955] 1 All E.R. 463, Barry J.
31. Mason v. Williams & Williams [1955] 1 W.L.R. 549; [1955] 1 All E.R. 808, Finnemore J.
32. McDonald v. B.T.C. [1955] 1 W.L.R. 1323; [1955] 3 All E.R. 789, Pilcher J.
33. Burgess v. Union Castle [1955] 1 Lloyd's Rep. 262, Devlin J.
34. Davison v. Apex Scaffolding [1956] 1 Q.B. 551, [1956] 1 All E.R. 473, 485 F, C.A.
35. Moore v. R. Fox [1956] 1 Q.B. 596; [1956] 1 All E.R. 182, C.A.
36. Buckingham v. Daily News [1956] 2 Q.B. 534; [1956] 2 All E.R. 904, C.A.
37. Quinn v. Horsfall: [1956] 1 W.L.R. 652: [1956] 2 All E.R. 467, C.A.
38. Kilgollan v. W. Cooke [1956] 1 W.L.R. 527; [1956] 2 All E.R. 294, C.A.
39. Jones v. Crosville Motor Services [1956] 3 All E.R. 417, Hallett J.
40. Harman v. Mitcham Works *The Times*, June 22, 1955; [1955] C.L.Y. 1894, C.A.
41. Heapy v. Cheshire C.C. (1955) 105 L.J. 410; [1955] C.L.Y. 1895, Donovan J.
42. Martin v. A. B. Dalzell [1956] 1 Lloyd's Rep. 94, C.A.
43. Cusack v. T. & J. Harrison [1956] 1 Lloyd's Rep. 101, C.A.
44. Thompson v. Rea [1956] 1 Lloyd's Rep. 249, McNair J.
45. Hill v. Wm. H. Muller [1956] 1 Lloyd's Rep. 281, Hilbery J.
46. Bastable v. Eastern Electricity Board [1956] 1 Lloyd's Rep. 586, C.A.
47. Newnham v. Tagart Morgan, *The Times*, July 20, 1956; [1956] C.L.Y., 3506, C.A.
48. Automatic Woodturning v. Stringer [1957] A.C. 544; [1957] 1 All E.R. 90, H.L.
49. Quinn v. Cameron [1958] A.C. 9; [1957] 1 All E.R. 760, H.L.
50. Morris v. Cunard [1956] 2 Lloyd's Rep. 132, Pilcher J.; [1956] 2 Lloyd's Rep. 583, C.A.
51. Gledhill v. Liverpool Abattoir [1957] 1 W.L.R. 1028; [1957] 3 All E.R. 117, C.A.
52. Parkes v. Smethwick Corporation (1957) 121 J.P. 415; [1957] C.L.Y. 2425, C.A.
53. Roberts v. T. Wallis [1958] 1 Lloyd's Rep. 29, Barry J.
54. Graves v. J. & E. Hall [1958] 1 Lloyd's Rep. 100, Barry J.
55. Fitzpatrick v. Crichton [1958] 1 Lloyd's Rep. 154, Ashworth J.
*56. Davie v. New Merton Board Mills [1959] 1 All E.R. 346, H.L.
57. Tomlinson v. Ellerman's Wilson [1959] 1 Lloyd's Rep. 141, Lord Parker C.J.
58. Hodgson v. P.L.A. [1959] 1 Lloyd's Rep. 389, Gorman J.
59. Davies v. Manchester Ship Canal [1960] 2 Lloyd's Rep. 11, C.A.

* This decision is largely *reversed* by the Employers' Liability (Defective Equipment) Act 1969. See cases in Chap. 15, (1) (d).

60. Christmas v. Blue Star [1961] 1 Lloyd's Rep. 95, Paull J.
61. Close v. Steel Company of Wales [1962] A.C. 367; [1961] 2 All E.R. 953, H.L.
62. Harriman v. Martin [1962] 1 W.L.R. 739; [1962] 1 All E.R. 225, C.A.
63. Leslie v. Metcalf Motor Coasters [1962] 2 Lloyd's Rep. 357, Paull J.
64. Patterson v. Flower Line [1963] 2 Lloyd's Rep. 310, Sachs J.
65. Stanbrook v. Waterlow [1964] 1 W.L.R. 825; [1964] 2 All E.R. 506, C.A.
66. Machray v. Stewart & Lloyds [1964] 3 All E.R. 716, McNair J.
67. Dimmock v. B.R.B. [1965] C.L.Y. 2709, Stephenson J.
68. Littley v. Fairey (1965) 109 S.J. 512; [1965] C.L.Y. 2707, Thompson J.
69. Bissett v. L. & G. [1965] 2 Lloyd's Rep. 93, Hinchcliffe J.
70. Taylor v. Rover [1966] 1 W.L.R. 1491; [1966] 2 All E.R. 181, Baker J.
71. Bradford v. Robinson Rentals [1967] 1 W.L.R. 1491; [1967] 2 All E.R. 181, Rees J.
72. Lovelidge v. Anselm Olding [1967] 2 Q.B. 351; [1967] 1 All E.R. 459, Widgery J.
73. Bell v. Arnott (1967) 111 S.J. 438; 2 K.I.R. 825, C.A.
74. Pearce v. Round Oak Steel Mills [1969] 1 W.L.R. 595; [1969] 3 All E.R. 680, C.A.
75. Richardson v. Stephenson Clark [1969] 3 All E.R. 705, Nield J.
76. Kerry v. Carter [1969] 1 W.L.R. 1372; [1969] 3 All E.R. 723, C.A.
77. McAdam v. Denholm [1968] 2 Lloyd's Rep. 511, C.A.
78. Sumner v. P.L.A. [1974] 2 Lloyd's Rep. 92, Mocatta J. (see Chap. 15, (6) **21**).
79. Osarak v. Hawker Siddeley, *The Times*, October 29, 1982; [1982] C.L.Y. 2124, Comyn J.
80. James v. Durkin, *The Times*, May 25, 1983; [1983] C.L.Y. 2541, Michael Davies J.
81. Calder v. H. Kitson Vickers Ltd [1988] I.C.R. 232; [1988] C.L.Y. 1952, C.A. (see Chap. 15(1), (b) **17**).
82. Bowman v. Harland & Wolff plc [1992] I.R.L.R. 349; [1992] C.L.Y. 3222, Carswell J., N.I. (see Chap. 15, (2)(j)**12**).
83. Gunter v. John Nicholas and Sons (Port Talbot) Ltd [1993] P.I.Q.R.P 67; [1993] C.L.Y. 2938, C.A.
84. McSherry v. British Telecommunications; Lodge v. British Telecommunications [1992] 3 Med. L.R. 129; [1992] C.L.Y. 1552, H.H. Judge Byrt Q.C. (see Chap. 15, (4)(b) **31**).
85. Mughal v. Reuters Ltd [1993] I.R.L.R. 571; *The Times*, November 10, 1993, H.H. Judge Prosser Q.C. (see Chap. 15 (4) (3) **32**).

U1. *Barker v. Ashmore Benson* (1952) C.A. 408.
U2. *Cross v. Imperial Paper Mills Ltd* (1953) C.A. 32.
U3. *Morgan v. Post Office* (1953) C.A. 266.
U4. *Goulding v. Ministry of Works* (1955) C.A. 175 A.
U5. *Parkes v. Ramoneur Co. Ltd* (1956) C.A. 198.
U6. *Hoare v. Blue Star Garages Ltd* (1957) C.A. 95.
U7. *Rippin v. M.C.C.* (1957) C.A. 108.
U8. *Smith v. Gomme* (1957) C.A. 182.
U9. *Wall v. Barker* (1957) C.A. 305.
U10. *Hillman v. N.C.B.* (1959) C.A. 259 A.
U11. *Farman v. S.W. Gas Board* (1961) C.A. 384 A.
U12. *Duncan v. Robinson Brothers* (1961) C.A. 178.
U13. *Bill v. Fisher and Ludlow* (1961) C.A. 376 A.
U14. *Warren v. Scruttons* (1962) C.A. 343.
U15. *O'Connor v. Gerrard* (1964) C.A. 30.
U16. *Woolcock v. Hathaway* (1964) C.A. 290.
U17. *Holden v. Cox* (1966) C.A. 14.
U18. *Ford v. Higgins* (1968) C.A. 432 A.
U19. *Mirchandani v. Pyrene* (1968) C.A. 256.
U20. *Gilmour v. Stanton & Staveley* (1968) C.A. 97.
U21. *Wallman v. Lawson* (1968) C.A. 50.
U22. *Reynolds v. B.S.C.* (1977) C.A. 128.
U23. *Mallick v. Allied Schools* (1980) C.A. 328.
U24. *Saunders v. S.E. Electricity Board* (1981) C.A. 0525.
U25. *Barnsley v. Grand Metropolitan Hotels* (1981) C.A. U.B. 97.
U26. *Crawford v. Post Office* (1984) C.A. 45 (see Chap. 15, (2)(a) **U5**).

U27. *Halewood v. A.E. O'Hore & Partners Ltd* (1984) C.A. 972 in (See Chap. 15, (6) **U13**).
U28. *Arthur v. Geevor Tin Miner Ltd* (1986) C.A. 417 (see Chap. 15, (6) **U14**).
U29. *Graham v. Esso Petroleum Ltd* (1986) C.A. 614 (see Chap. 15, (2) (a) **U8**).
U30. *Harvey v. Compair Industries Ltd* (1986) C.A. 870, (see Chap. 15, (5) **U13**).
U31. *Thomson v. Peglers Ltd* (1986) C.A. 522 (see Chap. 15, (2) (h) **U7**).
U32. *Weir v. Bedford Commercial Vehicles* (1988) C.A. 574 (see Chap. 15, (6) **U15**).
U33. *Simox v. B.S.C.* (1988) C.A. 769 (see Chap. 15, (2)(d) **U15**).
U34. *Bidwell v. North East Essex H.A.* (1988) C.A. 798 (see Chap. 15, (2) (a) **U10**).
U35. *Armstrong v. B.S.C.* (1989) C.A. 118 (see Chap. 15, (2) (1) **U11**).
U36. *Smith v Post Office* (1989) C.A. 931 (see Chap. 15, (6) **U16**).
U37. *Treacher v. B.B.C.* (1992) C.A. 136 (see. Chap. 15, (6) **U17**).

(7) Protective Equipment

(*N.B.* See also the cases listed as Examples, below. Some of the processes referred to in the cases on goggles are now specified processes under the Protection of Eyes Regulations 1974, *q.v.*)

Provision—left available in foreman's office–goggles 1
PROVISION—AVAILABLE IN STORE IF WANTED—BARRIER CREAM........ 2
Goggles—one-eyed man hammering rusty bolts—duty to provide 3
PROVISION—MEANING GENERALLY—MUST BE READILY AND OBVIOUSLY AVAILABLE 4
PROVISION—INSTRUCTIONS TO USE—MATERIAL AVAILABLE—BARRIER CREAM........ 5
Provision—material available—but no warning or encouragement to use—dust masks .. 6
Provision—issuing goggles to senior hand for distribution........ 7
Lifeline—for work outboard ship 8
Safety belt—safety net—for descending dry dock........ 9
Provision—safety spats 10
Goggles—for chipping chase in brick wall........ 11
REQUEST BY PLAINTIFF TO PROVIDE—EMPLOYER NOT AUTOMATICALLY BOUND TO COMPLY—GLOVES TO UNPACK SOFTWOOD CASES 12
Provision—safety spats—making them available sufficient in the case of an experienced man 13
Provision—scope of obligation varies from case to case 13
Provision—available if asked for—guard rail for ship's bunk........ 14
Barrier cream—efficacy doubted........ 15
Dermatitis from cement—no adequate precautions 16
SAFETY SPATS IN FOUNDRY—AVAILABLE—NOTICES UP SAYING SO—PLAINTIFF UNABLE TO READ—SUFFICIENT PRECAUTIONS TAKEN 17
Cancer from oil—no adequate medical advice or examinations........ 18
Dermatitis from brick dust—no washing facilities—thereby increasing risk of disease—but actual cause thereof unknown 19
Goggles—splinters commonly flying—but not regarded as danger—removing alum.... U1
Goggles—no higher duty owed to plaintiff wearing glasses U1
Gloves—men not wearing unless told to do so........ U2
Some protection provided—but not 100 per cent.—glass penetrating glove U3
Some protection provided—but not 100 per cent.—reasonable—jagged edges of steel sheets U4
Goggles not fitting 100 per cent. closely U5
Protective equipment not fitting properly—duty on man to take initiative........ U5

1. Finch v. Telegraph Co. [1949] 1 All E.R. 452; [1949] W.N. 57, Devlin J.

Defendants under statutory and common law duty to provide goggles—foreman hung pair of goggles in his office 30 feet away—he did not make this known to the men generally and plaintiff did not know where they were—*Held*, this was not a providing, and that goggles should either be "put in a place where they come easily and obviously to hand" or the workman "should be given clear directions where he is to get them" (454 F). Approved in **2**.

2. Clifford v. Charles Challen [1951] 1 K.B. 495; [1951] 1 All E.R. 72, C.A.

Synthetic glue likely to cause dermatitis—government notice put up warning of danger and specifying precautions which included the use of barrier cream—plaintiff later transferred to another department where no notice up but glue still used—cream was available in store if wanted—the foreman said he was not a great believer in it himself—*Held*, this was not a providing, and defendants should, at very least, have had the cream in the shop itself, "and the foreman should have seen, so far as he could, that the men used it" (75 A). The Lord Justice also said (74 G) that the foreman must keep men up to mark and not tolerate any slackness in safety precautions, but these dicta have been criticised in **5**, *q.v.* **1** approved.

3. Paris v. Stepney B.C. [1951] A.C. 367; [1951] 1 All E.R. 42, H.L.

Held, (3–2) that defendants were under a duty to provide goggles for one-eyed man hammering rusty bolts under car, even though probably no such duty existed for two-eyed men. See Chap. 15, (2)(b)**3**.

4. Norris v. Syndic [1952] 2 Q.B. 135; [1952] 1 All E.R. 935, C.A.

Question at issue was whether plaintiff was guilty of a breach under the Factories Act 1937, s. 119, in failing to use an "appliance provided"—the appliance was a perfectly proper guard to a power press which plaintiff for a number of years had been in the habit of not replacing when making sample presses after testing—defendants were liable under Factories Act 1937, ss. 14, 16, and at common law, but had defendants "provided" guard merely by fitting it to machine, without any instructions for its use?—*Held*, they had, and plaintiff had been guilty of a breach of Factories Act 1937, s. 119. Romer L.J. said "provide" meant "supply" or "furnish" (940 D), but added that a thing could not be "provided" unless it was readily and obviously available, *i.e.* placed ready to the workman's hand (941 E). Somervell L.J. (938 E) said the duty of providing something and the duty of ordering it to be used were two different things, and here the appliance was "at hand and available", and plaintiff knew about it, so it was "provided". On the other hand, "it may well be that if one is dealing with an appliance of general use like a lamp, it is not provided . . . unless its use is by instructions related to that operation" (938 C).

5. Woods v. Durable Suites [1953] 1 W.L.R. 857; [1953] 2 All E.R. 391, C.A.

Plaintiff, an experienced workman of 56, was instructed in how to use barrier cream and a government notice was also posted in similar terms—adequate supplies of materials were available—but plaintiff without defendants' knowledge ceased to take the precautions and got dermatitis—plaintiff in his claim relied chiefly on dicta of Denning L.J. in **2** about a foreman having to see that precautions were observed—*Held*, that **2** (*Clifford v. Challen*) could not be applied to present facts and that that decision did not mean that foreman was legally liable if he did not stand over workman to ensure precautions observed. It was *said* (395 E) that the basis of **2** was that the foreman there did not himself believe in the use of barrier cream—and perhaps because plaintiff there was a young trainee—*Held*, defendants not liable.

6. Crookall v. Vickers Armstrong [1955] 1 W.L.R. 659; [1955] 2 All E.R. 12, Glyn-Jones J.

Steel foundry—known risk of silicosis—masks available but no attempt to induce men to wear them—*Held*, defendants liable. Judge said that it was not enough to provide masks and leave it to men to decide whether to wear, but that employers must take all reasonable steps, by warning, encouragement and exhortation, to seek to persuade men to do so (16 C-E). See Chap. 15, (2)(d)**5**.

7. Stacey v. Ellerman's Wilson Line [1955] 1 Lloyd's Rep. 36, Pilcher J.

Held, defendants not liable.

8. Honeyman v. Orient S.N. [1955] 2 Lloyd's Rep. 27, Hilbery J.

Held, defendants liable.

9. Hurley v. Sanders [1955] 1 W.L.R. 470; [1955] 1 All E.R. 833, Glyn-Jones J.

Held, defendants liable for not providing safety equipment for access down steep altar courses of dry dock. *N.B.* To some extent the decision in this case may have turned on onus of proof. See Chap. 15, (5)**9** and also Chap. 15, (3)**10**.

10. Thorpe v. Qualcast [1955] C.L.Y. 1896, H.L.

Plaintiff a pattern moulder in iron foundry—splashes foot with molten metal when not wearing safety spats—evidence was that defendants did to knowledge of plaintiff provide safety spats free of charge, but plaintiff did not wear them because he had good foundry boots of his own—*Held*, reversing C.A., no evidence on which it could be said that defendants were negligent in failing to provide or to instruct plaintiff to wear spats.

11. Welsford v. Lawford Asphalte Co. [1956] C.L.Y. 5984, Diplock J.

Held, although the general practice was not to provide goggles, the danger was so obvious that defendants were liable for failing to provide.

12. Hardy v. Briggs Motor, *The Times*, March 19, 1957; [1957] C.L.Y. 2427, C.A.

Held, defendants not liable for failing to provide gloves, despite plaintiff's previous request to be provided.

13. Qualcast v. Haynes [1959] A.C. 743; [1959] 2 All E.R. 38, H.L.

Plaintiff an experienced moulder injured by molten metal splashing on his legs—he alleged that defendants were at fault in not providing spats to protect him—defendants had in their stores spats which to plaintiff's knowledge could be had for the asking, and strong boots were available on payment—*Held*, that on these facts no failure of duty by the defendants had been established. Lord Keith (43 B): "In considering whether there is a common law duty on an employer to provide something, the scope of the obligation must vary with the circumstances of the case . . . The spats being available, there was in my opinion no failure of duty on the part of the employers to provide spats for this workman."

14. Lawson v. Thompson Shipping Co. [1959] 2 Lloyd's Rep. 547, Paull J.

Held, defendants not liable.

15. Watson v. Ready Mixed Concrete, *The Times*, January 18, 1961, Edmund Davies J.

Plaintiff fitter employed 1956 and 1957 by defendants—hands often in contact with cement, oil and grease—had had dermatitis previously—1957 got skin disease of hands, which judge found was constitutional ezcema—*Held*, therefore, defendants not liable. *Obiter* judge *referred* to evidence of doctor who said that the value of barrier cream (which defendants had not provided) was presumptive only and had not been proved scientifically, and that some experts considered it might do more harm than good.

16. Snell v. John Shelbourne (1965) 109 S.J. 270; [1965] C.L.Y. 2723, Streatfeild J.

Held, defendants liable for failing to warn plaintiff (an experienced worker) of danger of dermatitis, failing to provide adequate washing facilities and failing to encourage plaintiff to take precautions.

17. James v. Hepworth & Grandage [1967] 2 All E.R. 829, C.A.

Held, defendants not liable, as safety spats were available, and there were notices up saying so (which plaintiff could not read). In addition, some men could be seen by plaintiff wearing spats; and there was a view, reasonably held, in the factory that there were advantages in not wearing them.

18. Stokes v. Guest Keen [1968] 1 W.L.R. 1776; [1968] C.L.Y. 2701, Swanwick J.

19. McGhee v. N.C.B. [1973] 1 W.L.R. 1; [1972] 3 All E.R. 1008, H.L.

Held, defendants liable, as it was sufficient, where the actual cause of the injury was unknown, that defendants' breach of duty had materially increased the risk of such injury.

U1. Dane v. Alumina Co. Ltd (1952) C.A. 250

Plaintiff struck in eye while removing alum from dish—splinters often flew off but not regarded as a danger—only accident of this kind—no goggles—since accident men still do not want goggles for this work—*Held*, defendants not negligent in failing to provide goggles—*Held*, also, no particular duty owed to plaintiff because he wore glasses.

U2. Halstad v. Wiles (1953) C.A. 37

Fellmongering—gloves needed—defendant bought and issued gloves—but plaintiff and other men took them off unless told to wear them—*Held*, defendant not liable.

U3. Prince v. G.E.C. Ltd (1955) C.A. 339 A

Plaintiff employed by defendants in making bulbs—glass spike penetrated gloves provided for use with result that finger amputated few years later—glass spikes not common experience of this operation—glass sometimes penetrated gloves of workers but easily taken out and no serious consequences—*Held*, that, inasmuch as the time of the accident was the relevant time, defendants not liable.

U4. Brown v. Austin Motor Co. Ltd (1956) C.A. 336

Plaintiff employed by defendants—cut on forearm when putting steel sheets with jagged edges into press—men often cut on hands and arms—sometimes stitches necessary—complaints that armlets provided but defendants did not insist on their use to protect forearms—(gloves also provided)—armlets not effective—because no protection against severe blow—objected to by men because made arms hot—*Held* defendants not negligent. *Clifford v. Challen & Sons Ltd.* **2** distinguished as in that case barrier cream effective to prevent dermatitis. Denning L.J. (3): "You have to measure the risk which is involved and take into account the precautions which are suggested, the expense of precautions, the effectiveness of them, and the practicability of them, in order to see whether the employer ought to use them or not. The common law does not go so far as the Factories Act. It does not say that no man must ever be injured and the employer must pay damages if he is ... "

U5. Davidson v. Clayton Aniline Co. Ltd (1957) C.A.

Plaintiff employed by defendants as process worker's serviceman—breaking up caustic soda with sledgehammer when particle went into eye as goggles fitted less closely about nose than usual—defendants took steps to guard against risk of injury to eye—selected this type of goggles after much experiment—largely accepted in various trades as good form of protection and approved by Works Council—issued to men under penalty of loss of three days' pay if not worn—first accident from 1953 when these goggles introduced—no injury to eyes of workmen wearing goggles for 20 years—every person whose work necessitated wearing goggles given printed form of notice under Factories Act 1937, setting out effect of Chemical Works Regulations 10 and 17—*Held*, defendants not liable—no reason to foresee goggles might not fit adequately—took reasonable care to prevent injury. Sellers L.J. (13 E): "The longer I sit in these courts the more satisfied I am that safety in industry does require co-operation on the part of the workpeople as well as care by the employers. In this case, although I recognise that there is no allegation made against the workman and none was necessary, if in fact the workman had got a pair of goggles which were too big for him, it was open to him to get them altered. The contrary position would have been readily recognised by him. If he had been handed a pair of goggles which were too tight and were uncomfortable, he would have been the first one to complain. He knew that the purpose of these goggles was to protect his eyes, and he could easily have said they were too large, if so they were."

U6. Baker v. Harrison (1958) C.A. 146

Dermatitis from machine-cleaning solvent—Rozalex No. 1 provided—satisfactory as very few cases of dermatitis—later on Rozalex No. 8 was produced as improvement on No. 1—defendants did not know of its existence—travelling salesman introduced Rozalex No. 9 to defendants which was another improvement on No. 1—defendants did not adopt No. 9 promptly—*Held*, defendants not negligent in failing to know about or adopt Rozalex No. 8 or in failing to adopt Rozalex No. 9 more promptly. Jenkins L.J. (11 B): "If an employer has provided a form of protection which has proved eminently satisfactory over a long period of years, I do not think he is to be charged with breach of his duty merely because he fails to make himself aware of some new protection which may work even more satisfactorily."

U7. McNally v. Frigidaire Ltd (1959) C.A. 114 A

Dermatitis from oil used in sheet-metal work—known risk—barrier cream used which was impervious to oil—but which was bound to come off skin as fingers worked—gloves also provided—changed approximately every two days—but were primarily to protect against cuts and were not oilproof—*Held*, defendants not liable.

U8. Wilson v. Nuffield Metal Products (1960) C.A. 206

Armlets provided but frequently were not worn—defendants issued a safety booklet urging employees to use the protective equipment issued—but did not exhort them directly to wear the armlets—*Held*, following *Qualcast v. Haynes* **13**, defendants not liable.

U9. Hartley v. Howard and Bullough (1961) C.A. 150

Dermatitis from non-soluble mineral oil—barrier cream and washing facilities provided—but there had been a number of previous casualties and employees including plaintiff had become slack about washing—*Held* (upholding C.C.J.), defendants liable, but plaintiff one-third to blame. Holroyd Pearce L.J.: "One knows that insidious dangers are more easily forgotten by workmen than dramatic and obvious dangers. The prudent employer will do his best to keep the thought of insidious dangers alive in the minds of men, whether by notices or instructions or in any other way that may help to that end, particularly so when it seems from a heavy incidence of the disease that precautions are being forgotten" (7 F).

U10. Clifford v. Bristol Aeroplane (1961) C.A. 1a

Dermatitis through washing components in paraffin—defendants provided (a) weekly inspection of hands by nursing sister, (b) barrier cream, (c) gloves, and (d) hot washing water—*Held*, defendants not liable, as reasonable precautions taken.

U11. Craig v. Humber (1962) C.A.

Dermatitis from hot paraffin—*Held*, defendants liable for (a) not warning plaintiff of danger, (b) not supplying adequate washing facilities, and (c) not notifying plaintiff barrier cream was available.

U12. Pellicci v. Jeyes (1964) C.A. 6

Plaintiff employed to fill containers of Sanilav—85 per cent sodium bisulphate—which on contact with water produces sulphuric acid—dermatitis resulted from contact between the powder and abrasion in hand—*Held*, defendants liable, as they should have known that abrasions were frequent owing to the nature of the work.

U13. Tees v. Walters Engineering (1984) C.A. 573

As plaintiff tried to free bush which had jammed on drill, small piece of metal flew into his eye. He had asked for but had not been provided with safety spectacles—*Held*, there was a nexus between what plaintiff was doing when injured and defendant's duty to provide spectacles—there was a clear breach of common law duty on defendants' part.

Examples

Safe

Dermatitis: plaintiff hypersensitive 2
GUARD: PLAINTIFF NOT KEEPING ADJUSTED . 4
Dermatitis: no known risk 7
Goggles: none to hammer rusty bolts 8
DERMATITIS: CAUSED BY WOOD DUST......... 9
Safety belt: none for window cleaner 10
BARRIER CREAM: AVAILABLE 11
Dermatitis: from cement: risk unknown 13
Goggles: issuing to senior hand 16
Safety spats: sufficiently provided 21
Respirator: none for metal-grinding 23
Safety net: none to erect staging in ship at sea 24
Gloves: none for sorting old rags 27
GLOVES: NONE TO UNPACK SOFTWOOD CASE.. 28
Gumboots: size 10 boots for size $8\frac{1}{2}$ man 30
Shoes: no rope-soled shoes for oily engine-room floor 31
Goggles: none to break concrete with mechanical pick 33
Safety spats: making available in stores 34
GOGGLES: NONE TO CLEAN DOCK WALL...... 35
SAFETY SPATS: AVAILABLE: AND NOTICES UP SAYING SO 39
Goggles: none to cut earthenware pipes with chisel............................ 40
Protective headgear: none for oxyacetylene cutting inside boiler.......... 41
GOGGLES: NONE TO CHIP BRICKWORK 44
Dermatitis from cement: no gloves: building site 45
Goggles: none to remove component after welding................................. 47
Dermatitis from oil coolant: plaintiff constitutionally susceptible............ 49
CARPENTER: NO NEED TO PROVIDE GAUNTLETS 56

Unsafe

RIDGE-SOLED BOOTS PROVIDED TO PREVENT SLIPPING: NO FURTHER DUTY AS TO INSTRUCTION OR WARNING 57
Dust extractor: none for metal dust.... 1
Goggles: merely hanging in office 3
Goggles: none unloading rotten seeds 5
BARRIER CREAM: IN STORES MERELY 6
Goggles: none for one-eyed man hammering 8
Goggles: none to hammer metal mandrel.. 12
Lifeline: none to work outboard ship. 14
Masks: not encouraging men to wear 15
Safety belt: none to go down dry dock 17
GUARD: NONE ON MILLING CUTTER 18
GUARD: NONE AGAINST WIRE BEING EJECTED 19
Goggles: none for one-eyed plaintiff chopping wood 20
Goggles: none for chipping brick wall 22
No lifeline: trawler trawling in storm . 25
Goggles: none for cutting steel piping.. 26
Goggles: none for carborundum wheel 29
CRAWLING-BOARDS: NONE FOR ASBESTOS ROOF.. 32
Dermatitis from cement: no proper precautions 36
CRAWLING-BOARDS: NONE ON PARTLY SHEETED SLOPING ROOF 37
Dress: operating unfenced power tool with loose tie 38
Molten metal: no safety box 42
Dermatitis from detergents: gloves up to wrist only.................................. 43
Dermatitis from brick dust: no washing facilities........................ 46
Earmuffs: none for 115–120 decibels . 48
Goggles: none for inexperienced man striking mild steel with hard steel hammer.. 50

Safe

Goggles: none for planing railway wheels U1
Safety belts: none for work on top of gasholder U2
Goggles: none for removing alum U3
Goggles: none for plaintiff holding spanner while fellow employee struck it U6
Goggles: none for twisting wood strips in vice U7
Dermatitis from paraffin: no protective equipment U8
Goggles: none for mechanical removal of metal burrs U10
Goggles: none for carrying lime putty U11
Gloves: provided but use not "insisted on" for handling aerated bottles U12
Goggles: none to break coal U14
Gloves: none for pouring bitumen U15
Spats for molten metal: some slight danger of metal getting inside spatsv U16
Dermatitis from paraffin: reasonable precautions U20
Weil's Disease: no safeguards in workroom occasionally visited by rats ... U22
Helmet or visor: none when sheet of glass breaks on cooling U27
Dermatitis: from trichlorethylene U28
Bump cap: none for engine driver inspecting cramped interior of engine U29

Unsafe

GOGGLES: PROVIDED BUT HABITUALLY NOT WORN: EMPLOYERS ACQUIESCING IN NON-USER 51
Dermatitis from glue: no gloves or cream: no instructions 52
EARMUFFS: NONE FOR GUN-TESTER 53
Shatter-proof spectacles: none to loosen rusty nut with wrench 54
Ear protection: none for shipyard worker 55, 60
Asbestos dust: no breathing equipment or protective clothing 58
GOGGLES:—ON THE FACTS, EMPLOYER UNDER DUTY TO PROVIDE INTO HANDS OF EMPLOYEE 59
WINDOW CLEANER: NO ANCHOR POINT FOR HARNESS 61
Goggles: none to chisel brass insets out from metal U4
Safety rope: provided for workman on quarry ledge but no insistence on its use U5
Goggles: none for pneumatic drilling of concrete U9
Barrier cream: none for transformer oil U13
Mask: none to protect against molten particles falling from furnace U17
Goggles: none to hammer medium carbon steel U18
Dermatitis from oil: lax precautions .. U19
Dermatitis from paraffin: reasonable precautions not taken U21
Dermatitis from sodium bisulphate U23
Goggles: none to free rusted nut with chisel U24
Goggles: unsuitable through always misting up U24
Lorry tyre: no cage to inflate from 45 to 60 lbs U25
Helmet: none for volunteer fire fighter U26

1. Franklin v. Gramophone Co. [1947] 1 K.B. 542; [1947] 1 All E.R. 353.
2. Clayton v. Caledonian Stevedoring (1948) 81 Ll.L.R. 332.
3. Finch v. Telegraph Construction [1949] 1 All E.R. 452; [1949] W.N. 57, Devlin J.
4. Beal v. Gomme (1949) 65 T.L.R. 543; [1949] W.N. 235, C.A.
5. Edwards v. Fred Leyland [1951] 1 Lloyd's Rep. 184, Donovan J.
6. Clifford v. Charles Challen [1951] 1 K.B. 495; [1951] 1 All E.R. 72, C.A.

7. Coleman v. Harland and Wolff [1951] 2 Lloyd's Rep. 76, Barry J.
8. Paris v. Stepney Borough Council [1951] A.C. 367; [1951] 1 All E.R. 42, H.L.
9. Ebbs v. James Whitson [1952] 2 Q.B. 877; [1952] 2 All E.R. 192, C.A.
10. General Cleaning Contractors v. Christmas [1952] 2 All E.R. 1110, H.L.
11. Woods v. Durable Suites [1953] 1 W.L.R. 857; [1953] 2 All E.R. 391, C.A.
12. Griffiths v. R. H. Green & Silley Weir [1955] 1 Lloyd's Rep. 190, Ormerod J.
13. Harvey v. N.Z. Shipping Co. [1955] 1 Lloyd's Rep. 251, Pilcher J.
14. Honeyman v. Orient S.N. [1955] 2 Lloyd's Rep. 27, Hilbery J.
15. Crookall v. Vickers Armstrong [1955] 1 W.L.R. 659; [1955] 2 All E.R. 12, Glyn-Jones J.
16. Stacey v. Ellerman's Wilson [1955] 1 Lloyd's Rep. 36, Pilcher J.
17. Hurley v. Sanders [1955] 1 W.L.R. 470; [1955] 1 All E.R. 833, Glyn-Jones J.
18. Quinn v. Horsfall [1956] 1 W.L.R. 652, [1956] 2 All E.R. 467, C.A.
19. Kilgollan v. W. Cooke [1956] 1 W.L.R. 527; [1956] 2 All E.R. 294, C.A.
20. Heapy v. Cheshire C.C. (1955) 105 L.J. 410; [1955] C.L.Y. 1895, Donovan J.
21. Thorpe v. Qualcast [1955] C.L.Y. 1896, H.L.
22. Welsford v. Lawford Asphalte Co. [1956] C.L.Y. 5984, Diplock J.
23. Quinn v. Cameron [1958] A.C. 9; [1957] 1 All E.R. 760, H.L.
24. Winstanley v. Athel Line [1956] 2 Lloyd's Rep. 424, Hallett J.
25. Lyell v. Boyd Line [1956] 2 Lloyd's Rep. 660, Willmer J.
26. Paling v. Marshall [1957] C.L.Y. 2420, Davies J.
27. Adamson v. Bickle Bros. [1957] C.L.Y. 2426, Pearson J.
28. Hardy v. Briggs Motor *The Times*, March 19, 1957; [1957] C.L.Y. 2427, C.A.
29. Nolan v. Dental Manufacturing [1958] 1 W.L.R. 936; [1958] 2 All E.R. 449, Paull J.
30. Houghton v. Perkins [1958] 1 Lloyd's Rep. 626, Donovan J.
31. Ali v. Ellerman & Bucknall S.S. Co. [1958] 1 Lloyd's Rep. 630, Slade J.
32. Jenner v. Allen West [1959] 1 W.L.R. 554; [1959] 2 All E.R. 115, C.C.
33. Walsh v. Allweather Co. [1959] 3 W.L.R. 1; [1959] 2 All E.R. 589, Glyn-Jones J.
34. Qualcast v. Haynes [1959] A.C. 743; [1959] 2 All E.R. 38, H.L.
35. Johnson v. Cammell Laird [1963] 1 Lloyd's Rep. 256, C.A.
36. Snell v. John Shelbourne (1965) 109 S.J. 270; [1965] C.L.Y. 2723, Streatfeild J.
37. Donaghey v. O'Brien [1966] 2 All E.R. 822, C.A.
38. Lovelidge v. Anselm Olding [1967] 1 All E.R. 459, Widgery J.
39. James v. Hepworth & Grandage [1967] 2 All E.R. 829, C.A.
40. Sheridan v. Durkin, *The Times*, January 12 1967; [1967] C.L.Y. 2708, Nield J.
41. Dowler v. Rye-Arc [1967] 1 Lloyd's Rep. 554, James J.
42. Cochrane v. Colvilles, 1968 S.L.T. 48; [1968] C.L.Y. 2698, Sheriff Ct.
43. Voller v. Schweppes (1969) 113 S.J. 898, C.A.
44. Hobbs v. Robertson [1970] 1 W.L.R. 980; [1970] 2 All E.R. 347, C.A.
45. Riddick v. Weir Housing Corp., 1970 S.L.T. 71, First Div.
46. McGhee v. National Coal Board [1973] 1 W.L.R. 1; [1972] 3 All E.R. 1008, H.L.
47. Hay v. Dowty Mining [1971] 3 All E.R. 1136, Mackenna J.
48. Berry v. Stone Manganese [1972] 1 Lloyd's Rep. 182; (1971) 12 K.I.R. 13, Ashworth J.
49. Darvill v. Hampton (1973) 13 K.I.R. 275, Rees J.
50. Payne v. Bennie (1973) 14 K.I.R. 395; [1973] C.L.Y. 2323, Shaw J.
51. Bux v. Slough Metals [1973] 1 W.L.R. 1358; [1974] 1 All E.R. 262, C.A.
52. Litherland v. Schreibers (1974) 18 Man. Law 7; [1974] C.L.Y. 2334, May J.
53. McCafferty v. Metropolitan Police District Receiver [1977] 1 W.L.R. 1073; [1977] 2 All E.R. 756, C.A.
54. Pentney v. Anglian Water Authority [1983] I.C.R. 464; [1983] C.L.Y. 2566, Comyn J.
55. Thompson v. Smith Shiprepairer [1984] Q.B. 405; [1984] 1 All E.R. 881, Mustill J. (see, *e.g.* Chap. 15, (2)(a) **24**).
56. Grioli v. Allied Building Company Ltd, *The Times*, April 10, 1985; [1985] C.L.Y. 1152/3, C.A. (see Chap. 15, (2)(h) **15**).
57. Smith v. Scot Bowyer Ltd, [1986] 1 R.L.R. 315; *The Times*, April 16, 1986, C.A. (see Chap. 15, (2)(d) **35**).
58. Bryce v. Swan Hunter [1988] 1 All E.R. 659, [1987] 2 Lloyds Rep. 426, Phillips J. (see Chap. 15, (2)(a) **27**).

59. Crouch v. British Rail Engineering [1988] I.R.L.R. 404; *The Times*, March 10, 1988, C.A. (see Chap. 15, (2)(a) **28**).
60. Baxter v. Harland & Wolff plc [1990] I.R.L.R. 516; [1991] C.L.Y. 1878, N.I.C.A. (see Chap. 15, (2)(a) **29**).
61. King v. Smith, *The Times*, November 3, 1994; [1994] C.L.Y. 2284, C.A. (see Chap. 15, (2)(c) **24**).

U1. *Palmer v. Wagon Repairs* (1951) C.A. 204.
U2. *Firth v. Newton Chambers* (1951) C.A. 268.
U3. *Dane v. Alumina Co.* (1952) C.A. 250.
U4. *Savine v. Hall Telephone Accessories Ltd* (1952) C.A. 409.
U5. *Martin v. Watkins* (1953) C.A. 81.
U6. *Bennett v. Francis Morton & Co. Ltd* (1953 C.A. 274 B.
U7. *Fuller v. Hordern-Richmond* (1955) C.A. 18.
U8. *Dibley v. Welbecson Press Ltd* (1955) C.A. 238.
U9. *Balkman v. Mowlem (John) Co. Ltd* (1956) C.A. 100 A.
U10. *Sharp v. C.A.V.* (1956) C.A. 130.
U11. *Smith v. H.J. Chard & Sons* (1957) C.A. 42.
U12. *Herbert v. Tizer Ltd* (1957) C.A. 210.
U13. *Kilday v. South Wales Electricity Board* (1957) C.A. 319 A.
U14. *King v. Direct Supply Coal Co.* (1960) C.A. 7.
U15. *Doyley v. Brigg* (1960) C.A. 35.
U16. *Thomas v. Richard Thomas and Baldwins* (1960) C.A. 37.
U17. *Thomas v. John Summers* (1960) C.A. 173.
U18. *Jenkins v. Kirk* (1960) C.A. 211.
U19. *Hartley v. Howard* (1961) C.A. 150.
U20. *Clifford v. Bristol Aeroplane* (1961) C.A. 1a.
U21. *Craig v. Humber* (1962) C.A. 107.
U22. *Clayton v. Worcester Royal Porcelain* (1963) C.A. 136 A.
U23. *Pellicci v. Jeyes* (1964) C.A. 6.
U24. *Denman v. Gibson* (1965) C.A. 263.
U25. *Wallman v. Lawson* (1968) C.A. 50.
U26. *Burrough v. Berkshire Fire Authority* (1971) C.A. 40.
U27. *Tyson v. Pilkingtons* (1974) C.A. 135.
U28. *Stephens v. Midland Metal* (1974) C.A. 227.
U29. *Shaw v. B.R.B.* (1980) C.A. 902.

(8) Negligence of Fellow Employee

1. Flaherty v. A. E. Smith Coggins (1951) 95 S.J. 685; [1951] C.L.C. 6775

Plaintiff member of gang handling heavy crate—dropped on plaintiff—cause unexplained—*Held*, it was for plaintiff to establish cause, and as he had failed to do so, action must be dismissed.

2. Smith v. Crossley Bros (1951) 95 S.J. 655; [1951] C.L.C. 6831, C.A.

Held, defendants not liable, as practical joke was an act of wilful misbehaviour which defendants could not reasonably have foreseen. Considered in **18**.

3. Coppin v. Butlers Wharf [1952] 2 Lloyd's Rep. 307, Pearson J.

Straw in hold of ship concealing dangerous hole—*Held*, the clearing of the straw did not require a system laying down, and was a matter for the gang, and hence defendants not liable. It is not clear whether gang, of which plaintiff was a member, were considered negligent or not—perhaps because negligence does not appear to have been alleged against plaintiff's "common employees".

4. Stapley v. Gypsum [1953] A.C. 663; [1953] 2 All E.R. 478, H.L.

Plaintiff and fellow worker both to blame for not taking down dangerous part of roof—*Held*, plaintiff could recover against employers for fault of fellow worker. (*N.B.* Plaintiff's share of contributory negligence was fixed at 80 per cent., since he was also guilty of subsequent negligence.) Applied in **16**.

5. Bull v. L.C.C., *The Times*, January 29, 1953; [1953] C.L.Y. 1463, McNair J.

6. O'Leary v. Glen Line [1953] 1 Lloyd's Rep. 601, Byrne J.

Two dock labourers swinging bales into net—one lets go his grip—consequent injury to plaintiff, the other—*Held*, defendants not liable: "It is just one of those things that will happen, no matter how careful people may be" (603).

7. Connor v. Port of Liverpool Stevedoring [1953] 2 Lloyd's Rep. 604, Gerrard J.

Plaintiff and X employed by defendants to load a sling—their *joint* responsibility, as judge found—due to bad stowage on their part, part of load comes off and strikes plaintiff—*Held*, as plaintiff and X *jointly* responsible, defendants must be vicariously liable for X, and liability would be apportioned 75 per cent. against plaintiff, 25 per cent. against defendants.

8. Judson v. B.T.C. [1954] 1 W.L.R. 585; [1954] 1 All E.R. 624, C.A.

Foreman ganger follows plaintiff into path of oncoming train—*Held*, defendants not liable. Lord Goddard C.J. said he found *Stapley v. Gypsum* **4** "very difficult to understand" (627 B), but the present case was different in that the foreman was not a ganger for the purpose of seeing that plaintiff walked in one place rather than another, and that nothing the ganger did contributed to plaintiff's accident. Singleton L.J. (629 A): "I do not think the negligence of one is mixed up with the negligence of the other, as was said to be the case with *Stapley v. Gypsum.*"

9. Ash v. Maltby [1954] 1 Lloyd's Rep. 336, Hilbery J.

Plaintiff's hand caught when defendants' servant (plaintiff's fellow employee) gives crane driver signal to lift too early—*Held*, defendants liable: "The same standard (*i.e.* that of contributory negligence) must be applied in considering whether a fellow worker has been guilty of negligence towards another workman . . . " (338, col. 2), and at (339 J) cites dictum of Lawrence J. in *Flower v. Ebbw Vale Steel Co.* [1934] 2 K.B. 132 at 139, which was expressly approved by Lord Wright in *Caswell v. Powell Duffryn* [1940] A.C. 152 at 174, as being as equally applicable to negligence of fellow worker as to contributory negligence: "It is not for every risky thing which a workman in a factory may do in his familiarity with the machinery that a plaintiff ought to be held guilty of contributory negligence." *But* now see *Staveley v. Jones* **15**.

10. Leathley v. Mersey Insulation [1954] 1 Lloyd's Rep. 349, C.A.

Held, defendants not liable, apparently because although system involved some risk it was normal and usual, and could not be termed unsafe.

11. Catherall v. Cunard S.S. [1954] 2 Lloyd's Rep. 303, Jones J.

12. Chattaway v. Maltby [1954] 2 Lloyd's Rep. 424, Hilbery J.

Held, defendants not liable: " ... it is setting an artificially high standard to say that this failure at this time with the hook to hit that sack and to make the small error that Champion did make is negligence" (427).

13. Simmons v. Bovis [1956] 1 W.L.R. 381; [1956] 1 All E.R. 736, Barry J.

Held, defendants liable.

14. Schofield v. Glen Line [1955] 2 Lloyd's Rep. 351, Glyn-Jones J.

Two men manhandling tea chest towards plaintiff's trolley when it falls—*Held*, defendants not liable: "He (plaintiff) invites me to draw the inference that one or other or both must have been negligent. ... This involves the proposition that whenever cargo ... falls, it follows that the dock labourers must have been negligent. This is inconsistent with plaintiff's own evidence ... He has not infrequently found ... that as he seeks to pick up cargo the package may slip; and he was certainly not prepared to admit ... he had been negligent" (353–354). Judge went on to say chest might have fallen by negligence or by misadventure, but not proved which.

15. Staveley Iron and Chemical Co. v. Jones [1956] A.C. 627; [1956] 1 All E.R. 403, H.L.

Lord Tucker (414 A), with whom Lords Cohen and Porter concurred: " ... I do not consider that ... the standard (of care) can differ according to whether the workman is being sued personally or his employer is being sued in respect of his acts or omissions in the course of his employment. It is true that there may be cases such as those involving breach of statutory duty, where an employer ... cannot be heard to say, as against his own servant, that some risky act due to familiarity ... amounts to contributory negligence. In this respect it is possible that the same act may have different consequences when the injured man is the plaintiff suing his employers, and where the employer is being sued by a third party (including another employee) in respect of the same act or omission ... This doctrine cannot be used to require any modification in the standard of care required from a workman in relation to his fellow servants or other third parties or the resulting liability of his employers."

16. Williams v. Port of Liverpool Stevedoring [1956] 1 W.L.R. 551; [1956] 2 All E.R. 69, Lynskey J.

Gang of six, including plaintiff, adopt improper system of stowage—*Held*, defendants vicariously liable for negligence of other five, and liability would be apportioned 50:50. **4** applied.

17. Allen v. Glen Line [1956] 1 Lloyd's Rep. 51, Roxburgh J.

A badly stowed bag falls and strikes plaintiff—plaintiff and two others have been stowing—not known who stowed bag in question—*Held*, it was impossible to say any particular person had been negligent, and it may well have been plaintiff himself.

18. Hudson v. Ridge Manufacturing Co. [1957] 2 Q.B. 348; [1957] 2 All E.R. 229, Streatfeild J.

Plaintiff injured by practical joke of co-employee X—X had been repeatedly warned by defendants against such conduct—*Held*, defendants liable, not vicariously for X's tort, but for failing to provide reasonably competent fellow workmen. **2** distinguished because in that case defendants could not foresee danger.

19. Vincent v. P.L.A. [1957] 1 Lloyd's Rep. 103, C.A.

Fellow employee dropped heavy bale of rubber which or part of which struck platform of scales projecting a 4lb. weight into the air which hit plaintiff—*Held*, this accident not reasonably foreseeable by a reasonably prudent employee and therefore defendants not liable.

20. Lee v. John Dickinson (1960) 110 L.J. 317, Pilcher J.

Plaintiff fell down stairs through being pushed from behind by a surge of other workers leaving the workroom when a bell sounded—*Held*, defendants liable.

21. Bell v. Blackwood, 1960 S.C. 11; 1960 S.L.T. 145, 1st Div.

Held, defendants liable.

22. Morgan v. A.E. Smith Coggins [1961] 1 Lloyd's Rep. 92, C.A.

Railman wrongly gave winchman order to heave—plaintiff's finger caught—railman not called—*Held*, that the fact that the railman did the wrong thing prima facie established negligence, and that as railman had not been called to show that it was a mere error of judgment, defendants were liable.

23. Phillips v. Elder Dempster [1961] 1 Lloyd's Rep. 211, Howard J.

Plaintiff and B employed by defendants to unload wooden crates bound with metal strips—B and plaintiff put hooks in strip and pulled—the strip broke and plaintiff fell—it was found that B s act did not contribute to plaintiff's injury—but, assuming that it had and that it constituted negligence—*Held obiter*, defendants not liable for negligence of B, because the system of work was safe, and the two men did not themselves "create a general dangerous situation, but used their discretion in performing an incidental task in the unloading" (218, col. 1). *Williams* **16** and *Stapley* **4** distinguished.

24. Sidwell v. British Timken (1962) 106 S.J. 243; [1962] C.L.Y. 1137, C.A.

Injury to plaintiff caused by playful pat from fellow worker on buttocks—*Held*, defendants not liable as act outside course of employment.

25. Barry v. Cleveland Bridge Co. [1963] 1 All E.R. 192, Lyell J.

Employers were held 50 per cent. liable for defects in wire used to hoist raft—but, *semble*, if only cause of accident had been riding on raft, it would have been a case of all three agreeing to flout orders, and plaintiff would have failed entirely.

26. Alderton v. Lamport and Holt [1963] 2 Lloyd's Rep. 541, Edmund Davies J.

Fellow employee of plaintiff dropped a crate of oranges—plaintiff slipped on one—judge said that if the evidence had shown that the fellow employee had got the crate onto his shoulder and then let it drop, that would undoubtedly point to negligence on his part—on the other hand, if the crate, while the fellow employee was trying to hoist it onto his shoulder, had caught on another crate or some extraneous projection and as a result had been dropped because the employee could not control it, it would not be negligence—he also said that the dropping of a crate was not *res ipsa loquitur* of itself—*Held*, in the result, defendants not liable, as there was no balance of probability on the evidence as to which way the crate had come to be dropped.

27. I.C.I. v. Shatwell [1965] A.C. 656; [1964] 2 All E.R. 999, H.L.

Two experienced shotfirers, who were brothers, tested an electric circuit for shotfiring, without withdrawing to shelter—breach of rules and statutory duty (which lay on the shotfirers, not on the employers)—*Held*, in an action by shotfirer George alleging that the employers were vicariously liable for the fault of shotfirer James: (a) (Lord Radcliffe dissenting), applying *Stapley* **4**, James' conduct was a cause of George's injury, but (b) on the facts *volenti* was a defence to the claim: "George was clearly acting without any constraint or persuasion" (Lord Pearce, 1013 G). "Each knew the risk he ran; each accepted it quite voluntarily" (Lord Donovan, 1017 B). Lord Pearce (Lord Radcliffe concurring) said that *volenti* was not available as a defence where the employer was in breach of his statutory duty (1013 B); but here the duty was on the shotfirers. Nor where the employer was vicariously in breach of some statutory duty through the neglect of some person of superior rank to the plaintiff whose commands the plaintiff was bound to obey (1013 C). As far as common law negligence was concerned. Lord Pearce said that *volenti* applied if there was a genuine full agreement, free from any kind of pressure, to assume the risk of loss. Negligent working by a whole gang, as in *Williams* **16**, might be difficult for the application of *volenti*, because there was an overall duty on the employer to provide a safe system and because it was difficult for one man to stand out against the gang (1013 D–E). Lord Pearce *reserved* for future consideration whether, so far as *volenti* and statutory duty were concerned, it was correct to arrive at the same view by holding that a breach of regulation laid on "a person in charge" did not create a vicarious liability in the employer of such person.

28. Aberan v. Philip Leonard, *The Times*, December 3, 1965; [1965] C.L.Y. 2692, Browne J.

Held, defendants not liable.

29. O'Reilly v. National Rail and Tramway [1966] 1 All E.R. 499, Nield J.

Plaintiff, being urged by co-employee to try hitting shell with sledgehammer, did so—*Held*, that although co-employee was negligent, defendant employers were not liable, because the act was outside the scope of employment and was *volenti* within *Shatwell* **27**, and there was no similar previous behaviour by co-employee which could have warned defendants. *Smith v. Crossley* **2** *applied.*

30. Bolt v. William Moss (1966) 110 S.J. 385; [1966] C.L.Y. 1102, Cantley J.

Held, defendants not liable.

31. Chapman v. Oakleigh (1970) 114 S.J. 432; 8 K.I.R. 1063, C.A.

Plaintiff schoolboy worked for defendants during holidays—he was instructed to obey orders of fellow-employees—three of the latter instructed him to put his hand up a meat-grinding machine, and then turned it on—*Held*, defendants liable, as plaintiff had been instructed to obey all instructions, and the argument that the employees were not acting in the course of their employment could not avail defendants.

32. Coddington v. International Harvester (1969) 113 S.J. 265; 6 K.I.R. 146, Ormrod J.

Practical joker, described as a "character" with a propensity for such jokes, but until the accident "in no way dangerous except in a remote theoretical sense", kicked a tin of burning paraffin—*Held*, employers not liable, as there was no evidence that the previous conduct had caused any danger or reasonable apprehension thereof. **2** and **18** considered.

33. Wood v. Duttons Brewery (1971) 115 S.J. 186; [1971] C.L.Y. 7937, C.A.

Fellow employee persuaded P to drink bottle, pretending it was beer—former thought it was detergent, but it was in fact caustic soda—*Held*, employers not liable, as they could not have foreseen fellow employee's action.

34. Hugh v. N.C.B., 1972 S.C. 252, O.H.

In breach of regulations and despite reasonable efforts by defendants to prevent practice, plaintiff and others jumped off moving train in mine—plaintiff injured in ensuing rush—*Held*, applying *Shatwell* **27**, plaintiff was *volens* and the action failed.

35. Harrison v. Michelin Tyre Co. Ltd [1985] I.C.R. 696; [1985] 1 All E.R. 918, Comyn J.

An employee at defendant's factory, for what he saw as a joke, pushed truck some 2 in. outside the bounds of a marked passageway under a duckboard on which plaintiff was standing. Duckboard tipped up—plaintiff fell and injured. Considering whether defendant vicariously liable, Comyn J. asked whether incident was "part and parcel of the employment in the sense of being incidental to it although and albeit unauthorized or prohibited" or "so divergent from the employment as to be plainly alien to and wholly distinguishable from the employment"—*Held*, on the facts, the former applied and thus defendant was vicariously liable.

36. Aldred v. Nacanco [1987] I.R.L.R. 292; [1987] C.L.Y. 1367, C.A.

In washroom of defendant's premises, employee X pushed slightly unstable washbasin against plaintiff's thigh, to startle her. Plaintiff turned quickly and in doing so injured her back which was known to defendant to be vulnerable—*Held*, defendant not liable because:

(a) Place of work not unsafe—not reasonably foreseeable that condition of washbasin might cause injury.
(b) X's act was unauthorised and wrongful, unconnected with X's employment, for which defendant not vicariously liable. *Per* Lawton L.J. (at p 295, paragraph 15): " ... the correct principle of law ... is that set out in the 18th edition of *Salmond on Torts* at p. 437 ... : ' ... a master is responsible not merely for what he authorizes his servant to do, but also for the way in which he does it. If a servant does negligently that which he was authorized to do carefully, or if he does frandulently that which he was authorized to do honestly, or if he does mistakenly that which he was authorized to do correctly, his master will answer for that negligence, fraud or mistake. On the other hand, if the unauthorized and wrongful act of the servant is not so connected with the authorized act as to be a mode of doing it, but is an independent act, the master is not responsible: for in such a case the servant is not acting in the course of his employment, but has gone outside of it'.". *Per* Lord Donaldson M.R. (at 295–296) the test in *Salmond* (above) is to be preferred to that formulated by Comyn J. in *Harrison v. Michelin Tyre Co. Ltd*, (**35** above).

37. McCready v. Securicor [1991] N.I. 229; [1994] C.L.Y. 5218, C.A. N.I.

Two employees of defendant playing on trolleys used at their work. While doing so, one's hand was crushed when the other closed a vault door on it—*Held*, defendant not liable—door was closed by employee engaged in a prank, independent of any act he was authorised to do. *Aldred v. Nacanco* (**36** above) followed.

U1. Shipley v. British Moulded Hose (1955) C.A. 165

Plaintiff and S jointly engaged in taking down some piping—admittedly dangerous system employed—S up ladder when he dislodges pipe which falls on plaintiff—although plaintiff was S's superior, S had insisted on the system and had overborne plaintiff—*Held*, S (and therefore defendants) negligent. No contributory negligence.

U2. Pickard v. N.C.B. (1961) C.A. 165

Stampede to get into pit cage about to go up—plaintiff injured—*Held*, defendants not liable, as (a) stampede not foreseeable, and therefore no failure of system, and (b) the men stampeding were not doing an authorised act in an unauthorised way, but were doing a wholly unauthorised act, and therefore defendants not vicariously liable.

U3. Wigley v. Dunlop (1968) C.A. 32

"On a footing of vicarious responsibility, it must be shown that the agent-servant-representative was himself personally negligent, having regard to his knowledge, his experience, his means of foreseeing danger to another workman or neighbour ... " (Winn L.J., 9 E).

U4. Bowden v. Ministry of Defence (1982) C.A. U.B. 531

N and O known to be at loggerheads with each other—altercation in tea room. N took teapot and threw it. It hit plaintiff. A supervisor was there but did nothing—*Held*, applying *Hudson* **18**, defendants liable for the failure of the supervisor to intervene. *N.B.* The supervisor was not called to give evidence.

U5. Jones v. Combined Optical Industries (1984) C.A. 240

Male employee came into slight physical contact with small lightly built female employee who was off balance and fell. Had she not been off balance, degree of contact would have been insufficient to cause her to fall—*Held*, in absence of something in nature of deliberate barge, mere physical contact would not constitute negligence.

U6. Jewkes v. Howe (1984) C.A. 926

Plaintiff, engaging in friendly horseplay with first defendant, held out ball-point pen as if it was a sword or dagger. First defendant struck plaintiff's hand with his foot. Inner part of pen flew out and struck plaintiff's eye—*Held*, neither first defendant nor his employer second defendant liable.

U7. O'Donnell v. D.F. O'Donnell & Sons (Birmingham) Ltd (1985) C.A. 581

Plaintiff, wearing green welding goggles, used oxyacetylene equipment to cut an accumulator shaft. He then withdrew to allow a fellow employee to use a hammer and chisel on the accumulator. The fellow employee began to do so after plaintiff had removed his welding goggles but before he had put on clear goggles intended to protect him from flying metal splinters. A splinter flew into plaintiff's right eye—*Held*, defendant vicariously liable for the negligence of the fellow employee.

U8. Alsford v. British Telecommunications plc (1986) C.A. 979

Plaintiff, telephone operative, ascended ladder to examine junction box at top of pole. Ladder had been left lashed at top but not at bottom by fellow employee. About to descend ladder again, plaintiff unlashed the top. Ladder twisted as he descended, and he fell—*Held*, defendant vicariously liable for negligence of fellow employee in leaving ladder unlashed at bottom when plaintiff's subsequent actions were foreseeable. Plaintiff two-thirds to blame.

U9. Hopkinson v. N.C.B. (1987) C.A. 1261

Two workmen tried to get derailed train back on rails using pull lift, the chain on which snagged. Plaintiff came to help and in doing so put his hand close to snagged chain, which suddenly unsnagged, injuring plaintiff's finger—*Held*, defendant liable. The two men admitted it would have been better not to allow the chain to snag. Once it had done so, there was a foreseeable risk of its suddenly unsnagging, presenting a danger to anyone in the vicinity. Plaintiff 75 per cent. to blame for putting his hand in a position of danger.

U10. Clarkson v. Greater Manchester C.C. (1989) C.A. 794

Plaintiff, fireman, was trying to rescue a baby from the bedroom of a house on fire. The sub-officer, in charge of the team, hosed water onto a fire burning in the hall and staircase area. This resulting steam displaced hot and burning vapours from the fire upwards into the bedroom where they enveloped plaintiff, who was severely burned. The displacement phenomenon was known to the sub-officer—*Held*, defendant liable.

Examples

Liable

Lifting unusual hatch cover: no warning	2
Winchman lowering hook onto plaintiff	3
Fire brigade: ladder left dangerous	4
Crane driver: lowering load on plaintiff	5
Crane driver: jerking load up so that it swings	7
EXPOSING NAKED LIGHT NEAR PETROL	9
Shotfirer: firing prematurely	10
Crane driver: lowering hook on man	11
Two men loading sling: object falls off	12
Deckhand dropping pin in block	13
Crane signaller: ordering lift too soon	15
Crane driver: keeping sling hanging over hatch	17
Crane driver: lowering load too fast into hold	21
CRANE DRIVER: KNOCKING PLAINTIFF TO DECK WITH SLING	24

Not liable

Crane driver: crushing man in unexpected position	1
Two men swinging bags: one lets go his hook	6
Two men swinging bales: one lets go grip	8
Two men lifting bacon: one lets go grip	14
FOUR MEN ERECTING TENT: ONE LETS GO GRIP	16
Fitter chiselling metal: sliver flies back	18
Docker rolling paper reel into plaintiff: warning	19
Two men hooking sack: hook of one not grips	20
One man placing pipe on platform: rolls off	22
Two men moving lino roll: fingers of plaintiff caught	23
Crane driver: slewing and luffing into plaintiff in hold	27

* Judge held co-employee was negligent, but employers were not liable.

Liable

Hitting chisel too hard U11
Chargehand: not warning plaintiff following him of oil patch on floor. U13
Practical joke: young employee told to obey all fellow employees: told to put hand in spout of machine U14
Altercation between employees: lack of supervision: plaintiff injured by flying teapot U16
Employee using hammer and chisel before another had put on goggles. U20
Nurse spilling water and failing to clear it up U21
Employee leaving ladder unlashed at bottom U22
Employees allowing chain to snag U23
Fireman causing vapours to be displaced, burning another U24

1. Spain v. Ocean Steamship Co. (1949) 83 Ll.L.R. 188 Sellers J.
2. Campbell v. P.L.A [1952] 1 Lloyd's Rep. 399 Gorman J.
3. Spalding v. Bradley Forge [1952] 1 Lloyd's Rep. 461, Lloyd-Jacob J.
4. Bull v. L.C.C. *The Times*, January 29, 1953; [1953] C.L.Y. 1463, McNair J.
5. Ashton v. M.D.H.B. [1953] 1 Lloyd's Rep. 230, Gorman J.
6. Sowerby v. Maltby [1953] 1 Lloyd's Rep. 462, Stable J.
7. Gray v. Docks Executive [1953] 1 Lloyd's Rep. 558, Parker J.
8. O'Leary v. Glen Line [1953] 1 Lloyd's Rep. 601, Byrne J.
9. Dunk v. Hawker Saunders *The Times*, October 27, 1953; [1953] C.L.Y. 2508, C.A.
10. England v. N.C.B. [1954] A.C. 403; [1954] 1 All E.R. 546; H.L.
11. Ould v. Butlers Wharf [1953] 2 Lloyd's Rep. 44, Gorman J.
12. Connor v. Port of Liverpool Stevedoring [1953] 2 Lloyd's Rep. 604, Gerrard J.
13. Brown v. Elder Dempster [1953] 2 Lloyd's Rep. 667. Barry J.
14. Pasfield v. Hays Wharf [1954] 1 Lloyd's Rep. 150, Hilbery J.
15. Ash v. Maltby [1954] 1 Lloyd's Rep. 336, Hilbery J.
16. Sims v. T. & J. Harrison [1954] 1 Lloyd's Rep. 354, C.A.
17. Barry v. B.T.C. [1954] 1 Lloyd's Rep. 372, Parker J.
18. Packman v. Harland & Wolff [1954] 1 Lloyd's Rep. 432, Hilbery J.
19. Perry v. Convoys [1954] 2 Lloyd's Rep. 258, Jones J.
20. Chattaway v. Maltby [1954] 2 Lloyd's Rep. 424, Hilbery J.
21. Bagshaw v. P.L.A. [1954] 2 Lloyd's Rep. 572, Ashworth J.
22. Hughes v. McGoff & Vickers [1955] 1 W.L.R. 416; [1955] 2 All E.R. 291; Ashworth J.
23. Briggs v. Shaw Savill [1955] 1 Lloyd's Rep. 39, Pilcher J.
24. Davey v. H. W. Howes [1955] 1 Lloyd's Rep. 95, C.A.
25. Barker v. Thomas Orford [1955] 1 Lloyd's Rep. 196, Ashworth J.
26. Simmons v. Bovis [1956] 1 W.L.R. 381; [1956] 1 All E.R. 736, Barry J.
27. Hayzer v. G.S.N. [1955] 1 Lloyd's Rep. 591, Hilbery J.
28. Staveley Iron & Chemical v. Jones A.C. 627; [1956] 1 All E.R. 403; [1956] A.C. 627, H.L.
29. Williams v. Port of Liverpool Stevedoring [1956] 2 All E.R. 69, Lynskey J.
30. Smithers v. B.I.S.N. [1955] 2 Lloyd's Rep. 67, Lord Goddard C.J.
31. Schofield v. Glen Line [1955] 2 Lloyd's Rep. 351, Glyn-Jones J.; [1955] 2 Lloyd's Rep. 719, C.A.
32. Dixon v. J. E. Charlton Ltd. [1955] 2 Lloyd's Rep. 509, Barry J.
33. Burnell v. B.T.C. [1955] 2 Lloyd's Rep. 549, C.A.

34. Neicho v. Maltby [1955] 2 Lloyd's Rep. 574, Barry J.; [1956] 1 Lloyd's Rep. 191, C.A.
35. Rossi v. P.L.A. [1956] 1 Lloyd's Rep. 478, Lynskey J.
36. Norcott v Glen Line [1956] 2 Lloyd's Rep. 108, Pilcher J.
37. Lilly v. N.Z. Shipping [1956] 2 Lloyd's Rep. 157, Pilcher J.
38. Kemp v. P.L.A. [1956] 2 Lloyd's Rep. 312, Gorman J.
39. Arter v. Scruttons [1956] 2 Lloyd's Rep. 349, Cassels J.
41. Lott v. Horsley Smith [1956] 2 Lloyd's Rep. 410, Glyn-Jones J.
42. Eggleston v. P.L.A. [1956] 2 Lloyd's Rep. 612, Ormerod J.
43. Flatman v. J. Fry [1957] 1 Lloyd's Rep. 73, Paull J.
44. Benbow v. N.Z. Shipping [1957] 1 Lloyd's Rep. 95, Devlin J.
45. Parsons v. A. W. King [1957] 1 Lloyd's Rep. 123, Stable J.
46. Griffin v. P.L.A. [1957] 1 Lloyd's Rep. 238, Stable J.
47. Driscoll v. Lange Bell [1957] 1 Lloyd's Rep. 377, Byrne J.
48. Pike v. Trinity Wharf [1957] 1 Lloyd's Rep. 122, Hilbery J.
49. Saitch v. Glen Line [1957] 2 Lloyd's Rep. 362, Pilcher J.
50. Hopwood v. Fruit Lines [1958] 1 Lloyd's Rep. 28, Elwes J.
51. White v. Ben Line Steamers [1958] 1 Lloyd's Rep. 541, Paull 1.
52. Bovell v. P.L.A. [1958] 2 Lloyd's Rep. 191, Lord Goddard C.J.
53. Ashford v. Scruttons [1958] 2 Lloyd's Rep. 223, C.A.
54. Graham v. Copthall [1958] 2 Lloyd's Rep. 366, Ashworth J.
55. Willis v. Unimarine [1958] 2 Lloyd's Rep. 436, Diplock J.
56. Crush v. Harland & Wolff [1959] 1 Lloyd's Rep. 41, Gorman J.
57. Wood v. North Thames Gas Board [1959] 1 Lloyd's Rep. 101, Gorman J.
58. King v. New Fresh Wharf [1959] 1 Lloyd's Rep. 344, Paull J.
59. Alexander v. John Wright [1959] 2 Lloyd's Rep. 383, Havers J.
60. Moss v. P.L.A. [1959] 2 Lloyd's Rep. 657, Havers J.
61. Bell v. Blackwood Norton, 1960 S.C. 11; 1960 S.L.T. 145, 1st Div.
62. Morgan v. Smith Coggins [1961] 1 Lloyd's Rep. 92, C.A.
63. Barry v. Cleveland Bridge [1963] 1 All E.R. 192, Lyell J.
64. I.C.I. v. Shatwell [1965] A.C. 656; [1964] 2 All E.R. 999; H.L.
65. Barram v. London & Southampton Stevedoring [1963] 1 Lloyd's Rep. 269, Glyn-Jones J.
66. Monticelli v. Scruttons [1963] 1 Lloyd's Rep. 362, Donovan L.J.
67. Alderton v. Lamport and Holt [1963] 2 Lloyd's Rep. 541, E. Davies J.
68. Horsley v. Collins [1965] 1 W.L.R. 1359; [1965] 2 All E.R. 423, Nield J.
69. Ryan v. New Fresh Wharf [1965] 1 Lloyd's Rep. 43, Lawton J.
70. Aberan v. Philip Leonard, *The Times*, December 3, 1965; [1965] C.L.Y. 2692, Browne J.
71. O'Reilly v. National Rail and Tramway [1966] 1 All E.R. 499, Nield J.
72. Brooks v. British Railways Board [1966] 1 Lloyd's Rep. 392, Edmund Davies J.
73. Campin v. P.L.A. [1966] 1 Lloyd's Rep. 398, Marshall J.
74. Brawn v. P.L.A. [1967] 2 Lloyd's Rep. 378, Swanwick J.
75. Treadway v. Dike [1967] 1 Lloyd's Rep. 564, Paull J.
76. Hopkins v. Shaw Savill [1968] 1 Lloyd's Rep. 103, Roskill J.
77. Cahill v. Metropolitan Terminals [1968] 2 Lloyd's Rep. 418, Roskill J.
78. Barrett v. Hay's Wharf [1968] 2 Lloyd's Rep. 491, Thompson J.
79. Rawding v. London Brick Co. (1970) 9 K.I.R. 194, James J.*
80. Bowden v. Barbrooke (1973) 15 K.I.R. 232; [1973] C.L.Y. 1223, Waller J.**
81. Rodway v. P.D. Wharfage [1973] 2 Lloyd's Rep. 511, Wien J. (one-third contributory negligence).
82. Harrison v. Michelin Tyre Co. Ltd. [1985] I.C.R. 696; [1985] 1 All E.R. 918, Comyn J. (see Chap. 15, (8) **35**).
83. Darby v. G.K.N. Screws & Fasteners Ltd [1986] I.C.R. 1; [1986] C.L.Y. 2266, Peter Pain J. (see Chap. 15, (5) **23**).
84. Aldred v. Nacanco [1987] I.R.L.R. 292; [1987] C.L.Y. 1367, C.A. (see Chap. 15, (8) **36**).

* Reversed by C.A. (1971) 4 K.I.R. 207 without this point being considered.
** Hammering masonry nails is now a specified process under the Protection of Eyes Regulations 1974.

85. Clowes v. N.C.B., *The Times*, April 23, 1987; [1987] C.L.Y. 2565, C.A. (see Chap. 15, (3) **23**).
86. Smith v. Stages [1989] A.C. 928; [1989] 1 All E.R. 833, H.L. (see Chap. 15 (1) (b) **19**).
87. McCready v. Securicor [1991] N.I. 229; [1994] C.L.Y. 5218, C.A. N.I.
U1. *Bennett v. Francis Morton & Co. Ltd* (1953) C.A. 274 B.
U2. *Prescott v. Hattersley Bros Ltd* (1954) C.A. 45.
U3. *Williams v. Turners Asbestos Cement Co.* (1954) C.A. 168.
U4. *Clark v. B.T.C.* (1955) C.A. 5.
U5. *Robinson v. Dewhurst* (1955) C.A. 319.
U6. *Wright v. N.C.B.* (1956) C.A. 74.
U7. *Dent v. Big Ben Films Ltd* (1956) C.A. 183.
U8. *Hadler v. Reed & Co. Ltd* (1957) C.A. 53.
U9. *Campion v. Notley* (1959) C.A. 187.
U10. *Fletcher v. Steel Company of Wales* (1960) C.A. 248.
U11. *Carpenter v. Telehoist* (1961) C.A. 228.
U12. *Deacon v. Metropolitan Cammell* (1965) C.A. 126.
U13. *Jones v. William Press* (1966) C.A. 108 B.
U14. *Chapman v. Oakleigh* (1970) C.A. 175.
U15. *Lawson v. Doxford and Sunderland* (1974) C.A. 234.
U16. *Bowden v. Ministry of Defence* (1982) C.A. U.B. 531.
U17. *O'Connor v. United Biscuits* (1982) C.A. U.B. 542.
U18. *Jones v. Combined Optical Industries* (1984) C.A. 240 (see Chap. 15, (8), **U5**).
U19. *Jewkes v. Howe* (1984) C.A. 926 (see Chap. 15, (8) **U6**).
U20. *O'Donnell v. D.F. O'Donnell & Sons (Birmingham) Ltd* (1985) C.A. 581 (see Chap. 15, (8) **U7**).
U21. *Cousins v. Lambeth, Southwark and Lewisham Area H.A.* (1986) C.A. 225 (see Chap. 15, (3) **U6**).
U22. *Alsford v. British Telecommunications plc* (1986) C.A. 979 (see Chap. 15, (8) **U8**).
U23. *Hopkinson v. N.C.B.* (1987) C.A. 1261 (see Chap. 15, (8) **V9**).
U24. *Clarkson v. Greater Manchester C.C.* (1989) C.A. 794 (see Chap. 15, (8) **U10**).

16. EMPLOYER'S LIABILITY—STATUTORY DUTY

Introductory Notes

1. Except in these Introductory Notes, standard abbreviations for Acts and Regulations are used throughout this chapter, as follows:

Statutes

C.M.A. 1911	Coal Mines Act 1911 (now repealed)
F.A.	Factories Act (various years, of which only the 1961 Act (in part) is still in force)
M.Q.A. 1954	Mines and Quarries Act 1954
O.S.R.P.A. 1963	Offices, Shops and Railway Premises Act 1963

Regulations

B.R. 1948	Building (Safety, Health and Welfare) Regulations 1948 (now revoked)
C.S.R. 1956	Coal and other Mines (Sidings) Regulations 1956
C.(G.P.)R. 1961	Construction (General Provisions) Regulations 1961
C.(L.O.)R. 1961	Construction (Lifting Operations) Regulations 1961
C.(W.P.)R. 1961	Construction (Working Places) Regulations 1966
D.R. 1934	Docks Regulations 1934 (now revoked)
E.R. 1908	Electricity Regulations 1908 (now revoked)
G.R. 1947	General Regulations 1947 (now revoked)
H.M.M.R. 1928	Horizontal Milling Machines Regulations 1928
L.R. 1906	Locomotives and Waggons (Used on Lines and Sidings) Regulations 1906
O.U.M.R. 1938	Operations at Unfenced Machinery Regulations 1938
S.R. 1931	Shipbuilding Regulations 1931 (now revoked)
S.S.R. 1960	Shipbuilding and Shiprepairing Regulations 1960
W.M.R. 1974	Woodworking Machines Regulations 1974

2. Due to the absence of any recent relevant cases, certain sections of this chapter in the Third Edition have not been reproduced. There has also been some renumbering and a section on miscellaneous regulations has been added. The following table provides cross-reference between the two editions:

Third Edition	*This Edition*
16(1)(a) and (b)	16(1)(a) and (b)
16(1)(c)	—
16(1)(d)	16(1)(c)
16(1)(e)	16(1)(d)
16(1)(f)	16(1)(e)
16(2)(a) to (j)	16(2)(a) to (j)
16(3)(a) to (c)	16(3)(a) to (c)
16(4)(a)	16(4)(a)
16(4)(b)	—
16(4)(c)	16(4)(b)
16(4)(d) to (f)	—
16(4)(g)	16(4)(c)
16(4)(h)	16(4)(d)
16(4)(j)	—
16(5)(a) to (j)	16(5) a to (j)
16(6)(a) to (g)	16(6)(a) to (g)
16(7)(a) to (f)	16(7)(a) to (f)
16(8)	—
16(9)(a) to (j)	16(8)(a) to (j)
16(10)(a) to (e)	16(9)(a) to (e)
16(11)	16(10)
16(12)	16(11)
16(12A)	16(12)
16(13)	16(13)
16 (13A)	16 (14)
16 (14)	16 (15)
16 (15) (a), (b)	—
16 (15) (c)	16 (16) (a)
16 (15) (d)	16 (16) (b)
16 (16)	16 (17)
—	16 (18)

3. Some sections of the Third Edition contained one or more cases under one or more sections or regulations of the provisions listed below, which ceased to have effect many years ago.

(A) Building (Safety, Health and Welfare) Regulations 1948;
(B) Coal Mines Act 1911;
(C) Factories Act 1937;
(D) General Regulations 1947;

(E) Grinding of Metal Regulations 1925;
(F) Shipbuilding Regulations 1931;
(G) Woodworking Machines Regulations 1922.

Such cases have not always been retained. The sections from which omissions have been made are indicated by reference back to this Introductory Note.

4. Cases decided under the Electricity Regulations 1908 have been retained. These, however, were revoked with effect from April 1, 1990 by the Electricity at Work Regulations, 1989 and will now only rarely concern the courts.

5. Cases decided under the Docks Regulations 1934 have been retained. These, however, were revoked with effect from January 1, 1989 by the Docks Regulations 1988 and will now only rarely concern the courts.

6. Cases decided under one or more of the provisions of the Factories Act 1937 or 1959 (repealed by the Factories Act 1961) have been retained *if*:

(a) one or more of the provisions were re-enacted in the 1961 Act; *and*
(b) one or more such re-enactments remain in force or, if repealed, were repealed not later than 1989.

The following table provides cross-references to all the 1937 and 1959 Act provisions referred to in the retained cases:

1937 Act	*1959 Act*	*1961 Act*
1		1
4		4
13		13
14		14
15		15
16		16
17		17
20		20
21		21
22 (1)–(6)		22
22 (7)		23
22 (8) (9)		25 (1) (2)
22 (10)		24
22 (11)		25 (4)
23		26
24		27
25	4	28
26		29
28		31
42		58
43		59
47		63 (now repealed)
49		65
139		163
151		175
152		176

7. The following provisions, *inter alia*, were repealed or revoked and replaced by The Manual Handling Operations Regulations 1992 with effect from January 1, 1993:

(a) Mines and Quarries Act 1954, s. 93;
(b) Factories Act 1961, s. 72;
(c) Offices, Shops and Railway Premises Act 1963, s. 23 (subject to specified exceptions);
(d) Construction (General Provisions) Regulations 1961, reg. 55.

8. The following provisions, *inter alia*, were repealed or revoked and replaced by the Personal Protective Equipment at Work Regulations 1992, with effect from January 1, 1993:

(a) Factories Act 1961, s. 65;
(b) Iron and Steel Foundries Regulations 1953, reg. 8;
(c) Shipbuilding and Shiprepairing Regulations 1960, regs. 73 and 74;
(d) Protection of Eyes Regulations 1974.

9. The following provisions, *inter alia*, are repealed or revoked and replaced by The Workplace (Health, Safety and Welfare) Regulations 1992, with effect from January 1, 1996, subject to the exceptions stated at the end of this Note:

(a) Factories Act 1967, ss. 1–7, 18, 28, 29, 57–60 and 69;
(b) Offices, Shops and Railway Premises Act 1963, ss. 4–16;
(c) Horizontal Milling Machines Regulations 1928 (in total);
(d) Iron and Steel Foundries Regulations 1953 (in total);
(e) Woodworking Machines Regulations 1974, reg. 10–12.

The exceptions are these:

(a) Workplaces coming into use for the first time after December 31, 1992, and modifications, extensions and conversions to existing workplaces started after December 31, 1992 must conform to the 1992 Regulations as soon as they come into use.
(b) Regulation 17(2) of the 1992 Regulations (requiring suitable traffic routes in a workplace) applies so far as is reasonably practicable to any workplace which is *not* a new workplace or a modification, extension or conversion with effect from January 1, 1993 (see reg. 17(5)).

10. The following provisions, *inter alia*, were repealed or revoked and replaced by The Provision and Use of Work Equipment Regulations 1992, with effect, from January 1, 1993, or from January 1, 1997 in relation to work equipment first provided for use before the former date:

(a) Mines and Quarries Act 1954, ss. 81(1) and 82;
(b) Factories Act 1961, ss. 12–17 and 19;
(c) Offices, Shops and Railway Premises Act 1963, s. 17;
(d) Horizontal Milling Machines Regulations 1928, the exemptions and regs. 2–7;
(e) Operations at Unfenced Machinery Regulations 1938. (in total);
(f) Iron and Steel Foundries Regulations 1953, reg. 5;
(g) Shipbuilding and Shiprepairing Regulations 1960, reg. 67;
(h) Construction (General Provisions) Regulations 1961, regs. 42, 43 and 57;
(i) Woodworking Machines Regulations 1974, regs. 1(2), 1(3), certain definitions in reg. 2 reg. 3(2) and regs. 5–9, 14–19, 21–38, and 40–43.

(1) Duty Generally

*(a) Who Can Sue.**

Provision	*See also Intro Notes*	*Plaintiff*	*Defendant*	*Relevant words*	*Sue or no*	
F.A. 1937, s. 26	6,9	Employee of independent contractor	Occupier	"Where any person has at any time to work"	Yes	1
"	"	INDEPENDENT CONTRACTOR (IN PERSON)	OCCUPIER	"	YES	2
D.R. 1934, reg. 37	5	Workman not employed in process	Stevedore	"Hold accessible to any person employed in process"	No	3
D.R. 1934, reg. 1	"	Ship's officer not employed in process	Dock authority	"Safety of persons employed in process"	No	4
F.A. 1937, s. 26	6,9	Employee of independent contractor	Occupier	"Where any person has at any time to work"	Yes	5
D.R. 1934, reg. 9	5	Superintendent	Shipowner	"For the use of persons employed in the process"	Yes	6
E.R. 1908, reg. 9	4	FIREMAN	OCCUPIER	"PERSON EMPLOYED"	No	7
F.A. 1937, s. 49	5,8	Employee of independent contractor	Occupier	"Person employed in the process"	No	8
L.R. 1906, reg. 14	—	"	"	"Person employed"	Yes	9
E.R. 1908, reg. 1	4	Workman not employed by occupier	Occupier	"Person employed"	Yes	10
F.A. 1937, s. 14	6,10	Man doing private work in own time	Occupier	"Person employed or working on the premises"	No	11

* Abbreviations are explained in Introductory Note 1. See also Introductory Notes 3(A), (B), (F) and (G).

Provision	*See also Intro Notes*	*Plaintiff*	*Defendant*	*Relevant words*	*Sue or no*	
D.R. 1934, reg. 1	5	Workman employed in processes going on private errand	Occupier	"Person employed in the processes"	No	12
D.R. 1934	"	Ship's engineer	Shipowner	"Person employed in the processes"	No	13
F.A. 1937, s. 26	6,9	**Independent contractor (in person)**	**Occupier**	**"Where any person has at any time to work"**	**Yes**	14
D.R. 1934, reg. 37	5	Person employed in process but trespassing	Shipowner	"Hold accessible to any person employed in the process"	No ?	15
F.A. 1937, s. 14	6,10	Employee on frolic	Occupier	"Every person employed . . . in the premises"	Yes	16
F.A. 1961, s. 14	10	Employee on frolic	Occupier	"Every person employed . . . in the premises"	Yes	17
E.R. 1908, reg. 1	4	Employee of independent contractor	Another contractor (on building operation)	"As if . . . any person undertaking any such operations . . . were the occupier"	Yes	18
"	"	"	Occupier of building site		No	"
F.A. 1961, s. 29(1)	9	Employee washing teacup in lavatory	Occupier	"Where any person has at any time to work"	No	19
F.A. 1961, s. 14	10	Employee using machine when not authorised	Occupier	"Every person employed . . . in the premises"	Yes	20
F.A. 1961, s. 29(1)	9	Fireman	Occupier	"Where any person has at any time to work"	No	21
O.S.R.P.A. 1963	"	Shop customer	Shop owner	S. 16 (floors)	No	22

Provision	See also Intro Notes	Plaintiff	Defendant	Relevant words	Sue or no	
C.(G.P.)R. 1961, reg. 3 and C.(W.P.)R. 1966, reg. 3	–	Employee of sub-contractor	Main contractor	"as affect him or any workman employed by him"	No	23
O.S.R.P.A. 1963, s. 16	9	**Employee on frolic trespassing**	**Occupier**	**(No specific words)**	**Yes**	24
C.(G.P.)R. 1961, reg.3	–	Working sub-contractor	Main contractor	"Every contractor . . . to use plant in a manner which complies"	No	25
C.(W.P.)R. 1966, reg. 28	–	Working sub-contractor (in name only)	Main contractor	"as affect any workman employed by him"	Yes	26
C.(W.P.)R. 1966	–	Working sub-contractor	Main contractor	"as affect any workman employed by. him"	No?	27
C.(L.O.)R. 1961, reg. 3(1)	–	Employee whose services hired out	General employer	". . . employer . . . undertaking . . . operation to which . . . Regulations apply . . ."	Yes	28
C.(W.P.)R. 1961, reg. 3(1)	–	Self-employed painting sub-contractor	Painting contractor	"as affect any workman employed by him"	No	29
F.A. 1961, s. 29(1)	9	Contractor's employee	Factory occupier	"where any person has at any time to work	Yes	30
C.(W.P.)R. 1966, reg. 3(1)	–	Casual worker	Employer	"every employer of workmen"	Yes	31
C.(G.P.)R. 1961, reg. 3	–	Employee whose services hired out	General employer	"employer . . . who . . . uses any plant and equipment"	Yes	32

1. Whitby v. Burt Boulton [1947] 1 K.B. 918; [1947] 2 All E.R. 324, Denning J.

Held, that the occupier of a factory was liable to employee of window cleaner for breach of F.A. 1937, s. 26. Approved by C.A. in **2** (on this point).

2. Lavender v. Diamints [1949] 1 K.B. 585; [1949] 1 All E.R. 532, C.A.

Held, that occupier of factory was liable to independent contractor in person (a window cleaner) for breach of F.A. 1937, s. 26; **1** approved on this point. *Obiter per* Tucker L.J. (535 E) the duty of an occupier under the whole of Part 2 of Factories Act (12–40) was wider than merely a duty to the employees of occupier. *Approved* in **14**.

3. Harvey v. Royal Mail Line (1949) 65 T.L.R. 286n., Hallett J.

Decided in 1941—breach of D.R. 1934, reg. 37—welder fell down open hatch left open by stevedores—*Held*, plaintiff could not sue under D.R. 1934, because he was not employed in connection with the processes, and reg. 37 expressly refers to the hatch of a hold accessible to any person employed, which by definition means any person employed in the processes.

4. Kininmouth v. William France Fenwick (1949) 65 T.L.R. 285; 82 Ll.L.R. 768, Hilbery J.

Breach of D.R. 1934, reg. 1—wireless officer slips on china clay on jetty—*Held*, could not sue, as reg. 1 provides the approaches are to be maintained with due regard to the safety of the persons employed, *i.e.* by definition employed in the processes, and therefore reg. 1 was only intended to protect such persons, and plaintiff could not sue.

5. Woodhead v. Whincup [1951] 1 All E.R. 387, 115 J.P. 97, McNair J.

Held, occupier of factory liable under F.A. 1937 to servant of independent contractor.

6. Dawson v. Euxine Shipping [1953] 1 W.L.R. 287; [1953] 1 All E.R. 299, McNair J.

Plaintiff a lighterman superintending loading of ship—*Conceded* that he was a person employed ("in the process," by extended definition) for the purpose of the D.R. 1934.

7. Hartley v. Mayoh [1954] 1 Q.B. 383; [1954] 1 All E.R. 375, C.A.

Defendant occupiers of factory in breach of E.R. 1908, made under Factories Acts—plaintiff a fireman coming onto premises to put out fire—*Held*, not within the ambit of the Regulations, as he was not a person employed.

8. Whalley v. Briggs Motors [1954] 1 W.L.R. 840; [1954] 2 All E.R. 193, Streatfeild J.

P employed by X an independent contractor in D's factory to break up concrete with a mechanical pick, being a process within F.A. 1937, s. 49—sues D—*Held*, that P, *qua* D, was not a person "employed in the process", since the words only referred to persons employed by the occupier in the processes of the occupier.

9. Stanton Ironworks v. Skipper [1956] 1 Q.B. 255; [1955] 3 All E.R. 544, D.C.

Case stated under the L.R. 1906, reg. 14—duty on occupier towards persons employed—injury to lorry driver employed by independent: contractor—*Held*, offence committed by D under F.A. 1937, s. 133 (since repealed).

10. Massey-Harris-Ferguson v. Piper [1956] 2 Q.B. 396; [1956] 2 All E.R. 722, D.C.

Prosecution of factory occupier under E.R. 1908, reg. 1 (inadequate switch)—duty owed to "persons employed"—*Held*, the words "persons employed" applied to all men working in the factory, it being immaterial by whom they were employed. *Hartley* **7** distinguished because the fireman there "was no more employed in a factory than a constable who might be called in to quell a disturbance or arrest a thief."

11. Napieralski v. Curtis [1959] 1 W.L.R. 835; [1959] 2 All E.R. 427, Havers J.

Plaintiff was injured on a circular saw while doing private work after factory hours—*Held*, *inter alia*, he could not sue under F.A. 1937 because he was neither "employed", nor was he "working on the premises" within the meaning of that term.

12. Wilczek v. Gardiner and Tidy [1959] 1 Lloyd's Rep. 91, Pearson J.

Plaintiff a carpenter on a wharf—he was "employed in the processes" of loading, etc., because on a few occasions he assisted in moving timber by crane into a vessel in the course of his duties—he went to get hot coals from the firebox of a crane—no authority to do so—*Held*, he could not sue under the D.R. 1934, because his expedition could not reasonably be regarded as ancillary to the occasions when he was engaged in the processes.

13. Hayhurst v. F. J. Everard [1961] 1 Lloyd's Rep. 538, Diplock J.

"Person employed in the processes"—D.R. 1934—*Held*, did not include a ship's engineer.

14. Wigley v. British Vinegars [1964] A.C. 307; [1962] 3 All E.R. 161, H.L.

Held, that the words "any person" in s. 26(2) of the F.A. 1937 included an independent contractor and (*obiter*) his employee cleaning windows in a factory. *Lavender v. Diamints* **2** approved: "A policeman who enters a factory in pursuit of a felon, or a fireman who enters to put out a fire, is not within the section, although he is a 'person' and he is 'working.' I think one must exclude, for example, the film actor who enters a factory where a scene in which he is playing is to be shot . . . In my view, the true distinction is between those who are to work for the purposes of the factory and those who are not" (Lord Kilmuir, 164 H, other four Law Lords concurring).

15. Henry v. Mersey Ports Stevedoring [1963] 2 Lloyd's Rep. 97, C.A.

Plaintiff dock worker was sent by employing stevedores to an unlit tween deck, where he fell down unfenced hatch—he sued, *inter alios*, the shipowner for breach of D.R. 1934, reg. 37 (hatches in accessible holds to be fenced)—Widgery J. ([1963] 1 Lloyd's Rep. 365) found that the plaintiff was a trespasser but was still protected by reg. 37, since the hold was "accessible"—Held, by C.A., however, that he was not a trespasser, but said *obiter* that if he had been, he would not have been entitled to claim for breach of the regulation. Sellers L.J. (106, col. 1): " . . . the Regulations, as far as I know, have never been applied in favour of a trespasser."

16. Uddin v. Associated Portland Cement Manufacturers [1965] 2 Q.B. 582; [1965] 2 All E.R. 213, C.A.

In order to catch a pigeon, plaintiff went up a long steel ladder, and leaned over an unfenced shaft set 4 feet 6 in. above platform floor and on top of long metal casing—arm caught—*Held*, that plaintiff came within the category of "every person employed . . . in the premises", even though he was on a frolic, and therefore could sue (80 per cent. contributory negligence).

17. Allen v. Aeroplane and Motor Castings [1965] 1 W.L.R. 1244; [1965] 3 All E.R. 377, C.A.

Fencing case—dangerous nip—not known what plaintiff was doing in order to get his hand trapped—county court judge concluded that he was on a frolic of his own—*Held*, following *Uddin* **16**, this was irrelevant and defendants were liable. Diplock L.J. (379 H): "It is unnecessary to show that the employee was injured in the course of his employment; it is sufficient that he should be employed at the premises."

18. Fisher v. C.H.T. [1966] 2 Q.B. 475; [1966] 1 All E.R. 88, C.A.

Plaintiff, employed by plasterers, was injured through touching a live wire in ceiling—liability was mainly decided at common law, but question also arose as to who was liable under E.R. 1908, reg. 1 (protection of conductors)—the place was a restaurant owned by D1, operated under licence by D2, and being re-decorated by D3—D2 were at the same time doing electrical repairs themselves, and their employee was responsible for making the wire live—D1 and D2 were both occupiers at common law (see Chap. 10, (1) **9**)—*Held*, D2 were liable under the regulations as the notional occupiers of a factory by virtue of F.A. 1961, s. 127(4), but that D1 was not liable (nor, semble, D2) as occupiers. The liability of D3 was said to be debatable, as it was not clear whether D3 were (as D2 clearly were) "persons undertaking the operations" within s. 127(4).

19. Cockady v. British Siddeley (1965) 115 L.J. 661; [1965] C.L.Y. 1652, Barry J.

20. Leach v. Standard Telephones [1966] 1 W.L.R. 1392; [1966] 2 All E.R. 523, Browne J.

21. Flannigan v. British Dyewoods, 1969 S.L.T. 223, O.H.; 1970 S.L.T. 285, I.H.

22. Reid v. Galbraiths Stores, 1970 S.L.T. 83, O.H.

23. Smith v. George Wimpey [1972] 2 Q.B. 329; [1972] 2 All E.R. 723, C.A.

Held, overruling *Upton v. Hipgrave* [1965] 1 All E.R. 6 and *Baron v. French* [1971] 3 All E.R. 1111, and approving *Bunker v. Charles Brand* [1969] 2 Q.B. 480 and *Taylor v. Sayers* [1971] 1 All E.R. 934. The ratio of the decision was that the debated words "as affect him" had been brought in, and brought in only, to fill the previous lacuna whereby a working sub-contractor could not be prosecuted if he himself worked in breach of regulations.

24. Westwood v. Post Office [1974] A.C. 1; [1973] 3 All E.R. 184, H.L.

Uddin **16** approved.

25. Jones v. Minton (1973) 15 K.I.R. 309; [1974] C.L.Y. 2599, Thompson J.

26. Ferguson v. John Dawson [1976] 1 W.L.R. 1213; [1976] 3 All E.R. 817, C.A.

Plaintiff had agreed to work for defendant main contractors as a working sub-contractor for labour only—but in all other respects, judged by all available tests, was working under a contract of service—*Held*, that the reality was what mattered, and that he could sue as a person "employed".

27. Massey v. Crown Life [1978] 1 W.L.R. 676; [1978] 2 All E.R. 577, C.A.

Unfair dismissal case, in the course of which the Court of Appeal *referred* to *Ferguson* **26** without enthusiasm. Lord Denning M.R. *said* (581 C): "In most of these cases I expect it will be found that the parties do deliberately agree for the man to be self-employed or 'on the lump'. It is done especially so as to obtain the tax benefits. When such an agreement is made, it affords strong evidence that that is the real relationship. If it is so found the man must accept it. He cannot afterwards assert that he was only a servant."

28. Williams v. West Wales Plant Hire Co. [1984] 1 W.L.R. 1311; [1984] 3 All E.R. 397, C.A.

Plaintiff's employers hired out his services, and the crane he operated, to a builder. During the building operation, crane fell over due to collapse of earth. Plaintiff claimed, *inter alia*, that his employers were in breach of C.(L.O.)R. 1961, reg. 11(1)—*Held*, employer liable. They were "undertaking" a building operation within meaning of reg. 3(1), because through the plaintiff their employee they were actively engaged in a building operation.

29. Page v. Read (1984) 134 New L.J. 723; [1984] C.L.Y. 1203, Stocker J.

30. Dexter v. Tenby Electrical Accessories Ltd [1991] Crim. L.R. 839; *The Times*, March 11, 1991, D.C.

See Chap. 16, (5)(h) **43** for further details.

31. Galek's Curator Bonis v. Thomson, 1991 S.L.T. 29; [1991] C.L.Y. 4432

So *held*, in relation to the part of reg. 3(1) dealing with the alteration of any scaffold.

32. Morris v. Breaveglen Ltd [1993] I.C.R. 766; [1993] P.I.Q.R. P294, C.A.

Defendant supplied plaintiff to S under labour-only sub-contract, requiring defendant, *inter alia*, to insure against employer's liability, indemnify S against all such claims and perform all obligations placed on employers by statute or common law, though in practice S controlled plaintiff's work. Plaintiff instructed by S to tip soil from a dumper truck in area in part of which was steep, unprotected overhang. Truck went over the edge, probably because plaintiff inadvertently took foot off clutch—he had not been trained properly in driving dumper truck—*Held*, *inter alia*, that through the plaintiff, defendant was "using" the truck within meaning of C.(G.P.)R. 1961, reg. 3, and was thus liable for admitted breaches of regs. 32 and 37.

*(b) Who Can Be Sued**

Regulation	*See also Intro. Notes*	*Operation*	*Defendant*		*Whether liable*
F.A. 1937, s. 26	6,9	Unsafe access down side of dry dock	Dock owners	1	Yes
D.R. 1934, reg. 20	4	Unsafe rope not belonging to defendants	Stevedore employers	2	No
F.A. 1937, s. 26	6,9	Unsafe access caused by independent contractor	Factory occupier	3	Yes
E.R. 1908	4	UNSAFE SWITCH UNDER CONTROL OF POWER COMPANY	FACTORY OCCUPIER	4	Yes
F.A. 1937, ss. 25, 26	6,9	Faulty plank supplied by independent contractor	Factory occupier	5	Yes
F.A. 1937, s. 17	6,10	Dangerous machinery	Seller	6	No
F.A. 1937, s. 26	6,9	Breach caused by independent contractor	Factory occupier	7	Yes
F.A. 1937, s. 26	"	Breach of Factories Act on ship under repair in dry dock	Dock owners	8	Yes
F.A. 1937, s. 17	6,10	INSTALLING SHAFTS AND GEARING WHICH CONTRAVENE SECTION	OCCUPIER	9	No
F.A. 1937, s. 17	6,10	SUPPLYING SHAFTS AND GEARING WHICH CONTRAVENE SECTION	SUPPLIER	9	?

* Abbreviations are explained in Introductory Note 1. See also Introductory Notes 3(A), (B) and (F).

1. Rippon v. P.L.A. [1940] 1 K.B. 858; [1940] 1 All E.R. 637, Tucker J.

Unsafe access down side of dry dock to ship therein—*Held inter alia*, dock owners were occupiers for purposes of F.A. 1937, ss. 25 and 26. *Followed* in **9**.

2. O'Melia v. Freight Conveyors [1940] 4 All E.R. 516, Croom-Johnson J.

Defendants supplied a sound rope—it disappeared and another one was substituted in circumstances unknown—the second rope was partly severed—defendants were sued under D.R. 1934, reg. 20.—*Held*, however, since under the duties provisions the obligation was only cast on the "owner of the plant and machinery used in the processes", defendants were not liable, as the second rope was not theirs.

3. Whitby v. Burt Boulton [1947] K.B. 918; [1947] 2 All E.R. 324, Denning J.

Held, that where a breach of F.A. 1937, s. 26 occurred while a contractor was carrying on a building operation therein, the occupier would be liable (but he received 100 per cent, indemnity from the contractor, who was liable for faulty system at common law). *But* in *Lavender v. Diamints* [1949] 1 K.B. 585; [1949] 1 All E.R. 532, C.A. Tucker L.J. said that he wished to reserve the point whether F.A., 1937, s. 26 applied to building operations carried on in a factory. *Applied* in **7**.

4. Heard v. Brymbo Steel Works [1947] K.B. 692; 80 Ll.L.R. 424, C.A.

Explosion at switchboard due to faulty conductor—*Held*, employers liable. Another cause of the accident was that an electricity switch at the factory, which was under the control of the power company, was also faulty—*Held*, employers were also liable for this under E.R. 1908 (see at 698, top).

5. Hosking v. De Havilland [1949] 1 All E.R. 540; 83 Ll.L.R. 11, Lewis J.

Held, employers liable under F.A. 1937, ss. 25(1) and 26(1) for faulty plank provided in factory of employers by an independent contractor. **3** *applied.*

6. Biddle v. Truvox [1952] 1 K.B. 101; [1951] 2 All E.R. 835, Finnemore J.

Held, seller of dangerous machinery under no statutory liability in third party proceedings.

7. Whincup v. Woodhead [1951] 1 All E.R. 387; 115 J.P. 97, McNair J.

Held, following **3** and applying F.A. 1948, s. 14(4), that a factory occupier was bound to observe duty under F.A. 1937, s. 26 when an independent contractor was carrying on a building operation in a factory. (The independent contractor was also liable under the B.R. 1948).

8. Welch v. Admiralty [1952] 2 Lloyd's Rep. 520, Havers J.

Ship under repair in dry dock pursuant to licence agreement with dock owners—*Held*, following **1**, that the dock owners were the occupiers for the purpose of F.A. 1937, s. 26 since they had only granted a licence to the repairers to use the dock.

9. Uddin v. Associated Portland Cement Manufacturers [1965] 2 Q.B. 582; [1965] 2 All E.R. 213, C.A.

Case was mainly fought on s. 14—but plaintiff argued that in any event the occupier of the factory was also liable under F.A. 1937, s. 17 (which deals with the construction and sale of machinery) for installing machinery which did not conform with the section—*Held*, not, as the section was solely concerned with the duty of the supplier. Whether a supplier would be liable in damages under this section was not directly discussed, but *Biddle v. Truvox* **6** is authority for saying that he would be liable to a penalty only.

*(c) Rules of Construction**

		See also Introductory Notes
CONSTRUCTION AGAINST CREATING OFFENCES PREFERRED	1	6
Object of Acts to protect workmen—to be construed accordingly	2	–
CONSTRUCTION AGAINST CREATING OFFENCES IS A RULE OF LAST RESORT	3	–
OBJECT OF ACTS TO PROTECT WORKMEN—TO BE CONSTRUED ACCORDINGLY	4	6
CONSTRUCTION AGAINST CREATING OFFENCES PREFERRED	5, 6	–
Construction which would make process impracticable—adopted—fencing of grindstone	7	6, 10
WORDS TO BE CONSTRUED ACCORDING TO THEIR TRADE MEANING	8	–
Construction which would make process impracticable—to be rejected—securing coal face	9	6
Legislature presumed to endorse construction previously given	10	10
ORDINARY FAMILIAR WORDS—TO BE DETERMINED BY ORDINARY STANDARDS OF COMMON SENSE RATHER THAN BY DICTIONARIES—"STAIRCASE"	11	–
ORDINARY FAMILIAR WORDS—TO BE CONSTRUED BY COMMON SENSE RATHER THAN BY "ATTEMPTS AT DEFINITION OR PHILOSOPHICAL DISCUSSION"—PART OF MACHINERY	12	–
LEGISLATURE PRESUMED TO ENDORSE CONSTRUCTION PREVIOUSLY GIVEN	13	6, 10
Construction not be strained in favour of awarding compensation	14	–
Legislation presumed to endorse construction previously given	U1	–

1. Burns v. Terry [1951] 1 K.B. 454; [1950] 2 All E.R. 987, C.A.

Somervell L.J. (991 D. Cohen L.J. concurring) adopted dictum of Lord Simonds in *L.N.E.R. v. Berriman* [1946] A.C. 278; [1946] 1 All E.R. 255, 270, citing passage from judgment of Lord Esher M.R. in *Tuck v. Priester* (1887) 19 Q.B.D. 629, 638: "We must be very careful in construing that section, because it imposes a penalty. If there is a reasonable interpretation which will avoid the penalty . . . we must adopt that construction. If there are two reasonable constructions we must give the more lenient one." But the Lord Justice (991 E) also pointed out that in *Berriman* Lord Wright has said he did not think this rule applied to the F.A. 1937 and similar Acts.

2. Harrison v. N.C.B. [1951] A.C. 639; [1951] 1 All E.R. 1102, H.L.

Lord Porter (1107 F): "It was suggested . . . that the C.M.A. 1911 is a measure imposing criminal liability, and therefore should be interpreted as throwing no greater burden on the employer than its words compel. It has however to be remembered that this Act is also a remedial measure passed for the protection of the workman, and must therefore be read so as to effect the object so far as the wording fairly and reasonably permits."

* Abbreviations are explained in Introductory Note 1.

3. McCarthy v. Coldair [1951] 2 T.L.R. 1226; [1951] W.N. 590, C.A.

Denning L.J.: "So far as the Factories Acts are concerned, the rule (*i.e.* construction to be against creating offences) is only to be applied when other rules fail. It is a rule of last resort."

4. Norris v. Syndie [1952] 2 Q.B. 135; [1952] 1 All E.R. 935, C.A.

Denning L.J. (939 D): "... the Act (*i.e.* F.A. 1937) is intended to prevent accidents to workmen, and I think it should be construed so as to further that end." The Lord Justice also referred with approval to dicta in **2** and **3** above.

5. Rees v. Bernard Hastie [1953] 1 Q.B. 328; [1953] 1 All E.R. 375, C.A.

Somervell L.J. at 377 A: "To my mind, that is a natural construction. Even if the other construction were possible, this is a schedule which created offences, and the natural construction should clearly prevail for the benefit of a person against whom a breach is alleged."

6. Summer v. Priestley [1955] 1 W.L.R. 1202; [1955] 3 All E.R. 445, C.A.

Singleton L.J. (447 A): "If one considers the question of construction alone, it is necessary to remember that this is a penal regulation."

7. John Summers v. Frost [1955] A.C. 740; [1955] 1 All E.R. 870, H.L.

Held, that the fact that secure fencing as prescribed by F.A. 1937, s. 14 would make the grindstone in question commercially unusable could not be allowed to affect the obligation to fence, which was absolute.

8. Jenner v. Allen West [1959] 1 W.L.R. 554; [1959] 2 All E.R. 115, C.A.

Question was what was meant by "crawling boards"—*Held*, that the meaning should be interpreted in the light of its meaning in the building trade. Dictum of Lord Esher M.R. in *Unwin v. Hanson* [1891] 2 Q.B. 115, 119 applied: "If the Act is one passed with reference to a particular trade, business or transaction, and words are used which everybody conversant with that trade, business or transaction knows and understands to have a particular meaning in it, then the words are to be construed as having that particular meaning, though it may differ from the common or ordinary meaning of the words."

9. Gough v. N.C.B. [1959] A.C. 698; [1959] 2 All E.R. 164, H.L.

Question was whether duty of securing sides of working place in coal mine extended to coal face—*Held*, yes, as the key to the question lay in what was meant by "securing," and it was possible to read that word in such a way that there was no breach in bringing down the face deliberately. Lord Reid (169 G, Lord Morton concurring): "I would agree with this argument to the extent that Parliament cannot have intended altogether to prevent the winning of coal, and that nothing in the Act can be read in such a way as to produce this result."

N.B. One distinction between this case and **7** is that in **7** liability arose under the Factories Acts, where the Minister had a dispensing power under F.A. 1937, s. 60, to modify the obligations of the Act.

10. Hamilton v. N.C.B. [1960] A.C. 633; [1960] 1 All E.R. 76, H.L.

Question was whether "properly maintained" in M.Q.A. 1954, s. 81(1) imported an absolute obligation—*Held*, yes, following *Smith v. Cammell Laird* [1939] 4 All E.R. 381, where the word was "maintained" alone. Lord Simmonds (78 G): "It is difficult to suppose that the legislature, knowing from *Smith's* case what meaning must be attributed to the word 'maintain' alone, thought to give it a different meaning by adding the word 'properly.'"'

11. Kimpton v. Steel Company of Wales [1960] 1 W.L.R. 527; [1960] 2 All E.R. 274, C.A.

Held, that a set of three steel steps leading up to a platform was not a staircase, since although the set could be brought within the dictionary definition, in ordinary common sense it was not.

12. Cherry v. International Alloys [1961] 1 Q.B. 136; [1960] 3 All E.R. 264, C.A.

The question was whether a factory truck constituted factory machinery—*Held*, not. Sellers L.J. (266 H) said that he adopted the view of the Master of the Rolls in *Rogers v. News of the World*, to the effect that "the construction of the words, which are ordinary English words, must be determined by common sense, and that any attempt at definition, or philosophical discussion, should be avoided." *But* see now Chap. 16, (6) (b) **18**, where this decision was *overruled*.

13. Mitchell v. Westin [1965] 1 W.L.R. 297; [1965] 1 All E.R. 657, C.A.

In 1955 (*Richard Thomas and Baldwins* (Chap. 16, (6) (f) **5**) H.L. decided that the words "in motion or in use"—in F.A. 1937, s. 16 must be given a restricted meaning—on June 22, 1961, F.A. 1961, repeating s. 16, received Royal Assent—*Held*, per Pearson L.J. (664 B) and Salmon L.J. (666 B) that thereby Parliament acknowledged that they did mean the words to have some restricted meaning. *But* Salmon L.J., while agreeing that H.L. intended the words to have some restricted meaning, pointed out that H.L. "did not reach any measure of unanimity on what that special meaning was." In this connection, C.A. had interpreted the *Richard Thomas* decision in *Knight v. Leamington Spa* (Chap. 16, (6) (f) **6**), which was decided on May 16, 1961. Pearson L.J. *said* he doubted whether, in view of the proximity of dates, this latter decision could be said to have been endorsed by the legislature.

14. Haigh v. Charles Ireland [1974] 1 W.L.R. 43; [1973] 3 All E.R. 1137, H.L.

"A court is not entitled to place a strained meaning on the words it (F.A. 1961) uses so as to provide an alternative way of serving this social purpose (*i.e.* of providing compensation in cases where there has been no causative fault on the part of anyone) instead of its primary purpose of laying down under penal sanctions specific precautions which must be taken . . . " (Lord Diplock, 1147 H, three other Law Lords concurring).

U1. Palmer v. Shirley and Warbey Box Co. (1965) C.A. 193

"After the decision in the H.L. (*Richard Thomas, supra*) the Factories Act 1961 was passed which re-enacted sections 14 and 16 in exactly the same words . . . Parliament . . . since they repeated the words, must be taken to have accepted the decision . . . as correctly interpreting their intention" (Salmon L.J., 3 F).

*(d) Special and General Provisions**

			See also Intro. Notes
SPECIAL REGULATIONS DO NOT MODIFY GENERAL DUTY IF NOT AN EXHAUSTIVE CODE NOR DEAL WITH PARTICULAR PART OF MACHINE	1	H.M.M.R. 1928	6,9,10
Special regulations may modify absolute general duty	2	**Generally**	6,10
EXEMPTION UNDER SPECIAL REGULATIONS—DOES NOT ALSO EXEMPT FROM GENERAL DUTY	3	H.M.M.R. 1928	6,9,10
Special sections dealing with cranes (and probably lifts) do not oust general duty to fence	4	**F.A. 1961**	10

1. Benn v. Kamm [1952] 2 Q.B. 127; [1952] 1 All E.R. 833, C.A.

Horizontal milling machine—plaintiff injured by a dangerous part other than the cutter—H.M.M.R. 1928 only deal with fencing the cutter—*Held*, that the Regulations were not an exhaustive code nor did they modify F.A. 1937 with regard to parts other than the cutter, and therefore defendants liable under F.A. 1937, s. 14. Followed in **3** and in *Dickson v. Flack* (Chap. 16, (6) (e) **3**.

2. John Summers v. Frost [1955] A.C. 740; [1955] 1 All E.R. 870, H.L.

Held, by H.L. that special regulations made under F.A. 1937, s. 60, could modify the absolute duty laid down by s. 14.

3. Quinn v. Horsfall [1956] 1 W.L.R. 652; [1956] 2 All E.R. 467, C.A.

Horizontal milling machine which, because used for automatic profiling, was exempt from fencing under H.M.M.R. 1928—Regulations contained a proviso saying that nothing in the exemption should prejudice the application of the Factories Act—*Held*, that defendants were under duty to fence under F.A. 1937, s. 14. C.A. gave no real indication of what would have been the position, if there had been no proviso, except the citation from Somervell L.J., *ante*, that "this depends on the wording of the Regulations."

4. B.R.B. v. Liptrot [1969] 1 A.C. 136; [1967] 2 All E.R. 1072, H.L.

Question was whether the general obligation to fence dangerous parts of machinery applied to a mobile crane—one of the arguments put up was that there were special sections in F.A. 1961 dealing with cranes (and with lifts and hoists), and that therefore these things fell outside the general obligation to fence machinery—*Held*, not so. Lord Dilhorne thought that lifts and hoists might fall in a special and exclusive code, because the group of sections dealing therewith contained a power (s. 25(4)—now repealed) to the Minister to dispense with the requirements of this group of sections if he was satisfied it would in special circumstances be unreasonable to enforce them, but he said this

* Abbreviations are explained in Introductory Note 1. See also Introductory Notes 3(B), (E) and (G).

did not apply to the crane group of sections, because it contained no sections similar to s. 25(4): see 1076 I. Lord Reid thought that the argument as a whole was so improbable that he would have to be satisfied that some of the special sections were either inconsistent or at least difficult to reconcile with the general section (1079 F). Lord Hodson thought that if the Minister, under powers given by the special sections, had made regulations which were inconsistent with the general section, the argument could have substance, but that was not the case here (1082 A). Lord Guest said that the special section dealing with cranes dealt with construction and maintenance (s. 27), leaving the general section (s.14) to apply to fencing (1084 I). Lord Pearson said that *Carrington* (Chap. 16, (7) (c) **8**) was rightly decided and was sufficient for the proposition that the general duty still existed side by side with the special section.

*(e) Limitation to Particular Class of Injury**

			See also Intro. Notes
PROTECTION FROM DUST—DUTY LIMITED TO INJURIES CAUSED BY INADEQUATE VENTILATION	1	F.A. 1937, s. 4(1)	6,9
FAULTY ELECTRIC CABLE—BREAKING WHEN PULLED—DUTY NOT LIMITED TO INJURIES CAUSED ELECTRICALLY	2	E.R. 1908, REG. 6	4
MATERIAL FLYING OUT OF UNFENCED MACHINE—FENCE WOULD INCIDENTALLY HAVE KEPT MATERIAL IN	3	F.A. 1937, s. 14	6,10
No mask provided against visible dust—mask would incidentally have protected against injurious invisible dust which at time was unknown danger	4	F.A. 1937, s. 47(1)	6
Protection from dust—duty limited to injuries caused by inadequate ventilation	5	**F.A. 1937, s. 4(1)**	6,9
ELECTRICAL PART OF LIFTING MACHINE FAULTY—PLAINTIFF MISTAKENLY PRESSING BUTTON TILL THUMB RUPTURED	6	F.A. 1961, s. 27(1)	—
Noise from machine injuring plaintiff—may be breach of duty to keep workplace safe	7	F.A. 1961, s. 29(1)	9
Dematitis from contracted coolant—employers in breach of duty to keep place of work safe	8	F.A. 1961, s. 29(1)	"
Noise-induced deafness—employers in breach of duty to keep place of work safe	9	F.A. 1961, s. 29(1)	"

* Abbreviations are explained in Introductory Note 1. See also Introductory Notes 2 and 3(A) and (B).

Vibration while finger—employer not in breach of duty to keep place of work safe (but liable at common law)	10	F.A. 1961, s. 29(1)	9

1. Ebbs v. James Whitson [1952] 2 Q.B. 877; [1952] 2 All E.R. 192, C.A.

Dust from monsonia wood causing dermatitis—*Held*, no claim under F.A. 1937, s. 4(1), as this section was only concerned with protecting employees by ventilation. *Approved* by H.L. in **5**.

2. Gatehouse v. John Summers [1953] 1 W.L.R. 742; [1953] 2 All E.R. 117, C.A.

Electrician pulls at an electric cable on a crane, which breaks at a joint, so that he falls and is killed—*Held*, defendants liable under reg. 6, as cable was not of proper mechanical strength and it was immaterial that the injury was not electrically caused.

3. Kilgollan v. W. Cooke [1956] 1 W.L.R. 527; [1956] 2 All E.R. 294, C.A.

Wire ejected from machine—defendants were intending to fit guard under F.A. 1937 to keep people out—such guard would also incidentally have kept wire in—*Held*, no action for breach of statutory duty lay, because the injury was not of the kind against which F.A. 1937 was designed to protect plaintiff, and hence the injury was not caused by the breach. See *also* **4**.

4. Richards v. Highway Ironfounders [1957] 1 W.L.R. 781; [1957] 2 All E.R. 162, Pearson J.

See Chap. 16, (7) (d) **10**—judge appears to have assumed that if defendants, in pursuance of their duty to protect against visible but non-injurious dust, had only had available Mark IV respirators which incidentally safeguarded also against the then unknown invisible injurious dust, defendants would have been liable if they had failed to provide Mark IV respirators for a man who was injured by the invisible dust. But *quaere* in view of **3**.

5. Nicholson v. Atlas Steel [1957] 1 W.L.R. 613; [1957] 1 All E.R. 776, H.L.

A case which turned mainly around the duty to protect from dust under F.A. 1937, s. 47(1)—but Lord Simonds (779 F, Lords Oaksey and Morton concurring) appears to have approved the decision in **1.** (*N.B.* The decision in **1** was also applied by Devlin J. in *Graham v. C.W.S.* (Chap. 16, (7) (d) **8**) although the judge left open the question whether s. 4(1) conferred any right of civil action at all.)

6. Evans v. Sanderson (1968) 4 K.I.R. 115; [1965] C.L.Y. 1597, C.A.

In breach of F.A. 1961, s. 27(1) (good construction, etc., of all parts of lifting machines) the electrical contactors of a crane were defective—plaintiff, thinking control buttons were faulty, mistakenly pushed them until tendon in thumb ruptured—*Held*, that the injury was caused by the defect, and defendants were liable.

7. Carragher v. Singer Manufacturing Co., 1974 S.L.T. (Notes) 28

Held, that the duty to keep a workplace safe could apply to excessive noise emitted from a machine. In *Berry v. Stone Manganese* [1972] 1 Lloyd's Rep. 182 the point had been left open.

8. Yates v. Rockwell Graphic Systems Ltd [1988] I.C.R. 8; [1988] C.L.Y. 1739, Steyn J.

See Chap. 16, (5) (e) **16** for further details.

9. Baxter v. Harland & Wolff plc [1990] I.R.L.R. 516; [1991] C.L.Y. 1878, N.I.C.A.

See Chap. 16, (5) (e) **17** for further details.

10. Bowman v. Harland Wolff plc [1992] I.R.L.R. 349; [1992] C.L.Y. 3222, Carswell J., N.I.

See Chap. 16, (5) (e) **18** for further details.

(2) Standard of Care Generally

*(a) "Dangerous"**

(*N.B.* Most of the cases in which the meaning of the word "dangerous" has arisen are fencing cases, which are set out in Chap. 16, (6) (a). This subsection contains a selection of cases illustrating the meaning of "dangerous" generally under the statutory code.)

		See also Intro. Notes
Danger to the careless as well as to the careful must be anticipated	1	–
DANGER MEANS ORDINARY AND NOT EXCEPTIONAL DANGER	2	–
Danger from extravagant carelessness cannot be anticipated	3	–
Danger to the careless as well as to the careful must be anticipated	4	–
Danger may not include ordinary transient hazards	5	–
EXPERIENCED MEN MUST BE PROTECTED AS WELL AS INEXPERIENCED	6	4
DANGER INCLUDES DANGER TO THE UTTERLY STUPID AND NEGLIGENT	7	–
BLETCHLEY FLETTON TEST RESTATED—TO READ "REASONABLY FORESEEABLE CAUSE OF INJURY"—RATHER THAN "POSSIBLE CAUSE OF INJURY"	8	10

1. Walker v. Bletchley Flettons [1937] 1 All E.R. 170, du Parcq J.

"In considering whether machinery is dangerous, it must not be assumed that everyone will always be careful. A part of a machine is dangerous if it is a possible cause of injury to anybody acting in a way in which a human being may reasonably be expected to act in circumstances which may be reasonably expected to occur" (175 F). *Approved* by H.L. in **4**. See *also* comments of Divisional Court in **3**.

2. Hutchinson v. London and North Eastern Railway [1942] 1 K.B. 481; [1942] 1 All E.R. 330, C.A.

Question was whether a lookout should have been provided for railway gangers—defendants said that the duty only arose when some exceptional danger arose, *e.g.*, abnormally short visibility—*Held*, not so, and the words "danger likely to arise" referred to all ordinary danger, and defendants therefore liable.

* Abbreviations are explained in Introductory Note 1.

3. Carr v. Mercantile Produce [1949] 2 K.B. 601; [1949] 2 All E.R. 531, D.C.

Dictum of du Parcq J. in **1** cited with approval, but Divisional Court point out that the judge added: "Nobody expects human beings to be so extravagantly careless as to touch some part of the machine which is not only not difficult to avoid, but which is actually difficult to get near."

4. John Summers v. Frost [1955] A.C. 740; [1955] 1 All E.R. 870, H.L.

On the question whether the machine in question was dangerous, Lord Simonds said that the dictum of du Parcq J. in **1** gave "as precise a definition as can be hoped for," if read in conjunction with the dictum of Lord Cooper in *Mitchell v. North British Rubber*, 1945 S.C.(J.) at 73, as follows: "(A machine is dangerous . . . if) in the ordinary course of human affairs danger may reasonably be anticipated from its use unfenced, not only to the prudent, alert and skilled operative, but also to the careless or inattentive worker whose inadvertent or indolent conduct may expose him to risk of injury or death from the unguarded part." Lord Oaksey agreed with Lord Simonds, and Lord Reid also approved the above two dicta, which therefore have the approval of a majority of the House of Lords.

5. Cowhig v. Port of London Authority [1956] 2 Lloyd's Rep. 306, Pearce J.

Held, that a part of a dock road was not "dangerous" merely because there was a hosepipe laid across it.

6. Murfin v. United Steel [1957] 1 W.L.R. 104; [1957] 1 All E.R. 23, C.A.

No insulating screen as required by E.R. 1908, reg. 24 "where necessary to prevent danger"—defendants argue that there was no danger, as the apparatus was in a room set apart under reg. 15, into which only experienced men could enter—*Held*, no defence, because experienced men just as liable to lapses as inexperienced.

7. Uddin v. Associated Portland Cement Manufacturers [1965] 2 Q.B. 582; [1965] 2 All E.R. 213, C.A.

Lord Pearce (217 C): "There is nothing to justify the view that the (F.A. 1937) intended its protection for only the slightly stupid or slightly negligent and intended to withdraw all protection from the utterly stupid and utterly negligent."

8. Rodgers v. London Brick Company (1970) 8 K.I.R. 843; [1970] C.L.Y. 1713, C.A.

Question was whether machinery was dangerous within M.Q.A. 1954, s. 82(1)—*Held*, by C.A., on the facts, it was a freak accident, and that there was no liability (the rising bar at the rear of a tractor embedded in clay at the bottom of a clay pit had been raised by P in order to attach a drag line, which had caused the clay on which P was standing to shift, which in turn caused P to lose his balance and catch his foot between the bar and some gland nuts on the tractor). C.A. said that machinery was dangerous if it was a reasonably foreseeable cause of injury to anybody acting in a way in which a human being might be reasonably expected to act in circumstances which might reasonably be expected to occur. This is the *Bletchley Fletton* **1** test, with the substitution of "reasonably foreseeable cause of injury" for "possible cause of injury." This stems directly from Lord Reid's dictum in *Summers* **4** at 883. But in that case Lord Simonds (Lord Oaksey concurring) and Lord Keith approved the original formula, provided that Lord Cooper's dictum in *Mitchell v. North British* was read in conjunction: this dictum (see **4**, where it is quoted) goes to the way in which the worker may be expected to act, rather than to the cause of injury. Therefore *Summers* does not conclude the matter. Subsequently there have been cases where, in turn, each formula has been used. In the cases contained in Chap. 16, (2) (b) ("safe") *Sheppey* **4** and *Trott* **9** were ones where "possible" was used, while in *Croft* **U2** "reasonable" was firmly stipulated. *Smart* **U3** is more consistent with "possible," *Woods* **13** with "reasonable." Under Chap. 16, (2) (c) ("secure") Lord Denning in *Brown* **15**, sitting in H.L., used the word "possible," and in *Soar* **17** he said that he adhered to the formula as used by du Parcq J., *i.e.* "possible".

*(b) "Safe"**

		See also Intro. Notes
TEST FOR DANGEROUS MACHINERY—NOT A CONCLUSIVE GUIDE TO "SAFE"	1	–
"SAFE" INCLUDES GUARDING AGAINST THE UNLIKELY AS WELL AS THE LIKELY	2	–
"SAFE" MEANS GUARDING AGAINST DANGER WHICH IS BOTH APPRECIABLE AND FORESEEABLE	3	–
Test for dangerous machinery—is a good guide to "safe"	4	–
Test of "safe" must cater for men of experience—who may be careless.	4	–
TEST OF "SAFE" WILL VARY ACCORDING TO CIRCUMSTANCES	5	6, 9
"Safe" means unlikely to cause harm or injury	6	–
DOES NOT INCLUDE DUTY TO GUARD AGAINST ORDINARY INCIDENTS OF LIFE	7	6, 9
"Safe" includes ability to stand up to lighthearted user	8	–
TEST FOR DANGEROUS MACHINERY—IS THE PROPER TEST FOR "SAFE"	9	–
"Cannot safely be done"—building regulations—test is foreseeability ...	10	–
"CANNOT SAFELY BE DONE"—BUILDING REGULATIONS—TEST IS AS FOR DANGEROUS MACHINERY	11	–
Extraneous and isolated dangers do not make a safe place unsafe	12	–
"CANNOT SAFELY BE DONE"—ACCIDENT MUST BE FORESEEABLY LIKELY—RATHER THAN FORESEEABLY POSSIBLE	13	–
"CANNOT SAFELY BE DONE"—STEEL ERECTOR SITTING ASTRIDE A BEAM	13	–
Place of work—must be safe *qua* place—not *qua* equipment brought onto it for a particular operation	14	–
"Cannot safely be done"—building regulations—meaning	U1	–
Test depends on whether real risk foreseeable—test must cater for the careless	U2	–
Definition in McCarthy approved	U3	–

1. Slayford v. Harland & Wolff (1948) 82 Ll.L.R. 160, C.A.

Held, that the test for dangerous machinery laid down in *Walker v. Bletchley Flettons* (Chap 16, (6) (a) **1**) was not a conclusive guide to what is "safe" as regards safe means of access. *But* see **4** and **9**.

2. McCarthy v. Coldair [1951] 2 T.L.R. 1226; [1951] W.N. 590, C.A.

Ten-foot ladder was placed at a proper angle for plaintiff—unfooted—it slipped—*Held*, that there not merely a slight but a substantial risk it would slip, and therefore was not a safe means of access: " 'Safe' means safe for all contingencies that may reasonably be foreseen, unlikely as well as likely, possible as well as probable."

* Abbreviations are explained in Introductory Note 1.

3. Moodie v. Furness Shipbuilding [1951] 2 Lloyd's Rep. 600, C.A.

Insufficient headroom on staging at top of ladder—deceased banged head and fell fatally—*Held*, not safe means of access (S.R. 1931, reg. 1). Denning L.J. (605): "In order that a means of access should be safe, it seems to me that it must be free from any danger which is both appreciable and foreseeable."

4. Sheppey v. Matthew T. Shaw [1952] 1 T.L.R. 1272; [1952] W.N. 249, Parker J.

Plaintiff a steel erector was put on to painting steel girders which he had erected—to get there he slid along the top edge of the one boom and under purlins—fell—*Held*, this was not safe access (B.R. 1948, reg. 5). "Reference has been made to passages in decided cases where the duty is said to be to provide reasonably safe means of access. For myself, with great deference, I get little help from adding the word 'reasonably.' It is not in the regulations. If it is used in contra-distinction to 'absolutely safe,' I can understand it; but if it is intended to mean 'safe for anybody acting reasonably,' in the sense of taking full precautions for their own safety, I cannot agree with it . . . These regulations are intended to safeguard workmen against acts which, owing to the frailty of human nature, continually occur of carelessness or inadvertence, and whatever epithet one applies here to the word 'safe,' I think it must mean a degree of safety which to some extent, at any rate, foresees the fact that human beings . . . will from time to time . . . not exercise a very high degree of care for their own safety" (1274). The judge then went on to paraphrase the *Walker v. Bletchley Flettons* test (see Chap. 16 (6) (a) **1**), transposing "unsafe access" for "dangerous part of machinery," and continued: "In considering whether a means of access is safe, it would be right to consider the employment of the people who are going to do the work. It may be that access would be safe, say, for a steel erector, where it would not be safe for a lawyer; but one must not carry that too far, because otherwise . . . you would be testing the safety of the access by the skill of people to avoid danger. I think that in considering safety you must assume that the means of access will be used by a person experienced in the particular trade in question, and in my view the means in the present case was not safe for a steel erector. I say that in spite of the evidence . . . of the men concerned, who thought this was child's play" (1275). *Approved* by C.A. in **9**.

5. Moncrieff v. Swan Hunter [1953] 2 Lloyd's Rep. 149, C.A.

Plaintiff lowering himself by rope onto third sill of dry dock—*Held*, no failure to provide access. Denning L.J. (150): "In considering . . . 'safe means of access,' it is very necessary to bear in mind the nature of the place, the experience of the man, and the general practice in the industry. As Pritchard J. said on one occasion, you cannot expect the floor of a dock to be as free from obstruction as a dance floor . . . It has often been said that (F.A. 1937, s. 26) adds very little to the common law duty of the employer."

6. Clayton v. Russell [1953] 2 Lloyd's Rep. 692, Donovan J.

" 'Safe' means 'unlikely to cause harm or injury' " (695).

7. Thomas v. Bristol Aeroplane [1954] 1 W.L.R. 694; [1954] 2 All E.R. 1, C.A.

Early morning snowfall which was not swept away from factory approaches—*Held*, defendants not liable. Morris L.J. (4A): "The risks which resulted that morning were no more than the risks which form a part of the ordinary incidents of life to which all are subject." *N.B.* This case was brought under F.A. 1937, s. 26 where the duty is qualified by a "reasonably practicable" proviso.

8. Cottrell v. Vianda S.S. [1955] 2 Lloyd's Rep. 450, Devlin J.

Ladder into hold broke—defendants allege that this happened because plaintiff was playing the fool—*Held*, defendants liable, because a ladder to be safe must be able to stand a degree of lighthearted use.

9. Trott v. W.E. Smith [1957] 1 W.L.R. 1154; [1957] 3 All E.R. 500, C.A.

Steel erector had to walk along a 3-foot girder without handhold to gain access to place of work—*Held*, not safe access, and defendants liable. Test propounded by Parker J. in **4** approved, as follows: "In considering whether the means of access provided is safe or unsafe, it must not be assumed that everyone will always be careful. A means of access is unsafe if it is a possible cause of injury to anybody acting in a way a human being may reasonably be expected to act in circumstances which may reasonably be expected to occur" (505 B, Jenkins L.J).

10. Connolly v. McGee [1961] 1 W.L.R. 811; [1961] 2 All E.R. 111, Paull L.

11. Curran v. William Neill & Son [1961] 1 W.L.R. 1069; [1961] 3 All E.R. 108, 111G, C.A.

12. Amis v. Smith's Dock Co. [1963] 1 Lloyd's Rep. 181, Veale J.

Gangway intrinsically safe—became unsafe by reason of shot blasting in vicinity—*Held*, the means of access did not thereby become unsafe: "I do not think that a safe access becomes unsafe as an access by reason of an isolated and extraneous act of negligence which is committed at or near it" (187, col. 1).

13. Woods v. Power Gas Corporation (1969) 8 K.I.R. 834; [1970] C.L.Y. 247, C.A.

Question was whether work could safely be done (within C.(G.P.)R. 1961, reg. 7(2)) (now replaced by C.(W.P.)R. 1966, reg. 7) by a steel erector sitting astride a girder—he was inserting bolts when he fell—*Held*, there was no breach, as sitting astride a girder was a familiar position for a skilled steel erector. Davies L.J., applying dicta in *Connolly* **10**, *Curran* **11** and *Edgar* **U1**, said that the accident must be foreseeably likely rather than foreseeably possible (5 B in C.A. transcript 402 of 1969).

14. Evans v. Sant [1975] Q.B. 626; [1975] 1 All E.R. 294, D.C.

Laying water main—testing equipment was brought onto site which for some reason built up a dangerous pressure, causing main to blow up—*Held*, "certainly in criminal proceedings," no breach of C.(W.P.)R. 1966, reg. 6(2) (duty to make and keep safe place at which person works).

U1. Edgar v. Manchester Slate Co. (1961) C.A. 409

"Cannot safely be done" (B.R. 1948, reg. 5)—Sellers L.J. (8 F): "I think the regulation contemplates a degree of danger so great that no reasonable employer would require his workman to face it because of foreseeable accident. It involves consideration of the extent of the danger and the likelihood of injury occurring."

U2. Croft v. Lockheed Hydraulic (1964) C.A. 110

Question was whether a means of access was safe—Salmon L.J. (4 B): "The test to be applied seems to me to be whether an employer ought reasonably to have foreseen that the means of access constituted a real risk of injury to his employee: *Summers v. Frost* (Chap. 16, (2) (a) **4**). In considering this question the employer must not assume his workmen are paragons of prudence, nor indeed that they will at all times use reasonable care for their own safety. On the other hand, he need not approach the problem on the basis that they are suicidal lunatics. He must assume merely that they are ordinary human beings and may behave in the way that common experience shows that they do sometimes behave in the course of their work . . . The test is not whether the bare possibility of injury is reasonably foreseeable: see Lord Reid in *Summers*, p. 764. A bare possibility of injury may exist however safe the access."

U3. Smart v. Young (1968) C.A. 66

Definition of "safe" in *McCarthy* **2** applied.

*(c) "Secure" and "Securely"**

(*N.B.* This subsection contains those cases where the words "secure" and "securely" have been judicially considered. Reference should also be made to the fencing cases in Chap. 16, (6) (d) and the mining cases in Chap. 16, (13), where cases which merely illustrate the application of the principles are also set out.)

* Abbreviations are explained in Introductory Note 1.

1. Chasteney v. Michael Nairn [1937] 1 All E.R. 376, D.C.

"It is to be observed that the words are 'securely fenced,' and not somewhat securely fenced" (Lord Hewart C.J., 379).

2. Vowles v. Armstrong Siddeley [1938] 4 All E.R. 796, C.A.

Held, that the duty to provide secure fencing was absolute. This case was relied on by C.A. in **6** as very nearly direct authority for the proposition that foreseeability is a factor in "securely fenced."

3. Caulfield v. Pickup [1941] 2 All E.R. 510, Asquith J.

Fall of stone from roof of mine—*Held*, that this in itself proved that roof was not secure.

4. Hodgson v. British Arc Welding [1946] K.B. 302; [1946] 1 All E.R. 95, Hilbery J.

Held, that the fact that a plank in a staging was warped meant that the staging was not "securely constructed."

5. Edwards v. N.C.B. [1949] 1 K.B. 704; [1949] 1 All E.R. 473, C.A.

Fall in travelling road of mine due to latent defect known as glassy slant—*Held*, that the road was not "secure."

6. Burns v. Terry [1951] 1 K.B. 454; [1950] 2 All E.R. 987, C.A.

Plaintiff went up a ladder to clear a shelf of some chocolate beans—the ladder slipped and plaintiff put out his hand which got caught in a cogged pulley wheel—*Held*, that this was not reasonably foreseeable, and therefore there was no breach of the duty to fence the wheel "securely." *Approved* by H.L. in **12**.

7. Smith v. Chesterfield Co-op. Society [1953] 1 W.L.R. 370; [1953] 1 All E.R. 447, C.A.

Lord Goddard C.J. (448 H) cited extract from judgment of Lord Normand in *Lyon v. Don Brothers*, 1944 S.C.(J.) 5: " . . . the standard to be observed is a fence which will prevent accidents occurring in circumstances which may reasonably be anticipated, but the circumstances which may be anticipated reasonably include a great deal more than the staid, prudent, well-regulated conduct of men diligently attentive to their work, and the occupiers of factories are bound to reckon on the possibility of conduct very different from that. They are bound to take into account the possibility of negligent, ill-advised or indolent conduct on the part of their employees, and even of frivolous conduct, especially where young persons are employed." And at 449 F the Lord Chief Justice included "folly, in direct disobedience of orders" as within the zone of contemplation of the employer.

8. Charles v. S. Smith [1954] 1 W.L.R. 451; [1954] 1 All E.R. 499, Hilbery J.

Machine with perspex cover which could be lifted—*Held*, not securely fenced, as it was "not enough that it is provided with a means of achieving security" (501 H).

9. Pugh v. Manchester Dry Docks [1954] 1 W.L.R. 389; [1954] 1 All E.R. 600, Donovan J.

Held, no defence that machine would be unusable if securely fenced.

10. Marshall v. Gotham [1954] A.C. 360; [1954] 1 All E.R. 937, H.L.

Fall of roof of mine due to latent defect known as slickenside—*Held*, not secure. Lord Tucker (943 G): "I agree that the word 'secure' does not involve security from the effects of earthquake or an atom bomb, but I think it must involve security from all the known geological hazards inherent in mining operations." *Applied* in **11**. See **14**.

11. Jackson v. N.C.B. [1955] 1 W.L.R. 132; [1955] 1 All E.R. 145, Hallett J.

Plaintiff shotfirer in breach of regulations left his bag of explosives near where he was firing shot—result was bag exploded and brought down roof—*Held*, applying dictum of Lord Tucker in **10**, the roof was secure against all ordinary hazards, and defendants not liable. The judgment contains a review of a number of cases on "secure," including an unreported decision of same judge, namely *Hayes v. N.C.B.* (1952), where a man was being carried out on a stretcher, and the stretcher party pushed a tub aside so as to dislodge a prop, which brought roof down, and it was held that the roof was secure. The judge also indicated (149 B) that the foreseeability test applied in the fencing cases (*e.g.* in **6**) was applicable also in mining cases.

12. John Summers v. Frost [1955] A.C. 740; [1955] 1 All E.R. 870, H.L.

Plaintiff injured on a grindstone which was fenced by a hood except for an arc about 7in. long at grinding face—more fencing would have made it commercially unusable—*Held*, it was not securely fenced, as there was an absolute duty to fence so that there was no longer a reasonably foreseeable risk of injury to the workman using the machine, even though he was careless or inattentive. **6** *approved*.

13. Jones v. Richards [1955] 1 W.L.R. 444; [1955] 1 All E.R. 463, Barry J.

"A fence which depends for its efficacy on the memory and concentration of a single workman is not in truth a sufficient and secure fence" (470 B).

14. Gough v. N.C.B. [1959] 2 W.L.R. 658; [1959] 2 All E.R. 164, H.L.

Question was whether duty to secure extended to coal face—*Held*. yes, once it was realised that "secure" meant secure against accidental or unintended falls only, and did not include deliberate bringing down of coal face. Lord Tucker (172 A) repeated his formula in **10**, saying that deliberate bringing down was not a geological hazard.

15. Brown v. N.C.B. [1962] A.C. 574; [1962] 1 All E.R. 81, H.L.

Duty to keep road and working place secure (M.Q.A. 1954, s.48)—*Held*, that "secure" meant:

(a) "A physical condition of stability which will ordinarily result in safety" (Lord Radcliffe, 85 H, Lord Simonds and Lord Reid concurring);
(b) It must not be "a possible cause of injury to anybody acting in a way in which a human being may be expected to act in circumstances which may be reasonably expected to occur" (Lord Denning, 89 G).

16. Tinto v. Stewart and Lloyds, 1962 S.L.T. 314, O.H.

Unfenced gangway affording secure foothold in all ordinary circumstances—explosion sending forth flames and smoke round gangway—*Held*, foothold did not thereby become insecure within F.A. 1937, s. 26(2)

17. Soar v. N.C.B. [1965] 1 W.L.R. 886; [1965] 2 All E.R. 318, C.A.

"I am still inclined to think that the test laid down by du Parcq J. in *Walker v. Bletchley Fletton* (see Chap. 16, (6) (a) **1**) is as good as any" (Lord Denning M.R., 321 A).

*(d) "Practicable" and "Reasonably Practicable"**

			See also Intro. Notes
R.P.§	**Period of risk very short**	1	—
PRACTICABLE	DICTIONARY DEFINITIONS	2	—
R.P.	FACTORS TO BE TAKEN INTO ACCOUNT	3	—
R.P.	ONUS LIES ON DEFENDANT	4	—
R.P.	INCONVENIENCE OF PRECAUTION NO DEFENCE	5	—
A.P.M.‡	MUST HAVE REGARD TO EXISTING STATE OF KNOWLEDGE	6	—
Practicable	Dictionary definitions	7	—
R.P.	**Fall of roof—slickenside—leading case**	8	—
R.P.	Standard not to be so high as to impose undue burden on industry—threshing machine	9	—
A.P.M.	DANGER UNKNOWN AT MATERIAL TIME	10	—
A.P.M.	Masks—employer must take steps to induce men to wear	11	—
A.P.M.	FOUNDRY DUST—DANGER UNKNOWN AT TIME	12	—
R.P.	TWO ALTERNATIVES—ONE UNREASONABLE	13	—
R.P.	Onus on defendants—provision of gangway	14	—
Practicable	Official publication calling attention to danger	15	—
A.P.S.†	To remove inflammable powder from vat—defendant unaware that powder there	16	—
R.P.	SAME AS COMMON LAW STANDARD—MINING CASE	17	—
R.P.	HIGHER THAN COMMON LAW STANDARD—SAFE ACCESS	18	—
R.P.	**Onus on defendants—who must call evidence—sides of coal mine**	19	—
PRACTICABLE AND R.P.	DISTINGUISHED	20	—
PRACTICABLE	HIGHER STANDARD THAN AT COMMON LAW	21	—
Practicable	Contrasted with reasonably practicable	22	—
Impracticable	Contrasted with not reasonably practicable	23	—
R.P.	**Onus of proof is on defendant**	24	9
R.P.	**Risk of injury only a remote possibility**	25	—
PRACTICABLE	DEGREE OF KNOWLEDGE REQUIRED—EMPLOYER MUST CONSIDER RELEVANT TECHNICAL LITERATURE AND OFFICIAL SAFETY PAMPHLETS	26	—

* Abbreviations are explained in Introductory Note 1.
§ R.P. = Reasonably practicable.
‡ A.P.M. = All practicable measures.
† A.P.S. = All practicable steps.

R.P.	RARITY OF PREVIOUS ACCIDENTS—PREVALENCE GENERALLY OF SYSTEM USED—ARE BOTH FACTORS IN FAVOUR OF DEFENCE	27	—
Practicable and r.p.	Distinguished	28	—
R.P.	CONSIDERED IN CONTEXT OF EFFORTS TO CLEAR SNOW AND ICE	29	9
R.P.	*No higher duty than at common law*	U1	6,9
R.P.	*Higher standard than at common law*	U2	
R.P.	*Where safeguard practicable, defendants must show they have given proper consideration thereto*	U3	—
R.P.	*Onus on plaintiff?*	U4	9
R.P.	*Defendants must call evidence*	U5	—
R.P.	*No breach if no reason to suspect danger*	U6	—
R.P.	*What defendant has to prove*	U7	—
R.P.	*Foreseeability—standard is higher than at common law*	U7	

1. Coltness Iron Co. v. Sharp [1938] A.C. 90; [1937] 3 All E.R. 593, H.L.

Case under the C.M.A. 1911, s. 102(8)—a machinery cover had been removed for a short time for testing after repair—*Held*, not reasonably practicable to avoid the breach. Lord Atkin (593 H): "The time of non-protection is so short, and the time, trouble and expense of any other form of protection is so disproportionate that I think the defence is proved." *Approved* by Lord Oaksey in **8**.

2. Lee v. Nursery Furnishings [1945] 1 All E.R. 387; [1945] W.N. 57, C.A.

" 'Practicable' is defined in the *Oxford English Dictionary* as 'capable of being carried out in action' or 'feasible' " (Lord Goddard C.J., 389 H).

3. Edwards v. N.C.B. [1949] 1 K.B. 704; [1949] 1 All E.R. 743, C.A.

Latent defect in coal mine—glassy slant—question whether it was reasonably practicable to avoid breach—*Held*, defendants liable, as they had not proved it was not reasonably practicable. "Reasonably practicable" is narrower than "physically possible," and implies a computation between quantum of risk on the one hand and time trouble and expense of safeguards on the other, and if the defendant can show a gross disproportion (very small risk against great safeguards), he discharges that onus. *See* now **8**, leading H.L. case.

4. McCarthy v. Coldair [1951] 2 T.L.R. 1226; [1951] W.N. 590, C.A.

Held, onus of proving not reasonably practicable lies on defendant.

5. Street v. B.E.A. [1952] 2 Q.B. 399; [1952] 1 All E.R. 679, C.A.

Singleton L.J. (685 F): "The duty (*i.e.* not reasonably practicable) . . . cannot be met by saying: 'Well, it was not very convenient.' Those are not the words of the section."

6. Adsett v. K. and L. Steelfounders [1953] 1 W.L.R. 773; [1953] 2 All E.R. 320, C.A.

Foundry dust causing pneumoconiosis—in 1942 defendants had installed a new type of extractor plant—plaintiff alleged that had it had been installed earlier he would not have caught disease—defendants had in fact been the first to instal this type of extractor—*Held*, that, in deciding whether "all practicable measures" had been taken, one must have regard "to the state of knowledge at the time, and particularly to the knowledge of scientific experts" (Singleton L.J., 322 D), and that according to this test the claim failed. *Approved* by C.A. in **12**. *But* see **11**.

7. Knight v. Demolition Co. [1953] 1 W.L.R. 981; [1953] 2 All E.R. 508, Parker J.

Accidental collapse of brick arch during demolition—definition of "practicable" given in **2** applied, and also that cited in **6**: "possible to be accomplished with known means or resources." *N.B.* C.A. subsequently affirmed decision on common law grounds, without considering liability in statutory duty.

8. Marshall v. Gotham [1954] A.C. 360; [1954] 1 All E.R. 937, H.L.

Fall of roof in mine due to latent defect known as slickenside, for which there was no known method of detection—in accordance with ordinary practice roof was not supported—it was quite a "possibility" that a hydraulic prop would have diverted fall so as to prevent death of deceased but no more than that—otherwise defendant could only have timbered mine throughout—*Held*, defendant not liable, as not reasonably practicable to secure roof against fall. Lord Oaksey (939 D) approved Lord Atkin's dictum in **1**, and (939 G) approved following passage of Jenkins L.J. in C.A.: " ... 'reasonably practicable' ... is no more and no less than what is capable of being done to make roofs and sides secure within the limits of what it is reasonable to do, and it cannot be reasonable to do more than that which it appears necessary and sufficient to do according to the best assessment of what is necessary and sufficient that can be made at the relevant time, that is (immediately before the accident)." Lord Reid (942 F) said that there "may well be precautions which it is practicable, but not reasonably practicable to take," and that in deciding what was reasonably practicable, "if a precaution is practicable, it must be taken unless, in the whole circumstances, it would be unreasonable. And as men's lives may well be at stake, it should not lightly be held that to take a practicable precaution is unreasonable." Lord Tucker (944 H): " ... when one finds that the risk of slickenside is very remote and that the suggested measures are of an elaborate nature and would only result in a 'possibility' ... I do not consider that a finding against the respondents (defendants) is justified."

9. Jones v. Richards [1955] 1 W.L.R. 444; [1955] 1 All E.R. 463, Barry J.

"One must always guard against making industry impossible and against slowing down production by setting unduly high standards or by placing wholly unreasonable requirements on the makers and owners of machinery of this kind" (470 D)—*Held*, however, defendants were liable.

10. Gregson v. Hick Hargreaves [1955] 1 W.L.R. 1252, [1955] 3 All E.R. 507, C.A.

Foundry dust causing silicosis—until then no one realised that dust might contain silica—*Held*, defendants liable, because there was "a substantial quantity of ordinary visible dust" (Jenkins L.J., 514 H), and they could have taken "practicable measures" to protect plaintiff against it, it being "irrelevant whether the dust is known or believed to be noxious or not" (515 D). On this basis, current state of knowledge of *danger* appears to be irrelevant when considering what is "practicable," or perhaps all substantial quantities of dust are to be deemed potentially dangerous by the statute even if current knowledge is quite the contrary. Parker L.J. however (516) said that "practicable" only included measures which were feasible in the light of current knowledge; and (516 H) that the danger to be guarded against was the danger that silica would be inhaled, and that defendants were liable for not taking all practicable measures against this danger—but if the danger was then unknown, how could it be practicable in this sense to guard against it? Singleton L.J. (513

D) applied the same reasoning as Jenkins L.J. *N.B.* No other cases seem to have been cited to the court.

11. Crookall v. Vickers Armstrong [1955] 1 W.L.R. 659; [1955] 2 All E.R. 12, Glyn-Jones J.

Steel foundry—known risk of silicosis—masks available for anyone who asked for them—but attempts to induce men to wear them were half-hearted—*Held*, defendants liable, as "all practicable measures" included the provision of masks and the taking of steps by the defendants to induce men to wear them.

12. Richards v. Highway Ironfounders [1955] 1 W.L.R. 1049; [1955] 3 All E.R. 205, C.A.

N.B. This case was heard before **10**. Foundry dust causing silicosis—danger unknown at the time—*Held*, new trial must be held on question as to whether defendants had taken all practicable measures. As to this phrase, the court approved dictum of Singleton L.J. in **6** (current state of knowledge to be taken into account) (see Lord Evershed M.R., 209 I), and it would appear that the question posed by the court was whether, if the defendants had taken all practicable precautions against the ordinary dust, such measures would have included the provision of a mask which incidentally would have given protection against the then unknown danger from silica, and to what extent such protection would have been effective (Lord Evershed M.R., 211 E).

13. Walsh v. N.C.B. [1956] 1 Q.B. 511; [1955] 3 All E.R. 632, C.A.

Boulder falling from roof in coal mine—*Held, inter alia*, it was not reasonably practicable to avoid the breach, as there were only two alternatives, spragging up the boulder and blowing it out, and defendants had chosen the former because they judged, correctly, the latter to be unreasonable.

14. Walter Wilson v. Summerfield [1956] 1 W.L.R. 1429; [1956] 3 All E.R. 550, D.C.

15. Balfour v. Wm. Beardmore, 1956 S.L.T. 205, O.H.

Pneumoconiosis in foundry—*Held*, that since the publication of the interim report of the Committee on Dust in Steel Foundries in 1944, defendants could not plead that they could not reasonably have foreseen the danger, and therefore were liable for failing to take practicable precautions.

16. Williams v. Holliday (1957) 107 L.J. 378; [1957] C.L.Y. 1408, Davies J.

Inflammable powder in shaft of vat—defendants unaware that powder was there—*Held*, liable for failing to take all practicable steps to remove it.

17. Jones v. N.C.B. [1957] 2 Q.B. 55; [1957] 2 All E.R. 155, C.A.

Denning L.J. (161 E): "This (the issue of reasonably practicable) is closely allied to the issue at common law . . . So close indeed are these issues that we think that, if the Board are exempt from liability at common law, they will be exempt under section 102(8) [of C.M.A. 1911] also . . . ".

18. Trott v. W. E. Smith [1957] 1 W.L.R. 1154; [1957] 3 All E.R. 500, C.A.

Safe access case under B.R. 1948, reg. 5—steel girder 3 in. wide—*Held*, defendants liable for breach of statutory duty (issue at common law not decided). Jenkins L.J. (504 A): "The regulation here specifically enjoins the provision of safe means of access so far as is reasonably practicable. That seems to me to place on the employer a stricter obligation than is laid on him in relation to comparable matters by the general duty of reasonable care at common law."

19. Gough v. N.C.B. [1959] A.C. 698; [1959] 2 All E.R. 164, H.L.

At trial defendants contended successfully there was no breach of duty to secure sides—called no evidence on "reasonably practicable"—H.L. having held there was a breach—*Held*, further (3–2) that case could not be remitted to hear such evidence, and that defendants having called no evidence on issue were liable.

20. Brown v. N.C.B. [1961] Q.B. 303; [1960] 3 All E.R. 594, C.A.

Pearce L.J. (609 F): "The word 'reasonably' has a slight tendency to modify the word 'practicable.' I respectfully agree with the words of Lord Reid in *Marshall v. Gotham* **8**: 'But, in my judgment, there may well be precautions which it is "practicable," but not "reasonably practicable" to take." ' *N.B.* This case subsequently went to the House of Lords: [1962] 1 All E.R. 81.

21. Sanderson v. N.C.B. [1961] 2 Q.B. 244; [1961] 2 All E.R. 796, C.A.

"But the boundaries of practicability are wider than the boundaries of reasonable care; and over the boundaries of reasonable care the defendants never by their evidence tried to go" (Donovan L.J., 800 H).

22. Moorcroft v. Thomas Powells [1962] 1 W.L.R. 1447; [1962] 3 All E.R. 741, D.C.

"It seems to me that 'practicable' must impose a stricter standard than 'reasonably practicable.' It may be that certain matters that one would take into consideration if the words were 'reasonably practicable,' such matters as the cost and the like, have to be eliminated" (Lord Parker C.J., 746 C).

23. Jayne v. N.C.B. [1963] 2 All E.R. 220, Veale J.

Coal-mining case—judge said that gap between impracticable and impossible was not wide, but was wider than that between impracticable and not reasonably practicable. He included under impracticable cases of danger unknown at the time; and where removal of one danger might create another greater. As examples where avoidance of danger would be practicable but not reasonably practicable, he instanced cases where precautions would involve heavy cost or where risk was of limited duration.

24. Nimmo v. Alexander Cowan [1968] A.C. 107; [1967] 3 All E.R. 187, H.L.

Safe "so far as is reasonably practicable" (F.A. 1961, s. 29)—*Held*, (3–2) onus of proof was on defendants.

25. Jenkins v. Allied Ironfounders [1970] 1 W.L.R. 304; [1969] 3 All E.R. 1609, H.L.

Scrap from casting knocked or falling to floor during movement—it would have been possible to have a system of contemporaneous raking or sweeping—*Held*, however, since the risk of injury was only a remote possibility, such a system was not reasonably practicable.

26. Cartwright v. G.K.N. Sankey (1973) 14 K.I.R. 349; [1973] C.L.Y. 1445, C.A.

Noxious fumes—alleged breach of F.A. 1961, s. 63 (now repealed) to take "all practicable measures"—trial judge held that there was insufficient indication of danger from contemporary medical and other literature to establish liability—but in 1965 the Ministry had published pamphlet (Dust and Fumes in Factory Atmospheres) which contained ceiling limits—*Held*, in the light of currently available means of knowledge, and in particular the pamphlet, defendants had failed to take all practicable measures. An employer who was required to take all practicable measures was under a duty to consider the relevant medical and other literature on the subject, and in particular any relevant safety pamphlets.

27. Thompson v. Bowaters [1975] K.I.L.R. 47; [1975] C.L.Y. 1427, C.A.

Plaintiff on top of stack of bales, 21 feet high hooking bales to crane—fell in circumstances he could not remember—plaintiff alleged that defendants should have had a system of taking off inner bales first—thus producing a "parapet" of safety—judge found that this would have been reasonably practicable—*Held*, not so, because the rarity of such accidents and the prevalence in the industry of the system employed alike made the "parapet" system not reasonably practicable.

28. Sanders v. Lloyd [1982] I.C.R. 360; [1982] C.L.Y. 1365, Drake J.

29. Gitsham v. C. H. Pearce and Sons [1992] P.I.Q.R. P57; *The Times*, February 11, 1991, C.A.

Plaintiff slipped on snow and ice when crossing road on defendant's six-acre weather-exposed site in harsh weather conditions. Defendant treated snow and ice by mechanical salt and sand spreader—process should have finished by time of accident—*Held*, defendant not in breach of F.A. 1961, s. 29(1) or negligent. Even if relevant area had not been treated (as to which trial judge made no finding) judge was entitled to find that defendant was doing everything reasonably practicable, taking into account severity of weather and size of site. *Per* Stocker L.J.: "The fact that the system might for one reason or another have been running late does not itself in my view establish that the system was not being properly put into effect."

U1. Mazorriaga v. Willis (1957) C.A. 195

Hodson L.J. (2 F): "(F.A., 1937 s. 26) does not add much to the common law duty to take reasonable care, at any rate in cases between master and servant" (quoting Denning L.J. in *McCarthy v. Coldair* **4**).

U2. Welch v. Summers (1958) C.A. 108

Plaintiff fell from vertical fixed ladder with awkward hand-rail—*Held*, defendants liable under F.A. 1937, s. 26(1) ("safe access so far as reasonably practicable") but *not* liable at common law.

U3. Sweet v. N.C.B. (1959) C.A. 124

Collapse of support girder—breach of G.R. 1947, reg. 6(3)—defendants say not reasonably practicable to avoid breach—*Held*, defendants liable, as they had not discharged onus on them: the evidence showed that safeguards were "practicable," but defendants had never really considered them at this particular place.

U4. Bell v. Dorman Long (1963) C.A. 80

Duty to keep floors free from obstruction "so far as is reasonably practicable" (F.A. 1961, s. 29)—*Held*, *per* Pearson L.J. that onus of proof on the proviso was on plaintiff, and, *per* Sellers L.J., that the overall obligation was on plaintiff, but in the circumstances the question was one which was mainly in the knowledge of the defendants. *But* see **4**—and also **3** and **19**, which latter were however cases under C.M.A. 1911.

U5. Vaughan Williams v. B.A.C. (1968) C.A. 301

"Occupiers of factories had better take warning from *Nimmo* **24** that (in cases involving a reasonably practicable provision) they are unlikely to be able to sustain the onus of proof which lies on them unless they are prepared to put their own witnesses in the witness box" (Diplock L.J., 5 B).

U6. Hunter v. Thompson (1967) C.A. 310

"I cannot believe it is 'reasonably practicable' to take any steps to make and keep a place safe if he has no reason to suspect it may be unsafe" (Salmon L.J., 15 D).

U7. Williams v. Painter (1968) C.A. 224. Also in (1968) 5 K.I.R. 224, C.A.

Winn L.J. (4 E) said that defendants had to establish that it was not practicable to avoid the state of affairs complained of by any measure which was (a) practicable, *i.e.* capable of being taken and (b) would not involve such expense or other effort and exertion in time and labour as would be unreasonable. On foreseeability, Winn L.J. (4 C–D) said: "It is true, I think (and I do not think more than this can be said) that no question of what is reasonably practicable can arise unless the particular danger is one which is capable of being foreseen. I do not, however, accept the proposition submitted that it is only if a reasonable man ought in the circumstances to have foreseen a particular danger that the obligation is imposed by this statutory provision".

*(e) "Efficient"**

			See also Intro. Note
Lighting "poor"—can still be "efficient"	1	D.R. 1934, reg. 3	5
"Efficiently lighted"—defined	2	D.R. 1934, reg. 3	"
"Efficient" means efficient in relation to what is being done	3	D.R. 1934, reg. 12	"

1. Kerridge v. Port of London Authority [1952] 2 Lloyd's Rep. 142, Donovan J.

"Lighting can be efficient, that is adequate to enable work to be done in safety—even though it may be poor" (145).

2. Cowhig v. Port of London Authority [1956] 2 Lloyd's Rep. 306, Pearce J.

Hosepipe lying across part of dock road at night—*Held*, defendants not liable. "Efficiently lighted" meant "reasonably well lighted for the purpose for which the light is there."

3. Edwards v. A/S Lundegaard [1958] 2 Lloyd's Rep. 193, 197, Pearson J.

* Abbreviations are explained in Introductory Note 1. See also Introductory Notes 3(C) and (G).

(f) "Provided" and "Available"*

1. O'Mahoney v. Press [1948] 92 S. J. 311; [1948] C.L.C. 3971, Atkinson J.

Held, occupiers of factory not liable for breach of statutory duty.

2. Finch v. Telegraph Construction [1949] 1 All E.R. 452; [1949] W.N. 57, Devlin J.

Goggles were hung up on a hook in foreman's office—evidence that neither plaintiff nor most employees knew where they were—*Held*, that to constitute a providing goggles must be in place where they come easily and obviously to hand or plaintiff must be given clear directions where to get them.

3. Farquhar v. Chance Bros. [1951] W.N. 422; (1951) 115J.P. 469, D.C.

Held, no breach of statutory duty. *Applied* in **7**.

4. Norris v. Syndic Manufacturing [1952] 2 Q.B. 135; [1952] 1 All E.R. 935, C.A.

The question at issue was whether plaintiff was guilty of a breach under F.A. 1937, s. 119 in failing to use an "appliance provided"—the appliance was a perfectly proper guard to a power press, which plaintiff for a number of years had been in the habit of not replacing when making sample presses after testing—defendants were liable under F.A. 1937, ss. 14–16 and also at common law, because the system of work was unsafe—but had defendants "provided" guard merely by fitting it to machine, without any sufficient instructions as to its use?—*Held*, they had, and plaintiff was guilty of a breach of F.A. 1937, s. 119. Romer L.J. said "provide" meant "supply" or "furnish" (940 D), but added that a thing could not be "provided" unless it was readily and obviously available, *i.e.* placed ready to the workman's hand (941 E). Somervell L.J. (938 E) said that the duty of providing something

* Abbreviations are explained in Introductory Note 1. See also Introductory Note 3(G).

and the duty of ordering it to be used were two different things, and here the appliance was "at hand and available," and plaintiff knew about it, so it was "provided." On the other hand, "it may well be that if one is dealing with an appliance of general use like a lamp, it is not 'provided' . . . unless its use is by instructions related to that operation" (938 C).

5. Roberts v. Dorman Long [1953] 1 W.L.R. 942; [1953] 2 All E.R. 428, C.A.

Held that a safety belt 10 minutes' walk away was too far away to be "available."

6. Nolan v. Dental Manufacturing Co. [1958] 1 W.L.R. 936; [1958] 2 All E.R. 449, Paull J.

Held, no provision: "I am satisfied that no goggles were provided in any real sense of the word. An old pair of goggles was somewhere in the machine shop, probably hanging by one particular grinder of a different type, which the foreman said he did consider dangerous. In addition, there was one pair of goggles in the stores, quite close to where the carborundum wheel was. As however there were at least three or four carborundum wheels, of the same kind as the one on which plaintiff was working at the time of the accident, and all of them might be in operation at the same time, it cannot possibly be said that goggles were provided for use by toolsetters on these grinders. Further. I am satisfied there were no adequate notices as to goggles being available . . . " (451 B).

7. Ginty v. Belmont Building Supplies [1959] 1 All E.R. 414, Pearson J.

Defendants under a duty to provide duckboards—they made an arrangement with X for X to supply them—X kept them in a store near plaintiff's place of work (considerably less than 50 yards away)—plaintiff was told that he could help himself—*Held*, this was a sufficient providing: "It is a very material circumstance here that the boards had to be used in different places. They must be nearby; they must be shown to the person requiring them and placed at his disposal; he must know that they are there for him to use, and he must know that he can put them where he wants" (422 G). **3** *applied.*

8. Aylmer v. Vickers Armstrong [1963] 1 Lloyd's Rep. 148, C.A.

Question whether safe means of access were provided (under S.R. 1931, reg. 1) when there was a transient slippery object thereon—*Held*, defendants not liable, as (*per* Lord Denning M.R. at 150) "provided" means the original provision. Maintenance means the subsequent maintenance of it in an efficient state and good repair. Danckwerts L.J. concurred in above, but Russell L.J. said that in his view providing was to be regarded as a continuous process; the latter however concurred in the decision on the ground that a place could remain safe despite transient obstructions.

9. Bux v. Slough Metals [1973] 1 W.L.R. 1358; [1974] 1 All E.R. 262, C.A.

Held, applying dictum of Romer L.J. in **4**, defendants had provided the goggles (which C.A. also found were "suitable"). But C.A. held defendants were liable at common law for failing to take reasonable steps to ensure that goggles were worn (see Chap. 15, (2)(e) **22**).

10. Smith v. British Aerospace [1982] I.C.R. 98; [1982] C.L.Y. 1368, C.A.

Defendants supplied safe means of access up to staging. Plaintiff instead used unsafe access (a set of portable steps) recently set up by other employees. Management could reasonably have anticipated the use of the unsafe route, but did not condone it—*Held*, defendants not liable. They had not supplied or adopted the unsafe means of access, and accordingly had not "provided" it for the purpose of F.A. 1961, s. 29. If an employer had not supplied the dangerous means of access, it had to be shown that "he appreciated that the particular structure was in fact being used as a means of access and . . . was content that his workmen should continue so to use it." It was not sufficient to make an employer liable merely because he can "reasonably anticipate that a man may, for his own purposes, use a particular piece of apparatus to gain access to a workplace" (Griffiths L.J. 106).

*(g) Construction and Material**

			See also Intro. notes
Of sound construction and properly maintained—meaning	1	F.A. 1937, s. 25	6, 9
OF SOUND MATERIAL—ABSOLUTE DUTY—LIFT OR HOIST	2	F.A. 1937, s. 22	6
GOOD CONSTRUCTION—NOT MEAN FIT FOR PARTICULAR PURPOSE	3	F.A. 1937, s. 23	6
Of good construction, etc. and free from patent defect—latter phrase does not qualify earlier part	4	F.A. 1937, s. 24	6
GOOD CONSTRUCTION—NOT MEAN FIT FOR PARTICULAR PURPOSE	5	F.A. 1937, s. 23	6
SOUND CONSTRUCTION—MEANS WELL MADE ONLY	6	F.A. 1937, s. 25	6, 9
Of good construction, etc.—obligation extends to dismantling as well as to use of scaffold	7	S.S.R. 1960	–
Of good construction—obligation extends to design and lay-out as well as structural soundness	8	C. (W.P.) R. 1966	–

1. Mayne v. Johnstone and Cumbers Ltd [1947] 2 All E.R. 159; 207 L.T. 199, Lynskey J.

Held, words meant "of such construction and so maintained as to be fit for the work which it is anticipated is to be done on it" (159 G).

2. Whitehead v. James Scott [1949] 1 K.B. 358; [1949] 1 All E.R. 245, C.A.

3. Beadsley v. United Steel [1951] 1 K.B. 408; [1950] 2 All E.R. 872, C.A.

Suitable lifting tackle available—but defendants' employee used lifting tackle which though well made was unsuitable for job—plaintiff killed—*Held*, defendants not liable under s. 23(1) (a), as "good construction" simply meant "well made," and did not imply the tackle must be suitable for any particular purpose.

4. McNeil v. Dickson, 1957 S.C. 345, Lord Wheatley.

Jib fell due to metal fatigue—latent defect—defenders argued that "free from patent defect" in F.A. 1937, s. 24(1) qualified the preceding words in the subsection, and allowed latent defect as a defence—*Held*, not so.

5. Gledhill v. Liverpool Abattoir [1957] 1 W.L.R. 1028; [1957] 3 All E.R. 117, C.A.

Held, following **3**, that "good construction" meant "well made," and a chain did not cease to be of good construction merely because it was unsuitable for a particular purpose—*Held*, also following *Latimer v. A.E.C.* (Chap. 16, (2) (h) **7**), that "properly maintained" in F.A. 1937, s. 24(1) meant that it

* Abbreviations are explained in Introductory Note 1.

was the "sound construction", etc., which had to be maintained, and this does not import any requirement as to suitability.

6. Hawkins v. Westinghouse (1959) 109 L.J. 89; [1959] C.L.Y. 1287, C.A.

Held, "sound construction" merely meant "well made," and imposed no obligation in respect of a difference in height between a manhole cover and a grating.

7. Graham v. Greenock Dockyard, 1965 S.L.T. 61; [1965] C.L.Y. 2654, Ct. of Sess.

8. Smith v. Davies (1969) 5 K.I.R. 320, Cooke J.

*(b) Maintenance and Repair**

		See also Intro Notes
"Maintained"—absolute duty	1	–
"Repair"—whether includes routine oiling of permanent way	2	–
"Of sound construction and properly maintained"—meaning	3	–
"Properly maintained in efficient working order"—absolute duty—lift or hoist	4	–
"Repair"—routine painting of ship by crew	5	–
"Repair"—anti-fouling paint on ship	6	–
"Maintenance" of floor—transient conditions not included duty to maintain	7	9
"Maintenance" of floor—oil and water coming on due to sudden storm	7	9
"MAINTENANCE" OF DOCK APPROACHES—WOODEN PLATFORM FALLING ON DECEASED	8	5
"MAINTENANCE" OF ACCESS—TEMPORARY OBSTRUCTION OF FLOOR	9	–
"REPAIR"—INSPECTION OF PERMANENT WAY TO SEE WHAT REPAIRS NEEDED	10	–
"Repair"—anti-fouling paint on ship	11	–
"REPAIR"—MEANS PUTTING BACK INTO GOOD CONDITION SOMETHING WHICH HAS FALLEN INTO BAD	12	–
"MAINTENANCE" OF FLOOR—HOW FAR DUTY ABSOLUTE	13	–
"Maintenance" of floor—transient danger—patch of ice on cold store floor	14	–
"REPAIR OR MAINTENANCE"—MAKING A PROFILE OF GUTTER ON ROOF	15	–
"Maintained"—absolute duty—ladder	16	–
"Repair"—tightening loose fishplates and knocking in loose keys	17	–
"PROPERLY MAINTAINED"—MEANING OF TERM	18	–
"Repair"—railway lengthman inspecting line and adjusting where required	19	–
"Properly maintained"—absolute duty—winch in mine	20	10

* Abbreviations are explained in Introductory Note 1.

1. Smith v. Cammell Laird [1939] 4 All E.R. 381, H.L.

"Maintained in such a condition as to ensure the safety of all persons employed"—loose plank in staging—*Held*, duty absolute.

2. London and North Eastern Railway v. Berriman [1946] A.C. 278; [1946] 1 All E.R. 255, H.L.

Held, not work of repair: "It (repair) contains some suggestion of putting right that which has gone wrong. It does not include the mere keeping in order by oiling, brushing or cleaning something which is otherwise in perfect repair and only requires attention to prevent the possibility of its going wrong in the future" (Lord Porter at 267 C).

3. Mayne v. Johnstone and Cumbers Ltd [1947] 2 All E.R. 159; 207 L.T. 199, Lynskey J.

Held, words meant "of such construction and so maintained as to be fit for the work which it is anticipated is to be done on it" (159 G).

4. Galashiels Gas Co. v. O'Donnell [1949] A.C. 275; [1949] 1 All E.R. 319 H.L.

5. Taylor v. Ellerman's Wilson Line [1952] 1 Lloyd's Rep. 144, Ormerod J.

Ship owned by first defendants was in dry dock of second defendants for repairs—while being repaired crew of ship do routine painting of ship—no connection with repairs—deceased member of crew while painting falls from staging which if regulations applied would not have complied therewith—*Held*, this was not work of repair or construction, but of maintenance, and therefore Regulations did not apply. *Distinguished* in **6** and **11**.

6. Day v. Harland & Wolff [1953] 1 W.L.R. 906; [1953] 2 All E.R. 387, Pearson J.

Held, following **2**, that, since "to repair" was, broadly, "to remedy defects," the work of applying anti-fouling paint was a work of repair. **5** *distinguished* on its facts. *Followed* in **11**.

7. Latimer v. A.E.C. [1953] A.C. 643; [1953] 2 All E.R. 449, H.L.

Oil and water coming onto floor due to sudden storm—*Held*, the duty to maintain referred to the general condition and soundness of construction, and not to some transient and exceptional condition such as the oil and water in question, and therefore defendants not liable under F.A. 1937, s. 25(1). *N.B.* F.A. 1961, s. 28(1) now adds a duty to keep floors, passages and gangways free, so far as is reasonably practicable, from any substance likely to cause persons to slip, so that in similar cases there is now an additional criterion. The decision, of course, remains an authority as regards the duty to *maintain* floors *Applied* in **8, 9, 14.18** and **20**.

8. Woods v. W. H. Rhodes [1953] 1 W.L.R. 1072; [1953] 2 All E.R. 658, C.A.

Wooden platform propped against sliding door of dock shed—collapses on deceased when he opens door—*Held*, following **7**, that the duty to maintain dock approaches under D.R. 1934, reg. I did not extend to articles temporarily brought onto the floor of the approach or working place.

9. Levesley v. Thomas Firth [1953] 1 W.L.R. 1206; [1953] 2 All E.R. 866, C.A.

Steel packing piece projecting into marked way of factory floor—*Held*, following **7**, that as it was only there temporarily, and as "the time involved was very short" defendants not liable for not maintaining safe access.

10. Judson v. B.T.C. [1954] 1 W.L.R. 585; [1954] 1 All E.R. 624, C.A.
Held, not "repairing."

11. Hurley v. Sanders [1955] 1 W.L.R. 470; [1955] 1 All E.R. 833, Glyn-Jones J.

Held, following **6**, this was work of repair.

12. Walsh v. N.C.B. [1956] 1 Q.B. 511; [1955] All E.R. 632, C.A.

Lord Evershed M.R. (610 B): " 'Repair,' in its ordinary context, indicates the putting back into good condition of something that, having been in good condition, has fallen into bad condition"; and (640 G): "If defendants established that that which they did not do was, though practicable, unreasonable, they should be taken to have established that that alternative was not reasonably practicable.

13. Payne v. Weldless Steel [1956] 1 Q.B. 196; [1955] 3 All E.R. 612, C.A.

Factory floor case where plaintiff failed on facts and C.A. refused to disturb finding of county court judge—question revolved round whether floor was "properly maintained"—plaintiff's counsel argued this was an absolute obligation, relying on *Galashiels* **4.** C.A. agreed but said that in that case lift was admittedly unsafe, and therefore there was no defence to an absolute obligation. *But* first one had to establish it was not "efficient" (which meant not efficient from safety point of view), see 615 B (Hodson L.J.) and 613 G (Denning L.J.), and this was a question of degree.

14. Davie v. Port of London Authority [1955] 1 Lloyd's Rep. 135, Pilcher J.

Held, that a patch of ice on the floor of a cold store was a transient danger, and therefore, following **7**, there was no breach of statutory duty (but defendants were liable at common law).

15. Sumner v. Priestly [1955] 1 W.L.R. 1202; [1955] 3 All E.R. 445, C.A.

Held, Regulations did not apply, as this was not repair or maintenance, but rather making preparation for making a new gutter

16. Jones v. Crosville Motor Services [1956] 1 W.L.R. 1425; [1956] 3 All E.R. 417, Hallett J.

Held, following **1**, duty absolute.

17. Reilly v. B.T.C. [1957] 1 W.L.R. 76; [1956] 3 All E.R. 857, Donovan J.

Held, danger likely to arise, and defendants therefore liable for not providing lookout—*Held*, also, that this was a "work of repair." *Approved* on latter by H.L. in **19.**

18. Gledhill v. Liverpool Abattoir [1957] 1 W.L.R. 1028; [1957] 3 All E.R. 117, C.A.

Held, following **7**, that it was the "sound construction", etc., which had to be properly maintained.

19. Cade v. B.T.C. [1959] A.C. 256; [1958] 2 All E.R. 615, H.L.

Held, approving **17**, this was work of repair.

20. Hamilton v. N.C.B. [1960] A.C. 633; [1960] 1 All E.R. 76, A.C.

Winch tipped forward due to the absence of stells—the absence could have been due to act of stranger or latent defect—*Held*, this was immaterial, as the obligation in M.Q.A. 1954, s. 81(1) that all parts of machinery shall be "properly maintained" was absolute. *Latimer v. A.E.C.* **7** and *Galashiels v. O'Donnell* **4** considered and approved.

21. Hall v. Fairfield Shipbuilding, 1962 S.L.T. 206, O.H.

Some lengths of metal rod fell from bench onto passage—plaintiff put foot on one and fell—*Held*, defendants liable under s. 28(1), F.A. 1961 as the rod was "a substance likely to cause persons to slip," and the defendants had failed to keep the passage free therefrom.

22. Aylmer v. Vickers Armstrong [1963] 1 Lloyd's Rep. 148, C.A.

' "Provide' means the original provision. 'Maintenance' means the subsequent maintenance of it in an efficient state and in good repair" (Lord Denning M.R., 150, Danckwerts L.J. concurring). But Russell L.J. said that provision was to be regarded as a continuing process.

23. Chalmers v. N.C.B., 1963 S.L.T. 358; [1963] C.L.Y. 2306, O.H.

Colliery pumpman injured by excessive internal pressure of pump when dismantling same—defendants claimed that, as plaintiff was maintaining the pump at the time, they were not in breach of their statutory duty of maintenance—*Held*, defendants liable, as their duty to maintain pump in good condition was absolute and continuous, and in any event plaintiff was not maintaining, but investigating a fault.

U1. Shelley v. Binn's Ltd (1956) C.A. 65 A.

Held, defendants not liable.

*(j) Miscellaneous**

				See also Intro. Note
Required to proceed	Area meant	1	D.R. 1934, r. 12	5
Accessible	Defined	1	D.R. 1934, r. 37	5
Fence	What constitutes	1	"	5
Effective measures	Absolute duty	2	F.A. 1937, s. 24	6
EXAMINATION OR ADJUSTMENT	NOT TESTING AFTER TOOL-SETTING	3	F.A. 1937, s. 16	6,10
EFFECTIVE SCREEN	MUST PREVENT PARTICLES GETTING ROUND	4	F.A. 1937, s. 49	6,8
SUITABLE GOGGLES	MUST FIT PERSON USING	4	"	6,8
PLANT	CUTTING OFF BOLTS—WIDE MEANING OF WORD		F.A. 1937, s. 49	"
LIKELY TO BE INJURIOUS	NOT INCLUDE PERSON WITH IDIOSYNCRASY	6	F.A. 1937, s. 47	6
Where work is being carried on	Plaintiff going back to get tools	7	D.R. 1934 r.42	5
Required to proceed	"	7	"	5
Reasonable	Previous practice of defendant no criterion	8	D.R. 1934, r.2	5
All practicable measures	Danger unknown at time	9	F.A. 1937, s.47	6
Likely to be injurious	"	9	"	6
QUALIFIED DUTY	GENERAL STANDARD MUST ALLOW FOR LAPSES BY EXPERIENCED AS WELL AS INEXPERIENCED	10	E.R. 1908 REGS. 15, 24	4
Ship	Floating structure for pumping sludge	11	D.R. 1934	5
Adequate strength	Rope breaking	12	F.A. 1937, 23	6
PATENT DEFECT	MEANS OBSERVABLE AS OPPOSED TO OBSERVED	13	M.Q.A. 1954, s. 81	10
No lifting tackle . . . shall be used	Unauthorised use of wire rope—which breaks	14	F.A. 1937, s.23	6
Has to work	Two alternative places	15	F.A. 1961, s.29(2)	9
Required to pass	**Two alternative routes**	16	**C.S.R. 1956, r.20**	—
HAS TO WORK	TWO ALTERNATIVE PLACES	17	B.R. 1948, REG. 31(3) C.(G.P.)R. 1961 REG. 7(1)	—
Plant	**Not article brought to factory to be processed**	18	**F.A. 1961, s.31(4)**	—
REQUIRED TO LIFT	ASSISTANTS OFF ILL	19	O.S.R.P.A. 1963, s.23	8

* Abbreviations are explained in Introductory Note 1. See also Introductory Notes 3(A) and (E).

1. Henaghan v. Rederiet Forangirene [1936] 2 All E.R. 1426, Lewis J.

Held, (a) "required to proceed" in reg. 12(c) did not necessarily mean "ordered to proceed" but included any place where a workman might properly go for ropes, etc.; (b) "accessible" in reg. 37(a) meant accessible without reasonable let or hindrance, and (c) "fence" in reg. 37(a) is a fence situated in close proximity to a single hatch.

2. Lotinga v. N.E. Marine Eng. Co. [1941] 2 K.B. 399; [1941] 3 All E.R. 1, D.C.

Plaintiff working near a travelling crane—F.A. 1937, s. 24(7)—*Held,* absolute duty.

3. Nash v. High Duty Alloys [1947] 1 K.B. 377; [1947] 1 All E.R. 363, C.A.

Held, testing after tool setting was not examination or adjustment, and therefore machine must be fenced.

4. Lloyd v. F. Evans and Sons [1951] C.L.C. 3949; [1951] W.N. 306, C.A.

Held, (a) screen which allowed bits of metal to get round into plaintiff's eyes was not an "effective screen," though of recognised type, and (b) goggles were "unsuitable" which though suitable for work did not fit plaintiff closely.

5. Watts v. Enfield Rolling Mills [1952] 1 All E.R. 1013; 1 T.L.R. 733, C.A.

Held, that an aircraft engine was included in "other plant" for the purposes of s. 49. *Overruled* in **18**.

6. Ebbs v. James Whitson [1952] 2 Q.B. 877; [1952] 2 All E.R. 192, C.A.

Sandpapering monsonia wood—dust which gave plaintiff dermatitis because he had a particular idiosyncrasy—*Held,* plaintiff could not claim in these circumstances the dust was "likely to be injurious," since his case was one of personal idiosyncrasy (and perhaps because there was only one other recorded case of dermatitis from such cause—see 193A).

7. Wenborn v. Harland & Wolff [1952] 1 Lloyd's Rep. 255, Sellers J.

Plaintiff employed by ship repairers went back to 'tween deck after finishing work there in order to get his tools and move them to a place of safety—at the time there was no repair work going on there but repairers were doing work in engine room—plaintiff fell down open unlighted hatch—*Held,* (a) the Regulations as a whole applied, because owing to the work in the engine room the ship was still under repair: *aliter* probably if the work for the day had ceased and the ship had moved out of dry dock (261); (b) plaintiff was not "required to proceed" to, nor was "work being carried on" in, the 'tween decks, and therefore the duties as to access (reg. 1) and lighting (reg. 42) did not apply; and (c) plaintiff in going back was not a trespasser. **1** considered under (b). Defendants 25 per cent., plaintiff 75 per cent. to blame.

8. Hayward v. Port of London Authority [1954] 2 Lloyd's Rep. 363, McNair J.

On the question whether means of escape from a dock for persons immersed was "reasonably adequate," defendants argued that since they had had a standard practice since 1904, this must be taken to be reasonable. To this judge said (370, col. 1): "This argument if accepted would lead to the conclusion that the dock authorities are to be the sole judges of the extent of the obligation imposed on them by the regulation. I accordingly reject the argument though I am prepared to accept that the practice of other good authorities may be some evidence of reasonableness."

This case subsequently went to the House of Lords (see Chap. 16, (9)(b) **4**), but above dictum was not commented on, except that Lord Tucker, in the course of the argument reported at p. 6, col. 1, appears to have agreed therewith.

9. Richards v. Highway Ironfounders [1957] 1 W.L.R. 781; [1957] 2 All E.R. 162, Pearson J.

See Chap. 16,(7) (d) **10**.

10. Murfin v. United Steel [1957] 1 W.L.R. 104; [1957] 1 All E.R. 23, C.A.

Defendants were arguing that as the room in question was reserved to experienced electricians an insulating screen was not necessary—*Held*, liable because "there is just as much risk of an experienced man falling or slipping when he is working as there is of an inexperienced man doing so"(27 C).

11. Cook v. Dredging Company [1958] 1 Lloyd's Rep. 334, Jones J.

12. Milne v. Wilson, 1960 S.L.T. 162, O.H.

Held, "adequate strength" related, not to the designed load of a rope, but to the actual load being carried.

13. Sanderson v. N.C.B. [1961] 2 Q.B. 244; [1961] 2 All E.R. 796, C.A.

Held, that the meaning of "patent" in "patent defect" was objective, not subjective, and that it meant "observable" and not "observed"—if a defect occurred in darkness, it could nonetheless be patent, if it was apparent on inspection, as, *e.g.* with a lamp.

14. Barry v. Cleveland Bridge [1963] 1 All E.R. 192, Lyell J.

For full details see Chap. 16 (7) (c) **13**—a heavy raft was being lifted by crane by its four wire loops—these loops were for mooring and not for lifting, and their use for lifting was unauthorised—*Held*, the user constituted a breach by defendants, who were held 50 per cent. liable.

15. Davies v. John G. Stein, 1965 S.L.T. 169; [1965] C.L.Y. 1651, Ct. of Sess.

Plaintiff attempting to start machine 11 feet above ground—he stood on some slippery planks and fell—he could, less conveniently, have stood on floor of loft above—*Held*, the planks did not constitute a place where he "had to work" within F.A. 1961, s. 29(2).

16. Smith (or Westwood) v. N.C.B. [1967] 1 W.L.R. 871; [1967] 2 All E.R. 593, H.L.

Shunter at coal mine was caught by passing train which he was accompanying as part of his duty—the route he was taking was impeded and unsafe, and defendants would be liable under Coal Mines Sidings Regulations 1956, reg. 20, if the route was one along which he was "required to pass"—there was another safe route along the top of a bank—*Held*, that defendants were liable, as the plaintiff was required to pass along the route taken. Lord Guest (599 A) said that the word "required" must take its meaning from the context, and that *Henaghan* **1** showed it did not mean ordered, nor did it have to be shown that the route taken was taken as a matter of necessity; it was enough if what he was doing in taking the route was reasonably incidental to the performance of his duties as a shunter. Lord Pearce (601 B) based his opinion on the fact that the route was a "normal" one for a shunter carrying out the duty of accompanying the train.

17. Kendrick v. Cozens & Sutcliffe (1968) 5 K.I.R. 469; [1968] C.L.Y. 334, C.A.

Steel erector burning steel from a ladder—because sparks were falling on his hands, he moved to an adjacent roof, which was fragile—*Held*, plaintiff did not "have to work" from roof, as, following **15**, the words must be given their natural meaning which inferred an order or compulsion, and therefore no breach of statutory duty. *But* defendants were held 25 per cent liable at common law.

18. Haigh v. Charles Ireland [1974] 1 W.L.R. 43; [1973] 3 All E.R. 1137, H.L.

Held, overruling *Watts* **5**. "If it is there as part of the apparatus for use in carrying on the industrial process undertaken on those premises, it is 'plant' within the meaning of the Act even though it may be temporarily out of use or in the course of installation, repair or removal. If it is there for the purpose of being subjected to that industrial process . . . it is not 'plant'" ' (Lord Diplock, 1148 D, three other Law Lords concurring).

19. Black v. Carricks [1980] I.R.L.R. 448; [1980] C.L.Y. 919, C.A.

Bakers shop—bread trays usually moved by two women but manageress on her own, the assistants being off ill. She phoned her superior who instructed her to get on with her job as best she could, and if she needed help to ask a customer. Manageress injured herself lifting tray unaided—*Held*, she had not been "required" to lift the tray, and therefore defendants not liable. The word "required" connoted that she could not have performed the task adequately in the circumstances in any manner which would not have necessitated lifting the weight she did (*per* Shaw L.J., 451). Here, on the facts, it was implicit that if she could not manage a load by herself, she could either leave it or seek assistance from a customer.

(3) Proof

*(a) Onus of Proof**

		See also Intro. Notes
PLAINTIFF MUST PROVE INJURY CAUSED AS WELL AS PROVE BREACH—TUBERCULOSIS ALLEGED TO COME FROM DUST FROM SHOEMAKING	1	–
"REASONABLY PRACTICABLE" PROVISO—ONUS OF PROOF IS ON DEFENDANTS	2,3	–
BREACH PROVED—MANNER OF ACCIDENT UNKNOWN—ONUS OF PROOF—ALLEGED FLYING BOLT	4	6,8
"Reasonably practicable" proviso—onus of proof is on defendants	5	–
Knowledge of precautions much more within defendants' knowledge—irrelevant to shift ordinary onus from plaintiff	5	–
Breach proved—manner of accident unknown—onus of proof—object falling from unboarded platform	6	–
"Reasonably practicable" proviso—onus of proof is on defendants	7	–
Plaintiff must prove injury caused by breach as well as prove breach	8	–

* Abbreviations are explained in Introductory Note 1.

1. Mist v. Toleman [1946] 1 All E.R. 139, C.A.

Held, onus being on plaintiff to prove *nexus*, he had failed to do so. See *Bonnington Casting v. Wardlaw* **8**.

2. Edwards v. N.C.B. [1949] 1 K.B. 704; [1949] 1 All E.R. 743, C.A.

3. McCarthy v. Coldair [1951] W.N. 590; [1951] 2 T.L.R. 1226, C.A.

4. Watts v. Enfield Rolling Mills [1952] 1 All E.R. 1013; [1951] 1 T.L.R. 733, C.A.

Eye injury—no goggles—*Could* have been caused by a flying bolt (in breach of F.A. 1937, s. 49)—but no proof that it was, or was not—*Held*, claim failed. Denning L.J. (1017 D) said a plaintiff must prove two things: first, that his injury was caused by a relevant danger (*i.e.* one the statutory duty was intended to guard against), and secondly, that there was a breach of statutory duty intended to guard against this very danger. If both of these are proved, the proper inference is that the breach was the cause of the injury, unless the occupier proves that it was not. He went on to say that the judge could have *inferred* that plaintiff had been struck by bolt, but as he did not do so, plaintiff had failed to prove first requisite. *But* see now *Bonnington Castings v. Wardlaw* **8** where H.L. not accept above and say that onus always on plaintiff.

5. Marshall v. Gothan [1954] A.C. 360; [1954] 1 All E.R. 937, H.L.

Metalliferous Mines Regulations 1938 (now revoked)—"shall, so far as may be reasonably practicable, be observed"—*Held, per* Lords Tucker, Cohen and Keith, Lords Oaksey and Reid being silent, this wording put the onus of establishing not reasonably practicable on defendants. Lord Tucker (943 F) said, Lord Cohen (945 A) concurring: "I do not consider that the fact that the difficulty or ease of doing what is necessary to maintain safety is so much more within the knowledge of the management than of their work-people (to quote the dicta in the judgments of C.A. in *Callaghan v. Kidd*

[1944] 1 All E.R. 527 and *McCarthy v. Coldair* [1951] 2 T.L.R. 1228 ...) is, in itself, a sufficient justification for shifting an onus which normally lies on plaintiff."

6. Hughes v. McGoff & Vickers [1955] 1 W.L.R. 416; [1955] 2 All E.R. 291 Ashworth J.

Pipe fell off a platform and fatally injured deceased—platform was not adequately boarded to comply with B.R. 1948—*Held*, the failure to provide toeboards, "in the absence of any other explanation," was a cause of the accident (297 A), and defendants were therefore liable. *N.B.* This decision may be doubtful on this point since *Bonnington* **8**.

7. Walter Wilson v. Summerfield [1956] 1 W.L.R. 1429; [1956] 3 All E.R. 550, D.C.

8. Bonnington Castings v. Wardlaw [1956] A.C. 613; [1956] 1 All E.R. 615, H.L.

Dictum in *Vyner v. Waldenburg* [1945] 2 All E.R. 547 to effect that proof of breach by plaintiff shifts onus to defendants to disprove causation *overruled*. "It would seem obvious in principle that a plaintiff must prove not only negligence or breach of duty, but also that such fault caused, or materially contributed to, his injury ... I would only add that, in at least two subsequent cases, *Mist v. Toleman* **1** and *Watts v. Enfield Rolling Mills* **4**, the Court of Appeal, being powerless to overrule a decision of that court, were driven to find distinctions which did not appear to me to be satisfactory ... " (Lord Reid, 618 C-H). Lord Keith (621 G) said the correct principles were laid down in *Caswell v. Powell Duffryn* [1939] 3 All E.R. 722 and *Stimson v. Standard Telephones* [1939] 4 All E.R 225. *But see Nicholson v. Atlas Steel* **9**.

9. Nicholson v. Atlas Steel [1957] 1 W.L.R. 613; [1957] 1 All E.R. 776, H. L.

Pneumoconiosis from silica dust in foundry—ventilation found to be inadequate, in breach of F.A. 1937, s.4(1)—*Held*, this meant (Lord Simonds, 781 H) deceased was exposed to a greater degree of risk than he need have been, and since the excess was not so negligible as to come within the *de minimis* rule, this excess was one material cause of death, and defendants liable. Lord Simonds (779) F, Lords Oaksey and Morton concurring): " ... if the statute prescribes a proper system of ventilation by the circulation of fresh air so as to render harmless so far as practicable all fumes dust and other impurities that may be injurious to health ... and if it is proved that there is no system, or only an inadequate system, of ventilation, it requires little further to establish a causal link between the default and the illness due to noxious dust of a person employed in the shop. Something is required as was held in *Wardlaw's* case **8**. I was a party to that decision and would not in any way resile from it. But it must not be pressed too far." Lord Cohen (782 I) applied Lord Reid's test in **8** by asking whether "on a balance of probabilities the breach of duty caused or materially contributed" to the injury.

10. Clarkson v. Modern Foundries [1957] 1 W.L.R. 1210; [1958] 1 All E.R. 33, Donovan J.

Held, defendants liable for full damage (pneumoconiosis from dust), as—following *Bonnington* **8**—"if it was impossible to distinguish between innocent and guilty dust in the matter of liability ... it was equally impossible to distinguish between them in the matter of quantum of damages" (36 F).

11. Beizcak v. N.C.B. [1965] 1 W.L.R. 518; [1965] 1 All E.R. 895, Karminski J.

Fall in mine—manager not called to give evidence—under M.Q.A. 1954, s.48(2), manager was under a duty, for the purpose of enabling him to take necessary steps to secure mine, of taking necessary steps to obtain relevant information—*Held*, onus in this respect was on defendants, and as manager had not been called, they were liable. Dictum of Lord Grant in *Sinclair v. N.C.B.*, 1963 S.C. 586, 593, applied: "The steps which he took or failed to take and the information which he obtained or failed to obtain are matters peculiarly within the knowledge of the manager. It seems reasonable that the onus of averring and proving them should be cast on the manager and not on the pursuer."

12. Allen v. Aeroplane and Motor Castings [1965] 1 W.L.R. 1244; [1965] 3 All E.R. 377, C.A.

Fencing case—plaintiff proved dangerous nip and injury to hand resulting therefrom—but county court judge rejected his account of how he came to get injury and concluded he was on a frolic of his own—*Held*, defendants were liable. The plaintiff was "a person employed at the premises," and a duty was owed to him, and defendants were liable if they failed to fence and by their failure caused injury, even though the exact way in which the injury took place was unknown. Dictum to this effect in *Stimson v. Standard Telephones* [1939] 4 All E.R. 225 *approved.*

13. Garner v. John Thompson (1968) 112 S.J. 1006; 6 K.I.R. 1, C.A.

Plaintiff gave evidence that ladder slipped while he was on it, but gave no evidence as to cause of it slipping—defendants called no evidence—*Held*, defendants liable, as the slipping was prima facie evidence ladder was unsafe under F.A. 1961, s. 29. *cf* **U2**.

14. Nimmo v. Alexander Cowan [1968] A.C. 107; [1967] 3 All E.R. 187, H.L.

15. Gitsham v. C.H. Pearce & Sons [1992] P.I.Q.R. P57; *The Times*, February 11, 1991, C.A.

For further details see Chap. 16, (2) (d) **29**.

16. Harper v. Mander and Germain Ltd, *The Times*, December 28, 1992; [1993] C.L.Y 2014, C.A.

Held, once it had been established that an employee's accident had been caused by an accumulation of slippery paste on a duckboard, they were in breach of F.A. 1961, s. 28(1) unless they pleaded and proved that it was not reasonably practicable to keep the duckboard free at all times from the slippery substance.

17. Larner v. British Steel plc [1993] I.C.R. 551; [1993] 4 All E.R. 102, C.A.

Metal structure supporting a roller collapsed onto plaintiff's leg due to fracture in structure not detected by engineer and fitter who had examined structure shortly before accident. Plaintiff claimed breach of F.A. 1961, s.29(1)—*Held*;

(a) Since defendants had not pleaded or contended that it was not reasonably practicable to make plaintiff's place of work safe, such a conclusion was not open to the Court, burden of proof on this issue being on defendant.
(b) To establish breach of s.29(1), plaintiff did not have to prove the danger was reasonably foreseeable. The test of safety was a strict one.
(c) Accordingly, breach of s.29(1) established.

U1. Vaughan Williams v. B.A.C (1968) C.A. 301

So *said* by Diplock L.J. (see Chap. 16, (2)(d) **U4**).

U2. Hodgkinson v. Enfield Standard (1971) C.A. 378

Ladder slipped sideways—it was of good construction, properly footed, etc.—accident probably occurred because plaintiff leaned over too far—*Held*, no breach of F.A. 1961, s.29(1)—*Garner* **13** was distinguished on the ground that there the defence had called no evidence to negative the charge of unsound construction, unduly slippery floor, defective suckers, etc.—and accordingly in that case, the defendants having called no evidence, could not escape liability.

U3. Bowes v. Sedgefield D.C. (1980) C.A. 818

*(b) Causation**

		See also Intro. Notes
BREACH PROVED—CAUSE OF INJURY UNKNOWN—BUT INFERRED DUE TO BREACH ..	1	–
BREACH PROVED—CAUSE OF INJURY UNKNOWN—NO INFERENCE THAT BREACH A CAUSE	2	6,8
TWO COMPETING CAUSES—FAULTY SCAFFOLD—AND PLAINTIFF'S OWN EPILEPSY.....	3	–
BREACH OF NO CAUSATIVE EFFECT—DUE TO PLAINTIFF'S OWN MISCONDUCT..........	4	–
Breach proved—cause of injury unknown—but inferred due to breach	5	–
BREACH OF LITTLE CAUSATIVE EFFECT—DUE TO PLAINTIFF'S OWN MISCONDUCT......	6	–
Plaintiff must prove both breach and that damage caused thereby........	7	–
Breach—no adequate means of escape from dock water—whether drowning to be inferred as due to breach	8	–
Rule that plaintiff must prove both breach and causation not to be pressed too far	9	6,9
BREACH PROVED—CAUSATION ATTRIBUTED "ON A BALANCE OF PROBABILITIES".....	10	–
Continuing breach—part outside limitation period—defendants liable for whole damage caused	11	–
BREACH PROVED—PLAINTIFF MUST ALSO PROVE THAT COMPLIANCE BY DEFENDANTS WOULD PROBABLY HAVE PREVENTED ACCIDENT	12	–
BREACH PROVED—AND THAT INJURY DUE TO BREACH—BUT MANNER OF ACCIDENT UNKNOWN	13	–
BREACH PROVED—PLAINTIFF INJURED WHEN MISTAKENLY TRYING TO OPERATE DEFECTIVE MACHINE	14	–
BREACH PROVED—AND THAT INJURY WOULD NOT HAVE HAPPENED BUT FOR BREACH—BUT MANNER OF ACCIDENT UNFORESEEABLE........	15	–
Breach proved—cause of injury unknown—but breach materially adding to risk of injury........	16	–
HUMAN INTERVENTION BETWEEN BREACH OF STATUTORY DUTY AND INJURY—WHAT PLAINTIFF MUST PROVE	17	–
Breach proved—creates or increases risk of injury to workman—workman then suffers such injury—defendant liable	18	6,8,9
Necessity to prove causal connection between breach and accident	19	–
Collapse of scaffold—necessary to prove this is due to condition of scaffold or parts thereof rather than acts of vandals	20	

* Abbreviations are explained in Introductory Note 1.

1. Smithwick v. N.C.B. [1950] 2 K.B. 335; 66 T.L.R. (Pt. 2) 173, C.A.

Aperture giving access to unfenced machinery—dangerous—deceased found dead near-by—cause of accident unknown—*Held*, that it could be inferred that the want of fencing was one of the causes.

2. Watts v. Enfield Rolling Mills [1952] 1 All E.R. 1013; [1952] 1 T.L.R. 733, C.A.

Eye injury—no goggles—*Could* have been caused by a flying bolt (in breach of F.A. 1937, s. 49)—but no proof that it was, or was not—*Held*, claim failed. Denning L.J. (1017 D) said a plaintiff must prove two things: first, that his injury was caused by a relevant danger (*i.e.* one that the statutory duty was intended to guard against), and, secondly, that there was a breach of a statutory duty intended to guard against this very danger. If both of these are proved, the proper inference is that the breach was the cause of the injury, unless the occupier proves that it was not. He went on to say that the judge could have inferred that the plaintiff had been struck by the bolt, but as he did not do so, the plaintiff had failed to prove the first requisite. But see now H.L. decision in **7**, where H.L. did not accept the above, and said that onus was always on the plaintiff.

3. Cork v. Kirby Maclean [1952] 2 All E.R. 402; [1952] W.N. 399, C.A.

Plaintiff fell from scaffold in epileptic fit—defendants were unaware that he was an epileptic—but there was no guard rail or toeboards—which might have saved him—*Held*, this was not a question of onus of proof, but of two contributing causes, neither of which was too remote, and liability ought to be apportioned equally, so that defendants were 50 per cent. liable.

4. Norris v. William Moss [1954] 1 W.L.R. 346; [1954] 1 All E.R. 324, C.A.

Scaffold under erection—one upright slightly out of vertical—hence breach of Regulations if B.R. 1948, reg. 10 applies—plaintiff tries to remedy matters in a manner which is "fantastically wrong"—causes scaffold to collapse—*Held*, the accident was not caused by a breach (if any) by defendants, but by plaintiff's own conduct, and claim failed. See also the cases in Chap. 4, (1)(d).

5. Hughes v. McGoff and Vickers [1955] 1 W.L.R. 416; [1955] 2 All E.R. 291, Ashworth J.

Defendants were installing electrical conduit pipes in a factory under construction—a 12-foot pipe placed on a platform fell off and fatally injured deceased, who was employed by defendants—*Held*, that there was a breach of B.R. 1948, reg. 24(1) (failure to provide toeboards), and that this failure, "in the absence of any other explanation" (297 A), was a cause of the accident, and therefore defendants were liable. *N.B.* This decision is now perhaps doubtful, since it was or may have been based on *Vyner v. Waldenburg* [1945] 2 All E.R. 547, C.A., which has since been overruled by H.L. in **7**.

6. Hodkinson v. Henry Wallwork [1955] 1 W.L.R. 1195; [1955] 3 All E.R. 236, C.A.

Unfenced transmission belt 9 feet above ground—breach—plaintiff, unauthorised, went up ladder to adjust stoppage—in doing so he acted in defiance of accepted practice—*Held*, that the breach in failing to fence was a cause of the accident, though only to the extent of 10 per cent.

7. Bonnington Castings v. Wardlaw [1956] A.C. 613; [1956] 1 All E.R. 615, H.L.

Dictum in *Vyner v. Waldenburg* [1945] 2 All E.R. 547, C.A. to the effect that proof of breach by plaintiff shifts onus to defendant to disprove causation *overruled.* Lord Reid (618 C-H): "It would seem obvious in principle that the plaintiff must prove not only negligence or breach of duty, but also that such fault caused or materially contributed to his injury . . . I would only add that in 'at least two subsequent cases, *Mist v. Toleman* (Chap. 16(3)(a) **1**) and *Watts v. Enfield Rolling Mills* **2**, the Court of Appeal, being powerless to overrule a decision of that court, were driven to find distinctions which did not appear to me to be satisfactory." *But* see also **11**.

8. Hayward v. Port of London Authority [1956] 2 Lloyd's Rep. 1, H.L.

Lord Tucker (9, col. 2: probably *obiter*, as decision proceeded on other grounds, as to which see Chap. 16, (9) (b) **4**): "If the case had stood there, . . . I should have found no difficulty in deciding in favour of the appellant (plaintiff) both on the question of the breach of the regulation and on causation. When I find that the law requires some means of support to be afforded to a man in peril of drowning and I find none has been provided, I should not have great difficulty in drawing the inference that had support been afforded . . . there was a reasonable probability that a man who had learnt to swim in his youth might have availed himself of it, unless there was cogent evidence that he would have drowned in any event." Lord Jowitt appears to have agreed with this, while the other three Lords were non-committal.

9. Nicholson v. Atlas Steel [1957] 1 W.L.R. 613; [1957] 1 All E.R. 776, H.L.

Pneumoconiosis from silica dust in foundry—ventilation found to be inadequate in breach of F.A. 1937, s. 4(1)—*Held*, this meant (Lord Simonds, 781 H) that deceased was exposed to a greater degree of risk than he need have been, and since the excess was not so negligible as to come within the *de minimis* rule, this excess was one material cause of death, and defendants were liable. Lord Simonds (779 F, Lords Oaksey and Morton concurring): " . . . if the statute prescribed a proper system of ventilation . . . and if it is proved that there is no system, or only an inadequate system, of ventilation, it requires little further to establish a causal link between that default and the illness . . . Something is required, as was held in *Wardlaw's* case **7**. I was a party to that decision and would not in any way resile from it. But it must not be pressed too far." Lord Cohen (782 I) applied Lord Reid's test in **7** by asking whether "on a balance of probabilities the breach of duty caused or materially contributed to the injury."

10. Clarke v. E. R. Wright and Son [1957] 1 W.L.R. 1191; [1957] 3 All E.R. 486, C.A.

First defendants, in breach of B.R. 1948 reg. 21, failed to take any steps to satisfy themselves that a scaffold to be used by the plaintiff, their employee, was stable—the second defendants, who erected the scaffold, were in any event liable to plaintiff for the subsequent collapse—*Held*, applying Lord Reid's test in **7**, that the plaintiff had made it appear that, "on a balance of probabilities, the breach of duty caused, or materially contributed to, his injury," and therefore the first defendants were liable.

11. Clarkson v. Modern Foundries [1957] 1 W.L.R. 1210; [1958] 1 All E.R. 33, Donovan J.

Pneumoconiosis from dust—continuing breach, part of which fell outside the limitation period—*Held*, defendants liable for the full damage, since, following **7**," if it was impossible to distinguish between innocent and guilty dust in the matter of liability . . . it was equally impossible to distinguish between them in the matter of the quantum of damages" (36 F).

12. Corn v. Weir's Glass [1960] 2 All E.R. 300, C.A.

Plaintiff on a building operation overbalanced and fell over open side of stairs while carrying large sheet of glass—fall of 3 feet to ground—open side unprotected—because fall was less than 6 feet 6 in. plaintiff could not rely on B.R. 1948, reg. 27(2) (absence of guard rail)—sued under B.R. 1948, reg. 27(1) (absence of hand-rail), of which defendants were admittedly in breach—*Held*, defendants not liable because, applying *Bonnington Castings* **7** and *Clarke v. E. R. Wright* **10**, plaintiff had not proved that the breach of duty on a balance of probabilities caused or materially contributed to his injury (Devlin L.J., 306 D). "The rule requires the plaintiff to show that if before the accident the regulation had been complied with, his injury probably would not have occurred, and this test of probability means, I think, that the court should consider independently of the accident how the employer would probably have complied with the regulation if he had done as he ought. If there are two or more ways in which he might have done so and one would, on the facts of the accident, have protected the plaintiff and the others would not have protected him and if no one can say that any one way is more likely to have been chosen than the others, then the plaintiff as a matter of probability fails" (306 E). Applying the above to the facts, it was held that it was conjectural whether a hand-rail, assuming it was likely to have been put on the open side, would have withstood the plaintiff if he had fallen against it.

13. Allen v. Aeroplane and Motor Castings [1965] 1 W.L.R. 1244; [1965] 3 All E.R. 377, C.A.

Fencing case—plaintiff proved dangerous nip and injury resulting therefrom, but county court judge rejected his account of how he came by his injury and concluded that plaintiff was on a frolic—*Held*, that even so defendants would still owe a duty to plaintiff, and, owing a duty, they would be liable if there was a failure to fence which caused injury, even though the exact way in which the injury took place was unknown. Dictum to this effect in *Stimson v. Standard Telephones* [1939] 4 All E.R. 225 *approved.*

14. Evans v. Sanderson (1968) 4 K.I.R. 115; [1968] C.L.Y. 1597, C.A.

In breach of F.A. 1961, s. 27(1) (good construction, etc., of all parts of lifting machines) the electrical contactors of a crane were defective—plaintiff, mistakenly, thought button was at fault and ruptured thumb pressing it—*Held*, injury was caused by the defect, and defendants were liable.

15. Millard v. Serck Tubes [1969] 1 W.L.R. 211; [1969] 1 All E.R. 598, C.A.

Drilling machine emitted a coil of swarf which having caught plaintiff's hand dragged it in—defendant's expert admitted that machine was dangerous and ought to have been fenced—but the manner of the accident was, on the judge's findings, unforeseeable—*Held*, following *Allen* **14**, this was immaterial, and defendants were liable. Impliedly *approved* by H.L. in *Callow* (Chap. 16(6)(b) **20**): see latter at 645 H.

16. McGhee v. N.C.B. [1973] 1 W.L.R. 1; [1972] 3 All E.R. 1008, H.L.

Lack of washing facilities—amounting to breach of duty at common law—this, plus conditions of working in brick dust, materially increased risk of dermatitis—but, in the present state of medical knowledge it could not be said that plaintiff's dermatitis was not due to some other cause—*Held*, defendants liable, as it was enough that the breach of duty should have materially contributed to the injury, which in this case it had by materially increasing the risk of such injury.

17. McGovern v B.S.C. [1986] I.C.R. 608; [1986] I.R.L.R. 411, C.A.

Plaintiff tripped on displaced toe-board on walkway 20 metres below which molten metal was being moved, bent down to move it so no one else would trip on it, and injured his back because the board was jammed—*Held,*

(a) Defendant in breach of absolute duty imposed by C(W.P.)R. 1966, reg. 30(2) to keep gangway free from unnecessary obstruction.
(b) Where, as here, there had been some human intervention (by plaintiff himself or a third party) between breach of statutory duty and injury, plaintiff had to prove that the intervention:
  (i) was a natural and probable consequence of the breach; and
  (ii) had not broken the chain of causation.

Here, he had done so, having regard to height of walkway and occasional presence of molten metal beneath it.

(c) Reg. 30(2) was intended to protect workmen against risk of injury, and was not confined to preventing risks resulting from colliding with or tripping over an obstruction.

18. Bryce v. Swan Hunter Group plc [1988] 1 All E.R. 659; [1987] 2 Lloyd's Rep. 426, Phillips J.

Deceased worked as painter in shipyards from time to time between 1937 and 1942, 1946 and 1950 and 1958 and 1970. Limited exposure to asbestos dust during first period, substantial exposure during second and third. Died of mesothelioma in 1981, as a result of exposure to asbestos dust. Widow sued three former employers, for whom deceased had worked for total of 399 days in 1947, between 1958 and 1962 and in 1970—*Held,*

(a) Having regard to Factories Inspectorate literature between 1932 and 1956 defendants should have appreciated at times of plaintiff's employments by them that exposure to asbestos dust was likely to be injurious to employees, and were under a duty at common law, of which they were in breach, to reduce though not altogether to prevent such exposure.
(b) Defendants also in breach of ss. 4(1) F.A. 1937 and/or 1961 which applied successively to shipyards and required defendants to " ... render harmless so far as practicable ... dust ... that may be injurious to health generated in ... work carried on ... ".
(c) Because ships' compartments in which plaintiff worked were not "workrooms", s. 4(1) did not also require defendants to maintain adequate ventilation.
(d) Defendants also in breach of duties arising successively under F.A. 1937, s. 47(1) and S.S.R. 1960, reg. 53(2) because they had failed to take all practicable measures to protect persons employed against inhalation of dust likely to be injurious to them.
(e) Deceased's additional exposure to asbestos dust due to defendants' breaches of duty was significant, but less than he would have experienced in any event during his working life.
(f) Widow could not prove on balance of probabilities that additional fibres inhaled by deceased due to breaches of duty of any one of the defendants caused the mesothelioma: neither could any defendant prove to same standard that its breaches of duty were not at least a contributory cause of the mesothelioma.
(g) Widow entitled to invoke principle in *McGhee v. N.C.B.* **16** that if conduct of a particular kind creates or increases a risk of injury to another, and a defendant owes to a plaintiff a duty not to conduct himself in that way, then if defendant is in breach of such duty and plaintiff suffers such injury, the injury is taken to have been caused by the breach of duty even though the existence or extent of the contribution made by the breach cannot be ascertained.
(h) In the instant case, defendants' breaches of duty increased risk of deceased's developing mesothelioma, whether by adding to the number of possible initiators of the condition or producing cumulative effect on reduction of deceased's body defence mechanism. Deceased

in fact developed mesothelioma. Each defendant must accordingly be taken to have caused the mesothelioma by its breach of duty.

19. Galek's Curator Bonis v. Thomson, 1991 S.L.T. 29; [1991] C.L.Y. 4432

Held, in an action relying on that part of C.(W.P.)R. 1966, reg. 3(1) which requires every contractor and employer of workmen who "alters any scaffold to comply with such of . . . these Regulations as relate to the . . . alteration of scaffolds" it is necessary to prove that the alterations in the scaffold were causally connected with the accident.

20. Campbell v. Glasgow C.C., 1991 S.L.T. 616; [1991] C.L.Y. 4433

See Chap. 16, (8) (d) **6** for further details.

21. Gunter v. John Nicholas & Sons (Port Talbot) Ltd [1993] P.I.Q.R. P67; [1993] C.L.Y. 2938, C.A.

Plaintiff's right hand came into contact with unguarded wood cutter which had continued to revolve for some $3\frac{1}{2}$ minutes after machine switched off—*Held*, by trial judge, defendants negligent in failing is provide brake for cutter (not challenged on appeal) and in breach of W.M.R. 1974, reg. 5, but declined to make a finding as to position of plaintiff's hand when it came into contact with cutter—*Held*,

(a) On the evidence, a guard complying with reg. 5 would have left $1\frac{3}{4}$ inches of cutter exposed. Having declined to determine position of plaintiff's hand, judge cannot have found that breach of reg. 5 was causative of the accident.
(b) Plaintiff, experienced machinist and familiar with machine, two-thirds to blame for failing to observe cutter was still moving.

U1. Lancaster v. Wigan Brick Co. (1960) C.A. 1

Transmission shaft insecurely fenced because fence did not completely protect it—deceased removed this fence—*Held*, defendants not liable, as their breach did not cause the accident.

U2. Pettitt v. Layfield Oura (1961) C.A. 136 A

Inhalation of trichlorethylene fumes—county court judge found ventilation inadequate for purposes of F.A. 1937, s. 4, but that plaintiff had intentionally leaned over tank and inhaled fumes, and that against conduct of this nature good ventilation would have been of no effect—and therefore, following *Bonnington* **7**, plaintiff had not proved injury was due to breach—*Held*, by C.A., this was right, and defendants not liable. *Cf. Jones* v. *Lionite Specialities* (Chap 15 (2)(b) **U1**).

U3. Stephenson v. Whittal Builders Co. Ltd (1981) C.A. U.B. 132

Plaintiff, experienced joiner, securing asbestos sheeting to shed roof. P climbed onto roof when unnecessary and fell through asbestos sheet. Defendants conceded "technical" breach of C.(W.P)R. 1966, reg. 36(1).—*Held*, that the defendants were not liable, as the plaintiff's negligence was the sole cause of the accident. The plaintiff was sufficiently experienced not to require instruction how to carry out his work. His decision to climb onto the roof was unforeseeable and (*per* Ormrod L.J., 7) "there is no duty on employers to instruct or remind employees of the terms of regulations which do not appear to be relevant to the job in hand and which no reasonable employer could have thought were relevant ... ".

*(c) Whether Plaintiff Would Have Used Safeguard if Provided**

		See also Intro. Note
IT DOES NOT LIE IN MOUTH OF DEFENDANT TO SAY PRECAUTION WOULD HAVE BEEN OF NO USE	1, 2, 3	–
NOT FOR DEFENDANT TO SAY THAT FENCING WOULD NOT HAVE AVOIDED ACCIDENT	4	–
Plaintiff must prove that defendant's breach caused the accident	5	–
If requisite safeguard not provided, easy to infer that failure to provide was a cause of the damage	6	–
Rule that plaintiff must prove causation not to be pressed too far	7	–
Plaintiff must prove that he would have used safeguard if it had been provided	8	–
Overstatement to say that it does not lie in mouth of defendant to say that precaution would not have been used	9	–
Plaintiff must prove he would have used safeguard if provided	10, 11	6,9
Finding that plaintiff would not have used safeguard must be based on evidence	12	–
PLAINTIFF UNABLE TO READ NOTICE SAYING SAFETY SPATS AVAILABLE—BUT MAKING NO ENQUIRIES—FEW MEN IN FACTORY WEARING THEM	13	–
No proper scaffolding—plaintiff giving uncontroverted evidence that he would probably have used it if provided	14	–
PLAINTIFF MUST SHOW HE WOULD HAVE USED SAFEGUARD IF PROVIDED	15	–
Plaintiff failing to satisfy judge that he would have used goggles if provided	U1	–

1. Bonham-Carter v. Hyde Park Hotel [1948] W.N. 89; (1948) 64 T.L.R. 177, L.C.J.

But see now **10** and **11**.

2. Roberts v. Dorman Long [1953] 1 W.L.R. 942; [1953] 2 All E.R. 428, C.A.

Lord Goddard C.J. (432 C): "If a person who had to make an inquiry fails to do so, he cannot be heard to say: 'But even if I had, it would have led to no useful results.' So, I think, that if a person is under a duty to provide safety belts or other appliances and fails to do so, he cannot be heard to say: 'Well, if I had done so, they would not have been worn'." *Approved* by Parker L.J. in **3.** *Applied* by Singleton L.J. in **4.** *Overruled* in **10.**

3. Drummond v. British Building Cleaners [1954] 1 W.L.R. 1434; [1954] 3 All E.R. 507, C.A.

Dictum in **2** approved by Parker L.J. at 513 H. *But* see **10** and **11.**

* Abbreviations are explained in Introductory Note 1.

4. Williams v. Sykes and Harrison [1955] 1 W.L.R. 1180; [1955] 3 All E.R. 225, C.A.

Plaintiff very foolishly set a machine belt (unfenced) in motion and proceeded to clean it—defendants allege that there would still have been an accident if there had been fencing—*Held*, applying **2** and dicta in *Stapley* v. *Gypsum* (Chap. 15, (8) **4**), that this would be mere surmise, and that "if speculations are being indulged in, they ought not to be those most favourable to the party in default" (235 F), and that therefore defendants liable (but only for 20 per cent.). *But* see **10** and **11.**

5. Bonnington Castings v. Wardlaw [1956] A.C. 613; [1956] 1 All E.R. 615, H.L.

Held, that the onus of proof throughout was on the plaintiff, both to prove the breach and that the plaintiff had thereby suffered damage, and that it was not enough to prove the breach and a possibility that the injury might have been caused by the breach. As a result, the decisions in **1–4** above, in so far as they depend on the dicta cited, may be doubtful now. *But* see **7.** *Applied* in **10.**

6. Hayward v. Port of London Authority [1956] 2 Lloyd's Rep. 1, H.L.

Lord Tucker (9, col. 2: probably *obiter*, as the decision turned on other grounds, as to which see Chap. 16, (9) (b) **4**): "When I find that the law requires some means of support to be afforded to a man in peril of drowning, and I find none has been provided, I should not have great difficulty in drawing the inference that had support been afforded . . . there was a reasonable probability that a man who had learned to swim in his youth might have availed himself of it, unless there was cogent evidence that he would have drowned in any event." Lord Jowitt appears to have agreed with this, but the other three Lords were non-committal.

7. Nicholson v. Atlas Steel [1957] 1 W.L.R. 613; [1957] 1 All E.R. 776, H.L.

Lord Simonds, after saying that if a system is required and none is set up, it required little further to establish a causal link between that default and the illness of the plaintiff, went on to say (779 G): "Something is required, as was held in *Wardlaw's* case **5**. I was a party to that decision and would not in any way resile from it. But it must not be pressed too far."

8. Nolan v. Dental Manufacturing [1958] 1 W.L.R. 936; [1958] 2 All E.R. 449, Paull J.

Held, following **5**, that as plaintiff had failed to prove that he would have worn goggles if they had been provided; therefore defendants were not liable for breach of statutory duty.

9. Qualcast v. Haynes [1959] A.C. 743; [1959] 2 All E.R. 38, H.L.

Lord Denning (46 G): "But this (*i.e.* principle as enunciated in **2**) is an overstatement. The judge *may* infer the omission to be the cause, but he is not bound to do so. If at the end of the day, he thinks that, whether the duty was omitted or fulfilled, the result would have been the same, he is at liberty to say so."

10. McWilliams v. Sir William Arrol & Co. [1962] 1 W.L.R. 295; [1962] 1 All E.R. 623, H.L.

Fatal fall of steel erector not wearing safety belt—in breach of duty at common law and under F.A. 1937, s. 26(2) defendants had withdrawn safety belts some days before accident—substantial evidence to the effect that deceased would not have worn a safety belt if one available—*Held*, defendants not liable since (a) plaintiff had not proved that deceased would have worn a safety belt if provided, and therefore had not proved that the breach caused the accident (*Roberts v. Dorman*

Long **2** overruled and *Bonnington Castings v. Wardlaw* **5** applied), and (b) there was no duty on the employers to instruct or exhort the deceased to wear a safety belt.

11. Wigley v. British Vinegars [1964] A.C. 307; [1962] 3 All E.R. 161. H.L.

Held, that claim failed because plaintiff had not established that deceased would have used a safety belt if hooks on windows provided. *McWilliams v. Sir William Arrol* **10** followed.

12. Ross v. Associated Portland Cement [1964] 1 W.L.R. 768; [1964] 2 All E.R. 452, H.L.

Plaintiff had used a ladder to repair cableway—mobile tower should have been provided—*Held*, the principle in *McWilliams* **10** could not avail defendants, as there was no evidence to establish that plaintiff would not have used mobile tower if available (Lord Guest 459 B, Lord Upjohn 461 G, and Lord Donovan 464 A).

13. James v. Hepworth & Grandage [1968] 1 Q.B. 94; [1967] 2 All E.R. 829, C.A.

Held, the only inference from the facts that plaintiff made no enquiries about the contents of the notice (which he could not read) and that few men in the factory wore spats was that if he had known they were available he would not have worn them.

14. O'Donnell v. Murdoch Mackenzie [1967] 3 K.I.R. 299; [1967] C.L.Y. 333, H.L.

Plaintiff drilling hole from concrete window sill 4 feet by 5 feet with hammer that tended to stick in hole—he gave evidence that if proper scaffolding had been provided, he would probably have used it—*Held*, the failure to provide scaffolding was the cause of the accident and defendants were liable for breach of C. (G.P.) R. 1961, reg. 7(2) (now C (W.P.) R. 1966, reg. 7).

15. Bux v. Slough Metals [1973] 1 W.L.R. 1358; [1974] 1 All E.R. 262, C.A. See judgment of Edmund Davies L.J. at 270 F.

U1. Denman v. Gibson (1965) C.A. 263

Judge expressly made no finding as to whether plaintiff would have used goggles if provided—*Held*, plaintiff could not succeed without such a finding in his favour (common law case).

(4) Defences

(a) Contracting Out

1. Lavender v. Diamints [1949] 1 K.B. 585; [1949] 1 All E.R. 532, C.A.

Independent contractor injured cleaning window—*Held*, occupier could not contract out of the F.A. liability under terms of contract with independent contractor.

2. I.C.I. v. Shatwell [1965] A.C. 656; [1964] 2 All E.R. 999, H.L.

Held, volenti was a defence to claim of each based on breach of statutory duty of the other, because "the employer was not himself in breach of any statutory duty and was not vicariously in breach of any statutory duty through the neglect of some person of superior rank to the plaintiff and whose commands the plaintiff was bound to obey (or who had some special and different duty of care)." (Lord Pearce. 1013 C).

3. Hugh v. N.C.B. [1972] S.C. 252; [1977] C.L.Y. 2051, Lord Keith, O.H.

In breach of Regulations and despite reasonable efforts by defendants to stop practice, plaintiff and others jumped off moving train in mine—plaintiff injured in ensuing rush—*Held*, applying *Shatwell* **2**, plaintiff was *volens* and action failed.

*(b) Delegation to Third Party**

		See also Intro. Note
APPARATUS CONTROLLED BY THIRD PARTY—IN FACTORY	1	4
Third party undertaking statutory duty—shipowners	2	–
SUB-CONTRACTING—PERFORMANCE OF STATUTORY DUTY CANNOT BE AVOIDED BY	3	–
Sub-contracting—statutory duty can in some cases be avoided by	4	–

1. Heard v. Brymbo Steel Co. [1947] K.B. 692; (1948) 177 L.T. 251, C.A.

Case under E.R. 1908, which imposes the duty of observance on the occupier—one of the causes of the accident was a faulty switch in the factory, which was under the control of the power company—*Held*, occupier/employer liable under Regulations.

2. Jerred v. Dent [1948] 2 All E.R. 104; 81 Ll.L.R. 412, Atkinson J.

Shipowners assure stevedores that they have performed latter's statutory duty of securing hatch covers—*Held*, shipowners 90 per cent., stevedores 10 per cent. to blame.

3. Mulready v. Bell [1953] 2 Q.B. 117; [1953] 2 All E.R. 215, C.A.

Breach of B.R. 1948, reg. 31(1) by roofing sub-contractor—*Held*, that contractor was liable, on the ground that having undertaken to perform the work he could not avoid the duty which went with it by sub-contracting. *But* see now **4**.

4. Donaghey v. Bolton and Paul [1968] A.C.1.; [1967] 2 All E.R. 1014, H.L.

Failure by plaintiff to use crawling boards, contrary to B.R. 1948 reg. 31(3)—defendant main contractors had sub-contracted the work in question to plaintiff's employers (who were uninsured and had no assets)—question was whether the defendants owed statutory duty to plaintiff or whether the fact of sub-contracting had cast the whole of the duty on plaintiff's employers—*Held*, defendants were liable. All the Law Lords said that the question in such cases was whether a duty had ever attached to the defendant, and this turned on the wording of the particular regulations concerned. Here the relevant regulation was **4** (ii) (duty to comply with such requirements of

* Abbreviations are explained in Introductory Note 1.

(various regulations) "as relate to any work, act or operation performed or about to be performed" by the defendant). Accordingly, if the extent of the sub-contracting was such that the defendant never in any real sense "performed" the work, he would not come under any duty at all. In the present case this was not so, as the defendant had retained sufficient control over the work to be "performing" it. Dicta in *Mulready* **3** to the effect that a person could never avoid statutory duty by sub-contracting disapproved as being too wide.

*(c) Breach by Employer but Plaintiff's Default Real Cause**

		% v. plaintiff	*See also Intro. Notes*
UNFOOTED LADDER—PLAINTIFF ERECTING AND GOING UP	1	100	–
SCAFFOLD SLIGHTLY OUT OF VERTICAL—PLAINTIFF TRYING TO STRAIGHTEN	2	100	–
Defective ladder—plaintiff foreman borrowing	3	99	–
Guard—plaintiff failing to put in position	4	33	–
DEFECTIVE EQUIPMENT—PLAINTIFF CHARGEHAND USING	5	20	–
CRAWLING BOARDS—PLAINTIFF IN CHARGE NOT USINGV	6	66	–
Unguarded machine—plaintiff deliberately inserting hand	7	100	–
Unguarded machine—constant use of inching button—plaintiff keeping hand too close to cylinder while cleaning	8	66	–
Inadequately guarded saw—plaintiff using it when neither authorised nor competent to do so—and failing to adjust it as well as it could be	9	75	–
INADEQUATELY GUARDED MACHINE—PLAINTIFF'S FINGER INADVERTENTLY SLIPPING UNDER GUARD	10	0	–
REPLACING GUARD INCORRECTLY—AFTER REPLACING CUTTER—PLAINTIFF NOT TRAINED TO ACT	11	100	–
UNGUARDED MACHINE—HOLDING RAG TO BELT OF MACHINE TO STOP GREASE SPREADING	12	100	10
Unguarded scaffold—plaintiff overbalancing	U1	100	–
Opening in floor—plaintiff falling down	U2	100	6, 9
Unguarded machine—plaintiff deliberately inserting hand.	U3	50	–
No working platform—plaintiff not using planks instead	U4	100	–
Defective ladder—plaintiff knowingly using	U5	80	–
Unguarded machine—plaintiff cleaning in motion	U6	50	6, 10
Share of blame under 10 per cent.—to be disregarded	U7		6, 10
Unguarded machine—plaintiff adjusting in motion	U7	100	6, 10
Inadequately guarded machine—removing fence entirely	U8	100	–
No rule that plaintiff's share of blame to be limited to 50 per cent.	U9		10

1. Manwaring v. Billington [1952] 2 All E.R. 747; [1952] W.N. 467, C.A.

Plaintiff went up an unsecured and unfooted ladder—had been told not to by defendants—plaintiff had also erected ladder—breach of B.R. 1948, regs. 29(3) and (4) by defendants as a result—*Held*, plaintiff's contributory negligence was real and sole cause, and defendants not liable.

* Abbreviations are explained in Introductory Note 1.

2. Norris v. Wm. Moss [1954] 1 W.L.R. 346; [1954] 1 All E.R. 324, C.A.

Scaffold under erection—one upright slightly out of vertical—hence breach of Regulations *if* reg. 10 applies—plaintiff tries to remedy matters in a manner which is "fantastically wrong"—causes scaffold to collapse—*Held*, the accident was not caused by a breach (if any) by defendants, but by plaintiff's own conduct, and claim failed.

3. Johnson v. Croggan [1954] 1 W.L.R. 195; [1954] 1 All E.R. 121, Pilcher J.

Held, obiter, because plaintiff defeated on delegation and *ex turpi causa, q.v.*, that plaintiff's share of blame would be 99 per cent. (126A).

4. Jones v. Richards [1955] 1 W.L.R. 444; [1955] 1 All E.R. 463, Barry J.

"... a workman who fails to use a guard which he knows ought to be used ... is responsible and responsible to a very substantial degree" (472 B). Threshing machine case—plaintiff aged 18—*Held*, one-third to blame.

5. Davison v. Apex Scaffolds [1956] 1 Q.B. 551; [1956] 1 All E.R. 473, C.A.

Collapse of scaffold causing death of chargehand erector—due to use of "foreign" coupler which was defective through having too long a bolt—defendants admittedly in breach of statutory duty, and also negligence (485 F) for having mixed a "foreign" coupler with their own—question was whether deceased was himself to blame, either at common law or for his own breach of statutory duty under B.R. 1948, reg. 4—four allegations were made against deceased:

(a) he should have rejected the coupler as a foreigner;
(b) he should have discovered the bolt was too long;
(c) he should have followed an alleged drill of coupling the vertical first;
(d) he should have put in a second coupler as a safety precaution.

Singleton L.J. said (481 I) that deceased was in breach of statutory duty under (c) and (d); Jenkins L.J. said (486 H) that deceased was guilty of contributory negligence under (a), but did not go into question of whether this contributory negligence was at common law or breach of statutory duty; Hodson L.J. said no contributory negligence at all—*Held*, as a result, deceased 20 per cent. to blame.

6. Jenner v. Allen West [1959] 1 W.L.R. 554; [1959] 2 All E.R. 115, C.A.

Roof work—deceased falls fatally—breach of B.R. 1948, reg. 3(3)(a) by defendants in failing to provide crawling boards—and by both deceased and defendants in that crawling boards were not used—deceased was in charge of the work—but it was an awkward task and although he had done roofing work (though a leading plumber) he had not done a task of these dimensions before—he knew in general boards should be used—but there was no evidence he had been instructed to use them, or that he had been instructed in the Regulations—*Held*, that deceased two-thirds to blame, and defendants one-third. *Approved* in Chap. 16, (4)(d) **U8**.

7. Rushton v. Turner Bros [1960] 1 W.L.R. 96; [1959] 3 All E.R. 517, Ashworth J.

Fibre-crushing machine consisting of rotating pan with cover which when lifted stopped the machine—the machine could be cleaned this way—but the method usually employed and which plaintiff did employ was to open a trap-door underneath and put hand in—machine here was unguarded—plaintiff put hand in when machine in motion—fingers crushed—plaintiff had been warned orally and in writing not to touch machine in motion—he could have stopped it to clean it—*Held*, although there was a statutory breach the real cause was plaintiff's own negligence and defendants were not liable. *Doubted* by Devlin L.J. in **U8**.

8. Kelly v. John Dale [1965] 1 Q.B. 185; [1964] 2 All E.R. 497, Winn J.

9. Leach v. Standard Telephones [1966] 1 W.L.R. 1392; [1966] 2 All E.R.523, Browne J.

Plaintiff, being neither authorised nor competent to use a metal cutting saw, did so and lost thumb—saw could not be adjusted to be wholly safe—but plaintiff failed to adjust it as well as it could be—*Held*, it was not a case where the conduct of the plaintiff was the sole cause, and defendants were 25 per cent. liable.

10. Stocker v. Norprint (1971) 115 S.J. 58; 10 K.I.R. 10, C.A.

Plaintiff's finger inadvertently slipped under guard of inadequately fenced labelling machine—judge found for defendant on ground that plaintiff's conduct was sole cause—*Held*, not so, where as here plaintiff had made an accidental error, and defendants were 100 per cent. liable.

11. Lineker v. Raleigh [1980] I.C.R. 83; [1980] C.L.Y. 1269, C.A.

Held, defendants not liable. Plaintiff was not trained to change cutter (of horizontal milling machine) and should not have done it. It was incorrect to say that, where in such circumstances there was a breach of statutory duty, there was something like a *res ipsa loquitur* situation or a shifting of the burden of proof to the defendants to establish that the breach was not the cause of the accident.

12. Jayes v. I.M.I. (Kynoch) Ltd [1985] I.C.R. 155; [1985] C.L.Y. 2330, C.A.

Plaintiff, an experienced supervisor, held rag to stop grease spreading from belt of a machine being tested without guards after attention to a lubrication problem. Rag became caught, and plaintiff's finger pulled into machine and partially amputated. Plaintiff claimed breach of F.A. 1961, s. 14 and O.U.M.R. 1938, reg. 5. He admitted he had done a very foolish thing—*Held*, there was no principle of law that there could not be a case of 100 per cent. contributory negligence, even when the intention of the statute concerned is, *inter alia*, to protect against folly on the part of workmen. There comes a point at which the degree of fault is so great that the Court ceases to make fine distinctions, and holds that, in practical terms, the fault is entirely that of the plaintiff. Assuming that there had been breaches of statutory duty, the judge was entitled to take that view of this case.

U1. Morris v. William Willett (1952) C.A. 133

Plaintiff overbalanced on scaffold—no guard rail, in breach of B.R. 1948—*Held*, defendants not liable, as guard rail would not have prevented accident.

U2. Caswell v. Morris Motors Ltd (1952) C.A. 213

Plaintiff fell into pit enabling men to work underneath cars—at night—no work on cars being carried on—*Held*, despite breach of F.A. 1937, s. 25(3) (fencing of openings in floor), defendants not liable, as real cause was plaintiff's contributory negligence.

U3. Cross v. Segal (1952) C.A. 257

Plaintiff puts his hand behind bars to adjust insecurely fenced transmission belt in motion—a conscious and deliberate act on the part of plaintiff—*Held*, 50:50.

U4. Edmunds v. Sir Alfred McAlpine & Son Ltd (1952) C.A. 365

Plaintiff laying concrete floor at factory—no working platform in accordance with B.R. 1948, reg. 22—plaintiff ordered and warned by foreman to use planks provided—plaintiff deliberately did not use planks—*Held*, defendants not liable—cause of accident not absence of platform but solely conduct of plaintiff.

U5. Kelly v. Thomas & Edge (1953) C.A. 266 A

Ladder with rung missing—known to plaintiff—breach of B.R. 1948, reg. 27 by defendants in providing and in allowing user—breach of reg. 14 by plaintiff in using—*Held*, applying *Stapley v. Gypsum* (Chap. 4(1)(b) 4) provision and use were "so closely mixed up" that responsibility ought to be shared: plaintiff 80 per cent., defendants 20 per cent. to blame. *N.B.* Other ladders were available for plaintiff to use.

U6. Burrows v. Metal Box Co. (1956) C.A. 347

Plaintiff minder of colour printing machine—had to clean rollers from time to time—no fence—warned that must stop machine to clean it—practice in factory not to stop machine to clean rollers, though dangerous, to save trouble—men knew they should not clean machine when running—*Held*, defendants in breach of F.A. 1937, s. 14—50 per cent. contributory negligence against plaintiff for doing not only what told not to do but also what no sensible person would do.

U7. Powell v. Reddihough (1957) C.A. 151

Plaintiff technician of great experience—employed by third party to repair defendants' machines—hand crushed while adjusting roller—*Held*, that, although defendants in breach of F.A. 1937, s. 14 real cause was plaintiff's own conduct, *or* alternatively defendants' share of blame was under 10 per cent. and therefore should be disregarded.

U8. Lancaster v. Wigan Brick Co. (1960) C.A. 1

Inadequate fence to transmission shaft—deceased removed fence entirely—*Held*, subsequent accident was wholly attributable to act of deceased, and defendants not liable for breach of statutory duty in failing to fence. Devlin L.J. (13 F) said, however: "If it is once proved that the breach of the statute played a causative part, even a small one, in bringing about the injury, I am not sure that the employer can wholly escape liability." He reserved for future consideration and correctness of the decision in *Rushton v. Turner* 7.

U9. Lynch v. Key Engineering (1971) C.A. 84

Salmon L.J. (6 C): "One ought not to approach a case of this kind on the basis that, once it has been shown against a defendant that he is in breach of section 14 of the Act (*i.e.* the fencing provisions), then you must rigidly apply a rule that in no circumstances can the plaintiff be as much as 50 per cent. to blame." *N.B.* The plaintiff was acting both foolishly and contrary to instructions in relation to a dangerous nip.

*(d) Breach of Employer Caused Solely by Act of Plaintiff**

		% v. plaintiff	See also Intro. Notes
GUARD—PLAINTIFF REMOVING	1	20	—
UNFOOTED LADDER—PLAINTIFF ERECTING AND GOING UP	2	100	—
Defective ladder—plaintiff foreman borrowing	3	99	—
DEFECTIVE SCAFFOLD COUPLER—PLAINTIFF CHARGEHAND USING	4	20	—
GENERAL RULE WHEN PLAINTIFF'S BREACH THEREBY PUTS DEFENDANT IN BREACH	4		—
Crawling boards—plaintiff failing to use	5	100	—
General rule when plaintiff's breach thereby puts defendant in breach	5		—
CRAWLING BOARDS—PLAINTIFF FAILING TO USE	6	66	—
Task beyond competence of plaintiff	7		—
UNFOOTED LADDER—PLAINTIFF GOING UP	8	50	—
Test is whose conduct caused the breach—plaintiff using ladder instead of mobile tower	9	33	6, 9
Where statutory duty solely on defendants, plaintiff cannot fail altogether	9	—	6,9
UNFOOTED LADDER—PLAINTIFF CHARGEHAND GOING UP	10	100	—
GUARD—PLAINTIFF REMOVING	11	100	—
Not switching off power—setting mould in press—with guard removed	12	100	—
TRESTLE WITH LATENT DEFECT—PLAINTIFF FOREMAN BORROWING TO CONSTRUCT SCAFFOLD	13	0	—
Crawling boards—plaintiff failing to use—provided by defendant main contractors—but use not insisted on by plaintiff's employers—who were sub-contractors	14	25	—
Employer is liable unless he takes all reasonable steps to prevent breaches by employees	15	50	—
Guard—plaintiff repairing machine—and requesting machine be run after guard had been removed	16	100	—
Not switching off power—tool setter working on unguarded machine	17	100	10
PLAINTIFF FAILING TO LOCK WHEELS OF OR FIT OUTRIGGER TO A MOBILE TOWER SCAFFOLD	18	100	—
PLAINTIFF CHOOSING TO WORK FROM UNFENCED PLATFORM, WHEN FORKLIFT TRUCK WITH CAGE AVAILABLE	19	100	9
Defective rope for scaffold—plaintiff using	U1	50	–
Guard—plaintiff removing	U2	90	–
Dangerous part of machinery—plaintiff making adjustment so as to make spindle dangerous	U3	50	–
Guard—plaintiff removing	U4	100	6, 10
Guard—plaintiff removing	U5	100	"
Unfooted ladder—plaintiff foreman going up	U6	100	–

* Abbreviations are explained in Introductory Note 1.

		% v. plaintiff	See also Intro. Note
Crawling boards—plaintiff failing to use	U7	100	–
Guard—plaintiff removing	U8	75	–
Unfooted ladder—plaintiff going up	U9	50	–
Defective bosun's chair—made by plaintiff	U10	50	–
Defective plank—plaintiff used as gangway	U11	100	6, 9
Ladder—dangerously placed	U12	100	9
Ladder—unlashed—used by chargehand	U13	78	–
Onus of proof in such cases	U13		–
Guard—plaintiff removing	U14	100	–
Unfooted ladder—plaintiff knowing it could be secured by hook	U15	100	–
Unfooted ladder—plaintiff going up when assistant has gone away to phone	U16	50	–
Putting hand in machine—thinking it had stopped	U17	25	10
Issuing written instructions about regulations—but not ensuring instructions carried out	U18	50	–
Fragile roof—plaintiff uneccessarily climbing onto it	U19	100	–

1. Norris v. Syndic [1952] 2 Q.B. 135; [1952] 1 All E.R. 935, C.A.

Plaintiff removes guard and fails to replace—*Held, inter alia*, contributory negligence, but as defendants had set a bad example, plaintiff only 20 per cent. to blame.

2. Manwaring v. Billington [1952] 2 All E.R. 747; [1952] W.N. 467, C.A.

Plaintiff went up an unsecured and unfooted ladder—had been told not to by defendants—plaintiff had also erected ladder—breach of B.R. 1948, regs. 29(3) and (4) by defendants as a result—*Held*, plaintiff's contributory negligence was real and sole cause, and defendants not liable.

3. Johnson v. Croggan [1954] 1 W.L.R. 195; [1954] 1 All E.R. 121, Pilcher J.

Held (*obiter*) that plaintiff's share of blame would be 99 per cent. (126 A).

4. Davison v. Apex Scaffolds [1956] 1 Q.B. 551; [1956] 1 All E.R. 473, C.A.

Collapse of scaffold causing death of chargehand erector—due to use of "foreign" coupler which was defective through having too long a bolt—defendants admittedly in breach of statutory duty, and also negligence (485 F) for having mixed a "foreign" coupler with their own—question was whether deceased was himself to blame, either at common law or for his own breach of statutory duty under B.R. 1948, reg. 4—four allegations were made against deceased:

(a) he should have rejected the coupler as a foreigner;
(b) he should have discovered the bolt was too long;
(c) he should have followed an alleged drill of coupling the vertical first;
(d) he should have put in a second coupler as a safety precaution.

Singleton L.J. said (481 I) that deceased was in breach of statutory duty under (c) and (d); Jenkins L.J. said (486 H) that deceased was guilty of contributory negligence under (a) but did not go into question of whether this contributory negligence was at common law or breach of statutory duty;

Hodson L.J. said no contributory negligence at all—*Held*, as a result, deceased 20 per cent. to blame: "The deceased and defendants are both in breach of statutory duty . . . and defendants' breach was brought about by the deceased's breach; that is to say, the deceased . . . at once committed a breach of his own statutory duty and put defendants in breach of theirs. In these circumstances I cannot for my part see how plaintiff can succeed merely on proof of defendants' breach of statutory duty . . . In my view, it must be necessary for plaintiff . . . to go on and prove that the breach of statutory duty . . . was in some degree due to defendants' negligence over and above their statutory responsibility for a mere innocent breach of the regulations. The inquiry on which one must embark thus does not differ greatly from the inquiry necessary in a case where the issue is one of negligence or no negligence at common law." The Lord Justice went on to say (485 F) that in this case there was such negligence by defendants. Compared in **5**.

5. Ginty v. Belmont Building Supplies [1959] 1 All E.R. 414, Pearson J.

Roof work—duckboard provided for plaintiff—but not used—plaintiff falls—as a result both plaintiff and defendant (the latter as a result of plaintiff's failure to use duckboard) were in breach of B.R. 1949, reg. 31(3)(a)—*Held*, that in a case like this the true test was not to be measured by whether there had been delegation or not, but by asking whose fault in substance was it?; and applying this test the fault in substance was wholly that of plaintiff, and accordingly defendants were not liable. Compare **4**. *Approved* in **U8**.

6. Jenner v. Allen West [1959] 1 W.L.R. 554; [1959] 2 All E.R. 115, C.A.

Roof work—deceased falls fatally—breach of B.R. 1948, reg. 31(3)(a) by defendants in failing to provide crawling boards—and by both deceased and defendants in that crawling boards were not used—deceased was in charge of the work—but it was an awkward task and although he had done roofing work (though a leading plumber) he had not done a task of these dimensions before—he knew in general boards should be used—but there was no evidence he had been instructed to use them, or that he had been instructed in the Regulations—*Held*, that deceased two-thirds to blame, and defendants one-third. *Approved* in **U8**.

7. Byers v. Head Wrightson [1961] 1 W.L.R. 961; [1961] 2 All E.R. 538, Elwes J.

Plaintiff, a chargehand steel erector, constructed, with two other men, a plank bridge over a depression or trench on a building site for the purpose of moving a heavy mobile welding set—the plank bridge constituted a scaffold within B.R. 1948 and was defective in that it was unstable—in transit the welding set had tilted and injured the plaintiff—*Held*, that the defendants were liable, notwithstanding that the breach of the B.R. 1948 resulted from the acts of the plaintiff, because "the task of appraising what was necessary was not within the competence of the plaintiff" (543 A): "What counsel for the defendants is doing is tantamount to faulting a Corporal for not measuring up to the standard of a trade-qualified Staff-Sergeant" (543 I).

8. McMath v. Rimmer Brothers [1962] 1 W.L.R. 1; [1961] 3 All E.R. 1154, C.A.

Unfooted ladder—plaintiff ganger (*i.e.* chargehand) went up a ladder during unauthorised absence of labourer who should have been footing—breach of B.R. 1948, reg. 29(4)—*Held*, there was a breach both by plaintiff and defendant, but plaintiff's fault was not co-extensive with that of defendants for the defendants additionally were responsible for the absence of the labourer, and that defendants were 50 per cent. liable. *Ginty v. Belmont* **5** *approved*; *Jenner v. Allen West* **6** *applied*.

9. Ross v. Associated Portland Cement Manufacturers [1964] 1 W.L.R. 768; [1964] 2 All E.R. 452, H.L.

Plaintiff a chargehand steel erector lent to defendant factory occupiers in order, *inter alia*, to repair an overhead net held up by cables—the loan was more or less a permanent one (461 B) but he was not an expert at this particular work, which D's engineer told him to do and left him to carry out in his own way—plaintiff discussed ways and means with mate, and in default of something better being available he selected a ladder—the proper method was to use a mobile tower, and the use of a ladder was admittedly dangerous—hence there was a clear breach of F.A. 1937, s. 26, as amended by F.A. 1959, s. 5 (safe place of work)—but was the breach wholly plaintiff's fault within the principle laid down in *Ginty* **5**?—defendants called no evidence, and Nield J. held it wholly plaintiff's fault, mainly because (so it appears) plaintiff was sufficiently expert for defendants to be entitled to leave it to him to decide what to do and to come to their chief engineer if he wanted help or equipment (455 B)—H.L., while not dissenting from the test in *Ginty* **5** emphasised that the question really was whose conduct caused the breach (Lord Reid 455 H, Lord Guest 458 I)—*Held*, applying this question, defendants were two-thirds liable. The reasons for this decision were as follows:

(a) Lord Reid: Defendants failed to take proper steps to see that proper equipment was available, and they were not entitled to leave all decisions to a man of plaintiff's limited skill (456 D).
(b) Lord Guest: The working place was unsafe and this was a cause of the accident. It was also a breach of the obligation laid on defendants by s. 26. Defendants could not escape liability by saying that plaintiff chose an unsafe working place (458 H).
(c) Lord Upjohn: In *Ginty* **5** there was a duty on both the defendants and the plaintiff. Here the sole statutory obligation is on the defendants. In such cases, unless defendants' share of the blame is *de minimis*, the plaintiff cannot fail altogether (460 H).
(d) Lord Donovan in terms (463 H) had same reasons as Lord Reid.
(e) Lord Simonds concurred generally (453 G).

10. Hammill v. Camborne Water Co. (1964) 108 S.J. 335; [1964] C.L.Y. 374, C.A.

Held, plaintiff's breach co-extensive with that of defendants, since it was his duty to see that the Regulations were observed, and his claim therefore failed.

11. Mitchell v. Westin [1965] 1 W.L.R. 297; [1965] 1 All E.R. 657, C.A.

To tighten screw on collar of lathe, plaintiff removed guard, and then, to turn lathe to expose screw, switched machine on and off in a short jerk—*Held*, machine not "in motion" (see Chap. 16, (6)(f) **11**), but even if it was, plaintiff would have been taking a risk which was "unnecessary and unjustified" (Pearson L.J., 665 E), as he could have turned the lathe by hand, and in such circumstances would have been wholly to blame.

12. Horne v. Lec Refrigeration [1965] 2 All E.R. 898, Cantley J.

Power accidentally switched on by trailing lead of electric drill—which deceased was using to set new mould in press—guard had had to be removed for this purpose—*Held*, deceased solely to blame, as it was not a repetitive job, and he ignored the established safety drill by leaving most of the power switches on, so that press operated when the trailing lead caught a switch on the press.

13. Quinn v. Green [1966] 1 Q.B. 509; [1965] 3 All E.R. 785, C.A.

Collapse of scaffold trestle due to latent defect—plaintiff foreman had borrowed trestles and planks from other contractors and inspected them carefully—defendant employers were admittedly in

breach of B.R. 1948 reg. 5 (suitable scaffolds to be provided) and reg. 7(1) (scaffolds to be of good construction, etc.)—but was plaintiff himself in breach?—if so, since C.A. thought that there was no negligence or contributory negligence at common law, plaintiff's breach would probably be co-terminous with that of defendants, so that, following *Ginty* **5**, his right to recover would either be extinguished or reduced—*Held*, plaintiff was not in breach. Reg. 5 imposed a duty on employers only. Salmon L.J. thought that the same applied to reg. 7(1), but he said he was bound to the contrary by *Davison* **4**. Even so, because the facts were different, the plaintiff here was not in breach. In *Davison* **4** the plaintiff had used a defective coupler to construct the scaffold. Here, "it was not because of anything the plaintiff did in erecting the scaffolding that the scaffolding collapsed. The scaffolding collapsed because it was not of sound material or adequate strength" (791 E). Salmon L.J. went on to say that the decision in *Davison* **4** had been arrived at on three grounds, with the first two of which he agreed: (a) contributory negligence in selecting coupler; (b) breach of reg. 4 in failing to co-operate with employers in carrying out their duties; and (c) breach of reg. 7(1) in failing to construct scaffold properly. The latter, however, only applied to acts done in erecting scaffolds, and its scope "was not to be extended" (791 D). Willmer L.J. said that the ratio of *Davison* **4** was really under reg. 4, and that since it was plaintiff's duty to construct the scaffold being erected, he was in breach in failing to fulfil that duty (794 C).
N.B. Ginty **5** was distinguished because there the duty (a failure to use ladders) was on the plaintiff, and by his breach the employers were co-terminously put in breach.

14. Donaghey v. Boulton & Paul [1968] A.C. 1; [1967] 2 All E.R. 1014, H.L.

Crawling boards provided by main contractors—but not used by plaintiff—who was employed by sub-contractors—main contractors were held by H.L. to be under statutory duty to ensure that crawling boards were used (B.R. 1948 reg. 31(3)—for reasons see Chap. 16,(4)(**b**) **4**)—on this basis question was whether the plaintiff was solely liable on the principle laid down in *Ginty* **5**—*Held*, no, and plaintiff only 25 per cent. liable, as there were two main causes of the accident, the plaintiff's failure to use the boards and the failure of the foreman employed by plaintiff's own employers (*i.e.* the sub-contractors) to insist on their use; this latter cause had nothing to do with the plaintiff's own conduct, so that his share of the responsibility should be judged according to his own failure only.

15. Boyle v. Kodak [1969] 1 W.L.R. 661; [1969] 2 All E.R. 439, H.L.

Employee failed to lash ladder at top before mounting (which could have been done)—employers assumed that he would know the Regulations—*Held*, employers 50 per cent. liable.

16. Cope v. Nickel Electro [1980] C.L.Y. 1268, Sheldon J.

17. Humphreys v. Silent Channel [1981] C.L.Y. 1209, French J.

P, an experienced tool setter, failed to switch off power before working on machine—which was unguarded—admitted breach of F.A. 1961, s. 14(1)—*Held*, sole cause of accident was P's negligent failure to isolate machine.

18. Baker v. T. Clarke (Leeds) Ltd [1992] P.I.Q.R. P 262; [1993] C.L.Y. 2019, C.A.

Plaintiff, highly experienced foreman electrician, erected a mobile tower scaffold without locking the wheels or using outriggers. Working from a platform 10 feet high, he exerted too much horizontal force and the scaffold toppled. The trial judge found defendant in breach of C.(W.P.)R. 1966, regs. 6,7, 15(1) and 15(3), but plaintiff 50 per cent. to blame—*Held*, by Court of Appeal, that defendant's beaches were caused entirely by plaintiff's omissions. He was experienced, knew of the Regulations, and was aware of the risks he was running. *Per* Stuart-Smith L.J. at P 267: " . . . it is not necessary . . .

for an employer to tell a skilled and experienced man at regular intervals things of which he is well aware unless there is reason to believe that the man is failing to adopt the proper precautions or, through familiarity, becoming contemptuous of them. There is no evidence that this was the position here . . . It was plainly a matter . . . where they had to leave the individual decision to the common sense of the skilled experienced man on the site." Accordingly, the plaintiff's claim failed.

19. Walsh v. Crown Decorative Products [1993] P.I.Q.R. P 194; [1994] C.L.Y. 2293, C.A.

Plaintiff, experienced plumber, was asked to attend to leak in steam line 14 feet above floor level—chose to work from unfenced ladder platform, though fork-lift truck with cage was available—slipped and fell $7\frac{1}{2}$ feet from platform—alleged breach of F.A. 1961, s. 29(2)—*Held*, defendant not liable because:

(a) plaintiff had not *had* to work on platform, since he could have used truck with cage; therefore condition precedent to application of s. 29(2) not satisfied;
(b) even if s. 29(2) did apply, defendant had complied with it by providing truck with cage;
(c) where as here, it was reasonable to leave it to an employee to choose equipment from which to work, and he decides to work from equipment which places employer in breach of s. 29(2), such breach does not entitle employee to claim damages.

U1. Crawford v. Erection Services (1953) C.A. 254

Plaintiff used faulty suspension rope for scaffold—thereby defendants were in breach of B.R. 1948—defendants had done nothing to indicate better rope was available—plaintiff should have seen defect—*Held*, 50:50.

U2. Taylor v. Cass (1954) C.A. 262

Sand-mixing machine—plaintiff tipped guard over to make it virtually useless—defendants knew this was done but foreman never expressly prohibited it—plaintiff knew it was contrary to instructions—*Held*, plaintiff 90 per cent. to blame for contributory negligence, *inter alia*.

U3. Davies v. Metropolitan Vickers (1955) C.A. 162

Held, 50 per cent. contributory negligence.

U4. Elworthy v. New Merton Board Mills Ltd (1956) C.A. 169

Plaintiff engineer sent by employers to overhaul engine of mobile crane at defendants' premises—iron platform round engine—plaintiff ran engine for half an hour to test it—did not replace guards—plaintiff then went onto platform—plaintiff slipped and foot came into contact with revolving part of engine—*Held*, defendants not liable. Technically in breach of F.A. 1937, s. 14, but damages not recoverable as wholly fault of plaintiff—defendants had no control over work.

U5. Woods v. Crittall Manufacturing Co. Ltd (1957) C.A. 46

Plaintiff boiler man—water-operated pump—plaintiff started pump with cover off—wiping off water with rag—rag slipped and hand trapped in machinery—plaintiff experienced and competent—acting on own initiative—knew what he was doing and that running a risk—plaintiff person to whom defendants entitled to leave day-to-day work of looking after boilers in factory—*Held*, plaintiff cannot recover for breach of F.A. 1937, ss. 14 and 16, as state of affairs brought about by plaintiff himself.

U6. Smith v. R. Smith (Horley) Ltd (1957) C.A. 273 A

Plaintiff foreman steel erector employed by defendants—raising trusses in roof—fell from ladder 12 feet 6 in. long which was not secured or footed—plaintiff experienced man and job well within his capacity—*Held*, defendants in breach of B.R. 1948, reg. 29(4)—plaintiff in breach of B.R. 1948, reg. 4—plaintiff's breach operated to put defendants in breach—defendants not liable as plaintiff's breach effective cause of accident.

U7. Lockett v. Blackwell Stanistreet (1960) C.A. 6

Deceased fell through roof which was fragile—technical breach of B.R. 1948 by defendants in that deceased was not using crawling boards—but real cause was deceased's disobedience in not using the boards he had been told to use—*Held*, defendants not liable.

U8. Biles v. Decca (1960) C.A. 196

Plaintiff an experienced fitter took guard off machine and worked it unguarded for one and a half hours on production—accident—*Held*, defendants 25 per cent. to blame, as their foreman was on the spot at the time and could have seen, and stopped, what plaintiff was doing. Plaintiff 75 per cent. to blame. *Ginty v. Belmont* **5** and *Jenner v. Allen West* **6** approved.

U9. Boden v. Moore (1961) C.A. 197 A (also (1961) 105 S.J. 510)

Plaintiff painter working from unfooted ladder fell when ladder twisted—breach of B.R. 1948, reg. 29(4)—question was whether, as in *Manwaring* **2** and *Ginty* **5**, defendants' breach was a vicarious breach through plaintiff's own act and co-extensive with his own breach, or whether some of the blame could be attributed to defendants, as in *Jenner* **6**—*Held*, defendants 50 per cent. liable, as they had neither communicated the regulations to the plaintiff, nor given any express instructions, but it had also been a frequent practice, of which defendants were aware, for employees to work from unfooted ladders:

> "The regulations are mandatory, and an employer is in breach if they are broken. Precautions approved by general experience are not a substitute for the regulations. The employer must take all such steps as he can to see that the regulations are carried out. Unless he has done so, it is as a rule impossible for him to say that accidents resulting from a breach are solely the fault of the workman" (Holroyd Pearce L.J. at 7 E).

U10. Poplawski v. Jan Victor (1963) C.A. 7

Plaintiff employed by defendants to paint outside of house—he made a boatswain's chair from rope of his own—with the help of his workmate, who was senior to him, hoisted himself up—but rope eventually broke—clear breach of B.R. 1948 brought about by plaintiff's own conduct—but senior workmate was present and knew—*Held*, 50:50.

U11. Hudson v. Acme Flooring Co. (1963) C.A. 70 (also (1963) 107 S.J. 234)

Plaintiff laid down a defective plank to bridge a small gap—plank broke—*Held*, assuming (which was doubted) that plank was a gangway within F.A. 1937, s. 25(3) yet, applying *Ginty* **5**, defendants had done nothing which was not co-extensive with plaintiff's wrongful act, which had brought about the whole of the technical statutory default of the defendants. Defendants not liable.

U12. Ross v. Lloyd Lawrence (1963) C.A. 117

Deceased sent to repair safety net of aerial ropeway—leant ladder against net to get up—highly dangerous—defendants, who were the occupiers and not the employers, thereby in breach of F.A. 1961, s. 29—*Held*, applying *Ginty* **5**, defendants not liable.

U13. Millington v. Redpath Brown (1967) C.A. 157

Erection of steel girder framework—to get up—plaintiff chargehand used unlashed ladder, erected by persons and in circumstances unknown—*Held, per* Salmon L.J., 19 A, in such a case, defendants, being in breach of statutory duty, had, in order to escape liability altogether, to prove that the breach was exclusively the fault of the plaintiff; owing to the doubt about where the ladder had come from, they had failed to do this, and were 22 per cent. liable.

U14. Rogers v. Keen (1968) C.A. 396

U15. Redling v. Hoisting Appliance (1973) C.A. 135

Plaintiff erected and went up a ladder which was not securely fixed—in breach of C. (W.P.) R. 1966, reg. 32(2)—but ladder had a hook, as the plaintiff knew, and could have been secured—*Held*, defendants not liable, as breach was solely brought about by act of plaintiff.

U16. Milson v. Strachan and Henshaw (1973) C.A. 356

Plaintiff goes up unfooted ladder—breach of C. (W.P.) R. 1966—someone had been available to foot ladder—but had gone away, as plaintiff thought, to phone—*Held*, 50:50, as if the defendants did not provide someone to foot ladder, they must "clearly and specifically" warn him against the risk of going up by himself.

U17. Fowler v. C.E.G.B. (1974) C.A. 224

Plaintiff, cleaning out hopper, unscrewed cover and put hand in—thinking impeller had stopped—it had not—*Held*, applying *Boyle* **15**, defendants liable under F.A. 1961, s. 14—25 per cent. contributory negligence.

U18. Hunt v. G.L.C. (1977) C.A. 136

Painting from planking with access ladder—breaches of C. (W.P.) R. 1966, regs. 6(1), 32(2) and 35(5)(a)—all brought about by plaintiff's conduct in setting up the ladder—the defendants had issued plaintiff and other employees with cards telling what their duties under C. (W.P.) R. 1966 were—but they did not do what they could to see that the instructions were carried out—in particular the changehand said he would not have criticised the set-up as erected—*Held*, following *Boyle* **15**, plaintiff's fault was not co-terminous with that of the defendants, and liability would be apportioned 50:50.

U19. Stephenson v. Whittal Builders Co. Ltd (1981) C.A. U.B. 132

Plaintiff, experienced joiner, securing asbestos sheets to shed roof. Climbed onto roof when unnecessary and fell through asbestos sheet. Defendants conceded "technical" breach of C. (W.P.) R. 1966, reg. 36(1)—*Held*, that the defendants were not liable, as the plaintiff's negligence was the sole cause of the accident. The plaintiff was sufficiently experienced not to require instruction how to carry out his work. His decision to climb onto the roof was unforeseeable and (*per* Ormrod L.J. p. 7) "there is no duty on employers to instruct or remind employees of the terms of regulations which do not appear to be relevant to the job in hand and which no reasonable employer could have thought were relevant . . . ".

(5) Safety of Means of Access and Workplaces Generally

*(a) Meaning of "Access"**

			See also Intro. Notes.
Place of work or access—cannot be both at same time	1	F.A. 1937, s. 26	6, 9
Place of work or access—moving from one workplace to another	2, 4	F.A. 1937, s. 26	6, 9
Place of work or access—work on roof	3	F.A. 1937, s. 26	6, 9
Two routes—one unsafe	5	S.R. 1931, reg. 1	—
Access must be to place of work—not to place where employee under no duty to go	6	F.A. 1937, s. 26	6, 9
Access must be to place of work—not route to canteen	7	F.A. 1937, s. 26	6, 9
Place of work or access—cannot be both at same time	8	F.A. 1937, s. 26	6, 9
Place of work or access—work on roof	8	F.A. 1937, s. 26	6, 9
"Access" to hold of ship—means perpendicular access only—not include area round coamings	9	D.R. 1934, reg. 11	5
Place of work or access—moving material twenty feet	10	F.A. 1937, s. 26	6, 9
Two routes—one unsafe—access to hold	11	D.R. 1934, reg. 11	5
"Access" means access to specific place only—fireman going onto asbestos roof to put out fire not using "means of access"	12	F.A. 1937, s. 26	6, 9
Adjacent danger—duty extends thereto	13	S.R. 1931, reg. 1	5
Pushing truck into shed—not means of access	14	F.A. 1937, s. 26	6, 9
Ship under repair in dry dock—whether deck is means of access	15	**F.A. 1937, s. 26**	6, 9
Ship being painted from pontoon—deck is means of access	16		—
Place of work or access—cannot be both—plaintiff going to get shovel—treads on nail in plank	17	F.A. 1961, s. 29	9

* Abbreviations are explained in Introductory Note 1.

"Access" to hold of ship—means perpendicular access only—does not apply to state of tween deck at bottom of ladder	18	D.R. 1934, reg. 11	5
TWO ROUTES—ONE UNSAFE—LATTER BEING A SET OF STEPS SET UP BY WORKMEN—BUT NOT ADOPTED BY EMPLOYER—NOT "PROVIDED" BY EMPLOYER	19	F.A. 1961, s. 29	9
Duty to provide safe means of access—does not apply to roadways on which vehicle might be driven round a quarry	20	M.Q.A. 1954 s. 109	–
Stepping from top of boxes onto platform—whether platform means of access egress	21	F.A. 1961, s. 29 (1)	9
Getting into "bowels" of large machine not "access"	U1	F.A. 1937, s. 26	6, 9
Ladder—plaintiff going up to fetch down documents from shelf	U2	F.A. 1937, s. 26	6, 9
Wheeling barrow across yard—not "access"	U3	F.A. 1937, s. 26	6, 9
Place of work or access—cannot be both at same time	U4		–
Two routes—plaintiff arriving early—main entrance closed—chooses makeshift route	U5	F.A. 1937, s. 26	5, 6, 9
Two routes—one safe	U6		–

1. Lovell v. Blundells [1944] 1 K.B. 502; [1944] 2 All E.R. 53, 57 F, Tucker J.

2. Callaghan v. Fred Kidd [1944] K.B. 560; [1944] 1 All E.R. 525, C.A.

Plaintiff while moving from one grindstone to another 15 yards away tripped on some iron bars which had been put there—*Held*, defendants liable for not maintaining safe access.

3. Whitby v. Burt Boulton [1947] K.B. 918; [1947] 2 All E.R. 324, Denning J.

Plaintiff was removing a corrugated iron sheet from a roof when the timbers collapsed—*Held*, defendants had failed to provide a safe means of access to plaintiff's place of work. *Doubted* and *not followed* by Divisional Court in **8**.

4. Hopwood v. Rolls-Royce (1947) 176 L.T. 514, C.A.

Plaintiff and workmate carrying cylinder from one place of work to another—route reduced to 4 feet wide by aeroplane cylinders lying about—plaintiff falls—*Held*, the route plaintiff was taking was a means of access, and defendants liable because it was not safe. See **8**.

5. Donovan v. Cammell Laird [1949] 2 All E.R. 92; 82 Ll.L.R. 642, Devlin J.

"It may well be that where there are two routes to a place of work, each equally likely to attract a workman, the section is not complied with unless both are made safe, but where, as in this case, there is one safe route and the workman chooses another, which it cannot be reasonably anticipated that he would choose, I do not think there can be any obligation in respect of the second route" (89 G).

6. Dryland v. London Electrical (1949) 99 L.J. 665, C.A.

Plaintiff erecting aerial on roof—went over to remove old aerial—no instructions to do so—*Held*, plaintiff in going over was not using a means of access.

7. Davies v. De Havilland [1951] 1 K.B. 50; [1950] 2 All E.R. 582, Somervell L.J.

Held, semble, route to canteen was not a means of access.

8. Dorman Long v. Hillier [1951] 1 All E.R. 357; 115 J.P. 113, D.C.

Work removing sheets from roof—*Held*, following **4** and not following **3**, a workman moving about on a roof was not using roof as means of access, but as his place of work. Devlin J. also suggested, as Lord Greene M.R. had suggested in **4**, that a place could not be a place of work and a means of access at the same time. (*N.B.* **1**, which was direct authority for this proposition, was not cited.) *Followed* in **10**.

9. Carvil v. Hay [1954] 2 Lloyd's Rep. 381, Ct. of Sess., I.H.

10. Prince v. Carrier Engineering [1955] 1 Lloyd's Rep. 401, Parker L.J.

Held, following **4** and **8**, plaintiff was at his place of work during whole movement of frames: "I find it too artificial to say that there were two branches of work, one picking up the window frames and the other putting them down twenty feet away" (405, col. 1).

11. Cottrell v. Vianda S.S. [1955] 2 Lloyd's Rep. 450, Devlin J.

Two ladders into hold—one iron and one wooden—plaintiff uses wooden one which breaks—defendants say, *inter alia* that plaintiff should have used iron one, which was the access provided—*Held*, defendants liable, because plaintiff was reasonably justified in regarding the wooden ladder as a means of access.

12. Machin v. Cravens (1958) 108 L.J. 633; [1958] C.L.Y. 1319, Salmon J.

Held, no breach of F.A. 1937, s. 26, as the section only related to access to a specific place, and a fire might have occurred anywhere on the premises.

13. Davies v. J. L. Thompson [1960] 1 Lloyd's Rep. 22, C.A.

Ladder sound in itself—but with extraneous obstruction close to it—*Held*, this could in law constitute a breach of S.R 1931, r. 1 (safe means of access), but on the facts did not.

14. Newberry v. Joseph Westwood [1960] 2 Lloyd's Rep. 37, Donovan J.

Held, that the place was not a means of access within s. 26, so far as concerned the plaintiff who was pushing a truck, but was the place of work itself.

15. Gardiner v. Admiralty Commissioners [1964] 1 W.L.R. 590; [1964] 2 All E.R. 93, H.L.

Plaintiff had to carry boiling pitch across the deck of a ship under repair—*Held*, the deck constituted a means of access, notwithstanding that it was part of the object which was being repaired.

16. Day v. Harland & Wolff [1967] 1 Lloyd's Rep. 136, Waller J.

N.B. New trial was ordered by C.A. because of fresh evidence being discovered.

17. Taylor v. Coalite Oils (1967) 3 K.I.R. 315; [1968] C.L.Y. 1605, C.A.

Held, the place of the accident was the means of access to plaintiff's work, and not his place of work. It could not be both.

18. McCarthy v. Hellenic Lines [1968] 1 Lloyd's Rep. 537; [1968] C.L.Y. 2650, Willis J.

Held, following *Carvil* **9**.

19. Smith v. British Aerospace [1982] I.C.R. 98; [1982] C.L.Y. 1368, C.A.

Defendants supplied safe means of access up to staging. Plaintiff instead used unsafe access (a set of portable steps) recently set up by workmen and was injured. Management could reasonably have anticipated the use of the unsafe route, but did not condone it—*Held*, explaining statement of Devlin J. in *Donovan* **5** and distinguishing *Cottrell* **11**, defendants were not liable. They had not supplied or adopted the unsafe means of access, and accordingly had not "provided" it for the purpose of s.29. If an employer has not supplied the dangerous means of access, it must be shown that he "appreciated that the particular structure was in fact being used as a means of access and . . . was content that his workmen should continue so to use it." It was insufficient to make an employer liable merely because he can "reasonably anticipate that a man may, for his own purposes, use a particular piece of apparatus to gain access to a workplace" (Griffith L.J., 106).

20. English v. Cory Sand & Ballast Company Ltd, *The Times*, April 2, 1985; [1985] C.L.Y. 2178, Stocker J.

See Chap. 16, (13) **29** for further details.

21. Harrison v. R.B. Tennent, 1992 S.L.T. 1060; [1992] C.L.Y. 5821

A welder descended from the top of boxes where he had been working, to a platform, at which he fell through a damaged board—*Held*, the platform was a means of egress, and was within F.A. 1961, s. 29(1).

U1. Fraser v. Peek Frean (1951) C.A. 175

Large machine—plaintiff a fitter had to get inside it for maintenance work—getting out he slipped—sued under F.A. 1937, s. 26 (access)—*Held*, defendants not liable, as s. 26 did not apply to "the bowels of a machine."

U2. Stockton v. Metropolitan Vickers Electrical Co. Ltd (1951) C.A. 203

Held, place of work, and not means of access.

U3. Andrews v. Ministry of Supply (1951) C.A. 332

Plaintiff wheeling barrow of clinkers in yard—picks up hosepipe to move it—while doing so trips over heap of mortar—*Held,* no breach of F.A. 1937, s. 26, because *inter alia,* plaintiff was not on a means of access. Somervell L.J. applied (5A) test of Lord Greene M.R. in *Hopwood v. Rolls-Royce* **4:** "That (*i.e.* the interpretation of F.A. 1937, s. 26 proposed) would exclude movements taken while doing one operation or set of operations, and would confine the section to cases where it can truly be said that if a man is moving from one branch of his work to another branch of his work, his route in doing so is a means of access."

U4. Werndly v. D. Napier Ltd (1961) C.A. 147

Ormerod L.J. (4 E) expressed the view that, contrary to some Scottish decisions, a place could not both be a means of access and a place of work. Test put forward by Lord Greene M.R. in *Hopwood v. Rolls-Royce* **4** *applied.*

U5. Richards v. N.A.A.F.I. (1964) C.A. 16 A

Plaintiff arrived early and main door was locked—he followed another employee in through a makeshift route and fell—*Held,* assuming that the makeshift route was such as by itself might constitute a breach, there was yet no breach, because D had provided a safe means which P could have used if he had chosen to wait. *Cottrell* **11** was *considered:* Sellers L.J. (7 A) said that, although D were probably liable at common law because the wooden ladder was defective, he did not think the decision was correct in blaming D for breach of statutory duty, for D.R. 1934 reg. 11 required safe access to be provided to the hold, and this was done by means of the iron ladder—albeit there was also unsafe access to the same hold via the hatch with the wooden ladder. Pearson L.J. (11 A) agreed with this, but Russell L.J. (11 E) said that he could not accept that "if an employer actually provided two means of access, one safe and one unsafe, the section is complied with"—*Held,* also, that there was no liability at common law because, as in *Bolton v. Stone* (Chap. 2, (3) **1**), this was a case where injury was only a remote possibility (10 D).

U6. Kelly v. Structural Painters (1969) C.A. 88

Two routes to roof of building site—one via main staircase—other via an unlashed ladder (not belonging to defendants)—plaintiff used latter—*Held,* that as defendants had neither authorised nor encouraged plaintiff to use ladder, defendants not liable. *Donovan* **5** *applied.*

*(b) Meaning of "Floor"**

			See also Intro. Notes
Planking on gantry of crane—is a "floor"	1	F.A. 1937, s. 25	6, 9
SILL OF DRY DOCK—IS A "FLOOR"	2	F.A. 1937, s. 25	"
SAND SURFACE OF FACTORY—IS A "FLOOR"	3, 4	F.A. 1937, s. 25	"

* Abbreviations are explained in Introductory Note 1.

PLANKING OF STEEL GANTRY—NOT A "FLOOR"	5	F.A. 1937, s. 25	"
Entrance to wharf shed—of beaten earth—not a "floor"	6	F.A. 1937, s. 25	"
Open air woodyard—with unmade earthen surface	7	F.A. 1937, s. 25	"
FACTORY ROAD—NOT A "FLOOR, PASSAGE OR GANGWAY"	8	F.A. 1961, s. 28(1)	9
DUCKBOARD—IS A "FLOOR"	9	F.A. 1961, s. 28(1)	"
Outside yard—not a "floor"	U1		–

1. Morris v. Port of London Authority (1950) 84 Ll.L.R. 564, Pritchard J.

Held, "floor" includes floorboard of gantry on crane.

2. Taylor v. Green (R. & H.) and Silley Weir [1951] 1 Lloyd's Rep. 345, C.A.

Held, semble, that the sill of a dry dock was a "floor." But a dry dock itself is not an "opening in a floor" (*Bath v. B.T.C.* (Chap. 16, (5)(d) **5**)).

3. Harrison v. Metropolitan Vickers [1954] 1 W.L.R. 324; [1954] 1 All E.R. 404, C.A.

Held, the sand surface was a floor, and defendants liable for hole therein.

4. Harper v. Manchester Ship Canal, *The Times*, January 20, 1954; [1954] C.L.Y. 1314, C.A.

Plaintiff fell from a steel gangway over sand bed in foundry into hole in the sand—*Held*, the sand was a floor, and defendants were liable under F.A. 1937, s. 25(3).

5. Tate v. Swan Hunter [1958] 1 W.L.R. 39; [1958] 1 All E.R. 150, C.A.

Held, defendants not liable.

6. Newberry v. Joseph Westwood [1960] 2 Lloyd's Rep. 37, Donovan J.

Held, entrance from wharf to shed consisting of beaten earth was not a "floor" or "passage" or "gangway" within F.A. 1937, s. 25(1).

7. Sullivan v. Hall Russell, 1964 S.L.T. 192, Ct. of Sess.

Held, not a floor.

8. Thornton v. Fisher & Ludlow [1968] 1 W.L.R. 655; [1968] 2 All E.R. 241, C.A.

9. Harper v. Mander and Germain Ltd, *The Times*, December 28, 1992; [1993] C.L.Y. 2014, C.A.

U1. Mullinder v. Gasel (1960) C.A. 209

Semble, an outside yard in a factory is not a "floor."

*(c) Meaning of "Gangway" and "Passage"**

			See also Intro. Notes
Plank—is a "gangway"	1	F.A. 1937, ss. 25 and 26	6, 9
Entrance of beaten earth to shed—not a "gangway"	2	F.A. 1937, s. 25	"
Duckboard on which plaintiff working—not a gangway	3	B.R. 1948, reg. 27	–
Deals supporting Youngman boards—not a gangway	4	B.R. 1948, reg. 27	–
FACTORY ROAD—NOT A GANGWAY	5	F.A. 1961, s. 28	9
DUCKBOARD—CAN BE "GANGWAY" OR "PASSAGE"	6	F.A. 1961, s. 28	"
Country path within curtilage of factory	U1	*F.A. 1937, s. 25*	6, 9

1. Hosking v. De Havilland [1949] 1 All E.R. 540; 83 Ll.L.R. 11, Lewis J.

Plaintiff walking across plank (laid, incidentally, by independent contractor) which breaks—*Held*, plank was a gangway and employers were liable both under F.A. 1937, ss. 25(1) and 26(1).

2. Newberry v. Joseph Westwood [1960] 2 Lloyd's Rep. 37, Donovan J.

3. Regan v. G. & F. Asphalt [1967] 2 K.I.R. 666; [1967] C.L.Y. 370, Blain J.

4. Howitt v. Alfred Bagnall [1967] 2 Lloyd's Rep. 370; [1967] C.L.Y. 372, Waller J.

5. Thornton v. Fisher & Ludlow [1968] 1 W.L.R. 655; [1968] 2 All E.R. 241, C.A.

6. Harper v. Mander and Germain Ltd, *The Times*, December 28, 1992; [1993] C.L.Y. 2014, C.A.

U1. Legg v. Allen West & Co. Ltd (1957) C.A. 74

Held, not a "gangway."

*(d) Meaning of "Opening" in Floor or Ground**

			See also Intro. notes
Inspection pit—is "opening in floor"	1, 2	F.A. 1937, s. 25	6,9
OPEN SPACE AT END OF BAY—NOT "OPENING IN FLOOR"	3	F.A. 1937, s. 25	"
HOLE IN SAND SURFACE OF FACTORY FLOOR—IS "OPENING IN FLOOR"	4, 6	F.A. 1937, s. 25	"
DRY DOCK—NOT "OPENING IN FLOOR"	5	F.A. 1937, s. 25	"

* Abbreviations are explained in Introductory Note 1.

SUNKEN TANK—PROBABLY NOT "OPENING IN GROUND"	7	B.R. 1948, REG. 77	–
SPACE AT EDGE OF STEEL GANTRY PLANKING—PROBABLY NOT "OPENING IN FLOOR"	8	F.A. 1937, s. 25	6, 9
Small ladle pit in foundry—is "opening in floor"	9	F.A. 1961, s.28	9
BAY AT EDGE OF FACTORY FLOOR—NOT "OPENING IN FLOOR"	10	F.A. 1961, ss.28(4), 29	"
Teagle opening—at end of warehouse floor	U1	*F.A. 1937, s. 25*	6, 9
Gap between platforms—not an opening in floor	U2	*F.A. 1937, s. 25*	"

1. Barrington v. Kent Rivers Catchment Board [1947] 2 All E.R. 782; 64 T.L.R. 35.

2. Griffin v. London Transport Executive [1950] 1 All E.R. 716; [1950] W.N. 152.

3. Street v. B.E.A. [1952] 2 Q.B. 399; [1952] 1 All E.R. 679, C.A.

Plaintiff falls down unguarded open space at end of a bay—*Semble*, plaintiff did not fall down an opening in the floor, but over the edge of the floor (864 A).

4. Harrison v. Metropolitan Vickers [1954] 1 W.L.R. 324; [1954] 1 All E.R. 404, C.A.

Held, the sand surface was a floor, and defendants liable for hole therein.

5. Bath v. B.T.C. [1954] 1 W.L.R. 1013; [1954] 2 All E.R. 542, C.A.

Held, a dry dock could not be regarded as an opening in a floor: "Where words are, as the words of section 25 (3) are, perfectly familiar, all one can do is to say whether or not one regards them as apt to cover or describe the circumstances in question in any particular case" (Somervell L. J., 543 C).

6. Harper v. Manchester Ship Canal, *The Times*, January 20, 1954; [1954] C.L.Y. 1314, C.A.

Plaintiff fell from a steel gangway over sand bed in foundry into a hole in the sand—*Held*, the sand was a floor, and defendants were liable under s. 25(3).

7. Knight v. Lambrick Contractors [1957] 1 Q.B. 562; [1956] 3 All E.R. 746, C.A.

8. Tate v. Swan Hunter [1958] 1 W.L.R. 39; [1958] 1 All E.R. 150, C.A.

Held, defendants not liable.

9. Sanders v. Lloyd [1982] I.C.R. 360; [1982] C.L.Y. 1365, Drake J.

Plaintiff twisted ankle in ladle pit in foundry floor—pit 30 inches by 17 inches by 8 inches—*Held*, that pit was an "opening in a floor" for the purpose of s. 28(4), even though a person could not fall into it, and that defendants were liable for failing to cover same (as to which see Chap. 16, (5)(h)**35**), but were not negligent at common law.

10. Allen v. Avon Rubber Co. Ltd [1986] I.C.R. 695; [1987] I.R.L.R. 22, C.A.

Plaintiff depressed wrong pedal on forklift truck and reversed it over edge of bay let into factory floor. Pallets which would usually have been stacked in bay against the edge so as to prevent accidental falls, had been removed for stocktaking—*Held,*

(a) Defendants not in breach of F.A. 1961 s 28(4) by failing to fence bay. Edge of bay was also edge of factory floor, thus bay was not opening in floor.
(b) Defendants in breach of F.A.1961, s 29(1) and negligent, in failing to provide safe place of work. Barrier could have been placed at edge at modest cost. Infrequency of plaintiff's exposure to danger from the edge did not diminish the danger when present.
(c) Plaintiff 50 per cent. to blame.

U1. Kenny v. Hutchinson (1959) C.A. 2

Question whether this was an opening in a floor discussed but not decided.

U2. McHarg v. Stewarts and Lloyds (1963) C.A. 61

Conveyor belt 4 feet wide in shed—on each side were raised platforms—*Held,* the gap between the platforms where the belt was did not constitute an "opening in a floor."

*(e) Meaning of "Workroom," "Working Place", "Working Platform" and "Place"**

			See also Intro. Notes
"Working place"—must be reasonably localised	1	B.R. 1926, reg. 15	–
"Working platform"—must be part of scaffolding, and not main structure	2	B.R. 1948, reg. 22	–
"Working place"—includes temporary flat roof	3	B.R. 1948, reg. 2(1)	–
"WORKROOM"—DOES NOT INCLUDE BOILER ROOM	4	F.A. 1937, s. 47	6
"Temporary platform"—refers to time platform is there, not to user thereof	5	B.R. 1948, reg. 24 (5) (d)	–
"Working place"—restricted in meaning to places akin to working platforms	6	**B.R. 1948, reg. 24(1)**	–
"Working place"—place where plaintiff actually is working	7	M.Q.A. 1954, s. 49	–
"WORKING PLACE"—MAY INCLUDE FLAT ROOF UNDER CONSTRUCTION	8	B.R. 1948, REG. 24	–
"WORKING PLACE"—MAY INCLUDE FLOOR OF BUILDING UNDER DEMOLITION	9	C.(W.P.)R. 1966, REG. 28	–
"Place at which person works"—must be safe *qua* place—not *qua* equipment brought there for a particular operation	10	C(W.P.)R. 1966, reg. 6	–

* Abbreviations are explained in Introductory Note 1.

"WORKING PLACE"—JOB ON ROOF TAKING 10–15 MINUTES—TIME IS SUFFICIENTLY APPRECIABLE TO MAKE PLACE A "WORKING PLACE"	11	C(W.P.)R. 1966, reg. 28	–
"Working place"—may include structure within workshop—fire engine cab being fitted out	12	F.A. 1961, s. 29	9
"Place at which person works"—may be unsafe *qua* essential equipment kept permanently at workplace—compressed air sprayer	13	F.A. 1961, s. 29(1)	"
"WORKING PLACE"—MUST BE SAFE QUA PLACE—DOES NOT CEASE TO BE SAFE BECAUSE PLAINTIFF CARRIED OUT REPAIR TO PLACE NEGLIGENTLY	14	F.A. 1961, s. 29(1)	"
Ships' compartments in which painter working not "workrooms"	15	F.A. 1937 and 1961, s. 4(1)	6,9
Ambit of "place" explained—not confined to floor space	16	F.A. 1961, s. 29(1)	9
"Place" covers not only fabric of but also atmosphere and conditions within the workplace	17	F.A. 1981, s. 29(1)	9
Vibration from caulking hammer—no breach of statutory duty—"place" not dangerous	18	(F.A. 1961, s. 29(1))	9
Forklift truck (seat of which was insecure) held not a "place"	19	F.A. 1961, s. 29(1)	9
Forklift truck held to be a "place"—**19** not followed	20	F.A. 1961, s. 29(1)	9

1. Field v. Perry's [1950] 2 All E.R. 521; [1950] W.N. 320, Devlin J.

Held, that a night watchman's tour of duty could not be regarded as his "working place." *Approved* in **6**.

2. Hutchinson v. Cocksedge [1952] 1 All E.R. 696, Croom-Johnson J.

Plaintiff was on a steel platform drilling holes—the platform was to be part of the building when finished—*Held*, this was not a "working platform" within B.R. 1948, reg. 22, as it was not part of the scaffolding.

3. George Ball v. Sills (1954) 118 J.P. 519; [1954] C.L.Y. 354, D.C.

Workman was working on a building operation on flat upper floor which was temporarily the roof when he fell off unguarded edge—*Held*, this was a working place within B.R. 1948, reg. 24(1). See **6**.

4. Brophy v. Bradfield [1955] 1 W.L.R. 1148; [1955] 3 All E.R. 286, C.A.

Held, that F.A. 1937, ss. 4 and 47 only applied to protect people in "work-rooms," and a boiler room in the circumstances of the case was not a workroom. (*N.B.* Plaintiff had no known business to be in boiler room.)

5. Westcott v. Structural and Marine Engineers [1960] 1 W.L.R. 349; [1960] 1 All E.R. 775, Lord Parker C.J.

Plaintiff fell from a concrete roof where he was erecting a steel chimney—question was whether the roof was a "temporary platform" within B.R. 1948, reg. 24(5)(d), so as to exempt defendants from duty to provide guard rail—*Held*, not, and defendants therefore liable, because "temporary" does not refer to the fact that the platform is only used temporarily, but that it is only there temporarily (777 G).

6. Gill v. Donald Humberstone [1963] 1 W.L.R. 929; [1963] 3 All E.R. 180, H.L.

Creosoting of felt covering of roof which sloped gently at 19 degrees—plaintiff working from ladder laid on roof when, in order to move ladder, he put foot on roof, slipped and fell—he alleged breach of B.R. 1948, reg. 24, in that he fell from working place which had no guard rail—*Held*, reg. 24 did not apply, since he was not at a "working place" at all within the meaning of the regulation; the term had to be construed in its context and was restricted to a place similar to, and having the characteristics of, a working platform. **1** approved. **3** was commented on without approval or disapproval of the decision, since the facts were "obscure"; but the view expressed by Lord Goddard C.J. that a working place ordinarily meant a place where a man was working was assented to, except where (as here) the meaning was qualified by the context.

7. Venn v. N.C.B. [1967] 2 Q.B. 557; [1967] 1 All E.R. 149, Veale J.

"It is the place where he is actually working which is also the place where he has been set to work or in which he may be expected to be" (156 A).

8. Kelly v. Pierhead [1967] 1 W.L.R. 65; [1967] 1 All E.R. 657, C.A.

Held, distinguishing *Gill v. Humberstone* **6**, that a flat roof could, and in this case did, constitute a "working place," so as to require guard rails.

9. Boyton v. Willment [1971] 1 W.L.R. 1625; [1971] 3 All E.R. 624, C.A.

Demolition—one wall removed—and parts of each floor, leaving passageways along which men could move to demolish and throw down material—plaintiff fell from edge of a passageway on the side where the wall had been removed—*Held*, following *Kelly* **8**, he was at a working place within C(W.P.)R. 1966, reg. 28. Buckley L.J. (628 J) said that the passageways were left in order to provide the employees with a space from which they could carry out their work of removing the debris, they were areas of defined and limited extent, and they were not areas where the men would merely work transiently for the time being and then pass on; and as a result they had all the characteristics of a "working place." Edmund Davies L.J. emphasised that the demolition workers were engaged on work in the area concerned for "an appreciable period of time," which in turn was emphasised by Lord Devlin in *Gill* **8** as an important factor in deciding the question.

10. Evans v. Sant [1975] Q.B. 626; [1975] 1 All E.R. 294, D.C.

Laying water main—testing equipment was brought onto site which for some reason produced a dangerous pressure, causing main to blow up—*Held*, "certainly in criminal proceedings," no breach of C.(W.P.)R. 1966, reg. 6(2) (duty to make and keep safe place at which person works).

11. Ferguson v. John Dawson [1976] 1 W.L.R. 1213, C.A.

Throwing scaffolding boards down from roof—12 to 14 boards in all—job taking 10 to 15 minutes—*Held*, this was an appreciable time, so that, following **6**, **8** and **9**, the place where the plaintiff was throwing down the boards was a "working place" within C. (W.P.)R. 1966, reg.28(1).

12. Cox v. Angus (H.C.B.) [1981] I.C.R. 683; [1981] C.L.Y. 1212, Lloyd J.

Held, that a fire engine cab being fitted out in D's workshop was itself a working place, and that it was irrelevant that the structure was temporary: "If the thing on which, or in which, a person is working is sufficiently large, it can itself be the place where he is working, even though it forms part of or is in a larger place."

13. Nixon v. Searle [1982] C.L.Y. 2122, Tudor Evans J.

P injured when lid blew off compressed air sprayer which was kept permanently in, and as an essential part of, the working place—*Held*, applying ratio in *Evans* **10**, defendants liable for breach of F.A. 1961, s.29(1), and also in negligence.

14. Wilson v. Wallpaper Manufacturers [1982] C.L.Y 1364, C.A.

15. Bryce v. Swan Hunter Group plc [1988] I All E.R. 659; [1987] 2 Lloyds Rep. 426; Phillips J.

See Chap. 16, (3)(b) **18** for full details.

16. Yates v. Rockwell Graphic Systems Ltd [1988] I.C.R. 8; [1988] C.L.Y. 1739, Steyn J.

From 1956, plaintiff's hands were regularly in contact with contaminated coolant, from which arose a known and substantial risk of dermatitis. Notices warned employees regularly to wash their hands and use barrier cream, but there was no system of inspecting or cleaning the coolant until 1987. Plaintiff developed dermatitis in 1978—*Held*, defendants liable at common law and for breach of F.A. 1961, s.29(1). *Per* Steyn J. at 14, "place" in s.29 (1) did not simply mean the floor space within a factory: "One has to have regard to the permanently installed machinery and the regular activities carried on in the factory in order to decide whether the place is safe." Reasonably practicable steps were available to make the place safe, namely regular inspection and cleaning of coolant such as was introduced in 1987.

17. Baxter v. Harland & Wolff plc [1990] I.R.L.R. 516; [1991] C.L.Y. 1878, N.I. C.A.

Held, finding employees in breach of s. 27 of Factories (Northern Ireland) Act 1938 (equivalent of F.A. 1961, s.29 (1)) in industrial deafness case. *Yates* **16** followed.

18. Bowman v. Harland & Wolff plc [1992] I R.L.R. 349; [1992] C.L.Y. 3222, Carswell J., N.I.

Plaintiffs were employed at defendant's Belfast shipyard from the 1950s and 1960s onwards—regularly used hand-held caulking hammers, vibration from which caused them to suffer from Raynaud's Phenomenon, also known as "vibration white finger"—*Held*, defendant liable in negligence but plaintiffs also claimed, *inter alia*, a breach of s. 30(1) of Factories (Northern Ireland) Act 1965 (identical to F.A. 1961, s.29 (1)). Carswell J. dismissed this claim: "In order to make the place of work unsafe the danger has to come from something which makes the place itself dangerous . . . When a caulker commences . . . operating his caulking hammer on a piece of metal . . . the danger of physical harm from the vibration thereby created comes solely from that operation and is limited to himself . . . In a case such as the present the operation may create danger but the place itself is not unsafe."

19. McFaulds v. Reed Corrugated Cases, 1993 S.L.T. 670; [1993] C.L.Y. 5358

20. Gunion v. Roche Products, *The Scotsman,* October 19, 1994; [1994] C.L.Y. 5887

Plaintiff's hand became trapped in door of forklift truck—*Held,* the truck was a "place" within s.29 (1). There was nothing in the Act to suggest that "place" and "plant" were mutually exclusive.

*(f) Safety of Means of Ascent**

			See also Intro. Notes
Ladder—latent corrosion in screws of rung—"maintained"	1	F.A. 1937, s. 25	6,9
Safe access—means (*i.e.* ladders) available but not in position	2	F.A. 1937, s. 25	6,9
Safe access—gap of 4 feet 6 in.—ladders available	3	"	6.9
SAFE—MEANS OF ACCESS—"SAFE" EXPLAINED	4	"	"
SAFE ACCESS—UNMANNED LADDER SLIPPING	4	"	"
Safe means of access—not trestles for getting up to platform	5	S.R. 1931, reg. 1	–
Dry dock—rough ground and débris—no guard rail round altar steps	6	F.A. 1937, s. 26	6,9
ACCESS—TO SILL OF DRY DOCK	7	"	"
ACCESS—STATUTORY DUTY SAME AS COMMON LAW—TEST MUST HAVE REGARD TO SURROUNDING CIRCUMSTANCES	7	"	"
Ladder—"adequate strength"—rung breaking	8	B.R. 1948, reg. 29	–
staircase—whether two handrails required—"condition of surface" and "special circumstances"	9	F.A. 1937, S. 25	6.9
Access to hold—two ladders—one unsafe	10	D.R. 1934, regs. 11, 47	5
Safe access—lighthearted user—access must be strong enough to withstand	10	D.R. 1934, reg. 11	"
Safe access—steep altar courses of drydock	11	S.R. 1931, reg. 1.	–
Safe access—not a descent of 2 feet 6 in. from one staging to another with a gap between staging and ship	12	"	–
Safe access—not a ladder with rope wound round rung	13	D.R. 1934, reg. 11	5
HAND-RAIL ON STAIRS—WHETHER MUST BE SUCH AS TO PREVENT FALLING OVER OPEN SIDE	14	B.R. 1948, REG. 27	–

* Abbreviations are explained in Introductory Note 1. See also the cases in Chap. 16,(8)(f).

STAIRS—INCLUDES UNCOMPLETED STAIRS	14	B.R. 1948, REG. 27	–
STAIRCASE—NOT A SET OF THREE STEEL STEPS UP TO PLATFORM	15	F.A. 1937, s. 25	6,9
LADDER—OBSTRUCTING PROJECTION 6 IN. AWAY FROM SIDE	16	S.R. 1931, REG. 1	–
LADDER UNFOOTED AND UNSECURED—NO INSTRUCTIONS BY EMPLOYERS—EMPLOYERS RELY ON PLAINTIFF	17	B.R. 1948, REG. 5	–
Gangway to barge plank 20 in. wide with no hand-rail	18	F.A. 1937, s. 26	6.9
Staircase—not a ramp over steps	19	F.A. 1937, s. 25	6,9
Broken step in transit shed	20	"	"
Ladder—propped against cableway	21	**F.A. 1937, s. 26**	"
LADDER—CHARGEHAND GOING UP UNFOOTED	22	B.R. 1948, REG. 29	–
LADDER—SLIPPING—IS PRIMA FACIE EVIDENCE OF UNSAFETY	23	F.A. 1961, s. 29	9
Ladder—mounting before lashed at top—employer has duty to see regulations enforced	24	**B.R. 1948, reg. 29**	–
Ladder—from deck to quay—suspended on wires instead of resting on its wheels	25	D.R. 1934, reg. 9	5
PORTABLE SET OF STEPS—UNSAFE AND SET UP BY EMPLOYEES—OTHER SAFE MEANS OF ACCESS AVAILABLE	26	F.A. 1961, s. 29	9
Ladder "affords a means of access or egress" if used as such, even if not put there for that purpose	27	C.(W.P.)R. 1966, reg. 32	–
Unlit steel staircase	28	F.A. 1961, s. 29(1)	9
Vertical ladder without loops	29	F.A. 1961, ss. 5, 29(1)	"
Ladder—kept available for getting up to and down from crane	U1	*F.A. 1937, s. 26*	6.9
Fixed ladder—ending at platform level—hand-rail up to that level	U2	"	"
Staircase—not three steps	U3	*F.A. 1937, s. 25*	"
Ladder—insecurely placed by plaintiff	U4	*B.R. 1948, reg. 5*	–
Ladder—insecurely placed by plaintiff	U5	*B.R. 1948, reg. 29*	–
Ladder—unfooted	U6	"	–
Aluminium ladder—no rubber feet	U7	"	–
Ladder—slipping—breach not proved	U8	*F.A. 1961, s. 29*	9
Temporary steps instead of ladder—risers 16 inches deep at top—safe	U9	"	"
Unfooted ladder—plaintiff's mate going away to phone	U10	*C.(W.P)R. 1966, reg. 32*	–
Staircase—not three stone steps leading to yard	U11	*F.A. 1961, s. 28*	9
Unfastened and unfooted ladder used as regular means of access	U12	*F.A. 1961, s. 29*	"

1. Cole v. Blackstone [1943] K.B. 615; (1943) 59 T.L.R. 374, Macnaghten J.

Held, "maintained" as defined by s. 152(1) imported an absolute duty to ensure ladder in an efficient state. *Followed* in **10**.

2. O'Mahony v. Press (1948) 92 S.J. 311; [1948] C.L.C. 3971, Atkinson J.

Held, occupiers of factory not liable for breach of statutory duty.

3. Farquar v. Chance Bros [1951] W.N. 442; 115 J.P. 469, D.C.

Held, no breach of statutory duty.

4. McCarthy v. Coldair [1951] W.N. 590; [1951] 2 T.L.R. 1226, C.A.

Ten-foot ladder was placed at proper angle for plaintiff—it slipped—*Held*, that there was not merely a slight but substantial risk it would slip, and therefore not a safe means of ascent: ' "Safe' means safe for all contingencies that may reasonably be foreseen, unlikely as well as likely, possible as well as probable." See Chap. 16(2) (b) **2**.

5. Daniels v. Frederick Leyland [1951] 1 Lloyd's Rep. 59, Pritchard J.

Held, defendants liable for not providing ladder to get up to platform, so that plaintiff had to mount by the trestles.

6. Welch v. Admiralty [1952] 2 Lloyd's Rep. 520, Havers J.

Plaintiff a ship's painter (not employed by defendants) going along side of dry dock in order to get to place of work when he stumbles on a piece of debris on rough ground and falls headlong down altar steps to bottom—*Held*, there should have been a guard rail round altar steps, particularly in view of rough ground, and defendants liable under F.A. 1937, s. 26(1) (access).

7. Moncrieff v. Swan Hunter [1953] 2 Lloyd's Rep. 149, C.A.

Plaintiff lowering himself by rope onto third sill of dry dock—*Held*, no failure to provide safe access. Denning L.J. at 150: "In considering . . . 'safe means of access,' it is very necessary to bear in mind the nature of the place, the experience of the man and the general practice in the industry. As Pritchard J. said on one occasion you cannot expect the floor of a dock to be as free from obstruction as a dance floor . . . It has often been said that F.A. 1937, s. 26, adds very little to the common law duty of the employer . . . ".

8. Johnson v. Croggan [1954] 1 W.L.R. 195; [1954] 1 All E.R. 121, Pilcher J.

Held, ladder not of "adequate strength." *But* plaintiff was defeated on delegation, *ex turpi causa* and contributory negligence, *q.v.*

9. Harris v. Rugby Portland Cement [1955] 1 W.L.R. 648; [1955] 2 All E.R. 500 C.A.

Piece of grease deposited on top stair—nearby was a hatchway from which grease was issued—*Held*, there was nothing in the "condition of the surface" and no "special circumstances" which were "specially liable to cause accidents" and therefore defendants not liable.

10. Cottrell v. Lianda S.S. [1955] 2 Lloyd's Rep. 450, Devlin J.

Two ladders into hold—one iron and one wooden—plaintiff uses wooden one which breaks—defendants say (a) that plaintiff should have used the iron one, which was the access "provided" and (b) that he was playing the fool on the ladder—*Held*, defendants liable, because (a) plaintiff was reasonably justified in regarding it as a proper means of access, and (b) a ladder, to be "safe," must be able to withstand some degree of lighthearted user.

11. Hurley v. Sanders [1955] 1 W.L.R. 470; [1955] 1 All E.R. 833, Glyn-Jones J.

Defendants ship repairers had sub-contracted work of applying anti-fouling paint to plaintiff's employers—plaintiff had to descend steep altar courses of dry dock to get at ship's bottom—slipped in doing so—*Held*, following *Day v. Harland & Wolff* (Chap. 16, (2)(h) **6**), this was work of "repair," and the access was not safe (for reasons, see Chap. 15, (5) **9**).

12. Smith v. London Graving Dock [1956] 1 Lloyd's Rep. 186, Lord Goddard C.J.

13. Mace v. R. & H. Green & Silley Weir [1959] 2 Q.B. 14; [1959] 1 All E.R. 655, Lord Parker C.J.

14. Corn v. Weir's Glass [1960] 1 W.L.R. 557; [1960] 1 All E.R. 300, C.A.

Plaintiff on a building operation overbalanced and fell over open side of stairs while carrying large sheet of glass—fall of 3 feet to ground—open side unprotected—defendants not in breach of B.R. 1948, reg. 27(2) (guard rail) because fall of less than 6 feet 6 in. but were in breach of B.R. 1948, reg. 27(1), in that no hand-rail was provided—*Held*, that "hand-rail" here did not mean something which would serve as a guard rail (although in cases under F.A. 1937, s. 25(2), it probably did), and as plaintiff had not proved that a hand-rail *simpliciter* would have prevented his injuries (see Chap. 16, (3) (b) **12** for fuller details), defendants not liable—*Held*, also, that "stairs" included uncompleted stairs.

15. Kimpton v. Steel Company of Wales [1960] 1 W.L.R. 527; [1960] 2 All E.R. 274, C.A.

16. Davies v. J. L. Thompson [1960] 1 Lloyd's Rep. 22, C.A.

Held, safe.

17. Boden v. Moore (1961) 105 S.J. 510, C.A.

Held, 50:50.

18. Moor v. Greenhithe Lighterage [1961] 1 Lloyd's Rep. 149, Elwes J.

Held, that a gangway to a barge in a barge yard (which constituted a factory) consisting of a plank 20 in. wide with no hand-rail was not safe access within F.A. 1937, s. 26(1), and defendants were liable.

19. Roast v. Nortic Electrical (1961) 111 L.J. 598; [1961] C.L.Y. 3523, Thesiger J.

Held, ramp laid over steps leading to warehouse was not a "staircase" within F.A. 1937, s. 25(1). *But* defendants were liable at common law.

20. Fisher v. Port of London Authority [1962] 1 All E.R. 358, Stevenson J.

Held, defendants liable for breach of F.A. 1937, s. 25(1).

21. Ross v. Associated Portland Cement Manufacturers [1964] 1 W.L.R. 768; [1964] 2 All E.R. 452, H.L.

Held, unsafe.

22. Hammill v. Camborne Water Co., (1964) 108 S.J. 335; [1964] C.L.Y. 374, C.A.

Held, plaintiff's breach co-extensive with that of defendants, since it was his duty to see the Regulations were observed, and his claim failed.

23. Garner v. John Thompson (1968) 112 S.J. 1006; *The Times*, November 28, 1968, C.A.

Plaintiff standing on ladder which slipped—he called no evidence as to why it slipped—defendants called no evidence at all—*Held*, proof of slipping was prima facie evidence of unsafety under F.A. 1961, s.29, and defendants were liable. *cf.* **U8**.

24. Boyle v. Kodak [1969] 1 W.L.R. 661; [1969] 2 All E.R. 439, H.L.

Held, breach of Regulations, and employers 50 per cent. liable for failing to take reasonable steps to prevent employee committing breach.

25. Watson v. Ben Line [1971] 2 Lloyd's Rep. 269, Bridge J.

Held, ladder safe.

26. Smith v. British Aerospace [1982] I.C.R. 98; [1982] C.L.Y. 1368, C.A.

Held, employers not liable. For details see Chap. 16, (5)(a) **19**.

27. Lanigan v. Derek Crouch Construction Ltd, 1985 S.L.T. 346 n.

28. Davies v. Massey Ferguson Perkins [1986] I.C.R. 580; [1986] C.L.Y. 1539, Evans J.

Plaintiff on night shift missed footing when descending outside steel staircase, the light at the bottom of which was not working—stumbled and injured back—*Held*, defendant in breach of duty under F.A. 1961, s. 5(1) to maintain sufficient and suitable lighting, which was absolute. Also in breach of F.A. 1961, s. 29(1)—system for repairing lighting defects once reported was satisfactory, but for discovering and reporting defects was not, dependent on periodic patrols of parts of factory site by security guard or reports of defects by individual workmen. On available evidence, plaintiff had not proved that defendant negligent at common law.

29. Sloan v. Almond Fabrication, 1992 S.L.T. 114; [1992] C.L.Y. 5820

Held, a near vertical ladder, 22 feet high, with no protective loops, by which access was gained to the driving cab of a crane in a factory, was not a safe means of access, either at common law or under F.A. 1961, s. 29(1).

U1. Senior v. Fowler (1952) C.A. 69

Held, safe means of access.

U2. Cole v. Berk & Co. Ltd (1956) C.A. 76

Held, defendants not liable.

U3. Rogers v. News of the World Ltd (1958) C.A. 295

U4. Forsdike v. Meek (1963) C.A. 92

Fall from ladder which plaintiff had positioned insecurely—*Held*, no breach of B.R. 1948, reg. 5, as work would have been safe if ladder securely placed. *But* defendants were partly liable at common law for failing to give proper instructions how to place ladder.

U5. Finn v. Sprosson (1964) C.A. 100

Held, although this constituted a breach by defendants, plaintiff himself was entirely responsible, and defendants were not liable. *N.B.* Ladder in this case was less than 10 feet long.

U6. Parsons v. Porter (1964) C.A. 116

Plaintiff fell from unfooted ladder more than 10 feet long—the employee who should have footed it had gone away—*Held*, 50:50. Defendants were liable for employee's failure to foot, and plaintiff because he took no steps to see that ladder was secured at base.

U7. Shanton v. Cynamid of Great Britain (1964) C.A. 246

No rubber feet on aluminium ladder, which slips—*Held*, employers one-third liable, and plaintiff two-thirds for sending away assistant who should have footed ladder.

U8. Hodgkinson v. Enfield Standard (1971) C.A. 378

Ladder slipped sideways—it was of good construction, properly footed, etc.—accident probably occurred because plaintiff leaned over too far—*Held*, no breach of F.A. 1961, s. 29(1). *Garner* **23** *distinguished*, on the ground that there the defence had called no evidence to negative the chance of unsound construction, unduly slippery floor, defective suckers, etc.

U9. Plant v. English Electric (1972) C.A. 317

U10. Milsom v. Strachan and Henshaw (1973) C.A. 356

Plaintiff going up unfooted ladder—thereby breach of C. (W.P.) R. 1966—someone had been available to foot ladder—but had gone away, as plaintiff thought, to phone—*Held*, 50:50, as if defendants did not provide someone to foot ladder, they must warn him "clearly and specifically" against risk of going up by himself.

U11. Mardy v. Hawker Siddeley (1977) C.A. 75

Held, applying **15** and **U3**.

U12. Smith v. B.R.B. (1985) C.A. 577

Employees regularly had to gain access to storage area 10 feet above ground level, using any available ladder. Plaintiff was injured when unfastened and unfooted ladder he was using for this purpose slipped—*Held*, defendants liable in negligence and in breach of F.A. 1961, s. 29—means of access were unsafe—a permanently fastened ladder, or means of easily fastening a ladder, were called for—it was plainly foreseeable that men would use an insecure ladder. Plaintiff 50 per cent to blame, for stopping on a rung above the level of the storage area, knowing the ladder to be insecure.

*(g) Safety of Elevated Places**

			See also Intro. Notes
Plank—breaking	1	F.A. 1937, s. 26	6.9
ROOF—MADE OF BRITTLE ASBESTOS	2	F.A. 1937, s. 26	"
Roof—gutter with duckboards removed	3	F.A. 1937, s. 26	"
Gangway—ordinarily secure—adjacent explosion	4	F.A. 1937, s. 26	"
Ladder—window cleaner	5	**F.A. 1937, s. 26**	"
Gangway—ordinarily secure—adjacent shotblasting	6	F.A. 1937, s. 26	"
Staging—dismantling—obligation as to good construction etc., continues	7	S.R. 1960, reg. 17 (1)	–
Concrete window sill 4 feet by 5 feet—to drill hole in wall with heavy and awkward hammer	8	**C.(G.P.)R. 1961, reg. 7 (2)**	–
STEEL ERECTION—STEEL ERECTOR SITTING ASTRIDE BEAM	9	C.(G.P.)R., 1961, REG. 7 (2)	–
Platform 4 feet high—with rail 4 feet high surrounding it—plaintiff working on bus—falls under rail	10	F.A. 1961, s. 29	9
STACK OF BALES 21 FEET HIGH—PLAINTIFF ON TOP HOOKING BALES TO CRANE—IS SAFE	11	F.A. 1961, s. 29	"
ELEVATED WALKWAY—DISPLACED TOE-BOARD—ABSOLUTE DUTY IMPOSED BY AND SCOPE OF REG. 30 (2)	12	C.(W.P.)R., 1966, REG. 30 (2)	–
PLAINTIFF WORKING ON UNFENCED PLATFORM—DID NOT HAVE TO DO SO, SINCE FORKLIFT TRUCK WITH CAGE AVAILABLE—DEFENDANT NOT LIABLE	13	F.A. 1961, s. 29 (2)	9
Ladder as place of work—F.A. 1961 s. 29 (2) applies	U1	F.A. 1961, s. 29	"
Using fork lift truck to replace light—safe without guard rail	U2	F.A. 1961, s. 29	"

1. Hosking v. De Havilland [1949] 1 All E.R. 540, Lewis J.

Plaintiff walking across plank (laid, incidentally, by independent contractor) which breaks—*Held*, plank was a gangway and employers were liable both under ss. 25(1) and 26(1).

2. Lavender v. Diamints [1949] 1 K.B. 585; [1949] 1 All E.R. 532, C.A.

Held, not a safe means of access for plaintiff (a window cleaner).

3. Whincup v. Woodhead [1951] 1 All E.R. 387, McNair J.

Held, not safe access.

* Abbreviations are explained in Introductory Note 1. See also Introductory Notes 3 (A) and (F), and the cases in Chap. 16(8)(d), (e) and (g).

4. Tinto v. Stewart and Lloyds, 1962 S.L.T. 314, O.H.

Unfenced elevated gangway affording secure foothold in all ordinary circumstances—explosion sending forth flames and smoke round gangway—*Held*, foothold did not thereby become insecure within F.A. 1937, s. 26(2).

5. Wigley v. British Vinegars [1964] A.C. 307; [1962] 3 All E.R. 161, H.L.

Deceased window cleaner employed as independent contractor to clean factory windows—he was provided by factory occupier with a sound ladder, from which he fell—window was a pivoted one, so that deceased had to use one hand to press against window while cleaning other portion with other hand—*Held*, no breach of F.A. 1937, s. 26(2), because the ladder afforded a secure foothold and if necessary handhold within the meaning of the section; the place from which he was liable to fall was the ladder, which provided secure foothold and handhold

6. Amis v. Smith's Dock Company [1963] 1 Lloyd's Rep. 181, Veale J.

Gangway intrinsically safe—became unsafe by reason of shotblasting in vicinity—*Held*, the means of access did not thereby become unsafe.

7. Graham v. Greenock Dockyard, 1965 S.L.T. 61; [1965] C.L.Y. 2654, Ct. of Sess.

8. O'Donnell v. Murdoch Mackenzie, 1967 S.C.(H.L.) 63; 3 K.I.R. 299, H.L.

Held, not safe.

9. Woods v. Power Gas Corporation (1969) 8 K.I.R. 834; [1970] C.L.Y. 247, C.A.

Held, the work was safe, as sitting astride a steel girder to insert bolts was a familiar position for a skilled steel erector.

10. McClymont v. Glasgow Corporation, 1971 S.L.T. 45, Ct. of Sess.

Held, defendant liable under F.A. 1961, s. 29, as the gap under rail could well have been filled with wire mesh, but 75 per cent. contributory negligence.

11. Thompson v. Bowaters [1975] K.I.L.R. 47; [1975] C.L.Y. 1427, C.A.

So held, the decision turning mainly on the fact that, due to the rarity of accidents in the industry of this sort and to the prevalence of the system used, it was not reasonably practicable to adopt better methods.

12. McGovern v. B.S.C. [1986] I.C.R. 608; [1986] I.R.L.R. 411, C.A.

See Chap. 16, (3)(b) **17** for further details.

13. Walsh v. Crown Decorative Products [1993] P.I.Q.R. P.194; [1994] C.L.Y. 2293, C.A.

See Chap. 16, (4)(d) **19** for further details.

U1. Shanton v. Cynamid of Great Britain (1964) C.A. 246

Said by Willmer L.J. (4 D), *obiter*, that F.A. 1961, s. 29(2) applies to a place of work on a ladder, on the authority of *Wigley* **5**.

U2. Gale v. Westinghouse (1969) C.A. 57

*(h) Safety at Ground Level**

			See also Intro. Note
OBSTRUCTION—IRON BARS ON FLOOR	1	F.A. 1937, s. 26	6, 9
Collapse—floor gives way under weight of Jack	2	F.A. 1937, s. 25	6, 9
OBSTRUCTION—REDUCING WIDTH OF GANGWAY	3	F.A. 1937, s. 26	6, 9
Collapse—edge of gantry floor breaking	4	F.A. 1937, s. 25	6, 9
Slipping—grease and/or rainwater in depression	5	F.A. 1937, s. 25	6, 9
OBSTRUCTION—AIR LINE ON SILL OF DOCK	6	F.A. 1937, ss. 25, 26	6, 9
Tripping—rough ground and debris round dry dock	7	F.A. 1937, s. 26	6, 9
Slipping—oil and water coming on due to sudden storm	8	**F.A. 1937, s. 25**	6, 9
OBSTRUCTION—PROJECTING ON TO MARKED GANGWAY	9	F.A. 1937, s. 26	6, 9
OBSTRUCTION—TO BE EXPECTED ON DOCK FLOORS	10	F.A. 1937, s. 25	6, 9
SLIPPING—EARLY MORNING SNOW ON FACTORY APPROACH	11	F.A. 1937, s. 26	6, 9
OBSTRUCTION—GROOVE AND LOOSE STEEL PLATE ON FLOOR	12	F.A. 1937, s. 25	6, 9
Slipping—patch of ice on cold store floor	13	F.A. 1937, s. 25	6, 9
TRIPPING—MANHOLE COVER AND GRATING AT DIFFERENT HEIGHTS	14	F.A. 1937, s. 25	6, 9
TRIPPING—RIDGE OF SAND ON FLOOR	15	F.A. 1937, ss. 25, 26	6, 9
Maintenance—meaning of "properly maintained"	16	F.A. 1937, s. 25	6, 9
Slipping—metal rod on floor	17	F.A. 1959, s. 4	6, 9
Obstruction—piece of dunnage on warehouse floor	18	F.A. 1961, ss. 28/29	9
SLIPPING—FLOOR OF SAUSAGE FACTORY	19	F.A. 1959, s. 4	6, 9
Obstruction—vertical angle iron projecting above floor level—part of fixed machine	20		–
Obstruction—two heavy plates lying at angle on factory floor—slippery through covering of slag dust	21		–

* Abbreviations are explained in Introductory Note 1. See also Introductory Note 3 (F).

Slipping—metal plate covered with film of slag dust	21		–
Obstruction—rod in passageway—alleged failure to instruct employees not to throw or deposit things	22		–
OBSTRUCTION—MOULD PLACED ON FLOOR OF GANGWAY	23		–
OBSTRUCTION—PAPER REELS STORED ON FLOOR	24	F.A. 1961, s. 28	9
OBSTRUCTION—TROLLEY PARTIALLY IN GANGWAY	25	F.A. 1961, s. 28	9
Slipping—viscous fluid leaking—plaintiff slipping while clearing up	26	F.A. 1961, s. 28	9
Slipping—water coming on passage after heavy rain	27	F.A. 1961, s. 28	9
Obstruction—pile of scrap metal Knocked off castings	28	**F.A. 1961, s. 28**	9
Obstruction—not reasonably practicable to remove in time	28	**F.A. 1961, s. 28**	9
SLIPPING—CANTEEN WORKER SLIPPING ON WATER ON FLOOR—STANDARD OF CARE THE SAME UNDER BOTH SECTIONS	29	F.A. 1961, ss. 28,29	9
Screw on floor	30	F.A. 1961, s.28	9
Tripping on wire on factory floor	31	F.A. 1961, s.28	9
Slipping—factory yard—snow and slush not cleared by 11 a.m.—defendants liable	32	F.A. 1961, s.29	9
Slipping—ice on car park—by foot-path into factory	33	F.A. 1961, s.29	9
Floor of fire engine cab being fitted out—loose piping	34	F.A. 1961, s.29	9
Small opening in floor—requirement to fence includes requirement to cover	35	F.A. 1961, s.28 (4)	9
SLIPPING—OIL ON FLOOR—ONUS ON DEFENDANTS TO SHOW REASONABLE STEPS TAKEN TO PREVENT IT GETTING THERE	36	F.A. 1961, s. 28	9
OBSTRUCTION—NOT ANGLE IRON PROPERLY STORED AT SIDE OF ROAD	37	M.Q.A. 1954, s. 34	–
ICE ON FACTORY CAR PARK—SLIPPING	38	F.A. 1961, s.29(1)	9
Hole in floor—coloured tape around	39	F.A. 1961, s.29(2)	9
Slipping—ice in front of factory door	40	F.A. 1961, s.29(1)	9
BAY AT EDGE OF FACTORY FLOOR—NO BARRIER—DEFENDANT LIABLE	41	F.A. 1961, s.29(1)	9
SHIPPING—SNOW AND ICE IN LARGE WEATHER-EXPOSED CAR PARK—DEFENDANT NOT LIABLE	42	F.A. 1961, s.29(1)	9

Contractor's employee falling through defective roof—whether knowledge of defect must be proved—meaning of "has to work"	43	F.A. 1961, s.29(1)	9
METAL STRUCTURE COLLAPSING ONTO PLAINTIFF—DEFENDANT LIABLE	44	F.A. 1961, s.29(1)	9
Yarn tied across passageway as "practical joke"—defendant not liable	45	F.A. 1961, ss.28, 29(1)	9
Machine tipping over—defendant liable even though accident not reasonably foreseeable	46	F.A. 1961, s.29(1)	9
Slipping—soapy material regularly flowing on to floor	U1	*F.A. 1937, s.25*	6,9
Slipping—smooth steel plate in passage	U2	*F.A. 1937, s. 26*	6, 9
Obstruction—steel plates on slag floor of factory	U3	*F.A. 1961, s. 29*	9
Slipping—grease on floor	U4	*F.A. 1961, s. 28*	9
Slipping—grease on floor	U5	*F.A. 1961, s. 28*	9
Obstruction—bobbins projecting over white line of gangway—22 feet left between lines	U6	*F.A. 1961, s. 28*	9
Gap in passage—having to go through it sideways	U7	*F.A. 1961, s. 29*	9
Slipping—grease spot from overhead crane	U8	*F.A. 1961, s. 28*	9
Slipping—grease on floor	U9	*F.A. 1961, s. 28*	9
Slipping—ice on factory path—no steps taken for 24 hours	U10	*F.A. 1961, s. 29*	9
Slipping—wax applied to, but not wiped off, floor	U11	*O.S.R.P.A. 1963, s. 16*	9
Obstruction—not trolley on floor of depot	U12	*F.A. 1961, s. 28*	9
Obstruction—not brick protruding 2 inches in walkway of mine	U13	*M.Q.A. 1954, s. 34*	–
Swarf—swept at end of day	U14	*F.A. 1961, s. 29*	9
Knowledge of plaintiff that floor unsafe—how far relevant	U15	*F.A. 1961, s. 28*	9
Floor—sweeping twice a day	U16	*F.A. 1961, s. 29*	9
Obstruction—metal tray protruding one foot into passageway	U17	*F.A. 1961, s. 28*	9
Obstruction—box on floor—reducing width of gangway	U18	*O.S.R.P.A. 1963, s. 16*	9
Slipping—floor of w.c. wet—defendants liable	U19	*O.S.R.P.A. 1963, s. 16*	9
Slipping—ice on factory path—in early a.m.—gritting washed away by rain earlier in night	U20	*F.A. 1961, s. 29*	9

Obstruction—not boxes of components—or loose rocker cover—visible and stored	U21	*F.A. 1961, s. 28*	9
Floor—pile of swept rubbish left standing	U22	*F.A. 1961, s. 28*	9
Road in mine covered with ice and snow	U23	*M.Q.A. 1954, s. 34*	–
Power socket bolted to floor—not an "obstruction"	U24	*O.S.R.P.A. 1963, s. 16*	9
Corner of floor tile standing $\frac{1}{4}$ inch proud	U25	*F.A. 1961, s. 29(1)*	9
Rail $3\frac{1}{2}$ inches wide giving egress down to floor	U26	*F.A. 1961, s. 29(1)*	9
Swarfega on floor	U27	*F.A. 1961, s. 28(1)*	9
Wooden batten on ill-lit floor	U28	*F.A. 1961 s. 28(1)*	9
Metal grating protruding $\frac{1}{2}$ inch	U29	*F.A. 1961, ss. 28(1), 29(1)*	9
Pallets protruding 2 feet into main gangway	U30	*F.A. 1961, s. 28(1)*	9
Exerting force while standing on step-ladder	U31	*F.A. 1961, s. 29(1)*	9
Plug on floor of aisle	U32	*F.A. 1961, s. 28(1)*	9
Moving large sheet of glass in confined space—defendant not liable	U33	*F.A. 1961, s. 29(1)*	9
Manoeuvring heavy steel member in confined space—defendant liable	U34	*F.A. 1961, s. 29(1)*	9
Snow and ice on factory car park—policy decision by defendant not to clear same	U35	*F.A. 1961, s. 29(1)*	9
Cast iron radiator stored beneath table	U36	*F.A. 1961, ss. 28(1), 29(1)*	9

1. Callaghan v. Fred Kidd [1944] 1 K.B. 560, C.A.

Plaintiff while moving from one grindstone to another 15 yards away tripped on some iron bars which had been put there—*Held*, defendants liable for failing to maintain safe means of access.

2. Mayne v. Johnstone & Cumbers Ltd [1947] 2 All E.R. 159, Lynskey J.

Deceased was installing a heavy machine when the floor supporting the jack gave way—*Held*, that words in s. 25(1) "of sound construction and properly maintained" meant so constructed and maintained as to be fit for the work which it is anticipated is to be done on it, and applying this test defendants were liable.

3. Hopwood v. Rolls-Royce (1947) 176 L.T. 514, C.A.

Held, that an access which had been reduced by 4 feet wide by two aeroplane cylinder heads was not "safe" for plaintiff and workmate carrying a 4-foot-long cylinder head weighing 89 lb.

4. Morris v. Port of London Authority (1950) 84 Ll.L.R. 564, Pritchard J.

Held, defendants liable.

5. Davies v. De Havilland [1951] 1 K.B. 50; [1950] 2 All E.R. 582, Somervell L.J.

Held, defendants not liable.

6. Taylor v. R. & H. Green and Silley Weir [1951] 1 Lloyd's Rep. 345, C.A.

Held, that the sill, which was part of the floor of the dock, was properly maintained, and no liability under s. 25(1) or 26(1).

7. Welch v. Admiralty [1952] 2 Lloyd's Rep. 520, Havers J.

Plaintiff a ship's painter (not employed by defendants) going along side of dry dock in order to get to place of work when he stumbles on a piece of debris on rough ground and falls headlong down altar steps to bottom—*Held*, there should have been a guard rail round altar steps, particularly in view of rough ground, and defendants liable under F.A. 1937, s. 26(1) (access).

8. Latimer v. A.E.C. [1953] A.C. 643; [1953] 2 All E.R. 449, H.L.

Oil and water coming onto floor due to sudden storm—*Held*, the duty to maintain referred to the general condition and soundness of construction, and not to some transient and exceptional condition such as the oil and water in question, and therefore defendants not liable under F.A. 1937, s. 25(1). *N.B.* F.A. 1961, s. 28(1) now adds a duty to keep floors, passages and gangways free from obstructions and substances likely to cause persons to slip, so that in similar cases there is now an additional criterion. The decision, of course, remains an authority on the duty to *maintain* floors. *Applied* in **9** and **13.**

9. Levesley v. Thomas Firth [1953] 1 W.L.R. 1206; [1953] 2 All E.R. 866, C.A.

Steel packing piece projecting into marked way of factory floor—*Held*, following **8**, that as it was only there temporarily, and as "the time involved was very short," defendants not liable for not maintaining safe access.

10. Moncrieff v. Swan Hunter [1953] 2 Lloyd's Rep. 149, C.A.

Plaintiff lowering himself by rope onto third sill of dry dock—*Held*, no failure to provide safe access. Denning L.J. at 150: "In considering . . . 'safe means of access,' it is very necessary to bear in mind the nature of the place, the experience of the man and the general practice in the industry. As Pritchard J. said on one occasion you cannot expect the floor of a dock to be as free from obstruction as a dance floor . . . It has often been said that F.A. 1937, s. 25, adds very little to the common law duty of the employer . . . ".

11. Thomas v. Bristol Aeroplane [1954] 1 W.L.R. 694; [1954] 2 All E.R. 1, C.A.

Held, defendants not liable: "The risks which resulted that morning at that time from the vagaries of the weather were no more than the risks which form a part of the ordinary incidents of daily life to which all are subject" (Morris L.J., 4 A).

12. Payne v. Weldless Steel [1956] 1 Q.B. 196; [1955] 3 All E.R. 612, C.A.

Groove in floor, with steel plate in it which tipped as plaintiff walked across—county court judge found for defendants—*Held*, findings should not be disturbed. Plaintiff argued first that the test under s. 25(1) was not so much safety as efficiency, to which C.A. replied that "maintained" in its context had safety as its underlying conception (616 D); and secondly that the duty was absolute, to which C.A. agreed but said there was a question of degree first, namely, whether the floor was so maintained "as to be safe for persons using" it (613 E).

13. Davie v. Port of London Authority [1955] 1 Lloyd's Rep. 135, Pilcher J.

Held, that a patch of ice on the floor of a cold store was a transient danger, and therefore, following **8**, there was no breach of statutory duty (but defendants were liable at common law).

14. Hawkins v. Westinghouse (1959) 109 L.J. 89, C.A.

Held, defendants not liable for breach of statutory duty.

15. Graham v. Distington Engineering *The Guardian*, December 15, 1961; [1961] C.L.Y. 5932, C.A.

Plaintiff tripped on ridge of sand in factory—*Held*, employers liable since once plaintiff had established there was a ridge of sand there and he had fallen on it, the onus shifted to defendants to prove their servant was not negligent in failing to clear it up; and since they had failed to do this, they were therefore liable.

16. Fisher v. Port of London Authority [1962] 1 All E.R. 458, Stevenson J.

So held at 461 F, applying test in *Payne v. Weldless Steel* **12**.

17. Hull v. Fairfield Shipbuilding, 1962 S.L.T. 206, O.H.

"Substance likely to cause persons to slip"—F.A. 1959, s. 4 (now F.A. 1961, s. 28)—*Held*, "substance" included a length of metal rod which had fallen from one of the benches.

18. Aiken v. Port of London Authority [1962] 2 Lloyd's Rep. 30, Paull J.

Piece of dunnage on warehouse floor—*Held*, no breach of F.A. 1937, s. 25 or 26 (as amended by F.A. 1959, s. 4) or common law—*Held*, however, defendants liable for bad lighting.

19. Graham v. H. Lyons [1962] 3 All E.R. 281, C.A.

Plaintiff slipped on slippery substance on floor of sausage factory—prima facie breach of F.A. 1937, s. 25(1), as amended by F.A. 1959, s. 4 (now F.A. 1961, s. 28)—"shall, so far as is reasonably practicable, be kept free from any obstruction and from any substance likely to cause persons to slip"—*Held*, that defendants had a good system for cleaning floor, and the employees carried out the system, so far as was reasonably practicable, and defendants were not liable.

20. Drummond v. Harland Engineering, 1963 S.L.T. 115, Ct. of Sess.

Piece of vertical angle iron projecting $\frac{1}{2}$ in. above floor, being part of a fixed machine—*Held*, that since angle iron was part of a fixture in the premises, it could not be an obstruction.

21. Dorman Long v. Bell [1964] 1 W.L.R. 333; [1964] 1 All E.R. 617, H.L.

Plaintiff slipped when treading on the upper of two heavy plates lying at angle on floor and covered with film of slag dust—*Held*, defendants liable (with 50 per cent. contributory negligence), as the plates were an obstruction (618 G), and on the balance of probabilities it was reasonably practicable to have removed them. Lord Reid, the other Lords concurring, said (618 I) that the danger arose from a combination of the slope of the plates and the slippery film, and that it was immaterial whether the slippery substance was or was not actually in contact with the floor, since the duty applied to all slippery substances on which anyone on the floor was likely to step.

22. Fairfield Shipbuilding v. Hall [1964] 1 Lloyd's Rep. 73, H.L.

Plaintiff trod on a metal rod lying in a factory passageway and fell—there was no evidence as to how the rod came to be there—it could have fallen by accident from a bench or barrow, or it could have been put or left on floor by an employee—defendant, *inter alia*, contended that their duty under F.A. 1961, s. 28 (1) only arose when a danger had got onto the floor, and did not extend to preventing objects getting onto the floor—this contention was rejected (75, col. 1)—plaintiff claimed that it would have been reasonably practicable to have kept floor clear by issuing instructions (which was not done) to employees not to leave or throw objects on floors—*Held*, (3–2) that, in view of the absence of evidence as to how the piece of metal came to be on the floor, it could not be said that such instructions would, on a balance of probabilities, have averted the danger.

23. Churchill v. Louis Marx (1964) 108 S.J. 334; [1964] C.L.Y. 1523, C.A.

Mould placed on floor of factory, this being a convenient and proper place for it—*Held*, not an obstruction, as an obstruction was something which had no business to be and ought reasonably not to be where it was.

24. Pengelley v. Bell Punch [1964] 1 W.L.R. 1055; [1964] 2 All E.R. 945, C.A.

Reels of paper in storeroom—smaller reels on racks—larger reels on floor in front of rack—plaintiff, getting a small reel, twisted his knee in between two larger ones—*Held*, not an obstruction. "In this section an 'obstruction' is something on the floor which has no business to be there, and which is a source of risk to persons using the floor" (Lord Denning M.R., 946 H). "The expression 'floors' in this context . . . is in my view limited to those parts of the factory floor on which workmen are intended or likely to pass and repass" (Diplock L.J., 947 E).

25. Marshall v. Ericsson Telephones [1964] 1 W.L.R. 1367; [1964] 3 All E.R. 609, C.A.

Held, applying *Pengelley* **24** and *Churchill* **23**, not an obstruction.

26. Vinnyey v. Star Paper [1965] 1 All E.R. 175, Cumming Bruce J.

Held, defendants not liable.

27. Taylor v. Gestetner (1967) 2 K.I.R. 133; [1967] C.L.Y. 1642, Paull J.

Held, defendants liable.

28. Jenkins v. Allied Ironfounders [1970] 1 W.L.R. 304; [1969] 3 All E.R. 1609, H.L.

Plaintiff walking backwards while moving a heavy casting from one pile to another tripped over an excrescence of scrap (known as a gate) which had been knocked or fallen from a previous casting—these gates would be covered by the pile of castings until the castings were moved away—*Held*, the gates were not an obstruction when covered by the pile, because at such time the pile consisted of objects properly put on the floor, and so could not constitute an obstruction; but when the castings themselves were removed, the gates remaining then became an obstruction—*Held*, however, that the defendants were not liable, for it was not reasonably practicable in the time interval (which was less than an hour, and perhaps only a few minutes) to have a system to remove the gates; the only way would have been contemporaneous raking, which would have been possible, but not reasonably practicable, in all the circumstances.

29. Ashdown v. Jonas Woodhead (1975) 118 S.J. 578; [1975] K.I.L.R. 27, C.A.

Canteen worker slipped on pool of water on floor of canteen—she sued under both s. 28 and s. 29—county court judge found that the defendants by employing a good man to clean floors had discharged their s. 28 duty ("so far as reasonably practicable keep floors free from substances likely to cause persons to slip"), but were in breach of s. 29 ("so far as reasonably practicable keep the place of work safe")—*Held*, the standard of care was the same under both sections, and since the defendants had discharged their duty under s. 28 by employing a competent cleaner, it followed that they were not liable under s. 29 either.

30. Gillies v. Glynwed, 1977 S.L.T. 97; [1977] C.L.Y. 2048, Ct. of Sess.

Held, obstruction, but not reasonably practicable to remove.

31. Bennett v. Rylands Whitecross [1978] I.C.R. 1031; [1978] C.L.Y. 1458, Kilner Brown J.

Held, defendants liable, as they had not proved it was not reasonably practicable to keep floor clear.

32. Bell v. Vaughan [1979] C.L.Y. 1299, Hodgson J.

33. Woodward v. Renold [1980] I.C.R. 387; [1980] C.L.Y. 1274, Lawson J.

Held, defendants liable, distinguishing *Thomas* **11**. Defendants' practice was to grit the footpath leading to the factory, but not the car park itself, but it was obvious that employees using the car park would converge on the area near the footpath, so that at least that part of the car park should have been gritted.

34. Cox v. Angus (H.C.B.) [1981] I.C.R. 683; [1981] C.L.Y. 1212, Lloyd J.

Held, the duty under s. 29 (1) to make and keep every place of work safe covered transient dangers, unlike the duty to provide and maintain a safe means of access. As the pipe could have been removed from the cab before P was injured (by inadvertently stepping on it), D was in breach of duty (and was negligent at C.L.). *But* 50 per cent. contributory negligence.

35. Sanders v. Lloyd [1982] I.C.R. 360; [1982] C.L.Y. 1365, Drake J.

Held, that "fencing" under s.28(4) included covering, and that it was practicable for the opening (a small ladle pit in a foundry) to be covered.

36. Johnston v. Caddies Wainwright [1983] I.C.R. 407; [1983] C.L.Y. 1686, C.A.

P slipped on small patch of oil on factory floor. D operated proper cleaning system. D called no evidence to show that the oil got onto the floor without fault on their part—*Held*, following *Williams v. Painter* **U8**, D were liable, as they had not disproved a breach of s. 28 (1): "Once it is proved that there is a slippery substance on a factory floor on which the plaintiff had slipped, it is, I think, then for the defendants to show that they have taken all reasonable precautions, first, to prevent that slippery substance being on the floor at all, and then, secondly, to clear it off the floor . . . It may be, of course, that in most cases the second aspect of that duty is more important, but the dual nature of the obligation which does arise under s. 28 still remains." (May, L.J., 413 D). As the defendants failed to call evidence to show how the oil got onto the floor, they had failed to establish that they had taken all reasonable precautions to prevent the oil getting there.

37. Jennings v. N.C.B. [1983] I.C.R. 636; [1983] C.L.Y. 2412, C.A.

For details see Chap. 16,(13) **27**.

38. Fildes v. International Computers [1984] C.L.Y. 2316, C.A.

Plaintiff slipped on ice on factory car park one acre in area, during several days' freezing weather. Only way to make car park safe would have been to cover it with sand and salt twice a day. Defendant did not treat car park at all, but gave priority to more frequently used areas elsewhere on its premises—*Held*, defendants not in breach of F.A. 1961, s. 29 (1) and not liable in negligence.

39. Rigg v. Central Electricity Generating Board, *The Times*, February 23, 1985; [1985] C.L.Y. 1529, Pain J.

Held, that the erection of coloured tape around a hole in the floor, which would warn the plaintiff of the danger but not prevent him from falling in, was within the means required by s. 29 (2) for ensuring the safety a person liable to fall more than two metres, where it was not practicable to erect a fence around the hole.

40. Darby v. G.K.N. Screws & Fasteners Ltd [1986] I.C.R. 1; [1986] C.L.Y. 2266, Peter Pain J.

After snowy night, plaintiff slipped on untreated ice in front of a door to defendant's factory, just before 7.45 a.m. shift. Salt-spreading gang came on duty at 7.30 a.m. and salted most used and dangerous parts first—*Held*, defendants neither negligent nor in breach of duty under F.A. 1961, s. 29 to provide safe means of access—had taken all reasonably practicable steps by its system, and no basis for finding that any individual employee had negligently failed to salt the relevant area earlier.

41. Allen v. Avon Rubber Co. Ltd [1986] I.C.R. 695; [1987] I.R.L.R. 22, C.A.

For further details see Chap. 16, (5) (d) **10**.

42. Gitsham v. C.H. Pearce & Sons [1992] P.I.Q.R. P57; *The Times*, February 11, 1991, C.A.

For further details see Chap. 16, (2) (d) **29**.

43. Dexter v. Tenby Electrical Accessories Ltd [1991] Crim.L.R. 839; *The Times*, March 11, 1991, D.C.

Employee of contractor engaged to do work at factory fell through defective roof. Factory occupier charged with breach of F.A. 1961, s. 29(1) which required provision of safe means of access to every place at which "any person has at any time to work"—*Held*, (a) "any person" would include the contractor's employee; (b) occupier could be in breach of s. 29(1) though blameless and without knowledge of the contravention; (c) *per* Lloyd L.J., the construction of "has . . . to work" in *Kendrick v. Cozens & Sutcliffe* (Chap. 16, (2) (j) **17**) was too restrictive. By analogy to *Smith v. N.C.B.* (Chap. 16, (2) (j) **16**) a person "had to work" at a place if to do so was reasonably incidental to the performance of his duty.

44. Larner v. British Steel plc [1993] I.C.R. 551; [1993] 4 All E.R. 102, C.A.

See Chap. 16, (3) (a) **17** for further details.

45. McLean v. Remploy, 1994 S.L.T. 687; [1994] C.L.Y. 5886

Plaintiff fell over length of yarn tied across passageway by fellow employee as practical joke—*Held*, defendant not in breach of F.A. 1961, ss. 28 and 29. Though the yarn was an obstruction and rendered passage unsafe, defendant had proved it was not reasonably practicable to have removed it before accident.

46. Neil v. Greater Glasgow H.B., 1994 S.C.L.R.; [1994] C.L.Y. 5888

Plaintiff injured when part of machine at which he was working tipped over—*Held*, defendant in breach of F.A. 1961, s. 29(1) even though accident not reasonably foreseeable, because it would have been reasonably practicable to clamp machine to floor.

U1. Shelley v. Binns (1956) C.A. 65 A

Held, defendants not liable for any fault in system provided for cleaning but were liable for negligence of cleaners in failing to do their work.

U2. Kennedy v. Massey (1960) C.A. 31

Held, not safe, and defendants liable.

U3. Bell v. Dorman Long (1963) C.A. 80

Two steel plates 4 in. deep and overlapping each other lying on slag floor of factory—*Held*, these were an obstruction within F.A. 1961, s. 29 and defendants liable (but 50 per cent. contributory negligence against plaintiff). Sellers L.J. (7 A): "The idea of obstruction seems to be, from its customary definition, something which creates a situation where the way becomes more or less impassable or at any rate where it makes the passage more difficult." Pearson L.J. (15 B) said that in his view the word "obstruction" in the section connoted some element of risk.

U4. Lappin v. Dorman Long (1964) C.A. 109

Black grease on floor of lathe-fitting shop—coming from rollers and parts brought in during work—defendants employed a man from 8 a.m. to 4 p.m. to keep floor clean—plaintiff slipped during night shift at 2 a.m.—*Held*, defendants not liable, as they had done all that was reasonably practicable (Diplock L.J. *dubitante*).

U5. Taylor v. Executors of James Mills (1964) C.A. 238

"In the course of operations which were conducted in the rolling mill it was inevitable that oil and grease should get on the floor. The removal of oil and grease is not such a simple operation as when there is some other kind of debris to be dealt with. Grease and oil are awkward things to remove; and one cannot really have such operations going on continuously while work is being done for all 24 hours of the day" (Danckwerts L.J., 7 A).

U6. Martin v. Pirelli (1967) C.A. 266 A

Held, obstruction within F.A. 1961, s. 29. 50 per cent. contributory negligence.

U7. Matthews v. K. & L. (1968) C.A. 255

Narrow gap in passage through which plaintiff had to go sideways carrying load—*Held*, access awkward, but not unsafe. Definition of "safe" in *Trott* (Chap. 16 (2) (b) **9**) *applied.*

U8. Williams v. Painter (1968) C.A. 224. (Also in (1968) 5 K.I.R. 487, C.A.)

Slip on grease spot falling from overhead crane—*Held*, defendants liable under F.A. 1961, s. 28, for the onus was on them to establish it was not reasonably practicable to avoid the state of affairs by any measure which was (a) practicable, *i.e.* capable of being taken, and (b) would not involve such expense and other effort and exertion in time and labour as would be unreasonable (4 E); and defendants had not discharged this onus. On foreseeability in relation to reasonably practicable, Winn L.J. said (4 C-D): "It is true, I think (and I do not think more than this can be said), that no question of what is reasonably practicable can arise unless the particular danger is one which is capable of being foreseen. I do not, however, accept the proposition submitted that it is only if a reasonable man ought in the circumstances to have foreseen a particular danger that the obligation is imposed by the statutory provision."

U9. Bristow v. Richard Johnson (1972) C.A. 128

Floor dangerously slippery from grease—which it was impracticable to remove—*Held*, reversing trial judge, defendants liable because they had failed to prove that serrated (instead of smooth) steel plates to form floor and/or duckboards were not reasonably practicable.

U10. Bielups v. B.S.C. (1972) C.A. 280

Held, defendants liable. *Thomas* **11** distinguished because there the fall was sudden.

U11. Hull v. Liverpool Police (1973) C.A. 74 A

Plaintiff P.C. in refreshment room of police station—writing out statement—slipped on floor—which to knowledge of everyone was slippery with wax—which has been applied, but not wiped off—*Held*, breach of O.S.R.P.A. 1963, s. 16 (which is equivalent to F.A. 1961, s. 28), because it would have been reasonably practicable to avoid the danger by, *e.g.* putting the room out of bounds during the relevant period of an hour or two.

U12. Humphries v. Selfridges (1974) C.A. 373

Held, trolley on floor of receiving area of depot did not constitute an "obstruction." *Pengelley* **24** *applied.*

U13. McCann v. N.C.B. (1975) C.A. 113

Brick protruding 2 in. in well-lit tub-track (which was also a walk-way) of mine—*Held*, not an "obstruction" within M.Q.A. 1954, s. 34(1)(b), C.A. approved definition of "obstruction" by Wien J. as follows: "I consider the word "obstruction" in its ordinary sense means something which hinders a person or impedes his progress or makes a walking way less passable . . . Clearly an obstruction on the decided cases means something which has no business to be on the floor and which ought not reasonably to be there. In other words it is an object whose presence on the floor might cause an accident and that object serves no useful purpose at all."

U14. Pouney v. Burman (1975) C.A. 422

Steel and aluminium swarf from three or four lathes—plaintiff cuts leg thereon—swarf only swept at end of each day—*Held*, by C.A., they would not disturb decision of county court judge that sweeping should have been more frequent.

U15. Clarke v. B.S.C. (1975) C.A. 461

Scarman L.J. (10 A): "If the condition of a floor is unsafe it does not help the defendant to establish that the plaintiff knew that it was unsafe. But if the question at issue be whether the floor was safe or unsafe, then the plaintiff's knowledge . . . is relevant. . . . It is relevant in two ways. The statutory and common law duty to an employee is, as stated by Denning L.J. in *Payne* **12**, a duty to keep a floor in good repair so as to be safe for persons using it. It is relevant therefore . . . to see what *is* the knowledge of the person using it . . . Secondly, knowledge is also relevant . . . when one sees how persons have behaved in the past. If employees with that knowledge have not made any complaint . . . then it is clearly open to the judge to take that factor into account."

U16. Oldham v. Associated British Hat Manufacturers (1976) C.A. 219

Loop of twine on floor—floor was swept twice a day and employees were instructed to pick up bits and pieces they saw—*Held*, even if this was an obstruction, defendants had done all that was reasonably practicable. *N.B.* Defendants called no evidence, having obtained all they wanted in cross-examination.

U17. Mortimer v. Catton & Co. Ltd (1981) C.A. 125

Plaintiff decided to move heavy metal tray left protruding one foot into passageway—*Held*, that as the tray was not a foreseeable source of danger, it did not constitute an obstruction under s.28(1). It did not become an obstruction because the plaintiff was tempted to meddle with it and thereby put himself at risk.

U18. Hughes v. British Airways (1977) C.A. 399 A

Box of mail on floor—gangway gap between box and a table was $4\frac{1}{2}$ feet. Plaintiff tripped over box when carrying tray of letters—*Held*, box could be an "obstruction," even though there was a sensible business purpose for it to be there (Megaw L.J. 5D), and on the facts was. Defendants liable.

U19. Iceton v. Durham A.H.A. (1979) C.A. 460

U20. Allen v. International Harvester (1981) C.A. 131

Held, defendants not liable, as they had taken all proper steps, and the real cause was that it had unforeseeably started to freeze again at about 5.30 a.m. *Thomas* **11** applied.

U21. Betts v. British Leyland (1981) C.A. U.B. 59

Held, applying *Pengelley* **24** and *Marshall* **25**, not an obstruction, as the component boxes and the rocker cover were reasonably stored and readily visible in their positions.

U22. Thompson v. Swan Hunter (1982) C.A. U.B. 547

Held, defendants liable.

U23. Selby v. English Clays Lovering and Pochin Co. (1983) C.A. 367

The plaintiff slipped on a road in a mine which was covered with ice and snow—*Held*, there was a breach of M.Q.A. 1954, s. 34(1)(b) which provided that the floor of such a road "... shall be kept ... in such a condition that any persons ... who use that ... road can tread it with safety ... ". The regulation referred to the condition of the fabric of the floor, and would not be breached merely by the presence of extraneous matter on the floor of the road, such as a banana skin. It would be breached, however, if the floor was covered with snow and ice, or flooded with water.

U24. Sommerville v. Rowntree Mackintosh Ltd (1984) C.A. 556

Plaintiff tripped over power socket bolted to floor of recently vacated office. Socket had been used to plug in electrical equipment—*Held*, defendant not in breach of O.S.R.P.A. 1963, s.16. Socket was not an "obstruction" within s.16 unless and until defendant had decided to use floor in such a way as not to require socket.

U25. Pickford v. Control Data (1984) C.A. 720

Plaintiff tripped on 2 feet square tile, one corner of which was "something not more than $\frac{1}{4}$ inch proud" of the adjacent tiles. There were 5,500 such tiles on the floor, which was heavily used. Defendant relied on those using the floor to report loose tiles, which were then promptly attended to. No evidence that anyone had noticed anything wrong with the tile in question before the accident, and no evidence of any previous tripping accident—*Held*, defendants not liable in negligence and not in breach of F.A. 1961, s.29.

U26. Metcalf v. Cleveland Bridge and Engineering Co. Ltd (1986) C.A. 626

Plaintiff stepped down from a platform 32 in. above factory floor level onto a rail $3\frac{1}{2}$ in. wide which was 13 in. above floor level. This was the commonly used means of egress from the platform. On this occasion, plaintiff's foot slipped and he fell—*Held*, defendants not in breach of F.A. 1961, s.29 (1).

U27. Chrost v. B.S.C. (1987) C.A. 575

Plaintiff slipped on Swarfega that had fallen from a wall dispenser. His job was to clean the floor—*Held*, defendant not negligent and not in breach of F.A. 1961, s.28(1). Some Swarfega would have got on floor even had the dispenser been located over the sinks.

U28. Barker v. Brook Motors Ltd (1987) C.A. 996

Plaintiff tripped over wooden batten on floor of a passage in defendant's factory. Passage was ill-lit but plaintiff had not switched on the light—*Held*, defendant liable in negligence and for breach of F.A. 1961, s.28 (1). Plaintiff 50 per cent. to blame.

U29. Thompson v. Yorkshire Imperial Metals Ltd (1988) C.A. 239

Plaintiff tripped on piece of metal grating which protruded $\frac{1}{2}$ in. above adjoining piece—*Held*, defendant not in breach of F.A 1961, ss.28 and 29.

U30. Dilley v. British Leyland Cars Ltd (1988) C.A. 555

Forklift truck driver struck stack of pallets protruding about 2 feet into main gangway, and injured his left hand—*Held*, defendant not in breach of F.A. 1961, s. 28(1). Pallets created no foreseeable danger. The cause of the accident was plaintiff's error of judgement.

U31. Dwyer v. Welsh Water Authority (1988) C.A. 1009

Plaintiff stood on step-ladder to free a blockage of coke or coal in a conveyor, using 12-foot bar which became jammed. Plaintiff pulled bar as hard as he could—bar suddenly freed, and plaintiff fell, bringing step-ladder with him. A solid working platform surrounded by a cage would have prevented the accident and could have been provided at insignificant expense—*Held*, defendant negligent and in breach of F.A. 1961, s. 29(1). Accident circumstances were foreseeable. Plaintiff one-third to blame, for failing to take the greatest possible precautions to see he would not lose his balance if bar came away.

U32. Formby v. Ripaults Ltd (1988) C.A. 1114

Plaintiff was injured when stepping onto a plug on the floor of an aisle along which she was pushing a small trolley—*Held*, defendant in breach of F.A. 1961, s. 28(1). Defendant had a good system for clearing up items which had fallen onto the floor, but no evidence of any system to prevent errant plugs getting onto the floor.

U33. Carzana v. West 'N' Welsh Windows Ltd (1989) C.A. 343

Glass-cutter was moving large sheet of glass in confined space when it struck part of a glass rack and shattered—*Held*, defendant neither negligent nor in breach of F.A. 1961, s. 29(1). Place of work not unsafe.

U34. Ditchfield v. Mabey and Johnson Ltd (1989) C.A. 1098

Welder rolled steel member weighing 175 lbs over to gain access to another part of it. Crushed his thumb between it and a previously welded member which restricted available work space—*Held*, defendant liable in negligence and in breach of F.A. 1961, s. 29(1)—failed to provide crane to remove previously welded member and provided workplace so restricted in space as to present a foreseeable risk of the kind of accident that happened. Plaintiff 25 per cent. to blame—should have checked whether there was room to roll the member.

U35. Johnson v. Rolls Royce Ltd (1989) C.A. 1123

Plaintiff slipped on ice in factory car park. Defendant had made a policy decision not to clear ice and snow in their car parks—*Held*, defendant in breach of F.A. 1961, s. 29(1).

U36. Shore v. Royal Ordnance plc (1989) C.A. 1177

When plaintiff lifted a table at defendant's factory a cast iron radiator stored beneath the table fell on him—*Held*, defendant not liable at common law—no foreseeable danger. Not in breach of F.A. 1961, s. 28—radiator was not an obstruction—and not in breach of s. 29.

*(j) Safety of Foothold**

"Adequate foothold"—sitting across a moving girder	1	–
Ladder	2	6, 9
Secure foothold—means intrinsically secure in ordinary conditions	3	6, 9

* Abbreviations are explained in Introductory Note 1.

1. Roberts v. Dorman Long [1953] 1 W.L.R. 942; [1953] 2 All E.R. 428, C.A.

Held, that a man who was required to sit astride a girder as it was being moved had not got "foothold," which in its ordinary meaning meant standing ground (430 F)—*Held*, further that having safety belts at a point 10 minutes' walk away was not making them "available."

2. Wigley v. British Vinegars [1964] A.C. 307; [1962] 3 All E.R. 161, H.L.

Deceased window cleaner employed as independent contractor to clean factory windows—he was provided by occupier with a sound ladder, from which he fell—window was a pivoted one, so that deceased had to use one hand to press against window while cleaning other portion with other hand—not wearing safety belt but had brought one with him—however, window had no hooks on it—there was evidence that it was not usual for window cleaners to use a safety belt when working from a ladder—*Held*, no breach of F.A. 1937, s. 26(2) because the ladder afforded a secure foothold and if necessary handhold within the meaning of the section, for the place from which he was liable to fall was the ladder, which provided secure foothold and handhold.

3. Tinto v. Stewart and Lloyds, 1962 S.L.T. 314, O.H.

Elevated unfenced factory gangway of steel plate in good condition—explosion causing flames and smoke in vicinity of gangway—*Held*, defendants not liable under F.A. 1937, s. 26(2) (secure foothold), as the foothold under all ordinary circumstances was secure.

(6) Fencing of Machinery

*(a) "Dangerous"**

* Abbreviations are explained in Introductory Note 1.

Accident records—largely irrelevant	11	–
Action by factory inspectors—largely irrelevant	11	–
NIP BETWEEN CONVEYOR BELT AND ROLLER	12	–
Mechanical clothes press in laundry	13	–
Nip between conveyor belt and drum—danger to cleaners but not to operator	14	–
Trapdoor giving access to unguarded part of machine underneath	15	–
Electric drill shattering and flying out—not reasonably foreseeable	16	–
Feeding hopper of plastics grinding machine	17	–
Sack hoist—nip between hoist and aperture	18	–
DANGER INCLUDES DANGER TO THE UTTERLY STUPID AND UTTERLY NEGLIGENT	19	6,10
REVOLVING SHAFT—ON TOP OF STRUCTURE 4 FEET HIGH—REACHED BY ASCENDING STEEL LADDER TO PLATFORM	19	6,10
Flexible driving shaft of hand power tool—unfenced for last 3 inches—is dangerous	20	–
Stationary carrier arm—felt milling machine	21	–
Hot press for trubenising collars	U1	–
Piece of metal placed on rails to brake trucks	U2	–
Revolving spindle of drill—metal projecting 1 inch—due to plaintiff not fitting it properly	U3	–
Mobile welding machine	U4	6,10
Complaints of factory inspectors—relevant	U5	–
Previous accidents—relevant	U5	–
Part of machine falling outside guard	U6	6,10
Engine of mobile crane under repair	U7	6,10
Cleaning unfenced rollers in motion—warned not to do so	U8	–
Outlet chute of vegetable cutting machine—plaintiff putting hand up	U9	–
Coupling box disintegrating and flying out of rolling mill	U10	–
Nip between wire rope and pulley attached to coal cutter	U11	–
Effect of no complaint by factory inspector	U11	–
Nature of evidence to which court will look on issue of "dangerous"	U11	–
Tool on tool post—near moving chuck	U12	–
Feeding paper into machine for making doyleys	U13	–

1. Walker v. Bletchley Flettons [1937] 1 All E.R. 170, du Parcq J.

Plaintiff going to toolbox of mechanical excavator slipped and was caught by wheel of machine—*Held*, dangerous: "In considering whether machinery is dangerous, it must not be assumed that everyone will always be careful. A part of a machine is dangerous if it is a possible cause of injury to anybody acting in a way in which a human being may reasonably be expected to act in circumstances which may be reasonably expected to occur" (175 F). *Applied* in **8** and **10**. *Approved* by H.L. in **11**. See amplifying comment of Divisional Court in **9**.

2. Chasteney v. Michael Nairn [1937] 1 All E.R. 376, D.C.

Held, dangerous.

3. Findlay v. Newman Hender [1937] 4 All E.R. 58, D.C.

Workman injured replacing belt on mill gearing 12 feet above ground—*Held*, dangerous.

4. Sutherland v. James Mills [1938] 1 All E.R. 283, D.C.

Gear wheels of electrically driven reeling machine—*Held*, dangerous and irrelevant on this issue that workman had been warned not to put hand near them.

5. Fowler v. Yorkshire Electric Power [1939] 1 All E.R. 407, Lawrence J.

Held, dangerous.

6. Stimson v. Standard Telephones [1940] 1 K.B. 342; [1939] 4 All E.R. 225, C.A.

Held, dangerous.

7. Wood v. L.C.C. [1940] 2 K.B. 642; [1940] 4 All E.R. 149, Wrottesley J.

Aperture in electric mincing machine just wide enough for young girl's hand—*Held*, dangerous. (*N.B.* This case was reversed on other grounds—[1941] 2 All E.R. 230, C.A.)

8. Kinder v. Camberwell B.C. [1944] 2 All E.R. 315, D.C.

Held, applying **1**, dangerous, because "in the ordinary course of human affairs danger might reasonably be anticipated from the use of the machine without protection."

9. Carr v. Mercantile Produce [1949] 2 K.B. 601; [1949] 2 All E.R. 531, D.C.

Dough machine with hopper–hopper $11\frac{1}{4}$ in. deep, upper $6\frac{1}{4}$ in. being a funnel in shape—two rings 5 in. and $1\frac{5}{8}$ in. in diameter at bottom of funnel—fingers could only come into contact with worm at bottom if hand forced through rings—magistrate found not dangerous—*Held*, there was ample evidence for him to do so. Dictum in **1** cited, but Divisional Court pointed out that in that case the judge added: "Nobody expects human beings to be so extravagantly careless as to touch some part of the machine which is not only not difficult to avoid, but which is actually difficult to get near." At 605, bottom, Lord Goddard C.J. said that the fact that no complaint had ever been made by a factory inspector was "at least some evidence that in the opinion of a duly qualified person no accident is reasonably likely to occur." But this latter dictum is now doubtful. See **11**. But dictum was *followed* in **U11**.

10. Smithwick v. N.C.B. [1950] 2 K.B. 335; [1950] 2 T.L.R. 173, C.A.

Case under the C.M.A. 1911, s. 55—unfenced conveyor belt machinery—aperture giving access thereto—question was whether possibility that, if the conveyor belt was held up, workman would look inside aperture—*Held*, yes, and machine dangerous.

11. John Summers v. Frost [1955] A.C. 740; [1955] 1 All E.R. 870, H.L.

Plaintiff injured on grindstone which was fenced by a hood except for an arc about 7 in. long at grinding face—more fencing would have made the grindstone commercially unusable—*Held*, not securely fenced (see Chap. 16, (6) (d) **10** for details). On the question whether the machine was dangerous, Lord Simonds (873 E) said that the dictum of du Parcq J. in **1** gave as precise a direction as can be hoped for, if read in conjunction with the dictum of Lord Cooper in *Mitchell v. North British Rubber*, 1945 S.C.(J.) 69 at 73, *i.e.*: "(A machine is dangerous if . . .) in the ordinary course of human affairs danger may reasonably be anticipated from its use unfenced, not only to the prudent, alert and skilled operative, but also to the careless or inattentive worker whose inadvertent or indolent conduct may expose him to risk of injury or death from the unguarded part." Lord Oaksey agreed with Lord Simonds, and Lord Reid (882–883) also approved the above two dicta, which therefore have the approval of a majority of H.L. *Burns v. Terry* (Chap. 16 (6) (d) **5**), which laid down the test of reasonable foreseeability, was expressly approved by Lords Keith and Reid, and impliedly so by the others. Lord Reid (883 C) further defined the test to be applied by citing from the judgment of Lord Cooper referred to above the following addition: "The question is not whether the occupiers of the factory knew it was dangerous; nor whether a factory inspector had so reported; nor whether previous accidents had occurred; nor whether the victims of these accidents had been contributorily negligent. The test is objective and impersonal." Lord Keith (890 B) agreed with this, and (890 A) said that the record of accidents and the acquiescence of factory inspectors could carry no weight, "unless possibly in marginal cases." *Applied* in **14**.

12. Williams v. Sykes and Harrison [1955] 1 W.L.R. 1180; [1955] 3 All E.R. 225, C.A.

Held, dangerous.

13. Humphreys v. North Liverpool Hospital M.C. [1956] C.L.Y. 3455, Diplock J.

Held, not dangerous, and defendants not liable for failing to fence.

14. Dunn v. Birds Eye Food [1959] 2 Q.B. 265; [1959] 2 All E.R. 403, D.C.

Unfenced nip—safe to the operator—but a reasonably foreseeable cause of injury to night cleaning staff in that they might try to clean while in motion—*Held*, applying **11**, dangerous.

15. Rushton v. Turner Bros [1960] 1 W.L.R. 96; [1959] 3 All E.R. 517, Ashworth J.

Held, dangerous, but 100 per cent. contributory negligence by plaintiff, and defendants therefore not liable. See Chap. 16 (4) (c) **7** for details in respect of plaintiff's contributory negligence.

16. Close v. Steel Company of Wales [1962] A.C. 367; [1961] 2 All E.R. 953, H.L.

Bit of electric drill shattered and piece entered eye of plaintiff—*Held*, that the bit was not a dangerous part of machinery. The drill was a well-known machine used in homes as well as factories, and although a bit occasionally shattered, there was no evidence of previous accidents, the fragments being so small and light that they usually went only a few inches. Test of Wills J. in *Hindle v. Birtwistle* [1897] 1 Q.B. 192 applied: "Machinery or parts of machinery is and are dangerous if in the ordinary course of human affairs danger may reasonably be anticipated from the use of them without protection."

17. Woodley v. Mason Freer [1963] 1 W.L.R. 1409; [1963] 3 All E.R. 636, D.C.

Plastics grinding machine with top feeding hopper and side feed—injury to operator when manually pressing struck material down hopper—warning had been given against doing this—and hopper had once had protective bars across mouth—*Held*, reversing magistrates, machine was dangerous according to the only inference which could be drawn from the primary facts.

18. Irwin v. White Tomkins and Courage [1964] 1 W.L.R. 387; [1964] 1 All E.R. 545, H.L.

Held, there was evidence on which a jury could find that a sack hoist with an open window or aperture into which a man could insert his head produced a dangerous nip, and so constituted dangerous machinery.

19. Uddin v. Associated Portland Cement Manufacturers [1965] 2 Q.B. 582; [1965] 2 All E.R. 213, C.A.

In order to catch a pigeon, plaintiff went up a steel ladder and leaned over a shaft set on top of a metal cabinet 4 feet 6 in. high on a metal platform—*Held*, plaintiff, being within the words "every person . . . employed in the premises," was within the scope of F.A. 1937, s. 14, and since the shaft was dangerous, he could recover (but 80 per cent. contributory negligence). Lord Pearce (217 C-E): "The occupier may exculpate himself . . . by showing that only a piece of unforeseeable folly could create danger in some particular piece of machinery, and that therefore it could not be called dangerous . . . Once however it has been shown to be dangerous and to have needed fencing, it seems to me that he should be potentially liable to all employees who suffer from that failure. There is nothing to justify the view that the Act of 1937 intended its protection for only the slightly stupid or slightly negligent, and intended to withdraw all protection from the utterly stupid and utterly negligent."

20. Lovelidge v. Anselm Olding [1967] 2 Q.B. 351; [1967] 1 All E.R. 459, Widgery J.

21. Hindle v. Joseph Porritt [1970] 1 All E.R. 1142; [1970] C.L.Y. 1067, Brabin J.

Plaintiff's hand was caught while moving felt in felt milling machine—as a result he hit his shoulder against the stationary carrier arm—*Held*, defendants not liable.

U1. Lonie v. Rego Clothiers Ltd (1952) C.A. 303

Held, dangerous (but 66 per cent. contributory negligence).

U2. Read v. Medhurst Whites Ltd (1953) C.A. 215 A

Held, not "part of machinery" and defendants not liable when plaintiff's fingers caught.

U3. Davies v. Metropolitan Vickers Electrical Co. Ltd (1955) C.A. 162

Held, dangerous (but 50 per cent. contributory negligence).

U4. McGuinness v. Sulzer Bros. (London) Ltd (1955) C.A. 196 A

Plaintiff's fingers caught by revolving fan when attempting to remove burning material from inside machine—flap preventing workman coming into contact with machine down—flap could be lifted up—*Held*, no breach of F.A. 1937, s. 14 or 16.

U5. Noce v. Standard Motor Co. Ltd (1955) C.A. 270

Lord Evershed M.R. (4) said that dictum of Lord Cooper in *Mitchell v. North British Rubber Co.*, 1945 S.C. 69 as approved by H.L. in *Summers v. Frost* **11**, meant that record of accidents and/or action by factory inspectors was relevant on question whether machinery was dangerous.

U6. Bevan v. Steel Co. of Wales (1955) C.A. 381

Plaintiff's hand injured when part of machine fell out of its correct position so that it came below guard—*Held*, no breach of F.A. 1937, s. 14.

U7. Elworthy v. New Merton Board Mills (1956) C.A. 169

Plaintiff engineer repairing engine of crane—took guard off and left engine running—came back—slipped—*Held*, breach of F.A. 1937, s. 14, but 100 per cent. contributory negligence, so defendants not liable.

U8. Burrows v. Metal Box Co. (1956) C.A. 347

Plaintiff, minder of colour printing machine—had to clean rollers from time to time—no fence—warned that must stop machine to clean it—practice in factory not to stop machine to clean rollers, through dangerous, to save trouble—men knew they should not clean machine when running—*Held*, defendants in breach of F.A. 1937, s. 14–50 per cent. contributory negligence against plaintiff for doing not only what told not to do also what no sensible person would do.

U9. Rippin v. M.C.C. (1957) C.A. 108

Held, defendants not liable, as plaintiff's conduct unforeseeable. (*N.B.* This was a case at common law, as machine was being used at a school.)

U10. Paterson v. Darlington & Simpson Rolling Mills Ltd (1958) C.A. 314

Held, not dangerous.

U11. Williams v. N.C.B. (1959) C.A. 110

Nip between wire rope and pulley attached to coal cutter moving at $\frac{1}{2}$ m.p.h.—*Held*, not dangerous; Lord Goddard said that in so holding he took into account:

(a) no expert or mine-worker's inspector had been called to say it was dangerous;
(b) no previous accident on any of 200 similar machines;
(c) no complaint by Inspector of Mines (following dictum in *Carr* **9**).

U12. Johnson v. Dowty Rotol (1962) C.A. 406

Plaintiff's hand caught in chuck—drew it away sharply so that back of wrist struck tool on tool post—*Held*, chuck in itself not a dangerous piece of machinery, but the tool on the tool post, having regard to its proximity to the chuck, was, and defendants were liable.

U13. Harwood v. Cross Paperware (1975) C.A. 120

Feeding paper into machine for making doilies—plaintiff allowed her hand to be carried by paper into mouth of narrow felt covered aperture formed by two narrow slats—two fingers bruised—*Held*, reversing county court judge, not "dangerous" part of machinery.

(b) "Machinery" and "Part of Machinery"*

* Abbreviations are explained in Introductory Note 1.

1. Thurogood v. Van den Berghs [1951] 2 K.B. 537; [1951] 1 All E.R. 682, C.A.

Held, obiter, that if the place where a factory fan was being repaired had been a factory (which it was not), the fan would not have had to be fenced, since it was not machinery being used in a factory, but was being repaired therein.

2. Parvin v. Morton Machine Co. [1952] A.C. 515; [1952] 1 All E.R. 670, H.L.

Held, the machinery only meant machinery used for production, and did not include machinery which was produced in the factory.

3. Williams v. Sykes & Harrison [1955] 1 W.L.R. 1180; [1955] 3 All E.R. 225, C.A.

Held, dangerous part of machinery.

4. Bullock v. G. John Power [1956] 1 W.L.R. 171; [1956] 1 All E.R. 498, C.A.

Wire being wound onto an electric drum which was fenced—loose end of wire rode up over guard and killed deceased—*Held*, applying *Nicholls* (Chap. 16(6)(e) **1**), the wire was "material" and not "part of machinery," and therefore defendants not liable. *But* see **6**.

5. Kilgollan v. W. Cooke [1956] 1 W.L.R. 527; [1956] 2 All E.R. 294, C.A.

Piece of wire (part of material) flies out—*Held*, defendant under no duty to fence under F.A. 1937, s. 14. *Nicholls* (Chap. 16(6)(e) **1**) *applied.*

6. Hoare v. Grazebrook [1957] 1 W.L.R. 638; [1957] 1 All E.R. 470, Lynskey J.

Vertical borer around which the component, which was attached to the machine, revolved—dangerous nip thereby created—in which plaintiff caught his hand—*Held*, defendant liable, following the unreported decision of Finnemore J. in *Lenthall v. Gimson*: "If danger does exist from the operation of the machine and if a part becomes dangerous from the operation of the machine, it seems to me that it is a 'dangerous part' of the machinery, and the fact that it is not dangerous when no operation is taking place is quite irrelevant" (474 B). *Approved* by H.L. in **20**.

7. Lewis v. High Duty Alloys [1957] 1 W.L.R. 632; [1957] 1 All E.R. 740, Ashworth J.

Automatic planing machine which carried block being planed back and forth under a "bridge" from which a plane projected—plaintiff was trapped between block and bridge (the latter being static)—*Held*, the bridge could not be regarded as a dangerous part of machinery, since it was not dangerous *per se*, and it was only the conjunction of it and the block which was dangerous. *Disapproved* by H.L. in **20**.

8. Rutherford v. R. E. Glanville [1958] 1 W.L.R. 415; [1958] 1 All E.R. 532, C.A.

Carborundum wheel disintegrates at high speed—known danger—drives hood up so that hood cuts plaintiff's wrist—*Held*, distinguishing *Nicholls* (Chap. 16,(6)(e) **1**), the duty to fence included a duty to fence parts of machinery flying out, and the fact that it was the hood and not the part which struck plaintiff was immaterial, so that defendants were liable for failure to fence.

9. Dunn v. Birds Eye Food [1959] 2 Q.B. 265; [1959] 2 All E.R. 403, D.C.

Held, part of machinery.

10. Cherry v. International Alloys [1960] 1 Q.B. 136; [1960] 3 All E.R. 264, C.A.

Overruled in **18**.

11. Eaves v. Morris Motors [1961] 2 Q.B. 385; [1961] 3 All E.R. 233, C.A.

Milling of bolt heads—vice held bolts and carried them forward under rotating cutting wheels and then back again—cutting wheels guarded—plaintiff was about to remove two bolts which had been returned by vice when the machine repeated without plaintiff pulling starting-handle—plaintiff hurriedly removed hand and cut it on a burr on bolt head—*Held*, defendants not liable as:

(a) the bolt was material and not machinery: *Bullock v. G. John Power* **4** and *Nicholls v. Austin* (Chap. 16(6)(e) **1**) applied;
(b) A dangerous nip between material and machinery could constitute a dangerous part of machinery (applying *Hoare v. Grazebrook* **6** and not following *Lewis v. High Duty Alloys* **7**), yet here, on the facts, the repeating of the machinery was not reasonably foreseeable, and therefore the nip was not dangerous. See **U2**.

12. Quintas v. National Smelting Co. [1961] 1 W.L.R. 401; [1961] 1 All E.R. 630, C.A.

Held, aerial ropeway and moving buckets suspended therefrom were not "machinery" within F.A. 1937, s. 14.

13. Irwin v. White Tomkins & Courage [1964] 1 W.L.R. 387; [1964] 1 All E.R. 545, H.L.

New machinery was being installed in a factory—which included seven sack hoists—at least one sack hoist was complete, though not yet in commercial use—deceased was in charge of the installation and was running this hoist—probably to test it—he climbed onto an incomplete conveyor belt and put his head through "window"—was struck by a descending bar—defendants contended that, as the hoist had not been taken into use, no obligation to fence arose—*Held*, not so, on the facts: "Machinery means machinery which has been installed as part of the equipment of the factory" (*per* Lord Reid, 547 G). Here, although much of the machinery being installed was still in course of erection, the hoist in question had been installed, and constituted an independent machine in its own right. *Parvin* **2** only applied to exclude machinery which was being produced in the factory. *N.B.* The dividing line would seem to be that all machinery which (a) has been (as opposed to is being) installed, (b) as part of the equipment of the factory is within the obligation to fence; otherwise, not. See *Liptrot* **18**.

14. Baxter v. Central Electricity Generating Board [1965] 1 W.L.R. 200; [1964] 2 All E.R. 815, Ashworth J.

Now *quaere*: see *Liptrot* **18**.

15. Midland & Low Moor Iron v. Cross [1965] A.C. 343; [1964] 3 All E.R. 752, H.L.

Metal bars being fed between rollers—lower rollers were power driven—upper ones were free to revolve—plaintiff's hand caught in nip between upper roller and bar—machine admittedly not dangerous until a bar was fed in—*Held*, upper roller was a dangerous part of machinery, because one must have regard to the upper roller "when doing its ordinary work" (Lord Reid, 755 C). Dictum of Holroyd Pearce L.J. in *Eaves* **11** cited with approval by three Law Lords: "It is not the nature of the material and it is not the material itself which causes the danger. The danger is caused by the design of the machine itself working normally with harmless material." *N.B.* The case where the workpiece was moving and the relevant part of machinery stationary was reserved for future consideration, as to which see now *Callow* **20**.

16. Pearce v. Stanley-Bridges [1965] 1 W.L.R. 931; [1965] 2 All E.R. 594, C.A.

A platform rising by compressed air came close as it rose to the end of a factory structure, creating a narrow gap—*Held*, there was no obligation to fence. *Irwin* **13** distinguished, because there the moving and the stationary part belonged to the same machine, while here the gap was between the moving part of a machine and "some extraneous object" (*N.B.* Claim would in any event have failed on foreseeability). Probably approved in *Callow* **20**.

17. Lovelidge v. Anselm Olding [1967] 2 Q.B. 351; [1967] 1 All E.R. 459, Widgery J.

Held, the hand power tool was machinery, and its unfenced shaft part of machinery. *Haynes v. John Hunt* (unreported, Blain J.) distinguished, where a similar tool was held not to be machinery. Judge based himself on *ratio decidendi in Liptrot* [1966] 2 All E.R. 247, C.A., where mobile crane was held to be machinery. *N.B. Liptrot* **18** went to H.L., where ratio was somewhat differently expressed, but would still seem to cover decision.

18. B.R.B. v. Liptrot [1969] 1 A.C. 136; [1967] 2 All E.R. 1072, H.L.

Plaintiff got caught between revolving body of mobile crane and wheel of chassis—*Held*, following *Cherry* **10**, that mobile crane was outside fencing provisions—but alternatively the Judge found that if fencing provisions did apply there was an unfenced dangerous part—on appeal these latter findings were not challenged until too late, so that only question in H.L. was whether mobile objects such as cranes were within the obligation to fence—*Held*, overruling *Cherry* **10**, that they were. The machine itself did not have to be fenced as a machine, but if it had dangerous parts (which was here doubtful), then they had to be fenced. *N.B.* as a result, in the case of factory vehicles, the dividing line would seem to be between the danger of factory accidents (against which there must be fencing) and the danger of traffic accidents (see Lord Pearson at 1087 B). Another argument put forward by the defendants was that the general fencing provision did not apply because the special provisions relating to cranes formed a separate and exclusive code. This argument was rejected, but Viscount Dilhorne (1076 I) said that he saw the force of a similar argument in relation to the special provisions relating to hoists. This was not referred to in the other speeches, so that in all probability the force of the decision in *Irwin* **13**, which was based on the provisions of the Northern Ireland Act and in which the point about a special and exclusive code does not appear to have been taken, remains intact, both in its general application and in special relation to hoists.

19. Millard v. Serck Tubes [1969] 1 W.L.R. 211; [1969] 1 All E.R. 598, C.A.

A machine which was drilling a hole in metal emitted a coil of swarf—which caught plaintiff's hand and dragged it into machine—*Held*, defendants liable for failing to fence. *N.B.* Accident happened in "an entirely unforeseeable way," but C.A. said that this, in the circumstances, was immaterial, because the drill had been admitted by defendant's expert to be dangerous and unfenced, and the mere fact that a machine which should have been fenced produced an accident in an unforeseen way which fencing would have obviated was no answer. This decision seems to have been impliedly approved by H.L. in *Callow* **20**. See latter at 645 H.

20. F. E. Callow v. Johnson [1971] A.C. 335; [1970] 3 All E.R. 639, H.L.

Metal workpiece revolved in machine—machine had a cutting tool attached to a boring bar, which moved forward imperceptibly as cutting proceeded—plaintiff's hand trapped in nip between boring bar and moving workpiece—*Held*, defendants liable: "Once it is accepted that a nip is dangerous within (F.A. 1961) s. 14, it seems to be immaterial whether it is caused by two moving parts or by a moving part in juxtaposition with a stationary part." *Hoare* **6** *approved* and *applied*. Later on, Lord Hailsham L.C. examined an argument based on analogies drawn from a headman's axe or a motor car pinning someone against a wall, the argument being that it could not be said that the wall or the execution block were dangerous parts; the L.C. said that he agreed, but only because the axe and the block, and the car and the wall, were not parts of the same thing or of the same complex, but independent entities which came into juxtaposition either adventitiously (in the case of the wall) or by deliberate action (in the case of the block). This line of reasoning would seem to go some way to support the decision in *Pearce* **16**.

21. Hindle v. Joseph Porritt [1970] 1 All E.R. 1142, Brabin J.

Held, the stationary part of the machine (a carrier arm) against which shoulder was thrown was not a dangerous part of machinery; it was just part of the machine. It would in any event have been idle to fence it, because then the plaintiff would have been thrown against the fence instead. *N.B.* This case antedates *Callow* **20**.

22. Ballard v. Ministry of Defence [1977] I.C.R. 513; [1977] C.L.Y. 1402, C.A.

Engine, a product of the factory, being tested—plaintiff and another reversed the fan blades so as to warm the factory during a power cut while it was being tested—*Held*, following *Parvin* **2** and *Irwin* **13**, the engine remained a product of the factory and the temporary ancillary benefit of providing warm air did not make it equipment which required to be fenced.

23. Wearing v. Pirelli [1977] 1 W.L.R. 48; [1977] 1 All E.R. 339, H.L.

Held, it was immaterial that the plaintiff's hand was brought into contact with the material encasing the drum rather than with the drum itself, and defendants were liable.

24. Mirza v. Ford Motor Co. [1981] I.C.R. 757; [1981] C.L.Y. 1210, C.A.

Held, not part of machinery. *Per* Ormrod L.J., the section did not apply to machinery or a part of machinery to which the concept of fencing was inapposite, such as the safety hook of a crane. *Per* Brandon L.J. and Hollings J., the term "part of machinery" was to be interpreted according to its ordinary and natural meaning, and the safety hook was not covered by the term so interpreted.

25. Johns v. Martin Simms [1983] I.C.R. 305; [1983] 1 All E.R. 127, Lawson J.

26. T.B.A. Industrial Products Ltd, v. Lainé [1987] I.C.R. 75; [1987] C.L.Y. 1854, D.C.

Held, that "machinery" in F.A. 1961, s. 14(1) did not include machinery in the process of installation or which was the product of the manufacturing process at a factory; but did include a machine installed for modification, testing and development which, if successful, would result in its being used in the manufacturing process.

U1. Read v. Medhurst Whites (1953) C.A. 215 A

Held, not part of machinery.

U2. Bill v. Fisher & Ludlow (1961) C.A. 376 A

Power press fed with continuous metal strip by feeding machine—press stamped metal 45 times a minute—each time this happened the continuous strip between press and feeding machine, which were 6 feet apart, arched up and subsided—just below strip was a girder joining the two machines and on this girder a block of wood 18 inches long had been put to stop clanging—plaintiff had to mind two pairs of these machines—to reach lever on distant pair he used to stoop and reach below girder—while doing so he put his hand on wooden block and it was caught in the nip between metal strip and block—*Held*,

(a) defendants liable at common law for failing to fence nip, the danger of which was reasonably foreseeable; but
(b) defendants not liable for breach of statutory duty as neither the block nor the girder were "machinery".

As to (b) Holroyd Pearce L.J. said (8 C) he accepted that when one part of a machine moved against an immobile part, both were machinery and both were dangerous, but here neither girder nor block (nor strip metal) were machinery. He approved *Hoare v. Grazebrook* **6** and disapproved *Lewis v. High Duty Alloys* **7**. *Eaves v. Morris Motors* **11** was explained thus (10 B):

> "So far as the burr or sharpness of the bolt was concerned, the bolt could not . . . be equated to the block since it was the sharpness or danger in the material and not the danger from the machinery itself which caused the accident. But in so far as any dangerous nip might be created between a stationary part of the machine and the bolts, which were being carried in the normal way by the force of the machinery so designed to carry them, the danger would be in the machinery and not in the quality or nature of the material."

(c) Transmission Machinery

1. Deane v. Edwards [1941] 2 All E.R. 274, Wrottesley J.

Plaintiff a garage hand operating a lift actuated by an electric motor—hand gets caught in the rope loop connecting lift to motor—*Held*, this was transmission machinery, and should have been fenced.

2. Richard Thomas & Baldwins v. Cummings [1955] A.C. 321; [1955] 1 All E.R. 285, H.L.

Plaintiff repairing a mechanical grindstone, the fencing of which had for this purpose been removed—in manually pulling the pulley belt his hand got trapped—*Held*, no liability, because although it was transmission machinery it could not be said that a machine was in motion when it was manually pulled for the purpose of repair.

*(d) "Securely Fenced"**

1. Chasteney v. Michael Nairn [1937] 1 All E.R. 376, D.C.

Lord Hewart C.J. at 379 A: ... "It is to be observed that the words are 'securely fenced' and not somewhat securely fenced."

* Abbreviations are explained in Introductory Note 1.

2. Vowles v. Armstrong Siddeley [1938] 4 All E.R. 796, C.A.

Held, that the duty to fence, once it arises, is absolute.

3. Dennistoun v. Greenhill [1944] 2 All E.R. 434, D.C.

Justices found machine was "securely fenced in the best known method at the time having regard to the work it had to do"—*Held*, this was not the test, and the finding was irrelevant to the question whether the machine was without qualification securely fenced. *Per* Viscount Caldecote L.C.J.: "If fencing is only secure in so far as it is all that is possible if the machine is to be used at all, that is not securely fencing" (437 E).

4. Smith v. Morris Motors [1950] 1 K.B. 194; [1949] 2 All E.R. 715, D.C.

Held, in deciding what was meant by "securely fenced," one has to look at the machine at the actual time of the accident, and if there was no fence, then, there was a breach; further, section 16 gives a sort of definition, or explanation, of what is meant by secure fencing. "Section 14 imposes the duty and section 16 defines its extent . . . " (Lynskey J.). (The references are to F.A. 1937.)

5. Burns v. Joseph Terry [1951] 1 K.B. 454; [1950] 2 All E.R. 987, C.A.

Plaintiff, in order to clear a shelf of some chocolate beans, went up a ladder—the ladder slipped sideways—plaintiff put out his hand and it got caught in a cogged pulley wheel. Hilbery J. held this was not reasonably foreseeable—*Held*, Denning L.J. dissenting, this was the right test, relying on **2** in some part, and defendant not liable. *Approved* by H.L. in **10**.

6. Smith v. Chesterfield Co-op. Society [1953] 1 W.L.R. 370; [1953] 1 All E.R. 447, C.A.

Bakery rolling machine—guard was provided, but girl could get her hand under it, as plaintiff did—*Held*, not securely fenced (60 per cent. contributory negligence). Lord Goddard C.J. (448 H) cited Lord Normand's dictum in *Lyon v. Don Brothers*, 1944 S.C.(J.) 5: "It can appositely be said that the standard to be observed is a fence which will prevent accidents from occurring in circumstances which may reasonably be anticipated, but the circumstances which may reasonably be anticipated include a great deal more than the staid, prudent, well-regulated conduct of men diligently attentive to their work, and the occupiers of factories are bound to reckon on the possibility of conduct very different from that. They are bound to take into account the possibility of negligent, ill-advised or indolent conduct on the part of their employees, and even of frivolous conduct, especially where young persons are concerned." And at 449 F Lord Goddard included "folly, in direct disobedience of orders" as within the zone of contemplation of the employer.

7. Charles v. S. Smith [1954] 1 W.L.R. 451; [1954] 1 All E.R. 499, Hilbery J.

Plaintiff employed at a machine with a perspex cover which could be lifted and which served as a guard—plaintiff lifted cover to feel inside, and while doing so involuntarily set the machine in motion with his leg—*Held*, (a) machine was not securely fenced, for it is not enough that "it is provided with a means of achieving security" (501 H), and (b), following *Cummings v. Richard Thomas and Baldwins* [1953] 2 All E.R. 43, C.A., there was also a breach of F.A. 1937, s. 16, since the only distinction was that in that case plaintiff's action was voluntary, whereas here it was involuntary (but *quaere* now this second ground, as *Cummings* was reversed by H.L. (see chap. 16(6)(f) **5**) on wider grounds).

8. Pugh v. Manchester Dry Dock [1954] 1 W.L.R. 389; [1954] 1 All E.R. 600, Donovan J.

Grinding machine—*Held*, no defence that machine would be unusable if fenced to prevent all contact. See **10**.

9. Jones v. Richards [1955] 1 W.L.R. 444; [1955] 1 All E.R. 463, Barry J.

Case under Threshing Machines Act 1878—*Held*, defendant liable: "A fence which depends for its efficacy on the memory and concentration of a single workman is not in truth a sufficient and secure fence" (470 B).

10. John Summers v. Frost [1955] A.C. 740; [1955] 1 All E.R. 870, H.L.

Plaintiff injured on a grindstone which was fenced by a hood except for an arc about 7 in. long at grinding face—more fencing would have made it commercially unusable—*Held*, it was not securely fenced, as there was an absolute duty to fence so that there was no longer a reasonably foreseeable risk of injury to the workman using the machine, even though he was careless or inattentive. **5**, which laid down the test of reasonable foreseeability, was expressly approved by Lords Reid and Keith, and impliedly so by the others.

11. Hodkinson v. Henry Wallwork [1955] 1 W.L.R. 1195; [1955] 3 All E.R. 236, C.A.

Held, that an unfenced transmission belt 9 feet above ground was not in such a position to be as safe as if fenced, and therefore breach of F.A. 1937, s. 13.

12. Boryk v. N.C.B., 1959 S.C. 1, I.H.

Coal cutting machine with unfenced picks—picks struck a wood tree—causing tree to be thrown against plaintiff—*Held*, defendants liable for failing to fence under C.M.A. 1911, s. 55, as the obligation to fence was not limited merely to the prevention of injury by direct contact with dangerous machinery.

13. Quintas v. National Smelting Co. [1960] 1 W.L.R. 217; [1960] 1 All E.R. 104, Devlin J.

Hand-rail of two rails 3 feet high to fence a moving cableway—gap of 18 inches in hand-rail—plaintiff went through gap and was struck by moving bucket—*Held*, not securely fenced, because, applying dicta of Lord Porter in *Carroll v. Barclay* (Chap. 16, (6)(e) **2**) and Lord Morton in *Summers v. Frost* **10** fencing must be such as to deter a man willing to run a minor risk and take a short cut, and therefore defendants liable (but 75 per cent. contributory negligence). Decision *reversed* by C.A. (see [1961] 1 All E.R. 630) on other grounds, without comment on above proposition.

14. Johnson v. J. Stone [1961] 1 W.L.R. 849; [1961] 1 All E.R. 869, Hinchcliffe J.

Plaintiff cutting castings with a bandsaw—the casting came into contact with an insecurely fenced pulley, which fractured and fell on plaintiff—*Held*, the duty to fence extended to fencing against tools and workpieces coming into contact with machinery, and defendants were therefore liable. Impliedly *overruled* in *Sparrow* **16**.

15. Close v. Steel Company of Wales [1962] A.C. 367; [1961] 2 All E.R. 953, H.L.

Bit of electric drill shattered and piece entered eye of plaintiff—*Held*, that "securely fenced" meant that a dangerous part should be securely fenced for the purpose of preventing the body of the operator coming into contact with the machinery, and therefore defendants not liable. *Nicholls v. Austin* (Chap. 16, (6)(e) **1**) and *Carroll v. Andrew Barclay* (Chap. 16, (6)(e) **2**) *followed.*

16. Sparrow v. Fairey Aviation [1964] A.C. 1019; [1962] 3 All E.R. 706, H.L.

Plaintiff scraping burrs from revolving component—scraping tool caught jaws of revolving lathe which held component and got out of control—plaintiff's hand thrown against some (but not a "dangerous") part of the machine—the jaws themselves were admittedly dangerous parts of machinery—*Held*, defendants not liable, because, following *Close* **15**, the only duty under the statute was to fence against contact of the worker with dangerous parts of the machine. *Semble*, contact with the clothing of a workman would come within the statute, but contact with a tool held by him did not.

17. Baxter v. Central Electricity Generating Board [1965] 1 W.L.R. 200; [1964] 2 All E.R. 815, Ashworth J.

Held, machine was securely fenced within B.R. 1948, reg. 85 (which did not contain any proviso about examination similar to F.A. 1961, s. 16): "One contemplates secure fencing as a protection for workpeople when they are operating machinery, and no one could suggest for one moment that this heater was a danger to anyone so long as it was being used as the makers intended" (819 G).

18. Uddin v. Associated Portland Cement Manufacturers [1965] 2 Q.B. 582; [1965] 2 All E.R. 213, C.A.

Man leaned over shaft to catch a pigeon—*Held*, defendants liable, but 50 per cent, contributory negligence.

19. Allen v. Aeroplane and Motor Castings [1965] 1 W.L.R. 1244; [1965] 3 All E.R. 377, C.A.

County court judge found that plaintiff was on a frolic of his own in getting his hand trapped—*Held*, that even so defendants were liable.

20. Foster v. Flexile Metal (1967) 4 K.I.R. 49; [1968] C.L.Y. 1589, Paull J.

Held, machinery not fenced within meaning of Act.

21. Millard v. Serck Tubes [1969] 1 W.L.R. 211; [1969] 1 All E.R. 598, C.A.

Held, defendants were liable, even though the exact manner of the accident could not be foreseen: "Once the two questions: Is the machinery dangerous? Is there a duty to fence it? have been answered in the affirmative, foreseeability is no longer relevant. If it is then proved that the plaintiff has suffered an injury by some part of his body coming into contact with the machinery and that this would not have occurred if the defendants had complied with their statutory duty, the defendants are liable" (Salmon L.J., 600 A). *Cf.* the cases in Chap. 16, (1)(e). Impliedly *approved* by H.L. in *Callow* (Chap. 16, (6)(b) **20**): see Lord Hailsham's speech at 645 H.

22. Wearing v. Pirelli [1967] 1 W.L.R. 48; [1967] 1 All E.R. 339, H.L.

Revolving drum—on which rubber material was fed—and then worked by plaintiff—while doing so, his tool jerked so that his hand was brought into contact with the revolving material—*Held*, defendants liable, as it was immaterial that the plaintiff's hand was caught by the revolving material rather than with the actual drum itself.

23. Scott v. Kelvin Concrete, 1993 S.L.T. 935; [1993] C.L.Y. 5356

Trying to repair a press, plaintiff climbed inside it via its hopper, and accidentally caused it to operate. Press had been designed with safety features including a key control (which had been wired out) and fences connected to safety switches (which had been taped up). The hopper could be reached without passing through any fences—*Held*, employer in breach of F.A. 1961, s. 14. Had the press been properly fenced with gates with interlock switches, it could not have operated while someone was inside it carrying out a repair.

U1. Bankhead v. De Havilland Aircraft Co. Ltd (1954) C.A. 318

Plaintiff's hand caught in machine—to save machine being out of action for a few days foreman had directed system of work whereby guards removed and piece of wood of insufficient length used—*Held*, defendants in breach of F.A. 1937, s. 14.

U2. Lancaster v. Wigan Brick Co. (1960) C.A. 1

Transmission shaft about 1 foot 4 in. above floor level—protected by a wooden barrier 3 feet 2 in. high—but unprotected on top—*Held*, not securely fenced, but defendants not liable because breach had nothing to do with the accident.

*(e) Fencing Against Things Flying Out**

		See also Intro. Notes
Material flying out—no duty to fence	1	6, 10
Broken machinery flying—whether duty to fence exists	2	–
MACHINERY FLYING OUT—KNOWN DANGER—DUTY TO FENCE	3	6, 10
MATERIAL EJECTED—NO DUTY TO FENCE—WIRE BEING WOUND ONTO DRUM	4	–
MATERIAL FLYING OUT—NO DUTY TO FENCE—PIECE OF WIRE	5	6, 10
MACHINERY FLYING OUT—KNOWN DANGER—CARBORUNDUM WHEEL—DUTY TO FENCE	6	–
Material or machinery flying out—no duty to fence	7	–

* Abbreviations are explained in Introductory Note 1.

1. Nicholls v. Austin [1946] A.C. 493; [1946] 2 All E.R. 92, H.L.

Woodworking machine—claim under F.A. 1937, s. 14—offcut flies out—*Held*, no duty under F.A. 1937, s. 14, to fence against dangerous articles or material ejected. *Applied* in **4** and **5**. *Followed* in **7**.

2. Carroll v. Andrew Barclay [1948] A.C. 477; [1948] 2 All E.R. 386, H.L.

Machine belt breaks and flies out—*Held*, F.A. 1937 did not impose any duty to fence against such danger. Lord Porter (486): "Fencing in my opinion means the erection of a barricade to prevent any employee from making contact with the machine, not an enclosure to prevent broken machinery from flying out." *But* Lord du Parcq (486–487), Lord Simon concurring (482), said that, if machines were dangerous because fragments or loose parts were sometimes ejected from them, then the obligation to fence might arise.

3. Dickson v. Flack [1953] 2 Q.B. 464; [1953] 2 All E.R. 840, C.A.

Part of vertical moulding machine flies out, this being a recognised danger—*Held*, defendants liable, *interalia*, for breach of F.A. 1937, s. 14. The decision was based in part on the fact that the danger of a part flying out was a recognised one. See **2**, where this question was discussed, but not decided. *Disapproved* in **7**.

4. Bullock v. G. John Power [1956] 1 W.L.R. 171; [1956] 1 All E.R. 498, C.A.

Wire being wound onto an electric drum which was fenced—loose end of wire rode up over guard and killed deceased—*Held*, applying **1**, the wire was "material" and not "part of machinery," and therefore defendants not liable. *But* see *Hoare* (Chap. 16, (6)(b) **6**).

5. Kilgollan v. W. Cooke [1956] 1 W.L.R. 527; [1956] 2 All E.R. 294, C.A.

Piece of wire (part of material) flies out—*Held*, defendant under no duty to fence under F.A. 1937, s. 14. **1** *applied.*

6. Rutherford v. R. E. Glanville [1958] 1 W.L.R. 415; [1958] 1 All E.R. 532, C.A.

Carborundum wheel disintegrates at high speed—known danger—drives hood up so that hood cuts plaintiff's wrist—*Held*, distinguishing **1**, the duty to fence included a duty to fence parts of machinery flying out, and the fact that it was the hood and not the part which struck plaintiff was immaterial, so that defendants were liable for failure to fence. *Disapproved* in **7**.

7. Close v. Steel Company of Wales [1962] A.C. 367; [1961] 2 All E.R. 953, H.L.

Bit of electric drill shattered and a piece entered eye of plaintiff—*Held*, defendants not liable—even if bit was dangerous, the obligation to fence did not extend to requiring fencing against parts of the machinery (or parts of the material) flying out. *Dickson v. Flack* **3**, *Newnham v. Taggart Mo* (unreported) and *Rutherford v. Glanville* **6** *disapproved. Nicholls v. Austin* **1** *followed* and *approved. But* Lord Goddard (961 D) said that if a machine had a known tendency to throw out parts of the machine or of the material, the absence of a shield might well make defendants liable at common law.

*(f) When Fencing Must Be Maintained**

		See also Intro. Notes
Exposure for cleaning—machine never fenced at all	1	–
TESTING AFTER TOOLSETTING—WHETHER "EXAMINATION OR ADJUSTMENT"	2	–
MACHINERY ATTENDANT—POSITION OF TOOLSETTER	2	–
Meaning of section 16	3	6, 10
Machinery "in motion"—plaintiff involuntarily setting unguarded machine in motion	4	"
Machinery "in motion"—whether includes manual movement of machine under repair	5	–
GUARD REMOVED FOR ADJUSTMENT OF MACHINE—SLOW ROTATION BY INCHING BUTTON—NOT "IN MOTION"	6	6, 10
Machinery "in motion"—inching button—young person cleaning roller of printing machine	7	6
New machinery—being worked for testing purposes—hoist	8	–
MACHINERY "IN MOTION"—PRINTING MACHINE MOVING IN SHORT JERKS AT SPEED—PREPARATORY TO MAIN OPERATION	9	–
Machinery "in use"—fan heater under examination and repair—being run with guard removed	10	6, 10
MACHINERY "IN MOTION"—SWITCHING LATHE ON AND THEN IMMEDIATELY OFF—TO EXPOSE AND GET AT SCREW ON COLLAR	11	–
"In motion or in use"—setting new mould in press—power accidentally switched on	12	–
"In motion or in use"—inching button—while cleaning rollers	13	–
"In motion or in use"—resetting with tool holder crawling forward in lowest gear	14	–
"IN MOTION"—INCHING BUTTON—SLOWLY ROTATING PRINTING PRESS	15	–
Maintenance electrician working on machine—wrongly thinking power switched off	U1	6, 10
Machine unfenced for adjustment by toolsetter	U2	"
Machine unfenced for adjustment—accidental slow rotation—not "in motion"	U3	–
"In motion"—inching button—plaintiff inadvertently pressing	U4	–
"In motion"—uncovenanted stroke by drop hammer—not "in motion"	U5	–

1. Atkinson v. Baldwins (1938) 158 L.T. 279, D.C.

Lord Hewart C.J. (281, bottom): "... although no doubt if a man has failed to fence at all, he cannot be heard to say that he is not liable on the ground that the fence has been removed for repair."

2. Nash v. High Duty Alloys [1947] K.B. 377; [1947] 1 All E.R. 363, C.A.

Held, testing after toolsetting was not examination or adjustment, and therefore machine must be fenced—*Held*, also that a toolsetter had to be certificated like any other machinery attendant, though he was exempt from the clothing, etc. provisions of reg. 5.

* Abbreviations are explained in Introductory Note 1.

3. Smith v. Morris Motors [1950] 1 K.B. 194; [1949] 2 All E.R. 715, D.C.

Lynskey J. (at 200, middle): "Section 14 imposes the duty, and section 16 defines its extent ... " (References are to F.A. 1937.)

4. Charles v. S. Smith [1954] 1 W.L.R. 451; [1954] 1 All E.R. 499, Hilbery J.

Plaintiff employed at a machine with a perspex cover which could be lifted, and which served as a guard—plaintiff lifted cover to feel inside, and while doing so, his leg involuntarily set the machine in motion—*Held*, defendants liable, because (a) machine was not securely fenced, for it was "not enough that it was provided with a means of achieving security" (501 H), and (b), following *Cummings v. Richard Thomas* [1953] 2 All E.R. 43, there was also a breach of F.A. 1937, s. 16, since the only difference between the two cases was that here plaintiff's action was involuntary, whereas in *Cummings* it was voluntary. *But quaere* this second ground now, since *Cummings* has been reversed by H.L. see **5**.

5. Richard Thomas and Baldwins v. Cummings [1955] A.C. 321; [1955] 1 All E.R. 285, H.L.

Plaintiff repairing a mechanical grindstone, the fencing of which had for this purpose been removed—in manually pulling the pulley belt his hand got trapped—*Held*, no liability, because although it was transmission machinery, it could not be said that a machine was in motion when it was being manually pulled for the purpose of repair.

6. Knight v. Leamington Spa Courier [1961] 2 Q.B. 253; [1961] 2 All E.R. 666, C.A.

Inching button pressed to rotate printing rollers for cleaning—guard lifted—dangerous nip—plaintiff's fingers caught in nip—*Held*, defendants not liable, because the use of the inching button, which produced only a slow rotation, did not constitute the machinery being "in motion or in use" within F.A. 1937, s. 16. *Richard Thomas and Baldwins v. Cummings* **5** *applied.*

7. Kelly v. John Dale [1965] 1 Q.B. 185; [1964] 2 All E.R. 497, Winn J.

Held, following *Knight* **6** and *Dodd v. Ben Capper* **U3**, machine was not "in motion or use," but defendants were liable under second limb of F.A. 1937, s. 20 (young persons not to clean machinery if thereby exposed to risk of injury from any moving part).

8. Irwin v. White Tomkins and Courage [1964] 1 W.L.R. 387; [1964] 1 All E.R. 545, H.L.

Held, the sack hoist, being dangerous machinery, had to be fenced, notwithstanding that it had not been taken into commercial use. Lord Hodson (549 G) said that he saw no justification for drawing a distinction between machinery which had actually been brought into commercial use and the same machinery being run in a normal manner preparatory to commercial use.

9. Stanbrook v. Waterlow [1964] 1 W.L.R. 825; [1964] 2 All E.R. 506, C.A.

Heidelberg printing machine—normally fenced—but, when being set up for next run, was mechanically rotated for very short distances, using the main starting lever—causing machine to rotate at 40 r.p.m. within seconds—*Held*, machine was "in motion"—slow movement by hand or by an inching button was not "in motion," but movement at speed, as here, was.

10. Baxter v. Central Electricity Generating Board [1965] 1 W.L.R. 200; [1964] 2 All E.R. 815, Ashworth J.

B.R. 1948, reg. 4: duty on employer "using" machinery to fence same in accordance with reg. 85—this was treated as equivalent to the duty to fence machinery "in use" under F.A. 1937, s. 16—calor gas fan heater was being used to dry out machinery—it was not working properly—to investigate fault, plaintiff ran it with guard removed—*Held*, applying the *ratio decidendi* in *Cummings* **5** and *Knight* **6**, heater was not "in use" at the time, but was under examination or repair. *Held*, also, that in any event heater did not constitute machinery: see Chap. 16, (6)(b) **14**.

11. Mitchell v. Westin [1965] 1 W.L.R. 297; [1965] 1 All E.R. 657, C.A.

To tighten screw on collar of lathe, plaintiff removed guard and switched on and then at once off, in order to turn lathe and expose screw—he could have done it by hand—*Held*, machine was not "in motion," as there was only an intermittent movement, no evidence of high speed, and no substantial movement comparable to ordinary running. The Court approved the statement of Holroyd Pearce L.J. in *Knight* **6** as to the effect of the decision of H.L. in *Cummings* **5**, as follows:

> " . . . (*Cummings* **5**) is authority for the proposition that the words 'in motion or in use' connote the substantial movement of its normal working, or if it is not at the time achieving its normal purpose, some movement reasonably comparable to its normal working . . . The slow sporadic rotation or intermittent movement . . . intended to place it more advantageously for cleaning or repair is not normal motion or use within the section . . . "

12. Horne v. Lee Refrigeration [1965] 2 All E.R. 898, Cantley J.

Held, machine was not "in use," applying dictum of Upjohn L.J. in *Knight* **6**, as it was not being used for any commercial purpose; but it was "in motion," applying dictum of Pearson L.J. in *Mitchell* **11**, as the press moved in the same way as its normal working. *But* claim failed because the sole fault causing the accident was that of the deceased (see Chap. 16, (4) (d) **12**).

13. Finnie v. John Laird, 1967 S.L.T. 48; [1967] C.L.Y. 2727, Ct. of Sess.

Held, machinery not "in motion" or "in use".

14. Foster v. Flexile Metal (1967) 4 K.I.R. 49; [1968] C.L.Y. 1589, Paull J.

Semble, machinery not in motion or in use.

15. Normille v. News of the World (1975) 119 S.J. 301; 18 Man.Law 3, C.A.

Held, following *Knight* **6** and *Mitchell* **11**, press not "in motion or use".

U1. Goodman v. Key & Whiting Ltd (1951) C.A. 156

Plaintiff maintenance electrician—sent by employer to service machine at defendants' factory—plaintiff erroneously assumed power was off—while plaintiff was working on machine operator started it up—plaintiff thereby injured—*Held*, defendants liable under F.A. 1937, s. 14 (but 60 per cent. contributory negligence).

U2. Broughton v. Joseph Lucas Ltd (1958) C.A. 330 A

Plaintiff toolsetter employed by defendants—plaintiff testing machine—put in hand to make slight adjustment—uncovenanted stroke—plaintiff's hand injured—*Held*, defendants in breach of F.A.

1937, s. 16—toolsetters thought immune from F.A. 1937, s. 16, until C.A. decision in **2**—defendants drew clear attention of everyone concerned to obligation by putting up notice and getting all toolsetters including plaintiff to sign copy of notice—unpopular as slowed down work affecting bonus—defendants took no steps by disciplinary insistence or rearrangement of wages or time to make it practicable for precautions to be carried out—defendants 75 per cent. to blame—25 per cent. contributory negligence against plaintiff.

U3. Dodd v. Ben Capper (1961) C.A. 368

Plaintiff replacing roller in printing machine—unintentionally pressed button which momentarily caused slow rotation—*Held*, following *Knight v. Leamington Spa Courier* **6**, defendants not liable, as machine not "in motion".

U4. Palmer v. Shirley and Warbey Box Co. (1965) C.A. 193

Held, following *Knight* **6** and *Dodd v. Ben Capper* **U3**, defendants not liable.

U5. Hanson v. Thomas Smith (1966) C.A. 208

*(g) Young Persons**

		See also Intro. Note
No young person to work at prescribed machines—duty is on employer—not on employee	1	6
Cleaning bacon slicer—young person rotating blade contrary to instructions—absolute prohibition	2	–
Cleaning cylinder of printing machine—applying rag while cylinder still in motion—contrary to instructions	3	–

1. McCafferty v. Brown, 1950 S.C. 300; 1950 S.L.T. 366, O.H.

Plaintiff a young person within F.A. 1937, s. 21 (no young person to work at prescribed machines, etc.)—while working at such a machine, hand got caught therein—defendants argued that plaintiff was himself in breach of s. 21—*Held*, not so, and defendants wholly liable, as the duty was solely on the occupier to prevent breach. See also *Shearer v. Harland Wolff* [1947] N.I. 102, to like effect.

2. Dewhurst v. Coventry Corporation [1969] 3 W.L.R. 249; [1969] 3 All E.R. 1225, D.C.

Prosecution under O.S.R.P.A. 1963, s. 18 (similar to F.A. 1961, s. 20)—employee under 18 had been shown how to clean slicer without rotating blade—but did latter because it was quicker—*Held*, offence proved, because s. 18(1) imposed absolute prohibition, if the operation exposed the employee to a risk of injury from a moving part. See also *Kelly* Chap. 16, (6) (f) **7**).

3. Denyer v. Charles Skipper [1970] 1 W.L.R. 1087; [1970] 2 All E.R. 382, C.A.

Young person was instructed to clean cylinder of printing machine by wiping it, then inching cylinder round and, when stationary, cleaning the further surface exposed—contrary to instructions

* Abbreviations are explained in Introductory Note 1.

he applied rag while cylinder was still moving—*Held*, defendants liable, but 50 per cent. contributory negligence.

(7) Factories

*(a) Meaning of "Factory"**

(*N.B.* See also Examples at end of subsection.)

		See also Intro. Notes
Persons who are employed–not students at technical institute	1	–
Adapting for sale—includes compressing waste paper	2	–
Factory under construction—can constitute factory	3	6, 10
ARTICLE—INCLUDES COAL-GAS	4	6
Running repairs and minor adjustments—defined	5	–
SHOP—ADAPTING FOR SALE DONE ON PREMISES—NOT A FACTORY	6	–
SEPARATE FACTORY—MAINTENANCE BUILDING IN FACTORY	7	–
PURPOSE INCIDENTAL TO MAIN PROCESS—MAINTENANCE BUILDING	7	–
FACTORY UNDER CONSTRUCTION—TARPAULIN DIVIDING OFF PART IN USE	8	6
Purpose incidental to main process—not administrative staff canteen	9	6
Purpose incidental to main process—includes industrial canteen	10	–
BY WAY OF TRADE—CLUB GARAGE	11	–
Repairing or washing—bus depot	12	–
Persons who are employed—does not include prisoners	13	–
RATING CASES—MUST RECEIVE SAME CONSTRUCTION	14	–
Adapting for sale—sorting and grading furs	15	–
PURPOSE INCIDENTAL TO MAIN PROCESS—NOT APRON OUTSIDE HANGER	16	6
Shop—bacon slicing done in backroom—is a factory	17	–
Article—includes water	18	–
Purpose incidental to main process—pump house and filter house in water pumping station	18	–
ADAPTING FOR SALE—NATURAL DRYING OF TIMBER	19	–
Purpose incidental to main process—water pump house in factory	20	–
PURPOSE INCIDENTAL TO MAIN PROCESS—OFFICES AND LIBRARY USED IN CONJUNCTION WITH PHOTOGRAPHIC DARK ROOM	21	6
Curtilage—two contiguous open areas	22	6
Making of an article—assembly of steel parts in the open	22	6
Article—not radio waves emitted from studio	U1	
Derelict site within factory precincts—not part of factory	U2	

1. Weston v. L.C.C. [1941] 1 K.B. 608; [1941] 1 All E.R. 555, Wrottesley J.

Held, not a factory: "... Parliament did not intend by the words 'persons who are employed' to cover scholars, pupils and learners" (560 B).

* Abbreviations are explained in Introductory Note 1.

2. Kinder v. Camberwell B.C. [1944] 2 All E.R. 315, Lord Caldecote C.J.

Held, premises factory, as compressing waste-paper a process of adapting for sale.

3. Barrington v. Kent Rivers Catchment Board [1947] 2 All E.R. 782; 64 T.L.R. 35, Hilbery J.

Building of workshop—machinery in building, but not assembled or fixed—walls and roof (apparently) built—during installation of plant plaintiff was employed to inspect a lorry—he fell down uncovered inspection pit—*Held*, that as plaintiff was doing one of the processes set out in F.A. 1937, s. 151, the place was a factory, and therefore plaintiff could recover (under s. 25(3)).

4. Cox v. Cutler [1948] 2 All E.R. 665; [1948] W.N. 345, C.A.

Held, (a) coal-gas was an "article" within F.A. 1937, s. 151, but (b) a blitzed gasholder which no longer did or could hold gas was not a gasholder or part of a gas factory. See **12**.

5. Griffin v. London Transport [1950] 1 All E.R. 716; [1950] W.N. 152, Lord Goddard C.J.

6. Joyce v. Boots Cash Chemists [1951] 1 All E.R. 682n.; [1951] W.N. 176, C.A.

Held, not a factory, for the manual labour used was for a purpose incidental only to the substantial purpose for which the premises were used.

7. Thurogood v. Van den Berghs [1951] 2 K.B. 537; [1951] 1 All E.R. 682, C.A.

Plaintiff, an electrician, was testing an electric fan in the maintenance building of a margarine factory—the building was separate from the main factory in which the fan ordinarily was sited—*Held*, the processes in the maintenance building were incidental to the main purpose of the factory, and that accordingly it was not a separate factory (when the fan, being machinery not used, but being repaired, therein, would not have been required to be fenced), but part of the main factory, so that the requirement to fence applied.

8. Street v. British Electricity Authority [1952] 2 Q.B. 399; [1952] 1 All E.R. 679, C.A.

Factory under construction—part in use—tarpaulin divides part in use from part not in use—*Held*, part not in use was to be deemed not to be part of factory, under F.A. 1937, s. 151(6). *Followed* in **24**.

9. Thomas v. British Thomson-Houston [1953] 1 W.L.R. 67; [1953] 1 All E.R. 29, Havers J.

Cleaner employed by defendants injured in administrative-staff restaurant—*Held*, not part of the factory, because although within the curtilage and therefore within the definition of factory under F.A. 1937, s. 151(1), it was excluded by s. 151(6) as being "solely used for some purpose other than the processes carried on in the factory." Judge used as one test whether the restaurant was essential for the welfare of the *industrial* workers.

10. Luttman v. I.C.I. [1955] 1 W.L.R. 980; [1955] 3 All E.R. 481, Jones J.

Held, canteen was part of factory, following the rating case, *London Co-operative v. S. Essex Assessment Committee* [1941] 3 All E.R. 252, as approved by C.A. in **8**, because the use of the canteen was a purpose incidental to the processes of manufacture, and was therefore not a place solely used for some purpose other than the processes.

11. Automobile Proprietary v. Brown [1955] 1 W.L.R. 573; [1955] 2 All E.R. 214, C.A.

Held, that a limited company established for the purpose of running a club (the R.A.C.) was not functioning "by way of trade" in operating premises for the repair and maintenance of its own vehicles. (Rating case.)

12. Jones v. Crosville Motor Services [1956] 1 W.L.R. 1425; [1956] 3 All E.R. 417, Hallett J.

Held, bus depot where only washing of windows and minor running repairs carried out not a factory. It was argued that it was because it came within (b) of the main definition ("repairing or washing of any article") but judge said that the exclusion in paragraph (vi) of the additional definitions ("not being premises where only cleaning, washing, running repairs . . . carried out") was meaningless in that case, and he was inclined to think that the reason was that "for purposes of gain" in the main definition must mean direct gain, although from the cases, including rating cases (which could afford assistance in construction, as appeared from **18**, 686 C-H), this in general was doubted (as indirect gain seemed to be included also), but in the present case there seemed no other way of reconciling (b) of the main definition with the exclusion to paragraph (vi) of the additional definitions.

13. Pullen v. Prison Commissioners [1957] 1 W.L.R. 1187; [1957] 3 All E.R. 470, Lord Goddard C.J.

Held, not a factory, as there was no relationship of master and servant, and no employment for wages. **2** *applied.*

14. Fatstock Marketing v. Morgan [1958] 1 W.L.R. 357; [1958] 1 All E.R. 646, C.A.

On the relationship between Factory Act and rating cases Sellers L.J. (655 D) cited with approval dictum of Scrutton L.J. in *Bailey v. Potteries Electric Traction* [1931] 1 K.B. 385, 393: "It must be borne in mind that if you exclude a hereditament from derating because there is no manufacturing process carried on in it, you are depriving the workmen of the protection of the Factory Acts, as well as the employer of the benefit of derating."

15. Hudson's Bay Co. v. Thompson [1960] A.C. 926; [1959] 3 All E.R. 150, H.L.

Fur skins were received from individual trappers and were then sorted and graded into lots of uniform quality for sale—the skins as received were received in bales—*Held*, the bale was the unit to be considered and not individual skins, and the process carried on amounted to an adapting for sale of the bales. (Rating case.)

16. Walsh v. Allweather Co. [1959] 2 Q.B. 300; [1959] 2 All E.R. 589, C.A.

Concrete apron outside hanger which was being used by defendant employers as a factory—plaintiff was engaged on breaking concrete with a mechanical pick—piece of concrete entered his eye—*Held*, the apron did not constitute a factory because, although it was within the "close curtilage or precincts of" the hangar, it was "a place solely used for some purpose other than the processes carried on in the factory" within F.A. 1937, s. 151(6), and therefore was deemed not to be a factory.

17. McLeavy v. Liptons [1959] C.L.Y. 1284, Finnemore J.

Bacon-slicing machine in backroom of grocer's shop—room used to receive, unpack and treat goods for retail sale—*Held*, room was a factory.

18. Longhurst v. Guildford Water Board [1963] A.C. 265; [1961] 3 All E.R. 545, H.L.

Accident in pump house of Water Board—premises comprised land and two buildings, a filter house and a pump house—*Held*, the premises were not a factory, because:

(a) the water in the filter beds was "an article," and therefore the filter house was a factory; but
(b) the pump house was used for a different process, namely pumping water to consumers, from the process carried on in the filter house, and therefore the pump house was not part of the factory constituted by the filter house.

Lord Reid (547 D): "The word 'article' itself appears to me to be capable of meaning anything corporeal."

19. Buncombe v. Baltic Sawmills [1961] 1 W.L.R. 1181; [1961] 3 All E.R. 272, C.A.

Held, storage of timber so that the timber dried itself naturally was not an adapting for sale.

20. Newton v. John Stanning [1962] 1 W.L.R. 30; [1962] 1 All E.R. 78, D.C.

Factory containing a pump house—the pump house was an essential part of the work—*Held*, pump house part of the factory.

21. Paul Popper v. Grimsey [1963] 1 Q.B. 44; [1962] 1 All E.R. 864, C.A.

Photographic business—premises on second floor with corridor in middle—on one side were ancillary offices and a library of negatives, on the other were the dark room and the glazing room—*Held*, the whole premises were a factory, as prima facie they came within F.A. 1937, s. 151 (1), because "the existence of a manufacturing activity in the close or precinct will make the whole of the premises a factory, unless some particular part of the premises is excluded by the terms of section 151 (6)"—which was not the case here.

22. Barry v. Cleveland Bridge Co. [1963] 1 All E.R. 192, Lyell J.

Steel erectors had the non-exclusive use of two areas—areas were contiguous, save for an access road which intersected them—one area was used for a factory process, *i.e.* the making of an article, and the other for storing the articles—*Held*, both areas were within the close curtilage or precincts of the factory, for "a close need not have any boundary wall or fence" (195 I)—*Held*, further, the assembly on a quay of steel parts to make larger components such as booms constituted the making of an article within F.A. 1937, s. 151 (1)

U1. Granada T.V. v. Kerridge (1963) C.A. 67

Rating case—T.V. studio—the occupiers made electrical impulses which were emitted in waves—*Held*, this did not constitute an "article," which, to apply dictum of Lord Reid in *Longhurst* **18**, had to be "something corporeal, something you can see and get hold of"—*Held*, also, T.V. studio was not an electrical station within F.A. 1901, 6 Sched. 6, para. 20.

U2. Armstrong v. B. S. C. (1989) C.A. 118

Security officer patrolling derelict site within precincts forming a factory tripped over debris on ground—*Held*, defendant not liable. F.A. 1961, s. 29 (1) excluded by s. 175 (6), which provides that "where a place situate within the . . . precincts forming a factory is solely used for some purpose other than the processes carried on in the factory, that place shall not be deemed to form part of the factory for the purposes of this Act . . . ".

Examples

Factory

- Dry dock with ship in ... 1
- Garage ... 4
- Industrial canteen ... 5
- Compressing waste paper ... 7
- Industrial canteen ... 8
- Factory under construction ... 9
- Egg packing station ... 10
- ENGINEER TESTING CONCRETE ... 12
- Testing aeroplane propellers ... 13
- Tram repair shop ... 14
- TESTING ELECTRIC FAN ... 18
- PROCESSING SPARE PARTS ... 19
- Industrial canteen ... 23
- SLAUGHTHERHOUSE ... 28
- SLAUGHTERHOUSE ... 29
- **Sorting and grading furs** ... 30
- Slicing bacon in shop backroom ... 32
- **Water filter house** ... 33
- Barge moored at repair yard ... 34
- Pump-house in factory ... 36
- Dock transit shed ... 37
- Photographic dark room ... 38
- Assembling steel parts in open ... 39
- Office block: used for designing engines ... 40
- **Workshop at back of shop: repairing TV sets** ... 41
- Hospital workshop ... 42
- Film studio: in which films made and scenery adapted ... 44

Not a Factory

- Technical institute ... 2
- KITCHEN IN INSTITUTION ... 3
- Ship in wet dock ... 6
- BLITZED GASHOLDER ... 11
- SHIP UNDER REPAIR AT JETTY ... 15
- Milk-cooling depot ... 16
- CHEMIST'S SHOP ... 17
- FACTORY UNDER CONSTRUCTION ... 20
- STORING AND ARRANGING STOCK ... 21
- Administrative staff canteen ... 22
- Disused part separated off by sheeting ... 24
- CLUB RUNNING GARAGE ... 25
- Bus depot ... 26
- Prison workshop ... 27
- APRON OUTSIDE HANGER ... 31
- **Water pump-house** ... 33
- DRYING TIMBER NATURALLY ... 35
- Premises used to produce and deliver T.V. programmes ... 43
- *Television studio* ... U1
- *Hospital laundry: loading bags on open space just outside laundry* ... U2
- *Testing crane in disused factory* ... U3
- *Workshop attached to school physics laboratory* ... U4

1. Rippon v. P.L.A. [1940] 1 K.B. 858; [1940] 1 All E.R. 637, Tucker J.
2. Weston v. L. C. C. [1941] 1 K.B. 608; [1941] 1 All E.R. 555, Wrottesley J. *Applied* in **27**.
3. Wood v. L. C. C. [1941] 2 K.B. 642; [1941] 2 All E.R 230, C.A.
4. Deane v. Edwards [1941] 2 All E.R. 274, Wrottesley J. See also [1941] 3 All E.R. 331, C.A.
5. London Co-op v. S. Essex A. C. [1942] 1 K.B. 53; [1941] 3 All E.R. 252, D.C. (Rating case.) *Applied* in **23**.
6. Lovell v. Blundells [1944] K.B. 502; [1944] 1 All E.R. 53, Tucker J.

7. Kinder v. Camberwell B. C. [1944] 2 All E.R. 315, Lord Caldecote C. J.
8. Simmonds v. Assessment Committee [1944] K.B. 231; [1944] 1 All E.R. 264, D.C. (Rating case.)
9. Barrington v. Kent Rivers C. B. [1947] 2 All E.R. 782; 64 T.L.R. 35, Hilbery J.
10. A. Richardson v. Middlesbrough A. C. [1947] K.B. 958; [1947] 1 All E.R. 884, D.C. (Rating case.)
11. Cox v. Cutler [1948] 2 All E.R. 665; [1948] W.N. 345, C.A.
12. Hendon Corporation v. Stanger [1948] 1 K.B. 571; [1948] 1 All E.R. 377, C.A.
13. Acton B. C. v. Middlesex A. C. [1949] 2 K.B. 10; [1949] 1 All E.R. 409, D.C. (Rating case.)
14. Griffin v. London Transport [1950] 1 All E.R. 716; [1950] W.N. 152, Lord Goddard C.J.
15. Chatburn v. Manchester Dry Docks (1950) 83 Ll.L.R. 1, C.A.
16. Wiltshire C. V. C. v. London Co-op. [1950] 1 All E.R. 937; 1 T.L.R. 1016, D.C. (Rating case.)
17. Joyce v. Boots Cash Chemists [1951] 1 All E.R. 682n; [1951] W.N. 176, C.A.
18. Thurogood v. Van den Berghs [1951] 2 K.B. 537; [1951] 1 All E.R. 682, C.A.
19. Cockram v. Tropical Preservation Co. [1951] 2 K.B. 827; [1951] 2 All E.R. 520, C.A. (Rating case.)
20. Street v. B. E. A. [1952] 2 Q.B. 399; [1952] 1 All E.R. 679, C.A. *Applied* in **24**.
21. Davis Cohen v. Hall [1952] 1 All E.R. 157; [1952] W.N. 33, C.A. (Rating case.)
22. Thomas v. B. T. H. [1953] 1 W.L.R. 67; [1953] 1 All E.R. 29, Havers J.
23. Luttman v. I. C. I. [1955] 1 W.L.R. 980; [1955] 3 All E.R. 481, Jones J.
24. Prince v. Carrier Engineering [1955] 1 Lloyd's Rep. 401, Parker L.J.
25. Automobile Proprietary v. Brown [1955] 1 W.L.R. 573; [1955] 2 All E.R. 214, C.A. (Rating case.)
26. Jones v. Crosville [1956] 1 W.L.R. 1425; [1956] 3 All E.R. 417, Hallett J.
27. Pullen v. Prison Commissioners [1957] 1 W.L.R. 1187; [1957] 3 All E.R. 470, Lord Goddard C.J.
28. Gledhill v. Liverpool Abattoir [1957] 1 W.L.R. 1028; [1957] 3 All E.R. 117, C.A.
29. Fatstock Marketing v. Morgan [1958] 1 W.L.R. 357; [1958] 1 All E.R. 646, C.A. (Rating case.)
30. Hudson's Bay Co. v. Thompson [1960] A.C. 926; [1959] 3 All E.R. 150, H.L. (Rating case.)
31. Walsh v. Allweather [1959] 2 Q.B. 300; [1959] 2 All E.R. 589, C.A.
32. McLeaby v. Liptons (1959) 228 L.T. 195; 109 L.J. 667, Finnemore J.
33. Longhurst v. Guildford Water Board [1963] A.C. 265; [1961] 3 All E.R. 545, H.L. (Rating case.)
34. Moor v. Greenhithe Lighterage [1961] 1 Lloyd's Rep. 149, Elwes J.
35. Buncombe v. Baltic Sawmills [1961] 1 W.L.R. 1181; [1961] 3 All E.R. 272, C.A.
36. Newton v. John Stanning [1962] 1 W.L.R. 30; [1962] 1 All E.R. 78, D.C. (Rating case.)
37. Fisher v. P. L. A. [1962] 1 W.L.R. 234; [1962] 1 All E.R. 458, Stevenson J.
38. Paul Popper v. Grimsey [1963] 1 Q.B. 44; [1962] 1 All E.R. 864, D.C. (Rating case.)
39. Barry v. Cleveland Bridge [1963] 1 All E.R. 192, Lyell J.
40. Powley v. Bristol Siddeley [1966] 1 W.L.R. 729; [1965] 3 All E.R. 612, Megaw J.
41. J. & F. Stone Lighting v. Haygarth [1968] A.C. 157; [1966] 3 All E.R. 539, H.L.
42. Bromwich v. National E. N. T. Hospital [1980] I.C.R. 450; [1980] 2 All E.R. 663, Cantley J.
43. Ulster T. V. v. Comr. of Valuation [1980] 5 N.I.J.B.; [1980] C.L.Y. 1986, N.I.C.A.
44. Dunsby v. B. B. C., *The Times*, July 25, 1983; [1983] C.L.Y. 1687, Peter Pain J.

U1. *Granada T. V. v. Kerridge* (1963) C.A. 67.
U2. *Pilkington v. Mersey R. H. A.* (1978) C.A. 717.
U3. *Bacon v. Union Cold Storage* (1979) C.A. 128.
U4. *Mallick v. Allied Schools* (1980) C.A. 328.

*(b) Meaning of "Occupier" under Factories Act**

		See also Intro. Notes
Switchboard under construction by independent contractor—factory owner is nevertheless the occupier thereof	1	–
Factory can only have one occupier	2	–

* Abbreviations are explained in Introductory Note 1.

1. Turner v. Courtaulds [1937] 1 All E.R. 467, D.C.

Held, that a factory owner who was "making an additional section to the switchboard" of the factory was the occupier thereof, even though at the time it was still under construction by an independent contractor.

2. Smith v. Cammell Laird [1940] A.C. 242; [1939] 4 All E.R. 381, H.L.

3. Rippon v. Port of London Authority [1940] 1 K.B. 858; [1940] 1 All E.R. 637, Tucker J.

Unsafe access down side of dry-dock—*Held*, dock owners were occupiers for purpose of F.A. 1937, ss. 25 and 26, while ship repairers were notional occupiers for purpose of Shipbuilding Regulations (reg. 1)—*Held* dock owners 75 per cent., ship repairers 25 per cent., to blame. *Followed* in **6**.

4. Meigh v. Wickenden [1942] 2 K.B. 160; [1942] 2 All E.R. 68, D.C.

Held, receiver for debenture holders occupier because he was complete master of the affairs of the company. "The occupier's responsibility under the Act does not depend on proof of personal blame or even upon knowledge of the contravention" (Lord Caldecote C.J.).

5. Cox v. Cutler [1948] 2 All E.R. 665; [1948] W.N. 345, C.A.

Scott L.J. (688 C) and Wrottesley L.J. (670 E) and Wynn-Parry J. (674 A) all cite with approval definition of occupier given by Lord McLaren in *Ramsey v. Mackie* (1904) 7 F. (Ct. of Sess.) 106, 109: " 'Occupier' plainly means the person who runs the factory . . . , who regulates and controls the work that is done there . . ."

6. Welch v. Admiralty [1952] 2 Lloyd's Rep. 520, Havers J.

Held, following **3**, that dock owners were Factories Act occupiers, since they had only granted a licence to repairers to use dock.

7. Whalley v. Briggs Motors [1954] 1 W.L.R. 840; [1954] 2 All E.R. 193, Streatfeild J.

Plaintiff employed by X, an independent contractor in defendants' factory, to break up concrete with a mechanical pick, being a process within F.A. 1937, s. 49—sues defendants—*Held*, that X and not defendants was the notional occupier by virtue of F.A. 1937, s. 139 (owner of machine used in factory deemed to be occupier in relation to persons employed by him)—therefore claim failed.

8. Robinson v. R. Durham and Sons, *The Times*, June 10, 1992; [1992] C.L.Y. 2221, H. H. Judge Stroyan Q.C. *Held*, a heavy goods vehicle is a "machine moved by mechanical power" for the purposes of F.A. 1961, s. 163, (replacing F.A. 1937, s. 139) if used in a factory. Thus the vehicle's owner or hirer would be deemed to be the occupier of the factory *vis-à-vis* his own employees.

*(c) Lifting Tackle and Lifting**

			See also Intro. Notes
Travelling crane may be "dangerous machinery"—duty to fence	1	F.A. 1937, s.14	6, 10
"FREE FROM PATENT DEFECT"—MARKESHIFT SLING COMPRISING CHAINS OF UNEQUAL LENGTH, SPRUNG HOOKS AND KNOTS IN CHAINS	2	F.A. 1937, s. 23(1)	6
TRAVELLING CRANE—COMES WITHIN 20 FEET OF PLACE OF EMPLOYMENT—BUT HITS TOOL AND NOT WORKMAN	3	F.A. 1937, s. 24(7)	"
"OF SOUND MATERIAL"—LIFT OR HOIST—ABSOLUTE DUTY	4	F.A. 1932, s. 22(1)	"
"Properly maintained in efficient working order"—absolute duty	5	"	"
"GOOD CONSTRUCTION"—NOT MEAN FIT FOR PARTICULAR PURPOSE	6	F.A. 1937, s. 23(1)	"
PARTS AND WORKING GEAR" OF LIFTING MACHINE—ELECTRIC CABLE TAKING CURRENT TO CRANE MAGNET	7	F.A. 1937, s. 24(1)	"
"Overhead travelling crane"—not include a crane travelling on rails on ground	8	F.A. 1937, s. 24(7)	6, 10
Definitions of various types of cranes	8	F.A. 1937, s. 24	"
Travelling crane may be "dangerous machinery"—duty to fence	8	F.A. 1937, s. 14	"
"GOOD CONSTRUCTION—NOT MEAN FIT FOR ANY PARTICULAR PURPOSE	9	F.A. 1937, s. 23(1)	6
"PROPERLY MAINTAINED"—MEANS MERELY THAT THE "GOOD CONSTRUCTION", ETC., MUST BE MAINTAINED	9	F.A. 1937, s. 24(1)	"
Prevent . . . contact . . . with moving part of lift"—absolute duty—plaintiff putting hand through outer door	10	F.A. 1937, s. 22(3)	"
"Free from patent defect"—does not qualify preceding phrases—jib breaking through metal fatigue	11	F.A. 1937, s. 24(1)	"
"Adequate strength"—must be adequate to actual, rather than designed, load	12	F.A. 1937, s.23(1)	6
No lifting tackle . . . shall be used"—rusty mooring wire used to lift raft—use not authorised by occupier	13	"	"
MANUAL LIFTING—145 LBS. UNAIDED	14	F.A. 1961, s.72	7

* Associations are explained in Introductory Note 1.

"RAISING . . . MATERIALS—INCLUDES USE OF CRANE AND HOOK TO LEVER UP SCAB ADHERING TO FOUNDRY FLOOR	15	F.A. 1961, s.26	–
"PARTS AND WORKING GEAR" OF LIFTING MACHINE—INCLUDES ELECTRICAL CONTRACTORS TAKING CURRENT TO CRANE MACHINERY	16	F.A. 1961, s.27	–
ELECTRICAL DEFECT IN CRANE—PLAINTIFF MISTAKENLY PRESSING ACTUATING BUTTON TILL THUMB RUPTURED	16	"	–
MANUAL LIFTING—ONE-LEGGED MAN	17	F.A. 1961, s.72	7
Fork-lift truck—is not a "hoist or lift"	18	F.A. 1961, s.22	–
"Employed to lift carry or move"—doing work which involves moving object—person is "employed" to move it—unless told he must not do so single handed	19	**F.A. 1961, s. 72**	7
Turning over stillage 1–1¼ cwt.—too heavy for woman	19	"	"
85 lbs. for two women—is "likely to cause injury"	20	O.S.R.P.A. 1963, s.23	"
MANUAL LIFTING—HEAVY BREAD TRAY UNAIDED	21	"	"
EXERTING FORCE OF ABOUT 100 LBS—NO BREACH OF STATUTORY DUTY	22	F.A. 1961, s.72	"
"EMPLOYED TO LIFT OR MOVE"—"TO HIM"—"LIKELY"—MEANINGS CONSIDERED	22	"	"
LIFTING BATCHES OF TILES EACH WEIGHING 25 LBS—EMPLOYER NOT LIABLE—SCOPE OF S. 72 EXPLAINED—MEANING OF "TO HIM" CONSIDERED	23	"	"
"Part . . . of lifting machine"—includes operating switch	U1	*F.A. 1937, s. 24(1)*	6
"Teagle opening"—meaning	U2	*F.A. 1937, s.22(10)*	"
Manual lifting—140 lbs. unaided	U3	*C.(G.P.) R. 1961, reg. 55*	–
"Employed to lift"—employee left to select safe load	U4	*F.A. 1961, s.72*	7
Lifting cartous each weighting 24 lbs—defendant not liable	U5	"	"
Moving metal weighing 54 lbs—defendant not liable	U6	"	"
Two employees lifting 240 lbs—defendant not liable	U7	"	"
Lifting nylon roll weighing 123 lbs—defendant not liable	U8	"	"

1. Fowler v. Yorkshire Electric Power [1939] 1 All E.R. 407, Lawrence J, and jury

Plaintiff on ladder put hand on track of overhead travelling crane—crane struck hand—*Held*, crane and track were dangerous machinery within F.A. 1901, s. 10(1)(*c*) (now re-enacted in F.A. 1937, s. 14), and defendants liable. See *also* **8**.

2. Dawson v. Murex [1942] 1 All E.R. 483, C.A.

Held, or rather admitted (see 488 B), there was a breach.

3. Holmes v. Hadfields [1944] K.B. 274; [1944] 1 All E.R. 235, C.A.

Plaintiff's place of employment consisted of a platform and girder, part in and part out of the 20 feet radius of travelling crane—plaintiff stood outside 20 feet area, but crane hit tool of plaintiff lying within 20 feet area which struck plaintiff—*Held*, defendants liable, as prohibition against coming within 20 feet of place of employment was an absolute one.

4. Whitehead v. James Stott [1949] 1 K.B. 358; [1949] 1 All E.R. 245, C.A.

Held, absolute duty, and latent defect no defence.

5. Galashiels Gas Co. v. O' Donnell [1949] A.C. 275; [1949] 1 All E.R. 319, H.L.

6. Beadsley v. United Steel [1951] 1 K.B. 408; [1950] 2 All E.R. 872, C.A.

Suitable lifting tackle available—but defendants' employee used lifting tackle which though well made was unsuitable for job—deceased killed—*Held*, defendants not liable under F.A. 1937, s. 23(1)(*a*), as "good construction" simply meant "well made," and did not imply the tackle must be suitable for any particular purpose.

7. Gatehouse v. John Summers [1953] 1 W.L.R. 742; [1953] 2 All E.R. 117, C.A.

Held, the electric cable was no "part" of the lifting machine, and therefore F.A. 1937, s. 24, did not apply.

8. Carrington v. John Summers [1957] 1 W.L.R. 504; [1957] 1 All E.R. 457, Streatfeild J.

Held, that "overhead travelling crane" meant a crane which travels overhead, and not an overhead crane which travels, and therefore excluded a crane which travelled along rails on the ground, even though it was an overhead crane in the sense (which judge thought was the proper test) that the lifting mechanism was at a height higher than that to which the load could be raised. Various definitions of other types of crane also suggested—*Held*, also that the fact that there were special provisions in F.A. 1937, s. 24 (7), for overhead travelling cranes did not exclude the general duty to fence under F.A. 1937, s. 14. See **1**.

9. Gledhill v. Liverpool Abattoir [1957] 1 W.L.R. 1028; [1957] 3 All E.R. 117, C.A.

Held, following **6**, that "good construction" meant "well made," and a chain did not cease to be of good construction merely because it was unsuitable for a particular purpose—*Held*, also, following *Latimer v. A.E.C.* (Chap. 16, (5) (h) **8**), that "properly maintained" in F.A. 1937, s. 24 (1), meant that it was the "sound construction," etc., which had to be maintained, and this does not import any requirement as to suitability.

10. Blakeley v. C. & H. Clothing [1958] 1 W.L.R. 378; [1958] 1 All E.R. 297, Lynskey J.

Held, absolute duty and defendants liable.

11. McNeil v. Dickson, 1957 S.C. 345, Lord Wheatley

Held, a plea of latent defect in the form of metal fatigue was irrelevant, as the words "free from patent defect" did not qualify the preceding phrases.

12. Milne v. Wilson, 1960 S.L.T. 162, O.H.

Rope sling breaks—claim that rope not of adequate strength—defendants plead that "adequate" meant sufficient to carry designed load only—*Held*, not so, and that actual load being carried had to be considered. Defendants liable.

13. Barry v. Cleveland Bridge Co. [1963] 1 All E.R. 192, Lyell J.

Plaintiff and two fellow-employees lifting a heavy raft by crane from quayside into water—plaintiff and one fellow-employee, contrary to permitted practice, were riding on raft when one of the four wire loops of raft, into which the lifting chains had been fitted, broke and plaintiff went into the water—the quay area was a factory, and the wire loops on the raft were for mooring only and not for lifting, as plaintiff and fellow-employees knew—wire loops were rusty and patently defective—*Held*, the use of such lifting tackle was a breach of F.A. 1937, s. 23(1)(a) inasmuch as use was not confined to uses authorised by employer, and employers therefore liable—*Held*, further, that taking into account disobedience of plaintiff in riding on raft and his part in the breach as to user of lifting tackle, plaintiff could only recover 50 per cent. *Aliter, semble*, if only cause had been riding on raft, when it would have been a case of all three agreeing to flout orders, and plaintiff would have failed entirely.

14. Kinsella v. Lebus (1963) 108 S.J. 14, C.A.

Held defendants not liable, on the ground (as explained, though not necessarily approved, in *Brown* **19**) that it was not too heavy for a man to lift a jig weighing 145 lbs. on to a press. In so far as the decision may have been on the ground that plaintiff was not employed to lift the jig by himself, because he had help available, decision was *disapproved* in **19**. But plaintiff *won* at common law: see Chap. 15, (4)(a) **13**.

15. Ball v. Richard Thomas & Baldwins [1968] 1 W.L.R. 192, [1968] 1 All E.R. 389, C.A.

16. Evans v. Sanderson (1968) 4 K.I.R. 115; [1968] C.L.Y. 1597, C.A.

In breach of F.A. 1961, s. 27(1) (all parts of lifting machine to be of good construction etc.) electrical contactors of crane were defective—plaintiff, mistakenly, thought button was faulty and pressed it until his thumb ruptured—*Held*, (a) not following dictum to contrary in *Gatehouse* **7**, the contactors were parts of the crane, and (b) the injury was caused by the defect, so that defendants were liable.

17. Peat v. Muschamp (1969) 7 K.I.R. 469; [1970] C.L.Y. 900, C.A.

One-legged man lifting chains—weight was all right for an ordinary man—plaintiff had been told to get help if he wanted it—and help was available—*Held*, defendants not in breach of statutory duty. *But* see now *Brown* **19**, where this decision is probably *disapproved* by H.L.

18. Oldfield v. Reed & Smith [1972] 2 All E.R. 104, Lawton J.

19. Brown v. Allied Ironfounders [1974] 1 W.L.R. 527; [1974] 2 All E.R. 135, H.L.

Painting stillages weighing 1–1¼ cwt.—in order to paint them they had to be turned over—it was admitted that turning over a stillage was too heavy for a woman—normal practice was for two women to turn them—but sometimes one did it by herself—plaintiff could have had help if she wanted—and she knew that turning them single-handed was a departure from normal practice—but she did not know, and had not been told, that she must not turn them by herself—plaintiff injured while turning stillage—*Held*, she was employed to paint the stillages, and as painting them involved turning them, she was therefore employed to turn them, and "not having been told not to turn them by herself . . . she cannot . . . be said to have been doing something which she was not employed to do, when she turned them single handed" (Lord Dilhorne, 139 B, three other Law Lords concurring). Viscount Dilhorne (140 E) *said* that the test was what the plaintiff was employed to do. If he was told that he must not lift an object without assistance, then he was not employed to do so; if on the other hand, it was left to him to decide and he decided to lift it himself, then he was employed to do so. *Kinsella* **14** and *Peat* **17** both considered, and in so far as their ratio was that plaintiff had been left to get help, readily available, if he required it, both were *disapproved.*

20. Hamilton v. Western S.M.T., 1977 S.L.T. 66, O.H.

21. Black v. Carricks [1980] I.R.L.R. 448; [1980] C.L.Y. 919, C.A.

Issue was whether the plaintiff manageress of a bakery shop whose assistants were off ill and who was injured lifting a bread tray which was normally moved by two was "required" to lift the same within O.S.R.P.A. 1963, s.23—*Held*, she was not (see Chap. 16,(14) **4** for details). The Court *said* that the word "employed" in s.72(1) of the Factories Act 1961 was of similar application to "required", though wider; and that in considering either phrase a court had to consider not only the weight of the object and the physique of the employee but all other surrounding circumstances. In this connection *Kinsella* **14** was a decision on its own facts and should no longer be cited.

22. Bailey v. Rolls Royce (1971) Ltd [1984] I.C.R. 688; [1984] C.L.Y. 2282, C.A.

Plaintiff injured back exerting force of about 100 lbs when manoeuvering a component. Plaintiff, to defendants' knowledge, had exhibited predisposition to back injury—*Held*:

(a) Defendant not liable in negligence—on the evidence, under no duty to stop plaintiff from doing the job, warn him of risk of injury or instruct him to ask for help, in view of the extent of the risk of injury and the extent of likely injury should the risk materialise.
(b) On the evidence defendant not in breach of F.A. 1961, s.72(1), as to which:
  (i) a person was "employed to lift or move" a load so heavy as to be likely to injure him only if his work necessarily involved the lifting or moving of such a load, and not if his work involved the selection by him of a safe load to lift or move;
  (ii) "to him" referred is the particular employee involved;
  (iii) "likely" meant more probable than not, the test being objective and unrelated to the employer's actual or constructive knowledge of the risk of injury.

23. Whitfield v. H. R. Johnson (Tiles) Ltd, [1990] 3 All E.R. 426; [1990] I.R.L.R. 525, C.A.

Plaintiff was required each day to lift between about 270 and 360 batches of tiles each weighing about 25 lbs from trolley onto conveyor belt. Was vulnerable to back injury because of congenital condition of which defendant knew nothing, but had had no previous problems with the lifting until, one day, she felt pain in back and leg when lifting—*Held*, defendants not negligent and not in breach of F.A. 1961, s. 72, which applied only where the likelihood of injury arose from the weight of the load, having regard to the sex, build, physique and other obvious or known characteristic of the employee, and all relevant circumstances such as the nature of the object lifted, and the available grip, foothold and space. The words "to him" in s. 72 did not require the court to have regard to an employee's characteristics of which his employer was unaware. *Bailey v. Rolls Royce (1971) Ltd* **22** should not be interpreted as ruling otherwise.

U1. Bradley v. Thomas and Baldwins Ltd (1952) C.A. 32

U2. Kenny v. Hutchison (1959) C.A. 2

Meaning of "teagle opening" discussed.

U3. Moran v. Kitching (1969)

Plaintiff was instructed to move angle iron weighing 140 lbs—it was not strongly disputed that this was a breach of C.(G.P.)R. 1961, reg. 55 (which is in similar terms to F.A. 1961, s. 72)—*Held*, that plaintiff was 25 per cent. negligent himself in not trying to get help.

U4. Pilkington v. Mersey R.H.A. (1978) C.A. 717

P injured back lifting 113 lb laundry bag—*Held*, no breach of s. 72, as this was a case where P could properly be left to select what was a safe load to him. *Dicta* of Lord Dilhorne (to the contrary) in *Brown* **19** disapproved, and dictum of Lord Kilbrandon (to the effect that if the work did not necessarily involve moving injuriously heavy weights it could often be left to the employee to make up the load to be moved) preferred.

U5. Chessum v. Lesley U.K. Sales Ltd (1984) C.A. 669

Plaintiff injured elbow lifting cartons each weighing 24 lb from pallet onto workbench. She decided to do this work in absence of a male porter who would normally do it—*Held*, defendant not in breach of F.A. 1961, s. 72. The injury was caused not by the weight of any carton but by repetitive flexing of the elbows. Defendants not liable at common law either—system of work not unsafe.

U6. Turner v. British Leyland (U.K.) Ltd (1984) C.A. 698

U7. Shaw v. Cleveland Bridge & Engineering Co. Ltd (1985) C.A. 1060

Plaintiff was injured lifting a pipe weighing 240 lb assisted by a mate—*Held*, defendant not negligent and not in breach of F.A. 1961, s. 72. Pipe was not too heavy to be lifted by two persons.

U8. Frank v. Halls Barton Ropery (1990) C.A. 369

Plaintiff aged 23 injured back when he bent down to lift a two-wheel barrow containing rolls of nylon weighing 123 lbs—*Held*, defendant not liable in negligence and not in breach of F.A. 1961, s. 72.

*(d) Dust and Fumes**

			See also Intro. Notes
DUST FROM SHOEMAKING—TUBERCULOSIS—PROOF OF NEXUS	1	F.A. 1937, s. 47(1)	6
LIKELY TO BE INJURIOUS—NOT INCLUDE PERSON WITH IDIOSYNCRASY	2	F.A. 1937, s. 47(1)	6
WOOD DUST CAUSING DERMATITIS—DUTY TO PROTECT AGAINST INHALATION ONLY	2	F.A. 1937, s. 47(1)	6
EFFECTIVE AND SUITABLE PROVISION—REFER TO VENTILATION ONLY	2	F.A. 1937, s. 4(1)	6.9
ALL PRACTICABLE MEASURES TO REMOVE DUST—MUST HAVE REGARD TO EXISTING STATE OF KNOWLEDGE	3	F.A. 1937, s. 47(1)	6
All practicable measures—masks—employers must take steps to induce men to wear	4	F.A. 1937, s. 47(1)	6
ALL PRACTICABLE MEASURES—DANGER UNKNOWN IN CURRENT STATE OF KNOWLEDGE.	5	F.A. 1937, s. 47(1)	6
SUBSTANTIAL QUANTITY OF DUST—BELIEVED HARMLESS—EXTENT OF DUTY TO PROTECT..	5	F.A. 1937, s. 47(1)	6
FUMES IN BOILER ROOM—NOT A "WORKROOM"	6	F.A. 1937, ss. 47(1), 4(1)	6, 9
ALL PRACTICABLE MEASURES—DANGER UNKNOWN AT TIME—SUBSTANTIAL QUANTITY OF DUST	7	F.A. 1937, s. 47(1)	6
EXHAUST APPLIANCES—OBLIGATION ONLY ARISES WHEN DUST ORIGINATES FROM FIXED POINT	7	F.A. 1937, s. 47(1)	6
Effective and suitable provision—refers to ventilation only—not to general duty to render dust harmless	8	F.A. 1937, s. 4(1)	6, 9
Ventilation—whether failure gives right of action	8	F.A. 1937, s. 4(1)	6, 9
Prevent dust accumulating—refers to deposits of dust only	8	F.A. 1937, s. 47(1)	6
Effective and suitable provision—refers to ventilation only—not to general duty to render dust harmless	9	**F.A. 1937 s. 4(1)**	6, 9

* Abbreviations are explained in Introductory Note 1. See also Introductory Note 3(E).

Ventilation—whether failure gives right of action	9	**F.A. 1937 s. 4(1)**	6, 9
Inadequate ventilation—may be a material cause of pneumoconiosis	9	**F.A. 1937 s. 4(1)**	6, 9
Swing frame grinders—not portable grinding machines	9	**F.A. 1937 s. 4(1)**	6, 9
All practicable measures—danger unknown at time—substantial quantity of dust	10	F.A. 1937, s. 47(1)	6
Likely to be injurious—"substantial quantity of dust"—duty only arises if defendants knew or ought to have known	10	F.A. 1937, s. 47(1)	6
Incidental safeguard—respirator giving protection against known dust giving incidental protection against unknown injurious dust	10	F.A. 1937, s. 47(1)	6
All practicable steps—to remove inflammable powder from tank before welding—defendants unaware powder there	11	F.A. 1937, s. 28(4)	6
Continuing breach—part outside limitation period—pneumoconiosis from foundry dust	12	F.A. 1937, s. 4(1)	6, 9
Inhalation over long period—how far action statute-barred	13	F.A. 1937, s. 4(1)	–
Dust from foundry sand—danger recognised since 1950	14	F.A. 1961, s. 63(1) (now repealed)	–
INJURIOUS FUMES—SAFETY PAMPHLET ISSUED IN 1965	15	F.A. 1961, s. 63(1) (now repealed)	–
ALL PRACTICABLE MEASURES—DEGREE OF KNOWLEDGE REQUIRED—EMPLOYER MUST CONSIDER RELEVANT MEDICAL AND TECHNICAL LITERATURE—AND SAFETY PAMPHLETS	15	F.A. 1961, s. 63(1) (now repealed)	–
Dust in cotton mill—from carding and brush stripping—producing byssinosis	16	F.A. 1961, ss. 4, 63 (now repealed) and 1	9
Asbestos dust—shipyard painter later dying of mesothelioma—defendant liable	17	F.A. 1937, ss. 4(1), 47(1) F.A. 1961, s. 4(1) S.S.R. 1960, reg. 53(2)	6, 9
Carbon monoxide poisoning	U1	*F.A. 1937, s. 47*	6
Pneumoconiosis from "innocent" dust—minimal addition from "guilty" dust	U2	*F.A. 1937, s. 47*	6
Fumes—trichlorethylene—inadequate ventilation—but plaintiff addict to inhaling	U3	*F.A. 1937, s. 4(1)*	6, 9

Rubbing slipstones on fine sand—silicosis	U4	*F.A. 1937, s. 47(1)*	6
Oxygen leak from pipe of cutter—confined space	U5	*S.R. 1960, reg. 48(1)*	–

1. Mist v. Toleman [1946] 1 All E.R. 139, C.A.

Held, onus being on plaintiff to prove nexus, he had failed to do so. See *Bonnington Castings v. Wardlaw* (Chap. 16 (3) (a) **8**).

2. Ebbs v. James Whitson [1952] 2 Q.B. 877; [1952] 2 All E.R. 192, C.A.

Sandpapering monsonia wood—dust which gave plaintiff dermatitis because he had a particular idiosyncrasy—*Held*, claim failed, because under F.A. 1937, s. 47, (a), the quantity was not substantial, (b) it was not likely to be injurious to persons employed, since the plaintiff's case was one of personal idiosyncrasy (and perhaps because there was only one recorded case of dermatitis from such cause—193 A), and (c), *per* Hodson L.J. at 196 A, s. 47 was only directed to protecting persons against inhalation; and claim under s. 4 failed because the section was only directed to protecting persons employed by ventilation, and lack of ventilation played no part in this particular accident. *Applied* in **8**. See *also* **9**, where H.L. appear to have approved this interpretation of s. 4(1).

3. Adsett v. K. & L. Steelfounders [1953] 1 W.L.R. 773; [1953] 2 All E.R. 320, C.A.

Tipping sand in foundry and shovelling it through a grid onto a conveyor belt—dust used to rise through grid, and gave plaintiff pneumoconiosis—defendants installed a new type of extractor plant in 1942—plaintiff alleged if it had been installed earlier he would not have got disease—defendants had in fact been the first to instal this type of extractor—*Held*, that, in deciding whether "all practicable measures" had been taken, "one must have regard to the state of knowledge at the time, and, particularly to the knowledge of scientific experts," and according to this test, claim failed (322 D. Singleton L.J.). *But* see **5**. *Approved* by C.A. in **7**.

4. Crookall v. Vickers Armstrong [1955] 1 W.L.R. 659; [1955] 2 All E.R. 12, Glyn-Jones J.

Steel foundry—known risk of silicosis—masks available for anyone who asked for one—but attempts to induce the men to wear them were half-hearted—*Held*, that "all practicable measures" included the provision of masks, and the taking of steps by defendants to induce men to wear them, and defendants were therefore liable.

5. Gregson v. Hick Hargreaves [1955] 1 W.L.R. 1252, [1955] 3 All E.R. 507, C. A.

Iron foundry—dust causing silicosis—until then no one realised that the dust might contain silica—plaintiff on appeal did not argue the "likely to be injurious" limb (probably because of **2**), but said that he should have been protected against "a substantial quantity of dust" under the second limb—*Held*, defendants liable, because there was a substantial quantity of "ordinary, visible dust" (Jenkins L.J. 514 H), and they could have taken practicable measures to protect plaintiff against it, it being "irrelevant whether the dust is known or believed to be noxious or not" (515 D). Once it became known that the dust was noxious, defendants' duty under the first limb ("likely to be injurious") came into operation (514I). On this basis, current state of knowledge *of danger* appears to be irrelevant when what is "practicable" is being considered, or perhaps all substantial quantities of dust are to be deemed potentially dangerous by the statute even if current knowledge is quite to the contrary. Parker L.J. however (516) said that "practicable" only included measures which were feasible in the light of current knowledge, and he then went on to say that the danger to be guarded against was a danger that silica would be inhaled (516 H) and that defendants were liable for not taking all practicable measures against this danger—but if the danger was unknown in the then state of knowledge, how was it "practicable" (as defined) to guard? Singleton L.J. (513 D) applied the same reasoning as Jenkins L.J., *ante*. *N.B.* No other cases seem to have been cited to the Court.

6. Brophy v Bradfield [1955] 1 W.L.R. 1148; [1955] 3 All E.R. 286, C.A.

Held, ss. 4 and 47 only applied to protect persons in workrooms, and a boiler-room was not a workroom, and therefore claim failed.

7. Richards v. Highway Ironfounders [1955] 1 W.L.R. 1049; [1955] 3 All E.R. 205, C.A.

(This case was heard before **5**.) Substantial quantity of dust given off in foundry—contained silica, but unknown at material time—*Held*, case must go back for new trial as to whether defendants had taken "all practicable measures". As to this phrase, the court approved dictum of Singleton L.J. in **3** (current state of knowledge to be taken into account—Evershed M.R., 209 I), and it would appear that the question posed by the court was whether, if defendants had taken all practicable measures to protect against the ordinary dust, such measures would have included the provision of a mask of a type which, incidentally, would have given protection against the then unknown danger from silica, and to what extent such protection would have been effective. (See Evershed M.R., 211 E—*Held*, also the obligation to supply exhaust appliances only arose when the dust came from a definable and fixed point of origin, and not when, as here the dust came from anywhere and everywhere all over the foundry floor. See *also* **10**—result of *new trial*.

8. Graham v. Co-operative Wholesale Society [1957] 1 W.L.R. 511; [1957] 1 All E.R. 654, Devlin J.

Plaintiff contracted dermatitis from mahogany dust—an unknown risk at time—he sued at common law and under F.A. 1937, ss. 4(1) and 47(1)—*Held*, defendants not liable. Under s. 4(1) judge left open question of whether an action lay, but said that the section on its proper construction, following **2** merely imposed a duty to ventilate, which defendants had done; and under s. 47(1) the duty (apart from a duty to prevent inhalation) was merely a duty to prevent dust accumulating as a deposit, and it could not be said that the dust which got onto the plaintiff's skin was a deposit in this sense. As to s. 4(1) see **9**.

9. Nicholson v. Atlas Steel Foundry [1957] 1 W.L.R. 613; [1957] 1 All E.R. 776, H.L.

Held, that inadequate ventilation meant that silica dust remained suspended in atmosphere longer than it should, thus exposing plaintiff to additional risk, and defendants liable—*Held*, also that swing frame grinders were not portable grinding machines for the purpose of a certificate of exemption under Grinding of Metals Regulations 1925, reg. 1. The proposition of **2** and **8** that F.A. 1937, s. 4(1), refers to ventilation only is supported by the dictum of Lord Simonds (779 F, Lords Oaksey and Morton concurring) saying: " ... if the statute prescribes a proper system of ventilation by the circulation of fresh air so as to render harmless, etc ... "

10. Richards v. Highway Ironfounders [1957] 1 W.L.R. 781; [1957] 2 All E.R. 162, Pearson J.

Case of silica dust in foundry—new trial had been ordered C.A. in **7**—judge found that a substantial quantity of ordinary visible dust had been given off plus a quantity of invisible injurious dust of which defendants at material time neither were not ought to have been aware—to protect against ordinary visible dust defendants could have provided various types of respirators but only one, the Mark IV, which was comparatively cumbersome, would have incidentally protected against the injurious invisible dust—*Held*, defendants not liable for failing to take all practicable measures. Judge said that, owing to the "practicable" qualification the phrase "likely to be injurious" meant that defendants must have had actual or constructive knowledge to be liable and the same must apply to the alternative limb "substantial quantity of dust" (applying **2** and **5**). He then went on to deal with "practicable measures" which defendants ought to have taken against the only hazard to which in view of the above the statute then applied, namely the ordinary, visible dust; and he concluded that defendants would probably have supplied less cumbersome respirators than the Mark IV, and that if Mark IVs had been provided the men would probably not have worn them. Judge seems incidentally to have assumed that if Mark IVs had been the only protection available against the ordinary dust, defendants would have been liable, even though the protection thus given against the real mischief, the invisible dust, would have been purely incidental and not in pursuance of any statutory obligation to protect against such dust. See 166 E-H. But query whether this is correct in view of *Kilgollan v. W. Cooke* (Chap 16(1) (e)**3**).

11. Williams v. Holliday (1957) 107 L.J. 378; [1957] C.L.Y. 1408, Davies J.

Held, the shaft of the vat was "plant, tank or vessel" and defendants, although unaware powder there, liable for not taking all practicable steps to remove it.

12. Clarkson v. Modern Foundries [1957] 1 W.L.R. 1210; [1958] 1 All E.R. 33, Donovan J.

Held, plaintiff could recover whole damage—see Chap. 16,(3) (a) **10**.

13. Cartledge v. Jopling [1963] A.C. 758; [1963] 1 All E.R. 341 H.L.

Decision in effect *reversed* by Limitation Act 1963.

14. Wallhead v. Ruston and Hornsby (1973) 14 K.I.R. 285; [1973] C.L.Y. 737, Bagnall J.

Plaintiff worked in iron foundry from 1924 to 1964—during which time he developed bronchitis and emphysema—this condition was not caused, but was aggravated, by dust from the foundry sand—in 1950 a book was issued which led to the danger becoming generally recognised—*Held*, that from 1950 on defendants were in breach of statutory duty to take all practicable measures. Damages assessed accordingly.

15. Cartwright v. G.K.N. Sankey (1973) 14 K.I.R. 349; [1973] C.L.Y. 1445, C.A.

Arc welder exposed to injurious fumes—judge dismissed action because insufficient indication of danger from medical and other literature—but in 1965 Ministry issued pamphlet (Dust and Fumes in Factory Atmospheres) which contained ceiling limits—*Held*, it was the duty of an employer, when required to take "all practicable measures," to consider the relevant medical and other technical literature and also any relevant official safety pamphlets, and having regard particularly to the 1965 pamphlet, defendants were here liable.

16. Brooks v. J. & P. Coates [1984] 1 All E.R. 702; [1984] C.L.Y. 1012, Boreham J.

P employed in D's cotton mill from 1935 to 1965. P regularly exposed to dust from carding and brush stripping and as a result developed bronchitis and in 1979 byssinosis was diagnosed—*Held*,

(a) D were in breach of s. 4. They had known that the dust could cause byssinosis, but had failed prior to 1963 to render the dust harmless by adequate ventilation, although it was practicable for them to have done so. Proof of actual or constructive knowledge of the danger was a prerequisite to liability under s. 4.

(b) D were in breach of s. 63. The dust was both substantial and offensive. D had failed to take all practicable precautions to protect P from inhaling the dust (by the provision of a respirator) and/or to prevent the dust from accumulating and/or to fit exhaust appliances: "I take practicable in this context to mean a precaution which could be taken . . . without practical difficulty" (718 G).

(c) "There was no breach of s. 1. 'Clean' had to depend on the nature of the processes, and absolute cleanliness could not be achieved when spinning cotton. Furthermore, it was doubtful if s. 1 related to dust produced in the course of a process carried on in the factory.

17. Bryce v. Swan Hunter Group plc [1988] 1 All E.R. 659; [1987] 2 Lloyds Rep. 426, Phillips J. See Chap. 16,3(b) **18** for full details.

U1. Wickwar v. Bryant and Stenner (1959) C.A. 33 A

Appeal from jury verdict that plaintiff contracted carbon monoxide poisoning—*Held*, that there was evidence to support verdict. In course of long judgment Morris L.J. went in detail into the circumstances in which such poisoning could arise.

U2. James v. Austin Motor (1959) C.A. 55

Fettling shop—pneumoconiosis caused by dust in atmosphere generally—defendants' process had also contributed some similar dust—but not in any proportion which was material—*Held*, defendants not liable.

U3. Pettit v. Layfield Oura (1961) C.A. 136 A

Inhalation of trichlorethylene fumes—inadequate ventilation—but plaintiff had intentionally leaned over tank to inhale and against conduct of this nature good ventilation would have been of no effect—*Held*, therefore, following *Bonnington* (Chap. 16,(3)(b) **7**), that defendants not liable, as plaintiff had not proved injury was due to breach. For two other cases of inhaling trichlorethylene fumes, which did not turn on statutory duty, see *Jones v. Lionite* (Chap. 15(2)(b) **U1**) and *Peebles v. Armstrongs Patents* (Chap. 15(2)(d) **U5**).

U4. Nash v. Parkinson Cowan (1962) C.A. 121

Held, defendants not liable under F.A. 1937, s. 47(1) or at common law, because danger at the time not foreseeable by "a reasonably informed employer."

U5. Cram v. Ryton Marine (1976) C.A. 424

Shipbuilding—plaintiff and others remedying bulkhead plate in small compartment—oxygen leak from their cutter—plaintiff swished a compressed air pipe about for a time—then struck an arc to do the burning—residual oxygen immediately ignited—*Held*, defendants liable for breach of S.R. 1960, reg. 48(1) (ventilation).

(e) Goggles and Eyes

(*N.B.* The corresponding section in the Third Edition contained a number of cases decided prior to the coming into force on April 10, 1975 of the Protection of Eyes Regulations 1974. These cases have not been retained. The 1974 Regulations were revoked with effect from January 1, 1993 by the Personal Protective Equipment at Work Regulations 1992.)

NO DUTY ON EMPLOYER TO IDENTIFY THE PROCESSES FOR WHICH EYE PROTECTORS SHOULD BE WORN 1

1. Coe v. Port of London Authority, *The Times*, May 16, 1988; [1988] C.L.Y. 1738, C.A.

Held, Protection of Eyes Regulations 1974 impose no duty on an employer to identify for an employee provided with eye protectors pursuant to the Regulations the processes for which reg. 11 requires the employee to wear protectors.

(f) Welfare Provisions*

			See also Intro. Notes
DUTY TO PROVIDE "SUITABLE ACCOMMODATION" FOR CLOTHING—WHETHER ACTION LIES IF CLOTHING STOLEN	1	F.A. 1937, S. 43	6, 9
Inadequate washing facilities—dermatitis	2	F.A. 1937, s. 42(1)	"
LIGHTING—EMPLOYEE ARRIVING EARLY AND GOING TO SWITCH ON MORE LIGHTS—TRIPS—NO STATUTORY BREACH	3	F.A. 1961, S. 5	9
LIGHTING—FACTORY ROAD UNLIT IN EARLY MORNING—LIGHTING INSTALLED IN ROAD AND AVAILABLE	4	"	"
Unlit steel staircase—duty to light is absolute	5	"	"
Duty to provide "clean" factory—whether action lies for spilt sulphuric acid	U1	*F.A. 1937, s. 1*	6, 9
Lighting—factory road unlit	U2	*F.A. 1961, s. 5*	9

1. McCarthy v. Daily Mirror [1949] 1 All E.R. 801; 65 T.L.R. 501, C.A.

"Suitable accommodation" to be provided for clothing (F.A. 1937, s. 43)—*Held*, that the risk of theft was an element to be taken into account in deciding what was "suitable".

2. Reid v. Westfield Paper, 1957 S.C. 218, I.H.

Held, an action would lie. *Clifford v. Charles Challen* [1951] 1 K.B. 495; [1951] 1 All E.R. 72; C.A., in so far as dicta therein indicate the contrary, not followed.

3. Lane v. Gloucestershire Engineering [1967] 1 W.L.R. 767; [1967] 2 All E.R. 293, C.A.

4. Thornton v. Fisher & Ludlow [1968] 1 W.L.R. 655; [1968] 2 All E.R. 241, C.A.

Cleaner going to work at 6.45 a.m. tripped over coil of wire on factory road—*Held*, the lighting which could have been turned on was not "effective" within F.A. 1961, s. 5(1) until turned on, and on the

* Abbreviations are explained in Introductory Note 1.

facts the natural lighting was insufficient, as it was half light and the plaintiff would be likely to miss obstructions such as the one in question. Defendants liable.

5. Davies v. Massey Ferguson Parkins [1986] I.C.R. 580; [1986] C.L.Y. 1539, Evans J.

See Chap. 16, (5)(f) **28** for further details.

U1. Oakley v. Steel Co. of Wales (1960) C.A. 179 A

Sulphuric acid spilled on concrete—causing plaintiff to slip—plaintiff sued at common law and under F.A. 1937, s. 1 (clean state of factory)—*Held* by Cassels J., plaintiff succeeded under both heads, but C.A., finding common law liability proved, *said* it was not necessary to consider the claim under s. 1.

U2. Davison v. Vauxhall Motors Ltd (1990) C.A. 174

Plaintiff slipped on loose gravel and/or tripped on defect in surface of roadway at defendant's factory, as she was leaving in the dark—*Held*, defendant in breach of F.A. 1961, s. 5(1). The road was unlit, but should have been sufficiently well lit to alert pedestrians to such hazards.

(8) Building

(a) *"Building Operations" and "Works of Engineering Construction"**

* Abbreviations are explained in Introductory Note 1.

1. Lavender v. Diamints [1949] 1 K.B. 585, 593; [1949] 1 All E.R.532, C.A.

2. Hutchison v. Cocksedge [1952] 1 All E.R. 696, Croom-Johnson J.

Plaintiff a steel erector employed by defendants who made plant for sugar beet factories—plaintiff was required to drill holes in a metal casing 17 feet from ground—he ascended to a steel platform which was to be part of the building when finished—it had no railings—plaintiff fell off—*Held*, defendants were not engaged on a building operation, but on providing plant for a building, and therefore action failed. *Applied* in **5**.

3. Knight v. Demolition Co. [1953] 1 W.L.R. 981; [1953] 2 All E.R.508, Parker J.

Collapse of a brick arch forming retort block during demolition—first question was, was it a building or plant?—*Held*, even if it was plant, it was also a building. Parker J. pointed out that reg. 2 excluded many unlikely structures, such as lattice-work structures to support electric light, from being buildings, which indicated that a wide definition was envisaged (511 B). *N.B.* This case went to appeal [1954] 1 All E.R. 711, where decision was affirmed on issue of common law liability, and the above issues were in consequence not considered.

4. Elms v. Foster Wheeler [1954] 1 W.L.R. 1071; [1954] 2 All E.R. 714, C.A.

Plaintiff engaged on installing steam generating plant in a power station, for which girders and joists had to be erected to provide galleries, staircases and floors operating the plant—*Held*, this constituted the construction of a building, and was therefore a building operation. *Applied* in **6**, *q.v.*, and in **10**.

5. Copeland v. R. & H. Green and Silley Weir [1954] 2 Lloyd's Rep. 315, Finnemore J.

Plaintiff working on a 20 foot scaffold screwing a metal casing to the flue funnel of a factory—part of work of "putting up" new apparatus for dealing with exhaust fumes—*Held*, this was plant, rather than the construction or structural alteration of a building and therefore not a building operation. **2** *applied*; decision of Sellers J. in *Street v. B.E.A.* [1952] 2 Q.B. 399 (which latter went to C.A. on another point) and **3** and **4** *considered*, but *distinguished* on facts.

6. Hughes v. McGoff and Vickers [1955] 1 W.L.R. 416; [1955] 2 All E.R. 291, Ashworth J.

Defendants were installing electrical conduit pipes in a factory under construction—a 12-foot pipe placed on a platform fell off and fatally injured deceased, who was employed by defendants—*Held*, applying **4**, this was a building operation. In following **4** on the question of building operations judge said there were two tests: that of Somervell L.J., which was whether defendants were engaged on the construction of a building or were merely putting something into a building; and that of Romer L.J., which was to ask whether a building was being constructed, and whether defendants were contributing to the construction of that building. On both tests the operation in question was a building operation (295 B-H).

7. Sumner v. Priestley [1955] 1 W.L.R. 1202; [1955] 3 All E.R. 445, C.A.

Held, Regulations did not apply, as this was not repair or maintenance, but rather making preparation for making a new gutter. *Distinguished* in **15** and **18**.

8. Simmons v. Bovis [1956] 1 W.L.R. 381; [1956] 1 All E.R. 736, Barry J.

Lift being installed in building under construction—main contractor responsible for scaffolding—but sub-contractor's man erects a makeshift scaffold in lift onto which plaintiff, employed by main contractor, steps and falls because it is grossly defective—*Held*, applying test of Romer L.J. in **6**, this was a building operation.

9. McGuire v. Power Gas Corporation [1961] 2 All E.R. 544, Salmon J.

"It seems to me that it is quite possible for a structure to be a building . . . notwithstanding that it is not enclosed by walls and a roof, and is not one of the more ordinary forms of buildings. The proviso itself suggests that the word 'building' is used in a very wide sense . . . "

10. Byers v. Head Wrightson [1961] 1 W.L.R. 961; [1961] 2 All E.R. 538, Elwes J.

Held, following **4** and **9**.

11. Baxter v. Central Electricity Generating Board [1965] 1 W.L.R. 200; [1964] 2 All E.R. 815, Ashworth J.

12. Horsley v. Collier and Catley [1965] 1 W.L.R. 1359; [1965] 2 All E.R. 423, Nield J.

Plaintiff excavator driver employed by defendants on excavating site for pumping station—10 feet from the side of the excavation there was to be a building to house pump motors—while plaintiff was in excavation (which was 20–25 feet deep) another employee lobbed down hammer, hitting plaintiff on head—*Held*, the Court had to look at the principal object of the operations, and here it was *preparation for the building* of a pumping station (427 B). Such preparation included "necessary but ancillary work in connection with an intended building" (426 H); and as plaintiff was doing such work in the excavation at the time, (albeit that the direct purpose of the latter was to house a pumping well and not to facilitate the erection of a building) the operation was a building operation.

13. Ritchie v. James Russell, 1966 S.L.T. 244; [1966] C.L.Y. 1106, Ct. of Sess.

14. Price v. Claudgen [1967] 1 W.L.R. 575; [1967] 1 All E.R. 695, H.L.

"If someone replaces a burnt-out wire or mends a break in a wire in a neon installation on a building, it does not seem to me that it can reasonably be said that he is repairing a building. Both before and after such operation of replacement or repair the building will be the same; neither its structure nor its condition will be affected" (Lord Morris of Borth-y-Gest, 698 D).

15. O'Brien v. U.D.E.C. (1968) 112 S.J. 311; 5 K.I.R. 449, C.A.

Held (2–1) cleaning trusses preparatory to painting part of the operation of redecoration, and hence a building operation. *Summer* **7** *distinguished.*

16. Morter v. Electrical Installations (1969) 6 K.I.R. 130; [1969] C.L.Y. 317, Donaldson J.

17. British Transport Docks v. Williams [1970] 1 W.L.R. 652; [1970] 1 All E.R. 1135, D.C.

18. Vineer v. Doidge [1972] 1 W.L.R. 893; [1972] 2 All E.R. 794, C.A.

Plaintiff on scaffold measuring windows of house under construction for glazing—*Held*, this was a building operation. *Sumner* **7** *distinguished*, mainly (but perhaps not entirely) because there there was no building under construction, so that the only question was whether the work was repair or maintenance.

19. Shepherd v. Pearson Engineering, 1980 S.C. 268; [1982] C.L.Y. 2161, O.H.

Held, that a ship was not a "work of engineering construction" as it was not a "steel or reinforced concrete structure" within F.A. 1961, s. 176(1) as extended by the Engineering Construction (Extension of Definition) Regulations 1960.

20. Bowie v. Great International, *The Times*, May 14, 1981; [1981] C.L.Y. 1207, C.A.

21. Cullen v. N.E.I. Thompson, 1992 S.L.T. 1105; [1992] C.L.Y. 5251

Held, the construction in a yard of part of a bridge for erection elsewhere was a "work of engineering construction", thus the Construction (Working Places) Regulations 1966 applied to it.

U1. Kelsey v. Babcock & Wilcox (1958) C.A. 29 B

Held, that putting hot water system in a power station under construction was a building operation.

U2. Thompson v. British Oxygen (1965) C.A. 35. Also 109 S.J. 194, C.A.

Brackets to carry pipes were being fixed to girders in factory—*Held*, applying *Elms* **4**, *Hughes* **6** and *Baxter* **11**, this was a building operation. Lord Denning M.R. (3 F-4 A): "Those cases show that the "construction of a building" includes the construction of the several parts of a building; and further that a building comprises not only the walls and the roof but also all the equipment which is an essential and integral part of it ... Quite generally, it includes plant which is so essential to the building and so integral a feature of it that the building and plant can be reckoned as one structure. But it does not include plant or machinery which is not an essential or integral part of the building, such as presses on a factory floor."

U3. Williams v. S.W.E.B. (1976) C.A. 423 B

Held, applying *Price* **14**, that bringing a new electric cable to a line of houses to provide off-peak electricity was not repair or maintenance of a building, and therefore was not a building operation.

U4. Tucker v. Hampshire C.C. (1986) C.A. 99

*(b) Duties**

Factory occupier—whether liable for breach of Factories Act caused by independent building contractor	1,2	
Who can be sued—"as affect him or any workman employed by him"—main contractor liable to sub-contractor's employee	3	C.(G.P)R,1961:reg.3
WHO CAN BE SUED—WHO IS OCCUPIER FOR PURPOSE OF ELECTRICITY REGULATIONS	4	
Who can be sued—"as relate to any work ... performed"—main contractor liable for omissions of sub-contractor for labour only	5	**C.(G.P.)R 1961 reg. 3**
Main contractor—sub-contracting for labour only—will usually still be performing the work	5	"
WHO CAN BE SUED—"AS AFFECT ANY WORKMAN EMPLOYED BY HIM"—MAIN CONTRACTOR NOT LIABLE TO SUB-CONTRACTOR IN PERSON	6	
Who can be sued—"as affect him or any workman employed by him"—main contractor not liable to sub-contractor's employee	7	C.(G.P.)R. 1961, reg. 3
Duty of scaffolding contractor—includes duty to ensure access across site safe for employees	8	C.(G.P.)R. 1961, regs. 3, 6
Who can be sued—"as affect him or any workman employed by him"—main contractor not liable to sub-contractor for labour only	9	C.(W.P.)R. 1966, reg. 3
Who can be sued—"as affect him or any workman employed by by him"—main contractor liable to sub-contractor's employee	10	"
WHO CAN BE SUED—AS AFFECT HIM OR ANY WORKMAN EMPLOYED BY HIM"—MAIN CONTRACTOR NOT LIABLE TO SUB-CONTRACTOR'S EMPLOYEE	11	"
Who can be sued—main contractor not liable to working sub-contractor for unguarded machine—"every contractor ... to use plant ... in a manner which complies"	12	C.(G.P.)R. 1961, reg. 3
Who can sue—independent contractor cannot sue for breach of C.(W.P.)R. 1966	13	C.(W.P.)R. 1966, reg. 3
WHO CAN SUE—WORKING SUB-CONTRACTOR IN NAME ONLY—IS ABLE TO SUE AS EMPLOYEE	14	

* Abbreviations are explained in Introductory Note 1. See also Introductory Note 3(A), and Chap. 16, (1)(a) and (b).

1. Whitby v. Burt Boulton [1947] K.B. 918; [1947] 2 All E.R. 324, Denning J.

Held, yes. *Followed* in **2.** *But* in *Lavender v. Diamints* [1949] 1 K.B. 585; [1949] 1 All E.R. 532, C.A., Tucker L.J. said that he wished to keep the point open.

2. Whincup v. Woodhead [1951] 115 J.P. 97; [1951] 1 All E.R. 387, McNair J.

Held, following **1** and applying F.A. 1948, s. 14 (4), (now repealed) that an occupier would be liable for breaches of Factories Act occurring while an independent building contractor was carrying on building operation in factory.

3. Upton v. Hipgrave [1965] 1 W.L.R. 208; [1965] 1 All E.R. 6, Marshall J.

Breach of C.(G.P.)R. 1961, reg. 46 (falling materials)—duty on every contractor, etc., to comply with such of the requirements "as affect him or any workman employed by him"—plaintiff was employed by sub-contractors and sued his own employers (who were clearly liable) and also the main contractors—*Held*, that the latter were liable, because the requirement of reg. 46 "affected" them. *Overruled* by *Smith* **11**.

4. Fisher v. C.H.T. [1966] 2 Q.B. 475; [1966] 1 All E.R. 87, C.A.

Live wire in ceiling—touched by plastering employee—issue was mainly on common law negligence, but question also arose as to who was liable under the E.R. 1908, reg. 1 (protection of conductors)—premises were owned by D1, operated under licence by D2, who were also doing electrical repairs, and being redecorated by D3, who were plaintiff's employers—at common law D1 and D2 were both occupiers—*Held*, D2 liable as the notional occupiers of a factory under F.A. 1961, s. 127 (4). Neither D1 nor, it seems, D2 were liable as occupiers. The liability of D3 was left undecided, as it was not clear whether they were persons "undertaking the operations" within s. 127, as D2 clearly were. (E.R. 1908, reg.1 and F.A. 1961, s. 127(4) have both since been repealed.)

5. Donaghey v. O'Brien; Donaghey v. Boulton and Paul [1968] A.C.1; [1967] 2 All E.R. 1014, H.L.

Breach of B.R. 1948, reg. 31 (no crawling boards)—as a result employee of sub-contractor for labour only is injured—question is whether main contractors are liable for breach—*Held,* the proper test was to apply the wording of reg. 4 (now C.(G.P.)R. 1961, reg. 3(1)(b)): were the main contractors performing the work or operations in the course of which the employee was injured?—*Held,* by this test, main contractors liable, as they were responsible for seeing that materials and safety apparatus were available, and their foreman was there to keep an eye on what was going on (Lord Reid, 1023 B). *Aliter,* it would seem if the sub-contract had by its scope excluded the main contractors from any part in the work or operations; but it would seem that, in a sub-contract for labour only, such a state of affairs would be rare, if not impossible.

6. Barry v. Black-Clawson (1966) 2 K.I.R. 237; [1967] C.L.Y. 2678, C.A.

Erection of gantry by defendants—collapse of standards supporting guard rail due to hidden defect—sub-contractor of defendants in person thrown as a result—*Held,* defendants owed no duty under B.R. 1948, as the plaintiff was a sub-contractor in person.

7. Bunker v. Charles Brand [1969] 2 Q.B. 480; [1969] 2 All E.R. 59, O'Connor J.

Breach of C.(G.P.)R. 1961, reg. 7 (safe means of access)—plaintiff was employed by sub-contractors, and sued main contractors—duty was to comply with such of the requirements "as affect him or any workman employed by him"—*Held,* not following *Upton* **3**, the main contractor was not liable. *Approved* by C.A. in *Smith* **11**.

8. Smith v. Vange [1970] 1 W.L.R. 733; [1970] 1 All E.R. 249, MacKenna J.

9. Taylor v. Sayers [1971] 1 W.L.R. 561; [1971] 1 All E.R. 934, Orr J.

Held, following **7**, main contractors not liable to sub-contractor for labour only. *Approved* by C.A. in *Smith* **11**.

10. Baron v. B. French [1971] 3 All E.R. 1111, Bagnall J.

Overruled in Smith **11**.

11. Smith v. George Wimpey [1972] 2 Q.B. 329; [1972] 2 All E.R. 723, C.A.

Held, for the reasons given in *Bunker* **7**. *Bunker* **7** and *Taylor* **9** approved. *Upton* **3** and *Baron* **10** *overruled.*

12. Jones v. Minton (1973) 15 K.I.R. 309; [1974] C.L.Y. 2599, Thompson J.

Main contractor had suggested to working sub-contractor that he should see if a disused mixer would start—the regular mixer had broken down—the disused mixer had no guard, so that sub-contractor was injured—*Held,* main contractor owed no duty under C(G.P.)R. 1961, regs. 3 and 42.

13. Clare v. Whittaker [1976] I.C.R. 1; [1976] C.L.Y. 1884, Judge Fay

14. Ferguson v. John Dawson [1976] 1 W.L.R. 1213, C.A.

Claim for failing to guard side of working place (C.(W.P.)R. 1966, reg. 28)—duty only owed by defendants if plaintiff was employed under a contract of service—plaintiff had been engaged as a "lump" worker—but in all other respects had been working as if under a contract of service—the defendants provided the tools, they told him what to do, they could move him from site to site, and the site agent of the defendants could dismiss him—*Held*, that whatever the label put by the parties on their relationship, in truth the plaintiff was working under a contract of service and accordingly could sue.

15. Massey v. Crown Life [1978] 1 W.L.R. 676; [1978] 2 All E.R. 576, C.A.

Unfair dismissal case, in the course of which the Court of Appeal *referred* to *Ferguson* **14** without enthusiasm. Lord Denning M.R. *said* (581 C): "In most of these cases I expect it will be found that the parties do deliberately agree for the man to be 'self-employed' or 'on the lump'. It is done especially so as to obtain the tax benefits. When such an agreement is made, it affords strong evidence that that is the real relationship. If it is so found the man must accept it. He cannot afterwards assert that he was only a servant."

16. Kealey v. Heard [1983] 1 W.L.R. 573; [1983] 1 All E.R. 973, Mann J.

Defendant decided to convert properties into flats. Instead of engaging a general contractor, he engaged specialist tradesmen individually, including plaintiff, a self-employed plasterer. Plaintiff injured when planks on scaffold erected by unknown workman collapsed—*Held*, that the defendant was not a contractor within the meaning of reg. 3 since that term referred to a person who himself undertook building operations, whereas the defendant had merely hired independent contractors who had undertaken the building operations. He did not, therefore, owe the duties set out in the Regulations. However, the defendant was held liable in negligence: see Chap. 7(2)(d) **30**.

17. Williams v. West Wales Plant Hire Co. [1984] 1 W.L.R. 1311; [1984] 3 All E.R. 397, C.A.

Plaintiff's employers hired out his services and the crane he operated, to a builder. During the building operation, crane fell over due to collapse of earth. Plaintiff claimed, *inter alia*, that his employers were in breach of C.(L.O.)R. 1961, reg. 11(1)—*Held*, employer liable. They were "undertaking" a building operation within meaning of reg. 3(1), because through the plaintiff their employee they were actively engaged in a building operation.

18. Page v. Read (1984) 134 New L.J. 723; [1984] C.L.Y. 1203, Stocker J.

U1. Grosvenor v. Gerrard (1954) C.A. 19

Deceased employed by defendants as general roof maintenance man—fell at place on roof where no reason for him to be—*Held*, defendants not liable, as no duty owed under B.R. 1948 or at common law.

U2. Jackson v. Miller Buckley (1978) C.A. 525

U3. Laurence v. Bartholomew (1982) C.A. 289

*(c) Access**

(*N.B.* See also, more generally, cases in Chap. 16, (5). For Ladders, see Chap. 16, (8)(f), and for Roof Work, see Chap. 16, (8)(g).)

Duty to provide	Sub-contractor—no duty to provide for	1
Duty to provide	To all workplaces—not merely scaffolds	2
What is safe	Plank 6 in. from ground	2
What is safe	Sliding along girde	3
What is safe	Full definition	3
WHAT IS SAFE	WALKING ALONG 3-IN. GIRDER	4
WHAT IS SAFE	WALKING ALONG STEEL RAFTER	5
MEANING OF STAIRS	INCLUDES UNCOMPLETED STAIRS	6
HAND-RAIL ON STAIRS	HAND-RAIL NEED NOT SERVE AS GUARD RAIL	6
GUARD RAIL ON STAIRS	MAY BE NECESSARY TO PROVIDE UPPER AND LOWER RAIL	7
LADDER TO ROOF	DOOR TO ROOF WITH KEY BUT NO HANDLE—PLAINTIFF FALLS WHILE SHUTTING DOOR	8
Access across site to Scaffold	Scaffolding sub-contractor owes duty to own employee to see such access safe	9
SAFE ACCESS	NOT GUTTER ALONG BOTTOM OF FRAGILE ASBESTOS ROOF	10
Access to shaft	Includes going down it and working at the edge of it	11
Two routes—one safe	*Defendants not liable because they had not authorised or encouraged use of unsafe route*	U1
Safe access	*Temporary steps with 16-inch risers—safe*	U2
Broken Glass in Window frame	*Defendant not liable—had not provided frame as means of access*	U3

1. Vaughan v. Building Estates [1952] 2 Lloyd's Rep. 231, McNair J.

2. Brown v. Troy [1954] 1 W.L.R. 1181; [1954] 3 All E.R. 19, Gerrard J.

Plaintiff falls off plank 6 in. from ground—claims it was not "safe access" to his place of work—*Held*, that duty of employer under B.R. 1948, reg. 5 was to provide safe access not only to scaffolds but to all places of work, but on the facts the plank did constitute safe access.

3. Sheppey v. Matthew T. Shaw (1952) 1 T.L.R. 1272; [1952] W.N. 249, Parker J.

Plaintiff a steel erector put onto painting steel girders which he had erected—to get there he slid along top edge of one boom and under purlins—fell—*Held*, this was not safe access: "Reference has been made to passages in decided cases where the duty is said to be to provide reasonably safe means of access. For myself, with great deference, I get little help from adding the word 'reasonably.' It is not in the regulations. If it is used merely in contradistinction to 'absolutely safe,' I can understand it; but if it is intended to mean 'safe for anybody acting reasonably,' in the sense of taking full precautions for their own safety, I cannot agree with it . . . These regulations are intended . . . to safeguard workmen against acts which, owing to the frailty of human nature, continually occur of carelessness or inadvertence, and whatever epithet one applies here to the word 'safe,' I think it must mean a degree of safety which to some extent, at any rate foresees the fact that human beings . . . will

* Abbreviations are explained in Introductory Note 1.

from time to time . . . not exercise a very high degree of care for their own safety" (1274). *Approved* by C.A. in **4**.

4. Trott v. W.E. Smith [1957] 1 W.L.R. 1154; [1957] 3 All E.R. 500, C.A.

Held, defendants liable. Test propounded by Parker J. in **3** approved: "In considering whether the means of access provided is safe or unsafe, it must not be assumed that everyone will always be careful. A means of access is unsafe if it is a possible cause of injury to anybody acting in a way a human being may be reasonably expected to act in circumstances which may be reasonably expected to occur" (505 B, Jenkins L.J.).

5. Ryan v. Redpath Brown [1959] 109 L.J. 120; [1959] C.L.Y. 336, C.A.

Deceased an experienced steel erector lost his balance when going from working platform along steel rafter to help fellow employee—*Held*, defendants not liable under B.R. 1948, reg. 5 (now C.(W.P.)R. 1966, reg. 7) as the test was to ask whether there was a possibility of injury to the deceased acting in the way he might reasonably have been expected to act in circumstances which might reasonably have been expected to occur. *Cf.* **3** and **4**. One distinction is that here deceased may not have been using rafter as access; he left his working platform to help a fellow workman, so that the issue was not access, but whether his work could be "safely" performed without a scaffold.

6. Corn v. Weir's Glass [1960] 1 W.L.R. 577; [1960] 2 All E.R. 300, C.A.

Plaintiff on a building operation overbalanced and fell over open side of stairs while carrying large sheet of glass—fall of 3 feet to ground—open side unprotected—defendants not in breach of B.R. 1948, reg. 27(2) (guard rail) because fall less than 6 feet 6 in.—but were in breach of reg. 27(1), in that no hand-rail was provided—*Held*, that "hand-rail" here did not mean something which would serve as a guard rail (although in cases under F.A. 1937, s. 25(2) (now F.A. 1961, s. 28(2)), it probably did) and as plaintiff had not proved that a hand-rail *simpliciter* would have prevented his injuries (see Chap. 16, (3)(b) **12** for fuller details), defendants not liable—*Held*, also, that "stairs" included uncompleted stairs.

7. Astell v. London Transport Board [1966] 1 W.L.R. 1047, [1966] 2 All E.R. 748, C.A.

Held, that B.R. 1948, reg. 27(2) contemplated that two guard rails, an upper and a lower, might be necessary and in this case defendants were liable for failing to provide a lower rail.

8. Jenkins v. Norman Collison [1970] 1 All E.R. 1121, C.A.

Held, unsafe access, but two-thirds contributory negligence.

9. Smith v. Vange [1970] 1 W.L.R. 733; [1970] 1 All E.R. 249, MacKenna J.

10. Byrne v. E.H. Smith [1973] 1 All E.R. 490, C.A.

11. Gardiner v. Thames Water Authority, *The Times*, June 8, 1984; [1984] C.L.Y. 1230, Tuder Evans J.

So held, in relation to the proviso to C.(G.P.)R. 1961, reg. 13.

U1. Kelly v. Structural Builders (1969) C.A. 88

U2. Plant v. English Electric (1972) C.A. 317

U3. Angell v. W.F. Button & Son Ltd (1987) C.A. 624

Demolition worker cut his knee on broken glass in a window frame when climbing down from a roof—*Held*, defendant not liable in negligence or for breach of C.(W.P.)R. 1966, reg. 6(2)—defendant had not provided or adapted the window frame as a means of access/egress.

*(d) Scaffolds**

(*N.B.* For Ladders, see Chap. 16, (8)(f) and for Working Places and Platforms see Chap. 16, (8)(e).)

Safely be done	**Concrete window sill to drill hole**	1	**C.(W.P.)R. 1966, reg. 7**
Good construction	Includes design and lay-out as well as structural soundness	2	C.(W.P.)R. 1966, reg. 9
SAFELY BE DONE	STEEL ERECTOR SITTING ASTRIDE MAIN BEAM	3	C.(W.P.)R. 1966, REG. 7
CAPABLE OF BEING USED	SCAFFOLD NOT CAPABLE OF BEING USED AS A SCAFFOLD—BUT ABLE TO BE USED FOR PURPOSES CONNECTED WITH THE WORK	4	C.(W.P.)R. 1966, REG. 16
SATISFY SELF THAT SCAFFOLD STABLE	EMPLOYER SENDING PLAINTIFF TO OUT-SITE—TO MEASURE WINDOWS	5	C(W.P.)R. 1966, reg. 23
Regulation 9	Applies to partly dismantled scaffold	6	C.(W.P.)R. 1966, reg. 9
Regulation 9	Does not apply where scaffold collapses due to act of vandals	6	C(W.P.)R. 1966, reg. 9
Regulation 15	Applies only to complete scaffolds	6	C(W.P.)R. 1966, reg. 15

1. O'Donnell v. Murdoch Mackenzie (1967) 3 K.I.R. 299; [1967] C.L.Y. 333, H.L.

Plaintiff drilling hole in wall from concrete window sill 4 feet by 5 feet, some 10 feet above ground—the correct tool was a pugger, but all that was provided was a heavier jack-hammer which tended to stick in hole—*Held*, this was work which could not safely be done from sill, and defendants were liable.

* Abbreviations are explained in Introductory Note 1. See also Introductory Note 3(A).

2. Smith v. Davies (1969) 5 K.I.R. 320; [1969] C.L.Y. 319, Cooke J.

3. Woods v. Power Gas Corporation (1969) 8 K.I.R. 834; [1970] C.L.Y. 247, C.A.

Question was whether work could safely be done (within C.(G.P.)R. 1966, reg. 7(2), now replaced by C.(W.P.)R. 1966, reg. 7) by a steel erector sitting astride a girder in order to insert bolts—*Held*, there was no breach, as sitting astride a girder was a familiar position for an experienced steel erector. Davies L.J. said that the accident must be foreseeably likely rather than foreseeably possible.

4. Skelton v. A.V.P. Developments (1970) 8 K.I.R. 927; [1970] C.L.Y. 249, C.A.

Plaintiff was standing on a trestle doing work on a ceiling—on reaching end of trestle, he put his foot on the bar of a partly dismantled scaffold to get extra purchase—with the obvious result—the scaffold was sufficiently dismantled to be incapable of use as a scaffold—*Held*, defendants liable (but 25 per cent. contributory negligence), because it was still capable of being used for a purpose connected with the work—which was what the regulation meant.

5. Vineer v. Doidge [1972] 1 W.L.R. 893; [1972] 2 All E.R. 794, C.A.

Employers sent plaintiff to a site to measure windows—but did nothing to assure themselves about the scaffolds, except to leave it to the plaintiff himself—*Held*, liable. Roskill L.J. (798 E) considered whether the employers had delegated their duty to plaintiff as their "competent agent," and said not, as there was no express creation of a relationship of principal and agent for this purpose.

6. Campbell v. Glasgow C.C., 1991 S.L.T. 616; [1991] C.L.Y 4433

Held, inter alia:

(a) C.(W.P.)R. 1966, reg. 9 (providing for the construction and material of "every scaffold and every part thereof") applied to a partly dismantled scaffold, but not where a scaffold collapsed due to the acts of vandals rather than the condition of the scaffold or the parts thereof.
(b) C.(W.P.)R. 1966, reg. 15 (providing for the stability of scaffolds) applied only to completed scaffolds.

(e) Working Places and Platforms*

Place at which any person habitually employed	Temporary floor in lift shaft—used to store materials	1	C.(G.P.)R. 1961, reg. 46
WORKING PLACE	MAY INCLUDE UPPER FLOOR OF BUILDING UNDER DEMOLITION....	2	C.(W.P.)R. 1966, REG. 28
Working platform	Not beams on upper floor of house under construction....	3	C.(W.P.)R. 1966, reg. 24

* Abbreviations are explained in Introductory Note 1. See also Introductory Note 3(A). It may be convenient to bear in mind that, by extended definition of scaffold, a working platform is always a scaffold, but a working place is not necessarily so, and is not defined in the Regulations.

Place at which a person works	Loading platform—slippery furnace waste—liable..........	3	C.(W.P.)R. 1966, reg. 6(2)
Place at which a person works	Duty only extends to safety of place *qua* place..................	4	"
Place at which a person works	Laying water main—danger from testing equipment brought onto site.................	5	"
Working platform	May include permanent part of building..........................	6	C.(W.P.)R. 1961

1. Byrne v. Truscon, 1967 S.L.T. 159; [1967] C.L.Y. 2717, Ct. of Sess.

Plaintiff, building labourer, was storing wood on temporary floor of lift shaft, when material fell on him from above—temporary floors were used from time to time as convenient places to store materials—*Held*, that the test was not whether the plaintiff was employed at the place habitually, but whether it was a habitual place of employment or a contemplated place of employment where men would work habitually, not casually, and that on the evidence this was such a place.

2. Boyton v. Willment [1971] 1 W.L.R. 1625; [1971] 3 All E.R. 624, C.A.

Demolition—one wall removed—and parts of each floor, leaving passageways where men could bring and throw down material—plaintiff fell from the edge of a passageway adjacent to the removed wall—*Held*, he was at a working place. All L.JJ. attached importance to the fact that the work was not of a transient nature, but would engage the men in the area for an appreciable period of time. Buckley L. J. (628 J), giving the first judgment, also said that the passageways, in addition to being left so that men could carry out their work on them, were areas of defined and limited extent, so that, together with the non-transient nature of the work, they had all the characteristics of a working place.

3. Buist v. Dundee Corporation, 1971 S.L.T. 76; [1972] C.L.Y. 2391, Ct. of Sess.

4. Busby v. Watson (1972) 13 K.I.R. 498; [1972] C.L.Y. 2321, Forbes J.

5. Evans v. Sant [1975] Q.B. 626; [1975] 1 All E.R. 294, D.C.

Laying water main—testing equipment was brought on to site which for some reason produced a dangerous pressure, causing main to blow up—*Held*, no breach of duty to keep place safe: " . . . where as in the present instance, you start with a place safe in every degree, and the only thing which renders it unsafe is the fact that equipment brought on to it for a particular operation, and being used for a particular operation on a particular day, produces an element of danger, it seems to me that that is not enough to justify the allegation, certainly in criminal proceedings, that the place itself has not been made safe" (Lord Widgery C.J. 301G).

6. Gardiner v. Thames Water Authority, *The Times*, June 8, 1984; [1984] C.L.Y. 1230, Tuder Evans J.

Held, inter alia, that "working platform" in regs. 24 and 28 applied not only to a structure erected to provide a man with a place of work, but also to a permanent part of a building if that part (a) was used as a place of work and (b) was a "working platform" in the ordinary sense.

*(f) Ladders**

(*N.B.* See also, more generally, Chap. 16, (5)(f).)

Adequate strength	Rung breaking	1
UNFOOTED	PLAINTIFF GOING UP	2
UNFOOTED	PLAINTIFF GOING UP—NO INSTRUCTIONS FROM EMPLOYERS	3
UNFOOTED	PLAINTIFF CHARGEHAND GOING UP	4
Unlashed	**Possible to lash before mounting**	5
	Employer must do all he can be reasonably expected to do to secure compliance with regulations	5
Rung missing	*Plaintiff knowingly using same*	U1
Unfooted	*Foreman going up*	U2
Insecurely placed	*Plaintiff going up*	U3
Unfooted	*Plaintiff's assistant going away*	U4
No rubber feet	*Aluminium ladder*	U5
Unhooked	*Plaintiff going up—when he knew he could secure same with hook*	U6
Unfooted	*Plaintiff's assistant having gone away*	U7
Unfooted	*Plaintiff unable to find someone to help, though asked to do so*	U8

1. Johnson v. Croggan [1954] 1 W.L.R. 195; [1954] 1 All E.R. 121, Pilcher J.

Held, ladder not of "adequate strength." *But* plaintiff was defeated on delegation, *ex turpi causa* and contributory negligence, *q.v.* See also the D.R. 1934 case of *Cottrell v. Vianda* (Chap. 16, (5) (f) **10**), where it was held that a ladder, to be safe, must be able to stand up to some lighthearted user.

2. McMath v. Rimmer Brothers [1962] 1 W.L.R. 1; [1961] 3 All E.R. 1154, C.A.

Unfooted ladder—plaintiff ganger (*i.e.* chargehand) went up a ladder during unauthorised absence of labourer who should have been footing it—breach of B.R. 1948, reg. 29(4)—*Held*, there was a breach both by plaintiff and defendants, but plaintiff's fault was not coextensive with that of defendants, for the defendants additionally were responsible for the absence of the labourer, and that defendants were 50 per cent. liable.

3. Boden v. Moore (1961) 105 S.J. 510, C.A.

Held, 50:50.

4. Hammill v. Camborne Water Co. (1964) 108 S.J. 335; [1964] C.L.Y. 374, C.A.

Held, plaintiff's breach was co-extensive with that of the defendants, since it was his duty to see that the Regulations were observed, and claim failed.

5. Boyle v. Kodak [1969] 1 W.L.R. 661; [1969] 2 All E.R. 439, H.L.

Plaintiff went up long ladder—which could have been lashed at the top before mounting—plaintiff and defendants both thereby in breach—*Held*, plaintiff's breach was not co-extensive with that of the

* Abbreviations are explained in Introductory Note 1.

defendants, since the latter were under a duty to do all they could reasonably be expected to do to ensure compliance with the Regulations, and they ought to have instructed the plaintiff that where it was practicable to lash a ladder at the top before mounting this should be done—*Held*, 50:50.

U1. Kelly v. Thomas and Edge (1953) C.A. 266

Plaintiff knew rung missing but used same—other ladders available—*Held*, defendants 20 per cent., plaintiff 80 per cent., to blame.

U2. Smith v. R. Smith (Horley) Ltd (1957) C.A. 273 A

Plaintiff foreman steel erector employed by defendants—raising trusses in roof—fell from ladder 12 feet 6 in. long which was not secured or footed—plaintiff experienced man and job well within his capacity—*Held*, defendants in breach of B.R. 1948, reg. 29 (4)—plaintiff in breach of B.R. 1948, reg. 4—plaintiff's breach operated to put defendants in breach—defendants not liable, as plaintiff's breach effective cause of accident.

U3. Finn v. Sprosson (1964) C.A. 100

Held, although this constituted a breach by the defendants, the plaintiff was entirely responsible, and defendants were not liable.

U4. Parson v. Porter (1964) C.A. 116

Plaintiff fell from long unfooted ladder—the employee who should have footed it had gone away—*Held*, 50:50. Defendants were liable for failure of the employee to foot, and plaintiff for failing to take any steps to see that ladder was secured at its base.

U5. Shanton v. Cynamid (1964) C.A. 246

Held, Defendants liable. But 66 per cent. contributory negligence v. plaintiff for sending away an assistant who should have footed ladder.

U6. Redling v. Hoisting Appliance (1973) C.A. 135

Plaintiff erected and went up ladder which was not secure fixed—breach of C. (W.P.) R. 1966, reg. 32 (2)—but ladder had a hook, as plaintiff knew, and could have been secured—*Held*, defendants not liable as breach was solely brought about by act of plaintiff.

U7. Milsom v. Strachan and Henshaw (1973) C.A. 356

Plaintiff went up unfooted ladder—someone had been available to foot ladder—but had gone away, as plaintiff thought, to phone—*Held*, 50:50, as if the defendants did not provide someone to foot ladder, they must "clearly and specifically" warn the person concerned of the danger of going up by himself.

U8. Freeman v. Brockhouse Berry Ltd (1984) C.A. 1001

Plaintiff climbed unlashed and unfooted ladder to repair shutter. Had been told by his foreman to ask another employee H to foot the ladder. Plaintiff could not find H, though H was in a nearby annexe where plaintiff could have found him had he looked. Ladder slipped and plaintiff fell—*Held*, defendant not in breach of C. (W.P.) R. 1966, reg. 32 (3).

*(g) Roofs, Girders and Joisting**

Crawling boards	None used—fall through gap in sloping roof	1	C. (W.P.) R. 1966, reg. 35
"Open joisting"	Beams to receive neolith—in house under construction	2	C. (W.P.) R. 1966, reg. 33
Passing/working near fragile material	Employer's duty to provide safeguards is absolute	3	C. (W.P.) R. 1966, reg. 36(2)

1. McInally v. Price, 1971 S.L.T. 43, Ct. of Sess.

Defendants argued that as plaintiff had not fallen off edge of sloping rood the regulation did not apply (which used to be the case under B.R. 1948, reg. 31(1))—*Held*, C. (W.P.) R. 1966, reg. 35(4) was not so limited in its application, and defendants were liable for not providing crawling boards.

2. Buist v. Dundee Corporation, 1971 S.L.T. 76; [1972] C.L.Y. 2391, Ct. of Sess.

Held, the beams were not "open joisting," as they were not laid to support the floor of the house but to receive a neolith involved in the construction of the second floor.

3. Briggs Amasco Ltd v. Thurgood, *The Times*, July 30, 1984; [1984] C.L.Y. 1231, D.C.

Held, reg. 36(2) imposes an absolute duty to provide one or more of the means specified of preventing persons falling through fragile material. The words "reasonably practicable" qualified the standard or degree of the means to be provided.

*(h) Excavations and Demolitions**

Ambit of reg. 14(2) considered	1	C.(G.P)R. 1961, reg. 14(2)
Excavating trench 6 feet deep—timber available—but several miles away	U1	*C.(W.P.)R 1966, reg. 8*
Gas fitter—falling into hole in street—defendant not liable	U2	*C(W.P.)R 1966, reg. 6(2)*

1. Blackman v. C. J. Pryor (Earth Moving Contractors) Ltd, *The Times*, July 5, 1994; [1994] C.L.Y. 3373, Ognall J.

Held, reg. 14(2), which provides that "no . . . plant or equipment shall be placed or moved near the edge of any excavation (or) pit . . . where it is likely to cause a collapse of the side of the excavation (or) pit . . . " applies to the top of an excavation pit but not to the floor or bottom of such a pit.

U1. Hamlett v. East (1973) C.A. 175

Side of trench 6 feet deep collapsed—killing ganger in charge—employers had timber available, but several miles away—the need to dig 6 feet deep had arisen unexpectedly—*Held*, employers liable for breach of duty to provide and use timber, but deceased 25 per cent. liable in going on instead of phoning for timber to be sent.

* Abbreviations are explained in Introductory Note 1. See also Introductory Note 3(A).

U2. Taylor v. British Gas Corporation (1986) C.A. 906

An experienced gas fitter was dealing with a gas leak in a residential street. When stepping backwards out of the hole he was excavating he fell into another nearby hole about 3 feet deep—*Held*, defendant not liable in negligence and not in breach of C.(W.P.)R. 1966, reg. 6(2). The place of work was not unsafe. Alternatively, if place was unsafe, the erection of barrier between the closely proximate holes was not reasonably practicable, and was not normal practice.

(j) Miscellaneous*

Fencing machinery—hand power tool—with 7-foot shaft—unfenced for last 3 inches	2	C.(G.P.)R. 1961, reg. 42
"Loose materials"—means only materials required for use on the site	2	C.(G.P.)R. 1961, reg. 48
Fencing machinery—"works or uses"—running machine to clean same—machine is being "worked"	3	C.(G.P.)R. 1961, reg. 42
Whether plant or equipment being "worked" or "used"—fan in engine of excavator being examined whilst engine running	4	C.(G.P.)R. 1961, reg. 3
"Shaft"—could include well-hole	5	C.(G.P.)R. 1961, reg. 13
Removal of well covering—is not "formation of . . . shaft"	5	C.(G.P.)R. 1961, proviso to reg. 13
"Access" to shaft—includes going down it and working at the edge of it	5	C.(G.P.)R. 1961, proviso to reg. 13
Provision of safety nets, sheets, belts or other equipment—when duty arises	5	C.(W.P.).R. 1966, reg. 38
ELEVATED WALKWAY—DISPLACED TOEBOARD—ABSOLUTE DUTY IMPOSED BY AND SCOPE OF REG. 30(2)	6	C.(W.P.)R. 1966, REG. 30(2)
Manual lifting—140 lbs. unaided—breach but 25 per cent. contributory negligence for not getting help	U1	*C.(G.P.)R. 1961, reg. 55*
Electric cable—exposed during roadworks—but left unprotected—plaintiff penetrates same while digging	U2	*C.(G.P.)R. 1961, reg. 44*
Bolt lying on passageway floor	U3	*C.(G.P.)R. 1966, reg. 48(2)*
Plaintiff lifting pavement cornerstone weighing 220 lbs—but not employed to do so	U4	*C.(G.P.)R. 1961, reg. 55*
Overloaded crane—both employer and employee in breach of regulation	U5	*C.(L.O.)R. 1961, reg. 31*
"Chasing" cut into floor of building under construction	U6	*C.(W.P.)R. 1961, reg. 6(2)*
Folding step-ladders	U7	*C.(W.P.)R. 1966, regs. 6(2), 18, 32(7)*

1. Lovelidge v. Anselm Olding [1967] 2 Q.B. 351; [1967] 1 All E.R. 459, Widgery J.

Held, tool constituted machinery, and should have been fenced.

* Abbreviations are explained in Introductory Note 1. See also Introductory Note 3(A).

2. Morter v. Electrical Installations (1969) 6 K.I.R. 130, Donaldson J.

3. Smith v. Watson, [1977] S.L.T. 204; [1977] C.L.Y. 1399, High Ct. of Justiciary

4. Johns v. Martin Simms [1983] I.C.R. 305; [1983] 1 All E.R. 127, Lawson J.

Held, that the words "works" or "uses" embrace not only the commercial or industrial operation of a machine for its designed purpose but any operation thereof for whatever purpose which involves the activation of the machine itself, including for the purpose of ordinary maintenance and adjustment.

5. Gardiner v. Thames Water Authority, *The Times*, June 8, 1984; [1984] C.L.Y. 1230, Tudor Evans J.

So held, in relation to reg. 13 and the proviso thereto. In relation to reg. 38 (which is expressed to apply only if compliance with other specified regulations is impracticable)—*Held*, that reg. 38 did not apply if (a) none of the other specified regulations applied, or (b) if one or more of them did apply but had not been breached. Thus for example, reg. 38 would not apply if (a) the defendant was exempted from compliance with reg. 28(1) and 33 by regs. 28(4) and 34, respectively; or (b) the defendant proved that it was not reasonably practicable to make a place of work safe, so that he was not in breach of reg. 6(2).

6. McGovern v. B.S.C. [1986] I.C.R. 608, [1986] I.R.L.R. 411, C.A.

See Chap. 16, (3)(b) **17** for further details.

U1. Moran v. Kitching (1969) C.A. 288

U2. Laurence v. Bartholomew (1982) C.A. 289

Held, defendants liable.

U3. Reader v. B.S.C. (1985) C.A. 848

Plaintiff stepped on substantial bolt lying on floor in a passageway, and alleged a breach of C.(G.P.)R. 1961, reg. 48(2)—*Held*, assuming the bolt to be "loose material", it did not "restrict unduly the passage of persons" and the regulation did not therefore require defendant to move it.

U4. Walker v. Reigate and Banstead B.C. (1986) C.A. 312

Plaintiff lorry driver was injured lifting a pavement cornerstone weighing 220 lbs in the course of unloading it from his lorry. The normal practice was to roll such stones along the floor of the lorry—*Held*, defendant not negligent and not in breach of C.(G.P.)R 1961, reg. 55. Plaintiff was employed to move the cornerstone, not to lift it.

U5. McGrath v. St. Mary's (Plant Hire) Ltd (1987) C.A. 604

Crane-driver injured when his over-loaded crane toppled over. Audible overload warning system had failed to operate—*Held*, plaintiff and defendant were both in breach of C.(L.O.)R. 1961, reg. 31—respectively one-third and two-thirds to blame.

U6. Hodgson v. Shepherd Engineering Services Ltd (1987) C.A. 1194

Experienced electrician, having descended a ladder, caught his foot in a "chasing" cut into the floor of the building under construction at which he was working. The chasing, 4–6 in. wide and about 2 in. deep, had been cut into the floor to take wires and cables at a later stage of construction. It was clear to see and the plaintiff was aware of its presence. Chasings were regular features of buildings under construction—*Held*, defendant not in breach of C.(W.P.)R. 1966, reg. 6(2). It had not been proved that the site was unsafe.

U7. Marshall v. Liverpool C.C. (1990) C.A. 350

Plaintiff and colleague stood on separate trestles to paint a ceiling. One of the legs of colleague's trestle went through a floorboard and he lost his balance, bringing down plaintiff's trestle. The defective floorboard could not have been detected by inspecting or walking on it. Plaintiff's foreman had inspected the premises—*Held*, defendant not in breach of C.(W.P.)R. 1966, reg. 6(2)—all reasonably practicably steps had been taken—but the trestles were being used as folding step-ladders and defendants in breach of regs. 18 and 32(7).

(9) Docks

*(a) Duties**

* The Reputations refered to in all these cases are the Docks Regulations 1934, as to which see Introductory Note 5.

1. Hawkins v. Thames Stevedoring (1936) 80 S.J. 387; [1936] 2 All E.R. 472, Atkinson J.

Held, that a workman employed on lagging pipes while processes were being carried on could sue under D.R. 1934. This decision has been criticised and may not be consistent with *Hartley* (Chap. 16 (1) (a) **7** and *Stanton* (Chap. 16 (1)(a) **9**). See **5** and **6**.

2. Yorke v. British and Continental S.S. Co. (1945) 78 L1.L.R. 181, C.A.

Held, D.R. 1934 had no extraterritorial effect, even if ship British—*Held*, however, defendants liable at common law.

3. Grant v. Sun Shipping Co. [1948] A.C. 549; [1948] 2 All E.R. 238, H.L.

Action by dock labourer (not employed by either defendant) against shipowners and ship repairers—repairers had left a hatch uncovered and unlit, and plaintiff fell down it—plaintiff sued shipowners for breach of statutory duty and at common law, and repairers at common law—shipowners also blamed repairers for breach of statutory duty—*Held*, *per* Lord du Parcq, with whose reasons Lord Uthwatt and (probably) Lord Porter expressly agreed:

(a) shipowners liable at common law, because they had the duty as invitors, and it was not enough to tell and/or rely on repairers to make secure, they must take steps themselves;
(b) shipowners liable under reg. 12 (failure to light), the duty being on them;
(c) repairers liable at common law, for plainly dangerous act in leaving hatch uncovered and unlit;
(d) repairers liable under reg. 37 (failure to cover hatch), the duty being on them.

As to (d), this ground has been criticised, as the repairers were not carrying out any of the "processes," so that no duty could be on them.

4. Jerred v. Dent [1948] 2 All E.R. 104; 81 Ll.L.R. 412, Atkinson J.

Shipowners assure stevedores that they have performed the statutory duty of the latter of securing hatch covers—they had not in fact done so—*Held*, shipowners 90 per cent. to blame, stevedores 10 per cent.

5. Harvey v. Royal Mail (1949) 65 T.L.R. 286n., Hallet J.

Decided in 1941—breach of reg. 37 (hatch) in Part IV—welder falls down hatch left open by stevedores—*Held*, plaintiff could not sue under D.R. 1934 because he was not employed in connection with the processes, and reg. 37 expressly refers to the hatch of a hold "accessible to any person employed," which by definition means any person employed in the processes. This case and **6** are at variance with **1**.

6. Kininmonth v. William France, Fenwick (1949) 65 T.L.R. 285; 82 Ll.L.R. 768, Hilbery J.

Breach of reg. 1 (regular approach)—wireless officer slips on china-clay on jetty—*Held*, could not sue, as reg. 1 provides that the approaches are to be maintained with due regard to the safety of persons employed, which by definition in D.R. 1934 means persons employed in the processes, and therefore reg. 1 was only intended to protect such persons, and plaintiff could not sue. See **5**.

7. Cook v. Dredging Co. [1958] 1 Lloyd's Rep. 334, Jones J.

8. Graves v. J. & E. Hall [1958] 2 Lloyd's Rep. 100, Barry J.

Refrigeration condenser being removed from ship for repair—*Held*, not "goods," and therefore D.R. 1934 did not apply: "It is quite clear that ship's stores can properly be described as goods. I refer to the case of *Hayward v. P.L.A.* [1955] 1 Lloyd's Rep. 211 (see Chap. 16 (9)(b)**4** . . . I think "goods" in these regulations can only refer to merchandise of some kind, be it part of the ship's cargo or part of the stores of the ship . . . I think it would be an unreasonable interpretation to interpret the words "unloading moving and handling goods" as having any reference to moving or handling part of the ship's machinery or plant" (111, col. 1).

9. Mace v. R. & H. Green & Silley Weir [1959] 2 Q.B. 14; [1959] 1 All E.R. 655, Lord Parker C.J.

Held, that inasmuch as in *Manchester Ship Canal v. D.P.P.* [1930] 1 K.B. 547 and also in **1**, replacing hatch covers had been held to be part of the process of unloading (and/or loading) as being ancillary thereto, so also was the work of clearing up spillage after unloading.

10. Wilczek v. Gardiner and Tidy [1959] 1 Lloyd's Rep. 9, Pearson J.

Plaintiff a carpenter working as an invitee on defendants' wharf—he was "employed in the processes" because on a few occasions he assisted in moving timber (which constituted "goods") by crane into a vessel in the course of his duties—he went to get hot coals from the firebox of defendant's crane—slipped on wharf while doing so—no authority to take the coals—*Held*, he could not sue under D.R. 1934, because his expedition could not reasonably be regarded as ancillary to the occasions when he was engaged in the processes.

11. Hayhurst v. F. J. Everard [1961] 1 Lloyd's Rep. 539, Diplock J.

Held, that ship's engineer could not sue under D.R. 1934, not being a "person employed in the processes"—*Held*, that the process of loading did not commence merely because hatch covers had been removed before the vessel got to the wharf.

12. Henry v. Mersey Ports Stevedoring [1963] 2 Lloyd's Rep. 97, C.A.

Plaintiff dock worker sent by employing stevedores to a 'tween deck which was in darkness—fell down open hatch—trial judge found plaintiff was trespassing at the time—C.A. reversed this finding, but *said obiter* that if he had been trespassing, he would not have been protected by D.R. 1934.

13. Coughlin v. Thames & General Lighterage [1967] 2 Lloyd's Rep. 418; [1968] C.L.Y. 2729, Roskill J.

In breach of reg. 42 hatch beams not adequately secured to prevent displacement—stevedores were unloading barge—*Held*, both bargeowners and stevedores liable for breach of regulation, as both were carrying on the processes.

14. Mullis v. U.S. Lines [1969] 1 Lloyd's Rep. 109, Browne J.

*(b) Docks and Quays**

1. Chappell v. A. E. Smith (1947) 80 Ll.L.R. 92, Sellers J.

Wheel of bogie catches in gap between railway lines—*Held*, this did not mean that the means of access were unsafe, and defendants were not guilty of any breach of reg. 1 (means of access).

2. Murrin v. Convoys [1951] 2 Lloyd's Rep. 82, Streatfeild J.

Held, defendants not liable, as on the facts the lighting was adequate.

3. Kerridge v. Port of London Authority [1952] 2 Lloyd's Rep. 142, Donovan J.

"Lighting can be efficient—that is adequate to enable the work to be done—even though it may be poor."

4. Hayward v. Port of London Authority [1956] 2 Lloyd's Rep. 1, H.L.

Held, defendants not liable for any breach of reg. 2 (reasonably adequate means of escape from water). The reasons for this decision differ: Lords Jowitt and Tucker said that the interval of 300 feet between escape ladders was by itself unreasonable and would have been a breach resulting in liability but for the fortuitous presence of a pontoon which was near enough to be reasonably adequate; Lord Oaksey said that 300 feet did not constitute a breach; Lords Radcliffe and Evershed expressed no opinion on this point.

* See Introductory Note 5. Abbreviations are explained in Introductory Note 1.

5. Johnson v. British Transport Commission [1956] 2 Lloyd's Rep. 207, Donovan J.

Held, that the structure in question, which was a platform 3 feet 6 in. high, was a bridge, but not a footway over a bridge, which was something different from the bridge itself.

6. Cowhig v. Port of London Authority [1956] 2 Lloyd's Rep. 306, Pearce J.

Held, that a part of a dock road was not dangerous merely because there was a hosepipe across it, and that "efficiently lighted" meant "reasonably well lighted for the purpose for which the light is there"—*Held*, defendants not liable.

7. Bush v. Colonial Wharves [1958] 1 Lloyd's Rep. 533, Pearson J.

Held, defendants liable (but 40 per cent. contributory negligence).

8. Wilczek v. Gardiner and Tidy [1959] 1 Lloyd's Rep. 91, Pearson J.

Plaintiff alleged that the berthing edge of a dock should have been fenced under reg. 1 (duty to maintain "dangerous parts or edges of a dock, wharf or quay")—*Held*, (a) the word "dangerous" qualified the word "edges" as well as "parts," and (*obiter*) (b) an unfenced berthing edge was not dangerous because its existence was obvious and well known, and in any event it would not be practicable to fence it.

9. Jarvis v. Hay's Wharf [1967] 1 Lloyd's Rep. 329, Mocatta J.

10. Carter v. Port of London Authority [1974] 1 Lloyd's Rep. 583; [1974] C.L.Y. 2603, Cantley J. (*obiter*)

*(c) Gangways**

		D.R. 1934
Ladder—"of sound material"—one rung missing	1	reg. 9
Gangway—provision not reasonably practicable	2	reg. 9
Safe access to ship—whether defendants discharge whole duty by providing gangway	3	reg. 9
Safe gangway provided—plaintiff using Jacob's ladder instead	4	reg. 9
Gangway—secondary duty on employers—when arising	5	reg. 50
Two ladders provided—one unsafe	6	reg. 11
"Safe access"—ladder—must be strong enough to withstand light-hearted user	6	reg. 11
Gangway—provision alleged to be not reasonably practicable—onus on defendants	7	reg. 9
DUNNAGE AT BOTTOM OF GANGWAY—SLIPPING	8	REG. 9
"Safe access"—ladder from deck to quay—suspended on two wires—instead of resting on its wheels	9	reg. 9

* See Introductory Note 5. Abbreviations are explained in Introductory Note 1.

1. Leeson v. Gardner, 1947 S.L.T. 264, Ct. of Sess.

2. O'Brien v. Granford [1951] 1 Lloyd's Rep. 414, Donovan J.

Approved in **7**.

3. Dawson v. Euxine Shipping [1953] 1 W.L.R. 287; [1953] 1 All E.R. 299, McNair J.

Plaintiff a lighterman superintending loading of ship—slipped on gangway—alleged that cross treads of gangway were defective—it was conceded that plaintiff was a person employed—defendants argued that as they had provided a gangway which complied with reg. 9 (a) they had fulfilled the whole of their statutory duty of providing safe access—*Held*, not so, and that reg. 9 (a) prescribed what must be done in addition to providing safe access—*Held*, on the facts, plaintiff failed.

4. Lowe v. Scruttons [1953] 1 Lloyd's Rep. 432, Hilbery J.

Plaintiff dock labourer falls off Jacob's ladder which was improperly secured—there was safe access aft—plaintiff failed to prove that defendants had anything to do with the Jacob's ladder. (*N.B.* They were sued under the default provisions of reg. 50 as employers)—*Held*, defendants not liable.

5. Hayward v. Glen Line [1955] 2 Lloyd's Rep. 142, Finnemore J.

Held, that the secondary duty on employers to comply with regs. 9, 10 and 12 arose "as soon as possible after the employer knew or ought to have known, that there was a breach of statutory duty by the person responsible" (145, col. 2).

6. Cottrell v. Vianda S.S. [1955] 2 Lloyd's Rep. 450, Devlin J.

Two ladders into hold—one iron and one wooden—plaintiff uses wooden one which breaks—defendants say (a) that plaintiff should have used iron one, which was the access "provided," and (b) that plaintiff was playing the fool on the ladder—*Held*, defendants liable, because (a) plaintiff was reasonably justified in regarding it as a proper means of access, and (b) a ladder, to be "safe," must be able to withstand some degree of light-hearted user. *Doubted* as to (a) in *Richards* (Chap. 16, (5) (a) **U5**).

7. Walter Wilson v. Summerfield [1956] 1 W.L.R. 1429; [1956] 3 All E.R. 550, D.C.

Held, that the onus was on the defendants to establish that it was not reasonably practicable to provide a gangway, and as they had failed to discharge onus, they were guilty of a breach (although they had provided ladder under reg. 9 (b)). **2** *approved.*

8. Winstanley v. T. & J. Harrison [1968] 2 Lloyd's Rep. 119, C.A.

Held, reversing Ct. of Passage judge, defendants liable.

9. Watson v. Ben Line [1971] 2 Lloyd's Rep. 269; [1971] C.L.Y. 7791, Bridge J.

Held, safe.

*(d) Ship**

		D.R. 1934
"Required to proceed"—area meant	1	reg. 12 (c)
"Accessible"—defined	1	reg. 37 (a)
"Fence"—what required to constitute	1	reg. 37 (a)
Hatch cover of intermediate deck—loading onto—not a deck stage	2	regs. 36, 38
Hatch uncovered and unlit—shipowners liable for lighting—repairers for covering	3	**regs. 12, 37**
Hatch covers and lights—duty not to remove applies to all such—whether required by Regulations or not	3	**reg. 45**
Access from hold—safe ladder	4	
"Stage"—not a tier of drums being loaded—slippery	5	reg. 36 (c)
"Guard against accident by shoring or otherwise"—only aimed at preventing cargo falling over	5	reg. 41
Insufficient lighting—not replacing bilge boards	6	regs. 12, 37
Hatch cover giving way	7	
FENCING OF FRICTION GEARING—WINCH—"SO FAR AS IS PRACTICABLE WITHOUT IMPEDING SAFE WORKING"	8	REG. 26
Hatch signaller—employed but absent	9	reg. 43
Duty to employ signaller—may be on more than one person	9	reg. 9
Lighting—reg. 3 does not apply to lighting a ship	9	reg. 3
Lighting and access—secondary duty on employers—"within shortest time practicable"	9	regs. 50, 12
"Short interruption of work"—not $2\frac{1}{2}$ hours	10	reg. 37 (a)
Safe access to hold—duty additional to duty to provide ladder of specified type	11	regs. 11 (1), 11(2)
Safe access to hold—safe ladder	11	reg. 11 (2)
Access to hold—duty limited to perpendicular access—not include pile of coal round coamings	12	reg. 11
Lighting—secondary duty on employers—when arising	13	regs. 50, 12
Gangway—secondary duty on employers—when arising	13	regs. 50, 9
Access to hold—two ladders—one unsafe	14	regs. 11, 47
"Safe" access—light hearted user—access must be strong enough to withstand	14	reg. 11
LIGHTING—SECONDARY DUTY ON EMPLOYERS—WHEN ARISING	15	REGS. 50, 12
"MOTOR"—FENCING—NOT INCLUDE STEAM WINCH	16	REG. 26
Lighting—"efficient" means efficient in relation to work being done	17	reg. 12
Lighting—temporary lighting in hold inadequate	18	reg. 12
Access to hold—rope wound round rung	19	reg. 11 (1)
Access to the hold "in which work is being carried on"—work means work on the "processes"	19	reg. 11 (1)
HATCH COVERS—DUTY NOT TO REMOVE AND TO REPLACE EXTENDS ONLY TO HATCH COVERS "REQUIRED TO BE PROVIDED"—NOT TO ALL HATCH COVERS	20	REG. 45

* See Introductory Note 5. Abbreviations are explained in Introductory Note 1.

Ladder from hold—insufficient headroom................................	21	reg. 11
INSUFFICIENT LIGHTING—UNFENCED HATCH ON 'TWEEN DECK.............	22	REGS. 12, 37
Access to hold—slipping on split seed on 'tween deck at foot of ladder..	23	reg. 11

1. Henaghan v. Rederiet Forangirene [1936] 2 All E.R. 1426, Lewis J.

Held, (a) "required to proceed" in reg. 12 (c) did not necessarily mean "ordered to proceed," but included any place where a workman might properly go for ropes, etc., (b) "accessible" in reg. 37 (a) meant accessible without reasonable let or hindrance, and (c) "fence" in reg. 37 (a) is a fence situated in close proximity to a single hatch.

2. Hanlon v. Port of Liverpool Stevedoring [1937] 4 All E.R. 39, Lewis J.

Excessive weight loaded onto hatch cover of intermediate deck—*Held*, hatch cover not a deck stage for the purpose of reg. 36, but if cargo was to be loaded onto hatch cover on intermediate deck, cover must be strong enough to bear cargo in order to comply with reg. 38.

3. Grant v. Sun Shipping Co. [1948] A.C. 549; [1948] 2 All E.R. 238, H.L.

Action by dock labourer (not employed by either defendant) against shipowners and ship repairers—repairers had left a hatch uncovered and unlit, and plaintiff fell down it—plaintiff sued shipowners for breach of statutory duty and at common law and repairers at common law—shipowners also blamed repairers for breach of statutory duty—*Held*, *per* Lord du Parcq, with whose reasons Lord Uthwatt and (probably) Lord Porter expressly agreed:

(a) shipowners liable at common law, because they had duty to plaintiff as invitors, and it was not enough to tell and/or rely on repairers to make safe, they must take steps themselves;
(b) shipowners liable under reg. 12 (failure to light), duty being on them;
(c) repairers liable at common law, for plainly dangerous act in leaving hatch uncovered and unlit;
(d) repairers liable under reg. 37 (failure to cover hatch), duty being on them.

(As to (d) see Chap. 16(9)(a)**3**.)

It was also *held* (*obiter*), at 561, that the ban in reg. 45 on removing hatch covers, lights "or other things whatsoever required by these regulations to be provided" extended to *all* hatch covers, lights, etc., and "required by these regulations . . . " only governed "other things." *But* see **20**.

4. Bryan v. General Steam Navigation [1951] 1 Lloyd's Rep. 495, Lynskey J.

5. Sullivan v. Antwerp S.S. Co. [1952] 1 Lloyd's Rep. 555, Jones J.

6. Byrne v. Clan Line [1952] 2 Lloyd's Rep. 598, Ormerod J.

7. Rysdale v. Blackfriars Lighterage [1952] 2 Lloyd's Rep. 31, Barry J.

Held, defendants liable.

8. Ritchie v. Irving [1953] 1 All E.R. 37; [1952] 2 Lloyd's Rep. 387, C.A.

Winch not securely fenced—*Held*, on the facts, it was so fenced "so far as is practicable without impeding safe working of ship".

9. Johnson v. Beaumont [1953] 2 Q.B. 184; [1953] 2 All E.R. 106, McNair J.

Accidental failure of light in hold during discharge—signaller employed by second defendants (who also employ crane-driver and have general control of unloading) goes to get new bulb—while doing so, crane lowers grab onto plaintiff's foot in hold—plaintiff employed as a trimmer by first defendants—*Held*, following *Ashworth* (Chap. 16, (9) (e) **3**), there was a breach of reg. 43 (duty to employ hatch signaller) by both defendants, since they were both "by their workmen carrying on the processes," but there was no breach of reg. 3, since that regulation did not apply to the lighting of a ship, nor was there a breach of regs. 12–50 by first defendants, since the failure of the light was a sudden accident and prompt steps were taken to put it right (though not by first defendants).

10. Gray v. Dock Executive [1953] 1 Lloyd's Rep. 558, Parker J.

11. Cheeseman v. Orient S.N. [1954] 2 Lloyd's Rep. 231, Slade J.

12. Carvil v. Hay [1954] 2 Lloyd's Rep. 380, Ct. of Sess, I.H.

13. Hayward v. Glen Line [1955] 2 Lloyd's Rep. 142, Finnemore J.

Held, that the secondary duty on employers to comply with regs. 9,10 and 12 arose "as soon as possible after the employer knew or ought to have known, that there was a breach of statutory duty by the person responsible" (145, col. 2).

14. Cottrell v. Vianda SS. [1955] 2 Lloyd's Rep. 450, Devlin J.

Two ladders into hold—one iron and one wooden—plaintiff uses wooden one which breaks—defendants say (a) that plaintiff should have used the iron one, which was the access "provided" and (b) that he was playing the fool on the ladder—*Held*, defendants liable, because (a) plaintiff was reasonably justified in regarding it as a proper means of access, and (b) a ladder, to be "safe," must be able to withstand some degree of light-hearted user. *Doubted* as to (a) in *Richards* Chap. 16 (5) (a) **U5**).

15. Simons v. W.H. Rhodes [1956] 1 W.L.R. 642; [1956] 2 All E.R. 569, C.A.

Poor lighting on ship causing accident to plaintiff stevedore employed by first defendants—*Held*, first defendants equally liable with second defendants, because although the duty to light only fell on first defendants "as soon as possible after they knew or ought to have known" of second defendants' failure (574 A), yet here first defendants' men knew all about the poor lighting, and "so ought the management" (Singleton L.J. at 574 G).

16. Shanley v. West Coast Stevedoring [1957] 1 Lloyd's Rep. 391, C.A.

17. Edwards v. A/S Ludegaard [1958] 2 Lloyd's Rep. 193, 197, Pearson J.

18. Lynch v. Furness Withy [1958] 2 Lloyd's Rep. 360, Diplock J.

19. Mace v.R. & H. Green & Silley Weir [1959] 2 Q.B. 14; [1959] 1 All E.R. 655, Lord Parker C.J.

Held, that the words in reg. 11(1) "where work is being carried on" meant work on the processes, and not just any sort of work—*Held*, also that the ladder with rope round rung was not a safe means of access, and defendants therefore liable.

20. Cockerill v. William Cory [1959] 2 Q.B. 194; [1959] 2 All E.R. 561, C.A.

Deceased fell into hold—the hatch covers had been partly removed for loading and not replaced—after loading vessel began to move to a buoy—deceased after loading had gone onto hatch to uncoil wire and had slipped—the coamings were 5 feet high (so reg. 37 (a) did not apply to require replacement)—did reg. 45 apply (all "such" things to be restored immediately)?—"such" things included under the regulation " . . . gear, ladder, hatch covering, . . . or other things whatsoever *required by these regulations to be provided*"—*Held*, these last words governed all the antecedent words and not merely "other things," and since (because the coamings were over 2 feet 6 in. high) there was no regulation requiring a hatch covering to be provided, there was therefore no obligation under reg. 45 to replace hatch coverings, and therefore defendants not liable. Dicta to the contrary in **3** *not followed.*

21. Wilkins v. William Cory [1959] 2 Lloyd's Rep. 98, Gorman J.

Held, defendants liable.

22. Henry v. Mersey Ports Stevedoring [1963] 2 Lloyd's Rep. 97, C.A.

Plaintiff dock worker was sent by employing stevedores to a 'tween deck which was in darkness—fell down open hatch—*Held*, shipowners were liable for breach of reg. 37 (accessible hatch unfenced), but not for breach of reg. 12 (lighting of places where processes being carried on), since employers should not have sent plaintiff to 'tween deck. *N.B.* Both employers and shipowners were found liable at common law.

23. McCarthy v. Hellenic Lines [1968] 1 Lloyd's Rep. 537, Willis J.

Plaintiff bumped his knee going down ladder to 'tween deck—and then at bottom bent to rub knee, but slipped on spilt seeds—*Held*, no breach of reg. 11 (access to holds), because, applying *Carvil* **12**, the regulation only applied to perpendicular access. No liability at common law either.

*(e) Moving Cargo**

		D.R. 1934
Hatch cover of intermediate deck—loading onto—not a deck stage	1	regs. 36, 38
Rope—no rope to be used unless . . . etc.—defective rope substituted for sound rope	2	reg. 20
HATCH SIGNALLER—EMPLOYED BUT ABSENT	3	REG. 43
"Unloading cargo"—removing dunnage	4	reg. 43
"Stage"—not a tier of drums being loaded—slippery	5	reg. 36 (c)
"Guard against accident by shoring or otherwise"—only aimed at preventing cargo falling over	5	reg. 41
"GUARD AGAINST ACCIDENT BY SHORING"—WHERE HANDLING CANNOT BE CARRIED OUT SAFELY UNAIDED—FALL OF BALE FROM TIER ...	6	REG. 41
FENCING OF FRICTION GEARING—WINCH—"SO FAR AS IS PRACTICABLE WITHOUT IMPEDING SAFE WORKING"	7	REG. 26
Hatch signaller—employed but absent	8	reg. 43
Duty to employ signaller—may be on more than one person.	8	reg. 9

* See Introductory Notes 3(A) and 5. Abbreviations are explained in Introductory Note 1.

1. Hanlon v. Port of Liverpool Stevedoring [1937] 4 All E.R. 39, Lewis J.

Excessive weight loaded onto hatch cover of intermediate deck—*Held*, hatch cover not a deck stage for the purpose of reg. 36, but if cargo was to be loaded onto hatch cover on intermediate deck, cover must be strong enough to bear cargo in order to comply with reg. 38.

2. O'Melia v. Freight Conveyors [1940] 4 All E.R. 516, Croom-Johnson J.

Defendants supplied a second rope—it disappeared and another one was substituted in circumstances unknown—the second rope was partly severed—*Held*, since under duties the obligation under reg. 20 was only cast on "the owner of the plant and machinery used in the processes", defendants were not liable, as the rope was not theirs.

3. Ashworth v. McQuirk [1944] K.B. 1; [1943] 2 All E.R. 446, C.A.

Defendants employed a signaller who temporarily left hatch—*Held*, defendants liable. *Followed* in **8**.

4. Spalding v. Bradley Forge [1952] 1 Lloyd's Rep. 461, Lloyd-Jacob J.

Held, that removing dunnage was not unloading cargo, but a wholly separate operation, carried out for convenience of shipowners.

5. Sullivan v. Antwerp S.S. Co. [1952] 1 Lloyd's Rep. 555, Jones J.

6. Walker v. Bowaters Paper Mills [1952] 2 Lloyd's Rep. 299, C.A.

Bale on top tier falls down during discharge—*Held*, reg. 41 had no application, because the work could be carried out safely unaided, and "unaided" meant "unaided by some method of securing the stack" (*per* McNair J. in first court, at 301).

7. Ritchie v. Irving [1953] 1 All E.R. 37; [1952] 2 Lloyd's Rep. 387, C.A.

Winch not securely fenced—*Held*, on the facts, it was so fenced "so far as is practicable without impeding safe working of ship."

8. Johnson v. Beaumont [1953] 2 Q.B. 184; [1953] 2 All E.R. 106, McNair J.

Accidental failure of light in hold during discharge—signaller employed by second defendants (who also employ crane driver and have general control of unloading) goes to get new bulb—while doing so, crane lowers grab onto plaintiff's foot in hold—plaintiff employed as a trimmer by first defendants—*Held*, following **3**, there was a breach of reg. 43 (duty to employ hatch signaller) by both defendants, since they were both "by their workmen carrying on the processes," but there was no breach of reg. 3, since that regulation did not apply to the lighting of a ship, nor was there a breach of regs. 12–50 by first defendants, since the failure of the light was a sudden accident and prompt steps were taken to put it right (though not by first defendants).

9. Smith v. Port Line [1955] 1 W.L.R. 514; [1955] 2 All E.R. 297, C.A.

Plaintiff lighterman standing on barge in arc of crane when struck thereby—crane driver had an unrestricted view into hold—*Held*, in view of this, proviso (i) to reg. 43 was satisfied and there was no need to have signaller even if crane driver's view of where plaintiff was was obstructed.

10. Hill v. Wm. H. Muller [1956] 1 Lloyd's Rep. 281, Hilbery J.

"... the sort of aid the regulation is for is shoring or something other than shoring of a like kind, that is to say, artificial and not merely human" (284, col. 2).

11. Dawes v. Scruttons [1956] 1 Lloyd's Rep. 490, Havers J.

"I think it ('unaided') means not merely without the assistance of some other man, but without the assistance of some shoring or precautions of that character" (491, col. 2).

12. Shanley v. West Coast Stevedoring [1957] 1 Lloyd's Rep. 391, C.A.

13. Bamber v. Union Castle [1956] 2 Lloyd's Rep. 552, Devlin J.

Cargo being landed onto deck near hatchway—*Held*, no signaller required under reg. 43, as regulation was directed to cargo being hoisted through a hatch.

14. Gibson v. Skibs [1966] 2 All E.R. 476, Cantley J.

15. Coughlin v. Thames & General Lighterage [1967] 2 Lloyd's Rep. 418; [1968] C.L.Y. 2729, Roskill J.

U1. Cornforth v. Felixstowe Docks (1974) C.A. 306

Held, signaller no longer "employed," and therefore defendants liable for breach of reg. 43.

(10) Electricity*

		E.R. 1908
"So placed and safeguarded to prevent danger"	1	reg. 2
"Such special precautions as may be necessary to prevent danger"—testing and research—failure of automatic safety device—duty not absolute	2	reg. 4
"So maintained as to prevent danger"—conductor causing short circuit	3	reg. 1
Apparatus controlled by third party—liability of employer	3	
Separation of live section by screen—removal of screen during test	4	regs. 18 (d), 1
"Of proper construction as regards mechanical strength"—joint of cable breaking when pulled—deceased falling result	5	reg. 6
"Danger" from shock burn "or other injury"—*ejusdem generis*	6	reg. 26
"So placed and safeguarded as to prevent danger as far as reasonably practicable"—bare overhead wires of travelling electric crane	7	reg. 2
Danger to persons employed—includes danger to servant of independent contractor	8	reg. 1
Disconnected switch—constitutes "apparatus" not "so worked as to prevent danger"	8	reg. 1
Screen—whether necessary to prevent danger—in room where only experienced men allowed	9	regs. 15, 24
"Danger"—experienced men just as liable to have lapses as inexperienced	9	
Unaccompanied work—cleaning live plant when forbidden	10	reg. 28
Building operation—who is liable for breach of Electricity Regulations	11	reg. 1
Overhead live conductor—electrician slipping so that hand touched wire	12	reg. 2
"Conduct their work in accordance with these Regulations"—meaning	13	Duties

1. Long v. Kirk (1938) 82 S.J. 256; [1938] 1 All E.R. 142, D.C.

Held, these words were absolute, and did not permit "what some people may think to be a moderate amount of danger to somebody else."

2. Proctor v. Johnson [1943] K.B. 553; [1943] 1 All E.R. 565, C.A.

Fatal accident through deceased coming into contact with a high voltage research and testing apparatus—defendant had used an automatic safety device (which had failed) and had also instructed deceased to use an earthing rod (which he had not done)—*Held*, defendant had complied with reg. 4.

* See Introductory Note 4. Abbreviations are explained in Introductory Note 1.

3. Heard v. Brymbo Steel Works [1947] K.B. 692; (1948) 177 L.T. 251. C.A.

Explosion at switchboard due to faulty conductor—*Held*, employers liable. Another cause of the accident was that a switch at the factory, which was under the control of the *power company*, was also faulty—*Held*, employers were liable for this also under E.R. 1908.

4. Barcock v. Brighton Corporation [1949] 1 K.B. 339; [1949] 1 All E.R. 251, Hilbery J.

Explosion because plaintiff removed a shuttered lid when carrying out test—*Held*, probably *obiter* that duty had been delegated to plaintiff, but plaintiff recovered at common law for unsafe system.

5. Gatehouse v. John Summers [1953] 1 W.L.R. 742; [1953] 2 All E.R. 117, C.A.

Electrician pulls at an electric cable on a crane, which breaks at a joint, so that he falls and is killed—*Held*, defendants liable under reg. 6, as cable was not of proper mechanical strength and it was immaterial that injury was not electrically caused.

6. Lake v. London Electricity Board [1955] 1 All E.R. 324, Parker L.J.

Held," or other injury "referred *ejusdem generis* to injury due to electrical energy.

7. Garrett v. Thomas Borthwick [1955] 1 Lloyd's Rep. 532, Jones J.

Held, on the facts, defendants not liable.

8. Massey-Harris-Ferguson v. Piper [1956] 2 Q.B. 396; [1956] 2 All E.R. 722, D.C.

Held, defendants liable for having a switch which appeared to be connected to overhead wire, but in fact was inoperative.

9. Murfin v. United Steel [1957] 1 W.L.R. 104; [1957] 1 All E.R. 23, C.A.

No insulating screen as required by reg. 24—defendants plead it was not necessary adequately to prevent danger, because it was in room set apart under reg. 15, which only experienced men could enter—*Held*, no defence, because experienced men just as liable to have lapses as inexperienced.

10. Knight v. Colvilles, 1963 S.C. 26; [1964] C.L.Y. 1268, Ct. of Sess.

Deceased employed to clean dead plant—he switched on a transformer, and in breach of orders cleaned it—electrocuted—*Held*, no breach of reg. 28 (men to work accompanied where experience needed to avoid danger), as deceased was only employed to clean dead, and therefore safe, plant.

11. Fisher v. C.H.T. [1966] 2 Q.B. 475; [1966] 1 All E.R. 87, C.A.

Plaintiff, employed by plasterers (D3), was injured touching a live wire in the ceiling—liability was mainly decided at common law, but the question also arose as to who was liable under reg. 1 (protection of conductors)—the place was a restaurant owned by D1, operated under licence by D2, and being re-decorated by D3—D2 were at the same time doing some electrical repairs of their own, and their employee was responsible for the wire being live—D1 and D2 were both occupiers at common law—*Held*, D2 liable under E.R. 1908 as notional occupiers of a factory by virtue of F.A. 1961, s. 127(4), but that D1 were not liable (nor, it would seem, D2) as actual occupiers. The liability of D3 was left undecided, as it was not clear whether they were "persons undertaking the operations" within s. 127(4)—as D2 clearly were.

12. Howell v. A.P.V. Paramount (1967) 111 S.J. 809; [1967] C.L.Y. 2718, C.A.

Held, defendants not in breach of reg. 2 (guarding of live conductors) because it was not reasonably practicable to guard the wire.

13. Turner v. A.E.I. (1971) 11 K.I.R. 1, Waller J.

Plaintiff, in accordance with normal practice, was working on dead side of fuse box without isolating the live side—received shock—employers were in breach of their duty, but was plaintiff in breach of his duty to "conduct his work in accordance with the regulations "?—*Held*, no, because in this case no actual method of work had been prescribed by the Regulations, so that it could not be said that the plaintiff, who was doing work precisely as required by his employers, was in breach.

(11) Horizontal Milling Machines*

		H.M.M.R. 1928
REGULATIONS NOT AN EXHAUSTIVE CODE	1	
FENCING—DEFENDANTS MUST COMPLY WITH FACTORY ACTS—EXCEPT FOR CUTTERS	1	3
FENCING—AUTOMATIC PROFILING—EXEMPTED PROCESS—DEFENDANTS UNDER NO DUTY UNDER FACTORY ACTS TO FENC	2	
Fencing—only required when cutter in motion	3	regs. 3, 6
Stopping appliance—clutch out of order—stop buttom situated on right—plaintiff working on left	U1	*reg. 4*

1. Benn v. Kamm [1952] 2 Q.B. 127; [1952] 1 All E.R. 833, C.A.

Horizontal milling machine—plaintiff injured by a dangerous part other than the cutter—H.M.M.R. 1928 only dealt with fencing the cutter—*Held*, that the Regulations were not an exhaustive code nor did they modify F.A. 1937, with regard to parts other than the cutter, and therefore plaintiff could succeed under s. 14. *Followed* in **2**.

2. Quinn v. Horsfall [1956] 1 W.L.R. 652; [1956] 2 All E.R. 467, C.A.

Horizontal milling machine which, because for automatic profiling, was exempt from fencing under H.M.M.R. 1928—Regulations contained a proviso saying that nothing in the exemption should prejudice the application of F.A. 1937—*Held*, that defendants were under duty to fence under s. 14. C.A. gave no real indication of what would have been the position, if there had been no proviso, except the citation from Somervell L.J., *ante*, that "this depends on the wording of the regulations."

3. Morris Motors v. Hopgood [1957] 1 Q.B. 30; [1956] 3 All E.R. 467, D.C.

Milling machine with movable jig which moved forward under power onto the cutters—as it moved forward it passed through gap in guard which it then completely closed—the cutters only started to revolve when the jig was through gap—workman left his hand in front of jig so that it was carried

* See Introductory Notes 9 and 10. Abbreviations are explained in Introductory Note 1.

onto the cutters as they began to revolve—*Held*, no breach, as reg. 3 requiring fencing must be read in conjunction with reg. 6 requiring the cutters to be fenced when in motion, and since there was a proper fence when the cutters were in motion, therefore no offence.

U1. Carey v. Howard and Bullough (1956) C.A. 21 A

Held, defendants liable.

(12) Iron and Steel*

	Reg.		Liable or not
Pouring aisle—insufficiently defined—and not wide enough	1	6(2)	Yes
Plaintiff working within 12 feet of spout	U1	5	*Yes*

1. Hawkins v. Ian Ross [1970] 1 All E.R. 180, Fisher J.

U1. Lewis v. Matthew Swain (1969) C.A. 129 (unreported)

(13) Mines and Quarries

(*N.B.* (1) The corresponding section in the Third Edition contained a number of cases under the following provisions, which are no longer in force:
Metalliferous Mines Regulation Act 1872
Coal Mines Act 1911
General Regulations 1913
Explosives in Coal Mines Order 1934
Metalliferous Mines General Regulations 1938
Quarrier General Regulations 1938
General Regulations 1947
Coal Mines (Explosives) Order 1951
Coal Mines (Explosives) Regulations 1956
Coal and Other Mines (Managers and Officials) Regulations 1956
Coal Mines (Support) Regulations 1956
These cases have not been retained.

(2) With one exception, references in the right-hand column in the introductory section below are to the Mines and Quarries Act 1954 (M.Q.A. 1954). "C.S.O. 1956" is an abbreviation for the Coal and Other Mines (Sidings) Order 1956.

(3) Some of the sections of the M.Q.A. 1954 referred to below have been or will be repealed, as follows:

s. 31—by the Mines (Shafts and Winding) Regulations, 1993 with effect from April 1 1993 or, in the case of tin or tin ore mines, January 1, 1996

s. 34—by the Mines (Safety of Exit) Regulations 1988

* The Regulations referred to are the Iron and Steel Foundries Regulations, 1953, as to which see Introductory Notes 8, 9 and 10.

ss. 81, 82—See Introductory Note 10

ss. 88, 89—by the Management and Administration of Safety and Health at Mines Regulations 1993, except for their application to quarries by M.Q.A. 1954, s. 115.

"Properly maintained"—absolute duty—winch	1	**s. 81(1)**
PATENT DEFECT—MEANS OBSERVABLE AS OPPOSED TO OBSERVED	2	s. 81
OBSTRUCTION IN ROAD—NOT A TAUT HAULAGE ROPE	3	s. 34
"Secure"—meaning of	4	**s. 48**
Manager—duty to keep mine secure—extent	4	**s. 48**
"To secure"—meaning of	5	s. 108
"Competent person"—meaning of	5	
Maintenance—colliery pump—pumpman injured investigating fault	6	
"SECURE"—"NECESSARY STEPS"—FALL THROUGH LATENT DEFECT—INCIPIENT BEDDING PLANE	7	s. 48(1)
"Secure"—"necessary steps"—steps taken must be one or other of the two steps prescribed	8	**s. 48(1)**
Tram—shackler run down by	9	s. 41(2)
"Secure"—"necessary steps"—manager not called as witness—onus is on defendants to prove that manager took all steps to inform himself as to steps necessary to secure mine	10	s. 48
Onus of proof—insecure mine—defendants must call manager to prove that he took all necessary steps to inform himself as to what steps needed to secure mine	10	s. 48
"SECURE"—"NECESSARY STEPS"—DANGER MUST BE FORESEEABLE	11	s. 48
Re-setting roof supports at coal face—H girders—bent girder "springing" when prop removed	12	ss. 51 (3), 81 (1)
"Apparatus"—probably does not include a roof girder	12	s. 81 (1)
Barrier against falling down shaft—only required to guard against risk of falling from surface entrance—not from inside shaft	13	s. 31 (2)
"Working place"—defined	14	s. 48
"Every place where any mineral is worked"—cannot be a place which is not a "working place"	14	s. 49
Fall—is prima facie evidence that manager is in breach of statutory duty	14	s. 48
"Required to pass"—normally safe route obstructed—alternative route available	15	**C.S.O. 1956, reg. 20**
"Close and effective supervision"—cannot be said to be exercised by manager who is ignorant of operation being carried out	16	s. 103
"Impracticable" proviso—manager unaware operation in question being carried out	16	s. 157
"Duty of every manager . . . to secure that . . . operations are so carried on as to avoid danger from falls"—absolute duty	16	s. 108

1. Hamilton v. N.C.B. [1960] A.C. 633; [1960] 1 All E.R. 76, H.L.

Winch tipped forward due to the absence of stells—the absence could have been due to act of stranger or latent defect—*Held*, this was immaterial, as the obligation in M.Q.A. 1954, s. 81(1), that all parts of machinery shall be "properly maintained" was absolute.

2. Sanderson v. N.C.B. [1961] 2 Q.B. 244; [1961] 2 All E.R. 796, C.A.

Hooks from an endless conveyor belt became unfastened and caught plaintiff's leg—defendants said that (a) this was not a "patent defect" within M.Q.A. 1954, s. 81(1), since there was no evidence as to when the hooks became unfastened and it might have been at a time immediately before the accident when there was no one who could have seen it, and (b) it was "impracticable" to remedy the defect—*Held*, defendants liable—the defect was patent, in the sense of the "observable" (as opposed to "observed"), and it was immaterial that it occurred in darkness, for it would have been apparent on inspection with a lamp—and further the defendants had failed to prove that it was impracticable to remedy the defect, inasmuch as all they had proved was that the accident could have happened without their negligence.

3. Cook v. N.C.B. [1961] 1 W.L.R. 1192; [1961] 3 All E.R. 220, C.A.

Taut haulage rope running between rails of haulage track—plaintiff tripped crossing rails—*Held*, this was not an "obstruction" within M.Q.A. 1954, s. 34(1) and defendants not liable. The test was whether there was "something not in its proper place in the ordinary course of things, something which should not have been there at all" (223 C, Lord Evershed M.R.).

4. Brown v. N.C.B. [1962] A.C. 574; [1962] 1 All E.R. 81, H.L.

Tub dislodges girder so that stone falls from roof—plaintiff electrician summoned to remove an electric lamp from the fallen girder—on arrival plaintiff while looking for a tool in bag was hit by second fall of stone—*Held*, defendants not liable under M.Q.A. 1954, s. 48(1), because the duty imposed by s. 48(1) was a duty "to exercise care and skill—the highest degree of care and skill that a competent manager could exercise" (Lord Reid at 83 I), or because (*per* Lord Radcliffe at 86 F) the manager's duty was to ask himself what steps were required to keep the road secure, and to answer that question "in the light of the best obtainable information as to the circumstances, geophysical or otherwise, that he is to deal with and knowledge of skilled and up to date engineering science and practice." Applying these tests, the defendants had not been in breach of duty. As to the meaning of "secure" Lord Radcliffe (85 H) said it meant a physical condition of stability which would ordinarily result in safety, while Lord Denning (89 G) said that a roof was not secure if it was "a possible cause of injury to anybody acting in a way in which a human being may reasonably be expected to act in circumstances which may be reasonably expected to occur."

5. Brazier v. Skipton Rock [1962] 1 W.L.R. 471; [1962] 1 All E.R. 955, Winn J.

Plaintiff shotfirer in quarry—saw projecting rock above his place of work—thought that if it fell it would fall clear—he was wrong—*Held*, defendants liable, as being in breach of M.Q.A. 1954, s. 108(1) (*i.e.* manager's duty to secure that operations so carried on as to avoid danger from falls), because "to secure" meant to achieve the result that the operations were so carried on as to avoid danger from falls. Dictum of Holroyd Pearce L. J. in *Brown v. N.C.B.* [1960] 3 All E.R. 607 applied. But this case has subsequently been to House of Lords, where dictum was not referred to. Meaning of "competent person" also considered.

6. Chalmers v. N.C.B. 1963, S.L.T. 358; [1963] C.L.Y. 2206, O.H.

Colliery pumpman injured by fault in pump when investigating same—defendants say that, as plaintiff was engaged in maintaining pump at the time, they were not in breach of their statutory duty to maintain—*Held*, not so, as duty of defendants to maintain was absolute and continuous, and in any event plaintiff was not maintaining pump at the time, but only investigating fault.

7. Tomlinson v. Beckermet [1964] 1 W.L.R. 1043; [1964] 3 All E.R. 1, C.A.

Fall in haematite ore mine due to latent defect known as incipient bedding plane—no known way of discovering same—*Held*, defendants not liable. *Brown* **4** *applied*. "How could the mine manager take the necessary steps under the section if there was nothing to tell him that any steps were necessary" (Davies L. J., 10 I).

8. Stein v. O'Hanlon [1965] A.C. 890; [1965] 1 All E.R. 547, H.L.

Clay mine—fall of clay from side of road—due to foreseeable insecurity from adjacent shotfiring—manager claimed that best mining practice was to test and trim the sides, which he was having done, rather than to support—*Held*, M.Q.A. 1954, s. 48 imperatively required that "where insecurity has come to light or is expected, the manager must adopt one or other of the two prescribed methods (controlling movement or supporting). . . . " and therefore defendants were in breach.

9. Jones v. N.C.B. [1965] 1 W.L.R. 532; [1965] 1 All E.R. 221, Nield J.

Held, defendants were not liable for breach of statutory duty (but were at common law) because "running away" in s. 41 (2) meant unintended and therefore uncontrolled movement, which was not so in this case.

10. Beizcak v. N.C.B. [1965] 1 W.L.R. 518 [1965] 1 All E.R. 895, Karminski J.

So held, following dictum of Lord Grant in *Sinclair v. N.C.B* 1963 S.C., 586, 593 where he said that "the steps which he took or failed to take are matters peculiarly within the knowledge of the manager. It seems reasonable and logical that the onus of averring and proving them should be cast upon the manager and not the pursuer".

11. Soar v. N.C.B. [1965] 1 W.L.R. 886; [1965] 2 All E.R. 318, C.A.

Held, defendants not liable, as no danger could be anticipated. Lord Denning M. R. said that the roof was secure by the *Bletchley Fletton* test (see Chap. 16, (2) (a) **1**); Danckwerts and Winn L.JJ. decided issue on the ground that preventive measures, being unforeseeable, could not be "necessary."

12. Grimstead v. N.C.B. [1965] 1 W.L.R. 1252; [1965] 3 All E.R. 446, Milmo J.

Held, defendants not liable, as there had been no breaches of s. 51(3) (suitable materials to be readily available) or of s. 81 (1) (apparatus to be free from patent defect). *Semble*, the girder was not "apparatus" within the meaning of the section.

13. Rodgers v. N.C.B. [1966] 1 W.L.R. 1559; [1966] 3 All E.R. 124, Waller J.

14. Wenn v. N.C.B. [1967] 2 Q.B. 557; [1967] 1 All E.R. 149; Veale J.

Held, that a working place was "the place where he is actually working which is also the place where he has been set to work or in which he may be expected to be" (156 A), and accordingly a place where the withdrawal of supports had commenced, but the intended fall had taken place at a stage earlier than intended, was still a working place. "Because any disturbance of support creates some risk, and because safety precautions will take into account this risk . . . it does not, in my judgment, follow that an unintended fall inside a working place becomes an intended fall outside a working place" (158 H)—*Held*, also, that "every place where any mineral is worked" could not include a place which was not a working place—*Held*, further, that a fall was *some* evidence of a breach of s. 48(1)(154C).

15. Smith (or Westwood) v. N.C.B. [1967] 1 W.L.R. 871; [1967] 2 All E.R. 593, H.L.

Shunter at coal mine was caught and killed by passing train—route on which he was travelling was unsafe, and defendants would be liable if deceased had been "required to pass" by that route—unsafe because partly blocked by obstruction—*Held*, deceased was, in the circumstances, "required to pass" by the route he chose, because he was "accompanying" the train in accordance with his duty—*Held*, also, that the defendants were liable at common law for allowing the route, normally safe, to become obstructed, and failing to give any warning thereof.

16. Sanderson v. Millom Hematite [1967] 3 All E.R. 1050; 3 K.I.R. 264, Cantley J.

Plaintiff, being told, after fall of rain, to get on with work, went to work at quarry face—neither manager nor deputy knew he would be at that place—fall of rock from face—*Held*, defendants in breach of s. 103 (1), in that manager could not claim to be exercising close etc. supervision when he did not even know that plaintiff was working at face, and that it was practicable for him to have known and exercised supervision—*Held*, also that the duty under s. 108 (1) of the manager to secure that operations shall be carried out so as to avoid danger from falls was an absolute duty, subject only to the practicability proviso in s. 157; the latter put the onus on defendants, who had on the evidence failed to discharge it, and were therefore liable under this section as well.

17. Robson v. N.C.B. [1968] 3 All E.R. 159, Waller J.

Plaintiff, an experienced miner, was trying to move a conveyor motor—to do this he set a steel strut into the limestone roof—when pressure was put on the strut, it bit into the roof, loosening it so that a little later a stone fell and injured plaintiff—a deputy had inspected the place at a time when the strut was erected, but had made no comment—the proper method would have been to put a wooden lid between the strut and the roof—*Held*, defendants not liable, for, following *Brown* **4** and *Stein* **8**, liability depended on foreseeability, and the defendants' manager (on whom the duty rested) could not have foreseen that plaintiff would adopt the method he did. The fact that the deputy saw the improper method in operation was immaterial, for it did not affect the foresight to be imputed to the manager.

18. Collier v. Hall and Ham River (1968) 4 K.I.R. 628; [1968] C.L.Y. 2693, Waller J.

Held, defendants liable.

19. Lister v. N.C.B. [1970] 1 Q.B. 228; [1969] 3 All E.R. 1077, C.A.

Held, that s. 34(1)(a) dealt with the construction of the road and its maintainance, and that s. 34 (1) (b) with objects and obstructions in the roadway, and that the two limbs were mutually exclusive.

20. Rodgers v. London Brick Co. (1970) 8 K.I.R. 843; [1970] C.L.Y. 1713, C.A.

For details, see Chap. 16, (2) (a) **8**.

21. McFarlane v. N.C.B., 1974 S.L.T. 16; [1974] C.L.Y. 2349, O.H.

Falls from roof—not known to manager—if known would have suggested roof insecure—*Held*, defendants liable, since the manager must be deemed to have all the relevant information necessary for a decision as to whether the roof was likely to fall, and the question whether insecurity was foreseeable depended on the existence of such information.

22. Anderson v. N.C.B., 1970 S.C. 42; [1970] C.L.Y. 2350, Ct. of Sess.

Two strippers working to bring down coal from a "nose"—*Held*, duty to keep working place secure did not apply, since it was the purpose of the operation in question to cause the coal to fall.

23. Hill v. N.C.B. 1976 S.L.T. 261; [1977] C.L.Y. 2007 Ct. of Sess.

Shotfiring on night shift—next day plaintiff struck by falling stone—*Held*, that, although the defect might have been undetectable, the shotfiring could have caused the roof to become disturbed, and the defendants were in breach of duty in failing to inspect after shotfiring.

24. Thompson v. N.C.B. [1982] I.C.R. 15; [1982] C.L.Y. 2019, C.A.

Deceased employed primarily as pump attendant and tippler operator. Occasionally he worked as a wagon lowerer if there was shortage of labour and had not had adequate instruction as a wagon lowerer and was not competent to do the job unsupervised. Being conscientious, he responded to a tannoy message for a wagon lowerer and was killed while lowering wagons—*Held*, Watkins L.J. expressing no view, the deceased was "employed" as a wagon lowerer, and, as he was not properly trained and was unsupervised, defendants were in breach of s. 88—*Held*, also, by Dunn L.J. (20 E–21 B) that, subject to s. 157, s. 88 imposed a strict and unqualified duty which did not depend on foreseeability.

25. McMullen v. N.C.B. [1982] I.C.R. 148; [1982] C.L.Y. 2121, Caulfield J.

26. Storey v. N.C.B. [1983] I.C.R. 156; [1983] 1 All E.R. 375, Mustill J.

Deceased killed while riding on mineral conveyor. Defendants prohibited practice and made provision for fining those guilty of it but employees and even on occasions deputies and officials continued the practice. Fines were imposed very infrequently and only in small sums—*Held*, that, although the defendants had not been negligent at common law, they had not "enforced" the rules and were liable for breach of statutory duty (but 75 per cent. contributory negligence): "Given that the defendants did all that they could be expected as regards bringing the rules, and the reasons for them, to the attention of their workers, did they go on to "enforce" them? In my judgment they did not. If exhortation failed, as it did, sanctions would be required. These did not in any real sense exist" (380 J).

27. Jennings v. N.C.B. [1983] I.C.R. 636; [1983] C.L.Y. 2412, C.A.

Plaintiff took "snap" at edge of road. Materials stored there ready for use. Plaintiff caught foot on angle iron and was injured—*Held*, that, even though s. 34 applied to the full width of the road, the angle iron was not an "obstruction" as it was reasonably stored there and was not a foreseeable danger to persons reasonably using the road—*Held*, also that the defendants had not been negligent.

28. Hammond v. N.C.B. [1984] 1 W.L.R. 1218; [1984] 3 All E.R. 321, C.A.

Due to unstable bind above a coal seam being worked, falls from sections of newly-exposed roof occurred in the wake of a mechanical coal cutter. As plaintiff observed the repair of a resulting roof cavity by packing it with timber, a second fall occurred from the cavity and plaintiff was injured. He alleged breaches of M.Q.A. 1954, ss. 48 and 49—*Held*,

(a) At time of first fall from cavity, place beneath it was not a "working place" within s. 48, because no one could be expected to have been working there at that time.
(b) At time of second fall, place beneath it was a working place, but fall was not foreseeable and defendant, who had proved it was impracticable to prevent it, had a defence under s. 157.
(c) Read together, s. 49(1) and (5) only required provision and maintenance of roof support in accordance with support rules of mine. There was no evidence of any breach of such rules.

29. English v. Cory Sand Ballast Company Ltd, *The Times*, April 2, 1985; [1985] C.L.Y. 2178, Stocker J.

Held, in relation to M.Q.A. 1954, that:

(a) The duty imposed by s. 108(1) on quarry manager to secure that quarrying operations were so carried on as to avoid danger from falls referred to falls of materials from the quarry face and not to the fall of persons over the edge of the quarry face.
(b) The duty imposed by s. 109 to provide and maintain safe means of access to every place at a quarry at which any person had to work related to the part of the quarry at which quarrying was being carried on, and did not apply to roadways on which vehicles might be driven round the quarry.

30. Mettam v. British Coal Corporation, *The Times*, July 23, 1988, [1988] C.L.Y. 2278, C.A.

Held, mine manager's duty under M.Q.A. 1954, s. 48(1) is not absolute. It requires him to apply the highest skill and care to obviate potential dangers which are foreseeable in the light of information obtained by him pursuant to s. 48(2) as to the state of the mine, and of skilled and up-to-date engineering science and practice. (*Brown v. N.C.B.* **4** applied.)

31. Hanks v. British Coal Corporation, *The Times*, February 14, 1989; [1989] C.L.Y. 2402, C.A.

U1. Lloyd v. N.C.B. (1968) C.A. 393

Obiter, per Edmund Davies L.J. (18 E), a sloping pile of debris resting against a side would not constitute a side of a working place within s. 48(1) of M.Q.A. 1954.

U2. McCann v. N.C.B. (1975) C.A. 113

U3. Richardson v. N.C.B. (1980) C.A. 160

Plaintiff injured by fall from coal face. The issue in the appeal was whether the plaintiff was required to give particulars of the defendants' alleged failure to comply with M.Q.A. 1954, s. 48(1). Bridge L.J. made the following *comments* on the onus of proof on the defendant: "The admitted fall from the face which injured the plaintiff raises a *prima facie* case of a breach of section 48(1). This can only be rebutted by the defendants if they can show that the manager took the necessary steps to obtain the relevant information under section 48(2) and in the light of that information used all due skill and care to keep the face secure under section 48(1), but that the circumstances of the particular fall resulting in injury to the plaintiff were not such as might reasonably be expected to occur so as to give rise to a foreseeable danger." Otherwise the defendants must fall back on the "reasonably practicable" proviso of s. 157.

(14) Offices, Shops and Railway Premises*

* Abbreviations are explained in Introductory Note 1. See also Introductory Notes 7, 9 and 10.

1. Reid v. Galbraith's Stores, 1970 S.L.T. 83, O.H.

Held, that the provisions of O.S.R.P.A. 1963 dealing with the safety of floors were for the protection of staff and not shop customers.

2. Westwood v. Post Office [1974] A.C. 1; [1973] 3 All E.R. 184, H.L.

Lift motor room—from which employees in telephone exchange were excluded—deceased, a telephone exchange employee, used the room to gain access to the roof, in order to have a break—room had defective trap door—*Held,* the lift motor room was, as a result of statutory definition, part of the office premises, and there was therefore a breach of statutory duty in failing to ensure floor soundly constructed, etc.—*Held,* irrelevant that deceased was trespassing, since he was a person "employed to work in office premises," and this, *per* Lord Kilbrandon, brought him within the class of persons to whom a duty was owed (although the Act contained no general statement of duties owed). *Uddin* (Chap. 16, (1) (a) **16**) *approved—Held,* further, that there was no contributory negligence since any fault by deceased was that of trespass rather than negligence.

3. Oxfordshire C.C. v. Oxford University, *The Times,* December 10, 1980; [1980] C.L.Y. 920, D.C.

Held, rooms in a library used for clerical/editorial/administrative work could constitute "office premises",provided (a) the area was sufficiently defined or definable, (b) it was an area in which people were employed, and (c) its sole or principal use was as office premises.

4. Black v. Carricks [1980] I.R.L.R. 448; [1980] C.L.Y. 919, C.A.

P manageress of D's bakery shop—assistants all unexpectedly off ill—bread trays normally moved by two women—P phoned superior who instructed her to get on with her job as best she could and, if she needed help, to ask a customer—P injured lifting tray by self—*Held,* P not "required" to lift the tray, and therefore D not in breach of O.S.R.P.A. 1963, s.23. The word "required" connoted that P could not have performed the task adequately in the circumstances in any manner which would not have necessitated lifting the weight she did (*per* Shaw L.J., 451). Here, on the facts, it was implicit that, if she could not manage a load by herself, she could either leave it or seek assistance from a customer.

5. Osarak v. Hawker Siddeley, *The Times,* October 29, 1982; [1982] C.L.Y. 2124, Comyn J.

Held, defendants in breach of O.S.P.R.A. 1963, s.23 (and negligent).

6. Wray v. G.L.C. [1987] C.L.Y. 2560, Michael Ogden Q.C., sitting as a Judge of the High Court.

Held, O.S.R.P.A. 1963, s.14(2) imposes absolute liability. Thus the plaintiff established a breach of the section when one of the legs of the chair on which he was sitting broke, even though the plaintiff failed to establish that the defendant knew of the defect.

7. Bell v. D.H.S.S., *The Times*, June 13, 1989; [1989] C.L.Y. 2547, Drake J.

Defendant provided hot water for employees to make drinks in kitchen on top floor of four-storey office block. Spillages from mugs or cups carried thence to employees' places of work were common. Defendant's bulletins regularly encouraged staff to take more care. Plaintiff slipped on liquid probably spilt by another employee on imitation marble floor outside lift with manually operated door—*Held,*

(a) on the evidence, defendant's system of inspection was reasonable, however;
(b) defendant negligent and in breach of duties under s. 2 of Occupiers' Liability Act 1957 and O.S.R.P.A. 1963, s. 16(1) because:
   (i) set against history of spillages, entreaties in bulletins did not discharge defendant's duties;
   (ii) defendant should have provided distribution point for hot water on each floor, appropriate saucers, cups and trays and a suitable non-slip surface over the imitation marble.

8. McSherry v. British Telecommunications; Lodge v. British Telecommunications [1992] 3 Med. L.R. 129; [1992] C.L.Y. 1552, H. H. Judge Byrt Q.C.

Plaintiffs developed repetitive strain injury in course of employment as data processing officers—*Held,*

(a) Defendant liable in negligence. Plaintiffs' condition caused by repetitive movements of unsupported hands and arms. Strain aggravated because defendant's bonus system caused plaintiffs to push themselves to limit; by plaintiffs' poor posture which defendants should have corrected; and by seating which was unsuitable because not properly adjustable.
(b) Defendant also in breach of O.S.R.P.A. 1963, s. 14 relating to the provision of suitable seating.

U1. Hull v. Liverpool Police (1973) C.A. 74A

Plaintiff P.C. went to refreshment room of police station to write out statement—slipped on floor—which to everyone's knowledge was slippery with wax applied but not wiped off—*Held,* breach of O.S.R.P.A. 1963, s.16, which could have been avoided by, *e.g.* putting room out of bounds during the relevant period of an hour or two.

U2. Hughes v. British Airways (1977) C.A. 399A

Box of mail on floor—gangway gap between box and a table was 4'–4½'. Plaintiff tripped over box when carrying tray of letters—*Held,* box could be an "obstruction", even though there was a sensible business purpose for it to be there (Megaw L.J., 5D), and on the facts was an obstruction. Defendants liable. *N.B.* See also cases in Chap. 16, (5)(h).

U3. Iceton v. Durham Area H.A. (1979) C.A. 490

U4. Hodgson v. Surrey C.C (1986) C.A. 13

Secretary raised seat of chair provided for her and tightened a screw to secure it, but failed to locate screw in a channel in which, unknown to her, it was needed to locate to obtain the correct purchase. Seat suddenly descended as she was sitting on it, and she injured her lower back—*Held*, defendant in breach of the absolute provisions of O.S.R.P.A. 1963, s.14(2). Plaintiff not responsible for the breach.

U5. Sadler v. Central Dairy Products (1989) C.A. 270

Plaintiff descending steep staircase carrying tray, caught foot on chute obstructing staircase. Plaintiff had given instructions that the chute should be looked up out of the way when not in use—*Held*, defendant in breach of O.S.R.P.A. 1963, s.16(1). Plaintiff 25 per cent. to blame.

U6. Disney v. South Western Egg Products (1993) C.A. 938

Plaintiff carried tray of loaves down ramp with 1:4 slope at shop where she worked, to which the loaves had been delivered. She slipped on a few seeds from loaves she had carried by hand immediately beforehand. Ramp was swept after deliveries complete and items delivered had been carried into the shop—*Held*, defendant not negligent and not in breach of O.S.R.P.A. 1963, s. 16.

(15) Railways

		Prevention of Accidents Regulations 1902
"DANGER LIKELY TO ARISE"—WORDS NOT LIMITED TO EXCEPTIONAL DANGER—GANGERS REPAIRING LINE	1	REG. 9
"Repair" of permanent way—routine oiling	2	**reg. 9**
Lookout—one man outside tunnel—inadequate	3	reg. 9
"REPAIR" OF PERMANENT WAY—INSPECTION TO SEE WHAT REPAIRS NEEDED	4	REG. 9
Engine pushing wagons—no "efficient means" taken to obviate risk	5	Regulations for Factory Engines 1901 reg. 14
"Danger likely to arise"—two men repairing way with spanner requiring two men	6	Regulations, 1902, reg. 9
"Danger likely to arise"—patrolling lengthman—trains going at 15 m.p.h	7	**reg. 9**
"Work of repair"—lengthman inspecting and adjusting where required	7	**reg. 9**
POINT LEVERS—"PARALLEL TO ADJACENT LINES, OR IN SUCH OTHER POSITION AND BE OF SUCH FORM, AS TO	8	REG. 5

"DANGERS LIKELY TO ARISE"—TEST IS OBJECTIVE—GANGER AND TWO MEN SENT TO DO THREE-MAN JOB—ON LINE WHERE UNSCHEDULED TRAINS MIGHT (AND DID) RUN	9	REG. 9
RAILWAY RULE BOOK—EFFECT OF—GANGER FAILING TO APPOINT LOOK-OUT—AND BEING HIMSELF RUN DOWN	9	REG. 9
Ganger walking in permanent way	U1	
Duty to warn—does not include duty to ensure warning received	U2	
"Danger likely to arise"—ganger repairing line	U3	
Unexpected train—shunter walking long track—no duty on board to warn	U4	*reg. 9*
Wagon being shunted—goods guard checking train on adjacent line—duty on board to warn	U5	*reg. 9*

1. Hutchinson v. London and North Eastern Railway [1942] 1 K.B. 481; [1942] 1 All E.R. 330, C.A.

Three gangers repairing line—no lookout—clear day with visibility one mile in one direction and 440 yards in other—run down by express—defendants say duty to provide lookout only arises where some exceptional danger, *e.g.*, abnormally short visibility, arises—*Held*, not so, and that the words "danger likely to arise" referred to all ordinary danger, and defendants therefore liable.

2. London and North Eastern Railway v. Berriman [1946] A.C. 278; [1946] 1 All E.R. 255, H.L

Held, not work of repair: "It (repair) contains some suggestion of putting right that which has gone wrong. It does not include the mere keeping in order by oiling, brushing or cleaning something which is otherwise in perfect repair and only requires attention to prevent the possibility of its going wrong in the future" (Lord Porter at 267 C).

3. Dyer v. Southern Ry. [1948] 1 K.B. 608; [1948] 1 All E.R. 516, Humphreys J.

Held, that, to comply with the rule, "apparatus reasonably effective or persons effective for the purpose required" must have been provided, and one man outside a tunnel, where he could neither see nor hear effectively, was not a compliance, and therefore defendants liable.

4. Judson v. British Transport Commission [1954] 1 W.L.R. 585; [1954] 1 All E.R. 624, C.A.
Held, not work of "re-laying or repairing."

5. Stanton Ironworks v.Skipper [1956] 1 Q.B. 255; [1955] 3 All E.R. 544, D.C.

6. Reilly v. British Transport Commission [1957] 1 W.L.R. 76; [1956] 3 All E.R. 857, Donovan J.

Held, danger likely to arise, and defendants therefore liable for not providing lookout *Held*, also that this was a "work of repair." *Approved* on latter by H.L. in **7**.

7. Cade v. British Transport Commission [1959] A.C. 256; [1958] 2 All E.R. 615, H.L.

Lengthman walking along line to inspect and to knock in any loose keys and tighten loose fishplates—trains only going at 15 m.p.h.—*Held*, approving **6** and applying the dicta in **2**, this was work of repair, but danger was not likely to arise, and therefore defendants not liable for failing to provide lookout.

8. Hicks v. British Transport Commission [1958] 1 W.L.R. 493; [1958] 2 All E.R. 39, C.A.

Held. that the words "parallel, etc." and "in such other position and be of such form" were alternative obligations, and if the first was satisfied by having the lever working in a plane parallel to the line, the regulation was complied with without recourse to the second.

9. Keaney v. B.R.B. [1968] 1 W.L.R. 879; [1968] 2 All E.R. 532, C.A.

Ganger and two men were detailed by sub-inspector to renew bolts at a certain joint—night-time—it was a three-man job, and while it was proceeding ganger was run down by a train—the train had been diverted by signalman from adjacent line—it was accepted that railwaymen should know that unexpected trains could come along line at any time—*Held*, defendants were liable under r. 9 of the Prevention of Accident Regulations 1902 for not providing a look-out, as "danger was likely to arise"; the danger, *per* Davies L.J. (358 I) was objective, and the question did not turn on whether the Board thought or should have thought that danger was likely to arise. The defendants relied on r. 234 (d) of their Rule Book in exculpation. This provided that it was the ganger's duty to post the look-out—*Held*, that this did not exculpate the defendants. They did not discharge their duty by making rules, and the making of such a rule was simply the machinery by which they sought to carry out their duty. The crucial question was whether the ganger's failure to comply with r. 234 (d) was the sole cause of the breach of the Prevention of Accident Regulations 1902 (Davies L.J., 538–539), and on the facts it was not, for the sub-inspector had sent only three men to do a three-man job, so that no fourth man was available as a look-out. 50 per cent. contributory negligence.

U1. Lloyd v. British Transport Commission (1961) C.A. 128

Plaintiff lengthman run down by engine while walking in 4-feet way of a track—this was a very common practice in daytime and defendants must have known of it to the point of acquiescence, notwithstanding it was in breach of Rules—but plaintiff was walking at first light in weather which was foggy with rain—*Held*, defendants not liable as they could not be taken to have acquiesced in practice in such conditions.

U2. Pounder v. South Durham Steel (1961) C.A. 52

Regulation 16 of Locomotive and Wagons on Sidings Regulations prohibits movement of wagons "until warning has been given by the person in charge to persons whose safety is likely to be endangered"—plaintiff argued that this imported a duty to ensure that the warning was received—*Held*, not so, and defendants not liable. Devlin L.J. (9 D): "There is no obligation on defendants to ensure that such a warning is heard and understood. Provided it is a reasonable and adequate warning, they have discharged their duty."

U3. Arthur v. B.R.B. (1963) C.A. 156

Gang working in northbound express track near Wolverton on Euston line—at approach of south-bound express most of gang stepped onto pathway—but deceased continued working and a north-bound express ran him down—question was whether a lookout was needed—*Held*, no, as no "danger likely to arise." Tests propounded by Lord Morton in *Cade* 7 applied, *viz.* (a) site of accident, (b) amount and speed of traffic (c) the nature of the work and (d) experience of deceased. In addition, judge took into account the rule, which was enforced in practice, that on the approach of a train the gang had to move onto pathway; and (*per contra*) C.A. thought it relevant that gang were considerably spread out at the time. There had never been such an accident on this stretch, and the foreman with 30 years' experience had never thought it necessary to have a lookout man. This last factor was probably critical in what C.A. said was a borderline decision.

U4. Sankey v. B.R.B. (1963) C.A. 214

Held, no duty on board to warn gangers or shunters of unusual or late-running trains. This view seems impliedly to have been accepted in *Keaney* **9** also.

U5. Savage v. B.R.B. (1965) C.A. 310 A

Goods guard was checking his train at night as it went slowly past him in goods yard—run down by wagon shunted on adjacent line—*Held*, defendants liable, as they should have warned him of wagon being shunted (no contributory negligence).

(16) Shipbuilding*

(a) Safety of Access

1. Day v. Harland & Wolff [1967] 1 Lloyd's Rep. 136, Waller J.

N.B. This decision was set aside by C.A. by reason of fresh evidence being discovered.

2. Mullard v. Ben Lines [1970] 1 W.L.R. 1414; [1971] 2 All E.R. 424, C.A.

Held, defendant liable, *inter alia*, under S.S.R. 1960, reg. 6 (safe access). One-third contributory negligence.

3. Williams v. Swan Hunter Shipbuilders Ltd, *The Times*, March 24, 1988; [1988] C.L.Y. 1752, C.A.

Held, a three-foot hinged extension linking the end of a ship's gangway to the quayside did not form part of a "main gangway giving general access to a vessel" and did not therefore need to be fitted with a handrail pursuant to S.S.R. 1960, reg. 7.

U1. James v. Swan Hunter Shipbuilders Ltd (1990) C.A. 887

Plaintiff engaged in construction of frigate. Other workmen removed planks giving access to plaintiff's place of work. He, expecting planks still to be there, stumbled and was injured—*Held*, defendant in breach of S.S.R. 1960, reg. 6. Plaintiff 25 per cent. to blame.

* Abbreviations are explained in Introductory Note 1. See also Introductory Notes 3(F) and 10.

(b) Lighting, Staging and Other Regulations

Staging—dismantling—obligation as to construction and material continues	1	S.S.R. 1960, reg. 17
HATCH—UNFENCED AND UNLIT—PLAINTIFF GOING IN WITHOUT TORCH	2	S.S.R. 1960, REGS. 26, 69
"Reason to apprehend" fumes—duty is subjective	3	S.S.R. 1960, regs. 50, 51
Inhalation of injurious dust—asbestos—workman later dying of mesothelioma	4	S.S.R. 1960, reg. 53(2)
Sling—application of 1960 Regulations	5	S.S.R. 1960, reg. 42
"Adequate protection for the hands"—explained	6	(S.S.R. 1960, reg. 73)
Ventilation—oxygen leaking from pipe of cutter	U1	*S.S.R.* 1960, *reg.* 48(1)

1. Graham v. Greenock Dockyard, 1965 S.L.T. 61; [1965] C.L.Y. 2654, Ct. of Sess.

2. Mullard v. Ben Line [1970] 1 W.L.R. 1414; [1971] 2 All E.R. 424, C.A.

'Tween deck hatch left open—unfenced and unlit—plaintiff riveter in passing by to fetch a tool fell through it—clear breaches of regs. 6 (access), 26 (fencing hatches) and 69 (lighting)—trial judge held plaintiff liable for 50 per cent, contributory negligence—*Held*, the assessment of contributory negligence would be reduced to 33 per cent., as the plaintiff's momentary error in stepping into the darkened area without a torch was not to be judged too harshly against the defendants' flagrant and continuing breach of the Regulations, which were designed to guard against precisely this type of accident.

3. Bishop v. Starnes [1971] 1 Lloyd's Rep. 162, Dunn J.

4. Bryce v. Swan Hunter Group plc [1988] 1 All E.R. 659; [1987] 2 Lloyds Rep 426, Phillips J. See Chap. 16(3)(b) **18** for full details.

5. Forsyth's Curator Bonis v. Govan Shipbuilders Ltd, 1988 S.L.T. 321

Held, reg. 42 applies to a sling whether or not it is being actually used for a lift.

6. Bowman v. Harland Wolff plc [1992] I.R.L.R. 349; [1992] C.L.Y. 3222, Carswell J., N.I.

The plaintiffs were employed at the defendant's Belfast shipyard from the 1950s, and 1960s, onwards and regularly used hand-held pneumatic caulking hammers, the vibration from which caused them to suffer from Raynaud's Phenomenon, also known or "vibration white finger"—*Held* defendant liable in negligence but plaintiffs also claimed, *inter alia*, a breach of reg. 72 of the Shipbuilding and Shiprepairing Regulations (Northern Ireland) 1971 (identical to S.S.R. 1960, reg. 73) which provides that "adequate protection for the hands shall be available for all persons employed when ... engaged in machine caulking ... "—*Held*, that regulation was directed to the protection of the hands against direct trauma from hazards such as sharp edges of metal, and was not intended to cover risks such as vibration from the normal use of caulking machines.

U1. Cram v. Ryton Marine (1976) C.A. 424

Plaintiff and others remedying bulkhead plate in small compartment—leak of oxygen from pipe of their cutter—to clear it, plaintiff swished a compressed air pipe about for a short time—then struck an arc to do the burning—residual oxygen immediately ignited—*Held*, defendants liable for breach of reg. 48(1) (ventilation).

(17) Woodworking*

1. Gunter v. John Nicholas & Sons (Port Talbot) Ltd [1993] P.I.Q.R. P67; [1993] C.L.Y. 2938, C.A.

See Chap. 16, (3) (b) **21** for further details.

2. Arbuckle v. A.H. McIntosh & Co., 1993 S.L.T. 857; [1993] C.L.Y. 5355

Held, the duty of a sawyer using a circular saw under reg. 14(1)(a) to "use and keep in proper adjustment the guards ... provided in accordance with these Regulations" arose only when the employers had provided a properly adjusted guard for the saw.

(18) Miscellaneous Regulations

1. R. v. A1 Industrial Products plc [1987] I.C.R. 418; [1987] 2 All E.R. 368, C.A.

Held, for the purposes of F.A. 1961 and The Asbestos Regulations 1969, a "process" did not include a single operation such as the demolition of a kiln or the removal of disused machinery. (*N.B.* overruled in *Nurse v. Morganite Crucible Ltd* **2**.

* Abbreviations are explained in Introductory Note 1. See also Introductory Notes 3, 4, 9 and 10.

2. Nurse v. Morganite Crucible Ltd [1989] A.C. 692; [1989] 1 All E.R. 113, H.L.

Held, "process" for the purpose of the application of the Asbestos Regulations 1969 meant "any operation or series of operations being an activity of more than minimal duration". Thus the Regulations applied to the demolition of brick driers, the roof panels of which contained asbestos. *R v. A1 Industrial Products plc* **1** overruled.

3. Mearns v. Lothian R.C., 1991 S.L.T. 338; [1991] C.L.Y. 5693

Plaintiff injured when awkwardly shaped valve weighing 98 lbs slipped as he carried it up a ladder on vessel on which he worked—no one else immediately avaîlable to help him, and defendant had given no instruction what to do if no assistance—*Held*, a safe system of work would involve telling employee not to perform such a task himself but to seek assistance—defendents negligent and in breach of statutory duty to provide safe system of work under Merchant Shipping (Health and Safety: General Duties) Regulations 1984, reg. 4(2)(a). Plaintiff 50 per cent. to blame.

4. MacMillan v. Wimpey Offshore Engineers and Constructors, 1991 S.L.T. 515; [1991] C.L.Y. 5073

Regulation 32(2) of the Offshore Installations (Operational Safety, Health and Welfare) Regulations 1976 provides, *inter alia*:

> "It shall be the duty of the employer of an employee employed by him for work on or near an offshore installation to ensure that the employee complies with any provision of those Regulations imposing a duty on him . . . ".
>
> Regulation 32 (3) (a) provides, *inter alia*:
>
> "It shall be the duty of every person while on or near an offshore installation not to do anything likely to endanger the safety or health of himself or other persons on or near the installation . . . ".

Held, (a) reg. 32 (2) places an absolute responsibility on an employer, imposing vicarious liability for the default of an employee and a direct duty to guarantee compliance with the Regulations by employees, even when they were not actually working; (b) the Regulations are concerned to protect workmen at all times on or near an installation, and not just while working; (c) Accordingly, the Regulations could be relied on by the plaintiff who claimed that his head had been battered against a metal skip by the defendant's foreman.

5. Hewett v. Alf Brown's Transport Ltd [1992] I C.R. 530; [1992] P.I.Q.R. P199, C.A.

The Court of Appeal upheld the finding of Otton J. that a man exposed to lead dust for at most an hour a day composed of three or four intermittent and equally spread periods throughout the working day, the degree and intensity of the exposure being below any envisaged by the approved Code of Practice "Control of Lead at Work", had not experienced "significant" exposure to the dust. Thus his employers would not have been bound by reg. 8 of the Control of Lead at Work Regulations 1980 to provide him with protective clothing.

6. Edgson v. Vickers plc, [1994] I.C.R. 510; [1994] C.L.Y. 2276, Jeffrey Burke Q.C.

17. LIABILITY OF SERVANT TO MASTER

1. Gregory v. Ford [1951] 1 All E.R. 121; 67 L.Q.R. 288, Byrne J.

Negligent driving by servant—failure of master to insure—*Held*, "a servant is of course liable at the suit of his master for damage which is the result of the servant's negligence,' but no indemnity in present case because the damage flowed from breach of implied term by master in failing to insure. See Chap 15,(1) (b) **2**. *Sed quaere* in view of **4**.

2. Jones v. Manchester Corporation [1952] 2 Q.B. 852; [1952] 2 All E.R. 125, C.A.

Death of patient caused by negligence of young anaesthetist—as the hospital authorities should not have left the administration of the anaesthetic to someone so inexperienced, and had thereby contributed to the damage—*Held*, hospital not entitled to indemnity and contribution should be four-fifths against hospital, one-fifth against anaesthetist.

3. Semtex v. Gladstone [1954] 1 W.L.R. 945; [1954] 2 All E.R. 206, C.A.

Negligent driving by sèrvant—master had insured—*Held*, following **1**, that although there was an implied term that master would insure against Road Traffic Act liability (so that servant should not be called on to perform illegal act), there was no implied term that master should indemnify, and therefore master could claim from servant the third-party damages for which he was vicariously liable. *Approved* in **4**.

4. Lister v. Romford Ice Co. [1957] A.C. 555; [1957] 1 All E.R. 125, H.L.

Held, (3–2) servant liable to indemnify master, as it was an implied term servant should use reasonable care, which he had not, and he was therefore liable for breach, since there was no countervailing implied term against master, except a duty to insure as required by law (with which master had complied). **3** approved. But see **5**.

5. Harvey v. O'Dell [1958] 2 Q.B. 78; [1958] 1 All E.R. 657, McNair J.

Servant S a storekeeper employed by M on an outside job, in connection with which he used his own motor-car in the course of his employment—S negligently had accident—M sues S for contribution and indemnity—*Held*, there was no contractual right to indemnity arising from the conditions of service, as the implied term laid down by H.L. in **4** only extended "to the performance of those duties which the S expressly or impliedly professes to possess at the time when he enters the conditions of service" (667 A *et seq.*), but that M had a right of contribution under the Law Reform (Married Women and Joint Tortfeasors) Act 1935 (since superseded by the Civil Liability (Contribution) Act 1978), which, since M's liability was purely vicarious, should be 100 per cent.

6. Superlux v. Plaisted *The Times*, December 12, 1958; [1958] C.L.Y. 195, C.A.

Defendant, employed by plaintiff as a salesman, left 14 vacuum cleaners in a car outside his house all night—cleaners all stolen—*Held*, defendant, being in a responsible position, was under a duty to safeguard plaintiff's property, and, having been negligent, was liable.

18. PROFESSIONS, TRADES AND INSTITUTIONS

(1) Accountants, Auditors and Receivers and Other Financial Advisers

1. Candler v. Crane Christmas [1951] 2 K.B. 164; [1951] 1 All E.R. 426, C.A.

Held, that defendants in the absence of fraud, contract or fiduciary relationship, had no liability for careless misrepresentation. *Overruled* in *Hedley Byrne v. Heller* (Chap. 18 (2) **8**), *q.v.*

2. De Savary v. Holden Howard, *The Times*, January 12, 1960; [1960] C.L.Y. 2112, Barry J.

Creditors appointed defendant accountant to investigate affairs of plaintiff's companies—defendant was paid by plaintiff—the accounts produced were not accurate and in consequence plaintiff took on commitments which resulted in loss—*Held*, there was no contract between plaintiff and defendant and therefore defendant was not liable for any negligent misstatement, and in any event defendant was not negligent. *But* see now *Hedley Byrne v. Heller* (Chap. 18, (2)**8**), which indicates that, if defendant had been negligent, he probably would have been liable.

3. Fogg v. Gaulter [1960] C.L.Y. 2500; 110 L.J. 718, Lancaster Palatine Court

Accountants without authority disclosed to third party copies of income tax returns made by a client—*Held*, that the accountants were in breach of their duty, and were liable for damage that ensued.

4. Luscombe v. Roberts (1962) 106 S.J. 373; [1962] C.L.Y. 2008, Megaw J.

Solicitor transferred large sums of money from clients' to office account—defendant accountant regularly certified accounts in order—*Held*, defendants had been negligent, but were not liable as real cause of loss arose from plaintiff's own dishonesty.

5. Re Thomas Gerrard [1968] Ch. 455; [1967] 2 All E.R. 525, Pennycuick J.

Invoice dates altered so as to bring receipts into current period, thereby inflating profit for such period—auditors accepted managing director's assurances as sufficient explanation for alterations—made no further investigation—*Held*, negligence—*Held*, also, that standards of reasonable care for auditors were higher now than 60–70 years ago.

6. Dimond v. Hamilton [1969] N.Z.L.R. 609, N.Z.C.A.

Held, a special relationship existed, and that an action would lie.

7. Scott v. MacFarlane [1978] 1 N.Z.L.R. 553; [1979] C.L.Y. 1884, N.Z.C.A.

By an error the accounts as certified by company auditors overstated the assets. In reliance, *inter alia*, on the accounts the plaintiffs took over the company—*Held*, no special relationship existed, and auditors were therefore not liable. Richmond P *said* that a special relationship ought not to be found to exist unless the maker of the statement was or ought to have been aware that his advice would be made available to and be relied on by a particular person for a particular transaction. Considered in *Caparo* (**17**).

8. Standard Chartered Bank v. Walker [1982] 1 W.L.R. 1410; [1982] 3 All E.R. 938, C.A.

For further details see Chap. 7, (1)(a)**19**.

9. JEB Fasteners Ltd v. Marks Bloom & Co. [1983] 1 All E.R. 583: [1983] C.L.Y. 2534, C.A.

Held, auditors not liable. Distinguished in *Caparo* (**17**).

10. Owen Investments Ltd v. Bennett Nash Wolf and Co. (1984) 134 New L.J. 887; [1984] C.L.Y. 2279, Dennis Henry Q.C., sitting as a deputy judge.

Accountants retained to advise concerning possible purchase of company and setting off company's losses against plaintiff's profits—*Held*, liable for failure to advise upon effect of stock relief claw-back on company's ceasing to trade.

11. Inland Revenue Commissioners v. Hoogstraten [1985] Q.B. 1077; [1984] 3 All E.R. 25, C.A.

Sequestrator appointed by court, *inter alia*, to manage defendant's estate; it was conceded there was sufficient proximity to give rise to a duty of care—*Held*, notwithstanding they were officers of the court, there was no reason why they should be immune from suit.

12. American Express International Banking Corp v. Hurley [1985] 3 All E.R. 564; [1985] C.L.Y. 313, Mann J.

Receiver appointed by bank—*Held*, liable to guarantor of company's debt for failing to take reasonable care in obtaining true market value of equipment sold by him.

13. Lloyd Cheyham & Co. Ltd v. Littlejohn & Co. [1987] BCLC 303; [1987] C.L.Y. 318, Woolf J.

Plaintiff injected capital into trailer rental company on basis of audited accounts; auditors conceded duty of care owed—*Held*, no breach of duty in respect of manner in which cost of replacing tyres was dealt with.

14. Whiteoak v. Walker (1988) 4 BCC 122; [1988] C.L.Y. 2423, Terence Cullen Q.C.

Auditors of limited company valued shares for purpose of sale by minority to majority shareholder pursuant to articles—*Held*, the auditors had not fallen below the requisite standard, namely that of a reasonably competent chartered accountant in general practice acting as an auditor.

15. Huxford v. Stoy Hayward & Co. (1989) 5 BCC 421; [1989] C.L.Y. 2538, Popplewell J.

Accountants investigated and reported on company's affairs & subsequently advised receivership—*Held*,

(a) no duty of care owed to shareholders or guarantors and doubtful whether any owed to directors for reports prepared for company's bankers;
(b) duty of care owed to directors and doubtful whether any owed to shareholders and guarantors in monitoring the company's affairs;
(c) duty of care owed to company and directors but not to guarantors in advising receivership.

In any event no breach.

16. Al Saudi Banque v. Clarke Pixley [1990] Ch. 313, [1989] 3 All E.R. 361, Millett J.

Bankers alleged auditors of limited company had been negligent in their examination of and reporting upon the company's accounts as a result of which they had lent or continued to lend moneys to the company which was in fact insolvent—*Held*, on a preliminary issue, that whether the bankers were potential or actual creditors at the time the auditors reported there was no sufficient proximity to give rise to a duty of care being owed.

17. Caparo Industries PLC v. Dickman [1990] 2 A.C. 605; [1990] 1 All E.R. 568, H.L.

The plaintiffs alleged that auditors of the accounts of a public limited company were negligent in certifying them and that the plaintiff in reliance thereon had purchased additional shares in a bid to take the company over and had suffered loss—*Held*, on a preliminary point, nothing in the Companies Act 1985 suggested that the accounts were prepared and sent to members for any purpose other than to enable them to exercise their class rights in general meeting and they were not supplied to assist individual shareholders to help them decide whether to invest in the company; although it was foreseeable that individual shareholders or others might use and rely upon such accounts in deciding whether to invest in or lend to the company and hence suffer loss if they were negligently certified, in the absence of knowledge of the auditors, actual or to be inferred, that the plaintiff as an individual or member of an identifiable class would be likely to rely on the accounts in undertaking a specific transaction or transactions there was no sufficient "proximity" to establish a duty of care and in the circumstances no such duty was owed to the plaintiff either as a shareholder or as a member of the public at large.

18. Knight v. Lawrence [1991] 1 E.G.L.R. 143; [1991] C.L.Y. 2655, Sir Nicholas Browne-Wilkinson V.C.

Receivers appointed by lenders under the Law of Property Act 1925, s. 109 of the rents and profits of tenanted properties charged by owner to secure loan—*Held*, receivers in breach of duty of care owed to owner by reason of their failure to serve rent review notices in time.

19. James McNaughton Paper Group Ltd v. Hicks Aderson & Co. [1991] 2 Q.B. 113; [1991] 1 All E.R. 134, C.A.

Plaintiffs negotiate take-over of a group of companies—the group instruct accountants to prepare accounts—draft accounts showing a loss were repaired and sent by group to plaintiffs. Accountants thereafter advised plaintiffs that the group was breaking even or doing marginally worse. Take-over completed and errors in accounts found—*Held*, no duty of care owed by accountants to plaintiffs, there being no sufficient proximity. *Caparo* (**17**) followed.

20. Morgan Crucible Co PLC v. Hill Samuel & Co. Ltd [1991] Ch. 295; [1991] 3 All E.R. 148, C.A.

For details see Chap. 18, (7) **3**.

21. Berg Sons & Co. Ltd v. Adams (1992) BCC 661; [1993] C.L.Y. 2982, Hobhouse J.

Held, company's auditors were negligent in not qualifying their certificate to the accounts and were thereby in breach of their contract with and duty owed to the company but it was not reasonably foreseeable that such failure would cause loss or damage to the company or its members in the circumstance and no loss was caused by such breach—*Held*, further, although it was foreseeable that creditor banks would rely on the accounts to some extent, no duty of care was owed to them (*Caparo* (**17**) relied on); in any event, any loss, being inability to recover on four bills, not caused by any breach.

22. Deloitte Haskins & Sells v. National Mutual Life Nominees Ltd [1993] A.C. 774; [1993] 2 All E.R. 1015, P.C., New Zealand.

Auditors held under no liability at common law to trustee of company receiving unsecured deposits for failure to report, pursuant to statutory obligations, of company's probable insolvency, or for failure to realise company insolvent earlier; in any event, no loss proved to have been caused.

23. Downsview Nominees Ltd v. First City Corporation Ltd [1993] A.C. 295; [1993] 3 All E.R. 626, P.C.

A first debenture holder and a receiver and manager appointed by him owe no general duty in negligence to subsequent encumberances to take reasonable care in the exercise of powers and in dealing with assets, any duties being owed in equity to act in good faith.

24. West Wiltshire D.C. v. Garland [1993] Ch. 409; [1993] 4 All E.R. 246, *Morritt J.*; (1995) 2 W.L.R. 439, C.A.

Defendant officers of local authority claimed against the auditor of the local authority appointed by the audit commission in negligence and for negligent misrepresentation.—*Held*, it was not fair, just or reasonable to impose a duty of care on the auditors for the benefit of officers (for loss of employment and its benefits) at common law when no statutory liability had been imposed. On appeal it was further held arguable that the auditors owed a duty of care at common law as well as a duty under statute to the local authority itself: *Spring v. Guardian Assurance* (Chap. 18, (4) **20**) and *Henderson v. Merrett* (Chap. 18, (4) **21**) considered.

25. Galoo Ltd v. Bright Grahame Murray [1994] 1 W.L.R. 1360, C.A.

Third plaintiff agreed to acquire 5 per cent of second plaintiff which had a subsidiary, the first plaintiff. The price was to be determined by reference to audited accounts. Subsequently third plaintiff lent moneys to first and second plaintiffs and acquired more shares in second plaintiff. It was alleged the first and second plaintiffs' auditors had been negligent in auditing the accounts; first and second plaintiffs claimed they had suffered loss by continuing to trade at loss; this claim struck out—auditors' assumed negligence not causative of loss, merely providing opportunity for loss to be incurred. Third plaintiff's claim for loss resulting from lending moneys and making further share purchase struck out—*Caparo* **17** applied—claim for loss by making original purchase not struck out—auditors allegedly provided accounts to third plaintiffs knowing how the price was to be calculated—*Morgan Crucible* **20** relied on.

26. Anthony v. Wright, The Independent September 27, 1994; [1994] C.L.Y. 3335, Lightman J.

Plaintiffs invested in limited company—the company held these moneys as trustee for them but its directors fraudulently misused those funds—the plaintiffs' claim against the company's auditors for negligent failure to discover the fraud was struck out as no duty of care was owed.

27. Eagle Trust PLC v. SBC Securities Ltd The Independent 28/9/94 (1994) C.L.Y. 3351, Arden J.

Defendent advised plaintiff company as to the structure of an offer the plaintiff was making for another public company; the defendant also arranged for a rights issue & cash alternative offer underwritten by another company to be sub-underwritten; held: the defendant owed no duty of care as financial adviser in respect of its decision qua underwriter to accept particular persons as sub-underwriters.

U1. Jackson v. King (1955) C.A. 42

Allegation of negligence against accountant failed—no part of accountant's duty to investigate leases without being instructed to do so, especially when solicitors are engaged.

U2. Devlin v. Mobey (1988) C.A. 816

The company accountant gave impression to potential purchaser of company that it was not only solvent but viable—*Held*, liable to purchaser in negligence—*Hedley Byrne* (Chap. 18, (2) **8**) applied.

(2) Banks

1. Welch v. Bank of England [1955] Ch. 508; [1955] 1 All E.R. 811, Harman J.

A complex case resulting from the forgery and fraudulent conversion of trust funds by a trustee—question arises whether plaintiff's claim against bank (between whom there is the relationship of banker and customer) is barred by her own negligence—*Held*, negligence as a defence must amount to conduct estopping plaintiff or alternatively to ratification by her.

2. Baker v. Barclays Bank [1955] 1 W.L.R. 822; [1955] 2 All E.R. 571, Devlin J.

Held, defence not established and defendants liable.

3. Midland Bank v. Seymour [1955] 2 Lloyd's Rep. 147, Devlin J.

Held, breach of duty by bank.

4. Nu-Stilo Footwear v. Lloyds Bank, *The Times*, June 19, 1956; [1956] C.L.Y. 676, Sellers J.

Action for conversion of cheques—defence of good faith and no negligence—plaintiff had a secretary M who opened an account with defendants in the name of a non-existent person, B—B was represented as a freelance agent—M then passed a number of cheques drawn on plaintiff's bank through B's account—the cheques were for large amounts inconsistent with B's alleged occupation and some were third party cheques—*Held*, defendants had been negligent in not making inquiries and therefore claim succeeded.

5. Evans v. Midland Bank *The Times*, November 21, 1956; [1956] C.L.Y. 5807, Lord Goddard C.J.

Cashier lobbed a parcel of 5,000 £1 notes weighing 12½ lbs at customer which injured customer in eye—*Held*, defendants liable.

6. Woods v. Martins Bank [1958] 1 W.L.R. 1018; [1958] 3 All E.R. 166, Salmon J.

Held, defendants liable.

7. Orbit Mining Co. v. Westminster Bank [1963] 1 Q.B. 794; [1962] 3 All E.R. 565, C.A.

Held, on the facts, defendants not liable.

8. Hedley Byrne v. Heller [1964] A.C. 465; [1963] 3 All E.R. 575, H.L.

Alleged negligence in credit status report given by bankers—*Held*, such negligence could give rise to liability in tort, if there was a special relationship (for meaning of which see Chap. 19(1) **1**), but here there was no duty because there was an express disclaimer of responsibility, and also, *semble* (*per* Lords Reid, Morris and Hodson), the special relationship did not on the facts exist, and the bankers' only duty was to act honestly. **6** *approved.*

9. Universal Guarantee v. National Bank of Australasia [1965] 1 W.L.R. 691; [1965] 2 All E.R. 98, P.C.

M, employed by P and being authorised by P to sign and endorse cheques, drew cheques on fictitious payees, forged the endorsements, then added his own endorsement per pro. P, and paid them into P's account, abstracting for himself the equivalent amount of cash to be paid in, and falsifying the cash and cheque totals in the carbon paying-in slips—*Held*, bank not liable for the loss.

10. Burnett v. Westminster Bank [1966] 1 Q.B. 742; [1965] 3 All E.R. 81, Mocatta J.

Held, cheque had been wrongly debited and bank must pay back. The issue turned mainly on the question whether the customer had been given sufficient notice of computerisation and of its effect that all cheques would be applied to the account printed on them.

11. Marfani v. Midland Bank [1968] 1 W.L.R. 956; [1968] 2 All E.R. 573, C.A.

Employee of drawer of cheque took it and posing as payee opened new account into which he paid cheque—then drew the proceeds—bank had obtained one favourable reference from a person who previously (but not this time) had been reliable—*Held*, bank not liable.

12. Schioler v. Westminster Bank [1970] 2 Q.B. 719; [1970] 3 All E.R. 177, Mocatta J.

13. Mutual Life Ltd v. Evatt [1971] A.C. 793; [1971] 1 All E.R. 150, P.C.

Held, (3–2) that no action lay, because the basis of the cause of action was the holding out of skill and competence to advise, and there was here no allegation that the insurance company either carried on the business of giving such advice or held themselves out as doing so. See, more generally, cases in Chapter 19.

14. Kenton v. Barclays Bank [1977] C.L.Y. 189, Judge Leonard.

15. Mason v. Bank of Nova Scotia (1980) 10 B.L.R. 77; [1981] C.L.Y. 1250, High Ct. of Ont.

16. Bartlett v. Barclays Bank [1980] 1 All E.R. 139, Brightman J.

Held, that it was a trustee's duty to conduct trust business with the care that a reasonably prudent businessman would extend to his own affairs. Moreover, a professional corporate trustee, such as a bank, owed a higher standard of care and was liable for loss caused to a trust by neglect to exercise the special care and skill which it professed to have.

17. Commonwealth Trading Bank of Australia v. Sydney Wide Stores (1981) 148 C.L.R. 304; [1984] C.L.Y. 165 High Ct. of Aust.

18. Standard Chartered Bank v. Walker [1982] 3 All E.R. 938; 1 W.L.R. 1410, C.A.

Held, that a debenture holder was not in general responsible for the acts of a receiver appointed by it, but if it interfered or gave directions to the receiver, then it was under a duty towards the company and the guarantors to use reasonable care. For further details see Chap. 7(1)(a) **19**.

19. O'Hara v. Allied Irish Banks (1985) B.C.L.C. 52; [1984] C.L.Y. 2297, Harman J.

20. Thackwell v. Barclays Bank Plc, The Times December 5, 1984; [1984] C.L.Y. 174, Hutchison J.
Held, bank negligent in failing to make inquiry of payee of cheque where circumstances of presentation were unusual—however, payee could not recover because bank could rely on maximum *ex turpi causa non oritur actio* to defeat payee's claim.

21. Cornish v. Midland Bank Plc [1985] 3 All E.R. 513; [1985] C.L.Y. 2324, C.A.

Where a bank chooses to advise a customer as to the nature and effect of a mortgage in favour of the bank prior to its execution by that customer, the bank was under a duty not negligently to misstate its effect—*Held*, breach of duty in failing to advise mortgage covered future as well as present advances.

22. American Express International Banking Corp. v. Hurley [1985] 3 All E.R. 564; [1985] C.L.Y. 313, Mann J.

See Chap. 18, (1) **12**.

23. Tai Hing Cotton Mill Ltd v. Liu Chong Hing Bank Ltd [1986] A.C. 80; [1985] 2 All E.R. 947, P.C.

A customer's duty to his bank in relation to forged cheques was to exercise due care in drawing his cheques so as not to facilitate fraud or forgery and to inform his bank at once of any unauthorised cheques of which he became aware. There was nothing to the advantage of the law's development in searching for a liability in tort where the parties were in a contractual relationship. It was not accepted that the parties' mutual obligations in tort could be any greater than those to be found expressly or by necessary implication in their contract.
See *Henderson v. Merrett* (Chap. 19(a) **22**).

24. Royal Bank Trust Co. (Trinidad) Ltd v. Pampellone [1987] 1 Lloyd's Rep. 218; [1987] C.L.Y. 2576, P.C.

Bankers gave reference to plaintiff in respect of a finance company to effect that "all our reports indicate that this company may be regarded as trustworthy for its ordinary business engagements"—on another occasion they orally informed him of a recent credit report and gave him brochures in respect of a deposit-taking company. In reliance thereon the plaintiff alleged he placed moneys with those companies—*Held*, bankers not liable—there was no tendering of advice and no reliance thereon.

25. Redmond v. Allied Irish Banks [1987] *Financial Law Reports* 307; [1987] C.L.Y. 198, Saville J.

Plaintiff paid in cheques at Manchester branch marked "not negotiable—account payee only" to the credit of his account at a branch in Ireland—he was not payee but cheques were endorsed on back—he drew against uncleared cheques—cheques fraudulently put into circulation and when fraud discovered bank debited his account with the amount paid out—*Held*, the banker/customer relationship created no duty to warn against or advise on the risks inherent in carrying through that which the customer wanted to do—no duty owed in tort—in any event the bank had warned him.

26. Yuen Kun Yeu v. Att.-Gen. of Hong Kong. [1988] A.C. 175; [1987] 2 All E.R. 705, P.C.

The commissioner of deposit-taking companies registered a company as a deposit-taking company pursuant to a Hong Kong ordinance—*Held*, did not owe a duty of care to depositors with the company who lost their money when it went into liquidation. Foreseeability of harm alone was not sufficient to create a duty of care—a close and direct relationship of proximity had to be shown. In the instant case, the circumstances to be considered included the fact that protection of depositors was only one purpose of the ordinance, such protection was by way of criminal and registration sanctions, risks to would-be depositors had to be balanced against those to existing depositors if deregistration recurred, lack of day-to-day management control by the commissioner and any duty owed would be to all would-be depositors.

For the future it should be recognised that the two-stage test in *Anns v. Merton L.B.C.* (chap. 18(6) **13** was not to be regarded as in all circumstances a suitable guide to the existence of a duty of care.

27. Minories Finance Ltd v. Arthur Young; Johnson Matthey P.L.C. v. Arthur Young [1989] 2 All E.R. 105; [1989] C.L.Y. 150, Saville J.

Plaintiff claimed damages against their auditors—auditors claimed indemnity/contribution from Bank of England under the Civil Liability (Contribution) Act 1978 for breach of duty of care owed to plaintiff to carry out its supervisory functions over U.K. banks with reasonable skill and care—*Held*, not just, fair or reasonable to impose such a duty.

28. Davis v. Radcliffe [1990] 1 W.L.R. 821; [1990] 2 All E.R. 536, P.C.

Finance Board via Treasurer of Isle of Man issued and renewed licenses to the Savings & Investment Bank Ltd which was eventually wound up with loss of deposits—*Held*, no duty of care owed to the plaintiff depositors. Case indistinguishable for all practical purposes from *Yuen Kun Yeu v. Att-Gen of Hong Kong* **26**.

29. Lloyd's Bank PLC v. Waterhouse (1991) 21 Fam. Law 23; [1992] C.L.Y. 2200, C.A.

30. Barclays Bank PLC v. Quincecare Ltd [1992] 4 All E.R. 363; [1988] C.L.Y. 177, Steyn J.

A director and chairman of a company instructed company's bankers to transfer funds from the company's account to solicitors, which funds the chairman then misappropriated—*Held*, the bankers owed a duty in both contract and tort to the company to exercise reasonable care and skill in and about the transfer but not liable as not put on inquiry by the circumstances as to whether in fact the transaction was truly authorised by the company.

31. Morgan Crucible Co. PLC v. Hill Samuel & Co. Ltd [1991] Ch. 295; [1991] 3 All E.R. 148, C.A.

For details see Chap. 18, (7) **3**.

32. Barclays Bank PLC v. Khaira [1992] 1 W.L.R. 623; [1992] C.L.Y. 215, Thomas Morison QC.

Defendant alleged duty owed by bank to advise her to seek independent legal advice to explain the nature and effect of a legal charge over a dwelling-house before she signed the charge—she was not a customer at the branch where she signed—*Held*, no duty in contract or tort owed (husband's notice of appeal struck out [1993] 1 Family L.R. 343; [1994] C.L.Y. 3536).

U1. Bentel v. Barclays Bank International Ltd (1985) C.A. 950

Bank in error treated plaintiff as non-resident and therefore permitted to deal on Johannesburg Stock Exchange—subsequent inquiry showed Bank of England consent required, which took three years to obtain. Plaintiff claimed that but for their breach of contract or negligence in making that error consent would have been obtained in one year and claimed two years loss of dealing—*Held*, bank not liable.

U2. Lloyds' Bank PLC v. Cobb (1991) C.A. 1225

Bank, in examining details of commercial project before deciding whether to make a loan to their customer, did not, in the absence of evidence that the customer was seeking their advice, assume any duty of care to him. Summary judgment given for bank.

U3. Midland Bank PLC v. Hubbard (1993) C.A. 180

Wife executed legal charge on matrimonial home which was in her sole name in favour of bank after bank manager had explained that the charge was to secure borrowing in accordance with arrangements agreed with her husband and that the worst scenario would be the sale of the house—*Held*, bank not in breach of duty.

(3) Barristers

1. Rondel v. Worsley [1969] 1 A.C. 191; [1967] 3 All E.R. 993, H.L.

Held, a barrister is not liable for professional negligence in the conduct of a case. This immunity probably extends to work done while litigation is pending, but probably not to other advisory work or to work in drafting documents; but the exact limits in this context are not certain.

2. Biggar v. McLeod [1978] N.Z.L.R. 9; [1979] C.L.Y. 2111, N.Z.C.A.

Client alleged barrister misinformed her as to terms of settlement he advised she should accept—*Held*, barrister immune from suit, as settlement related to conduct of litigation.

3. Saif Ali v. Sydney Mitchall [1980] A.C. 198; [1978] 3 All E.R. 1033, H.L.

Counsel negligently advised on joinder of defendants and negligently settled pleadings in accordance therewith. The action against the proper defendants became time-barred—*Held*, (3–2) counsel liable. The proper test was *stated* to be that expressed by McCarthy P in *Rees v. Sinclair* [1974] 1 N.Z.L.R. 180 at 187, as follows:

> "Each piece of before-trial work should, however, be tested against the one rule: that the protection only exists where the particular work is so intimately connected with the conduct of the cause in Court that it can fairly be said to be a preliminary decision affecting the way that cause is to be conducted when it comes to a hearing."

4. Matthew v. Maughold Life Assurance Co. Ltd, *The Times*, February 19, 1987, [1987] C.L.Y. 2563, C.A.

Barrister, in reconsidering a tax-saving scheme previously advised by him, was entitled to assume that the lay client's solicitor was monitoring the matter and he was not under a duty to explain it further.

(4) Brokers including Insurers

1. United Mills Agencies v. R. E. Harvey [1952] 1 All E.R. 225n.; 1 T.L.R. 149, McNair J.

2. Fraser v. Furman [1967] 1 W.L.R. 898; [1967] 3 All E.R. 57, C.A.

Held, broker liable. Case turns mainly on meaning of clause that "insured shall take reasonable care" to avoid liability.

3. Central B.C. Planers v. Hocker [1970] 9 D.L.R. (3d) 689; [1970] C.L.Y. 1880, British Columbia Supreme Court

4. Osman v. J. Ralph Moss [1970] 1 Lloyd's Rep. 313, C.A.

5. Fine's Flowers v. General Accident (1974) 49 D.L.R. (3d) 641; [1970] C.L.Y. 2326, Ontario High Court

Held, broker liable for not warning owner of horticultural business of risk of plants freezing if a water pump failed.

6. Cherry Ltd. v. Alliance Insurance [1978] 1 Lloyd's Rep. 274; [1978] C.L.Y. 1695, Cantley J.

7. McNealy v. Pennine Insurance [1978] R.T.R. 285; [1978] C.L.Y. 1694, C.A.

8. Woolcott v. Excess Insurance (No. 2) [1979] 2 Lloyd's Rep. 210; [1979] C.L.Y. 1519, Cantley J.

9. Stafford v. Conti [1981] 1 All E.R. 691; [1981] 1 Lloyd's Rep. 466, Mocatta J.

Held, following *Whitehouse v. Jordan* (Chap. 18(11) **22**), that as a broker cannot always be right in his advice as to the commodities futures market, which is unpredictable, an error of judgment is not necessarily negligent. Losses are not in themselves evidence of negligence, and strong evidence is required to establish negligence in respect of an individual transaction.

10. The Arta [1983] 2 Lloyd's Rep. 405; [1983] C.L.Y. 2550, Leggatt J.

Held, charterer's brokers were negligent (but the chain of causation was broken by the subsequent negligence of the owner's brokers).

11. Merrill Lynch Futures Inc. v. York House Trading Ltd, The Times, May 24, 1984; [1984] C.L.Y. 2288, C.A.

Held, losses made on the commodity market were not of themselves evidence of negligence.

12. Markappa Inc. v. N.W. Spratt Ltd; The Arta [1985] 1 Lloyd's Rep. 534; [1985] C.L.Y. 3162, C.A.

Shipbrokers held liable to shipowners for negligent misstatement which induced them to enter into a charterparty—chain of causation not broken by subsequent negligent failure of shipowner's agent to inform them of matters which might have led them to repudiate the contract.

13. Forsikringsaktieselskapet Vesta v. Butcher [1986] 2 All E.R. 488; [1986] C.L.Y. 366, Hobhouse J.; [1988] 3 W.L.R. 565, C.A.

Insurance brokers acting for Norwegian insurance company, placed reinsurance with London underwriters—*Held*, liable not only in contract but also for breach of duty of care in failing to act on telephone call from insurance company that a term of the reinsurance was unacceptable. Deduction for contributory negligence permissible albeit claim laid in contract (appeal on a different point to H.L. dismissed [1989] A.C. 852).

14. Banque Keyser Ullman S.A. v. Skandia (U.K.) Insurance Co. Ltd [1991] 2 A.C. 249; [1990] 2 All E.R. 947, H.L.

Bankers made loans to third party, repayment being covered by insurance policies—unknown to them manager of Lloyd's brokers placing the insurance on the bankers' behalf deceived them by insuing false cover notes—such deceit became known to the insurers' senior underwriter—*Held*, insurers not liable for breach of any duty to disclose such knoweledge to the bankers—in any event such breach not causative of loss.

15. Duncan Stevenson MacMillan v. A.W. Knott Becker Scott Ltd [1990] 1 Lloyd's Rep. 98; [1990] C.L.Y. 2717, Evans J.

Clients suffered loss as a result of the negligence of their Lloyd's brokers (in liquidation)—such brokers, due to the negligence of their E & O brokers, were not insured—*Held*, E & O brokers not liable to Lloyd's brokers' clients, albeit they would be liable at the suit of the liquidator.

16. Harvest Trucking Ltd v. Davis [1991] 2 Lloyd's Rep. 638; [1991] C.L.Y. 2649, Judge Diamond

Held, the duty of care owed by an insurance intermediary, is similar to that owed by a broker and includes the duty to ensure that the assured was made aware of any new and onerous or unusual terms which were conditions precedent to recovery under the policy.

17. Punjab National Bank v. De Boinville [1992] 1 W.L.R. 1138; [1992] 3 All E.R. 104, C.A.

Held, insurance broker owes a duty of care to the specific person whom he knows is to become an assignee of an insurance policy, at all events if that person actively participates in giving instructions for the insurance to the broker's knowledge.

18. Bank of Nova Scotia v. Hellenic Mutual War Risks Association (Bermuda) Ltd [1990] 1 Q.B. 818; [1989] 3 All E.R. 628, C.A.

Insurers of ships failed to inform bankers who had advanced moneys to shipowners on security of the ships of circumstance which entitled them to repudiate liability—bankers in ignorance advance more money—bankers claimed, *inter alia*, in tort for breach of a duty to inform of such matter—C.A. reversed trial judge's finding that he would, if necessary, find liability for breach of duty to speak ([1988] 1 Lloyd's Rep. 514). H.L. [1992] 1 A.C. 233 did not deal with point.

19. Youell v. Bland Welch & Co. Ltd (No. 2) [1990] 2 Lloyd's Rep. 431, Phillips J.

Brokers arranging reinsurance failed to inform insurers that, unlike the original insurance, the reinsurance on offer and subsequently effected was subject to a 48-month cut-off clause, or to take appropriate action once they knew there was a risk of the period of reinsurance being exceeded—*Held*, their duties did not lie exclusively in contract, there being concurrent remedies in contract and tort, and the brokers were in breach of duty of care—the insurers' own negligence in failing to notice the clause did not break the chain of causation but amounted to contributory negligence to the extent of 20 per cent.

20. Spring v. Guardian Assurance PLC [1994] 3 W.L.R. 354; [1994] 3 All E.R. 129, H.L.

—*Held*, (by a majority) insurance company and company selling the former's policies owed a duty of care on *Hedley Byrne* principles when giving a reference in respect of a person being the former's agent and the latter's ex-employee.

21. Henderson v. Merrett Syndicates Ltd. [1994] 3 W.L.R. 761; [1994] 3 All E.R. 506, H.L.

Managing agents of Lloyd's names owed a duty of care in tort to their names to exercise care and skill and so as not to cause economic loss—names were at liberty to pursue remedy in tort even if there was available a contractual remedy—contractual provisions did not in the instant case preclude names from doing so. For further details see Chap. 19, (a) **22**.

U1. Daniels v. Marx (1963) C.A. 251

Shares bought for the account—brokers failed to sell before end of account—*Held*, brokers liable, but only nominal damages, as shares had subsequently risen.

U2. Samani v. Walia (1994) C.A. 534

Defendant insurance broker did not check client's proposal form—had he done so he would have observed client had failed to declare previous claims and refusal of previous insurers to renew insurance—*Held*, defendant liable to client when new insurers after a fire claim repudiated for non-disclosure.

(5) Estate Agents, Valuers, Surveyors, Auctioneers and the Like

1. Buckland v. Watts (1968) 112 S.J. 841; [1968] C.L.Y. 3721, C.A.

2. Daisley v. Hall (1972) 225 E.G. 1553; [1972] C.L.Y. 2311, Bristow J.

3. Lees v. English & Partners (1977) 242 EG 295; [1977] C.L.Y. 2024, May J.

4. Sing v. Hilyer & Hillyer (1979) 251 E.G. 95; [1979] C.L.Y. 134, Forbes J.

Auctioneers sold house at auction—attempted to procure buyer's name and address, but he vanished. House subsequently sold for lower sum. Vendor sued auctioneers in negligence, *inter alia*, for difference in price—*Held*, defendants were not negligent in failing to secure name and address. A purchaser had never vanished before in defendants' auctions, a resale at that time would have been difficult and furthermore the defendants had no power to coerce the purchaser.

5. Yianni v. Edwin Evans [1982] Q.B. 438; [1981] 3 All E.R. 592, Park J.

Plaintiffs decided to buy a house for £15,000 if could obtain building society mortgage for £12,000. Applied to Halifax Building Society for mortgage. Halifax instructed defendants to carry out survey and prepare valuation for them. Plaintiffs required to pay survey fee to Halifax. Halifax's documents contained warning that any mortgage advance did not imply any warranty as to the reasonableness of the purchase price, but plaintiffs did not read warning. Defendants knew that most prospective purchasers of lower priced houses relied on their building society's valuation and did not instruct an independent surveyor. Defendants advised Halifax that house was adequate security for loan of £12,000. In reliance, Halifax advanced plaintiffs £12,000 (without revealing contents of defendant's report to them), and plaintiffs completed purchase. Plaintiffs would not have purchased had they not believed on basis of defendants' valuation that the house was worth at least £12,000. In fact, defendants negligently failed to notice serious defects in foundations and house was worth little more than its site value—*Held*, that the defendants were liable in negligence to the plaintiffs. It was within the defendants' reasonable contemplation that the plaintiffs would rely on their valuation which was communicated to them by the Halifax's offer of a mortgage advance of £12,000 and that carelessness in valuing the house would cause the plaintiffs loss. Accordingly, they owed the plaintiffs a duty of care under *Hedley Byrne v. Heller* (Chap. 19,(a) **1**) and were in breach of that duty. There were no policy factors negativing liability. Approved in *Smith v. Eric S. Bush* Chap. 18,(13) **54**).

6. Edmonds v. Andrew & Ashwell (1982) 261 E.G. 53; [1982] C.L.Y. 18, Barry Chedlow Q.C. as D.C.H.J.

Prospective purchasers occupied premises for some time and then withdrew from sale—*Held*, that estate agents had not been negligent.

7. Fryer v. Bunney (1982) 263 E.G. 1083; [1982] C.L.Y. 2163, Official Referee.

8. Bradshaw v. Press (1983) 263 E.G. 565; [1983] C.L.Y. 47, C.A.

Extent of duty of estate agent *discussed*—*Held*, on the facts, estate agent (reversing trial judge) not liable.

9. Computastaff Ltd v. Ingledew Brown Bennison & Garrett (1983) New L.J. 598, [1983] C.L.Y. 2574

Held, estate agents negligent.

10. Nahhas v. Pier House (Cheyne Walk) Management Ltd [1984] E.G. Digest 849; [1984] C.L.Y. 2320, Dennis Henry Q.C.

Held, surveyors acting as managing agents of a block of flats and their principals liable for negligent system of recruitment as a result of which porter with recent criminal record was employed and thereafter stole jewellery from plaintiff's flat.

11. Garland v. Ralph Pay & Ransom [1984] E.G. Digest 867; [1984] C.L.Y. 2328, Nicholls J.

Held, selling agents of mortgagee in breach of a duty of care to property developer mortgagor in failing to market property properly but, although a higher price could have been obtained, no loss suffered by reason of agreement between mortgagor and mortgagee forgiving indebtedness on terms.

12. Stevenson v. Nationwide Building Society [1984] E.G. Digest 934; [1985] C.L.Y. 2295, J. Wilmers Q.C.

Plaintiff's claim against building society for negligent mortgage valuation by employee of shop property which partly spanned river failed—*Held*, disclaimer of liability reasonable under Unfair Contract Terms Act 1977: bet see *Smith v. Eric S. Bush* (Chap. 18, (13) **54**).

13. Hooberman v. Salter Rex [1985] 1 E.G.L.R. 144; [1985] C.L.Y. 2328, Judge Smout Q.C.

Structural survey with respect to proposed purchase of maisonette—failure to report on defect in felt upstand—*Held*, liable in breach of contract for failure to exercise due skill and care.

14. Alchemy (International) Ltd v. Tattersalls Ltd [1985] 2 E.G.L.R. 17; [1985] C.L.Y. 135, Hirst J.

Successful bidder for plaintiff's colt at auction repudiated bid—auctioneer decided not to put up for sale again that day but delayed for two days—*Held*, not negligent in so delaying. Principles in *Maynard* (Chap. 18, (11) **25**) followed.

15. Palacath Ltd v. Flanagan [1985] 2 All E.R. 161; [1985] C.L.Y. 2315, Mars Jones J.

Surveyor appointed by President of the Royal Institution of Chartered Surveyors to act as an expert and not as an arbitrator in determining rent under rent review clause in a lease—*Held*, not immune from suit of landlord alleging negligence in such determination.

16. Spriggs v. Sotheby Parke Bernet & Co. Ltd [1986] 1 E.G.L.R. 13; [1986] C.L.Y. 136, C.A.

Diamond placed by plaintiff with auctioneers for sale stolen whilst in their care—CA. did not accept the system for viewing of jewellery was a reasonably safe system in the circumstances or that such system was functioning properly—*Held*, however, exclusion clause excluded liability.

17. Predeth v. Castle Phillips Finance Co. Ltd [1986] 2 E.G.L.R. 144; [1986] C.L.Y. 2232, C.A.

Mortgagee in possession instructed chartered surveyor to value property at its lowest valuation—the property had already been sold subject to contract—subsequent sales of the property occurred at significantly higher prices—*Held*, surveyor not in breach of contract or under a duty to advise as to true market value.

18. G.P. & P. Ltd v. Bulcraig & Davies [1986] 2 E.G.L.R. 148; [1986] C.L.Y. 2285, John Gorman Q.C.

Held, solicitors who acted for clients in and about obtaining lease liable for failure to discover that planning permission limited use of part of premises as offices in connection with the printing trade—*Held*, surveyors acting for those clients in finding those premises not liable. Appeal to C.A. ([1988] 1 E.G.L.R. 138) concerned only with quantum and costs.

19. Sutcliffe v. Sayer [1987] 1 E.G.L.R. 155; [1987] C.L.Y. 2596, C.A.

Surveyor instructed to prepare valuation report—*Held*, he was not in breach of contract or general duty of care, his valuation being reasonably accurate—he was not under a duty to warn of difficulties of resale.

20. Nash v. Evens & Malta [1988] 1 E.G.L.R. 130; [1988] C.L.Y. 2464, Ewbank J.

Building society instructed valuer to value flat for mortgage purposes—valuer assumed wrongly, that walls were solid brick—plaintiffs bought flat but on subsequent resale cracks were observed which were due to rusting wall ties of cavity wall construction—*Held*, no cracks visible at original valuation and hence no breach of duty of care.

21. R.L. Polk & Co. (Great Britain) Ltd v. Edwin Hill & Partners [1988] 1 E.G.L.R. 142; [1988] C.L.Y. 2418, Judge Lewis Hawser Q.C.
Assumed defendant chartered surveyor and architects were negligent in and about contruction of perimeter fence to development and which started to lean during first plaintiff's ownership which was when the cause of action arose—second plaintiff then acquired development—*Held*, second plaintiff knew or ought to have known of defect at time of acquisition and hence not entitled to sue.

22. Davies v. Parry [1988] 1 E.G.L.R. 147; [1988] C.L.Y. 2457, McNeill J.

Held, valuer instructed by building society liable to purchaser in negligence for failing to notice cracks in dwelling house or realise the real possibility of settlement or other structural damage—*Held*, further, liability not avoided by various written warnings that the report was a valuation only or that there might be defects which only a structural survey would reveal—no contributory negligence by plaintiff.

23. Strover v. Harrington [1988] 1 E.G.L.R. 173; [1988] C.L.Y. 489, Sir Nicholas Browne-Wilkinson V.C.

Particulars of sale and answers to inquiries before contract stated house on main drainage as did report of surveyors retained by plaintiff. Estate agents prior to sale informed plaintiff's solicitors that particulars were incorrect in that house was not on main drainage; the solicitors did not tell plaintiff who only found out after completion—*Held*, surveyor not negligent, being entitled to rely on what he was told by vendor—the vendor's solicitors' misrepresentation was not causative of loss—the plaintiff's solicitors' failure to inform was the cause of the loss and any remedy would be against them.

24. McIntyre v. Herring Son & Daw [1988] 1 E.G.L.R. 231; [1988] C.L.Y. 3213, E.A. Machin Q.C.

Long leaseholders were entitled to acquire freeholds under Leasehold Reform Act 1967 if rateable value reduced to £1,500 or less. Negotiation with the district valuer could not achieve such reduction—chartered surveyors did not believe such could be obtained on appeal to local valuation court and did not advise as to merits of appeal—*Held*, on preliminary issue as to liability only, that surveyors in breach of duty whereby leaseholders were deprived of opportunity of deciding whether to appeal or not.

25. Green v. Ipswich B.C. [1988] 1 E.G.L.R. 239; [1988] C.L.Y. 2456, Judge Fox-Andrews Q.C.

Purchaser of dwelling-house sued building society mortgage valuers and local authority offering improvement grants on basis that each had separately made statements that settlement was slight and required little remedial work—*Held*, neither defendant negligent and in any event the local authority owed no duty of care save to the extent it assumed such a duty by its schedule of defects.

26. Tenenbaum v. Garrod [1988] 2 E.G.L.R. 178, C.A.

Plaintiff was found to have instructed valuer to value premises at low value in order to aid negotiations for purchase—his offer to purchase was refused and property sold for higher price elsewhere—*Held*, claim of lost chance to purchase by reason of low valuation not sustainable.

27. Druce Investments Ltd v. Thaker [1988] 2 E.G.L.R. 229, Kenneth Jones J.

Estate agent's claim for commission. Defendant's allegations of mistatement as to competing offers of purchase and ability to resell at a profit rejected.

28. Wallshire Ltd v. Aarons [1989] 1 E.G.L.R. 147; [1989] C.L.Y. 2578, Hywel Moseley Q.C.

Independent surveyor appointed by the president of RICS to determine as an expert what rent should be on review—*Held*, not negligent.

29. Miro Properties Ltd v. J. Trevor & Sons [1989] 1 E.G.L.R. 151; [1989] C.L.Y. 2569, Recorder Bernstein Q.C.

Structural surveyors admitted liability in tort for negligence—*Held*, fact that plaintiff was not in existence when negligent statement was made was immaterial, since it was made with the intention that it be passed on to persons both as individuals and as agents of the plaintiff company when the same came into existence; issue of reliance on negligent advice resolved in plaintiff's favour.

30. Cross v. David Martin & Mortimer [1989] 1 E.G.L.R. 154; [1989] C.L.Y. 2589, Phillips J.

Chartered surveyors agreed to provide plaintiffs with House Buyers' Report and Valuation—*Held*, negligent in reporting.

31. Smith v. Eric S. Bush; Harris v. Wyre Forest D.C. [1990] 1 A.C. 831; [1989] 2 All E.R. 514, H.L.

See Chap. 18, (13) **54**.

32. Eley v. King & Chasemore [1989] 1 E.G.L.R. 180; [1989] C.L.Y. 2590, C.A.

Plaintiff instructed defendants to survey house and advise on structural condition—*Held*, not negligent.

33. Thomas Miller & Co. v. Richard Saunders & Partners [1989] 1 E.G.L.R. 267, Rougier J.

Held, surveyors in breach of a contractual duty of care in handling rent review but breach not causative of loss.

34. Rajdev v. Becketts [1989] 2 E.G.L.R. 144; [1989] C.L.Y. 2579, R.A.K. Wright Q.C.

Surveyor appointed to act for underlessee of shops premises with respect to rent review clause—*Held*, negligent in failing to make representations within the time fixed by expert appointed to determine rent.

35. Beresforde v. Chesterfield B.C. [1989] 2 E.G.L.R. 149; [1989] C.L.Y. 2565, C.A.

Plaintiffs claimed that second defendant building society in making mortgage offer to them negligently misstated the value of the property and that the general standard of construction was not satisfactory—*Held*, that despite what was said by Lords Templeman and Griffiths in *Smith v. Eric S. Bush*. (Chap. 18, (13) **54**) the claim was arguable and would not be struck out.

36. Gibbs v. Arnold Son & Hockley [1989] 2 E.G.L.R. 154; [1990] C.L.Y. 3307, Stephen Desch Q.C.

Valuation report prepared by valuer instructed by building society which disclosed old movement in the house and some need for timber repairs—house owners sued on basis of subsequent engineers report which disclosed that underpinning and more substantial timber repairs and other works were necessary—*Held*, valuer's original views were basically correct and there was no breach of duty.

37. Hipkins v. Jack Cotton Partnership [1989] 2 E.G.L.R. 157; [1990] C.L.Y. 1567, Scott Baker J.

Insurance company, the plaintiff's employer, instructed surveyor to prepare a valuation and a structural report on dwelling-house—*Held*, negligent in failing to note partially patched up cracks and in failing to be put an inquiry by them, the lie of the land and the situation of the house.

38. Bere v. Slades [1989] 2 E.G.L.R. 160; [1990] C.L.Y. 3306, Judge Newman Q.C.

Purchasers of dwelling-house sued mortgage valuation valuers whose report was prepared for a building society—the walls were of concrete construction which was unstable—purchasers conceded such instability was not directly discoverable on inspection—*Held*, neither the cracks existing at the date of inspection nor other signs should have led the valuers to call for further investigation.

39. Roberts v. Hampson & Co. [1990] 1 W.L.R. 94; (1989) 2 All E.R. 504, Ian Kennedy J.

Surveyors prepared valuation survey report for building society with copy to proposed purchasers—it noted a limited amount of damp and a certain amount of rot—in fact there was a considerable amount of dry rot—*Held*, although such a survey did not normally require movement of furniture or lifting of carpets and was limited in extent, a surveyor would have to spend longer than was usual on such a survey if the case required it—if there was specific ground for suspicion and the trail of suspicion led behind furniture or under carpets, he should take reasonable steps to follow the trail until he had all the information which it was reasonable for him to have before making his valuation—in this case, the surveyor should have tested further than he did for dampness.

40. Whalley v. Roberts & Roberts [1990] 1 E.G.L.R. 164; [1990] C.L.Y. 3305, Auld J.

Bungalow had been built with sloping floors the obviousness of which the builder had sought to camouflage—valuers instructed by bank for purposed mortgage loan to plaintiffs did not note or report on the slope—*Held*, not in breach of duty owed to plaintiffs.

41. Allen v. Ellis & Co. [1990] 1 E.G.L.R. 170; [1990] C.L.Y. 3322, Garland J.

Surveyor retained by plaintiffs to carry out structural survey of property which they then purchased—*Held*, negligent in advising garage and its roof was in satisfactory condition when roof was at end of its useful life and brittle—*Held*, plaintiffs entitled to damages for cost of repair, diminution in value and personal injury when husband fell through roof.

42. Howard v. Horne & Sons [1990] 1 E.G.L.R. 272; [1990] C.L.Y. 1568, Judge Bowsher Q.C.

Valuers instructed by building society to carry out mortgage valuation and by intended purchasers to prepare a "House Buyer's Report"—*Held*, negligent in reporting on state of wiring. Damages awarded on basis of value of lost opportunity to negotiate a reduction in purchase price rather than normal measure.

43. Lloyd v. Butler [1990] 2 E.G.L.R. 155; [1991] C.L.Y. 2656, Henry J.

Valuer engaged by building society to carry out mortgage valuation—*Held*, liable to purchaser in failing to report on true state of roof, wet rot in windows, woodworm and defects in wiring and central heating.

44. Beaumont v. Humberts [1990] 2 E.G.L.R. 166; [1991] C.L.Y. 2657, C.A.

Plaintiff's claim against surveyor that he was negligent in advising bank as to reinstatement value of property being purchased by him failed, the reasons being variously no duty of care owed, no reliance on surveyor's advice, no negligence and no damage.

45. Luxmoore-May v. Messenger May Baverstock [1990] 1 W.L.R. 1009; [1990] 1 All E.R. 1067, C.A.

Plaintiffs alleged auctioneers and valuers negligently failed to recognise and advise them as to the potential value of two paintings of fox hounds—they were valued by the auctioneers' consultant, an independent contractor, at between £30 & £40, sold at the auctioneer's auction for £840 and subsequently sold at Sotherbys as being the work of George Stubbs for £88,000—*Held*, (a) the duty assumed by the auctioners was to express a considered opinion as to sale value and to that end take further appropriate advice, (b) the standard to be expected was that of provincial auctioneers, as they were, (c) a personal duty of care having been assumed, it was not discharged by employing an independent contractor unless he himself was not personally negligent, and (d) the consultant had not in the circumstances been proved negligent.

46. Lough Eske Holdings Ltd v. Knight Frank & Rutley [1991] E.G.C.S. 18; [1991] C.L.Y. 105, Cresswell J.

Plaintiffs alleged that on estate agents' negligent advice two Irish estates had been sold at too low a price—*Held*, estate agents had been negligent only in not advising an expert valuation of the standing timber but since the plaintiffs would not have been prepared to pay for such a valuation at the time and there was only one interested purchaser there was no loss and damages of £1 were awarded—counter claim for fees allowed.

47. Knight Frank & Rutley v. Randolph [1991] 1 E.G.L.R. 46; [1992] C.L.Y. 90, McPherson J.

Vendor alleged that but for estate agents negligence or breach of contract a higher price would have been obtained—*Held*, no negligence or breach and agents entitled to their fees.

48. Watts v. Morrow [1991] 1 E.G.L.R. 150; [1992] C.L.Y. 1548 Judge Bowsher Q.C.

Held, structural survey negligent by reason of failure to point out that many of the items reported on required immediate attention. (Appeal on quantum only [1991] 4 All E.R. 937.)

49. Watson v. Lane Fox & Partners [1991] 2 E.G.L.R. 21; [1992] C.L.Y. 3224, Potts J.

Held, estate agents not negligent or in breach of contract in selling property at price achieved or in failing to get a higher price from an underbidder.

50. Henley v. Cloke & Sons [1991] 2 E.G.L.R. 141; [1992] C.L.Y. 1547, Judge Thayne Forbes Q.C.

Surveyor carried out mortgage valuation for bank—he noticed distortion in front bay windows which he concluded, correctly, was of long standing—he made no reference to this in his report—he also failed to observe or report on a defective drain—copy of report sent to purchasers—*Held*, negligent and property worth less than value advised.

51. Beaton v. Nationwide Building Society [1991] 2 E.G.L.R. 145; [1992] C.L.Y. 3207, Neil Butterfield Q.C.

Surveyor, employee of building society, carried out mortgage valuation on dwelling—he reported on structural movement which he considered was a risk which could be accepted—purchaser proceeded partly in reliance on report and partly on own assessment—*Held*, negligent in concluding further movement was not a risk—disclaimer notice held unreasonable under Unfair Contract Terms Act 1977—notice under the Building Societies Act 1962, s. 30, did not exclude duty of care.

52. Hacker v. Thomas Deal & Co. [1991] 2 E.G.L.R. 161; [1992] C.L.Y. 3215, Judge Fawlus.

Purchaser of property in Belgravia alleged negligence/breach of contract in carrying out a structural survey by failing to report on dry rot—*Held*, not negligent—not proved surveyor should have detected signs at time of inspection which should have led him to conclude dry rot was present at time of inspection.

53. Civic Structures Ltd v. Clark Quinney & Co. [1991] 2 E.G.L.R. 165; [1992] C.L.Y. 3207, Leonard J.

Properly developers alleged estate agents were negligent/in breach of contract in advising on the yield to be expected from a development—it was found the estate agents had gratuitously passed on an opinion of a third party as to the yield, as the plaintiff knew—*Held*, no reliance on estate agents and no negligence.

54. Sears Investment Trust Ltd v. Lewis's Group Ltd [1992] R.A. 262; *The Times*, September 22, 1992, Harman J.

Valuers on instructions of plaintiff's parent company pursued an appeal against the rateable value of the plaintiff's Glasgow store. Following an agreement to transfer the store to the defendants, the plaintiffs told valuers to take instructions from defendants as to appeal. Appeal was successful and valuers obtained repayment of excess rates which were paid to the defendants—*Held*, valuers as from the date of change owed no duty of care or loyalty to the plaintiffs—claim for damages in negligence dismissed.

55. P.K. Finans International (U.K.) Ltd v. Andrew Downs & Co. Ltd [1992] 1 E.G.L.R. 172; [1992] C.L.Y. 3216, Sir Michael Ogden Q.C.

Copy of valuation of a property being converted into a nursing home was supplied to licensed deposit takers who lent on the security of the property. The valuer stated he had made oral inquiries but no official search as to planning consents—*Held*, not negligent in not advising that planning consents should be verified—if there had been negligence, then deposit takers contributorily negligent in failing to instruct solicitors to verify the same.

56. Heatley v. William H. Brown Ltd [1992] 1 E.G.L.R. 289; [1992] C.L.Y. 1549, Judge Bowsher Q.C.

Structural surveyor held to be negligently in breach of contract; in view of the detailed terms of the contract there was no room for liability in tort. *Tai Hing* Chap. 18, (2) **23** followed.

57. Peach v. Iain G. Chalmers & Co. [1992] 2 E.G.L.R. 135; [1992] C.L.Y. 5658, Lord Caplan, C. of Sess.

Held, valuers instructed by bank for mortgage purposes liable to purchasers for misdescription of method of construction.

58. Hiron v. Pynford South Ltd [1992] 2 E.G.L.R. 138; [1993] C.L.Y. 2997, Judge Newey Q.C.

Structural engineer advised insurers of property as to its underpinning—building surveyor likewise advised owners—each pursuant to contract—*Held*, in neither case was there owed in addition a duty in tort—further the engineer did not owe a duty of care to the owners.

59. Mount Banking Corporation Ltd v. Brian Cooper & Co. [1992] 2 E.G.L.R. 142; [1992] C.L.Y. 3213, R.M. Stewart Q.C.

Held, Valuation for bank of open market value of building on the security of which money was lent was within acceptable range of figures a competent valuer using due skill and care would reach.

60. Kerridge v. James Abbott & Partners [1992] 2 E.G.L.R. 162; [1993] C.L.Y. 2995, Judge Hordern Q.C.

Structural survey for purchasers of house—*Held*, not liable for failing to advise there was a real risk that dry not was present in concealed timbers under the roof.

61. Allied Trust Bank Ltd v. Edward Symmons & Partners (1994) 1 E.G.L.R. 165, N. Clarke Q.C.

Property developer sought loan from bank for purchase and conversion of house into flats and provided valuation report to the bank which, *inter alia*, gave an open market value which included the additional amount it was anticipated prospective purchasers would pay for the prospect of obtaining planning permission—*Held*, surveyors not in breach of duty to bank inso doing.

62. Letgain Ltd v. Supercement Ltd [1993] E.G.C.S. 184; (1994) 07 E.G. 192, C.A.

Held, property consultants not in breach of contract in not advertising property for sale as instructions were to put on market quietly—in any event, price achieved within acceptable range of values.

63. Muldoon v. Mays of Lillput Ltd [1993] 1 E.G.L.R. 43; [1993] C.L.Y. 2984; Judge Zucker Q.C.

Held, estate agents not negligent in advising sale at a particular value, there being no evidence that the property was included in any development scheme which would have justified a higher valuation.

64. Private Bank & Trust Co. Ltd v. S (U.K.) Ltd [1993] 1 E.G.L.R. 144; [1993] C.L.Y. 2998, Judge Rice

Owners of property instructed valuers—copy of valuation sent to plaintiff who lent in reliance thereon—*Held*, valuation not negligent.

65. Macey v. Debenhan Tewson & Chinnocks [1993] 1 E.G.L.R. 149; [1993] C.L.Y. 2996, Andrew Blackett-Ord Q.C.

Plaintiff alleged surveyor had been negligent in advising him to pay too much for a property—action dismissed.

66. C.I.L. Securities Ltd v. Brian Champion Long [1993] 2 E.G.L.R. 164; [1994] C.L.Y. 3386, John Mowbray Q.C.
Held, surveyors negligent and in breach of contract in advising landlord as to amount achievable on rent reviews of leased premises.

67. Zubaida v. Hargreaves [1993] 2 E.G.L.R. 170, Judge Zucker Q.C.

Surveyor appointed as independent expert to determine appropriate rent of premises tenanted by plaintiff—*Held*, not negligent. C.A. dismissed appeal (1995) 1 E.G.L.R. 127.

68. Preston v. Torfaen B.C. (1994) 65 B.L.R. 1; [1994] C.L.Y. 3398, C.A.

Plaintiffs were subsequent purchasers of a house built on land which the defendant surveyors had advised the local authority was suitable to carry foundations for a housing estate—*Held*, not liable for cracks allegedly due to faulty design of foundations/soil conditions, the case not falling within any special category outside the *Hedley Byrne* principle which would entitle recovery for economic loss or in the absence of reliance.

69. McCullagh v. Lane Fox & Partners Ltd (1994) 08 E.G. 118; *The Times*, January 25, 1994, Colman J.

Estate agent's particulars negligently misstated area of ground—disclaimer of liability in particulars—subsequent oral misrepresentation of same matter in partial reliance on which plaintiff purchased—*Held*, liable for oral representation but no loss caused.

70. Matto v. Rodney Broom Associates (1994) 2 E.G.L.R. 163; [1994] N.P.C. 40, C.A.

Held, structural surveyor liable to purchaser for negligent performance of contract in that his reports failed to address the likelihood of movement in the distant as well as the more immediate future.

71. Axa Equity & Law v. Goldsack & Freeman [1994] 1 E.G.L.R. 175; [1994] C.L.Y. 3387, Judge Marr Johnson
Valuers instructed to value leasehold flat for remortgage purposes—subsequent default by borrowers and forced sale—alleged negligent overvaluation—*Held*, valuation at very top of permissible bracket and claim failed.

72. Marc Rich & Co. A.G. v. Bishop Rock Marine Co. Ltd (1995) 3 W.L.R. 227, H.L.

Surveyor employed by classification in society was allegedly negligent in permitting a vessel after repairs to continue her journey with the consequent loss of cargo—it was assumed the loss of the cargo was foreseeable and constituted physical damage to goods and was the result of carelessness by the surveyor. *Held*: (4–1) assuming sufficient "proximity", it was not just, fair or reasonable to impose a duty of care on the society in favour of the cargo owner. *Caparo* (Chap. 18, (1) **17**) and *Murphy v. Brentwood D.C.* (Chap. 18, (13) **66**) applied.

73. Helmclub v. Pepper Fox [1994] N.P.C. 81; [1994] C.L.Y. 3396, Judge Paul Baker Q.C.

Plaintiff claimed he had suffered loss by relying on overvaluation of his property contained in letter written by surveyor—*Held*, letter could not be read as a formal valuation and he had not relied on it.

U1. Conn v. Munday (1955) C.A. 295

Defendant surveyor—failed to go into cellar while surveying house—there was woodworm in cellar—*Held*, defendant negligent.

U2. Cunningham v. Herbert Fulford & Chorley (A Firm) (1958) C.A. 59

Held, estate agents not liable, as on the facts he had taken reasonable care in inquiring into the tenant's suitability.

U3. Ezekiel v. McDade (1994) C.A. 1373

Held, surveyor negligent in failing to notice and report on unacceptable position of heavy concrete purlin in roof.

U4. Sneesby v. Goldings (A Firm) (1994) C.A. 1463

Held, surveyor negligent in carrying out building society survey.

(6) Architects, Engineers, Builders and the Like

(*N.B.*: In *Murphy v. Brentwood D.C.* [1991] 1 A.C. 398, (see Chap. 18, (13) **66**), it was held that *Anns v. Merton London B.C.* **13** "was wrongly decided as regards the scope of any private law duty of care resting upon local authorities in relation to their function of taking steps to secure compliance with building byelaws or regulations & should be departed from … *Dutton v. Bognor Regis Urban District Council*" **10** "should be overruled as should all cases subsequent to *Anns* which were decided in reliance on it" *per* Lord Keith. In the light of that decision, cases listed here which were decided after *Dutton* and prior to *Murphy* need to be treated with caution in so far as they relied or may have relied upon those earlier decisions.

1. Clayton v. Woodman [1962] 2 Q.B. 533; [1962] 2 All E.R. 33, C.A.

Building work which involved the cutting of a chase—plaintiff bricklayer suggested to architect a different way of doing the work—architect refused to vary the specification—the chase was cut in unsafe manner and plaintiff was injured—it could have been cut safely—*Held*, architect not liable, for all that he had done was to refuse to vary the specification.

2. Clay v. Crump [1964] 1 Q.B. 533; [1963] 3 All E.R. 687, C.A.

Demolition—architect passed a wall as safe which was not—one month later the same fell on plaintiff, who was employed in rebuilding—*Held*, applying *Hedley Byrne v. Heller* (Chap. 18, (2) **8**), architect liable.

3. Bagot v. Stevens Scanlon [1966] 1 Q.B. 197; [1964] 3 All E.R. 577, Diplock L.J.

Preliminary point of law—as to whether time ran from the date of the last act of negligence alleged or from the date when damage first occurred—if action lay in contract, the former was correct, and action would be time-barred—*Held*, action lay in contract only. Dictum of Greer L.J. in *Jarvis v. May Davies* [1936] 1 K.B. 399 at 405 *applied* and *Clark v. Kirby Smith* (Chap. 18, (15) **10**) *followed*.

4. Quinn v. Burch [1966] 2 Q.B. 370; [1966] 2 All E.R. 283, C.A.

Building contractor failed to provide step-ladder as stipulated—sub-contractor for labour only used unsafe and unfooted trestle instead—*Held*, only duty of main contractor lay in contract, and the injuries were not the result of breach of contract, but of plaintiff's own decision to use the trestle.

5. Moresk Cleaners v. Hicks [1966] 2 Lloyd's Rep. 338, Official Referee

6. Heaven v. Mortimore (1968) 205 E.G. 767; [1968] C.L.Y. 2660, C.A.

Builder had built houses negligently so that cracks appeared—builder became ill, and son on his behalf took out some trial bore holes to discover extent of damage—he filled them in negligently, and damage resulted—before Karminski J. ([1967] C.L.Y. 2676) son argued that the only duty was contractual, and that any contractual relationship lay between father and house owners only—judge held that the duty lay in tort as well, and applied *Wagon Mound* to hold son liable both in negligence and nuisance—C.A. affirmed judgment—*Held*, son liable in negligence.

7. Driver v. Willett [1969] 1 All E.R. 665, Rees J.

8. Worboys v. Acme Investment (1969) 119 New L.J. 332; *The Times*, March 26, 1969, C.A.
Held, that in the absence of expert evidence it could not be said to be so glaring an omission as to constitute negligence.

9. Brickfield Properties v. Newton [1971] 1 W.L.R. 862; [1971] 3 All E.R. 328, C.A.

10. Dutton v. Bognor Regis U.D.C. [1972] Q.B. 373; [1972] 1 All E.R. 462, C.A.

Overruled: see *Murphy* (Chap. 18, (13) **66**).

11. Bourne v. McEvoy (1975) 237 E.G. 496; [1976] C.L.Y. 1862, Bristow J.

X, selling property to Y, consulted L on dry rot treatment—X and Y had agreed to share the cost of any work done—X commissioned L to do the work—*Held*, applying *Dutton* **10**, L owed a duty to Y (even though they did not know of their existence), but on the facts there was no breach of duty.

12. Sutherland v. Maton [1976] J.P.L. 753; [1976] C.L.Y. 87, Cobb J.

Plaintiff bought three-year-old house—which subsided four years later due to negligence of builder—the only survey carried out had been by building society at time of purchase by plaintiff—this had recommended that the cause of a crack be investigated—*Held*, that in the circumstances, having regard to the recent date when house was built, plaintiff acted reasonably in not having a full survey, and builder was liable.

13. Anns v. Merton London B.C. [1977] 2 W.L.R. 1024; [1977] 2 All E.R. 492, H.L.

Cracks in flats due to defective foundations—plaintiff occupiers claimed that the local authority were liable, inasmuch as they had either failed to inspect the foundations (in the exercise of their functions under the Public Health Act 1936, now (but not then) replaced by the Public Health Act 1961) or had been negligent in approving them after inspection—the case was argued as a preliminary point on these assumptions—*Held*, that ordinarily, but subject to provisos, the local authority would be liable for negligent inspection, but not for failing to inspect at all. *Dutton* **10** was approved as a decision, but on grounds which were generically different to those of the judgments in *Dutton*. In *Dutton* the general tenor of the judgments was to treat the issue as an extension of the *Hedley Byrne* principle. But in the present case (perhaps because a failure to inspect, in addition to negligent inspection, was also in issue) the **H.L.** approached the matter differently. Lord Wilberforce (three other Law Lords concurring) said that, by the basic proximity test and by the absence of any special considerations negativing liability, a duty of care would ordinarily arise, but the existence of that duty in law had to be considered in the light of the scheme of the Public Health Act 1936, inasmuch as in most similar statutes there were areas of policy or "discretion," and decisions in these areas could not, ordinarily and subject to provisos, be challenged in the courts. Largely overruled in *Murphy* (Chap. 18, (13) **66**).

14. William Hill Organisation Ltd v. Bernard Sunley & Sons Ltd (1982) 22 B.L.R. 1; [1982] C.L.Y. 252, C.A.

Plaintiffs engaged defendants to construct office block under RIBA form of contract—clause 24 defined circumstances in which final certificate to be conclusive evidence work properly carried out and completed in accordance with contract. A conclusive final certificate was issued. Many years later, serious defective workmanship was discovered. Plaintiffs. *inter alia* sought to circumvent the final certificate by suing defendants in negligence—*Held*, that as the contract circumscribed the boundaries of the duty of care and defined its content, the plaintiffs were not entitled to claim a remedy in tort wider than the obligations assumed by the defendants under the contract: "It is not open to the plaintiffs in effect to disregard those clauses of the contract which provided for the conclusive effect of the Final Certificate but to claim a remedy for breaches which were only capable of ascertainment by reference to the contract itself." (Cumming-Bruce L.J. at 29). In principle, as Lord Roskill suggested in *Junior Books v. Veitchi* (Chap. 1 (3) (a) 11), an exclusion clause in a contract may be relevant in determining the duty of care in tort.

15. Dillingham v. Downs (1972) 13 Build.L.R. 97; [1980] C.L.Y. 1899, Sup. Ct. of N.S.W.

Held, that the mere fact that the parties were in a pre-contractual relationship at the time when the duty was alleged to have arisen did not in itself preclude the existence of a duty of care on the part of the building owner in disclosing special site conditions, but on the facts there had been no breach of any such duty.

16. Oldschool v. Gleeson (1976) 4 Build.L.R. 103; [1980] C.I.Y. 218, Judge Stabb Q.C.

Collapse of party wall during redevelopment. Contractors agreed to indemnify and claimed contribution from the consulting engineers, alleging *inter alia*, that the engineeers owed them a duty of care in relation to design and/or supervision—*Held*, that:

(a) collapse was not due to a design fault;
(b) the engineeers' duty of supervision did not extend to instructing the contractors as to the manner in which they were to execute the work;
(c) a consulting engineer or architect did owe the contractor a duty of care in respect of supervision of the work, but that duty was limited by the assumption that the contractor acted at all times as a competent contractor, and the duty in no way extended into the area of how the work was to be carried out; and
(d) a breach of duty was not proved.

17. Hone v. Benson [1977] C.L.Y. 2062, Judge Fay Q.C.

The defendants, being husband and wife, built a restaurant, in which they and/or a plumber working for them installed a hot water system. Some months later they sold the premises to P. In an action brought by P he alleged that (a) the defendants when building restaurant knew that they might soon sell it; (b) the hot water system was negligently designed and installed; and (c) after conveyance the system malfunctioned, causing physical damage and loss—*Held*, the allegations if proved would make the defendants liable.

18. Batty v. Metropolitan Property [1978] Q.B. 554; [1978] 2 All E.R. 445 C.A.

D2 (builders) built a house for D1 (property developers) on an unstable hillside. D1 later sold same to Mr and Mrs P. A landslip occurred, damaging part of garden and causing Mrs P significant mental distress. It was then discovered that a further landslide could at any time, and would within 10 years cause house to collapse. As a result house was valueless. Such danger should have been apparent to a reasonably competent property developer and/or builder. Defendants argued that no cause of action arose in respect of the house until it was itself damaged or was "in such a state as to present present or imminent danger to the health or safety of the occupier" (456 E). To this Megaw L.J. (the other 2 L.JJ. concurring) *said* (457 G—458 B) that there was already physical damage in the shape of the landslip onto the garden and on a wider view, there was in fact imminent danger to health or safety at the time the action was brought—*Held*, both defendants liable, D1 in contract and tort, and D2 in tort. Doubted in *D & F Estates* **63**.

19. Abrams v. Ancliffe [1978] 2 N.Z.L.R. 420; [1979] C.L.Y. 213, N.Z.Sup.Ct.

P, a builder, estimated to D for certain work. Later he received specifications from D's architect and realised that the work was more extensive than he had thought but said nothing to D about his misgivings. D frequently inquired about the final price, without reply, despite this D allowed the work to begin. Costs escalated above the original estimate—*Held*, P owed a duty of care in giving estimate, and was in breach thereof in not telling D of his misgivings before committing himself to the work.

20. B.L. Holdings v. Wood (1979) 123 S.J. 570; [1980] C.L.Y. 1868, C.A.

Planning permission without prior development permit only available for office development up to 10,000 square feet. Planning officer advised architect that certain areas such as the car park would not count in the 10,000 square feet and planning permission was duly granted but this advice was wrong, and the permission was later found to be void—*Held*, reversing trial judge, architect not liable to his client, as in the circumstances he was entitled to assume that the local authority knew their job as regards planning and to accept their assurances.

21. Balcomb v. Wards Construction (1981) 259 E.G. 765; [1981] C.L.Y. 197, Sir Douglas Frank Q.C. as D.H.C.J.

Builders engaged structural engineers to advise on foundations of proposed houses. Engineers failed to appreciate risk of heave due to removal of trees which had been abstracting moisture from soil. As a result, foundations were inadequate and plaintiffs houses suffered damage. Builders admitted liability to plaintiff—*Held*, applying *Batty* **18** that the engineers were negligent in relation to both the plaintiffs and the builders. The engineers were not entitled to a contribution from the builders as the latter had discharged their duty of care by employing engineers to advise them on matters outside their own expertise.

22. Sutcliffe v. Chippendale & Edmundson (1982) 18 Build.L.R. 149; [1982] C.L.Y. 232, H.H. Judge Stabb Q.C.

23. Townsend v. Cinema News (1982) 20 Build. L.R. 118; [1983] C.L.Y. 255, C.A.

Held, architects liable to building owner. The measure of damages was the cost of the work required to make the premises comply with the byelaws—*Held*, also, that the architects were liable to indemnify the builders against their liability to the owner.

24. Eames v. North Hertfordshire D.C. (1982) 18 Build.L.R. 58; [1982] C.L.Y. 242, H.H. Judge Fay Q.C.

25. Newham B.C. v. Taylor Woodrow Anglian (1982) 19 Build.L.R. 99; [1983] C.L.Y. 249, C.A.

Held, that the defendants had not been negligent. They had made adequate inquiries before using a system which had been in use for 20 years and was based upon fundamental principles of building. The defendants were, however, held liable for breach of contract.

26. Junior Books v. Veitchi [1983] A.C. 520; [1982] 3 All E.R. 201, H.L.

For details see Chap. 1(3)(a) **11**. Considered in *D. & F. Estates* (**63**); explained in *Murphy* (Chap. 18, (13) **66**).

27. Brunswick Construction v. Nowlan (1983) 21 Build.L.R. 27; [1983] C.L.Y. 276, Supreme Ct. of Canada

Held, that the builders should have recognised the defects in the design and knowing that the owner was relying on the design, ought to have warned the owner of the defects.

28. Bluett v. Woodspring D.C. [1983] J.P.L. 242; [1983] C.L.Y. 2513, Judge Stabb Q.C.

29. Acrecrest v. Hattrell [1983] Q.B. 260; [1983] 1 All E.R. 17, C.A.

Overruled in *Peabody* **31**.

30. Dove v. Banhams Patent Locks Ltd [1983] 1 W.L.R. 1436; [1983] 2 All E.R. 833, Hodgson J.

31. Peabody v. Parkinson [1985] A.C. 210; [1984] C.L.Y. 2298, H.L.

Held, local authority not liable. For details see Chap. 18, (13) **29**.

32. Rimmer v. Liverpool C.C. [1984] 2 W.L.R. 426; [1984] 1 All E.R. 930, C.A.

For details, see Chap 10(8)(a)**22**.

33. Twins Transport Ltd v. Patrick & Brocklehurst (1984) 25 B.L.R. 65; [1984] C.L.Y. 395, Judge Lewis Hawser Q.C.

First defendant, property developer, agreed with plaintiff to design and construct building—second defendant agreed with first defendant to design and construct roof, their contract containing exclusion clause. Roof defective due to poor design and poor workmanship which proper supervision by the second defendants of their sub-contractors would have revealed. Agreed second defendant's duty to plaintiff lay only in tort—*Held*, exclusion clause not effective as between the two defendants and second defendants liable in negligence to plaintiff, irrespective of exclusion clause, for economic loss being cost of repair of roof.

34. Jackson v. Bishop (1984) 48 P. & C.R. 57; [1984] C.L.Y. 3625, C.A.

Purchasers of land claimed, *inter alia*, against developers of estate in negligence for causing misleading plans to be annexed to the conveyance—*Held*, developers liable. *Batty* **18** relied on, (which is now doubted—see D and F. Estates **63**).

35. Southern Water Authority v. Lewis & Duvivier (1984) 27 B.L.R. 111; [1984] C.L.Y. 239, Judge Smout Q.C.

Owner of sewerage scheme built pursuant to a contract made with its predecessor sued sub-contractors in tort for negligent design, supply and installation of equipment—*Held*, although in ordinary course of events there was sufficient proximity between a sub-contractor and a building owner who had suffered damage, the issuing of take-over certificates in effect excluded all liability in tort.

36. Cynat Products Ltd v. Landbuild (Investment & Property) Ltd [1984] 3 All E.R. 513; [1984] C.L.Y. 2283, Judge Sir William Stabb Q.C.

Steelwork of roof collapsed due to faulty design—*Held*, first defendant, who had agreed to have works properly designed and carried out, liable for breach of contract and of duty of care (such primary duty being non-delegable)—*Held*, further, second defendant who had agreed to design and supervise construction in breach of contract and duty—*Held*, further, the local authority was at fault: having granted building regulation approval subject to receipt of steelwork details and having inspected the work (the design of which had been altered in the interim) they should have insisted on details being provided.

37. Wimpey Construction U.K. Ltd v. D.V. Poole [1984] 2 Lloyd's Rep. 499; [1984] C.L.Y. 2340, Webster J.

Builders claimed that a failure by them to take into account long-term factors affecting soil conditions (namely, softening of clay) in the design of a quay wall was negligent and they were therefore entitled to indemnity under a policy of insurance—*Held*, they had not been negligent.

38. Shui On Construction Co. Ltd v. Shui Kay Co. Ltd [1984–1985] 1 Const. L. J. 305; [1986] C.L.Y. 215, H.K. High Court, Hunter J.

Main contractors alleged that the architects and engineers owed them a duty to exercise reasonable skill and care in the performance of their functions pursuant to the contract and a duty to act fairly and impartially in the performance of those functions—*Held*, claim would not be struck out.

39. Equitable Debenture Assets Corporation Ltd v. William Moss Group Ltd [1984] 1 Const. L.J. 131; [1985] C.L.Y. 221, Judge Newey Q.C.

Architect employed to design and supervise erection of curtain walling to be erected by sub-contractor—*Held*, architect owed to employer a duty of care in negligence as well as in contract to precisely the same extent—in the absence of agreement he could not delegate such duties to others—although he could not be criticised for adopting the system of curtain walling, he was aware that the workmanship of the sub-contractor and/or the design was at fault and should have discovered what was wrong and prepared a scheme to put it right—*Held*, further, main contractor must have known that the skills required to build the walling in accordance with the design were beyond that of the average fitter and was therefore in breach of implied term in contract and of a duty of care in negligence owed to employer and architect to inform the architect of design defects known to them.

40. Ketteman v. Hansel Properties Ltd [1984] 1 W.L.R. 1274; (1985) 1 All E.R. 352, C.A.

Judge at first instance found in favour of plaintiff houseowners in claim for negligence in relation to defective foundations against builders and architects—*Held*, by C.A., local authority was also negligent in inspection of foundations and that the nature of cracks in the wall and the likelihood of progressive damage meant there was an imminent danger to health or safety and therefore liability. *Anns* **13** applied. Proceedings in H.L. (1987) A.C. 189 on limitation point only.

41. Low v. R. J. Haddock Ltd (1985) 6 Con. L.R. 122; [1985] C.L.Y. 213, Judge Newey Q.C.

Builder built two semi-detached houses near to oak tree all on land owned by him—land on which tree stood subsequently dedicated as highway—*Held*, builder not liable in negligence or nuisance for damage to foundations caused by moisture abstraction as he could not have been expected to foresee that highway authority would allow the tree to get to such a size as to cause damage. *Held*, further, authority, although it could not initially have foreseen such damage, later became aware of the risk and was negligent in failing to take steps to avert it by reducing size of tree.

42. Southern Water Authority v. Lewis & Duvivier (No. 2) [1984–1985] 1 Const.L.J. 74; [1985] C.L.Y. 2331, Judge Smout Q.C.

Consulting engineers claimed sub-contractor for sewerage works owed a duty of care to them in relation to the quality and fitness of the sub-contract works and that they were entitled to recover as damages the damages and interest they were liable to pay the water authority for their failure property to supervise the sub-contract works—*Held*, no duty of care owed—in any event the damages sought were irrecoverable as being pure economic loss. Claim under the Law Reform (Married Women and Tortfeasors) Act 1935, s. 6(1)(c), also failed.

43. Victoria University of Manchester v. Hugh Wilson and Lewis Womersley and Pochin (Contractors) Ltd [1985] 2 Con.L.R. 43; [1985] C.L.Y. 220, Judge Newey Q.C.

Ceramic tile cladding to reinforced concrete building in due course fell off to a large extent. The following findings were made:

(a) The architect owed similar duties in contract and tort and should have warned the plaintiffs of the dangers inherent in the new method of fixing adopted—the design was defective and inspection inadequate.
(b) The sub-contractor did not adequately fix the tiles—the plaintiff's clerk of works failed to exercise proper care in not seeing such defects.
(c) The contributory negligence of architect and clerk of works was no defence to plaintiff's claim against main contractor in contract for sub-contractor's faults.
(d) Main contractor was under a duty by virtue of an implied term to warn of defects in design they believed existed but were not in breach of that duty. *Equitable Debenture* **39** followed.
(e) Architect did not owe a duty of care to the main contractor in relation to inspection of the sub-contractor's work.
(f) Sub-contractor owed main contractor a duty in tort as well as in contract to fix the tiles properly.
(g) Sub-contractor owed a duty in tort of negligence to the plaintiffs—*Junior Books* **26** relied on.

44. Perry v. Tendring D.C. [1985] 1 E.G.L.R. 260; [1985] C.L.Y. 192, Judge Newey Q.C.

For details see Chap. 18, (13) **31**.

45. Kensington & Chelsea & Westminster Area H.A. v. Wettern Composites Ltd [1985] 1 All E.R. 346; [1985] C.L.Y. 212, Judge Smout Q.C.

Held, architects for hospital extension negligent in supervision of fixing of mullions—*Held*, structural engineers not negligent.

46. Southern Water Authority v. Carey [1985] 2 All E.R. 1077; [1985] C.L.Y. 195, Judge Smout Q.C.

See *Southern Water Authority* **35** and **42**.

47. London Congregational Union Inc. v. Harriss & Harriss [1985] 1 All E.R. 335; [1985] C.L.Y. 189, Judge Newey Q.C.

Held, architects negligent in their design of drainage arrangement. C.A. [1988] 1 All E.R. 15 concerned only on limitation point.

48. Shankie-Williams v. Heavey [1986] 2 E.G.L.R. 139; [1986] C.L.Y. 2272, C.A.

Dry rot specialist inspected, treated for and gave a guarantee in respect of dry rot in a ground floor flat for owner of whole property—*Held*, he owed a duty of care to a subsequent purchaser of the flat but, assuming he was negligent, such was not causative of loss.

49. Coleman Street Properties Ltd v. Denco Miller Ltd (1986) 31 B.L.R. 32; [1986] C.L.Y. 223, Lawson J.

A builder's negligence was the cause of fire in air-handling units at premises of which first plaintiffs were owners and second plaintiffs were tenants—*Held*, the contract with the tenants did not exempt builder from liability—*Held*, further, builder liable to owners and tenants in negligence and in tenants' case in breach of contract for loss and damage to premises and equipment.

50. Imperial College of Science & Technology v. Norman & Dawbarn (1987) 8 Con.L.R. 107; [1987] C.L.Y. 233, Judge Smout Q.C.

Held, architects of 12-storey block liable in negligence for failure to take reasonable steps in their design and supervision to guard against penetration of water principally by reason of inadequate weathering strips and the failure to require water-proof grout, which materially and substantially contributed to the dangerous condition of exterior ceramic tiling—*Held*, not liable for failure to give warning as to life of the tiling itself.

51. Nye Saunders & Partners v. Alan E. Bristow (1988) 37 B.L.R. 92; [1988] C.L.Y. 2421, C.A.

Architect provided houseowner with estimate of likely cost of renovation prepared by an independent quantity surveyor—*Held*, architect in breach of duty in not warning houseowner of likely effect of inflation on the final cost of the work.

52. Welsh Health Technical Services Organisation v. Haden Young (1988) 37 B.L.R. 130; [1988] C.L.Y. 2442, Macpherson J.

Nominated sub-contractor tendered on basis that employer or main contractor would bear sole risk of loss or damage by fire—sub-contractor's employee negligently caused damage by fire—*Held*, prima facie sub-contractor owed a duty of care to the employer not to cause damage to the works or to persons or property or pure economic loss (*Junior Books* **26** relied on) but employer's assumption of liability for fire negatived scope of duty.

53. Audsley v. Leeds C.C., *The Times*, June 2, 1988; [1988] C.L.Y. 2458, Judge Herrod Q.C.

Negligent builder and local authority inspector—*Held*, no cause of action against local authority as safety and health not affected (see *Anns* **13**)—further, in absence of assignment of the cause of action against the builder, the plaintiff, who had no proprietary interest in the property when the cause of action accrued, was barred from proceeding

54. Pratt v. George J. Hill Associates (1988) 38 B.L.R. 25; [1988] C.L.Y. 2411, C.A.

Plaintiff entered into contract with manifestly unreliable builder on recommendation of architect—*Held*, at first instance, architect in breach of duty. Appeal concerned with quantum only.

55. George Hawkins v. Chrysler (U.K.) Ltd and Burne Associates (1988) 38 B.L.R. 36; [1988] C.L.Y. 2428, C.A.

Employer retained engineers to design and supervise installation of showers at their foundry—engineers consulted others as to a suitable flooring material. Employee slipped on floor and was injured—employer alleged engineers in breach of term that they would use reasonable care and skill in the selection and use of flooring material—*Held*, not negligent.

56. Ernst & Whinney v. Willard Engineering (Dagenham) Ltd, (1988) 40 B.L.R. 67, Judge John Davies Q.C.

Consulting engineers designed and sub-contractors installed air-conditioning system in building for freeholders. Subsequent lessee sues both in negligence—*Held*, assuming negligence and breach of contracts with freeholders, it was not just or reasonable to impose liability in tort—in any event, the claim was for pure economic loss. (*Junior Books* **26** and *Anns* **13** considered).

57. Simaan General Contracting Co. v. Pilkington Glass Ltd (No. 2) [1988] Q.B. 758; [1988] 1 All E.R. 791, C.A.

Defendants supplied green double-glazed panels to others who incorporated them in a building as sub-contractors—building owner withheld moneys due to main contractor on the ground that the colouring was inconsistent—*Held*, the defendants owed no duty of care to the main contractors for such pure economic loss (*Junior Books* **26** distinguished).

58. Greater Nottingham Cooperative Society Ltd v. Cementation Piling & Foundations Ltd [1989] Q.B. 71; [1988] 2 All E.R. 971, C.A.

Negligent piling operations by nominated sub-contractor caused physical damage to adjoining premises for which liability admitted. Employer claimed damages for economic loss, namely, that caused by delay in deciding how to proceed to completion of piling work, additional cost to employers under main contract and for loss and expense claims caused by delay under the main contract—*Held*, no liability (there being no breach of the collateral agreements between sub-contractor and employer which did not relate to manner of carrying out work)—there was no assumption of responsibility by sub-contractor for economic loss—any duty of care to prevent such loss was negated and, as a matter of policy, no such liability arose.

59. University of Warwick v. Sir Robert McAlpine (1988) 42 BLR 1; [1989] C.L.Y. 219, Garland J.

Third defendant recommended a process of resin bonding to overcome problems of defective ceramic tile cladding and became a sub-contractor for the remedial work—*Held*, sub-contractor knew or ought to have known of the risk of damage being caused by the resin to the tiles and was in breach of duty of care in not warning the employer—the damage was not purely economic loss, (*Simaan* **57** and *Greater Nottingham* **58** considered).

60. Surrey Heath B.C. v. Lovell Construction Ltd (1988) 42 BLR 25; [1989] C.L.Y. 218, Judge Fox-Andrews Q.C.

Building owner claimed against main contractor in contract and tort and against sub-contractor in tort for loss and damage caused by fire negligently caused by sub-contractor—*Held*, as against main contractor there was no room for a parallel duty in tort since the contract expressly dealt with the subject-matter of the claim and the claim in tort failed and there could be no claim for loss and damage save that recoverable in contract. The sub-contractor conceded a duty was owed to take reasonable care to avoid direct damage to the owner's property—*Held*, sub-contractor liable for such damage and consequential costs so far as such sums were not recoverable by insurance—no recovery allowed for pure economic loss. (Appeal 48 B.L.R. 108 on various points but not against principal findings.)

61. Stormont Main Working Men's Club & Institute Ltd v. J. Roscoe Milne Partnership (1988) 13 Con. L.R. 127; [1990] C.L.Y. 393, Judge Bowsher Q.C.

Architects conceded it was a term of engagement by the plaintiffs that they would exercise all due professional skill and care and that they owed a duty of care in acting as their architects—*Held*, not liable for not designing alterations so that pillars were removed so as to facilitate the playing of competition snooker—the plaintiffs did not intend to create such facilities at the time of instruction and the architects were not to be criticised for interpreting instructions as limited to obtaining planning permission for an extension catering for whatever improvements to games facilities were practicable.

62. Michael Salliss & Company Ltd v. E.C.A. Calil (1988) 4 Const. L.J. 125; [1988] C.L.Y. 2420, Judge Fox-Andrews Q.C.

Contractor claimed architects owed it a duty of care to use all proper professional skill and care in the preparation of specifications and drawings, in authorising extensions to the contract period and in ensuring the work would be carried out continuously—further, to certify any extension with reasonable expedition—*Held*, no duty owed in respect of preparation of plans and specifications or as to whether or not a survey should be carried out or a variation be ordered—but the architects did owe a duty to act impartially in respect of such matters as certificates and extensions of time and in so far as damage could be established as having been caused by their unfairness in respect of matters about which, under the contract, they were required to act impartially, damages were recoverable and were not too remote.

63. D. & F. Estates Ltd v. Church Commissioners for England [1989] A.C. 177; [1988] 2 All E.R. 992, H.L.

The plaintiff was tenant of a flat in a block built some time previously by the defendant main contractor—his sub-contractor had carried out defective plasterwork in the flat as a result of which it became loose and partly fell down. The plaintiff's claim for the cost of replastering failed as being a claim for pure economic loss—there was no room for the application of the *Donoghue v. Stevenson* principle where a hidden defect in a permanent structure was discovered before any injury to the person or damage to property other than the structure had occurred (*Dutton* (**10**) and *Anns* **13** considered; *Batty* **18** doubted).

64. University Court of the University of Glasgow v. William Whitfield (1989) 42 B.L.R. 66; [1989] C.L.Y. 2539, Judge Bowsher Q.C.

University sued architect for negligent advice and design of art gallery whereby leaks and condensation occurred—*Held*, architect under a duty in contract and tort to exercise all due and proper professional care and skill and he was in breach thereof. (Limitation point resolved in university's favour.)—*Held*, further, architect was not entitled to contribution from the main contractor as (a) main contractor did not owe to the university a duty in tort to warn it of defects in the architect's design and (b) main contractor did not owe the architect a duty of care to warn him of his defective design, the loss claimed being pure economic loss, namely, the architect's liability to the university.

65. Gray v. T.P. Bennett & Son (1990) 43 B.L.R. 63; [1990] C.L.Y. 393, Judge Sir William Stabb Q.C.

Builder deliberately concealed the fact that he had hacked off concrete nibs on reinforced concrete panels which nibs were to provide support for brick facing panels—this was done to accommodate misalignment of concrete panels with brick work—*Held*, architects, engineers and clerk of works not negligent in not checking alignment—in any event such failure was not causative of loss by reason of the deliberate wrongdoing of the builders and it was not foreseeable that he would act thus—*Held*, builder liable in contract and tort.

66. Pacific Associates Inc. v. Baxter [1990] 1 Q.B. 993; [1989] 2 All E.R. 154, C.A.

Consulting engineers were appointed by employer to supervise works to be performed by contractors pursuant to contract made with employer. Contractor claimed engineers' negligent failure to certify delay and expense to which it was entitled under the contract had caused loss and damage—the contractor had previously settled a claim for loss and expense against the employer. Statement of claim struck out because:

(a) Given the contractual framework, in particular provisions enabling the contractor to recover loss and expense against the employer, there was no express or implied voluntary assumption of a duty of care with consequential liability for precuniary loss by the engineers in favour of the contractor—in those circumstances there was no reliance by the contractor on any such assumption by the engineers: *Hedley Byrne* distinguished.
(b) In any event, no duty of care should be imposed on the enginees towards the contractor.
(c) In any event, a clause in the contract exempting the engineers from liability prevented the imposition of any such liability on the engineers in favour of the contractor: *Sallis* **62** and *Shui On* **38** referred to.

67. Leon Engineering & Construction Co. Ltd v. Ka Duk Investments Co. Ltd (1990) 47 B.L.R. 139; [1990] C.L.Y. 236, Hong Kong High Court, Bokhary J.

Main contractors sought to join architects in action on the ground that they owed to them and were in breach of a duty of care to give proper, timely and impartial consideration to their claims and to issue all certificates in strict accordance with the terms of the contract—*Held*, following *Pacific Associates* **66**, no such duty owed.

68. Cosgrove & Cosgrove v. Weeks (1989) 14 Con. L.R. 119; [1990] C.L.Y. 3795, Judge Newey Q.C.

Dwelling-house owners alleged against developers and builders of the estate in which their house lay that other houses had been negligently built with inadequate foundations—as a result their house had been "blighted". They also made a claim in breach of contract in respect of their own house—*Held*, claim would not be struck out as disclosing no reasonable cause of action.

69. Norwich C.C. v. Harvey (1989) 1 W.L.R. 828; [1989] 1 All E.R. 1180, C.A.

Owner of swimming pool complex contracted with builder for extension—owner accepted risk of fire—roofing sub-contractor's employee negligently caused fire—*Held*, any duty of care otherwise owed to the owner by the builder did not arise in the contractual circumstances.

70. Richard Roberts Holdings Ltd v. Douglas Smith Stimson Partnership (1990) 46 B.L.R. 50; [1990] C.L.Y. 392, Judge Newey Q.C.

Plaintiffs claimed against architects in breach of contract and negligence for recommending and permitting an unsuitable lining for an effluent tank—no fee was charged for this part of the architects' services and they were in fact ignorant in the field of linings—*Held*, liable in contract and tort, it being part of their remit to find out about the quality of lining required from others if they did not know themselves. Contractors also held liable in contract and tort for poor design and workmanship.

71. Kijowski v. New Capital Properties Ltd (1990) 15 Con. L.R. 1; [1990] C.L.Y. 398, Judge Esyr Lewis Q.C.

Held, *inter alia*, that differential settlement in house was due to the builders's negligent failure to take reasonable care in and about the construction of the house and as such gave rise to a danger to the safety or health of the occupant—the plaintiff was not contributorily negligent in not having a survey carried out of the house when he purchased it.

72. Frost v. Moody Homes Ltd; Hoskisson v. Donald Moody Ltd (1990) 6 Const. L.J. 43; [1990] C.L.Y. 3253, Judge Newey Q.C.

Plaintiffs purchased house or estate developed by first and second defendants who employed engineer to design and advise about foundations, in particular the presence and removal of an apple tree—cracks subsequently appeared in house—*Held*, (a) engineer not negligent and assuming (without deciding) he owed a duty to the plaintiffs in negligence he was not in breach of it, nor was he in breach of duty to or contract with the first and second defendants, (b) first and second defendants were in breach of contract for failing to make first-floor joints sufficiently strong and to connect drainage correctly and also negligent—they were not liable for design of foundations by the engineer, a competent independent contractor, and (c) the structural engineer acting on behalf of the plaintiffs and their insurer was negligent in assessing that expensive foundation works were necessary and that broke the chain of causation of damage. (*D. & F. Estates* **63** considered). (Accrual and limitation of cause of action also considered.)

73. Department of the Environment v. Thomas Bates & Son, Ltd [1991] 1 A.C. 499; [1990] 2 All E.R. 943, H.L.

Builders pursuant to contract with lessees constructed a building complex part of which was sublet to the plaintiffs. Subsequently roof leaked due to defective workmanship—concrete pillars were also found to be sub-standard and prevented the full designed use of the building. The plaintiffs claimed builders owed them a duty to use reasonable skill and care in building the complex. At first instance builders were found liable for the defective roof but not liable for the strengthening off the pillars, there being no imminent danger to health or safety, the cost of such remedial works being pure economic loss—the decision concerning the latter claim was confirmed on appeal. (*Murphy v. Brentwood D.C.* (Chap. 18, (13) **66**) applied.)

74. Portsea Island Mutual Co-operative Society Ltd v. Michael Brashier Associates (1990) 6 Const. L.J. 63; [1990] C.L.Y. 3292, Judge Newey Q.C.

Architect designed supermarket premises for developer who had agreed to lease them to the plaintiffs. Sometime after completion brick slips forming part of the exterior began to fall—before any injury or damage occurred, the plaintiffs removed the unsafe slips and carried out remedial work—defects in car park wall which posed no risk of injury or damage were also put right—*Held,* architect was in breach of duty of care owed to plaintiffs in respect of the brick slips but in the light of Lord Brandon in *Junior Books* **26** and of *D. & F. Estates* **63** the condition of the slips rendering them liable to fall could not be relied upon as recoverable damage. However, it did not seem fair that the plaintiffs should be treated as not having suffered damage because they removed the dangerous slips at some expense to themselves but would have suffered damage had they left them to fall on an employee or lower part of the building and therefore they could recover as economic loss the cost of removing brick slips and other work necessary to render the wall safe (relying on *Junior Books* (Lord Brandon) and *D.O.E. v. Thomas Bates* **73**) but not the cost of recladding the wall—*Held,* further, no duty of care owed in respect of the car park wall.

75. Anderson v. Benson [1991] E.G.C.S. 75; [1992] C.L.Y. 3196, C.A.

Architect engaged to design and supervise construction of extension to ground-floor flat—extension higher than planned to avoid tree roots—thus partially obscured window of first-floor flat—*Held,* architect was in breach of his duty to tell ground-floor flat owner that roof would be higher than planned and that others might have rights to enforce—the cost of compromise with the first-floor flat owner was a foreseeable and recoverable loss.

76. Pfeiffer v. E. & F. Installations [1991] 1 E.G.L.R. 162, C.A.

Heating engineer instructed to inspect heating plant at house plaintiff proposed to buy—failure to discover cracks in heat exchanger—*Held,* whether the case was put in contract or tort the duty was to test and inspect and report with the reasonable skill and care to be expected of a competent heating engineer—*Held,* liable.

77. Warner v. Basildon Development Corporation (1991) 7. Const. L.J. 146; [1992] C.L.Y. 3197, C.A.

Subsequent purchasers of a dwelling-house sued the builder—*Held,* builder was negligent and in breach of duties imposed by the Building Regulations as regards the foundations—as a result, the house suffered from defects which rendered it less valuable but which did not pose any risk of personal injury or damage to property other than the house—*Held,* on basis of *D. & F. Estates* **63**, builder not liable.

78. Alcock v. Wraith (1992) 59 B.L.R. 16; [1992] C.L.Y. 3264, C.A.

Owners of terrace house employ independent contractor to re-roof using tiles instead of slates—difficulty in effecting and failure to effect waterproof join with neighbour's roof—*Held*, owners under non-delegable duty to ensure the roofing work was done with proper care.

79. Lancashire s Cheshire Association of Baptist Churches Inc. v. Howard & Seddon Partnership (1993) 65 B.L.R. 21; [1993] C.L.Y. 2980, Judge Kershaw Q.C.

Plaintiff's claim against architect in contract and tort for negligent design—contract claim statute-barred—*Held*, (a) in law there could be a duty of care actionable in the tort of negligence where the parties were in a contractual professional relationship but not in all such cases, and (b) on the evidence, the submission of drawings did not equate to a statement (express or implied) as to the technical qualities of the building, nor did the plaintiffs rely on them as such, any reliance being upon the earlier implied term that the architect would prepare technically sound designs—*Hedley Byrne* therefore did not apply and there could be no recovery for the economic loss. *Midland Bank v. Hett Stubbs (Chap. 18, (15)* **22**) followed: *Tai Hing* (Chap. 18, (2) **23**) and *Junior Books* **26** considered.

80. Lindenberg v. Canning (1994) 62 B.L.R. 147; [1994] C.L.Y. 321, Judge Newey Q.C.

Builder demolished walls shown as non-load-bearing on plan—*Held*, breach of implied term to exercise care as should have realised the possibility of damage and sought clarification from plaintiff's surveyor or put up temporary props—*Held*, further, not in breach of duty in negligence on *Hedley Byrne* principles nor liable on *Donoghue v. Stevenson* principles as no injury to person or property—damages reduced by 75 per cent. by reason of surveyor's wrongly showing walls as non-load-bearing.

81. Barclays Bank PLC v. Fairclough Building Ltd, (1995) P.I.Q.R. P152; (1995) 5 C.L. 253, C.A.

Contract to carry out maintenance work as building; sub-contractor undertakes to do part of the work including cleaning of asbestos roofs—cleaning of roofs sub-sub contracted—*Held*, sub-subcontractor was in breach of contract in failing to take precautions which a careful and competent contractor would have taken whereby the sub-contractor had suffered economic loss, namely damages payable to the main contractor—*Held*, further, applying *Henderson v. Merrett Syndicates* (Chap. 18(4) **21**) the sub-subcontractor, as a skilled contractor undertaking maintenance work, assumed responsibility to the sub-contractor no less than did a financial or other professional adviser undertaking work and as such owed a concurrent duty in tort to avoid causing economic loss by failing to exercise the care and skill of a competent contractor—*Held*, further, in such circumstances it was permissible to reduce (by half) the damages suffered by the sub-contractor under the Law Reform (Contributory Negligence) Act 1945 on the ground that the damage was suffered partly as a result of the sub-contractor's own fault in that it also failed, as it ought, to have appreciated the risk of contamination from asbestos dust.

82. Cardy & Son v. Taylor [1994] 38 Con.L.R. 79; [1994] C.L.Y. 324, Judge Bowsher Q.C.

Employer counterclaimed damages for, *inter alia*, defective design against contractor who joined unqualified architect, who had designed alterations to premises, as third party—*Held*, duty of care owed by an architect was the same whether he was qualified or not—contractor not guilty of contributory negligence in failing to check the architect's survey or in failing to conduct his own survey.

U1. Haston v. G. & M.W.V. (1981) C.A. 513

Architect designed drink shelf at height of 4 feet around pillar in bar. Plaintiff stood up from chair by pillar and violently banged head on shelf—*Held*, that the architect was not liable as the risk of accident, though foreseeable, was remote: "Foreseeability of risk of danger is not in itself the test of professional negligence; the nature of the risk, the gravity of the danger, if any, must be considered before concluding that there has been a breach of professional duty in the light of the standards of the profession." (Ormrod L.J., 8–9).

U2. Gravenall v. H. V. Jones & Co. Ltd (1985) C.A. 100

Installer of oil-fired burner negligent in failing to tighten joints on either side of fire valve properly as a result of which oil leaked—*Held*, maintenance contractor in breach of contract as well.

U3. Eckersley v. Binnie & Partners (1988) C.A. 137

Massive explosion in underground chamber of waterworks system due to presence of methane, causing loss of life—*Held*, consulting engineers should have foreseen the possibility of accumulation of methane and were liable—*Held*, contractors and operators not liable.

U4. Easter v. The Richies & Blythin Partnership (1991) C.A. 206

Architects retained to design house and obtain planning permission but not to supervise construction. House not built in accordance with approved drawings and had to be rebuilt—*Held*, architects not in breach of contract or negligent in failing to provide sufficiently accurate or detailed drawings.

(7) Company Directors

1. The Thomas Saunders Partnership v. Harvey [1990] Trading Law Reports 78; [1990] C.L.Y. 4312, Thayne Forbes Q.C.

Plaintiff architects asked defendant director of proposed sub-contractors whether floor supplied by them met certain criteria and were assured by him that it did—it did not—*Held*, director liable in deceit and also owed a duty of care as he had special skill and knowledge in the relevant field and had assumed personal responsibility for the accuracy of his statement—*Hedley Byrne* applied—*Held*, liable to make contribution under Civil Liability (Contribution) Act 1978.

2. Al-Nakib Investments (Jersey) Ltd v. Longcroft [1990] 1 W.L.R. 1390; [1990] 3 All E.R. 321, Mervyn Davies J.

A parent company formed a subsidiary to exploit information storage and retrieval system and offered shares in both companies to existing shareholders by means of a prospectus—the plaintiffs subscribed. In addition, in reliance on prospectus and/or subsequent interim reports they bought further shares in the market in subsidiary. Their claim against the directors of both companies for negligent misstatement in the prospectus and reports was struck out in so far as it related to shares bought in the market as the purposes for which prospectus and reports were respectively made were to enable shareholders to decide whether or not to subscribe and to inform them of the activities of the subsidiary and therefore no duty of care owed beyond that. *Caparo* (Chap. 18, (1) **17**) applied.

3. Morgan Crucible Co. PLC v. Hill Samuel & Co. Ltd [1991] Ch. 295; [1991] 3 All E.R. 148, C.A.

In response to chairman of public limited company issuing a profit forecast supported by its accountants and bankers, plaintiffs increased bid for the company and were successful. Plaintiffs subsequently claimed that, in making such statements, the directors, accountants and bankers severally owed them a duty of care—*Held*, claim would not be struck out—it was arguable there was sufficient proximity as to give rise to a duty of care. *Caparo* (Chap. 19, (1) **17**) distinguished.

(8) Dentists

1. Fish v. Kapur [1948] 2 All E.R. 176; 64 T.L.R. 328, Lynskey J.

Held, not *res ipsa loquitur*, and plaintiff offering no evidence of negligence, action failed.

2. Garner v. Morrell [1953] C.L.Y. 2538; *The Times*, October 31, C.A.

Held, that accident called for an explanation from defendant, and since it had been found throat pack was too short, defendant's explanation broke down, and plaintiff was entitled to succeed.

3. Tanswell v. Nelson [1959] C.L.Y. 2254; *The Times*, February 11, McNair J.

Face swelling after extraction of teeth—defendant dentist consulted doctor who diagnosed an abscess—in fact it was osteomyelitis—*Held* dentist not liable, as he was entitled to rely on opinion of doctor.

4. O'Neill v. Kelly [1961] C.L.Y. 5977; *The Times*, December 15, Davies L.J.

Held, dentist not negligent.

5. Lock v. Scantlebury [1963] C.L.Y. 2415; *The Times*, July 25, Paull J.

Dislocation of jaw during extraction—not discovered then or in subsequent visits for six months—*Held*, dentist negligent.

6. Heath v. Berkshire H.A. [1992] 3 med L.R. 57; 8 B.M.C.R. 57, Mantell J.

See Chap. 18(11) **47**.

U1. Young v. Partridge (1956) C.A. 240

Scaling teeth—electric brush slipped and cut plaintiff's tongue—plaintiff sitting in proper position—head and tongue motionless—*Held*, defendant negligent. Not case of *res ipsa loquitur* but burden on plaintiff—plaintiff showed negligence by proving that undergoing straightforward operation, no risk, given modicum of skill, injured though did not move. Reference made to *Fish* v. *Kapur* **1**, which was distinguished as there is always possibility of fracture of jaw resulting from extraction of tooth—and unreported case of *Potter* v. *Buxton* (December 6, 1948) where fragment of tooth allowed to go down throat during extraction, under anaesthetic, and it was held that this did not establish negligence.

U2. Fletcher v. Bench (1973) C.A. 313

Wisdom tooth extraction—fracture of jaw—and burr of drill broken and left in bone—but no X-rays taken until eleven days later—*Held*, circumstances were so strong that the onus had passed to the defendant to prove he had used due care, which he had failed to do, and was liable.

(9) Hairdressers

1. Dobbin v. Waldorf [1937] 1 All E.R. 331, Mr. Commissioner Procter

Plaintiff had bleached hair and because of this defendant's permanent wave was liable to damage her hair—*Held*, defendant liable for not warning plaintiff and for not carrying out a test.

2. Parker v. Oloxo [1937] 3 All E.R. 524, Hilbery J.

Held, hairdresser liable for hair dye which was irritant to anyone who was susceptible—*Held*, manufacturer also liable.

3. Watson v. Buckley [1940] 1 All E.R. 174, Stable J.

Hair dye contained 10 per cent. instead of 4 per cent. chromic acid—causes dermatitis—*Held*, hairdresser liable in contract and distributor liable in tort. The hairdresser would probably not have been liable in tort, as the distributor had advertised the substance as safe and thus precluded the likelihood of intermediate examination. The distributor was liable because he was not dealing with an established manufacturer of repute, but with an agent who had "emerged from Spain", and he therefore ought to have exercised care to see that the product was safe.

(10) Innkeepers and the Like

1. Bonham-Carter v. Hyde Park Hotel (1948) 64 T.L.R. 177; [1948] W.N. 89, L.C.J.

Defendant, a common inn, gave plaintiff a room which had what was "in substance" a communicating door with another room—protected only by a turnbuckle which was easy to force—and which was forced by a thief—plaintiff had asked for door to be locked, but it was not—defendants had exhibited statutory notice, so were only liable for negligence—*Held,* turnbuckle was so inadequate as to be negligence.

2. Olley v. Marlborough Court [1949] 1 K.B. 532; [1949] 1 All E.R. 127, C.A.

Bucknill L.J. at 543 bottom (on question of whether common inn): "A house used as a private hotel, that is to say, for the reception of persons who desire to go and live there, appears not to be an inn" (citing *Halsbury* (2nd ed.), Vol. 18, p. 138). Plaintiff, a guest, hung her bedroom key on hook in reception office—later stolen and thief gets into plaintiff's bedroom—*Held,* defendants were liable for negligence unless they showed they had taken reasonable care to guard key, which on the evidence they had not done—*Held,* further, that defendants could not rely on exempting notice displayed in plaintiff's bedroom, because the contract had been made before plaintiff could see the notice.

3. Gee Walker v. Friary Hotel [1950] 1 T.L.R. 59; [1950] W.N. 6, C.A.

Car stolen from park while guest who intended to stay night having dinner—*Held*, innkeeper liable unless he could show loss due to negligence of guest, which on the facts he failed to do.

4. Williams v. Linnitt [1951] 1 K.B. 565; [1951] 1 All E.R. 278, C.A.

Common inn—plaintiff goes there for evening drink—parks car in car park—notice in car park exempting defendant from liability—car stolen—*Held*, (a) plaintiff was a "traveller" and hence entitled to protection given by common law to guest at common inn, (b) the exempting notice had no effect, since the Innkeepers Act did not apply to carriages, which included cars, and (3) the car park was *infra hospitium*: therefore defendant liable.

5. Watson v. People's Refreshment House Association [1952] 1 K.B. 318; [1952] 1 All E.R. 289, Devlin J.

Held, that runway of petrol station, being across road and not usually used as a car park, was not *infra hospitium*, and that innkeeper in giving permission to park had not thereby extended the *hospitium*.

6. Bell v. Travco Hotels [1953] 1 Q.B. 473, [1953] 1 All E.R. 638, C.A.

Held, defendants not liable: "The mere fact that plaintiff slipped on some stones which had become polished owing to ordinary wear in this drive is no justification for holding that this was a dangerous place" (Lord Goddard C.J. at 639 H).

7. Seccombe v. Clarke Baker (1953) 103 L.J. 624; [1953] C.L.Y. 1783, Judge Thomas.

Held, following *Winkworth v. Raven* [1931] 1 K.B. 652, defendant not liable in the absence of negligence.

8. Gates v. Dorchester Hotel, *The Times*, March 7, 1953; [1953] C.L.Y. 1789, McNair J.

Held, defendants a common inn.

9. Gresham v. Lyon [1954] 1 W.L.R. 1100, [1954] 2 All E.R. 786, McNair J.

Theft of luggage from locked boot of car parked for night in garage yard of common inn—*Held*, defendant not liable because (a) applying dicta from **4** and **5** there was no implied invitation (as distinct from permission) by defendant to leave luggage (as distinct from car itself) in garage yard, which was 300 yards from hotel, and (b) plaintiff's own act in leaving luggage in car constituted a failure to take reasonable care, to which the loss was due.

10. Williams v. Owen [1955] 1 W.L.R. 1293; [1956] 1 All E.R. 104, Finnemore J.

Fire in hotel garage destroying plaintiff's car—*Held*, no absolute liability as this only extended to loss or theft of goods, not to damage to them, and in any event the 1776 Act would have curtailed absolute liability, and since there was no negligence claim failed.

11. Edwards v. West Herts Group Management Committee [1957] 1 W.L.R. 415; [1957] 1 All E.R. 541, C.A.

See Chap. 15, (1) (b) **6**—duty of boarding-house keepers to safeguard property of guests *discussed obiter*.

12. Samuel v. Westminster Wine Co., *The Times*, May 16, 1959; [1959] C.L.Y. 173, Thesiger J.

Plaintiff arriving late for dinner at hotel left her mink coat in an anteroom where there were other women's coats and which previously had been used as a supervised cloakroom—no attendant present—coat stolen—*Held*, defendants liable for negligence as bailees for reward.

13. Adams v. Trust Houses [1960] 1 Lloyd's Rep. 380, Mr. Comr. Fenton Atkinson

Hotel resident left his car for the night in hotel garage—garage in charge of night porter—during the night car was taken out by porter and wrecked—porter had in fact had five previous convictions and had been to prison—before engaging him hotel proprietor had spoken on the telephone to a member of the staff at a hotel where the porter had previously been employed for a few months—received a reply to the effect that there appeared no reason to doubt his honesty—*Held, obiter*, that having regard to the opportunities for dishonesty available to an untrustworthy night porter the lack of precautions taken in engaging the night porter in question amounted to negligence on the part of the proprietor.

14. Cooper v. Dempsey (1961) 105 S.J. 320; [1961] C.L.Y. 482, C.A.

Plaintiff took car to defendant garage for repairs—defendant left car in his car park with ignition key in switch and doors unlocked and without supervision—car stolen and damaged in crash—*Held*, defendant liable.

15. Houghland v. R. R. Low [1962] 1 Q.B. 694; [1962] 2 All E.R. 159, C.A.

Motor coach trip—suitcase of plaintiff put in boot—lost—*Held*, the failure of defendants to return the suitcase established a prima facie case in negligence, and as this had not been rebutted, defendants were liable.

16. British Road Services v. Arthur V. Crutchley [1968] 1 All E.R. 811, C.A.

17. Presvale v. Sutch and Searle [1967] 1 Lloyd's Rep. 131, Roskill J.

18. Council of City of Sydney v. West (1967) 114 C.L.R. 481; [1967] C.L.Y. 172, High Ct. Aust.

Owner parked car and received ticket exempting liability in wide terms, and providing that ticket had to be presented to obtain delivery of car—an unauthorised person took the car by presenting a bogus ticket—*Held*, defendants were liable, because the act of the attendant in permitting the thief to take the car was an unauthorised delivery by him, and not mere negligence in relation to some matter authorised by the contract, and secondly because the defendants had undertaken to deliver the vehicle only on presentation of the proper ticket, and had released it without such presentation.

19. Kott v. Gordon Hotels [1968] 2 Lloyd's Rep. 228, Fenton Atkinson J.

20. Carroll v. Garford, *The Times*, November 22, 1968; [1968] C.L.Y. 2649, Paull J.

21. Transmotors v. Robertson [1970] 2 Lloyd's Rep. 224, Mocatta J.

Theft of load in transit—driver claimed he had been attacked and load hijacked—*Held*, carriers as bailees had to prove on a balance of probabilities that they had used all reasonable care, which involved proving that the load had not been stolen by the driver, and as they had not discharged this burden, they were liable.

22. McGeough v. Don Enterprises [1984] 1 W.W.R. 256; [1984] C.L.Y. 2299, Canada, Saskatchewan Q.B.

Visitor to cocktail bar had previously been evicted by bartender for being a nuisance. He returned and after being told to leave appeared to do so but instead stabbed customer in lounge—*Held*, operator of hotel lounge not liable.

23. Munro v. Porthkerry Park Holidays Estates, *The Times*, March 9, 1984; [1984] C.L.Y. 2305, Beldam J.

The scope of a licensee's duty of care extended to a duty to guard against danger arising from a customer's inability to take care of himself because of excessive consumption of alcohol—*Held*, licensee not liable for death of customer who deliberately climbed over fence and fell down cliff—there was no evidence he was so inebriated that he was incapable of taking care of himself or that licensee should have appreciated such was the case.

24. Chordas v. Bryant (Wellington) (1988) 91 A.L.R. 149; [1990] C.L.Y. 3275, Fed. Ct. of Australia

Customer at hotel bar struck and injured by another—*Held*, hotel not liable—the other customer's intoxication not such as to lead reasonably prudent manager to remove him.

25. Reilly v. Ryan [1991] 2 I.R. 247; [1992] C.L.Y. 3263

U1. Hughes v. Laing (1960) C.A. 190

Held, defendant liable.

U2. Gallagher v. Jones (1985) C.A. 251

Plaintiff chucked out of public house by landlord—*Held*, landlord had used no more force than necessary and not liable for resultant injury.

U3. Brocken v. Allied Breweries Ltd (1987) C.A. 1252

Plaintiff walked through passageway to leave public house and stepped on a glass and was injured—*Held*, no liability as safe system of operating service of drinks and collection of glasses which had not been departed from.

(11) Medical

The law relating to medical negligence has expanded substantially since the first cases where included, and the cases set out are for the most part concerned with general principles such as causation, standard of care, informed consent, status, etc. Cases which are decided on their own facts have been included in the examples section.

Standard of care due_acting in accordance with general and approved practice 1

Diathermy treatment—inadequate warning to patient of danger of too much heat 2
PROOF OF NEGLIGENCE—PLAINTIFF NEED NOT PROVE PARTICULAR DOCTOR OR NURSE NEGLIGENT 3
Intoxicated patient—need to examine closely 4
INEXPERIENCED ANAESTHETIST 5

1. Whiteford v. Hunter (1950) 94 S.J. 758; [1950] W.N. 553, H.L.

Plaintiff claimed damages resulting from erroneous diagnosis of defendant that he had cancer of the bladder—the argument revolved mainly round whether defendant should have used one or other of two special cystoscopes, neither of which he had and both of which at the time were difficult to obtain—*Held*, in the circumstances he was not negligent, approving the dictum of Maugham L.J. in *Marshall v. Lindsey C.C.* [1935] 1 K.B. 516 at 540 that "a defendant charged with negligence can clear himself if he shows that he acted in accordance with general and approved practice".

2. Clarke v. Adams (1950) 94 S.J. 599; [1950] C.L.C. 6673, Slade J.

Patient receiving diathermy treatment not warned adequately of danger if apparatus gives out too much heat, and of need to call out if this happens—*Held*, defendant negligent.

3. Cassidy v. Ministry of Health [1951] 2 K.B. 343; [1951] 1 All E.R. 574, C.A.

Operation on fingers—rigid splint for 14 days—hand found to be useless owing to too tight and too prolonged bandaging—*Held*, that this raised a prima facie case of negligence against defendants, which defendants had not displaced by evidence, and that it was not necessary for plaintiff to prove that a particular doctor or nurse was negligent, as all the people by whom he was treated were servants of defendants.

4. Wood v. Thurston [1951] C.L.C. 6871; *The Times*, May 25, 1951, Pritchard J.

Drunk man brought to hospital with history of having been under a moving lorry—he had 18 broken ribs, broken collar bone and badly congested lung from which he died next day—house surgeon pleaded he did not examine more closely in view of deceased's dulled reaction to pain and inability to give any account of what had happened—*Held*, defendant should have been even more careful, and if he had used stethoscope he would almost certainly have found deceased's true condition.

5. Jones v. Manchester Corporation [1952] 2 Q.B. 852; [1952] 2 All E.R. 125, C.A.

Death of patient caused by inexperience of anaesthetist—*Held*, hospital liable not only for her negligence but also for entrusting dangerous operation to her.

6. Daniels v. Heskin (1953) 87 I.L.T. 189; [1954] C.L.Y. 2288, Supreme Court of Eire.

Defendant when stitching plaintiff broke a piece of needle which remained in her—he decided not to operate at once but to wait two months—warned maternity nurse to keep eye on her and inform him if she suffered any pain—*Held*, defendant was under no absolute duty to warn plaintiff about needle or about the course he intended to pursue.

7. Roe v. Ministry of Health [1954] 2 Q.B. 66; [1954] 2 All E.R. 131, C.A.

Local anaesthetic by injection in hospital—ampoule is bathed in phenol to sterilise—it contains undetectable cracks caused by some mishandling in hospital—phenol gets into ampoule, and when injected causes paralysis—anaesthetist and nurses sued—*Held*, not liable, because at the material time the risk of undetectable cracks was not medically appreciated, so that therefore the anaesthetist was not liable, nor were the nurses liable for mishandling, for they had no reason to foresee invisible cracks as a consequence of mishandling. On the general topic of medical negligence Denning L.J. said (139 D): "We should be doing a disservice to the community at large if we were to impose liability for everything that happens to go wrong . . . We must insist on due care for the patient at every point, but we must not condemn as negligence that which is only a misadventure." Cited in **9** by judge in addressing jury.

8. Hatcher v. Black, *The Times*, July 2, 1954; [1954] C.L.Y. 2289, Denning L.J. and jury.

Plaintiff, a singer, operated on by defendant, for thyroidectomy—after operation her left vocal chord is paralysed—plaintiff alleged that before operation her doctor, defendant, had advised her the operation involved no risk—Denning L.J. *told* jury they must not find surgeon guilty merely because one of the risks inherent in an operation took place; with regard to the doctor jury must decide whether doctor told her no risk or merely prevaricated to stop her worrying—*verdict* for both defendants.

9. Bolam v. Friern Hospital Management Committee [1957] 1 W.L.R. 582; [1957] 2 All E.R. 118, McNair J. and jury.

Plaintiff sustained fractures while having electro-convulsive treatment to which he had consented—alleged defendants negligent in not warning of risk, not using relaxant drugs or manual control—*Verdict*, not guilty. Judge said, as to warning, plaintiff must show he would have refused treatment if warned; and as to other allegations defendants not negligent if they acted in accordance with practice accepted as proper by a responsible body of medical men skilled in that particular art, merely because there is another body taking opposite view. **7** cited.

10. Crivon v. Barnet Hospital Management Committee, *The Times*, November 19, 1958; [1958] C.L.Y. 2283, C.A.

One pathologist diagnosed carcinoma, but the head of the department took a different view—*Held*, first pathologist not negligent merely because another pathologist took a different view.

11. Newton v. Newtons Model Laundry *The Times*, November 3, 1959; [1959] C.L.Y. 2256; Salmon J.

Plaintiff was taken to hospital after falling 12 feet onto concrete—he was examined and sent home—in fact he had fractures of (a) patella, (b) nose and (c) wrist—*Held*, doctor was negligent in not diagnosing (a)—but not in not diagnosing (b) and (c).

12. Junor v. McNicol, *The Times*, March 26, 1959; [1959] C.L.Y. 2255, H.L.

House surgeon sued for failing to give sufficient penicillin—consultant in charge of case, under whose directions defendant acted, had ordered some—but defendant had not heard this order—defendant, on own initiative, gave some—but in insufficient quantity—*Held*, not liable, for house surgeon's duty was to carry out consultant's directions unless manifestly wrong, and all defendant had done was to show some initiative and care over and above instructions.

13. Corder v. Banks, *The Times*, April 9, 1960; [1960] C.L.Y. 2185, McNair J.

Held, defendant liable.

14. Chapman v. Rix, *The Times*, December 22, 1960; [1960] C.L.Y. 2186, H.L.

Butcher wounded abdomen boning meat with knife—saw defendant doctor at hospital who told him that it was a surface wound and he should see his own doctor in the evening—in fact peritoneum was ruptured and butcher later died—*Held*, (3–2) that the failure of defendant to communicate directly with plaintiff's doctor was not negligence: but *aliter semble*, if defendant had not told plaintiff himself to see own doctor.

15. Coles v. Reading Hospital Management Committee, *The Times*, January 31, 1963; [1963] C.L.Y. 2356, Sachs J.

Deceased died of tetanus after a crush injury to finger—finger at time covered in dust and dirt—deceased went to cottage hospital, where wound was cleansed, and he was told to go to a proper hospital, where he would have had anti-tetanus injection—but no one impressed on him the reason for or the importance of going—and he did not go—*Held*, cottage hospital authorities were liable. Judge referred to "difficulties of communication" when a patient was transferred under the National Health Service scheme from one hospital to another, and said that the responsibility for ensuring that a proper system of communication existed in such cases rested on whoever was in charge of the hospital—*Held*, also, that a G.P. whom deceased later saw and who failed to give anti-tetanus injection was negligent.

16. Stevens v. Bermondsey Hospital Management Committee, *The Times*, May 16, 1963; [1963] C.L.Y. 2414, Paull J.

Accident—negligent diagnosis by hospital casualty officer—as a result plaintiff unaware of true extent of disability and settled claim against tortfeasor for much less than real value—*Held*, the difference between the settlement figure and the real figure was not recoverable from the casualty officer, since a doctor's duty was limited to the sphere of medicine, and unless he examined with a view to legal liability, such liability was outside the sphere of his duty.

17. Barnett v. Chelsea Hospital Management Committee [1969] 1 Q.B. 428; [1968] 1 All E.R. 1068, Nield J.

Three nightwatchmen drank tea which made them vomit—they went to the casualty department of the local hospital—the casualty officer, on being told of the complaints by a nurse, did not see the men, but told them to go home and call in their own doctors—some hours later one of them died from arsenical poisoning—*Held*, (a) the casualty department officers owed a duty of care in the circumstances; (b) the casualty doctor had been negligent in not seeing them, but (c) even if he had, it was improbable that the only effective antidote could have been administered in time to save the deceased, and therefore the defendants were not liable.

18. Male v. Hopmans (1967) 64 D.L.R. (2d) 105; [1968] C.L.Y. 2714, Ont. C.A.

General consent to treatment—doctor feared serious infection and osteomyelitis, and decided to use drug, without specific consent, with known possible side effects of impairing hearing and kidneys—*Held*, doctor not at fault in this respect, but he was liable for failing to carry out recommended tests before using the drug.

19. Robinson v. Post Office [1974] 1 W.L.R. 1176; [1974] 2 All E.R. 737, C.A.

Issue was whether the way in which a doctor had injected a test dose of serum was *novus actus interveniens* to an accident sustained by plaintiff (see **X**), but the judgment of Orr L.J. contains detailed reference to the risks of, and precautions to be observed with, the injection of anti-tetanus serum generally.

20. Chatterton v. Gerson [1981] Q.B. 432; [1981] 1 All E.R. 257, Bristow J.

Two unsuccessful operations to relieve pain—resulting in numbness of right leg. Plaintiff did not allege negligence in the performance of the operations, but claim was based on failure by the doctor to explain the full implications of the operative treatment, so that (a) there was negligence, in as much as the failure to explain meant that the plaintiffs could not make an informed decision as to having, the operations, and (b) there was trespass, in as much as there was no real consent—*Held*, on the facts, defendant doctor not liable. As to (a), "there is no obligation on the doctor to canvass with the patient anything other than the inherent implications of the particular operation he intends to carry out. He is certainly under no obligation to say that if he operates incompetently he will do damage. The fundamental assumption is that he knows his job and will do it properly. But he ought to warn of what may happen by misfortune however well the operation is done, if there is a real risk of misfortune inherent in the procedure ... In what he says any good doctor has to take into account the personality of the patient, the likelihood of the misfortune, and what in the way of warning is or the particular patient's welfare" (266 F). As to (ii), "once the patient is informed in broad terms of the nature of the procedure which is intended, and gives her consent, that consent is real, and the cause of action on which to base a claim for failure to go into risks and implications is negligence, and not trespass" (265 E). Here, as there was no real risk that the plaintiff would develop the serious complications which she did, the defendant was not negligent in failing to warn her of the risk. Even if she had been warned, she still might have accepted the operation.

21. Whitehouse v. Jordan [1981] 1 W.L.R. 246; [1981] 1 All E.R. 267, H.L.

Baby suffered severe brain damage during trial of forceps delivery. Obstetrician was alleged to have pulled too long and too hard on the forceps. Court of Appeal held that, even if this were so, it amounted only to an error of clinical judgment and as such was not negligence in law—*Held*, the obstetrician had not been negligent. However, an error of judgment by a surgeon would constitute negligence if it resulted from a failure to measure up to the standard of the ordinary skilled surgeon exercising and professing to have the special skill of a surgeon.

22. McKay v. Essex Area.H.A. [1982] 2 Q.B. 1166; [1982] 2 All E.R. 771, C.A.

For details see Chap. 1(2)(a)**14**.

23. Clark v. MacLennan [1983] 1 All E.R. 416; [1983] C.L.Y. 2548, Peter Pain J.

Plaintiff developed severe stress incontinence following childbirth. Operation on bladder was performed one month after birth. Normal practice was not to perform such operation until at least three months after birth in order to the risk of haemorrhage—plaintiff did suffer haemorrhaging during operation. This caused the operation to fail and plaintiff was left with permanent stress incontinence. The question was whether the haemorrhage causally resulted from operating only one month after birth—*Held*, defendants were liable, as the onus of proof had shifted to them and they had failed to discharge it: "It seems to me that it follows from *McGhee* (3–3) that where there is a situation in which a general duty of care arises and there is a failure to take a precaution, and that very damage occurs against which the precaution is designed to be a protection, then the burden lies on the defendant to show that he was not in breach of duty as well as to show that the damage did not result from his breach of duty" (427 G).

24. Maynard v. West Midlands Regional H.A. [1984] 1 W.L.R. 635; *The Times*, May 9, 1983, H.L.

Facts immaterial, save that there was an allegedly wrong diagnosis followed by treatment which was harmful—both sides called respectable medical evidence as to whether the diagnosis and treatment was right or wrong. The judge preferred the plaintiff's medical evidence, and found for the plaintiff—*Held*, this was wrong, and the defendants were not liable: "I have to say that a judge's 'preference' for one body of distinguished professional opinion to another also professionally distinguished is not sufficient to establish negligence in a practitioner whose actions have received the seal of approval of those whose opinions, truthfully expressed, honestly held, were not preferred . . . In the realm of diagnosis and treatment negligence is not established by preferring one respectable body of professional opinion to another. Failure to exercise the ordinary skill of a doctor (in the appropriate speciality, if he be a specialist) is necessary" (Lord Scarman, 639 G–H).

25. Hills v. Potter [1983] 3 All E.R. 716; [1983] C.L.Y. 5276, Hirst J.

Plaintiff underwent "elective" operation designed to cure deformity of neck. Operation performed properly but, due to small inherent risks, plaintiff was left paralysed from the waist down. Defendant gave her general advice as to risks and prospects of operations but he did not go into great detail. Defendant's advice was in accordance with practice of reasonable body of practitioners in field. Plaintiff alleged that the defendant was negligent in failing to explain the full implications of the operation—*Held*, following *Bolam* **9**, *Maynard* **24** and *Chatterton* **20**, that the defendant had not been negligent. He owed the same standard of care in relation to the giving of information as to an operation as in relation to diagnosis and treatment, namely to act in accordance with a practice accepted as proper by a responsible body of skilled practitioners in the same field, and this the defendant had done. Even had she had a fuller explanation of the risks, it is possible that she would have elected to have the operation—*Held*, also that the plaintiff had given a true consent to the operation and that the American doctrine of "informed consent" could only be incorporated in English law as a result of a decision of an appellate court. See now *Sidaway* **29**.

26. Freeman v. Home Office [1984] 1 All E.R. 1036; [1984] C.L.Y. 3570, C.A.

Held, a prisoner in one of HM prisons is not rendered incapable of consenting to medical treatment by virtue of his imprisonment—*obiter*, doctrine of informed consent no part of English law.

27. Harrington v. Essex Area H.A., *The Times*, November 14, 1984; [1984] C.L.Y. 2325, Beldam J.

In a medical negligence action, the plaintiff had not discharged the burden of proof if he could not lead the court to select one of two possible explanations for complications occurring to him after operation.

28. Emeh v. Kensington, Chelsea And Westminster H.A. [1985] Q.B. 1012; [1984] 3 All E.R. 1044, C.A.

Sterilisation operation negligently performed. Child subsequently born deformed. Important case on damages, but question as to whether *novus actus interveniens*—*Held*, plaintiff could recover damages, because the purpose of the sterilisation was the avoidance of another child; compensatable loss suffered by the plaintiff as a result of negligent sterilisation extended to any reasonably foreseeable financial loss caused directly by the unexpected pregnancy. The plaintiff's decision not to have an abortion was not a *novus actus* or failure to mitigate her loss because the Health Authority, by its negligence, had confronted P with a dilemma which she had sought to avoid by having the sterilisation.

29. Sidaway v. Bethlem Royal Hospital Governors [1985] 2 WLR 480; [1985] 1 All E.R. 643, H.L.

The plaintiff underwent a neck operation to cure a pain in her shoulders and neck which had been persistent, on the advice of the defendant's surgeon. In accordance with practice of reasonable body of medical opinion, surgeon did not warn plaintiff of risk of spinal cord damage, which was very slight (less than 1 per cent.) but which risk if materialised would produce injury ranging from the mild to the very severe. Operation performed with reasonable skill and care, but resulting in spinal cord damage for plaintiff and severe disablement—*Held*;

(a) (Lord Scarman dissenting) A doctor's liability for failure to warn the patient of the risks inherent in the operation as part of treatment recommended by him was assessed in accordance with the practice of a responsible body of medical opinion (*i.e* test as in *Bolam* **9**) Although the doctrine of "informed" consent was not part of English law, and decision on risks to be disclosed was largely a matter of clinical judgment, the disclosure of a risk of serious adverse consequence may be so obviously necessary for patient to make informed choice that no reasonably prudent doctor would fail to disclose it.
(b) (per Lord Templeman) Doctor was under a duty to provide a patient with the information necessary for balanced judgment in deciding whether to submit to treatment, but this was subject to the doctor's overriding duty to have regard to the best interests of the patient, which included deciding the terms in which the information should be couched.

30. Thake v. Maurice [1986] Q.B. 644; [1986] 2 W.L.R. 337

Plaintiff husband had a vasectomy operation performed which subsequently failed because of recanalisation of *vas deferens*, allowing plaintiff wife to become pregnant. Both Ps sued alleging breach of contractual guarantee that operation would be successful and breach of duty of care, in failing to warn of small risk of failure—*Held*, dismissing claim for breach of contractual guarantee, the defendant was under a clear duty to give a warning that plaintiff husband faced small risk of becoming fertile again; by failing to advise accordingly, plaintiff wife, not appreciative of pregnancy risk, dismissing possibility when periods missed, and therefore deprived of opportunity to seek abortion at an early stage.

31. Wilsher v. Essex Area H.A. [1988] 2 W.L.R. 557; [1988] 1 All E.R. 871, H.L.

Plaintiff infant was born prematurely and in a poor condition, and treated in special care baby unit at defendant Hospital, suffering from oxygen deficiency. Junior doctor inserted a catheter into a vein rather than an artery—action checked by senior registrar who did not notice mistake and plaintiff received excess dose of oxygen, which was not monitored. As a result, it was alleged that plaintiff developed incurable condition of the retina and near blindness.—*Held*, on appeal to the House of Lords, that notwithstanding any negligence (as found by the Court of Appeal) where the plaintiff's injury was attributable to a number of possible causes, the combination of defendant's breach of duty and P's injury did not give rise to a presumption that defendant had caused the injury. The burden remained on the plaintiff to prove a positive link between such negligence and his injury, although in certain circumstances the link could be inferred from the evidence. However, the plaintiff had failed to discharge the burden of proof to establish the causal link between the retinal condition suffered and the excess oxygen dose, as the condition was attributable to a number of other possible causes. See also Chap. 3, (3).

32. Barr v. Southern Health and Social Services Board [1987] C.L.Y. 2711

Birth injury. Mother was suffering from pre-eclampsia, and claimed midwife not present at birth. P born with umbilical cord around its neck—*Held*, negligence not proved on the facts—P had failed to prove that his injury had been caused by asphyxia in turn consequential on pre-eclampsia of mother.

33. Worster v. City And Hackney H.A., *The Times*, June 22, 1987; [1987] C.L.Y. 2619, Garland J.

Sterilsation operation failed. P had signed a consent form and question arose as to whether this was an assurance of success—*Held*, that form was not an assurance of success in the operation.

34. Hotson v. East Berkshire H.A. [1987] A.C. 750; [1987] 3 W.L.R. 232, H.L.

Delayed dignosis by defendant Health Authority in respect of 13-year-old boy presenting with injured hip (5 days). Subsequently, a severe condition and restrictive disability developed and P claimed negligence on basis that condition was caused by delay in diagnosis—*Held*, by judge of first instance, that plaintiff was 75 per cent. likely to develop the condition, but the delay denied the plaintiff of a 25 per cent. chance of recovery, whereby he was entitled to damage. C.A. upheld judge at first instance on question of causation, but was overturned on appeal to the House of Lords, where it was held that the question of causation, that is, whether it was the fall or the delay in diagnosis that caused the serious condition, was to be determined on a balance of probabilities. Questions concerning loss of a chance could not arise where the damage had already been sustained before the duty fell to be considered. (This case is also important in the context of *causation* generally.)

35. Gold v. Haringey H.A. [1988] Q.B. 481; [1987] 2 All E.R. 888 C.A.

Plaintiff underwent a sterilisation operation on the day after the birth of her third child, which subsequently failed, leading to fourth pregnancy and birth. Plaintiff informed that the operation would be irreversible—but was not warned of the risk of failure, or referred to the possibility of husband's vasectomy—*Held*, hospital not liable. There was no distinction between the duty and standard of care in a therapeutic and non-therapeutic context; the standard of care was that of the ordinary skilled member of the profession, and depended on whether or not there was a substantial body of responsible doctors who would not have given such a warning or advice. In 1979, such a substantial body existed, and accordingly the *Bolam* **9** test was applied.

36. Kay v. Ayshire and Arran Health Board [1987] 2 All E.R. 417 H.L.

Infant plaintiff admitted to hospital suffering from pneumococcal meningitis, and during treatment negligent overdose of penicillin was given. Recovered from meningitis, but found to be suffering from deafness—*Held*, hospital not liable, because it could not be ascertained from two competing causes of damage, the meningitis, or the overdose, which had been responsible. It was necessary first to prove that a tortious cause was capable of causing and likely to have caused the damage before a presumption in favour of the injured plaintiff could be made, in accordance with *McGhee v. N.C.B. (supra).*

37. Sa'd v. Robinson (1989) 4 B.M.L.R. 131, Leggatt J.

Infant plaintiff suffers irreversible brain damage from anoxia after complicated sequence of events instigated by her sucking hot tea from the spout of the pot. Various defendants sued—*Held*, two general practitioners negligent in failing to refer P as soon as condition and first symptoms were reported by parents, because respiratory problems should have been foreseen as a consequence of sucking hot tea, and an immediate referral to hospital should have been made, but paediatrician not negligent at hospital in not summoning an anaesthetist, as this was within the scope of her discretion.

38. Knight v. Home Office [1990] 3 All E.R. 237; [1990] 140 New L.J. 210, Pill J.

Prisoner commits suicide when detained in prison hospital. Had been in remand prison awaiting transfer to mental hospital, and was known to have suicidal tendencies—*Held* standard of care provided for mentally ill prisoner in prison hospital was not as high as that required in a special psychiatric hospital, and prison staff were not negligent in failing to keep deceased under constant observation. 15-minute observations were what ordinary skilled medical staff in their position would have undertaken, (*Wilsher* and *Bolam* applied).

39. Ellis v. Wallsend District Hospital [1990] 2 Med L.R. 103; [1991] C.L.Y. 2667, C.A.

Surgeon failed to warn P of risks of operation (paraplegia), negligently. Question aose as to whether this failure was causative of the subsequent injury—*Held* the court must consider subjectively whether a negligent failure to warn a patient of the risks of treatment was causative of the injury. Here the question to be asked was whether this patient would have undergone the procedure if she had known of the risks.

40. Goorkani v. Tayside Health Board [1991] S.L.T. 94; [1991] C.L.Y. 4879

Drug treatment to prevent eye deterioration; failure to warn that infertility was a possible consequence—*Held*, failure to warn amounted to negligence, but since it had not been proved that any different course of treatment would have been adopted if the patient had been so warned, the damage as a consequence of the failure to warn was restricted to distress and anxiety to patient from discovering possibility of infertility.

41. Rance v. Mid- Downs H.A. [1991] 2 W.L.R. 159, Brooke J.

P's child born suffering from spina bifida which it was alleged, was a condition which should have been detected *in utero* by ultrasound scan—*Held* no cause of action could lie in negligence because procedure which P alleged should have been taken, that is abortion, would have been unlawful under the Infant Life (Preservation) Act 1929, s. 1, as the foetus at 27 weeks was a child capable of being born alive.

42. Bentley v. Bristol & Western H.A. (No. 2) [1991] 3 Med. L.R. 1 [1992] C.L.Y. 3244, Hirst J.

Sciatic nerve paralysed during hip replacement. Probable cause was damage by traction or stretching of the nerve—*Held* D negligent on principle of *res ipsa loquitur.*

43. Thornton v. Nicol [1992] 3 Med. L.R. 41; [1992] C.L.Y. 3236, McPherson J.

Sick child not referred by general practitioner to hospital—*Held,* no negligence, because it could not be said that the child was so ill that any reasonable doctor would have referred her to hospital.

44. Burgess v. Newcastle H.A. [1992] Med. L.R. 224; [1992] C.L.Y. 3240, Turner J.

A surgeon acting in accordance with accepted medical opinion was not negligent in performance of operation.

45. Hughes v. Waltham Forest H.A. [1991] 2 Med. L.R. 155; [1992] C.L.Y. 3247, C.A.

Damages claimed by widow on behalf of deceased husband who died during gallstone operation. Question arose as to whether deceased should have been sent for specialist investigation and should not have been discharged before normality of tests results had been established—*Held,* treatment in accordance with accepted practice by responsible body of medical opinion.

46. Coyne v. Wigan H.A. [1992] 2 Med. L.R. 301; [1992] C.L.Y. 3231, Rose J.

P suffered brain damage through hypoxia—had been extubated and reintubated post-operatively—argued *res ipsa loquitur.* D argued that hypoxia had been caused by silent regurgitation of gastric contents—*Held,* judgment for P. On evidence, silent regurgitation could not have occurred without laryngeal or broncho-spasm being apparent, and failure to notice would have amounted to negligence.

47. Heath v. Berkshire H.A. [1992] 3 Med. L.R. 57; 8 B.M.L.R. 57, Mantell J.

P suffered permanent damage to the lingual nerve during an operation to remove wisdom teeth. D argued that damage was unavoidable risk of operation (unavoidable manipulation of the retractor), and P in turn, that if this was so she should have been warned of the risk before consenting to the operation—*Held,* on balance of probabilities there had been a want of care on the part of the oral surgeon, who had cut into the lingual nerve, but there had been no lack of informed consent.

48. Davis v. Barking H.A. [1993] 4 Med. L.R. 85; [1993] 12 C.L. 490, McCullough J.

P suffers non-negligent injury during operation, but sues for assault on basis that had not consented to form of treatment. *Obiter dicta* remarks that if the information on which the consent to an operation was given was insufficient, liability in negligence could arise.

49. Moore v. Worthing District H.A. [1993] 3 Med. L.R.; [1993] 5 C.L. 304, Owen J.

Plaintiff underwent mastoidectomy and subsequently suffered ulnar nerve lesions—claimed lesions caused by negligence of surgeon and anaesthetist—*Held*, D not liable. Maxim of *res ipsa loquitur* did not apply as medical accident could have occurred without negligence on part of D, and in fact did.

50. Marsden v. Bateman [1993] 4 Med. L.R. 181; [1994] 1 C.L. 262, Rose J.

Baby born with brain damage alleged, to have been caused by hypoglaecemia after birth as a result of D's negligence—*Held*, no negligence in failing to diagnose hypoglaecemia, on the grounds that readings from dextro sticks, video of foetus, and absence of signs of spasticity were contra-indications. Further, there was no evidence of coma, convulsions or apnoea, and on balance it was impossible to say that hypoglaecemia had caused condition.

51. Saunders v. Leeds Western H.A. [1993] 4 Med. L.R. 355; [1994] C.L.Y. 2320

P suffers cardiac arrest whilst under anaesthesia. *Res ipsa loquitur alleged—Held*, a fit heart does not stop under anaesthesia without negligence. *Res ipsa loquitur* applied. P does not need to show the cause of the arrest, as D had offered no explanation which would not involve negligence.

52. Bolitho v. City and Hackney H.A. [1993] P.I.Q.R. P334, [1993] 4 Med. L.R. 381, C.A. [1994] C.L. 286/332

P discharged from hospital care with respiratory difficulties. Clear evidence of failure on part of medical staff at hospital to provided prompt attendance and negligence admitted. The question arose as to whether it would have been reasonable to intubate P in any event—*Held*, that there was no evidence to establish that the reasonably competent doctor would have intubated P.

53. Defreitas v. O'Brien, *The Times*, February 7, 1995, C.A.

A responsible body of medical practitioners, in accordance with Bolam (**9**) principles, need not be substantial, as long as opinions reasonably held.

U1. Patel v. Adyha (1985) C.A. 168

General practitioner failed to detect a tubercular spine condition—*Held*, a proper examination would have revealed the need to obtain specialist advice, and therefore doctor was negligent.

U2. Lobley v. Nunn (1985) C.A. 823

Infant P suffered irreparable brain damage in course of being treated for rare condition—epiglottitis. Condition had deteriorated after receptionist declined to let child "jump the queue" at doctor's surgery—*Held*, doctors in practice not vicariously liable and receptionist not negligent in any event. There had been nothing in the situation which presented to the receptionist to alert her to the need for immediate attention.

U3. Gauntlett v. Northampton H.A. (1985) C.A. 835

P was in patient at a mental hospital who was allowed to got to lavatory unaccompanied. Some knowledge that P might have had matches with her, on part of D's nursing staff. P set fire to herself and sustained injury—*Held*, D not liable. Requisite standard of supervision had been provided, and causation not established in any event.

U4. Bull v. Devon Area H.A. (1989) C.A. 235

Unacceptably long interval between birth of first and second twin led to brain damage of second through *intra partum* asphyxia. *Res ipsa loquitur* applied—*Held*, hospital liable. The system should have been able to manage the premature labour of twins, if this had involved calling a registrar or consultant in such circumstances.

U5. Walker v. Semple (1993) C.A. 573

Held, D's erroneous diagnosis of schizophrenia and hypomania did not constitute negligence because it was reached upon information which might well have misled the ordinary competent doctor into mistaken diagnosis. *Bolam* test applied.

Examples

(i) Operations and Injections

Liable

- Swab left in body 1
- Injection piercing sciatic nerve 2
- Injection: cocaine instead of procaine 3
- Injection: faulty asepsis: paralysis 4
- Drainage tube left in body 5
- ANAESTHESIA: INEXPERIENCED ANAESTHETIST 6
- Injections: overdose: 34 doses of streptomycin instead of 30 11
- **Swab left in body** 14
- **Penicillin injection: not ascertaining from medical records whether patient allergic** 17
- Legal abortion: failure to terminate pregnancy 18
- Anterior colporraphy: performed too early after childbirth 20
- Hysterectomy: damage to ureter.... 25
- *Anaesthesia: no qualified anaesthetist present* U1
- *Gas gangrene: after operation on foot of healthy youth* U2

Not Liable

- BLOOD TRANSFUSION: CAUSING BRACHIAL PALSY 7
- INJECTION: CRACKED AMPOULE CAUSING PARALYSIS 8
- Thyroidectomy: causing paralysis of left vocal chord...................... 9
- Hysterectomy: allegedly unnecessary 10
- ANAESTHESIA: PATIENT INJURED IN PROCESS 12
- Injection in spine: paralysis........... 13
- Eye operation: retina cut 15
- Injection: needle breaking and part staying in buttock............... 16
- **Obstetrician: trial of forceps delivery** 19
- Ear operation: damage to facial nerve 21
- Sterialisation: pre-operative D and C procedure not carried out 22
- Anaesthetist: patient experiencing awareness during operation....... 23
- Sterialisation: post-operative check not preformed 24
- Fibroma believed to be cyst removed from knee-footdrop........ U3
- Vasectomy—two zerosperm counts—advice to plaintiff U4

1. Dryden v. Surrey C.C. [1936] 2 All E.R. 535, Finlay J.
2. Caldiera v. Gray, *The Times*, February 15, 1937.

3. Collins v. Herts. C.C. [1947] K.B. 598; [1947] 1 All E.R. 633, Hilbery J.
4. Voller v. Portsmouth Corp. [1947] C.L.C. 6869; *The Times*, April 30, 1947, Atkinson J.
5. Hocking v. Bell [1948] W.N. 21.
6. Jones v. Manchester Corporation [1952] 2 Q.B. 852; [1952] 2 All E.R. 125, C.A.
7. Crawford v. Charing Cross Hospital, *The Times*, December 8, 1953; [1953] C.L.Y. 2518, C.A.
8. Roe v. Ministry of Health [1954] 2 Q.B. 66; [1954] 2 All E.R. 131, C.A.
9. Hatcher v. Black, *The Times*, July 2, 1954, [1954] C.L.Y. 2289, Denning L.J. and jury.
10. Breen v. Baker, *The Times*, January 27, 1956; [1956] C.L.Y. 6013, Barry J.
11. Smith v. Brighton H.M.C., *The Times*, May 2 1958; [1958] C.L.Y. 2261, Streatfeild J.
12. Williams v. N. Liverpool H.M.C., *The Times*, January 17, 1959; [1959] C.L.Y. 2252, C.A.
13. Moore v. Lewisham H.M.C., *The Times*, February 5, 1959; [1959] C.L.Y. 2253, Barry J.
14. Cooper v. Nevill, *The Times*, March 10, 1961; [1961] C.L.Y. 5951, P.C.
15. White v. Westminster Hospital, *The Times*, October 26, 1961; [1961] C.L.Y. 5954, Thompson J.
16. Brazier v. Ministry of Defence [1965] 1 Lloyd's Rep. 26, McNair, J.
17. Chin Keow v. Government of Malaysia [1967] 1 W.L.R. 813, P.C.
18. Scuriaga v. Powell (1979) 123 S.J. 406; [1979] C.L.Y. 1882, Watkins J.
19. Whitehouse v. Jordan [1981] 1 W.L.R. 246; [1981] 1 All E.R. 267, H.L.
20. Clark v. MacLennan [1983] 1 All E.R. 416; [1983] C.L.Y. 2548, Peter Pain J.
21. Ashcroft v. Mersey Regional H.A. [1983] 2 All E.R. 245; [1983] C.L.Y. 2558, Kilner Brown J.
22. Venner v. North East Essex H.A., *The Times*, February 21, 1987; [1987] C.L.Y. 2602, Tucker J.
23. Taylor v. Worcester & District H.A. [1991] 2 M.L.R. 215; [1992] C.L.Y. 3230, McKinnon J.
24. McLennan v. Newcastle H.A. [1992] 3 M.L.R. 215; [1992] C.L.Y. 3246.
25. Hendy v. Milton Keynes H.A. (No.2) [1992] 3 M.L.R. 119; [1992] C.L.Y. 3238, Jowitt J.

U1. Lomax v. Slack (1952) C.A. 23.
U2. Thompson v. West Midlands R.H.A. (1978) C.A. 410.
U3. Mose v. West Hertfordshire H.A. (1987) C.A. 1199.
U4. Palmer v. Eadie (1987) C.A. 571.

Examples

(ii) Treatment and Diagnosis

Liable

Infectious disease caught in hospital: puerperal fever 1
Diathermy: no warning of danger if apparatus got too hot 3
SPLINT: LEFT ON TOO LONG AND TOO TIGHT 4
Intoxicated casualty patient: not using stethoscope: congested lung undiscovered 5
INHALER: PROPPED ON LAP OF CHILD AND SPILLING 6
Casualty patient: failure to diagnose fractures 10
Post-operative patient sent home: no arrangement to receive phone messages about condition 12

Not liable

Erroneous diagnosis of cancer: cystoscope not used 2
Dettol: strong solution causing dermatitis 7
Electro-convulsive therapy: fracture during treatment 8
ERRONEOUS DIAGNOSIS OF CANCER 9
Insufficient penicillin: given by house surgeon defendant working under consultant 11
Casualty patient—wound in abdomen: house surgeon failing to inform G.P. of his findings after sending patient home 13
HOSPITAL ORTHOPAEDIC PATIENT: SUICIDE FROM GROWING DEPRESSION 20

1. Heafield v. Crane, *The Times*, July 31, 1937, Singleton J.
2. Whiteford v. Hunter (1950) 94 S.J. 758; [1950] W.N. 553, H.L.
3. Clarke v. Adams (1950) 94 S.J. 599; [1950] 1 C.L.C. 6673, Slade J.
4. Cassidy v. Ministry of Health [1951] 2 K.B. 343; [1951] 1 All E.R. 574, C.A.
5. Wood v. Thurston [1951] 1 C.L.C. 6871; *The Times*, May 25, 1951, Pritchard J.
6. Cox v. Carshalton H.M.C., *The Times*, March 29 1955; [1955] C.L.Y. 1852, C.A.
7. Smith v. St. Helier H.M.C., *The Times*, May 10 1956; [1956] C.L.Y. 5964, Devlin J.
8. Bolam v. Friern H.M.C. [1957] 1 W.L.R. 582; [1957] 2 All E.R. 118, McNair J. and jury.
9. Crivon v. Barnet H.M.C. *The Times*, November 19, 1958; [1958] C.L.Y. 2283, C.A.
10. Newton v. Newtons Model Laundry, *The Times*, November 3, 1959; [1959] C.L.Y. 2256, Salmon J.
11. Junor v. McNicol, *The Times*, March 26, 1959, H.L.
12. Corder v. Banks, *The Times*, April 9, 1960; [1960] C.L.Y. 2185, McNair J.
13. Chapman v. Rix, *The Times*, December 22, 1960, H.L.
14. McCormack v. Redpath Brown, *The Times*, March 24, 1961; [1961] C.L.Y. 5952, Paull J.
15. Chute Farms v. Curtis, *The Times*, October 10, 1961; [1961] C.L.Y. 5987, Elwes J.
16. Coles v. Reading H.M.C., *The Times*, January 31, 1963, Sachs J.
17. Hucks v. Cole (1968) 112 S.J. 483; [1968] C.L.Y. 2716, C.A.
18. Selfe v. Ilford H.M.C., *The Times*, November 26, 1970; [1970] C.L.Y. 1852, Hinchcliffe J.

19. Langley v. Campbell, *The Times*, November 6, 1975; [1975] C.L.Y. 2317, Cusack J.
20. Hyde v. Tameside Area. H.A., *The Times*, April 16, 1981; [1981] C.L.Y. 1854, C.A.
21. Blyth v. Bloomsbury H.A., *The Times*, May 24, 1985; [1985] C.L.Y. 232, Leonard J.
22. Gardner v Mountfield (1989) 5 B.M.L.R., Scott Baker J.
23. Scott v. Bloomsbury H.A. (1989) 7 B.M.L.R. 77, Brooke J.
24. Prendergast v. Sam and Nee [1989] C.L.Y. 2545.
25. Rance v. Mid-Downs H.A. [1991] 1 All E.R. 801, Brooke J.
26. Cavanagh v. Weston H.A. [1992] 3 Med.L.R. 49; [1992] C.L.Y. 3242, McPherson J.
27. Bovenzi v. Kettering H.A. [1992] 3 Med.L.R. 293; [1992] C.L.Y. 3237, Nolan J.
28. Christie v. Somerset H.A. [1992] Med.L.R. 75; [1992] C.L.Y. 1543, Sir Michall Ogden Q.C.
29. Defreitas v. O'Brien [1993] 4 Med.L.R. 281; [1994] 2 C.L. 372, H.H.J. Burt.
30. Durrant v. Burke [1993] 4 Med.L.R. 258; [1994] 1 C.L. 263, H.H.J. Fallon.
31. Stockdale v. Nicholls [1993] 4 Med.L.R. 191; [1994] 1 C.L. 264, Otton J.
32. Hucks v. Cole [1994] C.L. 287/333, C.A.

U1. Landau v. Werner (1961) 105 S.J. 1008; (1961) C.A. 395 A.
U2. Rouse v. Kensington etc. Area H.A. (1982) C.A. U.B. 396.
U3. Kong v. King (1987) C.A. 366.
U4. Connelly v. Wigan A.H.A. (1994) C.A. 317.

(12) Prisons and Asylum Keepers

1. Holgate v. Lancashire Mental Hospitals Board [1938] 4 All E.R. 19, Lewis J. and jury

Mental defective detained in criminal lunatic institution—many convictions for assault—while released on licence he made serious assault on female plaintiff—jury *found* the Board, the superintendent and the acting superintendent all guilty of negligence.

2. Ellis v. Home Office [1953] 2 Q.B. 135; [1953] 2 All E.R. 149, C.A.

H was a mental defective in prison hospital—prison officer left hospital block, leaving cell doors open—H then attacked P—*Held*, defendants not liable, since although they owed a duty of care they had no reason to think H was more dangerous or more violent than an ordinary prisoner.

3. D'Arcy v. Prison Commissioners, *The Times*, November 17, 1955; [1955] Crim.L.R. 56, Barry J. and jury

Plaintiff serving preventive detention has his throat cut by three fellow prisoners—jury *find* defendants 95 per cent. to blame, plaintiff 5 per cent.

4. Smith v. Hale, *The Times*, October 27, 1956; [1956] C.L.Y. 5940, Ormerod J.

Approved school—throwing of home-made arrows—*Held*, defendants had taken all reasonable steps to prevent practice, and not liable.

5. Pullen v. Prison Commissioners [1957] 1 W.L.R. 1187; [1957] 3 All E.R. 470, Lord Goddard C.J.

Claim by prisoner for breach of statutory duty under the Factories Acts—*Held*, prison commissioners not liable, as the prison workshop was not a factory, there being no relationship of master and servant and no employment for wages.

6. Davis v. Prison Commissioners, *The Times*, November 21, 1963; [1963] C.L.Y. 2866, McKenna J.

Prisoner injured at work—prison commissioners, while disclaiming any relationship of master and servant, *accepted* that they had a responsibility for the safety of the prisoner which was similar to that arising from the relationship of master and servant—*Held*, on the facts, the defendants were not liable.

7. Home Office v. Dorset Yacht Co. [1970] A.C. 1004; [1970] 2 All E.R. 294, H.L.

Held, that the Borstal authorities owed a duty of care in respect of the control and supervision of their inmates, and that if in breach of such duty inmates were allowed to escape they would be liable to owners of property in "proximity".

8. Ferguson v. Home Office, *The Times*, October 8, 1977, Caulfield J.

9. Egerton v. Home Office [1978] Crim.L.R. 494, May J.

Sexual offender, recently taken off segregation, was attacked in lavatory—*Held*, defendants knew that plaintiff was likely to be attacked and reasonable steps should have been taken to prevent it, but the particular attack in the particular place could not reasonably have been foreseen.

10. Vicar of Writtle v. Essex C.C. (1979) 77 L.G.R. 656; [1979] 1 C.L.Y. 1865, Forbes J.

Held, following *Dorset Yacht Co.* **7**, the local authority owed a duty of care in respect of the control and supervision of the inmates of the home, and, if in breach of such duty an inmate was allowed to escape, the authority would be liable for foreseeable damage caused by the inmate to the owners of property in "proximity." For details, see Chap. 7, (1)(a)**15** and Chap. 1(4)(c)**13**.

11. Freeman v. Home Office [1984] 1 All E.R. 1036; [1984] C.L.Y. 3570, C.A.

12. Porterfield v. Home Office, The Independent, March 9, 1988; [1988] C.L.Y. 2436, Roch J.

Prisoner assaulted by another unknown prisoner; he claimed assault was result of negligent supervision and inadequate protection—*Held,* not liable.

13. Steele v. Northern Ireland Office [1988] 12 N.I.J.B.I.; [1989] C.L.Y. 2706, N.I., Kelly J.

Sex offender attacked whilst on remand—*Held,* duty on defendant to exercise reasonable care for prisoner's safety *a fortiori* where sex offender—breach of duty found but reduced by one-third for plaintiff's contributory negligence in failing to heed advice given to him that he needed protection.

14. Knight v. Home Office [1990] 3 All E.R. 237; [1991] C.L.Y. 2654, Pill J.

Deceased who was mentally disturbed was remanded to prison pending transfer to hospital—he was known to have suicidal tendencies and to be violent and was therefore kept in a cell where observed every $\frac{1}{4}$ hour—he hung himself—*Held,* the standard of care to be exercised in a prison hospital was not required to be as high in all respects or for all purposes as that appropriate to a psychiatric hospital outside prison—in all the circumstances negligence not established.

15. H. v. Secretary of State for the Home Department (1992) 136 S.J. 140 (Case Reports); [1992] C.L.Y. 3210, C.A.

Due to negligence of prison authorities, a prisoner's previous convictions for sexual offences became known and he had to be removed from association under rule 43—*Held,* following *R. v. Deputy Governor of Parkhurst Prison, ex p. Hague* [1992] 1 A.C. 58 (not summarised in this work as not a negligence case) the damage resulting did not give rise to a claim in negligence.

16. Forde v. Home Office [1994] 4 C.L. 221, Judge McLean

Due to negligence of prison officer, prisoner's previous sexual offences made known to other inmates as a result of which he was assaulted by them—*Held,* defendant liable. Alternative claim that governor should have transferred plaintiff rejected.

U1. Size v. Shenley Hospital (1970) C.A. 30

U2. Gauntlett v. Northampton H.A. (1985) C.A. 835

In patient at mental hospital set fire to T-shirt when unaccompanied in washroom—*Held,* defendants not liable for failure of sufficient supervision—prior incident where patient's husband handed in matches which patient had threatened to use to set light to herself would have had no effect upon patient being allowed to washroom on her own.

U3. Palmer v. Home Office (1988) C.A. 285

Prisoner stabbed in lavatory with scissors from adjacent tailor's workshop wielded by category A co-prisoner who worked there as a cleaner—*Held*, defendants not negligent in giving co-prisoner work there and continuing to do so after he had previously been found in possession of some blades.

(13) Public Officers

(*N.B.*: In *Murphy v. Brentwood D.C.* [1991] 1 A.C. 398 (see **66** below) it was held that *Anns v. Motor London B.C.* (**5** below) "was wrongly decided as regards the scope of any private law duty of care resting upon local authorities in relation to their function of taking steps to secure compliance with building byelaws or regulations & should be departed from ... *Dutton v. Bognor Regis Urban District Council*" **2** "should be overruled as should all cases subsequent to *Anns* which were decided in reliance on it" *per* Lord Keith. In the light of that decision, cases listed here which were decided after *Dutton* and prior to *Murphy* need to be treated with caution in so far as they relied or may have relied upon those earlier decisions.)

1. Ministry of Housing v. Sharp [1970] 2 Q.B. 223; [1970] 1 All E.R. 1009, C.A.

Registrar of local land charges issued erroneous clear certificate to purchaser—who thus got title free from incumbrance registered by plaintiff ministry—error was due to failure of a clerk to search properly—*Held*, registrar was under no absolute statutory duty to issue an accurate certificate, though possibly he might have been in breach of a statutory duty to use reasonable care, if (which was not the case) he had acted negligently—*Held*, further, there was sufficient "proximity" between the clerk and the incumbrancer to create a *Donoghue v. Stevenson* relationship and duty of care, and accordingly the clerk was liable for breach of that duty.

2. Dutton v. Bognor Regis U.D.C. [1972] Q.B. 373; [1972] 1 All E.R. 462, C.A.

Held, building surveyor and local authority liable. *Upheld as a decision in Anns* **5**, but on somewhat different grounds. Overruled in *Murphy* **66** and all cases based on it post-*Anns* **5**.

3. Bryson v. Northumbria Police [1977] C.L.Y. 2042, Reeve J.

Held, on the facts, defendants not liable.

4. Rutherford v. Att.-Gen. [1976] 1 N.Z.L.R. 403; [1976] C.L.Y. 1870, Hamilton Supreme Ct.

5. Anns v. Merton London B.C. [1977] 2 W.L.R. 1024; [1977] 2 All E.R. 492, H.L.

Foundations of building defective—assumed for argument that local authority had either failed to carry out its function under the Public Health Act 1936 (now replaced by the Public Health Act 1961) of inspecting them or had been negligent in carrying out the inspection—*Held*, (a) council would not be liable for failure to inspect unless (i) it had not exercised its discretion properly as to the making of inspections, and (ii) it had failed to exercise reasonable care in its acts or omissions to secure that the by-laws concerning foundations would be complied with; and (b) it would be liable for negligent inspection if the inspector, having assumed the duty of inspecting and acting otherwise than in the bona fide exercise of any discretion under the statute, failed to take reasonable care in the inspection. Lord Wilberforce (three other Law Lords concurring) said that, as a result of the *Dorset Yacht* case (Chap. 1, (2) (a) **7**), the existence of a duty of care no longer depended on bringing the case within some existing precedent. *In general*, the question was now to be approached in two stages: the first question was whether there was a sufficient relationship of proximity or neighbourhood such that in the reasonable contemplation of the defendant carelessness by him might cause damage to another; and secondly, whether there were any considerations, such as arose in the "economic loss" cases (see Chap. 1, (3) (a)), which ought to negative or limit or reduce the scope of the duty or the class of person to whom it was owed. But in the *particular* case of a public body discharging functions under statute, these tests were not enough, since the powers and duties of the public body were definable in terms of public and not private law. It was usual for the statutes which applied in such cases to contain a large area of policy, which the courts called "discretion," and the exercise of which could not, in general, be called in question in the courts, so long as the decision was made responsibly and for reasons which accorded with the statutory purpose. But also many statutes presupposed the practical execution of policy decisions, so that in addition to the area of policy or discretion there was (although the distinction was largely a matter of degree) an "operational area" as well, and the more operational a power or duty might be, the easier it was to superimpose on it a common law duty of care. Applying these principles Lord Wilberforce reached the conclusions set out above. The liability for negligent inspection (as opposed to non-inspection) was because inspection, once embarked on, was in the operational area, though there could be a discretionary element in its exercise (*e.g.* as to time and manner and techniques), and a plaintiff alleging negligence would have to prove that the conduct complained of was not within the limits of a discretion bona fide exercised before he could begin to rely on a common law duty of care.

Considered in *Peabody* **29**. Distinguished in *Curran* **43**. Largely overruled in *Murphy* **66**.

6. Trappa v. District of Surrey (1978) 95 D.L.R. (3d) 107; [1979] C.L.Y. 1890, Br.Col.Sup.Ct.

7. Hallett v. Nicholson 1979 S.C. 1; [1981] C.L.Y. 1859, Ct. of Sess.

Two guests died in hotel fire. Their personal representatives sued hoteliers. Hoteliers blamed area fire authority. Authority had inspected hotel in accordance with duties under Fire Precautions Act 1971 but had not advised hoteliers not to reopen pending carrying out of recommended precautions, nor applied under section 10(2) for an order prohibiting use of hotel for overnight guests, nor advised interim fire precautions—*Held*, that the fire authority was not liable. Acts or omissions by a statutory authority in the course of an improper exercise of its statutory duties or powers which infringed the rights of third parties might be actionable. For the exercise of a statutory duty to be improper, it must be either not authorised by statute or not made bona fide in the interests of the public within the limits of any statutory discretion: *Anns* **5** and *Dorset Yacht Co.* (Chap. 1, (2)(a) **7**) applied. However, the local authority's failure to advise the hoteliers not to re-open or to obtain an order under section 10(2) was wholly within the area of its discretion under the 1971 Act, and it was under no duty to advise on interim precautions.

8. Marsh v. Betstyle & G.L.C.D [1979] C.L.Y. 1875, Judge Hawser Q.C.

9. Harris v. Demolition Contractors [1979] 2 N.Z.L.R. 166 [1980] C.L.Y. 198, N.Z.Sup.Ct.

10. Stewart v. East Cambridgeshire D.C. (1979) 252 E.G. 1105; [1980] C.L.Y. 1879, Sir Douglas Franks Q.C.

House built on old gravel pit—severe cracking. Building inspector had seen boreholes during construction which appeared sufficient to him—*Held*, inspector not liable. He owed a duty under

Anns **5**, but he was not a professionally qualified expert, and he was not required to do the work of a structural engineer by, *e.g.* sinking further boreholes.

11. Worlock v. Saws (1981) 260 E.G. 920; [1982] C.L.Y. 2148, Woolf J.

Now *superseded* by decision in C.A. **22.**

12. Belvedere Motors v. King (1981) 260 E.G. 813; [1982] C.L.Y. 2144, Kenneth Jones J.

Held, that the defendant had not been negligent: "In this case the defendant can only be guilty of negligence if it can be shown that he has omitted to consider some matter which he ought to have considered, or that he has taken into account some matter which he ought not to have taken into account, or in some way has failed to adopt the procedure and practice accepted as standard in his profession and has so failed to exercise the care and skill which he, on accepting the appointment, held himself out as possessing" (at 814).

13. Culford Metal v. E.C.G.D. *The Times*, March 25, 1981; [1981] C.L.Y. 2752, Neill J.

Export Credits Guarantee department (a government department) gave negligent advice to exporter. In reliance thereon, exporter did not insure against the risk of non-payment by foreign importer—*Held*, E.C.G.D. liable for loss due to absence of insurance cover.

14. Dunlop v. Woollahra M.C. [1981] 2 W.L.R. 693; [1981] 1 All E.R. 1202, P.C.

The defendant council passed two statutory resolutions imposing building restrictions which the plaintiff alleged caused him loss. The plaintiff obtained declarations that one resolution was *ultra vires* and the second void because the defendants had failed to give the plaintiff a proper hearing before passing the resolution. The plaintiff then claimed damages for (a) as regards the first resolution, breach of duty of care to ascertain that the resolution was *intra vires*, and (b) as regards the second, breach of duty of care to give the plaintiff a proper hearing—*Held*, as to (a), that on the facts there had been no breach of duty of care, if one was owed, but Privy Council felt considerable *doubt* as to whether any such duty was owed—*Held*,as to (b), the failure to accord a proper hearing could not amount to a breach of a duty of care sounding in damages: "The effect of the failure is to render the exercise of the power void and the person complaining of the failure is in as good a position as the public authoirity to know that that is so. He can ignore the purported exercise of the power. It cannot affect his legal rights" (Lord Diplock, 1209 J).

15. Lyons v. Boote and Maidstone C.C. [1982] 262 E.G. 981; [1982] C.L.Y. 2125, Drake J.

So held, the judge saying that the principles in *Anns* **5** can properly be applied to the provisions of the Planning Acts for the giving of approval to plans.

16. Potter v. Mole Valley D.C. and Surrey D.C., *The Times*, October 22, 1982; [1982] C.L.Y. 2266, French J.

Held, D1 (who appear to have been the drainage authority, although this is not expressly stated) were not liable within the principle in *Anns* **5** for failing to use their statutory powers under the Land Drainage Act 1976 to abate flooding, as their failure to act did not arise from any improper motive but was a bona fide decision within the area of the authority's discretion. See also Chap. 1, (3)(b) **13**.

17. Page Motors v. Epsom and Ewell C.C. (1982) 80 L.G.R. 337; [1982] C.L.Y. 2267, C.A.

See Chap. 2, (1)**10**.

18. Haig v. Hillingdon L.B. (1982) 19 Build. L.R. 143; [1983] C.L.Y. 278, Judge Fay Q.C.

Builder (subsequently going into liquidation) altered an approved design for an extension to a first floor maisonette above a shop by putting in softwood joists instead of a rolled steel joist. As a result the structure was not capable of sustaining the load imposed. The defendant council appreciated the importance of the steel joist to the stability of the structure, but their surveyor failed to inspect same or detect the alteration—*Held*, defendant council liable, it being no excuse in the circumstances that the builder had failed to notify the council before covering up the joists.

19. Dennis v. Charnwood B.C. [1983] Q.B. 409; [1982] 3 All E.R. 486, C.A.

Plaintiffs commissioned builder to construct house on site of former sandpit. Plan provided for house to be supported on concrete raft. Plan approved by local authority who ought to have known that the raft was inadequate as a foundation for the house. Serious damage to house resulting therefrom—*Held*, local authority liable. "A local authority is under a duty to take reasonable care in deciding whether plans required by the building regulations are defective . . . A local authority is only liable for breach of duty if it fails to exercise reasonable care in the performance of its statutory functions and as a result allows the erection of a building which has defects likely to cause damage or discomfort to the occupier, defects which a prudent local authority exercising its statutory powers would have required to be eliminated" (Templeman L.J., 493 D-E). Distinguished in *Investors in Industry* **38**.

20. Rivers v. Cutting [1982] 1 W.L.R. 1146; [1982] 3 All E.R. 69, C.A.

Plaintiff abandoned car on motorway. Under the Removal and Disposal of Vehicles Regulations 1968, reg. 4, police arranged for garage to tow vehicle away. Car damaged while being towed. Issue was whether the police were vicariously liable for the negligence of the garage—*Held*, police were under a duty to use reasonable care in choice of independent contractor to tow car away, but were not liable for his negligence in carrying out the work.

21. Bluett v. Woodspring D.C. [1983] J.P.L. 242; [1983] C.L.Y. 2513, Judge Stabb Q.C.

22. Worlock v. Saws (1983) 265 E.G. 774; [1983] C.L.Y. 2521, C.A.

Held, (a) the council was liable to the owner for failing to detect defective foundations: "If an inspector misconstrues the regulations in such circumstances, I do not consider that the local authority upon whom the duty of care rests can shelter behind the building inspector's error, however reasonable, and say that they themselves were not negligent" (Goff L.J., 730). The council should have advised their inspectors as to the application of the regulation to the work in question; and (b) even if it could be proved that the local authority were aware of the inexperience of the builder, that was irrelevant to their duty of supervision. There was no reason to depart from the conventional apportionment of 75 per cent. against the builder and 25 per cent. against the local authority.

23. Acrecrest v. Hattrell [1983] Q.B. 260; [1983] 1 All E.R. 17, C.A.

Overruled in *Peabody* **29**.

24. Fellowes v. Rother D.C. [1983] 1 All E.R. 513; [1983] C.L.Y. 2538, Robert Goff J.

Trial of preliminary issues of law in action alleging negligent exercise of statutory powers to carry out coast protection work. The judge reviewed the leading authorities, and in particular *Anns* **5**, and *said* (522 A): "From these authorities the following principles can . . . be derived. Where a plaintiff claims damages for negligence at common law against a public body or official purporting to act in pursuance of a power conferred by statute or other legislation, he can only succeed if he can show (1) that the act complained of was not within the limits of a discretion bona fide exercised under the relevant power, (2) that having regard to all the circumstances, including the legislation creating the relevant power, there was sufficient proximity to create a duty of care on the defendant to avoid damage to the plaintiff of the type complained of, and no ground for negativing (or reducing or limiting) such duty of care, (3) that it was reasonably foreseeable by the defendant, or by those for whom he was vicariously responsible, that the act complained of was likely to cause damage of the type in fact suffered by the plaintiff by reason of such act. In considering these questions, there is no rule that, merely because the defendant was acting under a statutory power as opposed to a statutory duty, liability is contingent on the defendant causing the plaintiff fresh or additional damage."

25. Marshall v. Osmond [1983] Q.B. 1034; [1983] 2 All E.R. 225, C.A.

See Chap. 13(2) **14**.

26. Rimmer v. Liverpool C.C. [1984] 1 All E.R. 930, C.A.

For details see Chap. 10(8)(a)**22**.

27. P. Perl (Exporters) Ltd v. Camden L.B.C. [1984] Q.B. 342; [1983] 3 All E.R. 161, C.A.

See Chap. 1, (3) (b) **15**.

28. Strable v. Dartford B.C. [1984] J.P.L. 329; [1984] C.L.Y. 3459, C.A.

Held, on a preliminary issue, that an individual injuriously affected by the refusal or granting of planning permission had no right of action for damages against the planning authority—in any event no negligence disclosed in the instant case.

29. Governors of the Peabody Donation Fund v. Sir Lindsay Parkinson & Co. Ltd [1985] A.C. 210; [1984] 3 All E.R. 529, H.L.

Plans, prepared by the plaintiff's architects and approved by the local authority, provided for the construction of a flexible system of drainage for a housing development on the plaintiff's land. In fact, a rigid system was installed by the builders on the architect's instructions. During installation the local authority's building inspector became aware of the change but did nothing. The plaintiffs sued the local authority for breach of duty of care by failing to warn them of the risk of economic loss unless a flexible system in accordance with the plans was installed—*Held*, although it might be reasonably foreseeable by the local authority that failure to invoke their powers to require compliance with the approved plans might involve economic loss to the plaintiffs, it was neither reasonable nor just to impose a liability on the local authority to indemnify the plaintiffs against such loss in the circumstances, in particular when the plaintiffs relied on the advice of architects, engineers and contractors—the local authority's power to require compliance was not for the purpose of safeguarding building developers against economic loss resulting from their failure to comply with approved plans. *Anns* (**5**) considered. *Acrecrest* (**23**) overruled.

30. S. v. Walsall M.B.C. [1985] 1 W.L.R. 1150; [1985] 3 All E.R. 294, C.A.

Child taken into care and boarded out to foster parents by local authority pursuant to statutory powers—there child suffered severe burns to feet—*Held*, relationship between child and local authority regulated solely by statutory scheme—foster parents therefore were not to be treated as its agents and it was not vicariously liable for the negligence of either foster parent.

31. Perry v. Tendring D.C. [1985] 1 E.G.L.R. 260; [1985] C.L.Y. 192, Judge Newey Q.C.

Houses built on land subject to long-term leave—*Held*, local authority, consulting engineers and builder not liable in negligence to purchasers as at time they acted they could not reasonably have known of the phenomenon.

32. Shaddock & Associates Pty v. Parramatta C.C. (No. 1) (1980–81) 150 C.L.R. 225; [1985] C.L.Y. 2304, High Court of Australia

Telephone and written inquiry of local authority as to road proposals—land purchased in reliance on answer that there were none—*Held*, local authority liable on *Hedley Byrne* principle.

33. Billam & Billam v. Cheltenham B.C. (1985) 3 Con.L.R. 99; [1986] C.L.Y. 198, Cyril Newman Q.C.

Plaintiffs were subsequent purchasers of house built partly on site of filled-in pond—*Held*, local authority were not negligent at planning permission stage in failing to discover the former existence of pond from old maps but building inspector had been negligent at foundation stage of building. *Anns* **5** relied on.

34. Rigby v. Chief Constable of Northamptonshire [1985] 1 W.L.R. 242; [1985] 2 All E.R. 985, Taylor J.

Police fired CS gas canister into gunsmith's shop to force out a psychopath who had broken into it—fire broke out as a result of canister's use—*Held*, police not negligent in not having or using a safer means of propulsion at that time but were negligent in firing the canister at a time when they knew no fire appliance was available to attend if fire broke out. Claim in *Rylands v. Fletcher* failed.

35. Low v. R. J. Haddock Ltd [1985] 6 Con. L.R. 122; [1985] C.L.Y. 213, Judge Newey Q.C.

See Chap. 18, (6) **41**.

36. Russell v. Barnet L.B.C. (1984) 83 LGR 152; [1985] C.L.Y. 2499 a, Tudor Evans J.

Lessees of house claimed subsidence damage caused by roots of trees which stood on adjoining pavement—highway authority, whilst not owners of trees, had statutory powers to maintain them and to prohibit them becoming a nuisance—*Held*, authority were or ought to have been aware of risk of tree roots causing damage and were liable not only in nuisance but also for breach of duty of care.

37. King v. Liverpool C.C. [1986] 1 W.L.R. 890; [1986] 3 All E.R. 544, C.A.

Tenant of local authority flat asked landlord to secure the flat above against vandals—any steps then taken were ineffective and as a result tenant's flat damaged by water ingress—*Held*, council not liable in negligence.

38. Investors in Industry Commercial Properties Ltd v. South Bedfordshire D.C. [1986] Q.B. 1034; [1986] 1 All E.R. 787, C.A.

The plaintiffs caused warehouses to be built on their land; the local authority passed plans and inspected and approved the foundation bases—the foundations proved inadequate—*Held*, the local authority in exercising their supervisory powers granted by statute owed no duty of care to an original building owner (albeit it might to a subsequent occupier) to ensure a building was erected in accordance with the relevant Building Regulations—it would not normally be just and reasonable to do so, in particular where it was incumbent on the building owner to ensure compliance and he had had and relied upon professional advisers. *Peabody* **29** applied. *Dennis v. Charnwood B.C.* **19** distinguished.

39. J.G.F. Properties Ltd v. Lambeth B.C. [1986] 1 E.G.L.R. 277; [1986] C.L.Y. 2281, Judge Rubin

Alleged negligence of local authority in reply to inquiries by purchaser's solicitors by failure to disclose planning blight affecting the properties to be purchased—*Held*, form of reply not negligent.

40. Percival v. Walsall M.B.C. [1986] 2 E.G.L.R. 136; [1986] C.L.Y. 210, C.A.

Settlement occurred to dwelling held by occupiers under long lease—*Held*, local authority negligent in allowing house and extension to be built either not in accordance with approved or from inadequate plans but not liable as defects did not and would not pose danger to health or safety.

41. Stockley v. Knowsley M.B.C. [1986] 2 E.G.L.R. 141; [1986] C.L.Y. 2249, C.A.

Tenant of council flat informed them of a frozen pipe; they told her to turn stopcock off but through ignorance of its location she did not do so—*Held*, council liable to tenant for resultant damage—they should have stressed the importance of turning it off and have advised her how to go about it.

42. Bell v. Secretary of State for Defence [1986] Q.B. 322; [1985] 3 All E.R. 661, C.A.

Soldier received injury during horseplay from which he died—administrator of his estate alleged that but for negligent delay and shortcomings in examination and treatment he would have survived—*Held*, by a majority, that is so far as the acts or omissions alleged occurred whilst deceased was off duty (in this whilst at a civilian hospital), a certificate under *section 10 of* the Crown Proceedings Act 1947, did not preclude any cause of action. Overruled in *Pearce v. Secretary of State for Defence* (Chap. 4 (4) **2**).

43. Curran v. Northern Ireland Co-Ownership Housing Association Ltd. [1987] A.C. 718; [1987] 2 All E.R. 13, H.L.

The Northern Ireland Housing Executive awarded an improvement grant to the plaintiff's predecessor in title with which an extension to the house had been built—plaintiff's claim for negligent failure to ensure extension was properly built failed—*Held*, no duty of care owed: *Anns* **5** distinguished—the Executive had no powers of control over the building works, only a power to withhold grant moneys if it was not satisfied with the quality of the work.

44. Hambro Life Assurance PLC v. White Young & Partners [1987] 2 E.G.L.R. 159; [1987] C.L.Y. 2584, C.A.

Plaintiffs purchased but never themselves occupied a building constructed some time previously—it was conceded the defendant local authority had been negligent in giving Building Regulation approval and in inspecting progress of work and that there was present and imminent danger to health and safety of occupants/licences/visitors—*Held*, the plaintiffs were not part of the section of the public to whom any duty of care was owed, being merely owners and never having been occupiers of the property.

45. Christchurch Drainage Board v. Brown, *Daily Telegraph*, October 12, 1987; [1987] C.L.Y. 2591, P.C., New Zealand

In deciding whether to grant planning permission, a local authority referred applications to drainage board to advise concerning flood risks and the board habitually provided such details without express request—*Held*, board liable to a houseowner for loss for not properly checking flood levels pertinent to house for which planning permission granted.

46. Fry v. Robert A. Jackson (Builder & Contractor) Ltd and Guildford B.C. [1987] 7 Con. L.R. 97; [1987] C.L.Y. 241, Judge Newey Q.C.

Owners of two houses sued builder and local authority—builder took no part in trial and local authority conceded it owed a duty under the Building Regulations—*Held*, builder liable in breach of contract and on basis of *Dutton* **2** and *Anns* **5** in negligence in respect of faulty foundations—*Held*, further, following *Peabody* **29** and *Investors in Industry* **38**, the local authority's duty under the Regulations was owed only to owner occupiers unless (same in special circumstances) they were the "first builders" in the sense of having caused the buildings to be erected, the duty being limited to not causing danger to health or safety—there was such danger in the instant case and whilst there was no breach in the passing of plans, the building inspector had failed to exercise reasonable care when permitting a departure from the plans in respect of foundations.

47. James McKinnon v. Country & Metropoliton Developments Ltd (1987) 9 Con. L.R. 61; [1988] C.L.Y. 2432, Judge John Davies Q.C.

Plaintiff purchased duelling-house from builder—*Held*, on basis of *Dennis v. Charnwood* **19** and *Anns* **5** a local authority owed a duty of care in approving plans and over site inspection—*Held*, further, no breach over approval of plans but breach over inspecting foundations.

48. Kimbell v. Hart D.C. (1987) 9 Con. L.R. 118; [1987] C.L.Y. 242, Judge Smout Q.C.

Plaintiffs purchased 11-year-old house and sold prior to action—they claimed against local authority negligence over site inspection and securing compliance with Building Regulations, as a result of which subsidence had occurred—*Held*, no evidence that the subsidence damage constituted imminent danger to health or safety and therefore no cause of action had arisen under *Anns* **5** and *Jones v. Stroud D.C.* [1986] 1 W.L.R. 1141 (limitation case, not digested in this work); in any event, local authority had not been negligent.

49. Scott-Whitehead v. N.C.B. (1987) 53 P & C.R. 263; [1987] C.L.Y. 3866, Stuart Smith J.

Plaintiffs had licence from water authority to use river water to irrigate land owned and leased by them; due to working of coal board's mines, river water became excessively saline—*Held*, water authority in breach of duty of care for failing to warn plaintiffs that salinity might be dangerously high—*Held*, further coal board not liable.

50. Dear v. L.B. of Newham (1988) 20 H.L.R. 348; [1989] C.L.Y. 3140, C.A.

Local authority failed despite requests to remove rubbish taken from roof space of property tenanted by infant plaintiff's mother and deposited on adjoining balcony—infant climbed and fell from the rubbish suffering injury—*Held*, the rubbish was not house refuse within the meaning of the Public Health Act 1936 s. 72; had it been, the authority would have owed a duty of care to the plaintiff and have been in breach thereof.

51. Mc Nerny v. L.B. of Lambeth (1988) 21 H.L.R. 188; [1989] C.L.Y. 2152, C.A.

Held, no duty owed by landlord letting unfurnished flat which had not been negligently built but which suffered from condensation due to nature of use by occupant and lack of ventilation and manner of construction.

52. Rowling v. Takaro Properties Ltd [1988] A.C. 473; [1988] 1 All E.R. 163, P.L.

Minister of State refused, pursuant to statutory powers, to consent to the issue of shares in a New Zealand company to a foreign company—*Held*, assuming a duty of care was owed, the Minister had not acted negligently.

53. Green v. Ipswich B.C. [1988] 1 E.G.L.R. 239; [1988] C.L.Y. 2456, Judge Fox-Andrews Q.C.

See Chap. 18, (5), **25**.

54. Smith v. Eric. S. Bush; Harris v. Wyre Forest D.C. [1990] 1 A.C. 831; [1989] 2 All E.R. 514, H.L.

Two prospective purchasers of dwelling-houses relied on valuations (required by prospective mortgagees pursuant to statutory requirement) in deciding whether or not to purchase. In one case, the report was by an independent valuer to a building society with a copy disclosed to the purchaser—in the other, the report was by an employee of the lending local authority and no copy was disclosed—in both cases, there were disclaimers of liability and advice to purchasers to procure their own survey. Both valuers were negligent in and about their valuations and both purchasers suffered loss and damage in having repairs effected—*Held*

(a) In the absence of any disclaimer of liability the valuer valuing a house for mortgage purposes, knowing that the mortgagee will rely and the mortgagor will probably rely on the valuation and knowing that the purchaser/mortgagor has in effect paid for the valuation, is under a duty to exercise reasonable skill and care, such duty being owed to both parties to the mortgage for which the valuation was made.
(b) The disclaimers in both cases were notices within the meaning of the Unfair Contract Terms Act 1977 and had therefore to satisfy the requirement of reasonableness.
(c) It was not fair or reasonable to exclude liability in particular where the valuer was a professional man carrying out a valuation of a modest dwelling which should present no difficulty, he knew most purchasers relied on his valuation without an independent survey which most could not afford, he was paid for his services in effect by the purchaser, the purchaser trusted the mortgagees and their valuers, the valuer knew failure by him could be disastrous for the purchaser and the valuer was most likely to be covered by insurance and the purchaser had no effective power to object to the disclaimer.

Yianni (Chap. 18, (5) **5**) approved.

55. Jones v. Department of Employment [1989] Q.B. 1; [1988] 1 All E.R. 725, C.A.

Plaintiff alleged adjudication officer was negligent in not allowing him unemployment benefit (which he subsequently obtained on appeal) and claimed damages for the legal costs of appeal, for personal expenses and for worry, distress and inconvenience. Claim struck out—to allow a common law action for negligence would be to allow a challenge to the correctness of the adjudicating officer's decision, *i.e.* its finality, by a route other than that provided for by statutory provisions—*Held*, further, the officer's duty lay in the field of public law and was enforceable only by the statutory appeal procedure or judicial review (a public law remedy)—thus no duty of care owed in private law and it was not just or reasonable that there should be.

56. Hill v. Chief Constable of West Yorkshire [1989] A.C. 53; [1988] 2 All E.R. 238, H.L.

Allegation that, but for negligent police investigation of a series of murders, the murderer would have been apprehended before he also killed the plaintiff's daughter. Claim struck out—despite foreseeability of harm to such as the daughter, there was absent any such ingredient or characteristic as led to liability in *Dorset Yacht v. Home Office* (Chap. 18(12) **7**) or any other characteristic which would establish a duty of care—as a matter of public policy there should be immunity from suit on grounds similar to those appertaining to a barrister as set out in *Randel v. Worsley* (Chap. 19(3) **1**).

57. Calveley v. Chief Constable of the Merseyside Police [1989] A.C. 1228; [1989] 1 All E.R. 1025, H.L.

Various police officers claimed against their respective chief constables damages for variously anxiety, vexation, depressive illness and loss of overtime earnings during and due to periods of suspension or dismissal and allegedly due to the negligent conduct of investigations into their conduct carried out pursuant to regulations—*Held*, there was no cause of action either because the injury alleged was not reasonably foreseeable or was a claim for purely economic loss or it was contrary to public policy that any actionable duty of care should arise.

58. Mills v. Winchester Diocesan Board of Finance [1989] Ch. 428; [1989] 2 All E.R. 317, Knox J.

Plaintiffs and other local inhabitants were the assumed objects of a charitable trust and claimed damages against the Charity Commissioners for their assumed negligent advice to the first defendants as to the meaning of the trust, as a result of which the plaintiffs and others had suffered damage, injury and distress—*Held*, there was no sufficient proximity between the plaintiffs and the Commissioners, nor was it just or equitable for there to be a duty of care, in particular where there was a right of appeal against any action proposed on the basis of the Commissioners advice—*Hedley Byrne* of no application, there being no reliance on the advice by the plaintiffs.

59. Ryeford Homes Ltd v. Sevenoaks D.C. [1989] 2 E.G.L.R. 281; [1990] C.L.Y. 4443, Judge Newey Q.C.

Builders and developers claimed against local authority, *inter alia*, damages for negligence in and about (a) granting planning permission for houses to be built on raised land, (b) failing to ensure the houses were built in accordance with planning permission granted, and (c) connection with sewers—*Held*, such claims to be struck out, as no duty of care owed—claim for irrecoverable economic loss and/or limitation.

60. Seabrink Residents Association Ltd v. Robert Walpole Campion & Partners (1989) 14 Con. L.R. 62; [1990] C.L.Y. 394, Judge Esyr Lewis Q.C.

Plaintiffs alleged local authority negligent in not rejecting plans submitted to it by firm of engineers—*Held*, the duty under the Public Health Act 1936, s. 64(1) was to take reasonable care to ensure that plans for buildings submitted for approval complied with Building Regulations and were not otherwise defective (*Anns* **5** and *Dennis v. Charnwood B.C.* **19** followed)—such duty did not include walls, bridges or roads which were not part of a building and was owed only to resident occupiers whose safety or health was endangered by its breach and not to a limited company which owned the building—although the damage to the structure gave rise to a present or imminent danger to the safety of the individual occupiers, a failure to take reasonable care in passing the plans had not been established.

61. Clough v. Bussan [1990] 1 All E.R. 431; [1990] C.L.Y. 3278, Kennedy J.

Police knew of malfunctioning traffic lights—accident due to malfunction—*Held*, no duty of care owed. *Hill v. Chief Constable* **56** and *Yuen Kun Yeu v. Att. Gen. for Hong Kong* (Chap. 18, (2) **26**) applied.

62. Partington v. Wandsworth L.B.C; The Independent, November 8, 1989; [1989] C.L.Y. 2563, Schiemann J.

Plaintiff pushed over and thus injured by unpredictable mentally handicapped girl under the care of local authority supervisor—*Held*, although the authority was under a duty to take reasonable care to prevent such as the girl from injuring others, the nature of that duty could vary from person to person and from day to day depending on the mood of the handicapped person—in the circumstances, the authority not proved negligent.

63. R. v. H.M. Treasury, ex p. Petch [1990] C.O.D. 19; [1991] C.L.Y. 2724, Popplewell J.

The plaintiff, a former assistant secretary who suffered from psychiatric illness, was dismissed from the civil service—he claimed *inter alia*, damages for anxiety and distress caused by negligent delay in dealing with his claim for a pension—*Held*, *inter alia*, it was an implied term of the pension scheme that a decision thereunder would be made within a reasonable time—in private law, a claim for delay in dealing with a claim giving rise to injury did not of itself found a cause of action—it had to be shown that the defendants exceeded or abused their powers in the normal judicial review sense so that the act had to be shown to be *ultra vires* or to be in breach of a statutory duty—"negligence" is not to be taken in its ordinary sense of failing to take reasonable care—in the present case, the Minister owed the plaintiff a duty of care in common law negligence—there was foreseeability that delay would cause him some damage—there was a relationship of proximity between the parties "equivalent to contract" and it would not be unjust or unreasonable to impose such a duty of care—there was an implied duty owed to him under statute to consider his claim timeously however, on the facts, there had been no breach of duty.

64. Richardson v. West Lindsey D.C. [1990] 1 W.L.R. 522; [1990] 1 All E.R. 296, C.A.

Plaintiff bungalow owner submitted plans prepared by building draughtsman to local authority for Building Regulation approval—plans were approved but subsequent amended plans were neither rejected nor approved although all parties proceeded as if they were approved—roof built to amended plans defective—*Held*, no duty of care owed. *Investors in Industry* **38** followed. *Dennis v. Charnwood B.C.* **19** distinguished.

65. Kirkham v. Chief Constable of the Greater Manchester Police. [1990] 2 Q.B. 283; [1990] 3 All E.R. 246, C.A.

Police who took plaintiff's husband into custody knew of his suicidal tendencies but failed to pass such knowledge on to the prison authorities—as a result he succeeded in committing suicide—*Held*, negligent and liable in damages—defences of *volenti* and *ex turpi causa* rejected.

66. Murphy v. Brentwood D.C. [1991] 1 A.C. 398; [1990] 2 All E.R. 908, H.L.

Local authority approved plans for concrete raft foundation for a building pursuant to statutory obligation and after taking advice from independent consulting engineers. Plaintiff purchased the house—the raft was inadequately designed and cracks appeared in walls and gas and soil pipes cracked—plaintiff sold at a price taking account of the defects—*Held,* where defects which would render the structure dangerous are discovered in time to avert the possibility of injury or damage then the cost of repair or loss of value is pure economic loss and therfore irrecoverable—*Anns* **5** departed from in so for as it imposed any private law duty of care on local authorities in relation to their function of taking steps to secure compliance with byelaws and building regulations. *Dutton v. Bognor Regis U.D.C.* **2** overruled and all cases subsequent to *Anns* **5** decided in reliance on it. *Per* Lord Bridge: *Junior Books* (Chap. 1, (3)(a)**11**) understandable only on basis of a situation where, even in the absence of contract, there is a special relationship of proximity between a builder and a building owner which is sufficiently akin to contract to introduce the element of reliance, so that the scope of the duty of care owed by the builder to the owner is wide enough to embrace purely economic loss.

67. Hughes v. National Union of Mineworkers [1991] I.C.R. 669; [1991] 4 All E.R. 278, May J.

Claim by police officer against, *inter alios,* Chief Constable in negligence for causing, permitting or requiring him to take up a position in a police line without support from behind when facing a crowd of picketing miners at whose hands he suffered injury. Claim struck out—public policy required that senior police officers should not generally be liable to their subordinates who might be injured by rioters or the like for on-the-spot operational decisions taken in the course of attempts to control serious public disorder.

68. Surtees v. Kingston-upon-Thames B.C. [1991] 2 F.L.R. 559; [1992] C.L.Y. 3198, C.A.

Plaintiff placed in foster care by local authority—at two years old child sustained burn to foot in wash-basin by somehow activating hot tap whilst foster parent temporarily out of room—*Held,* (a) (Beldam L.J. dissenting) foster parents not negligent—duty owed same as for ordinary parent to his or her own children (b) as against authority, as a matter of causation claim bound to fail unless injuries deliberately inflicted—the occurrence of accidental injury by negligence could not be affected by the number of visits paid by the authority to the faster parents or the child, nor by the circumstances in which the child was boarded out unless urgent removal from the faster parents was required.

69. Targett v. Torfaen B.C. [1992] 3 All E.R. 27; [1992] C.L.Y. 3199, C.A.

Local authority landlord designed and built house let to plaintiff on weekly tenancy—plaintiff falls down inadequately lit steps to which no handrail and suffers injury—*Held,* liable—case indistinguishable from *Rimmer v. Liverpool C.C.* **26**, which had not been overruled by *Murphy* **66**.

70. Lonrho PLC v. Tebbit [1992] 4 All E.R. 282; [1992] C.L.Y. 2, C.A.

In the light of Monopolies and Mergers Commission report, plaintiff gave undertaking to the Secretary of State not to increase its shareholding in company it sought to take over. A subsequent Commission report concluded that the acquisition would not be contrary to the public interest—there was then delay by the Secretary of State in releasing the plaintiff from its undertaking by which time a rival bidder had been successful—*Held,* plaintiff's claim that there was a breach of duty to exercise the Secretary of State's duties and powers, in particular with regard to the undertaking, with reasonable care, would not be struck out as disclosing no reasonable cause of action.

71. Palmer v. L.B. of Harrow, *The Times*, April 22, 1992; [1992] 1 P.I.Q.R. P296, Potter J.

Local authority pursuant to statutory obligations sent children with special educational needs to a boarding school whose headmaster sexually abused them. It was alleged the authority was negligent in sending or allowing them to go there—*Held*, no duty of care owed.

72. Johnson v. Bournemouth B.C. [1992] E.G.C.S. 73; [1992] C.L.Y. 2650, C.A.

Plaintiff agreed to purchase lease, etc., of a hotel from owners, Dorset County Council. Approved form of enquiry to borough council stated replies where appropriate covered both district and county councils—answer referred to a policy statement which disclosed long-term plans for roads affecting property—oral inquiry received assurance that no development planned which would affect property—lease purchased—*Held*, on subsequent claim for damages inquiries not improperly answered and no liability.

73. Welsh v. Chief Constable of the Merseyside Police [1993] 1 All E.R. 692; [1993] C.L.Y. 2943, Tudor Evans J.

Plaintiff claimed damages against, *inter alios*, the Crown Prosecution Service alleging that they negligently failed to ensure magistrates' court was informed that two offences for which he was on bail had been taken into consideration in the Crown Court as a result of which he was arrested—*Held*, claim would not be struck out as disclosing no reasonable cause of action.

74. Alexandrou v. Oxford [1993] 4 All E.R. 328; [1990] C.L.Y. 3286, C.A.

Police attend shop premises in response to burglar alarm connected to station—failure to inspect rear of premises allowed burglars to escape with goods—*Held*, no sufficient special relationship between the shopkeeper and police to give rise to a duty of care—alternatively it was not fair or reasonable that the police should be under such a duty. *Hill v. Chief Constable* **56** followed.

75. Petch v. Customs & Excise Commissioners [1993] I.C.R. 789; [1994] C.L.Y. 1930, C.A.

Plaintiff alleged breakdown in health due to negligence of employers in causing him to be under excessive pressure of work and also by lack of care in furnishing information to the Treasury in respect of pension and injury benefit—conceded defendants owed him a duty to take reasonable care to ensure the duties allocated to him should not damage his health—*Held*, no breach of that duty.

76. Ancell v. McDermott [1993] R.T.R. 235; [1993] C.L.Y. 2958, C.A.

Police noticed spillage of diesel fuel on road but did not take steps to warn public of the danger—driver skidded thereon and accident resulted—*Held*, no duty of care owed, following *Hill v. Chief Constable* **56** and *Alexandrou v. Oxford* **74**.

77. R. v. L.B. of Lambeth, exp. Barnes (1993) 25 H.L.R. 140; [1993] C.L.Y. 2045, Rose J.

On application for judicial review by a homeless person, it was conceded the respondent was in breach of its duty under Housing Act 1985 to rehouse him—*Held*, applicant entitled to recover damages for breach of statutory duty—*Held*, further, on material before the court it was not established that the applicant had been negligently kept in temporary accommodation longer than was necessary to secure permanent accommodation but that eight months' unexplained silence could be categorised as negligence, for which applicant entitled to recover damages.

78. Ephraim v. Newham L.B.C. (1993) 91 L.G.R. 412; [1993] P.I.Q.R. P156, C.A.

Local authority pursuant to statutory duty advised plaintiff of where she might find accommodation—from that source she learnt of and found a room to rent in a house in multiple occupation—she there suffered injury due to inadequate fire precautions—*Held*, although sufficient degree of proximity, it was not fair, just or reasonable to impose a duty of care where the authority did not know of the inadequacy and where the imposition of such duty would oblige it to have inspected the property before giving such advice.

79. Barrett v. Ministry of Defence, (1995) 1 W.L.R. 1217, *The Times*, January 13 1995, C.A.

Held, defendant liable in negligence for death of naval airman who got so drunk that when unconscious he inhaled vomit and died—*Held*, no duty to prevent deceased from abusing alcohol as he did but there was a failure to provide adequate care or medical cover—deceased two-thirds contributorily negligent.

80. Holtom v. Barnet L.B.C., *The Times*, September 30, 1993; [1993] C.L.Y. 2855, Judge Oddie

Plaintiff under care of local authority treated, wrongly in the event, as mentally handicapped and severely subnormal—*Held*, on application to strike out, authority could be sued for being in breach of its obligations while it had been in *loco parentis* but not as local education authority—similarly, the plaintiff could not maintain an action against the school at which she was a pupil, it not being just or reasonable for it to owe the duty of care pleaded.

81. T. v. Surrey C.C., (1994) 4 All E.R. 577, *The Independent*, January 21, 1994; [1994] 2 C.L. 350, Scott Baker J.

Local authority recommending registered childminder to plaintiff's mother—*Held*, negligent in failing to inform her of a question mark as to her suitability and liable for brain injury caused by minder—*Held*, further, no common law duty owed in respect of failure to cancel registration pursuant to provisions of Nurseries and Childminders Regulation Act 1948: *held*, further, breach of statutory duty in not cancelling or suspending registration gave no private law remedy.

82. E. v. Dorset C.C. [1994] 3 W.L.R. 853; [1994] C.L.Y. 1878, C.A.

Held, it was at least arguable that a local education authority might be in breach of a duty of care owed to a child with special educational needs in assessing and providing therefor. But see now H.L. in (1995) 3 W.L.R. 152.

83. M. v. Newham L.B.C.; X (Minors) v. Bedfordshire C.C. [1994] 2 W.L.R. 554; [1994] C.L.Y. 4296, C.A.

Neither an action for breach of statutory duty nor (by a majority) one for common law negligence could be maintained by a child against a local authority in respect of acts or omissions for which the authority was responsible in the exercise of its functions under child care legislation. But see now H.L. in (1995) 3 W.L.R. 152.

84. Walker v. Northumberland C.C. [1994] N.L.J. 1659; [1994] C.L.Y. 2278, Colman J.

Held, local authority liable for mental breakdown of their employee, an area social services officer, caused by stress and pressures of work.

85. Lervold v. Chief Constable of Kent [1994] C.L.Y. 3385, C.A.

Plaintiff was lawfully arrested when his boat drifted ashore—whilst in detention his boat was looted and damaged by natural causes. His claim against the police that they owed a duty of care not struck out.

86. Elguzouli-Daz v. Commissioner of Police of the Metropolis; McBrearty v. Ministry of Defence (1995) 2 W.L.R. 173; [1994] C.L.Y. 3345, C.A.

Alleged negligence of Crown Prosecution Service for delay in deciding to abandon prosecutions; claims struck out as no duty of care owed either on ground that it was not fair, just & reasonable to impose such a duty—alternatively, the service was immune from liability in negligence. *Caparo* (Chap. 18, (1) **17**) and *Hill v. Chief Constable of West Yorkshire* **56** applied. *Welsh v. Chief Constable of the Merseyside Police* **73** distinguished.

87. Dear v. Thames Water (1994) 33 Con. L.R. 43; [1994] C.L.Y. 3405, Judge Bowsher Q.C.

The plaintiff claimed in negligence and nuisance against the water and local authorities for damage to his house caused by the ingress of foul and storm water resulting from the overflowing of two partially culverted streams—one of the streams was the responsibility of the National Rivers Authority who was not a party to the action—the other ran through private land and was not a public sewer. The claim in negligence was based on a negligent failure to carry out statutory duties (there was no claim for breach of statutory duty or for breach of strict liability)—*Held*, such common law duty and in any event negligence had not been established—claim in nuisance also failed.

U1. Marsden v. L.B. of Havering (1984) C.A. 114

Plaintiff injured when door knocker came away in hand due to defect of which landlord knew—*Held*, liable.

U2. Foy v. Dacorum B.C. (1987) C.A. 1001

Held, council not negligent over answers to inquiries as to existence of public path or byway over plaintiff's land or whether such was maintainable at public expense.

U3. King v. Liverpool C.C. (1990) C.A. 885

Plaintiffs' ground floor flat in block owned by council flooded by escape of water from loft—*Held*, landlord liable—*res ipsa loquitur.*

(14) Schoolmasters

(a) Supervision and Care

		Liable or not
P.T.—STUMBLE WHILE VAULTING	1	Yes
Playground—no teacher	2,4	No
FARMWORK—NO TEACHER	3	No
INDOOR GAME—"TOUCH" IN ROOM WITH GLASS PARTITION	5	Yes
P.T.—VAULTING—BOY AT END CATCHING	6	No
ATTACK BY CO-PUPIL—LUMP OF COKE FROM STACK	7	No
Picnic—pupil climbing up onto unlikely place	8	No
ATTACK BY CO-PUPIL—METAL BARS FROM PLAYGROUND SHED	9	No
FIGHTING—PLAINTIFF ACCIDENTALLY KNIFED IN LEG	10	No
Playground—pupil of six climbing up pipe	11	No
Classroom—leaving children of four alone for 10 minutes—escape onto road	12	Yes
Escape onto road by children of four—presumption of negligence	12	—
Attack by co-pupil—handicraft knife taken from unlocked cupboard	13	No
Attack by co-pupil—home-made arrow—approved school	14	No
Attack by co-pupil—with scissors during handicrafts	15	No
HOLIDAY HOME—PUPIL CLIMBING TREE BY LADDER AND JUMPING DOWN	16	Yes
POT OF HOT TEA—PUPIL OF 14 REQUIRED TO CARRY—SCALDED	17	No
PLAYGROUND—ROUNDERS—BAT PROHIBITED BUT USED	18	No
Attack by co-pupil—air pistol	19	No
Visit to zoo—wandering in unsupervised groups	20	No
Attack by co-pupil—piece of coke thrown in playground	21	No
Classroom—pupils squirting caustic soda—thinking it water	22	No
JUDO CLASS—STUDENT'S ARM BROKEN IN COMBAT	23	No
Morning break—horseplay	24	Yes
School bus—horseplay—no teacher on board	25	No
Letting child of five out too early—no parent to meet—is negligent	26	Yes
Girls aged eleven playing cricket unsupervised	27	No
PLAYGROUND—INFANTS THROWING SAND—JUST AFTER SCHOOL HOURS	28	No
P.T.—HANDSTAND—PUPIL UNFIT FOR P.T.—NO SUPERVISION	29	Yes
ART CLASS—SHARP-ENDED SCISSORS—BOY OF 7 INJURED USING THE SAME	30	Yes
TACKLING PUPILS AT RUGBY	31	Yes
Woodworking machine—pupil absent when demonstrated—injury on use	32	Yes
Trampoline accident at end of lesson after pupils told to finish	33	No
ACCIDENT PLAYING RUGBY	34	No
Pupil treated at school on basis that mentally handicapped and severely subnormal—wrongly in the event	35	No
Standard of care—that of a parent of 20 children	U1	—
Apparent injury to child—no steps taken beyond examination	U2	No
School bus—plaintiff allowed to cross unsupervised after leaving bus	U3	Yes

Marking of university examination papers—court has no jurisdiction to hear complaints	U4	No
Three boys of eight left to push heavy piano without supervision	U5	Yes
Children in road—Cub Scouts on treasure hunt in small groups—one group dashing out across suburban road	U6	No
Girls aged 15 knocking up at tennis in gymnasium unsupervised	U7	No
School taxi—taxi driver dropped off plaintiff at dangerous spot	U8	No
Fall from parallel bars in gym	U9	No
Stone thrown by pupil on geology expedition injures another	U10	Yes
Cadet on army assault course falls and breaks wrists	U11	No
Plaintiff at youth camp knocked down by minibus driven without authority	U12	No
Band saw machine causing injury—pupil had received instruction and supervision	U13	No
Nursery school pupil trapped thumb in nip between door and jamb of Wendy house	U14	No

1. Gibbs v. Barking Corporation [1936] 1 All E.R. 115, C.A.

Boy falls while vaulting—*Held*, defendants liable. "The games master does not seem to have acted with that promptitude which the law requires" (Slesser L.J., 116).

2. Rawsthorne v. Otley [1937] 3 All E.R. 902, Hilbery J.

Held, that the staff were not negligent in leaving the boys in the playground without supervision.

3. Camkin v. Bishop [1941] 2 All E.R. 713, C.A.

Schoolboys go out to do war work on local farm—*Held*, in strong language, headmaster under no duty whatever to provide supervision.

4. Ricketts v. Erith B.C. [1943] 2 All E.R. 629, Tucker J.

Held, not negligence.

5. Ralph v. London C.C. (1947) 63 T.L.R. 546, C.A.

Children playing "touch" in schoolroom with glass partition—plaintiff puts hand through glass—*Held*, that as a reasonably prudent parent would have contemplated danger defendants liable for not supervising game to prevent danger.

6. Wright v. Cheshire C.C. [1952] 2 All E.R. 789; [1952] W.N. 466, C.A.

Held, not negligent to have boy instead of master at end of line to catch.

7. Rich v. London C.C. [1953] 1 W.L.R. 895; [1953] 2 All E.R. 376, C.A.

Plaintiff a pupil injured by a lump of coke thrown by co-pupil and obtained from unfenced coke stack on playground—*Held*, defendants not liable—defendants' duty was to take such care "as a careful father would take of his boys"; the supervision was adequate, and it could not be said that a careful father would fence in a stack of coke.

8. Trevor v. Inc. Froebel Institute, *The Times*, February 11, 1954; [1954] C.L.Y. 2238, Sellers J.

Held, defendants not liable.

9. Driscoll v. Grattan Wilson [1954] C.L.Y. 2239, C.A.

Held, defendants not liable.

10. Clark v. Monmouthshire C.C. (1954) 118 J.P. 244; [1954] C.L.Y. 2240, C.A.

Held, defendants not liable. Denning L.J.: "The duty of a schoolmaster does not extend to constant supervision of all the boys all the time. That is not practicable. Only reasonable supervision is required." (Plaintiff was 13.)

11. Jeffrey v. L.C.C. (1954) 52 L.G.R. 521; [1954] C.L.Y. 2241, McNair J.

Plaintiff aged five years 10 months climbed from playground up water pipe on to glass roof through which he fell and died—*Held*, defendants not liable: " . . . it seems to me that school authorities . . . must strike some balance between the meticulous supervision of children every moment of the time when they are under their care, and the very desirable object of encouraging the sturdy independence of children as they grow up; and I think encouragement of sturdy independence and the ability to get on without detailed supervision must start at quite an early age."

12. Carmarthenshire C.C. v. Lewis [1955] A.C. 549; [1955] 1 All E.R. 565, H.L.

Two children of four left in classroom by mistress intending to be away a few minutes—she is away 10 minutes, as she has to tend to injured child—while she is away children escape into playground and thence onto road—causing traffic accident—plaintiff's husband killed—plaintiff sues school—*Held*, school authorities owed road users a duty of care in such circumstances, and that, though the mistress was not negligent, the escape onto the road through the playground raised a presumption of negligence, and as defendants had called no evidence to explain the escape, they had failed to discharge onus and were liable.

13. Suckling v. Essex C.C., *The Times*, January 27, 1955; [1955] C.L.Y. 1844, Vaisey J.

One pupil attacks another with a scorer knife (used for handicrafts) taken from unlocked cupboard—*Held*, defendants not liable.

14. Smith v. Hale, *The Times*, October 27 1956; [1956] C.L.Y. 5940, Ormerod J.

Held, defendants not liable as they had taken all reasonable steps to prevent arrow throwing.

15. Ellesmere v. Middlesex C.C., *The Times*, December 12, 1956; [1956] C.L.Y. 6025, Hallett J.

Held, defendants not liable.

16. Peters v. Hill, *The Times*, March 29, 1957; [1957] C.L.Y. 2367, C.A.

Held, defendant liable for not having adequate supervision to see that plaintiff, aged seven, came down the tree by the ladder, which was left accessible for children.

17. Cooper v. Manchester Corporation, *The Times*, February 13, 1959; [1959] C.L.Y. 2260, C.A.

Held, reversing trial judge, defendants not liable.

18. Price v. Caernarvonshire C.C., *The Times*, February 11, 1960; [1960[C.L.Y. 2145, C.A.

Held, defendants not liable, as use of bat prohibited, and prohibition observed when headmaster shortly before had visited yard.

19. Harris v. Guest, *The Times*, October 25, 1960; [1960] C.L.Y. 2146, Fenton Atkinson J.

Schoolboy aged 16 injured by an air pistol discharged by a fellow pupil during an unsupervised period at school—*Held*, school were not liable, as it would be too onerous to require that a class of 20 boys and girls aged about 16 should be constantly supervised.

20. Murphy v. Zoological Society, *The Times*, November 14, 1962; [1962] C.L.Y. 68, Fenton Atkinson J.

Visit of scout cubs to Whipsnade Zoo—35 boys and three adults in charge—plaintiff aged 10 and two boys visited lions' cage unaccompanied and climbed between the two guarding fences—one of them provoked lion which mauled plaintiff—*Held*, (a) zoo not liable, because boys trespassers, and further no lion had "escaped", and (b) Boy Scouts' Association not liable, because it was not negligent of those in charge to allow boys to split up into unsupervised groups, and in any event the Association was not vicariously liable for the acts of scout-masters and cub-mistresses.

21. Newton v. East Ham Corporation, *The Guardian*, July 11, 1963, Lord Parker C.J.

Boy of four in school playground injured by piece of coke thrown by older boy—a supervisor was present, but her attention was elsewhere—*Held*, defendants not liable, as there was no obligation to provide efficient supervision to watch all parts of the school playground at the same time.

22. Crouch v. Essex C.C. (1966) 64 L.G.R. 240; [1967] C.L.Y. 2739, Widgery J.

23. Conrad v. I.L.E.A. (1967) 111 S.J. 684; *The Times*, May 26, 1967, C.A.

24. Beaumont v. Surrey C.C. (1968) 66 L.G.R. 580; [1968] C.L.Y. 2726. Geoffrey Lane J.

Mixed secondary school of 900 pupils between 11 and 18—during morning break two teachers were allotted to clear the classrooms and supervise pupils in playground—on the day in question they were mainly engaged in clearing the classrooms—there was a nine-foot-long powerful piece of elastic which the P.T. master had discarded and put in an open waste bin—this was used in horseplay, and P's eye was injured—*Held*, school liable (a) for inadequate supervision and (b) for leaving elastic in open bin.

25. Jacques v. Oxfordshire C.C. (1968) 66 L.G.R. 440; [1968] C.L.Y. 2727, Waller J.

Plaintiff hit in eye by pellet fired in school bus—no adult, save driver, on board—discipline entrusted to two prefects—*Held*, school owed a duty of care, but on the facts were not liable.

26. Barnes v. Hampshire C.C. [1969] 1 W.L.R. 1563; [1969] 3 All E.R. 746, H.L.

27. Turner v. Somerset C.C. [1974] C.L.Y. 2581, Croom-Johnson J.

28. Good v. I.L.E.A. (1980) 10 Fam. Law 213; [1981] C.L.Y. 1830, C.A.

At end of school hours P, aged $6\frac{1}{2}$, and the rest of his class were escorted onto school playground where majority of pupils were collected by waiting parents. The rest (including P) would go to an adjacent play centre. On the playground was a pile of building sand, which was roped off and which pupils had been warned to keep away from (play centre was not quite ready to open). P and companion went away to the sand and the companion threw some at P, injuring his eye. No staff were present to witness the incident—*Held*, defendants not liable for want of supervision. No one could reasonably be expected to keep an eye on the children every minute of the day.

29. Moore v. Hampshire C.C. *The Times*, November 6, 1981; [1981] C.L.Y. 579, C.A.

Pupil disabled and unfit for P.T. Teacher advised of this but pupil persuaded teacher she was allowed to do P.T. No supervision of pupil who was injured attempting handstand—*Held*, case was indefensible.

30. Black v. Kent C.C. (1983) 82 LGR 39; The Times, May 23, 1983, C.A.

In art class chair of P aged 7 jogged and P was jabbed in eye by the sharp point of scissors he was using—*Held*, D liable. The use of sharp scissors in such a class involved appreciably greater risk of injury than the use of blunt scissors, and ought to be avoided unless there were valid reasons to the contrary.

31. Affutu-Nartoy v. Clarke, *The Times*, February 9, 1984; (1984) C.L.Y. 3391, Hodgson J.

32. Hoar v. Board of School Trustees (1984) 6 W.W.R. 143; [1985] C.L.Y. 2333, British Columbia C.A.

Pupil injured himself on wood-working machine; he had been absent when its use had been demonstrated—*Held*, school liable—50 per cent contributory negligence.

33. Bills v. State of South Australia (1985) 38 SASR 80; [1986] C.L.Y. 2286

At end of trampoline lesson, teacher told pupils to pack up and walked a short distance away—plaintiff mounted trampoline and was injured—*Held*, teacher not negligent.

34. Van Oppen v. Clerk to the Bedford Charity Trustees [1990] 1 W.L.R. 235; [1989] 3 All E.R. 389, C.A.

Pupil at school suffered severe spiral injury when playing rugby football—negligence was alleged on the part of the school in

(a) coaching & instruction (this was rejected by the trial judge (1989) 1 All E.R. 273 and not appealed from);
(b) failing to advise his father of the risks and of the need to insure,
(c) failing to insure themselves

Held, as to (b) and (c); it would be neither just nor reasonable to impose on the school a greater duty than that which rested on a parent, there was no such proximity between the school and the plaintiff as to give rise to a general duty to have regard to his economic welfare or, if there were, it was neither fair nor reasonable to impose such a duty

35. Holton v. Barnet L.B.C., The Times, September 30, 1993; [1993] C.L.Y. 2855, Judge Oddie

For details see Chap. 18(13) **80**.

U1. Nicholson v. Westmorland C.C., *The Times*, October 25, 1962; [1962] C.L.Y. 2087, C.A.

Held, that the test of reasonable care was that of a reasonably careful parent, but of a parent of 20 children.

U2. Davies v. Cornwall C.C. (1962) C.A. 308

Girl of six fell at school—fracture of leg—not reasonably discoverable by school staff at the time—girl was weeping, sweating and complaining of pain in her leg—beyond examining leg staff did nothing but allowed girl to walk to shop of an aunt close by—*Held*, not negligent not to have taken further steps (such as sending for parents or medical aid).

U3. Ellis v. Sayers Confectionery (1963) 61 L.G.R. 299; (1963) C.A. 56A

Plaintiff pupil, aged eight, deaf and dumb, run down while crossing road after leaving school bus—*Held*, lady in charge on bus was liable for not seeing it was safe for plaintiff to cross. 20 per cent. v. school, 80 per cent. v. vehicle (excessive speed).

U4. Thorne v. London University (1966) C.A. 79

U5. Street v. Hampshire C.C. (1969) C.A. 103

U6. Atherton v. Bentley (1970) C.A. 212

U7. Hopkins v. Birmingham Corporation (1974) C.A. 351

U8. Myton v. Woods and Essex C.C. (1980) C.A. 646

Education authority arranged with taxi firm to transport retarded child to and from school. Taxi driver set down child at dangerous spot and the child was injured—*Held*, that the authority were not vicariously liable for the driver's negligence. A reasonable parent would have engaged taxi firm and would not have supervised the driver.

U9. Walters v. Liverpool C.C. (1983) C.A. 609

10-year-old child, contrary to instructions, walked along one instead of both parallel bars in gymnasium and fell—*Held*, supervising teacher not negligent in failing to observe such disobedience in time.

U10. Porter v. City of Bradford M.C. (1985) C.A. 901

16½-year-old boy on voluntary geology expedition, having been told to stop rolling boulders down a path, while teacher out of sight threw stones into river, one of which caused head injury to fellow pupil—*Held*, defendants liable.

U11. Morgan v. Avonhurst School Educational Trust Ltd (1985), C.A. 982

Demonstration of army assault course by cadets—plaintiff lost grip on rope, fell and broke wrists—*Held*, defendants not liable.

U12. Mason v. Essex C.C. (1988) C.A. 295

Plaintiff knocked down and injured at youth camp by volunteer driving a minibus—volunteer knew not allowed to drive—*Held* accident did not occur in course of employment—defendants not liable.

U13. Watson v. Mid Glamorgan C.C. (1989) C.A. 971

15-year-old pupil injured right wrist on band saw machine in wood workshop—he had received instruction and been supervised in its use—*Held*, defendants not liable.

U14. Smart v. Gwent C.C. (1991) C.A. 397

Three-year-old child caught thumb in nip between door of Wendy house and jamb at nursery school—30 in class supervised by experienced teacher—*Held*, defendants not liable.

(b) State of Premises

		Liable or not
Room with glass partition—indoor game	1	Yes
ROOM WITH GLASS PARTITION—INDOOR GAME	2	Yes
Glass swing door—child left unattended in hospital	3	Yes
Room with thin glass panel—indoor game	4	Yes
Glass swing door—$\frac{1}{8}$ in. thick	5	Yes
GLASS ON PLAYGROUND—FROM BROKEN MILK BOTTLE	6	Yes
UNFENCED PRINTING MACHINE—SCHOOL LIABLE AT COMMON LAW	7	Yes
FLING WALL IN PLAYGROUND—BOY FALLING AGAINST	8	No
Glass door (in children's room of public house)—$\frac{1}{8}$ in. thick	U1	No
Glass windows—inadequately guarded during rough game	U2	Yes
Double swing doors—forearm trapped as swung closed	U3	No

1. Cahill v. West Ham Corporation (1937) 81 S.J. 630, Porter J.

Relay race indoors—boy put hand through glass partition—*Held*, defendants liable.

2. Ralph v. London C.C. (1947) 63 T.L.R. 546, C.A.

Playing "touch" in schoolroom—plaintiff put hand through glass partition—*Held*, defendants liable.

3. Gravestock v. Lewisham Hospital Management Committee, *The Times*, May 27, 1955; [1955] C.L.Y. 1853, Streatfeild J.

Girl patient aged nine—left unattended temporarily—ran into glass swing door—*Held*, defendants liable.

4. Lyes v. Middlesex C.C. (1962) 61 L.G.R. 443; [1962] C.L.Y. 2425, Edmund Davies J.

Fifteen-year-old schoolboy playing when hand went through glass panel in door—*Held*, (a) that panel was too thin and therefore was not "efficient" (b) the defendants were therefore in breach of School Grants Regulations 1951, reg. 5 and the Education Act 1944, s.10(2); (c) that the standard of care required of defendants was that of a careful parent applying his mind to school life, where there was more larking, rather than to home life; and that (d) applying this standard, defendants were liable.

5. Refell v. Surrey C.C. [1964] 1 W.L.R. 358; [1964] 1 All E.R. 743, Veale J.

Considered by C.A. in **U1**.

6. Martin v. Middlesborough Corporation (1965) 63 L.G.R. 385; [1965] C.L.Y. 2735, C.A.

7. Butt v. I.L.E.A. (1968) 66 L.G.R. 379; [1968] C.L.Y. 2724, C.A.

8. Ward v. Herts C.C., *The Times*, December 19, 1969; [1969] C.L.Y. 2473, C.A.

U1. Gurney v. Everards Brewery (1975) C.A. 518

Children's room in public house—double doors glazed from two feet 6 inches up with panels $7\frac{1}{2}$ in. by $10\frac{1}{2}$ in.—$\frac{1}{8}$ in. thick—panels had been there for over 30 years without incident—by 1966 British Standard Code of Practice C.P. 152 of 1966 required such panels to be of toughened glass—plaintiff aged nine put hand through panel during play—*Held*, defendants not liable. *Refell* **5** was distinguished on the facts, inasmuch as there (a) it was a swing door in a girls' school leading to the lavatory; (b) the panel was $8\frac{1}{4}$ in. by 15 in., and (c) the evidence showed that it was an obvious danger.

U2. Meadows v. Scout Association (1977) C.A. 52

U3. Meehan v. Lancashire C.C. (1988) C.A. 1006

(15) Solicitors

1. Richards v. Cox [1943] 1 K.B. 139; [1942] 2 All E.R. 624, C.A.

Managing clerk advised plaintiff wrongly on a difficult of motor insurance law—*Held*, negligent, as he should have consulted his principal or counsel.

2. Yager v. Toff [1944] 1 All E.R. 552, C.A.

Held, in general, no duty to warn client of approach of option date in lease.

3. Lake v. Bushby [1949] 2 All E.R. 964; [1950] W.N. 28, Pritchard J.

Held, negligence. Judge also said duty of solicitor arises *ex contractu* only.

4. Bailey v. Bullock [1950] 2 All E.R. 1167; [1950] W.N. 482, Barry J.

June 1947 plaintiff gave defendant instructions to obtain possession of house, December 1948 notice to quit served by defendant—March 1949 plaintiff consulted other solicitors—*Held*, negligence.

5. Griffiths v. Evans [1953] 1 W.L.R. 1424; [1953] 2 All E.R. 1364, C.A.

Held, in the circumstances of the case, not negligent, since plaintiff consulted defendant solely with regard to the quantum of compensation, and not generally.

6. Simmons v. Pennington [1955] 1 W.L.R. 183; [1955] 1 All E.R. 240, C.A.

Solicitor answers a requisition in "stock form"—saying that there are restrictive covenants and appear to have been breaches in the past, but no notice of breach has been served—in reality the covenants were obsolete but solicitor did not say so, and as a result purchaser rescinded—*Held*, this was not negligent, as the solicitor was following general practice (but see 243 H, it might well be negligence in future).

7. Goody v. Baring [1956] 1 W.L.R. 448; [1956] 2 All E.R. 11, Danckwerts J.

Held, negligence.

8. Dunn v. Fairs (1961) 105 S.J. 932; [1961] C.L.Y. 8501, Barry J.

Woman dying of cancer, shortly before death, bought annuity—did so because solicitor "caused or permitted" her to do so—administrator sued for loss to estate of woman—*Held*, solicitor owed no duty to administrator, and in any event he was not negligent, as to have disclosed reason for not purchasing annuity would have meant disclosing to her that she suffered from an incurable disease.

9. Gregory v. Tarlo (1964) 108 S.J. 219; *The Times*, March 6, 1964, McNair J.

Held, negligence, and awarded, in view of strength of claim, three-quarters of likely damages, plus 12 per cent. for resulting delay.

10. Clark v. Kirby Smith [1964] Ch. 506; [1964] 2 All E.R. 835, Plowman J. (see now **22**)

Failure to apply in time for new business lease—plaintiff claimed (a) for loss of new lease, (b) for cost of dilapidations which he had to pay, and (c) for costs of negotiating (b)—*Held*, that claim lay in contract, and items (b) and (c) accordingly could not be recovered, and were in any event the result of the plaintiff's own breach of covenant; and, as to (a) nominal damages only, because the plaintiff had produced no evidence as to the value, if any, which a new lease would have had.

11. Hill v. Harris [1965] 2 Q.B. 601; [1965] 2 All E.R. 358, C.A.

12. Bryant v. Goodrich (1966) 110 S.J. 108; [1966] C.L.Y. 11468, C.A.

Held, solicitor liable.

13. Attard v. Samson (1966) 110.S.J. 249; [1966] C.L.Y. 11481, Phillimore J.

14. Cook v. S. [1967] 1 W.L.R. 457; [1967] 1 All E.R. 299, C.A.

Held, error of judgment by counsel did not break chain of causation (see, for this, [1966] 1 All E.R. 248, Lawton J.)—*Held*, also, that plaintiff could not claim damages for nervous shock, for although such damages could be claimed in contract (as well as in tort), it was not in general a reasonably foreseeable consequence, and although the defendant might be liable if the plaintiff had a special propensity to nervous shock which was known to the defendant, it was not proved that the defendant here knew any more than that the plaintiff was a highly strung woman, which was not enough. See **21** and **22**.

15. Neushul v. Mellish (1967) 111 S.J. 399; (1967) 203 E.G. 27, C.A.

Plaintiff, a widow of 47, being infatuated with one F, wanted to lend him money, and she employed defendant solicitor to raise second mortgage on her house for this purpose—defendant gave plaintiff no advice on the dangers of the transaction—F, on receiving loan, left the country—*Held*, (2–1) defendant liable to plaintiff. *N.B.* Facts may have been somewhat special; for defendant had knowledge of F's affairs and was acting for him as well, and a bank manager had strongly advised plaintiff against the loan.

16. Rondel v. Worsley [1969] 1 A.C. 191; [1967] 3 All E.R. 993, H.L.

H.L. said *obiter* that the immunity of a barrister in the conduct of a case (see Chap. 18 (3) **1**) extended also to solicitors acting as advocates. The exact extent of this immunity in connection with work done before a hearing is not certain.

17. Buckland v. Mackesy (1968) 112 S.J. 841; [1968] C.L.Y. 3721, C.A.

Held, solicitor had sufficiently discharged his duty by warning purchaser of danger of signing contract before mortgage application approved.

18. Sykes v. Midland Bank [1971] 1 Q.B. 113; [1970] 2 All E.R. 471, C.A.

Held, defendants were negligent, but plaintiff could only recover 40s. nominal damages, since he had not shown that if he had been warned of the covenant he would have altered his conduct in entering into the lease.

19. Stinchcombe and Cooper v. Addison (1971) 115 S.J. 368; [1971] C.L.Y. 8033, Brightman J.

20. Collard v. Saunders [1971] C.L.Y. 11161, Mocatta J.

Held, D liable (but not for all the items of damage claimed).

21. Heywood v. Wellers [1976] Q.B. 446; [1976] 1 All E.R. 300, C.A. (see now **22**)

Owing to negligence of solicitors a husband was able to continue molesting plaintiff wife for a substantial period—causing her mental distress—*Held*, she could recover damages for such distress. Lord Denning M.R. (306 H) applied, as the test, the second rule in *Hadley v. Baxendale*, saying that the damage which the plaintiff suffered was certainly within the contemplation of the defendants. He also said that *Cook*, **14** though a different case, might need to be reconsidered. James L.J. (309 E) applied the test formulated by Lord Denning M.R. in *Cook* **14**, *i.e.* the line is to be drawn where in a particular case the "good sense" of the judge decides. Bridge L.J. (310 H) said that there was "a clear distinction to be drawn between mental distress which is an incidental consequence to the client of the misconduct of litigation by his solicitor, on the one hand, and mental distress on the other hand which is the direct and inevitable consequence of the solicitor's negligent failure to obtain the very relief which it was the sole purpose of the litigation to secure."

22. Midland Bank Trust Co. v. Hett Stubbs & Kemp [1979] Ch. 384; [1978] 3 All E.R. 571, Oliver J.

Held, applying *Esso v. Mardon* Chap. 1(5) **13**, and not following *Clark* **10** and dicta *Cook* **14** and *Heywood* **21**. More generally, see cases in Chap. 1, (5).

23. Mainz v. Dodd, *The Times*, July 21, 1978, Watkins J.

24. Power v. Halley (1978) 88 D.L.R. (3d) 981; [1979] C.L.Y. 2562, Nfld.Sup.Ct.

25. Ladenbau v. Crawley [1978] 1 W.L.R. 266; [1978] 1 All E.R. 682, Mocatta J.

26. Saif Ali v. Sydney Mitchell [1980] A.C. 198; [1978] 3 All E.R. 1033, H.L.

27. Ross v. Caunters [1980] Ch. 297; [1979] 3 All E.R. 580, Meggarry V.C.

Testator instructed his solicitor to draft will giving legacy to plaintiff. Through an oversight the solicitor allowed plaintiff's husband to attest the will—*Held*. (a) solicitor owed a duty of care to legatee (as to which see Chap. 7(1)(a) **16**), and (b) the fact that the claim was for financial loss alone was no bar (for details see Chap. 1(3)(a)**8**).

28. Rowe v. Turner Hopkins [1980] N.Z.L.R. 550; [1981] C.L.Y. 1852, N.Z. High Ct.

Held, that the solicitor had been negligent.

29. Seale v. Perry [1982] V.R. 193; [1983] C.L.Y. 2569, Supreme Ct. of Victoria

A solicitor failed to ensure that a will was executed in accordance with statutory provisions as a result of which intended beneficiaries received nothing—*Held*, by a majority, not following *Ross v. Caunters* **27**, that the solicitor did not owe a duty of care to the intended beneficiaries—*Held*, Also, that the intended beneficiaries had not suffered any loss recognisable in law.

30. Carradine Properties v. Freeman (1989) 5 Const. L.J. 267; [1990] C.L.Y. 3283, C.A.

Held, that the defendant solicitors were not liable in negligence for failing to enquire whether their experienced property developer client held a property owner's liability insurance policy. An experienced client may require less advice than an inexperienced one.

31. Computastaff Ltd v. Ingledew Brown Bennison & Garrett (1983) New L.J. 598; [1983] C.L.Y. 2574

Held, solicitors negligent.

32. R. P. Howard v. Woodman Matthews & Co. [1983] Com. L.R. 100; [1983] C.L.Y. 3611, Staughton J.

Held, that the solicitor had been negligent and was liable both to the company and to its effective "owner" who had suffered a separate loss.

33. Edward Wong Finance Co. v. Johnson, Stokes & Master [1984] 2 W.L.R. 1; [1983] C.L.Y. 3887, P.C.

Held, that the conveyancing practice known as a "Hong Kong style" completion which involves the purchasers' solicitors forwarding the purchase money to the vendor's solicitors on undertakings by the latter is negligent, because there is a foreseeable risk of the latter misappropriating the money.

34. McNamara v. Martin Mears & Co. (1983) 127 S.J. 69; [1983] C.L.Y. 3609, Peter Pain J.

Held, that it was the duty of a solicitor to make proper inquiries as to the assets and circumstances of the parties to a divorce before advising on a settlement figure. The defendants had failed to make such inquiries and were negligent. The measure of damage was the difference between the settlement which should have been advised and the settlement reached on the basis of the negligent advice.

35. Dogma Property Ltd v. Gale (1984) 134 New L.J. 453; [1984] C.L.Y. 2339, Kilner Brown J.

36. Raintree Ltd v. Holmes & Hills (1984) 134 New L.J. 522; [1984] C.L.Y. 336, Hobhouse J.

37. Trustee of Property of P.A.F. Foster v. Crusts [1986] BCLC 307; [1985] C.L.Y. 2309, Judge Finlay Q.C.

Solicitors failed to advise limited company to register charge under the Companies Act 1948 s. 95—*Held*, any duty owed to company also owed to guarantors of company's debt. Statement of claim not struck out.

38. Holmes v. H. Kennard & Son (1985) 49 P. & C.R. 202; [1985] C.L.Y. 2939, C.A.

Solicitor liable for relying on the form for withdrawing a caution, as vacating a notice registered at the Land Registry of a wife's interest in a property under the Matrimonial Homes Act 1967.

39. G.P. & P. Ltd v. Bulcraig & Davies [1986] 2 E.G.L.R. 148; [1986] C.L.Y. 2285, John Gorman Q.C.

Held, solicitors for plaintiffs in and about obtaining lease liable for failure to discover that planning permission limited use of part of premises as offices in connection with the printing trade—plaintiff's surveyor who helped find the premises not liable—appeal [1988] 1 E.G.L.R. 138 concerned quantum and costs only. See Chap. 18, (5) **18**.

40. County Personnel (Employment Agency) Ltd v. Alan R. Pulver & Co. [1987] 1 W.L.R. 916; [1987] 1 All E.R. 289, C.A.

Unusual rent review clause in underlease—solicitor should have advised underlessee not to proceed at least without further investigation—*Sykes v. Midland Bank Executor & Trustee Co. Ltd* **18** followed.

41. McClellan v. Fletcher (1987) 137 New L.J. 593; [1987] C.L.Y. 3559, Anthony Lincoln J.

Held, solicitor negligent in failing to ensure a life insurance policy had been taken out where the policy was part of the security in which a mortgage was advanced for purchase of house by deceased—deceased had lost the contingent interest in such policy less the premium payable—75 per cent deduction for deceased's contributory negligence in failing to pay premium.

42. Re A. (A Minor) (Costs) (1988) 18 Fam. Law 339; [1988] C.L.Y. 3371, C.A.

Solicitors negligent in not pursuing appeal expeditiously—personally liable in costs to opposing party.

43. Dutfield v. Gilbert H. Stephens & Sons (1988) 18 Fam Law 473; [1989] C.L.Y. 1740, Anthony Lincoln J.

Held, solicitors not liable in and about advice to wife in divorce proceedings as regards financial provision.

44. Clarke v. Bruce Lance & Co. [1988] 1 W.L.R. 881; [1988] 1 All E.R. 364, C.A.

Testator by will left freehold interest in a garage to the plaintiff and his wife—testator subsequently instructed solicitors to draw up option to purchase garage to lessees exercisable after testator's and his wife's death. On testator's death, plaintiff alleged solicitors should have advised testator that the granting of the option was misconceived, uncommercial and prejudiced the plaintiff—*Held*, no duty of care owed by solicitors to plaintiff. *Yuen Kun Yeu v. Att Gen. of Hong Kong* (Chap. 18, (2) **26**) followed: *Ross v. Caunters* **27** distinguished.

45. Hawkins v. Clayton (1988) 164 CLR 539; [1989] C.L.Y. 2560, High Ct. of Australia

Solicitors retaining deceased's will delayed attempts to find and inform executor for six years—*Held*, in breach of duty to take reasonable steps to find him and liable for loss suffered by estate due to delay.

46. Al-Kandari v. J. R. Brown & Co [1988] Q.B. 665; [1988] 1 All E.R. 833, C.A.

Solicitors acted for plaintiff's husband in proceedings between them—the solicitors held the husband's passport which was also that of the children who were in the custody, care and control of the plaintiff—*Held*, liable to plaintiff in damages for negligent failure to tell her that the passport was no longer under their control.

47. Somasundaram v. M. Julius Melchior & Co. [1988] 1 W.L.R. 1394; [1989] 1 All E.R. 129, C.A.

Plaintiff claimed in civil proceedings that solicitors had been negligent in persuading him to plead guilty in criminal proceedings and in mitigation. Claim struck out—plaintiff was seeking to attack in civil proceedings the final decision of a criminal court of competent jurisdiction *Hunter v. Chief Constable of the West Midlands Police* [1982] A.C. 529 applied.

48. Strover v. Harrington [1988] 1 EGLR 173; [1988] C.L.Y. 489, Sir Nicholas Brown-Wilkinson V.-C.

For details see Chap. 18, (5) **23**.

49. O'Boyle v. Leiper, The Times, January 26, 1990; [1990] C.L.Y. 3255, C.A.

Solicitors compromised claim by client for negligent mislaying of deeds which delayed completion of sale of property. Subsequent claim by client for contribution in proceedings brought by purchaser against him—*Held*, solicitors not liable to contribute.

50. Stratton Ltd v. Weston, The Financial Times, April 11, 1990; [1990] C.L.Y. 3295, Judge Hywel Moseley Q.C.

Tenant alleged solicitors negligent in failing to register agreement for lease upon learning of receivership of landlords—*Held*, not liable as registration would have served no purpose.

51. Lynne v. Gordon Doctors & Walton, The Times, June 17, 1991; [1991] C.L.Y. 2674, Phillips J.

A deceased mortgagee whose solicitors had allegedly failed to ensure his life was insured as part of the mortgage transaction did not suffer any loss thereby on his death. *McClellan* **41** distinguished.

52. Westway Homes Ltd v. Gore Wood & Co., The Times, July 9, 1991; [1991] C.L.Y. 3384, C.A.

Solicitor allegedly negligent in giving notice to vendor's solicitor instead of to vendor; summary judgment set aside—the solicitor's course of conduct rather than his state of mind had to be judged, namely whether no prudent solicitor would have so acted.

53. Smith v. Claremont Haynes & Co., The Times, September 3, 1991; [1991] C.L.Y. 3383, Judge Barnett Q.C.

54. Robins v. Meadows & Moran [1991] 2 E.G.L.R. 137; [1991] C.L.Y. 2673, Judge Bates Q.C.

Held, solicitors negligent in and about carrying out instructions to sell property and to terminate lease of frontage for advertising purposes, several notices to terminate being defective.

55. Corfield v. D.S. Bosher & Co. [1992] 1 E.G.L.R. 163; [1992] C.L.Y. 4098, Judge Crawford Q.C.

Solicitors failed to tell landlord that time limit for purposes of challenge under the Arbitration Act 1950, s. 23 was 21 days—landlord lost chance of successful appeal and fresh hearing as to amount due under rent review—*Held*, negligent.

56. Gran Gelato Ltd v. Richcliff (Group) Ltd [1992] Ch. 560; [1992] 1 All E.R. 865, Sir Donald Nicholls V.-C.

Held, first defendants liable for negligent answer to inquiries before lease given on their behalf by second defendant solicitors.—*Held*, further, that although there was a close and direct relationship between those solicitors and the plaintiff and foreseeability of loss, it would not be just fair or reasonable to impose a duty of care on the solicitors. *Caparo* (Chap. 18, (1) **17**) applied.

57. Neighbour v. Barker [1992] 2 E.G.L.R. 149, [1993] C.L.Y. 2989, C.A.

Plaintiff's claim against their solicitors for negligence/breach of contract in advising them to complete the purchase of a bungalow after serious defects were discovered—dismissed.

58. Whelton Sinclair v. Hyland [1992] 2 E.G.L.R. 158; [1993] C.L.Y. 2991, C.A.

Landlord served notice under Landlord and Tenant Act 1954 on assignee of lease—*Held*, solicitor had been instructed by assignee prior to expiry of time limit and hence liable for failure to serve counter-notice.

59. Palmer v. Durnford Ford [1992] Q.B. 483; [1992] 2 All E.R. 122, Simon Tuckey Q.C.

Plaintiff haulage contractor sued vendor and repairer of vehicle—claim abandoned at trial. Plaintiff claimed breach of contractual duty of care against his solicitor and expert in that action—*Held*, in so far as such claim sought to impugn the decision of the court which allowed abandonment of the claim it was struck out. *Hunter v. Chief Constable of the West Midlands Police* [1982] A.C. 529 applied.
(This part of decision doubted in *Walpole v. Partridge & Wilson* **71**.)

60. F. & G. Reynolds (Whitchurch) Ltd v. Joseph, *The Times*, November 6, 1992, [1992] C.L.Y. 4099, Scott Baker J.

61. Kecskemeti v. Rubens Rabin & Co., *The Times*, December 31, 1992; [1993] C.L.Y. 2987, Macpherson J.

Held, Beneficiary under a will entitled to succeed against testator's solicitors for their failure to draw will so that he received half proceeds of sale of properties. *Ross* (**27**) followed.

62. McManus Developments Ltd v. Barbridge Properties Ltd & Blandy & Blandy [1992] N.P.C. 49; [1992] C.L.Y. 3212, C.A.

Solicitors acted for property developers in purchase of property on which three houses were to be built; prior to completion a possible problem arose as to the precise line of the boundary—*Held*, solicitors negligent in not making further inquiry before completion. *Midland Bank v. Hett Stubbs* **22** followed.

63. Worboys v. Cartwright [1992] N.P.C. 106, J. Morritt Q.C.

Solicitors acting for plaintiff in sale of own farm and purchase of tenancy of another advised him that he had enforceable contract to purchase—*Held*, negligent in not advising prior to sale of his own farm that specific performance was not certain as the tenant had challenged his surveyors' purported authority to make the contract on his behalf.

64. Griffiths v. Dawson & Co. [1993] 2 F.L.R. 315; (1993) C.L.Y. 2986, Ewbank J.

65. Wood v. Law Society, *The Times*, July 30, 1993; (1993) C.L.Y. 3756, Otton J.

Held, the Law Society did not owe a duty of care to complainants at common law or in statute when exercising its investigative or disciplinary powers in respect of its members. Affirmed by C.A., *The Times*, March 2, 1995.

66. Clark Boyce v. Mouat [1993] 4 All E.R. 268; [1993] C.L.Y. 3750, P.C.

Solicitor acted both for plaintiff and for her son in a mortgage transaction between them—she declined to take independent advice—solicitor advised her of legal implications—*Held*, not liable to go further and advise as to wisdom of transaction to person in full possession of faculties.

67. Law v. Cunningham [1993] E.G.C.S. 126; [1994] 3 C.L. 396, Judge Bromley Q.C.

68. Mercantile Building Society v. J.W. Mitchell Dodds & Co. [1993] N.P.C. 99; [1994] C.L.Y. 4227, C.A.

Solicitors acted for client wishing to remortgage his property and for the building society which was willing to lend—*Held*, solicitors liable to building society for failure to make an independent check that the whole of the land was included in the registered title.

69. Forbouys v. Gadhavi [1993] N.P.C. 122; [1994] C.L.Y. 4236 J. Chadwick Q.C.

Held, solicitor not liable for failing to advise commercially experienced clients to await outcome of rent review clause in lease before proceeding.

70. Glantz v. Polikoff [1993] N.P.C. 145; [1994] C.L.Y. 4241, Judge Moseley Q.C.

Solicitor received from a third party a sum by way of deposit against the solicitor's undertaking to hold it until exchange of contracts in relation to a flat—by time the deposit was paid to purchaser, solicitor should have been aware of circumstances which would have caused a prudent man of business to stop before paying out the money—*Held*, not liable for breach of duty of care in negligence but liable in equity for breach of duty as trustee.

71. Walpole v. Partridge & Wilson [1994] Q.B. 106; [1994] 1 All E.R. 385, C.A.

Claim against solicitor for failing to act with due care and skill and expedition over appeal from Crown Court—appeal not pursued and hence loss of chance that fines and costs might have been remitted—*Held*, claim maintainable and not collateral attack upon a final decision of court or abuse of process. *Hunter v. Chief Constable of the West Midlands Police* [1982] A.C. 529 considered. *Palmer* **59** doubted.

72. Hemmens v. Wilson Browne [1994] 2 W.L.R. 323; [1993] 4 All E.R. 826, Judge Moseley Q.C.

Solicitor drew a document entitling client's mistress to call for payment of £110,000—document unenforceable and client refused to pay—*Held*, not fair, just or reasonable to impose duty of care on solicitor when client still alive and able, if he wished, to put matters right. *Ross* **27** and C.A's decision in *White* **76** distinguished. Claim failed on *Hedley Byrne* principles. *Caparo* (Chap. 19, (1) **17**) applied.

73. Reeves v. Thrings & Long [1993] E.G.C.S. 196; [1994] C.L.Y. 4230, C.A.

Alleged negligent failure by solicitor to advise purchaser of hotel that access to car park was by licence for which annual fee payable and determinable on six months notice—*Held*, by a majority, duty of solicitor discharged.

74. Haigh v. Wright Hassall & Co. [1994] E.G.C.S. 54; [1994] C.L.Y. 4231, C.A.

On assurance from intending purchasers of public house that they would bring in the deposit later that day, solicitors orally agreed exchange of contracts—deposit never furnished—*Held*, solicitors were not in the circumstances required to inquire further as to how well founded the assurance was and hence not liable.

75. Mortgage Express v. Bowerman & Partners, (1994) 2 E.G.L.R. 156; [1994] C.L.Y. 4232, Arden J.

A solicitor acting for both lender and borrower in a conveyance owed a duty to both to protect their interests and so should have informed both of information which put him on inquiry as to the accuracy of a valuation. Affirmed by C.A., *The Times*, August 1, 1995.

76. White v. Jones, (1995) 2 W.L.R. 187; [1995] N.L.J. 251, H.L.

Solicitors delayed the carrying out of testator's instructions to prepare a new will making bequests to his daughters who were not beneficiaries under his then existing will—testator died before instructions carried out—*Held*, (3–2) that tortious negligence on the lines proposed in *Ross v. Caunters* **27** was inappropriate to the present case and the principle in *Hedley Byrne* could not in the absence of special circumstances give rise on ordinary principles to an assumption of responsibility by the testator's solicitor towards an intended beneficiary but that in cases such as this there should be extended to the intended beneficiary a remedy under the *Hedley Byrne* principle by holding that the assumption of responsibility by the solicitor towards his client should be held in law to extend to the intended beneficiary who (as the solicitor could reasonably foresee) might, as a result of the solicitor's negligence, be deprived of his intended legacy in circumstances in which neither the testator nor his estate would have remedy against the solicitor. It was legitimate to extend the law to the limited extent proposed using the incremental approach by way of analogy advocated in *Caparo Industries PLC v. Dickman* (Chap. 18, (1) **17**).

U1. Stroud v. Franks (1956) C.A. 249

Dictum by Denning L.J. (3 C): "I would emphasise as strongly as I can that a case of negligence against a solicitor has to be fully proved. In the old days it used to be said that a professional man would not be liable unless there was gross negligence. We do not use that word nowadays, but, at any rate, it has got to be fully proved that he has neglected his duty to his clients."

U2. Klinger v. Beach (1958) C.A. 311 A

Plaintiff proprietors of night club—anxious to get special hours certificate—dealt with in Licensing Act 1953—defendant solicitors instructed by plaintiff—defendant not acquainted with procedure—failed to take proper steps—*Held*, defendant negligent as should have realised there would be statutory provisions and supplementary rules and regulations—defendant should have got hold of textbook on subject which was available and familiarised himself with sections in Act dealing with procedure for obtaining special hours certificate—but defendant not liable as negligence did not result in damage to plaintiff.

U3. Gattward v. Campbell (1960) C.A. 29

Solicitor acting for vendor and purchaser omitted to tell purchaser that vendor had refused to allow part of purchase money to stand out for seven days—*Held*, negligent.

U4. Aslan v. Clintons [1985] C.L.Y. Unreported Cases 71; C.A. 457

Property dealer claimed damages for failure by his solicitor to warn him of the danger of signing a contract for the sale of flats with vacant possession unless he was sure he could give such possession—*Held*, not liable (reported at first instance (1984) 134 New L.J. 584).

U5. Booth v. Davey (1988) C.A. 297

U6. Makris v. Howell-Jones & Partners (1991) C.A. 75

Held, solicitors negligent in accepting instructions from plaintiff where there was or was likely to be an acute conflict of interest between plaintiff and, W, an existing client.

U7. Livingston International Freight Ltd (T/A D.C. Andrews Ballantyre & Co.) v. Lawrence Jones (1994) C.A. 257

Pre-writ negligence established but negligence in causing plaintiff to defend legal proceedings not established. No damages proved to have been caused by pre-writ negligence.

(16) Union

1. Iwanuszezak v. General Municipal Boilermakers & Allied Trades Union [1988] I.R.L.R. 219; [1988] C.L.Y. 3581, C.A.

Member of defendant union was made redundant when shift pattern changed and he could no longer work comfortably due to poor sight. He claimed in contract and tort against union that it had failed to take reasonable care to protect his employment and protect his conditions of work by using, in effect, their negotiating power upon his employers. Claim struck out as disclosing no cause of action.

2. Stubbs v. Hunt & Wrigley [1992] 1 E.G.L.R. 17; [1992] C.L.Y. 134, Phillips J.

Dairy farmer's application to tribunal for a milk quota was unsuccessful—National Farmers Union advised against challenging it—admitted duty of care—*Held*, advice not negligent as any challenge would have been unsuccessful.

3. Hood v. National Farmers Union (1994) 01 E.G. 109; [1994] C.L.Y. 158, C.A.

Held, union's failure to advise member of the possibility of challenging a tribunal's decision by way of judicial review negligent—the chances were that there would have been an order for a rehearing as the tribunal had erred in law.

19. LIABILITY FOR NEGLIGENT MISSTATEMENTS

(*N.B.* This section only deals with cases where the question is whether liability arises in tort independently of contract. For cases where there is a concurrent duty in contract, see the appropriate headings in Chapter 18.)

(a) General Scope and Limits of Duty

1. Hedley Byrne v. Heller [1964] A.C. 465; [1963] 2 All E.R. 575, H.L.

Bankers' reference as to creditworthiness—given "without responsibility on our part"—assumed for argument to be negligent—no contract between giver and recipient of reference—but latter claimed that a duty of care was owed in tort—*Held*, a duty of care could be owed, provided there was a special relationship between the parties, which, *semble* (*per* Lords Reid, Morris and Hodson), there had not been on the facts, but in any event there had been a sufficient disclaimer of responsibility, which prevented any duty of care arising. The special relationship necessary to found a duty was defined as follows:

(a) Lord Reid (583 B): "Those relationships where it is plain that the party seeking information or advice was trusting the other to exercise such a degree of care as the circumstances required, where it was reasonable for him to do that, and where the other gave the information or advice when he knew or ought to have known that the inquirer was relying on him."
(b) Lord Morris (594 C) and Lord Hodson (601 B): "If, in a sphere in which a person is so placed that others could reasonably rely on his judgment or his skill or on his ability to make careful inquiry, a person takes it on himself to give information or advice to, or allows his information or advice to be passed on to, another person who, as he knows or should know, will place reliance on it, then a duty of care will arise."
(c) Lord Devlin (611 F): "Wherever there is a relationship equivalent to contract, there is a duty of care."
(d) Lord Pearce (617 G): "There is a duty of care created by special relationships which, though not fiduciary, give rise to an assumption that care as well as honesty is demanded."

The legal basis on which such a relationship existed in relation to the notion of proximity was *discussed.* Lord Reid (587 A) said that the basis rested on the inference of an undertaking to assume a duty of care. Lord Morris (594 B) said words to the same effect. Lord Devlin (608 C) said it arose out of proximity, but was confined to relationships equivalent to contract (611 F). Lord Pearce (617 G) said that it arose out of the assumption of a duty of care, and (615 H) any connection with the principle of proximity was purely by way of analogy. *N.B.* In the result, it would seem that the main criterion is assumption, rather than proximity.

2. Mutual Life Ltd. v. Evatt [1971] A.C. 793; [1971] 1 All E.R. 150, P.C.

Held, no duty owed because giving advice on investments was no part of the business of an insurance company (3–2). Lord Diplock, delivering the opinion of the majority, said that the duty would normally only arise where the advice was given by some person or company whose business "involves the giving of advice of a kind which calls for special skill and competence," and that the carrying on of such a business was the normal way in which a person let it be known that he claimed to possess such skill and competence. But he also approved *Anderson* Chap. 19 (b) **3**), and suggested that the basis of the duty there lay in the fact that the adviser had a financial interest in the transaction on which he gave the advice.

3. Dutton v. Bognor Regis U.D.C. [1972] 1 Q.B. 373; [1972] 1 All E.R. 462, C.A.

Overruled in *Murphy* (Chap. **18** (13) **66** as are all cases based on it post-*Anns* **5**.

4. Esso Petroleum v. Mardon [1976] Q.B. 801; [1976] 2 All E.R. 5, C.A.

Negligent estimate by Esso, owners of a new garage site, of likely petrol sales—thereby inducing M to enter into tenancy agreement for the site—the Misrepresentation Act 1967 was not then in force—*Held*, the negligent estimate was not only a breach of warranty, but was also a breach of the *Hedley Byrne* duty. On this latter question, Esso raised two main points: first, that where a contract resulted between the parties, their rights were governed by the law of contract, which superseded any duty under *Hedley Byrne.* All three L.JJ. said that the *Hedley Byrne* duty could co-exist with contractual duties which might supervene. Secondly, it was argued that, following *Mutual Life* **2**, the duty was only owed by someone who held himself out as carrying on the business or profession of giving advice. To this Lord Denning M.R. (16 A) said that the duty applied to someone who professed to have a special knowledge or skill, which would include the Esso representative making the estimate in the present case. Ormrod L.J. (21 G) accepted that the majority opinion in *Mutual Life* **2** limited the duty to persons holding themselves out as carrying on a business of giving advice, but said that on this point he preferred the minority opinion of Lords Reid and Morris, to the effect that the duty arose where the giving of the advice created a special relationship whereby the moral obligation was translated into a legal one. Shaw L.J. did not deal specifically with the point.

5. Anns v. Merton L.B.C. [1977] 2 W.L.R. 1024; [1977] 2 All E.R. 492, H.L.

Held, that, subject to certain provisos, a council surveyor who negligently approved foundations would be liable to a subsequent purchaser of the house. *N.B.* Unlike the judgments in *Dutton* **3**, the speeches of the H.L. did not deal with the issues as specifically arising under the principles in *Hedley Byrne* **1**, but on the criteria for the existence of a duty of care generally as expounded in the *Dorset Yacht* case (Chap. 1,(2) (a) **7**) (*i.e.* first, whether there is sufficient proximity or neighbourhood, and secondly, whether there are any special considerations negativing or limiting the duty of care or the class of persons by whom it is owed). Lord Wilberforce (three other Law Lords concurring), having decided that these criteria were satisfied, then went on to consider whether the scope of the statutory function exercisable by the county surveyor under the Public Health Act 1936 was such as to limit the existence of the duty of care which, on general principles, would arise. For fuller details of these matters, see Chap. 1,(2) (a) **10**. Largely overruled in *Murphy* (Chap. 18, (13) **66**).

6. The Busiris [1980] 1 Lloyd's Rep. 569; [1980] C.L.Y. 363, Parker J.

P purchased and agreed to resell fuel oil—inspection contract with D1—D4 (not in contractual relationship with P) made a negligent misstatement in a telex as to the nature of the inspection on which P acted. P suffered economic loss only—*Held*, in addition to D1 being liable in contract, D4 was also liable in tort, even though P only suffered economic loss. *Hedley Byrne* **1** applied.
N.B. This case went to the C.A., but on other issues only.

7. Yianni v. Edwin Evans [1982] Q.B. 438; [1981] 3 All E.R. 592, Park J.

Plaintiffs decided to buy a house for £15,000 if they could obtain building society mortgage for £12,000. P's applied to Halifax Building Society for mortgage. Halifax instructed defendants to carry out survey and prepare valuation for them. Plaintiffs paid survey fee to Halifax—Halifax documents contained warning that any mortgage advance did not imply any warranty as to the reasonableness of the purchase price, but plaintiffs did not read warning. Defendants knew that most prospective purchasers of lower-priced houses relied on their building society's valuation and did not instruct an independent surveyor. Defendants advised Halifax that house was adequate security for loan of £12,000. In reliance, Halifax advanced plaintiffs £12,000 (without revealing contents of defendant's report to them) and plaintiffs completed purchase. Plaintiffs would not have purchased had they not believed on basis of defendants' valuation that the house was worth at least £12,000. In fact, defendants negligently failed to notice serious defects in foundations and the house was worth little more than its site value—*Held*, that the defendants were liable in negligence to the plaintiffs. It was within the defendants' reasonable contemplation that the plaintiffs would rely on their valuation, which was communicated to them by the Halifax's offer of a mortgage advance of £12,000 and that carelessness in valuing the house would cause the plaintiffs loss. Accordingly, they owed the plaintiffs a duty of care under *Hedley-Byrne v. Heller* **1**, and were in breach of that duty. There were no policy factors negativing liability. Approved in *Smith v. Eric S. Bush* **16**.

8. Culford Metal v. E.C.G.D., *The Times*, March 31, 1981; [1981] C.L.Y. 2752, Neill J.

Negligent advice by E.C.G.D. (a government department) to exporter—in reliance on advice, exporter did not insure against risk of non-payment by foreign importer—*Held*, that E.C.G.D. were liable for loss due to absence of insurance cover.

9. Bluett v. Woodspring D.C. [1983] J.P.L. 242; [1983] C.L.Y. 2513, Judge Stabb Q.C.

10. Stevenson v. Nationwide Building Society [1984] E.G. Digest 934; [1985] C.L.Y. 2295, J. Wilmers Q.C.

Plaintiff's claim against building society for negligent mortgage valuation by employee of shop property which partly spanned river failed—*Held*, disclaimer of liability reasonable under Unfair Contract Terms Act 1977: but see *Smith v. Eric S. Bush* **16**.

11. Davies v. Parry [1988] 1 E.G.L.R. 147; [1988] C.L.Y. 2457, McNeill J.

For details see Chap. 18, (5) **22**.

12. Mills v. Winchester Dioceson Board of Finance [1989] Ch. 428; [1989] 2 All E.R. 317, Knox J.

Assumed objects of charitable trust claimed damages from the Charity Commissioners for their assumed negligent advice to trustees as to the meaning of the trust as a result of which the objects had suffered damage, injury and distress—*Held*, there was no sufficient proximity between the objects and the Commissioners, nor was it just or equitable for there to be a duty of care, in particular where there was a right of appeal against any action proposed on the basis of the Commissioners' advice—*Hedley Byrne* of no application, there being no reliance on the advice by the objects.

13. Chaudhry v. Prabhakar [1989] 1 W.L.R. 29; [1988] 3 All E.R. 718, C.A.

Unpaid agent of plaintiff advised purchase of VW car when should have realised there were defects & further enquiry necessary—*Held*, a duty of care arose where a party was asked for and gave gratuitous advice upon a matter within his particular skill or knowledge and who knows or ought to have known the person asking for the advice would rely and act upon it—liable.

14. Reid v. Rush & Tompkins Group PLC [1990] 1 W.L.R. 212; [1989] 3 All E.R. 228, C.A.

Plaintiff employee whilst working in Ethiopia, suffered injury in road traffic accident caused by a third party's negligence. He alleged his employers should either have taken out insurance to cover him against such eventuality or have advised him to do so himself, there being no compulsory third party motor insurance scheme in that country—*Held*, no term could be implied into the contract to provide or to advise taking out such insurance—there was no duty on a master to take reasonable care to protect a servant from suffering economic loss—there was no voluntary assumption of responsibility by the defendants towards the plaintiff under *Hedley Byrne* principles.

15. Al-Saudi Banque v. Clarke Pixley [1990] Ch. 313; [1989] 3 All E.R. 361, Millett J.

Held, no duty of care owed to bankers who allegedly lent or continued to lend moneys to company in reliance upon the audited accounts. Approved in *Capare* **18**.

16. Smith v. Eric S. Bush; Harris v. Wyre Forest D.C. [1990] 1 A.C. 831; [1989] 2 All E.R. 514, H.L.

Two prospective purchasers of dwelling-houses relied on valuations (required by prospective mortgagees pursuant to statutory requirement) in deciding whether or not to purchase. In one case the report was by an independent valuer to a building society with a copy disclosed to purchaser—in the other, the report was by an employee of the lending local authority and no copy was disclosed—in both cases there were disclaimers of liability and advice to customers to procure their own survey. Both valuers were negligent in and about their valuation and both purchasers suffered loss and damage in having repairs effected—*Held*,

(a) In the absence of any disclaimer of liability, the valuer valuing a house for mortgage purposes knowing that the mortgagee will and the mortgagor will probably rely on the valuation and that the purchaser/mortgagor has in effect paid for the valuation, is under a duty to exercise reasonable skill and care, such duty being owed to both parties to the mortgage for which the valuation was made.
(b) The disclaimers in both cases were notices within meaning of the Unfair Contract Terms Act 1977 and had therefore to satisfy the requirement of reasonableness.
(c) It was not fair or reasonable to exclude liability, in particular where the valuer was a professional man carrying out a valuation of a modest dwelling which should present no difficulty, he knew most purchasers relied on his valuation without an independent survey which most could not afford, he was paid for his services in effect by the purchaser, the purchaser trusted the mortgagees and their valuers, the valuer knew failure by him could be disastrous for the purchaser and the valuer is most likely to be covered by insurance and the purchaser has no effective power to object to the disclaimer. *Yianni* **7** approved.

17. Mariola Marine Corporation v. Lloyd's Register of Shipping (The "Morning Watch") [1990] 1 Lloyd's Rep. 547; [1991] C.L.Y. 2668, Phillips J.

Yacht surveyed on instructions of owner prior to sale—purchaser alleged he relied on survey in deciding to purchase, the same was negligent and he had thereby suffered economic loss—*Held*, although it was reasonably foreseeable that a purchaser would be influenced by the result of the survey, there was not in all the circumstances sufficient "proximity" to give rise to a duty of care. *Caparo* **18** and *Smith v. Eric. S. Bush* **16** considered.

18. Caparo Industries PLC v. Dickman [1990] 2 A.C. 605; [1990] 2 W.L.R. 358, H.L.

Defendant auditors audited the accounts of a public limited company, which accounts were sent to shareholders prior to the annual general meeting. The plaintiffs made various purchases of shares, some allegedly in reliance upon the audited accounts and allegedly suffered loss through their being innaccurate and misleading—*Held*, although such loss was foreseeable, in order to establish "proximity" in such a case it was necessary to prove "that the defendant knew that his statement would be communicated to the plaintiff, either as an individual or as a member of an identifiable class, specifically in connection with a particular transaction or transactions of a particular kind . . . and that the plaintiff would be very likely to rely on it for the purpose of deciding whether or not to enter upon that transaction or upon a transaction of that kind"; *per* Lord Bridge at 368 D. See also Lord Roskill—375E, Lord Oliver at 383 H—384E and Lord Jauncey at 405D—*Held*, further in the absence of particular knowledge, the auditors owed no duty of care to members of the public generally who relied upon the accounts in deciding to purchase shares and the statutory duties owed by auditors to shareholders was a duty owed to them as a body or class and did not extend to an individual, save as a member of the class in respect of some class activity. In the circumstances, no duty of care was owed. *Hedley Byrne* **1** and *Smith v. Eric S. Bush* **16** applied.

19. Beaton v. Nationwide Building Society [1991] 2 E.G.L.R. 145; [1992] C.L.Y. 3207, Neil Butterfield Q.C.

For details see Chap. 18, (5) **51**.

20. Petch v. Customs & Excise Commissioners [1993] I.C.R. 789; [1993] C.L.Y. 2945, C.A.

Held, following *Spring v. Guardian Assurance PLC* [1993] I.C.R. 412, C.A., defendant ex-employers did not owe plaintiff ex-employee a duty of care in formulating answers to Treasury questions about his work record—in any event no breach of any duty, if owed, and no damage caused. (*Quaere* whether this would now be followed, given decision of H.L. in *Spring* **21** below.)

21. Spring v. Guardian Assurance PLC [1994] 3 W.L.R. 354; [1994] 3 All E.R. 129, H.L.

Insurance company and company selling the former's policies—*Held*, by a majority, they owed a duty of care on *Hedley Byrne* principles when giving a reference in respect of a person being the former's agent and the latter's ex-employee.

22. Henderson v. Merrett Syndicates Ltd [1994] 3 W.L.R. 761; [1994] 3 All E.R. 506, H.L.

Various Names at Lloyds sought to establish liability in tort against various managing agents of their respective syndicates for losses suffered by them—some managing agents had a contractual relationship with the Names, others were sub-agents to the Names' own agents.—*Held*, notwithstanding the criticisms expressed in, *e.g. Smith v. Eric S. Bush* **16** and *Caparo* **18** about the concept of "assumption of responsibility" expressed in *Hedley Byrne*, there was no difficulty in applying the concept to those who performed services of a professional or quasi-professional nature—contract apart, in the present case there had plainly been such an "assumption" by the managing agents towards the Names in their syndicates, holding themselves out as possessing a special expertise to advise the Names on the suitability of risks to be underwritten, reinsurance and settlement of claims—the Names, as those agents well knew, relied on their expertise. Prima facie, a duty of care was owed, whether arising by way of analogy from categories of relationship already recognised as falling within the principle of *Hedley Byrne* or by a straight application of that principle. No problem therefore arose from the fact that the loss suffered was pure economic loss. Such tortious liability would arise irrespective of whether or not the services were rendered gratuitously or whether or not pursuant to contract, unless such liability was limited or excluded by contract by reason of the contract being inconsistent with such liability—a plaintiff who had available to him concurrent remedies in contract and tort might choose that remedy which appeared to him to be the most advantageous. In the present case, neither the context of the words "absolute discretion" in some of the contracts nor the fact that some of the managing agents were sub-agents modified or excluded the duty of care otherwise owed in tort, such duty being the same as that owed under the terms implied in the contracts, namely to exercise care and skill. It was likely that the present case was most unusual and it was not to be inferred from the instant case that other sub-agents would be held directly liable to the agent's principal in tort. *Hedley Byrne* **1** and *Midland Bank Trust v. Hett Stubbs* (Chap. 18, (15) **22**) applied. Observations in *Tai Hing* (Chap. 18, (2) **23**) considered—the issue in that case being whether a tortious duty of care could be established which was more extensive than that which was provided for under the relevant contract.

23. McCullagh v. Lane Fox & Partners Ltd (1994) 08 EG 118; [1994] C.L.Y. 114, Colman J.

For details see Chap. 19, (b) **86**.

24. White v. Jones, (1995) 2 W.L.R. 187; [1995] N.L.J. 251, H.L.

Solicitors delayed the carrying out of testator's instructions to prepare a new will making bequests to his daughters who were not beneficiaries under his then existing will—testator died before instructions carried out—*Held*, (3–2) that tortious negligence on the lines proposed in *Ross v. Caunters* Chap. 18(15) **27** was inappropriate to the present case and the principle in *Hedley Byrne* could not in the absence of special circumstances give rise on ordinary principles to an assumption of responsibility by the testator's solicitor towards an intended beneficiary but that in cases such as this there should be extended to the intended beneficiary a remedy under the *Hedley Byrne* principle by holding that the assumption of responsibility by the solicitor towards his client should be held in law to extend to the intended beneficiary who (as the solicitor could reasonably foresee) might, as a result of the solicitor's negligence, be deprived of his intended legacy in circumstances in which neither the testator nor his estate would have remedy against the solicitor. It was legitimate to extend the law to the limited extent proposed using the incremental approach by way of analogy advocated in *Caparo Industries PLC v. Dickman* **18**.

U1. British Gas Corp. v. Derbyshire C.C. (1981) C.A. U.B. 331

For details see Chap. 2, (9) **U3**.

(b) Particular Instances

		Liable or not
Banker—giving reference as to creditworthiness	1	?
ARCHITECT—PASSING WALL AS SAFE—SUBSEQUENT COLLAPSE	2	Yes
Agent—representation as to creditworthiness of principal	3	Yes
Accountant—preparing balance-sheet with a view to offer for shares of company being made	4	Yes
Safety consultant—passing hoist as safe	5	Yes
REGISTRAR OF LOCAL LAND CHARGES—MAY BE LIABLE FOR NEGLIGENT CLEAR CERTIFICATE	6	?
CLERK IN LOCAL LAND REGISTRY—MAKING NEGLIGENT SEARCH	6	Yes
Insurance company—advising on investments	7	No
LOCAL AUTHORITY—NEGLIGENTLY APPROVING FOUNDATIONS OF HOUSE	8	Yes
PETROL COMPANY—NEGLIGENTLY ESTIMATING LIKELY SALES OF NEW SITE TO PROSPECTIVE TENANT	9	Yes
Hire-purchase finance company—failing to register agreement	10	No
Minister—negligently issuing certificate of fitness for heavy goods vehicle	11	Yes
Landlord—gratuitously insuring premises—then failing to renew—but not informing tenant	12	No
Local authority—negligently approving foundations of house	13	Yes
Navigational equipment—wrongly recording position of undersea pipeline	14	Yes
Accountant—certifying company accounts—third party taking over company in reliance on accounts	15	No
Government department—export credits guarantee department—negligent advice to exporterv	16	Yes
Surveyor instructed by building society—may owe duty of care to mortgagor	17	Yes
ACCOUNTANT—PREPARING MISLEADING COMPANY ACCOUNTS—PURCHASER OF COMPANY ENCOURAGED THEREBY—BUT WOULD HAVE PURCHASED IN ANY EVENT	18	No
LOCAL AUTHORITY—NEGLIGENT INSPECTION OF FOUNDATIONS	19	Yes
Surveyor—mortgage valuation—disclaimer	20	No
Local authority—information as to road proposals	21	Yes
Local authority—negligent inspection at foundation stage—no negligence at planning permission stage	22	Yes & No
BANKER—DUTY NOT TO MISSTATE EFFORT OF MORTGAGE TO CUSTOMER	23	Yes
Local authority—whether duty owed to building owner	24	No
Architects and engineers—whether duty of care owed to main contractor	25	Arguable
Local authority—reply to inquiries by purchaser's solicitors	26	No
LOCAL AUTHORITY—NEGLIGENT AS TO PLANS BUT NO DANGER TO HEALTH OR SAFETY	27	No
DRY ROT SPECIALIST—TREATING AND GUARANTEEING FLAT FOR OWNER OF BLOCK—DUTY OWED TO SUBSEQUENT FLAT PURCHASER BUT NO BREACH	28	No
LOCAL AUTHORITY—WHETHER DUTY OWED TO BUILDING OWNER IN PASSING PLANS AND INSPECTION OF FOUNDATIONS	29	No

Solicitors—duty of care to guarantors	30	Arguable
Reference—duty of care but negligence not established	31	No
Local authority—duty to subsequent house purchaser over plans but no breach	32	No
Local authority—Building Regulation approval and site inspection—no negligence and no danger to health or safety	33	No
LOCAL AUTHORITY—WHETHER DUTY TO MERE OWNER OF PROPERTY REGARDING PLANS AND INSPECTION	34	No
Local authority—inspector permitting departure from plans—whether liable to owner-occupier	35	Yes
Drainage board—omission to check flood level data—whether liable to houseowner	36	Yes
Banker's reference and information—no tendering of or reliance on advice	37	No
Surveyor—valuation—assumed solid instead of cavity wall	38	No
Valuer—disclaimer as to report	39	Yes
Surveyor—statement as to settlement	40	No
Local authority—improvement grant—whether duty of care	40	No
Vendor—reply to pre-contract inquiry	41	No
Architect—whether duty of care to main contractor	42	Yes partly
BUILDING SOCIETY—ALLEGED MISSTATEMENT OF VALUE	43	Arguable
Building society mortgage valuation—whether breach of duty to house purchaser	44	No
Valuer—valuation and structural report	45	Yes
Valuer—mortgage valuation	46	No
Local authority—whether duty of care to builders and developers in respect of planning permission	47	No
Local authority—whether failure to take care in passing plans	48	No
Accountant—whether duty of care in reporting on company's affairs to shareholders, directors or guarantors	49	Partly but no breach
Bank of England—whether duty of care owed in supervision of U.K. banks	50	No
Architect—extent of liability to lessor of premises for faulty design	51	Yes, partly
Architect—whether duty of care owed to main contractor	52	No
Builder—whether liable to house owner for differential settlement	53	Yes
Valuer—failure to notice sloping floor—concealment by builder	54	No
Valuer—failure to report defects	55	Yes
SURVEYOR—ADVISING BANK AS TO REINSTATEMENT VALUE—WHETHER LIABLE TO PURCHASER	56	No
Director—whether liable for statement as to quality of company's product	57	Yes
Auditor—whether duty of care to lending bankers	58	No
Valuer—mortgage report—failure to follow trail of suspicion	59	Yes
LOCAL AUTHORITY—WHETHER DUTY OF CARE OWED IN APPROVING DEFECTIVE PLANS	60	No
Directors—whether liable for contents of prospectus and reports to subsequent purchasers of shares	61	No

CONSULTING ENGINEER—WHETHER DUTY OF CARE TO MAIN CONTRACTOR	62	No
Valuer—whether duty of care owed to purchaser for mortgage valuation report	63	Yes
Auditor—whether duty of care owed to public generally and individual shareholder	64	No
BUILDER—WHETHER LIABLE TO SUBSEQUENT PURCHASERS	65	No
Valuer—mortgage valuation report	66	Yes
Valuer—disclaimer—negligent mortgage valuation	67	Yes
ACCOUNTANT—WHETHER DUTY OF CARE TO PARTIES NEGOTIATING TAKE-OVER	68	No
DIRECTOR—WHETHER DUTY OF CARE OWED TO PARTY MAKING TAKE-OVER BID	69	Arguable
LOCAL AUTHORITY—WHETHER REPLY TO INQUIRIES IMPROPERLY ANSWERED	70	No
Valuer—whether negligent in failing to advise that planning consents be verified	71	No
Valuer—misdescription of method of construction in mortgage valuation	72	Yes
Structural engineer—instructed by insurers—whether duty of care to property owners	73	No
Auditors—whether duty of care to company's bankers—negligent certification of accounts	74	No
Valuer—rateable value appeal—whether duty of care to former principal where change of principals	75	No
INSURANCE BROKER—WHETHER DUTY OF CARE TO ASSIGNEE OF POLICY	76	Yes
Solicitor—whether duty of care owed to recipient of answers to inquiries	77	No
Valuer—method of valuation—whether negligent	78	No
Valuer—whether valuation negligent	79	No
Auditors—whether liable at common law for failure to realise or report on company's insolvency pursuant to statutory obligations	80	No
Auditors to local authority—whether duty owed to (a) authority or (b) its officers	81	(a) Yes (b) No
AUDITORS—WHETHER ASSUMED NEGLIGENCE CAUSATIVE OF LOSS TO COMPANY, ITS SUBSIDIARY OR PARTY AGREEING TO BUY SHARES	82	Yes & No
Reference—whether duty of care owed	83	Yes
Managing agent at Lloyd's—whether duty of care owed to Names	84	Yes
SURVEYOR—ADVISING LOCAL AUTHORITY—WHETHER LIABILITY TO SUBSEQUENT HOUSE PURCHASER	85	No
Estate agent—oral misrepresentation as to particulars—whether loss caused	86	No
Solicitor—whether duty of care to beneficiary	87	Yes
Local authority—whether negligent over answers to inquiries	U1	No
Accountant—whether liable to potential purchaser for giving impression company not only solvent but viable	U2	Yes
Statement during negotiations not within Hedley Byrne principle	U3	No
Banker—whether liable to customer over examining project before deciding to lend	U4	No
Computer equipment supplier—misrepresentation as to capability of equipment	U5	Yes
Coffee shop—misrepresentation of turnover	U6	Yes

1. Hedley Byrne v. Heller [1964] A.C. 465; [1963] 2 All E.R. 575, H.L.

Held, that because defendant bankers in giving a reference as to creditworthiness had sufficiently disclaimed responsibility, no duty of care could arise in any event. On the question whether, but for the disclaimer, a duty of care would have arisen, *semble* it would not have (*per* Lords Reid, Morris and Hodson). But Lords Pearce and Devlin indicated that it would turn on the facts brought out in evidence (the appeal being argued as a preliminary point of law).

2. Clay v. Crump [1964] 1 Q.B. 523; [1963] 3 All E.R. 687, C.A.

Held, architect liable to building worker who was injured by subsequent collapse.

3. Anderson v. Rhodes [1967] 2 All E.R. 850; [1967] C.L.Y. 2677, Cairns J.

Defendant, buying potatoes on commission for T, represented to sellers that T were all right for credit—incorrect and negligent—*Held*, the sellers could recover against defendant. *Hedley Byrne* **1** *followed. Approved in Mutual Life* **7**, on the ground that, although the defendant did not hold himself out as carrying on a business involving giving advice, the duty of care arose because he had a financial interest in the transaction on which he gave the advice.

4. Dimond v. Hamilton [1969] N.Z.L.R. 609; [1969] C.L.Y. 2462, N.Z.C.A.

5. Driver v. Willett [1969] 1 All E.R. 665; [1969] C.L.Y. 2409, Rees J.

Held, following *Clay* **2**, safety consultant liable.

6. Ministry of Housing v. Sharp [1970] 2 Q.B. 223; [1970] 1 All E.R. 1009, C.A.

Registrar of local land charges issued erroneous clear certificate to purchaser—who thus got title free from incumbrance registered by plaintiff ministry (being a charge for contingent repayment of development compensation)—the error was due to the failure of a clerk to search properly—*Held*, the registrar was under no absolute statutory duty to issue an accurate certificate, though possibly he might have been in breach of a duty to use reasonable care, if (which was not the case) he had acted negligently in issuing the certificate—*Held*, further, there was sufficient "proximity" between the clerk and the plaintiffs to create a *Donoghue v. Stevenson* duty of care, and accordingly the clerk was liable for breach of that duty.

7. Mutual Life v. Evatt [1971] A.C. 793; [1971] 1 All E.R. 150, P.C.

Held, (3–2) insurance company not liable for negligent investment advice, inasmuch as the *Hedley Byrne* duty would normally only arise where the advice was given by someone whose business "involves the giving of advice of a kind which calls for special skill and competence". *But* see comments in *Esso* **9**.

8. Dutton v. Bognor Regis U.D.C. [1972] 1 Q.B. 373; [1972] 1 All E.R. 462, C.A.

Overruled in *Murphy* (Chap. 18 (13) **66**) as are all cases based on it post-*Anns* (**13**).

9. Esso Petroleum v. Mardon [1976] Q.B. 801; [1976] 2 All E.R. 5, C.A.

Held, owners of new garage site were in breach of *Hedley* duty of care in negligently giving prospective tenant of site a false estimate of likely petrol sales. For detailed reasons for decision, see Chap. 19 (a) **4**—*Held*, it was immaterial that the tenant had as a result of the estimate entered into a contract of tenancy, inasmuch as the duty in tort still co-existed with the supervening contractual rights and duties. Also Lord Denning M.R. (16 A) qualified the limitations put on the duty in *Mutual Life* **7**, while Ormrod L.J. said that on this question he preferred the minority opinion given by Lords Reid and Morris (21 G).

10. Moorgate Mercantile v. Twitchings [1976] 3 W.L.R. 66; [1976] 2 All E.R. 641, H.L.

So held (3–2), *but* subsequently the rules of H.P. information have been changed, so that now members undertake to register *all* H.P. agreements concluded by them.

11. Rutherford v. A.G. [1976] 1 N.Z.L.R. 403; [1976] C.L.Y. 1870, Hamilton Sup.Ct.

12. Argy Trading v. Lapid Developments, *The Times*, September 29, 1976; [1976] C.L.Y. 1868, Croom-Johnson J.

13. Anns v. Merton L.B.C. [1977] 2 W.L.R. 1024; [1977] 2 All E.R. 492, H.L.

Held, council would be liable for negligent inspection of foundations by their surveyor. Unlike the judgments in *Dutton* **8**, the speeches of the H.L. dealt with the issues as to be decided according to the general criteria for the existence of a duty of care rather than as arising specifically under the *Hedley Byrne* line of cases (perhaps because there was a concurrent question as to whether the council would be liable if they failed to make any inspection at all), and in consequence the fuller details of the decision are set out at Chap 1, (2) (a) **10**. Largely overruled by *Murphy* (Chap. 18, (13) **66**).

14. Caltex Oil v. Willemstad [1977] C.L.Y. 2009; (1977) 51 A.L.J.R. 270, High Ct. of Australia

15. Scott v. MacFarlane [1978] 1 N.Z.L.R. 553; [1979] C.L.Y. 1884, N.Z.C.A.

By an error, accountants overstated the assets of a company in their certified accounts. In reliance, *inter alia*, on the accounts plaintiffs took over the company—*Held*, accountants not liable. Richmond P *said* that a special relationship (*i.e.* where responsibility for advice exists) ought not to be found to exist unless the maker of the statement was or ought to have been aware that his advice would be made available to and be relied on by a particular person for a particular transaction. Considered in *Caparo* (Chap. 19, (a) **18**).

16. Culford Metal v. E.C.G.D., *The Times*, March 25, 1981; [1981] C.L.Y. 2752, Neill J.

Export Credit Guarantee Department (a government department) gave negligent advice to exporter—in reliance thereon, exporter did not insure against the risk of non-payment by foreign importer. E.C.G.D. *Held* liable for loss due to absence of insurance cover.

17. Yianni v. Edwin Evans [1982] Q.B. 438; [1981] 3 All E.R. 592, Park J.

For details see Chap. 19(a) **7**. Approved in *Smith v. Bush* (Chap. 19, (a) **16**).

18. J.E.B. Fasteners v. Mark Bloom [1983] 1 All E.R. 583; [1983] C.L.Y. 2534, C.A.

Distinguished in *Caparo* (Chap. 19, (a) **18**).

19. Ketteman v. Hansel Properties Ltd [1984] 1 W.L.R. 1274; [1985] 1 All E.R. 352, C.A.

Held, local authority inspection of foundations was negligent (applying *Anns* **13**)—builders and architects had been found negligent at first instance. For further details see Chap. 18, (6) **40**.

20. Stevenson v. Nationwide Building Society [1984] E.G. Digest 934; [1985] C.L.Y. 2295, J. Wilmers Q.C.

See Chap. 19, (a) **10**.

21. Shaddock & Associates Pty v. Parramatta C.C. (No. 1) (1980–81) 150 C.L.R. 225; [1985] C.L.Y. 2304, High Court of Australia

Telephone and written inquiry of local authority as to road proposals—land purchased in reliance on answer that there were none—*Held,* local authority liable on *Hedley Byrne* principle.

22. Billam & Billam v. Cheltenham B.C. (1985) 3 Con L.R. 99, [1986] C.L.Y. 198, Cyril Newman Q.C.

For details see Chap. 18, (13) **33**.

23. Cornish v. Midland Bank PLC [1985] 3 All E.R. 513; [1985] C.L.Y. 2324, C.A.

See Chap. 18, (2) **21**.

24. Governors of the Peabody Donation Fund v. Sir Lindsay Parkinson & Co. Ltd [1985] A.C. 210; [1984] 3 All E.R. 529, H.L.

For details see Chap. 18, (13) **29**.

25. Shui On Construction Co. Ltd v. Shui Kay Co. Ltd (1984–5) 1 Const. L.J. 305; [1986] C.L.Y. 215, Hunter J, H.K. High Ct.

Main contractors alleged architects and engineers owed them a duty to exercise reasonable skill and care in the performance of their functions pursuant to the contract and a duty to act fairly and impartially in the performance of those functions—*Held,* claim would not be struck out.

26. J.G.F. Properties Ltd v. Lambeth B.C. [1986] 1 E.G.L.R. 277; [1986] C.L.Y. 2281, Judge Rubin

Alleged negligence of local authority in reply to inquiries by purchaser's solicitors by failure to disclose planning flight affecting the properties to be purchased—*Held,* form of reply not negligent.

27. Percival v. Walsall M.B.C. [1986] 2 E.G.L.R. 136; [1986] C.L.Y. 210, C.A.

Settlement occured to dwelling held by occupiers under long lease—*Held,* local authority negligent in allowing house and extension to be built either not in accordance with approval or from inadequate plans but not liable as defects did not and would not pose danger to health or safety.

28. Shankie-Williams v. Heavey [1986] 2 E.G.L.R. 139; [1986] C.L.Y. 2272, C.A.

See Chap. 18, (6) **48**.

29. Investors in Industry Commercial Properties Ltd v. South Bedfordshire D.C. [1986] Q.B. 1034; [1986] 1 All E.R. 787, C.A.

For details see Chap. 18, (13) **38**.

30. Trustee of Property of P.A.F. Foster v. Crusts [1986] B.C.L.C 307; (1985) C.L.Y. 2309, Judge Finlay Q.C.

Solicitors failed to advise limited company to register charge under the Companies Act 1948 s. 95—*Held*, any duty owed to company also owed to guarantors of company's debt. Claim not struck out.

31. Lawton v. B.O.C. Transhield Ltd [1987] I.C.R. 7; [1987] 2 All E.R. 608, Tudor Evans J.

Fomer employers allegedly gave inaccurate and unfair reference negligently—*Held*, sufficient proximity to give rise to a duty of care but negligence not established.

32. James McKinnon v. County and Metropolitan Developments Ltd (1987) 9 Con. L.R. 61; [1988] C.L.Y. 2432, Judge John Davies Q.C.

For details see Chap. 18, (13) **47**.

33. Kimbell v. Hart D.C (1987) 9 Con L.R. 118; (1987) C.L.Y. 242, Judge Smout Q.C.

For details see Chap. 18, (13) **48**.

34. Hambro Life Assurance PLC v. White Young & Partners [1987] 2 E.G.L.R. 159; [1987] C.L.Y. 2584, C.A.

For details see Chap. 18, (13) **44**.

35. Fry v. Robert A. Jackson (Builder & Contractor) Ltd and Guildford B.C. (1987) 7 Con. L.R. 97; [1987] C.L.Y. 241, Judge Newey Q.C.

For details see Chap. 18, (13) **46**.

36. Christchurch Drainage Board v. Brown, The Daily Telegraph October 12, 1987; [1987] C.L.Y. 2591, P.C.

For details see Chap. 18, (13) **45**.

37. Royal Bank Trust Co. (Trinidad) Ltd v. Pampellone [1987] 1 Lloyd's Rep. 218; [1987] C.L.Y. 2576, P.C.

Banker gave reference to plaintiff in respect of a finance company to effect that "all our reports indicate that this company may be regarded as trustworthy for its ordinary business engagements"—on another occasion they orally informed him of a recent credit report and gave him brochures in respect of a deposit taking company. In reliance thereon the plaintiff alleged he placed monies with those companies—*Held*, bankers not liable—there was no tendering of advice and no reliance thereon.

38. Nash v. Evens & Matta [1988] 1 E.G.L.R. 130; [1988] C.L.Y. 2464, Ewbank J.

For details see Chap. 18, (5) **20**.

39. Davies v. Parry [1988] 1 E.G.L.R. 147; [1988] C.L.Y. 2457, McNeill J.

For details see Chap. 18, (5) **22**.

40. Green v. Ipswich B.C. [1988] 1 E.G.L.R. 239; [1988] C.L.Y. 2456, Judge Fox-Andrews Q.C.

For details see Chap. 18, (5) **25**.

41 Cooper v. Tamms [1988] 1 E.G.L.R. 257; [1988] C.L.Y. 1710, P.J. Crawford Q.C.

Vendor's reply to inquiries before contract as to her knowledge of problems with damp and rot—rot subsequently found—*Held*, plaintiffs had placed no material reliance on the reply and their claim for misrepresentation failed—alternatively vendor had reasonable grounds to and did believe facts represented were true—*Held*, further, assumed duty of care on *Hedley Byrne* principles not breached.

42. Michael Sallis & Company Ltd v. E.C.A. Calil (1988) 4 Const. L.J. 125; [1988] C.L.Y. 2420, Judge Fox-Andrews Q.C.

Held, architect owes a duty to act impartially towards main contractor in respect of such matters as certificates and extensions of time and in so far as damage could be established as having been caused by unfairness in respect of matters about which under the contract they were required to act impartially damages were recoverable and not too remote—*Held*, no duty owed in respect of preparation of plans or specifications or as to whether a survey he carried out or a variation ordered.

43. Beresforde v. Chesterfield B.C. [1989] 2 E.G.L.R. 149; [1989] C.L.Y. 2565, C.A.

For details see Chap. 18, (5) **35**.

44. Gibbs v. Arnold Son Hockley [1989] 2 E.G.L.R. 154; [1990] C.L.Y. 3307, Stephen Desch Q.C.

For details see Chap. 18, (5) **36**.

45. Hipkins v. Jack Cotton Partnership [1989] 2 E.G.L.R. 157; [1990] C.L.Y. 1567, Scott Baker J.

For details see Chap. 18, (5) **37**.

46. Bere v. Slades [1989] 2 E.G.L.R. 160; [1990] C.L.Y. 3306, Judge Newman Q.C.

For details see Chap 18, (5) **38**.

47. Ryeford Homes Ltd v. Sevenoaks D.C. [1989] 2 E.G.L.R. 281; [1990] C.L.Y. 4443, Judge Newey Q.C.

For details see Chap. 18, (13) **59**.

48. Seabrink Residents Association Ltd v. Robert Walpole Campion & Partners (1989) 14 Con; L.R. 62; [1990] C.L.Y. 394, Judge Esyr Lewis Q.C.

For details see Chap. 18, (13) **60**.

49. Huxford v. Stoy Hayward & Co. (1989) 5 BCC 421; [1989] C.L.Y. 2538, Popplewell J.

See Chap. 18, (1) **15**.

50. Minories Finance Ltd v. Arthur Young; Johnson Matthey PLC v. Arthur Young [1989] 2 All E.R. 105; [1989] C.L.Y. 150, Saville J.

Plaintiff claimed damages against their auditors—auditors claimed indemnity/contribution from Bank of England under the Civil Liability (Contribution) Act 1978 for breach of duty of care owed to plaintiffs to carry out its supervisory functions over U.K. banks with reasonable skill and care—*Held*, not just, fair or reasonable to impose such a duty.

51. Portsea Island Mutual Cooperative Society Ltd v. Michael Brashier Associates (1990) 6 Const. L.J. 63; [1990] C.L.Y. 3292, Judge Newey Q.C.

Architect designed supermarket premises for developer who had agreed to lease them to plaintiffs—*Held*, architect was in breach of duty of care in respect of brick ships forming part of exterior and which were unsafe—*Held*, however, liable only for the cost of rendering wall safe but not the cost of recladding the wall. *Junior Books* (Chap. 18, (6) **26**) *D. & F. Estates* (Chap. 18, (6) **63**) and *Department of the Environment v. Thomas Bates* (Chap. 18, (6) **73**) referred to. For further details see Chap. 18, (6) **74**.

52. Leon Engineering & Construction Co. Ltd v. Ka Duk Investment Co. Ltd (1990) 47 B.L.R. 139; [1990] C.L.Y. 236, Bokhary J., H.K. High Court.

Main contractors sought to join architects in action on the ground they owed to them and were in breach of a duty of care to give proper, timely and impartial consideration to their claims and to issue all certificates in strict accordance with the terms of the contract—*Held*, following *Pacific Associates* (Chap. 18, (6) **66**), no such duty owed.

53. Kijowski v. New Capital Properties Ltd (1990) 15 Con.L.R.I; [1990] C.L.Y. 398, Judge Esyr Lewis Q.C.

Held, inter alia, differential settlement in house was due to builder's negligent failure to take reasonable care in and about its construction and as such gave rise to a danger to the safety or health of the occupant—plaintiff was not contributorily negligent in not having survey carried out at time of his purchase.

54. Whalley v. Roberts & Roberts [1990] 1 E.G.L.R. 164; [1990] C.L.Y. 3305, Auld J.

For details see Chap. 18, (5) **40**.

55. Lloyd v. Butler [1990] 2 E.G.L.R. 155; [1991] C.L.Y. 2656, Henry J.

For details see Chap. 18, (5) **43**.

56. Beaumont v. Humberts [1990] 2 E.G.L.R. 166; [1991] C.L.Y. 2657, C.A.

For details see Chap. 18, (5) **44**.

57. The Thomas Saunders Partnership v. Harvey [1990] Trading Law Reports 78; [1990] C.L.Y. 4312, Thayne Forbes Q.C.

Plaintiff architects asked defendant director of proposed sub-contractors whether floor supplied by them met certain criteria and were assured by him that it did—it did not—*Held*, director liable in deceit and also owed a duty of care as he had special skill and knowledge in the relevant field and had assumed personal responsibility for the accuracy of his statement—*Hedley Byrne* applied—*Held*, liable to make contribution under Civil Liability (Contribution) Act 1978.

58. Al-Saudi Banque v. Clarke Pixley [1990] Ch. 313, [1989] 3 All E.R. 361, Millett J.

No duty of care owed by auditors to bankers who allegedly lent or continued to lend money to the company in reliance on the audited accounts. Approved in *Caparo* (Chap. 19, (a) **18**). See Chap. 18, (1) **16**.

59. Roberts v. J. Hampson & Co. [1990] 1 W.L.R. 94; [1989] 2 All E.R. 504, Ian Kennedy J.

For details see Chap. 18, (5) **39**.

60. Richardson v. West Lindsey D.C. [1990] 1 W.L.R. 522; [1990] 1 All E.R. 296, C.A.

For details see Chap. 18, (13) **64**.

61. Al-Nakib Investments (Jersey) Ltd v. Longcroft [1990] 1 W.L.R. 1390; [1990] 3 All E.R. 321, Mervyn Davies J.

See Chap. 18, (7) **2**.

62. Pacific Associates Inc. v. Baxter [1990] 1 Q.B. 993; [1989] 2 All E.R. 159, C.A.

Consulting engineers appointed to supervise works to be performed by contractors under contract with employer. Contractor's claim that engineer's negligent failure to certify delay and expense to which it was entitled under its contract with employer had caused loss and damage. Claim struck out because (a) given contractual framework, in particular provisions enabling contractor to recover loss and expense agaisnt employer, there was no express or implied voluntary assumption of a duty of care by engineers with consequential liability for pecuniary loss in favour of contractor, there was no reliance by contractor on any such assumption—*Hedley Byrne* distinguished, (b) in any event no duty of care should be imposed, (c) clause in contract exempting engineers from liability prevented the imposition of any such liability. *Sallis* **42** and *Shui On* **25** referred to.

63. Smith v. Eric S. Bush; Harris v. Wyre Forest D.C. [1990] 1 A.C. 831; [1989] 2 All E.R. 514, H.L.

For details see Chap. 19, (a) **16**.

64. Caparo Industries PLC v. Dickman [1990] 2 A.C. 605; [1990] 1 All E.R. 568, H.L.

Defendants audited the accounts of a public limited company which were sent to shareholders prior to annual general meeting. The plaintiffs made various purchases of shares some allegedly in reliance upon the audited accounts; due to their being innaccurate and misleading loss was suffered—*Held*, no duty of care owed. See Chap. 19, (a) **18**.

65. Warner v. Basildon Development Corporation (1991) 7 Const. L.J. 146; [1992] C.L.Y. 3197, C.A.

Held, builder negligent and in breach of duties imposed by Building Regulations as regards house foundations. Defects affected value but did not pose risk of injury or damage save to the home itself—*Held*, on basis of *D. & F. Estates* (Chap. 18, (6) **63**) builder was not liable.

66. Henley v. Cloke & Sons [1991] 2 E.G.L.R. 141; [1992] C.L.Y. 1547, Judge Thayne Forbes Q.C.

For details see Chap. 18, (5) **50**.

67. Beaton v. Nationwide Building Society [1991] 2 E.G.L.R. 145; [1992] C.L.Y. 3207, Neil Butterfield Q.C.

For details see Chap. 18, (5) **51**.

68. James McNaughton Paper Group Ltd v. Hicks Anderson & Co. [1991] 2 Q.B. 113; [1991] 1 All E.R. 134, C.A.

See Chap. 18, (1) **19**.

69. Morgan Crucible Co PLC v. Hill Samuel & Co. Ltd [1991] Ch. 295; [1991] 3 All E.R. 148, C.A.

See Chap. 18, (7) **3**.

70. Johnson v. Bournemouth B.C. [1992] E.G.C.S. 73; [1992] C.L.Y. 2650, C.A.

For details see Chap. 18, (13) **72**.

71. P. K. Finans International (U.K.) Ltd v. Andrew Downs & Co. Ltd [1992] 1 E.G.L.R. 172; [1992] C.L.Y. 3216, Sir Michael Ogden Q.C.

Copy of valuation of property being converted into nursing home supplied to licensed deposit-takers who lent on security of property. Valuer stated he had made oral inquiries but no official search as to planning consents—*Held*, not negligent in not advising that planning consents should be verified—if there had been negligence, then deposit-takers contributorily negligent in failing to instruct solicitors to verify the position.

72. Peach v. Iain G. Chalmers & Co. [1992] 2 E.G.L.R. 135; [1992] C.L.Y. 5658, Lord Caplan, Crt. of Sess.

See Chap. 18, (5) **57**.

73. Hiron v. Pynford South Ltd [1992] 2 E.G.L.R. 138; [1993] C.L.Y. 2997, Judge Newey Q.C.

Structural engineer advised insurers of property as to its underpinning—*Held, inter alia*, he did not owe a duty of care to the owners. For further details see Chap. 18, (5) **58**.

74. Berg Sons & Co. Ltd v. Adams [1992] BCC 661; [1993] C.L.Y. 2982, Hobhouse J.

See Chap. 18, (1) **21**.

75. Sears Investment Trust Ltd v. Lewis's Group Ltd (1992) R.A. 262; *The Times*, September 22, 1992, Harman J.

Valuers on instructions off plaintiff's parent company pursued an appeal against the rateable value of the plaintiff's Glasgow store. Following an agreement to transfer the store to the defendants, the plaintiffs told the valuers to take instructions from the defendants as to the appeal. Appeal was successful and valuers obtained repayment of excess rates which were paid to the defendants—*Held*, valuers as from the date of change owed no duty of care or loyalty to the plaintiffs—claim for damages in negligence dismissed.

76. Punjab National Bank v. De Boinville [1992] 1 W.L.R. 1138; [1992] 3 All E.R. 104, C.A.

Held, insurance broker owes a duty of care to the specific person whom he knows is to become an assignee of an insurance policy, at all events if that person actively participates in giving instructions for the insurance to the broker's knowledge.

77. Gran Gelato Ltd v. Richcliff (Group) Ltd [1992] Ch. 560; [1992] 1 All E.R. 865, Sir Donald Nicholls V.C.

Held, first defendants liable for negligent answer to inquiries before lease given on their behalf by second defendant solicitors—*Held*, further, that although there was a close and direct relationship between those solicitors and the plaintiff and foreseeability of loss, it would not be just, fair or reasonable to impose a duty of care on the solicitors. *Caparo* (Chap.) 19, (a) **18**) applied.

78. Allied Trust Bank Ltd v. Edward Symmons & Partners [1993] E.G.C.S. 163, [1994] C.L.Y. 3394, Mr. Clarke Q.C.

For details see Chap. 18 (5) **61**.

79. Private Bank & Trust Co. Ltd v. S. (U.K.) Ltd [1993] 1 E.G.L.R. 144; [1993] C.L.Y. 2998, Judge Price

Owners of property instruct valuers—copy of valuation sent to plaintiff who lent in reliance thereon—*Held*, valuation not negligent.

80. Deloitte Haskins & Sells v. National Mutual Life Nominees Ltd [1993] A.C. 774; [1993] 2 All E.R. 1015, P.C.

See Chap. 18, (1) **22**.

81. West Wiltshire D.C. v. Garland [1993] Ch. 409; [1993] 4 All E.R. 246, Morritt J.

See Chap. 18, (1) **24**.

82. Galoo Ltd v. Bright Grahame Murray [1994] 1 W.L.R. 1360, C.A.

See Chap. 18, (1) **25**.

83. Spring v. Guardian Assurance PLC [1994] 3 W.L.R. 354; [1994] 3 All E.R. 129, H.L.

Insurance company and company selling the former's policies—*Held*, by a majority, they owed a duty of care when giving a reference in respect of a person being the former's agent and the latter's ex-employee.

84. Henderson v. Merrett Syndicates Ltd [1994] 3 W.L.R. 761, (1994) 3 All E.R. 506, H.L.

For details see Chap. 19, (a) **22**.

85. Preston v. Torfaen B.C. (1994) 65 B.L.R. 1; [1994] C.L.Y. 3398, C.A.

Plaintiffs were subsequent purchasers of a house built on land which the defendant surveyors had advised the local authority was suitable to carry foundations for a housing estate—*Held*; not liable for cracks allegedly due to faulty design of foundations and/or soil conditions, the case not falling within any special category outside the *Hedley Byrne* principle which would entitle recovery for economic loss or in the absence of reliance.

86. McCullagh v. Lane Fox & Partners Ltd (1994) 08 E.G. 118; [1994] C.L.Y. 114, Colman J.

Estate agents' particulars negligently misstated area of ground—disclaimer of liability in particulars—subsequent oral misrepresentation of same matter in partial reliance on which plaintiff purchased—*Held*, liable for oral representation but no loss caused.

87. White v. Jones (1995) 2 W.L.R. 187; [1995] N.L.J. 251, H.L.

For details see Chap. 19, (a) **24**.

U1. Foy v. Dacorum B.C. (1987) C.A. 1001

For details see Chap. 18, (13) **U2**.

U2. Devlin v. Mobey (1988) C.A. 816

U3. Glen-Mor Fashions Ltd v. Jaeger Company Shops Ltd (1991) C.A. 1195

Parties had negotiations with a view to entering a concession agreement—the defendants later abandoned them—*Held*, defendants not liable for economic loss allegedly caused by the plaintiff's reliance on a statement as such was not within the confines of the *Hedley Byrne* principle.

U4. Lloyds Bank PLC v. Cobb (1991) C.A. 1225

Bank in examining details of commercial project before deciding whether to make a loan to their customer, did not, in the absence of evidence that the customer was seeking their advice, assume any duty of care to him. Summary judgement given for bank.

U5. Professional Reprographic Services Ltd v. D.P.S. Typecraft Ltd (1993) C.A. 175

Held, suppliers of computer equipment negligent under *Hedley Byrne* principle for representing computer equipment was compatible with plaintiff's typesetting equipment.

U6. Thompson v. Ali (1994) C.A. 406

Held, defendants liable to purchaser of coffee shop for misrepresenting turnover figure.

20. MISCELLANEOUS

1. Sidey v. Olsen Bros [1984] C.L.Y. 2304, C.A.

Injury caused in coach accident due to latent defect of which previous owner aware—current owner not liable for failure to ask previous owner whether coach was satisfactory or whether there had been any problems.

2. Norwich General Trust v. Grierson [1984] C.L.Y. 2 306, Stocker J.

Mortgagees in possession allowed condition of premises to deteriorate due to vandalism—*Held*, they or their agents had been negligent and had a duty to take reasonable steps to protect the premises from vandalism.

3. Condon v. Basi [1985] 1 W.L.R. 866; [1985] 2 All E.R. 453, C.A.

Defendant, a local Sunday league footballer, lunged with studs showing 9 inches off the ground at plaintiff on the opposing side, after plaintiff had pushed the ball away—plaintiff broke right leg—defendant sent off. Court of Appeal upheld trial judge's decision that D was liable in negligence. *Per* Lord Donaldson M. R.: "... there is no authority as to what is the standard of care which governs the conduct of players in competitive sports generally and, above all, in a competitive sport whose rules ... contemplate ... physical contact between the players." There would be liability "if ... the defendant failed to exercise that degree of care which was appropriate in all the circumstances, or that he acted in a way to which the plaintiff cannot be expected to have consented ... The standard is objective, but objective in a different set of circumstances. Thus there will of course be a higher degree of care required of a player in a First Division football match than of a player in a local league football match."

4. Pawlack v. Doucette and Reinks [1985] 2 W.W.R. 588; [1985] C.L.Y. 2337, British Columbia Supreme Court

First defendant invited plaintiff to water ski. Knowing plaintiff had no experience, first defendant explained, from a position on shore, how plaintiff should position himself in water. Unidentified person on shore shouted "go". Second defendant operating tow-boat, who had not asked whether plaintiff was experienced, applied full power. Plaintiff grabbed at rope. His fingers became entangled and were severed—*Held, inter alia,*:

(a) First defendant negligent in failing properly to execute the supervisory role he had assumed.
(b) Second defendant negligent in failing to ascertain whether plaintiff experienced, and applying full power in response to shout from shore.
(c) Defence of *volenti non fit injuria* did not arise. Not an obvious and necessary risk that second defendant would accelerate before plaintiff ready and without establishing system of communication.
(d) Intervention of unidentified person did not affect or reduce liability of first and second defendants.
(e) Plaintiff 15 per cent. contributorily negligent in grabbing moving rope.
(f) First and second defendants 55 per cent and 30 per cent liable respectively. *N.B.* The approach to contribution would be different in England and Wales—see *Fitzgerald v. Lane*, summarised on a different point in Chap. 13, (1)(k) **30**.

5. Spry v. Plowright, The Times, March 14, 1988; [1988] C.L.Y. 2454, Boreham J.

Plaintiff, lady dancing teacher and defendant, both in their sixties, dancing when defendant fell because his foot failed to go forward. Plaintiff injured—*Held*, defendant not liable—had not danced in such a way that a reasonable person would have said he was putting plaintiff at risk: "Each case depended on its own facts. The age and agility of the plaintiff had to be considered. The case of a twenty-year old whirling his seventy-year old grandmother was very different from the present case where the age and agility of the two people concerned was similar."

6. Business Computer International Ltd v. Registrar of Companies [1988] Ch. 229; [1987] 3 All E.R. 465, Scott J.

7. C.B.S. Songs Ltd v. Amstrad Consumer Electronics PLC [1988] 1 A.C. 1013 at 1059, 1060; [1988] 2 All E.R. 484, H.L.

Plaintiffs alleged that defendants, by advertising and offering for sale hi-fi systems capable, *inter alia*, of recording at high speed from pre-recorded cassettes on to blank tapes, had authorised and invited members of the public to infringe their copyright and were, *inter alia*, in breach of a duty of care owed to them not to cause or permit purchasers to infringe copyright, alternatively not to facilitate by sale or advertisement such infringement—*Held*, defendants did not owe a duty to prevent, discourage or warn against infringement and were therefore not liable in negligence.

8. Davey v. Cosmos Air Holidays [1988] C.L.Y. 2561, Judge Neville

9. Debs v. Sibec Developments Ltd [1990] R.T.R. 91; [1990] C.L.Y. 4026, Simon Brown J.

See Chap. 1, (3) (b) **34**.

10. Cope v. Cassells [1990] C.L.Y. 3296, H. H. Judge Owen

Defendant, an Aikido—martial arts teacher, demonstrating a technique with plaintiff, a pupil—delivered what was intended as a shadow blow with his knee, but hit plaintiff in abdomen—*Held*, defendant not liable. Defendant had acted with appropriate care, and plaintiff should have contemplated the use of the shadow blow. Neither practice nor necessary to warn of such a move.

11. Parker-Tweedale v. Dunbar Bank PLC [1991] Ch. 26; [1990] 3 W.L.R. 767, C.A.

Plaintiff, who was entitled to a beneficial interest in property of which his wife was sole legal owner and mortgagor, claimed that the mortgagee, in exercising its power of sale, owed him an independent duty in tort to take reasonable care to obtain a proper price—*Held*, the duty owed by a mortgagee to a mortgagor was recognised by equity as arising out of the particular relationship between them and it was unnecessary and confusing for the duties to be expressed in terms of the tort of negligence—there was no room for the imposition of a further duty in tort to the beneficiary (the beneficiary's right being against the mortgagor)—in any event the price obtained was a proper price. *Cuckmere Brick Co. Ltd. v. Mutual Finance Ltd* [1971] Ch. 949 considered.

12. Feeny v. Lyall, 1991 S.L.T. 156; [1991] C.L.Y. 5298, O.H.

Plaintiff struck golf ball onto wrong fairway—when recovering it, was struck by ball driven by another golfer from the tee of that fairway—*Held*, had the other golfer seen P, P would have been 25 per cent. contributorily negligent for failing to check on the actions of golfers on that tee.

13. Mobil Oil Hong Kong Ltd & Dow Chemical (Hong Kong) Ltd v. Hong Kong United Dockyards Ltd: The Hui Lien [1991] 1 Lloyd's Rep. 309: [1992] C.L.Y. 3956, P.C.

The plaintiff jetty owners claimed that the breaking adrift of a ship and consequent damage to their jetty and shore installations was due to negligence of the defendants in failing to take proper precautions to safeguard the ship against typhoon—*Held*, damage was not pure economic loss and defendants in breach of duty owed to plaintiffs at common law.

14. Dodgeson v. Airtours [1992] C.L.Y. 3217, District Judge Duckworth

15. Gurtner v. Beaton [1993] 1 Lloyd's Rep. 369; *The Times*, March 23, 1992, C.A.

Plaintiffs passengers in light aircraft which crashed into a hillside approaching Dundee Airport, due to pilot's negligence. They sued, *inter alia*, the employers of J, the air traffic controller on duty, alleging that J should have realised pilot had made a substantial navigational error, and intervened—*Held*, J not liable. J entitled to assume that pilot was competent, and knew of let-down procedure and presence of high ground in vicinity. Pilot had been told of low cloud cover. Pilot never asked for assistance. J had no reason to suppose pilot would suddenly depart from let-down procedure and descend to dangerous level.

16. Morrell v. Owen, *The Times*, December 14, 1993; [1993] C.L.Y. 2957, Mitchell J.

Archary and discus competitions for paraplegic athletes held simultaneously in sports hall, divided by net. Stray discus hit net. Net billowed out and discus hit plaintiff, an archer on other side, on temple. Plaintiff unaware of discus event. Archers received no safety instructions and coaches had taken no special safety precautions—*Held*, archery and discus coaches liable. Accident was entirely foreseeable. Coaches owed a greater duty of care to participants than would have done had they been able-bodied.

17. Lewis v. Buckpool Golf club, [1993] S.L.T. (Sh. Ct.) 43; [1992] C.L.Y 6076

Defendant, a 24-handicap golfer, mishit ball from tee and struck plaintiff on adjacent green—*Held*, defendant liable. All he had to do was wait for plaintiff to finish putting. Risk of a golfer of defendant's level of skill mishitting not so small that a reasonable man would disregard it. There was no basis for a plea of *volenti non fit injuria*.

18. Wilson v. Best Travel Ltd [1993] 1 All E.R. 353; [1993] C.L.Y. 494, Phillips J.

Plaintiff holiday maker tripped and fell against a glass patio door and suffered injury when it broke—*Held*, tour operator not in breach of contract or duty in alleged failure to exercise reasonable skill and care to ensure the hotel was reasonably safe by regular and competent inspection.

19. Crane v. Kynoch [1994] C.L.Y. 3399, Judge Birks

Various allegations made as to negligent administration of anaesthetic and treatment of and advice concerning dog—although precise cause of death (from heart failure) was difficult to establish—*Held*, applying the *Bolam* test of professional negligence and *Mc Ghee* on the issue of causation some of the various breaches of duty had clearly contributed to the death and the claim did not fail because the experts had not been able to offer a firm conclusion as to the precise cause of death.

U1. Whitford v. Monkman (1983) C.A. 926

Held, defendant liable when his radio-controlled glider hit plaintiff in face.

U2. Denyer v. Heaney (1985) C.A. 983

Plaintiff whilst go-karting on holiday package tour was struck from behind by defendant's go kart—*Held*, defendant liable.

U3. Fowlston (T/A Britton House Stud) v. Witham Land and Leisure Services Ltd (1988) C.A. 442

Ultrasonic scan by probe into mare's rectum to see whether she was pregnant caused a partial tear and consequent peritonitis and death—*Held*, vet not negligent in failing to detect injury at time.

U4. Cartwright v. Halfpenny Green Parachute Centre Ltd (1989) C.A. 519

Parachutist on first jump collided with tractor—*Held*, defendants liable for the major hazard posed by tractor's presence.

U5. Butler v. Vann (1991) C.A. 702

15-year-old in motor cycle race got rope from improperly erected marker fence entangled in his rear wheel when he went off the track; he resumed the race without realising but had later to stop and unravel it but whilst doing so was hit by another competitor—*Held*, defendants liable—no contributory negligence by plaintiff resuming race without checking rear wheel or acting as he subsequently did.

INDEX